Stem Cell Biology and Regenerative Medicine

Volume 1519

Our understanding of stem cells has grown rapidly over the last decade. While the apparently tremendous therapeutic potential of stem cells has not yet been realized, their routine use in regeneration and restoration of tissue and organ function is greatly anticipated. To this end, many investigators continue to push the boundaries in areas such as the reprogramming, the stem cell niche, nanotechnology, biomimetics and 3D bioprinting, to name just a few. The objective of the volumes in the Stem Cell Biology and Regenerative Medicine series is to capture and consolidate these developments in a timely way. Each volume is thought-provoking in identifying problems, offering solutions, and providing ideas to excite further innovation in the stem cell and regenerative medicine fields.

Yaşar Murat Elçin
Editor

Biofabrication in Regenerative Medicine

Basic Technologies, Emerging Modalities, and Applications

Springer

Editor
Yaşar Murat Elçin
Tissue Engineering, Biomaterials and Nanobiotechnology Laboratory, Faculty of Science and Stem Cell Institute
Ankara University
Ankara, Türkiye

ISSN 2196-8985 ISSN 2196-8993 (electronic)
Stem Cell Biology and Regenerative Medicine
ISBN 978-3-032-30293-9 ISBN 978-3-032-30294-6 (eBook)
https://doi.org/10.1007/978-3-032-30294-6

This Springer imprint is published by the registered company Springer Nature Switzerland AG
The registered company address is: Gewerbestrasse 11, 6330 Cham, Switzerland

Preface

Biofabrication appears to be ushering in a new era in regenerative medicine. What was once considered a distant dream is slowly becoming a tangible reality. Exciting developments are underway in the fabrication of functional living tissues or organs in the laboratory. The field of tissue engineering and regenerative medicine, which emerged in the early 1990s, has undergone a revolutionary transformation in the last decade, particularly driven by advancements in 3D bioprinting technology. Traditional biofabrication methods, which have led to some progress in the development of biomimetic tissues, are evolving into unconventional new hybrid approaches offering innovative solutions for creating scalable and multi-component hierarchical tissues. This book offers a journey into the fascinating world of biofabrication in regenerative medicine, reflecting years of research into advanced technologies and approaches, and the determined efforts to translate this knowledge into applications. Each chapter aims to provide a comprehensive understanding of the multifaceted aspects of this groundbreaking field. The first chapters of the volume cover the fundamentals of biofabrication strategies, the various types of biomaterials used, and the properties of bioinks. Next, smart materials that translate physical cues into cellular responses and neovascularization strategies are discussed. Subsequent chapters describe state-of-the-art developments in the biofabrication of various tissues, including skin, tendons, trachea, bone, skeletal muscle, blood vessels, and the eye. The final chapters address current approaches, namely, 3D-engineered platforms for disease modeling and the role of deep learning and artificial intelligence in biofabrication for regenerative medicine.

I would like to extend my sincere thanks to Merry Stuber, senior editor of the Stem Cell Biology and Regenerative Medicine series, for her support throughout this work, and to the production team for their extraordinary dedication in bringing this volume to life. I also express my gratitude to all the valuable authors who have contributed their scientific perspectives and expertise to this volume.

Ankara, Türkiye | Yaşar Murat Elçin

Preface

Contents

Contributors

Anas Abu-Dieh Department of Ophthalmology, CHU de Québec-Université Laval, Quebec City, QC, Canada

Hôpital Maisonneuve-Rosemont Research Center, Université de Montréal, Montreal, QC, Canada

Nureddin Ashammakhi Institute for Quantitative Health Science and Engineering, College of Human Medicine, Michigan State University, East Lansing, MI, USA

Paula Ávila-Fernández Department of Histology and Tissue Engineering Group, University of Granada, Granada, Spain

Instituto de Investigación Biosanitaria Ibs.GRANADA, Granada, Spain

Myriam Belaiche Institute of Biomedical Engineering, Université de Montréal, Montreal, QC, Canada

Nehar Celikkin Institute of Physical Chemistry, Polish Academy of Sciences, Warsaw, Poland

Jesús Chato-Astrain Department of Histology and Tissue Engineering Group, University of Granada, Granada, Spain

Instituto de Investigación Biosanitaria Ibs.GRANADA, Granada, Spain

Francesco Copes Laboratory for Biomaterials and Bioengineering, Canada Research Chair Tier I for the Innovation in Surgery, Department of Min-Met-Materials Engineering and Regenerative Medicine, CHU de Quebec Research Center, Laval University, Quebec City, QC, Canada

Giacomo Cortella Labs of Tissue Engineering & Nanomedicine, Department of Medicine, Surgery and Dentistry, University of Salerno, Fisciano, SA, Italy

Marco Costantini Institute of Physical Chemistry, Polish Academy of Sciences, Warsaw, Poland

Amrit Das Department of Ophthalmology, Université de Montréal, Montreal, QC, Canada

Ayşe Eser Elçin Tissue Engineering, Biomaterials and Nanobiotechnology Laboratory, Faculty of Science and Stem Cell Institute, Ankara University, Ankara, Türkiye

Stem Cell Institute, Ankara University, Ankara, Türkiye

Yaşar Murat Elçin Tissue Engineering, Biomaterials and Nanobiotechnology Laboratory, Faculty of Science and Stem Cell Institute, Ankara University, Ankara, Türkiye

Department of Chemistry, Faculty of Science, Ankara University, Ankara, Türkiye

Ahmed A. M. Elnour School of Chemistry and Chemical Engineering, Faculty of Engineering and Physical Sciences, The University of Southampton, Southampton, UK

Department of Biochemistry, Faculty of Medicine and Surgery, Dar Eloloum College of Science and Technology, Alamo Khartoum, Sudan

Faculty of Chemical and Process Engineering Technology, Universiti Malaysia Pahang Al-Sultan Abdullah (UMPSA), Pahang, Malaysia

Miguel Etayo-Escanilla Department of Histology and Tissue Engineering Group, University of Granada, Granada, Spain

Instituto de Investigación Biosanitaria Ibs. GRANADA, Granada, Spain

Nicole Fratini Department of Molecular Medicine, Sapienza University, Rome, Italy

National Research Council–Institute for Biomedical Technologies (CNR-ITB), Milan, Italy

Cesare Gargioli Department of Biology, University of Rome Tor Vergata, Rome, Italy

May Griffith Hôpital Maisonneuve-Rosemont Research Center, Université de Montréal, Montreal, QC, Canada

Centre de recherche du Centre hospitalier de l'Université de Montréal, Montreal, QC, Canada

Department of Ophthalmology, Université de Montréal, Montreal, QC, Canada

Institute of Biomedical Engineering, Université de Montréal, Montreal, QC, Canada

Waseem Haider School of Engineering and Technology, Central Michigan University, Mount Pleasant, MI, USA

Mohamed G. Hassan School of Chemistry and Chemical Engineering, Faculty of Engineering and Physical Sciences, The University of Southampton, Southampton, UK

Faustin Hategekimana Tissue Engineering, Biomaterials and Nanobiotechnology Laboratory, Faculty of Science and Stem Cell Institute, Ankara University, Ankara, Türkiye

Thi Thai Thanh Hoang Department of Orthopaedic Surgery, UC Davis Health, Sacramento, CA, USA

Nathaniel S. Hwang School of Chemical and Biological Engineering, The Institute of Chemical Processes, Seoul National University, Seoul, Republic of Korea

Institute of Engineering Research, Seoul National University, Seoul, Republic of Korea

Interdisciplinary Program in Bioengineering, Seoul National University, Seoul, Republic of Korea

BioMAX/N-Bio Institute, Institute of BioEngineering, Seoul National University, Seoul, Republic of Korea

Se Na Jang Department of PolymerNano Science and Technology and Polymer Materials Fusion Research Center, Jeonbuk National University, Jeonju-si, Jeonbuk, South Korea

Tae Hoon Kang Interdisciplinary Program in Bioengineering, Seoul National University, Seoul, Republic of Korea

Seyithan Kansız Tissue Engineering, Biomaterials and Nanobiotechnology Laboratory, Faculty of Science and Stem Cell Institute, Ankara University, Ankara, Türkiye

Department of Chemistry, Faculty of Science, Ankara University, Ankara, Türkiye

Gilson Khang Department of PolymerNano Science and Technology and Polymer Materials Fusion Research Center, Jeonbuk National University, Jeonju-si, Jeonbuk, South Korea

Department of Bionanotechnology and Bio-Convergence Engineering, Jeonbuk National University, Jeonju-si, Jeonbuk, South Korea

Gilson Khang Department of Bionanotechnology and Bio-Convergence Technology, Jeonbuk National University, Jeonju, Republic of Korea

Department of PolymerNano Science and Technology and Polymer Materials Fusion Research Center, Jeonbuk National University, Jeonju, Republic of Korea

Jung Hun Kim School of Chemical and Biological Engineering, The Institute of Chemical Processes, Seoul National University, Seoul, Republic of Korea

Institute of Engineering Research, Seoul National University, Seoul, Republic of Korea

Nakyung Kim Department of PolymerNano Science and Technology and Polymer Materials Fusion Research Center, Jeonbuk National University, Jeonju-si, Jeonbuk, South Korea

Sol Kim Microphysiological Systems Research Institute, Research Institute of Medical-Bio Convergence, Hallym University, Chuncheon, Republic of Korea

Soon Hee Kim Microphysiological Systems Research Institute, Research Institute of Medical-Bio Convergence, Hallym University, Chuncheon, Republic of Korea

Özge Lalegül-Ülker Tissue Engineering, Biomaterials and Nanobiotechnology Laboratory, Faculty of Science and Stem Cell Institute, Ankara University, Ankara, Türkiye

J. Kent Leach Department of Orthopaedic Surgery, UC Davis Health, Sacramento, CA, USA

Department of Biomedical Engineering, University of California, Davis, CA, USA

Grace Lin Hôpital Maisonneuve-Rosemont Research Center, Université de Montréal, Montreal, QC, Canada

Centre de recherche du Centre hospitalier de l'Université de Montréal, Montreal, QC, Canada

Fabio Maiullari Institute of Physical Chemistry, Polish Academy of Sciences, Warsaw, Poland

Diego Mantovani Laboratory for Biomaterials and Bioengineering, Canada Research Chair Tier I for the Innovation in Surgery, Department of Min-Met-Materials Engineering and Regenerative Medicine, CHU de Quebec Research Center, Laval University, Quebec City, QC, Canada

Sudarshini Nath Microphysiological Systems Research Institute, Research Institute of Medical-Bio Convergence, Hallym University, Chuncheon, Republic of Korea

Eylül Odabaş-Kansız Tissue Engineering, Biomaterials and Nanobiotechnology Laboratory, Faculty of Science and Stem Cell Institute, Ankara University, Ankara, Türkiye

Central Research Laboratory Application and Research Center, Ankara Yıldırım Beyazıt University, Ankara, Türkiye

Selçuk Öztürk Tissue Engineering, Biomaterials and Nanobiotechnology Laboratory, Faculty of Science and Stem Cell Institute, Ankara University, Ankara, Türkiye

Kırıkkale University, Faculty of Medicine, Department of Cardiology, Kırıkkale, Türkiye

Chan Hum Park Microphysiological Systems Research Institute, Research Institute of Medical-Bio Convergence, Hallym University, Chuncheon, Republic of Korea

Departments of Otorhinolaryngology-Head and Neck Surgery, Chuncheon Sacred Heart Hospital, School of Medicine, Hallym University, Chuncheon, Republic of Korea

Sunjae Park Department of PolymerNano Science and Technology and Polymer Materials Fusion Research Center, Jeonbuk National University, Jeonju-si, Jeonbuk, South Korea

Ketul C. Popat Department of Bioengineering, George Mason University, Fairfax, VA, USA

Giovanna Della Porta Labs of Tissue Engineering & Nanomedicine, Department of Medicine, Surgery and Dentistry, University of Salerno, Fisciano, SA, Italy

Yurii Promovych Institute of Physical Chemistry, Polish Academy of Sciences, Warsaw, Poland

David H. Ramos-Rodriguez Department of Orthopaedic Surgery, UC Davis Health, Sacramento, CA, USA

Marie-Claude Robert Hôpital Maisonneuve-Rosemont Research Center, Université de Montréal, Montreal, QC, Canada

Centre de recherche du Centre hospitalier de l'Université de Montréal, Montreal, QC, Canada

Department of Ophthalmology, Université de Montréal, Montreal, QC, Canada

Silvia Rodriguez-Fernandez Laboratory for Biomaterials and Bioengineering, Canada Research Chair Tier I for the Innovation in Surgery, Department of Min-Met-Materials Engineering and Regenerative Medicine, CHU de Quebec Research Center, Laval University, Quebec City, QC, Canada

Hee Sang Ro School of Chemical and Biological Engineering, The Institute of Chemical Processes, Seoul National University, Seoul, Republic of Korea

Aniruddha Vijay Savargaonkar School of Biomedical and Chemical Engineering, Colorado State University, Fort Collins, CO, USA

Şükran Şeker Tissue Engineering, Biomaterials and Nanobiotechnology Laboratory, Faculty of Science and Stem Cell Institute, Ankara University, Ankara, Türkiye

Hosoo Shin Department of PolymerNano Science and Technology and Polymer Materials Fusion Research Center, Jeonbuk National University, Jeonju-si, Jeonbuk, South Korea

Ramesh Singh Department of Bioengineering, George Mason University, Fairfax, VA, USA

Wojciech Swięszkowski Faculty of Materials Science and Engineering, Warsaw University of Technology, Warsaw, Poland

Maria Celeste Tirelli Institute of Physical Chemistry, Polish Academy of Sciences, Warsaw, Poland

Gökçe Uysal Stem Cell Institute, Ankara University, Ankara, Türkiye

Rafaelle Vinturelle Laboratory for Biomaterials and Bioengineering, Canada Research Chair Tier I for the Innovation in Surgery, Department of Min-Met-Materials Engineering and Regenerative Medicine, CHU de Quebec Research Center, Laval University, Quebec City, QC, Canada

Marina Volpi Faculty of Materials Science and Engineering, Warsaw University of Technology, Warsaw, Poland

Chapter 1
Three-Dimensional Bioprinting Technologies in Biofabrication

Ahmed A. M. Elnour, Mohamed G. Hassan, Waseem Haider, and Nureddin Ashammakhi

Abstract Biofabrication is an interdisciplinary field that combines biology and engineering to generate functional biological structures, providing a mechanism for the accurate placement of cells and biomaterials in three-dimensional (3D) space. The introduction of 3D bioprinting has been central to the realism with which constructs have been generated, allowing intricate structures to be recapitulated with precise control over the cell placement and material properties. Biocompatible bioinks form the foundation of biofabrication, allowing direct layering of cells and other components. Despite their importance, challenges persist, particularly in integrating the necessary vascular systems, managing the relationship between structure and function, and addressing unintended effects on cells during the printing process. This approach is crucial for advancing bioinks, as it allows for the integration of functional biopolymers, engineered structures, and cell-laden

A. A. M. Elnour (✉)
School of Chemistry and Chemical Engineering, Faculty of Engineering and Physical Sciences, The University of Southampton, Southampton, UK

Department of Biochemistry, Faculty of Medicine and Surgery, Dar Eloloum College of Science and Technology, Alamo, Khartoum, Sudan

Faculty of Chemical and Process Engineering Technology, Universiti Malaysia Pahang Al-Sultan Abdullah (UMPSA), Pahang, Malaysia
e-mail: aahe1u25@soton.ac.uk

M. G. Hassan
School of Chemistry and Chemical Engineering, Faculty of Engineering and Physical Sciences, The University of Southampton, Southampton, UK
e-mail: mghs1v19@soton.ac.uk

W. Haider
School of Engineering and Technology, Central Michigan University, Mount Pleasant, MI, USA
e-mail: haide1w@cmich.edu

N. Ashammakhi (✉)
Institute for Quantitative Health Science and Engineering, College of Human Medicine, Michigan State University, East Lansing, MI, USA
e-mail: ashammak@msu.edu

Y. M. Elçin (ed.), *Biofabrication in Regenerative Medicine*, Stem Cell Biology and Regenerative Medicine 1519, https://doi.org/10.1007/978-3-032-30294-6_1

hydrogel composites to achieve better control over intricate tissue designs. The rheological characteristics of bioinks, such as viscosity, shear-thinning properties, and viscoelasticity, are vital for achieving successful bioprinting results, as they directly impact printability, structural stability, and cell survival. The combination of bioprinting with microfluidic techniques marks a major breakthrough, enhancing the intricacy and functional abilities of 3D printed structures, thus broadening their potential uses. Currently, 3D bioprinting is applied in crucial fields such as regenerative medicine, drug screening, and advanced disease modeling. Nonetheless, the field encounters significant obstacles, especially in terms of scalability, vascularization of printed tissues, and successful translation of these technologies into clinical settings. This chapter outlines the future directions of biofabrication by examining current trends. It focuses on the creation of smart materials, engineering of multifunctional bioinks, optimization through artificial intelligence, and recent advancements in in vivo bioprinting methods. The aim is to produce functional and vascularized tissues and organs that replicate native tissues, paving the way for new possibilities in regenerative therapy and personalized medicine.

Keywords 3D bioprinting · Biomaterials · Disease modeling · Drug screening · Regenerative medicine and vascularization

Abbreviations

AI	Artificial intelligence
HA	Hyaluronic acid
TE	Tissue engineering
VN	Vagus nerve
AM	Additive manufacturing
ANN	Artificial neural networks
CAD	Computer-aided design
CCT	Controlled color temperature
DLP	Digital light processing
ECM	Extracellular matrix
EV	Extracellular vesicles
HTS	High-throughput screening
ISBP	Induced pluripotent stem cells
ML	Machine learning
YM	Yield management
ES	Embryonic stem
GelMA	Gelatin methacryloyl
MND	Motor Neuron Differentiation
MNM	Motor Neuron Maturation
NEM	Neural Expansion Medium
NIM	Neural Induction Medium

1.1 Introduction

Biofabrication is an emerging interdisciplinary field that combines the principles of biology, materials science, and engineering to create functional tissue structures for regenerative medicine. This process uses cells as fundamental building blocks and is inspired by the natural process of tissue organogenesis (Ashammakhi et al. 2019a). The technologies central to this field encompass additive manufacturing (AM), with a particular emphasis on three-dimensional (3D) printing and its specialized variant, 3D bioprinting (Abaci and Guvendiren 2024; Agarwal et al. 2022; Pountos et al. 2021; Seyedmahmoud et al. 2019; Sung et al. 2021; Taylor et al. 2024). These innovative methods provide outstanding control over the spatial arrangement of cell- or biomaterial-based constructs (Lamberger et al. 2024). Unlike traditional tissue engineering (TE) methods, which typically begin with pre-made scaffolds onto which cells are later added, biofabrication involves the direct incorporation of living cells into complex, user-defined, and custom-designed structures known as bioinks (Ashammakhi et al. 2019c; Marsh et al. 2023). This approach not only guides tissue development but also replicates the inherent diversity found in vivo (Ratnamani et al. 2022).

3D printing technology has been fundamental to the progress made in biofabrication. These tools are used to print cells and biomaterials precisely in a highly controlled, automated, layer-by-layer approach (Ramadan and Zourob 2021). 3D bioprinting is adopted in biomedical engineering owing to its application in the programmed production of bioinks enriched with growth factors, selective cell types, and biomaterials for tissue constructs (Piazza et al. 2021). This development has greatly improved our ability to fabricate patient-specific scaffolds for regenerative medicine, disease biology, and drug screening by achieving more consistent cellular and biomaterial deposition via bioink composition (Chimene et al. 2022).

TE and regenerative medicine are two areas that would benefit from 3D printing and 3D bioprinting as promising biofabrication technologies (Ashammakhi et al. 2021a, b; Pountos et al. 2023; Taylor et al. 2024). The facilities for building constructs increase internal architecture, such as native tissue, physiological relevance, and biomaterial functional integration (Rossi et al. 2024). Controlled composition and architecture are essential for the preparation of scaffolds to induce cell differentiation, fabricate tissues, and restore tissue functionality in vivo (Zhang et al. 2021a). Additionally, the ability to print with highly tunable bioinks (functional polymeric biomaterials, cells, and hydrogel co-cultures) has improved the fabrication of complex tissue and organ structures using three-dimensional (3D) printing techniques (Janarthanan and Noh 2018). The homogeneity of the bioinks produced here, especially in terms of rheological properties, printability, and cell viability, is critical for the successful printing and resulting quality of the bioprinted constructs (Adam Marsh et al. 2026; Mappa et al. 2023; Marsh et al. 2022). Therefore, biofabrication is a frontier in biomedical technology with groundbreaking potential in personalized medicine, tissue transplantation, and regenerative medicine, as well as for the development of sophisticated in vitro systems for research and pharmacology.

Immense progress has also been achieved in the field of bioinks and 3D bioprinting. Bioink formulations, which are historically based on hydrogels, are carefully prepared to improve cell viability, stimulate proliferation and differentiation, and preserve the architectural and mechanical integrity of printed constructs (Alzoubi et al. 2023). Natural polymers that are part of bioinks include collagen and gelatin (Ashammakhi et al. 2019c; Synofzik et al. 2024). To promote tissue regeneration, synthetic polymers such as polycaprolactone and polyethylene glycol can be modified with cell-adhesive molecules or growth factors. In addition, these polymers can be populated with living cells. The rheological properties of bioinks, including viscosity, shear-thinning behavior, and viscoelasticity, are crucial for ensuring printability and maintaining shape fidelity, which in turn supports cell viability in bioprinted structures (Bakhtiary et al. 2021). The shear-thinning nature of bioink allows it to flow from the print head when hydrostatic pressure is applied, and it remains stable once deposited. This property ensures minimal mechanical stress on cells while maintaining the ability to print effectively (Wu et al. 2020). Mathematical and computational simulation models have been employed to refine extrusion parameters and forecast the behavior of bioinks during 3D printing, thereby enhancing the resolution and consistency of printed structures (Rossi et al. 2024).

Despite these advancements, significant challenges persist in the field of biofabrication. One major hurdle is devising an efficient method to integrate functional blood vessels into bioprinted structures, which is crucial for the exchange of nutrients and oxygen as tissues increase in size (Ashammakhi et al. 2020; Dodda et al. 2025; Erdem et al. 2020; Hill et al. 2021). Additionally, in engineered tissues, the regulation of the relationship between form and function is often inadequate, and the crosslinking methods employed to stabilize bioinks can negatively affect cell viability and functionality (Cheng et al. 2024). Another key limitation is the lack of standardized methods for assessing the rheological properties and printability of bioinks. Variations in measurement tools and protocols hinder researchers from making meaningful comparisons of their findings across different studies or experimental contexts (Lamberger et al. 2024). Moreover, it ensures excellent printability, compatibility with biological systems, and robust crosslinked properties while preserving the bioactivity of the printed bioink (GhavamiNejad et al. 2020; Rammal et al. 2021; Wang et al. 2021).

Filling these knowledge gaps is necessary to advance biofabrication. The introduction of better bioinks with improved physical and biological properties, optimization of printing conditions, and standardization of characterization protocols may lead to successful functional and sustained integration into living tissues (Lai and Meagher 2024). The system-level relationships between bioink composition and its rheological and printability properties must be fully understood to guide the narrowing of optimal processing conditions for any TE or regenerative medicine application.

This chapter addresses a few questions: (I) What progress has been made so far, and what are the challenges in 3D printing/3D bioprinting? What effect do the rheological and mechanical properties of bioinks have on the printability, cell viability, and functionality of bioprinted constructs? How can the bioink formulation and printing procedures be optimized to obtain a designed complex tissue prototype with special characteristics? How can we promote the standardization of bioink characterization and printability testing to enhance reproducibility and comparability? We also discuss key existing challenges and knowledge gaps, such as vascularization, structure-function relationships, and standardization of characterization; strategies for formulation optimization and corresponding printing processes based on recent progress in materials science, computational modeling, and process engineering; as well as future research directions beginning to emerge toward clinical translation through the avenue of biofabrication.

To address these challenges, we propose the central hypothesis that bioinks can be rationally designed and optimized to print complex functional tissue constructs with enhanced printability, cell viability, and in vivo function by leveraging their rheological/mechanical performance. Furthermore, there is a need to establish standards for bioink characterization and printability evaluation to facilitate the reproducibility and scalability of various biofabrication technologies and help them be widely adopted in clinical and industrial applications.

This chapter explores the evolution of 3D printing and 3D bioprinting techniques in the realm of biofabrication. It delves into the fundamental concepts and methodologies, along with the specifics of AM for biological systems. The discussion includes the design, formulation, and characterization of bioinks, with particular emphasis on their rheological and mechanical properties. Additionally, it examines printability in relation to printing parameters and maps the process from curing to the final construct's suitability, addressing aspects such as vascularization and the integration of structure and function within the framework of standardization. This chapter also highlights the current limitations of each topic and subtopic, recent developments, future possibilities, and potential pathways for clinical and industrial applications.

1.2 Advances in Bioinks

The rapid advancement of bioprinting technologies necessitates corresponding progress in bioink formulations, which are crucial for creating structures with desired biological and mechanical characteristics. This development is significant as it directly influences the quality, functionality, and potential applications of bioprinted tissues and organs (Ciulla et al. 2023). Optimizing the rheological properties of bioinks is crucial for achieving successful printing results and enhancing positive biological effects, such as ensuring biocompatibility and supporting cell viability, which are vital for effective tissue regeneration (Lai and Wang 2023). To tackle the challenges associated with the extrusion-based bioprinting of hyaluronic acid, selecting the right bioink and process parameters is crucial (Askari et al. 2020). Achieving high-resolution bioprinting often involves a delicate balance between the viscosity of the bioink, speed of the print head, and size of the nozzle opening, as these are crucial factors (Lamberger et al. 2024). For instance, multicomponent hydrogels have emerged as appealing alternatives to overcome the limitations of single-component bio-inks. This blend of approaches leads to enhanced printability, shape accuracy, and biofunctionality (Cui et al. 2020), enabling the creation of intricate biomimetic settings that replicate the complexity of natural tissues, such as the extracellular matrix (ECM). Nevertheless, despite these advancements, there remains a considerable shortage of printable bioinks capable of maintaining long-term physiological functions (Ashammakhi et al. 2019b, c; Barrulas and Corvo 2023).

Specifically, employing disease-specific heart tissue bioinks derived from the decellularized ECM of both healthy and diseased tissues can present a novel approach to replicate in vivo physiology more accurately and gain a more detailed understanding of the mechanistic aspects of diseases (Ashammakhi et al. 2022; Rossi et al. 2024). Such a quest for better bioink integration resonates with the progress in microfluidic approaches for bioprinting, which allow precise manipulation of tiny amounts of liquid, cells, and molecules to assemble complex 3D patterns with high spatial resolution (Ciulla et al. 2023). In other words, bioinks are coaxially co-deposited with the sheath fluids of a cross-linker, which is composed of ultraviolet (UV)-initiated crosslinking of hydrogels, resulting in printed fibers for integrating microfluidic systems in conventional extrusion-based bioprinting. This convergence enables the manipulation of structural and compositional aspects during real-time printing (Ciulla et al. 2023). Despite the good definition enabled by microfluidic bioprinting, this approach is currently limited in industrial adoption due to the lack of available yield management (YM) technologies, and the mechanical properties of bioink materials have been inadequate to date (Askari et al. 2020). Consequently, novel bioink formulations with improved printability, biocompatibility, and biomimetic characteristics are urgently needed to fully exploit the potential of advanced 3D bioprinting methods in complex TE applications (Cheng et al. 2024). In addition, addressing the problem of printhead clogging due to particles and cellulosic materials contained in different bioinks is essential for maintaining both the quality of printing and the efficiency of the process (Iqbal et al. 2024). To address these challenges, it is essential to develop new bioinks with enhanced rheological characteristics and techniques to prevent particle aggregation, ensuring consistent material flow through nozzles. In addition to rheological behavior, biomaterials should be crafted with compositions that support cell proliferation during perfusion, while also possessing strong mechanical properties and structural integrity (Kafili et al. 2024). Integration of these advancements with 3D bioprinting technologies marks a major leap in the creation of intricate and functional tissue structures. This capability is crucial, particularly when designing tissues with vascular systems. Additionally, they allow for the precise handling and manipulation of small volumes (<100 μL) of liquids, cells, or biomaterials in a controlled manner (Ciulla et al. 2023). This comprehensive approach enables the development of layered micro-structures with intricate gradients that closely replicate the design of natural tissues (Mohammadi and Cidonio 2023). While microfluidics-based approaches provide precise, high-resolution control over the spatial distribution of cells, biomaterials, and signaling cues, numerous challenges remain in upscaling these intricate architectures toward larger 3D macro-assemblies (Ashammakhi et al. 2018a; Davoodi et al. 2020; Mohammadi and Cidonio 2023; Tavafoghi et al. 2021). However, the stiffness of micro fluidically fabricated constructs must be high enough to support well-defined complex structures without any (including multilayered) collapse for structural durability (Zhou 2017). Additional work is needed to address the problems in producing complex microvascular networks, which are essential for TE, as native organs have intricate structures with different cell types and physicochemical gradients that require effective nutrient and waste transport systems (Rahmati et al. 2020). Such systems are crucial for the viability and functioning of engineered tissues, preventing necrosis in thicker engineered constructs (Iqbal et al. 2024; Nwokoye and Abilez 2024). Thus, the development of more advanced processes that combine bioprinting with microfluidics is critical for generating complex 3D microvascular networks, which will allow mass transfer to large, viable tissue constructs (Zhou 2017). This usually requires the inclusion of advanced microfluidic systems and microscale technologies to generate dense beds of capillaries for efficient oxygen diffusion and nutrient exchange, which surpasses the limit of passive diffusion of approximately 200–250 μm in tissues (Fantini et al. 2024). Such improvements are essential for the long-term stability and physiological relevance of engineered tissues, especially when considering transplantation applications or the generation of more complex in vitro platforms (Ma et al. 2018).

The lack of working microvasculature continues to act as a major barrier to the development of thicker, physiologically relevant tissue constructs and pressures new strategies for overcoming hypoxia in implanted cell-laden tissues (Goldenberg et al. 2021; Vajda et al. 2021). This issue underscores the significance of teaching methods that integrate vascular networks into bioprinted products, allowing the delivery of vital nutrients and removal of waste, which are crucial for maintaining cell viability and function in larger tissues (Nwokoye and Abilez 2024). Despite significant in vitro advancements in developing microvascular networks, a considerable gap remains between these developments and the clinical need for enhanced vascularized tissues or organs (Zhang et al. 2020). This highlights the potential for developing advanced bioprinting methods that enable the creation of more complex materials with blood vessel-like structures (Iqbal et al. 2024). Nonetheless, the physiological relevance of these models is significantly undermined by the absence of native perfusable blood vessels, which are essential for delivering nutrients and oxygen and eliminating metabolic waste. This limitation becomes even more evident when working with structures that exceed the typical diffusion length scale of approximately 100–200 μm (Dobos et al. 2021; Zhao et al. 2022). This pressing issue necessitates the development of dependable vascularization methods. These methods focus on the geometric manipulation of biomaterials and other elements, including endothelial cells, smooth muscle cells, and growth factors, to stimulate the formation of new vessels with functional vascular structures within bioprinted tissue constructs (Shahabipour et al. 2019; Zhang et al. 2020).

One major challenge in TE is the vascularization of large 3D cell-scaffold structures generated through 3D bioprinting. Without blood vessels, the delivery of nutrients to cells is hindered beyond a range of roughly 100–200 μm, leading to low cell survival rates (Naghieh et al. 2017; Turnbull et al. 2020). This constraint demands the generation of functioning vasculature networks on the scale of both micrometers and millimeters within intricate structures, such as the liver, kidney, or heart, for perfusion and integration of grafts into the host vascular system (Miri et al. 2018). Therefore, the bottleneck of vascularization must be overcome to facilitate the clinical translation of bioprinted tissues and organs, as it heavily influences their long-term survival and function after implantation (Askari et al. 2020). One of the major hurdles for TE and regenerative medicine is the connection of a host functional vascular network to artificial tissues (Sriphutkiat et al. 2019). Strategies to address this include the use of isolated 3D printing of microvasculature, revascularizations strategies, and the addition of oxygen-generating particles (Ashammakhi et al. 2020; Erdem et al. 2020, 2022; Shahabipour et al. 2019); however, these approaches have their own difficulties in developing a perfusable network for wider applications (Goldenberg et al. 2021). Among them, sacrificial biomaterials to fabricate tubular lumen structures that can be further lined with endothelial cells and perfused are the most promising methods for vagus nerve stimulation engineering (Naghieh et al. 2017). While sacrificial bioprinting offers enhanced control over the shape of 3D printed lumens compared to the self-assembly of endothelial cells, it is limited by its inability to accurately replicate the small size of typical capillaries (Nwokoye and Abilez 2024). Furthermore, even with significant advancements in established biofabrication techniques, creating hierarchical vascular networks that are both perfusable and anatomically accurate, with diverse cellular compositions, remains a difficult task (Askari et al. 2020).

One key to overcoming this hurdle is the efficient differentiation of human pluripotent stem cells (hPSCs) into vascular cells (despite current challenges in reproducible lineage-specific differentiation and long-term retention of the mature cell phenotype), offering a viable platform to model diseases or employ drug screening (Nwokoye and Abilez 2024). Although seeding and encapsulation techniques can embed endothelial cells in scaffolds (Abukunna et al. 2025), randomly oriented, relatively non-interconnected vessels are typically obtained (Naghieh et al. 2017). In addition, there is a limited selection of biomaterials that can be used to develop these microchannels, and there is a lack of appropriate niches for endothelial cell functionality and network maturation (Shafiee et al. 2021). Therefore, the pursuit of new biomaterials that more closely replicate the ECM and encourage organized vascular network formation is ongoing. One approach to overcome these limitations is the fabrication of degradable sacrificial materials, improvement of hierarchical scaffold designs, and process optimization for clinical applications with improved functionality and efficiency for tissue regeneration and vascular research (Iqbal et al. 2024).

One widely used approach is to print sacrificial templates into materials such as agarose, gelatin, and pluronics. This provides a means to create complex microfluidic network structures inside cell-seeded hydrogels (Gold et al. 2018). These sacrificial inclusions are then removed after printing, leaving a lattice network of perfusable channels. Such a network can then be deendothelialized to recreate the working vasculature (Nwokoye and Abilez 2024). This allows for an unprecedented level of control over the morphological and dimensional features of these manufactured microvascular networks, which may be configured to resemble natural capillaries (Shafiee et al. 2021). Sugar-based sacrificial templating, including engineered sugar glasses, has been established as a powerful technique for fabricating 3D perivascular networks that can perfuse and branch within larger tissue constructs (Iqbal et al. 2024). Specifically, intricate bifurcating channels with a dome diameter as small as 150 μm can be generated via extrusion-based methods that emulate the hierarchical organization of natural vascular plexuses (Lim et al. 2019). Nonetheless, while the sacrificial templating method offers advantages for customizing and implementing desired vascular structures, there are significant obstacles to achieving successful cellular integration with sufficient long-term patency that meets clinical requirements (Iqbal et al. 2024), particularly in intricate organ systems. Additionally, sacrificial materials should be easily removable from regeneration sites, as their presence without degradation in regenerated tissues or their harsh extraction can compromise cellular viability and the integrity of the developed scaffolds (Iqbal et al. 2024).

1.2.1 Advances in Bioink Biomaterials

A. **Stimuli-Responsive Materials for Four-Dimensional (4D)-Bioprinting (4DBP)**

The advent of 4D printing technologies, which allow for temporal control and programming of the 3D printing process, has opened new possibilities for designing scaffolds that can alter their shape and biophysical properties in response to environmental changes (Ashammakhi et al. 2018a, b; Ashammakhi and Kaarela 2017; Pountos et al. 2023; Taylor et al. 2024). This adaptability is crucial for creating vascularized tissues, where the ability to respond in real-time to physiological signals is fundamental to the maturation of vessels and, to some extent, their long-term functionality (Ashammakhi et al. 2019e; Dodda et al. 2025; Miri et al. 2018).

However, the systematic description of bioink components, process parameters, and their associations with the biological properties of constructions is far from being fully defined (Miri et al. 2018). Therefore, it is necessary to standardize the protocols for rheological and mechanical characterization of bioinks in TE applications. These protocols would not only promote replicability but also facilitate predictions of processability. This landscape is further complicated by intrinsic biological response variability, which requires rigorous statistical analysis for the interpretation of experimental outcomes and evidence of materials' performance (Wang et al. 2021). Moreover, the interactions between bioink constituents, printing parameters, and post-printing maturation protocols are essential for designing the biological and mechanical behaviors of engineered tissues (Vyas et al. 2023). It is crucial to control these parameters to enable tissue mimicking and functionalization of 3D-bioprinted constructs for regenerative medicine (Alzoubi et al. 2023).

The critical elements of bioinks for 3D bioprinting biocompatibility, printability, and mechanical performance are key factors that influence cell viability and ensuing tissue formation (Agarwal et al. 2022; Ashammakhi et al. 2019b; Ashammakhi and Kaarela 2018; Potyondy et al. 2021). They presented that such properties are frequently opposing each other, and the improvement of one feature may be at the expense of the other, which requires a huge challenge in design and formulation (Bova et al. 2020). Recently, the focus has shifted to the development of stimuli-responsive bioinks that can respond adaptively to the in-vivo microenvironment and thus have been proposed as suitable candidates (Antezana et al. 2023). For example, novel smart hydrogels with mechanically tunable responses to stimuli, such as pH, temperature, or enzymatic activity, are under investigation to more closely mimic the dynamic nature of native tissues (Han et al. 2023). These adaptive materials are required for the design of bioinspired porous structures to control cell differentiation, tissue regeneration, and vascularization in a tunable temporal manner (Cui et al. 2018). This may include the addition of micro- and/or nanoparticle species to hydrogel matrices capable of transducing chemical or mechanical signals, which will increase the bioactivity and functionality of the tissue constructs.

A major shortcoming of the stimuli-sensitive materials reported to date is that they are deformed in a simple manner (e.g., encapsulation/folding) and are thus unsuitable for use in more complex physiological environments (Antezana et al. 2023). More advanced materials that can perform complex multi-mode reconfigurations, in a way that faithfully mimics the dynamic processes occurring in living biological systems, need to be developed (Ashammakhi et al. 2019c; Bakhtiary et al. 2021; Wu et al. 2020). The desire for such printed dynamic soft tissues has invigorated developments in 4D printing, a methodology in which intelligent materials inserted within 3D matrices can actuate and program morphing over time via computer-guided geometries (Vyas et al. 2023). Programmable shapeshifting in 4D bioprinted structures has significant potential for both TE and soft robotics applications; however, long-term mechanical stability to repeated shape changes is a critical area of study (Mathur et al. 2022).

In line with this, researchers have recently explored the use of naturally occurring biodegradable substances, such as cellulose and chitosan, to create sustainable 4D printable materials. These materials have the potential to reduce environmental impact while enhancing biocompatibility for applications in organ design and tissue regeneration (Antezana et al. 2023). Building on the capabilities of 3D bioprinting, 4D printing advances further by incorporating dynamic design elements into the printed structure. Over time, these structures can alter their shape, function, or properties in response to external stimuli, such as pH and temperature changes (Alanazi et al. 2025). This innovative method utilizes intelligent materials to construct dynamic biological systems that can self-fold, self-assemble, or transform as programmed, offering an unmatched capability to control tissue development and maturation (Miri et al. 2018).

For instance, hydrogel composite bioinks are employed in 4D biomimetic printing to create objects exhibiting intricate morphing behaviors. These structures can be altered to imitate the appearance of natural flowers and leaves when exposed to moisture (Miri et al. 2018). This moisture-sensitive behavior is especially advantageous for structures designed to operate in a watery environment (Miri et al. 2018). The adjustable characteristics of these materials facilitate the creation of intricate tissue TE scaffolds that closely resemble natural tissues and respond to physiological signals. This adaptability ultimately extends the lifespan of grafts and enhances functional recovery (Qu et al. 2023). The groundbreaking idea of 4D printing enables the creation of structures that not only replicate the original anatomical form but also adapt biomechanically, integrate with the host's microenvironment, and perform their intended functions (Askari et al. 2020). 4D printing enhances traditional 3D printing by utilizing smart materials that can alter their form when exposed to specific environmental triggers, thereby adding a temporal aspect to the printed items (Lai and Wang 2023). Therefore, polyplex-loaded 4D-bioprinted structures can be designed to emulate and respond to the complex physiological conditions found in-vivo, unlike static 3D scaffolds (Faber et al. 2023). Numerous "smart" materials, such as shape memory polymers and hydrogels, can transition from an origami form to a specific shape when activated by external elements such as humidity or ion concentration. This makes them particularly well-suited for use in regenerative medicine (Atila and Kumaravel 2023).

The idea of 4D printing permits us to encode intricate changes in shape into 3D structures that are composed of materials that are responsive to external stimuli, leading to their post-fabrication shaping or evolution (Mathur et al. 2022). Such a capability places 4D fabrication in the realm of rising technologies expected to impact biological applications by allowing the production of complex shapes with spatiotemporal guided control over structure and function in response to environmental cues, thus augmenting the natural tissue physiology process (Bonetti and Scalet 2024). Numerous materials have been used for 4D printing, including dielectric elastomers (Chen et al. 2023), shape memory polymers, and stimuli-responsive hydrogels (Ramezani and Ripin 2023), which are regarded as crucial for the development of 4D printing as a viable manufacturing technique in biomedical engineering. The stimulus responsiveness (e.g., to changes in temperature, pH, light, and magnetic fields) of these materials can be tuned, making them highly suitable for drug delivery, biosensing, and smart medical device applications (Imam et al. 2021). This methodology enables the "programming" of deformation into the material itself, thus negating the requirement for complex geometric features (Asciak et al. 2024). The motivation is the existence of material properties, such as shape memory, that cause some polymers to experience deformation in a reversible manner to return to equilibrium under certain conditions (Kanu et al. 2019). These smart materials are often exploited through mechanisms such as glass transition upon heating and transition from metastable state to stable state and can be controlled by the user for shape reconfiguration (Agarwal et al. 2022).

In addition, the advanced control of material behavior achievable with 4D printing will permit adaptive biomedical devices that can interact dynamically with biological conditions or environments, such as drug delivery systems triggering the release of therapeutics because of certain biomarkers (Antezana et al. 2023). The revolutionary idea of 4D printing involves creating materials that can change over time in response to varying conditions, such as temperature, light, or electric fields, thereby producing objects designed to undergo transformation during use (Antezana et al. 2023).

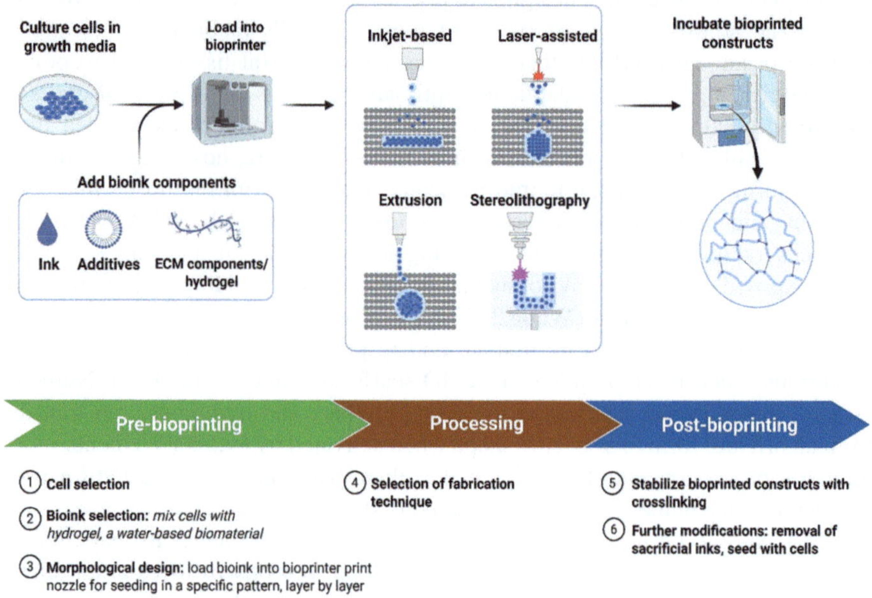

Fig. 1.1 Illustrates how bioprinting workflows improve bioink biomaterials

The innovation here lies in incorporating the time aspect into manufacturing processes and collaborating with leaders in the field of dynamic biomaterial elements and tissue structures that can be modified in vivo (Elhadad et al. 2023). The behavior of these stimuli-driven constructions enhances the utility of 4D printed materials in the fields of TE and regenerative medicine (Kim et al. 2024). The versatile characteristics of these adaptive materials broaden the scope of 4D printing to include applications in muscle and neural TE and advanced drug delivery systems. This capability facilitates the creation of intricate and dynamic biological structures that can replicate the body's natural microenvironment and interact effectively with host tissues for improved integration (Mathur et al. 2022). The attributes of 4D printing make it a superior technology compared to traditional manufacturing methods for creating and building configurations that can change dynamically (Mathur et al. 2022). The bioink biomaterial development using bioprinting is shown in Fig. 1.1.

1.2.2 Advances in Cellular Components

A. **Individual cells (primary cells, cell lines, stem cells, and induced pluripotent stem cells, iPSCs)**

Primary cells are isolated directly from living tissues and thus maintain high physiological relevance; however, they frequently possess only limited proliferative potential and require specialized culture conditions. Induced pluripotent stem cells (iPSCs) are a breakthrough that provides an unlimited source of patient-specific cells for differentiation into any desired cell lineage. This new technique bypasses the moral and immunological issues associated with embryonic stem (ES) cells (Ashammakhi et al. 2022; Bajada et al. 2008; Belk et al. 2020; Khademhosseini et al. 2020; Ziaran et al. 2025). In addition, developments in genome editing technology, including CRISPR/Cas9, have made it possible to make precise gene modifications in these stem cells, thereby expanding their therapeutic power and modeling diseases. These cellular building blocks are essential for developing advanced in vitro models of drug discovery and personalized medicine, that is, for microphysiological systems and organ-on-a-chip platforms (Zhang et al. 2023a, b). These sophisticated cell models permit better prediction of drug response and toxicity, less dependence on experimental animals, and faster development of novel therapeutic approaches (Bg et al. 2023). Proper regulation of differentiation and maturation is critical for generating tissues with appropriate architecture and mechanical properties (Antezana et al. 2023). Spheroidal and organotypic spheroid cultures at more complex level, cultured multi-cellular spheroids or organoids are formed by aggregation of cells from either stem cells or primary tissue explants, which introduce additional layers of physiological complexity as they recapitulate the architecture and function of the originating tissues (Hill et al. 2021; O'Hern et al. 2025). These complex cell assemblies that lie between traditional two-dimensional culture systems and intact organs are used extensively to provide improved models of disease, drug screening, and regenerative medicine (Lai and Wang 2023).

These next-generation multidimensional cellular systems, including cell self-assembly, biomaterials, and tubular microfluidic devices, are crucial for faithfully recapitulating the complex in vivo environments of both normal and diseased tissues (Bassi et al. 2021). To overcome the restricted conditions of conventional two-dimensional (2D) cell cultures that cannot mirror complex in vivo cellular crosstalk, environmental cues, and the physiology of 3D tissue architecture, innovative solutions have been proposed (Bassi et al. 2021; Fetah et al. 2019). The inclusion of hiPSCs is particularly important because it allows the generation of patient-derived systems with greater relevance to human physiology and pathophysiology, thus improving their predictive value for disease modeling and drug discovery (Masi et al. 2020). For example, the engraftment of breast epithelial cells using ECM extracts has yielded 3D ducts and milk protein expression, which cannot be achieved in 2D culture systems (Abady et al. 2024).

Moreover, advanced 3D in vitro systems, such as spheroids, organoids, and organs-on-a-chip, present more intricate models that more accurately replicate the complexity of living tissues. These models represent significant progress in preclinical drug testing and disease modeling compared to conventional 2D cell cultures (Bassi et al. 2021; Foglizzo et al. 2022). To successfully discover new drugs and develop disease models, it is crucial to precisely mimic the natural structure of tissues and cell shape. This can be accomplished through the biomimicry of 3D cellular models, particularly organoids (Fang and Eglen 2017; Silva-Pedrosa et al. 2023). Organoids hold great potential for exploring 3D tissue cultures that naturally develop into a variety of cell types, often mirroring organ systems (van Berlo et al. 2021). They serve as a strong alternative to 2D cultures, which cannot replicate the

3D microenvironment, thus offering enhanced relevance for disease modeling and drug testing (Gaetani and Chimenti 2023).

The development momentum of organoids is a result of the vision that they can transform science and medicine with models recapitulating the structural design and complex function of human organs (Zhang et al. 2024b). Organoids are more relevant to human immune responses and pharmacokinetic properties than traditional animal models, strengthening their utility in evaluating drug responses in humans and understanding disease mechanisms (Lee et al. 2021). Using feeder-dependent or feeder-free conditions (using the corresponding culture media), these 3D cultures, in particular organoids, can be cultured long-term because they have self-renewal and differentiation potential into distinct cell types obtained from either embryonic/adult stem cells or induced pluripotent stem cells (Aqeilan 2021). This feature allows the generation of tissue-like complex microenvironments and mimics in vivo interactions under laboratory conditions, making it a physiologically relevant tool for testing cell responses (Alnasser 2025). The shift from standard 2D cell cultures to more sophisticated 3D culture systems, such as organoids, constitutes significant progress in compensating for the inability of 2D models to mimic whole tissue microenvironments (Abbas et al. 2023). These robust 3D models present a more accurate mimic of organ function and disease, thus potentially refining the predictability of drug efficacy and toxicity screening (Alnasser 2025). Organoids are a type of 3D tissue-like construct generated through the self-organization, self-renewal, and differentiation potential of stem cells and provide anatomical and physiological close mimicry to organs (Matsui and Shinozawa 2021). This technology facilitates the creation of 3D structures that possess the shape, strength, and biological characteristics of an organ, serving as a bridge between in vivo and in vitro research (Mulaudzi et al. 2023). Overall, advances in cellular components are illustrated in Fig. 1.2.

B. **Cell aggregates (organoids, spheroids, assembloids)**

Organoids have proven to be extremely valuable in drug discovery, disease modeling, and regenerative medicine because of their ability to mimic the complexity of human organs (Han et al. 2024). These self-organizing systems derived from stem cells can accurately replicate the physiological characteristics of natural tissues, making them more suitable than traditional two-dimensional (2D) cell cultures for studying complex biological processes and developing new therapeutic approaches. They introduce patient-derived models for studying diseases, offering significant benefits over animal systems when examining both developmental and disease biology (Verstegen et al. 2025). The transition from two-dimensional cell culture techniques to advanced biofabrication using 3D organoid-on-a-chip technology exemplifies the significant advancements in biomedical research. This development enables precise control over cellular microenvironments and the construction of tissue structures, facilitating the creation of more accurate disease models and drug screening assays (Abady et al. 2024).

Organoids inherently form tissue-specific 3D structures, facilitating the exploration of developmental biology and understanding of disease mechanisms (Werschler

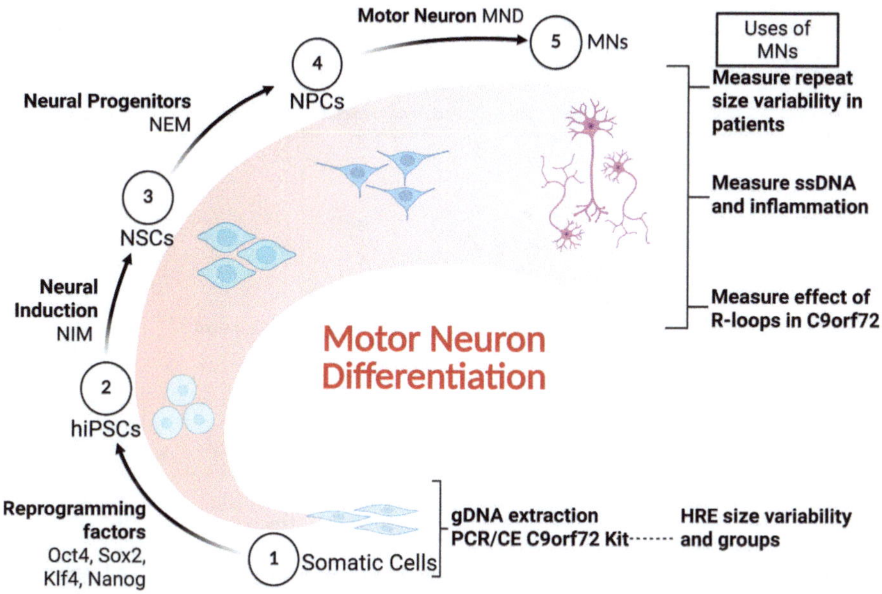

Fig. 1.2 Demonstration of the process of transforming induced pluripotent stem cells (iPSCs) into fully developed motor neurons associated with C9 or f72 hexanucleotide repeat expansion. *NIM* Neural Induction Medium, *NEM* Neural Expansion Medium, *MND* Motor Neuron Differentiation, *MNM* Motor Neuron Maturation

et al. 2024). This feature is crucial because 2D cell culture models fail to accurately represent in vivo environments, leading to inconsistencies in research findings (Mazrouei et al. 2020). While these models offer clear benefits as patient-specific models and have a structure that mimics living tissue, their potential for clinical application is limited because of their simpler complexity compared to human organs (Fan et al. 2025). One significant obstacle is the development of a vascular system; without an effective vascular network, the exchange of nutrients and oxygen is hindered, which can negatively impact the long-term viability and development of large organoids (Chaudhary and Chakraborty 2022). Consequently, the underdevelopment and inconsistency of organoid models hinder their broader use in disease modeling and regenerative medicine (Yao et al. 2024).

Nonetheless, the absence of standardized protocols limits their widespread use and hinders the ability to compare results across different research settings, potentially obstructing their integration into clinical practice (Arjmand et al. 2022; Pountos et al. 2019; Reyes et al. 2024; Taylor et al. 2024). Addressing these constraints is crucial for fully leveraging organoids in personalized medicine and drug development, including high-throughput screening and toxicology studies (Aqeilan 2021). Variability and consistency in organoids across different batches pose significant challenges, mainly due to variations in culture methods and cellular makeup (Aqeilan 2021). Moreover, the lack of key non-parenchymal cell

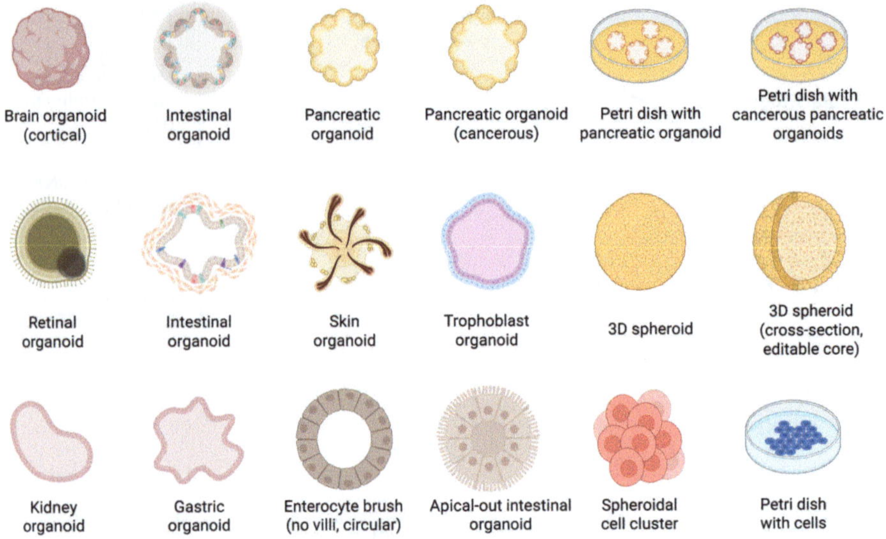

Fig. 1.3 Illustration of different cell aggregate types, including organoids and spheroids. (Figure produced by the authors using Biorender.com)

populations and functional vasculature in current organoid models might limit their degree of physiological relevance and long-term survival, leading to immature differentiation and an unrealistic representation of complex multifactorial pathologies (Childs 2024; Giorgetti et al. 2022). Several forms of cell aggregates, such as organoids and spheroids, are shown in Fig. 1.3.

C. ***Cell parts (membranes, extracellular vesicles [EVs])***

In particular, the lack of vasculature, immune populations, or proper neural innervation will be a hurdle to more closely model physiological complexity and function with organoids. This limitation has impaired their use in disease modeling and drug discovery (Ergün and Wörsdörfer 2022). Without these essential factors, organoids are limited in size and metabolism, which limits the study of organ-level interactions and systemic functions (Hu et al. 2024). In addition, the immune microenvironment of different tissues is difficult to recapitulate using organoids with complete simulation capability, which restricts their application for comprehensive modeling of immune-related diseases and drug responses (Huang et al. 2021). Moreover, the lack of 'standardized" procedures to compare generated organoid models hinders their general integration and translation in diverse research milieus (Bock et al. 2020). A limitation is that current organoids may mimic fetal tissues more than adult, fully developed organs, which influences disease modeling of adult-onset diseases and long-term drug responses (Rossi et al. 2018). Another limitation is the batch-to-batch variation in organoid production, which is commonly associated with inconsistencies in naturally generated ECM, such as Matrigel, making reproducibility and standardization between studies challenging (Mulaudzi et al. 2023). Together, these are the major challenges that clearly show the necessity of innovative bioengineered approaches, including highly controlled microfluidic systems and synthetic hydrogels, to overcome the constraints defined by conventional organoid culture conditions and move toward more precision for enhanced biomimetic and replicable models (Naderi-Meshkin et al. 2023). Biochemical and biophysical properties of designer matrices that allow specific control over these properties are needed to improve the self-organization and patterning of stem cells (Garreta et al. 2020). Novel synthetic hydrogels proved to some extent be able to circumvent the limitations associated with conventional matrixes, creating excellent physiological conditions for organoids growth and maturation as they led to an increase in available detectable lumen-like structures (Yao et al. 2024). Hence, these engineered matrices enable tunable manipulation of the biochemical and biomechanical cues that cause cells to self-organize, overcoming the challenge of generating heterogeneous organoids within non-defined natural hydrogels (Kim et al. 2023). Accordingly, new hydrogel formulations are being explored that more closely recapitulate the native ECM and provide greater control over substrate properties to guide organoid formation (Gan et al. 2023). In summary, these developments may help generate more sophisticated and unconventional organoid models that can better mimic physiological functions and related pathologies. The membranes, extracellular vehicles (EVs), and other cytosolic constituents are shown on Fig. 1.4.

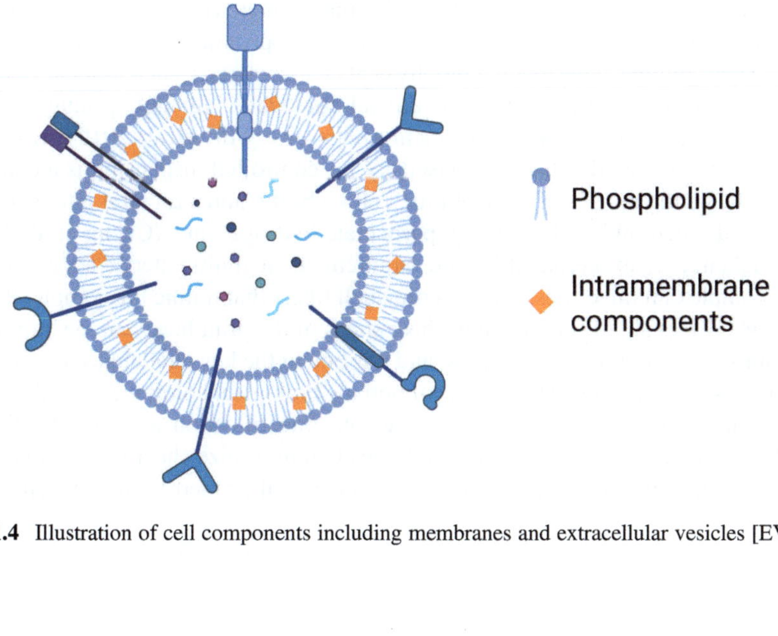

Fig. 1.4 Illustration of cell components including membranes and extracellular vesicles [EVs]

1.2.3 Advances in Additives

A. ***Biomolecules, pharmaceutical drugs, therapeutics, diagnostics***

The limitations of existing organoid models, including the lack of sufficient vascularization and innervation, further emphasize the need for better-described AM methods to increase structural complexity and function (Mulaudzi et al. 2023). New biofabrication techniques can overcome these limitations by incorporating vascular networks, stromal cells, and immune compartments into microphysiological systems, thereby creating models that more accurately mimic physiological processes (Huang et al. 2021). These sophisticated techniques frequently employ bioinks with specific viscoelastic properties and biocompatibility, enabling the precise printing of cells with meticulous control over microstructures (Traldi et al. 2023). This method allows the creation of hierarchical structures that replicate the intricate cellular patterns found in natural tissues, facilitating the development of physiologically relevant assemblies while reducing reactions from the host tissue (Garreta et al. 2020). Innovative solutions of this nature are essential for addressing issues related to size limitations and the delivery of nutrients and oxygen, which currently hinder the long-term sustainability and physiological makeup of larger organoids. Furthermore, integrating microfluidic devices with bioprinted structures enhances the control over the cellular microenvironment and nutrient supply, ultimately leading to the creation of more complex tissue models with improved functionality for disease modeling and drug testing. Nonetheless, producing clinical-grade constructs and adhering to Good Manufacturing Practices remain significant challenges in conducting long-term experiments with patient-derived tissues (Paradiso et al. 2022).

Smart hydrogels, a type of bioink, are becoming increasingly important for their role in the advancement and customization of 3D bioprinting (Nwokoye and Abilez 2024). These bioinks have distinct biophysical characteristics, such as ideal viscosity and mechanical strength, which are crucial for achieving high printability and maintaining cell viability to form functional tissues (Miri et al. 2019). However, obtaining the desired rheology and viscosity for controlled dispensing is a daunting task, as the gentle criteria of injectability, cell viability, and structural integrity must be satisfied when inkjet-3D printing particulate hydrogel inks (Cheng et al. 2024). This challenge is exacerbated by the requirement of multimaterial approaches to create complex architectures, such as core-shell fibers that mimic the complexities of the ECM (Hill et al. 2021). The high shear stress of the print head can be harmful to the viability and performance of cells, and it is one of the key challenges for retaining the fragile structure (Iqbal et al. 2024) of porcine biological components within these complicated bioinks. Therefore, the systematic identification and optimization of bioink formulations and printing technologies that minimize shear forces are critical for fabricating high-resolution, viable, and functional printed tissues (Cheng et al. 2024).

Furthermore, this problem is further complicated by the need to preserve cellular viability and phenotype during long-term cultures and large (bioreactor-size) constructs due to potential metabolic needs imposed by 3D structures as well as a possible development of nutrient gradients within them. Bioinks that better mimic the structure of living tissues are required for pharmaceutical drug discovery and toxicology screening to align high-fidelity tissue models with physiological responses and pathological conditions (Vyas et al. 2023). When formulating bioinks, it is crucial to achieve a balance between printability and biological requirements, such as cell encapsulation, growth, and differentiation (Agarwal et al. 2022).

To achieve precise jetting and accurate deposition, it is essential to meticulously manage factors such as viscosity and surface tension while ensuring a suitable biochemical and biomechanical environment for the encapsulated cells (Cheng et al. 2024). Despite significant progress, numerous obstacles must be overcome because of the inherent lack of mechanical properties in many natural biomaterials and the difficulties in replicating the complex biological and structural nature of the native ECM using current biofabrication methods (Rasouli et al. 2024).

For bioprinted constructs to achieve their therapeutic potential, especially in regenerative medicine, they must be able to integrate with host tissue to ensure not only the long-term survival of cells but also their functionality and differentiation (Alzoubi et al. 2023). This integration necessitates biomaterials that are specifically designed for in vivo degradation, are biocompatible, and can promote suitable cellular responses, such as vascularization and innervation, after implantation (Rossi et al. 2024). These stringent requirements pose a challenge in balancing the printability, mechanical properties, and biological functionality of the constructs, necessitating innovative approaches in bioink design and production (Santoso 2021). The need for versatile bioinks that can replicate the biological and mechanical characteristics of various tissue types, such as bone, brain, and blood vessels, is significant and currently unmet (Ashammakhi et al. 2019b, c; Valot et al. 2019). Furthermore, creating implants that can successfully integrate with tissues and endure over the long term after implantation remains a significant hurdle. This is particularly important for managing the immune response and mitigating the risk of fibrosis associated with implantation.

Despite these advancements, finding bioinks that can effectively facilitate cell differentiation and tissue development into functional structures suitable for in vivo implantation remains a challenge (Montero et al. 2019). In diagnostic fields such as high-throughput screening (HTS) and disease modeling, it is essential to create bioinks that can accurately mimic the unique microenvironment of a disease and the associated cellular reactions. This is frequently only achievable through accurate cues and mechanics that better replicate the fidelity of a pathological situation. These difficulties are being overcome through ongoing research to develop multicomponent bioinks in which stimuli-responsive polymers, growth factors, and decellularized ECM components can be combined to modulate the mechanical and biochemical cues that are essential for proper tissue formation and function (Rosellini et al. 2023).

B. ***Functional particles (iron, gold, oxygen generators)***

The integration of functional particles into bioinks also provides extra potential to improve mechanical properties, drug delivery capability, and biomimetic cues (Cheng et al. 2024). The selected fillers were intended to stabilize the matrix, potentially introduce specific topological characteristics, or offer magnetic or electrical properties that influence cell differentiation and arrangement (Cheng et al. 2024). Another viable approach involves the simultaneous printing of multiple bioinks, each with distinct compositions and characteristics to enhance biomimicry. This method aims to create an implanted tissue graft with controlled mechanical stiffness and selective cell growth promotion, while also concentrating on the targeted delivery of drugs or growth factors (Michel and Auzély-Velty 2020). These stringent requirements pose significant challenges in achieving a balance between the printability, mechanical characteristics, and biological functions of bioinks, necessitating innovative approaches for their design and production (Santos-Beato et al. 2022). Beyond biocompatibility and biodegradability, there is a growing demand for versatile bioinks that can be applied across various uses, aligning with the distinct biological and mechanical characteristics of different tissue types, such as bones, brains, and blood vessels (Valot et al. 2019). Looking ahead, the development of implants that enhance integration and ensure long-term success will remain a vital area of research, particularly from an immunological perspective. Additionally, there are ongoing concerns regarding fibrosis caused by viral attacks or the accumulation of cancer cells (Ciulla et al. 2023).

Nonetheless, creating bioinks that facilitate cell differentiation and maturation of tissues into genuine 3D structures suitable for implantation in living organisms remains a significant hurdle (Montero et al. 2019). In the realm of diagnostics, particularly from the standpoint of HTS and studies on the onset of diseases, it is crucial to create bioinks that accurately replicate the microenvironmental conditions associated with various diseases and their cellular responses. This often requires the integration of specific biochemical signals and mechanical characteristics to better simulate the disease state. To address these challenges, composite bioinks have been designed that incorporate stimuli-responsive polymers, growth factors, or decellularized ECM components to deliver the mechanical properties and biochemical cues essential for tissue development and functionality (Rosellini et al. 2023). Recent research has also explored the creation of smart bioinks, which can detect stimuli such as light or changes in pH as external triggers and modify the ECM structure to direct cells to form tissues in real time (Antezana et al. 2023).

Gold nanorods have been incorporated into gelatin methacrylate hydrogels to develop conductive bioinks for 3D bioprinting of cardiac tissues, and increased cell adhesion and synchronized contraction have been observed (Esmaeili et al. 2021). These electrically conductive bioinks, which can also be supplemented with microcarriers to improve the compressive strength of these tissues and provide targeted drug delivery capability, are critical for the development of engineered cardiac tissue with advanced levels of function (Valot et al. 2019). These novel substrates allow the fabrication of constructs that mimic native tissue arrangements and drive functional maturation essential for regeneration applications (Michel and Auzély-Velty 2020).

For example, incorporating gold nanorods into gelatin methacryloyl (GelMA) and alginate bioinks resulted in higher scaffold conductivity and electrical coupling in 3D printed cardiac patches (Wang et al. 2021). Outside cardiac applications, the rational addition of nanoparticles and other nanomaterials to bioinks to create nanocomposite bioinks is important for improving an array of TE constructs, such as bone, cartilage, dental, and cardiovascular tissues (Loukelis et al. 2023). Such nanocomposites (graphene, carbon nanotubes, or metal nanoparticles), as they present tunable mechanical properties and improved bioactivity and electrical conductivity (and therefore even more sophisticated cell-material interactions), may support tissue formation processes better than micro composites (Zhang et al. 2023a, b). For example, the addition of conductive nanoparticles (such as graphene, graphene oxide, and gold nanoparticles) can contribute to the development of electroactive tissues and facilitate electrical stimulation during culture, which is particularly important for cardiac, muscle, and neural tissues (Alizadeh et al. 2021; Michel and Auzély-Velty 2020). Moreover, the use of gold nanoparticles in hydrogel-based bioinks has been shown to increase the biocompatibility and bioactivity of the scaffold, inducing cell proliferation and differentiation through specific signaling pathways (Ashtari et al. 2019). The methods used before and after bioprinting are illustrated in Fig. 1.5.

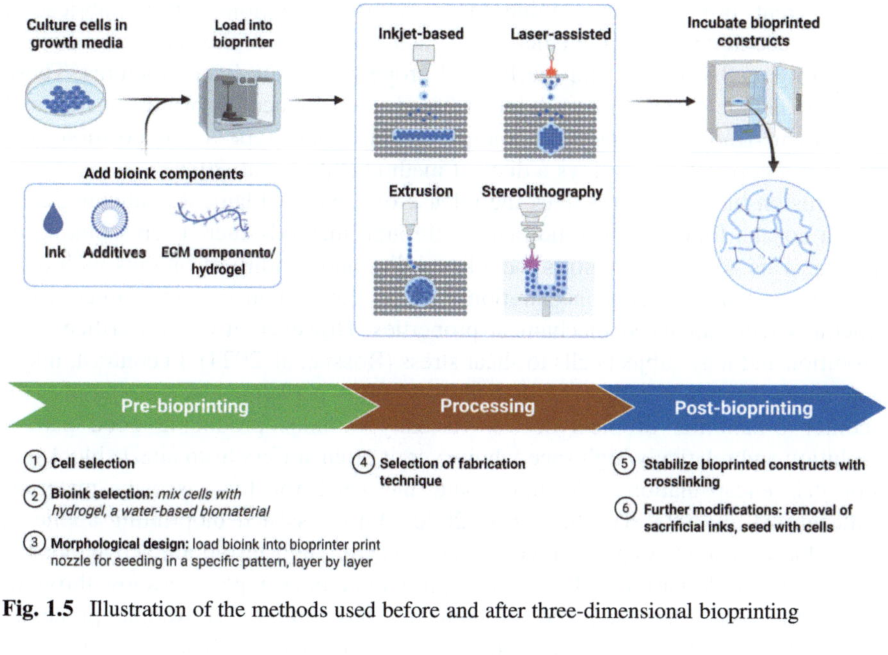

Fig. 1.5 Illustration of the methods used before and after three-dimensional bioprinting

1.3 Advances in Techniques

1.3.1 Conventional Bioprinting Techniques

Extrusion-based, inkjet, and laser-assisted bioprinting are typical bioprinting methods that serve as standard tools for generating 3D tissue microstructures, each with its own advantages in terms of resolution, cell viability, and material compatibility (Ashammakhi et al. 2019d). For instance, extrusion-based bioprinting can be very powerful in generating macroscopic structures because it processes a broad variety of bioink viscosities and cell concentrations, although it lacks precise control over the resolution and shear stress on cells. Inkjet bioprinting, on the other hand, offers high-throughput and excellent cell viability and is therefore a viable choice for patterning cells in 2D or fabricating thin tissue layers, albeit typically with low-viscosity bioinks and may be limited in producing intricate 3D structures (Cheng et al. 2024). The resolution-driven and cell placement requirements for complex microarchitectures can be attained by laser-assisted bioprinting; however, it is often slower and more expensive (Zhang et al. 2023a, b). Another technique is vat polymerization, including stereolithography and digital light processing (DLP), which can achieve high resolution and high throughput for oblique geometries but faces limitations in terms of the available photocurable bioinks and potentially cytotoxic photoinitiators. Each of these techniques has its own advantages and drawbacks; therefore, it is essential to carefully consider the biological application and desired characteristics of the tissue when selecting a bioprinting method. Despite the different principles that guide these diverse operations, all biofabrication methods encounter similar challenges in achieving a complex balance between printability, cell viability, and mechanical properties of the final structures. These methods include extrusion-based, inkjet-based, laser-induced forward transfer, and vat polymerization techniques, among others. Each type of deposition and processing application employs a distinct method (Iqbal et al. 2024).

Extrusion bioprinting involves the release of a bioink filament containing cells from a nozzle, followed by solidification through methods such as crosslinking or cooling. This approach supports the adaptability and rigidity of bioinks with high viscosity and dense cell concentrations, which can aid in creating larger tissue structures with enhanced mechanical properties. However, it often sacrifices fine resolution and may subject cells to shear stress (Rossi et al. 2024). In contrast, inkjet bioprinting (known as a drop-on-demand system) is performed by ejecting discrete picoliter-to-nanoliter droplets of low-viscosity bioinks, producing good pattern resolution and relatively high speed; however, it often suffers from nozzle blockage, poor cell encapsulation efficiency, and the need for low-viscosity materials (Antezana et al. 2023; Turnbull et al. 2020). Laser-assisted bioprinting applies a focused laser beam to expel cell-laden materials with high-resolution and avoids the problem of nozzle-based methods, although it sometimes experiences low throughput and the risk of laser-induced cell damage (Dias et al. 2020). Another process, VAT polymerization-based bioprinting, in which photoactivatable bioresins are cured layer-by-layer to create detailed 3D tissue structures (Jeznach et al. 2024), was first introduced in 1984 based on the selective solidification of a liquid prepolymer within a UV-curing is known to be capable of producing high-accuracy production. Among these, stereolithography and DLP process the liquid photopolymerizable resins one layer at a time to polymerize them with specifically targeted wavelengths of light, namely ultra-violet or visible (Perera et al. 2021).

The difference between these techniques lies in the method of material deposition. Nozzle deposition methods, such as extrusion and inkjet, work by physically extruding or forming drops, whereas optical-based methods, such as vat photopolymerization, rely on light-cured curing (Santoni et al. 2021). A comparative discussion of such techniques, their strengths, and drawbacks that impact their potential for TE applications are compared (Biondo et al. 2024; Elhadad et al. 2023). For example, extrusion-based biofabrication has gained significant commercial favor because it can accommodate various biocompatible materials and cell types that permit the fabrication of complex organs or structures (Jeznach et al. 2024). However, single printing processes, such as the most predominant process in extrusion bioprinting, may affect functional complexity despite approximating anatomical shapes because of their inability to represent the necessarily complicated structure of live tissues (Castilho et al. 2020). However, multimaterial bioprinting strategies are being pursued to address these limitations and enable the precise placement of multiple bioinks within a single structure to better replicate the heterogeneous composition of native tissues. Inkjet bioprinting, a variation of traditional methods, provides non-contact bioink droplet deposition at high speed, which is suitable for designing with high-resolution using low-viscosity biomaterials and accurate architectures (Vettori et al. 2020).

Although prescribing the rheological properties of bioinks for inkjet printing is an accurate method, it can also be harmful while developing cells and raises a key challenge in striking a balance between printability and cellular prerequisites (Carpio et al. 2021). Despite these developments, there is an inherent challenge in achieving biocompatibility and printability in a single bioink formulation: high viscosity formulations are mechanically robust but apply potentially damaging shear forces on embedded cells during extrusion (Vyas et al. 2023). Hydrodynamic biofabrication methods in combination with extrusion and electric field (electrohydrodynamic biofabrication) further extend the resolution to <1 μm allowing the possibly mimicking of complex microenvironments present in the ECM; however, cell compatibility and reproducibility still pose critical challenges (Castilho et al. 2020). Furthermore, the growing application of multi-principle biofabrication is addressing the limitations of single-based fabrication methods, resulting in the creation of intricate bio-structures with precisely controlled cellular and biomaterial compositions (Castilho et al. 2020). By integrating methods like melt spinning with extrusion-based biofabrication or suspended fabrication, these hybrid strategies aim to attain the precision and composition necessary for accurately replicating the structure and function of natural tissue (Castilho et al. 2020). Overall, given the advances in all aspects of this growing field (Ashammakhi et al. 2019e; Lai and Meagher 2024), we can confidently say that 3D-biomat will contribute significantly to driving synergistic technology development and integration, moving beyond technology-specific limitations while allowing for physiologically relevant levels of tissue complexity.

1.3.2 Emerging Methods

A. **Embedded bioprinting**

Mult technology biofabrication approaches, such as the integration of melt electrowriting and extrusion-based 3D bioprinting, are a major step forward in this regard, allowing the correlated color temperature or controlled color temperature (CCT) for the delivery of various cell types to improve the mechanical functionality of engineered constructs (Castilho et al. 2020). Melt electrospinning was used to deposit material onto the chondral matrix, while the bone component was printed using extrusion-based printing, and embedded layers of fibers were assured as architectural hierarchy (Castilho et al. 2020). An intriguing method is multitechnology, which integrates extrusion-based bioprinting with in-liquid (also known as droplet-based) printing to precisely arrange 3D cellular structures, like vascular networks, within a supporting bath (Castilho et al. 2020). The incorporation of microfluidic devices into extrusion-based bioprinting represents another advancement, greatly enhancing the vascularization of engineered tissues by mimicking physiological conditions on a microscale (Askari et al. 2020; Tavafoghi et al. 2021). This technical integration also enables the direct printing and patterning of cells within microfluidic chips to create biomimetic heterogeneous microenvironments (Askari et al. 2020). These hybrid fabrication techniques, which combine several processing stages, are gaining recognition as effective methods for enhancing the spatially precise seeding of engineered heterogeneous cell populations alongside various ECMs at different scales. This advancement aligns with the intricate multi-scale design and composition found in natural living tissues (Castilho et al. 2020). The field of biofabrication is becoming increasingly dynamic, with artificial intelligence (AI) serving as the key driver, surpassing the capabilities of parameterization and the integration of diverse technologies. This synergy enhances the reliability and functionality of bioprinted structures (Castilho et al. 2020). These combined approaches take advantage of the distinct properties of cell-laden hydrogels to create optimal cellular environments that support tissue growth and functionality within these complex structures (Hwangbo et al. 2024). The shift toward a multitechnology biofabrication strategy offers the potential to facilitate the creation of intricate tissues that cannot be achieved through single-process methods, marking a significant advancement in the realm of functional TE (Castilho et al. 2020).

By integrating these technologies, it becomes possible to create multilayered or multi-cellular structures that closely resemble the natural architecture, thereby enhancing functional performance in TE (Castilho et al. 2020). Advancements in

AI further support the shift toward multitechnology biofabrication (Castilho et al. 2020) and machine learning (ML) (Muniz Castro et al. 2021), which are anticipated to collectively enhance the programming of intricate biofabrication processes and the refinement of design parameters essential for the swift, high-volume production of functional living tissues (Castilho et al. 2020). AI can be utilized to examine how various materials interact in different settings, allowing for the optimization of 3D printing parameters that are customized for each patient. This process facilitates the selection of suitable biomaterials and bioink formulations that are specifically designed for particular uses (Cheng et al. 2024). Moreover, utilizing AI-driven algorithms for real-time online monitoring and feedback control during printing would be advantageous, as they can dynamically adjust an aerial computer-aided design (CAD) model to address the reduction in structural stability and cell viability (Castilho et al. 2020).

The rapid advancements in computation, driven by the transformative impact of big data and AI, are expected to streamline, simplify, automate, and support the design of biofabrication (Castilho et al. 2020). Integrating AI is crucial because current digital design tools and path generation software are often not user-friendly, given the complex control programming linked to advanced robot-based biofabrication systems (Castilho et al. 2020). Moreover, AI-based metamodels, including regression models and neural networks, can serve as rapid substitutes to align experimental data with computational modeling. This approach offers extensive design flexibility while maintaining precision for multi-tissue mechanistic models (Castilho et al. 2020). Integrating AI extensively will be crucial for creating innovative control strategies that can finely coordinate various manufacturing methods alongside adaptive process adjustments to achieve optimized tissue construct processing (Castilho et al. 2020).

In addition, the combination of machine vision and AI could reshape the online monitoring and control of bioprinting technology, which can solve the issue of accurate meshing between optical or laser profiling technology to multi-scale constructs for evaluation (Castilho et al. 2020). These platforms can robustly predict cellular response, printability, and scaffold quality, and accelerate the development of functional bioprinted tissue products (Jeznach et al. 2024). Moreover, ML can also be applied to optimize bioprinting parameters (e.g., bioink and printing conditions) to accelerate the fabrication of complex organ models and physiological in-vitro models (Shin et al. 2022). The incorporation of ML also includes the automation of quality control and standardization to lay the groundwork for robust biomanufacturing practices at scale (Antezana et al. 2023). This may lead to the development of adaptive control strategies for handling jobs with varying material or environmental characteristics, providing a means to maintain quality while minimizing waste.

In addition to process optimization, time-of-flight (ToF), and AI-assisted methodologies have dramatic impact on intelligent design of bioinks that are fundamental for immunological, tissue, and functional specificity seeking construction in 3D bioprinted constructs (Zhang et al. 2024a), internal advantage ML is intrinsically capable of high-resolution and reproducibility, as well as increased controllability of process-related parameters (Jeznach et al. 2024). Artificial neural networks (ANNs) models have been shown to outperform other tools for modeling drug release from 3D printed doses compared to alternative methods of ANNs models optimized for drug release prediction, suggesting that mean errors (±24.29 min) were negligible (Jeznach et al. 2024). Similarly, deep learning (a subtype of ML) is expected to significantly accelerate the fabrication and maturation of 3D bioprinted tissues and organs by automating workflows, ranging from medical image processing to post-printing modifications (Stapleton et al. 2020). These deep learning models can be subjected to a large amount of data so that optimal printing parameters can be determined, possible flaws in the bioink can be discovered, and subsequent changes in bio componential manipulation can be made to favor printability as well as cell survival simultaneously (Bonatti et al. 2022).

This sophisticated computation technique, particularly the Bayesian optimization approach, can identify better printing parameters faster than trial-and-error approaches, and hence will greatly promote bioprinting (Lamberger et al. 2024). Furthermore, ML techniques play an essential role in bioink printability assessment and optimization of printing parameters to fabricate porous structures for tissue regeneration (Jeznach et al. 2024). These sophisticated models can enhance our comprehension of the optimal rheological and mechanical characteristics of bioinks, which are crucial for successful extrusion, preventing scaffold collapse in intricate geometries, or accommodating various cell types (Jeznach et al. 2024). ML aids in forecasting the optimal parameters to produce drug delivery systems, which reduces material waste and leads to cost savings by optimizing the trial-and-error process of purification (Castillo-Henríquez et al. 2021). Moreover, the printability of bioinks can be quantitatively assessed using ML algorithms that consider factors like the rate at which the filament spreads. These algorithms can potentially determine an optimal combination of extrusion speed and printing resolution (Jeznach et al. 2024). The ability to predict also applies to the simulation of intricate rheological behaviors, like shear-thinning, which is essential for the extrusion of bioink. These simulations take into account factors such as weight fraction and shear rate to enhance the understanding of how materials behave during processing (Sarah et al. 2025). These advancements allow scientists to create bioinks with tailored printability and mechanical properties, which are crucial for preserving the shape and function of printed structures. For instance, Bayesian optimization techniques have been employed to fine-tune printing parameters like air pressure, printing speed, and nozzle temperature, resulting in the production of 3D printed polycaprolactone magnesium nanocomposite scaffolds with outstanding printability and resolution (Jeznach et al. 2024). This feature is specifically crafted to address the challenges of non-steady-state material behavior and the uncertainties inherent in 3D bioprinting processes (Alli et al. 2024a).

Iterative refining features of ML models enable them to adapt to complex data and discover hidden optimum structures for 3D printing, more than the classical empirical methodologies previously used (Alli et al. 2024a, b). With these models, print success can be estimated based on support placement to guide intelligently rather than empirically support the position to avoid print failure and reprints (Alli et al. 2024a, b). In addition, ML can distinguish and study geometric features in 3D and 4D printed objects, thus enabling the maintenance of their structural integrity even for complex design structures (Alli et al. 2024a, b). In addition, ML methods have played an important role in many scientific disciplines, such as medical image analysis and drug discovery, which are highly relevant to the complexity of treating multifactorial challenges and cross-correlations in scaffold fabrication and biomaterial–human body interactions within TE (Jeznach et al. 2024). In the field of material engineering, ML can be used to optimize the process-structure-property relationship, which will contribute to the rational design of scaffolds based on how the features of a material influence biological reactions (Jeznach et al. 2024). For example, ML has been used to optimize biomaterial design for printing ex-ante, and Bayesian optimization has been harnessed ex-situ to find the best possible print parameters based on process outcomes (Zanderigo et al. 2023). In conclusion, we assert that the widespread integration of AI/ML techniques into 3D printing and 3D bioprinting technologies will revolutionize the execution of AM iterations. This shift will move away from the existing trial-and-error methods toward processes that are driven by data and optimization. This groundwork will eventually enable a systematic approach to exploring and optimizing complex parameter spaces as we progress in material design and the production of bioconstruct (Alli et al. 2024a, b). The models facilitate an in-depth examination of the intricate relationships highlighted in literature, such as fabrication conditions, matrix characteristics, and biological reactions. This kind of data is crucial for designing scaffolds and making reliable predictions about interactions between materials and cells (Jeznach et al. 2024).

1.3.3 Combinatorial Approaches

A. ***Hybrid techniques***

Hybrid approaches incorporate various bioprinting technologies to enable the creation of multimaterial and multi-cellular structures, enhancing biofunctionality (Tavafoghi et al. 2021). This encompasses printing techniques, typically a mix of extrusion-based or inkjet methods, along with stereolithography techniques, enabling the creation of intricate shapes with varying cell densities and material arrangements (Cheng et al. 2024). To recreate the complex, customized multicellular structures and arrangements found in living organisms, which are essential for functional tissue substitutes and regenerative implants outside the body, these combined strategies are crucial (Ashammakhi et al. 2019a, b, c).

For instance, incorporating laser-assisted techniques into other bioprinting methods allows for highly precise placement of cells and biomaterials, which is essential for replicating the intricate microenvironment of tissues with a defined spatial resolution (Ashammakhi et al. 2019a). The incorporation of intelligent and biomimetic composite hydrogels within the framework of 4D bioprinting concepts elevates these hybrid characteristics to a more intricate level. This advancement facilitates stimuli-responsive processing for architectural shape transformation, offering new possibilities for medical applications (Malekmohammadi et al. 2021). Moreover, the combined technique of micro-extrusion and electrospinning enables the creation of robust structures that include challenging tissue interfaces, as demonstrated in both cartilage and pelvic floor TE (Tavafoghi et al. 2021).

These advanced hybrid bioprinting methods, especially in combination with microfluidic printheads, when integrated within extrusion-based bioprinters, allow for the controlled, high speed deposition of multiple bioinks in more complex spatiotemporal manners, which can generate gradients within printed constructs and single-cell encapsulation (Ashammakhi et al. 2018a, 2019c). Multimaterial bioprinting approaches, which involve different fabrication techniques, enable the fabrication of hybrid tissues with improved mechanical stability and bioactivity through the consecutive or simultaneous deposition of multiple bioinks (Tavafoghi et al. 2021). This advanced TE attempts to mitigate the requirement for a variety of tissue constructs that mimic the complex heterogenic characteristics of native biological systems, which cannot be achieved using a single bioink approach (Tavafoghi et al. 2021). Multi-cellular bioprinting, for instance, combines multiple biomaterials and several cell types, leading to higher complexity and structural features required in the construction of biomimetic constructs. This method is mainly based on a multi-nozzle system, in which layers of bioinks are deposited in succession (Ashammakhi et al. 2019c). Such a workflow offers the opportunity to spatially target differential cell types, ECM, and biomolecules, and therefore permits the bioprinting of highly complex tissue constructs on the print bed with high precision, as reported by others (Ashammakhi et al. 2019c). Nevertheless, the area of multimaterial 3D bioprinting is still in its infancy, and further investigation should be conducted to bring the technology from the lab bench to the clinic bedside as well as the industrial point of use (Tavafoghi et al. 2021). Microfluidics-based platforms and 3D printing integration provide promising strategies for layer-by-layer patterning, fast switching between different bioinks, and fabrication of complex multimaterial tissue constructs in much more complex structures that recapture the intricate networks present within native tissues (Tavafoghi et al. 2021). Nevertheless, the integration of different materials and cell types in a single construct is more challenging, mainly because of their fabrication processes. Overcoming these challenges is essential to mimic both the hierarchical structures and mechanical functions of native tissues (Ashammakhi et al. 2019a). Therefore, accurate control of the integration of different materials and cell types in biofabricated scaffolds is crucial to imitate the heterogeneity observed in native tissues, with recent improvements having been targeted at multilateral-dispensing systems that tailor spatial component distribution (Naghieh et al. 2017). These next-generation devices enable the precise manipulation of the placement of multiple cell types and biomaterials, which is necessary for geometrically complex structures and functional gradients required for the fabrication of advanced tissue models and regenerative therapies (Hassan et al. 2022). For instance, the coaxial micro-extrusion approach enables the production of a soft bioink shell containing cells and encapsulating a stiff core material, resulting in a good combination of mechanical strength and cellular viability

(Tavafoghi et al. 2021). In addition, such multimaterial systems allow for the integration of conductive materials, such as carbon nanotube inks, into cell-laden hydrogel structures, warranting constructs with improved electrical performance for cardiac TE applications (Ashammakhi et al. 2018a, b).

1.3.4 Ex Vivo, In Vivo, and In Situ 3D-Bioprinting

In situ 3D bioprinting takes place by directly targeting biomaterials and cells to a specific region in the body, instead of bioprinting outside and then implanting them within ex-vivo bioprinting as an implant after printing (Ashammakhi et al. 2019a; Ertas et al. 2021; Gaissmaier et al. 2005; Zhang et al. 2020). The second approach uses the native microenvironment of cells for tissue maturation, which avoids some of the associated safety risks of ex-vivo tissue culture and transplantation (Ashammakhi et al. 2019a).

The development of lightweight and compact in situ bioprinters, such as robotic arms or handheld units, is essential for the clinical application of in situ bioprinting Induced pluripotent stem cells (ISBP) in diverse surgical cases, even within sterile environments (Goldenberg et al. 2021). To overcome the constraints of on-site printing on non-flat surfaces and soft dynamic biological tissues, field-ready solutions are needed that rely on fast crosslinking bioinks with strong mechanical properties for direct incorporation (Ashammakhi et al. 2018a, b, 2019f).

One such innovation is the emergence of in situ skin printing systems cascading over a patient's damaged skin and depositing bioink directly at the same position for wound healing (Luo et al. 2023). Such systems frequently combine debridement, accurate 3D scanning, and modeling of wounds to tailor treatment to conditions, even for large skin lesions in difficult field settings (Luo et al. 2023). Another attractive field for in situ bioprinting is the potential of using multi-axis robots to achieve more accurate and multi-technique printing into complex multicompartmental constructs at the surgical site (Tavafoghi et al. 2021). For example, sophisticated systems have been devised to integrate laser scanning of injuries with cartridge-based delivery for personalized treatment regimens on a per-patient basis (Zhou et al. 2024).

Such integration also maximizes real-time adaptation to the wound and patient, thus improving the therapeutic performance of 3D printed bioconstruct (Zhang et al. 2024a). This streamlined approach eliminates the need for ex-vivo cell expansion or manipulation and integrates particulate technology with an in situ imprinting method for T cells. This leads to a faster treatment timeline and reduces the risk of cross-infection (Luo et al. 2023). Nonetheless, obstacles to the adoption of in situ bioprinting systems remain. Key issues in this field include the need for bioinks that possess enhanced mechanical properties, are biocompatible, and have controllable degradability to satisfy the requirements of various stages of tissue regeneration (Ashammakhi et al. 2019a; Turnbull et al. 2020). Furthermore, ensuring the long-term viability and functionality of in situ bioprinted structures under dynamic physiological conditions remains a significant challenge, necessitating ongoing advancements in biomaterials and printing technology. To validate the efficacy and safety of these innovative bioprinting techniques, multicenter studies should be conducted through well-structured preclinical or clinical trials. This effort should also be bolstered by the establishment of standardized protocols for material characterization, the optimization of printing parameters, and thorough biological assessments to guarantee dependable tissue integration and functionality (Ashammakhi et al. 2018a, b).

1.4 Current Challenges and Future Outlook

1.4.1 Challenges

A. ***Bioink-Related Challenges*** **(e.g.,** ***scalability, biocompatibility)***

The absence of a standardized bioink necessitates the use of tailored materials and specific cell-seeding densities. This variability complicates the comparison of experimental outcomes across different studies and hinders the standardization of bioprinting models (Datta et al. 2020). Developing and refining bioinks that are appropriate for various tissue types remains a significant challenge. It is difficult to balance the control of rheological and mechanical properties to maintain cell viability and functionality within printed tissues (Ashammakhi et al. 2019c). Therefore, creating new biomaterials that can replicate the complexity of the ECM and offer surface biochemistry and/or mechanics for cell growth and differentiation is essential for advancing biofabrication (Ashammakhi et al. 2019c). Additionally, understanding the long-term effects of bioprinted constructs within a physiological system, along with their stability and biocompatibility, presents a significant challenge. This is due to potential immunogenic responses that these bioink systems might trigger and their degradation rates. Furthermore, the small size of the tissue that can be fabricated using currently available microfluidic-integrated bioprinting systems is a major obstacle for scaling up to fabricate tissues at the human scale (Tavafoghi et al. 2021).

B. ***Technique-Related Challenges*** **(e.g.,** ***resolution, vascularization)***

Existing bioprinting techniques continue to encounter core challenges in achieving high-resolution, multimaterial printing while ensuring cell viability and functionality (Ashammakhi et al. 2019c). Overcoming these technical hurdles is essential for the widespread adoption of 3D bioprinting in clinical environments, particularly for creating living organ and tissue replacements (Alzoubi et al. 2023). A significant technical obstacle in 3D bioprinting is the inadequate vascularization within printed structures, which is crucial for improving the delivery of nutrients and oxygen to larger tissues (Hermida et al. 2020). Additionally, replicating cellular interactions and the intricate spatial arrangements of native tissues remains a challenge, especially when trying to emulate the complex microenvironments found in diseases like tumors, which are vital for advanced cancer research (Datta et al. 2020). Moreover, the creation of suitable bioinks, achieving industrial scalability, and reducing post-printing maturation times are still significant challenges in developing cancer-mimetic models (Unnikrishnan et al. 2021).

C. **Application-Specific Challenges**

One of the most significant application-specific obstacles is the lack of maneuverability to incorporate perfusable vascular networks within larger bioprinted structures that are required for nutrient and oxygen supply to avoid necrosis in thicker tissues (Datta et al. 2020). This difficulty is further exacerbated by the complex, wavy, hierarchical, and nonhomogeneous cellular arrangement observed in natural tissues, which cannot be cloned (Tavafoghi et al. 2021). Even with the improvement of biofabrication techniques, replicating in detail the complex native tissue microenvironment, composed of cell crosstalk and biomechanical signals, represents a major hurdle for functional tissue construct formation that can be used to replace or 3D model tissues in-vitro (Ashammakhi et al. 2019a). Natural biomaterials can have inadequate mechanical properties, whereas synthetic substitutes are often structurally undesirable, making it difficult to replicate the range of physical and biological attributes found in the native ECM (Rasouli et al. 2024).

These are major constraints that limit the clinical applicability of bioprinted tissues, especially in scenarios where intricate organ-like structures are necessary or when long-term functional stability is required (Tavafoghi et al. 2021). Additionally, there have been reports of inadequate nutrient supply to the implanted tissue due to insufficient perfusion. This highlights the importance of materials that offer not only mechanical strength but also architectural stability to facilitate proper in-vivo interactions post-implantation (Kasturi et al. 2023). Effective capillary development is also required to improve oxygen and nutrient delivery, as the distance for passive diffusion is up to 200–250 μm (Fantini et al. 2024). Furthermore, the lack of mature vasculature hampers functional and biomechanical integration with host circulation (Cui et al. 2018). A longer bioprinting time for larger organs can lead to cell survival loss in the initial printed sections because of extended exposure to non-ideal conditions (McCarthy et al. 2019). Furthermore, cells in the bioink suffer from shear stress during extrusion and thus die in several bioprinting processes. Therefore, it is necessary to optimize the printing parameters and nozzle designs (Naghieh et al. 2017).

1.4.2 Future Outlook

New printable and compatible bioinks with appropriate mechanical and biological features are required to overcome these constraints (Wang et al. 2021). Future research will probably focus on the use of stimuli-responsive materials and smart hydrogels that can dynamically change with the physiological environment, which could improve cell differentiation and tissue maturation (Antezana et al. 2023). In addition, achieving desirable bioink viscosity is important for their performance; a relatively high viscosity ink mechanically supports 3D printed construct stability but can be toxic to cells, whereas low-viscosity inks promote cell survival and proliferation but often result in lower mechanical strength of constructs (Ashammakhi et al. 2019c). To address this issue, multimaterial bioprinting strategies are currently under development, which enable the combination of biomaterials with different rheological properties and printing requirements for the assembly of hybrid scaffolds possessing enhanced mechanical and biological functionalities (Naghieh et al. 2017). Moreover, it is essential to incorporate superior mechanical strength and biological curing advanced bioinks for the development of constructs that can withstand physiological loading and support long-term tissue maturation and vascularization (Ashammakhi et al. 2019c).

Upcoming developments are likely to include bioinks containing complex biochemical cues for cellular self-assembly and vasculature development in a spatially and temporally defined manner (Ashammakhi et al. 2019c, Zhang et al. 2021a, b). Moreover, the next-generation landscape is expected to combine smart bioinks with nanoparticles and other functional additives integrated to improve properties such as antimicrobial effect and controlled drug release for therapeutic improvements (Naghieh et al. 2017).

3D bioprinting is expected to advance with ongoing research aimed at enhancing multimaterial and multi-nozzle printing systems. These systems will be able to deposit a variety of biomaterials and cell types with increased accuracy, aiding in the creation of intricate composite tissue structures that boast improved mechanical strength and high bioactivity (Tavafoghi et al. 2021). A crucial aspect of this development will be the integration and advancement of sophisticated robotics and AI, which are predicted to significantly influence print quality, speed, and automation. To address the challenge of scalability for broader clinical use, innovative strategies are required (Ashammakhi et al. 2019f). In addition, the combination of several fabrication methods in a single multifunctional printer (extrusion combined with inkjet or laser-induced forward transfer) will be necessary to obtain excellent organ printing quality suitable for clinical use (Jorgensen et al. 2020). The study of 4D bioprinting employing stimulus-responsive materials is an important step toward developing dynamic, shape-changing, or property-modifying constructs after printing. This ability will allow the creation of more complicated tissue and organ models (Ashammakhi et al. 2018a, b). There will also be great emphasis on furthering intraoperative bioprinting methods, especially when defect sizes are unknown or immediate surgery is required, including complex craniomaxillofacial reconstructions (Ashammakhi et al. 2018a, b). These methods have the advantage of direct tissue repair and regeneration, as they may eliminate some of the logistical concerns associated with ex-vivo construct maturation and transfer (Jorgensen et al. 2020).

Some on-site bioprinting approaches have been implemented for external organs, such as the skin (based on individual imaging data to fabricate special tissue architectures) (Miri et al. 2018). This individualized strategy avoids immunogenicity and transplant rejection and offers important advantages over traditional organ transplantation. In addition, this study illustrates the development of a bioprinter equipped with instant feedback (sensing and actuation) devices that enable adaptive process control and feedback during complex fabrication processes for improved quality assurance. The development of multi-axis robotic systems with integrated monitoring during printing using inspection sensors will improve reproducibility and enable direct fabrication onto complex anatomical surfaces (Castilho et al. 2020).

The article concludes by reflecting on the potential future advances of 3D bioprinting for applications beyond simple tissue constructs, but toward the generation of complex and vascularized organoids and microphysiological systems for drug screening and disease modeling. This development includes the generation of patient-specific implants and prostheses. Advanced imaging and AI-based design promise to have a potential impact on the improvement of functional outcomes and acceleration of the rehabilitation process (Ashammakhi et al. 2019a). Ultimately, the target is to produce clinically applicable bioprinted organs that are functionally efficacious, biomechanically like native organs, and contain integrated vasculature (Jorgensen et al. 2020). Ultimately, we aim to design living human constructs that resemble the biological and physical properties of natural tissues to repair tissue defects and replace organ structure and function (Ashammakhi et al. 2019a). As 3D bioprinting progresses to a stage where it can be applied in stem cell research, it will revolutionize regenerative medicine. This combined potential can be utilized to create tissue constructs that are capable of self-assembly and self-organization, possessing an inherent ability to repair (Chimene et al. 2022). This integration represents a move toward addressing some of the existing challenges in TE, such as immune rejection and inadequate integration, by leveraging the self-renewal and differentiation capabilities of stem cells within specifically bioprinted scaffolds. This approach to TE holds the promise of producing functional tissues that replicate the native 3D (3D) biology and native-like vasculature, thereby bringing the long-sought goal of creating transplantable organs within reach.

Moreover, the advancement of in-vivo maturation and vascularization of bioprinted constructs after implantation represents a cutting-edge research area. This is particularly crucial when addressing nutrient and oxygen transport issues in larger tissue constructs (Miri et al. 2019). To achieve clinical applicability, it is essential to tackle existing obstacles related to scalability, the long-term viability of bioprinted constructs, and their effective integration into the host (Fantini et al. 2024). Anticipated advancements include 4D and 5D bioprinting, which aim to create more intricate, tissue-like structures and organoids with greater precision (Ziaran et al. 2025). Additionally, computational modeling and AI-driven methods will be crucial for enabling real-time control of bioprinting, allowing for the adjustment of fabrication parameters to enhance both structural integrity and bioactivity (Castilho et al. 2020). This multifaceted approach will continue to propel the rational design of personalized, bioprinted constructions tailored to individual patients. Nonetheless, significant hurdles persist in creating anatomically accurate and fully functional organs with mature biological functions, especially concerning precise cell arrangement, effective cell differentiation, and strong vascularization (Abady et al. 2024; Ashammakhi et al. 2019a).

Acknowledgments NA acknowledges funding from the National Institutes of Health (1UG3TR003148-01), the American Heart Association (23IPA1053441), the Estonian Research Council (PRG1903), Michigan Translational Research and Commercialization Innovation Hub for AgBio (MTRAC AgBio, RG101700), Henry Ford Health, Department of Surgery (00679169), and Corewell Health Michigan State University Alliance grant. AMN acknowledges funding from the Sudastructure-MDH. Co. LTD (UIC251534).

Competing Interests The author(s) has no competing interests to declare that are relevant to the content of this manuscript.

References

Abaci A, Guvendiren M (2024) 3D bioprinting of dense cellular structures within hydrogels with spatially controlled heterogeneity [article]. Biofabrication 16(3):035027. https://doi.org/10.1088/1758-5090/ad52f1

Abady MM, Jeong JS, Kwon HJ, Assiri AM, Cho J, Saadeldin IM (2024) The reprotoxic adverse side effects of neurogenic and neuroprotective drugs: current use of human organoid modeling as a potential alternative to preclinical models. Front Pharmacol 15:1412188. https://doi.org/10.3389/fphar.2024.1412188

Abbas ZN, Al-Saffar AZ, Jasim SM, Sulaiman GM (2023) Comparative analysis between 2D and 3D colorectal cancer culture models for insights into cellular morphological and transcriptomic variations. Sci Rep 13(1):18380. https://doi.org/10.1038/s41598-023-45144-w

Abukunna FE, Aladdad AM, McLoughlin KJ, Thallapureddy K, Vierra M, Siddiqui Z, Kador KE (2025) Three-dimensional bioprinting of astrocytes and endothelial cells to direct retinal axon growth and vascularization [article]. Tissue Eng Part A. https://doi.org/10.1089/ten.tea.2024.0326

Adam Marsh EH-A, Theofania K, Romila M, Johnson V, Ross G, Tsamesidis I, Kontonasaki E, Bunn DM, Hammer N, Hankenson K, Spence D, Contag CH, Ashammakhi N, Chatzistavrou X (2026) A newovel bioactive glass-based hybrid multifunctional bioink with advanced enhanced cell viability properties for extrusion-based 3D bioprintingand antibacterial properties. Adv Healthc Mater

Agarwal K, Srinivasan V, Lather V, Pandita D, Vasanthan KS (2022) Insights of 3D bioprinting and focusing the paradigm shift towards 4D printing for biomedical applications. J Mater Res 38(1): 112–141. https://doi.org/10.1557/s43578-022-00524-2

Alanazi BN, Ahmed HA, Alharbi NS, Ebrahim NAA, Soliman SMA (2025) Exploring 4D printing of smart materials for regenerative medicine applications. Royal Society of Chemistry

Alizadeh P, Soltani M, Tutar R, Hoque Apu E, Maduka CV, Unluturk BD, Contag CH, Ashammakhi N (2021) Use of electroconductive biomaterials for engineering tissues by 3D printing and 3D bioprinting. Essays Biochem 65(3):441–466. https://doi.org/10.1042/EBC20210003

Alli YA, Anuar H, Bamisaye A, Manshor MR, Etafo NO, Bamidele MO, Rasheed MA, Olatunde SK, Akinfenwa AS, Lawal A (2024a) The appealing prospect of hydrogel in 3D/4D printing technology: overview and opportunities [review]. Polymer 315:127823. https://doi.org/10.1016/j.polymer.2024.127823

Alli YA, Anuar H, Manshor MR, Okafor CE, Kamarulzaman AF, Akçakale N, Nazeri FNM, Bodaghi M, Suhr J, Nasir NAM (2024b) Optimization of 4D/3D printing via machine learning: a systematic review. Elsevier BV

Alnasser SM (2025) From gut to liver: organoids as platforms for next-generation toxicology assessment vehicles for xenobiotics. BioMed Central

Alzoubi L, Aljabali AAA, Tambuwala MM (2023) Empowering precision medicine: the impact of 3D printing on personalized therapeutic. Springer

Antezana PE, Municoy S, Ostapchuk G, Catalano PN, Hardy JG, Evelson PA, Orive G, Desimone MF (2023) 4D printing: the development of responsive materials using 3D-printing technology. Pharmaceutics 15(12):2743–2743. https://doi.org/10.3390/pharmaceutics15122743

Aqeilan RI (2021) Engineering organoids: a promising platform to understand biology and treat diseases. Cell Death Differ 28(1):1–4. https://doi.org/10.1038/s41418-020-00680-0

Arjmand B, Rabbani Z, Soveyzi F, Tayanloo-Beik A, Rezaei-Tavirani M, Biglar M, Adibi H, Larijani B (2022) Advancement of organoid technology in regenerative medicine. Springer

Asciak L, Domingo-Roca R, Dow JR, Brodie R, Paterson N, Riches PE, Shu W, McCormick C (2024) Exploiting light-based 3D-printing for the fabrication of mechanically enhanced, patient-specific aortic grafts [article]. J Mech Behav Biomed Mater 154:106531. https://doi.org/10.1016/j.jmbbm.2024.106531

Ashammakhi N, Kaarela O (2017) Stimuli-responsive biomaterials: next wave. J Craniofacial Surg 28(7) https://journals.lww.com/jcraniofacialsurgery/fulltext/2017/10000/stimuli_responsive_biomaterials__next_wave.3.aspx

Ashammakhi N, Kaarela O (2018) Three-dimensional bioprinting can help bone. J Craniofacial Surg 29(1) https://journals.lww.com/jcraniofacialsurgery/fulltext/2018/01000/three_dimensional_bioprinting_can_help_bone.5.aspx

Ashammakhi N, Ahadian S, Fan Z, Suthiwanich K, Lorestani F, Orive G, Ostrovidov S, Khademhosseini A (2018a) Advances and future perspectives in 4D bioprinting. Wiley

Ashammakhi N, Hasan AZYS, Dokmeci M, Khademhosseini A (2018b) Microfluidic bioprinting
. Lab Chip

Ashammakhi N, Ahadian S, Pountos I, Hu S-K, Tellisi N, Bandaru P, Ostrovidov S, Dokmeci MR, Khademhosseini A (2019a) In situ three-dimensional printing for reparative and regenerative therapy. Biomed Microdevices 21(2):42. https://doi.org/10.1007/s10544-019-0372-2

Ashammakhi N, Hasan A, Kaarela O, Byambaa B, Sheikhi A, Gaharwar AK, Khademhosseini A (2019b) Advancing Frontiers in bone bioprinting. Adv Healthc Mater e1801048. https://doi.org/10.1002/adhm.201801048

Ashammakhi N, Ahadian S, Xu C, Montazerian H, Ko H, Nasiri R, Barros N, Khademhosseini A (2019c) Bioinks and bioprinting technologies to make heterogeneous and biomimetic tissue constructs. Mater Today Bio 1:100008. https://doi.org/10.1016/j.mtbio.2019.100008

Ashammakhi N, Ahadian S, Darabi MA, El Tahchi M, Lee J, Suthiwanich K, Sheikhi A, Dokmeci MR, Oklu R, Khademhosseini A (2019d) Minimally invasive and regenerative therapeutics. Adv Mater 31(1):e1804041. https://doi.org/10.1002/adma.201804041

Ashammakhi N, Darabi MA, Kehr NS, Erdem A, Hu S-k, Dokmeci MR, Nasr AS, Khademhosseini A (2019e) Advances in controlled oxygen generating biomaterials for tissue engineering and regenerative therapy. Biomacromolecules 21(1):56–72

Ashammakhi N, Hasan A, Kaarela O, Byambaa B, Sheikhi A, Gaharwar AK, Khademhosseini A (2019f) Advancing Frontiers in bone bioprinting. Wiley

Ashammakhi, N., Ahadian, S., Xu, C., Montazerian, H., Ko, H., Nasiri, R., Barros, N., & Khademhosseini, A. (2019g). Bioinks and bioprinting technologies to make heterogeneous and biomimetic tissue constructs

Ashammakhi N, Darabi MA, Kehr NS, Erdem A, Hu SK, Dokmeci MR, Nasr AS, Khademhosseini A (2020) Advances in controlled oxygen generating biomaterials for tissue engineering and regenerative therapy. Biomacromolecules 21(1):56–72. https://doi.org/10.1021/acs.biomac.9b00546

Ashammakhi N, GhavamiNejad A, Tutar R, Fricker A, Roy I, Chatzistavrou X, Hoque Apu E, Nguyen K-L, Ahsan T, Pountos I, Caterson EJ (2021a) Highlights on advancing Frontiers in tissue engineering. Tissue Eng Part B Rev 28(3):633–664. https://doi.org/10.1089/ten.teb.2021.0012

Ashammakhi N, Tamimi F, Caterson EJ (2021b) Three-dimensional bioprinting, oxygenated tissue constructs, and Intravital tissue regeneration. J Craniofacial Surg 32(7) https://journals.lww.com/jcraniofacialsurgery/fulltext/2021/10000/three_dimensional_bioprinting,_oxygenated_tissue.3.aspx

Ashammakhi N, GhavamiNejad A, Tutar R, Fricker A, Roy I, Chatzistavrou X, Hoque Apu E, Nguyen KL, Ahsan T, Pountos I, Caterson EJ (2022) Highlights on Advancing Frontiers in Tissue Engineering. Tissue Eng Part B Rev *28*(3):633–664. https://doi.org/10.1089/ten.TEB.2021.0012

Ashtari K, Nazari H, Ko H, Tebon P, Akhshik M, Akbari M, Alhosseini SN, Mozafari M, Mehravi B, Soleimani M, Ardehali R, Warkiani ME, Ahadian S, Khademhosseini A (2019) Electrically conductive nanomaterials for cardiac tissue engineering. Elsevier BV

Askari M, Naniz MA, Kouhi M, Saberi A, Zolfagharian A, Bodaghi M (2020) Recent progress in extrusion 3D bioprinting of hydrogel biomaterials for tissue regeneration: a comprehensive review with focus on advanced fabrication techniques. Royal Society of Chemistry

Atila D, Kumaravel V (2023) Advances in antimicrobial hydrogels for dental tissue engineering: regenerative strategies for endodontics and periodontics. Royal Society of Chemistry

Bajada S, Mazakova I, Richardson JB, Ashammakhi N (2008) Updates on stem cells and their applications in regenerative medicine. J Tissue Eng Regen Med 2(4):169–183. https://doi.org/10.1002/term.83

Bakhtiary N, Liu C, Ghorbani F (2021) Bioactive inks development for Osteochondral tissue engineering: a mini-review. Multidisciplinary Digital Publishing Institute

Barrulas RV, Corvo MC (2023) Rheology in product development: an insight into 3D printing of hydrogels and aerogels. Gels 9(12):986–986. https://doi.org/10.3390/gels9120986

Bassi G, Grimaudo MA, Panseri S, Montesi M (2021) Advanced multi-dimensional cellular models as emerging reality to reproduce in vitro the human body complexity. Multidisciplinary Digital Publishing Institute

Belk L, Tellisi N, Macdonald H, Erdem A, Ashammakhi N, Pountos I (2020) Safety considerations in 3D bioprinting using mesenchymal stromal cells [review]. Front Bioeng Biotechnol 8. https://doi.org/10.3389/fbioe.2020.00924

Bg PK, Mehrotra S, Marques SM, Kumar L, Verma R (2023) 3D printing in personalized medicines: a focus on applications of the technology. Mater Today Commun 35:105875–105875. https://doi.org/10.1016/j.mtcomm.2023.105875

Biondo M, Tomasello L, Giordano C, Arnaldi G, Pizzolanti G (2024) The promising approach of 3D bioprinting for diabetic foot ulcer treatment: a concise review of recent developments. Elsevier BV

Bock C, Boutros M, Camp JG, Clarke L, Clevers H, Knoblich JA, Liberali P, Regev A, Rios AC, Stegle O, Stunnenberg HG, Teichmann SA, Treutlein B, Vries RGJ (2020) The organoid cell atlas. Nature Portfolio

Bonatti AF, Vozzi G, Chua CK, Maria C (2022) A deep learning quality control loop of the extrusion-based bioprinting process. Int J Bioprint 8(4):620. https://doi.org/10.18063/ijb.v8i4.620

Bonetti L, Scalet G (2024) 4D fabrication of shape-changing systems for tissue engineering: state of the art and perspectives. Springer

Bova L, Billi F, Cimetta E (2020) Mini-review: advances in 3D bioprinting of vascularized constructs. BioMed Central

Carpio MB, Dabaghi M, Ungureanu J, Kolb M, Hirota JA, Moran-Mirabal J (2021) 3D bioprinting strategies, challenges, and opportunities to model the lung tissue microenvironment and its function. Frontiers Media, In

Castilho M, Ruijter M d, Beirne S, Villette CC, Ito K, Wallace GG, Malda J (2020) Multitechnology biofabrication: A new approach for the manufacturing of functional tissue structures? Elsevier BV, In

Castillo-Henríquez L, Castro-Alpízar J, Lopretti-Correa M, Vega-Baudrit J (2021) Exploration of bioengineered scaffolds composed of thermo-responsive polymers for drug delivery in wound healing [review]. Int J Mol Sci 22(3):1–25, Article 1408. https://doi.org/10.3390/ijms22031408

Chaudhary S, Chakraborty E (2022) Hydrogel based tissue engineering and its future applications in personalized disease modeling and regenerative therapy. Springer

Chen Y, Liu Y, Chen S, Zhang L, Rao J, Lu X, Ma Y (2023) Liver organoids: a promising three-dimensional model for insights and innovations in tumor progression and precision medicine of liver cancer [review]. Front Immunol 14:1180184. https://doi.org/10.3389/fimmu.2023.1180184

Cheng C, Williamson EJ, Chiu GTC, Han B (2024) Engineering biomaterials by inkjet printing of hydrogels with functional particulates. Springer

Childs CJ (2024) Interrogating stem cell niche factors in the developing human gut to advance in vitro models. Deep Blue (University of Michigan). https://doi.org/10.7302/23779

Chimene D, Deo KA, Thomas J, Dahle L, Mandrona C, Gaharwar AK (2022) Designing cost-effective open-source multihead 3D bioprinters. GEN Biotechnol 1(4):386–400. https://doi.org/10.1089/genbio.2022.0021

Ciulla MG, Massironi A, Sugni M, Ensign MA, Marzorati S, Forouharshad M (2023) Recent advances in the development of biomimetic materials. Multidisciplinary Digital Publishing Institute

Cui H, Miao S, Esworthy T, Zhou X, Lee S-J, Liu C, Yu Z-X, Fisher JP, Mohiuddin MM, Zhang LG (2018) 3D bioprinting for cardiovascular regeneration and pharmacology. Elsevier BV

Cui X, Li J, Hartanto Y, Durham M, Tang J, Zhang H, Hooper GJ, Lim KS, Woodfield TBF (2020) Advances in extrusion 3D bioprinting: A focus on multicomponent hydrogel-based bioinks. Wiley

Datta P, Dey M, Ataie Z, Unutmaz D, Özbolat İT (2020) 3D bioprinting for reconstituting the cancer microenvironment. Nature Portfolio, In

Davoodi E, Sarikhani E, Montazerian H, Ahadian S, Costantini M, Swieszkowski W, Willerth SM, Walus K, Mofidfar M, Toyserkani E, Khademhosseini A, Ashammakhi N (2020) Extrusion and microfluidic-based bioprinting to fabricate biomimetic tissues and organs. Adv Materials Technol 5(8):1901044. https://doi.org/10.1002/admt.201901044

Dias JR, Ribeiro N, Baptista-Silva S, Costa-Pinto AR, Alves N, Oliveira AL (2020) In situ enabling approaches for tissue regeneration: current challenges and new developments. Frontiers Media

Dobos A, Gantner F, Markovic M, Van Hoorick J, Tytgat L, Van Vlierberghe S, Ovsianikov A (2021) On-chip high-definition bioprinting of microvascular structures. Biofabrication 13(1): 015016. https://doi.org/10.1088/1758-5090/abb063

Dodda JM, Kunrath MF, Zhao LZ, Bodaghi M, Yousefi A, Ashammakhi N (2025) Autonomous Implants. Adv Mater e10702. https://doi.org/10.1002/adma.202510702

Elhadad AA, Rosa-Sainz A, Cañete R, Peralta E, Begines B, Balbuena M, Alcudia A, Torres Y (2023) Applications and multidisciplinary perspective on 3D printing techniques: recent developments and future trends. Materials Sci Eng: R: Rep 156:100760–100760. https://doi.org/10.1016/j.mser.2023.100760

Erdem A, Darabi MA, Nasiri R, Sangabathuni S, Ertas YN, Alem H, Hosseini V, Shamloo A, Nasr AS, Ahadian S, Dokmeci MR, Khademhosseini A, Ashammakhi N (2020) 3D bioprinting of oxygenated cell-laden gelatin Methacryloyl constructs. Adv Healthc Mater 9(15):e1901794. https://doi.org/10.1002/adhm.201901794

Erdem A, Haghniaz R, Ertas YN, Sangabathuni SK, Nasr AS, Swieszkowski W, Ashammakhi N (2022) Methods for fabricating oxygen releasing biomaterials. J Drug Target 30(2):188–199. https://doi.org/10.1080/1061186x.2021.1971235

Ergün S, Wörsdörfer P (2022) Organoids, Assembloids and Embryoids: new avenues for developmental biology, disease modeling, drug testing and toxicity assessment without animal experimentation. Organ 1(1):37–40. https://doi.org/10.3390/organoids1010004

Ertas YN, Vaziri AS, Abedi-Dorcheh K, Kazemi-Aghdam F, Sohrabinejad M, Tutar R, Rastegar-Adib F, Ashammakhi N (2021) Ian situ tissue engineering: A new dimension. In: Sheikh FA (ed) Engineering materials for stem cell regeneration. Springer, Singapore, pp 325–350. https://doi.org/10.1007/978-981-16-4420-7_13

Esmaeili H, Patino-Guerrero A, Hasany M, Ansari MO, Memić A, Dolatshahi-Pirouz A, Nikkhah M (2021) Electroconductive biomaterials for cardiac tissue engineering. Elsevier BV, In

Faber L, Yau A, Chen Y (2023) Translational biomaterials of four-dimensional bioprinting for tissue regeneration. IOP Publishing

Fan X, Hou K, Liu G, Shi R, Wang W, Liang G (2025) Strategies to overcome the limitations of current organoid technology - engineered organoids. SAGE Publishing

Fang Y, Eglen RM (2017) Three-dimensional cell cultures in drug discovery and development. In: SLAS Discovery: Advancing Life Sciences R&D. https://doi.org/10.1177/2472555217696795

Fantini DA, Yang G, Khanna A, Subramanian D, Phillippi JA, Huang NF (2024) Overcoming big bottlenecks in vascular regeneration. Nature Portfolio

Fetah KL, DiPardo BJ, Kongadzem E-M, Tomlinson JS, Elzagheid A, Elmusrati M, Khademhosseini A, Ashammakhi N (2019) Cancer modeling-on-a-Chip with future artificial intelligence integration. Small 15(50):1901985. https://doi.org/10.1002/smll.201901985

Foglizzo V, Cocco E, Marchiò S (2022) Advanced cellular models for preclinical drug testing: from 2D cultures to organ-on-a-Chip Technology. Multidisciplinary Digital Publishing Institute

Gaetani R, Chimenti I (2023) 3D cultures for modelling the microenvironment: current research trends and applications. Int J Mol Sci 24(13):11109–11109. https://doi.org/10.3390/ijms241311109

Gaissmaier C, Fritz J, Krackhardt T, Flesch I, Aicher WK, Ashammakhi N (2005) Effect of human platelet supernatant on proliferation and matrix synthesis of human articular chondrocytes in monolayer and three-dimensional alginate cultures. Biomaterials 26(14):1953–1960. https://doi.org/10.1016/j.biomaterials.2004.06.031

Gan Z, Qin X, Liu H, Liu J, Qin J (2023) Recent advances in defined hydrogels in organoid research. Elsevier BV

Garreta E, Kamm RD, Lopes SMCDS, Lancaster MA, Weiss R, Trepat X, Hyun I, Montserrat N (2020) Rethinking organoid technology through bioengineering. Nature Portfolio

GhavamiNejad A, Ashammakhi N, Wu XY, Khademhosseini A (2020) Crosslinking strategies for 3D bioprinting of polymeric hydrogels. Small 16(35):e2002931. https://doi.org/10.1002/smll.202002931

Giorgetti A, Gu Y, Suzuki K, Li M (2022) Editorial: Developmental models 2.0. Front Cell Dev Biol 10:1055139. https://doi.org/10.3389/fcell.2022.1055139

Gold KA, Gaharwar AK, Jain A (2018) Emerging trends in multiscale modeling of vascular pathophysiology: organ-on-a-chip and 3D printing. Elsevier BV

Goldenberg D, McLaughlin C, Koduru SV, Ravnic DJ (2021) Regenerative engineering: current applications and future perspectives. Frontiers Media

Han X, Saiding Q, Cai X, Xiao Y, Wang P, Cai Z, Gong X, Gong W, Zhang X, Cui W (2023) Intelligent vascularized 3D/4D/5D/6D-printed tissue scaffolds. Springer

Han X, Cai C, Deng W, Shi Y, Li L, Wang C, Zhang J, Rong M, Liu J, Fang B, He H, Liu X, Deng C-X, He X, Cao X (2024) Landscape of human organoids: ideal model in clinics and research. Elsevier BV

Hassan S, Gomez-Reyes E, Enciso-Martinez E, Shi K, Campos JG, Soria OYP, Luna-Ceron E, Lee MC, Garcia-Reyes I, Steakelum J, Jeelani H, Garcia-Rivera LE, Cho M, Cortes SS, Kamperman T, Wang H, Leijten J, Fiondella L, Shin SR (2022) Tunable and compartmentalized multimaterial bioprinting for complex living tissue constructs. ACS Appl Mater Interfaces 14(46):51602–51618. https://doi.org/10.1021/acsami.2c12585

Hermida MA, Kumar JD, Schwarz D, Laverty KG, Di Bartolo A, Ardron M, Bogomolnijs M, Clavreul A, Brennan PM, Wiegand UK, Melchels FP, Shu W, Leslie NR (2020) Three dimensional in vitro models of cancer: bioprinting multilineage glioblastoma models. Adv Biol Regul 75:100658. https://doi.org/10.1016/j.jbior.2019.100658

Hill J, Wildman RD, Mata Á (2021) Exploiting the fundamentals of biological organization for the advancement of biofabrication. Elsevier BV

Hu Y, Geng Q, Wang L, Wang Y, Huang C, Fan Z, Kong D (2024) Research progress and application of liver organoids for disease modeling and regenerative therapy. Springer

Huang Y, Huang Z, Tang Z, Chen Y, Huang M, Liu H, Huang W, Ye Q, Jia B (2021) Research Progress, challenges, and breakthroughs of organoids as disease models. Frontiers Media

Hwangbo H, Chae S, Kim W, Jo S, Kim GH (2024) Tumor-on-a-chip models combined with mini-tissues or organoids for engineering tumor tissues. Theranostics 14(1):33–55. https://doi.org/10.7150/thno.90093

Imam SS, Hussain A, Altamimi MA, Alshehri S (2021) Four-dimensional printing for hydrogel: theoretical concept, 4D materials, shape-morphing way, and future perspectives. Multidisciplinary Digital Publishing Institute

Iqbal MZ, Riaz M, Biedermann T, Klar AS (2024) Breathing new life into tissue engineering: exploring cutting-edge vascularization strategies for skin substitutes. Springer

Janarthanan G, Noh I (2018) Recent trends in bioinks for 3D printing. BioMed Central

Jeznach O, Tabakoglu S, Zaszczyńska A, Sajkiewicz P (2024) Review on machine learning application in tissue engineering: what has been done so far? Application areas, challenges, and perspectives. J Mater Sci 59(46):21222–21250. https://doi.org/10.1007/s10853-024-10449-2

Jorgensen A, Yoo JJ, Atala A (2020) Solid organ bioprinting: strategies to achieve organ function. American Chemical Society

Kafili G, Tamjid E, Simchi A (2024) The impact of mechanical tuning on the printability of decellularized amniotic membrane bioinks for cell-laden bioprinting of soft tissue constructs [article]. Sci Rep 14(1):29697. https://doi.org/10.1038/s41598-024-80973-3

Kanu NJ, Gupta E, Vates UK, Singh GK (2019) An insight into biomimetic 4D printing. Royal Society of Chemistry

Kasturi M, Mathur V, Gadre M, Srinivasan V, Vasanthan KS (2023) Three dimensional bioprinting for hepatic tissue engineering: from in vitro models to clinical applications. Springer

Khademhosseini A, Ashammakhi N, Karp JM, Gerecht S, Ferreira L, Annabi N, Darabi MA, Sirabella D, Vunjak-Novakovic G, Langer R (2020) Chapter 27 - embryonic stem cells as a cell source for tissue engineering. In: Lanza R, Langer R, Vacanti JP, Atala A (eds) Principles of tissue engineering, 5th edn. Academic Press, pp 467–490. https://doi.org/10.1016/B978-0-12-818422-6.00027-7

Kim DS, Kim D, Lim H, Youn J, Park T-E (2023) Scalable production of uniform and mature organoids in a 3D geometrically-engineered permeable membrane. Research Square (Research Square). https://doi.org/10.21203/rs.3.rs-3425714/v1

Kim D, Lee SJ, Lee D, Seok JM, Yeo SJ, Lim H, Lee JJ, Song JH, Lee K, Park WH, Park SA (2024) Biomimetic mineralization of 3D-printed polyhydroxyalkanoate-based microbial scaffolds for bone tissue engineering [article]. Int J Bioprinting 10(2):489–499. https://doi.org/10.36922/IJB.1806

Lai G, Meagher L (2024) Versatile xanthan gum-based support bath material compatible with multiple crosslinking mechanisms: rheological properties, printability, and cytocompatibility study [article]. Biofabrication 16(3):035005. https://doi.org/10.1088/1758-5090/ad39a8

Lai J, Wang M (2023) Developments of additive manufacturing and 5D printing in tissue engineering. J Mater Res 38(21):4692–4725. https://doi.org/10.1557/s43578-023-01193-5

Lamberger Z, Schubert DW, Buechner M, Cabezas NC, Schrüfer S, Murenu N, Schaefer N, Lang G (2024) Advanced optical assessment and modeling of extrusion bioprinting [article]. Sci Rep 14(1):13972. https://doi.org/10.1038/s41598-024-64039-y

Lee MO, Lee SG, Jung CR, Son YS, Ryu JW, Jung KB, Ahn JH, Oh JH, Lee HA, Lim JH, Kim J, Jang I, Choi J, Jung J, Park K, Lee B, Kim DS, Son MY, Cho HS (2021) Development of a quantitative prediction algorithm for target organ-specific similarity of human pluripotent stem cell-derived organoids and cells. Nat Commun 12(1):4492. https://doi.org/10.1038/s41467-021-24746-w

Lim KS, Baptista M, Moon S, Woodfield TBF, Rnjak-Kovacina J (2019) Microchannels in development, survival, and vascularisation of tissue analogues for regenerative medicine. Elsevier BV
Loukelis K, Helal ZA, Mikos AG, Chatzinikolaidou M (2023) Nanocomposite bioprinting for tissue engineering applications. Multidisciplinary Digital Publishing Institute
Luo Y, Xusong X, Gao Y, Ma J, Zhou X, Li Q, Yang H, Zhang B (2023) Development and application of a mechanical arm-based in situ 3D bioprinting method for the repair of skin wounds. Research Square (Research Square). https://doi.org/10.21203/rs.3.rs-3575253/v1
Ma J, Wang Y, Liu J (2018) Bioprinting of 3D tissues/organs combined with microfluidics. Royal Society of Chemistry
Malekmohammadi S, Aminabad NS, Sabzi A, Zarebkohan A, Razavi M, Vosough M, Bodaghi M, Maleki H (2021) Smart and biomimetic 3d and 4d printed composite hydrogels: opportunities for different biomedical applications [review]. Biomedicines 9(11):1537. https://doi.org/10.3390/biomedicines9111537
Mappa TA, Liu CM, Tseng CC, Ruslin M, Cheng JH, Lan WC, Huang BH, Cho YC, Hsieh CC, Kuo HH, Tsou CH, Shen YK (2023) An innovative biofunctional composite hydrogel with enhanced printability, rheological properties, and structural integrity for cell scaffold applications. Polymers (Basel) 15(15):3223–3223. https://doi.org/10.3390/polym15153223
Marsh A, Bunn D, Contag CH, Hammer N, Ashammakhi N, Chatzistavrou X (2022) New Hybrid Hydrogels for applications as bioinks in 3D printing implants. In: Tissue Engineering and Regenerative Medicine International Society (TERMIS), European Chapter Conference, Krakow, Poland. June 28–July 1, 2022
Marsh A, Apu EH, Bunn D, Contag C, Hammer N, Ashammakhi N, Chatzistavrou X (2023) New hybrid hydrogels for applications as BIOINKS in 3D printing implants. Tissue Eng A
Masi CD, Spitalieri P, Murdocca M, Novelli G, Sangiuolo F (2020) Application of CRISPR/Cas9 to human-induced pluripotent stem cells: from gene editing to drug discovery. BioMed Central
Mathur V, Agarwal P, Srinivasan V, Panwar A, Vasanthan KS (2022) Facet of 4D printing in biomedicine. J Mater Res 38(1):2–18. https://doi.org/10.1557/s43578-022-00779-9
Matsui T, Shinozawa T (2021) Human organoids for predictive toxicology research and drug development. Frontiers Media
Mazrouei R, Velasco V, Esfandyarpour R (2020) 3D-bioprinted all-inclusive bioanalytical platforms for cell studies. Sci Rep 10(1):14669. https://doi.org/10.1038/s41598-020-71452-6
McCarthy RR, Ullah MW, Booth P, Pei E, Yang G (2019) The use of bacterial polysaccharides in bioprinting. Elsevier BV
Michel R, Auzély-Velty R (2020) Hydrogel-colloid composite bioinks for targeted tissue-printing. American Chemical Society
Miri AK, Khalilpour A, Çeçen B, Maharjan S, Shin SR, Khademhosseini A (2018) Multiscale bioprinting of vascularized models. Elsevier BV
Miri AK, Mirzaee I, Hassan S, Mesbah Oskui S, Nieto D, Khademhosseini A, Zhang YS (2019) Effective bioprinting resolution in tissue model fabrication. Lab Chip 19(11):2019–2037. https://doi.org/10.1039/c8lc01037d
Mohammadi S, Cidonio G (2023) Unravelling hierarchical patterning of biomaterial inks with 3D microfluidic-assisted spinning: a paradigm shift in bioprinting technologies. Front Biomat Sci 2. https://doi.org/10.3389/fbiom.2023.1279061
Montero FE, Rezende RA, da Silva JVL, Sabino MA (2019) Development of a smart bioink for bioprinting applications. Front Mech Eng 5. https://doi.org/10.3389/fmech.2019.00056
Mulaudzi PE, Abrahamse H, Crous A (2023) Insights on three dimensional organoid studies for stem cell therapy in regenerative medicine. Springer
Muniz Castro B, Elbadawi M, Ong JJ, Pollard T, Song Z, Gaisford S, Perez G, Basit AW, Cabalar P, Goyanes A (2021) Machine learning predicts 3D printing performance of over 900 drug delivery systems. J Control Release 337:530–545. https://doi.org/10.1016/j.jconrel.2021.07.046

Naderi-Meshkin H, Cornelius VA, Eleftheriadou M, Potel KN, Setyaningsih WAW, Margariti A (2023) Vascular organoids: unveiling advantages, applications, challenges, and disease modelling strategies. BioMed Central

Naghieh S, Sarker MD, Izadifar M, Chen D (2017) Dispensing-based bioprinting of mechanically-functional hybrid scaffolds with vessel-like channels for tissue engineering applications—A brief review. Elsevier BV

Nwokoye PN, Abilez OJ (2024) Blood vessels in a dish: the evolution, challenges, and potential of vascularized tissues and organoids. Front Cardiovasc Med 11:1336910. https://doi.org/10.3389/fcvm.2024.1336910

O'Hern, C., Caywood, S., Aminova, S., Kiselev, A., Volmert, B., Cao, W., Wang, F., Dionise, M., Sewavi, M.-L., Skoric, M., Basrai, H., Mannering, F., Muniyandi, P., Popa, M., Boulos, G., Wolf, K., Brown, I., Nuñez-Regueiro, I., Huang, A.,... Aguirre, A. (2025). Human heart-macrophage assembloids mimic immune-cardiac interactions and enable arrhythmia disease modeling. Cell Stem Cell, 32(11), 1671–1690.e1613. doi: https://doi.org/10.1016/j.stem.2025.09.011

Paradiso A, Volpi M, Rinoldi C, Celikkin N, Negrini NC, Bilgen M, Dallera G, Pierini F, Costantini M, Święszkowski W, Farè S (2022) In vitro functional models for human liver diseases and drug screening: beyond animal testing. Royal Society of Chemistry

Perera K, Ivone R, Natekin E, Wilga C, Shen J, Menon JU (2021) 3D bioprinted implants for cartilage repair in intervertebral discs and knee menisci. Frontiers Media

Piazza ED, Pandolfi E, Cacciotti I, Fattore AD, Tozzi AE, Secinaro A, Borro L (2021) Bioprinting Technology in Skin, heart, pancreas and cartilage tissues: Progress and challenges in clinical practice. Multidisciplinary Digital Publishing Institute

Potyondy T, Uquillas JA, Tebon PJ, Byambaa B, Hasan A, Tavafoghi M, Mary H, Aninwene GE, Pountos I, Khademhosseini A, Ashammakhi N (2021) Recent advances in 3D bioprinting of musculoskeletal tissues. Biofabrication 13(2):022001. https://doi.org/10.1088/1758-5090/abc8de

Pountos I, Tellisi N, Ashammakhi N (2019) Three-dimensional bioprinting: safety, ethical, and regulatory considerations. In: Guvendiren M (ed) 3D bioprinting in medicine: technologies, bioinks, and applications. Springer, pp 191–203. https://doi.org/10.1007/978-3-030-23906-0_7

Pountos I, Tellisi N, Darabi MA, Erdem A, Mohamed T, Guvendiren M, Ashammakhi N (2021) 3D bioprinting. In: Atallah S (ed) Digital Surgery. Springer, pp 215–232. https://doi.org/10.1007/978-3-030-49100-0_16

Pountos I, Tellisi N, Ashammakhi N (2023) Chapter 10 – 4D printing for tissue engineering of smart constructs. In: Gonçalves G, Marques P, Mano J (eds) New trends in smart nanostructured biomaterials in health sciences. Elsevier, pp 325–349. https://doi.org/10.1016/B978-0-323-85671-3.00009-9

Qu G, Huang J, Gu G, Li Z, Wu X, Ren J (2023) Smart implants: 4D-printed shape-morphing scaffolds for medical implantation

Rahmati M, Silva EA, Reseland JE, Heyward CA, Haugen HJ (2020) Biological responses to physicochemical properties of biomaterial surface. Royal Society of Chemistry

Ramadan Q, Zourob M (2021) 3D bioprinting at the frontier of regenerative medicine, pharmaceutical, and food industries. Frontiers Media

Ramezani M, Ripin ZM (2023) 4D printing in biomedical engineering: advancements, challenges, and future directions. Multidisciplinary Digital Publishing Institute

Rammal H, GhavamiNejad A, Erdem A, Mbeleck R, Nematollahi M, Emir Diltemiz S, Alem H, Darabi MA, Ertas YN, Caterson EJ, Ashammakhi N (2021) Advances in biomedical applications of self-healing hydrogels. Mater Chem Front 5(12):4368–4400. https://doi.org/10.1039/D0QM01099E

Rasouli R, Sweeney CL, Frampton JP (2024) Heterogeneous and composite bioinks for 3D-bioprinting of complex tissue

Ratnamani MPC, Zhang X, Wang H (2022) A comprehensive assessment on the pivotal role of hydrogels in scaffold-based bioprinting. Multidisciplinary Digital Publishing Institute

Reyes DR, Esch MB, Ewart L, Nasiri R, Herland A, Sung K, Piergiovanni M, Lucchesi C, Shoemaker JT, Vukasinovic J, Nakae H, Hickman J, Pant K, Taylor A, Heinz N, Ashammakhi N (2024) From animal testing to in vitro systems: advancing standardization in microphysiological systems. Lab Chip 24(5):1076–1087. https://doi.org/10.1039/d3lc00994g

Rosellini E, Cascone MG, Guidi L, Schubert DW, Roether JA, Boccaccını AR (2023) Mending a broken heart by biomimetic 3D printed natural biomaterial-based cardiac patches: a review. Frontiers Media

Rossi G, Manfrin A, Lütolf MP (2018) Progress and potential in organoid research. Nature Portfolio

Rossi A, Pescara T, Gambelli AM, Gaggia F, Asthana A, Perrier Q, Basta G, Moretti M, Senin N, Rossi F, Orlando G, Calafiore R (2024) Biomaterials for extrusion-based bioprinting and biomedical applications. Front Bioeng Biotechnol 12:1393641. https://doi.org/10.3389/fbioe.2024.1393641

Santoni S, Gugliandolo SG, Sponchioni M, Moscatelli D, Colosimo BM (2021) 3D bioprinting: current status and trends—a guide to the literature and industrial practice. Bio-Des Manuf 5(1):14–42. https://doi.org/10.1007/s42242-021-00165-0

Santos-Beato P, Midha S, Pitsillides AA, Miller AF, Torii R, Kalaskar DM (2022) Biofabrication of the osteochondral unit and its applications: current and future directions for 3D bioprinting. SAGE Publishing

Santoso ZA (2021) The future of three-dimensional skin graft: a mini-review [article]. Bali Medical Journal 10(1):122–125. https://doi.org/10.15562/bmj.v10i1.2242

Sarah R, Schimmelpfennig K, Rohauer R, Lewis CL, Limon SM, Habib A (2025) Characterization and machine learning-driven property prediction of a novel hybrid hydrogel bioink considering extrusion-based 3D bioprinting. Gels 11(1):45–45. https://doi.org/10.3390/gels11010045

Seyedmahmoud R, Çelebi-Saltik B, Barros N, Nasiri R, Banton E, Shamloo A, Ashammakhi N, Dokmeci MR, Ahadian S (2019) Three-dimensional bioprinting of functional skeletal muscle tissue using gelatin Methacryloyl-alginate bioinks. Micromachines (Basel) 10(10):679

Shafiee S, Shariatzadeh S, Zafari A, Majd A, Niknejad H (2021) Recent advances on cell-based co-culture strategies for Prevascularization in tissue engineering. Frontiers Media

Shahabipour F, Ashammakhi N, Bonakdar S, Oskuee RK, Shokrgozar MA, Dehghani H, Khademhosseini A (2019) Key-points in engineering vascularized three-dimensional bioprinted bone constructs. Biofabrication

Shin J, Lee Y, Li Z, Hu J, Park SS, Kim K (2022) Optimized 3D bioprinting technology based on machine learning: A review of recent trends and advances. Multidisciplinary Digital Publishing Institute, In

Silva-Pedrosa R, Salgado AJ, Ferreira PE (2023) Revolutionizing disease modeling: the emergence of organoids in cellular systems. Multidisciplinary Digital Publishing Institute, In

Sriphutkiat Y, Kasetsirikul S, Ketpun D, Zhou Y (2019) Cell alignment and accumulation using acoustic nozzle for bioprinting. Sci Rep 9(1):17774. https://doi.org/10.1038/s41598-019-54330-8

Stapleton L, Zhu Y, Woo Y-p J, Appel E (2020) Engineered biomaterials for heart disease. Curr Opin Biotechnol 66:246–254. https://doi.org/10.1016/j.copbio.2020.08.008

Sung K, Patel Nisha R, Ashammakhi N, Nguyen K-L (2021) 3-dimensional bioprinting of cardiovascular tissues. JACC Basic Trans Sci 6(5):467–482. https://doi.org/10.1016/j.jacbts.2020.12.006

Synofzik J, Heene S, Jonczyk R, Blume C (2024) Ink-structing the future of vascular tissue engineering: a review of the physiological bioink design. Bio-Des Manuf 7(2):181–205

Tavafoghi M, Darabi MA, Mahmoodi M, Tutar R, Xu C, Mirjafari A, Billi F, Swieszkowski W, Nasrollahi F, Ahadian S, Hosseini V, Khademhosseini A, Ashammakhi N (2021) Multimaterial bioprinting and combination of processing techniques towards the fabrication of biomimetic tissues and organs. Biofabrication 13(4):042002. https://doi.org/10.1088/1758-5090/ac0b9a

Taylor S, Mueller E, Jones LR, Makela AV, Ashammakhi N (2024) Translational aspects of 3D and 4D printing and bioprinting. Adv Healthc Mater 13(27):2400463. https://doi.org/10.1002/adhm.202400463

Traldi C, Chiappini V, Menduti G, Tonda-Turo C, Boido M (2023) Advanced materials and biofabrication technologies to design in vitro functional central nervous system models. Frontiers Med Eng 1. https://doi.org/10.3389/fmede.2023.1270943

Turnbull G, Clarke J, Picard F, Zhang W, Riches P, Li B, Shu W (2020) 3D biofabrication for soft tissue and cartilage engineering. Elsevier BV

Unnikrishnan K, Thomas LV, Kumar RMR (2021) Advancement of scaffold-based 3D cellular models in cancer tissue engineering: an update. Frontiers Media

Vajda J, Milojević M, Maver U, Vihar B (2021) Microvascular tissue engineering—A review. Multidisciplinary Digital Publishing Institute

Valot L, Martínez J, Mehdi A, Subra G (2019) Chemical insights into bioinks for 3D printing. Royal Society of Chemistry

van Berlo D, Nguyen VVT, Gkouzioti V, Leineweber K, Verhaar MC, van Balkom BWM (2021) Stem cells, organoids, and organ-on-a-chip models for personalized in vitro drug testing. Curr Opinion Toxicol 28:7–14. https://doi.org/10.1016/j.cotox.2021.08.006

Verstegen MMA, Coppes RP, Béghin A, Coppi PD, Gerli M, Graeff ND, Pan Q, Saito Y, Shi S, Zadpoor AA, Laan LJWVD (2025) Clinical applications of human organoids. Nature Portfolio

Vettori L, Sharma P, Rnjak-Kovacina J, Gentile C (2020) 3D bioprinting of cardiovascular tissues for in vivo and in vitro applications using hybrid hydrogels containing silk fibroin: state of the art and challenges. Curr Tissue Microenviron Rep 1(4):261–276. https://doi.org/10.1007/s43152-020-00026-5

Vyas J, Shah I, Singh S, Prajapati BG (2023) Biomaterials-based additive manufacturing for customized bioengineering in management of otolaryngology: a comprehensive review. Frontiers Media

Wang Z, Wang L, Li T, Liu S, Guo B, Huang W, Wu Y (2021) 3D bioprinting in cardiac tissue engineering. Ivyspring International Publisher

Werschler N, Quintard C, Nguyen S, Penninger J (2024) Engineering next generation vascularized organoids. Elsevier BV

Wu Y, Wenger A, Golzar H, Tang XS (2020) 3D bioprinting of bicellular liver lobule-mimetic structures via microextrusion of cellulose nanocrystal-incorporated shear-thinning bioink. Sci Rep 10(1):20648. https://doi.org/10.1038/s41598-020-77146-3

Yao Q, Cheng S, Pan Q, Yu J, Cao G, Li L, Cao H (2024) Organoids: development and applications in disease models, drug discovery, precision medicine, and regenerative medicine. Wiley

Zanderigo G, Bracco F, Semeraro Q, Colosimo BM (2023) In-situ printability maps (IPM): A new approach for in-situ printability assessment with application to extrusion-based bioprinting. Bioprinting 36. https://doi.org/10.1016/j.bprint.2023.e00320

Zhang Y, Kumar P, Lv S, Xiong D, Zhao H, Cai Z, Zhao X (2020) Recent advances in 3D bioprinting of vascularized tissues. Mater Des 199:109398–109398. https://doi.org/10.1016/j.matdes.2020.109398

Zhang F, Liu J, He X, Wang R, Lu T, Zhang T, Liu Z (2021a) Preclinical evaluation of a novel 3D-printed movable lumbar vertebral complex for replacement: in vivo and biomechanical evaluation of goat model [article]. BioMed Resea Int 2021:2343404. https://doi.org/10.1155/2021/2343404

Zhang J, Wehrle E, Rubert M, Müller R (2021b) 3D bioprinting of human tissues: biofabrication, bioinks, and bioreactors. Multidisciplinary Digital Publishing Institute

Zhang S, Chen X, Shan M, Hao Z, Zhang X, Meng L, Zhai Z, Zhang L, Liu X, Wang X (2023a) Convergence of 3D bioprinting and nanotechnology in tissue engineering scaffolds. Multidisciplinary Digital Publishing Institute, In

Zhang S, Xu G, Wu J, Liu X, Fan YZ, Chen J, Wallace GG, Gu Q (2023b) Microphysiological constructs and systems: biofabrication tactics, biomimetic evaluation approaches, and biomedical applications. Wiley

Zhang H, Zhou X, Fang Y, Xiong Z, Zhang T (2024a) AI-driven 3D bioprinting for regenerative medicine: from bench to bedside. Elsevier BV

Zhang P, Tian W, Li P, Zhang F, Qu G, Du X, Liu G, Niu X (2024b) The application of custom 3D-printed prostheses with ultra-short stems in the reconstruction of bone defects: a single center analysis [article]. Front Bioeng Biotechnol 12:1349819. https://doi.org/10.3389/fbioe.2024.1349819

Zhao F, Sharma D, Sharma A, Hu L, Chen T-A, Voon S, Bayless K, Goldman J, Walsh A (2022) Perfusability and immunogenicity of implantable pre-vascularized tissues recapitulating native capillary network. Res Square (Research Square). https://doi.org/10.21203/rs.3.rs-2325499/v1

Zhou Y (2017) The recent development and applications of fluidic channels by 3D printing. BioMed Central

Zhou X, Luo Y, Gao Y, Ma J, Cai L, Zhou X, Li Q, Yang H, Zhang B (2024) Development and application of a mechanical arm-based in situ 3D bioprinting method for the repair of skin wounds. Deleted J 6(8). https://doi.org/10.1007/s42452-024-06043-5

Ziaran S, Danisovic L, Hammer N (2025) Editorial: tissue engineering and regenerative medicine: advances, controversies, and future directions. Front Bioeng Biotechnol 13:1568490. https://doi.org/10.3389/fbioe.2025.1568490

Chapter 2
Advanced Biomaterial Manufacturing for Regenerative Medicine: Emerging Non-printing and Additive Technologies

Aniruddha Vijay Savargaonkar, Ramesh Singh, and Ketul C. Popat

Abstract Biomaterials are essential in healthcare and regenerative medicine, with a range of fabrication methods available, including 3D bioprinting, additive manufacturing, and various non-printing technologies. Among these, 3D bioprinting is growing rapidly, driven by advances in printing precision, AI integration, and a pressing demand for customized, cell-laden tissue constructs that closely mimic native biology. However, other biomaterial fabrication techniques maintain unique advantages such as scalability, high-throughput production, simplicity, and superior extracellular matrix mimicry, making them indispensable for various regenerative applications. Therefore, this chapter provides a comprehensive overview of advanced biomaterial fabrication techniques for regenerative medicine, with primary emphasis on non-printing methods and additive manufacturing. Non-printing approaches, such as spinning methods, solvent casting, and self-assembly methods, enable scalable production of nanofibrous extracellular matrix mimics, injectable hydrogels, and porous scaffolds optimized for wound healing, soft tissue repair, and drug delivery. Additive manufacturing modalities, such as powder bed fusion, directed energy deposition, and vat photopolymerization, enable the creation of precise, patient-specific architectures with superior mechanical integrity for load-bearing implants.

Keywords Biomaterials · Nonprinting Methods · Additive Manufacturing · Regenerative Medicine

---

A. V. Savargaonkar
School of Biomedical and Chemical Engineering, Colorado State University, Fort Collins, CO, USA

R. Singh (✉) · K. C. Popat (✉)
Department of Bioengineering, George Mason University, Fairfax, VA, USA
e-mail: rsingh40@gmu.edu; kpopat@gmu.edu

Y. M. Elçin (ed.), *Biofabrication in Regenerative Medicine*, Stem Cell Biology and Regenerative Medicine 1519, https://doi.org/10.1007/978-3-032-30294-6_2

Abbreviations

AM	Additive Manufacturing
bis-GMA	bisphenol A-glycidyl methacrylate
BJT	Binder Jetting
CLIP	Continuous Liquid Interface Production
DED	Directed Energy Deposition
DLP	Digital Light Processing
DMLS	Direct Metal Laser Sintering
DNA	Deoxyribonucleic Acid
EBM	Electron Beam Melting
ECM	Extracellular Matrix
HA	Hydroxyapatite
PBF	Powder Bed Fusion
PCL	Polycaprolactone
PEGDA	Poly(ethylene glycol) diacrylate
PEO	Polyethylene Oxide
PLA	Polylactic Acid
PLLA	Poly l-lactide
PMMA	Polymethyl Methacrylate
PP	Polypropylene
PVA	Polyvinyl Alcohol
SBS	Solution Blow Spinning
SHS	Selective Heat Sintering
SLA	Stereolithography Apparatus
SLM	Selective Laser Melting
SLS	Selective Laser Sintering
TIPS	Thermally Induced Phase Separation
TTA	Trimethylolpropane triacrylate
UDMA	Urethane dimethacrylate
UHMWPE	Ultrahigh molecular weight polyethylene
VPP	Vat Polymerization
β-TCP	β-tricalcium phosphate

2.1 Introduction

Biomaterial manufacturing is at the core of regenerative medicine, offering new avenues to restore, replace, or regenerate damaged tissues and organs (Dzobo et al. 2018). These engineered materials provide a supportive, biologically active, and functional scaffold and construction (Qin et al. 2022). Biomaterials serve not only as passive structural supports but also as dynamic regulators of cellular behavior, closely mimicking the native extracellular matrix (ECM) in both composition and architecture (Mangani et al. 2025). This biomimicry is critical for guiding cell adhesion, proliferation, differentiation, and ultimately, tissue regeneration, making advanced manufacturing techniques integral to the success and translation of regenerative therapies (Chen et al. 2024). As the global burden of chronic wounds, degenerative diseases, and organ failure rises, the development of innovative biomaterial fabrication methods is urgently needed to overcome limitations of existing approaches and meet clinical demands.

The progression of biomaterial fabrication techniques is crucial in tackling current clinical challenges by enabling the creation of scaffolds specifically designed to meet the needs of various tissues. Advanced manufacturing methods now allow the production of materials that not only ensure biocompatibility and biodegradability but also exhibit enhanced mechanical strength and the capacity to actively interact with biological systems (Mirzaali et al. 2022). These developments support the incorporation of bioactive agents and living cells, fostering better tissue integration and improved function (Cong and Zhang 2025). Moreover, the interdisciplinary convergence of materials science, engineering, and biology has led to the design of multifunctional and responsive biomaterials that adapt to physiological conditions, enable controlled release of therapeutics, and promote regeneration (Shen et al. 2025; Vinchurkar et al. 2025). Therefore, investigating diverse fabrication strategies beyond conventional printing approaches is crucial for realizing novel regenerative therapies and meeting future medical demands.

Although 3D bioprinting has transformed scaffold fabrication by enabling precise architectural control, it is limited by factors such as a narrow range of usable materials, difficulties in preserving cell viability, and challenges in scaling up for clinical use (Gebeshuber et al. 2025). As a result, innovative non-printing and advanced additive manufacturing approaches are attracting interest due to their capability to fabricate complex and mechanically strong scaffolds that better incorporate biological components (Zhou et al. 2023; Do et al. 2015). This chapter provides a comprehensive review of innovative non-printing biomaterial fabrication techniques that show promise for regenerative medicine applications. It delves into the fundamental mechanisms, various fabrication methods, and strategies for incorporating cells and bioactive molecules, while also addressing critical challenges facing these approaches, with the aim of steering bio-fabrication toward more practical and effective clinical outcomes.

2.2 Non-printing and Additive Manufacturing

Non-printing and additive manufacturing (AM) methods both enable the production of scaffolds with improved mechanical properties and controlled structures, often without the issues associated with printing. Non-printing methods generally refer to traditional or emerging fabrication processes that do not rely on layer-by-layer material deposition (Baino et al. 2025). It involves fabrication techniques that form biomaterial scaffolds or structures without digitally controlled layer deposition. Examples include electrospinning to produce fibrous scaffolds and blow spinning for scalable fiber-based constructs. These methods often enable the continuous production of materials that mimic the native extracellular matrix morphology (Flores-Rojas et al. 2023). In contrast, additive manufacturing builds structures layer by

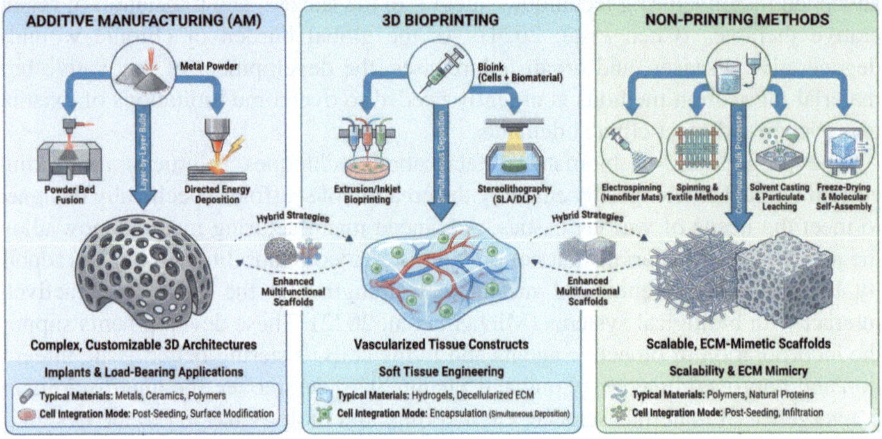

Fig. 2.1 Schematic representation of comparative biomaterial fabrication approaches; Additive manufacturing, 3D printing, and non-printing methods

layer from digital models, including methods such as powder bed fusion and directed energy deposition (Gibson et al. 2021a). AM can process a wide range of biomaterials, including polymers, metals, and ceramics, and can produce scaffolds with precise architectural control and patient-specific customization (Zhou et al. 2023; Kumar et al. 2025). Non-printing methods (e.g., spinning) offer scalability, while AM allows for the creation of geometrically intricate implants that are not possible with traditional molding or machining (Flores-Rojas et al. 2023) (Fig. 2.1).

2.3 Non-printing Manufacturing

Non-printing biomaterial manufacturing methods encompass a range of fabrication techniques that do not rely on the digital, layer-by-layer deposition characteristic of additive manufacturing (Baino et al. 2025). These methods can be classified into several categories according to their underlying physical processes.

2.3.1 Spinning Techniques

Spinning techniques play a pivotal role in the fabrication of fibrous scaffolds that closely mimic the architecture and function of the natural ECM (Flores-Rojas et al. 2023). These techniques facilitate the formation of high surface-area-to-volume nano-fibrous networks, providing scaffolds that support cell attachment, proliferation, and tissue regeneration (Kong et al. 2023). Key spinning methods include electrospinning, blow spinning, melt spinning, wet spinning, centrifugal spinning, and cell-spinning, each with distinct mechanisms, advantages, and applications

(Kong et al. 2023). These methods enable precise control over fiber morphology, porosity, and bioactivity using biocompatible polymers such as polycaprolactone (PCL), collagen, or silk fibroin.

2.3.2 Electrospinning

Electrospinning is one of the most established methods for producing ultrafine polymer fibers using an electric field. In a standard system, a high-voltage source is applied between a capillary containing the polymer fluid and a grounded collector, creating an intense electrostatic field. Once the electrostatic force exceeds the surface tension of the droplet at the needle tip, the droplet elongates into a cone, and a charged jet is expelled. As the solvent evaporates, the jet is stretched and thinned, ultimately forming solid fibers on the collector (Wang et al. 2025). This approach can process a wide range of materials, from synthetic polymers such as PCL and polylactic acid (PLA) to natural macromolecules, including collagen and chitosan, typically yielding porous nonwoven fibrous mats that resemble the extracellular matrix (Teng et al. 2025). Numerous variants have been developed, for example, coaxial electrospinning for generating core-shell fibers and melt electrospinning, which replaces solutions with polymer melts to eliminate the use of organic solvents (Mostofizadeh et al. 2023; Bachs-Herrera et al. 2021). Despite its versatility and suitability for ECM-like scaffold fabrication, electrospinning still faces key barriers such as the use of volatile organic solvents and relatively modest production rates compared with industrial throughput requirements (Flores-Rojas et al. 2023; Teng et al. 2025).

2.3.3 Blow Spinning (Solution Blow Spinning)

Solution blow spinning (SBS) relies on a fast-flowing gas stream rather than high voltage to produce fibers from polymer solutions (Carriles et al. 2023). Typically, the polymer solution is delivered through an inner nozzle, while compressed gas (such as air or nitrogen) exits from a surrounding outer nozzle. The shear forces and pressure gradient at the interface between the gas and the liquid stretches the emerging jet, which is drawn toward a collector and solidifies into fibers as the solvent evaporates. Because SBS does not require electrical components or conductive collectors, it is well-suited for portable or handheld devices and can be used to deposit fibers directly onto irregular or sensitive surfaces, including open wounds or tissue defects (Carriles et al. 2023). This enables the rapid in situ formation of conformal nanofibrous layers that can promote hemostasis, serve as protective dressings, and support tissue repair, while offering higher throughput compared to conventional electrospinning (Carriles et al. 2023).

2.3.4 Melt Spinning and Thermal Drawing

In melt spinning, a thermoplastic polymer is heated above its melting temperature and extruded through a spinneret to form continuous filaments, which are then cooled and solidified (Noh et al. 2023). Because the process does not involve any solvent, it eliminates concerns about residual solvent toxicity and is compatible with medical-grade polymers that can withstand elevated temperatures. However, only polymers with sufficient thermal stability and appropriate melt rheology can be used. An advanced derivative of this concept is thermal drawing, where a macroscopic perform comprising multiple components (for example, conductive fillers, optical materials, or microfluidic channels embedded in a polymer matrix) is thermally softened and drawn into slender fibers while preserving the internal architecture of the original preform (Bachs-Herrera et al. 2021; Wang et al. 2021a). This method enables the fabrication of multifunctional fibers that can simultaneously provide electrical conduction, optical guidance, and fluid transport, making them attractive for neural interfaces and other smart implantable devices capable of sensing, stimulation, and localized delivery (Liu et al. 2020).

2.3.5 Wet Spinning

Wet spinning represents a traditional and reliable approach for generating continuous filaments, particularly from polymers that are prone to degradation under heat, making them incompatible with melt-based processes. The method begins by dissolving the polymer in an appropriate solvent to create a viscous spinning dope, which is then forced through a spinneret into a coagulation bath containing a non-solvent liquid (Steppert et al. 2023). Fiber solidification occurs through phase inversion, where the original solvent diffuses into the bath, while the non-solvent penetrates the extrudate, or through dehydration effects within the bath, resulting in polymer precipitation. This process is ideal for handling natural polymers, such as collagen, silk fibroin, alginate, and cellulose, as well as synthetic polymers like PLA and PCL (Steppert et al. 2023). It yields durable, high-tenacity fibers well-suited for medical sutures, scaffolds in tissue repair, and large-volume production. Modern developments feature automated wet spinning systems that produce sponge-like meshes or hollow core-shell fibers for sustained release of antibiotics, proteins, or growth factors. Drawbacks include high energy demands, lengthy timelines, and the need for extensive rinsing to eliminate solvent remnants and contaminants, with post-processing stretching often applied to orient polymer chains and boost tensile strength. (Rocha et al. 2022).

2.3.6 Centrifugal Spinning

Centrifugal spinning, also known as rotary jet spinning or force-spinning, offers a fast, economical, and scalable method for producing micro- and nanofibers without relying on electrical fields. A polymer solution or melt is loaded into a spinneret that rotates at high speeds. Once centrifugal forces surpass surface tension and viscosity, the fluid ejects from the orifices as stretching jets that solidify upon solvent evaporation or cooling before reaching a collector (Marjuban et al. 2023). Key benefits in biomaterial production include compatibility with thick solutions and electrically non-conductive materials challenging for electrospinning, alongside superior output rates that support commercial scaling. Applications span tissue scaffolds made from materials like PCL, which enhance cell adhesion and growth, drug-eluting matrices that improve the bioavailability of insoluble compounds, and antimicrobial dressings for wound care. The technique also facilitates the alignment of nanofibers, which is advantageous for engineering musculoskeletal or neural tissues (Marjuban et al. 2023).

2.3.7 Cell-Spinning and Microfluidic Spinning

To directly incorporate living cells into fibrous constructs, microfluidic-based spinning strategies have been developed as gentle, water-based alternatives to traditional high-stress processes (Hong et al. 2019). In these systems, fluids are manipulated within microscale channels to continuously generate hydrogel fibers through mechanisms such as ionic crosslinking, enzymatic reactions, or light-initiated polymerization (Dores et al. 2025). Typically, a central stream containing cells and polymer precursors (for example, alginate, gelatin, or their derivatives) is enveloped by a sheath flow carrying crosslinking ions or initiators, causing solidification around the core and reducing the mechanical stress experienced by the cells (Dores et al. 2025). This configuration allows the production of cell-laden hydrogel microfibers with high cell viability and controlled composition, which can be assembled into three-dimensional tissue-like constructs, including perfusable or vascularized models. The laminar flow and geometric design of the microchannels also permit precise control over fiber architecture, enabling fabrication of core–shell, hollow, or Janus fibers, as well as spatial patterning of bioactive cues and therapeutic agents along or across the fiber cross-section (Dores et al. 2025).

2.4 Solvent-Based Fabrication Methods

Solvent-based approaches utilize differences in solubility and controlled phase changes to create highly porous scaffolds that facilitate tissue infiltration and growth.

2.4.1 *Solvent Casting Combined with Particulate Leaching*

This established process starts by dissolving a polymer in an appropriate solvent and blending it with porogen particles, such as sodium chloride or sugar crystals. The resulting mixture is poured into a mold, allowing the solvent to evaporate slowly. This is followed by immersion in water, which dissolves and removes the porogens, creating an interconnected network of pores within the solidified polymer matrix (Sola et al. 2019). The technique stands out for its simplicity and low cost, making it accessible for producing scaffolds suitable for bone or cartilage repair. However, it struggles with thicker constructions due to uneven solvent diffusion during drying, and incomplete porogen removal can leave behind traces of organic solvents that may pose biocompatibility risks (Sola et al. 2019).

2.4.2 *Phase Separation*

Phase separation methods, particularly thermally induced phase separation (TIPS), exploit the cooling of a homogeneous polymer solution to induce instability, thereby separating it into polymer-concentrated and solvent-rich phases. After phase demarcation, the solvent is extracted, yielding a scaffold featuring a nanofibrous structure with excellent pore interconnectivity (Zeinali et al. 2020). This enables the customization of pore dimensions and the incorporation of growth factors or other bioactive agents, making it ideal for soft tissue applications, such as skin or neural regeneration. TIPS offers superior control over morphology compared to other solvent methods; however, solvent residues and precise temperature management remain critical for achieving consistent outcomes (Zeinali et al. 2020; Zeinali et al. 2021).

2.4.3 *Freeze Drying (Lyophilization)*

Freeze drying fabricates porous matrices by rapidly freezing a polymer or hydrogel solution, then applying vacuum to sublimate the ice crystals directly from solid to vapor, using the crystals themselves as temporary porogen templates. Pore size and distribution depend on freezing conditions, such as cooling rate and polymer concentration, resulting in sponge-like architectures with tailored anisotropy (Katrilaka et al. 2023). Commonly applied to biopolymers like collagen, gelatin, or alginate, as well as advanced materials such as DNA hydrogels, this method excels in preserving bioactivity and supporting cell migration in applications like wound healing and cartilage engineering. Post-processing crosslinking often boosts structural integrity, addressing inherent mechanical fragility (Katrilaka et al. 2023).

2.5 Self-Assembly and Biomimetic Approaches

Self-assembly and biomimetic strategies provide cutting-edge methods for engineering biomaterials that replicate the hierarchical organization and dynamic responses of natural tissues (DiMaio et al. 2017; Wu et al. 2023a). Self-assembly is a bottom-up process that utilizes the spontaneous organization of molecular building blocks into stable, hierarchically structured formations driven by non-covalent interactions, including hydrogen bonding, π-π stacking, electrostatic forces, and hydrophobic effects (Kumar et al. 2018; Singh et al. 2017; Gupta et al. 2018). Molecular building blocks, such as peptides, proteins, polymers, and DNA, spontaneously form nanostructures like nanofibers, hydrogels, vesicles, and origami-folded scaffolds (Kosara et al. 2024; Menon et al. 2023). Biomimetic designs incorporate cues from the ECM, incorporating bioactive sequences that facilitate cell adhesion, enzymatic degradation, and signaling to guide tissue repair. These materials are highly modular and adaptable, allowing for precise adjustments to mechanical stiffness, degradation rates, and biofunctionality, which supports their use as injectable scaffolds for wound healing, 3D cell cultures, and targeted therapies (He et al. 2008; Mittal et al. 2021). Advances in peptide amphiphiles and protein modules further facilitate the creation of hierarchical assemblies that emulate natural fibril networks, thus improving regenerative outcomes in neural and cartilage applications (Singh et al. 2020a; Singh et al. 2018; Kesharwani et al. 2022).

2.5.1 Peptide Self-Assembly

Peptide self-assembly is an effective bottom-up method for creating biomaterials, using designed peptides that form nanofibers, gels, and matrices through weak intermolecular forces in biocompatible environments (Chen et al. 2019; Aldilla et al. 2020; Gelain et al. 2021; Levin et al. 2020; Das et al. 2025) Peptide sequences that often alternate between hydrophobic and charged residues initially overcome electrostatic barriers by adjusting the pH or adding salt, leading to a hydrophobic core and lateral β-strand alignment strengthened by hydrogen bonds and aromatic interactions. Peptides can be rationally designed to assemble into supramolecular hydrogels that mimic the ECM (Levin et al. 2020; Das et al. 2025). For example, peptides containing the diphenylalanine (FF) motif or those capped with aromatic groups (e.g., Fmoc, naphthalene) self-assemble into nanofibers via π-π stacking and hydrogen bonding. These structures are inherently biocompatible and biodegradable (Bakhtiary et al. 2023; Singh and Popat 2024).

Peptide amphiphiles stand out, combining lipid tails for micelle-like packing, central β-sheet domains for fiber elongation, and functional heads displaying motifs like RGD or MMP-cleavable sequences, yielding bundles of 5–10 nm fibers that entangle into shear-thinning hydrogels mimicking native ECM for in situ delivery

(Habibi et al. 2016; Hendricks et al. 2017). Peptide sequences can be engineered to form β-sheets, α-helices, or amphiphilic structures that respond to physiological stimuli, such as pH, ions, or enzymes, to trigger gelation in situ. Such smart biomaterials offer multiple benefits, exhibiting broad-spectrum antimicrobial activity that disrupts bacterial biofilms and promotes cell growth, collagen deposition, and neovascularization (Singh et al. 2018; Copling et al. 2023; Das and Das 2021; Singh et al. 2021; Swain et al. 2025). They are valuable for wound healing, where they can provide a moist environment, promote cell adhesion through motifs like RGD, and enable the sustained release of therapeutics (Bakhtiary et al. 2023).

2.5.2 Nucleic Acid (DNA) Hydrogels

DNA nanotechnology enables the programmable assembly of biomaterials through precise base pairing and Watson-Crick hybridization, creating rigid nanoscale architectures such as tiles, lattices, aptamer-functionalized networks, hydrogels, and DNA origami structures (Hoque and Rajaee 2017; Singh et al. 2023; Kansara et al. 2023; Singh et al. 2024). DNA hydrogels consist of DNA strands serving either as scaffolds or cross-linkers, constructed via branched DNA (X- or Y-shaped monomers), rolling circle amplification for ultra-long strands, or supramolecular motifs such as i-motifs and G-quadruplexes (Hanif et al. 2023; Yao et al. 2021). These hydrogels exhibit shear-thinning behavior and self-healing properties, facilitating the formation of injectable and moldable constructs with excellent biocompatibility and controlled degradation into harmless nucleotides that actively promote bone regeneration through mineral deposition. Functionalization with aptamers or ligands enhances cell adhesion, growth, and targeted movement, while the precise molecular architecture supports stem cell functions without toxicity, enabling their use in drug delivery and biosensing (Kosara et al. 2024; Hanif et al. 2023).

Beyond peptides and DNA, self-assembling biomaterials draw from a broad array of molecular families that organize into tissue-compatible scaffolds via non-covalent forces such as hydrophobic collapse, ionic pairing, and hydrogen bonding in biological settings (Mittal et al. 2021; Hendricks et al. 2017; Li et al. 2022; Zhuo et al. 2024). Naturally derived polysaccharides, including alginate, hyaluronan, chitosan, and modified celluloses, form water-rich gels through multivalent cross-linking, excelling in dermal healing and controlled release, while requiring composites for durability (Wang et al. 2021b; Tomić et al. 2023). Amphipthilic lipids and phospholipids further assemble into vesicular or tubular mimics of cell membranes for encapsulation and immunomodulation in soft tissues, whereas low-molecular-weight synthons, such as diphenylalanine derivatives or host-guest cyclodextrins, generate stiff nanotubes through aromatic interactions, which suit neural applications (Habibi et al. 2016).

2.6 Textile Techniques

Textile-based approaches, such as weaving, knitting, and braiding, have become crucial in biomaterial scaffold design, enabling the development of robust structures that can withstand mechanical loads in tissue engineering. These techniques assemble fibers, often created through wet spinning, electrospinning, or microfluidics, into organized, hierarchical structures that encourage directional cell alignment and tissue growth (Akbari et al. 2016; Ji et al. 2025). For example, fibers made using microfluidic spinning can be woven or coiled to create three-dimensional constructs with specific anisotropy, which is ideal for guiding regeneration in neural or muscular tissues. This precise fiber organization not only improves the structural strength but also boosts the biological performance of the scaffolds by mimicking the natural alignment of tissues (Ji et al. 2025).

2.7 Material Injection and Molding

Material Injection Injectable biomaterial formulations, especially hydrogels, provide a less invasive option for conforming to complex tissue voids and enabling localized therapeutic release. These systems typically exhibit shear-thinning behavior, where the viscosity decreases during syringe extrusion and rapidly reforms post-injection to maintain shape stability (Parvin et al. 2025; Chandel et al. 2024). Notable examples include tetrahedral DNA nanostructures and peptide-derived gels, which exhibit rapid structural recovery and endurance, supporting applications ranging from dermal repair to cardiac tissue restoration (Parvin et al. 2025). Portable applicators equipped with integrated mixing tips further simplify on-site deployment of dual-component systems, promoting immediate solidification upon tissue contact.

Molding The process involves pouring precursor solutions into custom molds, then solidifying them through crosslinking, gelation, or other triggers to create specific shapes (Emerson et al. 2022). This technique is ideal for producing patient-specific implants, such as ocular devices or orthopedic spacers. In advanced DNA-based gels, molding incorporates stimulus-responsive motifs, such as pH-sensitive i-motif sequences, to create shape-shifting materials that respond to environmental cues. Molding also works well with techniques like gas foaming, where porosity is formed during shape to improve nutrient diffusion and cell entry (Suamte et al. 2023) (Fig. 2.2).

2.8 Additive Manufacturing Technologies

Powder Bed Fusion uses layers of powdered metals, ceramics, or composites, fused by a laser or electron beam, to construct strong, load-bearing implants for orthopedics and dentistry. Directed Energy Deposition (DED) utilizes focused energy beams

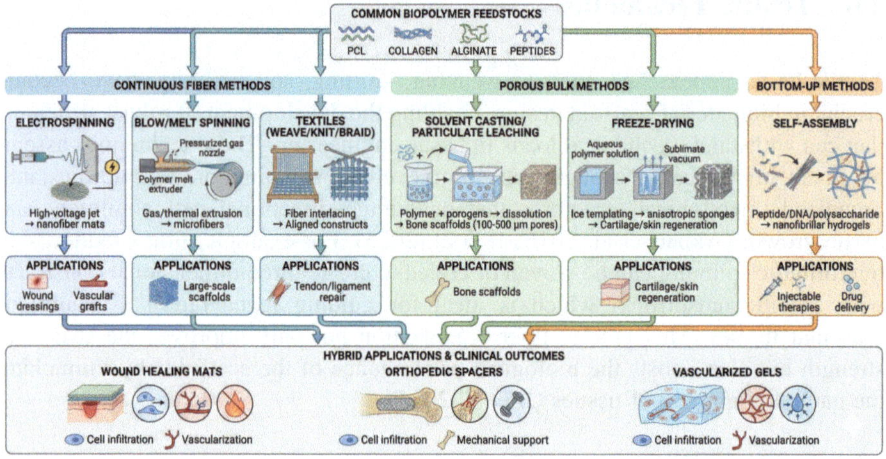

Fig. 2.2 Schematic representation of nonprinting techniques for biomaterial fabrications and applications

for site-specific deposition and repair of metal implants. Micro- and nano-additive methods, such as lithography and microfluidic-assisted fabrication, allow high precision and are being developed for delicate scaffold architectures in microtissue engineering.

2.8.1 Powder Bed Fusion (PBF)

PBF is one of the first commercialized AM processes. It was developed at the University of Texas at Austin in the United States (Gibson et al. 2020). It is a process that builds an object layer by layer using metal- or polymer-based materials powered by electricity (Joshua et al. 2024). It follows a set technique which involves the following steps:

1. **Slicing of model:** A 3D computer model is sliced using slicing software into individual layers.
2. **Spreading powder over the platform:** A thin layer of material, in powder form, is spread onto the build platform. The powder particles have a spherical shape and vary from 15 μm to 100 μm for different variations of PBF (Wegner 2021).
3. **Fusing of powder:** A laser or electron beam fuses the powder following the path as provided by the 3D model. This is a building with one layer.
4. **Lowering of the build platform:** After the first layer is completed, the build platform is lowered by the thickness of one layer. Steps 2–4 are repeated till all the layers of the model are completed.
5. **Post-processing:** The unused powders are collected and can be reused. If required, the object is heat-treated.

There are five types of PBF processes: (i) Selective Laser Sintering (SLS), (ii) Selective Laser Melting (SLM), (iii) Direct Metal Laser Sintering (DMLS), (iv) Selective Heat Sintering (SHS), and (v) Electron Beam Melting (EBM) (Dev Singh et al. 2021).

2.8.1.1 Selective Laser Sintering (SLS)

SLS uses heat and pressure to fabricate 3D models layer by layer. It is a very flexible technique and can create high-quality objects (Singh et al. 2020b). Powder is spread on the built platform, and a laser beam scans the powder selectively to fuse the particles based on the slicing data. This forms the first sintered layer, followed by the bed moving down, and the second layer powder is spread on the first layer (Dev Singh et al. 2021). This process is fast, accurate, and has minimal wastage. It has high application rates for biomedical purposes for pre-surgical planning, bone scaffolds for tissue engineering, and prosthetics (Singh et al. 2020b).

2.8.1.2 Selective Laser Melting (SLM)

SLM works similarly to SLS, with the difference being that it melts the powder particles instead of sintering (Dev Singh et al. 2021). This process enables the production of complex part geometries at a faster rate (Dev Singh et al. 2021). SLM has is also very precise and a minimum of 0.02 mm minimum thickness layer can be achieved (Singh et al. 2020b).

2.8.1.3 Direct Metal Laser Sintering (DMLS)

This technique is similar to SLS; however, it focuses more on sintering than full melting (Joshua et al. 2024). Compared to SLS, which has a minimum layer thickness of 0.08 mm, the minimum layer with DMLS is 0.1 mm (Singh et al. 2020b). It is a low-cost technique and finds applications in the aerospace and dental industries (Dev Singh et al. 2021; Singh et al. 2020b).

2.8.1.4 Selective Heat Sintering (SHS)

SHS is similar to SLS, but it has a thermal printhead instead of a powerful laser (Joshua et al. 2024). The layer is formed by the headed head touching the powder based on the sliced model (Dev Singh et al. 2021). This process is very low-cost and has great material adaptability; however, it can only be used with thermoplastic materials (Joshua et al. 2024). However, SHS has low printing speed and is unsuitable for high-temperature applications (Additive Manufacturing Research Group n.d.).

2.8.1.5 Electron Beam Melting (EBM)

EBM uses an electron beam instead of a laser to melt the powder particles. It operates under high vacuums to prevent oxidation, making it a favorable method for the aerospace, medical (orthopedic), and automotive industries (Dev Singh et al. 2021; Singh et al. 2020b). EBM has a high resolution, with layer thicknesses ranging from 50 μm to 150 μm (Joshua et al. 2024).

Materials As PBF sinters/melts the materials to form each layer of the sliced 3D model, the materials used should be able to melt and mold into shape (Gibson et al. 2020). Hence, for PBF, there are limited options for material selection available, primarily due to market demand and costs (Nouri et al. 2021). Even so, a wide range of materials can be used with PBF, including polymers, metals, and ceramics. When it comes to polymers, only thermoplastic polymers are compatible for use with PBF, with polyamide (commonly referred to as Nylon) being the most common material used for PBF (Gibson et al. 2020). Other polymers compatible with PBF include PEEK, Ultrahigh molecular weight polyethylene (UHMWPE), polypropylene (PP), polymethyl methacrylate (PMMA), PLA, PCL, and polyvinyl alcohol (PVA) (Nouri et al. 2021).

Metals are the most widely used class of materials with PBF due to their malleability. Any metal that can be welded can be used for PBF (Gibson et al. 2020). Metals are also widely used to fabricate biomaterials for orthopedic and dental applications (Gibson et al. 2020; Nouri et al. 2021). Metals powders widely used with PBF are stainless and tool steels, titanium, nickel, aluminum, cobalt-chrome, and their alloys (Joshua et al. 2024). When selecting metal powders for PBF, the weldability and castability of the metals, as well as the size and density of the powders, play a crucial role in determining the thickness and roughness of the layers (Nouri et al. 2021).

Benefits and Limitations Table 2.1 shows the advantages and disadvantages of PBF (Gibson et al. 2020; Joshua et al. 2024; Nouri et al. 2021) (Table 2.2).

Applications in Biomaterial Fabrication In the field of biomaterial fabrication, PBF is widely used, as it enables the production of both patient-specific and generic biomaterials (Joshua et al. 2024). Biomaterials fabricated using PBF include charcot joints, knee implants, hip implants, spinal cages, radial head prostheses, dental scaffolds and implants, heart valves, coronary stents, and orthopedic implants (Joshua et al. 2024; Wu et al. 2023b). In addition to the above-mentioned materials, implants can also be fabricated with the addition of bioactive compounds, such as hydroxyapatite (HA). It enables the higher bioactivity of implants used for bone regeneration (Nouri et al. 2021). When it comes to orthopedic applications, PBF, due to its layer-by-layer approach, enables the creation of biomimetic implants that replicate the micro- and nano-topography of bone.

Table 2.1 Summary of nonprinting methods

Method category	Key examples	Pore/fiber size	Primary applications
Spinning	Electrospinning, blow spinning	Nanoscale fibers	Wound healing, vascular grafts
Solvent-based	Casting/particulate leaching	100–500μm pores	Bone scaffolds
Freeze drying	Lyophilization	10–300μm pores	Cartilage, skin
Self-assembly	Peptide and DNA hydrogels	Nanoscale networks	Injectable therapies
Textile	Knitting, braiding	Macroscale aligned	Tendons, ligaments
Injection/ molding	Polymer molding	Variable	Bulk implants

Table 2.2 Advantages and disadvantages of Powder Bed Fusion Technique

Advantages	Disadvantages
Wide range of materials Advanced geometries are easier as loose powder can act as support material (mainly for polymer PBF) High precision Reduced waste	Longer time required to construct parts due to high preheating and post-processing times Multi-material parts are difficult to fabricate Accuracy and surface finish are inferior to liquid-based processes

2.8.2 Binder Jetting (BJT)

BJT is a form of additive manufacturing that is very similar to PBF, with the main difference being the use of a binder instead of laser/heat. Invented at MIT, the BJT uses binder droplets to form spherical agglomerates with powder, enabling the printing of layers. This is followed by a new layer of powder being spread on the build platform (Gibson et al. 2021b). After the complete model is printed, it is left in the powder bed to allow the binder to set. This is a highly scalable process at a considerably low cost, as simply increasing the number of printer nozzles would suffice (Gibson et al. 2021b). The quality of print depends on the interaction between the printed droplets in the powder (Ziaee and Crane 2019). A general process for BJT follows this sequence of steps:

1. A 3D model needs to be sliced, which can be used to print it layer by layer.
2. A thin layer of powder is spread on the build box.
3. A liquid binder is jetted on the layer of powder.
4. After binder deposition, the powder bed is heated to partially cure the layer and prepare the next spreading of powder. This step is crucial as it ensures a uniform temperature for each layer, facilitating adhesion while preventing cracking of the powder bed.

5. Following the drying of the binder, the powder bed is lowered by the thickness of one layer (usually 50 μm to 200 μm). This is followed by further powder deposition.
6. After the printing is complete, the model is left to dry in the powder bed and is usually further cured by heating in an oven at 180–200 °C.

Materials The first material to be used was a starch-based powder and a water-based binder. Currently, BJT can be used with all three classes of materials, i.e., metals, polymers, and ceramics (Gibson et al. 2021b; Ziaee and Crane 2019). Metals and their alloys form the bulk of the BJT materials, with stainless steels, Iron, cobalt-chromium alloy, and copper being some of the metals used extensively in BJT (Ziaee and Crane 2019). Polymers are used with BJT but have seen limited application due to the challenges involved with fabricating polymers into powder (Ziaee and Crane 2019). Polymers such as PMMA, PGA, PLA, PCL, and PEO (polyethylene oxide) have been printed using BJT (Gibson et al. 2021b; Ziaee and Crane 2019). Applications involving ceramics initially faced challenges due to the difficulty of machining them into powders (Ziaee and Crane 2019). To counter this limitation, BJT was modified to a slurry-based material, where layers of slurry were deposited and then dried, and a binder was used to selectively print the part shape (Gibson et al. 2021b).

Benefits and Limitations

Applications in Biomaterial Fabrication
BJT has a varied range of biomedical applications that are efficient in delivering anatomy-specific implants with favorable mechanical properties and biocompatibility, which can be achieved both in vitro and in vivo (Barui 2021). However, its usage is tied to the biocompatibility of the powder-binder systems used. PLLA (poly l-lactide), calcium phosphates, calcium silicate, and hydroxyapatite are some powders that are used with BJT (Ziaee and Crane 2019). However, as mentioned, due to the biocompatibility limitation, binder selection is constrained to pure water, chloroform, and acid-based binders (Ziaee and Crane 2019). BJT printed ceramic biomaterial scaffolds have also demonstrated a multifunctional ability in chemoprevention against cancerous cells, as well as in promoting osteoblast cell proliferation and differentiation (Barui 2021). In another study, a BJT printed ceramic scaffold with hydroxyapatite and calcium phosphate demonstrated enhanced osseointegration in a dog model in vivo (Igawa et al. 2006). BJT printed metallic biomaterials have also been extensively studied, with materials demonstrating increased cytocompatibility, favorable mechanical properties for orthopedic implants, and biomimetic microstructure (Barui 2021) (Table 2.3).

Table 2.3 Advantages and disadvantages of Binder Jetting Technique

Advantages	Disadvantages
Faster process as only a small fraction needs to be dispensed from the binder A wide array of materials is possible due to the modified slurry approach High-quality ceramic and metal parts No support structures are required during printing Bonding occurs at room temperature, hence preventing thermal defects like distortion, shrinkage, and cracks	Costly and higher post-processing needs like furnace operations or infiltration steps Poor mechanical properties (as-built condition), brittle, and highly porous Poor accuracy and surface finish

2.8.3 Directed Energy Deposition (DED)

According to the ASTM/ISO 52900 standard, DED is defined as "an additive manufacturing process in which focused thermal energy is used to fuse materials by melting as they are being deposited." (Ahn 2021) It can be used with a wide range of materials, which include polymers, ceramics, and metal powders (Gibson et al. 2021a). DED melts the material using a laser or electron beam as it is being deposited, which cools to form the model (Gibson et al. 2021a). It can work with both melt powder and wires (Gibson et al. 2021a). A DED process follows this series of steps: (Gibson et al. 2021a)

1. A deposition head, which is composed of laser optics, feed nozzle, and other equipment as required by the variation of the process, is used to deposit material on the substrate (flat plate or an existing part) where the new model is supposed to be built.
2. The feed (powder, wire) is injected into the melt pool with enough kinetic energy to defy gravity. This allows for deposition from different axes, enabling the collection of more complex parts.
3. The feed is then deposited on the substrate, followed by cooling (high for laser and low for electron beam).
4. Each pass of the deposition head creates a track, and each track overlaps about 25%, which ensures bonding and remelting of tracks.

Based on material feeding, there are two types: i) Powder-based DED, ii) Wire-based DED (Ahn 2021). Based on the source of energy, there are four main categories: i) Laser deposition, ii) Electron beam deposition, iii) Friction stir deposition, iv) Arc deposition (Gibson et al. 2021a).

2.8.3.1 Laser Deposition

One of the first commercialized processes, laser deposition utilizes a laser to build parts on a substrate. This setup can be used with multiple deposition heads as well as a multi-axis approach. The printing doesn't have to be performed on a planar surface and can be done on a tilting platform.

2.8.3.2 Electron Beam Deposition

This method, developed by NASA, is used to manufacture parts for the International Space Station (Banke 2006). This system utilizes an electron beam to melt material, conserving electrical resources, but it requires a vacuum environment to function. This setup can also be used in a multi-axis setting, and it is quicker and produces less waste material.

2.8.3.3 Arc Deposition

This method was devised by combining gas arc welding and multi-axis milling. It is a relatively low-cost technique with high deposition rates and has no limitations on the part size.

Materials DED can be used to print any material as long as it is stable in its molten form (Gibson et al. 2021a). Metals are easily processed unless they have high reflectivity, improper atmospheric preparation occurs, or bonding is inhibited by oxide formation (Gibson et al. 2021a). Similarly, ceramics are also difficult to use with DED as they are not stable during processing, and there is a risk of cracking due to rapid cooling (Gibson et al. 2021a).

Benefits and Limitations

Applications in Biomaterial Fabrication DED is used extensively to fabricate biomaterials, including those made from metals and ceramics. DED has been used to fabricate orthopedic implants, primarily for hip and dental implants, utilizing commercially pure titanium and the titanium alloy Ti6Al4V (Arias-González et al. 2021). DED has the unique quality of fabricating load-bearing implants with low modulus, which allows for enhanced osseointegration (Arias-González et al. 2021). Another material used to fabricate biomaterials with DED is CoCrMo, which is commonly employed in the fabrication of dental biomaterials (Arias-González et al. 2021) (Table 2.4).

2.8.4 Vat Polymerization (VPP)

VPP is a term used to describe a set of additive manufacturing techniques that involve a liquid photopolymer in a large tank, which is cured selectively to build

Table 2.4 Advantages and disadvantages of the Directed Energy Deposition Technique

Advantages	Disadvantages
Scaling up is easier Multi-axis Multi-material parts can be produced in a single build High deposition rates Fully dense parts with controllable microstructures	Poor resolution and surface finish High surface roughness Support structures are required for complex geometries

the model (Vladić et al. 2022). Photopolymerization is a chemical reaction in which a liquid transforms into a solid upon exposure to irradiation (Gibson et al. 2021c). This set of techniques follows the following strategy to print a part: (Bongiovanni and Vitale 2022).

1. The 3D model is processed by changing the orientation if required and adding extra support elements. This is followed by the slicing of the model.
2. The printer prints the model in the z-axis (height/depth) using a layer-by-layer approach as fed into it through the sliced model.
3. After the model printing is done, the model is rinsed in a wash solution to remove liquid resin.
4. Models undergo a post-processing step where the model is made more uniform through steps like bulk curing, support removal, grinding, polishing, painting, varnishing, coating, sterilization, inspection, and measurement, depending on the application of the printed part.

VPP can be categorized into three types: i) Stereolithography apparatus (SLA), ii) Digital light processing (DLP), iii) Continuous liquid interface production (CLIP) (Vladić et al. 2022).

2.8.4.1 Stereolithography Apparatus (SLA)

SLA is one of the oldest VPP processes, which is the most precise and is used to create finely detailed parts (Vladić et al. 2022). The parts are created when a UV laser, with a wavelength of 350–460 nm, polymerizes the resin. The part is created one layer at a time (Vladić et al. 2022).

Digital Light Processing (DLP) DLP is a layer-wise polymerization technique that utilizes a light source in the UV wavelength range to polymerize an entire layer of the object at once. Compared to SLA, DLP is faster because each layer is cured simultaneously (Vladić et al. 2022; Bongiovanni and Vitale 2022).

2.8.4.2 Continuous Liquid Interface Production (CLIP)

CLIP is an innovation that builds upon the conventional DLP. It utilizes digital projection with LEDs, as compared to a UV lamp, and features an oxygen-permeable window instead of a glass window. This allows for continuous object building as the platform can keep moving (Bongiovanni and Vitale 2022). CLIP prints objects continuously as opposed to other conventional methods; hence, issues with layer connection are eliminated, and a cohesive part is possible (Bongiovanni and Vitale 2022).

Materials Multifunctional acrylates and methacrylates are among the popular monomers used with VPP. Poly(ethylene glycol) diacrylate (PEGDA), urethane dimethacrylate (UDMA), bisphenol A-glycidyl methacrylate (bis-GMA), and trimethylolpropane triacrylate (TTA) are some examples of the same (Vladić et al. 2022). The photopolymer chemistry is categorized in the following manner: for free radical photopolymerization, acrylates are used, and for cationic photopolymerization, epoxy and vinyl ether-based resins are used (Gibson et al. 2021c).

Benefits and Limitations

Applications in Biomaterial Fabrication VPP is a favorable technique for biomaterial applications due to its ability to meet patient-specific, precise, and complex geometry requirements (Timofticiuc et al. 2024). VPP is primarily used in orthopedic, dental, and tissue engineering applications, including the development of scaffolds. The major class of materials used with VPP is inorganic materials, such as HA, zirconia, β-tricalcium phosphate (β-TCP), biphasic calcium phosphate (HA + β-TCP), and organic polymers, including poly (propylene fumarate), PCL, and PMMA (Timofticiuc et al. 2024) (Fig. 2.3, Tables 2.5 and 2.6).

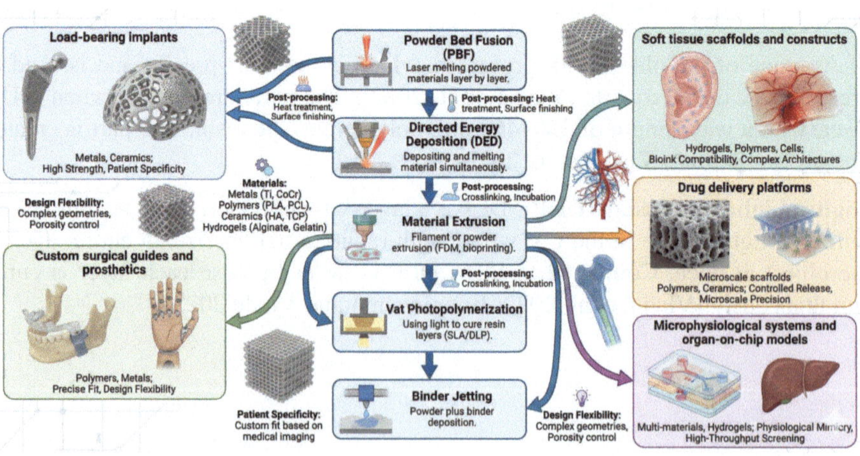

Fig. 2.3 Schematic representation of additive manufacturing techniques for biomaterials fabrication and applications

Table 2.5 Advantages and disadvantages of Vat Photopolymerization Technique

Advantages	Disadvantages
Fast production Best additive manufacturing technology for complex geometries Isotropic structure leads to predictable mechanical performance Resin can be reused - > low wastage Easily scalable	Only materials that can be used in resin form and are photosensitive are acceptable Parts are vulnerable to moisture, light, heat, and chemicals There is uncertainty about the long-term durability of the printed parts

A comparative summary of additive methods is given in Table 2.6

Table 2.6 A comparative summary of additive manufacturing, 3D bioprinting, and nonprinting techniques

Feature	Additive manufacturing	3D bioprinting	Non-printing
Core principle	Build materials layer by layer from 3D model data, contrasting subtractive methods by adding material gradually	Extends AM by adding living cells into bioinks for accurate placement of tissue-like structures	Encompasses subtractive removal, molding liquids, fiber drawing from solutions, and spontaneous molecular organization
Key techniques	Powder bed fusion (PBF), binder jetting (BJT), directed energy deposition (DED)	Extrusion (pneumatic or mechanical bioink dispensing); inkjet (droplet ejection); laser-assisted; volumetric (holographic)	Solvent casting with leaching; freeze-drying for porosity; electrospinning or blow spinning for nanofibers; self-assembly of DNA/peptides
Materials	Polymers (PLA, PCL); metals (titanium); ceramics (hydroxyapatite); composites	Cell-laden hydrogels (alginate, collagen); decellularized extracellular matrix	Polymers (PLGA, chitosan); DNA/peptide nanomaterials; solvents for spinning
Cell integration	Post-processing seeding due to harsh conditions, such as high temperatures	Direct encapsulation during printing for single-step integration	Post-seeding for spinning or freeze-drying may occur during the self-assembly or molding process
Advantages	Allows complex geometries and patient-specific designs from scans, with reduced waste	Provides cell-type spatial precision, automation, and microchannel vascular potential	Scalable throughput (e.g., blow spinning), ECM-like nanofibers, and simpler equipment requirements
Limitations	Surface roughness/stair-stepping, directional anisotropy, and high costs	Cell damage from shear, limited bioink options, and challenges in developing vascular networks	Poor internal architecture control, toxic solvents, and complex restricted geometries
Primary applications	Non-bioactive implants (joints, skull), surgical guides, prosthetics	Living tissues (skin, cartilage), disease models, organs-on-chips	Wound dressings, drug-releasing nanofibers/hydrogels, cell-attachment scaffolds

2.9 Conclusion

This chapter systematically explores the spectrum of biomaterial fabrication techniques essential for regenerative medicine, emphasizing non-printing methods alongside advanced additive manufacturing techniques. Non-printing approaches, ranging from electrospinning and blow spinning for nanofibrous ECM mimics to solvent casting, freeze-drying, textile engineering, molding, and self-assembly of peptides, proteins, polysaccharides, and lipids, offer foundational advantages in scalability, biocompatibility, and nanoscale fidelity, enabling high-throughput production of wound dressings, injectable hydrogels, and soft tissue scaffolds. These methods excel where continuous fiber networks or spontaneous molecular organization replicate native tissue microenvironments, though they often lack precision in complex geometries. Additive manufacturing extends capabilities through layer-by-layer construction via powder bed fusion, directed energy deposition, and vat photopolymerization, delivering patient-specific, mechanically robust implants with intricate lattices for load-bearing applications, such as bone regeneration. Comparative analyses reveal complementary strengths: non-printing for biological mimicry and volume production, AM for architectural control, and bioprinting for cellular precision.

Hybrid paradigms, such as electrospun coatings on AM scaffolds or self-assembled gels within printed lattices, emerge as optimal strategies to synergize these techniques, enhancing cell infiltration, vascularization, and functional integration. Future directions prioritize AI-optimized designs, in situ fabrication, regulatory standardization, and "living" responsive materials to overcome barriers related to scholarship, reproducibility, and translation. Ultimately, strategic selection and integration of these technique-focused methodologies will accelerate biomaterial scaffolds from benchtop prototypes to clinically viable regenerative therapies.

Acknowledgements AVS acknowledges Colorado State University for financial assistance and Dr. David Prawel of Colorado State University for his insightful discussion about the scope of Additive Manufacturing techniques. The RS is thankful to George Mason University for financial support.

Figures were generated or refined using a Gemini AI tool, and a brief description is provided of the extent of that use.

Conflicts of Interest The authors declared no conflict of interest.

Competing Interests The author(s) has no competing interests to declare that are relevant to the content of this manuscript.

References

Additive Manufacturing Research Group (n.d.) Powder bed fusion | additive manufacturing research group | Loughborough University." Accessed 8 Nov 2025. [Online]. Available: https://www.lboro.ac.uk/research/amrg/about/the7categoriesofadditivemanufacturing/powderbedfusion/

Ahn DG (2021) Directed energy deposition (DED) process: state of the art. Int J Precision Eng Manufact Green Technol 8(2):703–742. https://doi.org/10.1007/S40684-020-00302-7

Akbari M et al (2016) Textile technologies and tissue engineering: a path toward organ weaving. Adv Healthc Mater 5(7):751–766. https://doi.org/10.1002/ADHM.201500517

Aldilla VR et al (2020) Anthranilamide-based short peptides self-assembled hydrogels as antibacterial agents. Sci Rep 10(1):770. https://doi.org/10.1038/s41598-019-57342-6

Arias-González F et al (2021) Laser-directed energy deposition: principles and applications. In: Addit Manuf, pp 121–157. https://doi.org/10.1016/B978-0-12-818411-0.00003-3

Bachs-Herrera A, Yousefzade O, Del Valle LJ, Puiggali J (2021) Melt electrospinning of polymers: blends, nanocomposites, additives and Applications. Appl Sci *11*(4):1808. https://doi.org/10.3390/APP11041808

Baino F et al (2025) Recent trends in design, manufacturing and challenges of bone-like bioceramic scaffolds. Ceram Int 51(10):12355–12369. https://doi.org/10.1016/J.CERAMINT.2025.02.307

Bakhtiary N, Ghalandari B, Ghorbani F, Varma SN, Liu C (2023) Advances in peptide-based hydrogel for tissue engineering. Polymers *15*(5):1068. https://doi.org/10.3390/POLYM15051068

Banke J (2006) From nothing, something: one layer at a time - NASA. Accessed 12 Nov 2025. [Online]. Available: https://www.nasa.gov/aeronautics/from-nothing-something-one-layer-at-a-time/

Barui S (2021) 3D inkjet printing of biomaterials: principles and applications. Med Devices Sens 4 (1):e10143. https://doi.org/10.1002/MDS3.10143

Bongiovanni R, Vitale A (2022) Vat Photopolymerization. In: High resolution manufacturing from 2d to 3d/4d printing: applications in engineering and medicine, pp 17–46. https://doi.org/10.1007/978-3-031-13779-2_2/FIGURES/7

Carriles J, Nguewa P, González-Gaitano G (2023) Advances in Biomedical Applications of Solution Blow Spinning. Int J Molecular Sci 24(19):14757. https://doi.org/10.3390/IJMS241914757

Chandel AKS et al (2024) Injectable, shear-thinning, photocrosslinkable, and tissue-adhesive hydrogels composed of diazirine-modified hyaluronan and dendritic polyethyleneimine. Biomater Sci 12(6):1454–1464. https://doi.org/10.1039/D3BM01279D

Chen W et al (2019) Self-assembled peptide nanofibers display natural antimicrobial peptides to selectively kill bacteria without compromising Cytocompatibility. ACS Appl Mater Interfaces 11(32):28681–28689. https://doi.org/10.1021/acsami.9b09583

Chen Z et al (2024) Progress in biomaterials inspired by the extracellular matrix. Giant 19:100323. https://doi.org/10.1016/J.GIANT.2024.100323

Cong B, Zhang H (2025) Innovative 3D printing technologies and advanced materials revolutionizing orthopedic surgery: current applications and future directions. Front Bioeng Biotechnol 13:1542179. https://doi.org/10.3389/FBIOE.2025.1542179

Copling A et al (2023) Recent advances in antimicrobial peptide hydrogels. Int J Mol Sci 24 (8):7563. https://doi.org/10.3390/ijms24087563

Das S, Das D (2021) Rational Design of Peptide-based Smart Hydrogels for therapeutic applications. Front Chem 9. https://doi.org/10.3389/fchem.2021.770102

Das A, Vaghela D, Gupta S, Bhatia D, Biswas A (2025) Self-assembly of short peptides and DNA-based materials in precision biomedical applications. Supramolecular Mater:100123. https://doi.org/10.1016/j.supmat.2025.100123

Dev Singh D, Mahender T, Raji Reddy A (2021) Powder bed fusion process: a brief review. Mater Today Proc 46:350–355. https://doi.org/10.1016/J.MATPR.2020.08.415

DiMaio JTM, Doran TM, Ryan DM, Raymond DM, Nilsson BL (2017) Modulating supramolecular peptide hydrogel viscoelasticity using biomolecular recognition. Biomacromolecules 18 (11):3591–3599. https://doi.org/10.1021/acs.biomac.7b00925

Do AV, Khorsand B, Geary SM, Salem AK (2015) 3D printing of scaffolds for tissue regeneration applications. Adv Healthc Mater 4(12):1742. https://doi.org/10.1002/ADHM.201500168

Dores R, Oliveira MSN, Bimbo LM (2025) Microfluidic manufacture of composite fibers for biomedical applications. Adv Mater Technol 10(5):2400976. https://doi.org/10.1002/ADMT.202400976

Dzobo K et al (2018) Advances in regenerative medicine and tissue engineering: innovation and transformation of medicine. Stem Cells Int 2018:2495848. https://doi.org/10.1155/2018/2495848

Emerson AE, Mccall AB, Brady SR, Slaby EM, Weaver JD (2022) Hydrogel injection molding to generate complex cell encapsulation geometries. ACS Biomater Sci Eng 8(9):4002–4013. https://doi.org/10.1021/ACSBIOMATERIALS.2C00640

G. G. Flores-Rojas, B. Gómez-Lazaro, F. López-Saucedo, R. Vera-Graziano, E. Bucio, and E. Mendizábal, "Electrospun scaffolds for tissue engineering: a review," Macromol 2023, Vol 3, 3, pp. 524–553, Aug. 2023, doi:https://doi.org/10.3390/MACROMOL3030031

Gebeshuber IC, Khawas S, Sharma R, Sharma N (2025) Bioprinted scaffolds for biomimetic applications: a state-of-the-art Technology. Biomimetics 10(9):595. https://doi.org/10.3390/BIOMIMETICS10090595

Gelain F, Luo Z, Rioult M, Zhang S (2021) Self-assembling peptide scaffolds in the clinic. npj Regener Med 6(1):9. https://doi.org/10.1038/s41536-020-00116-w

Gibson I, Rosen D, Stucker B, Khorasani M (2020) Additive manufacturing technologies. In: Additive Manufacturing Technologies, pp 1–675. https://doi.org/10.1007/978-3-030-56127-7/COVER

Gibson I, Rosen D, Stucker B, Khorasani M (2021a) Directed energy deposition. In: Additive manufacturing technologies, pp 285–318. https://doi.org/10.1007/978-3-030-56127-7_10

Gibson I, Rosen D, Stucker B, Khorasani M (2021b) Binder Jetting. In: Additive Manufacturing Technologies, pp 237–252. https://doi.org/10.1007/978-3-030-56127-7_8

Gibson I, Rosen D, Stucker B, Khorasani M (2021c) Vat Photopolymerization. In: Additive manufacturing technologies, pp 77–124. https://doi.org/10.1007/978-3-030-56127-7_4

Gupta S, Singh R, Kumar V, Shukla P, Joshi KB (2018) Ornamentation of triskelion peptide Nanotori to produce gold nanoparticle (AuNP)-embedded peptide Nanobangles. Chem Asian J 13(21):3285–3295. https://doi.org/10.1002/asia.201801270

Habibi N, Kamaly N, Memic A, Shafiee H (2016) Self-assembled peptide-based nanostructures: smart nanomaterials toward targeted drug delivery. Nano Today 11(1):41–60. https://doi.org/10.1016/j.nantod.2016.02.004

Hanif W, Yadav I, Hasan E, Alsulaiman D (2023) Programmable all-DNA hydrogels based on rolling circle and multiprimed chain amplification products. APL Bioeng 7(4):46106. https://doi.org/10.1063/5.0169063/2918938

He Y et al (2008) Hierarchical self-assembly of DNA into symmetric supramolecular polyhedra. Nature 452(7184):198–201. https://doi.org/10.1038/nature06597

Hendricks MP, Sato K, Palmer LC, Stupp SI (2017) Supramolecular assembly of peptide Amphiphiles. Acc Chem Res 50(10):2440–2448. https://doi.org/10.1021/acs.accounts.7b00297

Hong J, Yeo M, Yang GH, Kim G (2019) Cell-electrospinning and its application for tissue engineering. Int J Molecular Sci *20*(24):6208. https://doi.org/10.3390/IJMS20246208

Hoque ME, Rajaee N (2017) Encoding Information in DNA: From Basic Structure to Nanoelectronics. American J Nanomater 5(2):51–58. https://doi.org/10.12691/ajn-5-2-2

Igawa K et al. (2006), "Tailor-made tricalcium phosphate bone implant directly fabricated by a three-dimensional ink-jet printer. Igawa K, Mochizuki M , Sugimori O, Shimizu K, Yamazawa K, Kawaguchi H, Nakamura K (eds) J Artificial Organs Springer 9(4):234–240, https://doi.org/10.1007/S10047-006-0347-Y

Ji H, Yang H, Li Z (2025) Application of Textile Technology in Vascular Tissue Engineering. *Textiles 5*(3):38. https://doi.org/10.3390/TEXTILES5030038

Joshua RJN et al (*2024*) Powder bed fusion 3D printing in precision manufacturing for biomedical applications: a comprehensive review. Materials *17*(3):769. https://doi.org/10.3390/MA17030769

Kansara K, Singh R, Yadav P, Mansuri A, Kumar A, Bhatia D (2023) Lipid modification of DNA tetrahedrons enhances cellular uptake, migration, and in vivo uptake. ACS Appl Nano Mater 6 (14):13443–13452. https://doi.org/10.1021/acsanm.3c02029

Katrilaka C et al (2023) Freeze-drying process for the fabrication of collagen-based sponges as medical devices in biomedical engineering. Materials *16*(12):4425. https://doi.org/10.3390/MA16124425

Kesharwani K et al (2022) Short peptide amphiphile nanostructures facilitate sunlight-induced nanowelding of gold nanosheets. Chem Commun 58(99):13815–13818. https://doi.org/10.1039/D2CC05392F

Kong B, Liu R, Guo J, Lu L, Zhou Q, Zhao Y (2023) Tailoring micro/nano-fibers for biomedical applications. Bioact Mater 19:328–347. https://doi.org/10.1016/J.BIOACTMAT.2022.04.016

Kosara S, Singh R, Bhatia D (2024) Structural DNA nanotechnology at the nexus of next-generation bio-applications: challenges and perspectives. Nanoscale Adv 6(2):386–401. https://doi.org/10.1039/D3NA00692A

Kumar V, Singh R, Joshi KB (2018) Biotin–avidin interaction triggers conversion of triskelion peptide nanotori into nanochains. New J Chem 42(5):3452–3458. https://doi.org/10.1039/C7NJ04248E

Kumar R, Mehdi H, Bhati SS, Arunkumar M, Mishra S, Lohumi MK (2025) A comprehensive review of advancements in additive manufacturing for 3D printed medical components using diverse materials. Discover Materials *5*(1):152. https://doi.org/10.1007/S43939-025-00349-W

Levin A, Hakala TA, Schnaider L, Bernardes GJL, Gazit E, Knowles TPJ (2020) Biomimetic peptide self-assembly for functional materials. Nat Rev Chem 4(11):615–634. https://doi.org/10.1038/s41570-020-0215-y

Li H, Mumtaz M, Isono T, Satoh T, Chen W-C, Borsali R (2022) Self-assembly of carbohydrate-based block copolymer systems: glyconanoparticles and highly nanostructured thin films. Polym J 54(4):455–464. https://doi.org/10.1038/s41428-021-00604-w

Liu Z, Ramakrishna S, Liu X (2020) Electrospinning and emerging healthcare and medicine possibilities. APL Bioeng 4(3):30901. https://doi.org/10.1063/5.0012309/23007

Mangani S et al (2025) Design and applications of extracellular matrix scaffolds in tissue engineering and regeneration. Cells *14*(14):1076. https://doi.org/10.3390/CELLS14141076

Marjuban SMH et al (2023) Recent advances in centrifugal spinning and their applications in tissue engineering. Polymers (Basel) 15(5):1253. https://doi.org/10.3390/POLYM15051253

Menon D, Singh R, Joshi KB, Gupta S, Bhatia D (2023) Designer, programmable DNA peptide hybrid materials with emergent properties to probe and modulate biological systems. Chembiochem 24(5). https://doi.org/10.1002/cbic.202200580

Mirzaali MJ, Moosabeiki V, Rajaai SM, Zhou J, Zadpoor AA (2022) Additive manufacturing of biomaterials—design principles and their implementation. Materials *15*(15):5457. https://doi.org/10.3390/MA15155457

Mittal A et al (2021) Self-assembly of carbohydrate-based small amphiphiles and their applications in pathogen inhibition and drug delivery: a review. Mater Adv 2(11):3459–3473. https://doi.org/10.1039/D0MA00916D

Mostofizadeh M, Pitcher ML, Sheikhi A (2023) Coaxial electrospinning. In: Electrospun and Nanofibrous Membranes: Principles and Applications, pp 105–126. https://doi.org/10.1016/B978-0-12-823032-9.00006-4

Noh S, Jung W, Sim S, Son HS, Choi JH, Koo J (2023) Effect of drawing conditions on crystal structure and mechanical properties of melt-spun Polylactic acid fibers. Fibers Polymers 24 (2):483–488. https://doi.org/10.1007/S12221-023-00091-1

Nouri A, Rohani Shirvan A, Li Y, Wen C (2021) Additive manufacturing of metallic and polymeric load-bearing biomaterials using laser powder bed fusion: a review. J Mater Sci Technol 94:196–215. https://doi.org/10.1016/J.JMST.2021.03.058

Parvin N, Joo SW, Mandal TK (2025) Injectable Biopolymer-Based Hydrogels: A Next-Generation Platform For Minimally Invasive Therapeutics. Gels *11*(6):383. https://doi.org/10.3390/GELS11060383

Qin J, Chen F, Wu P, Sun G (2022) Recent advances in bioengineered scaffolds for cutaneous wound healing. Front Bioeng Biotechnol 10:841583. https://doi.org/10.3389/FBIOE.2022.841583/FULL

Rocha J, Araújo JC, Fangueiro R, Ferreira DP (2022) Wetspun polymeric fibrous systems as potential scaffolds for tendon and ligament repair, healing and regeneration. Pharmaceutics 14 (11):2526. https://doi.org/10.3390/PHARMACEUTICS14112526

Shen X, Deng H, Lin J, Wang J, Liu Y, Mo S (2025) Biomaterial-driven regenerative drug delivery: a vicennial bibliometric landscape. Front Med (Lausanne) 12:1593985. https://doi.org/10.3389/FMED.2025.1593985/BIBTEX

Singh R, Popat KC (2024) Enhancing antibacterial properties of titanium implants through covalent conjugation of self-assembling Fmoc-Phe-Phe dipeptide on Titania nanotubes. ACS Appl Mater Interfaces. https://doi.org/10.1021/acsami.4c13885

Singh R, Gupta S, Kumar V, Joshi KB (2017) Hierarchical self-assembly of Diproline peptide into dumbbells and copper-ion-promoted robust discs. ChemNanoMat 3(9):620–624. https://doi.org/10.1002/cnma.201700129

Singh R, Kumar Mishra N, Kumar V, Vinayak V, Ballabh Joshi K (2018) Transition metal ion-mediated tyrosine-based short-peptide Amphiphile nanostructures inhibit bacterial growth. Chembiochem 19(15):1630–1637. https://doi.org/10.1002/cbic.201800220

Singh R, Mishra NK, Gupta P, Joshi KB (2020a) Self-assembly of a sequence-shuffled short peptide Amphiphile triggered by metal ions into terraced Nanodome-like structures. Chem Asian J 15(4):531–539. https://doi.org/10.1002/asia.201901715

Singh R et al (2020b) Powder bed fusion process in additive manufacturing: an overview. Mater Today Proc 26:3058–3070. https://doi.org/10.1016/J.MATPR.2020.02.635

Singh N, Singh R, Sharma S, Kesharwani K, Joshi KB, Verma S (2021) Transition-metal ion-mediated morphological transformation of pyridine-based peptide nanostructures. New J Chem 45(1):153–161. https://doi.org/10.1039/D0NJ04260A

Singh R, Yadav P, Naveena A H, Bhatia D (2023) Cationic lipid modification of DNA tetrahedral nanocages enhances their cellular uptake. Nanoscale 15(3):1099–1108. https://doi.org/10.1039/D2NR05749B

Singh R et al (2024) DNA tetrahedral nanocages as a promising nanocarrier for dopamine delivery in neurological disorders. Nanoscale 16(32):15158–15169. https://doi.org/10.1039/D4NR00612G

Sola A et al (2019) Development of solvent-casting particulate leaching (SCPL) polymer scaffolds as improved three-dimensional supports to mimic the bone marrow niche. Mater Sci Eng C 96:153–165. https://doi.org/10.1016/J.MSEC.2018.10.086

Steppert C, Steppert I, Bollinger T, Ebbinghaus T, Lang G, Scheibel T (2023) Biomimetic polymer fibers—function by design. Bioinspir Biomim 18(4):041003. https://doi.org/10.1088/1748-3190/ACDDC1

Suamte L, Tirkey A, Barman J, Jayasekhar Babu P (2023) Various manufacturing methods and ideal properties of scaffolds for tissue engineering applications. Smart Mater Manuf 1:100011. https://doi.org/10.1016/J.SMMF.2022.100011

Swain N et al (2025) Self-assembled short peptide Amphiphile-gold nanostructures: a novel approach for bacterial infection treatment. Chem Asian J 20(12). https://doi.org/10.1002/asia.202401852

Teng Y, Song L, Shi J, Lv Q, Hou S, Ramakrishna S (2025) Advancing electrospinning towards the future of biomaterials in biomedical engineering. Regener Biomater 12. https://doi.org/10.1093/RB/RBAF034

Timofticiuc IA et al (*2024*) Biomaterials adapted to vat photopolymerization in 3d printing: characteristics and medical applications. J Functional Biomater *15*(1):7. https://doi.org/10.3390/JFB15010007

Tomić SL, Babić Radić MM, Vuković JS, Filipović VV, Nikodinovic-Runic J, Vukomanović M (2023) Alginate-based hydrogels and scaffolds for biomedical applications. Marine Drugs *21* (3):177. https://doi.org/10.3390/MD21030177

Vinchurkar K et al (2025) Advances in sustainable biomaterials: characterizations, and applications in medicine. Discover Polymers 2(1):2. https://doi.org/10.1007/S44347-025-00014-8

Vladić G, Banjanin B, Kašiković N, Pavlović Ž (2022) Vat photopolymerization. In: Polymers for 3D printing: methods, properties, and characteristics, pp 65–74. https://doi.org/10.1016/B978-0-12-818311-3.00018-5

Wang Z et al (2021a) Advanced thermally drawn multimaterial fibers: structure-enabled functionalities. Adv Devices Instrumentation 2021. https://doi.org/10.34133/2021/9676470

Wang H, Deng H, Gao M, Zhang W (2021b) Self-assembled Nanogels based on ionic gelation of natural polysaccharides for drug delivery. Front Bioeng Biotechnol 9:703559. https://doi.org/10.3389/FBIOE.2021.703559/BIBTEX

Wang Q, Ji P, Bu T, Mao Y, He H, Ge N (2025) Recent Progress in the Application of Electrospinning Technology in the Biomedical Field. J Functional Biomater *16*(7):266. https://doi.org/10.3390/JFB16070266

Wegner A (2021) Introduction to powder bed fusion of polymers. Addit Manuf:33–75. https://doi.org/10.1016/B978-0-12-818411-0.00011-2

Wu W et al (2023a) Supramolecular hydrogel microspheres of platelet-derived growth factor mimetic peptide promote recovery from spinal cord injury. ACS Nano 17(4):3818–3837. https://doi.org/10.1021/acsnano.2c12017

Wu Y et al (2023b) An overview of 3D printed metal implants in orthopedic applications: present and future perspectives. Heliyon 9(7):e17718. https://doi.org/10.1016/J.HELIYON.2023.E17718

Yao C, Zhang R, Tang J, Yang D (2021) Rolling circle amplification (RCA)-based DNA hydrogel. Nature Protocols 16(12):5460–5483. https://doi.org/10.1038/s41596-021-00621-2

Zeinali R, Khorasani MT, Behnamghader A, Atai M, Del Valle L, Puiggalí J (*2020*) Poly (hydroxybutyrate-co-hydroxyvalerate) Porous Matrices from Thermally Induced Phase Separation. Polymers *12*(12):2787. https://doi.org/10.3390/POLYM12122787

Zeinali R, Del Valle LJ, Torras J, Puiggalí J (2021) Recent progress on biodegradable tissue engineering scaffolds prepared by Thermally-Induced Phase Separation (TIPS). Int J Molecular Sci *22*(7):3504. https://doi.org/10.3390/IJMS22073504

Zhou J, See CW, Sreenivasamurthy S, Zhu D (2023) Customized additive manufacturing in bone scaffolds—the gateway to precise bone defect treatment. Research 6:0239. https://doi.org/10.34133/RESEARCH.0239

Zhuo S, Liang Y, Wu Z, Zhao X, Han Y, Guo B (2024) Supramolecular hydrogels for wound repair and hemostasis. Mater Horiz 11(1):37–101. https://doi.org/10.1039/D3MH01403G

Ziaee M, Crane NB (2019) Binder jetting: a review of process, materials, and methods. Addit Manuf 28:781–801. https://doi.org/10.1016/J.ADDMA.2019.05.031

Chapter 3
Biomaterials for Biofabrication: Fundamentals, Innovations, and Future Perspectives

Sunjae Park, Se Na Jang, Nakyung Kim, Hosoo Shin, and Gilson Khang

Abstract Biofabrication represents a paradigm shift in regenerative medicine, transcending conventional tissue engineering approaches through precise spatiotemporal control of cellular and material organization. This technology enables the sophisticated simultaneous deposition of multiple cell types, growth factors, and biomaterials within three-dimensional constructs, moving beyond passive scaffolding to active engineering of biological systems.

This chapter presents a function-centered perspective on biomaterials, diverging from traditional chemical composition-based classifications to emphasize materials' capacity to "instruct" cellular fate. We explore three fundamental design principles: mechanically instructive materials leveraging mechanotransduction through stiffness and viscoelasticity, biochemically instructive materials utilizing peptide immobilization and growth factor delivery, and immunologically instructive materials modulating macrophage polarization for constructive tissue regeneration.

Advanced strategies including 4D biofabrication with time-dependent shape transformation and multi-signal integration through nanomaterial-reinforced hybrid bioinks are examined. We address critical challenges including standardized characterization methodologies, mechanistic understanding of material-cell interactions, and personalized therapeutic approaches utilizing high-throughput screening and artificial intelligence.

This chapter positions biomaterials as "intelligent therapeutic mediators," providing a new scaffold for advancing biofabrication technologies toward clinical translation and patient-specific regenerative medicine applications.

S. Park · S. N. Jang · N. Kim · H. Shin
Department of PolymerNano Science and Technology and Polymer Materials Fusion Research Center, Jeonbuk National University, Jeonju-si, Jeonbuk, South Korea

G. Khang (✉)
Department of PolymerNano Science and Technology and Polymer Materials Fusion Research Center, Jeonbuk National University, Jeonju-si, Jeonbuk, South Korea

Department of Bionanotechnology and Bio-Convergence Engineering, Jeonbuk National University, Jeonju-si, Jeonbuk, South Korea
e-mail: gskhang@jbnu.ac.kr

Y. M. Elçin (ed.), *Biofabrication in Regenerative Medicine*, Stem Cell Biology and Regenerative Medicine 1519, https://doi.org/10.1007/978-3-032-30294-6_3

Keywords Biofabrication · Biomaterials · Tissue Engineering · Regenerative Medicine · Mechanotransduction · Immunomodulation

Abbreviations

BMP-2	Bone Morphogenetic Protein -2
CCK-8	Cell Counting Kit-8
ECM	Extracellular Matrix
ELISA	Enzyme-Linked Immunosorbent Assay
FACS	Fluorescence Activated Cell Sorting
GO	Graphene Oxide
HAp	Hydroxyapatite
M1	M1 Macrophages
M2	M2 Macrophages
Micro-CT	Micro-Computed Tomography
MSCs	Mesenchymal Stem Cells
PLGA	Poly (lactic-co-glycolic acid)
RGD	Arginine-Glycine-Aspartic Acid
RT-PCR	Reverse Transcription Polymerase Chain Reaction
TAZ	Transcriptional Coactivator with PDZ-Binding Motif
VEGF	Vascular Endothelial Growth Factor
YAP	Yes-Associated Protein

3.1 Engineering Biomaterials for Advanced Biofabrication

3.1.1 From Structural Support to Precision Control

The field of tissue engineering has historically revolved around the synergistic interplay of three fundamental components: cells, scaffolds, and signaling molecules (Langer and Vacanti 1993). Conventional approaches entailed the seeding of various cell types onto pre-fabricated, porous scaffolds, with the expectation that this fundamental environment would guide tissue formation. However, these methods demonstrated a limited capacity to replicate the intrinsic complexity and microenvironment of native tissues (Hollister 2005; Atala et al. 2012).

The advent of biofabrication has precipitated a paradigm shift in the domain of tissue engineering, transcending the limitations of conventional methodologies to attain unparalleled levels of precision (Mironov et al. 2009; Groll et al. 2018). The fundamental principle of biofabrication entails the ability to exercise meticulous spatiotemporal control over the configuration of cells and materials within an engineered construct. Biofabrication is not merely a process of seeding cells onto a scaffold; it is a sophisticated process that demands precise execution (Murphy and

Atala 2014). This methodology has evolved into a multifaceted approach for the strategic, simultaneous deposition of multiple cell types, specific growth factors, bioceramic components, and distinct hydrogel formulations within a defined three-dimensional space (Kim et al. 2018; Ji and Guvendiren 2017).

These technologies ultimately provide the essential tools to precisely orchestrate cellular behavior, enabling the transition from providing passive structural support to actively engineering biological systems from the ground up. This fundamental shift in approach—from passive scaffolding to active, architectural design—is unequivocally the most pivotal and transformative contribution of biofabrication to the fields of tissue engineering and biomaterials (Moroni et al. 2018).

3.1.2 The Biofabrication: Technique-Dependent Biomaterial Design Considerations

While 3D bioprinting is arguably the most prominent technique within the biofabrication, the term itself encompasses a far broader spectrum of technologies (Baghdasaryan et al. 2024). Notable examples include electrospinning, used to fabricate nanofibrous scaffolds, and cell sheet engineering, a scaffold-free method where cells are cultured into contiguous sheets that are subsequently harvested for application (Xue et al. 2019; Okano et al. 1993; Ratner 2007).

Each fabrication technique imposes unique demands on the biomaterials utilized. The physicochemical properties required of a biomaterial are directly determined by the specific fabrication process it will undergo. For instance, materials employed as bioinks in extrusion-based bioprinting must exhibit shear-thinning rheological properties to ensure both smooth extrusion through the nozzle and rapid stabilization after deposition (Paxton et al. 2017; Gungor-Ozkerim et al. 2018). In a similar manner, polymers utilized in electrospinning must maintain stability when exposed to high-voltage electric fields (Xue et al. 2019).

While this chapter emphasizes versatile biomaterials with broad applicability across multiple techniques, it does so with full recognition that each fabrication process imposes its own distinct material requirements. A comprehensive understanding of these process-specific constraints is imperative for the effective selection and implementation of biomaterials in tissue engineering applications.

3.1.3 Key Characteristics of Biomaterials for Biofabrication

Biomaterials designed for biofabrication must meet a demanding array of requirements to successfully regenerate functional tissue constructs alongside living cells. The fundamental properties of these materials are such that they must demonstrate high bioactivity to promote cell survival and growth, maintain adequate structural integrity to preserve the intended architecture, and exhibit proper biological functionality (Eming et al. 2008; Chimene et al. 2016).

A fundamental challenge resides in recognizing that these essential properties do not function independently. Instead, they form an intricate web of interdependent relationships (O'brien 2011). For instance, chemical modifications intended to enhance mechanical properties may inadvertently compromise cytocompatibility (Van Den Bulcke et al. 2000). Conversely, efforts aimed at enhancing biodegradability have the potential to compromise structural stability (Portnov et al. 2017). This domino effect—where adjusting one characteristic triggers cascading changes throughout the system—represents one of the field's most significant challenges in achieving optimal material performance (O'brien 2011).

Consequently, the development of biofabrication biomaterials necessitates a comprehensive, systems-based design approach. Success is contingent not on the optimization of individual properties in isolation, but rather on the adoption of an integrative strategy that meticulously considers how each modification affects the entire material system (Balasubramaniyam et al. 2025). It is imperative to integrate comprehensive evaluation methodologies with systematic design approaches to mitigate the trade-offs associated with disparate material properties (Yang et al. 2021). This approach is indicative of the complex and integrated design thinking that characterizes modern biofabrication as an advanced scientific discipline (Table 3.1).

3.2 Design Principles for Bioactive Platforms Using Biofabrication

Traditional classification systems for biomaterials have primarily relied on categorizing them by their chemical composition (Hench and Polak 2002). This chapter, however, diverges from this conventional approach to propose a novel framework. The core of this new framework is a function-centric, systematic approach that focuses on the 'biological instructions' delivered by the biomaterial to the cell (Lutolf and Hubbell 2005).

Contemporary, next-generation biomaterials are no longer passive scaffolds that merely provide physical support. They have evolved into bioactive platforms capable of actively guiding cellular fate through a variety of biological signaling mechanisms (Langer and Tirrell 2004). Specifically, they can precisely guide cellular behavior and differentiation through mechanobiological signals (e.g., physical forces exerted on the cell) (Engler et al. 2006), biochemical signals (e.g., signaling molecules and growth factors) (Lee et al. 2011), and immunomodulatory signals (e.g., controlling the host immune response) (Franz et al. 2011).

This paradigm shift is poised to revolutionize the field of tissue regeneration. It is anticipated that by making the regenerative process more predictable and precisely controllable, these advanced biomaterials will dramatically enhance therapeutic efficacy (Khademhosseini and Langer 2016).

Table 3.1 Key characteristics and evaluation methods of biomaterials for biofabrication

Property	Definition	Target goal	Characterization
Biocompatibility	The ability to not cause harmful reactions (inflammation, toxicity, immune response) in the host	Minimal inflammatory response, suppression of fibrous capsule formation	ISO 10993 standard tests for cytotoxicity, sensitization, and implantation
Biodegradability	The ability to be degraded and metabolized/eliminated in the body	Degradation rate that matches the tissue regeneration rate, non-toxic degradation products	In vitro degradation tests (PBS, enzymes), in vivo mass loss and histological analysis after implantation
Mechanical properties	The ability to respond to physical forces such as stiffness, elasticity, and viscoelasticity	Mimic the mechanical properties of the target tissue (e.g., bone-GPa, muscle-kPa)	Tensile/compression tester, Rheometer
Processability	The ability to be fabricated into a desired three-dimensional structure	High printing precision, structural stability, high cell viability	Rheometer (viscosity, shear-thinning measurement), structural analysis after printing (microscopy, micro-CT)
Bioactivity	The ability to induce cell adhesion, proliferation, and differentiation	Promotion of specific cell behaviors (e.g., osteogenesis, angiogenesis)	Analysis of cell adhesion and proliferation (CCK-8, etc.), analysis of differentiation marker expression (RT-PCR, immunofluorescence staining)
Immunomodulatory function	The ability to modulate the host immune response in a regeneration-friendly manner	Induction of macrophage polarization from M1 (inflammatory) to M2 (regenerative)	Cytokine analysis after macrophage co-culture (ELISA), flow cytometry (FACS)

3.2.1 Mechanically Instructive Materials

Cells act as sophisticated mechanosensors, continuously probing and responding to their surrounding microenvironment (Ingber 2006; Kechagia et al. 2019). The complex process by which a material's physical properties dictate cellular morphology, motility, proliferation, and differentiation is known as mechanotransduction.

In biofabrication, the design of mechanically instructive materials centers on precisely engineering these mechanobiological cues to elicit targeted cellular responses (Vining and Mooney 2017; Adhikari et al. 2023). While early research primarily focused on static properties like stiffness or elastic modulus, recent trends have highlighted the quantitative understanding and control of dynamic properties—

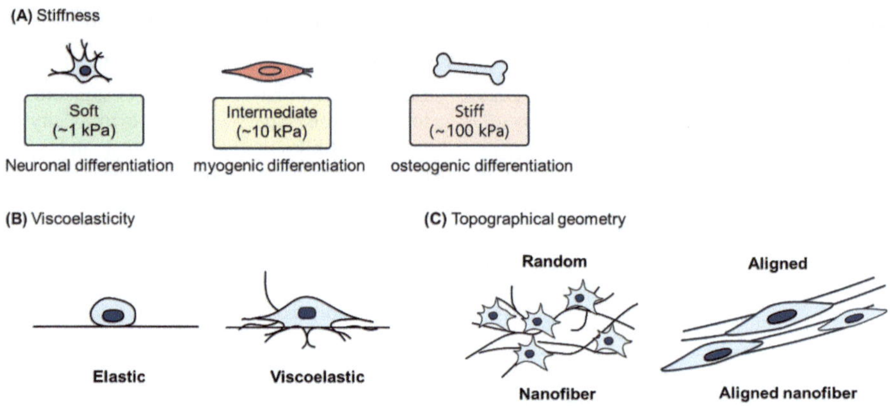

Fig. 3.1 Mechanotransduction pathways in biomaterial-guided cellular behavior: Schematic showing how mechanical cues from biomaterials (stiffness, viscoelasticity, topography)

such as viscoelasticity, relaxation time constants, and creep recovery—as critical elements for mimicking the precisely controlled environments of living tissues (Wang et al. 2022a; Saraswathibhatla et al. 2023) (Fig. 3.1).

- Stiffness: Stiffness, a measure of a material's resistance to deformation, is one of the most fundamental physical cue regulating cell behavior. For example, research by Engler et al. demonstrated that even under identical chemical and biological culture conditions, the differentiation pathway of mesenchymal stem cells (MSCs) varied with substrate stiffness, reflecting the native stiffness of brain (0.1–1 kPa), muscle (8–17 kPa), or bone tissue (25–40 kPa) (Engler et al. 2006). By mimicking these tissue-specific stiffness ranges, the intracellular YAP/TAZ mechanosensitive signaling pathway is activated, enabling the regulation of transcription factors within the nucleus (Dupont et al. 2011; Mohri et al. 2017).
- Viscoelasticity: Living tissues are not purely elastic; they exhibit viscoelasticity, meaning they gradually dissipate stress over time after being deformed by an external load. Cells are acutely sensitive to such dynamic mechanical environments. For example, research by Chaudhuri et al. showed that in alginate hydrogels with rapid stress relaxation, seeded cells spread, proliferated, and exhibited more robust osteogenic differentiation (Chaudhuri et al. 2016). From a biomaterial perspective, the essence of this mechanism is that the matrix does not simply resist the mechanical forces applied by the cell; instead, it restructures the local microenvironment through viscoelastic deformation and energy dissipation (Chaudhuri et al. 2020). Once the matrix compliantly remodels, cytoskeletal tension can be effectively established. This tension drives the translocation of mechanosensitive transcriptional regulators such as YAP/TAZ from the cytoplasm into the nucleus, promoting the expression of osteogenesis-related genes (Chaudhuri et al. 2016; Hu et al. 2024). Conversely, this entire process is suppressed in purely elastic materials with slow stress relaxation.

- Topography: In addition to bulk mechanical properties, the micro to nanoscale topography of a material's surface also acts as a potent physical cue (Teixeira et al. 2003; Bae et al. 2015). Notably, aligned nanofibrous scaffolds fabricated via electrospinning can guide cells like neurons or cardiomyocytes to elongate and form functional intercellular connections along the fiber direction (Li et al. 2002; Han et al. 2016). More recently, strategies using nanoimprint lithography to design nanopillars arranged at specific intervals have gained attention for their ability to precisely control the area and distribution of focal adhesions. For instance, it has been reported that on disordered nanostructures, focal adhesion formation is suppressed, biasing stem cells toward adipogenic differentiation. In contrast, on uniformly aligned nanopillar arrays, focal adhesions can fully mature, which in turn induces osteogenic differentiation (Dalby et al. 2007).

3.2.2 Biochemically Instructive Materials

Cells recognize biochemical cues present in the surrounding extracellular matrix (ECM), such as adhesive ligands, growth factors, and enzyme-sensitive cleavage sites (Hynes 2009). This recognition process regulates a wide range of physiological responses, including cellular differentiation, proliferation, and migration (Lutolf and Hubbell 2005; Hussey et al. 2018).

In biofabrication, a strategy is to precisely engineer these biochemical signaling systems to elicit desired cellular responses (Prestwich 2007). Recent research has moved beyond simple growth factor release to adopt more sophisticated approaches. This includes multidimensional signal control, such as optimizing ligand surface density, incorporating enzyme-responsive crosslinks, and implementing spatiotemporal concentration gradients (He et al. 2020; Rahimnejad et al. 2024).

- Peptide Immobilization: The immobilization of bioactive peptides is an effective method for mimicking the cell-binding functions of native ECM proteins (Hersel et al. 2003). By covalently bonding short amino acid sequences essential for cell adhesion to a material's surface, the interaction between cells and the material can be enhanced. The most widely studied example is the RGD peptide (Arginine-Glycine-Aspartic acid) (Pierschbacher and Ruoslahti 1984). This sequence acts as a key motif that specifically binds to integrin receptors on the cell surface, thereby mediating cell adhesion. For instance, one study demonstrated that incorporating RGD motifs into a poly (L-glutamic acid)-based injectable hydrogel significantly increased cell adhesion and proliferation rates by promoting active cell-matrix interactions (Celik et al. 2018). The strengths of this peptide-based strategy include its well-defined signaling, biochemical stability, and excellent experimental reproducibility. However, because these immobilized peptides are static and typically monofunctional, they have limitations in mimicking the dynamic, multistage process of tissue regeneration (Iqbal et al. 2023).

- Growth Factor and Drug Delivery: Growth factors provide biological signals that are considerably more potent than those from short peptides. For example, specific growth factors can directly control the differentiation of cell lineages and tissue formation processes: BMP-2 robustly induces osteogenic differentiation, while VEGF promotes angiogenesis (Yeh et al. 2024; Li et al. 2025). However, the clinical application of growth factors is constrained by several factors. High manufacturing costs, poor protein stability, and difficulties in controlling their release kinetics are primary examples. To overcome these limitations, early research focused on developing controlled-release technologies, such as systems utilizing PLGA (poly(lactic-co-glycolic acid)) nanoparticles (Kapoor et al. 2015; Semete et al. 2010; Mir et al. 2017) (Fig. 3.2).

3.2.3 Immunologically Instructive Materials

The initial interaction with the immune system is paramount for the successful function of any implantable biomaterial (Anderson et al. 2008). When a biomaterial is implanted in vivo, it first triggers an acute inflammatory response. If this response is not properly regulated, it can progress to a foreign body reaction and subsequent fibrous encapsulation, ultimately compromising the material's function. Consequently, recent research trends are shifting from passive, immune-evasive approaches to active strategies that harness the immune system to promote constructive tissue regeneration (Zhang et al. 2023; Kim et al. 2023).

The control of macrophage phenotype is a cornerstone of immunomodulatory strategies. Macrophages, which act as frontline sentinels of the immune system, can polarize into two primary phenotypes based on environmental cues. The first is the pro-inflammatory M1 phenotype, which eliminates pathogens and initiates inflammation. The second is the pro-regenerative M2 phenotype, which resolves inflammation and facilitates tissue repair (Vishwakarma et al. 2016; Baba et al. 2004).

For successful tissue regeneration, the phenotypic switching of these macrophages must occur at the appropriate time. That is, an initial M1-dominant phase is required to clear debris and initiate the inflammatory cascade, followed by a sequential switch to an M2-dominant phase to resolve inflammation and orchestrate tissue restoration (Brown et al. 2012). However, many conventional biomaterials problematically induce a chronic M1-dominant environment or, conversely, prolong M2 activation excessively, leading to over-activation of fibroblasts and subsequent fibrosis.

- Immunomodulation via Physical Properties: It is increasingly evident that the physical properties of a material alone can directly modulate macrophage behavior. Material stiffness, surface topography, and geometry all influence the immune response.

  In a representative study, Veiseh et al. demonstrated that immune responses could be controlled simply by tuning the size of alginate microcapsules (Veiseh

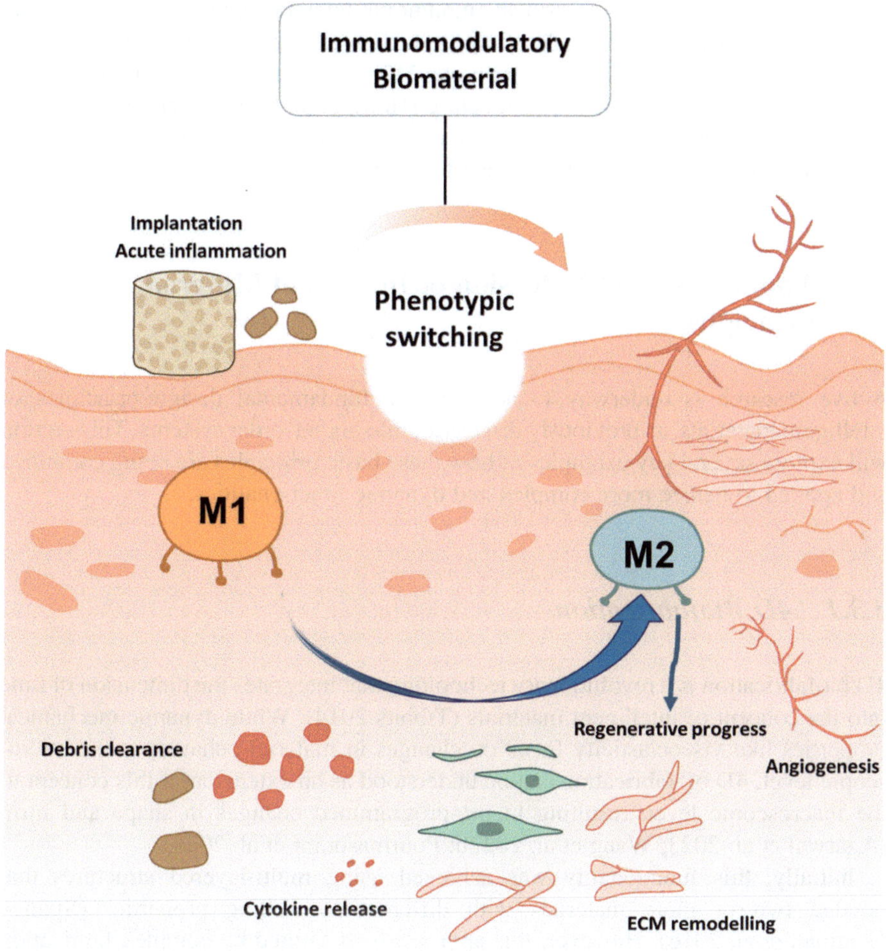

Fig. 3.2 Immunomodulatory strategies in biofabrication: from foreign body reaction to constructive tissue remodeling

et al. 2015). Large spherical capsules with diameters greater than 1.5 mm elicited a minimal foreign body reaction. In contrast, smaller capsules (below 0.5 mm) triggered severe fibrosis, accompanied by the infiltration of macrophages expressing both M1 and M2 markers. Furthermore, Zhang et al. utilized a zwitterionic polymer brush with nanoscale mixed positive and negative charges on its surface (Zhang et al. 2013). This surface chemistry dramatically suppressed protein adsorption, thereby preventing M1 macrophage activation and significantly reducing fibrous capsule formation (Lin et al. 2013).

- Immunomodulation via Chemical Properties and Degradation Products: The chemical composition of a material and the byproducts generated during its degradation also serve as critical immunomodulatory signals (Whitaker et al. 2021). For instance, certain decellularized extracellular matrix (dECM) materials are well-known to inherently promote M2 macrophage polarization, thereby fostering constructive tissue remodeling (Hong et al. 2020; Zhang et al. 2022). Thus, by appropriately designing a material's chemical characteristics, it is possible to guide the immune system to act beneficially for tissue regeneration.

3.3 Application and Extension of Intelligent Material Principles

Active research is underway to advance the fundamental design principles of intelligent materials, as previously discussed, into higher-order systems. This section will explore several key examples of how these basic principles are being combined and applied to realize more complex and dynamic functionalities.

3.3.1 4D Biofabrication

4D biofabrication is a revolutionary technology that integrates the dimension of time into the concept of intelligent materials (Tibbits 2014). While dynamic mechanical properties like viscoelasticity focus on changes in material behavior at the microscopic level, 4D biofabrication can be understood as an extension of this concept to the macroscopic level, resulting in pre-programmed changes in shape and form (Agarwal et al. 2023; Wang et al. 2022b; Pourmasoumi et al. 2023).

Initially, this functionality was achieved using multi-layered structures that bonded two or more materials with differential swelling properties (Sydney Gladman et al. 2016). However, this approach was limited by complex fabrication processes and issues with interlayer adhesion (Naficy et al. 2017). More recently, single-material-based 4D biofabrication strategies have been developed to overcome these challenges.

The method proposed by Aixiang Ding et al. is both simple and highly effective (Ding et al. 2022). It involves adding a UV absorber to a photopolymer solution along with a photoinitiator. When exposed to UV light, the absorber alters the penetration depth of the light, which in turn creates a crosslinking density gradient through the thickness of the hydrogel. Due to the principle that less crosslinked regions swell more, the hydrogel will spontaneously bend or fold into a pre-programmed shape the moment it is immersed in culture medium.

This capacity for spatiotemporal shape transformation is an essential function for moving beyond simple static scaffolds to recapitulating complex, dynamic phenomena, such as the processes of tissue development (Pramanick et al. 2025). Therefore, it is establishing itself as a core design principle for the development of next-generation instructive biomaterials.

3.3.2 *Multi-signal Integration: Hybrid Bioinks*

It is nearly impossible to optimally integrate all the previously discussed instructive signals—mechanical, biochemical, and immunological—within a single material (Pramanick et al. 2025). Natural polymer-based hydrogels, in particular, exhibit excellent biocompatibility but suffer from poor mechanical properties and low 3D printing fidelity (Bao et al. 2019; Zhao et al. 2023).

To overcome these limitations and effectively integrate multiple signals, one of the most promising strategies is the development of composite and hybrid bioinks that utilize nanomaterials as reinforcing agents (Sudheesh Kumar et al. 2012; Jaiswal et al. 2016; Mandal et al. 2017; Fan et al. 2013; Qi et al. 2015). The advantage of nanomaterials is that they not only enhance mechanical strength but can also provide biochemical cues themselves or act as delivery vehicles for other bioactive molecules.

For specific examples, graphene oxide (GO) possesses intrinsic bioactivity that promotes the osteogenic differentiation of stem cells, while hydroxyapatite (HAp) nanoparticles have a mineral composition very similar to native bone, providing strong osteoconductivity (Ramadas et al. 2017; Lee et al. 2015; Beiranvand et al. 2019). In a study by Zhang et al., the integration of graphene oxide into an alginate/gelatin bioink not only significantly improved printing fidelity but also resulted in a successful bone-mimicking scaffold with markedly enhanced osteogenic potential for mesenchymal stem cells (Zhou et al. 2017).

Such nanomaterial-based hybrid bioink technology makes it possible to simultaneously implement different types of biological signals within a single, integrated system. Therefore, it is regarded as a next-generation core platform technology capable of overcoming the fundamental limitations of conventional hydrogels.

3.4 Challenges and Future Directions

For the clinical trial of biofabrication technologies, it is critical not only to overcome technical barriers from a commercialization standpoint but also to systematically establish the fundamental concepts of materials science that underpin the field.

One of the most pressing challenges currently facing the field is the lack of methodologies for objectively measuring and quantifying biomaterial properties. We must move beyond ambiguous qualitative descriptors such as "soft," "fast stress-relaxing," or "immunomodulatory," and establish standardized methods to scientifically evaluate these characteristics. For example, the development of standardized protocols to precisely measure the mechanical properties that cells actually respond to and the creation of standard assays to assess a material's immunomodulatory capacity are problems that must be solved to enhance the scientific reliability of the field.

Another critical challenge is the need for a fundamental mechanistic understanding. While we know empirically through experimentation that certain materials induce specific cellular responses, the underlying principles governing these interactions often remain elusive. A core task for basic science is to elucidate how the physicochemical properties of a material modulate the complex intracellular signaling networks. Achieving this will necessitate the integration of systems biology approaches, such as genomics and proteomics, with data analysis powered by artificial intelligence.

To realize the ultimate goal of patient-specific, personalized therapies, we need the ability to predict how an individual patient will respond to a given biomaterial. This requires establishing universal material design principles that can account for and overcome patient-to-patient variability. Accomplishing this will likely require parallel efforts in high-throughput screening, utilizing libraries of materials against patient-derived cells.

3.5 Conclusion

Over the past several decades, the field of biomaterials has undergone a paradigm shift, evolving from the concept of passive scaffolds that support tissue engineering to that of intelligent, instructive media capable of actively orchestrating the entire process of tissue regeneration. Biofabrication technology stands as the key enabling tool to realize this potential in three-dimensional space.

This chapter moves beyond simple material classification to present three fundamental design principles—mechanical, biochemical, and immunological signaling—that are essential for designing the most effective biomaterials. We then discussed how these core principles can be extended into more complex systems and examined the fundamental challenges that must be addressed for the continued advancement of the field.

Acknowledgement This work was supported by the National Research Foundation of Korea (NRF) grant funded by the Korean government (MSIT) through the Korea–China (NSFC) Joint Research Program (IRIS No. RS-2024-NR121321) and the Korea–EU Joint Research Support Program (International Cooperation R&D) (Grant No. 2021K1A3A1A78097905; IRIS No. RS-2021-NR055663).

Competing Interests The author(s) has no competing interests to declare that are relevant to the content of this manuscript

References

Adhikari B, Stager MA, Krebs MD (2023) Cell-instructive biomaterials in tissue engineering and regenerative medicine. J Biomed Mater Res A 111(5):660–681

Agarwal K, Srinivasan V, Lather V, Pandita D, Vasanthan KS (2023) Insights of 3D bioprinting and focusing the paradigm shift towards 4D printing for biomedical applications. J Mater Res 38(1): 112–141

Anderson JM, Rodriguez A, Chang DT (2008) Foreign body reaction to biomaterials. Semin immunol.: Elsevier 20:86–100

Atala A, Kasper FK, Mikos AG (2012) Engineering complex tissues. Sci Transl Med 4(160): 160rv12–160rv12. https://doi.org/10.1126/scitranslmed.3004890

Baba Y, Pelayo R, Kincade PW (2004) Relationships between hematopoietic stem cells and lymphocyte progenitors. Trends Immunol 25(12):645–649

Bae WG, Kim J, Choung YH, Chung Y, Suh KY, Pang C et al (2015) Bio-inspired configurable multiscale extracellular matrix-like structures for functional alignment and guided orientation of cells. Biomaterials 69:158–164

Baghdasaryan O, Khan S, Lin JC, Lee-Kin J, Hsu CY, Hu CMJ et al (2024) Synthetic control of living cells by intracellular polymerization. Trends Biotechnol 42(2):241–252

Balasubramaniyam S, Rathinam T, Srinivasan M, Elumalai K (2025) Advanced 3D printing and multiscale technologies (Nano to macro) for personalized biomedical applications. Bioprinting 50:e00430

Bao Z, Xian C, Yuan Q, Liu G, Wu J (2019) Natural polymer-based hydrogels with enhanced mechanical performances: preparation, structure, and property. Adv Healthc Mater 8(17): 1900670

Beiranvand M, Farhadi S, Mohammadi A (2019) Graphene oxide/hydroxyapatite/silver (rGO/HAP/ag) nanocomposite: synthesis, characterization, catalytic and antibacterial activity. Int J Nano Dimens 10(2):180–194

Brown BN, Londono R, Tottey S, Zhang L, Kukla KA, Wolf MT et al (2012) Macrophage phenotype as a predictor of constructive remodeling following the implantation of biologically derived surgical mesh materials. Acta Biomater 8(3):978–987

Celik C, Mogal VT, Hui JHP, Loh XJ, Toh WS (2018) Injectable hydrogels for cartilage regeneration. In: Hydrogels: recent advances. Springer, pp 315–337

Chaudhuri O, Gu L, Klumpers D, Darnell M, Bencherif SA, Weaver JC et al (2016) Hydrogels with tunable stress relaxation regulate stem cell fate and activity. Nat Mater 15(3):326–334

Chaudhuri O, Cooper-White J, Janmey PA, Mooney DJ, Shenoy VB (2020) Effects of extracellular matrix viscoelasticity on cellular behaviour. Nature 584(7822):535–546

Chimene D, Lennox KK, Kaunas RR, Gaharwar AK (2016) Advanced bioinks for 3D printing: a materials science perspective. Ann Biomed Eng 44(6):2090–2102

Dalby MJ, Gadegaard N, Tare R, Andar A, Riehle MO, Herzyk P et al (2007) The control of human mesenchymal cell differentiation using nanoscale symmetry and disorder. Nat Mater 6(12): 997–1003

Ding A, Lee SJ, Ayyagari S, Tang R, Huynh CT, Alsberg E (2022) 4D biofabrication via instantly generated graded hydrogel scaffolds. Bioact Mater 7:324–332

Dupont S, Morsut L, Aragona M, Enzo E, Giulitti S, Cordenonsi M et al (2011) Role of YAP/TAZ in mechanotransduction. Nature 474(7350):179–183

Eming S, Smola H, Hartmann B, Malchau G, Wegner R, Krieg T et al (2008) The inhibition of matrix metalloproteinase activity in chronic wounds by a polyacrylate superabsorber. Biomaterials 29(19):2932–2940

Engler AJ, Sen S, Sweeney HL, Discher DE (2006) Matrix elasticity directs stem cell lineage specification. Cell 126(4):677–689

Fan J, Shi Z, Lian M, Li H, Yin J (2013) Mechanically strong graphene oxide/sodium alginate/polyacrylamide nanocomposite hydrogel with improved dye adsorption capacity. J Mater Chem A 1(25):7433–7443

Franz S, Rammelt S, Scharnweber D, Simon JC (2011) Immune responses to implants–a review of the implications for the design of immunomodulatory biomaterials. Biomaterials 32(28): 6692–6709

Groll J, Burdick JA, Cho D-W, Derby B, Gelinsky M, Heilshorn SC et al (2018) A definition of bioinks and their distinction from biomaterial inks. Biofabrication 11(1):013001

Gungor-Ozkerim PS, Inci I, Zhang YS, Khademhosseini A, Dokmeci MR (2018) Bioinks for 3D bioprinting: an overview. Biomater Sci 6(5):915–946

Han J, Wu Q, Xia Y, Wagner MB, Xu C (2016) Cell alignment induced by anisotropic electrospun fibrous scaffolds alone has limited effect on cardiomyocyte maturation. Stem Cell Res 16(3): 740–750

He W, Reaume M, Hennenfent M, Lee BP, Rajachar R (2020) Biomimetic hydrogels with spatial- and temporal-controlled chemical cues for tissue engineering. Biomater Sci 8(12):3248–3269

Hench LL, Polak JM (2002) Third-generation biomedical materials. Science 295(5557):1014–1017

Hersel U, Dahmen C, Kessler H (2003) RGD modified polymers: biomaterials for stimulated cell adhesion and beyond. Biomaterials 24(24):4385–4415

Hollister SJ (2005) Porous scaffold design for tissue engineering. Nat Mater 4(7):518–524

Hong JY, Seo Y, Davaa G, Kim H-W, Kim SH, Hyun JK (2020) Decellularized brain matrix enhances macrophage polarization and functional improvements in rat spinal cord injury. Acta Biomater 101:357–371

Hu W, Guo Z, Tang W, Long J (2024) Mechanoresponsive regulation of tissue regeneration during distraction osteogenesis. FASEB J 38(18):e70056

Hussey GS, Dziki JL, Badylak SF (2018) Extracellular matrix-based materials for regenerative medicine. Nat Rev Mater 3(7):159–173

Hynes RO (2009) The extracellular matrix: not just pretty fibrils. Science 326(5957):1216–1219

Ingber DE (2006) Cellular mechanotransduction: putting all the pieces together again. FASEB J 20(7):811–827

Iqbal S, Sohail M, Fang S, Ding J, Shen L, Chen M et al (2023) Biomaterials evolution: from inert to instructive. Biomater Sci 11(18):6109–6115

Jaiswal MK, Xavier JR, Carrow JK, Desai P, Alge D, Gaharwar AK (2016) Mechanically stiff nanocomposite hydrogels at ultralow nanoparticle content. ACS Nano 10(1):246–256

Ji S, Guvendiren M (2017) Recent advances in bioink design for 3D bioprinting of tissues and organs. Front Bioeng Biotechnol 5:23

Kapoor DN, Bhatia A, Kaur R, Sharma R, Kaur G, Dhawan S (2015) PLGA: a unique polymer for drug delivery. Ther Deliv 6(1):41–58

Kechagia JZ, Ivaska J, Roca-Cusachs P (2019) Integrins as biomechanical sensors of the microenvironment. Nat Rev Mol Cell Biol 20(8):457–473

Khademhosseini A, Langer R (2016) A decade of progress in tissue engineering. Nat Protoc 11(10): 1775–1781

Kim JH, Seol YJ, Ko IK, Kang HW, Lee YK, Yoo JJ et al (2018) 3D bioprinted human skeletal muscle constructs for muscle function restoration. Sci Rep 8(1):12307

Kim B, Pradhan L, Hernandez A, Yenurkar D, Nethi SK, Mukherjee S (2023) Current advances in immunomodulatory biomaterials for cell therapy and tissue engineering. Adv Ther 6(8): 2300002

Langer R, Tirrell DA (2004) Designing materials for biology and medicine. Nature 428(6982): 487–492

Langer R, Vacanti JP (1993) Tissue engineering. Science 260(5110):920–926. https://doi.org/10.1126/science.8493529

Lee K, Silva EA, Mooney DJ (2011) Growth factor delivery-based tissue engineering: general approaches and a review of recent developments. J R Soc Interface 8(55):153–170

Lee JH, Shin YC, Lee SM, Jin OS, Kang SH, Hong SW et al (2015) Enhanced osteogenesis by reduced graphene oxide/hydroxyapatite nanocomposites. Sci Rep 5(1):18833

Li WJ, Laurencin CT, Caterson EJ, Tuan RS, Ko FK (2002) Electrospun nanofibrous structure: a novel scaffold for tissue engineering. J Biomed Mater Res: An Official Journal of The Society for Biomaterials, The Japanese Society for Biomaterials, and The Australian Society for Biomaterials and the Korean Society for Biomaterials 60(4):613–621

Li S, Cai X, Guo J, Li X, Li W, Liu Y et al (2025) Cell communication and relevant signaling pathways in osteogenesis–angiogenesis coupling. Bone Res 13(1):45

Lin P, Lin C-W, Mansour R, Gu F (2013) Improving biocompatibility by surface modification techniques on implantable bioelectronics. Biosens Bioelectron 47:451–460

Lutolf MP, Hubbell J (2005) Synthetic biomaterials as instructive extracellular microenvironments for morphogenesis in tissue engineering. Nat Biotechnol 23(1):47–55

Mandal B, Rameshbabu AP, Soni SR, Ghosh A, Dhara S, Pal S (2017) In situ silver nanowire deposited cross-linked carboxymethyl cellulose: a potential transdermal anticancer drug carrier. ACS Appl Mater Interfaces 9(42):36583–36595

Mir M, Ahmed N, ur Rehman A (2017) Recent applications of PLGA based nanostructures in drug delivery. Colloids Surf B: Biointerfaces 159:217–231

Mironov V, Trusk T, Kasyanov V, Little S, Swaja R, Markwald R (2009) Biofabrication: a 21st century manufacturing paradigm. Biofabrication 1(2):022001

Mohri Z, Hernandez ADR, Krams R (2017) The emerging role of YAP/TAZ in mechanotransduction. J Thorac Dis 9(5):E507

Moroni L, Boland T, Burdick JA, De Maria C, Derby B, Forgacs G et al (2018) Biofabrication: a guide to technology and terminology. Trends Biotechnol 36(4):384–402

Murphy SV, Atala A (2014) 3D bioprinting of tissues and organs. Nat Biotechnol 32(8):773–785

Naficy S, Gately R, Gorkin R III, Xin H, Spinks GM (2017) 4D printing of reversible shape morphing hydrogel structures. Macromol Mater Eng 302(1):1600212

O'brien FJ (2011) Biomaterials & scaffolds for tissue engineering. Mater Today 14(3):88–95

Okano T, Yamada N, Sakai H, Sakurai Y (1993) A novel recovery system for cultured cells using plasma-treated polystyrene dishes grafted with poly (N-isopropylacrylamide). J Biomed Mater Res 27(10):1243–1251

Paxton N, Smolan W, Böck T, Melchels F, Groll J, Jungst T (2017) Proposal to assess printability of bioinks for extrusion-based bioprinting and evaluation of rheological properties governing bioprintability. Biofabrication 9(4):044107

Pierschbacher MD, Ruoslahti E (1984) Cell attachment activity of fibronectin can be duplicated by small synthetic fragments of the molecule. Nature 309(5963):30–33

Portnov T, Shulimzon TR, Zilberman M (2017) Injectable hydrogel-based scaffolds for tissue engineering applications. Rev Chem Eng 33(1):91–107

Pourmasoumi P, Moghaddam A, Nemati Mahand S, Heidari F, Salehi Moghaddam Z, Arjmand M et al (2023) A review on the recent progress, opportunities, and challenges of 4D printing and bioprinting in regenerative medicine. J Biomater Sci Polym Ed 34(1):108–146

Pramanick A, Hayes T, Sergis V, McEvoy E, Pandit A, Daly AC (2025) 4D bioprinting shape-morphing tissues in granular support hydrogels: sculpting structure and guiding maturation. Adv Funct Mater 35(5):2414559

Prestwich GD (2007) Simplifying the extracellular matrix for 3-D cell culture and tissue engineering: A pragmatic approach. J Cell Biochem 101(6):1370–1383

Qi X, Guan Y, Chen G, Zhang B, Ren J, Peng F et al (2015) A non-covalent strategy for montmorillonite/xylose self-healing hydrogels. RSC Adv 5(51):41006–41012

Rahimnejad M, Jahangiri S, Zirak Hassan Kiadeh S, Rezvaninejad S, Ahmadi Z, Ahmadi S et al (2024) Stimuli-responsive biomaterials: smart avenue toward 4D bioprinting. Crit Rev Biotechnol 44(5):860–891

Ramadas M, Bharath G, Ponpandian N, Ballamurugan A (2017) Investigation on biophysical properties of hydroxyapatite/graphene oxide (HAp/GO) based binary nanocomposite for biomedical applications. Mater Chem Phys 199:179–184

Ratner BD (2007) The catastrophe revisited: blood compatibility in the 21st century. Biomaterials 28(34):5144–5147

Saraswathibhatla A, Indana D, Chaudhuri O (2023) Cell–extracellular matrix mechanotransduction in 3D. Nat Rev Mol Cell Biol 24(7):495–516

Semete B, Booysen L, Lemmer Y, Kalombo L, Katata L, Verschoor J et al (2010) In vivo evaluation of the biodistribution and safety of PLGA nanoparticles as drug delivery systems. Nanomedicine 6(5):662–671

Sudheesh Kumar P, Lakshmanan V-K, Anilkumar T, Ramya C, Reshmi P, Unnikrishnan A et al (2012) Flexible and microporous chitosan hydrogel/nano ZnO composite bandages for wound dressing: in vitro and in vivo evaluation. ACS Appl Mater Interfaces 4(5):2618–2629

Sydney Gladman A, Matsumoto EA, Nuzzo RG, Mahadevan L, Lewis JA (2016) Biomimetic 4D printing. Nat Mater 15(4):413–418

Teixeira AI, Abrams GA, Bertics PJ, Murphy CJ, Nealey PF (2003) Epithelial contact guidance on well-defined micro-and nanostructured substrates. J Cell Sci 116(10):1881–1892

Tibbits S (2014) 4D printing: multi-material shape change. Archit Des 84(1):116–121

Van Den Bulcke AI, Bogdanov B, De Rooze N, Schacht EH, Cornelissen M, Berghmans H (2000) Structural and rheological properties of methacrylamide modified gelatin hydrogels. Biomacromolecules 1(1):31–38

Veiseh O, Doloff JC, Ma M, Vegas AJ, Tam HH, Bader AR et al (2015) Size-and shape-dependent foreign body immune response to materials implanted in rodents and non-human primates. Nat Mater 14(6):643–651

Vining KH, Mooney DJ (2017) Mechanical forces direct stem cell behaviour in development and regeneration. Nat Rev Mol Cell Biol 18(12):728–742

Vishwakarma A, Bhise NS, Evangelista MB, Rouwkema J, Dokmeci MR, Ghaemmaghami AM et al (2016) Engineering immunomodulatory biomaterials to tune the inflammatory response. Trends Biotechnol 34(6):470–482

Wang Y, Zhang Z, Yang Q, Cao Y, Dong Y, Bi Y et al (2022a) Immunoregulatory role of the mechanosensitive ion channel Piezo1 in inflammation and cancer. Molecules 28(1):213

Wang Y, Cui H, Esworthy T, Mei D, Wang Y, Zhang LG (2022b) Emerging 4D printing strategies for next-generation tissue regeneration and medical devices. Adv Mater 34(20):2109198

Whitaker R, Hernaez-Estrada B, Hernandez RM, Santos-Vizcaino E, Spiller KL (2021) Immunomodulatory biomaterials for tissue repair. Chem Rev 121(18):11305–11335

Xue J, Wu T, Dai Y, Xia Y (2019) Electrospinning and electrospun nanofibers: methods, materials, and applications. Chem Rev 119(8):5298–5415

Yang L, Pijuan-Galito S, Rho HS, Vasilevich AS, Eren AD, Ge L et al (2021) High-throughput methods in the discovery and study of biomaterials and materiobiology. Chem Rev 121(8): 4561–4677

Yeh CE, Chen WC, Chen CS, Hou WT, Li SJ, Hao YL et al (2024) Enhancing the angiogenesis and osteogenesis of low elastic modulus Ti-Nb-Zr-Sn alloy surface through grafting growth factors-containing gelatin nanoparticles. Surf Interfaces 46:104136

Zhang L, Cao Z, Bai T, Carr L, Ella-Menye JR, Irvin C et al (2013) Zwitterionic hydrogels implanted in mice resist the foreign-body reaction. Nat Biotechnol 31(6):553–556

Zhang Y, Zhu L, Hong J, Chen C (2022) Extracellular matrix of early pulmonary fibrosis modifies the polarization of alveolar macrophage. Int Immunopharmacol 111:109179

Zhang S, Yang H, Wang M, Mantovani D, Yang K, Witte F et al (2023) Immunomodulatory biomaterials against bacterial infections: Progress, challenges, and future perspectives. Innovations 4(6)

Zhao L, Zhou Y, Zhang J, Liang H, Chen X, Tan H (2023) Natural polymer-based hydrogels: from polymer to biomedical applications. Pharmaceutics 15(10):2514

Zhou X, Nowicki M, Cui H, Zhu W, Fang X, Miao S et al (2017) 3D bioprinted graphene oxide-incorporated matrix for promoting chondrogenic differentiation of human bone marrow mesenchymal stem cells. Carbon 116:615–624

Chapter 4
Rheological Properties and Printability Assessment of Bioinks from a Biofabrication Perspective

Seyithan Kansız, Faustin Hategekimana, Eylül Odabaş-Kansız, Ayşe Eser Elçin, and Yaşar Murat Elçin

Abstract Extrusion-based bioprinting has become the cornerstone of biofabrication due to its ability to process highly viscous bioinks and support high cell densities. This technology largely depends on the physicochemical properties of the bioinks which must ensure smooth extrusion, rapid solidification, and structural fidelity while preserving the cell viability. However, establishing standardized protocols for bioink formulation, printing parameters, post-processing, and the translation from small constructs to clinically relevant tissues and organs remain a major challenge, as it requires a comprehensive understanding and careful balancing of rheological properties and printability factors that critically influence bioprinting performance. This chapter systematically examines the rheological features of bioink functionality, including shear-thinning, viscoelasticity, yield stress, and thixotropy, and their interplay during extrusion-based bioprinting process. Advanced rheological characterization methods are also discussed as essential tools for quantifying

S. Kansız · Y. M. Elçin (✉)
Tissue Engineering, Biomaterials and Nanobiotechnology Laboratory, Faculty of Science and Stem Cell Institute, Ankara University, Ankara, Türkiye

Department of Chemistry, Faculty of Science, Ankara University, Ankara, Türkiye
e-mail: elcin@ankara.edu.tr

F. Hategekimana
Tissue Engineering, Biomaterials and Nanobiotechnology Laboratory, Faculty of Science and Stem Cell Institute, Ankara University, Ankara, Türkiye

E. Odabaş-Kansız
Tissue Engineering, Biomaterials and Nanobiotechnology Laboratory, Faculty of Science and Stem Cell Institute, Ankara University, Ankara, Türkiye

Central Research Laboratory Application and Research Center, Ankara Yıldırım Beyazıt University, Ankara, Türkiye

A. E. Elçin
Tissue Engineering, Biomaterials and Nanobiotechnology Laboratory, Faculty of Science and Stem Cell Institute, Ankara University, Ankara, Türkiye

Stem Cell Institute, Ankara University, Ankara, Türkiye

Y. M. Elçin (ed.), *Biofabrication in Regenerative Medicine*, Stem Cell Biology and Regenerative Medicine 1519, https://doi.org/10.1007/978-3-032-30294-6_4

bioink behavior under bioprinting-relevant conditions. Overall, this chapter provides a rational basis for the design of next-generation bioinks, enabling the development of structurally robust, biologically functional constructs for applications in tissue engineering and regenerative medicine.

Keywords 3D bioprinting · Extrusion-based bioprinting · Bioink · Rheological properties · Printability · Thixotropy · Shear-thinning · Viscoelasticity · Yield stress

Abbreviations

AA	Acrylic acid
BuMA	Butyl methacrylate
CMC	Carboxymethyl cellulose
CNF	Carbon nanofiber
CS	Chitosan
DEGMA	Di(ethylene glycol) methyl ether methacrylate
DMEM	Dimethylamino ethyl methacrylate
FUC	Fucoidan
GelMA	Gelatin methacrylate
GLA	Glutaraldehyde
GQD	Graphene quantum dot
HA	Hyaluronic acid
HAMA	Hyaluronic acid methacrylate
hiPSC-NPCs	Human induced pluripotent stem cell-derived neural progenitor cells
hMSCs	Human mesenchymal stem cells
hASCs	Human adipose-derived stem cells
HUVECs	Human umbilical vein endothelial cells
LCST	Lower critical solution temperature
LVR	Linear viscoelastic region
NFC	Nano fibrillated cellulose
OEGMA	Oligo(ethylene glycol) methyl ether methacrylate
PCL	Poly(caprolactone)
PEG	Poly(ethylene glycol)
PLA	Poly(lactic acid)
PLGA	Poly(lactic-co-glycolic acid)
TDS	Time-dependent solidification
UCST	Upper critical solution temperature
3D	Three dimensional

4.1 Introduction

Bioprinting refers to computer-assisted biofabrication approaches that enable the controlled spatial deposition of bioinks—typically consisting of biomolecules, living cells, and biodegradable materials—according to predefined three-dimensional (3D) architectures, with the aim of producing functional engineered tissue constructs (Cui et al. 2020; Vurat et al. 2020). To date, various 3D-printing techniques have been adopted to 3D-bioprinting applications including inkjet, laser-assisted, stereolithography, and extrusion-based printing. Among these techniques extrusion-based printing offers several practical advantages in bioprinting applications. Although inkjet and laser-assisted systems can achieve very high spatial resolution, they have basic limitations in terms of printing speed and the achievable size of the 3D-bioprinted constructs (Moroni et al. 2018; Gillispie et al. 2020). Stereolithography-based approaches, including digital light processing, can overcome some of these scale and speed limitations and may rival extrusion printing in overall fabrication efficiency. Nevertheless, these methods typically require large initial cell quantities because the entire resin volume must be populated prior to printing. In addition, stereolithography is generally limited to photo-crosslinkable materials (Gillispie et al. 2020; Derakhshanfar et al. 2018).

Extrusion-based 3D-bioprinting involves the continuous deposition of filamentous streams of a printable, cell-laden formulation that is first loaded into a printing cartridge (Kesti et al. 2015; Singh et al. 2026; Kansız et al. 2025). Bioink is extruded through a nozzle or ink reservoir via a compressed or screw system, and deposited onto a substrate in a sequential, layer-by-layer manner to build the desired 3D constructs. In literature, these deposited elements are commonly described as filaments, although terms such as strands or struts are also used. Many extrusion systems are equipped with multiple print heads, enabling the simultaneous deposition of different materials within a single construct. This capability allows the fabrication of structures with spatially defined variations in biomaterial composition, cell type, cell density, and incorporated bioactive cues (Ravanbakhsh et al. 2021). Compared with other bioprinting modalities, extrusion printing also supports the processing of bioinks containing relatively high cell concentrations. However, a major limitation of this technique is that cells experience mechanical stresses during extrusion, particularly shear forces generated as the bioink passes through the nozzle, which can negatively affect cell viability and function. Although extrusion bioprinting is compatible with a broader range of ink materials than other printing methods, one of its most frequently discussed challenges remains the limited number of suitable biomaterials, especially those formulated as bioinks. The main reason is that bioinks are required to balance multiple constraints at once, such as maintaining cell viability, providing a supportive microenvironment, and exhibiting suitable rheological properties for reliable 3D-bioprinting, which limits the number of materials that fulfill all criteria.

A bioink can be simply defined as a printable biomaterial formulation used in 3D-bioprinting that contains living cells and/or biologically active components, designed to be deposited layer-by-layer to fabricate tissue-like structures. They are typically formulated as aqueous hydrogel precursors in which cells are uniformly suspended. Therefore, they usually exhibit relatively low mechanical stiffness together with biochemical features that permit cell-mediated remodeling and matrix interaction. To date, various hydrogel precursors including gelatin, collagen, hyaluronic acid, silk fibroin, alginate, chitosan, κ-carrageenan, and their blends have been used to prepare bioink formulations. Although hydrogels of these biopolymers are well-known for their cytocompatibility, they usually suffer from some insufficient physicochemical properties such as rapid degradation rates, low mechanical properties to support shape fidelity, high swelling ratios, and rheological properties. Different cross-linking approaches like Michael addition, methacryl group mediated cross-linking, host-guest interactions and enzymatic cross-linking usually overcome these drawbacks. However, meeting proper rheological properties for developed bioink stands the major challenge in 3D-bioprinting applications. The bioink should possess shear-thinning property for extrusion, solidify rapidly following the extrusion step, and finally support the stacked structure with a proper yield stress. These properties should be in balance. For example, if a bioink has a high yield stress value, its extrudability requires high stress and affects the viability of the cell in post-printing. Therefore, different terms introduced into literature, *"printability window"* and "*biofabrication window*" each considers the optimal conditions for 3D-bioprinting results in terms of rheology, printability, and cell viability (Malda et al. 2013; Paxton et al. 2017).

This chapter describes the fundamental rheological requirements for extrusion-based 3D-bioprinting. First, the principles of extrusion-based bioprinting are introduced, followed by a presentation of the rheological context of the key stages of the printing process, including extrusion, solidification, and layer support. The subsequent section discusses the essential considerations for bioink development. Commonly used rheological characterization techniques and guidelines for interpreting their results are then outlined. In addition, parameters governed by bioink rheology—such as extrudability, filament uniformity, and shape fidelity—are comprehensively reviewed. Finally, current limitations and future perspectives are addressed. Overall, this chapter aims to provide a framework for the rational design of novel bioinks to achieve optimum bioprinting performance.

4.2 Extrusion-Based 3D-Bioprinting

Extrusion-based bioprinting is a prominent biofabrication technique that enables the controlled deposition of bioinks to produce 3D tissue-like constructs (Zhang et al. 2021). The method operates by forcing a bioink through a dispensing nozzle or needle using pneumatic pressure, mechanical pistons, or screw-driven systems. As the bioink exits the nozzle, it is deposited layer by layer according to a predefined digital model, allowing the formation of complex geometries with spatial control over cell distribution. A key feature of extrusion bioprinting is its ability to process materials with relatively high viscosity compared to droplet-based or laser-assisted methods (Cooke and Rosenzweig 2021). This enables the fabrication of mechanically stable structures and supports the printing of constructs with high cell densities. During printing, parameters such as extrusion pressure, nozzle diameter, temperature, and printing speed directly influence filament formation, resolution, and cell survival. In particular, excessive shear stress generated during extrusion may damage cells, making the optimization of bioink rheology and printing conditions essential for maintaining viability and function. Following deposition, printed filaments typically undergo physical or chemical crosslinking to stabilize the structure and preserve its shape. This solidification step may involve ionic interactions, temperature changes, enzymatic reactions, or photo-initiated polymerization, depending on the material system used. Through this combination of controlled extrusion and post-printing stabilization, extrusion-based bioprinting allows researchers to fabricate scaffolds and tissue models that approximate the architecture and microenvironment of native biological tissues (Jiang et al. 2019).

Because of its relative simplicity, compatibility with diverse biomaterials, and scalability, extrusion bioprinting has become one of the most widely used platforms in biofabrication approaches including tissue engineering, regenerative medicine, and in vitro disease modeling. Continued improvements in bioink design, nozzle engineering, and process control are expected to further advance the role of this technique in biomedical research and therapeutic development by increasing print resolution, cell viability, and functional maturation of printed constructs.

4.2.1 Extrusion

Extrusion is the process in which hydrogel-based bioink is forced through the nozzle to form filaments, which are deposited layer by layer to build complex tissue-like structures (Rau et al. 2023). The applied pressure must be sufficient to overcome the yield stress of the bioink and the flow resistance imposed by the nozzle. It is expected that the bioink should transit from solid-like phase (gel) to liquid-like phase (sol) for continuous flow. Different types of extruders have been utilized, including mechanical plunger, compressed air, and extrusion screws to generate pressure gradient for flow. However, the flow mechanism does not change regardless of the extruder (Malda et al. 2013). Screw-based extrusion systems are particularly advantageous for processing highly viscous biomaterials with viscosities about 10^4 Pa s (Schwab et al. 2020; Murphy and Atala 2014). Such mechanisms are therefore commonly preferred for the deposition of thermoplastic polymers, including PCL, PLA, and PLGA. Materials like hydrogels characterized with lower viscosity (typically below about 10^4 Pa s), piston-driven or pneumatic extrusion types are more frequently used (Kyle et al. 2017). Among these, pneumatic extruder systems dominate commercial bioprinting configurations due to their flexibility and operational simplicity. However, they often provide less precise control over deposition behavior, particularly when printing heterogeneous bioinks such as particle-filled composites or slurry-like bioink formulations. For all types of extruders, a continuous and uniform flow is achieved when the bioink flow rate is precisely matched to the translation speed of the printhead (Khalil and Sun 2007). A mismatch between these two parameters results in improper filament formation, ultimately leading to deflection and defects in the 3D-bioprinted construct.

4.2.2 Solidification

Solidification involves the state transition of the extruded bioink from a liquid-like state to a solid-like state after deposition. This step is crucial for maintaining the shape of the deposited filaments and minimizing unwanted excessive spreading or deformation. The material must solidify rapidly to maintain geometric accuracy and enable the successful building of successive layers. It requires careful consideration of the ink's rheological properties, such as yield-stress, resolidification (gelation) time, and curing time, as well as optimized printing parameters (Rau et al. 2023). Based on the solidification mechanism, the used bioinks are classified into shear yield-stress and time-dependent inks and the combination of the two. Yield-stress materials reversibly shift from solid-like to liquid-like behavior once the applied stress exceeds a critical threshold. Time-Dependent Solidification (TDS) inks transition from liquid-like to solid-like states upon deposition. Unlike yield-stress materials, this change is irreversible and typically needs an external chemical reaction or stimulus to initiate solidification (Rau et al. 2018). TDS could be achieved in different cross-linking approaches including guest-host interactions, physical mechanisms, or enzyme-mediated cross-linking.

4.2.3 Layer Support

Layer support refers to the ability of a deposited filament to withstand the mechanical load imposed by subsequently printed layers without undergoing yielding, buckling, lateral spreading, or excessive deformation (Duty et al. 2018; Romberg et al. 2021). This property is a key determinant of printability in extrusion-based bioprinting, as it directly influences the structural integrity, dimensional accuracy, and architectural stability of the fabricated construct throughout the layer-by-layer deposition process. Insufficient layer support can lead to progressive structural collapse, pore closure, or distortion of designed geometries, ultimately compromising both mechanical performance and biological functionality.

Effective layer support depends strongly on the viscoelastic and rheological characteristics of the bioink after deposition. In particular, the material must exhibit sufficiently high yield stress to resist plastic deformation under gravitational and stacking loads. At the same time, an adequate storage modulus is required to provide elastic resistance against compressive stress and to minimize the risk of filament buckling or collapse. Rapid structural recovery following extrusion further enhances stacking stability by enabling the printed filament to regain its mechanical strength before subsequent layers are deposited. Collectively, these material properties govern the load-bearing capacity of printed filaments and play a fundamental role in achieving reliable 3D construct formation. On the other hand, achieving both good extrudability and high shape fidelity is challenging, since the yield stress must be low enough to enable uniform filament extrusion while remaining sufficiently high to support the printed layers.

4.2.4 Rheological Factors Affecting Printability

Because extrusion bioprinting relies on extruding a bioink through a narrow nozzle, rheological properties of bioinks are primarily considered in relation to how they respond to the high shear conditions of the printing process. A range of rheological characterization methods can be used to evaluate printability-related properties, as most hydrogel-based bioinks exhibit non-Newtonian behavior. In contrast to Newtonian fluids, where viscosity remains constant and the relationship between shear stress and shear rate is linear, hydrogels commonly exhibit shear-thinning, characterized by a decrease of apparent viscosity with increasing shear rate. This characteristic is particularly advantageous for bioprinting, as it facilitates smooth extrusion through the nozzle while reducing the pressure required for flow and minimizing the shear stresses experienced by encapsulated cells. Other rheological behaviors, such as shear-thickening or rheopectic responses—where viscosity increases with shear rate or time are generally undesirable for extrusion bioprinting because they hinder flow, increase printing pressure, and may elevate mechanical stress on cells.

4.2.4.1 Shear-Thinning

Shear-thinning is a rheological property where the viscosity of a material decreases as the shear rate increases. Most materials widely used in extrusion based bioprinting such as concentrated polymer solutions, polymer melts, colloidal suspensions and partially cross-linked hydrogels exhibit this behavior (Schwab et al. 2020). The underlying mechanisms for shear-thinning behavior of bioinks vary across different classes of bioinks. Thermoplastic molten material exhibits inherent shear-thinning characteristics due to the molecular dynamics of long-chain macromolecules. High-molecular weight polymer chains are entangled and randomly oriented, forming a network that resists flow. Under applied shear stress, these chains progressively disentangle and orient along the direction of flow, reducing intermolecular interactions and consequently lowering the apparent viscosity. In bioinks formulated as colloidal dispersions, pastes, or particle-laden suspensions, shear-thinning behavior primarily originates from the shear-induced disruption of interparticle interactions within the solid phase (Wilson et al. 2017; Chimene et al. 2018). At rest, attractive forces and physical contacts between suspended particles generate a viscoelastic network that imparts structural rigidity to the material. When shear is applied, these interactions are temporarily weakened or broken, allowing the system to flow more readily. Once the stress is removed, the gradual reformation of particle-particle interactions recovers the viscoelastic network, thereby contributing to shape retention and structural stability after deposition. Most hydrogel systems typically exhibit shear-thinning behavior as a result of polymer chain disentanglement and macromolecular alignment along the direction of shear. This flow mechanism resembles that observed in polymer melts, with the key distinction that hydrogel systems contain a solvent phase that influences chain mobility, intermolecular interactions, and relaxation dynamics. At rest, these materials often display viscoelastic recovery and, in many cases, a measurable yield stress due to the presence of transient physical networks (Ouyang et al. 2016a). The shear-thinning response of hydrogel-based bioinks is largely affected by polymer concentration and molecular weight distribution (Cooke and Rosenzweig 2021). At low concentrations, intermolecular interactions are limited due to the large separation between chains. With increasing concentration, chain overlap becomes significant, promoting non-covalent intermolecular interactions. At high concentrations, this overlap can evolve into chain entanglement, resulting in the formation of a transient network that strongly influences rheological behavior.

4.2.4.2 Viscoelasticity and Yield Stress

Both viscoelasticity and yield stress are critical rheological properties that directly determine how well a bioink can be printed. Viscoelastic materials are materials that exhibit both viscous (fluid-like) and elastic (solid-like) behavior. It is commonly characterized by two fundamental parameters: the storage modulus (G'), representing the elastic component, and the loss modulus (G''), representing the viscous component of the material. G' quantifies the portion of mechanical energy that is stored and recoverable during deformation and is therefore directly related to the material's ability to maintain its shape and resist elastic deformation. In contrast, G'' reflects the energy dissipated as viscous flow, providing insight into the extent of structural rearrangement occurring within the material under applied stress. The relative magnitudes of G' and G'' provide a useful indicator of whether the material behaves predominantly as a solid-like or liquid-like system under given deformation conditions.

On the other hand, yield stress is defined as the minimum stress required for a material to transition from a solid-like state to a liquid-like state. This parameter is particularly important in extrusion-based bioprinting, as it governs both the initiation of flow through the nozzle and the ability of the deposited filament to retain its shape after printing. Like shear-thinning property it is directly related to molecular weight. For instance, Hájovská et al. reported that an increase in the molecular weight of alginate also led to an increase in the yield stress of GelMA/Alg bioinks (Hájovská et al. 2025). They reported stress values of 69 ± 16 Pa for G8A5VL (very low molecular weight), 327 ± 27 Pa for G8A5L (low molecular weight), and

538 ± 119 Pa for G8A5M (medium molecular weight). Bioink with an appropriate yield stress remains stable under low stresses, preventing spreading or collapse, while becoming flowable under higher stresses imposed during extrusion. More importantly, yield stress recovery (post-extrusion) is vital for layer stacking and dimensional accuracy.

4.2.4.3 Thixotropy

Thixotropy is defined as the time-dependent decrease in viscosity under constant shear stress, with subsequent structural recovery after stress removal. This reversible behavior originates from the progressive disruption and subsequent restoration of intermolecular networks within the bioink matrix, thereby allowing controlled flow during processing (Cooke and Rosenzweig 2021). As a consequence, thixotropic materials display characteristic hysteresis loops in their flow curves, where the enclosed area reflects the extent of structural breakdown (Calafel et al. 2025). Unlike instantaneous shear-thinning responses, thixotropy involves time-dependent microstructural evolution that can be deliberately tuned for specific bioprinting requirements. In particular, optimizing the recovery kinetics of thixotropic bioinks is critical to ensure adequate flow during extrusion while enabling rapid structural reformation to maintain printed geometry. This temporal aspect of rheology provides a valuable means of regulating material performance throughout both printing and subsequent maturation.

4.2.5 Rheological Characterization of Bioinks

Rheological characterization is essential for understanding how bioinks behave during extrusion-based printing. As the material moves from a resting state to strong shear inside the nozzle and then back to rest after deposition, its internal structure continuously evolves. Different rheological tests are used to monitor these changes (Fig. 4.1). For instance, shear measurements provide information about viscosity and shear-thinning behavior, which are closely related to the force required for extrusion. Oscillatory tests, such as amplitude and frequency sweeps, help determine the material's viscoelastic property and the point at which bioink begins to yield (flow). In addition, thixotropy experiments are useful for evaluating how rapidly bioink recovers its solid-like structure after deformation. It is an important factor that strongly influences shape retention once the filament is deposited. Considering these measurements together allows a more realistic interpretation of printing performance.

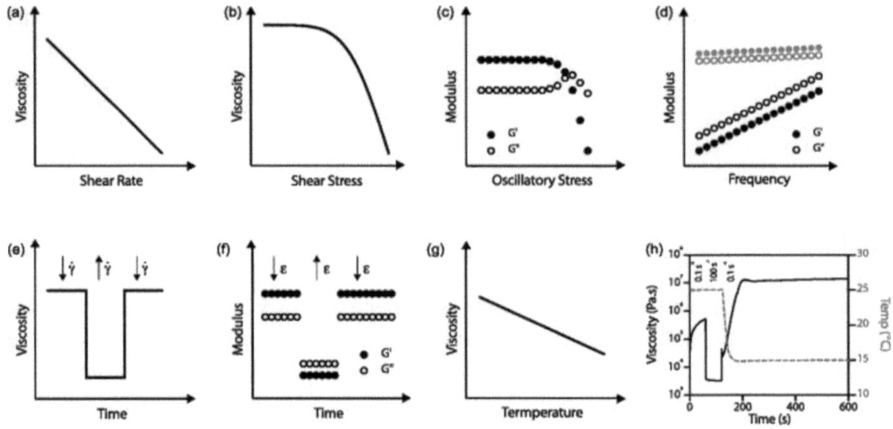

Fig. 4.1 Common rheological tests for bioinks include (a) shear rate sweep, (b) stress ramp, (c) oscillatory stress ramp (amplitude sweep), (d) frequency sweep of materials with different behaviors - solid-like gels (gray) and viscoelastic liquids (black), (e) rotational thixotropy (changing shear rate), (f) oscillatory thixotropy (changing oscillatory strain, ϵ), (g) rotational temperature sweep, and (h) an example of a thixotropy test (Cooke and Rosenzweig 2021)

4.2.5.1 Shear Rate Sweep

Shear rate sweep tests are among the most widely used rheological methods for characterizing fluid behavior, particularly for identifying deviations from Newtonian flow. In this test, the applied shear rate is progressively increased or decreased, often across several orders of magnitude, while the resulting shear stress is continuously measured. These data allow calculation of the apparent viscosity as a function of shear rate, providing insight into how the material responds to deformation under different flow conditions. Such measurements are especially important for complex fluids whose internal microstructure reorganizes under stress, leading to shear-thinning or, less commonly, shear-thickening responses. In the context of extrusion bioprinting, shear rate sweep tests are routinely performed to evaluate how a bioink will behave as it is forced through a nozzle. Many bioinks exhibit pronounced shear-thinning behavior, which is advantageous because it reduces the resistance to flow during extrusion while allowing the material to recover a higher viscosity after deposition. It can be quantitatively determined using power law model (Eq. 4.1), where η is viscosity (Non-Newtonian), k is the consistency index constant, $\dot{\gamma}$ is the shear rate, and n is the shear-thinning index, also called the flow index or power-law index. If $n < 1$, it indicates shear-thinning behavior of the bioink. On the other hand, $n > 1$ and $n = 1$ corresponds to shear-thickening behavior, a Newtonian fluid, respectively.

$$\eta = k\dot{\gamma}^{n-1} \tag{4.1}$$

In addition to the Power-Law model, Herschel-Bulkley has also been commonly used to determine shear-thinning properties of bioinks (Eq. 4.2). Unlike the Power-Law model, which characterizes flow behavior primarily through the flow index, the

Herschel-Bulkley model enables a more comprehensive interpretation of bioink response by incorporating yield stress, consistency, and shear-thinning parameters simultaneously. While the yield stress represents the minimum stress required to initiate flow, the consistency index reflects the overall resistance to flow and influences filament thickness and stacking stability. Also, the flow index describes the degree of shear-thinning behavior of the bioink. By combining these parameters, the Herschel-Bulkley model provides more physically meaningful data for evaluating both processability and structural fidelity in extrusion-based printing systems, making it particularly suitable for bioink characterization.

$$\tau = \tau_0 + \gamma k^n \tag{4.2}$$

4.2.5.2 Oscillatory Amplitude Sweeps

Oscillatory amplitude sweep tests are commonly employed to characterize the viscoelastic response of biomaterials. In an oscillatory amplitude sweep test, the storage and loss moduli of an ink are recorded while the oscillation amplitude is gradually increased at a constant frequency. Because stress and strain are inherently coupled, this procedure simultaneously probes the viscoelastic response under rising stress levels, which is why it may be described as a stress, strain, or amplitude sweep. In these measurements, the G' reflects the elastic, solid-like contribution, while the loss modulus G'' represents the viscous, liquid-like behavior. From these parameters, the complex viscosity, describing the frequency dependent resistance to deformation of a viscoelastic material, can also be determined. At low applied stresses or strains, both moduli remain essentially constant, defining the linear viscoelastic region (LVR), within which the internal structure of the material is preserved. As the imposed deformation increases beyond this region, a crossover point may occur where G'' exceeds G', often referred to as the critical strain or stress; this transition indicates the onset of structural breakdown and the shift toward flow-dominated behavior (Schwab et al. 2020). Such measurements are valuable for identifying characteristic points such as the apparent yield stress, corresponding to the end of the LVR, and the flow point associated with structural collapse. In extrusion bioprinting research, amplitude sweeps are therefore widely used not only to assess bioink stability but also to determine the yield stress at which transition from solid-like to fluid-like state occurs.

4.2.5.3 Frequency Sweeps

An oscillatory frequency sweep is commonly used to evaluate the viscoelastic (complex viscosity) response of a bioink by measuring its complex viscosity while the oscillation frequency increases at a fixed deformation amplitude. To relate these results to shear rate measurements, which report viscosity as a function of shear rate, researchers often examine whether the Cox-Merz rule is generally applied (Eq. 4.3)

(Cooke and Rosenzweig 2021; Mohamed Yunus and Parisi 2024). For many polymeric systems, the magnitude of the complex viscosity measured in oscillatory tests approximates the shear-rate viscosity when the angular frequency equals the shear rate. If this relationship is valid, oscillatory tests can be used to estimate flow behavior and extrusion performance. This approach is particularly useful in extrusion bioprinting because shear rates inside the nozzle frequently exceed 100 s^{-1}, a range that can be difficult to probe reliably with shear-rate experiments (Corker et al. 2019). Nevertheless, the Cox-Merz relationship is not universal and must be verified experimentally. For instance, suspensions containing increasing amounts of particulate fillers may follow the rule only within a limited concentration window; beyond that range, oscillatory measurements can significantly overestimate viscosity compared with steady-shear data. Therefore, both testing methods should be performed whenever possible to confirm whether the rule is valid for a given formulation. In cases where materials are extremely stiff or highly viscous, shear rate tests may produce unreliable data due to the large strains required, leaving oscillatory measurements as the only viable option-though under such conditions the Cox-Merz rule should not be assumed to apply.

$$\eta(\dot{\gamma}) = |\eta^*(\omega)|_{\dot{\gamma}=\omega} \tag{4.3}$$

4.2.5.4 Thixotropy Tests

Amplitude sweep tests identify the stress level at which a material transits from solid-like to liquid-like state, yet they do not reveal how quickly this transition takes place (Cooke and Rosenzweig 2021; Li et al. 2025). Also, they provide no information on the time required for the material to regain solid-like characteristics after flow, which corresponds to ink solidification. Therefore, thixotropy tests are used to evaluate the time-dependent structural recovery of bioinks and can be conducted in either rotational or oscillatory rheological modes to assess changes in G′ and G″. In extrusion bioprinting, thixotropic recovery is a critical parameter, as it determines how rapidly a bioink can rebuild its internal structure after extrusion to maintain filament stability and provide mechanical support to subsequent layers. A typical protocol consists of three stages: an initial low-shear (or low-strain) phase to characterize the material's rest structure, followed by a high-shear phase that simulates the extrusion step, and finally, a return to the original low-shear conditions to monitor recovery of the bioink which is essential for layer support (Calafel et al. 2025). Throughout the test, viscosity or moduli are recorded continuously, with particular attention paid to the recovery stage, where the time required for the material to regain its initial properties is determined. In oscillatory measurements, G′ generally dominates during low-stress conditions, indicating solid-like behavior, whereas G″ becomes dominant under high stress as the material transitions to a more fluid-like state. Because full structural recovery can be slow, recovery times are often reported based on the time needed to reach a defined fraction, commonly 80–90% of the initial value.

4.2.5.5 Temperature Sweeps

Temperature sweep tests are particularly valuable for bioinks composed of thermo-responsive biomaterials such as gelatin, collagen, and κ-carrageenan. In these experiments, viscosity or viscoelastic moduli are monitored as temperature is gradually increased or decreased, allowing identification of gelation, melting, or transition windows relevant to printing (Cooke and Rosenzweig 2021). Such information is essential for defining processing conditions in which extrusion can occur at manageable pressures while still preserving cell viability and structural fidelity after deposition. By determining temperature-dependent transitions, these measurements help establish operational ranges where a bioink remains sufficiently fluid for extrusion yet rapidly stabilizes once printed. Rheological tests can also be combined or programmed sequentially to reproduce realistic printing environments. For example, extrusion of a thermo-responsive bioink might involve storing it in a syringe at physiological temperature, exposure to high shear during extrusion, and subsequent recovery under lower temperature conditions on the print bed (Li et al. 2021). These stages can be simulated in a rheometer by coupling shear protocols with controlled temperature changes, enabling prediction of how quickly the material transitions from a liquid-like state during flow to a more solid-like structure after deposition. Such combined rheological simulations provide valuable insight into filament stabilization, gelation kinetics, and the overall reliability of the printing process (Table 4.1).

4.2.6 Printability Evaluation of Bioinks

Although numerous rheological techniques are available for bioink characterization, a persistent challenge in the field is the lack of standardized reporting methods (Rau et al. 2023). Extrusion involves complex interactions between yield stress, shear-dependent viscosity, elastic recovery, and nozzle geometry, yet different studies often report inconsistent parameter sets or use varying experimental configurations. Variability in rheometer geometries, gap settings, and testing protocols continues to limit direct comparison between datasets. As a result, the development of standardized characterization frameworks remains an important objective for improving reproducibility in extrusion bioprinting research. Therefore, assessment of printability represents a key stage in the development of any bioink formulation. Although the term printability is frequently used in the biofabrication literature, there is still no universally accepted definition that clearly determines when a material can be considered printable. One commonly cited description defines printability as the capacity of a bioink to be processed under specific printing conditions in a manner

Table 4.1 Rheological and printability results of different bioink compositions

Bioink composition	Cell sources	Application	Rheological findings (yield stress, storage modulus, printability, etc.)	Ref.
Cellulose nanofiber (CNF) backbone combined with Fucoidan (FUC) dissolved in 1.5% (v/v) acetic acid. The system was reinforced with hydrothermally synthesized nitrogen and sulfur co-doped graphene quantum dots (N,S-GQDs) at three concentrations (0.5%, 1%, and 1.5% v/v; designated as GQD1, GQD2, GQD3). $CaCl_2$ (2 wt%) was incorporated as a crosslinking agent to stabilize the hydrogel network.	L929 mouse fibroblasts	Skin tissue engineering - wound healing	All formulations exhibited non-Newtonian shear-thinning behavior suitable for extrusion bioprinting (shear rate range 10^{-2}-10^{2} s^{-1}). Viscosity increased in a concentration-dependent manner (GQD3 > GQD2 > GQD1 > control). Oscillatory frequency sweep analysis demonstrated that storage modulus (G′) remained consistently higher than loss modulus (G″) across 0.1–100 rad/s, confirming dominant elastic behavior and stable gel network formation. G′ increased with increasing GQD concentration, indicating enhanced mechanical reinforcement and improved post-printing shape fidelity. The hydrogel inks maintained structural integrity during extrusion (0.5 mm nozzle, 0.2 mL/h flow rate, 38 °C build plate)	Ciftci and Sillanpää (2026)
Nanofibrillated cellulose (NFC, 3 wt%) combined with sodium alginate (1 g per formulation) and water (0.5 g). Ionic crosslinkers incorporated directly into the ink as insoluble metal carbonates ($MgCO_3$, $CaCO_3$, $ZnCO_3$, $SrCO_3$) at 50, 100, and 150 µM per g NFC.	HUVECs	Tissue engineering – regenerative biomaterial scaffolds	All ink formulations exhibited pronounced shear-thinning behavior, with viscosities decreasing from ~3000–3500 pa s at low shear rates to below 1000 pa s at higher shear rates (0.1–100 s^{-1}). Carbonate type had minimal influence on flow curves, indicating matrix-dominated rheology	Peharda et al. (2026)

Post-printing in situ crosslinking was induced via acetic acid in a 50:50 ethanol-water medium, enabling gradual ion release and homogeneous ionic network formation			suitable for extrusion-based DIW printing. Oscillatory measurements showed dominant elastic behavior ($G' > G''$) across tested strains. $SrCO_3$-containing formulations displayed the highest storage and loss moduli, particularly at 150 μM concentration, indicating enhanced network reinforcement. Mechanical testing revealed Sr^{2+}-crosslinked scaffolds exhibited the highest tensile stress, modulus, and toughness, followed by Ca^{2+}, while Mg^{2+} promoted ductility with lower strength and Zn^{2+} resulted in brittle behavior	
Chitosan (CS, ~500 kDa) and acrylic acid (AA) blended at 1:10 ratio (2.05 g CS in 20.50 g AA +41.89 g DI water), followed by incorporation of 0.2% w/v glutaraldehyde (GLA) as chemical crosslinker and 1.0% w/v Darocur 1173 as photoinitiator. Pre-printing aging times were varied (5.0, 7.5, 10.0, and 12.5 min) prior to extrusion. Final dual crosslinking was achieved via Schiff base formation (GLA–CS) and UV-initiated polymerization of AA into poly(acrylic acid) (PAA), generating a double-network hydrogel	L-929 mouse fibroblasts	Skin tissue engineering - skin grafting / wound healing	Frequency sweep (0.1–100 Hz, 3% strain, 25 °C) showed $G' > G''$ for all aging conditions, indicating dominant elastic behavior suitable for extrusion printing. Tan δ remained below 1 (0.1–0.7 range), confirming gel-like character. Storage and loss moduli increased progressively with aging time due to enhanced crosslinking density. CSAA 7.5 min demonstrated optimal print fidelity (uniformity factor closest to 1), balancing viscosity and flow stability. Strand diameter decreased with increasing aging time (from 1.7 ± 0.3 mm at 5 min to 0.8 ± 0.2 mm at 12.5 min; nozzle diameter 0.41 mm), indicating improved shape retention	Wattanaeabpun et al. (2026)

(continued)

Table 4.1 (continued)

Bioink composition	Cell sources	Application	Rheological findings (yield stress, storage modulus, printability, etc.)	Ref.
4% (w/v) alginate +10% (w/v) carboxymethyl cellulose (CMC) + 16% (w/v) gelatin methacrylate (GelMA) in PBS; 0.25% (w/v) LAP photoinitiator. Dual crosslinking: UV (25 mW/cm^2, 60 s) + 0.1 M $CaCl_2$ (4 min).	Primary human fibroblasts; 1×10^6 cells/mL	Tissue engineering - gradient tissue regeneration	For 4% Alg–10% CMC–16% GelMA: Yield stress = 132 ± 25 Pa; crossover frequency: Not detected (NA); storage modulus $G' = 564 \pm 2$ pa; fiber diameter (FD) = 220 ± 10 μm; printability (Pr) = 0.93 ± 0.04; printing pressure = 165 kPa	Geevarghese et al. (2025)
Sacrificial bioink: 15% (w/v) gelatin in PBS loaded with HUVECs (5×10^6 cells/mL). Cell-laden embedding medium (MCCB supporting bath): Biphasic system composed of gelatin microgels (10% w/v, mechanically fragmented) as discrete phase + continuous low-viscosity hydrogel phase (primarily 5% w/v GelMA with 0.25% w/v LAP), mixed with HepG2 cells (1×10^7 cells/mL; rheology tested also at 3×10^7 cells/mL)	HepG2 hepatocellular carcinoma cells and HUVECs	Liver tissue engineering—Vascularized liver model	The MCCB supporting bath exhibited yield-stress behavior and shear-thinning properties described by the Herschel-Bulkley model. Yield stress ranged approximately from 0.9 to 7.2 pa depending on continuous-phase material. For 5% GelMA containing 3×10^7 cells/mL mixed with microgels, yield stress was ~2.2 Pa. Increasing cell density to 1×10^8 cells/mL reduced yield stress to ~1.17 Pa. Rheological tests confirmed $G' > G''$ for microgel phase and $G'' > G'$ for continuous phase under controlled temperature, enabling Bingham-like supporting behavior. The system showed self-healing recovery after high shear ($0.01\ s^{-1}$ - $10\ s^{-1}$ $0.01\ s^{-1}$) and temperature-responsive viscosity transition	Lv et al. (2025)

Carboxymethyl chitosan (either N, O-CMCS or O-CMCS; final concentration 1% or 3% w/v) combined with sodium alginate (1% or 3% w/v) and fibrinogen (10 or 20 mg mL^{-1}). Optimized formulation (B2) consisted of 1% (w/v) N, O-CMCS, 1% (w/v) alginate, and 20 mg mL^{-1} fibrin. Crosslinking was achieved using a $CaCl_2$/ thrombin/ chitosan solution to induce ionic and fibrin polymerization-based stabilization	hiPSC-NPCs; 2×10^6 cells mL^{-1}	Neural tissue engineering / in vitro neural modeling / drug screening platforms	All formulations exhibited shear-thinning behavior (0.01–90 s^{-1}). Tan δ values remained <1 across frequency sweeps (0.1–100 rad s^{-1}), indicating elastic-dominant behavior (G′ > G″). For the optimized B2 formulation: Viscosity at rest (shear rate = 1 s^{-1}): 269.13 pa s. storage modulus (G′ at 1 rad s^{-1}): 823.6 kPa; loss modulus (G″ at 1 rad s^{-1}): 133.2 kPa. Printability (Pr): 0.98 ± 0.01; extrusion pressure: ~8 kPa; B2 demonstrated uniform filament deposition, high shape fidelity, and stable lattice formation	Juraski et al. (2025)
Thermoresponsive PEG-based non-ionic triblock terpolymer $OEGMA300_{13}$-b-$BuMA_{22}$-b-$DEGMA_{12}$ (OBD), synthesized via group transfer polymerization. Bioink is 35% (w/w) in PBS. No additional cross linkers were used; gelation was temperature-induced (LCST-type physical gelation)	Primary human mesenchymal stem cells (hMSCs)	Tissue engineering - stem cell bioprinting platforms Soft tissue engineering—Cell-laden thermoresponsive scaffolds	Gel transition temperature ≈ 8 °C (35% w/w in PBS). Shear-thinning behavior confirmed at 37 °C (0.01–1000 s^{-1}). Yield point observed at shear rate ≈ 0.1 s^{-1}. Shear recovery test demonstrated rapid structural recovery (~20 s) with ~85% modulus retention after repeated high-strain cycles. Optimized printing parameters: 75 kPa extrusion pressure; 450 mm min^{-1} writing speed; 250 μm nozzle. Printability (Pr) ≈ 0.874 (layer stacking test). Estimated shear stress during printing ≈ 79 Pa	Zhang et al. (2025)

(continued)

Table 4.1 (continued)

Bioink composition	Cell sources	Application	Rheological findings (yield stress, storage modulus, printability, etc.)	Ref.
This study does not introduce a cell-laden bioink formulation; instead, it develops a xanthan gum–gelatin composite support bath material. The optimized support bath consists of 0.50–1.0% (w/v) xanthan gum combined with 0.25% (w/v) gelatin and $CaCl_2$ (15–50 mM). Benchmark materials (gelatin slurry 4.5%, Carbopol® 0.1%, Pluronic® F-127 25%) were comparatively evaluated	L929 murine fibroblasts	3D bioprinting technology - embedded bioprinting support bath Bioprinting methodology - multi-crosslinking compatible support system	For xanthan–gelatin composite: Yield stress: 0.18–2.9 pa (depending on xanthan concentration); zero-shear viscosity: 26.6–164 pa s; storage modulus (G'): ~10–70 pa; flow behavior index (n): 0.25–0.36 (shear-thinning behavior); viscosity recovery after shear: 79–95%. The material exhibited shear-thinning, low yield stress, elastic-dominant behavior ($G' > G''$), and rapid self-healing recovery-properties identified as essential for functional embedded bioprinting support baths	Lai and Meagher (2024)
4.5% (w/v) sodium alginate +4.5% (w/v) gelatin (250 bloom) + 4.5% (w/v) hyaluronic acid dissolved in PBS/DMEM; post-print ionic crosslinking with 0.5 M $CaCl_2$ (immersion), with optional $CaCl_2$ nebulization during printing	NIH/3 T3 murine fibroblasts; 1×10^6 cells/mL	Tissue engineering – hydrogel-based bioprinted scaffolds Printability modeling – creep-controlled layer optimization	Viscoelastic behavior characterized by elastic, inelastic, and viscous components; zero-shear viscosity decreased with increasing temperature (78.6 kPa·s at 21 °C - 2.38 kPa·s at 41 °C). Creep deformation significantly reduced with $CaCl_2$ nebulization (strand height loss 24 ± 11 µm vs. 193 ± 77 µm without nebulization). Arrhenius-type temperature dependence with activation energy $\approx 160 \pm 30$ kJ/mol	Palma et al. (2025)

Methacrylated κ-carrageenan with three different methacrylation degrees (κ-Car-L-MA, κ-Car-M-MA, κ-Car-H-MA). Composite formulations prepared by incorporating 2% (w/v) HAp particles. Bioinks prepared in PBS containing 1% (w/v) Irgacure 2959 photoinitiator and UV-crosslinked (365 nm)	hASCs, 2–3 × 10^6 cells/mL	Bone tissue engineering / Osteochondral-like bilayer constructs / mineralized tissue regeneration	All bioink formulations exhibited viscoelastic behavior with a defined linear viscoelastic region and gel-to-sol transition at characteristic yield strain. Temperature sweep showed gelation only for κ-car-H-MA (41.67 °C), reduced to 31.64 °C upon HAp incorporation. It was shown that methacrylation degree and HAp incorporation directly affects the Pr of 3D printed constructs. P_r value and yield stress of κ-car-M-MA-HAp were 1.04 ± 0.12 and 210.66 Pa	Kansız et al. (2025)

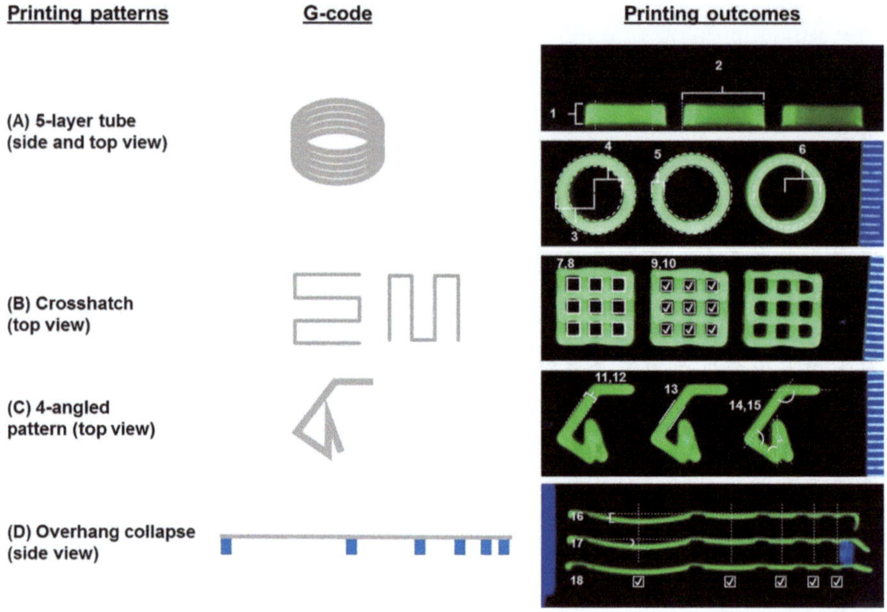

Fig. 4.2 Printability assessment used to evaluate bioink performance, including a five-layer tubular construct shown in side and top views to assess stacking stability and lumen integrity (**a**), two layer grid construct to examine filament continuity and pore accuracy (**b**), a four-angled pattern to evaluate directional control and corner fidelity during path changes (**c**), and an overhang structure to determine self-supporting ability, resistance to sagging, and post-deposition shape retention (**d**) (Gillispie et al. 2023)

that produces outcomes suitable for the intended application (Gillispie et al. 2020). Within the context of extrusion bioprinting, printability is generally understood to encompass adequate extrudability, continuous filament formation, and the ability to maintain structural integrity after deposition (Fig. 4.2). These factors together determine the dimensional accuracy of a printed construct relative to its digital design. In this framework, shape fidelity refers both to the ability of individual filaments to retain their geometry immediately after extrusion and to the capacity of the overall structure to preserve its intended architecture and is therefore closely related to what is sometimes described as printing accuracy.

4.2.6.1 Extrudability

Evaluation of filament formation and stacking capability represents an essential early step in predicting the shape fidelity of 3D constructs produced by extrusion-based printing. For successful deposition, the bioink must first begin to flow when the applied extrusion pressure exceeds its yield stress, allowing the material to transition from a solid-like state to liquid-like state. Extrudability can therefore be quantified by measuring the force required to dispense the bioink at a constant extrusion speed.

Bioinks with homogeneous composition typically produce stable extrusion forces, which in turn promote continuous and uniform filament formation. In contrast, the presence of particles, aggregates, or other structural heterogeneity can lead to fluctuations in the extrusion force over time, resulting in irregular flow and reduced consistency in the deposited filaments. Such variations may ultimately compromise filament uniformity and the overall geometric accuracy of the printed construct. Additionally, extrudability of bioinks is associated with nozzle size and the type. The extrusion of bioink is easier when the diameter of the nozzle is increased and the length of the nozzle is decreased (Hölzl et al. 2016). It is well known that higher extrusion pressures generate elevated shear stress within the nozzle, thereby increasing the shear stress to encapsulated cells. It directly affects the post-printing cell viability and the outcome of the procedure. For instance, Blasere et al. reported that cells subjected to low shear stress levels (<5 kPa) retained nearly unchanged membrane integrity, with viability remaining around 96%. However, exposure to higher shear stresses resulted in a noticeable decline in mean cell viabilities dropping to ~91% (5–10 kPa) and 76% (>10 kPa). They also reported cell viability of human mesenchymal stem cell post-printing viability, significantly decreased from 94% (4 kPa) to 92% (9 kPa), and 86% (18 kPa) (Blaeser et al. 2016). Consequently, successful bioprinting relies on balancing extrudability and cell viability, since the forces required for extrusion must be sufficient to drive flow while not exceeding the shear stress limits that cells can withstand.

4.2.6.2 Filament Uniformity

Another printability assessment is based on the evaluation of the morphology of extruded filaments. The filament drop test, in which material is extruded into open air instead of onto a printing surface. When the bioink lacks sufficient structural integrity, it tends to accumulate at the nozzle tip and form droplets, indicating that it is unlikely to support stable three-dimensional printing. In contrast, printable formulations typically produce a continuous and uniform filament. Some researchers have expanded this classification to also describe irregular, rough filaments formed by over-gelled bioinks, which exhibit uneven surfaces and poor uniformity. Gao et al. reported the filament uniformity as a function of tan (δ) (tan (δ) = G''/G') (Gao et al. 2018). Schaffner et al. reported that higher yield stress resulted in better filament uniformity (Schaffner et al. 2017). In this study, they prepared three different bioink formulations consisting of κ-carrageenan, hyaluronic acid and fumed silica at 3 wt%, 6 wt%, and 9 wt%. It was found that increased bioink concentration increases the yield stress in parallel with filament uniformity. Ouyang et al. introduced a quantitative parameter, *Pr* associated with the filament uniformity. It was defined by comparing the measured perimeter of a printed square pore (L) to that of an ideal square area (A) with the same dimensions. According to their criteria, a P_r value of 1 represents perfectly uniform extrusion lines, whereas values exceeding 1.1 indicate inadequate filament uniformity and poor printing precision (Ouyang et al. 2016b).

$$Pr = \frac{L^2}{16A} \tag{4.4}$$

For example, in a recent study, it was shown that both methacrylation degree and use of an additive directly affect the filament uniformity and P_r in 3D-printited grid structure (Kansız et al. 2025). This was explained by the effect of methacrylate groups and the additive in terms of weak interactions between the κ-carrageenan polymer chains resulting in the change in yield stress of the bioink.

4.2.6.3 Shape Fidelity

Due to their viscoelastic nature and limited mechanical stiffness, freshly deposited bioink filaments are prone to time-dependent deformation phenomena such as creeping, spreading, or collapse. Adjacent strands may merge, or stacked layers may lose the geometry if the material continues to flow after deposition (Schwab et al. 2020). Such effects typically arise when the yield stress or elastic modulus of the ink is insufficient to counteract external forces including gravity and surface tension. Ensuring rapid structural stabilization after extrusion is therefore essential for maintaining both filament integrity and layer separation. A very basic approach to examine filament coalescence consists of printing either parallel strands or patterns in which the spacing between filaments is progressively reduced. In meandering geometries, fusion typically initiates at the corners and expands as the distance between strands decreases or as the yield stress of the bioink becomes lower, eventually leading to complete merging and closure of the interfilament gaps (Wüst et al. 2014; Ahmadi Soufivand et al. 2023). Therefore, this test provides insight into the material's ability to reproduce fine structural features, such as small pores and sharp angles. High shape fidelity also requires the ability to fabricate structures with open pores or unsupported spans. In particular, preventing filaments sagging along the printing direction is critical when filaments bridge gaps between supporting features or when overhanging geometries are produced. Riberio et al. proposed filament-bridging tests, in which strands are printed across pillars separated by increasing distance (Ribeiro et al. 2018). The resulting deformation may be characterized by measuring the deflection angle or the area of sagging beneath the filament. These metrics reflect the balance between gravitational loading and the mechanical resistance of the material, which is governed largely by its yield stress and elastic modulus bioink. Indeed, higher yield stress values have been shown to correlate with reduced filament deflection. For very soft bioinks that cannot sustain long spans, simplified tests may instead evaluate the number of gaps a filament can traverse before breaking, providing an alternative measure of structural robustness during printing (Schwab et al. 2020; Mouser et al. 2020).

Recently Gillispie et al. reported a comprehensive study evaluating the rheological property and printability of various bioinks (Gillispie et al. 2023). The results showed that bioinks with high storage modulus and strong structural recovery generally achieved superior shape fidelity, yet several bioinks with moderate

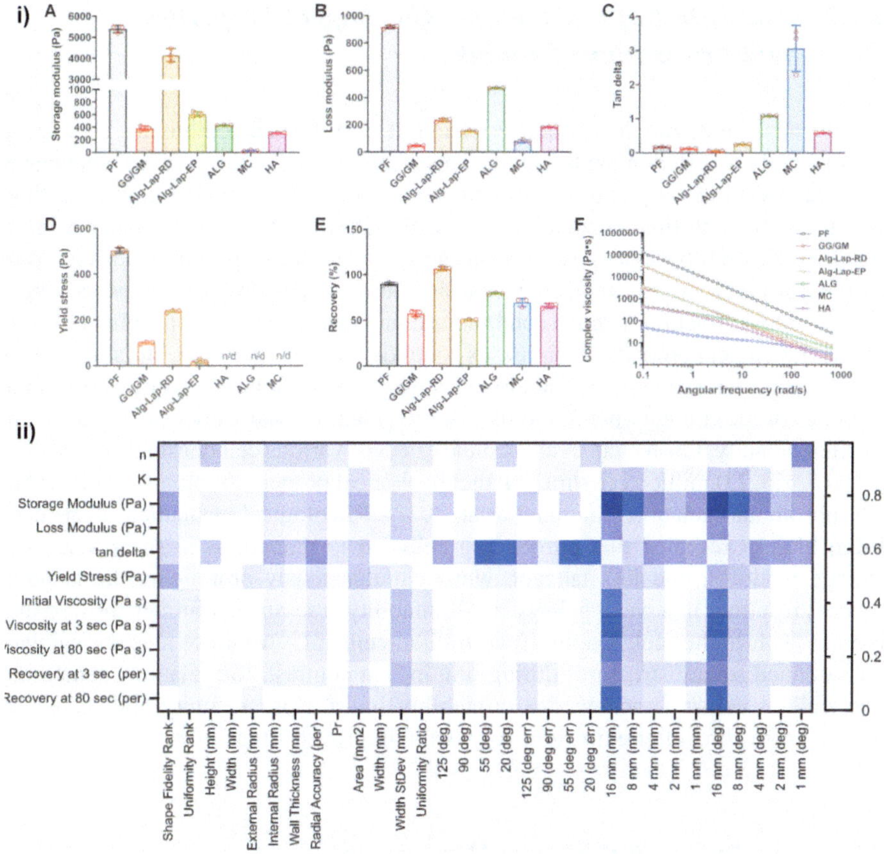

Fig. 4.3 Rheological evaluation of Pluronic F127 (PF), gellan gum-Gel-MA (GG/GM), Alginate-Laponite Rd. (Alg-Lap-RD), Alginate-Laponite EP (Alg-Lap-EP), Alginate (Alg), methylcellulose (MC), and hyaluronic acid (HA) **(i)**. Linear regression analysis between rheological parameters and bioink artifact printing outcomes **(ii)** (Gillispie et al. 2023)

elasticity also performed well, indicating that stiffness alone did not govern printability. Loss modulus showed little predictive value when considered independently, while low loss tangent often coincided with improved structural stability but failed to consistently distinguish high-performing inks. Yield stress broadly followed printing trends but could not be determined for some bioink formulations, further emphasizing methodological limitations of single-parameter assessment. By integrating hundreds of regression comparisons into a heatmap, the study demonstrated that printability arose from the combined interaction of viscoelastic balance, flow resistance, and recovery dynamics (Fig. 4.3). These findings reinforced the importance of multidimensional rheological characterization in guiding rational bioink design.

4.2.7 The Effect of Cells on the Rheological Properties and Printability of Bioinks

Comprehensive rheological characterization of fully formulated bioinks containing cells is rarely reported in the literature. This is largely due to the practical challenges associated with the large number of cells required for extensive rheological testing, which can be both time-consuming and costly. Despite these challenges, the influence of cells on bioink rheology remains an important factor in bioink design. From a physical perspective, cells can be considered as dispersed particles occupying a certain volume fraction within a continuous liquid phase. However, the effect of cells on the rheological property of bioinks is contradictory. For instance, in a study it was reported that the presence of chondrocytes increased both the viscosity and storage modulus of the collagen-based bioink prior to gelation (Diamantides et al. 2019). In a different study, Gosh et al. evaluated the effect of various cell densities of BMSCs, 0.1, 0.5, 1.0, 2.0 million cells/mL, on the rheological property of bioink composed of silk fibroin and gelatin (Majumder et al. 2022). Rheological evaluation of the cell-laden bioinks revealed that introducing cells led to reductions in shear viscosity, storage modulus, and loss tangent, while simultaneously prolonging the gelation process resulting in a weak gel system. Printability assessments further showed that bioinks with higher cell loading (two million cells/mL) were not able to maintain well-defined square structures during printing. In contrast, formulations containing one million cells/mL achieved a printability index close to unity and displayed reduced spreading after extrusion, suggesting improved shape fidelity.

4.3 Conclusion and Future Perspective

Despite the remarkable progress achieved in extrusion-based 3D bioprinting over the past decade, significant challenges remain before technology can reach its full potential in clinical and industrial applications. One of the most pressing limitations lies in the development of bioinks that simultaneously satisfy biological, mechanical, and rheological requirements. Current bioink systems often represent a compromise between printability and cell compatibility, where formulations optimized for extrusion stability may impose excessive shear stress on embedded cells, while cell-friendly materials often lack sufficient mechanical integrity for shape retention. Future research must therefore focus on designing multifunctional bioinks capable of dynamically adjusting their rheological behavior during different stages of the printing process. A promising direction involves the development of stimuli-responsive and smart biomaterials (Sadeghzade et al. 2026). Shear-thinning hydrogels with rapid self-healing capacity, reversible cross-linking mechanisms, or dual-stage gelation strategies can enable easier extrusion while preserving structural fidelity after deposition.

Another important future perspective concerns the integration of rheology with computational modeling and machine learning approaches. Predictive models that correlate rheological parameters with printability outcomes could significantly accelerate bioink development by reducing empirical trial-and-error experimentation. Coupling rheological datasets with process parameters such as nozzle geometry, extrusion pressure, and printing speed may enable the creation of digital twins of the printing process, allowing researchers to simulate and optimize constructs before fabrication. The incorporation of artificial intelligence into bioprinting workflows could thus transform biofabrication from an experience-driven practice into a data-guided engineering discipline. For instance, Zhot et al. used AI driven printability evaluation for the bioinks including GelMA, Alg, HAMA, and the blend of GelMA-HAMA (Zhou et al. 2026). This study demonstrated that integrating mechanistic understanding with interpretable AI models enables the rapid and reliable prediction of shape fidelity in embedded bioprinting systems. By coupling rheological signatures with support bath properties, the proposed framework substantially reduces experimental burden while providing physically meaningful design guidelines for printable bioinks.

Furthermore, the future of extrusion-based bioprinting will depend on advances in multi-material and hierarchical printing strategies. Native tissues possess complex spatial variations in composition, stiffness, and cellular organization, which cannot be reproduced using single-material constructs. Bioinks with tunable rheological behavior that allow controlled state (solid like-liquid like/liquid like-solid like) transitions during printing will be essential for the fabrication of functional, biomimetic tissues. In this context, the development of standardized rheological testing protocols will also be critical to ensure reproducibility and facilitate comparison between studies.

Competing Interests Y.M.E. is the founder and shareholder of Biovalda Health Technologies, Inc. (Ankara, Türkiye). The authors declare no competing financial interests in relation to this particular article. The authors are alone responsible for the content and writing of the paper.

References

Ahmadi Soufivand A, Faber J, Hinrichsen J, Budday S (2023) Multilayer 3D bioprinting and complex mechanical properties of alginate-gelatin mesostructures. Sci Rep 13:11253. https://doi.org/10.1038/s41598-023-38323-2

Blaeser A, Duarte Campos DF, Puster U, Richtering W, Stevens MM, Fischer H (2016) Controlling shear stress in 3D bioprinting is a key factor to balance printing resolution and stem cell integrity. Adv Healthc Mater 5:326–333. https://doi.org/10.1002/adhm.201500677

Calafel MI, Criado-Gonzalez M, Aguirresarobe R, Fernández M, Mijangos C (2025) From rheological concepts to additive manufacturing assessment of hydrogel-based materials for advanced bioprinting applications. Mater Adv 6:4566–4597. https://doi.org/10.1039/D5MA00019J

Chimene D, Peak CW, Gentry JL, Carrow JK, Cross LM, Mondragon E, Cardoso GB, Kaunas R, Gaharwar AK (2018) Nanoengineered ionic–covalent entanglement (nice) bioinks for 3D bioprinting. ACS Appl Mater Interfaces 10:9957–9968. https://doi.org/10.1021/acsami.7b19808

Ciftci F, Sillanpää M (2026) Bioactive 3D bioprinted n,s-graphene quantum dot reinforced nanocellulose/fucoidan scaffolds for wound healing. FlatChem 56:101008. https://doi.org/10.1016/j.flatc.2026.101008

Cooke ME, Rosenzweig DH (2021) The rheology of direct and suspended extrusion bioprinting. APL Bioeng 5:011502. https://doi.org/10.1063/5.0031475

Corker A, Ng HCH, Poole RJ, García-Tuñón E (2019) 3d printing with 2d colloids: designing rheology protocols to predict 'printability' of soft-materials. Soft Matter 15:1444–1456. https://doi.org/10.1039/C8SM01936C

Cui X, Li J, Hartanto Y, Durham M, Tang J, Zhang H, Hooper G, Lim K, Woodfield T (2020) Advances in extrusion 3D bioprinting: a focus on multicomponent hydrogel-based bioinks. Adv Healthc Mater 9:1901648. https://doi.org/10.1002/adhm.201901648

Derakhshanfar S, Mbeleck R, Xu K, Zhang X, Zhong W, Xing M (2018) 3D bioprinting for biomedical devices and tissue engineering: a review of recent trends and advances. Bioact Mater 3:144–156. https://doi.org/10.1016/j.bioactmat.2017.11.008

Diamantides N, Dugopolski C, Blahut E, Kennedy S, Bonassar LJ (2019) High density cell seeding affects the rheology and printability of collagen bioinks. Biofabrication 11:045016. https://doi.org/10.1088/1758-5090/ab3524

Duty C, Ajinjeru C, Kishore V, Compton B, Hmeidat N, Chen X, Liu P, Hassen AA, Lindahl J, Kunc V (2018) What makes a material printable? A viscoelastic model for extrusion-based 3D printing of polymers. J Manuf Process 35:526–537. https://doi.org/10.1016/j.jmapro.2018.08.008

Gao T, Gillispie GJ, Copus JS, Pr AK, Seol Y-J, Atala A, Yoo JJ, Lee SJ (2018) Optimization of gelatin–alginate composite bioink printability using rheological parameters: a systematic approach. Biofabrication 10:034106. https://doi.org/10.1088/1758-5090/aacdc7

Geevarghese R, Żur-Pińska J, Parisi D, Włodarczyk-Biegun MK (2025) A comprehensive protocol for hydrogel-based bioink design: balancing printability, stability, and biocompatibility. J Mater Chem B 13:13750–13768. https://doi.org/10.1039/D5TB00737B

Gillispie G, Prim P, Copus J, Fisher J, Mikos AG, Yoo JJ, Atala A, Lee SJ (2020) Assessment methodologies for extrusion-based bioink printability. Biofabrication 12:022003. https://doi.org/10.1088/1758-5090/ab6f0d

Gillispie GJ, Copus J, Uzun-Per M, Yoo JJ, Atala A, Niazi MKK, Lee SJ (2023) The correlation between rheological properties and extrusion-based printability in bioink artifact quantification. Mater Des 233:112237. https://doi.org/10.1016/j.matdes.2023.112237

Hájovská P, Kroneková Z, Cseriová Z, Ház A, Jančovičová V, Danišovič Ĺ, Žiaran S, Heydari A, Lacík I (2025) Tuning rheology and printability of gelatin methacryloyl/sodium alginate bioinks: the role of sodium alginate molar mass and sterilization. ACS Omega 10:49776–49793. https://doi.org/10.1021/acsomega.5c05476

Hölzl K, Lin S, Tytgat L, Van Vlierberghe S, Gu L, Ovsianikov A (2016) Bioink properties before, during and after 3D bioprinting. Biofabrication 8:032002. https://doi.org/10.1088/1758-5090/8/3/032002

Jiang T, Munguia-Lopez JG, Flores-Torres S, Kort-Mascort J, Kinsella JM (2019) Extrusion bioprinting of soft materials: an emerging technique for biological model fabrication. Appl Phys Rev 6:011310. https://doi.org/10.1063/1.5059393

Juraski AC, da Silva VA, Sharma R, Azzoni AR, Willerth SM (2025) Investigation of novel carboxymethyl chitosan-based bioinks for 3D bioprinting of neural tissues. Biomed Mater 20:035036. https://doi.org/10.1088/1748-605X/add6f9

Kansız S, Vurat MT, Parmaksiz M, Elçin AE, Elçin YM (2025) Methacrylated-κ-carrageenan/hydroxyapatite composite bioinks for extrusion-based bioprinting: physicochemical, rheological, mechanical, and in vitro biological investigations. Int J Biol Macromol 316:144745. https://doi.org/10.1016/j.ijbiomac.2025.144745

Kesti M, Müller M, Becher J, Schnabelrauch M, D'Este M, Eglin D, Zenobi-Wong M (2015) A versatile bioink for three-dimensional printing of cellular scaffolds based on thermally and photo-triggered tandem gelation. Acta Biomater 11:162–172. https://doi.org/10.1016/j.actbio.2014.09.033

Khalil S, Sun W (2007) Biopolyrner deposition for freefonn fabrication of hydrogel tissue constructs. Materi Sci Eng C 27:469–478. https://doi.org/10.1016/j.msec.2006.05.023

Kyle S, Jessop ZM, Al-Sabah A, Whitaker IS (2017) 'Printability' of candidate biomaterials for extrusion based 3D printing: state-of-the-art. Adv Healthc Mater 6:1700264. https://doi.org/10.1002/adhm.201700264

Lai G, Meagher L (2024) Versatile xanthan gum-based support bath material compatible with multiple crosslinking mechanisms: rheological properties, printability, and cytocompatibility study. Biofabrication 16:035005. https://doi.org/10.1088/1758-5090/ad39a8

Li Q, Zhang B, Xue Q, Zhao C, Luo Y, Zhou H, Ma L, Yang H, Bai D (2021) A systematic thermal analysis for accurately predicting the extrusion printability of alginate–gelatin-based hydrogel bioinks. IJB 7:3. https://doi.org/10.18063/ijb.v7i3.394

Li B, Huang C, Wang Z, Shi Z, Xu L, Huang S, Qu M, Xu Z, Zhang D, Guo B et al (2025) Modeling of extrusion 3D bioprinting precision considering the non-newtonian rheological dynamics of gelatin-chitosan hydrogels. ACS Appl Polym Mater 7:1257–1270. https://doi.org/10.1021/acsapm.4c02866

Lv W, Yu H, Aazmi A, Naren T, Cheng W, Yu M, Wang Z, Xu X, Yang H, Ma L (2025) Construction of complex three-dimensional vascularized liver tissue model in vitro based on a biphasic cell-laden embedding medium. Int J Extreme Manuf 7:035002. https://doi.org/10.1088/2631-7990/ada836

Majumder N, Mishra A, Ghosh S (2022) Effect of varying cell densities on the rheological properties of the bioink. Bioprinting 28:e00241. https://doi.org/10.1016/j.bprint.2022.e00241

Malda J, Visser J, Melchels FP, Jüngst T, Hennink WE, Dhert WJA, Groll J, Hutmacher DW (2013) 25th anniversary article: engineering hydrogels for biofabrication. Adv Mater 25:5011–5028. https://doi.org/10.1002/adma.201302042

Mohamed Yunus RA, Parisi D (2024) Scaling laws in polysaccharide rheology: comparative analysis of water and ionic liquid systems. Biomacromolecules 25:6883–6898. https://doi.org/10.1021/acs.biomac.4c01125

Moroni L, Boland T, Burdick JA, De Maria C, Derby B, Forgacs G, Groll J, Li Q, Malda J, Mironov VA et al (2018) Biofabrication: a guide to technology and terminology. Trends Biotechnol 36:384–402. https://doi.org/10.1016/j.tibtech.2017.10.015

Mouser VHM, Levato R, Mensinga A, Dhert WJA, Gawlitta D, Malda J (2020) Bio-ink development for three-dimensional bioprinting of hetero-cellular cartilage constructs. Connect Tissue Res 61:137–151. https://doi.org/10.1080/03008207.2018.1553960

Murphy SV, Atala A (2014) 3D bioprinting of tissues and organs. Nat Biotechnol 32:773–785. https://doi.org/10.1038/nbt.2958

Ouyang L, Highley CB, Rodell CB, Sun W, Burdick JA (2016a) 3D printing of shear-thinning hyaluronic acid hydrogels with secondary cross-linking. ACS Biomater Sci Eng 2:1743–1751. https://doi.org/10.1021/acsbiomaterials.6b00158

Ouyang L, Yao R, Zhao Y, Sun W (2016b) Effect of bioink properties on printability and cell viability for 3D bioplotting of embryonic stem cells. Biofabrication 8:035020. https://doi.org/10.1088/1758-5090/8/3/035020

Palma JH, Bertuola M, González-Wusener A, Arregui CO, Hermida ÉB (2025) Creep of alginate-gelatin-hyaluronic acid strands and cell viability after bioprinting. An Acad Bras Cienc 97:e20241453. https://doi.org/10.1590/0001-3765202520241453

Paxton N, Smolan W, Böck T, Melchels F, Groll J, Jungst T (2017) Proposal to assess printability of bioinks for extrusion-based bioprinting and evaluation of rheological properties governing bioprintability. Biofabrication 9(4):044107. https://doi.org/10.1088/1758-5090/aa8dd8

Peharda A, Lackner F, Steindorfer T, Fink J, Kotzbeck P, Kargl R, Kleinscheck KS, Mohan T (2026) Tailoring mechanical and functional properties of 3D-printed nanocellulose-alginate scaffolds via alternative ionic crosslinkers. Carbohydr Polym Technol Appl 13:101084. https://doi.org/10.1016/j.carpta.2026.101084

Rau DA, Herzberger J, Long TE, Williams CB (2018) Ultraviolet-assisted direct ink write to additively manufacture all-aromatic polyimides. ACS Appl Mater Interfaces 10:34828–34833. https://doi.org/10.1021/acsami.8b14584

Rau DA, Williams CB, Bortner MJ (2023) Rheology and printability: a survey of critical relationships for direct ink write materials design. Prog Mater Sci 140:101188. https://doi.org/10.1016/j.pmatsci.2023.101188

Ravanbakhsh H, Karamzadeh V, Bao G, Mongeau L, Juncker D, Zhang YS (2021) Emerging technologies in multi-material bioprinting. Adv Mater 33:2104730. https://doi.org/10.1002/adma.202104730

Ribeiro A, Blokzijl MM, Levato R, Visser CW, Castilho M, Hennink WE, Vermonden T, Malda J (2018) Assessing bioink shape fidelity to aid material development in 3D bioprinting. Biofabrication 10:014102. https://doi.org/10.1088/1758-5090/aa90e2

Romberg SK, Islam MA, Hershey CJ, DeVinney M, Duty CE, Kunc V, Compton BG (2021) Linking thermoset ink rheology to the stability of 3D-printed structures. Addit Manuf 37:101621. https://doi.org/10.1016/j.addma.2020.101621

Sadeghzade S, Nene A, Guo C (2026) Three-dimensional (3D) bioprinting based on microgel: design, properties, and applications. Curr Opinion Solid State Mater Sci 40:101248. https://doi.org/10.1016/j.cossms.2025.101248

Schaffner M, Rühs PA, Coulter F, Kilcher S, Studart AR (2017) 3D printing of bacteria into functional complex materials. Sci Adv 3:eaao6804. https://doi.org/10.1126/sciadv.aao6804

Schwab A, Levato R, D'Este M, Piluso S, Eglin D, Malda J (2020) Printability and shape fidelity of bioinks in 3D bioprinting. Chem Rev 120:10850–10877. https://doi.org/10.1021/acs.chemrev.0c00084

Singh YP, Moses JC, Kim MH, Gupta D, Pal V, Deniz ID, Gerhard EM, Ozbolat IT (2026) Three-tier framework for high-throughput biofabrication: integrating 3D bioprinting, assistive platforms, and translational opportunities. Bioact Mater 57:726–753. https://doi.org/10.1016/j.bioactmat.2025.11.024

Vurat MT, Ergun C, Elçin AE, Elçin YM (2020) 3D bioprinting of tissue models with customized bioinks. In: Bioinspired biomaterials: advances in tissue engineering and regenerative medicine, pp 67–84. https://doi.org/10.1007/978-981-15-3258-0_5

Wattanaeabpun S, Charoenthanakitkul D, Ariyachet C, Aumnate C, Hongrattanavichit I (2026) Influence of pre-printing aging time on the printability and performance of chitosan–polyacrylic acid double-network hydrogels for skin graft application. Int J Biol Macromol 342:150401. https://doi.org/10.1016/j.ijbiomac.2026.150401

Wilson SA, Cross LM, Peak CW, Gaharwar AK (2017) Shear-thinning and thermo-reversible nanoengineered inks for 3D bioprinting. ACS Appl Mater Interfaces 9:43449–43458. https://doi.org/10.1021/acsami.7b13602

Wüst S, Godla ME, Müller R, Hofmann S (2014) Tunable hydrogel composite with two-step processing in combination with innovative hardware upgrade for cell-based three-dimensional bioprinting. Acta Biomater 10:630–640. https://doi.org/10.1016/j.actbio.2013.10.016

Zhang YS, Haghiashtiani G, Hübscher T, Kelly DJ, Lee JM, Lutolf M, McAlpine MC, Yeong WY, Zenobi-Wong M, Malda J (2021) 3D extrusion bioprinting. Nat Rev Method Prime 1:75. https://doi.org/10.1038/s43586-021-00073-8

Zhang K, Constantinou AP, O'Connell C, Georgiou TK, Gelmi A (2025) A thermoresponsive peg-based methacrylate triblock terpolymer as a bioink for 3D bioprinting. J Mater Chem B 13:3593–3601. https://doi.org/10.1039/D4TB02572E

Zhou X, Zhang Z, Yu J, Ma L, Ma S, Wu B, Wang Z, Zhang T, Fang Y, Xiong Z (2026) AI-driven interpretation and prediction of embedded printability based on rheology. Bio-Des Manuf 9:63–79. https://doi.org/10.1631/bdm.2500456

Chapter 5
Translating Physical Cues into Cellular Responses: Material-Mediated Strategies in Biofabrication

Özge Lalegül-Ülker and Yaşar Murat Elçin

Abstract Cells exist within complex and constantly changing microenvironments shaped by the interplay of biochemical signaling and diverse physical cues, including mechanical loading, electrical potentials, magnetic fields, and acoustic stimulation. Although the biochemical regulation of tissue development and regeneration has been extensively explored, it is now evident that physical stimuli play a far more fundamental role than previously anticipated. Rather than serving as passive background factors, these cues play an active role in regulating cellular behavior, tissue homeostasis, and lineage specification. Cells interpret such signals through mechanotransductive and electromechanical pathways, enabling continuous adaptation of morphology, gene expression, and functional state. As this understanding has matured, recent advances in biofabrication have begun to move beyond purely passive scaffold designs. Increasing attention is now directed toward biomaterials that respond directly to physical stimuli and interact dynamically with their surrounding environment. These materials are designed not only to provide structural support, but also to convert external physical inputs into biologically meaningful signals. In this chapter, we summarize key classes of physically responsive biomaterials, including electrically conductive polymers, piezoelectric scaffolds, mechanically adaptable hydrogels, magneto-responsive systems, and ultrasound-activated composites. We discuss how such platforms allow spatially and temporally controlled modulation of the cellular microenvironment, supporting tissue regeneration across neural, musculoskeletal, cardiovascular, and vascular applications. We further examine how the integration of physical responsiveness into biomaterial design can help address limitations associated with conventional biochemical

Ö. Lalegül-Ülker
Tissue Engineering, Biomaterials and Nanobiotechnology Laboratory, Faculty of Science and Stem Cell Institute, Ankara University, Ankara, Türkiye

Y. M. Elçin (✉)
Tissue Engineering, Biomaterials and Nanobiotechnology Laboratory, Faculty of Science and Stem Cell Institute, Ankara University, Ankara, Türkiye

Department of Chemistry, Faculty of Science, Ankara University, Ankara, Türkiye
e-mail: elcin@ankara.edu.tr

Y. M. Elçin (ed.), *Biofabrication in Regenerative Medicine*, Stem Cell Biology and Regenerative Medicine 1519, https://doi.org/10.1007/978-3-032-30294-6_5

approaches, such as uncontrolled diffusion and off-target effects. Finally, current challenges and future perspectives related to the clinical translation of physically responsive biomaterials are outlined, highlighting their potential to actively and precisely regulate regenerative processes in real time.

Keywords Physically responsive biomaterials · Mechanotransduction · Biofabrication · Stimuli responsive hydrogels · Magnetosensitive scaffolds · Smart biomaterials · Piezoelectric biomaterials · Electromechanical signaling

Abbreviations

AgNWs	Silver nanowires
BMDMs	Bone marrow-derived macrophages
BTN	Amino-modified barium titanate
CNCs	Cellulose nanocrystals
CNTs	Carbon nanotubes
DBM	Decellularized bone matrix
DIW	Direct ink writing
FPLA	Flexible poly(lactic acid)
GelMA	Gelatin methacrylate
IVD	Intervertebral disc
LF-PEMF	Low-frequency pulsed electromagnetic field
LIPUS	Low-intensity pulsed ultrasound
MNPs	Magnetic nanoparticles
MSCs	Mesenchymal stem cells
OG	Oxidized gellan gum
PAN	Poly(acrylonitrile)
PANI	Poly(aniline)
P(CL-DLLA)	Poly(ε-caprolactone-D,L-lactide)
PEDOT:PSS	Poly(2,3-dihydrothieno-1,4-dioxin)-poly(styrenesulfonate)
PLCL	Poly(lactide-co-caprolactone)
PLLA	Poly(L-lactic acid)
PMMA	Poly(methyl methacrylate)
PNIPAM	Poly(N-isopropylacrylamide)
PTEGs	Piezo-triboelectric nanogenerators
PVA	Poly(vinyl alcohol)
PVDF-TrFE	Poly(vinylidene fluoride-trifluoroethylene)
SPIONs	Superparamagnetic iron oxide nanoparticles
TENGs	Triboelectric nanogenerators
3D	Three-Dimensional
4D	Four-Dimensional

5.1 Introduction

In living organisms, cells operate within dynamic environments where biochemical and physical stimuli continuously interact. Although the roles of growth factors, cytokines, and soluble signaling molecules in tissue development and regeneration are well established, accumulating evidence indicates that physical cues also exert a profound influence. Mechanical loading, shear stress, substrate stiffness, as well as electrical potentials, magnetic fields, and acoustic or gravitational forces have all been shown to contribute to the regulation of cellular behavior and the maintenance of tissue homeostasis (Tota et al. 2024; Nakaji-Hirabayashi et al. 2022; Holle et al. 2018).

Cells perceive and process these biophysical signals through a range of specialized mechanisms, including integrin-mediated adhesions, cytoskeletal reorganization, ion channel activity, and nuclear mechanotransduction pathways such as YAP/TAZ signaling. As a result, cells can adjust their morphology, gene expression profiles, migratory behavior, and lineage commitment in ways that are often highly tissue specific (Berdiaki et al. 2024; Uray and Uray 2021). Recognizing the central role of physical cues in native tissue environments, growing efforts are now directed toward the design of materials and constructs that extend beyond passive cellular support. This shift has given rise to the field of physically responsive biofabrication, which focuses on biomaterial systems capable of sensing and responding to mechanical, electrical, magnetic, or acoustic inputs to modulate biological function. In contrast to conventional scaffolds that primarily serve as inert carriers for cells or growth factors, physically responsive constructs are engineered to adapt their properties dynamically in response to external stimuli, enabling real-time regulation of the cellular microenvironment. Materials employed in physically responsive biofabrication encompass a diverse range of systems designed to interact with external physical stimuli. These include piezoelectric polymers capable of generating electrical signals in response to mechanical deformation, magneto-responsive hydrogels that can be actuated by applied magnetic fields, and ultrasound-responsive hydrogels that undergo localized deformation or induce microstreaming effects under acoustic stimulation. Through these mechanisms, such materials have been shown to promote cell alignment, enhance nutrient transport, and enable controlled drug release across different tissue engineering contexts (Chen et al. 2025; Guo et al. 2025; Manjua et al. 2025; Sikder et al. 2022; Parmaksiz et al. 2021).

Promising outcomes have been reported in several application areas. For instance, Xu et al. developed a bilayer nerve guidance conduit comprising an inner layer of PVDF-TrFE nanofibers coated with barium titanate nanoparticles and an outer thermoresponsive PNIPAM-based hydrogel (Xu et al. 2024a). Upon ultrasound stimulation, the piezoelectric nanofibers generated localized electric fields that promoted neurite outgrowth and guided axonal regeneration. At the same time, ultrasound-induced shrinkage of the hydrogel layer enabled controlled release of nerve growth factor, together resulting in enhanced peripheral nerve repair in a rat model (Xu et al. 2024a). Related concepts have also been explored using magnetic actuation strategies. Goodrich et al. reported a magneto-responsive hydrogel system incorporating magnetic nanostructures that allows dynamic mechanical modulation of the cellular microenvironment through externally applied alternating magnetic fields (Goodrich et al. 2023). In response to magnetic stimulation, the hydrogel undergoes controllable deformation, enabling the recreation of dynamic mechanical cues characteristic of native cell niches. Beyond its utility as a mechanobiology research platform, this system highlights the broader potential of magnetically responsive biomaterials for regulating cellular responses in tissue engineering applications (Goodrich et al. 2023).

One of the defining advantages of physically responsive materials is their capacity to connect biological systems with external, precisely controllable physical inputs. Advances in fabrication technologies, including 3D and 4D bioprinting as well as microfluidic platforms, now make it possible to spatially integrate responsive elements within complex architectures. These components can be activated remotely using non-invasive approaches, enabling dynamic and on-demand manipulation of engineered tissues. Importantly, such control can be applied not only during in vitro culture but also after implantation, allowing cellular activity to be regulated in real time in response to physiological or therapeutic demands (Murphy and Atala 2014; Sydney Gladman et al. 2016). Illustrative examples of this concept are beginning to emerge. Tai et al. developed a piezoelectric PVDF-TrFE scaffold designed to enhance peripheral nerve regeneration by converting mechanical stimuli into localized electrical signals (Tai et al. 2023). This mechanoelectrical coupling promoted Schwann cell activity and neurite outgrowth under in vitro conditions. In a rat injury model, the application of therapeutic shockwave–generated acoustic stimulation further supported axonal regeneration and functional recovery, demonstrating the therapeutic potential of mechanoelectrical stimulation without the need for implanted electrodes (Tai et al. 2023).

More broadly, the emergence of physically responsive materials has reshaped biofabrication strategies by offering solutions to key limitations associated with conventional biochemical approaches, including uncontrolled diffusion and the off-target effects of growth factors or small molecules (Municoy et al. 2020). In contrast to conventional biochemical approaches, physical stimuli such as mechanical, electrical, thermal, acoustic, or magnetic inputs can be applied with a high degree of spatial and temporal control. This capability enables dynamic and localized modulation of the cellular microenvironment, offering a level of precision that is difficult to achieve using diffusible biochemical factors alone. Notably, many physically responsive systems rely on intrinsic material properties, including piezoelectricity, magneto-responsiveness, or thermo-sensitivity, to elicit biological responses. By reducing or eliminating the need for exogenous bioactive agents, these materials may lower immunogenic risk, simplify formulation strategies, and potentially support more streamlined regulatory pathways (Municoy et al. 2020; Gelmi and Schutt 2021).

At the same time, important challenges must be addressed to enable broader translation of these approaches. Critical considerations include optimizing stimulation parameters such as intensity, frequency, and duration, while ensuring the long-term biocompatibility and stability of responsive materials. Additional complexity arises when integrating multiple modes of stimulation, for example through combined mechano-electrical or magneto-thermal strategies, as well as during efforts to scale these systems for clinical use. Moreover, the fundamental mechanisms by which different cell types sense and interpret physical cues, particularly within complex tissues such as the brain or myocardium, remain incompletely understood and warrant further investigation (Municoy et al. 2020; Dong and Malliaras 2025).

In this chapter, we focus on a range of smart material systems including piezoelectric polymers, conductive and magnetic hydrogels, and ultrasound-responsive composites that have been engineered to respond to physical stimuli within the biofabrication framework (Table 5.1). We explore their integration into scaffolds and bioprinted constructs, highlighting how these physically responsive platforms synergize with external cues to enhance tissue engineering outcomes in applications such as nerve regeneration, cardiac regeneration, bone repair, and vascular grafts. Furthermore, we discuss possible routes for advancing these systems toward clinical application, emphasizing the potential of these materials not only to recapitulate native tissue dynamics but also to actively modulate cellular behavior and regenerative processes in real time.

5.2 Biofabrication of Materials that Transduce Physical Stimuli

5.2.1 Electrically Conductive Polymers and Hydrogels

Electrically conductive biomaterials have become an important class of platforms in biofabrication for translating physical cues into cellular responses. In this context, the term conductive polymers encompasses both intrinsically conductive polymers such as polypyrrole, polyaniline, PEDOT:PSS as well as polymeric matrices rendered conductive through the incorporation of fillers, including carbon nanotubes, graphene-based materials, MXenes, or metallic nanoparticles.

A variety of biofabrication techniques, including 3D printing, electrospinning, photopatterning, and micropatterning, enable these intrinsically conductive or filler-modified materials to be organized with high precision into architectures that directly interface with cells. While intrinsically conductive polymers and hydrogels can efficiently transmit externally applied electrical stimulation to surrounding cells, composite systems enriched with conductive additives often provide additional advantages. These include improved mechanical robustness, enhanced printability, and greater long-term stability, thereby broadening their applicability across advanced biofabrication platforms. In recent years, these systems have been successfully employed to guide the growth and maturation of electrically responsive tissues such as cardiac, skeletal muscle, and neural constructs. By integrating conductive materials into biofabrication workflows, engineered tissues can be

Table 5.1 Overview of physically responsive biomaterials, fabrication approaches, and biological effects

Category	Materials / systems	Biofabrication method	Target application	Key outcomes	Refs.
Electrically conductive polymers and hydrogels	PEDOT: PSS hydrogel	3D bioprinting via DIW	Cardiac tissue—Epicardial interface	Conformal epicardial adhesion, Long-term stable electrophysiological monitoring, Low-voltage electrical modulation restoring cardiac rhythm	Wang et al. (2024)
	GelMA hydrogel + AgNWs	3D hydrogel fabrication	Skeletal muscle regeneration	Promoted aligned myotube formation, Restored ~95% of mucle mass and ~ 99% of contractile force under electrical stimulation	Xue et al. (2024)
	Electrospun PAN/PANI + nickel NPs	Electrospinning	Schwann cell proliferation Nerve regeneration	Schwann cell proliferation increased ~2.1 times	Wang et al. (2021a)
	Electrospun PAN/PANI + varying CNT scaffolds	Electrospinning	Neural differentiation of hADSCs	Higher CNT scaffold enabled advanced neural markers (β-tubulin III, MAP2) Low CNT guided early stage differentiation (nestin)	Khosravieh et al. (2024)
Magneto-responsive composites	DBM + MNPs / PEMF	Molding / freeze drying	Bone regeneration	Increased bone regeneration in critical-size rat cranial defect	Parmaksiz et al. (2021)
	PEGDA-GelMA hydrogel + aligned MNPs / SMF	Topographic anisotropy	Bone tissue engineering	Enhanced osteogenic differentiation of BMSCs via NOTCH signaling; accelerated bone regeneration in vivo	Tang et al. (2024)
	Fibrin hydrogel + MNPs /	In-situ enzymatic gelation / molding	Peripheral nerve regeneration	Increased NGF and VEGF expression Enhanced neurite outgrowth	Hong et al. (2024)

				Improved functional recovery in rat sciatic nerve defect model	
	PCl/PDA + MNPs / SMF	Melt extrusion 3D printing / dip coating	Bone regeneration	Enhanced osteogenic differentiation and mineralization	Zhuo et al. (2025)
Mechanically tunable scaffolds	3D porous silk fibroin scaffold	Nanofiber assisted-lyophilization	Tissue engineering	Enhanced cell compatibility through sheet content and tailored scaffold stiffness Directed stem cell differantiation by modulating scaffold mechanical properties	Bai et al. (2015)
	PNIPAM/methacrylic anhydride grafted chitosan + PLCL fillers	Mechanoactive hydrogel fabrication	Cartilage regeneration	Enhanced cartilage-like ECM deposition (Col II) Promoted cartilage formation through in situ applied mechanical stimuli by the scaffold	Gao et al. (2024)
Piezoelectric biopolymers and Nanogenerators	PVDF-TrFE coated PMMA	Dip coating / annealing	Bone regeneration	Promoted osteogenic cellular behavior in vitro Regulated BMDM immune response with shift toward pro-healing phenotype	Luo et al. (2022)
	Col films from bovine tendon	Solvent casting	Soft tissue engineering	Exhibited measurable piezoelectric response Maintained structural stability in PBS Confirmed potential for use as a piezoelectric biomaterial for biomedical applications	Andonegi et al. (2025)

(continued)

Table 5.1 (continued)

Category	Materials / systems	Biofabrication method	Target application	Key outcomes	Refs.
	Piezo-triboelectric charge nanogenerator patch	3D micro molding / spin coating	Cartilage regeneration	Promoted bone marrow stem cell migration, Ca^{2+} influx, and chondrogenic gene expression. Reduced osteophyte formation and enhanced cartilage regeneration in rat model	Zhang et al. (2025)
Ultrasound-responsive gels	Piezoelectric col/OG/BTN hydrogel	Composite hydrogel fabrication	Wound healing Immunomodulation Angiogenesis	Upregulated pro-angiogenic factors Enhanced endothelial cell migration/ tube formation Increased collagen deposition	Yan et al. (2025)
	Gelatin/ PVA hydrogel doped with piezoelectric (K,Na)NbO_3 (KNN) nanocrystals and rGO	Composite hydrogel fabrication	Neurovascular regeneration Diabetic wound healing	Increased endothelial cell angiogenesis Enhanced neurite outgrowth Improved local neurovascular regeneration Inhibited bacterial growth around wound site	Wang et al. (2025)

Abbreviations: *AgNWs* Ag NanoWires, *BMDM* Bone Marrow-*Derived* Macrophages, *BTN* Amino-modified barium titanate, *Col* Collagen, *DBM* Decellularized Bone Matrix, *DIW* Direct Ink Writing, *GelMA* Gelatin Methacrylate, *hADSCs* human Adipose tissue-Derived Stem Cells, *MNPs* Magnetic NanoParticles, *NPs* NanoParticles, *OG* Oxidized Gellan gum, *PEGDA* Poly(Ethylene Glycol) Diacrylate, *PLCL* Poly(Lactide-co-CaproLactone)

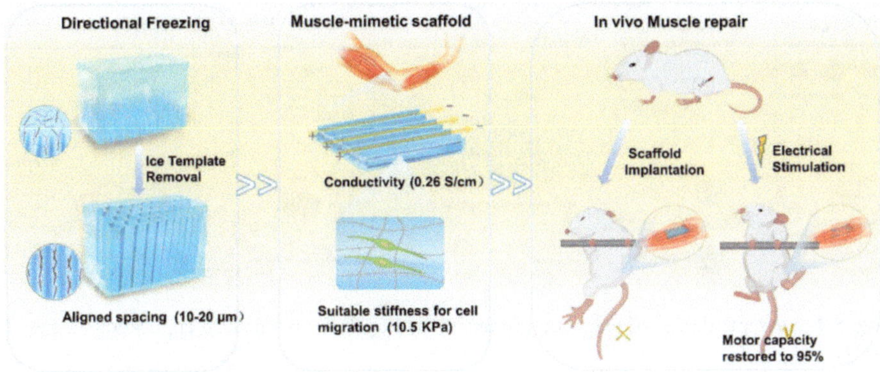

Fig. 5.1 GelMA–AgNW conductive hydrogel scaffolds combined with electrical signal for skeletal muscle repair (Xue et al. 2024)

designed to not only mimic the structural features of the extracellular matrix but also reproduce the electrophysiological signaling required for functional performance. Wang et al. reported the development of 3D printed PEDOT:PSS-based hydrogel bioelectronics via direct ink writing (DIW), which conformed to the epicardial surface for long-term stability (Wang et al. 2024). This implantable system enabled high-accuracy electrophysiological signal monitoring and low-voltage electrical stimulation, effectively restoring cardiac rhythm in a myocardial infarction model. As an example of electrically conductive nanocomposite scaffold engineered through conductive fillers, anisotropic GelMA–AgNW conductive hydrogel scaffolds were developed, promoting myotube alignment and restoring up to ~95% of muscle mass and ~ 99% of contractile function in a rat model under electrical stimulation (Fig. 5.1) (Xue et al. 2024). Wang et al. also developed electrospun PAN/PANI nanofibers doped with nickel nanoparticles, which exhibited a 6.4-fold increase in electrical conductivity compared to PAN/PANI alone (Wang et al. 2021a). Under electrical stimulation (100 mV cm^{-1} for 1 h/day over 5 days), the PAN/PANI/Ni scaffolds enhanced Schwann cell proliferation by approximately 2.1-fold, demonstrating the importance of optimizing scaffold conductivity for electrostimulation-mediated neural support. Thus, both intrinsically conductive polymers and conductive composites play a pivotal role in shaping the future of biofabrication-driven tissue engineering.

5.2.2 Magneto-Responsive Composites for Remote Modulation

Magneto-responsive composites have gained increasing attention as adaptable platforms for remotely modulating biological responses through the transduction of external magnetic fields into mechanical, thermal, or biochemical cues. Compared

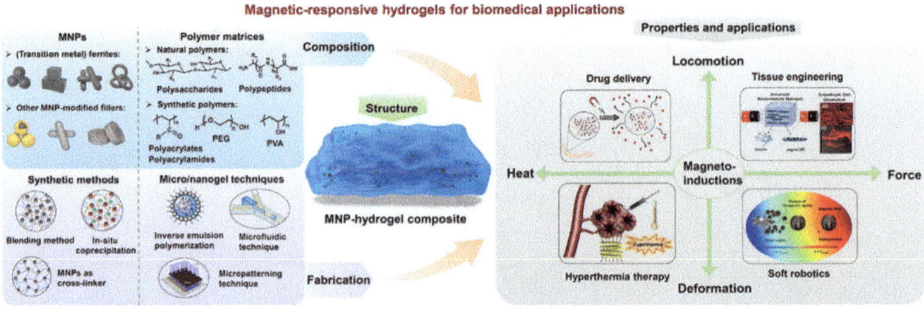

Fig. 5.2 Strategic design of magnetic-responsive hydrogels for biomedical applications (Li et al. 2021)

with optical stimulation, which is constrained by limited light penetration, or electrical approaches that typically require invasive electrodes, magnetic fields can penetrate deep tissue regions with minimal attenuation. This feature makes magnetic actuation particularly attractive for a wide range of biomedical applications. By incorporating SPIONs or related magnetic nanomaterials into polymeric matrices such as hydrogels, elastomers, or electrospun scaffolds, it becomes possible to achieve a high level of spatial and temporal control over biological processes. Through appropriate magnetic stimulation, these systems can influence cell behavior, regulate drug release, and support tissue regeneration in a controlled and non-invasive manner (Fig. 5.2).

The mechanisms through which magnetic stimulation modulates biological responses depend on both the characteristics of the applied magnetic field and the underlying material architecture. When exposed to alternating magnetic fields, SPIONs can generate localized heat through magnetothermal effects, a phenomenon that has been widely explored for on-demand drug release as well as cancer hyperthermia therapy. In other cases, static or low-frequency magnetic fields exert nanoscale torques on embedded nanoparticles, transmitting mechanical forces to the surrounding cellular environment. These forces can activate mechanosensitive ion channels or induce reorganization of cytoskeletal structures. Material design further influences how these effects are translated at the cellular level. In particular, anisotropic architectures in which magnetic particles are deliberately aligned during fabrication can provide directional guidance to cells. When combined with additional features such as surface topography, these systems may act synergistically to enhance cellular organization and functional outcomes.

Recent studies illustrate the broad biomedical potential of these systems. Tang et al. reported a magneto-anisotropic nanocomposite hydrogel that synergistically combined magnetic and topographic anisotropy, enhancing osteogenic differentiation of bone marrow stem cells through the NOTCH pathway and promoting bone regeneration in a rabbit defect model (Tang et al. 2024). As a representative in vivo study, Parmaksiz et al. developed a magneto-responsive DBM scaffold to assess its regenerative efficacy in a critical-size rat cranial defect model. The findings demonstrated a clear synergistic interaction between the magnetically functionalized graft and low-frequency pulsed electromagnetic field (LF-PEMF) stimulation, resulting in a statistically significant enhancement of new bone formation compared to controls (Parmaksiz et al. 2021). Beyond skeletal applications, magneto-responsive composites have also been investigated in neural tissue engineering. Hong et al. demonstrated that SPIONs-incorporated fibrin hydrogels within chitosan conduits facilitated neurite outgrowth in vitro and improved functional recovery in a rat sciatic nerve defect model (Hong et al. 2024). Taken together, these examples highlight how magneto-responsive composites can be designed to couple remote actuation with biologically meaningful outcomes. The ability to control these systems in a non-invasive manner makes them particularly attractive for applications in regenerative medicine, controlled drug delivery, and neuromodulation. At the same time, several practical challenges must be addressed, including the need to ensure long-term biocompatibility, achieve sufficient penetration depths for clinical relevance, and establish reliable strategies for nanoparticle dosing and standardization.

Looking ahead, increasing attention is being directed toward integrating magnetic actuation with complementary physical cues, such as electrical or mechanical stimulation. The development of such multimodal responsive platforms offers a promising route toward more faithfully reproducing the complexity of native tissue environments and enabling finer control over cellular behavior.

5.2.3 *Mechanically Tunable and Strain-Engineered Scaffolds*

Mechanically tunable scaffolds have gained significant attention in biofabrication as they allow precise modulation of the mechanical environment experienced by cells. Tissue-specific mechanical properties, such as stiffness, elasticity, and viscoelasticity, play critical roles in regulating cellular adhesion, proliferation, migration, and lineage-specific differentiation. For instance, neural tissues, particularly in the central nervous system, exhibit extremely low stiffness, typically on the order of 0.1–2 kPa (Sáez et al. 2023), while load-bearing tissues like cartilage and bone are orders of magnitude stiffer. Articular cartilage exhibits significantly higher stiffness compared to neural tissue, with compressive modulus values typically ranging from ~0.2 to 3 MPa (Chen et al. 2024; Petitjean et al. 2023). By designing scaffolds with adjustable mechanical features, it becomes possible to recreate physiologically relevant microenvironments and systematically investigate how mechanical cues are transduced into cellular responses. A common strategy to achieve tunability is through the modulation of polymer composition or crosslinking density in hydrogels. For example, silk fibroin-based scaffolds can be engineered by altering the β-sheet crystallinity to achieve a broad range of stiffness values, thereby directing mesenchymal stem cell (MSC) differentiation toward myogenic or endothelial lineages (Bai et al. 2015). Similarly, incorporation of nanofillers such as cellulose nanocrystals (CNCs) into poly(ε-caprolactone-D,L-lactide) (P(CL-DLLA)) networks has been reported as an elegant strategy to achieve fine-tuned mechanical properties. By simply adjusting CNC content, Young's modulus could be varied within the range of 5 to 15 MPa, creating a spectrum of stiffness conditions. This tunability was shown to elicit strikingly different cellular responses: softer scaffolds promoted neurite extension and survival of neuroblastoma cells, whereas stiffer constructs enhanced spreading and proliferation of dermal fibroblasts (Ustunel et al. 2021). These findings provide a compelling example of how scaffold mechanics alone, without additional biochemical modification, can direct cell-type specific behavior, highlighting the critical role of stiffness as a design parameter in tissue engineering. Additive manufacturing has further expanded the possibilities of strain-engineered scaffolds. Three-dimensional (3D) printing of viscoelastic polymers and composite inks has enabled the fabrication of scaffolds that not only vary stiffness spatially but also mimic dynamic mechanical loading conditions. A recent example involves 3D-bioprinted FPLA (flexible polylactic acid) scaffolds designed to model intervertebral disc (IVD) mechanics, where control of fiber spacing and porosity generated constructs with physiologically relevant viscoelastic properties. These scaffolds supported nucleus pulposus (NP) cell survival and matrix secretion, providing a functional platform for disc regeneration (Marshall et al. 2021).

Another important aspect of mechanically tunable scaffolds is their role in mechanotransduction studies. By systematically adjusting scaffold elasticity, researchers can investigate how integrins, focal adhesions, and cytoskeletal rearrangements translate mechanical signals into biochemical pathways. This knowledge directly informs the design of next-generation biofabrication strategies aimed at promoting functional tissue maturation. For instance, human MSCs cultured on soft substrates (e.g., ~1.37 kPa) tend toward adipogenic fate, while stiffer environments (~4.47 kPa) strongly induce osteogenic differentiation, mediated by ERK/JNK-dependent nuclear localization of TAZ (Hwang et al. 2015). Similarly, hydrogels stiffened in situ from ~3 to 30 kPa showed increased focal adhesion maturation and traction forces in hMSCs, emphasizing the dynamic control of mechanosensing (Guvendiren and Burdick 2012). Overall, mechanically tunable and strain-engineered scaffolds represent a versatile biofabrication strategy that bridges materials science and mechanobiology. By integrating tunable polymers, nanocomposites, and 3D printing technologies, it becomes possible to tailor the mechanical microenvironment in both static and dynamic contexts. This not only improves our understanding of mechanotransduction but also facilitates the development of clinically translatable constructs for musculoskeletal, neural, and cardiovascular applications. Future efforts will likely focus on multi-modal scaffolds that combine mechanical tunability with other stimuli-responsive features, thereby advancing the field toward truly biomimetic and adaptive tissue constructs.

5.2.4 *Piezoelectric Biopolymers and Nanogenerators*

Piezoelectric biomaterials have emerged as a powerful class of scaffolds that can convert mechanical stimuli into localized electrical cues, thereby bridging the gap between physical environments and bioelectrical regulation of cells. In natural tissues, many cell types, particularly those in bone, cartilage, neural, and muscular systems, are highly sensitive to electrical microenvironments. Harnessing piezoelectricity in engineered scaffolds thus offers a biomimetic approach to stimulate cell signaling without the need for external wired electrodes.

Classic piezoelectric polymers such as poly(vinylidene fluoride) (PVDF) and its copolymers (e.g., PVDF-TrFE) have been widely utilized in tissue engineering due to their stable piezoelectric coefficient, biocompatibility, and processability into fibrous or film structures (Luo et al. 2022; Ribeiro et al. 2015). More recently, biodegradable piezoelectric biomaterials such as poly(L-lactic acid) (PLLA), silk fibroin, and collagen-based composites have gained attention as alternatives to non-degradable polymers. For instance, PLLA demonstrates intrinsic piezoelectricity due to its helical chain structure and can generate significant shear piezoelectric constants, which are influenced by crystallinity and dipole alignment (Bai et al. 2024). Silk fibroin-based materials, although mainly recognized for their exceptional osteoconductive and structural properties, have also demonstrated β-sheet–mediated shear piezoelectricity. Zone-drawn silk films with high silk II (β-sheet) crystallinity exhibit shear piezoelectric coefficients as high as $d_{14} \approx -1.5$ pC/N, attributed to oriented β-sheets (Yucel et al. 2011). Additionally, recent studies have fabricated silk fibroin dry-spun fibers with tunable β-sheet content and achieved high piezoelectric output ($d_{33} \approx 3.24$ pm/V) and voltages (~27 V), which in turn promoted neurite extension in PC-12 cells, highlighting their potential in electroactive scaffold applications (Zhen et al. 2024). Additionally, cross-linked collagen films have been shown to exhibit measurable piezoelectric responses through aligned fibrillar organizations (Andonegi et al. 2025). By integrating these polymers into 3D scaffolds, cells can be exposed to continuous electrical stimulation under physiological mechanical loading, such as cyclic strain or body movement. A particularly promising direction involves the development of nanogenerators, such as triboelectric nanogenerators (TENGs) and piezo-triboelectric nanogenerators (PTEGs). These devices harvest biomechanical energy (e.g., joint motion, heartbeat, muscle contraction) and convert it into electrical outputs that can directly stimulate cells seeded within scaffolds. As a recent example, Zhang et al. reported a biodegradable PTEG patch that was able to convert joint motion into in situ electrical stimulation when implanted in an osteoarthritic rat model (Zhang et al. 2025). This electrical output was associated with increased calcium influx, upregulation of chondrogenic markers, enhanced stem cell recruitment, and a reduction in osteophyte formation, ultimately supporting improved cartilage matrix deposition. These findings suggest that integrating triboelectric and piezoelectric effects into biodegradable scaffolds may represent a promising strategy for cartilage repair.

Another emerging approach to improve piezoelectric performance is the incorporation of MXenes, a broad class of 2D materials derived from transition metal carbides, nitrides, and carbonitrides (e.g., Ti_3C_2Tx). MXenes exhibit high electrical conductivity, substantial surface area, and adaptable mechanical behavior, which make them attractive fillers to enhance the β-phase crystallinity and piezoelectric output of polymers such as PVDF-TrFE or PLLA (Wang et al. 2021b; Wu et al. 2024). These hybrid systems exemplify how piezoelectricity can be coupled with

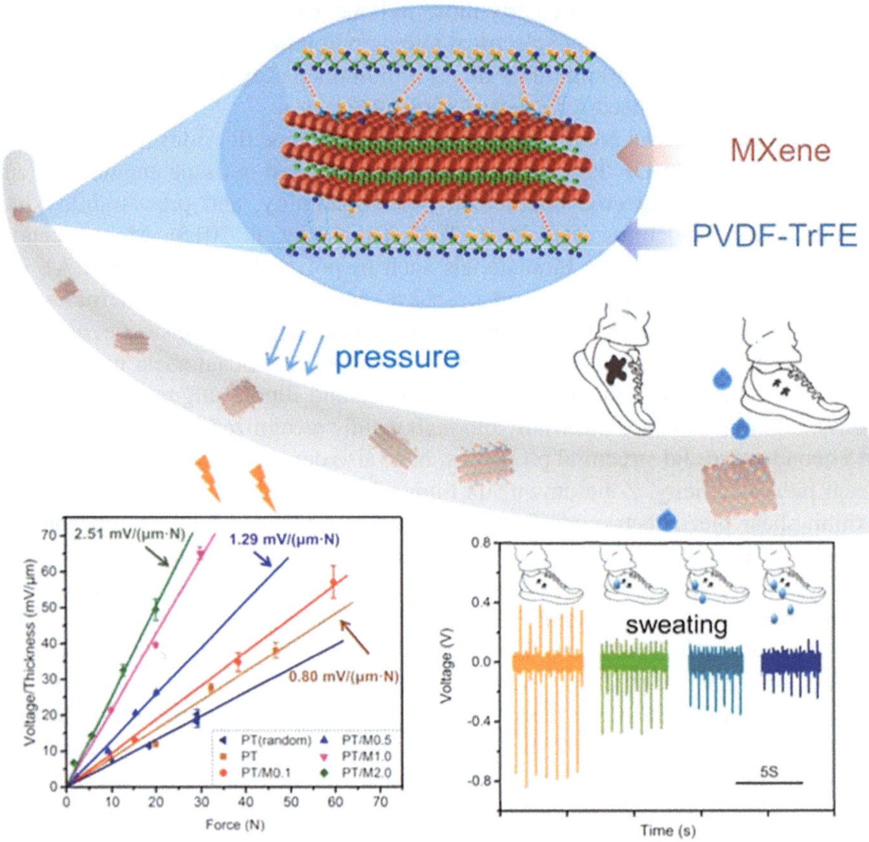

Fig. 5.3 The electrospun PVDF-TrFE/MXene composite film with good piezoelectric properties exhibits a good linear pressure-electrical signal response and the ability of sensing human daily activities (Wang et al. 2021b)

additional external physical stimuli to create multimodal bioelectronic scaffolds (Fig. 5.3). Indeed, piezoelectric scaffolds are increasingly combined with external physical cues to amplify their biological effects.

Ultrasound stimulation, for instance, can enhance the deformation of piezoelectric nanofibers, leading to higher local electric fields and improved cell responses. In a recent study, an ultrasound-activated piezoelectric hydrogel scaffold was developed, which generated localized electrical cues under ultrasonic stimulation. In vivo experiments showed that this stimulation promoted M2 macrophage polarization and enhanced angiogenesis, leading to significantly accelerated wound closure compared to control hydrogels (Yan et al. 2025). Overall, piezoelectric biopolymers and nanogenerators provide a unique platform for wireless, self-sustained electrical stimulation in tissue engineering. Their ability to couple mechanical loading with electroactive cellular responses makes them particularly suitable for regenerating load-bearing tissues (bone, cartilage, muscle) and electrically excitable tissues (nerve, myocardium). Future work is expected to place greater emphasis on biodegradable and multifunctional piezoelectric systems integrated with nanogenerators and responsive to external stimuli such as ultrasound, NIR, or magnetic fields, supporting progress toward clinically translatable and autonomous bioelectronic scaffolds.

5.2.5 *Ultrasound-Responsive Nanocomposites and Smart Gels*

Ultrasound (US) represents a uniquely translatable physical stimulus in regenerative medicine, offering non-invasive delivery, deep tissue penetration, and tunability of acoustic parameters. Its dual capacity acting as both a direct biomechanical cue and a remote activator of smart biomaterials renders it especially powerful in engineering dynamic and responsive scaffolds for tissue repair. At the cellular level, low-intensity pulsed ultrasound (LIPUS) exerts pro-regenerative effects by inducing subtle membrane displacement and calcium influx, which in turn activate key mechanotransduction pathways such as MAPK/ERK and PI3K/Akt. For example, LIPUS significantly increases phosphorylation of ERK1/2 and Akt, thereby promoting human amnion-derived MSC proliferation (Ling et al. 2017), and has been shown to enhance neurotrophic factor-induced neurite outgrowth via the ERK1/2–CREB–Trx-1 signaling axis (Zhao et al. 2016). These findings affirm LIPUS's capacity to independently modulate key cellular behaviors critical for tissue regeneration.

Beyond its intrinsic effects, ultrasound is increasingly leveraged to activate piezoelectric nanocomposites and hydrogel platforms, converting acoustic energy into bioelectric, chemical, or mechanical cues (Table 5.1). Yan et al. developed a collagen/oxidized gellan gum hydrogel enriched with $BaTiO_3$ nanoparticles (Fig. 5.4) (Yan et al. 2025). When exposed to ultrasound, this construct generated localized electrical signals that enhanced M2 macrophage polarization, promoted angiogenesis, and significantly accelerated wound healing, even encouraging hair follicle regeneration. Moreover, ultrasound has been used to boost scaffold performance beyond piezoelectricity. Wang et al. introduced an ultrasound-responsive hydrogel with enhanced electrokinetic behavior, demonstrating its capability to drive neurovascular regeneration in diabetic wounds through combined acoustic and ionic stimuli (Wang et al. 2025). Additional investigations have demonstrated that ultrasound can trigger precise drug release from smart hydrogels (Fig. 5.5). For example, Kubota et al. developed calcium alginate hydrogel microbeads incorporating tungsten particles to enhance acoustic sensitivity (Kubota et al. 2021). Under ultrasound stimulation, even without cavitation, these microbeads released encapsulated model drugs in a controlled manner, highlighting a mechanically driven, spatially resolved release mechanism. Collectively, ultrasound-responsive nanocomposites and smart

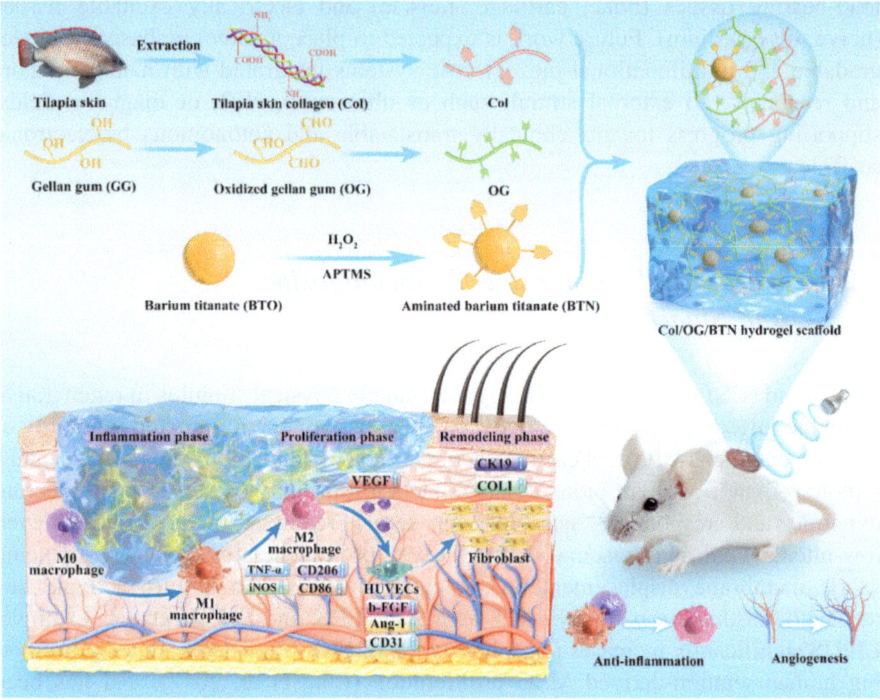

Fig. 5.4 Schematic diagram illustrates the preparation and wound healing mechanism of Col/OG/BTN hydrogel scaffolds (Yan et al. 2025)

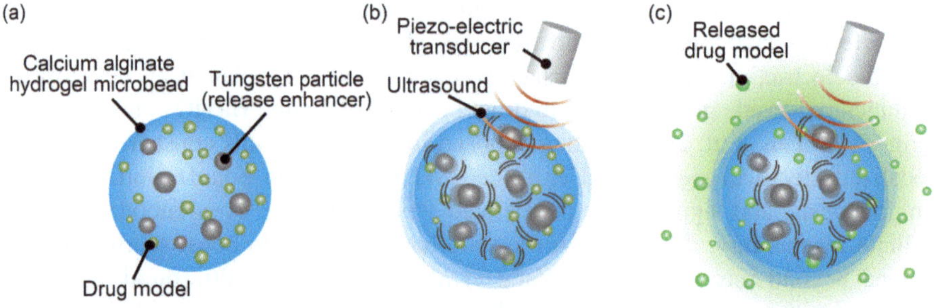

Fig. 5.5 Concept of the ultrasound-triggered drug release using vibration enhancer. (**a**) Hydrogel microbeads containing vibration enhancers and drug models. (**b**) Vibration enhancers in the hydrogel microbeads received the energy of applied ultrasound. (**c**) Drug models were released from hydrogel microbeads by the vibration of hydrogel microbeads and vibration enhancers (Kubota et al. 2021)

gels exemplify a new generation of biofabrication strategies, non-invasive, user-controllable, and multifunctional scaffolds. They enable precise orchestration of immunomodulatory, angiogenic, neurogenic, and regenerative processes, while aligning with existing clinical ultrasound infrastructure. Future research will focus on refining ultrasound parameters for safe, optimal activation, and tailoring material compositions for consistent, tissue-specific responses, moving toward fully adaptive, personalized regenerative therapies.

5.2.6 Hybrid Multi-modal Systems for Integrated Biophysical Stimulation

The development of hybrid multi-modal systems represents a logical next step in the evolution of physically responsive biomaterials, as it allows the integration of multiple biophysical cues into a single construct. While mono-modal systems, such as piezoelectric hydrogels, magneto-responsive scaffolds, or ultrasound-sensitive matrices, have each demonstrated promise in guiding specific aspects of cell fate, living tissues are intrinsically exposed to a highly dynamic environment where mechanical, electrical, thermal, and biochemical signals converge. Hybrid systems aim to recapitulate this complexity by combining different stimuli, thereby enabling synergistic and more physiologically relevant modes of regulation. One notable strategy involves the integration of magnetic and piezoelectric components into a single platform, generating so-called magneto-piezoelectric composites. In such systems, an externally applied magnetic field induces mechanical strain in magnetostrictive particles, which is subsequently transferred to the piezoelectric phase to produce localized electrical signals. Such dual-mode systems are attractive because they combine the deep tissue penetration and remote controllability of magnetic fields with the bioelectrical relevance of piezoelectric stimulation. Another line of investigation has focused on coupling photothermal agents with piezoelectric scaffolds. Hybrid photothermal–piezoelectric systems enable remote NIR irradiation to provide localized heating while simultaneously modulating mechanoelectrical outputs from piezoelectric components, offering spatiotemporal control over wound-relevant processes such as angiogenesis, immune regulation, and tissue regeneration (Chen et al. 2020). Importantly, the wavelength specificity of NIR light allows for non-invasive and tissue-penetrant activation, making such photo-piezoelectric hybrids attractive candidates for translational applications in cutaneous and musculoskeletal repair. Hybrid triboelectric–piezoelectric generators represent yet another compelling example of multi-modal platforms. By combining the surface charge accumulation of triboelectric materials with the strain-induced polarization of piezoelectric phases, these systems can harvest biomechanical energy from body movements more efficiently than either mechanism alone. Implantable hybrid tribo-electric nanogenerators have been shown to restore biomechanically driven electrical microenvironments in situ, activating mechano–electro–biochemical cascades that significantly accelerate critical-sized bone defect repair (Xu et al. 2024b). Such devices exemplify how energy-harvesting hybrids may offer clinically relevant solutions by reducing reliance on external power supplies or repeated interventions.

Ultrasound-triggered smart gels also lend themselves to hybridization, particularly when combined with thermo-responsive or mechano-electroactive components. Recent studies have demonstrated hydrogels that simultaneously respond to ultrasound-induced microstreaming and localized heating, thereby enabling both controlled drug release and piezoelectric stimulation. For instance, Xu et al. developed a thermoresponsive hydrogel embedded with aligned piezoelectric nanofibers that, upon ultrasound exposure, not only generated electrical signals to guide neurite outgrowth but also released neurotrophic factors in a temporally controlled fashion, collectively supporting functional recovery in a peripheral nerve injury model (Xu et al. 2024a). These results highlight how combining acoustic, thermal, and electrical modalities can achieve multi-layered control over tissue regeneration that more closely mimics the multifactorial nature of native healing.

The promise of hybrid multi-modal systems lies not only in their ability to reproduce the complexity of the native cellular microenvironment but also in the possibility of tailoring responses to specific therapeutic contexts. Nevertheless, challenges remain, including the need to fine-tune stimulation parameters across modalities, ensure long-term biocompatibility of increasingly complex material systems, and address regulatory hurdles associated with multifunctional constructs. Despite these obstacles, the progress made thus far strongly suggests that integrating multiple physical modes of stimulation into unified platforms offers a powerful strategy to advance biofabrication toward clinical translation.

5.3 Future Perspectives and Challenges

5.3.1 Material Selection, Biocompatibility, and Long-Term Function

Despite substantial advances in physically responsive biomaterials, material selection continues to represent a major challenge for long-term use and clinical translation (Öztürk et al. 2020). Responsive components including conductive fillers, magnetic nanoparticles, and piezoelectric phases are required not only to deliver reliable functional performance, but also to preserve biocompatibility and structural integrity under sustained mechanical or electromagnetic stimulation. Prolonged exposure to physical cues can lead to material fatigue, modifications in surface chemistry, or a gradual decline in responsiveness, all of which may alter cell–material interactions over time. Additional considerations arise when biodegradable responsive materials are employed. Degradation products can influence the local physicochemical environment, leading to pH fluctuations, immune activation, or changes in cellular behavior, underscoring the need for evaluation strategies that extend beyond short-term in vitro assays. Moving forward, greater emphasis on long-term in vivo studies, the development of fatigue-resistant material architectures, and degradation-aware design approaches will be essential to ensure sustained functionality while maintaining tissue homeostasis.

5.3.2 Standardization of Biophysical Stimulation Parameters

A further obstacle to the widespread adoption of physically responsive biofabrication is the absence of standardized stimulation protocols. Across the literature, key parameters including stimulus frequency, amplitude, duration, and temporal patterning are defined and applied in markedly different ways, which complicates direct comparison between studies and limits reproducibility. This challenge is further amplified by the fact that stimulation conditions optimized in vitro do not always translate effectively to in vivo settings, where tissue mechanics, signal attenuation, and dynamic biological feedback can differ substantially.

Addressing these issues will require greater emphasis on standardized reporting practices and the establishment of reference stimulation ranges, analogous to the dose–response frameworks commonly used for biochemical factors. Such efforts would improve cross-study comparability and help accelerate the maturation of physically responsive biofabrication technologies. At the same time, emerging adaptive stimulation strategies that adjust in response to real-time cellular feedback offer a compelling alternative to fixed-parameter approaches, with the potential to achieve more physiologically relevant and personalized modulation of engineered tissues.

5.3.3 Translation into Clinical Applications

The translation of physically responsive biomaterials into clinical practice offers considerable promise, while also introducing a set of practical and regulatory challenges. Activation strategies that are non-invasive or minimally invasive such as ultrasound, magnetic fields, or controlled mechanical loading are particularly appealing because they align well with existing clinical workflows and patient safety requirements. At the same time, regulatory pathways for multifunctional and dynamically responsive materials remain complex, as these systems often span the boundaries between medical devices, biologics, and active implantable technologies.

Beyond regulatory considerations, issues related to scalable manufacturing, reproducibility, and quality control must be carefully addressed to ensure consistency across responsive architectures and to meet clinical and industrial standards. Despite these hurdles, the capacity of physically responsive biomaterials to modulate cellular behavior without relying on exogenous growth factors positions them as strong candidates for next-generation regenerative therapies. More broadly, the ongoing shift from passive scaffolds toward adaptive, stimulus-responsive platforms capable of interacting with biological systems in real time has the potential to reshape biofabrication strategies and support the development of more personalized and precision-oriented regenerative medicine approaches.

Competing Interests Y.M.E. is the founder and shareholder of Biovalda Health Technologies, Inc. (Ankara, Türkiye). The authors declare no competing financial interests in relation to this particular article.

References

Andonegi M et al (2025) Piezoelectric properties of collagen films: insights into their potential for electroactive biomedical applications. Int J Biol Macromol 309:142799. https://doi.org/10.1016/j.ijbiomac.2025.142799

Bai S, Han H, Huang X, Xu W, Kaplan DL, Zhu H, Lu Q (2015) Silk scaffolds with tunable mechanical capability for cell differentiation. Acta Biomater 20:22–31. https://doi.org/10.1016/j.actbio.2015.04.004

Bai Y, Meng H, Li Z, Wang ZL (2024) Degradable piezoelectric biomaterials for medical applications. Med Mat 1(1):40–49. https://doi.org/10.1097/mm9.0000000000000002

Berdiaki A, Neagu M, Tzanakakis P, Spyridaki I, Pérez S, Nikitovic D (2024) Extracellular matrix components and mechanosensing pathways in health and disease. Biomolecules 14(9):1186. https://doi.org/10.3390/biom14091186

Chen Y, Ye M, Song L, Zhang J, Yang Y, Luo S et al (2020) Piezoelectric and photothermal dual functional film for enhanced dermal wound regeneration via upregulation of Hsp90 and HIF-1α. Appl Mater Today 20:100756. https://doi.org/10.1016/j.apmt.2020.100756

Chen Y, Saiding Q, Meng C, Cui W (2024) Engineering stiff and tough protein-based hydrogels: bridging the mechanical gap between muscle and cartilage. Matter 7(1):22–24. https://doi.org/10.1016/j.matt.2023.11.015

Chen W, Wei Y, Chang J, Hui Y, Ye J, Weng G et al (2025) Electrostimulation combined with biodegradable electroactive oriented nanofiber polycaprolactone/gelatin/carbon nanotube to accelerate wound healing. Mater Today Bio 31:101490. https://doi.org/10.1016/j.mtbio.2025.101490

Dong C, Malliaras GG (2025) Recent advances in stimuli-responsive materials and soft robotic actuators for bioelectronic medicine. Adv Mater:2417325. https://doi.org/10.1002/adma.202417325

Gao Y, Guo X, Wang X, Li D, Tang H, Zhao W et al (2024) Engineered mechanical dynamics in biomimetic hydrogel scaffold promotes phenotypic maintenance and cartilage formation of chondrocytes. Compos Part B 284:111665. https://doi.org/10.1016/j.compositesb.2024.111665

Gelmi A, Schutt CE (2021) Stimuli-responsive biomaterials: scaffolds for stem cell control. Adv Healthc Mater 10(1):2001125. https://doi.org/10.1002/adhm.202001125

Goodrich R, Tai Y, Ye Z, Yin Y, Nam J (2023) A magneto-responsive hydrogel system for the dynamic mechano-modulation of stem cell niche. Adv Funct Mater 33(2211288). https://doi.org/10.1002/adfm.202211288

Guo X, Gao Y, Yu J, Qiu S, Wang X, Wang S et al (2025) Dynamic mechanical stimulation of thermoresponsive nanofibers for activation of fibroblasts in skin repair. Adv Healthc Mater:2500277. https://doi.org/10.1002/adhm.202500277

Guvendiren M, Burdick JA (2012) Stiffening hydrogels to probe short-and long-term cellular responses to dynamic mechanics. Nat Commun 3(1):792. https://doi.org/10.1038/ncomms1792

Holle AW et al (2018) Cell–extracellular matrix mechanobiology: forceful tools and emerging needs for basic and translational research. Nano Lett 18(1):1–8. https://doi.org/10.1021/acs.nanolett.7b04982

Hong J, Wu D, Wang H, Gong Z, Zhu X, Chen F et al (2024) Magnetic fibrin nanofiber hydrogel delivering iron oxide magnetic nanoparticles promotes peripheral nerve regeneration. Regener Biomater 11:rbae075. https://doi.org/10.1093/rb/rbae075

Hwang JH, Byun MR, Kim AR, Kim KM, Cho HJ, Lee YH, Kim J, Jeong MG, Hwang S, Hong JH (2015) Extracellular matrix stiffness regulates osteogenic differentiation through MAPK activation. PLoS One 10(8):e0135519. https://doi.org/10.1371/journal.pone.0135519

Khosravieh ZF, Nekounam H, Asgari F, Haghighipour N (2024) Electrospun PAN/PANI/CNT scaffolds and electrical pulses: a pathway to stem cell-derived nerve regeneration. Biomed Phys Eng Express 10(5):055010. https://doi.org/10.1088/2057-1976/ad5e84

Kubota T, Kurashina Y, Zhao J, Ando K, Onoe H (2021) Ultrasound-triggered on-demand drug delivery using hydrogel microbeads with release enhancer. Mater Des 203:109580. https://doi.org/10.1016/j.matdes.2021.109580

Li Z, Li Y, Chen C, Cheng Y (2021) Magnetic-responsive hydrogels: from strategic design to biomedical applications. J Control Release 335:541–556. https://doi.org/10.1016/j.jconrel.2021.06.003

Ling L, Wei T, He L, Wang Y, Wang Y, Feng X, Zhang W, Xiong Z (2017) Low-intensity pulsed ultrasound activates ERK 1/2 and PI 3K-Akt signalling pathways and promotes the proliferation of human amnion-derived mesenchymal stem cells. Cell Prolif 50(6):e12383. https://doi.org/10.1111/cpr.12383

Luo Q, He X, Duan X, Liu H, Zhou Z, Cheng K (2022) A facile synthesis of P (VDF-TrFE)-coated-PMMA janus membranes for guided bone regeneration. Coatings 12(12):1947. https://doi.org/10.3390/coatings12121947

Manjua AC, Garrudo FF, Agostinho A, Gusmão A, Sanjuan-Alberte P, Ferreira FC, Gumuscu B (2025) Biomimetic model for electromagnetic modulation of cardiovascular cellular ınteractions on-chip. ACS Appl Bio Mater 8(8):7080–7094. https://doi.org/10.1021/acsabm.5c00798

Marshall SL et al (2021) Three-dimensional-printed flexible scaffolds have tunable biomimetic mechanical properties for intervertebral disc tissue engineering. ACS Biomater Sci Eng 7(12): 5836–5849

Municoy S, Alvarez Echazu MI, Antezana PE, Galdopórpora JM, Olivetti C, Mebert AM, Foglia ML, Tuttolomondo MV, Alvarez GS, Hardy JG (2020) Stimuli-responsive materials for tissue engineering and drug delivery. Int J Mol Sci 21(13):4724. https://doi.org/10.3390/ijms21134724

Murphy SV, Atala A (2014) 3D bioprinting of tissues and organs. Nat Biotechnol 32(8):773–785. https://doi.org/10.1038/nbt.2958

Nakaji-Hirabayashi T et al (2022) Enhanced proliferation and differentiation of human mesenchymal stem cells in the gravity-controlled environment. Artif Organs 46(9):1760–1770. https://doi.org/10.1111/aor.14251

Öztürk S, Ayanoglu FB, Parmaksiz M, Elçin AE, Elçin YM (2020) Chapter 11—clinical and surgical aspects of medical materials' biocompatibility. In: Mozafari M (ed) Handbook of biomaterials biocompatibility. Woodhead Publishing, pp 219–250. https://doi.org/10.1016/B978-0-08-102967-1.00012-8

Parmaksiz M, Lalegül-Ülker Ö, Vurat MT, Elçin AE, Elçin YM (2021) Magneto-sensitive decellularized bone matrix with or without low frequency-pulsed electromagnetic field exposure for the healing of a critical-size bone defect. Mater Sci Eng C 124:112065. https://doi.org/10.1016/j.msec.2021.112065

Petitjean N, Canadas P, Royer P, Noël D, Le Floc'h S (2023) Cartilage biomechanics: from the basic facts to the challenges of tissue engineering. J Biomed Mater Res A 111(7):1067–1089. https://doi.org/10.1002/jbm.a.37478

Ribeiro C, Sencadas V, Correia DM, Lanceros-Méndez S (2015) Piezoelectric polymers as biomaterials for tissue engineering applications. Colloids Surf B: Biointerfaces 136:46–55. https://doi.org/10.1016/j.colsurfb.2015.08.043

Sáez P, Borau C, Antonovaite N, Franze K (2023) Brain tissue mechanics is governed by microscale relations of the tissue constituents. Biomaterials 301:122273. https://doi.org/10.1016/j.biomaterials.2023.122273

Sikder P, Nagaraju P, Naganaboyina HP (2022) 3D-printed piezoelectric porous bioactive scaffolds and clinical ultrasonic stimulation can help in enhanced bone regeneration. Bioengineering 9(11):679. https://doi.org/10.3390/bioengineering9110679

Sydney Gladman A, Matsumoto EA, Nuzzo RG, Mahadevan L, Lewis JA (2016) Biomimetic 4D printing. Nat Mater 15(4):413–418. https://doi.org/10.1038/nmat4544

Tai Y, Tonmoy TI, Win S, Brinkley NT, Park BH, Nam J (2023) Enhanced peripheral nerve regeneration by mechano-electrical stimulation. npj Regener Med 8(1):57. https://doi.org/10.1038/s41536-023-00334-y

Tang S, Yan Y, Lu X, Wang P, Xu X, Hu K et al (2024) Nanocomposite magnetic hydrogel with dual anisotropic properties induces osteogenesis through the NOTCH-dependent pathways. NPG Asia Mater 16(1):16. https://doi.org/10.1038/s41427-024-00535-x

Tota M, Jonderko L, Witek J, Novickij V, Kulbacka J (2024) Cellular and molecular effects of magnetic fields. Int J Mol Sci 25(16):8973. https://doi.org/10.3390/ijms25168973

Uray IP, Uray K (2021) Mechanotransduction at the plasma membrane-cytoskeleton interface. Int J Mol Sci 22(21):11566. https://doi.org/10.3390/ijms222111566

Ustunel S et al (2021) Mechanically tunable elastomer and cellulose nanocrystal composites as scaffolds for in vitro cell studies. Mater Adv 2(1):464–476. https://doi.org/10.1039/D0MA00676A

Wang M, Tremblay PL, Zhang T (2021a) Optimizing the electrical conductivity of polyacrylonitrile/polyaniline with nickel nanoparticles for the enhanced electrostimulation of Schwann cells proliferation. Bioelectrochemistry 140:107750. https://doi.org/10.1016/j.bioelechem.2021.107750

Wang S, Shao HQ, Liu Y, Tang CY, Zhao X, Ke K, Bao RY, Yang MB, Yang W (2021b) Boosting piezoelectric response of PVDF-TrFE via MXene for self-powered linear pressure sensor. Compos Sci Technol 202:108600. https://doi.org/10.1016/j.compscitech.2020.108600

Wang F, Xue Y, Chen X, Zhang P, Shan L, Duan Q et al (2024) 3D printed implantable hydrogel bioelectronics for electrophysiological monitoring and electrical modulation. Adv Funct Mater 34(21):2314471. https://doi.org/10.1002/adfm.202314471

Wang F, Qiu J, Guan S, Chen S, Nie X, Fu Z, Yao FZ, Gong W, Wang K, Liu X (2025) An ultrasound-responsive hydrogel with piezoelectric-enhanced electrokinetic effect accelerates neurovascular regeneration for diabetic wound healing. Mater Today 84:48. https://doi.org/10.1016/j.mattod.2025.02.003

Wu Y, Yu Q, Zhou X, Ding W, Li X, Zhou P, Qiao Y, Huang Z, Wang S, Zhang J, Yang L, Zhang L, Sun D (2024) MXene-coated piezoelectric poly-L-lactic acid membrane accelerates wound healing by biomimicking low-voltage electrical pulses. Int J Biol Macromol 278:134971. https://doi.org/10.1016/j.ijbiomac.2024.134971

Xu D et al (2024a) Ultrasound-responsive aligned piezoelectric nanofibers derived hydrogel conduits for peripheral nerve regeneration. Adv Mater 36(28):2307896. https://doi.org/10.1002/adma.202307896

Xu D, Fu S, Zhang H, Lu W, Xie J, Li J et al (2024b) Ultrasound-responsive aligned piezoelectric nanofibers derived hydrogel conduits for peripheral nerve regeneration. Adv Mater 36(28):2307896. https://doi.org/10.1002/adma.202307896

Xue Y, Li J, Jiang T, Han Q, Jing Y, Bai S, Yan X (2024) Biomimetic conductive hydrogel scaffolds with anisotropy and electrical stimulation for in vivo skeletal muscle reconstruction. Adv Healthc Mater 13(4):2302180. https://doi.org/10.1002/adhm.202302180

Yan P, Zheng H, Liu P, Yan C, Zhao M, Ling S, Wang S, Liu C, Tan SH, Liang K, Teoh SH (2025) Ultrasound-activated piezoelectric hydrogel scaffold for synergistic immunomodulation and angiogenesis in accelerated wound healing. Acta Biomater 204:216. https://doi.org/10.1016/j.actbio.2025.08.006

Yucel T, Cebe P, Kaplan DL (2011) Structural origins of silk piezoelectricity. Adv Funct Mater 21(4):779–785. https://doi.org/10.1002/adfm.201002077

Zhang K, Wu Y, Li J, Cai X, Zhang C, Xu K, Wu J, Xu L, Hazarika D, Wan R, Chen C, Cao Z, Wang Y, Jin H, Yang Z, Dong S, Yan Y, Huang S, Feng G, Luo J, Wang ZL (2025) Biodegradable piezo-triboelectric charge nanogenerator patch for cartilage regeneration. ACS Nano 19:24747. https://doi.org/10.1021/acsnano.4c18811

Zhao L, Feng Y, Hu H, Shi A, Zhang L, Wan M (2016) Low-intensity pulsed ultrasound enhances nerve growth factor-induced neurite outgrowth through mechanotransduction-mediated ERK1/2–CREB–Trx-1 signaling. Ultrasound Med Biol 42(12):2914–2925. https://doi.org/10.1016/j.ultrasmedbio.2016.07.017

Zhen W, Chen J, Fan S, Zhang Y (2024) Piezoelectric fibers based on silk fibroin with excellent output performance. Chin Phys B 33(8):088701. https://doi.org/10.1088/1674-1056/ad51f5

Zhuo S, Zhang M, Zhang Y, Zhang X, Sang R, Fang X et al (2025) Osteogenesis induced by magnetic responsive composite scaffolds under a static magnetic field. Int J Bioprinting 11(3): 218–240. https://doi.org/10.36922/ijb.8351

Chapter 6
Platelet Rich Plasma and Platelet Lysate Biomaterials for Biofabrication: Advances, Applications, and Challenges

Şükran Şeker and Yaşar Murat Elçin

Abstract Platelet-derived biomaterials have emerged as promising candidates in regenerative medicine due to their autologous origin, rich biological content, and capacity to support tissue repair and cell function. Blood plasma derivatives used for fabrication of platelet-derived biomaterials such as platelet-rich plasma (PRP) and platelet lysate (PL) provide a natural source of growth factors, cytokines, and extracellular matrix proteins. These biomolecules exert significant regenerative effects by actively promoting cellular proliferation, migration, lineage-specific differentiation, angiogenesis, and collagen synthesis, thereby playing a pivotal role in the processes of wound healing and tissue regeneration. Owing to their inherent regenerative capacity, blood plasma derivatives have emerged as a highly promising autologous resource for integration into biomaterial-based strategies. Recent advances in biofabrication techniques have enabled the development of highly biocompatible and functional tissue constructs using PRP and PL. Biofabrication of platelet-derived biomaterials offers new insights and strategies for next-generation personalized regenerative medicine by integrating engineering innovation with biological functionality. This chapter aims to provide a comprehensive overview of current biofabrication strategies utilized in the development of platelet-derived biomaterials using PRP and PL, highlighting their applications in tissue engineering and regenerative medicine. The challenges in the biofabrication of platelet-derived biomaterials are also discussed along with possible solutions to these challenges.

Ş. Şeker
Tissue Engineering, Biomaterials and Nanobiotechnology Laboratory, Faculty of Science and Stem Cell Institute, Ankara University, Ankara, Türkiye

Y. M. Elçin (✉)
Tissue Engineering, Biomaterials and Nanobiotechnology Laboratory, Faculty of Science and Stem Cell Institute, Ankara University, Ankara, Türkiye

Department of Chemistry, Faculty of Science, Ankara University, Ankara, Türkiye
e-mail: elcin@ankara.edu.tr

Y. M. Elçin (ed.), *Biofabrication in Regenerative Medicine*, Stem Cell Biology and Regenerative Medicine 1519, https://doi.org/10.1007/978-3-032-30294-6_6

Keywords Platelet-derived biomaterials · Biofabrication · Platelet rich plasma · Platelet lysate · Tissue engineering scaffolds · Regenerative medicine

Abbreviations

Alg	Alginate
ECM	Extracellular Matrix
EGF	Epidermal Growth Factor
FBS	Fetal Bovine Serum
GelMA	Methacrylated Gelatin
GFs	Growth Factors
HA	Hyaluronic Acid
hASCs	Human Adipose Stem Cells
MSCs	Mesenchymal Stem Cells
PCL	Poly(ε-Caprolactone)
PDGF	Platelet-Derived Growth Factor
PEG	Polyethylene Glycol
PLMA	Methacrylated Platelet Lysate
PL	Platelet Lysate
PRP	Platelet-Rich Plasma
TGF-β	Transforming Growth Factor-β
VEGF	Vascular Endothelial Growth Factor
3D	Three-Dimensional

6.1 Introduction

Biofabrication is a transformative approach for engineering functional biomaterials that closely mimic the complexity of native tissues. By integrating advanced manufacturing techniques with biological components, biofabrication provides new opportunities to overcome the limitations of traditional biomaterial processing, offering precise spatial control over the organization of cells, growth factors (GFs), and extracellular matrix (ECM) components (Vyas et al. 2020).

Blood is a unique and autologous bioactive material that contains various proteins, GFs, and cytokines involved in wound healing, angiogenesis, and tissue remodeling. Blood products such as platelet-rich plasma (PRP) and platelet lysate (PL) have been used for decades in clinical applications to enhance tissue regeneration (Zhang et al. 2025). Among the various biomaterial sources, platelet-derived products have gained increasing attention due to their biocompatibility, autologous origin, and rich composition of GFs, and cytokines. Their intrinsic ability to modulate inflammatory responses, stimulate cell proliferation and tissue regeneration, and promote matrix deposition has positioned them as valuable building blocks for tissue engineering strategies (Ren et al. 2023). Blood, as a readily accessible and minimally invasive biological material, provides a unique natural source for developing next-generation scaffolds and bioinks. Recent advances in biofabrication technologies, particularly in crosslinking chemistry, and hybrid bioink formulations, have opened new frontiers to improve the physical, chemical, and biological properties of platelet-derived biomaterials (Del Amo and Andia 2023). By integrating these strategies, it is possible to create customizable, patient-specific constructs capable of recapitulating the dynamic nature of human tissues.

Despite these promising developments, several challenges continue to impede the widespread and standardized use of platelet-derived biomaterials. A primary limitation arises from donor variability and differences in platelet concentration, plasma composition, and clotting factor levels which can result in inconsistent mechanical and biological performance. Additionally, the mechanical stability and long-term durability of blood-based hydrogels are often inadequate for load-bearing or high-stress tissues. The lack of standardized processing and storage protocols further complicates reproducibility across laboratories and clinical studies (Şeker et al. 2025). To address these limitations, new standardization and fabrication strategies are needed that allow precise tuning of biochemical and mechanical properties of platelet-derived biomaterials.

Biofabrication serves as a platform for transforming platelet-derived materials into clinically translatable solutions. Driven by advanced manufacturing technologies, biofabrication enables the creation of patient-specific, bioactive constructs tailored for various regenerative applications including wound healing, vascular and bone regeneration (Zhao et al. 2022). However, the successful translation of these technologies from the laboratory to the clinic will require addressing key challenges in scalability, reproducibility, and regulatory compliance (Harley et al. 2021). This chapter aims to provide a comprehensive overview of biofabrication strategies for the development of platelet-derived biomaterials using PRP or PL for the next generation of personalized and functional regenerative therapies, emphasizing recent technological advances, biomedical applications and challenges.

6.2 PRP and PL: Biological Overview

Platelets are small, non-nucleated blood cells and normally circulate in an inactive state. They instantly migrate to and accumulate at the injured site after tissue damage. Upon exposure to thrombin and collagen, platelets become activated (Popescu et al. 2021), initiating the body's natural wound healing process (Fig. 6.1). Activation of platelets triggers the release of various bioactive molecules and GFs in their alpha granules (Santos et al. 2021). Tissue healing is a highly coordinated and complex process regulated by many cellular molecules, including GFs, cytokines, and chemokines, and generally consists of several overlapping phases. Each phase is precisely controlled through cell–cell interactions and

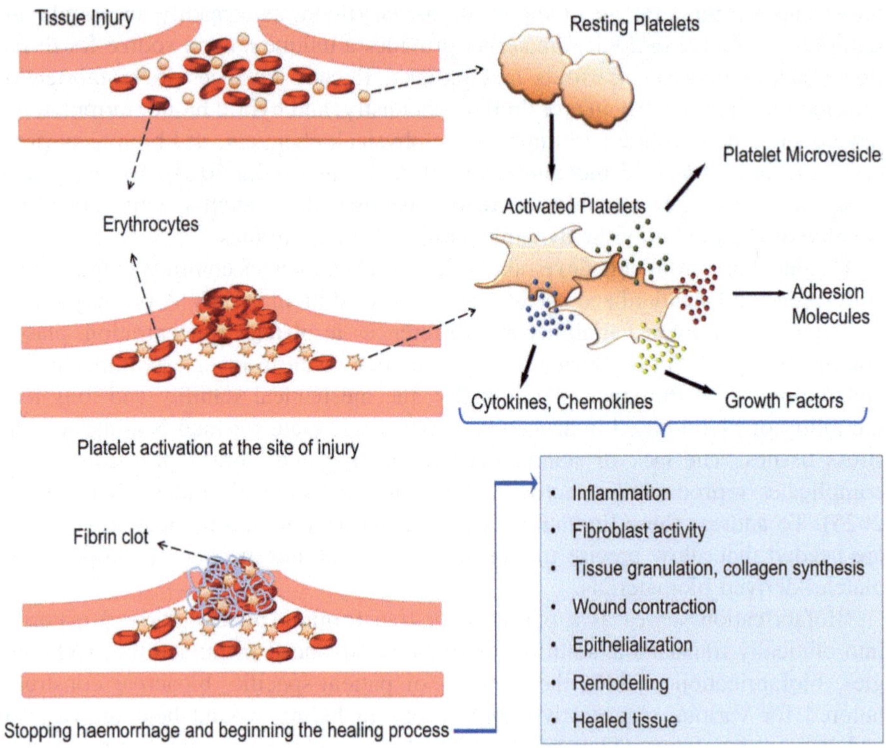

Fig. 6.1 Schematic illustration of platelet activation, fibrin clot formation and natural tissue healing process after a tissue injury. (Reprinted with permission from Ref. Şeker et al. 2025)

signaling pathways that collectively restore the integrity of the damaged tissue (Zhou et al. 2023).

PRP is an autologous blood derivative with a high concentration of platelets suspended in a small volume of blood plasma. Owing to its rich content of platelet-derived bioactive molecules including platelet-derived growth factor (PDGF), transforming growth factor-β (TGF-β), vascular endothelial growth factor (VEGF), and epidermal growth factor (EGF), PRP has been a potent biological agent in regenerative medicine for many years (Rath et al. 2025; Sánchez et al. 2025). PRP was first used in open-heart surgery to reduce excessive transfusion of homologous blood products in 1987, subsequently gaining widespread clinical adoption throughout the 1990s (Xue et al. 2020). In terms of tissue regeneration, PRP was initially applied in the field of dentistry in 1998 for maxillofacial bone regeneration (Buzalaf and Levy 2022). Since then, its utilization has expanded considerably, encompassing the treatment of both soft and hard tissues. PRP has long been used in liquid or gel forms for wound repair and tissue healing (Wu et al. 2022). PRP is prepared by centrifugation of whole blood samples in the density gradient centrifugation, or apheresis methods based on platelet collections selectively from the donor blood (He et al. 2022). PRP has a platelet concentration approximately ranging from

300,000 to 1,500,000 platelet in 1 mm^3 corresponding to ~5–7 times higher than that of circulating whole blood (Fang et al. 2020). This amount can be influenced by age, gender, and centrifugation or apheresis parameters. Platelets within platelet suspensions or PRP can be activated through mechanical approaches, including repeated freeze–thaw cycles or sonication, or via chemical stimuli, such as thrombin, or $CaCl_2$. Platelet membrane disruption (platelet lysis) triggered by mechanical or chemical activation facilitates the release of GFs. Mechanical activation is particularly advantageous due to its simplicity, efficiency, and cost-effectiveness (Pötter et al. 2021). Conversely, chemical activation with exogenous agents may result in adverse events, including peripheral thrombosis, myocardial infarction, or coagulopathies (Liebig et al. 2020). Furthermore, chemical activation promotes fibrin polymerization, resulting in the formation of a fibrin gel, whereas mechanical activation yields a cell-free PL following centrifugation to remove the residual platelet debris (Şeker et al. 2019).

PL can be considered as a promising alternative to PRP due to its enhanced stability, safety, and biological efficacy. Like PRP, PL contains a wide spectrum of platelet-derived bioactive molecules. The absence of intact platelets and leukocytes in PL minimizes the risk of immunogenic and pro-inflammatory reactions, thereby improving its safety profile (Da Fonseca et al. 2021). The cell-free nature of PL also allows for its use as a xeno-free supplement in cell culture systems, offering a reliable and ethically acceptable alternative to fetal bovine serum (FBS) (Anerillas et al. 2023). In addition, PL can be sterilized by filtration and stored at low temperatures without significant loss of bioactivity, providing superior stability and logistical advantages compared to freshly prepared PRP. Collectively, these properties make PL a more standardized, biocompatible, and practical blood product for regenerative medicine and therapeutic applications (Valtetsiotis et al. 2024).

6.3 Biofabrication Techniques for PRP/PL-Based Biomaterials

The field of regenerative medicine focuses on the development of biomaterials that can mimic the complexity and functionality of native tissues. Autologous human-derived materials are increasingly recognized as essential components in biomaterial design, as they provide superior biocompatibility and minimize immune reactions compared to allogeneic or synthetic alternatives; however, their availability is limited, arising both their value and the need for biomaterial strategies that maximize their efficient use in regenerative applications. Blood plasma derivatives have gained increasing attention in tissue engineering and regenerative medicine due to their bioactive properties, biocompatibility, and autologous nature (Huang et al. 2020; Şeker and Elçin 2024). These derivatives provide both biochemical and structural support to promote cell proliferation, migration, differentiation, and tissue remodeling (Shome et al. 2023).

PRP gels (or fibrin gels) are prepared by using some activators such as calcium chloride, ascorbic acid, collagen or thrombin (Soares et al. 2020; Zhang et al. 2022), produced through the conversion of fibrinogen to a three-dimensional (3D) fibrin network (Li et al. 2024). However, the use of activators to induce gelation results in a rapid and uncontrolled release of GFs, leading to a short duration of biological activity. The burst release may increase the risk of tissue hyperplasia during the early phase of wound healing, thereby reducing both the duration of PRP activity and its overall regenerative efficiency (Zhang et al. 2022).

PRP has been administered via injection at injury sites to enhance wound healing and tissue regeneration. However, the retention of PRP at the targeted site over extended periods may not always be feasible in clinical applications, often may require multiple local injections at specific intervals depending on the treatment protocol. The repetitive injections may result in significant fluctuations in GF concentrations within the target tissue, thereby reducing clinical predictability and increasing pain in the patient (Masoudi et al. 2016). One the other hand, one of the main limitations of PRP gels is their insufficient mechanical strength and stability for surgical handling and application. Due to their weak mechanical strengths and poor adhesion to tissue defects, the levels of tissue integration and healing capacity of PRP gels remain limited (Liu et al. 2017). Considering these limitations, PRP/PL-based scaffolds can provide sustained release of GFs at the damaged site, significantly enhancing the effectiveness of PRP on tissue healing. PRP/PL-based scaffolds can provide sustained release of GFs at the damaged site, significantly enhancing the efficiency of PRP on wound healing. PRP-loaded scaffolds enable the sustained release of GFs in PRP, providing controlled delivery platforms for prolonged release of autologous GFs, thereby potentially enhancing regenerative outcomes (Li et al. 2021). Consequently, this approach can effectively mitigate the initial uncontrolled and burst release of GFs typically observed with direct PRP applications. The integration of platelet-derived products into biofabrication technologies provides new frontiers in tissue engineering to produce customized platelet-derived scaffolds. This approach enables not only the controlled delivery of platelet-derived bioactive molecules but also the structural stability required for functional tissue regeneration (Del Amo et al. 2021). The biofabrication strategies that enable the blood components to be integrated into functional constructs provide unique control over structural, mechanical, and biological properties, thereby enhancing the therapeutic efficiency of platelet-derived biomaterials. The following sections focus on major biofabrication techniques for PRP/PL-based biomaterial engineering including 3D printing, electrospinning, microgel and microsphere fabrication, and crosslinking. Table 6.1 summarizes the main biofabrication strategies for the development of platelet-derived biomaterials.

Table 6.1 Some biofabrication strategies for PRP/PL-based biomaterials

Biomaterial	Biofabrication method	Outcome	Reference
PL-functionalized GelMA microspheres	Electrostatic microdroplet method	PL-GelMA microspheres promoted endothelial cell responses and angiogenesis in vitro, promising for vascularized regeneration	Zhang et al. (2021)
PL/cellulose nanocrystal scaffold	Crosslinking of aldehyde-modified CNCs with proteins	The cryogel scaffolds exhibited high microporosity, elasticity, and injectability, while enabling controlled release of platelet-derived GFs. They significantly enhanced osteogenic activity without external osteogenic supplements, and also promoted endothelial cell chemotaxis and marker expression, demonstrating pro-angiogenic potential	Ribeiro et al. (2022)
PL/HA-NH_2 scaffold	Crosslinking of proteins and HA-NH_2 via genipin	PL/HA-NH_2 scaffolds had interconnected macroporous structures, wide pore-size distribution, and typical viscoelastic behavior, and supported MSCs attachment, spreading and proliferation	Şeker et al. (2019)
PLMA hydrogel	Layer-by-layer 3D printing	First report of a 3D-printable PLMA bioink: Tunable mechanical properties by irradiation, good cell viability and proliferation in printed constructs	Min et al. (2021)
PGS/PLA/PRP electrospun nanofibers	Electrospinning of PGS/PLA/PRP fibers	The PGS/PLA/PRP electrospun fibers showed high cell viability in fibroblasts, macrophages, and endothelial cells, and promoted cell migration and faster wound closure. Incorporating PRP increased collagen production, reduced pro-inflammatory cytokines and increased anti-inflammatory cytokines and GFs	Heydari et al. (2024)
PRP-based microbeads	Fibrinogen polymerization and ionotropic gelation	MSCs-encapsulated microbeads were accelerated tissue repair, improved myofiber orientation, and reduced fibrosis compared to the control group in a rat VML model	Lalegül-Ülker et al. (2018)
Biomineralized PL/OD scaffold	Crosslinking of PL proteins with OD	Biomineralized PL/OD scaffolds showed mineral accumulation, high porosity, and suitable compressive strength. In vitro studies	Şeker et al. (2024b)

(continued)

Table 6.1 (continued)

Biomaterial	Biofabrication method	Outcome	Reference
		demonstrated that the scaffolds were non-toxic, hemocompatible, and supported human osteoblast attachment, spreading and viability	
PL/GelMA bioink	Extrusion-based bioprinting	The PL/GelMA bioink demonstrated suitable printability, shape fidelity, and tunable mechanical properties that can be matched to native skin tissue. It provided sustained release of bioactive GFs for up to two weeks, supporting high cell viability, good cell attachment, enhanced fibroblast proliferation, and increased ECM synthesis	Daikuara et al. (2021)
PL-rich plasma macroporous hydrogel (PLPMH)	Crosslinking of proteins with Alg using EDC and NHS	The PLPMH scaffold gradually released sphingosine-1-phosphate and proteins to recruit and polarize endogenous macrophages toward the anti-inflammatory M2 phenotype, induced long-term M2 infiltration, creating a local anti-inflammatory microenvironment, reducing inflammation, and enhancing cartilage regeneration in a rabbit defect model	Pan et al. (2021)
PRP/alginate/gelatin bioink	Extrusion-based bioprinting	PRP enhanced fibroblast and stem cell behavior, promoted endothelial tube formation, and modulated macrophage polarization. In in-vivo, PRP-enhanced bioinks accelerated high-quality wound closure, reduced inflammation, and improved angiogenesis compared with standard AG bioinks	Zhao et al. (2022)
hPL-loaded keratin hydrogel	Physical crosslinking	hPL-loaded keratin hydrogels supported cell attachment and proliferation, representing a promising platform for wound healing applications, offering tunable mechanical properties and sustained delivery of pro-regenerative biomolecules	Zuniga et al. (2022)
hPL aerogel	Supercritical fluid-based fabrication	The hPL aerogels exhibited notable mechanical stability, and offered improved handling compared to conventional liquid or	Tibourtine et al. (2024)

(continued)

Table 6.1 (continued)

Biomaterial	Biofabrication method	Outcome	Reference
		gel hPL formulations. The aerogels enabled sustained release of hPL-derived GFs. The released bioactive molecules promoted HUVEC migration, while the aerogels themselves supported fibroblast adhesion and proliferation	
PGS/PCL and PGS/ PGS-PCL nanofibrous membrane containing PRP	Coaxial electrospinning	The incorporation of PRP within the core and PGS within the shell significantly reduced the fiber diameter and the water contact angle, indicating markedly improved hydrophilicity and a more favorable surface for cellular attachment. The integration of PRP into the nanofiber architecture enhanced cell viability, and adhesion.	Shafizadeh et al. (2024)

Abbreviations: *PLMA* methacrylated platelet lysate, *PL* platelet lysate, *PGS* poly glycerol sebacate, *PLA* poly lactic acid, *VML* volumetric muscle loss, *OD* oxidized dextran, *Alg*, Alginate, GFs, growth factors, *ECM* extracellular matrix, *AG* alginate-gelatin, *hPL* human platelet lysate, *HUVEC* human umbilical vein endothelial cell, *PCL* polycaprolactone

6.3.1 3D Bioprinting

The integration of bioprinting technologies with blood plasma derivatives is a promising approach in regenerative medicine and tissue engineering. Recent advances in platelet-derived biomaterials have demonstrated the potential of platelet-based formulations as bioinks for regenerative applications (Ahlfeld et al. 2020). In one study, a transparent and printable human PL-based bioink was developed using fibrinogen and thrombin, resulting in a crosslinked fibrin network enriched with platelet-derived bioactive molecules. The resulting material exhibited excellent optical clarity, tunable viscoelasticity, and high biocompatibility, supporting epithelial cell adhesion and proliferation in corneal tissue models, thus offering a promising substitute for animal-derived or synthetic corneal scaffolds (Frazer et al. 2020). In another study, a biofunctional human-based nanocomposite bioink (HUink) reinforced by cellulose nanocrystals was developed using human PL (hPL) that provided a rich biochemical milieu for stem cell proliferation and differentiation. Cellulose nanocrystals in the bioink provided mechanical strength and stability of printed constructs, ensuring the fabrication of hierarchical, fibrillar 3D structures resembling native ECM (Mendes et al. 2019).

The incorporation of platelet-derived components into bioinks presents both opportunities and technical challenges. While PRP or PL provide a biologically rich milieu, they often lack the rheological properties required for precise extrusion printing. To address this limitation, hybrid formulations have been developed by blending blood derivatives with structural polymers such as alginate, gelatin, hyaluronic acid, or methacrylated gelatin (GelMA). These composites enhance viscosity and shape fidelity while retaining biological functionality. As an example, GelMA has been widely employed as a photo-crosslinkable carrier for PRP incorporation. Lian et al. (2024) developed PRP–GelMA hybrid hydrogels that leverage the mechanical tunability of GelMA and the biological activity of PRP. Upon photo-crosslinking, the composite hydrogels exhibited significantly enhanced compressive modulus and prolonged GF release, supporting endothelial cell network formation and accelerated wound closure in an in vivo model (Lian et al. 2024). A study explored an alginate–gelatin hydrogel system supplemented with PL to enhance the bioactivity of conventional bioinks. The platelet-derived bioactive molecules released from the resulting bioink promoted cell viability, proliferation, and ECM deposition, significantly improving the biological performance of alginate–gelatin scaffolds without compromising printability (Le et al. 2023). A study aimed to incorporate PRP into a GelMA hydrogel to generate a bioink suitable for 3D bioprinting of a structurally defined regenerative scaffold for cutaneous repair. The resulting 3D-bioprinted constructs exhibited structural, rheological, and mechanical characteristics comparable to that of GelMA-only scaffolds. Also, PRP-containing scaffolds enabled a sustained and controlled release of PRP-derived GFs for up to 14 days, and they displayed markedly enhanced angiogenic capacity relative to GelMA controls, without inducing a myofibroblastic phenotype in fibroblasts. This approach provided a means for integrating a patient's autologous GFs into a customized, 3D-bioprinted scaffold directly (Ibanez et al. 2021).

Methacrylated platelet lysate (PLMA) hydrogels exhibit tunable stiffness and crosslinking kinetics, allowing controlled encapsulation of cells and spatial patterning of bioactive cues within bioprinted constructs. In a such study, PLMA was dissolved in phosphate-buffered saline containing a photoinitiator and subsequently photo-crosslinked under ultraviolet irradiation. This process produced a fully human-derived, biomimetic hydrogel (PLMA hydrogel) generated via photopolymerization of PL for the first time. The results indicated that the elastic and structural properties of these hydrogels could be finely tuned by modulating either the concentration of PLMA or the degree of chemical modification (Santos et al. 2018).

Daikuara et al. (2021) developed a 3D-bioprinted dermal substitute using a cost-effective, growth-factor–rich bioink containing PL and GelMA (PLGMA bioink) (Fig. 6.2). The resulting bioink showed good printability, stable structure, and tunable mechanical properties matching native skin. It provided sustained release of biologically active GFs for up to two weeks, supporting cell viability, attachment, and proliferation of dermal fibroblasts. These growth factors also enhanced ECM production over time. The PLGMA bioink demonstrated strong potential for developing effective 3D-bioprinted skin tissue constructs (Daikuara et al. 2021).

In a recent study, a semi-occlusive wound dressing by integrating PRP into a sodium alginate-based hydrogel has been developed through 3D bioprinting to

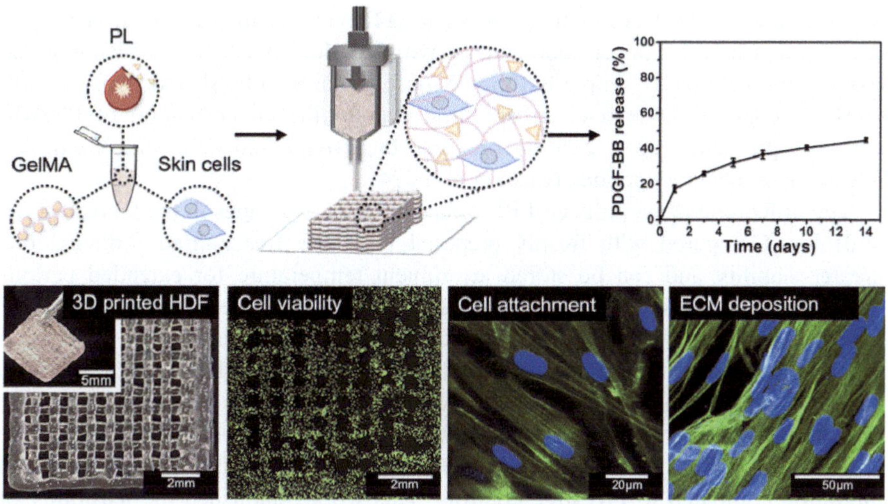

Fig. 6.2 Schematic illustration of the 3D bioprinting of PL-based skin tissue constructs through UV crosslinking. This fabrication process allows for proper cell encapsulation and the direct immobilization of GFs within the 3D-bioprinted construct. (Reprinted with permission from Ref. Daikuara et al. 2021)

ensure homogeneous distribution of bioactive components. The 3D-bioprinted scaffolds were specifically tailored to enhance tissue repair by promoting re-epithelialization, stimulating angiogenic activity, and supporting the remodeling of the ECM. In vivo experiments performed on a murine full-thickness wound model demonstrated that PRP-enriched dressings significantly accelerated wound contraction and epithelial closure, particularly during the early phases of healing. Histological evaluations further revealed an increased presence of capillary-like networks, a transition toward type I collagen predominance, and a reduction in inflammatory responses in PRP-treated wounds, collectively indicating a more advanced and functionally oriented regenerative process. Notably, the integration of PRP within the 3D-bioprinted hydrogel scaffold not only expedited structural repair but also contributed to the reestablishment of physiological skin-barrier integrity (De Almeida Barbosa et al. 2025).

6.3.2 Electrospinning

Electrospinning represents a versatile technique for fabricating nanofibrous scaffolds that mimic the ECM architecture while providing a high surface area for cell adhesion and bioactive molecule delivery. Integrating PRP and PL into electrospun scaffolds combines the mechanical and topographical advantages of nanofibers with the intrinsic regenerative potential of platelet-derived bioactive molecules (Heydari et al. 2024). Several incorporation strategies including direct blending of PRP/PL with polymer solutions, coaxial electrospinning for core–shell encapsulation, surface coating, and hybrid bilayer approaches have been developed. Direct blending and coating are technically simple but may expose proteins to harsh processing conditions. In contrast, coaxial electrospinning enables the encapsulation of PRP/PL within a protective core, helping preserve bioactivity and achieving controlled release over extended periods (Zhao et al. 2024).

The utilization of lyophilized PRP offers several advantages in the fabrication of scaffolds. Compared with freshly prepared PRP, the freeze-dried form exhibits greater stability and can be stored at ambient temperature for extended periods without significant loss of bioactivity. Accordingly, the use of lyophilized PRP may be regarded as an effective approach for the standardization and production of a ready-to-use and storable platelet-derived product (Andia et al. 2020). In a study, lyophilized PRP was incorporated into electrospun poly(ε-caprolactone) (PCL) nanofibers. The results showed that PRP-loaded nanofibers released bioactive proteins for up to 30 days, significantly enhancing fibroblast proliferation and migration compared to PRP-free controls. This work established the feasibility of maintaining GF activity following electrospinning, setting the stage for subsequent biofunctional nanofiber research (Sell et al. 2011). Cheng et al. (2018) employed coaxial electrospinning to encapsulate PRP within silk fibroin/PCL/polyvinyl alcohol core–shell fibers. The results showed sustained VEGF and PDGF release over 14 days and enhanced endothelial cell migration and angiogenic tube formation (Cheng et al. 2018). Cordenonsi et al. (2019) fabricated pullulan/sodium alginate (PUL/SA) electrospun nanofibers loaded with human PL for skin regeneration. Two strategies, incorporation and coating of PL, were performed to produce PL-based nanofiber. The incorporation of PL within the PUL/SA matrix did not markedly alter the morphology of nanofibers before crosslinking. Nevertheless, in the presence of PL, the crosslinking stage resulted in the formation of less sharp fibers due to increased hydrophilicity. In contrast, PL coating on the nanofibers led to a noticeable increase in their average diameter. Both preparation methods influenced the fiber size and elastic behavior of the resulting scaffolds. However, these morphological and mechanical variations had minimal impact on fibroblast attachment and proliferation. In particular, fibroblasts cultured on PL-containing fibers exhibited altered shapes and orientations. This cellular arrangement is indicative of a fibroblast-to-myofibroblast transition, which could contribute to improved wound healing outcomes (Cordenonsi et al. 2019). Likewise, Losi et al. (2020) investigated the wound healing potential of a bilayered fibrin/poly(ether)urethane scaffold incorporating PL fabricated through a combination of electrospinning and the spray phase-inversion technique. In vitro analyses revealed that the bilayered fibrin/poly(ether)urethane scaffold enabled a sustained release of biologically active platelet-derived bioactive molecules. Furthermore, the in vivo efficacy of the scaffold in promoting wound healing was assessed using a diabetic mouse model with full-thickness skin wounds. The results showed that wound closure on day 14 was significantly higher compared to PL-free scaffolds or commercial polyurethane films. Histological examination confirmed increased re-epithelialization and collagen deposition in tissues treated with PL- or GF-loaded scaffolds. These findings demonstrate that the bilayered fibrin/poly(ether)urethane scaffold incorporating PL effectively promoted in vivo wound repair, showed its potential in the clinical management of diabetic ulcers (Losi et al. 2020).

Heydari et al. (2024) investigated electrospun PGS/PLA nanofibers incorporated PRP to assess their potential in promoting in vitro wound healing (Fig. 6.3). The composite scaffold supported strong cell viability in fibroblasts, macrophages, and endothelial cells, and enhanced cell migration in scratch assays, indicating faster wound closure. PRP addition enhanced collagen production compared with PGS/PLA alone and decreased pro-inflammatory cytokines (IL-6, TNF-α) while increasing anti-inflammatory markers (IL-10, TGF-β), promoting an M2 macrophage response. The material also significantly stimulated angiogenesis by forming branching structures and tubular networks (Heydari et al. 2024).

Collectively, these studies demonstrate that electrospinning offers a robust platform for engineering platelet-based biomaterials with tunable bioactivity and mechanical properties. The combination of platelet-derived bioactive molecules with nanofibrous architecture provides a biomimetic environment supportive of tissue regeneration, while variations in polymer chemistry, spinning configuration, and post-processing allow for precise modulation of degradation and GF release profiles. Despite these advances, key challenges remain in maintaining GF stability during electrospinning, optimizing crosslinking to balance mechanical integrity and release kinetics. Also, harsh organic solvents commonly used for synthetic polymers may denature platelet proteins. Addressing these limitations through aqueous electrospinning and coaxial designs may be crucial for translating PRP/PL electrospun scaffolds from experimental prototypes to clinically viable regenerative therapies (Huang et al. 2020).

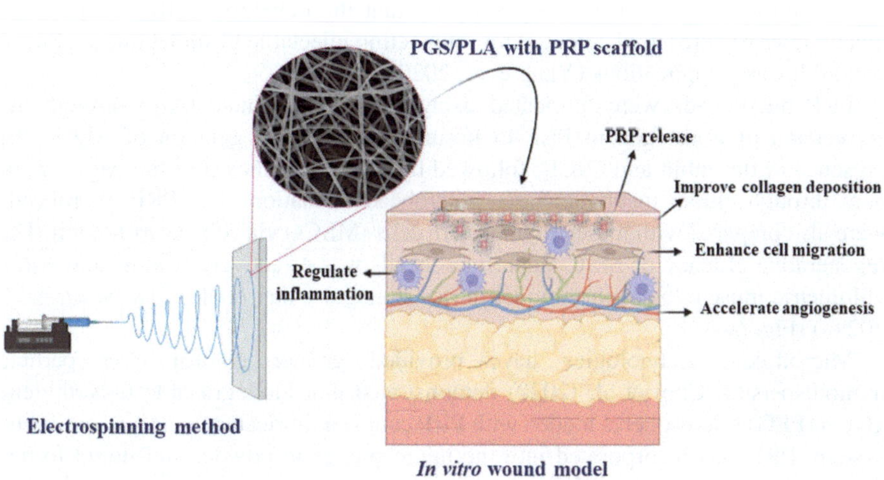

Fig. 6.3 Schematic representation of the fabrication of PGS/PLA-PRP fiber dressing. (Reprinted with permission from Ref. Heydari et al. 2024)

6.3.3 Microgel/Microsphere Fabrication

Studies have explored the incorporation of PRP and PL into microscale delivery platforms, such as microgels and microspheres for controlled release applications. The micron-sized structure of microgels and microspheres provides a large surface area-to-volume ratio and tunable porosity, which together facilitate controlled degradation, adjustable mechanical behavior, and customizable release kinetics of bioactive molecules. Also, the biological benefits of platelet-derived microgels and microspheres typically include sustained GF release, enhanced cellular responses, and improved tissue repair outcomes relative to unencapsulated PRP or PL (Liu et al. 2025). The encapsulation process protects free GFs from proteolytic degradation and thermal denaturation, while the gradual degradation of the polymer matrix ensures prolonged GF release. Moreover, these systems allow for minimally invasive administration through syringes, and their modularity facilitates combination with other scaffold architectures, such as electrospun meshes or molded hydrogels, to construct composite regenerative platforms (Yuan et al. 2024).

The fabrication of platelet-derived microgels and microspheres generally relies on several key strategies such as emulsion-based droplet formation, microfluidic droplet generation, ionotropic gelation, and photocrosslinking within dispersed microdroplets. In emulsion-based systems, aqueous solutions containing PRP or PL are emulsified into oil phases with biopolymers such as gelatin, alginate, or hyaluronic acid, followed by chemical or ionic crosslinking to solidify the droplets into discrete particles. Yang et al. (2020) successfully developed PRP-loaded gelatin microspheres that released platelet-derived bioactive molecules in a sustained manner using an emulsion crosslinking technique. The results demonstrated a prolonged release of VEGF for more than seven days. Furthermore, in vitro assays confirmed that the PRP-loaded microspheres promoted the proliferation and migration of L929 mouse fibroblast cells. This study suggests that the developed PRP-encapsulated gelatin microspheres hold potential for long-acting injectable formulations in clinical wound-healing applications (Yang et al. 2020).

PRP microbeads were fabricated using PRP and alginate (Alg) through the conversion of fibrinogen in PRP to fibrin and ionotropic gelation of Alg in the presence of thrombin and $CaCl_2$, followed by selective removal of the Alg component through citrate incubation after microbead formation. The PRP microbeads were also prepared with mesenchymal stem cells (MSCs) via cell encapsulation. The regenerative efficacy of MSC-laden microbeads was effectively demonstrated in a volumetric muscle loss injury model in rats (Lalegül-Ülker et al. 2018; Şeker et al. 2024a) (Fig. 6.4).

Microfluidic technologies have provided greater control over particle monodispersity. Choi et al. (2020) demonstrated that biodegradable polyethylene glycol (PEG) microspheres loaded with PRP could be fabricated using a microfluidic system. PRP was incorporated into the microspheres in powder and liquid forms. The resulting PRP-loaded PEG microspheres were systematically characterized in terms of their swelling behavior, mechanical modulus, degradation rate, and protein

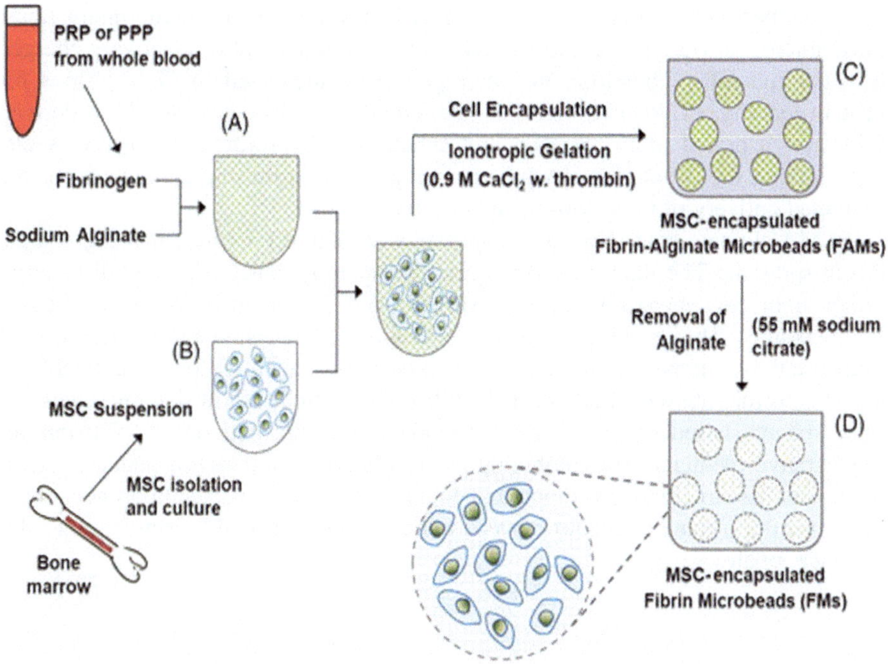

Fig. 6.4 Schematic illustration of the experimental steps of encapsulation of cells in PRP-derived microbeads. (Reprinted with permission from Ref. Lalegül-Ülker et al. 2018)

release profile as a function of PRP content and preparation method. Incorporation of powder PRP notably altered the physicochemical properties of the microspheres, with the most pronounced impact observed on their degradation behavior. Further analysis revealed that platelet aggregation and clot formation at the powder PRP formulation contributed to the altered microsphere degradation kinetics. The microfluidic PEG microsphere platform provided a promising delivery system for controlled PRP release, with potential applications in enhancing tissue regeneration, promoting wound healing, and mitigating tissue degeneration associated with osteoarthritis or intervertebral disc disease (Choi et al. 2020). Similarly, Mendes et al. (2020) fabricated PL-based microgels using microfluidic system with on-chip mixing of PL and norbornene-modified HA (NorHA) followed by photocrosslinking. The resulting PL-NorHA microgels had a hierarchical fibrillar network that facilitated sustained delivery of PL-derived proteins. PL in the PL-NorHA microgels further improved cellular interactions with the microgel network. Overall, the incorporation of PL-derived biomolecules promoted the bioactivity of the hydrogels, enabling the creation of dynamic, modular systems (Mendes et al. 2020).

Jooybar et al. (2019) developed hyaluronic acid (HA)-based microgels using a water-in-oil emulsion method. First, HA was functionalized with tyramine groups, and the resulting microdroplets were enzymatically crosslinked in the presence of hydrogen peroxide and horseradish peroxidase. Owing to electrostatic interactions, these microgels were particularly suitable for the entrapment of positively charged proteins and GFs. Therefore, the microgels were incubated in PL solutions for protein loading. PL-loaded microgels exhibited a sustained release of PL-derived GFs over a period of two weeks, and enhanced cell proliferation. These results indicate that the developed HA-based microgels are promising candidates for the sustained delivery of GFs (Jooybar et al. 2019).

PLMA/alginate core-shell microcapsules were initially fabricated using coaxial electrospraying. The microcapsules were subsequently collected, exposed to ultraviolet light for photocrosslinking, washed, and freeze-dried to obtain PLMA microsponges. The resulting microsponges supported adhesion and proliferation of human adipose-derived stem cells and demonstrated potential for the assembly of autologous microtissues (Ladeira et al. 2022). These studies show that microgels and microspheres based on PL or PRP provide a versatile and potent platform for regenerative medicine. By combining the biochemical richness of platelet derivatives with the structural and functional adaptability of micro-scale hydrogels, these systems offer a route to enable sustained, localized delivery of bioactive molecules in tissue repair.

6.3.4 Crosslinking

Despite their potent bioactivity, PRP and PL have some drawbacks such as weak mechanical stability, rapid degradation, and uncontrolled release of bioactive molecules, which limit their use as tissue scaffold. To address these limitations, the design of PRP- or PL-based tissue scaffolds using crosslinking has emerged as a promising strategy in biomaterial applications. Diverse crosslinking strategies have been developed to stabilize PRP/PL-based scaffold, regulate their degradation kinetics, and enable their incorporation into tissue-engineered scaffolds or injectable hydrogel systems. This approach enables local stabilization of proteins through the crosslinking within PRP/PL, thereby forming a PRP/PL-based scaffold. Through this method, PRP can simultaneously serve as both a structural scaffold material and an autologous source of GFs. Although studies on this approach are limited and very recent, it represents a potentially innovative pathway for the fabrication of PRP/PL-based scaffolds (Şeker et al. 2025).

Chemical crosslinking provides covalent stabilization of PL-based scaffolds through reactions between reactive amino, carboxyl, or hydroxyl groups in plasma proteins. An example of this strategy involves the development of an imine crosslinked, photo-crosslinkable hydrogel composed of o-nitrobenzyl alcohol (NB)-modified hyaluronic acid (HA-NB) and PRP. Upon light exposure, the reaction between aldehyde groups on HA-NB and amino groups of PRP proteins resulted in the formation of a PRP-based hydrogel on the tissue surface. The results revealed that photo-crosslinkable PRP hydrogel provided sustained and controlled release of

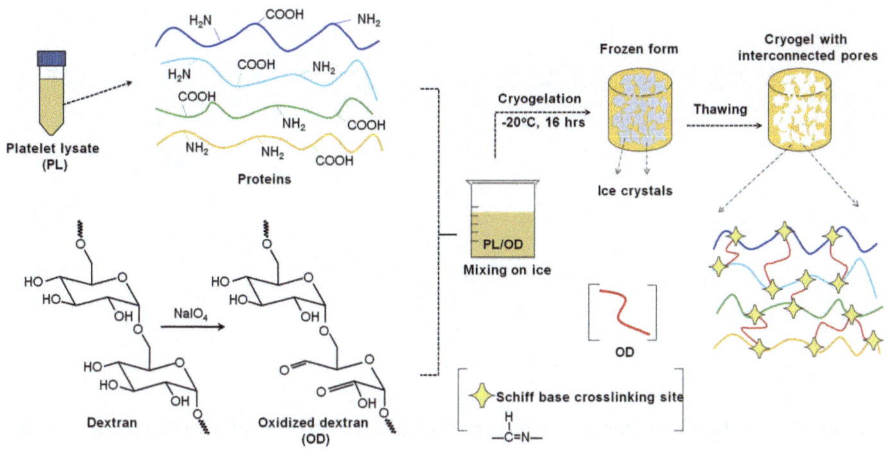

Fig. 6.5 Schematic illustration of preparation of macroporous PL/OD cryogels. (Reprinted with permission from Ref. Şeker et al. 2020)

GFs while demonstrating significantly enhanced adhesive strength to native cartilage tissue (Liu et al. 2017).

Another study developed the approach of crosslinking PL proteins with oxidized dextran (OD) to develop PL/OD cryogel scaffolds (Fig. 6.5). These PL-derived cryogels were fabricated by crosslinking between the amino groups of PL proteins and the aldehyde groups of OD. The findings indicated that the PL-derived cryogels showed an optimal microenvironment for human adipose stem cells. Furthermore, the PL/OD cryogel scaffolds underwent complete degradation within 90–240 days following subcutaneous implantation in rats, depending on the degree of OD crosslinking (Şeker et al. 2020). Successful biomineralization of PL/OD cryogels was also performed, and their potential as autologous bioactive scaffolds for bone tissue engineering was also demonstrated (Şeker et al. 2024b).

PL-derived cryogel scaffolds were prepared using aldehyde-modified cellulose nanocrystals, and biomineralized cellulose nanocrystals. This approach was designed to emulate the protein–mineral composite architecture of native bone ECM while capitalizing on the inherent bioactivity of platelet-derived GFs and cytokines. The resulting nanocomposite scaffolds exhibited high microporosity, elasticity, and excellent biocompatibility. Moreover, these scaffolds induced osteogenic differentiation of human adipose stem cells (hASCs) in the absence of osteogenic supplements, promoted endothelial cell chemotaxis, and demonstrated strong proangiogenic potential. The findings indicated that the mineralized cellulose nanocrystal-reinforced PL cryogel scaffolds can synergistically stimulate osteogenesis and angiogenesis, thereby representing a promising biomimetic platform for enhanced bone tissue regeneration (Ribeiro et al. 2022).

Genipin has been extensively used in biomaterials research and drug delivery fields as a natural crosslinking agent due to its remarkable biocompatibility and biodegradability, which can react with amine groups in protein backbones. Şeker

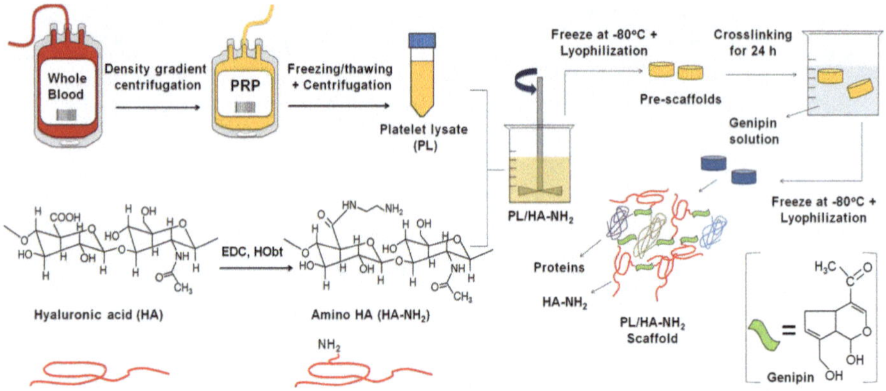

Fig. 6.6 Schematic illustration of the preparation of PL/HA-NH_2 scaffold. (Reprinted with permission from Ref. Şeker et al. 2019)

et al. (2019) fabricated a PL-derived scaffold composed of PL, amino-functionalized hyaluronic acid (HA–NH_2), and genipin (Fig. 6.6). The PL/HA–NH_2 scaffolds were fabricated by crosslinking the free primary amine groups of HA–NH_2 and PL proteins via genipin. The resulting PL/HA–NH_2 constructs supported MSC adhesion, spreading, and proliferation, indicating their potential as promising candidates for autologous tissue engineering applications (Şeker et al. 2019).

Min et al. (2021) developed PLMA hydrogels for 3D printing capable of rapid photo-crosslinking under UV light exposure. The resulting PLMA hydrogels exhibited controllable stiffness and degradation rates depending on UV exposure time and polymer concentration (Min et al. 2021). On the other hand, physical and ionic crosslinking strategies have also been exploited to generate PRP/PL-containing hydrogels that are easily processable and injectable. García-Orúe et al. (2022) demonstrated that oxidized alginate crosslinked with calcium ions could effectively entrap PRP, forming an injectable, shear-thinning hydrogel system. The composite showed gradual release of PDGF over several days, stimulating fibroblast migration and angiogenesis in vitro and in vivo (Garcia-Orue et al. 2022).

6.4 Current Limitations

Despite the therapeutic potential of PRP, its standardization remains challenging due to variability in preparation and activation methods. The clinical outcomes of PRP applications are basically dependent on the platelet concentration, as well as the levels and types of bioactive molecules that are central to key biological events such as cell proliferation, differentiation, chemotaxis, and tissue remodeling. However, the absence of a universally accepted protocol for PRP preparation and application method results in significant inconsistencies in clinical efficacy. This methodological diversity hampers the ability to compare studies and reproduce results, which has led to inconsistent findings across different investigations. Furthermore, depending on the preparation protocol, PRP may contain varying amounts of residual red blood cells and leukocytes, as well as occasionally small numbers of stem cells. These cellular components can vary across PRP samples, which is another factor that causes variation in PRP samples (Şeker et al. 2025).

Technical factors in centrifugation process such as rotor type, centrifuge type, speed, duration, and processing temperature are critical determinants of PRP composition. For instance, prolonged centrifugation may slightly enhance platelet recovery but simultaneously reduce leukocyte content in the plasma layer. Alternatively, low-temperature processing may suppress platelet activation and improve cellular viability, leading to considerable inter-batch variability in PRP formulations.

In addition to technical variables, donor-specific characteristics significantly influence PRP quality. Some factors such as the donor's age, gender, health, and physiological condition may impact the initial platelet concentration in the blood, and thereby affect the final GF and cytokine levels in the PRP products. Moreover, the method used to activate platelets may influence the duration of GF release. These differences may impact the regenerative capacity of PRP in clinical applications.

On the other hand, the degree and mechanism of crosslinking have profound effects on the biological performance of PRP/PL-based scaffolds. Increased crosslinking density typically enhances mechanical stiffness and reduces degradation, but may simultaneously restrict nutrient and waste diffusion and cell infiltration. Moderate crosslinking levels have been shown to maximize both structural integrity and cellular function (Şeker et al. 2020). Moreover, crosslinking may influence the release kinetics of platelet-derived bioactive molecules. Denser networks slow the diffusion of macromolecules, enabling sustained bioactivity over days or weeks. This sustained delivery is particularly advantageous for applications such as chronic wound healing or bone regeneration, where prolonged stimulation is required for tissue remodeling (Tsai et al. 2021).

6.5 Conclusions and Future Directions

To conclude, findings from early-stage clinical trials suggest that PRP and PL offer a safe and easily accessible source of autologous GFs. Given the inconsistencies in PRP formulations, developing novel preparation techniques that preserve the functionality of bioactive molecules would be advantageous in overcoming these limitations. As an alternative strategy, pooling PRP from multiple donors to reduce inter-individual variability or adopting standardized commercial hPL might improve consistency. However, such an approach would compromise the autologous nature of these therapies. The inconsistencies observed among PRP-based studies can potentially be resolved through systematic, high-throughput screening and advanced analytical characterization of PRP compositions. In this context, in-depth proteomic analysis of platelet-derived blood products could provide valuable insight, leading to more predictable and clinically effective outcomes. Therefore, future studies should prioritize well-structured, comprehensive investigations to determine the true clinical relevance and reliability of PRP-based therapies (Şeker et al. 2025).

From a biomaterial perspective, the absence of standardization in PRP content directly affects the reproducibility and quality of PRP-based tissue engineering scaffolds. Differences in scaffold characteristics such as degradation rate, porosity, and GF release dynamics may arise from this variability. It is well established that material-specific parameters like stiffness, biodegradability, pore size, and biological activity can influence the release behavior of GFs. As such, it is important to clearly report platelet concentration, GF composition and GF release profiles to improve reproducibility and facilitate comparisons across studies. Likewise, balancing mechanical performance with bioactivity remains a key design challenge. Over-crosslinking may reduce GF bioactivity or hinder cell-matrix interactions, while under-crosslinking may lead to early degradation. Despite current challenges, PRP and PL continue to show great potential as a personalized, autologous sources in the fabrication of scaffolds for tissue engineering and regenerative medicine.

Competing Interests Y.M.E. is the founder and shareholder of Biovalda Health Technologies, Inc. (Ankara, Türkiye). The authors have patent applications in relation to regenerative biomaterials. The authors declare no competing financial interests in relation to this particular article.

References

Ahlfeld T, Cubo-Mateo N, Cometta S, Guduric V, Vater C, Bernhardt A, Akkineni AR, Lode A, Gelinsky M (2020) A novel plasma-based BioINK stimulates cell proliferation and differentiation in bioprinted, mineralized constructs. ACS Appl Mater Interfaces 12(11):12557–12572. https://doi.org/10.1021/acsami.0c00710

Andia I, Perez-Valle A, Del Amo C, Maffulli N (2020) Freeze-drying of platelet-rich plasma: the quest for standardization. Int J Mol Sci 21(18):6904. https://doi.org/10.3390/ijms21186904

Anerillas LO, Wiberg M, Kingham PJ, Kelk P (2023) Platelet lysate for expansion or osteogenic differentiation of bone marrow mesenchymal stem cells for 3D tissue constructs. Regen Ther 24: 298–310. https://doi.org/10.1016/j.reth.2023.07.011

Buzalaf M a R, Levy FM (2022) Autologous platelet concentrates for facial rejuvenation. J Appl Oral Sci 30:e20220020. https://doi.org/10.1590/1678-7757-2022-0020

Cheng G, Ma X, Li J, Cheng Y, Cao Y, Wang Z, Shi X, Du Y, Deng H, Li Z (2018) Incorporating platelet-rich plasma into coaxial electrospun nanofibers for bone tissue engineering. Int J Pharm 547(1–2):656–666. https://doi.org/10.1016/j.ijpharm.2018.06.020

Choi MH, Blanco A, Stealey S, Duan X, Case N, Sell SA, Rai MF, Zustiak SP (2020) Microclotting of platelet-rich plasma upon loading in hydrogel microspheres leads to prolonged protein release and slower microsphere degradation. Polymers 12(8):1712. https://doi.org/10.3390/polym12081712

Cordenonsi LM, Faccendini A, Rossi S, Bonferoni MC, Malavasi L, Raffin R, Schapoval EES, Del Fante C, Vigani B, Miele D, Sandri G, Ferrari F (2019) Platelet lysate loaded electrospun scaffolds: effect of nanofiber types on wound healing. Eur J Pharm Biopharm 142:247–257. https://doi.org/10.1016/j.ejpb.2019.06.030

Da Fonseca L, Santos GS, Huber SC, Setti TM, Setti T, Lana JF (2021) Human platelet lysate—a potent (and overlooked) orthobiologic. J Clin Orthop Trauma 21:101534. https://doi.org/10.1016/j.jcot.2021.101534

Daikuara LY, Yue Z, Skropeta D, Wallace GG (2021) In vitro characterisation of 3D printed platelet lysate-based bioink for potential application in skin tissue engineering. Acta Biomater 123:286–297. https://doi.org/10.1016/j.actbio.2021.01.021

De Almeida Barbosa C, Gamba LK, Simeoni RB, Kocha MFV, Cardoso MA, Cunha RC, Guarita-Souza LC, Francisco JC, Fernandes BL (2025) Advanced 3D-printed hydrogel dressings incorporating platelet-rich plasma for accelerated skin repair. Tissue Barriers:2537992. https://doi.org/10.1080/21688370.2025.2537992

Del Amo C, Andia I (2023) Blood-derived biomaterials for tissue graft biofabrication by solvent-based extrusion bioprinting. Int J Bioprinting 9(5):762. https://doi.org/10.18063/ijb.762

Del Amo C, Perez-Valle A, Perez-Garrastachu M, Jauregui I, Andollo N, Arluzea J, Guerrero P, De La Caba K, Andia I (2021) Plasma-based bioInKs for extrusion bioprinting of advanced dressings. Biomedicine 9(8):1023. https://doi.org/10.3390/biomedicines9081023

Fang J, Wang X, Jiang W, Zhu Y, Hu Y, Zhao Y, Song X, Zhao J, Zhang W, Peng J, Wang Y (2020) Platelet-rich plasma therapy in the treatment of diseases associated with orthopedic injuries. Tissue EngPart B Rev 26(6):571–585. https://doi.org/10.1089/ten.teb.2019.0292

Frazer H, You J, Chen Z, Sayyar S, Liu X, Taylor A, Hodge C, Wallace G, Sutton G (2020) Development of a platelet Lysate–based printable, transparent biomaterial with regenerative potential for epithelial corneal injuries. Transl Vis Sci Technol 9(13):40. https://doi.org/10.1167/tvst.9.13.40

Garcia-Orue I, Santos-Vizcaino E, Sanchez P, Gutierrez FB, Aguirre JJ, Hernandez RM, Igartua M (2022) Bioactive and degradable hydrogel based on human platelet-rich plasma fibrin matrix combined with oxidized alginate in a diabetic mice wound healing model. Biomater Adv 135: 112695. https://doi.org/10.1016/j.msec.2022.112695

Harley WS, Li CC, Toombs J, O'Connell CD, Taylor HK, Heath DE, Collins DJ (2021) Advances in biofabrication techniques towards functional bioprinted heterogeneous engineered tissues: a comprehensive review. Bioprinting 23:e00147. https://doi.org/10.1016/j.bprint.2021.e00147

He M, Chen T, Lv Y, Song P, Deng B, Guo X, Rui S, Boey J, Armstrong DG, Ma Y, Deng W (2022) The role of allogeneic platelet-rich plasma in patients with diabetic foot ulcer: current perspectives and future challenges. Front Bioeng Biotechnol 10:993436. https://doi.org/10.3389/fbioe.2022.993436

Heydari P, Kharazi AZ, Shariati L (2024) Enhanced wound regeneration by PGS/PLA fiber dressing containing platelet-rich plasma: an in vitro study. Sci Rep 14(1):12019. https://doi.org/10.1038/s41598-024-62855-w

Huang Z, Wang W, Wang Q, Hojnacki T, Wang Y, Fu Y, Wang W (2020) Coaxial nanofiber scaffold with super-active platelet lysate to accelerate the repair of bone defects. RSC Adv 10(59):35776–35786. https://doi.org/10.1039/d0ra06305c

Ibanez RIR, Amaral RJFCD, Simpson CR, Casey SM, Reis RL, Marques AP, Murphy CM, O'Brien FJ (2021) 3D printed scaffolds incorporated with platelet-rich plasma show enhanced Angiogenic potential while not inducing fibrosis. Adv Funct Mater 32(10). https://doi.org/10.1002/adfm.202109915

Jooybar E, Abdekhodaie MJ, Karperien M, Mousavi A, Alvi M, Dijkstra PJ (2019) Developing hyaluronic acid microgels for sustained delivery of platelet lysate for tissue engineering applications. Int J Biol Macromol 144:837–846. https://doi.org/10.1016/j.ijbiomac.2019.10.036

Ladeira BM, Gomes MC, Custódio CA, Mano JF (2022) High-throughput production of microsponges from platelet lysate for tissue engineering applications. Tissue Eng Part C Methods 28(7):325–334. https://doi.org/10.1089/ten.tec.2022.0029

Lalegül-Ülker Ö, Şeker Ş, Elçin AE, Elçin YM (2018) Encapsulation of bone marrow-MSCs in PRP-derived fibrin microbeads and preliminary evaluation in a volumetric muscle loss injury rat

model: modular muscle tissue engineering. Artif Cells Nanomed Biotechnol 47(1):10–21. https://doi.org/10.1080/21691401.2018.1540426
Le TTV, Phan NTH, Tran HLB (2023) Alginate–gelatin hydrogel supplemented with platelet concentrates can be used as bioinks for scaffold printing. Asian Biomed 17(5):222–229. https://doi.org/10.2478/abm-2023-0063
Li J, Wang K, Bai X, Wang Q, Lv N, Li Z (2021) Enhanced regeneration of bone defects using sintered porous Ti6Al4V scaffolds incorporated with mesenchymal stem cells and platelet-rich plasma. RSC Adv 11(9):5128–5138. https://doi.org/10.1039/d0ra10215f
Li S, Dan X, Chen H, Li T, Liu B, Ju Y, Li Y, Lei L, Fan X (2024) Developing fibrin-based biomaterials/scaffolds in tissue engineering. Bioact Mater 40:597–623. https://doi.org/10.1016/j.bioactmat.2024.08.006
Lian S, Mu Z, Yuan Z, Shafiq M, Mo X, Mu W (2024) Methacrylated gelatin and platelet-rich plasma based hydrogels promote regeneration of critical-sized bone defects. Regen Biomater 11:rbae022. https://doi.org/10.1093/rb/rbae022
Liebig BE, Kisiday JD, Bahney CS, Ehrhart NP, Goodrich LR (2020) The platelet-rich plasma and mesenchymal stem cell milieu: a review of therapeutic effects on bone healing. J Orthop Res 38(12):2539–2550. https://doi.org/10.1002/jor.24786
Liu X, Yang Y, Niu X, Lin Q, Zhao B, Wang Y, Zhu L (2017) An in situ photocrosslinkable platelet rich plasma—complexed hydrogel glue with growth factor controlled release ability to promote cartilage defect repair. Acta Biomater 62:179–187. https://doi.org/10.1016/j.actbio.2017.05.023
Liu M, Ding J, Peng Y, Fang J, Zhao M, Zhang W, Chen H, Zhang J, Peng H, Wang Q (2025) Platelet-rich plasma-contained drug delivery systems to treat orthopedic injuries. Int J Pharm X 10:100372. https://doi.org/10.1016/j.ijpx.2025.100372
Losi P, Kayal TA, Buscemi M, Foffa I, Cavallo A, Soldani G (2020) Bilayered fibrin-based electrospun-sprayed scaffold loaded with platelet lysate enhances wound healing in a diabetic mouse model. Nano 10(11):2128. https://doi.org/10.3390/nano10112128
Masoudi EA, Ribas J, Kaushik G, Leijten J, Khademhosseini A (2016) Platelet-rich blood derivatives for stem cell-based tissue engineering and regeneration. Curr Stem Cell Rep 2(1):33–42. https://doi.org/10.1007/s40778-016-0034-8
Mendes BB, Gómez-Florit M, Hamilton AG, Detamore MS, Domingues RMA, Reis RL, Gomes ME (2019) Human platelet lysate-based nanocomposite bioink for bioprinting hierarchical fibrillar structures. Biofabrication 12(1):015012. https://doi.org/10.1088/1758-5090/ab33e8
Mendes BB, Daly AC, Reis RL, Domingues RM, Gomes ME, Burdick JA (2020) Injectable hyaluronic acid and platelet lysate-derived granular hydrogels for biomedical applications. Acta Biomater 119:101–113. https://doi.org/10.1016/j.actbio.2020.10.040
Min SJ, Lee JS, Nah H, Kim SH, Moon H, Reis RL, Kwon IK, Heo DN (2021) Development of photo-crosslinkable platelet lysate-based hydrogels for 3D printing and tissue engineering. Biofabrication 13(4):044102. https://doi.org/10.1088/1758-5090/ac1993
Pan X, Yuan S, Xun X, Fan Z, Xue X, Zhang C, Wang J, Deng J (2021) Long-term recruitment of endogenous M2 macrophages by platelet lysate-rich plasma macroporous hydrogel scaffold for articular cartilage defect repair. Adv Healthc Mater 11(6):e2101661. https://doi.org/10.1002/adhm.202101661
Popescu MN, Iliescu MG, Beiu C, Popa LG, Mihai MM, Berteanu M, Ionescu AM (2021) Autologous platelet-rich plasma efficacy in the field of regenerative medicine: product and quality control. Biomed Res Int 2021(1):4672959. https://doi.org/10.1155/2021/4672959
Pötter N, Westbrock F, Grad S, Alini M, Stoddart MJ, Schmal H, Kubosch D, Salzmann G, Kubosch EJ (2021) Evaluation of the influence of platelet-rich plasma (PRP), platelet lysate (PL) and mechanical loading on chondrogenesis in vitro. Sci Rep 11(1):20188. https://doi.org/10.1038/s41598-021-99614-0
Rath M, Spinnen J, Kuhrt LD, Priglinger E, Seika P, Runge D, Schubring S, Laue D, Wickert M, Erdem M, Ertel W, Shopperly LK (2025) Platelet-rich plasma a comprehensive review of isolation, activation, and application. Acta Biomater 204:52–75. https://doi.org/10.1016/j.actbio.2025.07.050

Ren S, Wang H, Ma S, Zhou J, Zhai J, Zhu Y, Chen S, Chen S, Jia K, Xu W, Zhou Y (2023) New strategy of personalized tissue regeneration: when autologous platelet concentrates encounter biomaterials. Front Bioeng Biotechnol 11:1297357. https://doi.org/10.3389/fbioe.2023.1297357

Ribeiro JP, Domingues RM, Babo PS, Nogueira LP, Reseland JE, Reis RL, Gomez-Florit M, Gomes ME (2022) Highly elastic and bioactive bone biomimetic scaffolds based on platelet lysate and biomineralized cellulose nanocrystals. Carbohydr Polym 292:119638. https://doi.org/10.1016/j.carbpol.2022.119638

Sánchez M, Ruiz JM, Pinel DM, Sánchez P, Fiz N, Guadilla J, Azofra J, Beitia M, Delgado D (2025) Increasing the concentration of plasma molecules improves the biological activity of platelet-rich plasma for tissue regeneration. Sci Rep 15(1):4523. https://doi.org/10.1038/s41598-025-88918-0

Santos SC, Custódio CA, Mano JF (2018) Photopolymerizable platelet lysate hydrogels for customizable 3D cell culture platforms. Adv Healthc Mater 7(23):e1800849. https://doi.org/10.1002/adhm.201800849

Santos RGD, Santos GS, Alkass N, Chiesa TL, Azzini GO, Da Fonseca LF, Santos AFD, Rodrigues BL, Mosaner T, Lana JF (2021) The regenerative mechanisms of platelet-rich plasma: a review. Cytokine 144:155560. https://doi.org/10.1016/j.cyto.2021.155560

Şeker Ş, Elçin YM (2024) Albumin-capped gold nanocluster-integrated human albumin scaffolds: a traceable, xeno-free and customizable template for autogenic tissue engineering applications. Process Biochem 143:256–265. https://doi.org/10.1016/j.procbio.2024.05.004

Şeker Ş, Elçin AE, Elçin YM (2019) Autologous protein-based scaffold composed of platelet lysate and aminated hyaluronic acid. J Mater Sci Mater Med 30(12):127. https://doi.org/10.1007/s10856-019-6334-7

Şeker Ş, Elçin AE, Elçin YM (2020) Macroporous elastic cryogels based on platelet lysate and oxidized dextran as tissue engineering scaffold: in vitro and in vivo evaluations. Mater Sci Eng C 110:110703. https://doi.org/10.1016/j.msec.2020.110703

Şeker Ş, Lalegül-Ülker Ö, Elçin AE, Elçin YM (2024a) Regeneration of volumetric muscle loss using MSCs encapsulated in PRP-derived fibrin microbeads. Methods Mol Biol 2939:221–230. https://doi.org/10.1007/7651_2024_533

Şeker Ş, Aral D, Elçin AE, Murat EY (2024b) Biomimetic mineralization of platelet lysate/oxidized dextran cryogel as a macroporous 3D composite scaffold for bone repair. Biomed Mater 19(2):025006. https://doi.org/10.1088/1748-605x/ad1c9a

Şeker Ş, Elçin AE, Elçin YM (2025) Current trends in the design and fabrication of PRP-based scaffolds for tissue engineering and regenerative medicine. Biomed Mater 20(2):022001. https://doi.org/10.1088/1748-605x/ada83f

Sell SA, Wolfe PS, Ericksen JJ, Simpson DG, Bowlin GL (2011) Incorporating platelet-rich plasma into electrospun scaffolds for tissue engineering applications. Tissue Eng A 17(21–22):2723–2737. https://doi.org/10.1089/ten.tea.2010.0663

Shafizadeh S, Heydari P, Kharazi AZ, Shariati L (2024) Coaxial electrospun PGS/PCL and PGS/PGS-PCL nanofibrous membrane containing platelet-rich plasma for skin tissue engineering. J Biomater Sci Polym Ed 35(4):482–500. https://doi.org/10.1080/09205063.2023.2299073

Shome S, Kodieswaran M, Dadheech R, Chevella M, Sensharma S, Awasthi S, Bandyopadhyay A, Mandal BB (2023) Recent advances in platelet-rich plasma and its derivatives: therapeutic agents for tissue engineering and regenerative medicine. Prog. Biomed. Eng. 6(1):012004. https://doi.org/10.1088/2516-1091/ad1338

Soares CS, Babo PS, Reis RL, Carvalho PP, Gomes ME (2020) Platelet-derived products in veterinary medicine: a new trend or an effective therapy? Trends Biotechnol 39(3):225–243. https://doi.org/10.1016/j.tibtech.2020.07.011

Tibourtine F, Canceill T, Marfoglia A, Lavalle P, Gibot L, Pilloux L, Aubry C, Medemblik C, Goudouneche D, Dupret-Bories A, Cazalbou S (2024) Advanced platelet lysate aerogels: biomaterials for regenerative applications. J Funct Biomater 15(2):49. https://doi.org/10.3390/jfb15020049

Tsai C, Young T, Chen G, Cheng N (2021) Developing a Glyoxal-Crosslinked chitosan/gelatin hydrogel for sustained release of human platelet lysate to promote tissue regeneration. Int J Mol Sci 22(12):6451. https://doi.org/10.3390/ijms22126451

Valtetsiotis, K., Di Martino, A., Brunello, M., D'Agostino, C., Poluzzi, R., Ferri, R., Mora, P., Traina, F., & Faldini, C. (2024). Platelet lysate for the treatment of osteoarthritis: a systematic review of preclinical and clinical studies. Musculoskelet Surg, 108(3), 275–288. doi: https://doi.org/10.1007/s12306-024-00827-z

Vyas C, Mishbak H, Cooper G, Peach C, Pereira RF, Bartolo P (2020) Biological perspectives and current biofabrication strategies in osteochondral tissue engineering. Biomanuf Rev 5(1). https://doi.org/10.1007/s40898-020-00008-y

Wu S, Guo W, Li R, Zhang X, Qu W (2022) Progress of platelet derivatives for cartilage tissue engineering. Front Bioeng Biotechnol 10:907356. https://doi.org/10.3389/fbioe.2022.907356

Xue Y, Su X, Jiang M, Yu Z, Yang H, Qin L, Giannoudis PV, Guo JJ (2020) Pure platelet-rich plasma facilitates the repair of damaged cartilage and synovium in a rabbit hemorrhagic arthritis knee model. Arthritis Res Ther 22(1):68. https://doi.org/10.1186/s13075-020-02155-6

Yang J, Zhou M, Li W, Lin F, Shan G (2020) Preparation and evaluation of sustained release platelet-rich plasma-loaded gelatin microspheres using an emulsion method. ACS Omega 5(42): 27113–27118. https://doi.org/10.1021/acsomega.0c02543

Yuan G, Yu C, Du X, Li D, Dou H, Lu P, Wu T, Hao C, Wang Y (2024) Injectable GelMA hydrogel microspheres with sustained release of platelet-rich plasma for the treatment of thin endometrium. Small 20(47):e2403890. https://doi.org/10.1002/smll.202403890

Zhang Q, Yang T, Zhang R, Liang X, Wang G, Tian Y, Xie L, Tian W (2021) Platelet lysate functionalized gelatin methacrylate microspheres for improving angiogenesis in endodontic regeneration. Acta Biomater 136:441–455. https://doi.org/10.1016/j.actbio.2021.09.024

Zhang Y, Wang Z, Deng Z, Wang Z, Song F, Zhu L (2022) Emerging delivery strategies of platelet-rich plasma with hydrogels for wound healing. Adv Polym Technol 2022:1–11. https://doi.org/10.1155/2022/5446291

Zhang G, Song Y, Zhuang T, Zhao Y, Pan Z, Pan Z (2025) Clinical application and research progress of platelet-rich plasma. Hematology 30(1):2549159. https://doi.org/10.1080/16078454.2025.2549159

Zhao M, Wang J, Zhang J, Huang J, Luo L, Yang Y, Shen K, Jiao T, Jia Y, Lian W, Li J, Wang Y, Lian Q, Hu D (2022) Functionalizing multi-component bioink with platelet-rich plasma for customized in-situ bilayer bioprinting for wound healing. Mater Today Bio 16:100334. https://doi.org/10.1016/j.mtbio.2022.100334

Zhao J, Chen L, Ma A, Bai X, Zeng Y, Liu D, Liu B, Zhang W, Tang S (2024) Recent advances in coaxial electrospun nanofibers for wound healing. Mater Today Bio 29:101309. https://doi.org/10.1016/j.mtbio.2024.101309

Zhou J, Liu Y, Liu X, Wan J, Zuo S, Pan T, Liu Y, Sun F, Gao M, Yu X, Zhou W, Xu J, Zhou Z, Wang S (2023) Hyaluronic acid-based dual network hydrogel with sustained release of platelet-rich plasma as a diabetic wound dressing. Carbohydr Polym 314:120924. https://doi.org/10.1016/j.carbpol.2023.120924

Zuniga K, Isaac A, Christy S, Wrice N, Mangum L, Natesan S, Burnett L, Christy R, Kowalczewski C (2022) Characterization of a human platelet lysate-loaded keratin hydrogel for wound healing applications in vitro. Int J Mol Sci 23(8):4100. https://doi.org/10.3390/ijms23084100

Chapter 7
Biofabrication Strategies for Neovascularization: Focusing on Lower Extremity Peripheral Arterial Disease

Selçuk Öztürk, Ayşe Eser Elçin, and Yaşar Murat Elçin

Abstract The establishment of a mature and functional vascular network through neovascularization is essential for delivering adequate oxygen and nutrients to sustain tissue viability and long-term integration. This represents a fundamental prerequisite for the treatment of lower extremity peripheral arterial disease (LE-PAD), as well as for broader regenerative medicine applications, including tissue and organ engineering. Neovascularization in LE-PAD remains challenging, particularly with conventional medical and surgical treatments, and regenerative medicine approaches, including stem cell-based therapies, growth factor delivery, and biomaterial platforms, have thus far shown limited clinical efficacy. Biofabrication-based strategies, including three-dimensional bioprinting, electrospinning, decellularized scaffolds, and multifunctional hydrogels, hold significant promise for achieving effective neovascularization of ischemic tissues, such as those affected in LE-PAD. By enabling spatiotemporal control over vascular architecture, rational engineering of cell–matrix interactions, and sustained, localized signaling, these approaches can promote stable and functional vessel formation with precisely controlled diameters tailored to specific physiological and hemodynamic requirements, thereby paving the way for personalized regenerative medicine therapies. This chapter first discusses these biofabrication strategies in the context of

S. Öztürk
Tissue Engineering, Biomaterials and Nanobiotechnology Laboratory, Faculty of Science and Stem Cell Institute, Ankara University, Ankara, Türkiye

Kırıkkale University, Faculty of Medicine, Department of Cardiology, Kırıkkale, Türkiye

A. E. Elçin
Tissue Engineering, Biomaterials and Nanobiotechnology Laboratory, Faculty of Science and Stem Cell Institute, Ankara University, Ankara, Türkiye

Stem Cell Institute, Ankara University, Ankara, Türkiye

Y. M. Elçin (✉)
Tissue Engineering, Biomaterials and Nanobiotechnology Laboratory, Faculty of Science and Stem Cell Institute, Ankara University, Ankara, Türkiye

Department of Chemistry, Faculty of Science, Ankara University, Ankara, Türkiye
e-mail: elcin@ankara.edu.tr

Y. M. Elçin (ed.), *Biofabrication in Regenerative Medicine*, Stem Cell Biology and Regenerative Medicine 1519, https://doi.org/10.1007/978-3-032-30294-6_7

LE-PAD. Then, key challenges to successful clinical translation are assessed, and future perspectives on the implementation of biofabrication strategies for LE-PAD and personalized regenerative medicine applications are outlined.

Keywords Neovascularization · Therapeutic angiogenesis · Peripheral arterial disease · Bioprinting · Biofabrication · Electrospinning · Hydrogels · Decellularization

Abbreviations

3D	Three-Dimensional
ATEV	Acellular Tissue-Engineered Vessel
CAD	Computer-Aided Design
CAM	Computer-Aided Manufacturing
CLTI	Chronic Limb Threatening Ischemia
CVD	Cardiovascular Disease
DES	Drug-Eluting Stent
DMOG	Dimethyloxalylglycine
DNA	Deoxyribonucleic Acid
EC	Endothelial Cell
ECM	Extracellular Matrix
EV	Extracellular Vesicle
FDA	Food and Drug Administration
FGF	Fibroblast Growth Factor
HA	Hyaluronic Acid
iPSC	Induced Pluripotent Stem Cell
LE-PAD	Lower Extremity Peripheral Artery Disease
P34HB	Poly(3-hydroxybutyrate-co-4-hydroxybutyrate)
PCL	Poly(caprolactone)
PEO	Poly(oxyethylene)
PPO	Poly(oxypropylene)
PTX	Paclitaxel
RNA	Ribonucleic Acid
SIS	Small Intestinal Submucosa
SMC	Smooth Muscle Cell
VEGF	Vascular Endothelial Growth Factor

7.1 Introduction

Lower extremity peripheral artery disease (LE-PAD) is a manifestation of systemic atherosclerosis affecting the arteries of the lower extremities. It is the third leading cause of atherosclerotic morbidity, following coronary heart disease and stroke.

LE-PAD is further associated with impairments in physical functioning and quality of life and, in its most severe form, chronic limb threatening ischemia (CLTI), with an increased risk of nonhealing wounds, tissue loss, and eventually amputation and limb loss (Criqui et al. 2021). Epidemiological data indicate a substantial global burden, with the number of individuals affected by LE-PAD increasing by 13.1% in high-income countries and 28.7% in low- and middle-income countries between 2000 and 2010 (Fowkes et al. 2013).

Treatment of LE-PAD primarily includes lifestyle modifications and pharmacological therapy; however, arterial revascularization is essential to prevent limb loss when CLTI develops. Endovascular therapies and open surgical bypass constitute the two major forms of revascularization in CLTI (Nordanstig et al. 2024). However, revascularization of these patients remains particularly challenging because the disease is diffuse and multilevel and extends beyond large conduit arteries to involve the distal and microvascular circulation. Lesions are often long and heavily calcified and affect below-the-knee vessels, limiting the feasibility and durability of both revascularization techniques (Kodama 2024; Öztürk 2025). Moreover, chronic ischemia creates a hostile tissue microenvironment characterized by inflammation, fibrosis, oxidative stress, and endothelial dysfunction, which collectively impair angiogenic and arteriogenic responses. As a result, restoration of proximal arterial patency does not consistently translate into effective tissue perfusion or wound healing (Kodama 2024; Öztürk 2025; Li et al. 2024). These challenges are further compounded by common comorbidities such as diabetes and chronic kidney disease, which exacerbate microvascular dysfunction and limit endogenous regenerative capacity. Together, these factors underscore the unmet clinical need for alternative strategies capable of inducing functional neovascularization and restoring perfusion of the lower extremities at the tissue level (Kandemir 2025).

Biologic and cellular therapies have been extensively investigated for the treatment of LE-PAD; however, results have been mixed in terms of improving outcomes, and no therapies have yet received approval from the Food and Drug Administration (FDA) or the European Medicines Agency (EMA) (Forster et al. 2018; Qadura et al. 2018). Incorporating biologics and cells with biomaterials, or employing biomaterial-alone approaches, represents an additional strategy to enhance vascularization, with promising results demonstrated in preclinical models (Qamar et al. 2023; Hernandez and Christman 2017). However, the clinical translation of biomaterial-based therapeutic strategies for LE-PAD remains limited. In a phase 1–2a study, sustained release of basic fibroblast growth factor (FGF) from gelatin hydrogel microspheres, delivered via a single intramuscular injection, improved blood flow in ischemic limbs, resulting in reduced rest pain and improvements in ankle–brachial index (ABI) and ulcer healing (Marui et al. 2007). Similar therapeutic efficacy was observed in a subsequent study using the same approach in patients with more severe LE-PAD (Kumagai et al. 2016).

The formation of new capillaries, referred to as neovascularization, is a highly coordinated and complex process involving multiple cell types and signaling molecules. Neovascularization occurs through three distinct yet interrelated mechanisms: vasculogenesis, angiogenesis, and arteriogenesis (Persson and Buschmann

2011). Vasculogenesis refers to the de novo formation of blood vessels during embryonic development, including the development of the fetal heart and vasculature from the yolk sac. This process is followed by angiogenesis, which involves the formation of new vascular structures from preexisting blood vessels and represents vascular remodeling during the postnatal period. In contrast, arteriogenesis arises from preexisting collateral arteries and serves to restore tissue perfusion when a major artery, such as a coronary or femoral artery, becomes occluded. Under normal physiological conditions, these collateral vessels have minimal functional significance; however, in response to stimuli such as hypoxia and increased shear stress, these vessels become activated and undergo rapid proliferation to restore oxygen and nutrient delivery to ischemic tissue, thereby acting as a natural bypass system and regulating the pressure gradient across obstructed arteries (Persson and Buschmann 2011). Angiogenesis and arteriogenesis, which biologically lead to vascular collateralization, are considered endogenous mechanisms that help preserve tissue viability during ischemia. For example, the presence of coronary collateralization has been recognized as a predictor of long-term survival in patients with coronary artery disease. However, these protective mechanisms alone are often insufficient to provide adequate oxygen delivery to ischemic tissues, and revascularization is therefore required (Spadaccio et al. 2022). Moreover, adequate vascularization is a critical prerequisite for successful tissue and/or organ engineering in regenerative medicine, not only for cardiovascular diseases (CVDs), as it enables oxygen and nutrient transport, metabolic waste clearance, and sustained viability and functional integration of engineered constructs. Tissue-engineered constructs exceeding a few millimeters in thickness are prone to central necrosis and poor engraftment as a result of limited oxygen and nutrient diffusion from adjacent vascular networks. Indeed, insufficient and delayed vascularization remains one of the primary rate-limiting steps in the clinical translation of tissue- and organ-engineered constructs. The lack of a rapidly perfused and hierarchically organized vascular network often leads to hypoxia, nutrient deprivation, and cell death within implanted constructs, ultimately compromising graft survival and functional integration. Consequently, the development of strategies that promote rapid and stable neovascularization has become a central focus in regenerative medicine and biofabrication research (Phelps and Garcia 2010). Functional microvasculature biofabrication strategies aim to create a complex signaling environment consisting of hollow lumens that allow blood flow, a hierarchically branched network topology, and biophysical and biochemical cues essential for tissue homeostasis (Fig. 7.1).

Neovascularization in LE-PAD is particularly challenging due to several interrelated factors. The ischemic tissue microenvironment is hostile, characterized by chronic hypoxia, persistent inflammation, fibrosis, and endothelial dysfunction, all of which impair endogenous vascular repair and limit responsiveness to proangiogenic stimuli (Cooke and Meng 2020). In addition, effective revascularization in skeletal muscle requires the formation of hierarchically organized vascular networks including arterioles, capillaries, and venules, rather than isolated capillary sprouting alone. For example, the normal reference diameters and structural characteristics of lower extremity arteries vary according to anatomical region, reflecting a

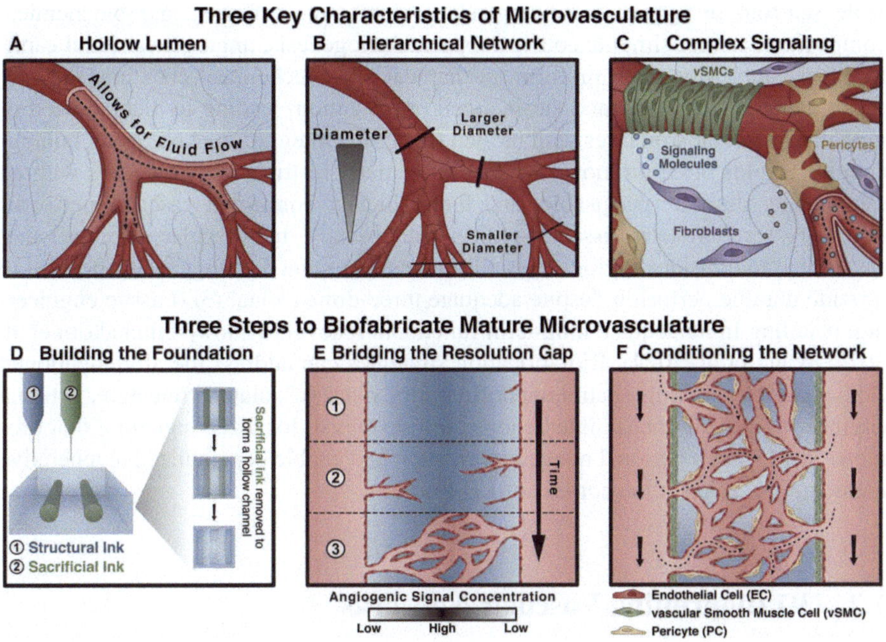

Fig. 7.1 Stages of functional microvasculature biofabrication: (**a**) the presence of a hollow lumen that enables blood flow; (**b**) a hierarchically branched network topology; and (**c**) a complex signaling environment composed of biophysical (fluid flow, ECM mechanics) and biochemical (diverse cell types, signaling molecules, matrix ligands) cues for tissue homeostasis. A three-stage approach can be used to accomplish these steps. (**d**) First, a basic, hollow network structure is created via extrusion-based bioprinting. (**e**) Second, proangiogenic signaling is applied to induce EC sprouting and network formation at the capillary scale. (**f**) Third, the network is matured with signals known to condition and stabilize nascent vascular networks, including the introduction of supporting cell types, i.e., vascular SMCs and pericytes). (Reproduced with permission from Seymour et al. 2022)

highly hierarchical vascular organization extending from large conduit arteries to small resistance vessels and capillary networks. Proximal arteries such as the iliac and femoral arteries exhibit larger diameters and distinct elastic and muscular properties, whereas distal popliteal and tibial arteries progressively transition to smaller-caliber, high-resistance vessels supplying skeletal muscle microcirculation (Struczewska et al. 2024; Lorbeer et al. 2018). This anatomical and functional heterogeneity presents a significant issue for therapeutic neovascularization through tissue engineering approaches, as effective revascularization requires reconstruction of multiscale, hierarchically organized vascular networks rather than uniform or capillary-only vessel formation (Laowpanitchakorn et al. 2024). Lower extremity tissues require blood vessels spanning multiple length scales, from large-caliber arterioles that regulate blood flow and pressure to dense capillary networks responsible for oxygen exchange, providing near-complete tissue coverage with an intercapillary spacing of less than 20 μm (Wang et al. 2024). Uniform and single-scale scaffold designs with homogeneous pore size, stiffness, and biochemical composition cannot simultaneously support arteriogenesis, angiogenesis, and capillary perfusion. Moreover, uniform mechanical and biochemical cues inadequately guide endothelial, mural, and stromal cell organization, leading to disorganized or immature vascular structures with limited functional integration. As a result, homogenous scaffolds often promote transient or spatially restricted angiogenesis without establishing durable, perfusable, and hierarchically connected vascular networks necessary for long-term tissue viability. Additionally, neovascular responses that are limited to transient angiogenesis without concomitant arteriogenesis often fail to provide durable perfusion despite adequate three-dimensional (3D) tissue engineering, resulting in inadequate long-term functional recovery (Laowpanitchakorn et al. 2024; Wang et al. 2024). Biofabrication strategies can address the aforementioned challenges by offering spatiotemporal control over vascular architecture, rational engineering of cell–matrix interactions, and sustained, localized signaling that promotes stable and functional neovascularization and enable personalized regenerative medicine therapies in the context of LE-PAD.

7.2 3D Bioprinting Vascular Networks

3D printing encompasses a range of additive manufacturing techniques that include extrusion-based printing, droplet-based printing, inkjet printing, laser-assisted printing, and light-based printing. Each technique is characterized by distinct operational principles, resulting in specific advantages and limitations with respect to bioink compatibility, cell viability, and structural complexity. These approaches differ in achievable resolution, fabrication speed, cost efficiency, and design constraints, which in turn influence their suitability for vascular tissue engineering applications (Yeo et al. 2023).

3D bioprinting can be classified into two main categories based on the method by which cells are incorporated into the printing material. In conventional approach, endothelial cells (ECs) are seeded onto a prefabricated structure following the printing process. In contrast, 3D bioprinting involves the direct incorporation of cells into the printing material to form a bioink, which is printed together with the biomaterial to generate vascular structures (Laowpanitchakorn et al. 2024). 3D bioprinting offers clear advantages over conventional vascular tissue engineering approaches by enabling precise spatial control over multiple cell types, biomaterials, and biochemical cues to create functional, perfusable, and hierarchically organized vascular networks. Unlike traditional scaffold-based or angiogenesis-driven strategies that rely on slow and poorly organized host-mediated vessel ingrowth, bioprinting allows the fabrication of predefined, lumenized, and multiscale vascular architectures integrating large-caliber vessels, arterioles, and capillaries within a single construct. This capability supports coordinated angiogenesis and arteriogenesis, improves endothelial maturation and vessel stabilization, and provides high reproducibility and design flexibility, making 3D bioprinting a powerful platform for engineering vascularized tissues with enhanced translational potential (Chae et al. 2023). Moreover, the field has evolved from 3D to four-dimensional bioprinting, in which printed constructs are designed to undergo controlled, time-dependent changes in shape, structure, or function in response to external or internal stimuli (Imrie and Jin 2025).

In vascular 3D printing and bioprinting, computer-aided design (CAD) and computer-aided manufacturing (CAM) enables the precise definition and fabrication of complex, hierarchically organized vascular architectures. CAD software is used to design lumenized and branched vessel geometries with controlled diameters, wall thicknesses, and branching angles, allowing recreation of multiscale vascular networks ranging from large-caliber conduits to microvascular features. These digital models can incorporate region-specific parameters, such as gradual diameter transitions and network density, which are critical for physiological flow regulation and perfusion. Through CAM, the CAD model is translated into printer-specific toolpaths by slicing the construct into layers and generating machine-readable instructions (e.g., G-code). This step governs deposition paths, extrusion pressure, feed rate, and spatial coordinates, ensuring accurate formation of perfusable channels and consistent layer-by-layer assembly. CAD/CAM workflows further enable spatial patterning of multiple inks including bioinks and cell types, supporting endothelialization, vessel maturation, and integration with surrounding tissues (Tomasina et al. 2019).

3D-bioprinting incorporates living cells during deposition and therefore requires special considerations owing to the sensitivity of cells to temperature fluctuations, mechanical forces such as high pressure and shear stress, as well as the pH and biocompatibility of the surrounding materials. In bioinks, the printing material should protect encapsulated cells from these external stresses during the printing process, while simultaneously maintaining printability and adequate shape retention (Laowpanitchakorn et al. 2024; Tomasina et al. 2019). Consequently, bioinks must exhibit appropriate rheological properties, including shear-thinning behavior and viscoelasticity, to enable smooth extrusion while minimizing cellular damage, along with controllable cross-linking mechanisms to ensure rapid shape fidelity, structural stability, and long-term functionality of printed vascular constructs. Bioinks can be broadly classified into two categories based on their origin: naturally derived bioinks, which are obtained from biological sources such as alginate, collagen, fibrin, gelatin, and hyaluronic acid (HA), and synthetic bioinks, which are engineered from defined polymeric materials (Tomasina et al. 2019). Naturally derived bioinks offer the intrinsic advantage of closely resembling the native cellular microenvironment, as they possess physicochemical properties similar to those of the extracellular matrix (ECM) or are direct components of the ECM itself (Gomes et al. 2008). However, these materials generally exhibit limited mechanical strength, resulting in mechanically weak 3D environments that provide insufficient structural support and mechanical cues for encapsulated cells (Tomasina et al. 2019). On the other hand, synthetic bioinks offer high reproducibility and wide availability and can be readily chemically modified, making them highly versatile and customizable for specific applications. They also exhibit tunable mechanical properties; however, they inherently lack cell-adhesive motifs, which limits direct cell–material interactions. Consequently, synthetic bioinks are frequently mixed with naturally derived polymers to enhance bioactivity while maintaining desirable mechanical performance (Tomasina et al. 2019). For example, Pluronic® is an amphiphilic triblock copolymer composed of polyoxyethylene (PEO) and polyoxypropylene (PPO) arranged in a PEO–PPO–PEO configuration. The PEO segments are hydrophilic, whereas the PPO segment is hydrophobic. Owing to its thermoreversible gelation behavior, Pluronic® undergoes a sol–gel transition in response to temperature changes, making it particularly well suited as a sacrificial ink for the fabrication of perfusable vascular networks (Wu et al. 2011). In vascular bioprinting, Pluronic® has been employed as a sacrificial biomaterial to support other biomaterials such as fibrin or gelatin (Kolesky et al. 2014; Kolesky et al. 2016). Hollow networks are usually created via common extrusion-based 3D bioprinting techniques, and endothelialization is performed after the hollow channels are formed (Fig. 7.2). Sacrificial inks are used to form a mold of the desired hollow space; this mold physically supports the surrounding ink when printing or casting is done around it. The sacrificial ink is removed following cross-linking of the surrounding ink, leaving a hollow lumen.

3D bioprinting of vascular structures has predominantly focused on the fabrication of small-diameter vessels, as large-diameter arterial disease in LE-PAD is typically managed using established surgical or endovascular revascularization procedures (Mir et al. 2023). Nevertheless, scaffold-free macrovascular structures, such as the aorta, can be biofabricated using 3D extrusion bioprinting through the layer-by-layer assembly of multicellular cylindrical aggregates, supported by hydrogel-based structures (Kucukgul et al. 2013). On the other hand, microextrusion bioprinting has been successfully employed to fabricate perfusable vascular networks with lumen diameters as small as 100 μm. It is the most commonly reported technique for small-diameter vascular printing and is compatible with a wide range of bioinks, including several naturally derived materials and virtually all synthetic bioinks used for scaffold fabrication (O'Connor et al. 2022). Laser-assisted bioprinting has already been used to fabricate microchannels with diameters as small as 5 μm, comparable to the smallest blood vessels in the human body, that can be successfully endothelialized. However, this technique is not well suited for large-diameter vascular fabrication (O'Connor et al. 2022; Arakawa et al. 2020). Similarly, stereolithography bioprinting is typically limited to a print resolution of ~300 μm, which restricts its ability to fabricate small-diameter vascular structures (O'Connor et al. 2022). Besides, the aforementioned 3D printing techniques can be applied to generate either scaffold-based or scaffold-free constructs. Scaffold-based bioprints typically utilize hydrogels composed of natural or synthetic polymers, whereas scaffold-free approaches rely on cellular aggregates, spheroids, decellularized ECM-derived materials, alginate hydrogels, or protein-based inks (Mir et al. 2023; Li et al. 2020). In addition, multimaterial bioprinting strategies enable the simultaneous deposition of multiple bioinks, allowing fabrication of complex vascular constructs with spatially heterogeneous composition and functionality (Mir et al. 2023). Additionally, in situ bioprinting represents another recent

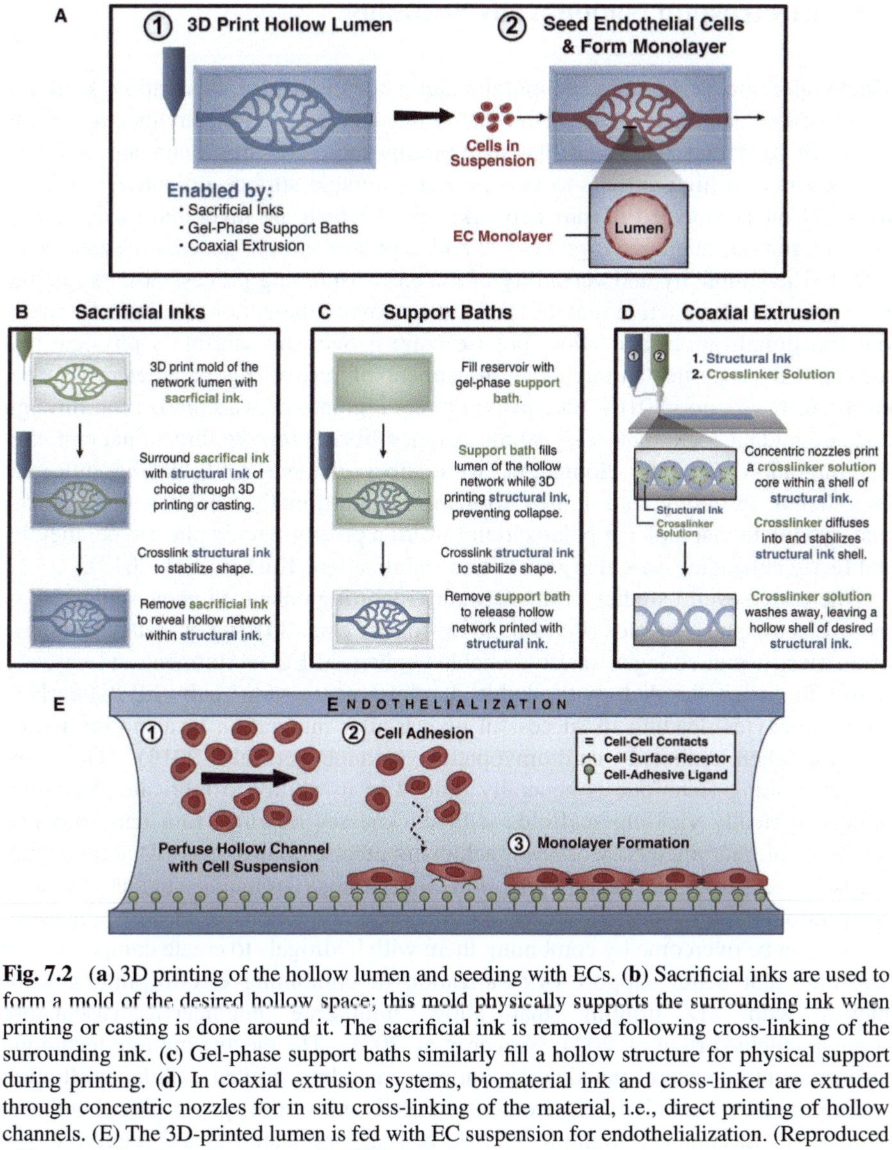

Fig. 7.2 (**a**) 3D printing of the hollow lumen and seeding with ECs. (**b**) Sacrificial inks are used to form a mold of the desired hollow space; this mold physically supports the surrounding ink when printing or casting is done around it. The sacrificial ink is removed following cross-linking of the surrounding ink. (**c**) Gel-phase support baths similarly fill a hollow structure for physical support during printing. (**d**) In coaxial extrusion systems, biomaterial ink and cross-linker are extruded through concentric nozzles for in situ cross-linking of the material, i.e., direct printing of hollow channels. (E) The 3D-printed lumen is fed with EC suspension for endothelialization. (Reproduced with permission from Seymour et al. 2022)

and versatile advancement in vascular biofabrication, enabling the direct deposition of biomaterials and cells onto the target tissue or organ and thereby eliminating the need for prefabricated constructs (Pagan et al. 2023).

7.3 Electrospun Nanofibrous Scaffolds

Electrospinning is an efficient biofabrication technique for fabricating scaffolds composed of nanometer-scale fibers that closely recapitulate the architecture of the native ECM. Electrospun scaffolds exhibit adjustable porosity, diameter, and degradation rate, a high surface-to-volume ratio, tunable surface properties, and can form 3D interconnected fibrous networks, all of which are favorable for EC adhesion, migration, angiogenic processes, and capillary morphogenesis (Nazeer et al. 2021). The simplicity and versatility of the electrospinning process also enable the incorporation of bioactive moieties to induce neovascularization, facilitate biomaterial functionalization, and allow precise control over the scaffold's physical and mechanical properties through the adjustment of processing parameters (Nazeer et al. 2021; Goonoo 2018). Electrospun fibers regulate neovascularization through contact guidance and matrix signaling. Aligned fibers promote directional endothelial migration and tube elongation, while fiber diameter and spacing influence endothelial sprouting and lumen formation. Additionally, electrospun matrices may modulate macrophage polarization toward a proangiogenic phenotype, thereby indirectly enhancing vascular growth and stabilization (Karkan et al. 2019).

There are several studies in the literature reporting enhanced neovascularization using electrospun scaffolds (Pu et al. 2015; Joanne et al. 2016). For instance, the use of an electrospun collagen scaffold enabled enhanced EC recruitment and vascular ingrowth when seeded with induced pluripotent stem cell (iPSC)-derived cardiomyocytes, leading to successful neovascular integration in a murine model of nonischemic-dilated cardiomyopathy (Joanne et al. 2016). However, electrospinning technique is generally limited in its ability to fabricate thick constructs, typically yielding scaffolds with thicknesses ranging from tens to a few hundreds of micrometers. Moreover, achieving precise control over 3D architecture, including scaffold dimensions and pore morphology, remains challenging with conventional approaches. However, the thickness limitations of electrospun membranes can be overcome by combining them with hydrogels to create composite, 3D scaffolds that better support vascularization or combining electrospinning techniques with 3D printing that allow multiscale engineered vasculature (Laowpanitchakorn et al. 2024; Nazeer et al. 2021). The electrospinning technique also encounters several practical limitations, including limited cellular infiltration and ingrowth, potential toxicity from residual solvents or post-processing chemicals, insufficient mechanical strength for load-bearing applications, and relatively low production throughput (Khorshidi et al. 2016). Cell infiltration in electrospun scaffolds can be improved by incorporating biological cues, increasing pore diameter, reducing fiber packing density, and applying advanced strategies such as cell electrospraying, multilayered constructs, and dynamic culture systems. In addition, combining electrospinning with complementary fiber fabrication methods can further enhance cellular ingrowth. Solvent-related toxicity can be mitigated by using cell-compatible solvents or adopting melt electrospinning approaches. Mechanical limitations, on the other hand, may be addressed by integrating inorganic phases into electrospun matrices, hybridizing electrospinning with other scaffold fabrication techniques, and applying post-processing modifications to reinforce scaffold strength and durability (Khorshidi et al. 2016).

Several electrospinning parameters, including porosity, pore size, fiber alignment, degradation rate, and scaffold stiffness, critically influence the angiogenic capacity of electrospun nanofibrous scaffolds (Nazarnezhad et al. 2022). Adequate porosity is essential for metabolite exchange and EC infiltration, with pore sizes of approximately 30–40 μm facilitating cell entry, while larger pores (>300 μm) are required to support robust neovessel ingrowth within the construct (Oliviero et al. 2012; Murphy and O'Brien 2010; Madden et al. 2010). Fiber alignment further plays a key role, as aligned nanofibers promote directional endothelial migration and organized neovessel formation (Gugutkov et al. 2017). In addition, slower polymer degradation rates are associated with enhanced cell recruitment and sustained vascularization (Sung et al. 2004). Scaffold mechanical properties are also important, as increased surface stiffness has been shown to enhance EC spreading, extension, and sprouting, collectively contributing to improved angiogenic outcomes (Mason et al. 2013).

In addition to promoting vascularization, electrospun scaffolds can exert additional therapeutic effects in CVDs, including LE-PAD (Broadwin et al. 2024). Owing to their inherent ability to mimic the native ECM, electrospun scaffolds can function as effective controlled drug delivery systems. A wide range of therapeutic agents including small molecules, growth factors, genes, and biologics can be incorporated into electrospun fibers using strategies such as direct blending, surface modification, coaxial electrospinning, and emulsion electrospinning, enabling spatially defined and sustained release profiles that enhance therapeutic efficacy in ischemic tissues (Zamani et al. 2013). Electrospun patches offer an advantageous platform for controlled drug delivery owing to their high surface area-to-volume ratio, tunable surface functionality, and favorable mechanical properties, including stiffness and tensile strength. These features support high drug loading and encapsulation efficiency, enable the co-delivery of multiple therapeutic agents, and allow controlled and sustained release profiles. Importantly, electrospinning is compatible with a broad spectrum of therapeutics, ranging from small hydrophobic and hydrophilic drugs to larger biomolecules such as proteins and nucleic acids. Collectively, these attributes make electrospun patches a versatile and cost-effective drug delivery strategy with significant potential for targeted therapy in myocardial and other ischemic tissues (Broadwin et al. 2024; Torres-Martínez et al. 2018).

Electrospinning technology also holds substantial therapeutic potential for the treatment of atherosclerosis and LE-PAD, particularly through the fabrication of drug-eluting stent (DES) coatings. Electrospun nanofibrous layers can be conformally deposited onto stent surfaces, providing an ECM-like interface and enabling controlled, sustained release of antiproliferative or anti-inflammatory agents. Preclinical studies in animal models have demonstrated that stents coated with drug-eluting electrospun materials reduce neointimal hyperplasia, improve endothelialization, and outperform bare-metal stents in limiting restenosis (Broadwin et al. 2024). The investigation of the effects of matrix elongation on the structural characteristics and drug release kinetics of poly(caprolactone) (PCL)-based and paclitaxel (PTX)-enriched electrospun matrices used as coatings for DES demonstrated that the arterial wall's capacity to retain and accumulate PTX resulted in prolonged local drug release in rabbit models. This suggests that electrospun stent coatings may achieve therapeutic efficacy with lower drug loading, potentially reducing the required PTX dose in DES applications (Nazarkina et al. 2021). A similar study using DES coated with an electrospun blend of PCL, human serum albumin, and PTX demonstrated reduced vascular trauma and significantly less neointimal hyperplasia compared with bare metal stents in rabbit iliac arteries (Kuznetsov et al. 2020). Incorporation of optimized concentrations of calcium silicate into aligned chitosan electrospun nanofibers yielded composite cardiac patch scaffolds that enhanced the expression of cardiac and angiogenic markers, promoted organized myofilament formation, and improved calcium signaling in neonatal rat cardiomyocytes, highlighting the potential of electrospun patch-based constructs to support neovascularization and functional cardiac tissue regeneration (Wang et al. 2019).

Studies have also demonstrated the angiogenic and regenerative efficacy of bioactive electrospun scaffolds in full-thickness wound defect models. For example, multifunctional electrospun poly(3-hydroxybutyrate-co-4-hydroxybutyrate) (P34HB) scaffolds with angiogenic and antibacterial properties have been developed as wound dressings (Li et al. 2023). Nanofibers were loaded with dimethyloxalylglycine (DMOG), a proangiogenic small molecule, and the antibiotic ciprofloxacin. Optical resolution photoacoustic micrographs revealed that mice treated with bioactive electrospun nanofiber scaffolds showed higher levels of neovascularization in wound defect areas, particularly in the early stages (Fig. 7.3).

7.4 Decellularized Biological Matrices

Decellularization is a biofabrication strategy that involves the removal of cellular components and genetic material from native tissues while preserving the 3D ECM architecture to yield a natural matrix with mechanical integrity. This method eliminates the need to design 3D vascular networks in vitro, as repopulation with appropriate human progenitor cells can be used to reconstruct permeable structures that retain a native 3D vascular architecture. In the context of LE-PAD, decellularized matrices may offer a uniquely biomimetic platform for promoting neovascularization within ischemic skeletal muscle, where endogenous regenerative capacity and angiogenic responsiveness are severely compromised (Broadwin et al. 2024; Tong et al. 2021). The decellularization technique relies on a combination of physical, chemical, and biological approaches to disrupt cellular membranes under immersive, agitative, and perfusive conditions. Physical treatments for decellularization include freeze-thaw cycles, high hydrostatic pressure, electroporation, supercritical and subcritical fluids, immersion with agitation, and perfusion-based methods. Chemical approaches involve the use of acids and bases, surfactants,

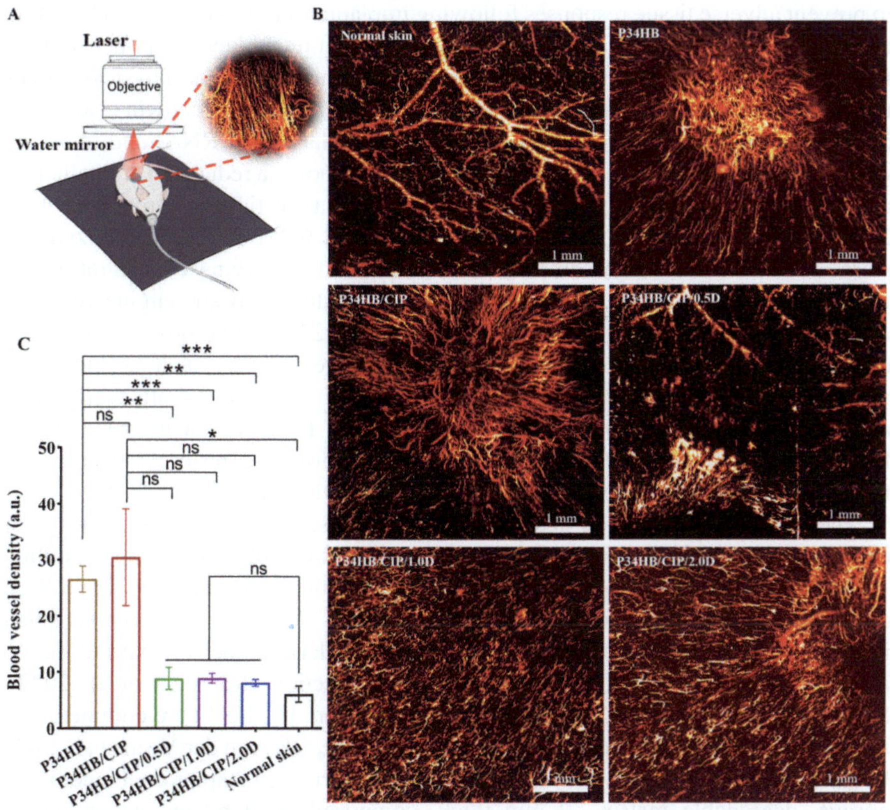

Fig. 7.3 Intravital imaging of angiogenesis within the skin wound defect by optical resolution photoacoustic microscopy (OR-PAM). (**a**) Schematic illustration of OR-PAM imaging in vivo. (**b**) The OR-PAM was used to scan animals on day 15 after undergoing or not undergoing the skin wound defect surgery. (**c**) Quantification of blood vessel density in the skin wound defect site by MATLAB. $**p < 0.01$, $***p < 0.001$ ($n = 5$). (Reproduced with permission from Li et al. 2023)

chaotropic agents, and osmotic stress to solubilize cellular components. On the other hand, biological decellularization strategies primarily rely on enzyme-based treatments that disrupt nucleic acids including deoxyribonucleic acid (DNA) and ribonucleic acid (RNA) and cell–matrix interactions by degrading proteins and other cellular constituents. Commonly used biological agents include trypsin, nucleases such as DNase and RNase, benzonase, and fetal bovine serum. These enzymatic agents are typically used in combination with ethylenediaminetetraacetic acid or surfactants to enhance decellularization efficiency by facilitating cell detachment and removal from tissues or organs (Wang et al. 2022).

For clinical applications, a properly decellularized scaffold should meet three fundamental criteria: (1) complete or near-complete removal of cellular components, (2) preservation of the native vascular architecture, and (3) conservation of the native ECM. In addition, all residual decellularization agents must be thoroughly removed to prevent adverse tissue responses following implantation (Saburi et al. 2022). With appropriate decellularization, decellularized ECM can retain key components of the native cellular microenvironment, including biochemical cues and physical signals that support cell recruitment, proliferation, and differentiation (Broadwin et al. 2024; Santschi et al. 2019). Moreover, because most cellular DNA, RNA, and immunogenic components are removed, decellularized ECM poses a reduced risk of eliciting an immune response compared with transplanted native tissues (Broadwin et al. 2024; Saburi et al. 2022). In addition, decellularized ECM can be lyophilized and stored as a powder, which can later be reconstituted at varying concentrations or formulated into hydrogels, bioinks, or coatings for diverse tissue engineering and regenerative medicine applications (Shi et al. 2023). Numerous studies have employed recellularization strategies in which target tissues, such as the heart, vessels, and even the aorta, are first decellularized while preserving their native architecture and ECM composition. Subsequently, ECs, mesenchymal cells, or fibroblasts are seeded onto the decellularized scaffolds to restore physiological function and biomechanical properties (Kim et al. 2016; Zhang et al. 2007).

The use of decellularized natural scaffolds represents a promising strategy for engineering complex, vascularized organs with potential clinical applicability. Accordingly, several commercially available decellularized constructs have been developed and are currently in use. For example, decellularized porcine small intestinal submucosa (SIS) has emerged as a particularly attractive scaffold due to its strong angiogenic potential in dermal reconstruction (Kargozar et al. 2022). SurgySIS® and OaSIS® (Cook Surgical, Bloomington, IN, USA) are commercially available decellularized matrices derived from porcine SIS (van der Veen et al. 2010; Urciuolo et al. 2019). Nevelia® (Symatese Biomateriaux, Chaponost, France) is a porous, degradable matrix ~2 mm thick, composed of stabilized native type I collagen of bovine origin, and has been shown to promote angiogenesis when used as a dermal substitute in patients with posttraumatic wounds. Histological and immunohistochemical analyses have demonstrated that Nevelia® supports accelerated neoangiogenesis and tissue regeneration, with newly formed tissue architecture closely resembling that of intact skin (De Angelis et al. 2018). CorMatrix® (CorMatrix Cardiovascular, Inc., Roswell, GA, USA) is another commercially available biological scaffold derived from decellularized porcine SIS and holds potential for cardiovascular applications (Mosala Nezhad et al. 2016). CorMatrix® has demonstrated enhanced vascularization and improved cardiac function in rodent models of myocardial infarction when surgically implanted as an epicardial patch over the infarcted region. Furthermore, in vitro studies indicate that interactions between human cardiac fibroblasts and the CorMatrix® scaffold elicit a robust, FGF-2-dependent and cell-mediated vasculogenic paracrine response that promotes functional blood vessel assembly (Mewhort et al. 2017). Implantation of the scaffold in eight patients during coronary artery bypass surgery resulted in increased regional myocardial perfusion, indicating a robust reparative potential in ischemic myocardium (Svystonyuk et al. 2020).

Decellularized ECM scaffolds also show promise for the treatment of LE-PAD. For instance, successful decellularization of the human iliac artery has recently been demonstrated, highlighting its potential as a clinically relevant scaffold for vascular graft applications in the treatment of LE-PAD. A perfusion-based decellularization protocol using enzymatic and detergent agents effectively removed cellular components while preserving the native ECM architecture, including organized collagen and elastin fibers. Recellularization with adipose tissue-derived stem cells demonstrated high cell viability, confirming scaffold bioactivity. Histological, mechanical, thermal, and ultrastructural analyses revealed retention of the hierarchical vascular structure, with increased stiffness indicative of adaptive ECM fiber realignment, and overall stability comparable to native tissue, supporting the suitability of these scaffolds for clinical vascular applications (Abad-Contreras et al. 2025). There are also several commercially available decellularized products that can be utilized for the treatment of LE-PAD. Artegraft® (LeMaitre Vascular, Inc., Brunswick, USA), a xenogeneic, cross-linked bovine carotid artery graft, has demonstrated excellent 5-year patency and limb salvage outcomes when used as a vascular conduit in lower extremity bypass surgery (Lindsey et al. 2018). CryoVein® (CryoLife, Inc., Kennesaw, USA), a cryopreserved saphenous vein allograft, has shown suboptimal patency but acceptable limb salvage rates in peripheral bypass surgery in patients with LE-PAD (Zehr et al. 2011; Hartranft et al. 2014). Other commercially available decellularized vascular products include Solcograft®, derived from the bovine carotid artery; ProCol®, obtained from the bovine mesenteric vein; and SynerGraft®, derived from the bovine ureter (Wang et al. 2022; Lin et al. 2018). However, the widespread utility of these synthetic vascular grafts has been limited due to suboptimal clinical outcomes, including graft-related thrombosis, infection, and aneurysm formation, with these complications being particularly pronounced in small inner-diameter vascular grafts. In addition, the lack of cellularity upon implantation and high production costs represents other limitations (Wang et al. 2022; Lin et al. 2018; Sharp et al. 2004). On the other hand, a decellularized vascular graft derived from porcine arteries, with surface modification for small-diameter arterial reconstruction, was used for below-the-knee arterial bypass surgery in three patients with diabetic lower limb ischemia. The procedure demonstrated favorable clinical outcomes, with a 100% primary patency rate at 6-month follow-up (Tong et al. 2021). It should be emphasized that autologous vessels continue to outperform decellularized vascular grafts and remain the optimal standard of care for surgical revascularization as bypass conduits in peripheral arterial trauma, owing to their superior patency rates and improved limb salvage outcomes (Reilly et al. 2019).

Despite its strong biomimetic potential, decellularization as a biofabrication strategy has important limitations. Batch-to-batch variability and incomplete decellularization can result in inconsistent biological performance and residual immunogenic components, whereas overly aggressive processing may disrupt essential ECM cues required for angiogenesis (Saburi et al. 2022; Xu et al. 2024; Kasravi et al. 2023). In addition, decellularized matrices, especially those derived from soft tissues, often exhibit limited mechanical strength and durability, necessitating reinforcement or combination with synthetic scaffolds for use in severely ischemic limbs (Saburi et al. 2022). While biologically instructive, decellularized ECM provides limited control over spatial vascular organization, restricting its ability to support hierarchical vessel formation (Golebiowska et al. 2024; Jin et al. 2025). These challenges are further compounded by the hostile ischemic microenvironment of LE-PAD, characterized by chronic inflammation, fibrosis, microangiopathy, and impaired progenitor cell recruitment (Kodama 2024; Öztürk 2025; Li et al. 2024; Cooke and Meng 2020), as well as by issues related to scalability, sterility, and regulatory translation (Jin et al. 2025; Rodriguez-Soto et al. 2022).

7.5 Multifunctional Hydrogels

Early studies on therapeutic neovascularization mostly focused on angiogenic growth factor delivery systems using biomaterial microspheres or scaffolds (Elçin et al. 1996; Elçin et al. 2001; Elçin and Elçin 2006; Demirdogen et al. 2010). These systems were used to create neovascularized cell transplantation beds for cell transplantation. Subsequently, combined applications with cells-seeded scaffolds were carried out for in vivo engineering of a variety of tissues (Elçin et al. 1999; Linn et al. 2003; Lalegul-Ulker et al. 2019). Previous studies involving cell transplantation or growth factor delivery aimed at therapeutic neovascularization have been relatively inadequate, primarily due to difficulties in stem cell engraftment and survival and the rapid release and enzymatic degradation of angiogenic factors after injection into affected tissues. In recent years, injectable biomaterial hydrogel-based therapies have shown therapeutic potential in preclinical models of CVD such as MI and LE-PAD (Ungerleider and Christman 2014). Hydrogels appear to have the ability to protect stem cells and support their viability during injection. They can also provide a sustained and localized delivery of angiogenic factors at the injection site (Li et al. 2021a).

Recently, research on injectable advanced multifunctional hydrogels combining various properties, including angiogenic properties, has attracted attention. These systems can be further developed to accommodate 3D bioprinting capabilities, giving the opportunity for use in 3D biofabrication. Li et al. developed a thermosensitive HA hydrogel bearing the cell adhesion peptide RGD, with antioxidant properties and skeletal muscle-matching stiffness. This hydrogel reduced intracellular reactive oxygen species levels and protected vessel-like structures against H_2O_2-induced damage in vitro, while also providing sustained release of vascular endothelial growth factor (VEGF) (Li et al. 2021b). When injected into ischemic rat hind leg muscle, the hydrogel reduced lipid oxidation, regulated oxidative-related genes, increased local blood flow in the muscle, and improved the running capacity of the subjects (Fig. 7.4).

It is thought that inflammation associated with oxidative stress may lead to the onset and progression of LE-PAD. In one study, a thermosensitive chitosan-gelatin hydrogel was designed as a carrier for ferulic acid, a natural phenolic compound, with antioxidant and angiogenic properties (Wang et al. 2020). The findings of this study demonstrated that the hydrogel could provide sustained ferulic acid release and also improved blood flow, muscle regeneration, and reduced inflammation in a

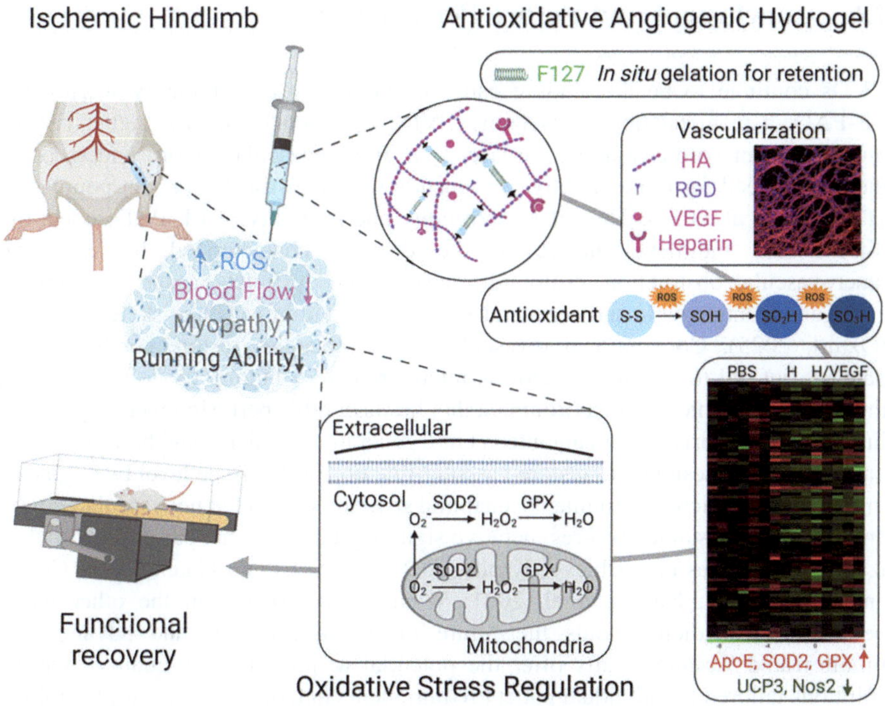

Fig. 7.4 Thermosensitive hyaluronic acid hydrogel-mediated oxidative stress regulation for functional recovery of rats with ischemic hindlimb. (Reproduced with permission from Li et al. 2021b)

mouse hind limb ischemia model. Lately, some studies appear to focus on developing functional hydrogels containing specific metal ions that possess proangiogenic properties. In one study, a trifunctional Sr/Si-containing composite hydrogel was designed for the treatment of lower extremity ischemic diseases, possessing properties that simultaneously enhance angiogenesis, regulate inflammation, and prevent muscle necrosis (Yuan et al. 2023). Sustained release of Sr^{2+} and SiO_3^{2-} ions from the injectable hydrogel was observed for 28 days, promoting proliferation of ECs and smooth muscle cells (SMCs) and localized neovascularization in vivo. In addition, the released ions facilitated the polarization of macrophages towards the regenerative M2 phenotype. Although further research is needed in this area, it is foreseeable that this treatment approach may offer advantages for LE-PAD patients due to the ease of production and minimally invasive application of cell-free injectable multifunctional hydrogels.

7.6 Conclusions and Future Perspectives

CVDs continue to be the leading cause of morbidity and mortality worldwide. LE-PAD, a manifestation of systemic CVD, is associated with a higher risk of mortality than coronary artery disease even after revascularization, underscoring the urgent need for more effective therapeutic strategies for this patient population (Takahara et al. 2024). The excess morbidity and mortality of LE-PAD reflect the diffuse and multilevel nature of the disease, characterized by extensive macrovascular obstruction, profound microvascular dysfunction, and an impaired endogenous angiogenic and regenerative response within ischemic skeletal muscle (Öztürk 2025). Conventional revascularization strategies restore conduit artery patency but fail to adequately address microcirculatory failure, tissue fibrosis, and the hostile ischemic microenvironment that limits durable perfusion recovery. These limitations have driven growing interest in regenerative medicine and biofabrication-based therapies designed to restore vascular function at the tissue level by engineering instructive microenvironments, enabling spatially controlled neovascularization, and providing sustained pro-regenerative signaling beyond what current revascularization approaches can achieve (Kandemir 2025; Phelps and Garcia 2010; Cooke and Meng 2020; Nazeer et al. 2021; Wang et al. 2025). On the other hand, personalized medicine holds the future of health sciences, and advances in biofabricated vascular grafts offer the potential to provide high-quality, durable solutions tailored to individual patient requirements in terms of vascular physiology and rheology. Biofabrication technologies, including 3D bioprinting, electrospinning, decellularization, and injectable multifunctional hydrogels, not only enable precise control over scaffold architecture, material composition, and biological signaling but also make possible to design patient-specific vascular constructs that better recapitulate native vascular structure and function (Laowpanitchakorn et al. 2024). In terms of personalized medicine, biofabrication technologies hold potential for neovascularization of individually engineered organs or tissues for various demands (Nazeer et al. 2021).

Given the limited efficacy of current revascularization strategies and medical therapies in LE-PAD, biomaterial-based approaches, particularly injectable biomaterials, have been extensively investigated. These biomaterials can be engineered to incorporate stem and/or progenitor cells, bioactive hydrogels, nanoparticles, growth factor-loaded microcapsules, or microcarriers, enabling localized and sustained therapeutic delivery within ischemic tissue (Qamar et al. 2023). The mechanical microenvironment plays a critical regulatory role in the formation and alignment of preformed vascular networks within engineered tissues, as well as in the ingrowth and remodeling of host blood vessels following implantation. Several factors, including material composition, mechanical and biochemical properties, degradation kinetics, porosity, and bioactive cargo, determine the neovascularization capacity of the delivered biomaterial in the ischemic tissue (Phelps and Garcia 2010). Optimization of biomaterial physical properties, including stiffness, surface roughness, anisotropy, porosity and pore size, as well as the incorporation of hollow channels, can significantly enhance vascularization in tissue-engineered constructs (Wang et al. 2024).

Biochemical strategies to enhance neovascularization of biomaterials in ischemic tissues predominantly rely on growth factor-based approaches. These growth factors include bFGF, VEGF, hepatocyte growth factor, platelet-derived growth factor, angiopoietins, ephrin, transforming growth factor-β, stromal cell-derived factor 1, and secreted protein acidic and rich in cysteine (Nazeer et al. 2021). However, the therapeutic application of growth factors has been limited by the complexity of biological injury and repair processes, as well as by intrinsic properties of the growth factors themselves, such as short half-life, limited tissue penetration, and the potential for off-target effects when these growth factors are systemically or locally administered. It should be emphasized that, despite their limitations, biomaterial scaffolds carrying growth factors represent a better delivery strategy compared to bolus injections or systemic administration (Qamar et al. 2023; Nazeer et al. 2021; Cheah et al. 2021). Such limitations can be addressed through various complementary strategies that enable precise control over the timing, sequence, dosage, and spatial localization of growth factor delivery within target tissues (Cheah et al. 2021). These strategies can be summarized as physical encapsulation for sustained local release with preserved bioactivity; affinity-based binding via electrostatic interactions between growth factors and scaffold components; ECM-mediated interactions; and heparin- or immobilized heparin-mediated affinity binding. On the other hand, high-affinity glycosaminoglycans further prolong growth factor retention, enhance stability, and protect against thermal denaturation, acidic pH inactivation, and proteolytic degradation. Direct covalent conjugation enables prolonged growth factor retention and controlled release. External stimulants such as ultrasound-triggered release from growth factor loaded microbubbles, magnetically induced release from hyperbranched dendrimers conjugated to nanoparticles, thermally triggered growth factor release from responsive hydrogels, light induced isomerization of photosensitive hydrogels, and electrically regulated growth factor delivery from conducting polymer-based hydrogels also allow dynamic and on-demand delivery of growth factors. Collectively, these external stimuli-responsive systems provide spatiotemporal control of growth factor presentation, thereby enhancing therapeutic efficacy while minimizing off-target effects such as cytotoxicity, hypotension, and excessive vascular leakage. Additionally, multiple and sequential growth factor delivery strategy more accurately recapitulates the in vivo microenvironment, where coordinated signaling by multiple factors is required for effective neovascularization (Wang et al. 2024; Nazeer et al. 2021; Cheah et al. 2021).

Mesenchymal stem/stromal cells have been the most investigated cellular therapy in CVDs as well as LE-PAD for their advantages such as availability to be obtained from a variety of tissues, well-defined characterization, and their angiogenic capacity (Öztürk et al. 2021a; Huang et al. 2024). Although cellular therapies have demonstrated an acceptable safety profile in clinical trials of LE-PAD, their therapeutic efficacy has been limited, outcome measures have been inconsistent, and none have yet progressed to routine clinical practice yet (Huang et al. 2024). On the other hand, acellular therapeutics such as extracellular vesicles (EVs) have successfully advanced into clinical trials for CVD. Notably, the first patient has already been enrolled in the SECRET-HF phase I trial evaluating the safety and feasibility of repeated injections of the EV-enriched secretome of cardiovascular progenitor cells differentiated from iPSCs in severe heart failure patients (Menasche et al. 2024). In terms of treatment of LE-PAD as well as other ischemic diseases by neovascularization through EV based approaches, there is encouraging preclinical data obtained from animal models. For instance, exosomes derived from human iPSC-derived mesenchymal stem cells promoted angiogenesis following injection into ischemic mouse limbs (Hu et al. 2015). For successful and effective clinical translation of EV-based approaches for the treatment of LE-PAD, further progress is required. Stem cells and/or EVs may also enhance the angiogenic efficacy of acellular carriers such as hydrogels (Huang et al. 2024; Dawes et al. 2025). For example, EV-embedded hydrogels offer several advantages, including controlled release of multiple angiogenic growth factors and bioactive molecules, disease-specific carrier customization, and improved local delivery. Moreover, such strategies pave the way for combinatorial approaches, rather than reliance on a single modality, to achieve effective neovascularization of ischemic tissues (Dawes et al. 2025).

Regenerative medicine therapies hold significant potential for addressing large-scale societal disasters, including earthquakes, pandemics, wars, and other mass-casualty events (Öztürk et al. 2021b; Öztürk et al. 2020; Tanriverdi et al. 2020). In this context, biofabricated, off-the-shelf vascular conduits represent a viable and scalable therapeutic option, offering immediate availability for functional vascular replacement. Symvess™, an acellular tissue-engineered vessel (ATEV), formerly referred to as the human acellular vessel, received FDA approval in December 2024 for use in adults as a vascular conduit for extremity arterial injury when urgent revascularization is required to prevent imminent limb loss and autologous vein grafting is not feasible (Rajani et al. 2025). This ATEV is a bioengineered human vascular tissue with a diameter of 6 mm and up to 40 cm of usable length, initially grown from human vascular cells. Following maturation, the engineered vessel undergoes decellularization, yielding an acellular, tubular human ECM. The scaffold supports host-mediated cellular repopulation after implantation, enabling progressive remodeling into a living vessel that closely recapitulates the structure, composition, and histology of a native human artery (Kirkton et al. 2019). It is stored under refrigerated conditions and can be made available to the surgeon almost immediately, as it does not require thawing or pre-use rinsing. This rapid availability without the need for autologous vein harvesting has the potential to significantly shorten time to revascularization in patients with traumatic extremity injuries (Rajani et al. 2025). Outcomes from both civilian patients and individuals with wartime extremity injuries in Ukraine have demonstrated encouraging results for ATEV when used to treat traumatic arterial injuries of the extremities (Lauria et al. 2022; Sokolov et al. 2023; Moore et al. 2025). A recent study, despite limited statistical power and short-term follow-up, suggested that key clinical outcomes including graft patency, amputation rates, conduit infection, need for reintervention, aneurysm or pseudoaneurysm formation, and mortality were comparable between the ATEV and autologous vein external controls (Rajani et al. 2025). A phase II study with up to 6 years of follow-up showed that the ATEV had infection resistance, mechanical performance, and immune tolerance comparable to autologous grafts in patients with advanced LE-PAD underscoring the long-term durability and clinical feasibility of ATEV in a high-risk limb-salvage population (Gutowski et al. 2023).

Future regenerative medicine strategies for LE-PAD will need to move beyond capillary-centric angiogenesis and deliberately prioritize arteriogenesis to achieve more robust perfusion recovery, improved limb salvage, and sustained functional outcomes. Although increasing capillary density may improve microcirculatory exchange, durable clinical recovery in LE-PAD will ultimately depend on the development of stable collateral arteries that can compensate for major arterial occlusions (Simons and Eichmann 2015). The future of neovascularization in LE-PAD will depend on our ability to move beyond incremental angiogenic approaches and embrace arteriogenesis-driven, biofabrication-enabled solutions that restore true conductance vessel function. Integrating advanced biomaterials, precision bioprinting, decellularized vascular matrices, and stimuli-responsive delivery systems offers an unprecedented opportunity to engineer therapies that are spatially controlled, mechanically informed, and biologically synchronized with the ischemic microenvironment. By coupling hemodynamic conditioning with immunomodulatory and pro-regenerative signaling, next-generation platforms can be designed not merely to induce vessel sprouting, but to orchestrate stable collateral artery formation and durable perfusion recovery. Targeting this vision will require interdisciplinary collaboration across vascular biology, materials science, bioengineering, and clinical and surgical medicine yet its realization holds the potential to fundamentally transform outcomes for patients with advanced LE-PAD. Importantly, advances achieved through biofabrication-driven neovascularization strategies in LE-PAD are poised to extend well beyond limb ischemia, establishing foundational design principles and scalable platforms capable of enhancing vascularization in engineered organs and complex tissues across the broader landscape of regenerative medicine.

Competing Interests Y.M.E. is the founder and shareholder of Biovalda Health Technologies, Inc. (Ankara, Türkiye). The authors declare no competing financial interests in relation to this particular article.

References

Abad-Contreras DE, Martinez-Ortiz AK, Martinez-Lopez V, Laparra-Escareno H, Martinez-Garcia FD, Perez-Calixto D, Vazquez-Victorio G, Sepulveda-Robles O, Rosas-Vargas H, Pina-Barba C et al (2025) Decellularization of human iliac artery: a vascular scaffold for peripheral repairs with human mesenchymal cells. Tissue Cell 93:102686. https://doi.org/10.1016/j.tice.2024.102686

Arakawa C, Gunnarsson C, Howard C, Bernabeu M, Phong K, Yang E, DeForest CA, Smith JD, Zheng Y (2020) Biophysical and biomolecular interactions of malaria-infected erythrocytes in engineered human capillaries. Sci Adv 6:eaay7243. https://doi.org/10.1126/sciadv.aay7243

Broadwin M, Imarhia F, Oh A, Stone CR, Sellke FW, Bhowmick S, Abid MR (2024) Exploring electrospun scaffold innovations in cardiovascular therapy: a review of electrospinning in cardiovascular disease. Bioengineering (Basel) 11. https://doi.org/10.3390/bioengineering11030218

Chae S, Ha DH, Lee H (2023) 3D bioprinting strategy for engineering vascularized tissue models. Int J Bioprint 9:748. https://doi.org/10.18063/ijb.748

Cheah E, Wu Z, Thakur SS, O'Carroll SJ, Svirskis D (2021) Externally triggered release of growth factors - a tissue regeneration approach. J Control Release 332:74–95. https://doi.org/10.1016/j.jconrel.2021.02.015

Cooke JP, Meng S (2020) Vascular regeneration in peripheral artery disease. Arterioscler Thromb Vasc Biol 40:1627–1634. https://doi.org/10.1161/ATVBAHA.120.312862

Criqui MH, Matsushita K, Aboyans V, Hess CN, Hicks CW, Kwan TW et al (2021) Lower extremity peripheral artery disease: contemporary epidemiology, management gaps, and future directions: a scientific statement from the American heart association. Circulation 144:e171–e191. https://doi.org/10.1161/CIR.0000000000001005

Dawes JS, Abdelaal M, Landmesser ME, Asgardoon MH, Waldron OP, Park JH, Jikaria N, Ravnic DJ (2025) Exosomes: the future of acellular nanotherapeutics in regenerative vascularization. Front Bioeng Biotechnol 13:1607605. https://doi.org/10.3389/fbioe.2025.1607605

De Angelis B, Orlandi F, Fernandes Lopes Morais D'Autilio M, Scioli MG, Orlandi A, Cervelli V, Gentile P (2018) Long-term follow-up comparison of two different bi-layer dermal substitutes in tissue regeneration: clinical outcomes and histological findings. Int Wound J 15:695–706. https://doi.org/10.1111/iwj.12912

Demirdogen B, Elçin AE, Elçin YM (2010) Neovascularization by bFGF releasing hyaluronic acid-gelatin microspheres: in vitro and in vivo studies. Growth Factors 28:426–436. https://doi.org/10.3109/08977194.2010.508456

Elçin AE, Elçin YM (2006) Localized angiogenesis induced by human vascular endothelial growth factor-activated PLGA sponge. Tissue Eng 12:959–968. https://doi.org/10.1089/ten.2006.12.959

Elçin YM, Dixit V, Gitnick G (1996) Controlled release of endothelial cell growth factor from chitosan-albumin microspheres for localized angiogenesis: in vitro and in vivo studies. Artif Cells Blood Substit Immobil Biotechnol 24:257–271. https://doi.org/10.3109/10731199609117438

Elçin YM, Dixit V, Lewin K, Gitnick G (1999) Xenotransplantation of fetal porcine hepatocytes in rats using a tissue engineering approach. Artif Organs 23:146–152. https://doi.org/10.1046/j.1525-1594.1999.06222.x

Elçin YM, Dixit V, Gitnick G (2001) Extensive in vivo angiogenesis following controlled release of human vascular endothelial cell growth factor: implications for tissue engineering and wound healing. Artif Organs 25:558–565. https://doi.org/10.1046/j.1525-1594.2001.025007558.x

Forster R, Liew A, Bhattacharya V, Shaw J, Stansby G (2018) Gene therapy for peripheral arterial disease. Cochrane Database Syst Rev 10:CD012058. https://doi.org/10.1002/14651858.CD012058.pub2

Fowkes FG, Rudan D, Rudan I, Aboyans V, Denenberg JO, McDermott MM, Norman PE, Sampson UK, Williams LJ, Mensah GA, Criqui MH (2013) Comparison of global estimates of prevalence and risk factors for peripheral artery disease in 2000 and 2010: a systematic review and analysis. Lancet 382:1329–1340. https://doi.org/10.1016/S0140-6736(13)61249-0

Golebiowska AA, Intravaia JT, Sathe VM, Kumbar SG, Nukavarapu SP (2024) Decellularized extracellular matrix biomaterials for regenerative therapies: advances, challenges and clinical prospects. Bioact Mater 32:98–123. https://doi.org/10.1016/j.bioactmat.2023.09.017

Gomes M, Azevedo H, Malafaya P, Silva S, Oliveira J, Silva G, Sousa R, Mano J, Reis R (2008) Natural polymers in tissue engineering applications. In: Tissue engineering. Elsevier, pp 145–192

Goonoo N (2018) Vascularization and angiogenesis in electrospun tissue engineered constructs: towards the creation of long-term functional networks. Biomed Phys Eng Express 4:032001. https://doi.org/10.1088/2057-1976/aaab03

Gugutkov D, Gustavsson J, Cantini M, Salmeron-Sanchez M, Altankov G (2017) Electrospun fibrinogen-PLA nanofibres for vascular tissue engineering. J Tissue Eng Regen Med 11:2774–2784. https://doi.org/10.1002/term.2172

Gutowski P, Guziewicz M, Ilzecki M, Kazimierczak A, Lawson JH, Prichard HL, Przywara S, Samad R, Tente W, Turek J et al (2023) Six-year outcomes of a phase ii study of human-tissue engineered blood vessels for peripheral arterial bypass. JVS Vasc Sci 4:100092. https://doi.org/10.1016/j.jvssci.2022.11.001

Hartranft CA, Noland S, Kulwicki A, Holden CR, Hartranft T (2014) Cryopreserved saphenous vein graft in infrainguinal bypass. J Vasc Surg 60:1291–1296. https://doi.org/10.1016/j.jvs.2014.05.092

Hernandez MJ, Christman KL (2017) Designing acellular injectable biomaterial therapeutics for treating myocardial infarction and peripheral artery disease. JACC Basic Transl Sci 2:212–226. https://doi.org/10.1016/j.jacbts.2016.11.008

Hu GW, Li Q, Niu X, Hu B, Liu J, Zhou SM, Guo SC, Lang HL, Zhang CQ, Wang Y, Deng ZF (2015) Exosomes secreted by human-induced pluripotent stem cell-derived mesenchymal stem cells attenuate limb ischemia by promoting angiogenesis in mice. Stem Cell Res Ther 6:10. https://doi.org/10.1186/scrt546

Huang NF, Stern B, Oropeza BP, Zaitseva TS, Paukshto MV, Zoldan J (2024) Bioengineering cell therapy for treatment of peripheral artery disease. Arterioscler Thromb Vasc Biol 44:e66–e81. https://doi.org/10.1161/ATVBAHA.123.318126

Imrie P, Jin J (2025) 4D bioprinting: keeping the technology alive. Macromol Mater Eng 310: 2400386. https://doi.org/10.1002/mame.202400386

Jin C, Zhang X, Jin Y, Chien PN, Heo CY (2025) Acellular extracellular matrix scaffolds in regenerative medicine: advances in decellularization and clinical applications. J Funct Biomater 16. https://doi.org/10.3390/jfb16100383

Joanne P, Kitsara M, Boitard SE, Naemetalla H, Vanneaux V, Pernot M, Larghero J, Forest P, Chen Y, Menasche P, Agbulut O (2016) Nanofibrous clinical-grade collagen scaffolds seeded with human cardiomyocytes induces cardiac remodeling in dilated cardiomyopathy. Biomaterials 80:157–168. https://doi.org/10.1016/j.biomaterials.2015.11.035

Kandemir H (2025) Treatment options for patients unsuitable for revascularization. In: Ebinç H, Öztürk S (eds) Approach to lower extremity peripheral artery diseases, pp 66–74

Kargozar S, Hosseini SA, Mozafari M (2022) Angiogenesis and vasculogenesis: status in tissue engineering. In: Biomaterials for vasculogenesis and angiogenesis. Elsevier, pp 1–13

Karkan SF, Davaran S, Rahbarghazi R, Salehi R, Akbarzadeh A (2019) Electrospun nanofibers for the fabrication of engineered vascular grafts. J Biol Eng 13:83. https://doi.org/10.1186/s13036-019-0199-7

Kasravi M, Ahmadi A, Babajani A, Mazloomnejad R, Hatamnejad MR, Shariatzadeh S, Bahrami S, Niknejad H (2023) Immunogenicity of decellularized extracellular matrix scaffolds: a bottleneck in tissue engineering and regenerative medicine. Biomater Res 27:10. https://doi.org/10.1186/s40824-023-00348-z

Khorshidi S, Solouk A, Mirzadeh H, Mazinani S, Lagaron JM, Sharifi S, Ramakrishna S (2016) A review of key challenges of electrospun scaffolds for tissue-engineering applications. J Tissue Eng Regen Med 10:715–738. https://doi.org/10.1002/term.1978

Kim JJ, Hou L, Huang NF (2016) Vascularization of three-dimensional engineered tissues for regenerative medicine applications. Acta Biomater 41:17–26. https://doi.org/10.1016/j.actbio.2016.06.001

Kirkton RD, Santiago-Maysonet M, Lawson JH, Tente WE, Dahl SLM, Niklason LE, Prichard HL (2019) Bioengineered human acellular vessels recellularize and evolve into living blood vessels after human implantation. Sci Transl Med 11. https://doi.org/10.1126/scitranslmed.aau6934

Kodama A (2024) Infrapopliteal surgical and endovascular intervention. Ann Vasc Dis 17:215–218. https://doi.org/10.3400/avd.ra.24-00070

Kolesky DB, Truby RL, Gladman AS, Busbee TA, Homan KA, Lewis JA (2014) 3D bioprinting of vascularized, heterogeneous cell-laden tissue constructs. Adv Mater 26:3124–3130. https://doi.org/10.1002/adma.201305506

Kolesky DB, Homan KA, Skylar-Scott MA, Lewis JA (2016) Three-dimensional bioprinting of thick vascularized tissues. Proc Natl Acad Sci USA 113:3179–3184. https://doi.org/10.1073/pnas.1521342113

Kucukgul C, Ozler B, Karakas HE, Gozuacik D, Koc B (2013) 3D hybrid bioprinting of macrovascular structures. Procedia Eng 59:183–192. https://doi.org/10.1016/j.proeng.2013.05.109

Kumagai M, Marui A, Tabata Y, Takeda T, Yamamoto M, Yonezawa A, Tanaka S, Yanagi S, Ito-Ihara T, Ikeda T et al (2016) Safety and efficacy of sustained release of basic fibroblast growth factor using gelatin hydrogel in patients with critical limb ischemia. Heart Vessel 31: 713–721. https://doi.org/10.1007/s00380-015-0677-x

Kuznetsov KA, Murashov IS, Chernonosova VS, Chelobanov BP, Stepanova AO, Sergeevichev DS, Karpenko AA, Laktionov PP (2020) Vascular stents coated with electrospun drug-eluting material: functioning in rabbit iliac artery. Polymers (Basel) 12. https://doi.org/10.3390/polym12081741

Lalegul-Ulker O, Şeker Ş, Elçin AE, Elçin YM (2019) Encapsulation of bone marrow-mscs in prp-derived fibrin microbeads and preliminary evaluation in a volumetric muscle loss injury rat model: modular muscle tissue engineering. Artif Cells Nanomed Biotechnol 47:10–21. https://doi.org/10.1080/21691401.2018.1540426

Laowpanitchakorn P, Zeng J, Piantino M, Uchida K, Katsuyama M, Matsusaki M (2024) Biofabrication of engineered blood vessels for biomedical applications. Sci Technol Adv Mater 25:2330339. https://doi.org/10.1080/14686996.2024.2330339

Lauria AL, Kersey AJ, Propper BW, Twerdahl EH, Patel JA, Clouse WD, Calderon DR, Rickett T, Rubin ZS, Rasmussen TE, White JM (2022) Preliminary experience with the human acellular vessel: a descriptive case series detailing early use of a bioengineered blood vessel for arterial repair. Ann Vasc Surg 87:100–112. https://doi.org/10.1016/j.avsg.2022.03.037

Li J, Wu C, Chu PK, Gelinsky M (2020) 3D printing of hydrogels: rational design strategies and emerging biomedical applications. MaterSci Eng: R: Rep 140:100543. https://doi.org/10.1016/j.mser.2020.100543

Li C, Kitzerow O, Nie F, Dai J, Liu X, Carlson MA, Casale GP, Pipinos II, Li X (2021a) Bioengineering strategies for the treatment of peripheral arterial disease. Bioact Mater 6:684–696. https://doi.org/10.1016/j.bioactmat.2020.09.007

Li C, Nie F, Liu X, Chen M, Chi D, Li S, Pipinos II, Li X (2021b) Antioxidative and angiogenic hyaluronic acid-based hydrogel for the treatment of peripheral artery disease. ACS Appl Mater Interfaces 13:45224–45235. https://doi.org/10.1021/acsami.1c11349

Li J, Chen JN, Peng ZX, Chen NB, Liu CB, Zhang P, Zhang X, Chen GQ (2023) Multifunctional electrospinning polyhydroxyalkanoate fibrous scaffolds with antibacterial and angiogenesis effects for accelerating wound healing. ACS Appl Mater Interfaces 15:364–377. https://doi.org/10.1021/acsami.2c16905

Li J, Varcoe R, Manzi M, Kum S, Iida O, Schmidt A, Shishehbor MH (2024) Below-the-knee endovascular revascularization: a position statement. JACC Cardiovasc Interv 17:589–607. https://doi.org/10.1016/j.jcin.2023.11.040

Lin CH, Hsia K, Ma H, Lee H, Lu JH (2018) In vivo performance of decellularized vascular grafts: a review article. Int J Mol Sci 19. https://doi.org/10.3390/ijms19072101

Lindsey P, Echeverria A, Cheung M, Kfoury E, Bechara CF, Lin PH (2018) Lower extremity bypass using bovine carotid artery graft (Artegraft): an analysis of 124 cases with long-term results. World J Surg 42:295–301. https://doi.org/10.1007/s00268-017-4161-x
Linn T, Erb D, Schneider D, Kidszun A, Elçin AE, Bretzel RG, Elçin YM (2003) Polymers for induction of revascularization in the rat fascial flap: application of vascular endothelial growth factor and pancreatic islet cells. Cell Transplant 12:769–778. https://doi.org/10.3727/000000003108747244
Lorbeer R, Grotz A, Dorr M, Volzke H, Lieb W, Kuhn JP, Mensel B (2018) Reference values of vessel diameters, stenosis prevalence, and arterial variations of the lower limb arteries in a male population sample using contrast-enhanced mr angiography. PLoS One 13:e0197559. https://doi.org/10.1371/journal.pone.0197559
Madden LR, Mortisen DJ, Sussman EM, Dupras SK, Fugate JA, Cuy JL, Hauch KD, Laflamme MA, Murry CE, Ratner BD (2010) Proangiogenic scaffolds as functional templates for cardiac tissue engineering. Proc Natl Acad Sci USA 107:15211–15216. https://doi.org/10.1073/pnas.1006442107
Marui A, Tabata Y, Kojima S, Yamamoto M, Tambara K, Nishina T, Saji Y, Inui K, Hashida T, Yokoyama S et al (2007) A novel approach to therapeutic angiogenesis for patients with critical limb ischemia by sustained release of basic fibroblast growth factor using biodegradable gelatin hydrogel: an initial report of the phase I-IIa study. Circ J 71:1181–1186. https://doi.org/10.1253/circj.71.1181
Mason BN, Starchenko A, Williams RM, Bonassar LJ, Reinhart-King CA (2013) Tuning three-dimensional collagen matrix stiffness independently of collagen concentration modulates endothelial cell behavior. Acta Biomater 9:4635–4644. https://doi.org/10.1016/j.actbio.2012.08.007
Menasche P, Renault NK, Hagege A, Puscas T, Bellamy V, Humbert C, Le L, Blons H, Granier C, Benhamouda N et al (2024) First-in-man use of a cardiovascular cell-derived secretome in heart failure. Case report. EBioMedicine 103:105145. https://doi.org/10.1016/j.ebiom.2024.105145
Mewhort HEM, Svystonyuk DA, Turnbull JD, Teng G, Belke DD, Guzzardi DG, Park DS, Kang S, Hollenberg MD, Fedak PWM (2017) Bioactive extracellular matrix scaffold promotes adaptive cardiac remodeling and repair. JACC Basic Transl Sci 2:450–464. https://doi.org/10.1016/j.jacbts.2017.05.005
Mir A, Lee E, Shih W, Koljaka S, Wang A, Jorgensen C, Hurr R, Dave A, Sudheendra K, Hibino N (2023) 3D bioprinting for vascularization. Bioengineering 10:606. https://doi.org/10.3390/bioengineering10050606
Moore EE, Curi M, Namias N, Kundi R, Lum YW, Fox CJ, Rajani RR, Rasmussen TE, Sokolov O, Niklason LE et al (2025) Bioengineered human arteries for the repair of vascular injuries. JAMA Surg 160:181–189. https://doi.org/10.1001/jamasurg.2024.4893
Mosala Nezhad Z, Poncelet A, de Kerchove L, Gianello P, Fervaille C, El Khoury G (2016) Small intestinal submucosa extracellular matrix (CorMatrix(R)) in cardiovascular surgery: a systematic review. Interact Cardiovasc Thorac Surg 22:839–850. https://doi.org/10.1093/icvts/ivw020
Murphy CM, O'Brien FJ (2010) Understanding the effect of mean pore size on cell activity in collagen-glycosaminoglycan scaffolds. Cell Adhes Migr 4:377–381. https://doi.org/10.4161/cam.4.3.11747
Nazarkina ZK, Chelobanov BP, Kuznetsov KA, Shutov AV, Romanova IV, Karpenko AA, Laktionov PP (2021) Influence of elongation of paclitaxel-eluting electrospun-produced stent coating on paclitaxel release and transport through the arterial wall after stenting. Polymers (Basel) 13. https://doi.org/10.3390/polym13071165
Nazarnezhad S, Kargozar S, Ramakrishna S (2022) Electrospun nanofibers for angiogenesis strategies. In: Biomaterials for vasculogenesis and angiogenesis. Elsevier, pp 383–414
Nazeer MA, Karaoglu IC, Ozer O, Albayrak C, Kizilel S (2021) Neovascularization of engineered tissues for clinical translation: where we are, where we should be? APL Bioeng 5:021503. https://doi.org/10.1063/5.0044027
Nordanstig J, Behrendt CA, Baumgartner I, Belch J, Back M, Fitridge R, Hinchliffe R, Lejay A, Mills JL, Rother U et al (2024) Editor's choice - European Society for Vascular Surgery (ESVS)

2024 clinical practice guidelines on the management of asymptomatic lower limb peripheral arterial disease and intermittent claudication. Eur J Vasc Endovasc Surg 67:9–96. https://doi.org/10.1016/j.ejvs.2023.08.067
O'Connor C, Brady E, Zheng Y, Moore E, Stevens KR (2022) Engineering the multiscale complexity of vascular networks. Nat Rev Mater 7:702–716. https://doi.org/10.1038/s41578-022-00447-8
Oliviero O, Ventre M, Netti PA (2012) Functional porous hydrogels to study angiogenesis under the effect of controlled release of vascular endothelial growth factor. Acta Biomater 8:3294–3301. https://doi.org/10.1016/j.actbio.2012.05.019
Öztürk S (2025) Revascularization in below-the-knee lesions. In: Ebinç H, Öztürk S (eds) Approach to lower extremity peripheral artery diseases, pp 58–65
Öztürk S, Elçin AE, Elçin YM (2020) Mesenchymal stem cells for coronavirus (COVID-19)-induced pneumonia: revisiting the paracrine hypothesis with new hopes? Aging Dis 11:477–479. https://doi.org/10.14336/AD.2020.0403
Öztürk S, Elçin AE, Elçin YM (2021a) Functions of mesenchymal stem cells in cardiac repair. Adv Exp Med Biol 1312:39–50. https://doi.org/10.1007/5584_2020_598
Öztürk S, Elçin AE, Koca A, Elçin YM (2021b) Therapeutic applications of stem cells and extracellular vesicles in emergency care: futuristic perspectives. Stem Cell Rev Rep 17:390–410. https://doi.org/10.1007/s12015-020-10029-2
Pagan E, Stefanek E, Seyfoori A, Razzaghi M, Chehri B, Mousavi A, Arnaldi P, Ajji Z, Dartora DR, Dabiri SMH et al (2023) A handheld bioprinter for multi-material printing of complex constructs. Biofabrication 15. https://doi.org/10.1088/1758-5090/acc42c
Persson AB, Buschmann IR (2011) Vascular growth in health and disease. Front Mol Neurosci 4:14. https://doi.org/10.3389/fnmol.2011.00014
Phelps EA, Garcia AJ (2010) Engineering more than a cell: vascularization strategies in tissue engineering. Curr Opin Biotechnol 21:704–709. https://doi.org/10.1016/j.copbio.2010.06.005
Pu J, Yuan F, Li S, Komvopoulos K (2015) Electrospun bilayer fibrous scaffolds for enhanced cell infiltration and vascularization in vivo. Acta Biomater 13:131–141. https://doi.org/10.1016/j.actbio.2014.11.014
Qadura M, Terenzi DC, Verma S, Al-Omran M, Hess DA (2018) Concise review: cell therapy for critical limb ischemia: an integrated review of preclinical and clinical studies. Stem Cells 36:161–171. https://doi.org/10.1002/stem.2751
Qamar SUR, Spahic L, Benolic L, Zivanovic M, Filipovic N (2023) Treatment of peripheral artery disease using injectable biomaterials and drug-coated balloons: safety and efficacy perspective. Pharmaceutics 15. https://doi.org/10.3390/pharmaceutics15071813
Rajani RR, Velez FF, Knight T, Kauffman L, Pascarella L, Malone DC, Rasmussen TE, Niklason LE, Parikh S (2025) Short-term performance of Symvess (acellular tissue engineered vessel-tyod) compared to external control data for autologous vein in treatment of extremity arterial injury. Trauma Surg Acute Care Open 10:e001814. https://doi.org/10.1136/tsaco-2025-001814
Reilly B, Khan S, Dosluoglu H, Harris L, O'Brien-Irr M, Lukan J, Dryjski M, Blochle R (2019) Comparison of autologous vein and bovine carotid artery graft as a bypass conduit in arterial trauma. Ann Vasc Surg 61:246–253. https://doi.org/10.1016/j.avsg.2019.05.017
Rodriguez-Soto MA, Polania-Sandoval CA, Aragon-Rivera AM, Buitrago D, Ayala-Velasquez M, Velandia-Sanchez A, Peralta Peluffo G, Cruz JC, Munoz Camargo C, Camacho-Mackenzie J et al (2022) Small diameter cell-free tissue-engineered vascular grafts: biomaterials and manufacture techniques to reach suitable mechanical properties. Polymers (Basel) 14. https://doi.org/10.3390/polym14173440
Saburi E, Jamialahmdi H, Samsami Y (2022) Three-dimensional (3D) angiogenic constructs. In: Biomaterials for vasculogenesis and angiogenesis. Elsevier, pp 273–300
Santschi M, Vernengo A, Eglin D, D'Este M, Wuertz-Kozak K (2019) Decellularized matrix as a building block in bioprinting and electrospinning. Curr Opin Biomed Eng 10:116–122. https://doi.org/10.1016/J.COBME.2019.05.003

Seymour AJ, Westerfield AD, Cornelius VC, Skylar-Scott MA, Heilshorn SC (2022) Bioprinted microvasculature: progressing from structure to function. Biofabrication 14:022002. https://doi.org/10.1088/1758-5090/ac4fb5

Sharp MA, Phillips D, Roberts I, Hands L (2004) A cautionary case: the synergraft vascular prosthesis. Eur J Vasc Endovasc Surg 27:42–44. https://doi.org/10.1016/j.ejvs.2003.09.015

Shi J, Teng Y, Li D, He J, Midgley AC, Guo X, Wang X, Yang X, Wang S, Feng Y et al (2023) Biomimetic tri-layered small-diameter vascular grafts with decellularized extracellular matrix promoting vascular regeneration and inhibiting thrombosis with the salidroside. Mater Today Bio 21:100709. https://doi.org/10.1016/j.mtbio.2023.100709

Simons M, Eichmann A (2015) Molecular controls of arterial morphogenesis. Circ Res 116:1712–1724. https://doi.org/10.1161/CIRCRESAHA.116.302953

Sokolov O, Shaprynskyi V, Skupyy O, Stanko O, Yurets S, Yurkova Y, Niklason LE (2023) Use of bioengineered human acellular vessels to treat traumatic injuries in the Ukraine-Russia conflict. Lancet Reg Health Eur 29:100650. https://doi.org/10.1016/j.lanepe.2023.100650

Spadaccio C, Nenna A, Rose D, Piccirillo F, Nusca A, Grigioni F, Chello M, Vlahakes GJ (2022) The role of angiogenesis and arteriogenesis in myocardial infarction and coronary revascularization. J Cardiovasc Transl Res 15:1024–1048. https://doi.org/10.1007/s12265-022-10241-0

Struczewska P, Razian SA, Townsend K, Jadidi M, Shahbad R, Zamani E, Gamache J, MacTaggart J, Kamenskiy A (2024) Mechanical, structural, and physiologic differences between above and below-knee human arteries. Acta Biomater 177:278–299. https://doi.org/10.1016/j.actbio.2024.01.040

Sung HJ, Meredith C, Johnson C, Galis ZS (2004) The effect of scaffold degradation rate on three-dimensional cell growth and angiogenesis. Biomaterials 25:5735–5742. https://doi.org/10.1016/j.biomaterials.2004.01.066

Svystonyuk DA, Mewhort HEM, Hassanabad AF, Heydari B, Mikami Y, Turnbull JD, Teng G, Belke DD, Wagner KT, Tarraf SA et al (2020) Acellular bioscaffolds redirect cardiac fibroblasts and promote functional tissue repair in rodents and humans with myocardial injury. Sci Rep 10:9459. https://doi.org/10.1038/s41598-020-66327-9

Takahara M, Soga Y, Iida O (2024) Lower extremity arterial disease vs. coronary artery disease: mortality differences after revascularization. Eur Heart J 45:1634–1643. https://doi.org/10.1093/eurheartj/ehae207

Tanriverdi AK, Polat O, Elçin AE, Ahlat O, Gurman G, Gunalp M, Oguz AB, Genc S, Elçin YM (2020) Mesenchymal stem cell transplantation in polytrauma: evaluation of bone and liver healing response in an experimental rat model. Eur J Trauma Emerg Surg 46:53–64. https://doi.org/10.1007/s00068-019-01101-9

Tomasina C, Bodet T, Mota C, Moroni L, Camarero-Espinosa S (2019) Bioprinting vasculature: materials, cells and emergent techniques. Materials (Basel) 12. https://doi.org/10.3390/ma12172701

Tong Z, Xu Z, Tong Y, Qi L, Guo L, Guo J, Gu Y (2021) Effectiveness of distal arterial bypass with porcine decellularized vascular graft for treating diabetic lower limb ischemia. Int J Artif Organs 44:580–586. https://doi.org/10.1177/0391398820980021

Torres-Martínez EJ, Cornejo Bravo JM, Serrano Medina A, Pérez González GL, Villarreal Gómez LJ (2018) A summary of electrospun nanofibers as drug delivery system: drugs loaded and biopolymers used as matrices. Curr Drug Deliv 15:1360–1374. https://doi.org/10.2174/1567201815666180723114326

Ungerleider JL, Christman KL (2014) Concise review: injectable biomaterials for the treatment of myocardial infarction and peripheral artery disease: translational challenges and progress. Stem Cells Transl Med 3:1090–1099. https://doi.org/10.5966/sctm.2014-0049

Urciuolo F, Casale C, Imparato G, Netti PA (2019) Bioengineered skin substitutes: the role of extracellular matrix and vascularization in the healing of deep wounds. J Clin Med 8. https://doi.org/10.3390/jcm8122083

van der Veen VC, van der Wal MB, van Leeuwen MC, Ulrich MM, Middelkoop E (2010) Biological background of dermal substitutes. Burns 36:305–321. https://doi.org/10.1016/j.burns.2009.07.012

Wang X, Wang L, Wu Q, Bao F, Yang H, Qiu X, Chang J (2019) Chitosan/calcium silicate cardiac patch stimulates cardiomyocyte activity and myocardial performance after infarction by synergistic effect of bioactive ions and aligned nanostructure. ACS Appl Mater Interfaces 11:1449–1468. https://doi.org/10.1021/acsami.8b17754

Wang CY, Hsiao CY, Tsai KL, Cheng YH (2020) Injectable thermosensitive chitosan-based hydrogel containing ferulic acid for treating peripheral arterial disease. J Tissue Eng Regen Med 14:1438–1448. https://doi.org/10.1002/term.3109

Wang X, Chan V, Corridon PR (2022) Decellularized blood vessel development: current state-of-the-art and future directions. Front Bioeng Biotechnol 10:951644. https://doi.org/10.3389/fbioe.2022.951644

Wang Y, Liu M, Zhang W, Liu H, Jin F, Mao S, Han C, Wang X (2024) Mechanical strategies to promote vascularization for tissue engineering and regenerative medicine. *Burns*. Trauma 12: tkae039. https://doi.org/10.1093/burnst/tkae039

Wang H, Lin F, Zhang Y, Lin Y, Gao B, Kang D (2025) Biomaterial-based vascularization strategies for enhanced treatment of peripheral arterial disease. J Nanobiotechnology 23:103. https://doi.org/10.1186/s12951-025-03140-4

Wu W, DeConinck A, Lewis JA (2011) Omnidirectional printing of 3D microvascular networks. Adv Mater 23:H178–H183. https://doi.org/10.1002/adma.201004625

Xu P, Kankala RK, Wang S, Chen A (2024) Decellularized extracellular matrix-based composite scaffolds for tissue engineering and regenerative medicine. Regener Biomater 11:rbad107. https://doi.org/10.1093/rb/rbad107

Yeo M, Sarkar A, Singh YP, Derman ID, Datta P, Ozbolat IT (2023) Synergistic coupling between 3D bioprinting and vascularization strategies. Biofabrication 16. https://doi.org/10.1088/1758-5090/ad0b3f

Yuan Y, Zhang Z, Mo F, Yang C, Jiao Y, Wang E, Zhang Y, Lin P, Hu C, Fu W et al (2023) A biomaterial-based therapy for lower limb ischemia using Sr/Si bioactive hydrogel that inhibits skeletal muscle necrosis and enhances angiogenesis. Bioact Mater 26:264–278. https://doi.org/10.1016/j.bioactmat.2023.02.027

Zamani M, Prabhakaran MP, Ramakrishna S (2013) Advances in drug delivery via electrospun and electrosprayed nanomaterials. Int J Nanomedicine 8:2997–3017. https://doi.org/10.2147/IJN.S43575

Zehr BP, Niblick CJ, Downey H, Ladowski JS (2011) Limb salvage with cryovein cadaver saphenous vein allografts used for peripheral arterial bypass: role of blood compatibility. Ann Vasc Surg 25:177–181. https://doi.org/10.1016/j.avsg.2010.07.020

Zhang WJ, Liu W, Cui L, Cao Y (2007) Tissue engineering of blood vessel. J Cell Mol Med 11: 945–957. https://doi.org/10.1111/j.1582-4934.2007.00099.x

Chapter 8
Skin Biofabrication

Paula Ávila-Fernández, Miguel Etayo-Escanilla, and Jesús Chato-Astrain

Abstract Skin biofabrication has emerged as a transformative strategy to overcome the limitations of conventional clinical approaches for managing skin defects. This chapter provides a comprehensive overview of the design and clinical translation of bioengineered skin substitutes, focusing on the three fundamental pillars of tissue engineering: cells, biomaterials, and bioactive molecules and their integration into advanced fabrication strategies. We discuss monolayer and multilayer models, highlighting their evolution from cultured epithelial autografts to complex bilayer constructs incorporating fibroblasts, melanocytes, and endothelial cells within biomimetic scaffolds. Special emphasis is placed on the translational pathway, including preclinical characterization and regulatory challenges under the Advanced Therapy Medicinal Product (ATMP) framework. Finally, clinically approved skin substitutes are classified by structural complexity, cellular origin, and intended use, illustrating their advantages, limitations, and impact on patient outcomes.

Keywords Tissue engineering · Biomaterials · Growth factors · Clinical translation · Advanced therapy medicinal products · Severe skin burns

Abbreviations

ATMP	Advanced Therapy Medicinal Products
bFGF	basic Fibroblast Growth Factor
CAlloK	Cultured Allogenic Keratinocytes
CEA	Cultured Epithelial Autografts
ECM	Extracellular Matrix
EGF	Epidermal Growth Factor
EMA	European Medicines Agency

P. Ávila-Fernández · M. Etayo-Escanilla (✉) · J. Chato-Astrain
Department of Histology and Tissue Engineering Group, University of Granada, Granada, Spain

Instituto de Investigación Biosanitaria ibs.GRANADA, Granada, Spain
e-mail: pavila@ugr.es; metayo@ugr.es; jchato@ugr.es

Y. M. Elçin (ed.), *Biofabrication in Regenerative Medicine*, Stem Cell Biology and Regenerative Medicine 1519, https://doi.org/10.1007/978-3-032-30294-6_8

ESEN	European Skin Engineering Network
GMP	Good Manufacturing Practice
MSCs	Mesenchymal Stem Cells
PCL	Polycaprolactone
PDGF	Platelet-derived Growth Factor
PGA	Polyglycolic Acid
RHE	Reconstructed Human Epidermis
STSGs	Split-thickness skin grafts
TGF-β	Transforming Growth Factor β
VEGF	Vascular Endothelial Growth Factor
3D	Three-dimensional

8.1 Introduction

The skin is the largest organ of the human body, accounting for approximately 15% of total body weight. Its integrity is essential for maintaining homeostasis, as it provides a dynamic barrier that prevents fluid loss, protects against pathogens, and regulates temperature. Although histologically complex, the skin can be broadly divided into two principal layers: the epidermis and the dermis. The epidermis, composed mainly of keratinocytes, ensures barrier function and rapid reepithelialization after injury, while the dermis, rich in fibroblasts, extracellular matrix (ECM), vasculature, and neural elements, confers mechanical strength and elasticity and supports vascularization and immune responses. Beyond its structural role, the skin performs critical physiological functions, including thermoregulation, sensory perception, immune surveillance, and protection against mechanical, chemical, and microbial insults (Arda et al. 2014; Kanitakis 2002).

A wide spectrum of pathological conditions can compromise skin integrity, ranging from acute injuries such as burns and traumatic wounds to chronic disorders including diabetic foot ulcers, venous leg ulcers, and pressure sores. These conditions represent a major clinical and socioeconomic burden worldwide. For example, burns alone account for an estimated 8.3 million new cases annually, with over 111,000 deaths globally, and remain the fourth most common type of trauma injury (Smolle et al. 2017; Yakupu et al. 2022). In severe burn patients, the limited availability of autologous donor sites remains a critical bottleneck, often resulting in prolonged hospitalization, increased infection risk, and high mortality rates. Current standard-of-care strategies, such as split-thickness autografts and allogeneic grafts, are frequently insufficient to restore full functionality and aesthetics, underscoring an urgent unmet need for advanced therapeutic solutions (Stewart et al. n.d.).

Over the past three decades, tissue engineering has emerged as a transformative approach to address these challenges by combining cells, biomaterials, and bioactive factors to generate functional skin substitutes(Langer and Vacanti 1993). Numerous artificial human skin models have been described in the literature, ranging from simple epidermal sheets to complex bilayered constructs incorporating dermal and epidermal components (Carriel et al. 2012; Dearman et al. 2021; Vig et al. 2017). These bioengineered tissues aim not only to achieve wound closure but also to restore the structural and functional properties of native skin. However, despite the proliferation of experimental models, only a limited number have successfully progressed from bench to bedside. The translational gap as Advanced Therapy Medicinal Products (ATMPs) is largely attributable to regulatory requirements imposed by the European Medicines Agency (EMA) and national competent authorities, to Compliance with Good Manufacturing Practice (GMP), rigorous quality control, and comprehensive preclinical and clinical validation significantly increase the complexity, cost, and timelines of product development (Egea-Guerrero et al. 2019; European Medicine Agency (EMA) 2025, 2017).

In this chapter, we will first provide an overview of the main biofabrication technologies currently employed for the generation of artificial human skin, and subsequently, we will examine clinically approved skin substitutes and discuss the key factors that enable successful translation into routine clinical practice.

8.2 Skin Biofabrication Technologies

8.2.1 Key Components

Tissue engineering relies on the interplay of three fundamental elements: cells, biomaterials, and bioactive molecules such as growth factors. These components act synergistically to recreate the structural and functional complexity of native tissues.

8.2.1.1 Cell Sources

The skin, as an organ, comprises two major tissue types: epithelial tissue forming the epidermis and connective tissue forming the dermis. This structural complexity dictates that bioengineered skin substitutes must incorporate multiple cell populations to achieve functional restoration. This structural heterogeneity requires the inclusion of multiple cell populations to achieve physiological relevance. The more biomimetic the intended construct, the greater the diversity of cell types needed, extending beyond keratinocytes and fibroblasts to include endothelial and immune cells.

Keratinocytes are the predominant cells of the epidermis and play a central role in restoring the barrier function of the skin. They are responsible for reepithelialization and the formation of stratified layers that prevent fluid loss and microbial invasion (Peña and Martin 2024). Isolation of keratinocytes typically begins with split-thickness skin biopsies or neonatal foreskin, which are enzymatically treated with trypsin or dispase to separate the epidermis from the dermis. The resulting cell suspension is filtered and plated in defined keratinocyte media. Alternatively, explant techniques allow keratinocytes to migrate from tissue fragments, although this method requires longer culture times (Chato-Astrain et al. 2021; Ortiz-Arrabal et al. 2023; Ścieżyńska et al. 2019). Once isolated, keratinocytes are expanded under conditions that maintain their proliferative capacity, commonly using serum-free media supplemented with epidermal growth factor and low calcium concentrations. The classic Rheinwald and Green method (Rheinwald and Green 1975), which employs a feeder layer of lethally irradiated 3 T3 fibroblasts, remains widely used to support keratinocyte growth and prevent senescence, although feeder-free systems have also been developed for clinical applications(Lenihan et al. 2014).

Fibroblasts, the principal cells of the dermis, synthesize ECM components such as collagen and elastin, providing mechanical strength and elasticity. They also secrete paracrine factors that influence keratinocyte differentiation and angiogenesis. Isolation of fibroblasts generally involves collagenase digestion of dermal tissue followed by centrifugation and plating in fibroblast-specific media (Goodarzi et al. 2020; Ningsih et al. 2024; Rittié and Fisher 2005). Cultured fibroblasts are typically maintained in monolayer until sufficient numbers are obtained for incorporation into scaffolds or hydrogels. These cells exhibit robust proliferative capacity and are relatively easy to expand, making them a cornerstone of dermal equivalent fabrication.

Melanocytes, located in the basal layer of the epidermis, are responsible for pigmentation and photoprotection through melanin synthesis. Their inclusion in biofabricated skin constructs is essential for achieving physiological color and protecting against ultraviolet radiation. As for keratinocytes, melanocytes can be isolated both using enzymatic digestion of epidermal tissue or by the explant-based methods. Once isolated, melanocytes require highly specific culture conditions to maintain their dendritic morphology and melanin-producing capacity (Cario and Taieb 2019). Traditional protocols often rely on co-culture with mitotically inactivated keratinocytes as feeder layers, which provide paracrine signals that prevent dedifferentiation and senescence (Goff et al. 2023; Ścieżyńska et al. 2021). However, recent advances have introduced serum-free, PMA-free media formulations supplemented with growth factors such as basic fibroblast growth factor (bFGF), endothelin-1, and cholera toxin, enabling feeder-free expansion under controlled conditions. Isolation of melanocytes often follows keratinocyte separation, using selective culture media enriched with growth factors such as basic bFGF and cholera toxin to promote melanocyte proliferation while inhibiting keratinocyte overgrowth. These cells require careful handling to maintain their dendritic morphology and melanin-producing capacity, which are critical for functional integration (Goff et al. 2023).

Endothelial cells are increasingly recognized as essential for overcoming one of the major limitations of engineered skin: delayed vascularization. Their inclusion promotes angiogenesis and improves graft survival by facilitating rapid inosculation with host vessels. Isolation of endothelial cells from dermal tissue involves enzymatic digestion followed by immunomagnetic bead sorting or fluorescence-activated cell sorting based on endothelial markers such as CD31 or VE-cadherin. These cells are cultured in specialized endothelial growth media and often co-cultured with fibroblasts to enhance vessel formation (Bourland et al. 2025; Hou et al. 2022).

Immune cells, particularly macrophages and dendritic cells, are being integrated into advanced skin models to replicate the immunological functions of native tissue. These cells contribute to cytokine signaling, pathogen defense, and tissue remodeling. Their inclusion is technically challenging because of the need to maintain viability and functionality in complex co-culture systems. Recent studies have demonstrated that macrophage incorporation into three-dimensional constructs enhances inflammatory response modeling and improves wound healing dynamics (Urciuolo et al. 2022; Wu et al. 2021).

The successful isolation and culture of these diverse cell types require stringent control of enzymatic digestion, media composition, and environmental conditions to preserve phenotype and functionality. As biofabrication technologies evolve, the integration of multiple cell populations will remain a key determinant of construct performance and translational success (Fig. 8.1).

8.2.1.2 Biomaterials

Biomaterials constitute the structural foundation of biofabricated skin substitutes, acting as three-dimensional frameworks that support cell adhesion, migration, and differentiation while guiding tissue organization. Their role extends beyond passive support; they actively influence cellular behavior through biochemical signals and mechanical cues. In skin biofabrication, biomaterials are broadly classified into natural polymers, which mimic ECM components, and synthetic polymers, which provide tunable mechanical properties and reproducibility. Increasingly, hybrid strategies combine both categories to achieve optimal bioactivity and structural integrity (Sheikholeslam et al. 2018; Yu et al. 2019).

Natural polymers are favored for their ability to replicate the biochemical complexity of the dermal ECM, which is essential for maintaining homeostasis, transmitting signals, and regulating cell proliferation. Collagen, the most abundant protein in the dermis, is the cornerstone of many scaffolds because of its inherent cell-binding motifs that facilitate fibroblast and keratinocyte adhesion (Chattopadhyay and Raines 2014; Wang et al. 2023). However, collagen hydrogels alone often exhibit poor mechanical strength and contraction, limiting their application in clinically demanding contexts. To overcome these limitations, cross-linking agents (Berasain et al. 2024; García-García et al. 2021; Li et al. 2025) and composite scaffolds have been developed, integrating multiple ECM-derived materials such as collagen–fibrin blends and agarose–collagen hydrogels, between others (Bindi et al. 2023; Sang et al. 2023). These combinations enhance biomechanical properties while preserving bioactivity, resulting in constructs that better mimic native tissue architecture and function. Another natural biomaterial widely used is fibrin; fibrin is particularly relevant for wound healing applications because of its intrinsic role in clot formation and angiogenesis. Fibrin as biomaterials has also poor mechanical properties, and it is overcome with composites one of those are fibrin–agarose

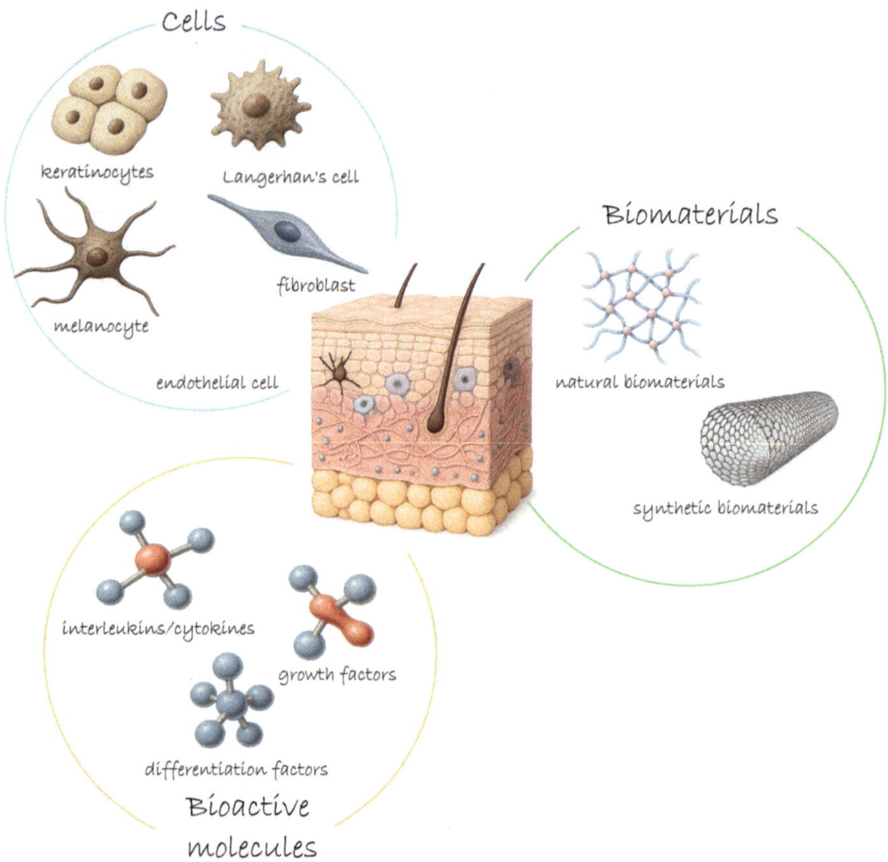

Fig. 8.1 Key components for designing an artificial skin substitute. The illustration depicts the three fundamental pillars of skin tissue engineering: cells, biomaterials, and bioactive molecules. Cells include those forming the epidermis (epithelial tissue) and the dermis (connective tissue), such as keratinocytes, fibroblasts, melanocytes, and endothelial cells. Biomaterials comprise natural and synthetic polymers that provide structural support and guide tissue organization. Bioactive molecules, including growth factors, regulate cell proliferation, differentiation, and angiogenesis. Together, these elements form the foundation for biofabricating clinically relevant skin substitutes

hydrogels have emerged as a particularly promising option for skin tissue engineering (Arribas-Arribas et al. 2023; Campos et al. 2020; Carriel et al. 2012; Martin et al. 2023). Fibrin provides a bioactive environment that promotes cell adhesion and angiogenesis, while agarose contributes structural stability and reduces contraction of the construct. This synergy addresses the limitations of fibrin alone, which is prone to rapid degradation and shrinkage. Fibrin–agarose scaffolds have demonstrated excellent biocompatibility in preclinical studies, supporting cellular infiltration, neovascularization, and controlled biodegradation without adverse systemic effects (Campos et al. 2020; Ionescu et al. 2020). Furthermore, this composite has progressed beyond the experimental stage: a bilayered fibrin–agarose skin substitute

(UGRSKIN model) has been clinically translated under hospital exemption for severe burns, with histological analyses confirming early epidermal maturation and dermal ECM organization in grafted patients (Egea-Guerrero et al. 2019; Martin et al. 2023).

Other natural polymers, such as hyaluronic acid, contribute hydration and viscoelasticity, while chitosan offers antimicrobial properties and structural support (Boateng et al. 2008). Decellularized dermal matrix represents the most biomimetic option, preserving native collagen and elastin architecture along with glycosaminoglycans and bound growth factors. After validated decellularization and lyophilization, these scaffolds provide an ideal platform for cell seeding and advanced tissue modeling, although standardization and immunogenicity testing remain critical for clinical use (Jansen et al. 2013).

In contrast, synthetic polymers such as polycaprolactone (PCL), polylactic acid (PLA), and polyglycolic acid (PGA) offer superior mechanical strength, scalability, and reproducibility. These materials can be processed into fibers, meshes, or porous scaffolds using techniques like electrospinning and three-dimensional (3D) printing, enabling precise control over architecture and porosity. Although synthetic polymers lack intrinsic bioactivity, they can be functionalized with peptides, growth factors, or nanoparticles to enhance cell adhesion and confer additional properties. Hybrid scaffolds combining natural and synthetic components are increasingly employed to leverage the advantages of both classes: natural polymers improve biocompatibility and cell signaling, while synthetic polymers provide structural integrity and durability. For example, alginate/gelatin hydrogels reinforced with PCL nanofibers have demonstrated enhanced healing in diabetic wound models, illustrating the clinical relevance of these composite strategies (Suamte et al. 2023).

Ultimately, the choice of biomaterials must balance biological mimicry, mechanical performance, and regulatory compliance. Natural polymers offer superior bioactivity but require reinforcement to overcome mechanical limitations, whereas synthetic polymers provide strength and scalability but demand functionalization to achieve cellular compatibility. The integration of these approaches represents a key trend in skin biofabrication, enabling the development of scaffolds that combine physiological relevance with translational feasibility.

8.2.1.3 Bioactive Molecules

The third pillar of skin biofabrication, alongside cells and biomaterials, is represented by bioactive molecules, primarily growth factors and cytokines. These signaling proteins orchestrate the complex processes of wound healing and tissue regeneration by regulating cell proliferation, migration, differentiation, and ECM deposition. In artificial skin models, the controlled delivery of bioactive molecules is essential to mimic the physiological microenvironment and accelerate integration with host tissue.

Growth factors such as epidermal growth factor (EGF), fibroblast growth factor (FGF), vascular endothelial growth factor (VEGF), platelet-derived growth factor

(PDGF), and transforming growth factor-beta (TGF-β) play pivotal roles in skin regeneration. EGF stimulates keratinocyte proliferation and migration, promoting rapid reepithelialization. FGF, particularly FGF-2, enhances fibroblast activity and angiogenesis, while VEGF drives vascularization, a critical step for graft survival. PDGF acts as a chemoattractant for fibroblasts and smooth muscle cells, supporting granulation tissue formation, and TGF-β regulates ECM synthesis and remodeling, contributing to scar formation and dermal stability (Barrientos et al. 2008; Bártolo et al. 2022; Yamakawa and Hayashida 2019).

Artificial skin substitutes often incorporate these molecules either through direct impregnation into scaffolds, controlled-release systems, or biological carriers such as platelet-rich plasma (PRP) and fibrin-based matrices. Despite their therapeutic potential, growth factor-based strategies face significant challenges. These molecules exhibit short half-lives, rapid diffusion from the application site, and susceptibility to proteolytic degradation, necessitating supraphysiological doses that increase cost and risk of adverse effects (Ren et al. 2019). To overcome these limitations, innovative approaches such as growth factor engineering, affinity-binding to biomaterials, and nanocarrier systems have been developed to prolong stability and achieve controlled release (Chato-Astrain et al. 2021, 2020; Chen et al. 2019; Gainza et al. 2014) Furthermore, combining multiple growth factors rather than single-agent delivery has proven synergistic, enhancing angiogenesis, keratinocyte migration, and ECM remodeling in engineered skin constructs (Park and Kim 2017).

8.2.2 *Biofabrication Approaches for Skin Substitutes*

The biofabrication of skin substitutes encompasses a spectrum of strategies aimed at replicating the structural and functional complexity of native skin. These approaches can be broadly categorized into monolayer skin models, which represent the simplest configuration, and multilayer skin models, which incorporate both epidermal and dermal components to achieve higher levels of biomimicry. In this section, we will first examine monolayer technologies, which form the foundation of epidermal engineering, before addressing multilayer constructs that aim to recreate full-thickness skin architecture.

8.2.2.1 Monolayer Skin Models

Monolayer skin models consist of a single layer of cells, typically keratinocytes, cultured on a two-dimensional substrate. These systems are technologically straightforward, requiring the isolation of keratinocytes from a small biopsy, expansion in defined media, and seeding onto a surface that supports adhesion and proliferation (Poumay and Faway 2023). The process begins with enzymatic dissociation of epidermal tissue using trypsin or dispase, followed by culture in serum-free media enriched with EGF and insulin to maintain proliferative capacity. Historically, the Rheinwald and Green method, which employs feeder layers of lethally irradiated 3 T3 fibroblasts, has been widely adopted to prevent premature differentiation and sustain keratinocyte growth (Rheinwald and Green 1975). More recent protocols have introduced xenogeneic-free systems using laminin-coated substrates and chemically defined media, improving safety and regulatory compliance (Tjin et al. 2020).

Among monolayer technologies, epidermal sheets, also known as cultured epithelial autografts (CEAs), are generated by expanding keratinocytes until confluence and lifting the cohesive cell layer from the culture surface. This requires careful handling to preserve sheet integrity, often using enzymatic detachment followed by flotation and transfer onto a supportive carrier (Wille et al. 2014). Self-assembly approaches have also been explored, where keratinocytes form continuous sheets without exogenous scaffolds, relying on their intrinsic ability to produce ECM components under optimized conditions (Climov et al. 2016).

Although monolayer models cannot replicate the 3D architecture or the complex cell–matrix interactions of native skin, they remain indispensable for early-stage research. They provide a reproducible and cost-effective platform for studying keratinocyte biology, epidermal barrier function, and disease mechanisms, as well as for preliminary testing of pharmacological agents and antiseptics under controlled conditions (Marsella et al. 2022; Ortega-Llamas et al. 2022). Their simplicity and scalability also make them foundational technologies for more advanced biofabrication strategies.

8.2.2.2 Multilayer Skin Models

Multilayer or 3D skin models represent a major step forward in biofabrication because they allow the recreation of a more physiologically relevant microenvironment compared to monolayer systems. These constructs enable complex interactions between cells and ECM, supporting processes such as stratification, differentiation, and angiogenesis. Most multilayer models aim to reproduce two of the three layers of native skin, the epidermis and dermis, forming full-thickness equivalents (FTE). However, some models exclusively replicate the epithelial layer, known as reconstructed human epidermis (RHE), which is widely used for toxicological testing and disease modeling (Desmet et al. 2017; Devaraj et al. 2025). RHE models permit keratinocyte stratification by culturing cells on semi-permeable membranes under air–liquid interface conditions (Rosdy and Clauss 1990). While these models are suitable for studying disorders confined to the epidermis, most tissue engineering strategies aim to incorporate a dermal component, given the fundamental role of the ECM in skin homeostasis and signaling (Phang et al. 2022; Wistner et al. 2023).

Technological approaches for generating multilayer skin models can be grouped into self-assembly systems, scaffold-based strategies, and 3D bioprinting techniques.

Self-assembly methods exploit the intrinsic capacity of cells to organize into tissue-like structures without exogenous scaffolds. Under optimized conditions, fibroblasts produce their own extracellular matrix, forming a dermal-like layer that can subsequently support keratinocyte seeding and stratification. These organoid systems are particularly valuable for modeling complex biological processes, including inflammatory responses and disease-specific phenotypes, as they provide a high degree of biomimicry (Chetprayoon et al. 2020; Dagher et al. 2022). However, their fabrication requires prolonged culture periods and precise control of biochemical cues to ensure matrix deposition and structural integrity.

Scaffold-based approaches remain the most widely used method for constructing multilayer skin models. Scaffolds provide a physical framework that supports cell adhesion, proliferation, and differentiation. Gel molding is a common technique, where natural biomaterials such as collagen, fibrin, agarose, and hyaluronic acid are dissolved to form a hydrogel. Fibroblasts are incorporated into the gel before polymerization, creating a dermal equivalent. Keratinocytes are then seeded on the surface and cultured at an air–liquid interface to promote epidermal stratification (Ávila-Fernández et al. 2024). This method is relatively simple and does not require specialized equipment, making it accessible for many research laboratories.

One limitation of traditional scaffold-based methods is their manual nature, which can lead to variability and low reproducibility. 3D bioprinting addresses these challenges by enabling precise spatial deposition of cells and biomaterials, resulting in highly reproducible and customizable constructs. Natural hydrogels such as collagen and fibrin and decellularized dermis ECM can be formulated as bioinks and combined with multiple cell types, including fibroblasts, keratinocytes, endothelial cells, and immune cells, to create complex tissue architectures(Quílez et al. 2020; Won et al. 2019). Among bioprinting modalities, extrusion-based printing is the most widely adopted due to its versatility and ability to handle viscous bioinks. However, despite its potential, the development of bioinks remains a major challenge. Bioinks must simultaneously meet conflicting requirements: they need to be biocompatible and supportive of cell viability, exhibit appropriate rheological properties for printing, and provide mechanical stability post-printing, all while ensuring controlled degradation and integration with host tissue (Peng et al. 2025; Weng et al. 2021). Achieving this balance often requires complex formulations and compromises between printability and biological performance, which continues to be a critical area of research (Fig. 8.2).

8.3 Clinically Approved Bioengineered Skin Substitutes: From ......Bench to Bedside

The translation of bioengineered skin substitutes from laboratory research to clinical application remains one of the most challenging steps in tissue engineering. While technological advances have enabled the development of increasingly biomimetic constructs, their clinical adoption is hindered by stringent regulatory requirements and the complexity of demonstrating safety, efficacy, and reproducibility. In Europe,

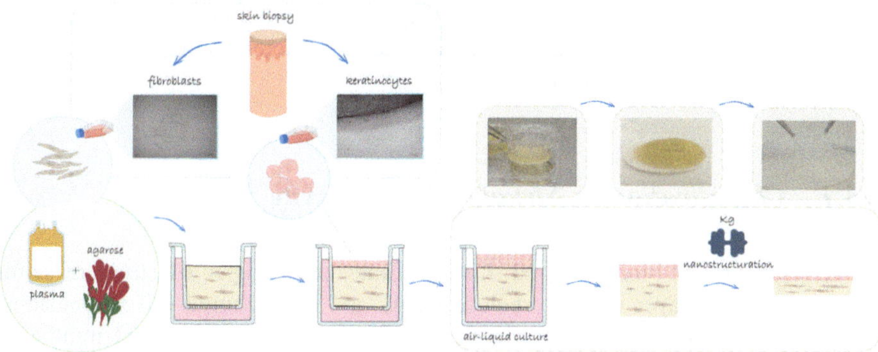

Fig. 8.2 Sequential biofabrication of a multilayered skin substitute based on the UGRSKIN model. The schematic illustrates the stepwise process for generating a bilayered construct: preparation of a fibrin–agarose dermal scaffold, embedding autologous fibroblasts within the matrix, and subsequent seeding of keratinocytes at the air–liquid interface to form a stratified epidermis

these products are classified as ATMPs under Regulation (EC) No 1394/2007, subjecting them to rigorous standards originally designed for large-scale pharmaceutical manufacturing. Compliance with GMP and Good Laboratory Practice (GLP) is mandatory, requiring specialized facilities, validated processes, rigorous quality controls, and comprehensive documentation throughout production and testing (Auxenfans et al. 2025; de la Cruz Valencia et al. 2025).

Before reaching the clinic, skin substitutes must undergo extensive preclinical characterization, including in vitro assays to confirm identity, purity viability, and potency, as well as in vivo studies in relevant animal models to evaluate integration, vascularization, and long-term safety (Campos et al. 2025). These studies are essential to predict clinical performance and to meet the expectations of national regulatory agencies, which demand robust evidence of product consistency and risk mitigation. However, the complexity of these constructs, often combining multiple cell types, biomaterials, and bioactive molecules, makes standardization difficult and prolongs development timelines. This translational bottleneck explains why, despite decades of research, only a limited number of bioengineered skin substitutes have achieved regulatory approval and routine clinical use in Europe (Auxenfans et al. 2025; European Medicine Agency (EMA) 2017).

Recognizing these challenges, European hospital-based laboratories producing skin substitutes for burn patients have established the European Skin Engineering Network (ESEN) and are actively collaborating under the COST Action CA23140 framework. This initiative aims to harmonize protocols, share expertise, and develop strategies to facilitate the safe and efficient translation of bioengineered skin products across Europe. By fostering collaboration and standardization, ESEN seeks to overcome regulatory and technical barriers, accelerating the availability of advanced skin substitutes for patients with severe burns and other extensive injuries.

In the following sections, we will briefly review the clinically approved skin substitutes, organized according to three criteria: structural complexity, cellular origin, and intended clinical use.

8.3.1 Classification by Structural Complexity

Clinically approved bioengineered skin substitutes are grouped by structural complexity into monolayer models, such as CEAs and non-cultured cell suspensions, which provide rapid epithelial coverage but lack dermal support, and multilayer models, which combine keratinocytes with fibroblasts in biomimetic scaffolds to restore both epidermal and dermal architecture.

8.3.1.1 Monolayer Skin Models

Cultured Epithelial Autografts

The clinical application of skin substitutes began with the development of CEAs in the late 1970s and early 1980s. Rheinwald and Green pioneered the technique of keratinocyte isolation and in vitro expansion, which made it possible to generate large sheets of autologous epidermis from a small skin biopsy (Rheinwald and Green 1975; Green et al. 1979). The first successful CEA transplantations were reported in 1981 at the Peter Bent Brigham Hospital (Boston, USA). These CEAs were applied to full-thickness burns in two adult patients, in combination with conventional meshed autografts, and reported successful adhesion to the wound beds and formation of a stratified epidermis resembling normal skin (O'Connor et al. 1981). Furthermore, 3 years later, it was demonstrated that these epithelial sheets can provide permanent coverage of extensive full-thickness burns in two pediatric patients (Gallico et al. 1984). CEAs provided, for the first time, the possibility of achieving permanent wound coverage in patients with insufficient donor skin, a scenario where just conventional split-thickness skin grafts (STSGs) were not feasible. On the one hand, with over 40 years of continuous operation, the "Centre Hospitalier Universitaire Vaudois" in Lausanne hosts the longest-running CEA program in Europe (Auxenfans et al. 2025; Déglise et al. 1987). They maintain the classic Rheinwald and Green method, producing keratinocyte sheets on 3 T3 fibroblast feeders and currently advancing toward formal regulatory approval in Switzerland. On the other hand, Lyon's 35-year program introduced a refined two-step enzymatic digestion (dispase and trypsin), human fibroblast feeder layers, and faster culture times (10–15 days) (Braye et al. 2005). Finally, in Paris optimized the original protocol by the introduction of human plasma-based epidermal substitute (hPBES), using inactivated donor plasma as a biological scaffold seeded with keratinocytes to create a fully human, biocompatible epidermal layer ready for clinical transplantation (Alexaline et al. 2019, 2015).

Despite the progress this technique represented for the treatment of large skin lesions, it has been limited by several well-documented drawbacks. On one hand, culturing cells into sheets may take 3 or 4 weeks (Green 1991), and these sheets need to be used within the shortest time as possible since delays reduce keratinocyte stem cell population, leading to poor engraftment and suboptimal wound healing (Barrandon and Green 1987; Pellegrini et al. 1999, 1998). In addition, it requires large-scale laboratory facilities and skilled laboratory personnel (Atiyeh and Costagliola 2007). On the other hand, the epithelial sheets are fragile, tear easily, and are difficult to manipulate without an effective carrier. Indeed, spontaneous blistering or avulsion due to minimal surface shearing forces is often observed beyond months after grafting (Ronfard et al. 2000; Sood et al. 2010) In addition, without a dermal component, CEAs show highly variability engraftment in burn care, with success ranging from poor to excellent, with mean epithelial take varying widely between 15% and 85% (Atiyeh and Costagliola 2007) Better results occur in wounds retaining dermal elements, such as partial-thickness burns (Auxenfans et al. 2025; Leary et al. 1992; Pellegrini et al. 1999). Histologic explanations for the low rate take have been attributed to delay in rete ridge formation and delayed maturation of the basement membrane (Ronfard et al. 2000).

Non-cultured Epithelial Autografts

As mentioned above, culturing stratified epidermal sheets is a complicated, labor-intensive and time-consuming process (Auxenfans et al. 2025). For this reason, in the mid-to-late 1990s, some research groups explored the idea of culturing many keratinocytes for transplantation onto the wound surface, thereby avoiding several steps in the process. In this regard, the Department of Plastic and Reconstructive Surgery at the Cologne Medical Center published the fundamental procedure for this method, focusing on the idea that keeping keratinocytes in a proliferative state by preventing them for confluence and stratifying in the culture could have positive effects when they are transplanted onto wounds (Stark and Kaiser 1994).

These approaches process a small biopsy from the patient to generate, instantly (Nuutila et al. 2023) or after a few passages (always splitting before reaching confluence) (Hartmann et al. 2007), a heterogeneous suspension of keratinocytes, melanocytes, and sometimes other epidermal cells that can be sprayed onto excised burn wounds. In some cases, the cell pellet is resuspended in a commercially available fibrinogen–thrombin tissue glue and sprayed onto the wound surface (Stark and Kaiser 1994). In some others, the cell suspension is mixed with cell culture (Hartmann et al. 2007), or with a ringer lactate solution prior to spray the wound surface (Gerlach et al. 2011).

Clinical studies indicate that non-cultured cell suspensions can reduce time to epithelialization in selected wounds, reduce donor-site requirements, and are more practical for early application compared with CEAs (Zweifel et al. 2008). However, outcomes depend on the wound depth and bed quality. Cell suspensions are usually most effective when applied to partial-thickness wounds or when used alongside meshed STSGs, rather than as a replacement for full-thickness skin loss on its own (Auxenfans et al. 2025; James et al. 2010). In addition, they normally show less structural integrity than sheet grafts. For example, Menon et al. (2013) found that patients using sprayed CEA with the modified Meek technique suffered hypertrophic scar formation, as would be expected in cases involving widely meshed autografts.

8.3.1.2 Multilayer Skin Models

The limitations of CEAs and cultured keratinocyte allografts have led to the development of more sophisticated skin substitutes, integrating not only keratinocytes but also fibroblasts and additional cellular components within biomimetic scaffolds. In this regard, the first bilayer autologous skin substitutes composed of a matrix containing autologous fibroblasts with autologous keratinocytes placed on top was developed by the University of Cincinnati in the late 1990s (Boyce et al. 1999). This paradigm shift is based on the understanding that effective skin regeneration requires functional epidermal–dermal interaction rather than purely epithelial coverage.

In the early 2000s, Meana and colleagues in Spain developed one of Europe's first hospital-based tissue-engineered skin substitutes, using fibrin as a 3D dermal scaffold in which autologous fibroblasts were embedded, and autologous keratinocytes were seeded on top to create a stratified epidermis (Meana et al. 1998). A multicenter clinical study later showed it provided effective, permanent coverage for severe burns with good functional and aesthetic results, but its clinical use declined after the 2009 European ATMP regulation introduced stricter GMP requirements (Gómez et al. 2011).

An important subsequent European contribution is the UGRSKIN substitute, developed by the Tissue Engineering Group at the University of Granada. This construct consists of a nanostructured fibrin–agarose dermal matrix containing autologous fibroblasts, overlaid with keratinocytes cultured at the air–liquid interface to generate a stratified epidermis (Carriel et al. 2012). In addition, it has already been accepted into clinical use under hospital exemption in Spain, where it has been successfully applied in more than 20 patients with severe burns. The translation and clinical implementation of UGRSKIN have been coordinated by the Andalusian Network for the Design and Translation of Advanced Therapies (And&Tat-RAdytTA), which now oversees transplantation activities. Today, UGRSKIN is recognized as an established ATMP and is officially included in the portfolio of services of the Spanish National Health System, marking a significant milestone in the integration of tissue-engineered skin into routine clinical practice (Egea-Guerrero et al. 2019; Martin et al. 2023).

In parallel, the Tissue Biology Research Unit, in collaboration with the Pediatric Burn Center at the University Children's Hospital Zurich, initiated preclinical testing of a bilayer autologous skin substitute composed of a mechanically compressed collagen hydrogel populated with fibroblasts and overlaid with keratinocytes (Braziulis et al. 2011; Schiestl et al. 2011). This construct, later named denovoSkin™, has successfully completed Phase 1 and Phase 2b clinical trials and is now advancing to a Phase 3 multicenter trial involving several European burn centers (Schiestl et al. 2025). To secure regulatory approval, part of the original research team established a spin-off company, making denovoSkin™ one of the few products with realistic prospects for marketing authorization in Europe. Meanwhile, the academic group at Zurich continues to refine the technology by incorporating additional cell types, such as melanocytes and endothelial cells, to create even more complex bilayer substitutes with enhanced physiological functionality (Auxenfans et al. 2025) (Fig. 8.3).

8.3.2 Classification by Origin

Beyond structural complexity, clinically approved skin substitutes can also be classified according to their cellular origin, as this factor directly influences

Fig. 8.3 Microscopic evaluation of the UGRSKIN model grafted in patients. Pre-grafting images show the multilayer fibrin–agarose skin substitute with a thin epithelial stratum and fibroblasts embedded within the biomaterial. Post-grafting evaluation in patients with severe burns demonstrated rapid remodeling and maturation into a highly stratified epidermis and a well-organized dermis, indicating quick biointegration and tissue remodeling. Microscopic images are stained with Alcian blue staining highlighting proteoglycans in blue. Scale bar: 50 μm

immunological compatibility, manufacturing logistics, regulatory requirements, and clinical application. Two main categories dominate: autologous and allogeneic products.

8.3.2.1 Autologous

Autologous substitutes, such as CEAs, keratinocyte sprays, and multilayer constructs, are derived from the patient's own cells, offering complete immunological compatibility and enabling permanent wound coverage (Auxenfans et al. 2014). However, their use in extensive burns is critically limited by time: patients often suffer from life-threatening conditions which require immediate coverage, yet the production of CEAs typically takes 2–4 weeks while more complex models take even longer. During this time, the patient remains at high risk of infection, fluid loss, and sepsis (Atiyeh and Costagliola 2007; Dearman et al. 2021; Zhang et al. 2021). This delay represents one of the most significant barriers to clinical success, as rapid wound closure is essential to reduce morbidity and mortality in massive burns (Merchant et al. 2025). Despite the amplification potential of keratinocytes, the time factor remains critical, and any delay in grafting reduces the proportion of clonogenic cells, compromising engraftment and long-term outcomes. The urgency of burn care underscores the need for accelerated manufacturing strategies for autologous constructs, an unmet challenge that has partly driven the development of allogeneic substitutes as an interim solution.

8.3.2.2 Allogeneic

Allogeneic substitutes, such as cultured allogeneic keratinocytes (CAlloK), provide readily available coverage for large burns and were introduced in the treatment of extensive burns soon after the autologous cultured keratinocytes (Auxenfans et al. 2014). They have been used in many centers as temporary biological dressings or to hasten reepithelialization while autologous cultures matured (De Luca et al. 1989). The extraction and expansion process mirrors that of autologous keratinocytes, but donor tissue is obtained from healthy volunteers, often surgical residues from procedures such as breast reduction or abdominoplasty, as in the Lyon Skin Substitute Bank (Auxenfans et al. 2014). A key advantage is that these cells can be cryopreserved, ensuring immediate availability compared to autologous constructs (Teepe et al. 1993; Yanaga et al. 2001).

However, allogeneic substitutes present important limitations, including the potential for immunogenic reactions, and the fact that they generally provide temporary coverage rather than permanent integration (Auxenfans et al. 2014). These risks, combined with regulatory constraints, have limited their widespread adoption as definitive treatments.

Beyond monolayer systems, allogeneic cells have also been incorporated into multilayer constructs. Allogeneic strategies have evolved to replace the slow-growing epithelial component with allogeneic mesenchymal stem cells (MSCs). These cells exhibit strong proliferative capacity and immunomodulatory properties, and under controlled conditions, they can differentiate into keratinocytes and other epidermal cell types (Martin-Piedra et al. 2019). This approach accelerates the manufacturing process and improves graft availability for patients in critical condition, while also supporting dermal regeneration and vascularization. Preclinical studies investigations suggest that MSC-based constructs could represent a promising alternative for next-generation skin substitutes, combining rapid production with enhanced biomimicry (Martin-Piedra et al. 2019).

8.3.3 Classification by Intended Use

Skin substitutes can also be categorized by their intended clinical purpose, which determines whether they serve as temporary coverage or aim for permanent integration.

8.3.3.1 Temporary Coverage

Temporary substitutes are designed to protect the wound and maintain a vascularized bed until definitive grafting is possible. They include CAlloK sheets, cadaveric allografts, and xenografts. These products provide immediate coverage, reduce fluid loss, and lower infection risk during the critical period between early excision and autologous graft availability. Clinical studies, including long-term retrospective series, indicate that their application can also speed donor-site healing, enabling repeated harvests of thin split-thickness grafts (Auxenfans et al. 2014). However, survival of allogeneic keratinocytes is transient, with reported persistence ranging from days to weeks depending on immune response and wound conditions (Wu et al. 1995; Zhao 1992). These substitutes therefore act as adjunctive therapies, bridging the gap until autologous solutions are ready.

8.3.3.2 Permanent Integration

Autologous constructs, including CEAs, keratinocyte sprays, and multilayer substitutes, are intended for definitive wound closure. They integrate with host tissue, restore epidermal and dermal architecture, and improve functional and aesthetic. For instance, a German team engineered a MatriDerm®-based composite skin autograft seeded with autologous fibroblasts and keratinocytes that closely mimicked healthy skin, and in clinical use on two patients with small full-thickness wounds, it achieved complete closure with positive outcomes(Golinski et al. 2009; Zöller et al. 2014). Despite these advantages, they face significant challenges: long culture times, strict GMP compliance, and limited ability to regenerate appendages or restore full

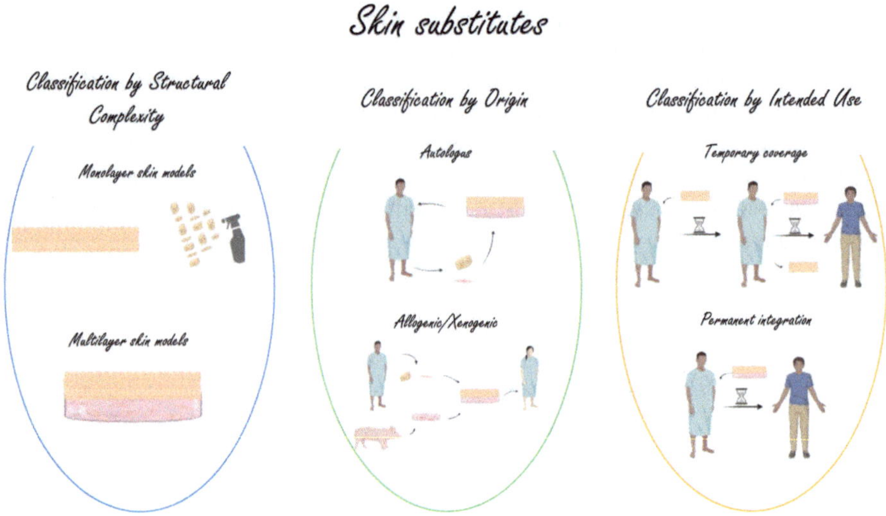

Fig. 8.4 Classification of clinically approved bioengineered skin substitutes. The diagram illustrates the three-tier classification framework applied to skin substitutes currently used in clinical practice. Products are organized by structural complexity (monolayer vs. multilayer constructs), cellular origin (autologous vs. allogeneic/xenogeneic) and intended clinical use (temporary coverage vs. permanent integration). This schematic highlights the diversity of strategies developed to address different clinical scenarios, from rapid wound protection in extensive burns to definitive reconstruction aimed at restoring long-term skin function

sensory function (Braziulis et al., 2011; Gómez et al. 2011; Martin et al. 2023). These constraints highlight the need for accelerated manufacturing strategies and innovative approaches to reduce production timelines while maintaining safety and efficacy (Dearman et al. 2021) (Fig. 8.4).

Acknowledgments This work was supported by the Spanish "Plan Estatal de Investigación Científica, Desarrollo e Innovación Tecnológica" (I+D+i) of the Spanish Instituto de Salud Carlos III, Ministry of Science, Innovation and Universities, Grant PI25/00002. Cofinanced by the European Union. Supported by grant DGP_PIDI_2024_00361, Consejería de Universidad, Investigación e Innovación, Junta de Andalucía, Spain, and and Programa FEDER Andalucía 2021-2027. Supported by Grant B-CTS-450-UGR20, Plan Propio de Investigación y Transferencia, Universidad de Granada and Consejería de Transformación Económica, Industria, Conocimiento y Universidades, Junta de Andalucía, Spain.

This research was also conducted as part of knowledge acquirement within the European Skin Engineering Network (ESEN) and by the European Cooperation in Science and Technology COST Action (CA23140 ESENBURN).

Competing Interests The author(s) has no competing interests to declare that are relevant to the content of this manuscript

References

Alexaline MM, Trouillas M, Nivet M, Bourreau E, Leclerc T, Duhamel P, Martin MT, Doucet C, Fortunel NO, Lataillade J-J (2015) Bioengineering a human plasma-based epidermal substitute with efficient grafting capacity and high content in Clonogenic cells. Stem Cells Transl Med 4: 643–654. https://doi.org/10.5966/sctm.2014-0155

Alexaline MM, Magne B, Zuleta Rodríguez A, Nivet M, Bacqueville D, Lataillade J-J, Trouillas M (2019) Influence of fibrin matrices and their released factors on epidermal substitute phenotype and engraftment. J Tissue Eng Regen Med 13:1362–1374. https://doi.org/10.1002/term.2879

Arda O, Göksügür N, Tüzün Y (2014) Basic histological structure and functions of facial skin. Clin Dermatol 32:3–13. https://doi.org/10.1016/j.clindermatol.2013.05.021

Arribas-Arribas B, Fernández-Muñoz B, Campos-Cuerva R, Montiel-Aguilera MÁ, Bermejo-González M, Lomas-Romero I, Martín-López M, Alcázar-Caballero RM, Del Mar Macías-Sánchez M, Campos F, Alaminos M, Gómez-Cía T, Gacto P, Carmona G, Santos-González M (2023) Nanostructured fibrin-agarose hydrogels loaded with allogeneic fibroblasts as bio-dressings for acute treatment of massive burns. Biomed. Pharmacother. Biomedecine Pharmacother. 168:115769. https://doi.org/10.1016/j.biopha.2023.115769

Atiyeh BS, Costagliola M (2007) Cultured epithelial autograft (CEA) in burn treatment: three decades later. Burns 33:405–413. https://doi.org/10.1016/j.burns.2006.11.002

Auxenfans C, Shipkov H, Bach C, Catherine Z, Lacroix P, Bertin-Maghit M, Damour O, Braye F (2014) Cultured allogenic keratinocytes for extensive burns: a retrospective study over 15 years. Burns 40:82–88. https://doi.org/10.1016/j.burns.2013.05.005

Auxenfans C, Valencia RG, Abdel-Sayed P, Alaminos M, Brunet J-F, Campos F, Chato-Astrain J, Carmona G, de Buys Roessingh A, Droz-Georget S, Farkas M, Fernandez Gonzalez A, Gönczi E, Huss F, Hartmann B, Heusi B, Karström A, Moiemen N, Sartoris G, Spranger A, Trouillas M, Rosas C, Vuola J, Woodtli V, Schiestl C, Böttcher S (2025) Laboratory-generated autologous skin substitutes for burn treatment in Europe: narrative review, experts' opinion, and legal considerations. Eur Burn J 6:30. https://doi.org/10.3390/ebj6020030

Ávila-Fernández P, Etayo-Escanilla M, Sánchez-Porras D, Fernández-Valadés R, Campos F, Garzón I, Carriel V, Alaminos M, García-García ÓD, Chato-Astrain J (2024) Spatiotemporal characterization of extracellular matrix maturation in human artificial stromal-epithelial tissue substitutes. BMC Biol 22:263. https://doi.org/10.1186/s12915-024-02065-y

Barrandon Y, Green H (1987) Three clonal types of keratinocyte with different capacities for multiplication. Proc Natl Acad Sci USA 84:2302–2306. https://doi.org/10.1073/pnas.84.8.2302

Barrientos S, Stojadinovic O, Golinko MS, Brem H, Tomic-Canic M (2008) Growth factors and cytokines in wound healing. Wound Repair Regen Off Publ Wound Heal Soc Eur Tissue Repair Soc 16:585–601. https://doi.org/10.1111/j.1524-475X.2008.00410.x

Bártolo I, Reis RL, Marques AP, Cerqueira MT (2022) Keratinocyte growth factor-based strategies for wound re-epithelialization. Tissue Eng Part B Rev 28:665–676. https://doi.org/10.1089/ten.TEB.2021.0030

Berasain J, Ávila-Fernández P, Cárdenas-Pérez R, Cànaves-Llabrés AI, Etayo-Escanilla M, Alaminos M, Carriel V, García-García ÓD, Chato-Astrain J, Campos F (2024) Genipin crosslinking promotes biomechanical reinforcement and pro-regenerative macrophage polarization in bioartificial tubular substitutes. Biomed Pharmacother 174:116449. https://doi.org/10.1016/j.biopha.2024.116449

Bindi B, Perioli A, Melo P, Mattu C, Ferreira AM (2023) Bioinspired collagen/hyaluronic acid/fibrin-based hydrogels for soft tissue engineering: design, synthesis, and in vitro characterization. J Funct Biomater 14:495. https://doi.org/10.3390/jfb14100495

Boateng JS, Matthews KH, Stevens HNE, Eccleston GM (2008) Wound healing dressings and drug delivery systems: a review. J Pharm Sci 97:2892–2923. https://doi.org/10.1002/jps.21210

Bourland J, Mayrand D, Tremblay N, Moulin VJ, Fradette J, Auger FA (2025) Isolation and culture of human dermal microvascular endothelial cells. Methods Mol Biol Clifton NJ 2922:85–96. https://doi.org/10.1007/978-1-0716-4510-9_7

Boyce ST, Kagan RJ, Meyer NA, Yakuboff KP, Warden GD (1999) THE 1999 CLINICAL RESEARCH AWARD cultured skin substitutes combined with integra artificial skin* to replace native skin autograft and allograft for the closure of excised full–thickness burns. J Burn Care Rehabil 20:453–461. https://doi.org/10.1097/00004630-199920060-00006

Braye F, Hautier A, Bouez C, Damour O (2005) Les substituts cutanés reconstruits en laboratoire: application au traitement des brûlés. Pathol Biol 53:613–617. https://doi.org/10.1016/j.patbio.2004.12.004

Braziulis E, Biedermann T, Hartmann-Fritsch F, Schiestl C, Pontiggia L, Böttcher-Haberzeth S, Reichmann E, Meuli M (2011) Skingineering I: engineering porcine dermo-epidermal skin analogues for autologous transplantation in a large animal model. Pediatr Surg Int 27:241–247. https://doi.org/10.1007/s00383-010-2777-0

Campos F, Bonhome-Espinosa AB, Chato-Astrain J, Sánchez-Porras D, García-García ÓD, Carmona R, López-López MT, Alaminos M, Carriel V, Rodriguez IA (2020) Evaluation of fibrin-agarose tissue-like hydrogels biocompatibility for tissue engineering applications. Front Bioeng Biotechnol 8:596. https://doi.org/10.3389/fbioe.2020.00596

Campos F, Carriel V, Bermejo-Casares F, Chato-Astrain J, Alaminos M (2025) Histological and histochemical methods for the evaluation of tissue engineered skin substitutes. Methods Mol Biol Clifton NJ 2922:249–265. https://doi.org/10.1007/978-1-0716-4510-9_19

Cario M, Taieb A (2019) Isolation and culture of epidermal melanocytes. Methods Mol Biol Clifton NJ 1993:33–46. https://doi.org/10.1007/978-1-4939-9473-1_3

Carriel V, Garzón I, Jiménez J-M, Oliveira A-C-X, Arias-Santiago S, Campos A, Sánchez-Quevedo M-C, Alaminos M (2012) Epithelial and stromal developmental patterns in a novel substitute of the human skin generated with fibrin-agarose biomaterials. Cells Tissues Organs 196:1–12. https://doi.org/10.1159/000330682

Chato-Astrain J, Chato-Astrain I, Sánchez-Porras D, García-García Ó-D, Bermejo-Casares F, Vairo C, Villar-Vidal M, Gainza G, Villullas S, Oruezabal R-I, Ponce-Polo Á, Garzón I, Carriel V, Campos F, Alaminos M (2020) Generation of a novel human dermal substitute functionalized with antibiotic-loaded nanostructured lipid carriers (NLCs) with antimicrobial properties for tissue engineering. J Nanobiotechnol 18:174. https://doi.org/10.1186/s12951-020-00732-0

Chato-Astrain J, Sánchez-Porras D, García-García ÓD, Vairo C, Villar-Vidal M, Villullas S, Sánchez-Montesinos I, Campos F, Garzón I, Alaminos M (2021) Improvement of cell culture methods for the successful generation of human keratinocyte primary cell cultures using EGF-loaded nanostructured lipid carriers. Biomedicine 9:1634. https://doi.org/10.3390/biomedicines9111634

Chattopadhyay S, Raines RT (2014) Review collagen-based biomaterials for wound healing. Biopolymers 101:821–833. https://doi.org/10.1002/bip.22486

Chen D, Hou Q, Zhong L, Zhao Y, Li M, Fu X (2019) Bioactive molecules for skin repair and regeneration: Progress and perspectives. Stem Cells Int 2019:6789823. https://doi.org/10.1155/2019/6789823

Chetprayoon P, Aueviriyavit S, Prateep A, Boonjing S, Maniratanachote R (2020) Multilayered fibroblasts constructed by accelerated cellular self-assembly and applications for regenerative medicine. ALTEX 37:75–84. https://doi.org/10.14573/altex.1904032

Climov M, Medeiros E, Farkash EA, Qiao J, Rousseau CF, Dong S, Zawadzka A, Racki WJ, Al-Musa A, Sachs DH, Randolph MA, Huang CA, Bollenbach TJ (2016) Bioengineered self-assembled skin as an alternative to skin grafts. Plast Reconstr Surg Glob Open 4:e731. https://doi.org/10.1097/GOX.0000000000000723

Dagher J, Arcand C, Auger FA, Germain L, Moulin VJ (2022) The self-assembled skin substitute history: successes, challenges, and current treatment indications. J Burn Care Res Off Publ Am Burn Assoc 44:S57–S64. https://doi.org/10.1093/jbcr/irac074

de la Cruz Valencia RG, Carmona Sánchez G, Auxenfans C, Brunet J-F, González AF, Woodtli V, Karström A, Trouillas M (2025) Quality controls of autologous skin products according to European GMP guidelines. Meth Mol Biol Clifton NJ 2922:325–334. https://doi.org/10.1007/978-1-0716-4510-9_25

De Luca M, Albanese E, Bondanza S, Megna M, Ugozzoli L, Molina F, Cancedda R, Santi PL, Bormioli M, Stella M, Magliacani G (1989) Multicentre experience in the treatment of burns with autologous and allogenic cultured epithelium, fresh or preserved in a frozen state. Burns 15:303–309. https://doi.org/10.1016/0305-4179(89)90007-7

Dearman BL, Boyce ST, Greenwood JE (2021) Advances in skin tissue bioengineering and the challenges of clinical translation. Front Surg 8:640879. https://doi.org/10.3389/fsurg.2021.640879

Déglise B, Benathan M, Frenk E, Krupp S (1987) Preliminary results of burn treatment using an autograft of cultured epidermis. Schweiz Med Wochenschr 117:1380–1383

Desmet E, Ramadhas A, Lambert J, Van Gele M (2017) In vitro psoriasis models with focus on reconstructed skin models as promising tools in psoriasis research. Exp Biol Med Maywood NJ 242:1158–1169. https://doi.org/10.1177/1535370217710637

Devaraj, Jain D, Maharana SK, Sawant P, Jain A (2025) Advancements in in vitro psoriasis models: relevance for drug discovery and therapeutic development. Int J Pharm 684:126097. https://doi.org/10.1016/j.ijpharm.2025.126097

Egea-Guerrero JJ, Carmona G, Correa E, Mata R, Arias-Santiago S, Alaminos M, Gacto P, Cuende N (2019) Transplant of tissue-engineered artificial autologous human skin in Andalusia: An example of coordination and institutional collaboration. Transplant Proc 51:3047–3050. https://doi.org/10.1016/j.transproceed.2019.08.014

European Medicine Agency (EMA), C. for A.T. (CAT) (2017) Guidelines on good manufacturing practice specific to advanced therapy medicinal products

European Medicine Agency (EMA), C. for A.T. (CAT) (2025) Guideline on quality, non-clinical and clinical requirements for investigational advanced therapy medicinal products in clinical trials

Gainza G, Pastor M, Aguirre JJ, Villullas S, Pedraz JL, Hernandez RM, Igartua M (2014) A novel strategy for the treatment of chronic wounds based on the topical administration of rhEGF-loaded lipid nanoparticles: in vitro bioactivity and in vivo effectiveness in healing-impaired db/db mice. J Control Release Off J Control Release Soc 185:51–61. https://doi.org/10.1016/j.jconrel.2014.04.032

Gallico GG, O'Connor NE, Compton CC, Kehinde O, Green H (1984) Permanent coverage of large burn wounds with autologous cultured human epithelium. N Engl J Med 311:448–451. https://doi.org/10.1056/NEJM198408163110706

García-García ÓD, El Soury M, González-Quevedo D, Sánchez-Porras D, Chato-Astrain J, Campos F, Carriel V (2021) Histological, biomechanical, and biological properties of Genipin-crosslinked decellularized peripheral nerves. Int J Mol Sci 22:E674. https://doi.org/10.3390/ijms22020674

Gerlach JC, Johnen C, Ottoman C, Bräutigam K, Plettig J, Belfekroun C, Münch S, Hartmann B (2011) Method for autologous single skin cell isolation for regenerative cell spray transplantation with non-cultured cells. Int J Artif Organs 34:271–279. https://doi.org/10.5301/IJAO.2011.6508

Goff PS, Castle JT, Kohli JS, Sviderskaya EV, Bennett DC (2023) Isolation, culture, and transfection of melanocytes. Curr Protoc 3:e774. https://doi.org/10.1002/cpz1.774

Golinski PA, Zöller N, Kippenberger S, Menke H, Bereiter-Hahn J, Bernd A (2009) Development of an engraftable skin equivalent based on matriderm with human keratinocytes and fibroblasts. Handchir. Mikrochir. Plast. Chir. Organ Deutschsprachigen Arbeitsgemeinschaft Handchir. Organ Deutschsprachigen Arbeitsgemeinschaft Mikrochir. Peripher Nerven Gefasse Organ V 41:327–332. https://doi.org/10.1055/s-0029-234132

Gómez C, Galán JM, Torrero V, Ferreiro I, Pérez D, Palao R, Martínez E, Llames S, Meana A, Holguín P (2011) Use of an autologous bioengineered composite skin in extensive burns: clinical and functional outcomes. A multicentric study. Burns 37:580–589. https://doi.org/10.1016/j.burns.2010.10.005

Goodarzi P, Aghayan HR, Payab M, Larijani B, Alavi-Moghadam S, Sarvari M, Adibi H, Khatami F, Heravani NF, Hadavandkhani M, Arjmand B (2020) Human fetal skin fibroblast isolation and expansion for clinical application. Methods Mol Biol Clifton NJ 2109:261–273. https://doi.org/10.1007/7651_2019_233

Green H (1991) Cultured cells for the treatment of disease. Sci Am 265:96–102. https://doi.org/10.1038/scientificamerican1191-96

Green H, Kehinde O, Thomas J (1979) Growth of cultured human epidermal cells into multiple epithelia suitable for grafting. Proc Natl Acad Sci 76:5665–5668. https://doi.org/10.1073/pnas.76.11.5665

Hartmann B, Ekkernkamp A, Johnen C, Gerlach JC, Belfekroun C, Küntscher MV (2007) Sprayed cultured epithelial autografts for deep dermal burns of the face and neck. Ann Plast Surg 58:70–73. https://doi.org/10.1097/01.sap.0000250647.39784.bb

Hou T, Du M, Gao X, An M (2022) Human vascular endothelial cells promote the secretion of vascularization factors and migration of human skin fibroblasts under co-culture and its preliminary application. Int J Mol Sci 23:13995. https://doi.org/10.3390/ijms232213995

Ionescu AM, Chato-Astrain J, Cardona Pérez J d l C, Campos F, Pérez Gómez M, Alaminos M, Garzón Bello I (2020) Evaluation of the optical and biomechanical properties of bioengineered human skin generated with fibrin-agarose biomaterials. J Biomed Opt 25:1–16. https://doi.org/10.1117/1.JBO.25.5.055002

James SE, Booth S, Dheansa B, Mann DJ, Reid MJ, Shevchenko RV, Gilbert PM (2010) Sprayed cultured autologous keratinocytes used alone or in combination with meshed autografts to accelerate wound closure in difficult-to-heal burns patients. Burns 36:e10–e20. https://doi.org/10.1016/j.burns.2008.11.011

Jansen LA, De Caigny P, Guay NA, Lineaweaver WC, Shokrollahi K (2013) The evidence base for the acellular dermal matrix AlloDerm: a systematic review. Ann Plast Surg 70:587–594. https://doi.org/10.1097/SAP.0b013e31827a2d23

Kanitakis J (2002) Anatomy, histology and immunohistochemistry of normal human skin. Eur J Dermatol EJD 12:390–399; quiz 400–401

Langer R, Vacanti JP (1993) Tissue engineering. Science 260:920–926. https://doi.org/10.1126/science.8493529

Leary T, Jones PL, Appleby M, Blight A, Parkinson K, Stanley M (1992) Epidermal keratinocyte self-renewal is dependent upon dermal integrity. J Invest Dermatol 99:422–430. https://doi.org/10.1111/1523-1747.ep12616134

Lenihan C, Rogers C, Metcalfe AD, Martin YH (2014) The effect of isolation and culture methods on epithelial stem cell populations and their progeny-toward an improved cell expansion protocol for clinical application. Cytotherapy 16:1750–1759. https://doi.org/10.1016/j.jcyt.2014.06.005

Li T, Zhou Z, Xie Y, Cai W, Zhu X, Jia Y, Zhang Z, Xu F, Huang G (2025) Engineering strong and tough collagen hydrogels and tissue constructs via twisting and crosslinking. Cell Rep Phys Sci 6:102454. https://doi.org/10.1016/j.xcrp.2025.102454

Marsella R, Ahrens K, Wilkes R (2022) Differences in behavior between Normal and atopic keratinocytes in culture: pilot studies. Vet Sci 9:329. https://doi.org/10.3390/vetsci9070329

Martin-Piedra MA, Alfonso-Rodriguez CA, Zapater A, Durand-Herrera D, Chato-Astrain J, Campos F, Sanchez-Quevedo MC, Alaminos M, Garzon I (2019) Effective use of mesenchymal stem cells in human skin substitutes generated by tissue engineering. Eur Cell Mater 37:233–249. https://doi.org/10.22203/eCM.v037a14

Martin-Piedra MA, Carmona G, Campos F, Carriel V, Fernández-González A, Campos A, Cuende N, Garzón I, Gacto P, Alaminos M (2023) Histological assessment of nanostructured fibrin-agarose skin substitutes grafted in burnt patients. A time-course study. Bioeng Transl Med 8:e10572. https://doi.org/10.1002/btm2.10572

Meana A, Iglesias J, Del Rio M, Larcher F, Madrigal B, Fresno MF, Martin C, San Roman F, Tevar F (1998) Large surface of cultured human epithelium obtained on a dermal matrix based on live fibroblast-containing fibrin gels. Burns J Int Soc Burn Inj 24:621–630. https://doi.org/10.1016/s0305-4179(98)00107-7

Menon S, Li Z, Harvey JG, Holland AJA (2013) The use of the meek technique in conjunction with cultured epithelial autograft in the management of major paediatric burns. Burns 39:674–679. https://doi.org/10.1016/j.burns.2012.09.009

Merchant M, Hu SB, Miller C, Ahmadi T, Garcia E, Smith MI (2025) Comprehensive Management of Severe Burn Injuries: a multidisciplinary approach from resuscitation to rehabilitation. Emerg Care Med 2:26. https://doi.org/10.3390/ecm2020026

Ningsih SS, Jusman SWA, Syaidah R, Nauli R, Fadilah F (2024) Efficient protocol for isolating human fibroblast from primary skin cell cultures: application to keloid, hypertrophic scar, and normal skin biopsies. Biol Methods Protoc 9:bpae082. https://doi.org/10.1093/biomethods/bpae082

Nuutila K, Katayama S, Laitinen A, Siltanen A, Patrikoski M, Valtonen J, Kankainen M, Kerkelä E, Kaartinen T, Juteau S, Korhonen M, Vuola J, Kankuri E (2023) ATMP-classified, scalable, autologous cell spray for the treatment of skin wounds and assessment of its effects on wound healing clinically and on a molecular level. Burns 49:1144–1156. https://doi.org/10.1016/j.burns.2022.09.006

O'Connor NE, Mulliken JB, Banks-Schlegel S, Kehinde O, Green H (1981) Grafting of burns with cultured epithelium prepared from autologous epidermal cells. Lancet 317:75–78. https://doi.org/10.1016/S0140-6736(81)90006-4

Ortega-Llamas L, Quiñones-Vico MI, García-Valdivia M, Fernández-González A, Ubago-Rodríguez A, Sanabria-de la Torre R, Arias-Santiago S (2022) Cytotoxicity and wound closure evaluation in skin cell lines after treatment with common antiseptics for clinical use. Cells 11:1395. https://doi.org/10.3390/cells11091395

Ortiz-Arrabal O, Bermejo-Casares F, Garzón I, Mesa-García M-D, Gómez-Llorente C, Alaminos M (2023) Optimization of human skin keratinocyte culture protocols using bioactive molecules derived from olive oil. Biomed Pharmacother 164:115000. https://doi.org/10.1016/j.biopha.2023.115000

Park U, Kim K (2017) Multiple growth factor delivery for skin tissue engineering applications. Biotechnol Bioprocess Eng 22:659–670. https://doi.org/10.1007/s12257-017-0436-1

Pellegrini G, Bondanza S, Guerra L, De Luca M (1998) Cultivation of human keratinocyte stem cells: current and future clinical applications. Med Biol Eng Comput 36:778–790. https://doi.org/10.1007/BF02518885

Pellegrini G, Ranno R, Stracuzzi G, Bondanza S, Guerra L, Zambruno G, Micali G, De Luca M (1999) The control of epidermal stem cells (HOLOCLONES) in the treatment of massive full-thickness burns with autologous keratinocytes cultured on FIBRIN1. Transplantation 68:868–879. https://doi.org/10.1097/00007890-199909270-00021

Peña OA, Martin P (2024) Cellular and molecular mechanisms of skin wound healing. Nat Rev Mol Cell Biol 25:599–616. https://doi.org/10.1038/s41580-024-00715-1

Peng W, Zhao Y, Ren B, He T, Li D, Zhang H, Du K, Wang B, Liu J (2025) Construction of a 3D bioprinted skin model for psoriasis research and drug evaluation. Biofabrication 17:4. https://doi.org/10.1088/1758-5090/adfe1d

Phang SJ, Basak S, Teh HX, Packirisamy G, Fauzi MB, Kuppusamy UR, Neo YP, Looi ML (2022) Advancements in extracellular matrix-based biomaterials and biofabrication of 3D Organotypic skin models. ACS Biomater Sci Eng 8:3220–3241. https://doi.org/10.1021/acsbiomaterials.2c00342

Poumay Y, Faway E (2023) Human epidermal keratinocytes in culture: a story of multiple recipes for a single cell type. Skin Pharmacol Physiol 36:215–224. https://doi.org/10.1159/000534137

Quílez C, de Aranda Izuzquiza G, García M, López V, Montero A, Valencia L, Velasco D (2020) Bioprinting for Skin. Methods Mol. Biol. Clifton NJ 2140:217–228. https://doi.org/10.1007/978-1-0716-0520-2_14

Ren X, Zhao M, Lash B, Martino MM, Julier Z (2019) Growth factor engineering strategies for regenerative medicine applications. Front Bioeng Biotechnol 7:469. https://doi.org/10.3389/fbioe.2019.00469

Rheinwald JG, Green H (1975) Serial cultivation of strains of human epidermal keratinocytes: the formation of keratinizing colonies from single cells. Cell 6:331–343. https://doi.org/10.1016/s0092-8674(75)80001-8

Rittié L, Fisher GJ (2005) Isolation and culture of skin fibroblasts. Methods Mol Med 117:83–98. https://doi.org/10.1385/1-59259-940-0:083

Ronfard V, Rives J-M, Neveux Y, Carsin H, Barrandon Y (2000) Long-term regeneration of human epidermis on third degree burns transplanted with autologous cultured epithelium grown on a fibrin matrix1,2. Transplantation 70:1588–1598. https://doi.org/10.1097/00007890-200012150-00009

Rosdy M, Clauss LC (1990) Terminal epidermal differentiation of human keratinocytes grown in chemically defined medium on inert filter substrates at the air-liquid interface. J Invest Dermatol 95:409–414. https://doi.org/10.1111/1523-1747.ep12555510

Sang S, Zhao Y, Shen Z, Cao Y, Cheng R, Yan Y, Jian A, Wang J (2023) Collagen-coated agarose-chitosan scaffold used as a skin substitute. Biotechnol Appl Biochem 70:1206–1216. https://doi.org/10.1002/bab.2432

Schiestl C, Biedermann T, Braziulis E, Hartmann-Fritsch F, Böttcher-Haberzeth S, Arras M, Cesarovic N, Nicolls F, Linti C, Reichmann E, Meuli M (2011) Skingineering II: transplantation of large-scale laboratory-grown skin analogues in a new pig model. Pediatr Surg Int 27:249–254. https://doi.org/10.1007/s00383-010-2792-1

Schiestl C, Neuhaus K, Meuli M, Farkas M, Hartmann-Fritsch F, Elrod J, Bressan J, Reichmann E, Böttcher-Haberzeth S (2025) Long-term outcomes of a cultured autologous Dermo-epidermal skin substitute in children: 5-year results of a phase I clinical trial. J Burn Care Res Off Publ Am Burn Assoc 46:326–334. https://doi.org/10.1093/jbcr/irae150

Ścieżyńska A, Nogowska A, Sikorska M, Konys J, Karpińska A, Komorowski M, Ołdak M, Malejczyk J (2019) Isolation and culture of human primary keratinocytes-a methods review. Exp Dermatol 28:107–112. https://doi.org/10.1111/exd.13860

Ścieżyńska A, Sobiepanek A, Kowalska PD, Soszyńska M, Łuszczyński K, Grzywa TM, Krześniak N, Góźdź A, Włodarski PK, Galus R, Kobiela T, Malejczyk J (2021) A novel and effective method for human primary skin melanocytes and metastatic melanoma cell isolation. Cancer 13:6244. https://doi.org/10.3390/cancers13246244

Sheikholeslam M, Wright MEE, Jeschke MG, Amini-Nik S (2018) Biomaterials for skin substitutes. Adv Healthc Mater 7. https://doi.org/10.1002/adhm.201700897

Smolle C, Cambiaso-Daniel J, Forbes AA, Wurzer P, Hundeshagen G, Branski LK, Huss F, Kamolz L-P (2017) Recent trends in burn epidemiology worldwide: a systematic review. Burns 43:249–257. https://doi.org/10.1016/j.burns.2016.08.013

Sood R, Roggy D, Zieger M, Balledux J, Chaudhari S, Koumanis DJ, Mir HS, Cohen A, Knipe C, Gabehart K, Coleman JJ (2010) Cultured epithelial autografts for coverage of large burn wounds in eighty-eight patients: the Indiana University experience. J Burn Care Res 31:559–568. https://doi.org/10.1097/BCR.0b013e3181e4ca29

Stark GB, Kaiser HW (1994) Cologne burn Centre experience with glycerol-preserved allogeneic skin: part II: combination with autologous cultured keratinocytes. Burns 20:S34–S38. https://doi.org/10.1016/0305-4179(94)90087-6

Stewart BT, Jeschke MG, Collins KA (n.d.) Epidemiology, risk factors, and prevention of burn injuries. UpToDate

Suamte L, Tirkey A, Babu PJ (2023) Design of 3D smart scaffolds using natural, synthetic and hybrid derived polymers for skin regenerative applications. Smart Mater Med 4:243–256. https://doi.org/10.1016/j.smaim.2022.09.005

Teepe RGC, Koch R, Haeseker B (1993) Randomized trial comparing cryopreserved cultured epidermal allografts with tulle-GRAS in the treatment of split-thickness skin graft donor sites. J Trauma Inj Infect Crit Care 35:850–854. https://doi.org/10.1097/00005373-199312000-00008

Tjin MS, Chua AWC, Tryggvason K (2020) Chemically defined and xenogeneic-free culture method for human epidermal keratinocytes on laminin-based matrices. Nat Protoc 15:694–711. https://doi.org/10.1038/s41596-019-0270-3

Urciuolo F, Passariello R, Imparato G, Casale C, Netti PA (2022) Bioengineered wound healing skin models: the role of immune response and endogenous ECM to fully replicate the dynamic of scar tissue formation in vitro. Bioeng Basel Switz 9:233. https://doi.org/10.3390/bioengineering9060233

Vig K, Chaudhari A, Tripathi S, Dixit S, Sahu R, Pillai S, Dennis VA, Singh SR (2017) Advances in skin regeneration using tissue engineering. Int J Mol Sci 18:789. https://doi.org/10.3390/ijms18040789

Wang Y, Wang Z, Dong Y (2023) Collagen-based biomaterials for tissue engineering. ACS Biomater Sci Eng 9:1132–1150. https://doi.org/10.1021/acsbiomaterials.2c00730

Weng T, Zhang W, Xia Y, Wu P, Yang M, Jin R, Xia S, Wang J, You C, Han C, Wang X (2021) 3D bioprinting for skin tissue engineering: current status and perspectives. J Tissue Eng 12: 20417314211028574. https://doi.org/10.1177/20417314211028574

Wille JJ, Burdge JJ, Park JY (2014) Methods for the preparation of an autologous serum-free cultured epidermis and for autografting applications. Methods Mol. Biol. Clifton NJ 1195:203–218. https://doi.org/10.1007/7651_2014_72

Wistner SC, Rashad L, Slaughter G (2023) Advances in tissue engineering and biofabrication for in vitro skin modeling. Bioprinting Amst Neth 35:e00306. https://doi.org/10.1016/j.bprint.2023.e00306

Won J-Y, Lee M-H, Kim M-J, Min K-H, Ahn G, Han J-S, Jin S, Yun W-S, Shim J-H (2019) A potential dermal substitute using decellularized dermis extracellular matrix derived bio-ink. Artif Cells Nanomed Biotechnol 47:644–649. https://doi.org/10.1080/21691401.2019.1575842

Wu J, Barisoni D, Armato U (1995) An investigation into the mechanisms by which human dermis does not significantly contribute to the rejection of Allo-skin grafts. Burns 21:11–16. https://doi.org/10.1016/0305-4179(95)90774-T

Wu P, Liang Y, Sun G (2021) Engineering immune-responsive biomaterials for skin regeneration. Biomater Transl 2:61–71. https://doi.org/10.3877/cma.j.issn.2096-112X.2021.01.008

Yakupu A, Zhang J, Dong W, Song F, Dong J, Lu S (2022) The epidemiological characteristic and trends of burns globally. BMC Public Health 22:1596. https://doi.org/10.1186/s12889-022-13887-2

Yamakawa S, Hayashida K (2019) Advances in surgical applications of growth factors for wound healing. Burns Trauma 7:10. https://doi.org/10.1186/s41038-019-0148-1

Yanaga H, Udoh Y, Yamauchi T, Yamamoto M, Kiyokawa K, Inoue Y, Tai Y (2001) Cryopreserved cultured epidermal allografts achieved early closure of wounds and reduced scar formation in deep partial-thickness burn wounds (DDB) and split-thickness skin donor sites of pediatric patients. Burns 27:689–698. https://doi.org/10.1016/S0305-4179(01)00008-0

Yu JR, Navarro J, Coburn JC, Mahadik B, Molnar J, Holmes JH, Nam AJ, Fisher JP (2019) Current and future perspectives on skin tissue engineering: key features of biomedical research, translational assessment, and clinical application. Adv Healthc Mater 8:e1801471. https://doi.org/10.1002/adhm.201801471

Zhang P, Zou B, Liou Y-C, Huang C (2021) The pathogenesis and diagnosis of sepsis post burn injury. Burns Trauma 9:tkaa047. https://doi.org/10.1093/burnst/tkaa047

Zhao YB (1992) Primary observation of prolonged survival of cultured epidermal allografts. Zhonghua Wai Ke Za Zhi 30:104–106, 125–126

Zöller N, Valesky E, Butting M, Hofmann M, Kippenberger S, Bereiter-Hahn J, Bernd A, Kaufmann R (2014) Clinical application of a tissue-cultured skin autograft: an alternative for the treatment of non-healing or slowly healing wounds? Dermatol Basel Switz 229:190–198. https://doi.org/10.1159/000362927

Zweifel CJ, Contaldo C, Köhler C, Jandali A, Künzi W, Giovanoli P (2008) Initial experiences using non-cultured autologous keratinocyte suspension for burn wound closure. J Plast Reconstr Aesthet Surg 61:e1–e4. https://doi.org/10.1016/j.bjps.2007.07.015

Chapter 9
Biofabricated 3D Tendon Constructs: A New Window into Tendon Physiology and Pathology

Giacomo Cortella and Giovanna Della Porta

Abstract Three-dimensional (3D) biofabrication technologies are revolutionizing tendon tissue engineering by enabling the creation of physiologically relevant extracellular matrix (ECM) microenvironments in vitro. Native tendon tissue is defined by a hierarchically organized, collagen-rich ECM and mechanosensitive cell populations, yet its complex architecture and limited regenerative capacity have historically constrained the study of both healthy and pathological conditions. Advances in 3D bioplotting and bioink engineering, particularly with methacrylated collagen (ColMA), now allow the fabrication of biomimetic constructs that recapitulate the structural, biochemical, and mechanical cues of tendon tissue. These engineered scaffolds support survival, proliferation, and tenogenic differentiation of human tendon stem/progenitor cells (TSPCs), facilitating dynamic ECM remodeling and de novo type I collagen deposition. When combined with controlled biochemical stimulation and perfusion-based bioreactor culture, 3D constructs reproduce fundamental aspects of tendon physiology, including cell–matrix interactions, ECM maturation, and mechanobiological adaptation. Moreover, these platforms provide a versatile testbed for modeling pathological processes such as inflammation, matrix degradation, fibrosis, and tissue degeneration under precisely tunable conditions. This chapter highlights the principles, bioink strategies, and bioprinting methodologies that underpin next-generation 3D tendon in vitro models, demonstrating their potential to advance tendon biology, disease modeling, regenerative medicine, and therapeutic screening.

Keywords Tendon biofabrication · Tendon tissue engineering · Biomimetic construct · Tendon stem/progenitor cells · Dynamic ECM remodeling · Bioreactor culture · Mechanobiology · Cell-matrix interactions · 3D tendon in vitro model

---

G. Cortella · G. Della Porta (✉)
Labs of Tissue Engineering & Nanomedicine, Department of Medicine, Surgery and Dentistry, University of Salerno, Fisciano, SA, Italy
e-mail: gdellaporta@unisa.it

Y. M. Elçin (ed.), *Biofabrication in Regenerative Medicine*, Stem Cell Biology and Regenerative Medicine 1519, https://doi.org/10.1007/978-3-032-30294-6_9

Abbreviations

ACL	Anterior Cruciate Ligament
CD73	Cluster of Differentiation 73
CD90	Cluster of Differentiation 90
CD105	Cluster of Differentiation 105
ColMA	Methacrylated Collagen
COMP	Cartilage Oligomeric Matrix Protein
DAPI	4′,6-diamidino-2-phenylindole
DCN	Decorin
ECM	Extracellular Matrix
FE-SEM	Field-emission scanning electron microscopy
GDF-5	Growth Differentiation Factor 5
HLA-DR	Human Leukocyte Antigen—DR Isotype
IL-6	Interleukin-6
MSCs	Mesenchymal Stromal/Stem Cells
NSAIDs	Nonsteroidal Anti-Inflammatory Drugs
PLGA-NPs	Poly(lactic-co-glycolic acid) Nanoparticles
qRT-PCR	Quantitative Real-Time Polymerase Chain Reaction
SEM	Scanning Electron Microscopy
TGF-β	Transforming Growth Factor-Beta
TNF	Tumor Necrosis Factor
TNMD	Tenomodulin
TSPCs	Tendon Stem/Progenitor Cells
VEGF	Vascular Endothelial Growth Factor

9.1 Tendon Pathologies: Clinical Implications, Economic Burden, and Unresolved Challenges

Tendon disorders represent a significant and often underappreciated health problem worldwide. Tendons are specialized connective tissues that connect muscles to bones, transmitting forces to facilitate movement. Their pathological conditions, commonly termed tendinopathies, include tendinitis, tendinosis, and tendon tears. The pathophysiology of these disorders is multifactorial (Sharma and Maffulli 2005; Sharma and Maffulli 2006; Kaux et al. 2011; Van Dijk et al. 2011; Nourissat et al. 2015). Mechanical overuse is a primary contributor, leading to microtrauma and collagen fiber disruption. Chronic overload may trigger maladaptive changes, including extracellular matrix degeneration, neovascularization, and altered tendon cell apoptosis. Biochemical factors such as imbalances in matrix metalloproteinases, inflammatory cytokines, and oxidative stress further exacerbate tissue damage (Gao et al. 2024; Xu et al. 2025).

The clinical manifestations of tendon pathology vary depending on the tendon involved. Commonly affected tendons include the rotator cuff, Achilles, patellar, and lateral elbow tendons. Patients typically present with pain, swelling, stiffness, and reduced function, which can significantly impair daily activities and athletic performance (Aicale et al. 2020; Magnan et al. 2014; D'Addona et al. 2017). Diagnostic evaluation relies on clinical examination, imaging modalities such as ultrasound or MRI, and sometimes histopathology in severe cases. Despite the high prevalence of tendon disorders, effective treatments remain limited. Conservative management, rest, physical therapy, nonsteroidal anti-inflammatory drugs (NSAIDs), and corticosteroid injections provide symptomatic relief but often fail to restore tendon integrity. Surgical intervention is required after rupture and reserved for severe tears or persistent symptoms but carries risks of complications and prolonged rehabilitation (Feng et al. 2024; Waterston et al. 1997; Ireland et al. 2001; Lui et al. 2010; Jelinsky et al. 2011; Fearon et al. 2013).

The economic burden of tendon disorders is substantial. Direct healthcare costs include outpatient visits, imaging, pharmacological treatments, physical therapy sessions, and surgical procedures. Indirect costs, often exceeding direct expenses, arise from work absenteeism, reduced productivity, and long-term disability. For instance, rotator cuff injuries and lateral epicondylitis contribute to significant workforce loss in both manual and office-based labor sectors. Epidemiological studies estimate that musculoskeletal tendon disorders account for billions in annual healthcare expenditure globally. Moreover, recurrent or chronic tendon pathology exacerbates long-term financial and social burdens, particularly in aging populations and professional athletes.

Despite advances in understanding tendon biology, several unresolved gaps persist. The exact mechanisms underlying chronic tendinopathy and failed healing responses remain unclear, limiting the development of targeted therapies (Bianchi et al. 2021; Foyt et al. 2018; Chae et al. 2022). There is a lack of standardized diagnostic criteria, leading to variability in clinical assessment and treatment outcomes (Gerami et al. 2022; Buerba et al. 2021). Current interventions primarily address symptoms rather than promoting tendon regeneration, highlighting the need for regenerative medicine approaches such as stem cell therapy, platelet-rich plasma, and gene therapy. Additionally, preventive strategies, including ergonomic modifications and early detection protocols, are underutilized in both occupational and athletic settings. Research on cost-effective management models is also insufficient, preventing the establishment of optimized care pathways that reduce both clinical and economic burdens.

9.2 The Need for Advanced Tendon In Vitro Models

As previously stated, tendon physiology is defined by a hierarchically organized extracellular matrix (ECM) and a population of mechanosensitive cells that preserve structural integrity under continuous mechanical load (Maffulli et al. 2023; Citro et al. 2023). The ECM of tendons is predominantly composed of aligned type I collagen fibers, proteoglycans, and glycoproteins, which together provide tensile strength and resilience. Tendon-resident cells, including tenocytes and tendon stem/progenitor cells (TSPCs), sense mechanical cues and respond by regulating ECM remodeling, thereby maintaining tissue homeostasis. The intricate structural organization, coupled with the dynamic interplay between resident cells and their surrounding matrix, is critical for tendon function. Traditional two-dimensional (2D) cell culture systems, however, fail to reproduce the complex architecture, spatial gradients, and mechanical environment of native tendon tissue. As a result, conventional in vitro models are limited in their ability to faithfully recapitulate tendon biology, investigate disease mechanisms, or predict regenerative outcomes following injury (Citeroni et al. 2020; Citro et al. 2023).

Recent advances in three-dimensional (3D) biofabrication offer transformative opportunities to overcome these limitations (Boularaoui et al. 2020; Sun et al. 2020; Singh et al. 2020; Zieliński et al. 2023; Parak et al. 2019; Cadamuro et al. 2023; Dec et al. 2024). Techniques such as bioprinting, bioplotting, and hydrogel-based scaffold engineering enable the creation of physiologically relevant microenvironments that more accurately mimic the structural, biochemical, and mechanical properties of native tendon ECM. These technologies allow precise control over scaffold architecture, fiber alignment, and matrix composition, supporting the recreation of microscale topographical cues, mechanical stiffness gradients, and biochemical signaling pathways. Consequently, 3D biofabricated constructs serve as highly predictive in vitro platforms for studying tendon development, pathology, and repair, bridging the gap between traditional in vitro assays by monolayer cultures and in vivo models.

Among the various 3D biofabrication strategies, bioprinting has emerged as a particularly promising approach in regenerative medicine and tissue engineering. By depositing cell-laden bioinks layer by layer, bioprinting enables unprecedented precision in scaffold architecture and spatial organization, facilitating the design of constructs that replicate tissue-specific features. The combination of bioinks, advanced bioprinters, and bioreactors represents a multidisciplinary approach in tissue engineering, allowing the fabrication of synthetic ECMs that function as physiologically and pathologically relevant 3D in vitro models. This integration supports not only the structural fidelity of engineered tissues but also the functional crosstalk between cells and their microenvironment.

Among the available bioinks, hydrogels have gained attention for their rapid crosslinking, high biocompatibility, and tunable bioactivity (Catoira et al. 2019; Billiet et al. 2012; Glowacki and Mizuno 2008; Meyer 2019; Osidak et al. 2024), especially for musculoskeletal applications (Ciardulli et al. 2021; Lamparelli et al. 2021; Ciardulli et al. 2020a). Methacrylated collagen (ColMA) is particularly attractive due to its ability to recapitulate the native composition and mechanical properties of tendon ECM (Gaudet and Shreiber 2012; Antoine et al. 2014; Pien et al. 2021; Amirrah et al. 2022; Noohi et al. 2023). The methacrylation process introduces reactive groups to the collagen backbone, enabling rapid photo-crosslinking and improving printability, which ensures precise scaffold architecture during the bioprinting process. Furthermore, ColMA supports cellular adhesion, proliferation,

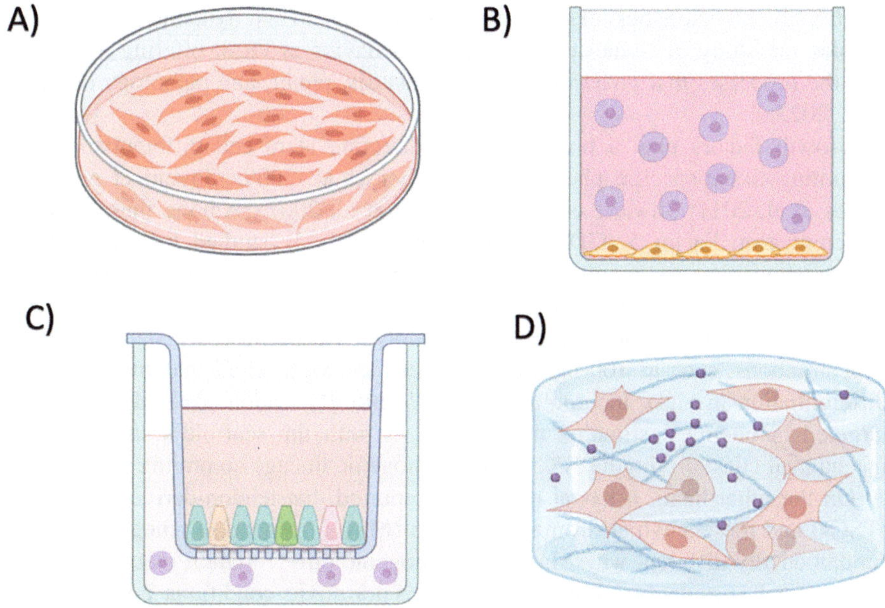

Fig. 9.1 Schematic representation of different in vitro culture models used for tendon in vitro research (**a**) Monolayer culture: Tendon stem cells (TSCs) or mesenchymal stromal cells (MSCs) grown on standard 2D plastic surfaces, allowing controlled assessment of basal cell behavior and early tenogenic responses. (**b**) Indirect or direct co-culture: Cells maintained in shared media or physical contact to study paracrine signaling, cell–cell communication, or interactions between TSCs and other tendon-relevant populations (e.g., fibroblasts, macrophages). (**c**) 3D scaffold-based model: Cells seeded within structured biomaterials (e.g., aligned fibers, hydrogels), providing physiological architecture and mechanical cues that support tenogenic differentiation and extracellular matrix production. (**d**) Advanced 3D environment: Multilayer, mechanically stimulated, or bioreactor-supported constructs that mimic tendon-like microenvironments more closely, enabling long-term maturation, matrix organization, and functional tissue development

and differentiation, fostering a microenvironment that closely mimics in vivo conditions. Despite these advantages, the use of pure ColMA in fully bioprinted scaffolds has been limited in the literature, with most applications relying on hybrid or composite materials. Developing a robust, reproducible pipeline for bioprinting ColMA alone would significantly broaden its applicability in tendon tissue engineering.

To fabricate a 3D bioengineered tendon model, cells must be incorporated within the scaffold matrix (see Fig. 9.1). The seeding of primary cells or stem cells into 3D constructs not only enhances physiological relevance but also facilitates cell–matrix interactions reminiscent of native tissue architecture. Within a 3D microenvironment, cells establish complex interactions with their neighbors and surrounding ECM, including cell–cell signaling and cell–matrix crosstalk (Clerici et al. 2023; Maffulli et al. 2000). These interactions influence key cellular processes such as proliferation, differentiation, and ECM remodeling, ultimately shaping the functional characteristics of engineered constructs. This dynamic environment enables the study of tissue-specific cellular behavior in vitro, offering a window into the processes that govern tendon homeostasis, repair, and pathology (Cortella et al. 2025a).

Growth factors play a pivotal role in directing stem cell differentiation and promoting tissue-specific phenotypes (Discher et al. 2009; Govoni et al. 2017; James et al. 2011; Shwartz et al. 2016; Zeng et al. 2007). Among these, Growth Differentiation Factor 5 (GDF-5) has been extensively studied for its ability to induce tenogenic gene expression. GDF-5 enhances the expression of tendon-related markers in human bone marrow-derived MSCs and Wharton's Jelly-derived MSCs, promoting commitment to a neo-tendon phenotype (Ciardulli et al. 2020b). Optimal concentrations, such as 100 ng/mL, have been shown to elicit maximal tenogenic differentiation in vitro. Incorporating GDF-5 into 3D tendon scaffolds provides a targeted biochemical stimulus that synergizes with the scaffold's structural and mechanical cues, driving hTSPCs toward tenogenic lineage commitment.

On the other hand, it has also recently reported that tendon-derived stem cells (TSCs) and mesenchymal/stromal stem cells (MSCs) respond to tenogenic cues in fundamentally different ways. In MSCs, tenogenic differentiation required specific biochemical stimulation, with GDF-7 under normoxic conditions producing the strongest induction of tenogenic proteins. These findings highlight those environmental cues in vitro, particularly physoxia, are sufficient to drive TSC tenogenesis, whereas MSCs rely more heavily on exogenous biochemical signals. This distinction is critical for optimizing tendon-focused regenerative strategies (Citro et al. 2025).

Beyond biochemical stimuli, the dynamic culture environment is also crucial for maintaining cell viability and supporting tissue maturation within 3D constructs. Perfusion bioreactors provide continuous medium flow, ensuring uniform nutrient delivery, waste removal, and oxygenation throughout the scaffold. This dynamic environment also facilitates mechanical stimulation, which is known to influence tendon cell behavior and ECM organization. By combining perfusion culture with GDF-5 supplementation, it is possible to create a physiologically relevant niche that promotes hTSPC proliferation, differentiation, and ECM deposition over extended culture periods.

9.3 Human Tendon Stem/Progenitor Cells: Features and Functions

A distinct population of tendon-resident stem/progenitor cells, commonly referred to hTSPCs, has recently been identified and extensively characterized. Importantly, they express tendon-specific markers and demonstrate the ability to generate tendon-like and enthesis-like tissues in vitro. First identified by *Bi* et al. in 2007, TSPCs were shown to reside within both human and mouse tendons, exhibiting classic stem cell characteristics such as clonogenicity, multipotency, and self-renewal capacity. These cells demonstrated superior proliferative potential compared to bone marrow-derived mesenchymal stromal cells (MSCs) and were capable of generating tendon-like tissues following extended in vitro expansion and in vivo transplantation. Since this seminal discovery, TSPCs have been recognized as a highly attractive cell source for tendon tissue engineering and regenerative medicine applications, offering a cellular foundation for studying both physiological and pathological tendon processes (Ciardulli et al. 2022; Yin et al. 2023; Clerici et al. 2025).

TSPCs were extracted from human tendon explants obtained from both healthy and pathological tissue samples. Surgeries were consistently performed within 3–5 days post-trauma, and TSPCs were immediately isolated to capture cells, during the initial stage of explanted tissue culture. Flow cytometry characterization confirmed that the isolated TSPCs retained a mesenchymal stem cell-like phenotype. Cells expressed canonical MSC surface markers, including CD90, CD73, and CD105, the latter being an accessory molecule for TGF-β signaling, while remaining negative for hematopoietic and immune markers such as CD45, CD34, and HLA-DR. Interestingly, TSPCs derived from pathological tissue exhibited positivity for CD14, a monocyte/macrophage lineage marker, highlighting potential phenotypic changes associated with injury or disease. These findings are consistent with previous reports and align with the definition provided by the International Society for Cellular Therapy for MSC-like populations, reinforcing the stem/progenitor status of TSPCs (Ciardulli et al. 2026).

Morphologically, TSPCs derived from healthy and pathological tissue also showed marked differences. Cells from healthy tendons displayed an elongated, fibroblast-like morphology and aligned along specific axes, reminiscent of native tendon architecture. Conversely, TSPCs extracted from pathological samples were smaller, more rounded, and featured thin dendritic projections around the perinuclear region, particularly evident after 14 days of culture. β-actin staining of the cytoskeleton at day 0 revealed that these morphological differences were already present immediately after isolation, suggesting that pathological TSPCs maintain an altered phenotype likely influenced by the diseased ECM or inflammatory milieu. This morphological distinction is indicative of phenotypic drift and may reflect impaired metabolic or reparative capacity, potentially contributing to the altered tissue organization observed in tendinopathic tendons (Ciardulli et al. 2022).

Beyond surface marker expression and morphology, TSPCs from healthy and pathological tendons exhibited distinct transcriptional and inflammatory profiles. At day 0, prior to any experimental treatment, pathological TSPCs displayed a slight but statistically significant downregulation of all tendon-specific genes, with the notable exception of decorin (DCN), an essential ECM component, which was upregulated. Decorin plays a critical role in regulating collagen fibrillogenesis and maintaining matrix organization, suggesting that pathological TSPCs may attempt to compensate for ECM disruption. In parallel, pathological TSPCs exhibited elevated expression of pro-inflammatory cytokines, including interleukin-6 (IL-6) and tumor necrosis factor (TNF), indicating that these cells actively participate in modulating inflammatory responses during tendon healing. These observations highlight the dual role of TSPCs: contributing to tissue regeneration while simultaneously orchestrating local immune responses (Cortella et al. 2025b).

Tenomodulin is also largely under expressed in pathological TSPC (Ciardulli et al. 2026). TNMD is a type II transmembrane glycoprotein whose extracellular domain contributes to the ECM, while a single transmembrane helix anchors it to the plasma membrane. This dual localization accounts for its detection in both ECM-rich fractions and membrane protein preparations. TNMD expression also varies across tendon types: energy-storing tendons such as the Achilles consistently exhibit higher TNMD levels than positional tendons (e.g., digital flexors), reflecting their greater mechanical loading and elastic function (Shukunami et al. 2016). As a result, TSCs derived from distinct anatomical sites may display different basal levels of TNMD in both healthy and diseased conditions. Although interindividual differences in TNMD abundance and glycosylation are likely, given variability in metabolism and mechanical loading, these aspects remain unexplored in human tendon tissues. In our previous work, diminished TNMD expression in TSCs derived from pathological tendons consistently correlated with ECM disorganization and reduced regenerative potential (Ciardulli et al. 2024), likely reflecting a disrupted tenogenic signaling environment in degenerative or overloaded tissues. As TNMD undergoes N-linked glycosylation within its C-terminal domain, this posttranslational modification is functionally important for protein folding, stability, and proper localization, as well as for supporting cell–matrix interactions. Evidence shows that reduced TNMD glycosylation compromises protein stability and alters its distribution, potentially impairing its regulatory functions in tendon homeostasis and ECM organization (Waterston et al. 1997). We therefore suggest that TNMD glycosylation is not simply a structural modification but a critical determinant of its biological activity and functional integrity in tendon tissue.

The process of tendon healing involves a tightly regulated sequence of overlapping phases: inflammatory, proliferative, and remodeling. In the early inflammatory phase, lasting only a few days post-injury, a fibrin clot forms at the wound site to provide temporary mechanical stability. Macrophages infiltrate the area to clear necrotic debris, while resident tenocytes begin to proliferate, particularly in the epitenon. During the proliferative phase, macrophages release growth factors that recruit additional reparative cells, and tenocytes deposit a provisional ECM, predominantly composed of type III collagen, which lacks the mechanical robustness of mature tendon tissue. In the final remodeling phase, which can extend from 1 to over 12 months, type I collagen deposition predominates, and the ECM is gradually aligned along the loading axis to restore tensile strength. Despite these orchestrated processes, repaired tendons frequently retain scar-like properties and fail to fully regain their native biomechanical characteristics (Jiang et al. 2025).

TSPCs are integrally involved in each stage of this healing cascade. In the inflammatory phase, TSPCs modulate local immune responses through cytokine secretion, as evidenced by the upregulation of IL-6 and TNF in pathological cells. During the proliferative stage, they contribute to matrix synthesis, while in the remodeling phase, they assist in generating organized type I collagen fibers. Importantly, TSPCs not only differentiate toward tenocyte lineages but also secrete chemotactic molecules and growth factors that recruit additional reparative cells, thus orchestrating a multicellular healing response. Their involvement underscores the unique regenerative potential of this population and highlights their value for in vitro modeling of tendon repair.

The ECM itself plays a critical role in regulating TSPC behavior, yet its influence remains incompletely understood. Tendon ECM is primarily composed of hierarchically organized type I collagen, which forms aligned fibrils that confer remarkable uniaxial tensile strength. Healthy tendons exhibit a predominance of type I collagen, whereas pathological tissues display increased type III collagen deposition. Type III collagen fibers are thinner, more disorganized, and associated with fibrotic and scarred tissue, leading to compromised mechanical properties. The presence of type III collagen at rupture sites is consistently linked to weakened tendon strength and impaired function. Notably, pathological TSPCs appear to reflect the ECM phenotype from which they were derived, exhibiting a more rounded, chondrocyte-like morphology, indicative of impaired matrix remodeling capacity. This correlation underscores the reciprocal interaction between resident progenitor cells and their surrounding ECM, highlighting the importance of engineering microenvironments that recapitulate native tendon architecture for effective in vitro modeling.

Since their initial discovery, TSPCs have been extensively characterized for their multipotent differentiation potential, including osteogenesis, adipogenesis, and chondrogenesis. However, the mechanisms by which TSPCs contribute to tendon-specific regeneration, particularly under pathological conditions, remain incompletely understood. Emerging evidence suggests that TSPCs can regulate inflammatory processes, commit to tenogenic lineages, and modulate ECM deposition in a context-dependent manner. This functional plasticity makes them a compelling cell source for tissue engineering, as they can be harnessed to study not only regenerative processes but also tendon pathologies such as tendinopathy, fibrosis, and chronic inflammation.

9.4 Contributions to 3D ColMA-Based Biofabrication

Given the limited reporting of pure ColMA scaffolds in the literature, *Della Porta and co-workers* developed an effective, reproducible workflow for generating a homogeneous, printable, and cell-compatible ColMA bioink. PhotoCol®, a commercially available methacrylated collagen formulation, is typically intended for manual extrusion rather than automated bioprinting (Cortella et al. 2025a, b). Overcoming this limitation required optimizing bioink formulation, printing parameters, and crosslinking protocols to achieve high-fidelity 3D constructs suitable for cellular studies. The resulting workflow aimed to enable the fabrication of bioengineered collagen scaffolds that could serve as robust in vitro models for studying tenogenic events in hTSPCs.

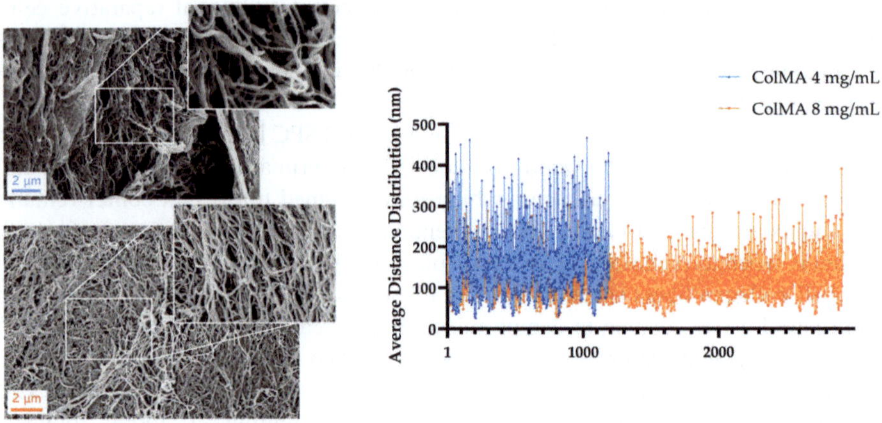

Fig. 9.2 Field-emission scanning electron microscopy (FE-SEM) images and average pore distribution distance of ColMA bioprinted scaffolds at two different concentrations. The two datasets shown in the plot on the right are related to Blue: ColMA 4 mg/mL and Orange: ColMA 8 mg/mL. Each color corresponds to measurements taken from collagen methacrylate (ColMA) samples at those respective concentrations, matching the two different microstructures shown in the SEM images on the left; adapted from (Cortella et al. 2025a)

Commercially available methacrylated collagen (PhotoCol®) has been described as offering compatibility with cell incorporation and manual extrusion. Despite handling ColMA during the bioplotting process presents notable technical challenges, primarily due to its unique thermal properties, which complicate precise control of hydrogel viscosity, the 3D in vitro models containing sensitive primary cells, such as human tendon stem/progenitor cells (hTSPCs), are particularly comfortable for future cell differentiation and growth. Optimal printability was observed at 8 mg/mL, which enabled proper crosslinking and high-resolution scaffold formation. Further optimization on printing speed and nozzle size was performed in a range of 5–10 mm/s with a nozzle gauges of 27–22 G, and the combination of 5 mm/s with a 22 G nozzle (0.70 mm internal diameter) was found to provide optimal outcomes. Under these conditions, needle blockages were avoided, and cell viability remained high, indicating that shear stress during extrusion was minimized. Morphological characterization of the printed scaffolds using field-emission scanning electron microscopy and pore average distances (Fig. 9.2) revealed that 8 mg/mL constructs possessed a higher number of pores, albeit smaller in size, compared to 4 mg/mL scaffolds. The mean distance among nearest neighboring pores was also reduced at the higher concentration. Given the enhanced printability and the retention of adequate void space for cell culture, 8 mg/mL is preferred.

hTSPCs were incorporated into the 3D ColMA scaffolds at a density of 1 × 10^6 cells/mL and successfully bioprinted with a high initial viability of 96%. The constructs were then cultured for 21 days in a perfusion bioreactor to ensure effective nutrient and waste exchange throughout the 3D environment. Medium supplementation with 100 ng/mL GDF-5 supported the promotion of tenogenic differentiation.

Under these dynamic conditions, cell viability remained consistently above 85% throughout the culture period. Morphologically, hTSPCs displayed elongated shapes by day 21, indicative of phenotypic maturation and adaptation to the 3D environment.

Cell behavior within the scaffolds was further evaluated using histological analyses with Sirius Red staining. Under polarized light, new collagen fibrils were clearly visible from day 7, suggesting active ECM remodeling by the embedded cells. Notably, the deposited collagen was predominantly type I, while type III collagen was largely absent. This observation is significant, as type I collagen is associated with structurally organized, functional tendon tissue, whereas type III collagen is often linked to injury, scar formation, and aging-related changes in tendon composition.

Gene expression analysis via qRT-PCR revealed dynamic patterns in tendon-related markers. Tenomodulin expression peaked at day 7, followed by a gradual decrease at days 14 and 21, reflecting temporal shifts in differentiation or scaffold remodeling. Type I collagen gene expression increased at day 14, coinciding with upregulation of other tendon-specific markers. Type III collagen exhibited statistically significant differences over time; however, immunofluorescence analysis detected type III collagen primarily at early time points and type I collagen only at later stages (day 21). Western blot analysis of tenomodulin showed a delayed increase at days 14 and 21, highlighting the complexity of gene–protein dynamics in 3D scaffolds.

Cytokine analysis of the culture medium further underscored the interplay between cellular behavior and scaffold environment. Traces of IL-1β were observed at all time points, while IL-6 and IL-8 exhibited a distinct temporal pattern, peaking at day 7 and declining by day 21 to levels of 54 pg/mL and 46 pg/mL, respectively. IL-6 is implicated in tendon disease and tears, while IL-8 contributes to ECM remodeling, biomechanical adaptation, and tissue homeostasis, as well as to pathological processes such as rheumatoid arthritis. The observed decline in IL-6 and IL-8 over time suggests a mitigation of their initial inflammatory roles, potentially influenced by GDF-5 supplementation and scaffold-induced microenvironmental cues.

Overall, this work established a robust, reproducible pipeline for bioprinting pure ColMA scaffolds with primary hTSPCs, demonstrating their potential as 3D in vitro models for studying tenogenic differentiation and tendon ECM remodeling. The optimized workflow overcomes prior limitations in hydrogel handling, printing resolution, and cell viability, providing a foundation for future studies. Beyond modeling physiological tendon development, this system can be adapted to investigate pathological hTSPCs, offering insights into biochemical changes associated with tendon disease and potential strategies to restore impaired cellular function. Future applications may include incorporation of nanoparticles or drug delivery systems within the 3D scaffolds to modulate cell behavior or enhance tissue regeneration, further expanding the versatility of ColMA-based biofabrication for tendon tissue engineering and regenerative medicine.

9.5 ColMA Scaffolds Functionalized with Nanocarriers for Development of Advanced In Vitro Microenvironment

By integrating aligned ECM architectures, biochemical cues, and three-dimensional culture conditions, an interactive platform providing critical extracellular signals that guide tenogenic differentiation and matrix organization can be organized. These models offer unprecedented opportunities to investigate dynamic cell–matrix interactions, early inflammatory responses, and ECM remodeling processes that are central to tendon homeostasis and pathology.

In particular, combining 3D bioplotted ColMA scaffolds with nanocarrier technology has emerged as a promising strategy to enhance the delivery and sustained release of growth factors while simultaneously providing a structurally and mechanically robust microenvironment. Traditional approaches, such as direct supplementation of growth factors in culture media, face significant limitations. Growth factors such as Growth Differentiation Factor-5 (GDF-5), a pivotal member of the Transforming Growth Factor-beta (TGF-β) superfamily, are prone to rapid degradation, which diminishes biological activity and necessitates repeated addition during media changes. Furthermore, the high concentration required to achieve effective tenogenic induction (100 ng/mL in our study) substantially increased culture costs and complicated experimental reproducibility. As an example, GDF-5 can be incorporated within bioresorbable polymeric carriers, specifically poly(lactic-co-glycolic acid) nanoparticles (PLGA-NPs), enabling controlled and sustained release of the peptide within a 3D collagen scaffold. This strategy ensures prolonged exposure of cells to the growth factor, optimizing tenogenic commitment while reducing both cost and variability associated with repeated supplementation. Various lipid nanoparticles carrying specific peptides/proteins or mRNA/gene therapies can be bioprinted within a 3D environment and evaluated for personalized or advanced nanomedicine applications. Potentially, all nanomedicine devices illustrated in Fig. 9.3 could be assembled within this 3D platform.

ColMA bioplotted scaffold was prepared adding lyophilized PLGA-NPs (Palazzo et al. 2021; Lamparelli et al. 2024) were resuspended in cell culture medium and incorporated into the collagen master mix (Fig. 9.4). This master mix was then bioplotted into three-dimensional scaffolds using an optimized extrusion-based printing protocol, achieving constructs with high structural fidelity and uniform distribution of both cells and nanoparticles (Cortella et al. 2025b). Perfusion bioreactors and dynamic loading systems can simulate physiological tensile forces, enhancing matrix deposition, collagen alignment, and functional maturation. These findings highlight that TSPC behavior is not solely genetically programmed but is profoundly modulated by the physical and biochemical context provided by the engineered niche. Dynamic perfusion culture was critical to the success of the system, providing continuous medium flow that ensures uniform nutrient and oxygen distribution while removing metabolic waste products (Hansmann et al. 2013; Gelinsky et al. 2015). This dynamic environment facilitates controlled release of

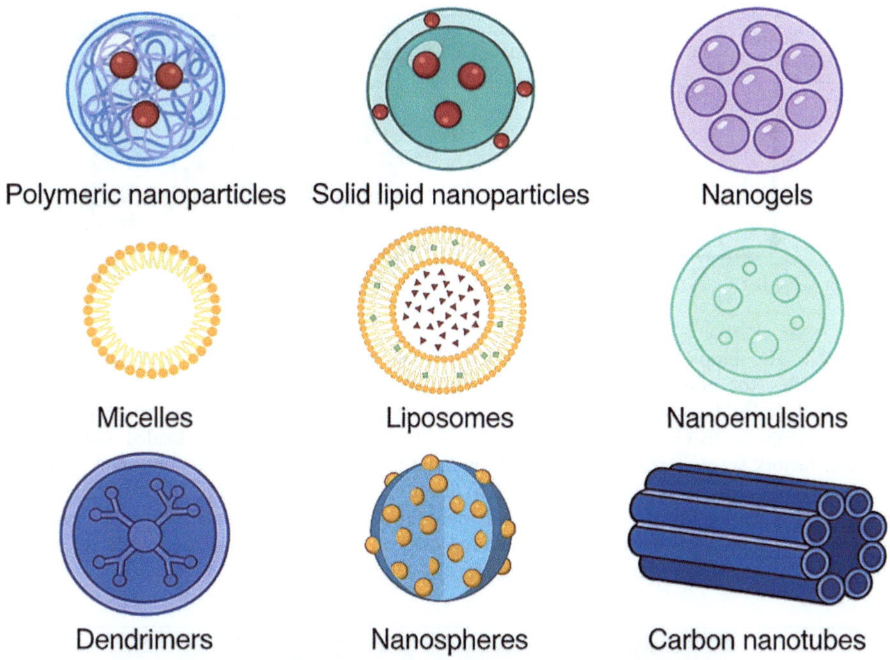

Fig. 9.3 Classification of potential nanoparticles for loading into 3D scaffolds. Schematic representation of various nanoparticle types that can be incorporated into bioplotted or hydrogel-based 3D in vitro models for controlled delivery of drugs, growth factors, or genetic material. These include polymer and solid lipid nanoparticles, nanogels, micelles, liposomes, nano-emulsions, dendrimers, nanospheres, and carbon nanotubes. The modular design of these nanoparticles allows tuning of release kinetics, bioactive molecule loading, and interactions with embedded cells, providing versatile platforms for advanced tissue engineering, regenerative medicine, and personalized therapy applications

GDF-5 from PLGA carriers and optimizes the biochemical milieu experienced by the cells (Cortella et al. 2025b).

Cellular behavior within the scaffold was further evaluated using histological and molecular techniques. Staining with specific antibodies revealed at confocal microscopy the progressive deposition of specific protein, for both healthy and pathological cells (Fig. 9.5). The deposited collagen was predominantly type I, consistent with the formation of structurally mature tendon ECM, whereas type III collagen was primarily observed at earlier time points and decreased over time. This trend aligns with the understanding that type I collagen is associated with functional tendon tissue, while type III collagen is typically linked to scar formation and tendon injury. These observations indicate that the 3D scaffold supports proper ECM remodeling, even in pathological cells, and promotes the deposition of high-quality collagen conducive to tendon regeneration. Tenomodulin secretion and deposition can be also observed much more effectively in a 3D environment than in a 2D approach, where only intracellular protein can be detected (Fig. 9.6).

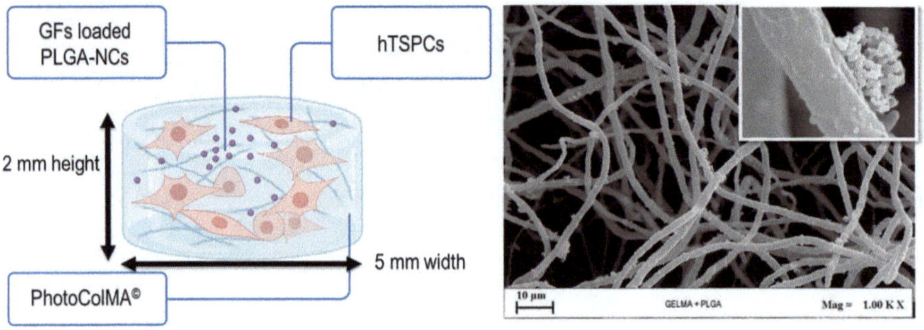

Fig. 9.4 3D bioplotted COLMA-based scaffold embedding TSPCs and incorporating nanoparticles for controlled growth factor delivery (**a**) Schematic representation of the 3D bioplotted scaffold composed of COLMA (methacrylated collagen) hydrogel, showing tendon stem/progenitor cells (TSPCs) encapsulated within the matrix. Nanoparticles loaded with selected growth factors are uniformly distributed throughout the construct to enable controlled, localized release during early culture and maturation. (**b**) Scanning electron microscopy (SEM) images of the bioplotted scaffold, illustrating the aligned microfibrous architecture and surface morphology. Nanoparticles appear as discrete deposits on the scaffold fibers, confirming successful integration into the 3D structure and providing an optimized interface for bioactive cue delivery

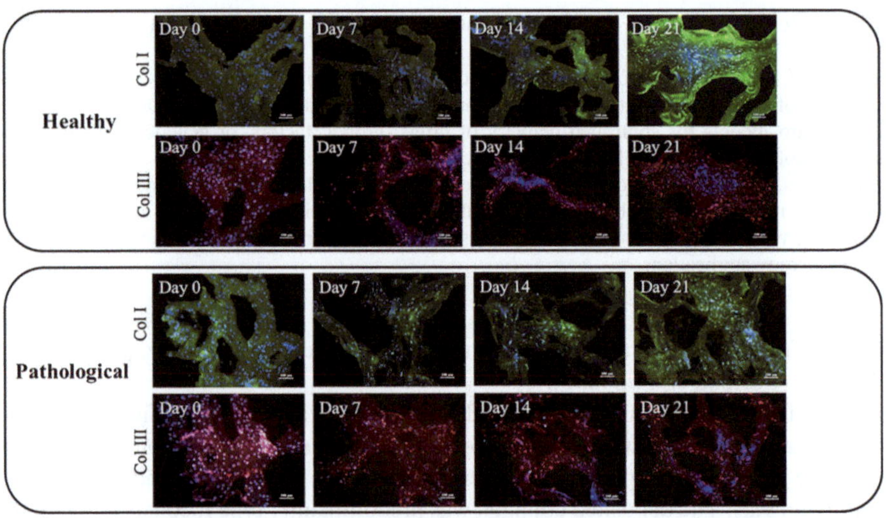

Fig. 9.5 Immunofluorescence analysis of collagen type I and type III in healthy and pathological TSPC cultures. Representative immunocytochemistry images showing tendon stem/progenitor cells (TSPCs) isolated from healthy (left panels) and pathological (right panels) tendon explants. Cells were stained for collagen type I (Col I) and collagen type III (Col III) to assess differences in extracellular matrix composition. Healthy TSPCs displayed robust Col I deposition with limited Col III expression, consistent with a balanced and organized matrix. In contrast, pathological TSPCs exhibited a marked increase in Col III signal, indicating a shift toward a disorganized and fibrosis-like matrix phenotype typically associated with tendon degeneration. Nuclei were counterstained with DAPI

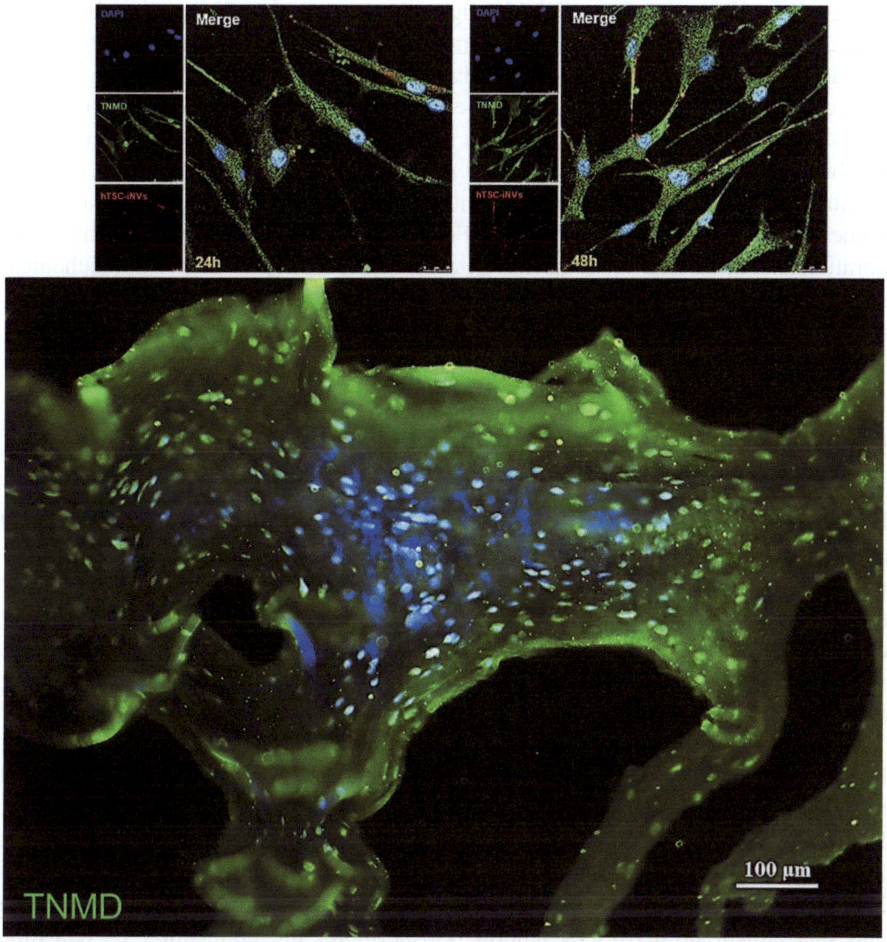

Fig. 9.6 Tenomodulin expression in TSPCs cultured in 2D versus 3D COLMA scaffolds. Representative immunofluorescence images showing tenomodulin (Tnmd, green) expression in tendon stem/progenitor cells (TSPCs) cultured on standard 2D monolayers (UPPER panels) compared with cells embedded within 3D COLMA scaffolds (LOWER panels). Nuclei were counterstained with DAPI (blue). While 2D cultures display limited and mostly perinuclear Tnmd signal, TSPCs in the 3D COLMA environment show enhanced and more organized tenomodulin expression, reflecting improved tenogenic differentiation and a more physiologically relevant extracellular matrix architecture

This approach demonstrates the feasibility of combining 3D bioplotted ColMA scaffolds with PLGA nanoparticle-mediated growth factor delivery to create a sophisticated in vitro platform for studying tendon pathology and regeneration. This approach offers several key contributions to the field of tendon tissue engineering. First, it establishes a reproducible methodology for fabricating 3D scaffolds with functionalized nanoparticles and pathological stem cells, which can serve as a platform for mechanistic studies of ECM remodeling, inflammatory responses, and tenogenic commitment. Second, it highlights the importance of integrating biochemical, mechanical, and structural cues to mimic the native tendon microenvironment. Third, the system provides a versatile platform for testing therapeutic interventions, including nanoparticle-mediated drug delivery, gene therapy approaches, or regenerative medicine strategies. Finally, this work underscores the potential of combining bioprinting and nanotechnology to create predictive, physiologically relevant in vitro models of tendon disease, facilitating translational research and the development of novel therapeutic strategies. Future developments may involve the incorporation of additional nanocarrier systems, co-culture models, or mechanical stimulation regimes to further enhance the fidelity of the in vitro tendon microenvironment, bridging the gap between laboratory models and in vivo conditions.

9.6 Future Outlook and Applications

By harnessing the unique properties of TSPCs within physiologically relevant 3D environments, researchers can elucidate the cellular and molecular mechanisms underpinning tendon homeostasis, injury response, and repair, paving the way for translational applications in musculoskeletal medicine. Unlike conventional 2D culture, which restricts cells to a planar surface, 3D scaffolds allow cells to interact with a surrounding ECM, engage in complex cell–matrix crosstalk, and align along fibrillar structures reminiscent of native tendon. First, the mechanical properties of 3D constructs, including stiffness, elasticity, and viscoelastic behavior, directly impact TSPC mechano-transduction. In addition to material complexity, advanced biomaterials and fabrication strategies are poised to further refine TSPC 3D culture. Methacrylate collagen remains a leading material due to its biocompatibility, but future developments may incorporate hybrid hydrogels combining collagen with elastin, fibrin, or glycosaminoglycans to more accurately replicate the biochemical and mechanical properties of tendon. Furthermore, the application of real-time imaging and biosensing technologies represents another transformative opportunity. Incorporating fluorescent reporters, mechanical strain sensors, and microelectrode arrays within 3D TSPC cultures could allow continuous monitoring of cell behavior, matrix remodeling, and electrophysiological responses. Coupled with high-resolution microscopy and computational modeling, these tools would enable a detailed understanding of how TSPCs sense and respond to mechanical, chemical, and inflammatory cues in 3D environments, providing predictive insights into tendon biology and disease progression.

On the other side, the combination of TSPC, 3D culture with advanced nanomedicine formulations, presents exciting possibilities. Nanocarrier and gene therapies nanosystems can provide sustained and localized delivery of growth factors, cytokines, or anti-inflammatory agents, enhancing differentiation efficiency and tissue regeneration. Functionalization of scaffolds with bioactive peptides or ECM-mimetic motifs could further modulate cell behavior, promote matrix deposition, and enhance scaffold integration with native tissues in translational applications. These strategies, combined with perfusion culture and controlled mechanical stimulation, are likely to yield increasingly sophisticated and predictive models of tendon biology, disease, and repair. As an example, growth factors such as GDF-5 (Ciardulli et al. 2020b) or TGF-β (Ciardulli et al. 2024), as well as hormones (Lamparelli et al. 2022), miRNA (Giordano et al. 2020), and other cells (Citeroni et al. 2020; Pinnarò et al. 2024; Scala et al. 2021) or gene therapies with mRNA drugs (Tello et al. 2025), have been already described to enhance tendon-specific ECM production. However, advanced studies by conventional supplementation in culture media is limited by rapid degradation, high cost, and nonuniform distribution. Encapsulation of growth factors within biodegradable nanoparticles, such as PLGA carriers as well as mRNA or protein within solid lipid nanoparticles, will enable more controlled and precise localized release directly within the 3D scaffold, maintaining bioactivity over extended periods. This strategy not only enhances tenogenic differentiation but also allows for fine-tuning of temporal and spatial signaling gradients, which are critical for replicating tendon developmental processes and pathological conditions in vitro.

Looking forward, one of the most promising directions in TSPC 3D culture is the development of disease-mimicking models. Tendon pathologies, including tendinopathy, age-related degeneration, and postinjury fibrosis, are associated with altered ECM composition, impaired mechano-transduction, and chronic inflammation. By incorporating pathological TSPCs into engineered scaffolds, researchers can recreate the cellular and molecular hallmarks of tendon disease in vitro. These models enable systematic investigation of the interplay between aberrant cell behavior, ECM remodeling, and inflammatory signaling, providing a platform for mechanistic studies and therapeutic screening. Integration of nanocarriers for growth factors, anti-inflammatory drugs, or gene modulators further expands the potential of these systems, allowing researchers to test regenerative interventions in a controlled and physiologically relevant context.

Another exciting future direction is the incorporation of multicellular complexity into TSPC 3D models. Tendon tissue is not composed solely of tenocytes and stem/progenitor cells; immune cells and neural components also contribute to tissue homeostasis, repair, and response to injury. Co-culturing TSPCs with endothelial cells, macrophages, or Schwann cells within 3D scaffolds could enable modeling of angiogenesis, immune modulation, and nerve–tendon interactions, thereby enhancing the physiological relevance of the model. Such integrated systems would be invaluable for dissecting the cellular crosstalk that occurs during tendon repair, degeneration, and chronic inflammation.

In the translational context, TSPC 3D culture platforms are likely to play an increasingly important role in personalized medicine. Patient-derived TSPCs can be incorporated into 3D scaffolds to model individual-specific tendon physiology and pathology, offering a powerful tool for drug screening, regenerative therapy optimization, and disease modeling. Future directions also include the integration of gene editing and synthetic biology tools to further manipulate TSPC behavior. Techniques such as CRISPR-Cas9 could be employed to modulate key transcription factors, signaling pathways, or mechanosensitive proteins within TSPCs, allowing for precise interrogation of the molecular drivers of tenogenesis, ECM remodeling, and pathological transformation. Coupling these approaches with 3D bioprinted models will provide a powerful platform to dissect causative relationships between genetic regulation and tissue-level outcomes.

Competing Interests The author(s) has no competing interests to declare that are relevant to the content of this manuscript.

References

Aicale R, Oliviero A, Maffulli N (2020) Management of Achilles and Patellar Tendinopathy: what we know, what we can do. J Foot Ankle Res 13:59. https://doi.org/10.1186/s13047-020-00418-8

Amirrah IN, Lokanathan Y, Zulkiflee I, Wee MFMR, Motta A, Fauzi MB (2022) A comprehensive review on collagen type I development of biomaterials for tissue engineering: from biosynthesis to bioscaffold. Biomedicine 10:2307. https://doi.org/10.3390/biomedicines10092307

Antoine EE, Vlachos PP, Rylander MN (2014) Review of collagen I hydrogels for bioengineered tissue microenvironments: characterization of mechanics, structure, and transport. Tissue Eng Part B Rev 20:683–696. https://doi.org/10.1089/ten.teb.2014.0086

Bianchi E, Ruggeri M, Rossi S, Vigani B, Miele D, Bonferoni MC, Sandri G, Ferrari F (2021) Innovative strategies in tendon tissue engineering. Pharmaceutics 13:89. https://doi.org/10.3390/pharmaceutics13010089

Billiet T, Vandenhaute M, Schelfhout J, Van Vlierberghe S, Dubruel P (2012) A review of trends and limitations in hydrogel-rapid prototyping for tissue engineering. Biomaterials 33:6020–6041. https://doi.org/10.1016/j.biomaterials.2012.04.050

Boularaoui S, Al Hussein G, Khan KA, Christoforou N, Stefanini C (2020) An overview of extrusion-based bioprinting with a focus on induced shear stress and its effect on cell viability. Bioprinting 20:e00093. https://doi.org/10.1016/j.bprint.2020.e00093

Buerba RA, Boden SA, Lesniak B (2021) Graft selection in contemporary anterior cruciate ligament reconstruction. JAAOS Glob Res Rev 5:e21.00230. https://doi.org/10.5435/JAAOSGlobal-D-21-00230

Cadamuro F, Nicotra F, Russo L (2023) 3D printed tissue models: from hydrogels to biomedical applications. J Control Release 354:726–745. https://doi.org/10.1016/j.jconrel.2023.01.048

Catoira MC, Fusaro L, Di Francesco D, Ramella M, Boccafoschi F (2019) Overview of natural hydrogels for regenerative medicine applications. J Mater Sci Mater Med 30:115. https://doi.org/10.1007/s10856-019-6318-7

Chae S, Choi Y-J, Cho D-W (2022) Mechanically and biologically promoted cell-laden constructs generated using tissue-specific bioinks for tendon/ligament tissue engineering applications. Biofabrication 14:025013. https://doi.org/10.1088/1758-5090/ac4fb6

Ciardulli MC, Marino L, Lovecchio J, Giordano E, Forsyth NR, Selleri C, Maffulli N, Della Porta G (2020a) Tendon and cytokine marker expression by human bone marrow mesenchymal stem cells in a hyaluronate/poly-lactic-co-glycolic acid (PLGA)/fibrin three-dimensional (3D) scaffold. Cells 9:1268. https://doi.org/10.3390/cells9051268

Ciardulli MC, Marino L, Lamparelli EP, Guida M, Forsyth NR, Selleri C, Della Porta G, Maffulli N (2020b) Dose-response tendon-specific markers induction by growth differentiation factor-5 in human bone marrow and umbilical cord mesenchymal stem cells. Int J Mol Sci 21:5905. https://doi.org/10.3390/ijms21165905

Ciardulli MC, Lovecchio J, Scala P, Lamparelli EP, Dale TP, Giudice V, Giordano E, Selleri C, Forsyth NR, Maffulli N et al (2021) 3D biomimetic scaffold for growth factor controlled delivery: an in-vitro study of Tenogenic events on Wharton's jelly mesenchymal stem cells. Pharmaceutics 13:1448. https://doi.org/10.3390/pharmaceutics13091448

Ciardulli MC, Scala P, Giudice V, Santoro A, Selleri C, Oliva F, Maffulli N, Della Porta G (2022) Stem cells from healthy and Tendinopathic human tendons: morphology, collagen and cytokines expression and their response to T3 thyroid hormone. Cells 11:2545. https://doi.org/10.3390/cells11162545

Ciardulli MC, Lovecchio J, Parolini O, Giordano E, Maffulli N, Della Porta G (2024) Fibrin scaffolds perfused with transforming growth factor-B1 as an in vitro model to study healthy and Tendinopathic human tendon stem/progenitor cells. Int J Mol Sci 25:9563. https://doi.org/10.3390/ijms25179563

Ciardulli MC, Lamparelli EP, Brongo S, Maffulli N, Della Porta G (2026) Bio-inspired lipid NanoVesicles (iNV) incorporating membrane proteins from healthy tendon stem cells for targeted protein restoration in Tendinopathic in-vitro model. Artif Cells Nanomedicine Biotechnol. 54(1):37–52. https://doi.org/10.1080/21691401.2025.2599071

Citeroni MR, Ciardulli MC, Russo V, Della Porta G, Mauro A, El Khatib M, Di Mattia M, Galesso D, Barbera C, Forsyth NR et al (2020) In vitro innovation of tendon tissue engineering strategies. Int J Mol Sci 21:6726. https://doi.org/10.3390/ijms21186726

Citro V, Clerici M, Boccaccini AR, Della Porta G, Maffulli N, Forsyth NR (2023) Tendon tissue engineering: an overview of biologics to promote tendon healing and repair. *J. Tissue Eng.* 14: 20417314231196275. https://doi.org/10.1177/20417314231196275

Citro V, Clerici M, Della Porta G, Maffulli N, Boccaccini AR, Dale TP, Forsyth NR (2025) Tenogenic cues are biochemically and environmentally distinct for tendon stem cells and mesenchymal/stromal stem cells. Stem Cells Int *2025*:9047956. https://doi.org/10.1155/sci/9047956

Clerici M, Citro V, Byrne AL, Dale TP, Boccaccini AR, Della Porta G, Maffulli N, Forsyth NR (2023) Endotenon-derived type II tendon stem cells have enhanced proliferative and Tenogenic potential. Int J Mol Sci 24:15107. https://doi.org/10.3390/ijms242015107

Clerici M, Ciardulli MC, Lamparelli EP, Lovecchio J, Giordano E, Dale TP, Forsyth NR, Maffulli N, Della Porta G (2025) Human tendon stem/progenitor cell-derived extracellular vesicle production promoted by dynamic culture. Artif Cells Nanomed Biotechnol 53:1–16. https://doi.org/10.1080/21691401.2025.2475099

Cortella G, Lamparelli EP, Ciardulli MC, Lovecchio J, Giordano E, Maffulli N, Della Porta G (2025a) ColMA-based bioprinted 3D scaffold allowed to study Tenogenic events in human tendon stem cells. Bioeng Transl Med 10:e10723. https://doi.org/10.1002/btm2.10723

Cortella G, Lamparelli EP, Lovecchio J, Giordano E, Maffulli N, Della Porta G (2025b) A 3D ColMA-based Tenogenic microenvironment unveils the behavior of tendon stem/progenitor cells (TSPCs) from Tendinopathic surgical explants. Bioengineering 12:1337. https://doi.org/10.3390/bioengineering12121337

D'Addona A, Maffulli N, Formisano S, Rosa D (2017) Inflammation in tendinopathy. Surgeon 15: 297–302. https://doi.org/10.1016/j.surge.2017.04.004

Dec P, Żyłka M, Burszewski P, Modrzejewski A, Pawlik A (2024) Recent advances in the use of stem cells in tissue engineering and adjunct therapies for tendon reconstruction and future perspectives. Int J Mol Sci 25:4498. https://doi.org/10.3390/ijms25084498

Discher DE, Mooney DJ, Zandstra PW (2009) Growth factors, matrices, and forces combine and control stem cells. Science 324:1673–1677. https://doi.org/10.1126/science.1171643

Fearon AM, Cook JL, Smith P, Scott A (2013) Gene expression in tenocytes suggests Degnerative tendon tears attempt to heal. Br J Sports Med 47:e2.44–e2.e2. https://doi.org/10.1136/bjsports-2013-092459.49

Feng S-M, Maffulli N, Oliva F, Saxena A, Hao Y-F, Hua Y-H, Xu H-L, Tao X, Xu W, Migliorini F et al (2024) Surgical Management of Chronic Achilles Tendon Rupture: evidence-based guidelines. J Orthop Surg 19:132. https://doi.org/10.1186/s13018-024-04559-5

Foyt DA, Norman MDA, Yu TTL, Gentleman E (2018) Exploiting advanced hydrogel technologies to address key challenges in regenerative medicine. Adv Healthc Mater 7(8):1700939. https://doi.org/10.1002/adhm.201700939

Gao Y, Sun W, Wang J, Zhao D, Tian H, Qiu Y, Ji S, Wang S, Fu Q, Zhang F et al (2024) Oxidative stress induces Ferroptosis in tendon stem cells by regulating Mitophagy through cgas-sting pathway. Int Immunopharmacol 138:112652. https://doi.org/10.1016/j.intimp.2024.112652

Gaudet ID, Shreiber DI (2012) Characterization of Methacrylated type-I collagen as a dynamic, photoactive hydrogel. *Biointerphases* 7:25. https://doi.org/10.1007/s13758-012-0025-y

Gelinsky M, Bernhardt A, Milan F (2015) Bioreactors in tissue engineering: advances in stem cell culture and three-dimensional tissue constructs. Eng Life Sci 15:670–677. https://doi.org/10.1002/elsc.201400216

Gerami MH, Haghi F, Pelarak F, Mousavibaygei SR (2022) Anterior cruciate ligament (ACL) injuries: a review on the newest reconstruction techniques. J Fam Med Prim Care 11:852–856. https://doi.org/10.4103/jfmpc.jfmpc_1227_21

Giordano L, Della Porta G, Peretti GM, Maffulli N (2020) Therapeutic potential of microRNA in tendon injuries. Br Med Bull 133:79–94. https://doi.org/10.1093/bmb/ldaa002

Glowacki J, Mizuno S (2008) Collagen scaffolds for tissue engineering. Biopolymers 89:338–344. https://doi.org/10.1002/bip.20871

Govoni M, Berardi AC, Muscari C, Campardelli R, Bonafè F, Guarnieri C, Reverchon E, Giordano E, Maffulli N, Della Porta G (2017) An engineered multiphase three-dimensional microenvironment to ensure the controlled delivery of cyclic strain and human growth differentiation factor 5 for the Tenogenic commitment of human bone marrow mesenchymal stem cells. Tissue Eng Part A 23:811–822. https://doi.org/10.1089/ten.tea.2016.0407

Hansmann J, Groeber F, Kahlig A, Kleinhans C, Walles H (2013) Bioreactors in tissue engineering—principles, applications and commercial constraints. Biotechnol J 8:298–307. https://doi.org/10.1002/biot.201200162

Ireland D, Harrall R, Curry V, Holloway G, Hackney R, Hazleman B, Riley G (2001) Multiple changes in gene expression in chronic human Achilles tendinopathy. Matrix Biol 20:159–169. https://doi.org/10.1016/S0945-053X(01)00128-7

James R, Kumbar SG, Laurencin CT, Balian G, Chhabra AB (2011) Tendon tissue engineering: adipose-derived stem cell and GDF-5 mediated regeneration using electrospun matrix systems. Biomed Mater 6:025011. https://doi.org/10.1088/1748-6041/6/2/025011

Jelinsky SA, Rodeo SA, Li J, Gulotta LV, Archambault JM, Seeherman HJ (2011) Regulation of gene expression in human tendinopathy. BMC Musculoskelet Disord 12:86. https://doi.org/10.1186/1471-2474-12-86

Jiang Y, Pattappa G, Lin D, Della Porta G, Rudert M, Shukunami C, Docheva D (2025) The role of Tenomodulin in the tendon repair process. Am J Physiol-Cell Physiol 329:C1075–C1084. https://doi.org/10.1152/ajpcell.00461.2025

Kaux J-F, Forthomme B, Goff CL, Crielaard J-M, Croisier J-L (2011) Current opinions on tendinopathy. J Sports Sci Med 10:238–253

Lamparelli EP, Lovecchio J, Ciardulli MC, Giudice V, Dale TP, Selleri C, Forsyth N, Giordano E, Maffulli N, Della Porta G (2021) Chondrogenic commitment of human bone marrow mesenchymal stem cells in a perfused collagen hydrogel functionalized with hTGF-B1-releasing PLGA microcarrier. Pharmaceutics 13:399. https://doi.org/10.3390/pharmaceutics13030399

Lamparelli EP, Ciardulli MC, Scala P, Scognamiglio M, Charlier B, Di Pietro P, Izzo V, Vecchione C, Maffulli N, Della Porta G (2022) Lipid Nano-vesicles for thyroid hormone encapsulation: a comparison between different fabrication technologies, drug loading, and an in vitro delivery to human tendon stem/progenitor cells in 2D and 3D culture. Int J Pharm 624: 122007. https://doi.org/10.1016/j.ijpharm.2022.122007

Lamparelli EP, Marino M, Scognamiglio MR, D'Auria R, Santoro A, Della Porta G (2024) PLA/PLGA Nanocarriers fabricated by microfluidics-assisted nanoprecipitation and loaded with rhodamine or gold can be efficiently used to track their cellular uptake and distribution. Int J Pharm 667:124934. https://doi.org/10.1016/j.ijpharm.2024.124934

Lui PP-Y, Chan L-S, Lee Y-W, Fu SC, Chan K-M (2010) Sustained expression of proteoglycans and collagen type III/type I ratio in a calcified tendinopathy model. Rheumatology 49:231–239. https://doi.org/10.1093/rheumatology/kep384

Maffulli N, Ewen SWB, Waterston SW, Reaper J, Barrass V (2000) Tenocytes from ruptured and Tendinopathic Achilles tendons produce greater quantities of type III collagen than tenocytes from Normal Achilles tendons: an in vitro model of human tendon healing. Am J Sports Med 28:499–505. https://doi.org/10.1177/03635465000280040901

Maffulli N, Cuozzo F, Migliorini F, Oliva F (2023) The tendon unit: biochemical, biomechanical, Hormonal Influences. *J Orthop Surg* 18:311. https://doi.org/10.1186/s13018-023-03796-4

Magnan B, Bondi M, Pierantoni S, Samaila E (2014) The pathogenesis of Achilles tendinopathy: a systematic review. Foot Ankle Surg 20:154–159. https://doi.org/10.1016/j.fas.2014.02.010

Meyer M (2019) Processing of collagen based biomaterials and the resulting materials properties. Biomed Eng Online 18:24. https://doi.org/10.1186/s12938-019-0647-0

Noohi P, Mahdavi SS, Abdekhodaie MJ, Nekoofar MH, Baradaran-Rafii A (2023) Photoreactive hydrogels based on type I collagen extracted from different sources as scaffolds for tissue engineering applications: a comparative study. Materialia 27:101651. https://doi.org/10.1016/j.mtla.2022.101651

Nourissat G, Berenbaum F, Duprez D (2015) Tendon injury: from biology to tendon repair. Nat Rev Rheumatol 11:223–233. https://doi.org/10.1038/nrrheum.2015.26

Osidak EO, Kozhukhov VI, Osidak MS, Domogatsky SP (2024) Collagen as bioink for bioprinting: a comprehensive review. Int J Bioprinting 6:270. https://doi.org/10.18063/ijb.v6i3.270

Palazzo I, Lamparelli EP, Ciardulli MC, Scala P, Reverchon E, Forsyth N, Maffulli N, Santoro A, Della Porta G (2021) Supercritical emulsion extraction fabricated PLA/PLGA micro/Nano carriers for growth factor delivery: release profiles and cytotoxicity. Int J Pharm 592:120108

Parak A, Pradeep P, du Toit LC, Kumar P, Choonara YE, Pillay V (2019) Functionalizing bioinks for 3D bioprinting applications. Drug Discov Today 24:198–205. https://doi.org/10.1016/j.drudis.2018.09.012

Pien N, Pezzoli D, Van Hoorick J, Copes F, Vansteenland M, Albu M, De Meulenaer B, Mantovani D, Van Vlierberghe S, Dubruel P (2021) Development of photo-Crosslinkable collagen hydrogel building blocks for vascular tissue engineering applications: a superior alternative to Methacrylated gelatin? Mater Sci Eng C 130:112460. https://doi.org/10.1016/j.msec.2021.112460

Pinnarò V, Kirchberger S, Künig S, Gil Cantero S, Ciardulli MC, Della Porta G, Blüml S, Elbe-Bürger A, Bochkov V, Stöckl J (2024) Oxidized phospholipids regulate tenocyte function via induction of Amphiregulin in dendritic cells. Int J Mol Sci 25:7600. https://doi.org/10.3390/ijms25147600

Scala P, Rehak L, Giudice V, Ciaglia E, Puca AA, Selleri C, Della Porta G, Maffulli N (2021) Stem cell and macrophage roles in skeletal muscle regenerative medicine. Int J Mol Sci 22:10867. https://doi.org/10.3390/ijms221910867

Sharma P, Maffulli N (2005) Tendon injury and tendinopathy: healing and repair. J Bone Jt Surg 87:187–202. https://doi.org/10.2106/JBJS.D.01850

Sharma P, Maffulli N (2006) Biology of tendon injury: healing, modeling and remodeling. J Musculoskelet Neuronal Interact 6(2):181–190

Shukunami C, Yoshimoto Y, Takimoto A, Yamashita H, Hiraki Y (2016) Molecular characterization and function of Tenomodulin, a marker of tendons and ligaments that integrate musculoskeletal components. Jpn Dent Sci Rev 52:84–92. https://doi.org/10.1016/j.jdsr.2016.04.003

Shwartz Y, Viukov S, Krief S, Zelzer E (2016) Joint development involves a continuous influx of Gdf5-positive cells. Cell Rep 15:2577–2587. https://doi.org/10.1016/j.celrep.2016.05.055

Singh S, Choudhury D, Yu F, Mironov V, Naing MW (2020) In situ bioprinting—bioprinting from benchside to bedside? Acta Biomater 101:14–25. https://doi.org/10.1016/j.actbio.2019.08.045

Sun W, Starly B, Daly AC, Burdick JA, Groll J, Skeldon G, Shu W, Sakai Y, Shinohara M, Nishikawa M et al (2020) The bioprinting roadmap. Biofabrication 12:022002. https://doi.org/10.1088/1758-5090/ab5158

Tello RP, Lamparelli EP, Ciardulli MC, Hirvonen J, Barreto G, Maffulli N, Della Porta G, Santos A, H. (2025) Hybrid lipid nanoparticles derived from human mesenchymal stem cell extracellular vesicles by microfluidic sonication for collagen I mRNA delivery to human tendon progenitor stem cells. Biomater Sci 13:2066–2081. https://doi.org/10.1039/D4BM01405G

Van Dijk CN, Van Sterkenburg MN, Wiegerinck JI, Karlsson J, Maffulli N (2011) Terminology for Achilles tendon related disorders. Knee Surg Sports Traumatol Arthrosc 19:835–841. https://doi.org/10.1007/s00167-010-1374-z

Waterston SW, Maffulli N, Ewen SW (1997) Subcutaneous rupture of the Achilles tendon: basic science and some aspects of clinical practice. Br J Sports Med 31:285–298. https://doi.org/10.1136/bjsm.31.4.285

Xu Z, Hou W, Zhang T, Chen R, Skutella T (2025) Exploring molecular and cellular signaling pathways: unraveling the pathogenesis of tendinopathy. J Orthop Transl 51:298–311. https://doi.org/10.1016/j.jot.2025.02.003

Yin H, Mao K, Huang Y, Guo A, Shi L (2023) Tendon stem/progenitor cells are promising reparative cell sources for multiple musculoskeletal injuries of concomitant articular cartilage lesions associated with ligament injuries. J Orthop Surg 18:869. https://doi.org/10.1186/s13018-023-04313-3

Zeng Q, Li X, Beck G, Balian G, Shen FH (2007) Growth and differentiation factor-5 (GDF-5) stimulates osteogenic differentiation and increases vascular endothelial growth factor (VEGF) levels in fat-derived stromal cells in vitro. Bone 40:374–381. https://doi.org/10.1016/j.bone.2006.09.022

Zieliński PS, Gudeti PKR, Rikmanspoel T, Włodarczyk-Biegun MK (2023) 3D printing of bio-instructive materials: toward directing the cell. Bioact Mater 19:292–327. https://doi.org/10.1016/j.bioactmat.2022.04.008

Chapter 10
Biofabrication Strategies for Tracheal Reconstruction: Conventional, 3D, and 4D Bioprinting Approaches

Soon Hee Kim, Sudarshini Nath, Sol Kim, Gilson Khang, and Chan Hum Park

Abstract Tracheal reconstruction is a major challenge due to the complex structure and mechanical demands of the trachea. Conventional surgical methods often face limitations in mechanical stability and tissue integration. Advanced biofabrication strategies offer promising alternatives, from non-3D-printed scaffold-free and scaffold-based approaches to 3D printing and 3D bioprinting using extrusion or digital light processing. Emerging 4D printing further enhances graft adaptability through stimuli-responsive materials. This chapter reviews these approaches, highlighting achievements, challenges in vascularization and integration, and future directions toward clinically viable tracheal therapies.

Keywords Trachea tissue engineering · Conventional fabrication · 3D printing · 3D bioprinting · 4D bioprinting · Trachea cartilage · Scaffold-free · Scaffold-based · Acellular scaffold

---

S. H. Kim (✉) · S. Nath · S. Kim
Microphysiological Systems Research Institute, Research Institute of Medical-Bio Convergence, Hallym University, Chuncheon, Republic of Korea
e-mail: shkim@hallym.ac.kr

G. Khang
Department of Bionanotechnology and Bio-Convergence Technology, Jeonbuk National University, Jeonju, Republic of Korea

Department of PolymerNano Science & Technology and Polymer Materials Fusion Research Center, Jeonbuk National University, Jeonju, Republic of Korea

C. H. Park (✉)
Microphysiological Systems Research Institute, Research Institute of Medical-Bio Convergence, Hallym University, Chuncheon, Republic of Korea

Departments of Otorhinolaryngology-Head and Neck Surgery, Chuncheon Sacred Heart Hospital, School of Medicine, Hallym University, Chuncheon, Republic of Korea
e-mail: hlpch@hallym.ac.kr

Y. M. Elçin (ed.), *Biofabrication in Regenerative Medicine*, Stem Cell Biology and Regenerative Medicine 1519, https://doi.org/10.1007/978-3-032-30294-6_10

Abbreviation

3D	Three-dimensional
4D	Four-dimensional
CAD	Computer-aided design
C-CVFIT	C-shape 3D-bioprinted biomimetic trachea
CHIM	Electrospun chitosan-based nanofiber membrane
CHyA-B	3D-printed PCL framework with collagen–hyaluronic acid matrices
CPCs	Cartilage progenitor cells
CSMA	Chondroitin sulfate methacryloyl
CVFIT	Cartilage–vascularized fibrous tissue-integrated trachea
dECM	Decellularized extracellular matrix
DIW	Direct ink writing
DLP	Digital light processing
DMD	Digital micromirror device
DTS	Decellularized tracheal scaffolds
ECM	Extracellular matrix
ElaMA	Elastin methacryloyl
FDM	Fused deposition modeling
GelMA	Gelatin methacryloyl
GMA	Glycidyl methacrylate
MSCs	Mesenchymal stem cells
O-CVFIT	O-shape tracheal constructs
p-CB	Photo-crosslinkable cartilage-specific bioink
PCL	Polycaprolactone
PEGDA-DTT	Poly (ethylene glycol) diacrylate- dithiothreitol
PGA	Polyglycolic acid
PGS	Poly(glycerol sebacate)
PLA	Polylactic acid
PLCL	Poly(L-lactide-co-ε-caprolactone)
PLGA	Poly(lactic-co-glycolic acid)
PLLA	Poly(L-lactide)
p-VFB	Photo-crosslinkable vascularized fibrous tissue-specific bioink
SFF	Solid freeform fabrication
Sil-MA	Methacrylated silk fibroin
SLA	Stereolithography
SLS	Selective laser sintering
TraCHIM	3D-printed biotracheal graft with an electrospun chitosan-based nanofiber membrane
TTE	Trachea tissue engineering
β-LG	β-lactoglobulin

10.1 Introduction

Cartilage is a specialized, avascular connective tissue with low cellularity that provides structural support, elasticity, and resistance to mechanical stress. Its unique mechanical properties, including shock absorption and resilience, are conferred by its extracellular matrix (ECM), which is rich in collagen type II and proteoglycans. These molecules enable water retention, thereby giving cartilage its characteristic viscoelastic behavior. There are three major types of cartilage—hyaline, elastic, and fibrocartilage—each differing in composition and anatomical location. Hyaline cartilage, the most prevalent type, is found at the ends of long bones, in the nose and larynx, and, most importantly, forming the C-shaped rings of the trachea that maintain airway patency and flexibility. Elastic cartilage, enriched with elastic fibers, provides the flexibility required for structures such as the auricle and epiglottis. Fibrocartilage, with its high collagen content, confers tensile strength and is localized in load-bearing sites such as the intervertebral discs and menisci (Hayes et al. 2001; Reina-Mahecha et al. 2023).

Cartilage regeneration remains a major clinical challenge due to its avascular nature and low intrinsic repair capacity. These limitations are especially critical in the trachea, where cartilage must provide structural support while enduring continuous airflow, mucociliary clearance, and dynamic mechanical stress. Extensive damage to the trachea, such as the loss of a long segment (over 50% in adults and 30% in children), makes direct surgical repair impossible. Traditional methods like metallic stents, silicone prostheses, and tissue grafts have been used, but they offer only temporary or incomplete fixes. These approaches are often plagued by complications such as re-narrowing, infection, and mechanical failure, and they struggle to fully integrate with the body (Haykal et al. 2014). These shortcomings have spurred growing interest in tissue engineering as a viable alternative for achieving durable tracheal regeneration.

Tissue engineering seeks to overcome these challenges by combining biodegradable scaffolds with living cells to restore both structure and function. While substantial progress has been achieved in orthopedic cartilage repair, translating these strategies to head and neck reconstruction is considerably more complex. Tracheal reconstruction, in particular, requires precise anatomical fidelity, long-term mechanical stability, and successful integration within an immunologically active environment that is constantly exposed to airflow and microbial challenges. These unique demands distinguish tracheal cartilage engineering from other cartilage repair applications and underscore the need for advanced biofabrication approaches (Liu et al. 2017).

Recent advances in three-dimensional (3D) printing technologies have revolutionized tissue engineering by enabling the fabrication of patient-specific scaffolds using biodegradable materials that mimic the mechanical properties of native cartilage. By integrating 3D printing with principles of regenerative medicine, customized tracheal constructs can be designed to recapitulate native architecture and mechanical function (Bartolo et al. 2022). 3D bioprinting has further advanced the field by directly incorporating living cells, such as chondrocytes or stem cells, within hydrogels to create biofunctional constructs. This approach enables precise spatial control over cell distribution and scaffold microarchitecture, thereby bridging the gap between engineering design and biological functionality. In the context of tracheal reconstruction, various 3D bioprinting modalities have been explored, including extrusion-based printing, photopolymerization techniques such as digital light processing (DLP), and hybrid systems that combine multiple printing strategies. From a tissue engineering perspective, different approaches have also been investigated, ranging from acellular scaffold constructs and scaffold-free systems to composite constructs where cells are seeded or placed within the scaffold. These strategies have significantly broadened the scope of biofabrication for airway reconstruction and have demonstrated the potential to generate patient-specific tracheal grafts with tailored structural and biological properties (Fishman et al. 2014). More recently, four-dimensional (4D) bioprinting has emerged as an extension of these advances, employing "smart" biomaterials capable of undergoing programmed changes in shape or function in response to external stimuli. Although still at an early preclinical stage with limited in vivo validation, 4D bioprinting holds promise for creating dynamic tracheal implants that can adapt to the host environment, reduce dependence on donor tissue, and mitigate immune rejection (Mathur et al. 2025).

Our laboratory has also pursued tracheal tissue engineering since 2018 using a variety of 3D printing technologies. We have regenerated tracheal constructs through PCL-based fused deposition modeling (FDM) printing (Park et al. 2018a), a 4-axis FDM printer (Park et al. 2018b), and photocurable hydrogel-based DLP (Kim et al. 2018, 2020a, 2021a; Hong et al. 2020) and extrusion printing (Lee et al. 2020), FDM-DLP hybrid printing (Lee et al. 2024), and further enhanced biocompatibility using 4D bioprinting approaches (Kim et al. 2020a). In addition, we have explored omentum culture of the fabricated construct to promote vascularization (Park et al. 2018a; Lee et al. 2024). Building on these experiences, this chapter will review recent advances in tracheal tissue engineering employing conventional methods, 3D printing, and 3D/4D bioprinting. By examining the key findings and limitations of each approach, it will provide new perspectives and propose future directions for clinical translation.

10.2 Overview of the Trachea

The trachea is a cylindrical airway located in the cervical and upper thoracic region that provides the main passage for airflow between the larynx and the lungs (Fig. 10.1). In adults, it measures approximately 11.8 cm in length and is supported by a series of C-shaped hyaline cartilage rings that maintain luminal patency. The posterior membranous wall, which lies adjacent to the esophagus, remains flexible to accommodate swallowing movements. The tracheal lumen is lined by a pseudostratified columnar epithelium containing goblet cells and motile cilia. Goblet cells produce mucus to entrap inhaled particles and pathogens, while the cilia propel

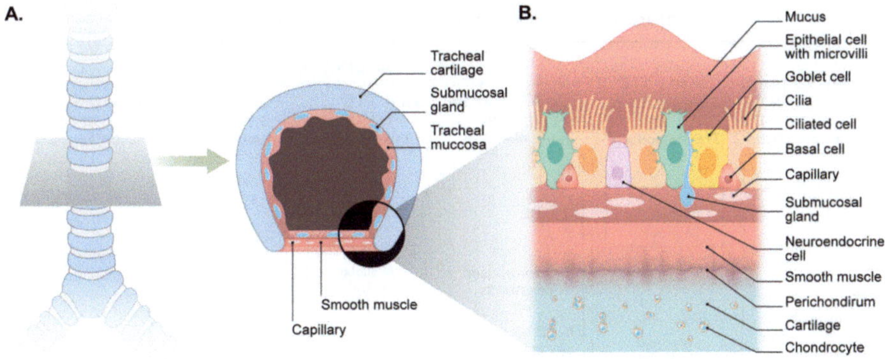

Fig. 10.1 Medical illustration of the anatomy of the trachea (Yeou and Shin 2025). (**a**) Cross section and (**b**) cell components of the trachea. (Permission: Reproduced with permission from S.H. Yeou, et al. Tissue-engineered tracheal reconstruction, Biomimetics 10 (7) (2025) 457, https://doi.org/10.3390/biomimetics10070457, © 2025 by the authors, Licensee MDPI, Basel, Switzerland under the terms and conditions of the Creative Commons Attribution (CC BY) license (https://creativecommons.org/licenses/by/4.0/))

the mucus upward toward the pharynx, thereby contributing to mucociliary clearance. In addition to filtration and defense, the trachea conditions inspired air by regulating its humidity and temperature, ensuring optimal gas exchange within the distal lung (Zhang et al. 2024; Kojima and Vacanti 2014; Yeou and Shin 2025).

Despite its robust structure, several pathological conditions can impair tracheal function. Tracheomalacia results from weakened cartilaginous support, leading to dynamic airway collapse, whereas tracheal stenosis arises from scar formation, prolonged intubation, or congenital malformations that narrow the lumen. Less frequently, primary or secondary tumors compromise the airway, often producing critical obstruction.

Surgical intervention remains the cornerstone of therapy for severe tracheal disease; however, it is technically demanding. Current options include segmental resection with end-to-end anastomosis or cartilage augmentation of localized stenoses. Selection of the procedure depends largely on lesion length and proximity to the larynx. Augmentation is generally favored in short-segment stenosis involving the subglottis, whereas resection and re-anastomosis are more effective for short lesions sparing the larynx. For extended stenoses, reconstructive strategies such as patch augmentation using fascia or pericardium or slide tracheoplasty are required. Importantly, resection with primary anastomosis is feasible only when the defect is less than ~50% of the adult trachea or ~30% of the pediatric trachea; longer resections risk excessive anastomotic tension and dehiscence. Since nearly half of clinically significant stenoses involve long segments, replacement tissues are often necessary to restore airway continuity (Ott et al. 2011).

Although direct anastomosis has long been regarded as the gold standard, its application is limited by the length of tissue that can be safely excised. Alternative palliative measures, such as endoscopic laser ablation or stent placement, can

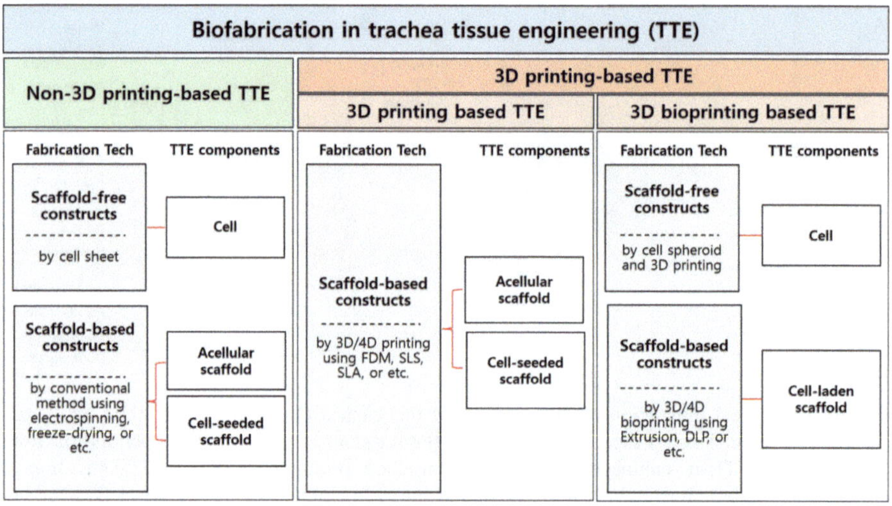

Fig. 10.2 Biofabrication methods in trachea tissue engineering (TTE). This review classifies biofabrication methods into two primary categories based on the use of 3D printing (non-3D printing vs 3D printing)

temporarily relieve obstruction but fail to provide durable repair. Investigational methods including the use of autografts, allografts, and prosthetic conduits have been attempted, however, each approach is hindered by complications (Azorin et al. 2006; Nakanishi et al. 1993). Synthetic prostheses are prone to extrusion, chronic inflammation, and poor tissue integration, while allogeneic transplantation is constrained by donor scarcity and immunological barriers.

These challenges underscore the urgent need for novel strategies. Tissue engineering has emerged as a promising avenue, integrating biological, engineering, and material science principles to develop functional tracheal substitutes. By employing regenerative cells seeded onto biocompatible scaffolds, this approach aims to circumvent immune rejection, overcome donor limitations, and enable the regeneration of structurally and mechanically competent tracheal cartilage. Such advances hold potential to transform the management of complex long-segment tracheal defects that remain inadequately addressed by conventional surgery (Fig. 10.2).

10.3 Trachea Tissue Engineering Using Non-3D-Printed (Conventional) Approaches

Tracheal defects resulting from congenital malformations, trauma, or disease present significant challenges that are often inadequately addressed by conventional surgery. This underscores the urgent need for novel strategies capable of restoring the structural and functional integrity of the airway. Tissue engineering has emerged as a promising avenue, integrating principles of biology, engineering, and materials science to create functional tracheal substitutes for subsequent implantation.

Early developments in tracheal tissue engineering largely paralleled advances in other organ systems, relying on both biomaterial scaffolds and cellular sources to support regeneration. Before the advent of modern 3D printing and 3D bioprinting technologies, these methods drew upon principles from regenerative medicine, biomaterials science, and surgical innovation. A pioneering study by Vacanti et al. (1994), which involved implanting polyglycolic acid (PGA) fibers seeded with chondrocytes into a rat model, demonstrated the feasibility of creating bioengineered airway grafts (Vacanti et al. 1994). This influential work catalyzed extensive efforts to design constructs capable of restoring both the structure and function of the trachea.

A wide variety of natural and synthetic biomaterials have since been explored for tracheal scaffolds (Baiguera et al. 2010). Naturally derived biomaterials—including elastic fibers, collagen, glycosaminoglycans, proteoglycans, gelatin, chitosan, hyaluronic acid, alginate, fibrin glue, DegraPol, and decellularized cartilage matrices—have been investigated for their ability to enhance cartilage formation in tracheal regeneration. Although these scaffolds offer excellent biocompatibility and support for neovascularization, constructs composed solely of natural materials generally fall short in providing the necessary mechanical strength and structural stability required for tracheal reconstruction (Jang et al. 2014; Schwarz et al. 2012). In contrast, synthetic polymers like PGA, poly(lactic-co-glycolic acid) (PLGA), and polycaprolactone (PCL) provide superior mechanical properties and tunable degradation profiles, although their limited bioactivity and potential to elicit immune responses remain challenges. To overcome these limitations, hybrid approaches that combine both natural and synthetic polymers have been investigated, aiming to balance mechanical performance with biological functionality.

The choice of cell source is equally important, as the native trachea is composed of heterogeneous tissues including cartilage, smooth muscle, epithelium, and vasculature (Kojima and Vacanti 2014). Autologous chondrocytes have been the most straightforward option due to their biocompatibility and reduced risk of rejection, but their limited availability and invasive harvesting procedures restrict clinical applicability (Kojima et al. 2002; Nomoto et al. 2013; Dennis et al. 2018; Chan et al. 2023). Mesenchymal stem cells (MSCs) have therefore attracted considerable interest because they can be obtained through minimally invasive methods and differentiated toward chondrogenic lineages (Lee et al. 2020; Xu et al. 2022; Sun et al. 2021; Zhang et al. 2022; Tang et al. 2023; Lu et al. 2025; Uchida et al. 2024). Moreover, co-culture strategies using MSCs in combination with chondrocytes have shown enhanced regenerative outcomes compared with monocultures (Kim et al. 2020b; Tsao et al. 2022). Collectively, scaffold composition and cell source must be carefully matched to replicate the structural and functional complexity of the native trachea.

In the early development of tracheal tissue engineering, fabrication methods such as solvent casting, freeze-drying, and electrospinning were used to produce porous matrices that could support cellular adhesion and growth. To replicate the tubular geometry of the trachea, approaches like molding with sacrificial templates and dip coating were explored.

From a tissue engineering perspective, three main strategies were employed. The first was the cell-only, or scaffold-free, approach, in which constructs such as cell sheets (Kanzaki et al. 2006; Wu et al. 2007a), spheroids (Uchida et al. 2024; Hamilton et al. 2019), or organoids (Gao et al. 2019; Knaneh-Monem et al. 2019) were used. This strategy avoided complications associated with biomaterial degradation but was limited by insufficient mechanical strength to endure airway stresses. The second approach involved cell–scaffold composites, where biodegradable scaffolds were seeded with chondrocytes, epithelial cells, or stem cells to accelerate cellularization and functional regeneration. Despite its potential, this method faced significant challenges, including low survival of transplanted cells and the practical difficulty of expanding patient-specific cells in vitro. The third strategy relied on scaffold-only, or cell-free, constructs. In this case, acellular scaffolds were implanted directly, depending on host cell infiltration and neovascularization to drive tissue repair. While this approach was simpler and less likely to provoke immune rejection, it frequently resulted in delayed and unpredictable regenerative outcomes. This section will explore these non-3D-printed approaches in detail, examining specific examples for each of the three tissue engineering strategies based on their key components (Fig. 10.3).

10.3.1 Scaffold-Free Approaches

Scaffold-free approaches in tracheal tissue engineering rely on the inherent ability of cells to self-assemble and organize into functional structures. By harnessing cellular interactions and extracellular matrix production, these methods aim to create constructs that more closely mimic native tissue. Such strategies reduce the risk of foreign-body responses and improve the integration of engineered grafts with host tissue. Ultimately, scaffold-free systems highlight the regenerative potential of cells themselves as the primary building blocks for airway reconstruction. Wu et al. developed a trachea-like cartilage graft by utilizing chondrocyte macroaggregates (Wu et al. 2007a). They developed a scaffold-free method for fabricating a tissue-engineered trachea. They isolated and expanded chondrocytes from rabbits, which were then seeded at a high density to form a cohesive cellular macroaggregate. This aggregate was wrapped around a silicon tube and implanted subcutaneously into the host rabbit to promote the formation of a cylindrical cartilage graft. After 8 weeks, the resulting tissue-engineered trachea successfully regenerated a cartilage-like structure with high expression of Type II collagen and proteoglycans, closely resembling native cartilage. This study demonstrates the feasibility of creating a functional tracheal graft using only cell aggregates, bypassing the need for an external scaffold.

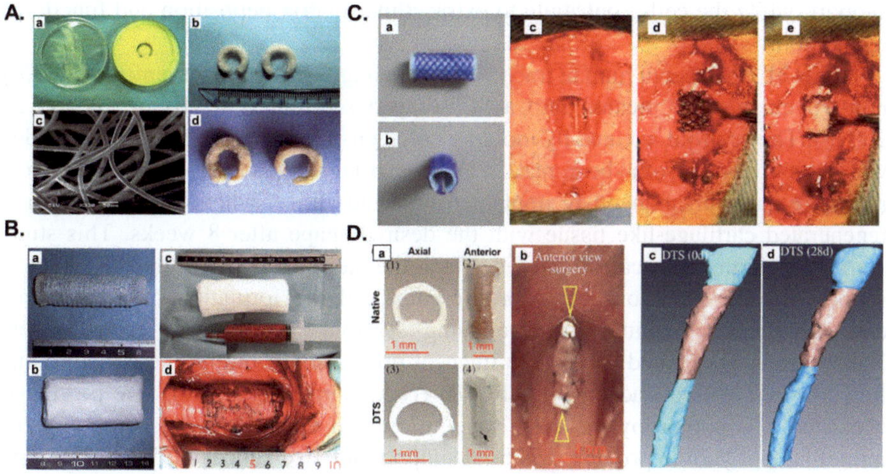

Fig. 10.3 Non-3D printing-based trachea tissue engineering. (**A**) Collagen-reinforced PLGA mesh: (a) PLGA preparation and C-shape mold, (b) collagen-reinforced mesh, (c) porous scaffold structure, (d) cartilage-like tissue in nude mice (Wu et al. 2007b). (**B**) In situ luminal remodeling prosthesis: (a) collagen layers, (b) polypropylene mesh with spiral stent, (c) preimplantation preparation, (d) canine tracheal reconstruction (Nakamura et al. 2009). (**C**) Three-layer composite scaffold with chondrocytes: (a–b) scaffold layers (collagen, PGA, copolymer mesh), (c–e) implantation in rabbits with gelatin sponge reinforcement (Komura et al. 2008). (**D**) Partially decellularized tracheal scaffold (DTS): (a) gross native vs DTS morphology, (b) in vivo implantation, (c) 3D reconstruction at day 28 (Liu et al. 2021). (Permission: (A) Reproduced with permission from W. Wu, et al. Engineering of human tracheal tissue with collagen-enforced poly-lactic-glycolic acid non-woven mesh: a preliminary study in nude mice, British Journal of Oral and Maxillofacial Surgery 45 (4) (2007) 272–278, https://doi.org/10.1016/j.bjoms.2006.09.004, Copyright © 2006 The British Association of Oral and Maxillofacial Surgeons. Published by Elsevier Ltd. All rights reserved, (B) Reproduced with permission from T. Nakamura, et al. In situ tissue engineering for tracheal reconstruction using a luminar remodeling type of artificial trachea, The Journal of thoracic and cardiovascular surgery 138 (4) (2009) 811–819, https://doi.org/10.1016/j.jtcvs.2008.07.072, Copyright © 2009 The American Association for Thoracic Surgery. Published by Mosby, Inc. All rights reserved. (C) Reproduced with permission from M. Komura, et al. An animal model study for tissue-engineered trachea fabricated from a biodegradable scaffold using chondrocytes to augment repair of tracheal stenosis, Journal of pediatric surgery 43 (12) (2008) 2141–2146, https://doi.org/10.1016/j.jpedsurg.2008.08.038, Copyright © 2008 Elsevier Inc. All rights reserved. (D) Reproduced with permission from L. Liu, et al. Regeneration of partially decellularized tracheal scaffolds in a mouse model of orthotopic tracheal replacement, Journal of Tissue Engineering 12 (2021) 20417314211017417, https://doi.org/10.1177/20417314211017417, © The Author(s) 2021 under the Creative Commons Attribution-NonCommercial 4.0 License)

10.3.2 *Scaffold-Based Approaches*

10.3.2.1 Cell-Seeded Scaffolds

In tracheal tissue engineering, the cell-seeded scaffold approach involves seeding various cell types, such as chondrocytes, epithelial cells, or stem cells, onto biocompatible scaffolds to promote tissue regeneration. The scaffold provides structural support, while the cells contribute to extracellular matrix deposition and functional restoration.

Wu et al. engineered human tracheal tissue using type I collagen-enforced PLGA non-woven mesh fabricated into a "C"-shaped scaffold (Fig. 10.3A; Wu et al. 2007b). The scaffold, created by molding collagen-coated PLGA fibers, was seeded with chondrocytes from sheep nasal septum cartilage. These cell-scaffold composites were then subcutaneously implanted into nude mice, where they successfully regenerated cartilage-like tissue with the desired shape after 8 weeks. This study demonstrated that the scaffold provides both the mechanical strength and biological support needed for chondrocyte proliferation and the formation of a functional cartilage matrix, making it a promising scaffold for tracheal reconstruction. Nakamura et al. created a biphasic tracheal prosthesis to mimic the structure and function of a native trachea (Fig. 10.3B) (Nakamura et al. 2009). The prosthesis consisted of a polypropylene mesh tube, reinforced with a spiraled polypropylene monofilament yarn to provide structural support and mechanical stiffness. This core was then coated with an atelocollagen layer through a multistep process, including surface activation and freeze-drying, to promote host tissue incorporation and ensure an airtight seal. When implanted in dogs, the group that received bone marrow-derived MSCs showed faster epithelialization and fewer complications, such as mesh exposure and luminal stenosis, compared to the peripheral blood group. This suggests that the scaffold's design, combined with stem cell therapy, is a promising strategy for effective tracheal regeneration. Komura et al. engineered a novel three-layer scaffold to address the complex requirements of tracheal cartilage regeneration (Fig. 10.3C) (Komura et al. 2008). The scaffold was designed with a specific material for each layer: an inner collagen sheet to promote the growth of epithelial cells, a middle PGA mesh to support new cartilage formation, and an outer l-lactide/ε-caprolactone copolymer mesh for elasticity. To create the regenerative grafts, they seeded these composite scaffolds with chondrocytes isolated from rabbits. The engineered constructs, along with a gelatin sponge that slowly released basic fibroblast growth factor (b-FGF), were then surgically implanted into a precise defect created in the rabbits' tracheas. They demonstrated its effectiveness in regenerating a functional airway within 3 months following implantation. Building on a previous scaffold-free technique (Wu et al. 2007a), Liu et al. utilized a scaffold-based approach to develop tissue-engineered tracheal cartilage grafts (Liu et al. 2010). They specifically used a PLGA copolymer scaffold combined with bone marrow MSC macroaggregates. The scaffold was prepared by disassembling commercially available sutures and then immersing the resulting fibers in rat tail collagen to create a porous structure. To form the graft, MSCs from rabbits were cultured to create macroaggregate sheets, which were then wrapped around the PLGA scaffold. These composites were incubated in a spinner flask for 4 weeks to promote chondrogenesis, or the formation of new cartilage tissue. The study successfully demonstrated that the MSC macroaggregates, under the influence of transforming growth factor-β, could fully degrade the PLGA scaffold and develop into a mature, autologous cartilage graft with evenly spaced lacunae. This innovative strategy offers an efficient way to fabricate ready-to-implant cartilage grafts for future animal studies.

10.3.2.2 Acellular Scaffolds

While cell-based strategies have demonstrated potential in various preclinical and clinical settings, it is often hindered by critical translational challenges, including lengthy cell culture periods, high costs, and stringent regulatory requirements. These limitations have prompted increasing interest in alternative approaches that do not require exogenous cell seeding. One such strategy is in situ tissue engineering, which capitalizes on the host's intrinsic regenerative capacity (Abdulghani and Mitchell 2019). In this approach, a cell-free scaffold is implanted directly into the defect site, where endogenous stem or progenitor cells are recruited to facilitate tissue regeneration. This reduces the need for complex in vitro manipulations, while bioactive cues embedded within the scaffold or delivered alongside the implant can further promote tissue ingrowth and vascularization. Decellularized extracellular matrix (dECM) scaffolds represent another cell-free strategy, offering native tissue architecture and biological signals that can support regeneration without pre-seeding (Abdulghani and Mitchell 2019; Ts et al. 2025). However, residual immunogenic or thrombogenic components within dECM remain concerns that require careful consideration. While not as widespread as other approaches, cell-free scaffold strategies have been explored for tracheal reconstruction in a handful of documented cases.

Hamaji et al. developed a composite tracheal scaffold and induce in situ vascularization by implanting it in the omentum (Hamaji et al. 2014). The researchers fabricated a cylindrical scaffold from a 0.8 mm-thick polypropylene mesh, a method described in a previous report, and implanted it into the omental sac of beagle dogs. They found that the omentum successfully formed a significantly thicker and more vascularized layer of connective tissue on the scaffold compared to the control group. While a coating of porcine atelocollagen further increased tissue thickness, it did not significantly enhance vascularization. The study concludes that this non-3D-printed approach is a feasible way to generate a functional, vascularized autologous tissue for tracheal reconstruction using the body's own regenerative capacity. Liu et al. developed partially decellularized tracheal scaffolds (DTS) to address long-segment tracheal defects while preventing collapse associated with complete decellularization (Fig. 10.3D) (Liu et al. 2021). Using sequential detergent treatments, all cell types except immunoprivileged chondrocytes were removed, preserving cartilage extracellular matrix and structural integrity. DTS were implanted orthotopically in a mouse model, where they supported epithelial and endothelial regeneration, improved chondrocyte viability, and restored native-like micromechanical properties by 28 days. These findings suggest that partial decellularization, which eliminates immunogenic cell types but retains chondrocytes and critical ECM components, provides a promising scaffold for functional tracheal replacement.

In summary, conventional, non-3D printing approaches to tracheal reconstruction including scaffold-free methods, cell-seeded scaffolds, and acellular scaffolds have laid a critical foundation for airway tissue engineering. Scaffold-free strategies exploit the intrinsic ability of cells to self-organize, minimizing immune responses and promoting graft integration; however, they are mechanically fragile, require temporary supports, and face challenges in scaling and vascularization. Cell-seeded scaffolds provide mechanical stability and support cellular growth, showing promise in preclinical and clinical studies, but achieving uniform vascularization and long-term structural integrity remains difficult. Acellular scaffolds circumvent the complexities of cell transplantation while offering structural and biological guidance; however, they often fail to replicate the anisotropic properties of native tracheal cartilage, balance rigidity with flexibility, and support consistent epithelialization or functional vascular networks. Collectively, these limitations—ranging from insufficient control over scaffold architecture and pore interconnectivity to challenges in directing cellular organization and biological signaling—underscore the need for more precise fabrication techniques. The experiences gained from conventional strategies have highlighted the critical importance of spatial and structural control, ultimately motivating the development of 3D printing and bioprinting technologies, which hold promise for overcoming these inherent limitations and achieving clinically translatable, mechanically robust, and biologically functional tracheal grafts.

10.4 Trachea Tissue Engineering Using 3D Printing

The introduction of solid freeform fabrication (SFF) (Crawford and Beaman 1999), also known as additive manufacturing, in the 1990s provided a powerful alternative to conventional scaffold fabrication methods such as solvent casting, freeze-drying, and electrospinning. By enabling the layer-by-layer construction of 3D structures with high precision, SFF laid the foundation for subsequent advances in tissue engineering. In the early 2000s, the adaptation of inkjet-based printers to deposit living cells instead of ink gave rise to 3D bioprinting (Sahoo and Tejaswini 2000). This breakthrough marked a paradigm shift, as it enabled the spatially controlled placement of cells, biomaterials, and bioactive factors to better replicate native tissue architecture and function.

In tracheal tissue engineering, 3D printing-based approaches can similarly be categorized according to the core tissue engineering elements employed: scaffold-free constructs and scaffold-based constructs. Initially, 3D printing in tracheal tissue engineering focused on scaffold-based strategies. The printed structures served either as stand-alone implants or as templates for subsequent cell seeding, essentially extending conventional tissue engineering methods. With the emergence of 3D bioprinting, however, scaffold–cell constructs could be fabricated in a single step using bioinks composed of hydrogel precursors and living cells, thereby opening new opportunities to reproduce the structural and biological complexity of the trachea.

In the following sections, we first examine tracheal reconstruction strategies based on simple 3D printing technologies such as fused deposition modeling (FDM), selective laser sintering (SLS), and stereolithography (SLA). We then highlight recent progress in 3D bioprinting approaches, including FDM- and DLP-based systems, which integrate both scaffolds and cells to achieve more functional outcomes.

10.4.1 *Scaffold-Based Approach (Acellular/Cell-Seeded Scaffolds)*

3D printing has emerged as a powerful technology in tissue engineering, enabling the fabrication of reliable and customizable scaffolds with patient-specific designs. Unlike conventional manufacturing, additive manufacturing allows precise control over key scaffold parameters, including size, geometry, and pore architecture, by integrating computer-aided design (CAD) software. This level of customization is particularly advantageous in regenerative medicine, where scaffold properties must closely match the biological and mechanical requirements of the target tissue. Various 3D printing techniques, such as FDM, SLS, SLA, electron beam melting (EBM), and so on, have been applied in the biomedical field, each offering distinct benefits in terms of material compatibility, resolution, and printing speed (Do et al. 2015; Kafle et al. 2021; Yang et al. 2018).

Polymers remain the most widely studied materials for 3D-printed scaffolds because they offer tunable mechanical properties, biodegradability, and biocompatibility. Biodegradable scaffolds are particularly attractive as they support tissue healing while gradually resorbing in the body, thus reducing the need for secondary surgeries and mitigating risks associated with permanent implants. Thermoplastic polymers such as PGA, PLGA, polylactic acid (PLA), and PCL have been widely investigated due to their structural similarity to native cartilage and their established use in biomedical applications (Valino et al. 2019). Among these biodegradable polymers, PCL has gained particular attention in recent decades as a long-term implantable biomaterial. PCL is a semicrystalline aliphatic polyester with favorable features such as biocompatibility, low toxicity of degradation products, and mechanical stability. Its slow degradation rate (2–4 years), although limiting for some soft tissue applications, is advantageous for long-term structural support in cartilage or tracheal reconstruction. Furthermore, PCL is easy to process because of its low melting point (59–64 °C) and high printability, making it suitable even for desktop-scale 3D printers (Woodruff and Hutmacher 2010). Given these properties, PCL has become the predominant material for fabricating tracheal scaffolds using 3D printing (Park et al. 2018b; Shai et al. 2024; She et al. 2021; Ghorbani et al. 2017; Yu et al. 2025; Shen et al. 2023; Khalid et al. 2023). These advantages make PCL particularly suitable for tracheal reconstruction. In the following sections, representative studies of tracheal reconstruction using different printing techniques and biomaterials will be discussed to highlight the progress and challenges in this field.

10.4.1.1 FDM-Based Fabrication

Invented by Crump in 1988, FDM is a form of 3D printing that uses material extrusion. The process begins by heating the material until it becomes a fluid. A nozzle then precisely deposits this flowing material onto a surface. By moving the nozzle and layering the extruded fluid, a 3D scaffold is built. The precision of the final product is directly tied to the quality and accuracy of the printing nozzle.

Park et al. fabricated a trachea scaffold using a 4-axis FDM technique, equipped with a rotating build platform and compared with conventional 3-axis FDM scaffolds (Park et al. 2018b). This system allowed printing while rotating the cylindrical construct, resulting in scaffolds with pore sizes and interconnectivity that closely matched CAD designs. The 4-axis PCL scaffolds also demonstrated superior mechanical strength and structural fidelity. When implanted into rabbit tracheal defect models, the constructs supported stable reconstruction, highlighting the potential of 4-axis FDM for producing accurate and mechanically reliable tracheal grafts. Khalid et al. developed a composite tracheal scaffold by integrating a 3D-printed PCL framework with collagen–hyaluronic acid (CHyA-B) matrices (Fig. 10.4A) (Khalid et al. 2023). The PCL component was fabricated through additive manufacturing into various structural designs to enhance strength, flexibility, and stability. These printed backbones were embedded within the freeze-dried CHyA-B scaffold to produce reinforced constructs. Mechanical performance was systematically evaluated, and the scaffolds were further tested for vascularization capacity in both in vitro and ex vivo settings. The combined approach demonstrated that the printed polymer structure supplied the necessary mechanical support, while the CHyA-B matrix sustained cellular growth and promoted angiogenesis, making the construct a promising candidate for tracheal replacement.

10.4.1.2 SLS-Based Fabrication

The principle of SLS was first proposed in 1986. An SLS system is typically composed of a laser, a powder bed, a piston that moves vertically, and a roller for spreading new powder layers. The process uses a computer-controlled laser to sinter (or fuse) the powder. The unfused powder surrounding the object acts as a natural support structure as the part is being built. SLS generally involves consolidating materials at a temperature below their melting point. In semisolid sintering, powder particles are only partially melted, creating a small amount of a liquid phase. This liquid then acts as a binder, joining the surrounding solid particles together to form a solid object. This method is particularly well-suited for low-melting-point polymers like PLA, PGA, poly(L-lactide) (PLLA), and PCL.

In the native trachea, C-shaped cartilage rings provide semirigid support, while the connecting fibrous membrane contributes collagen and vascular supply essential for epithelial renewal and infection defense. Inspired by this architecture, Wu et al. fabricated a three-layer elastomeric scaffold using 3D-printed PCL C-rings for

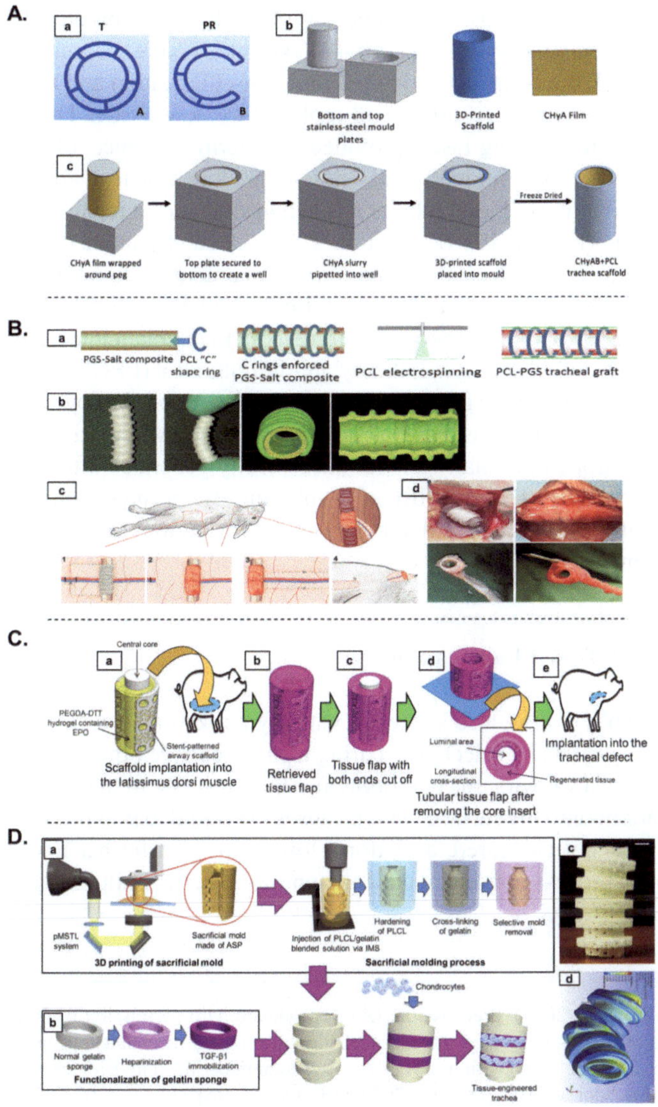

Fig. 10.4 Scaffold-based trachea reconstruction using 3D printing. (**A**) Reinforced CHyA-B composite scaffold fabricated by FDM: (a) Tubular (T) and partial ring (PR) designs, (b–c) schematic of composite fabrication combining CHyA film, CHyA-B slurry, and 3D-printed framework, followed by freeze-drying (Khalid et al. 2023). (**B**) SLS-based PGS-PCL elastomeric composite: (a) fabrication with SLS-printed C-shaped PCL rings and electrospun sheath, (b) micro-CT and gross views, (c) fascia wrapping for vascularized graft formation, (d) implantation and remodeling in vivo (Wu et al. 2019). (**C**) SLS-based tubular tissue flap: (a–d) fabrication and retrieval of scaffold–tissue constructs, (e) implantation into a segmental tracheal defect (Park et al. 2025). (**D**) SLA-based PLCL/gelatin bellows scaffold: (a–b) fabrication by indirect 3D printing with sacrificial mold and functionalization with heparin and TGF-β1, (c) gross morphology, (d) FEM simulation of luminal deformation under bending (Park et al.

mechanical stability combined with a porous poly(glycerol sebacate) (PGS) tube for elasticity and biodegradability (Fig. 10.4B) (Wu et al. 2019). Upon implantation in an animal model, the construct promoted rapid vascularization and host cell infiltration, with PGS gradually resorbed and replaced by new tissue. The integration of PCL rings into surrounding fascia provided long-term resilience, offering a promising alternative to conventional rigid, slow-degrading tracheal grafts. Park et al. developed a 3D printing-based tubular tissue flap strategy for repairing long segment tracheal defects (Fig. 10.4C) (Park et al. 2025). A stent-patterned airway scaffold was designed to provide radial strength while maintaining longitudinal flexibility, and its performance was evaluated through finite element analysis. The scaffold was fabricated using SLS with a removable central core to maintain lumen space and then loaded with poly (ethylene glycol) diacrylate-dithiothreitol (PEGDA-DTT) hydrogel containing erythropoietin (EPO) to promote vascularization. Following implantation into the latissimus dorsi muscle of Yucatan minipigs, a vascularized tubular tissue flap with a controlled luminal wall was successfully generated after 45 days. These findings demonstrate the feasibility of employing 3D-printed stent-patterned scaffolds to create pre-vascularized tubular grafts for future long segment tracheal reconstruction.

10.4.1.3 SLA-Based Fabrication

Stereolithography (SLA), also known as vat polymerization, is a 3D printing process that fabricates objects by selectively curing a photoreactive liquid resin. The process begins by filling a vat with this photopolymer liquid. A UV light source then shines a designed pattern onto the surface, which causes the liquid to polymerize and solidify. After each new layer is cured, a platform lowers the part further into the vat. This layer-by-layer process continues until the entire object is built. After printing, any

Fig. 10.4 (continued) 2015). (Permission: (A) Reproduced with permission from T. Khalid, et al. Development of tissue-engineered tracheal scaffold with refined mechanical properties and vascularization for tracheal regeneration, Frontiers in Bioengineering and Biotechnology 11 (2023) 1187500. https://doi.org/10.3389/fbioe.2023.1187500, Copyright © 2023 Khalid, Soriano, Lemoine, Cryan, O'Brien and O'Leary under the terms of the Creative Commons Attribution License (CC BY). (B) Reproduced with permission from W. Wu, et al. Fast degrading elastomer stented fascia remodels into tough and vascularized construct for tracheal regeneration, Materials Science and Engineering: C 101 (2019) 1–14, https://doi.org/10.1016/j.msec.2019.02.108, © 2019 Elsevier B.V. All rights reserved, (C) Reproduced with permission from J.H. Park, et al. Feasibility assessment of 3D printing-based tubular tissue flap in a porcine model for long segmental tracheal reconstruction, Tissue Engineering and Regenerative Medicine 22 (4) (2025) 469–479. https://doi.org/10.1007/s13770-025-00718-9, Copyright © 2025, The Author(s), (D) Reproduced with permission from J.H. Park, et al. A novel tissue-engineered trachea with a mechanical behavior similar to native trachea, Biomaterials 62 (2015) 106–115, https://doi.org/10.1016/j.biomaterials.2015.05.008, Copyright © 2015 Elsevier Ltd. All rights reserved) excess resin is drained away, leaving a complete 3D structure. Generally, this method utilizes either free-radical or cationic polymerization reactions to achieve solidification.

Park et al. introduced a tissue-engineered trachea combining structural and biological strategies to achieve native-like mechanical performance and cartilage regeneration (Fig. 10.4D) (Park et al. 2015). A hollow bellows-type scaffold was fabricated as the tracheal framework using a reliable 3D printing approach. To create a hollow bellows-type scaffold for the tracheal framework, the researchers used an indirect 3D printing method rather than direct printing. They first fabricated a mold with rectangular convolutions using an micro-SLA printer. Then, they injected a mixture of poly(L-lactide-co-ε-caprolactone) (PLCL, molar ratio 60:40) and gelatin into this mold to form the final structure. To promote chondrogenesis, gelatin sponges were chemically functionalized through heparinization and immobilization of TGF-β1, enabling sustained growth factor release and controlled degradation. The engineered trachea was constructed by inserting chondrocyte-seeded, functionalized gelatin sponges into the grooves of the bellows scaffold. Mechanical testing confirmed properties comparable to native trachea, and in vivo implantation demonstrated significant cartilage regeneration within the construct. This dual strategy, including 3D-printed mechanical framework combined with bioactive gelatin sponges, provides a promising substitute for tracheal stenosis repair.

Overall, basic 3D printing technologies such as FDM, SLS, and SLA have substantially advanced the fabrication of tracheal scaffolds by enabling patient-specific designs with controlled geometry and mechanical performance. FDM provides cost-effective production of mechanically robust frameworks, SLS allows fabrication of complex porous constructs with high strength, and SLA offers fine resolution and smooth surfaces that support favorable tissue interactions. However, a fundamental limitation of these techniques is their inability to directly print cell-laden structures, as the high processing temperatures (FDM, SLS) or the use of photoinitiators and UV light (SLA) is not compatible with living cells. Consequently, cell seeding must be performed as a secondary step, which often results in uneven cell distribution and delayed tissue integration. Future progress is likely to depend on hybrid approaches that combine the structural advantages of polymer-based scaffolds fabricated by these techniques with bioactive hydrogels or bioprinted cell-laden matrices. Such integration may overcome current drawbacks and bring basic 3D printing technologies closer to generating clinically relevant tracheal grafts.

10.5 Trachea Tissue Engineering Using 3D Bioprinting

3D bioprinting has emerged as a transformative technology by combining living cells with biomaterials in a highly controlled, layer-by-layer fabrication process. Unlike scaffold-based approach using basic 3D printing, 3D bioprinting enables the creation of constructs that not only reproduce the geometry of native tissues but also incorporate biological functionality from the outset. The process generally involves three coordinated steps: digital design based on medical imaging, automated deposition of cell-laden bioinks, and subsequent maturation in dynamic culture systems. Together, these steps make it possible to engineer tissues that possess both structural precision and biological relevance (Prasad et al. 2025).

For tracheal reconstruction, 3D bioprinting is particularly advantageous because the trachea requires tubular structures with mechanical robustness as well as the capacity for cellular integration and vascularization. 3D bioprinting strategies for this application can be broadly divided into two categories: scaffold-free constructs, which rely solely on cellular self-assembly, and scaffold-based constructs, in which cells are encapsulated within biomaterial-derived bioinks to provide both form and function. A range of 3D bioprinting modalities has been explored, including inkjet printing, extrusion systems, laser-assisted techniques, and photopolymerization. Among these, extrusion-based 3D bioprinting and DLP have become the predominant methods for tracheal graft fabrication. Extrusion printing offers flexibility in material selection and the ability to generate large, cell-laden tubular structures, whereas DLP provides high-resolution patterning and rapid printing speeds, albeit with more constraints on bioink formulations (Kačarević et al. 2018; Kim et al. 2024).

In 3D bioprinting, bioink plays a particularly critical role. While this chapter does not provide an exhaustive discussion of the various hydrogel precursors, cell types, and their specific properties or applications, these aspects have been extensively reviewed elsewhere (Zhang et al. 2024; Prasad et al. 2025; Choi et al. 2018; Taneja et al. 2022). In the following sections, we first outline the conceptual distinction between scaffold-free and scaffold-based tracheal constructs and then focus on extrusion and DLP 3D bioprinting as the principal approaches currently driving progress in the field of trachea tissue engineering.

10.5.1 Scaffold-Free Approaches (Kenzan Method)

To the best of our knowledge, the Kenzan method is almost uniquely applied to printing cell-only structures for tissue and organ reconstruction. The Kenzan method, developed by Prof. Koichi Nakayama of Saga University, is a scaffold-free 3D bioprinting technique that involves precisely placing cellular spheroids onto an array of fine needles (Fig. 10.5; Moldovan et al. 2017; Murata et al. 2020). The spheroids are positioned in a predefined 3D pattern, where they gradually fuse through natural cell–cell interactions and extracellular matrix deposition. Once sufficient tissue integrity is achieved, the construct is carefully removed from the needle array, yielding a scaffold-free tissue with controlled geometry. This method is particularly suited for generating tubular or hollow tissues, such as blood vessels and trachea, because it avoids the use of exogenous biomaterials while relying on the self-assembly capacity of cells.

Taniguchi et al. first demonstrated the feasibility of constructing a scaffold-free artificial trachea using a Bio-3D printing system in an inbred rat model (Taniguchi

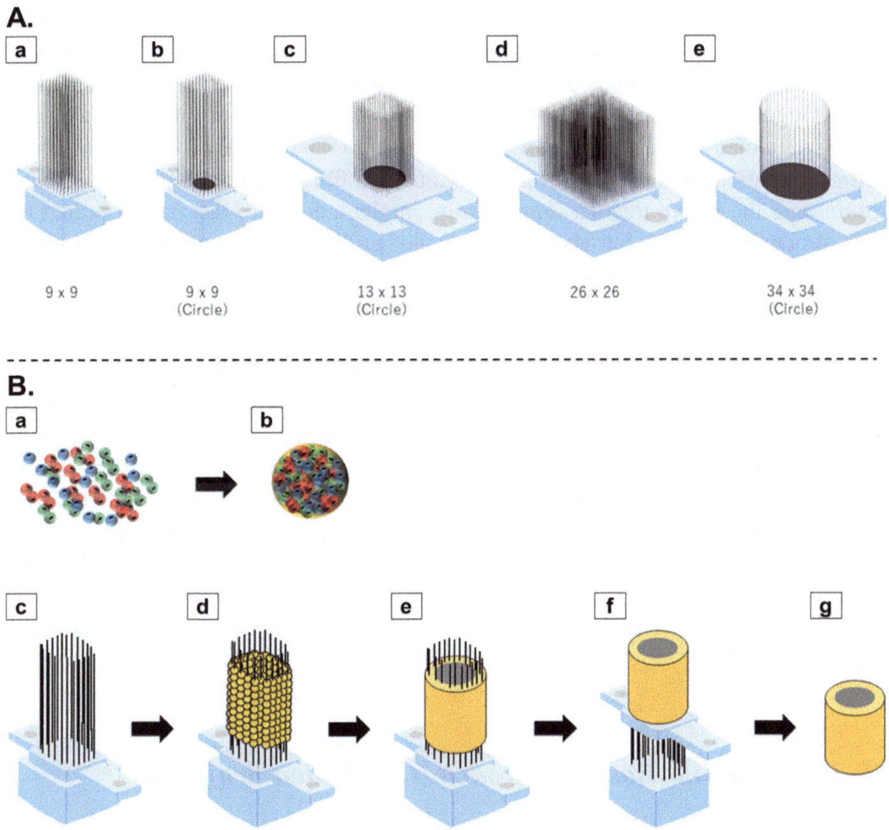

Fig. 10.5 Kenzan needle arrays and scaffold-free spheroid constructs. (**A**) Types of Kenzan needle arrays depending on applications (Murata et al. 2020) (a) urinary bladder and liver (rat), (b) peripheral nerve, trachea, and esophagus (rat), osteochondral tissue and blood vessels (minipig), (c) osteochondral tissue (minipig), (d) heart and liver (rat), (e) blood vessels (minipig), peripheral nerve (dog), and diaphragm (rat). (**B**) Spheroid-based bioink and scaffold-free construct fabrication using the Kenzan method (a, b) cell-only spheroids generated and cultured to produce extracellular matrix; (c–g) application of spheroids for scaffold-free bio-3D printing, including (c) preparation of the Kenzan platform, (d) automated skewering of spheroids onto microneedles, (e) fusion of spheroids during cultivation, (f) retrieval of the fused construct, and (g) maturation of the construct under tubular culture conditions. (Permission: Reproduced with permission from D. Murata, et al. Scaffold-free bio-3D printing using spheroids as "Bio-Inks" for tissue (Re-) construction and drug response tests. Advanced Healthcare Materials 9 (2020) 1901831, https://doi.org/10.1002/adhm.201901831, © 2020 The Authors. Published by WILEY-VCH Verlag GmbH & Co. KGaA, Weinheim under the terms of the Creative Commons CC BY license)

et al. 2018). Using spheroids composed of rat chondrocytes, MSCs, and lung microvessel endothelial cells, they successfully generated tubular grafts that possessed sufficient mechanical strength for transplantation and supported chondrogenesis and vasculogenesis in vivo. Building on this foundation, Machino et al. advanced the approach by applying the Kenzan method with human-derived cells, including chondrocytes, MSCs, fibroblasts, and HUVECs (Machino et al. 2019). Unlike the earlier study, where spheroids were generated from mixed rat cells, Machino et al. produced spheroids from different human cell types separately and arranged them precisely on needle arrays based on 3D configuration data. This strategy enabled the fabrication of more complex constructs that underwent bioreactor maturation to develop neo-cartilaginous and fibrous tubular structures closely resembling the native trachea. Importantly, implantation into rats demonstrated not only structural viability but also epithelial and capillary regeneration, representing a step closer to clinically relevant scaffold-free tracheal grafts.

Although scaffold-free tracheal constructs generated by the Kenzan method demonstrate the potential for functional airway regeneration, they are mechanically fragile at early stages and therefore require temporary silicone stents to prevent collapse and maintain airway patency. This reliance on synthetic supports partially undermines the "scaffold-free" concept and introduces risks such as airway irritation, inflammation, and stenosis. Nevertheless, the Kenzan method offers unique advantages, including the precise assembly of cell spheroids into predefined 3D geometries, promotion of natural cell–cell interactions, and the potential to achieve vascularized, patient-specific constructs without foreign scaffold materials. Furthermore, while stent-assisted implantation may be feasible in small animal models, scaling this approach to larger animals or clinical applications remains a major challenge.

10.5.2 Scaffold-Based Approach (Cell-Laden Scaffolds)

3D bioprinting technologies can be broadly categorized into four main types: inkjet, extrusion-based, laser-assisted, and photopolymerization 3D bioprinting. Inkjet 3D bioprinting ejects droplets of cell-laden bioink in a layer-by-layer manner, offering high resolution but often imposing mechanical stress on cells. Extrusion-based 3D bioprinting continuously extrudes viscous bioinks through a nozzle, making it suitable for large and robust constructs, though with lower resolution. Laser-assisted 3D bioprinting uses focused laser pulses to deposit microdroplets of bioink with excellent precision and high cell viability but requires costly equipment. Photopolymerization-based methods, such as digital light processing (DLP), employ light to crosslink photosensitive bioinks, enabling rapid fabrication of complex geometries but raising concerns of cytotoxicity. While inkjet and laser-assisted approaches are advantageous for creating thin layers or microstructures, tracheal tissue engineering typically demands mechanically resilient and large-scale constructs. Thus, extrusion-based 3D bioprinting and DLP have become the predominant techniques for tracheal graft fabrication, and the following section highlights representative studies using these two approaches.

10.5.2.1 Extrusion 3D Bioprinting

Extrusion-based 3D bioprinting is one of the most widely adopted techniques for fabricating complex tissue scaffolds. The method operates by using either pneumatic pressure or a piston to continuously push a bioink filament through a nozzle, building a 3D structure layer by layer. This approach offers the significant advantage of being able to handle a wide range of bioink viscosities, making it highly suitable for creating structurally rigid tissues like cartilage, which require robust mechanical properties. Moreover, the relatively gentle and room-temperature nature of the process minimizes stress on the cells, resulting in high cell viability. Despite its advantages, extrusion 3D bioprinting has notable limitations. Its primary drawback is low resolution, as the minimum feature size is constrained by the nozzle's diameter, making it challenging to create intricate microstructures such as vascular networks. Additionally, the mechanical stress on encapsulated cells during extrusion can significantly reduce viability, with some studies reporting a 40–80% decrease. To mitigate this, researchers use bioinks with specialized rheological properties. Shear-thinning bioinks, for example, become less viscous under the stress of extrusion, allowing them to flow more easily. Similarly, thixotropic bioinks temporarily lose viscosity while being printed but quickly regain their solid-like state afterward, ensuring the structural integrity of the printed construct. Extrusion-based 3D bioprinting has been expanded and applied in various forms, including multi nozzle extrusion, rod-supporting (4-axis) extrusion method, support bath-assisted extrusion 3D bioprinting, co-axial extrusion, and so on (Ramesh et al. 2021). Several adaptations of extrusion 3D bioprinting have been applied to create trachea-like structures.

Park et al. introduced a two-step extrusion-based 3D bioprinting strategy to fabricate a trachea-mimetic construct of clinically relevant dimensions with high cell viability (Fig. 10.6A; Park et al. 2021). First, a porous bellows-shaped scaffold was produced by conventional extrusion printing to provide the mechanical framework. Next, a rotational printing process was employed to selectively deposit cellular components, including cartilage rings on the exterior grooves and epithelial layers along the luminal surface. To enhance in vivo stability, the printed constructs were reinforced with a sinusoidal-patterned tubular mesh before implantation. Subcutaneous transplantation into nude mice demonstrated successful cartilage regeneration within the construct, confirming its potential for tracheal tissue engineering. Epithelial regeneration was not validated in this study. Hue et al. developed a 3D bioprinting strategy to create a cartilage–vascularized fibrous tissue-integrated trachea (CVFIT) by using two distinct photo-crosslinkable bioinks (Fig. 10.6B; Huo et al. 2022). The first, a cartilage-specific bioink (p-CB), was composed of gelatin methacryloyl, chondroitin sulfate, and cartilage acellular matrix and was loaded with chondrocytes. The second, a fibrous tissue-specific bioink (p-VFB), was made of hyaluronic acid methacrylate, 8-arm PEG-NHS, and dermal acellular matrix and contained fibroblasts. This innovative approach enabled the precise extrusion printing of alternating layers of cartilage and vascularized fibrous tissue rings, successfully fabricating the CVFIT. Hybrid photopolymerization ensured rapid crosslinking

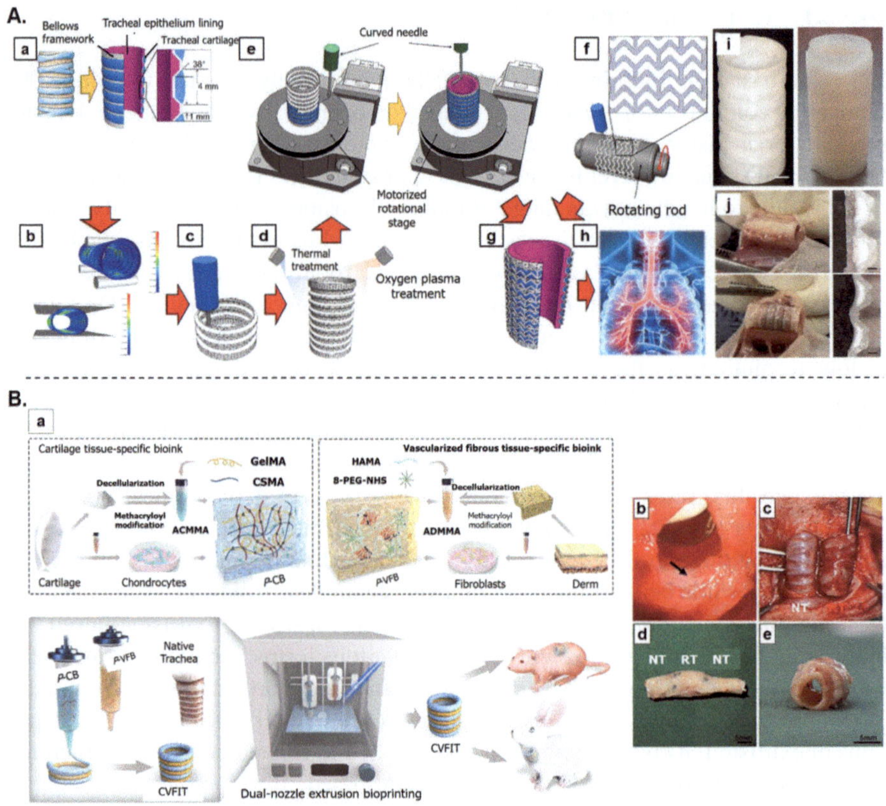

Fig. 10.6 Extrusion-based 3D bioprinting strategies for trachea tissue engineering. (**A**) Trachea-mimetic cellular construct of a clinically relevant size (a–h) Schematics of the two-step extrusion-based 3D bioprinting. Step 1 (a–d): (a) design based on canine trachea, (b) FEA for pore distribution, (c) fabrication of porous bellows framework, and (d) plasma treatment. Step 2 (e–h): (e) Rotational printing of cartilage rings and epithelial lining, (f) creation and (g) wrapping with SPTM, and (h) implantation into circumferential tracheal defect. (i) Photographs of construct (left) after rotational printing and (right) after wrapping with SPTM, j) retrieval of constructs with(Top)/without(bottom) SPTM after 8 weeks, showing preserved cartilage rings (Park et al. 2021). (**B**) Native-like trachea 3D bioprinting based on designable tissue-specific bioinks. (a) Schematic showing the design of cartilage- and vascularized fibrous tissue-specific bioinks and their use in 3D-bioprinting for creating CVFIT constructs. These were used for in vivo trachea reconstruction in nude mice and rabbits. (b–e) Segmental trachea reconstruction outcomes. (b) shows the well-vascularized inner wall of the regenerated trachea. (c) compares the regenerated trachea with a native trachea. (d–e) provide a gross view of the reconstructed tracheal segment 8 weeks after end-to-end anastomosis (Huo et al. 2022). (Permission: (A) Reproduced with permission from J.H. Park, et al. 3D bioprinting of a trachea-mimetic cellular construct of a clinically relevant size, Biomaterials 279 (2021) 121246, https://doi.org/10.1016/j.biomaterials.2021.121246, (B) Reproduced with permission from Y. Huo, et al. Functional trachea reconstruction using 3D-bioprinted native-like tissue architecture based on designable tissue-specific bioinks, Advanced Science 9 (2022) 2202181, https://doi.org/10.1002/advs.202202181,

and mechanical reinforcement, while amidation at the ring interfaces promoted firm integration between stiff and soft tissues. Subcutaneous implantation confirmed tissue-specific regeneration, and in situ reconstruction in tracheal defect models demonstrated both mechanical stability and physiological functionality. This approach highlights the feasibility of biomimetic, extrusion-based trachea reconstruction using multicomponent bioinks and cell-laden architectures. Building on their work with O-shaped tracheal constructs (O-CVFIT), Sun et al. developed a more advanced C-shaped 3D-bioprinted biomimetic trachea (C-CVFIT) that better mimics the natural human trachea and is designed for direct end-to-end anastomosis (Sun et al. 2024). They also used extrusion-based printing to create alternating rings of cartilage and vascularized fibrous tissue. The cartilage rings were made from a photo-crosslinkable hydrogel blend of gelatin methacryloyl and chondroitin sulfate methacryloyl (GelMA/CSMA), while the fibrous rings used gelatin methacryloyl and elastin methacryloyl (GelMA/ElaMA). This approach provides specific micro-environments suited for chondrocytes and fibroblasts. Compared with the previous O-shape design that required prematuration, the optimized C-shape structure enabled simplified printing paths, faster construct fabrication, and direct surgical implantation without intramuscular preimplantation. Subcutaneous implantation in mice confirmed tissue-specific regeneration, while segmental trachea reconstruction in rabbits demonstrated mechanical stability and physiological functionality. This study thus represents a step forward from the group's earlier CVFIT model, offering a one-step, clinically relevant surgical approach for segmental trachea repair using extrusion 3D bioprinting.

Collectively, extrusion-based 3D bioprinting provides a versatile platform for generating tracheal grafts, as it accommodates multiple biomaterials, supports high cell loading, and allows the fabrication of anatomically relevant hollow structures. Although challenges remain in replicating bifurcated airway geometries and ensuring long-term tissue integration, the adaptability of extrusion systems continues to make them highly promising for future clinical translation in tracheal tissue engineering.

10.5.2.2 DLP 3D Bioprinting

DLP-based stereolithography has recently emerged as a promising 3D bioprinting technology. This technique can be implemented in either top-down or bottom-up configurations. Compared with other approaches, DLP offers several distinct advantages. Since the projection system enables layer-by-layer polymerization of the bioink, the fabrication speed is markedly accelerated (~30 min, mm (Haykal et al. 2014)$\cdot s^{-1}$), whereas extrusion, inkjet, or laser micro-stereolithography typically proceed in a line-by-line manner. Importantly, the printing time for each layer remains constant, regardless of the structural complexity or lateral dimensions, and is determined only by the layer thickness. This rapid, nozzle-free process supports high cell survival rates (85–95%). Moreover, the use of a digital micromirror device (DMD), in which thousands of mirrors switch independently between on and off states to act as a dynamic photomask, enables resolutions as fine as 200 μm. However, one of the major limitations of this technique is the potential cytotoxicity arising from exposure to light (commonly UV) and the use of photoinitiators (Li et al. 2023). DLP 3D bioprinting has recently been explored for tracheal tissue engineering due to its ability to generate high-resolution constructs with precise geometry and homogeneous cell distribution.

DLP printing is not widely used because of the limited light-sensitive biomaterials to be applied. Kim et al. developed methacrylated silk fibroin (Sil-MA) to develop a DLP-printable bioink with high resolution, biocompatibility, and mechanical strength suitable for tissue engineering (Fig. 10.7A) (Kim et al. 2018). Sil-MA was synthesized by reacting degummed silk fibroin with glycidyl methacrylate (GMA), followed by purification and confirmation of methacrylation via NMR and FT-IR. Using Sil-MA (10–30%) with LAP photoinitiator, complex 3D constructs such as trachea, vessels, and organs were precisely fabricated, demonstrating excellent printability. Encapsulation of NIH/3 T3 fibroblasts and human chondrocytes within Sil-MA hydrogels confirmed high cytocompatibility and promoted cartilage tissue formation. Notably, the strong mechanical properties of Sil-MA allowed tracheal constructs to endure suturing and even enabled end-to-end anastomosis in a dog trachea model. Building on this earlier work, in the same group, Hong et al. applied Sil-MA bioink in a DLP 3D bioprinting system to fabricate trachea-like constructs (Fig. 10.7B) (Hong et al. 2020). The photocrosslinking process allowed rapid printing of cell-laden hydrogels with precise geometry and uniform cell distribution. In vitro studies using rabbit chondrocyte-laden Sil-MA hydrogels demonstrated high cell viability and cartilage formation over several weeks. For in vivo validation, a tracheal defect model in rabbits was employed. The printed Sil-MA constructs were sutured to the native trachea, where they remained structurally stable for 6 weeks posttransplantation. Moreover, the implanted hydrogels supported the regeneration of cartilage-like tissue and epithelial lining. These findings highlight the potential of Sil-MA-based DLP 3D bioprinting to generate mechanically stable and biologically functional tracheal grafts using only natural polymer-derived hydrogels, without the need for synthetic reinforcement.

Free radical polymerization has advanced hydrogel development, but printed hydrogels often suffer from high density for structural stability. This density can harm encapsulated cells by limiting their access to oxygen and nutrients. Tao et al. introduced a hybrid emulsion bioink designed for DLP-based 3D bioprinting, which enables in situ formation of macropores within tissue constructs (Tao et al. 2022). The system integrates a gelatin methacryloyl (GelMA)-based continuous phase with dextran droplets stabilized by β-lactoglobulin (β-LG) nanoparticles, ensuring structural stability during printing. Upon photopolymerization, dextran droplets could be selectively removed either in vitro or in vivo, leaving interconnected porous networks. This pore-forming strategy improved cell proliferation and spreading within the constructs, while maintaining high printability and geometric precision. When applied to tracheal 3D bioprinting, the porous constructs supported chondrocyte survival and maturation, ultimately promoting cartilage regeneration in a subcutaneous implantation model.

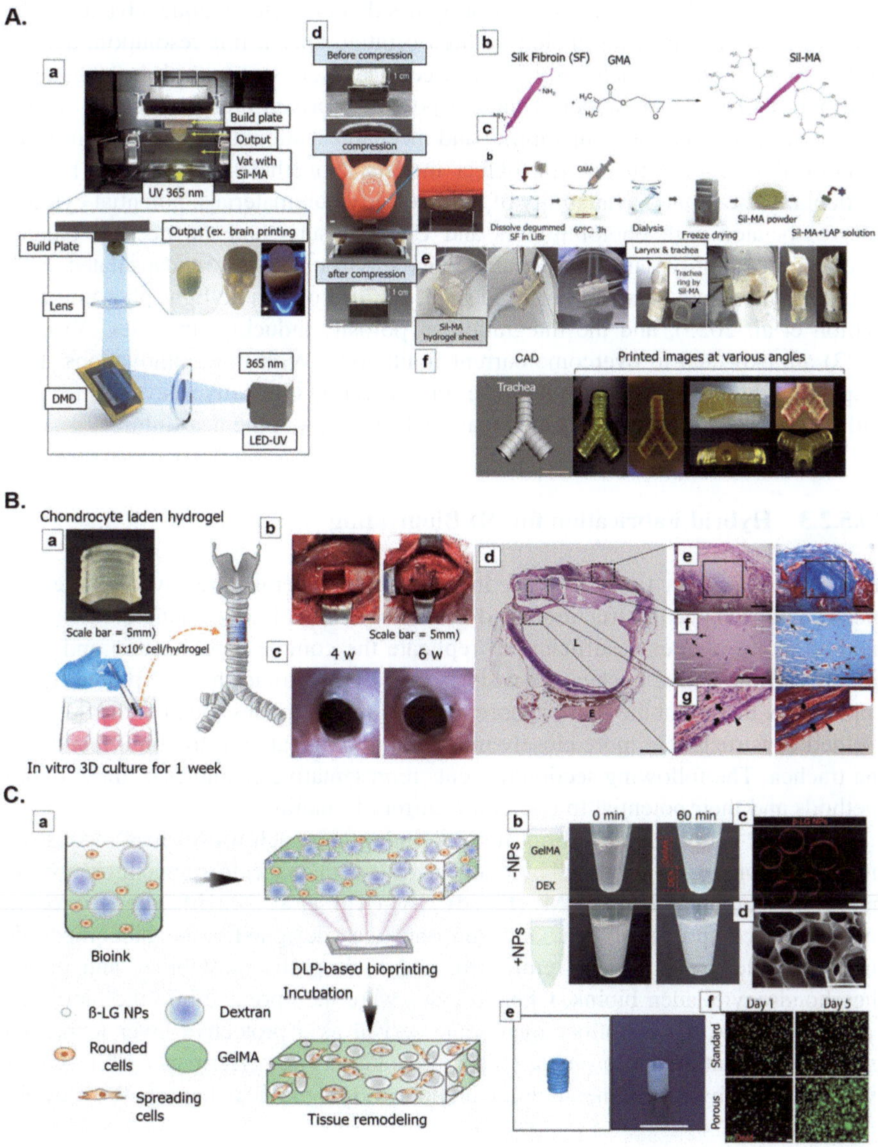

Fig. 10.7 DLP-based 3D bioprinting strategies for trachea tissue engineering. (**A**) DLP printing with photo-crosslinkable silk fibroin (Sil-MA): (a) Schematic of DLP 3D bioprinting using Sil-MA (DMD system). (b) Expected chemical structure of Sil-MA modified with GMA. (c) Bioink preparation process. (d) Sil-MA hydrogel showing high resilience under 7 kg compression. (e) Suturing of 3D-printed Sil-MA membrane and end-to-end anastomosis in dog trachea. (f) Trachea structure printed using Sil-MA bioink (Kim et al. 2018). (**B**) DLP-based trachea 3D bioprinting with chondrocytes: (a) Schematic of chondrocyte-laden Sil-MA hydrogel transplantation, cultured for 1 week. (b) Implantation into rabbit tracheal defect. (c) Endoscopic view showing progressive lumen recovery at 4 and 6 weeks. (d) Histology after 6 weeks confirming cartilage tissue formation. (e–g) H&E and MT staining showing epithelial extension, chondrocytes in

Collectively, DLP-based 3D bioprinting has demonstrated unique advantages for tracheal tissue engineering, including high printing speed, fine resolution, and the ability to generate geometrically precise, cell-laden constructs with homogeneous distribution. The development of natural polymer-derived bioinks such as Sil-MA has further enhanced biocompatibility and mechanical strength, enabling successful preclinical validation in tracheal defect models. Nonetheless, challenges remain, particularly the limited availability of light-sensitive biomaterials, potential cytotoxicity associated with photoinitiators and UV exposure, and the need to balance mechanical stability with a favorable microenvironment for encapsulated cells. Looking ahead, advances in bioink design, the use of visible-light photoinitiators (Tilton et al. 2023), and the integration of porosity-inducing strategies (Yi et al. 2022) are expected to overcome current limitations. With these innovations, DLP bioprinting holds considerable promise for generating clinically relevant, mechanically robust, and biologically functional tracheal grafts in the near future.

10.5.2.3 Hybrid Fabrication for 3D Bioprinting

The field of trachea tissue engineering still faces several unresolved challenges, including mechanical, structural, and biological limitations. A single fabrication method alone is often insufficient to replicate the complex architecture and functionality of the native trachea. To address this, recent studies have explored hybrid approaches that combine two or more fabrication techniques. Such strategies have yielded constructs that more closely mimic the biological and structural features of the trachea. The following section presents representative examples of these hybrid methods and their potential to overcome current limitations.

Kim et al. introduced a hybrid 3D bioprinting approach for tracheal reconstruction by combining a 3D-printed biotracheal graft with an electrospun chitosan-based nanofiber membrane (TraCHIM) (Fig. 10.8A) (Kim et al. 2021b). The electrospun membrane, composed of PCL and chitosan, was designed to be biocompatible, biodegradable, mechanically reinforced, and hydrophilic to stabilize and protect the chondrocyte-laden bioink. Chondrocytes were incorporated into the bioprinted construct, while the nanofiber membrane served as a protective layer to prevent bioink delamination and promote tissue integration. The performance of TraCHIM was evaluated by subcutaneous implantation in Sprague–Dawley rats for 2 weeks.

Fig. 10.7 (continued) lacunae, and new vessel formation (asterisk) (Hong et al. 2020). (Permission: Reproduced with permission from S.H. Kim, et al. Precisely printable and biocompatible silk fibroin bioink for digital light processing 3D printing, Nature communications 9 (1) (2018) 1620, https://doi.org/10.1038/s41467-018-03759-y, Copyright © 2018, The Author(s), (B) Reproduced with permission from H. Hong, et al. Digital light processing 3D printed silk fibroin hydrogel for cartilage tissue engineering, Biomaterials 232 (2020) 119679, https://doi.org/10.1016/j.biomaterials.2019.119679, © 2019 Elsevier Ltd. All rights reserved)

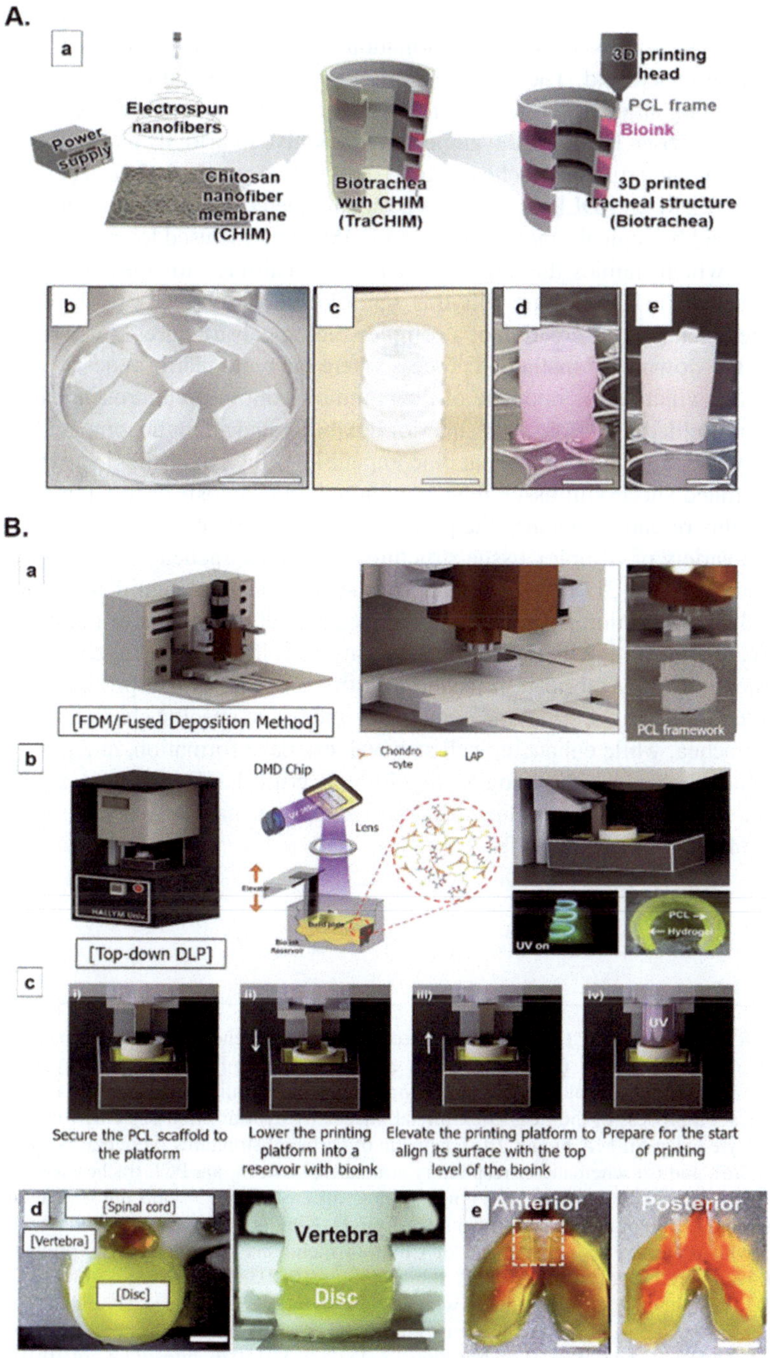

Fig. 10.8 Trachea reconstruction by 3D bioprinting reinforced with hybrid fabrication methods. (**A**) Electrospinning and FDM hybrid method: (a) Schematic of the fabrication of a 3D-printed PCL tracheal structure surrounded by an electrospun chitosan-based nanofiber membrane (CHIM).

Compared with controls, TraCHIM demonstrated enhanced survival of chondrocytes, improved cartilage formation, and more favorable degradation of the polymeric scaffold. These findings highlight the potential of protective hybrid 3D bioprinting strategies to accelerate functional cartilage regeneration for tracheal tissue engineering. Lee et al. developed an innovative hybrid 3D bioprinting method for creating an artificial trachea (Fig. 10.8B) (Lee et al. 2024). The technique integrates FDM and DLP to fabricate a bioengineered trachea with both structural integrity and biological function. First, an FDM printer is used to create a rigid PCL scaffold, which mimics the structure of tracheal cartilage for mechanical support. Subsequently, a DLP printer fills this scaffold with a chondrocyte-laden Sil-MA hydrogel, enabling the creation of a complex biological structure. This was achieved using a top-down DLP method, a process where the build platform descends into the resin tank, which is the opposite of the common bottom-up approach. This hybrid approach yielded a scaffold with superior flexibility and strength compared to a pure PCL scaffold, along with excellent biocompatibility. In vivo testing in a rabbit model demonstrated successful tissue regeneration without stenosis or inflammation. Ultimately, this research validates the potential of hybrid 3D bioprinting technology to create a variety of complex tissue structures as well as trachea.

Overall, hybrid 3D bioprinting approaches demonstrate significant promise for tracheal reconstruction by integrating the mechanical robustness of traditional scaffold materials with the biological functionality of cell-laden hydrogels. By combining complementary fabrication techniques, these strategies can produce constructs that better replicate the structural complexity and tissue-specific characteristics of the native trachea, while enhancing cell survival, cartilage formation, and graft integration. Such hybrid methodologies highlight a critical advancement in the field, offering a pathway toward clinically translatable, mechanically stable, and biologically functional tracheal grafts.

Fig. 10.8 (continued) (b) CHIM, (c) 3D-printed PCL frame, (d) chondrocyte-laden biotrachea, and (e) biotrachea with CHIM (TraCHIM) (Kim et al. 2021b). (**B**) FDM and DLP hybrid method: (a) 3D-printed PCL scaffold by FDM, (b) top-down DLP printing on the inner PCL scaffold, (c) fabrication process of the PCL–Sil artificial trachea by hybridization of FDM with DLP using chondrocyte-laden Sil-MA bioink, (d) schematic of vertebral structures (vertebral body, disc, and spinal cord), and (e) schematic of respiratory structures, showing the PCL trachea scaffold (white dotted line), bronchus (red ink), and lungs (yellow ink). Scale bar = 500 μm (Lee et al. 2024). (Permission: (A) Reproduced with permission from H. Kim, et al. Improved chondrogenic performance with protective tracheal design of Chitosan membrane surrounding 3D-printed trachea, Scientific reports 11 (1) (2021) 9258, https://doi.org/10.1038/s41598-021-88830-3, Copyright © 2021, The Author(s), (B) Reproduced with permission from J.S. Lee, et al. Hybrid 3D bioprinting for advanced tissue-engineered trachea: merging fused deposition modeling (FDM) and top–down digital light processing (DLP), Biofabrication 17 (1) (2024) 015026, https://doi.org/10.1088/1758-5090/ad92da, © 2024 The Author(s). Published by IOP Publishing Ltd under the terms of the Creative Commons Attribution 4.0 license)

10.6 Trachea Tissue Engineering Using 4D Printing

4D bioprinting, which introduces the temporal dimension into conventional 3D bioprinting, is emerging as a next-generation biofabrication technology. Unlike static 3D constructs, 4D-printed structures can undergo programmed transformations over time in response to external stimuli such as osmotic pressure, magnetic fields, heat, electrical currents, or light. This dynamic adaptability not only addresses many of the inherent limitations of 3D bioprinting but also enables the fabrication of complex, multilayered tissue architectures that more closely resemble native organs. The predominant transformation mechanism is shape change, allowing the creation of self-bending or morphing constructs that can improve functional performance and potentially facilitate minimally invasive surgical applications.

In specialized applications, such as tracheal scaffolds, there is a preference for nondegradable materials to mitigate risks associated with scaffold failure or migration. The development of personalized bioinspired 4D-printed scaffolds utilizing shape memory polymers (SMPs) represents a significant advancement in this area. These scaffolds can respond dynamically to external stimuli, providing a conformable fit and enhanced mechanical stability.

Zhao et al. investigated the application of shape memory polymers (SMPs) in the personalized 4D printing of bio-designed tracheal scaffolds (Fig. 10.9A) (Zhao et al. 2019). Utilizing a composite of shape memory PLA and Fe_3O_4, the researchers fabricated two bioinspired scaffolds through 4D printing, which can be temporarily deformed and then returned to their original shape when exposed to an alternating magnetic field. The design of the scaffolds, inspired by the microstructure of glass sponges, enhances their strength and stability, making them adaptable to varying environmental conditions within soft tissues. Mechanical testing demonstrated that the customized scaffolds possess high toughness, allowing them to deform alongside the trachea without sacrificing rigidity. The scaffolds successfully regained their initial shape within 35 s under an alternating magnetic field, confirming their functionality in vitro. This innovative approach highlights the potential of 4D bioprinting to create tailored, dynamic scaffolds for tracheal repair, offering a promising alternative to traditional scaffolding methods. Pandey et al. focused on the 4D bioprinting of biodegradable polymer blends, specifically PLA and PCL, utilizing the direct ink writing (DIW) technique (Pandey et al. 2022). The study investigates the shape-memory properties of different PLA/PCL compositions, where PLA acts as a fixed phase to retain the original shape, while PCL serves as a reversible phase to enable temporary shape transitions. Differential scanning calorimetry revealed that the glass transition temperature of the blends decreased with increased PCL content, optimizing the shape-fixity and recovery ratios, with the PLA70/PCL30 blend achieving 91% and 90%, respectively. The thermally activated tracheal scaffold made from this blend demonstrated excellent adaptability, fitting seamlessly within the lumen of a native trachea and maintaining a clear passage. This work highlights the potential of 4D bioprinting in creating personalized medical

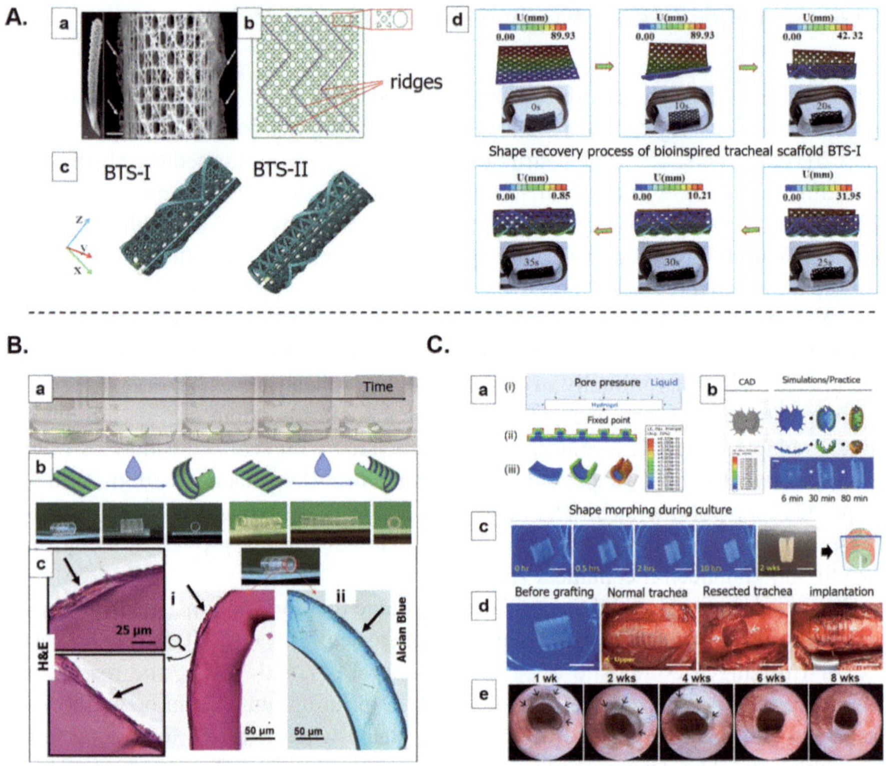

Fig. 10.9 4D printing-based trachea reconstruction using different stimuli. (**A**) (magnetic field stimuli) Shape memory PLA/Fe_3O_4 composite filament and bioinspired tracheal scaffold: (a) glass sponge skeleton and cage fragment, (b) plane graph of deployable tracheal scaffold (BTS-I), (c) initial configuration in ABAQUS, (d) magnetic field-induced actuation in vitro (Zhao et al. 2019). (**B**) (osmotic stimuli) Self-folding GPTMS scaffolds: (a) time-dependent self-folding, (b) folding direction controlled by printed line orientation, (c) histological assays after 21 d showing CPCs layer (H&E) and GAG deposition (Alcian Blue) (Chiesa et al. 2025). (**C**) (osmotic stimuli) 4D-bioprinted Sil-MA hydrogels: (a) FEA moisture swelling model (i–ii), (b) shape morphing via 4D printing and validation against FEA, (c) shape morphing during in vitro culture, (d) transplantation of 4D-bioprinted trachea, (e) bronchoscopic evaluation up to 8 weeks showing recovery of lumen and mucosa by week 6 (Kim et al. 2020a). (Permission: (A) Reproduced with permission from W. Zhao, et al. Personalized 4D printing of bioinspired tracheal scaffold concept based on magnetic stimulated shape memory composites, Composites Science and Technology 184 (2019) 107866, https://doi.org/10.1016/j.compscitech.2019.107866, © 2019 Elsevier Ltd. All rights reserved, (B) Reproduced with permission from I. Chiesa, et al. 4D bioprinted self-folding scaffolds enhance cartilage formation in the engineering of trachea, Advanced Materials Technologies 10 (6) (2025) 2401210, https://doi.org/10.1002/admt.202401210, © 2024 The Author(s). Advanced Materials Technologies published by Wiley-VCH GmbH under the Creative Commons CC-BY-NC license, (C) Reproduced with permission from S.H. Kim, et al. 4D-bioprinted silk hydrogels for tissue engineering, Biomaterials 260 (2020) 120281. https://doi.org/10.1016/j.biomaterials.2020.120281, © 2020 Elsevier Ltd. All rights reserved)

devices that can respond dynamically to physiological conditions, paving the way for innovative applications in tissue engineering.

Conventional 4D printing has largely relied on shape memory materials and external stimuli such as heat, magnetic fields, or electrical currents. However, these approaches often raise concerns regarding biocompatibility and introduce unnecessary complexity to the system. As a more cell-friendly alternative, osmotic-driven mechanisms offer a safer and simpler strategy for dynamic shape transformation. Hydrogels, with their intrinsic swelling capacity and tissue-like microenvironment, are particularly well-suited for this purpose, providing a biocompatible platform in which the culture medium itself can act as the stimulus. The following examples introduce representative examples of hydrogel-based osmotic 4D bioprinting.

This study by Chiesa et al. explored the innovative application of 4D bioprinting to engineer a self-folding gelatin-based bilayer scaffold for tracheal tissue engineering (Fig. 10.9B) (Chiesa et al. 2025). Utilizing the unique properties of the materials, the scaffold starts as a flat 2D structure and automatically transforms into a closed tubular shape upon hydration, mimicking the dynamic behavior of native tracheal tissue. An analytical model based on Timoshenko's beam thermostats was developed to predict the radius of curvature of the scaffold, ensuring precise control over its morphology. Various cell types, including airway fibroblasts, lung endothelial cells, and cartilage progenitor cells (CPCs), were seeded onto the scaffold in its flat configuration, where they retained their positions during the folding process and proliferated effectively. The study highlights that CPCs cultured on the 4D bioprinted scaffold exhibited improved differentiation into mature cartilage compared to those on traditional 2D flat scaffolds, indicating a responsive interaction with the scaffold's dynamic shape. This research underscores the potential of 4D bioprinting in creating complex tissue-engineered constructs that can adapt and function like natural tissues. Kim et al. explored a 4D bioprinting approach to fabricate a tissue-mimetic scaffold that dynamically responds to hydration stimuli (Fig. 10.9C) (Kim et al. 2020a). The researchers utilized silk fibroin hydrogel (Sil-MA) in a DLP printing method, allowing for the creation of bilayered constructs that could undergo controlled shape changes in physiological conditions. Thc study incorporated two cell types: human chondrocytes and human turbinate-derived MSCs, which were embedded within the hydrogel. An in vivo experiment was conducted using rabbits with tracheal damage, where the 4D bioprinted scaffolds were implanted. Over an 8-week period, the implants showed successful integration with the host trachea, resulting in the regeneration of epithelial and cartilage tissues at the targeted sites. This study underscores the potential of 4D bioprinting to create complex, biocompatible structures that can adapt to biological environments, paving the way for advancements in tissue engineering applications.

Overall, 4D printing holds considerable promise for advancing biomedical applications, particularly in the design of scaffolds that can adapt to anatomical variations and respond effectively to environmental changes, thereby improving their therapeutic potential. While still emerging, 4D bioprinting has demonstrated potential across various biomedical fields, including cartilage, trachea, muscle, kidney, and vascular networks. However, many existing studies have not sufficiently explored the interplay between design choices and the inherent limitations of 4D printing technologies in producing complex structures. Additionally, the majority of research has relied on short-term in vitro assessments, which often fail to provide insights into the long-term stability of shape transformations or their impact on cellular behavior and matrix deposition. Concerns regarding potential cell damage from certain fabrication methods must also be addressed.

10.7 Summary and Future Directions

This chapter reviewed diverse approaches to tracheal tissue engineering, ranging from conventional scaffold-based methods to advanced 4D bioprinting strategies. Conventional approaches have largely relied on synthetic polymers or dECM scaffolds, which are subsequently combined with cells or growth factors. Although these methods demonstrated initial feasibility, they remain limited in reproducing the anisotropic biomechanics of native cartilage, achieving long-term epithelialization and vascularization, and maintaining integration and durability after implantation.

To overcome these limitations, 3D printing technologies have been actively applied in tracheal reconstruction. Beyond acellular scaffold fabrication, 3D printing has enabled the creation of stent-like devices and customized molds to guide tissue formation. However, conventional molding and basic 3D printing approaches still face fundamental challenges, particularly in balancing rigidity and flexibility, establishing stable epithelial coverage and vascular networks, and ensuring mechanical reliability and immune compatibility in the long term.

3D bioprinting offers a significant advancement by enabling the simultaneous deposition of cells and biomaterials in anatomically relevant architectures. This approach has allowed the fabrication of C-shaped cartilage rings, smooth muscle, and mucosal layers either as separate components integrated after printing or as multi-material constructs printed in a single process. Extending this concept, 4D bioprinting introduces dynamic materials capable of altering shape or properties in response to environmental stimuli, offering new potential to address structural and functional limitations of static 3D-printed constructs.

One of the most critical challenges in tracheal regeneration remains vascularization. Strategies to address this include incorporation of angiogenic factors such as VEGF, preimplantation of scaffolds into vascularized tissues such as omentum or muscle, and in vitro pre-vascularization prior to implantation. Recent studies also highlight mechanically reinforced or biologically augmented scaffolds to enhance graft survival and integration.

Importantly, the trachea is not a simple tubular structure of cartilage alone but a complex composite organ consisting of cartilage rings, smooth muscle, mucosa, and dynamic biomechanical functions. Thus, reconstruction requires a holistic strategy that integrates biomaterials, cells, and advanced printing technologies and, in many cases, hybrid approaches. Despite remarkable progress, critical issues remain, including achieving the appropriate balance of mechanical strength and flexibility, minimizing immune rejection, and ensuring long-term vascular stability. Moreover, overly complex multi-material or multistep processes may pose challenges in clinical translation due to concerns in biocompatibility, standardization, and regulatory approval. Therefore, technological innovation must be accompanied by efforts to simplify and optimize manufacturing platforms with clinical applicability in mind.

A milestone achievement in this field was reported in 2024 by The Catholic University of Korea, where the world's first patient-specific 3D-bioprinted trachea—engineered with allogeneic adult stem cells—was successfully transplanted into a patient with otherwise untreatable tracheal defects. Six-month follow-up confirmed graft survival and integration, marking the first clinical translation of a bioengineered trachea (Yeou and Shin 2025). This success was possible only through close interdisciplinary collaboration across stem cell biology, biomaterials, engineering, regulatory science, GMP manufacturing, and clinical medicine.

In conclusion, tracheal reconstruction represents one of the most demanding goals in tissue engineering, requiring truly multidisciplinary innovation. Future research must focus on establishing functional vascularization and long-term graft integration while streamlining 3D bioprinting and regulatory processes into clinically realistic platforms. With these combined efforts, the field is poised to move from experimental proof-of-concept toward reproducible and safe clinical therapies.

Acknowledgments This research was supported by the Korean ARPA-H Project through the Korea Health Industry Development Institute (KHIDI), funded by the Ministry of Health and Welfare, Republic of Korea (RS- 2024-00512447); by the National Research Foundation of Korea (NRF), funded by the Ministry of Science and ICT, Republic of Korea (RS-2024-00360588); and by the Regional Innovation System and Education (RISE) program through the Gangwon RISE Center, funded by the Ministry of Education (MOE) and the Gangwon State (G.S.), Republic of Korea (2025-RISE-10-009).

Competing Interests The author(s) has no competing interests to declare that are relevant to the content of this manuscript.

References

Abdulghani S, Mitchell GR (2019) Biomaterials for in situ tissue regeneration: a review. Biomolecules 9(11):750

Azorin JF, Bertin F, Martinod E, Laskar M (2006) Tracheal replacement with an aortic autograft. Eur J Cardiothorac Surg 29(2):261–263

Baiguera S, Birchall MA, Macchiarini P (2010) Tissue-engineered tracheal transplantation. Transplantation 89(5):485–491

Bartolo P, Malshe A, Ferraris E, Koc B (2022) 3D bioprinting: materials, processes, and applications. CIRP Ann 71(2):577–597

Chan C, Liu L, Dharmadhikari S et al (2023) A multimodal approach to quantify chondrocyte viability for airway tissue engineering. Laryngoscope 133(3):512–520

Chiesa I, Esposito A, Vozzi G, Gottardi R, De Maria C (2025) 4D bioprinted self-folding scaffolds enhance cartilage formation in the engineering of trachea. Adv Mater Technol 10(6):2401210
Choi Y-J, Park JH, Jang J, Cho D-W (2018) 3D bioprinting technologies and bioinks for therapeutic and tissue engineering applications. J 3D Print Med 2(4):187–203
Crawford RH, Beaman JJ (1999) Solid freeform fabrication. IEEE Spectr 36(2):34–43
Dennis JE, Bernardi KG, Kean TJ, Liou NE, Meyer TK (2018) Tissue engineering of a composite trachea construct using autologous rabbit chondrocytes. J Tissue Eng Regen Med 12(3):e1383–e1391
Do AV, Khorsand B, Geary SM, Salem AK (2015) 3D printing of scaffolds for tissue regeneration applications. Adv Healthc Mater 4(12):1742–1762
Fishman JM, Lowdell M, Birchall MA (2014) Stem cell-based organ replacements—airway and lung tissue engineering. Semin Pediatr Surg:119–126
Gao B, Jing H, Gao M et al (2019) Long-segmental tracheal reconstruction in rabbits with pedicled tissue-engineered trachea based on a 3D-printed scaffold. Acta Biomater 97:177–186
Ghorbani F, Moradi L, Shadmehr MB, Bonakdar S, Droodinia A, Safshekan F (2017) In-vivo characterization of a 3D hybrid scaffold based on PCL/decellularized aorta for tracheal tissue engineering. Mater Sci Eng C 81:74–83
Hamaji M, Kojima F, Koyasu S et al (2014) Development of a composite and vascularized tracheal scaffold in the omentum for in situ tissue engineering: a canine model. Interact Cardiovasc Thorac Surg 19(3):357–362
Hamilton NJ, Hynds RE, Gowers KH et al (2019) Using a three-dimensional collagen matrix to deliver respiratory progenitor cells to decellularized trachea in vivo. Tissue Eng Part C Methods 25(2):93–102
Hayes DW, Brower RL, John KJ (2001) Articular cartilage: anatomy, injury, and repair. Clin Podiatr Med Surg 18(1):35–53
Haykal S, Salna M, Waddell TK, Hofer SO (2014) Advances in tracheal reconstruction. Plastic Reconstruct Surgery–Global Open 2(7):e178
Hong H, Seo YB, Lee JS et al (2020) Digital light processing 3D printed silk fibroin hydrogel for cartilage tissue engineering. Biomaterials 232:119679
Huo Y, Xu Y, Wu X et al (2022) Functional trachea reconstruction using 3D-bioprinted native-like tissue architecture based on designable tissue-specific bioinks. Adv Sci 9(29):2202181
Jang YS, Jang CH, Cho YB, Kim M, Kim GH (2014) Tracheal regeneration using polycaprolactone/collagen-nanofiber coated with umbilical cord serum after partial resection. Int J Pediatr Otorhinolaryngol 78(12):2237–2243
Kačarević ŽP, Rider PM, Alkildani S et al (2018) An introduction to 3D bioprinting: possibilities, challenges and future aspects. Materials 11(11):2199
Kafle A, Luis E, Silwal R, Pan HM, Shrestha PL, Bastola AK (2021) 3D/4D printing of polymers: fused deposition modelling (FDM), selective laser sintering (SLS), and stereolithography (SLA). Polymers 13(18):3101
Kanzaki M, Yamato M, Hatakeyama H et al (2006) Tissue engineered epithelial cell sheets for the creation of a bioartificial trachea. Tissue Eng 12(5):1275–1283
Khalid T, Soriano L, Lemoine M, Cryan S-A, O'Brien FJ, O'Leary C (2023) Development of tissue-engineered tracheal scaffold with refined mechanical properties and vascularisation for tracheal regeneration. Front Bioeng Biotechnol 11:1187500
Kim SH, Yeon YK, Lee JM et al (2018) Precisely printable and biocompatible silk fibroin bioink for digital light processing 3D printing. Nat Commun 9(1):1620
Kim SH, Seo YB, Yeon YK et al (2020a) 4D-bioprinted silk hydrogels for tissue engineering. Biomaterials 260:120281
Kim IG, Park SA, Lee S-H et al (2020b) Transplantation of a 3D-printed tracheal graft combined with iPS cell-derived MSCs and chondrocytes. Sci Rep 10(1):4326
Kim SH, Hong H, Ajiteru O et al (2021a) 3D bioprinted silk fibroin hydrogels for tissue engineering. Nat Protoc 16(12):5484–5532

Kim H, Lee JY, Han H et al (2021b) Improved chondrogenic performance with protective tracheal design of chitosan membrane surrounding 3D-printed trachea. Sci Rep 11(1):9258
Kim SH, Lee YJ, Lee JS, Ajiteru O, Lee OJ, Park CH (2024) Three-dimensional bioprinting using silk biomaterial ink: where we are trying to move? In: Silk-based biomaterials for tissue engineering, regenerative and precision medicine. Elsevier, pp 477–509
Knaneh-Monem H, Thornton ME, Grubbs BH, Warburton D, Grikscheit TC, Hochstim C (2019) Differential epithelial growth in tissue-engineered larynx and trachea generated from postnatal and fetal progenitor cells. Biochem Biophys Res Commun 510(2):205–210
Kojima K, Vacanti CA (2014) Tissue engineering in the trachea. Anat Rec 297(1):44–50
Kojima K, Bonassar LJ, Roy AK, Vacanti CA, Cortiella J (2002) Autologous tissue-engineered trachea with sheep nasal chondrocytes. J Thorac Cardiovasc Surg 123(6):1177–1184
Komura M, Komura H, Kanamori Y et al (2008) An animal model study for tissue-engineered trachea fabricated from a biodegradable scaffold using chondrocytes to augment repair of tracheal stenosis. J Pediatr Surg 43(12):2141–2146
Lee JS, Park HS, Jung H et al (2020) 3D-printable photocurable bioink for cartilage regeneration of tonsil-derived mesenchymal stem cells. Addit Manuf 33:101136
Lee JS, Jung H, Ajiteru O et al (2024) Hybrid 3D bioprinting for advanced tissue-engineered trachea: merging fused deposition modeling (FDM) and top–down digital light processing (DLP). Biofabrication 17(1):015026
Li W, Wang M, Ma H, Chapa-Villarreal FA, Lobo AO, Zhang YS (2023) Stereolithography apparatus and digital light processing-based 3D bioprinting for tissue fabrication. Iscience 26(2):106039
Liu L, Wu W, Tuo X et al (2010) Novel strategy to engineer trachea cartilage graft with marrow mesenchymal stem cell macroaggregate and hydrolyzable scaffold. Artif Organs 34(5):426–433
Liu Y, Zhou G, Cao Y (2017) Recent progress in cartilage tissue engineering—our experience and future directions. Engineering 3(1):28–35
Liu L, Dharmadhikari S, Shontz KM et al (2021) Regeneration of partially decellularized tracheal scaffolds in a mouse model of orthotopic tracheal replacement. J Tissue Eng 12: 20417314211017417
Lu Y, Shan Y, Zhu J et al (2025) Enhancing epithelial regeneration with gelatin methacryloyl hydrogel loaded with extracellular vesicles derived from adipose mesenchymal stem cells for decellularized tracheal patching. Int J Biol Macromol 284:137927
Machino R, Matsumoto K, Taniguchi D et al (2019) Replacement of rat tracheas by layered, trachea-like, scaffold-free structures of human cells using a bio-3D printing system. Adv Healthc Mater 8(7):1800983
Mathur V, Agarwal P, Kasturi M, Varadharajan S, Devi ES, Vasanthan KS (2025) Transformative bioprinting: 4D printing and its role in the evolution of engineering and personalized medicine. Discover Nano 20(1):1–57
Moldovan NI, Hibino N, Nakayama K (2017) Principles of the Kenzan method for robotic cell spheroid-based three-dimensional bioprinting. Tissue Eng Part B Rev 23(3):237–244
Murata D, Arai K, Nakayama K (2020) Scaffold-free bio-3D printing using spheroids as "bio-inks" for tissue (re-) construction and drug response tests. Adv Healthc Mater 9(15):1901831
Nakamura T, Sato T, Araki M et al (2009) In situ tissue engineering for tracheal reconstruction using a luminar remodeling type of artificial trachea. J Thorac Cardiovasc Surg 138(4):811–819
Nakanishi R, Shirakusa T, Mitsudomi T (1993) Maximum length of tracheal autografts in dogs. J Thorac Cardiovasc Surg 106(6):1081–1087
Nomoto M, Nomoto Y, Tada Y et al (2013) Bioengineered trachea using autologous chondrocytes for regeneration of tracheal cartilage in a rabbit model. Laryngoscope 123(9):2195–2201
Ott LM, Weatherly RA, Detamore MS (2011) Overview of tracheal tissue engineering: clinical need drives the laboratory approach. Ann Biomed Eng 39(8):2091–2113
Pandey H, Mohol SS, Kandi R (2022) 4D printing of tracheal scaffold using shape-memory polymer composite. Mater Lett 329:133238

Park JH, Hong JM, Ju YM et al (2015) A novel tissue-engineered trachea with a mechanical behavior similar to native trachea. Biomaterials 62:106–115

Park HS, Lee JS, Jung H et al (2018a) An omentum-cultured 3D-printed artificial trachea: in vivo bioreactor. Artif Cells Nanomed Biotechnol 46(sup3):1131–1140

Park HS, Park HJ, Lee J et al (2018b) A 4-axis technique for three-dimensional printing of an artificial trachea. Tissue Eng Regener Med 15(4):415–425

Park JH, Ahn M, Park SH et al (2021) 3D bioprinting of a trachea-mimetic cellular construct of a clinically relevant size. Biomaterials 279:121246

Park JH, Brown NE, Tucker SJ et al (2025) Feasibility assessment of 3D printing-based tubular tissue flap in a porcine model for long segmental tracheal reconstruction. Tissue Eng Regener Med:1–11

Prasad PR, Singh A, Gomes K, et al. (2025) 3D-bioprinting for lung and tracheal bioengineering: an overview

Ramesh S, Harrysson OL, Rao PK et al (2021) Extrusion bioprinting: recent progress, challenges, and future opportunities. Bioprinting 21:e00116

Reina-Mahecha A, Beers MJ, van der Veen HC, Zuhorn IS, van Kooten TG, Sharma PK (2023) A review of the role of bioreactors for iPSCs-based tissue-engineered articular cartilage. Tissue Eng Regener Med 20(7):1041–1052

Sahoo NK, Tejaswini G (2000) A review on bioprinting–its applications and future scope. J Mol Pharm Regul Aff 2(1)

Schwarz S, Koerber L, Elsaesser AF et al (2012) Decellularized cartilage matrix as a novel biomatrix for cartilage tissue-engineering applications. Tissue Eng Part A 18(21–22): 2195–2209

Shai S-E, Lai Y-L, Hung Y-W et al (2024) Long-term survival and regeneration following transplantation of 3d-printed biodegradable PCL tracheal grafts in large-scale porcine models. Bioengineering 11(8):832

She Y, Fan Z, Wang L et al (2021) 3D printed biomimetic PCL scaffold as framework interspersed with collagen for long segment tracheal replacement. Front Cell Dev Biol 9:629796

Shen Z, Sun F, Shan Y et al (2023) Construction of a novel cell-free tracheal scaffold promoting vascularization for repairing tracheal defects. Mater Today Bio 23:100841

Sun F, Lu Y, Wang Z, Shi H (2021) Vascularization strategies for tissue engineering for tracheal reconstruction. Regen Med 16(6):549–566

Sun Y, Huo Y, Ran X et al (2024) Instant trachea reconstruction using 3D-bioprinted C-shape biomimetic trachea based on tissue-specific matrix hydrogels. Bioact Mater 32:52–65

Taneja H, Salodkar SM, Parmar AS, Chaudhary S (2022) Hydrogel based 3D printing: bio ink for tissue engineering. J Mol Liq 367:120390

Tang H, Sun W, Liu X et al (2023) A bioengineered trachea-like structure improves survival in a rabbit tracheal defect model. Sci Transl Med 15(714):eabo4272

Taniguchi D, Matsumoto K, Tsuchiya T et al (2018) Scaffold-free trachea regeneration by tissue engineering with bio-3D printing. Interact Cardiovasc Thorac Surg 26(5):745–752

Tao J, Zhu S, Zhou N et al (2022) Nanoparticle-stabilized emulsion bioink for digital light processing based 3D bioprinting of porous tissue constructs. Adv Healthc Mater 11(12): 2102810

Tilton M, Camilleri ET, Potes MDA et al (2023) Visible light-induced 3D bioprinted injectable scaffold for minimally invasive tissue regeneration. Biomater Adv 153:213539

Ts M, Sasikumar S, Chameettachal S, Pati F (2025) Hybrid biofabrication of multilayered, self-supporting tracheal constructs using functionalized dECM hydrogels. ACS Appl Bio Mater 8(10):8845–8863

Tsao C-K, Hsiao H-Y, Cheng M-H, Zhong W-B (2022) Tracheal reconstruction with the scaffolded cartilage sheets in an orthotopic animal model. Tissue Eng Part A 28(15–16):685–699

Uchida F, Matsumoto K, Nishimuta M et al (2024) Fabrication of a three-dimensional scaffold-free trachea with horseshoe-shaped hyaline cartilage. Eur J Cardiothorac Surg 66(4):ezae336

Vacanti CA, Paige KT, Kim WS, Sakata J, Upton J, Vacanti JP (1994) Experimental tracheal replacement using tissue-engineered cartilage. J Pediatr Surg 29(2):201–205

Valino AD, Dizon JRC, Espera AH Jr, Chen Q, Messman J, Advincula RC (2019) Advances in 3D printing of thermoplastic polymer composites and nanocomposites. Prog Polym Sci 98:101162

Woodruff MA, Hutmacher DW (2010) The return of a forgotten polymer—Polycaprolactone in the 21st century. Prog Polym Sci 35(10):1217–1256

Wu W, Cheng X, Zhao Y, Chen F, Feng X, Mao T (2007a) Tissue engineering of trachea-like cartilage grafts by using chondrocyte macroaggregate: experimental study in rabbits. Artif Organs 31(11):826–834

Wu W, Feng X, Mao T et al (2007b) Engineering of human tracheal tissue with collagen-enforced poly-lactic-glycolic acid non-woven mesh: a preliminary study in nude mice. Br J Oral Maxillofac Surg 45(4):272–278

Wu W, Jia S, Chen W, Liu X, Zhang S (2019) Fast degrading elastomer stented fascia remodels into tough and vascularized construct for tracheal regeneration. Mater Sci Eng C 101:1–14

Xu Y, Dai J, Zhu X et al (2022) Biomimetic trachea engineering via a modular ring strategy based on bone-marrow stem cells and atelocollagen for use in extensive tracheal reconstruction. Adv Mater 34(6):2106755

Yang Y, Wang G, Liang H et al (2018) Additive manufacturing of bone scaffolds. Int J Bioprint 5(1):148

Yeou SH, Shin YS (2025) Tissue-engineered tracheal reconstruction. Biomimetics 10(7):457

Yi S, Liu Q, Luo Z et al (2022) Micropore-forming gelatin methacryloyl (GelMA) bioink toolbox 2.0: designable tunability and adaptability for 3D bioprinting applications. Small 18(25): 2106357

Yu YS, Kim DH, Park SH, Hwang Y, Lee JW, Kim SW (2025) Characteristics of 3D-printed Polycaprolactone tracheal scaffolds implanted in vivo. Tissue Eng Regener Med:1–10

Zhang B, Sun F, Lu Y et al (2022) A novel decellularized trachea preparation method for the rapid construction of a functional tissue engineered trachea to repair tracheal defects. J Mater Chem B 10(25):4810–4822

Zhang Y, Liu Y, Shu C et al (2024) 3D bioprinting of the airways and lungs for applications in tissue engineering and in vitro models. J Tissue Eng 15:20417314241309183

Zhao W, Zhang F, Leng J, Liu Y (2019) Personalized 4D printing of bioinspired tracheal scaffold concept based on magnetic stimulated shape memory composites. Compos Sci Technol 184(107866):10.1016

Chapter 11
Biofabrication Approaches and Technologies for Bone Tissue Engineering

Jung Hun Kim, Tae Hoon Kang, Hee Sang Ro, and Nathaniel S. Hwang

Abstract Bone tissue engineering has advanced rapidly with the advent of cutting-edge 3D printing technologies, enabling precise spatial control over scaffold architecture, material composition, and biological signal delivery. This chapter summarizes both conventional strategies and recent developments in biofabrication techniques applied to bone regeneration. It covers the range of technologies, materials, and resulting constructs used in these approaches and presents representative studies illustrating the translational pathway from in vitro modeling to large-animal validation. Also, the chapter discusses emerging trends in biofabrication aimed at future perspectives.

J. H. Kim
School of Chemical and Biological Engineering, The Institute of Chemical Processes, Seoul National University, Seoul, Republic of Korea

Institute of Engineering Research, Seoul National University, Seoul, Republic of Korea
e-mail: lkjh3160@snu.ac.kr

T. H. Kang
Interdisciplinary Program in Bioengineering, Seoul National University, Seoul, Republic of Korea
e-mail: tykhang@snu.ac.kr

H. S. Ro
School of Chemical and Biological Engineering, The Institute of Chemical Processes, Seoul National University, Seoul, Republic of Korea
e-mail: heesangro@snu.ac.kr

N. S. Hwang (✉)
School of Chemical and Biological Engineering, The Institute of Chemical Processes, Seoul National University, Seoul, Republic of Korea

Institute of Engineering Research, Seoul National University, Seoul, Republic of Korea

Interdisciplinary Program in Bioengineering, Seoul National University, Seoul, Republic of Korea

BioMAX/N-Bio Institute, Institute of BioEngineering, Seoul National University, Seoul, Republic of Korea
e-mail: nshwang@snu.ac.kr

Y. M. Elçin (ed.), *Biofabrication in Regenerative Medicine*, Stem Cell Biology and Regenerative Medicine 1519, https://doi.org/10.1007/978-3-032-30294-6_11

Keywords Bone tissue engineering · Biofabrication techniques · 3D printing · Functional bone regeneration · Clinical translation · Artificial intelligence-driven biofabrication

11.1 Introduction

Bone is a multifunctional, highly organized tissue that not only provides structural support for the body but also plays essential roles in hematopoiesis, mineral storage, immune regulation, and systemic metabolism (Hadjidakis and Androulakis 2006; Morgan et al. 2018; Takayanagi 2007). Damage caused by trauma, tumors, infection, or congenital defects remains a formidable clinical challenge, as conventional autologous and allogeneic bone grafts are constrained by donor scarcity, risk of immune rejection, infection, and imperfect anatomical matching (Alaribe et al. 2016). This unmet need has driven the evolution of bone tissue engineering (BTE), which integrates biomaterials, living cells, biochemical cues, and advanced manufacturing processes to regenerate functional bone (Koons et al. 2020).

In recent years, biofabrication has emerged as a transformative paradigm within BTE, shifting the focus from traditional material–cell combinations toward the spatially precise, multiscale replication of bone's structural and functional complexity. Biofabrication technologies—such as high-resolution 3D bioprinting, material deposition, patterning—enable the controlled replicating the distinct mechanical gradients and spatial heterogeneity between cortical and cancellous bone, as well as integrating vasculature and innervation into engineered constructs (Davoodi et al. 2020; Saadi et al. 2022).

This chapter presents a comprehensive overview of recent advances in biofabrication for bone tissue engineering, beginning with the biological and mechanical characteristics of bone, moving through biofabrication technologies that capture its complexity, and highlighting recent technologies. It further addresses standardized evaluation criteria for biofabricated bone constructs and outlines future trajectories—particularly the integration of artificial intelligence and predictive modeling—to guide the next generation of patient-specific, functionally optimized bone regeneration strategies.

11.2 Bone Biology and Biofabrication

Bone is maintained by a tightly coordinated network of osteoblasts/osteoclasts/osteocytes, bone marrow-resident mesenchymal stem cells, endothelial cells, and immune cells, which exchange biochemical and mechano-electrical signals (Hadjidakis and Androulakis 2006; Raggatt and Partridge 2010; Qin et al. 2020; Kusumbe et al. 2014). Moreover, at the organ level, the porosity of dense cortical bone and porous cancellous bone differs by five- to tenfold and the elastic modulus by more than tenfold (cortical bone 10–30 GPa, cancellous bone 0.2–3 GPa)

(Morgan et al. 2018; Beisekenov et al. 2025). To meet these diverse biological and mechanical requirements, bone regeneration must be conceived as a multidisciplinary design challenge that integrates cell biology, immunology, materials science, biomechanics, and advanced manufacturing technologies (Hench and Polak 2002; O'Brien 2011; Roseti et al. 2017). This section briefly summarizes the properties of bone tissue and the factors that should be considered in biomanufacturing strategies.

Bone is a physiological system maintained by the dynamic balance between various cells that participate to form a precisely coordinated tissue niche (Raggatt and Partridge 2010). These cells exchange biochemical signals and mechanical-electrical stimuli and drive bone homeostasis and regeneration (Bolamperti et al. 2022). In particular, osteocytes interpret mechanical loading through Wnt/β-catenin signaling (Qin et al. 2020) and coordinate remodeling by releasing mediators such as sclerostin (Winkler et al. 2003), RANKL, and other proteins (Schaffler and Kennedy 2012). Osteoblasts synthesize type I collagen matrix, secrete alkaline phosphatase to mineralize it, and can transition into lining cells or become embedded as osteocytes, also produce both RANKL and its decoy receptor OPG to control osteoclastogenesis (Zhu et al. 2024a). Osteoclasts, multinucleated cells derived from the monocyte–macrophage lineage, resorb bone via extracellular acidification and cathepsin K, and the balance between osteoblast/osteocyte-derived RANKL and OPG reciprocally regulates osteoclast activity under systemic (e.g., PTH) and local biochemical inputs (Teitelbaum 2000).

MSCs reside in perivascular niches of the periosteum and cancellous bone as separated using markers like CD105, CD90, CD73 (ISCT standard) stromal cells, where they differentiate toward osteoblasts in bone with Wnt signaling pathway (Fakhry et al. 2013) and, through their secretome (e.g., VEGF, IL-10, TGF-β, PGE_2), modulate angiogenesis and skew local immunity toward a pro-repair state (Han et al. 2022; Song et al. 2020). Endothelial cells not only build new vessels but also couple angiogenesis to osteogenesis by providing angiocrine signals (e.g., Notch ligands, VEGF/BMP/PDGF axes) that recruit and maintain osteogenic progenitors near type-H capillaries (Kusumbe et al. 2014; Sivaraj and Adams 2016). Macrophages orchestrate the temporal switch from an early M1-like program, debris, and pathogen clearance, TNF-α/IL-1β/IL-6 release, to an M2-like reparative state that promotes matrix deposition and revascularization via IL-4, IL-10, and TGF-β (Frade et al. 2023). Moreover, also various immune cells (T, neutrophil, dendritic cell, etc.) are involved in the bone immune environment (Takayanagi 2007).

The bone healing process involving these cells consists of four stages: inflammation immediately after injury, soft callus formation, hard callus formation, and remodeling (Einhorn and Gerstenfeld 2015). M1 macrophages and neutrophils that reach the site of injury attract MSCs and endothelial cells through initial inflammatory and cytokine signals, and MSCs then differentiate into osteoblasts to form callus tissue (Baht et al. 2018; Marsell and Einhorn 2011). During this period, angiogenesis, especially H-type blood vessel formation, occurs and the supply of oxygen and growth factors (Kusumbe et al. 2014). In the remodeling stage, osteoclast resorption and osteoblast formation occur simultaneously, and long-term tissue stability is maintained (Schindeler et al. 2008).

Therefore, biofabrication in bone tissue engineering should be understood as a precise design task that reproduces these biological, structural, mechanical, and immunological complex requirements. For example, to fabricate a bioengineered scaffold for bone applications, an extrusion-based fused deposition modeling (FDM) process can be selected. Using thermoplastics such as PCL or PLGA, the printer simultaneously introduces primary porous structure, thereby promoting cell infiltration and nutrient diffusion while meeting the physical-structural design targets (Winarso et al. 2022). Additional biochemical cues can be incorporated such as cell-adhesion motifs RGD through post-fabrication processing (Hersel et al. 2003), or β-TCP/hydroxyapatite microparticles can be dispersed to enable the slow release of Ca^{2+} fostering progenitor-cell attachment and osteogenic differentiation (Jeong et al. 2019). Immunomodulation and angiogenesis are also important considerations. Magnesium ions or anti-inflammatory chemicals can mitigate the host inflammatory response to the implant (Zhou et al. 2021). VEGF loading encourages endothelial-cell invasion, and co-printing endothelial cells with mesenchymal stem cells promotes vascular–osteogenic coupling. Additionally, continuous or stepwise transitions can be created via multi-nozzle printing, resin-blended digital light processing (DLP), or conical mixing techniques (Kuang et al. 2019; Mccauley and Bayles 2024). In this way, a biofabricated scaffold becomes more than a static structure; it must dynamically interact with biological systems at the cell, tissue, and organ levels to drive regeneration. Applying systematic design principles is therefore essential for ensuring the clinical integrity and long-term functionality of the construct and for advancing the practical translation of bone tissue engineering.

11.3 Biofabrication Strategies for Bone Tissue Engineering

As previously discussed, bone tissue is a complex tissue that simultaneously reflects its unique biological cellular composition, mechanical heterogeneity, hierarchical structure, immune response, and vascularization characteristics. Successfully regenerating it requires sophisticated fabrication strategies that can satisfy biological requirements while simultaneously providing mechanical stability and tissue integrity. In particular, biofabrication in bone tissue engineering is evolving beyond simple cell transplantation or material injection to integrate materials, cells, bioactive signals, and structural design to mimic living, functional bone tissue (Fig. 11.1). This chapter comprehensively covers the core manufacturing technology and materials used in biofabrication for bone regeneration, as well as the fabricated results and their applications (Fig. 11.2).

11.3.1 Core Biofabrication Technologies

Most biofabrication techniques focus on the creation of patient-specific scaffolds, fabricated layer by layer based on CAD models generated from medical images such

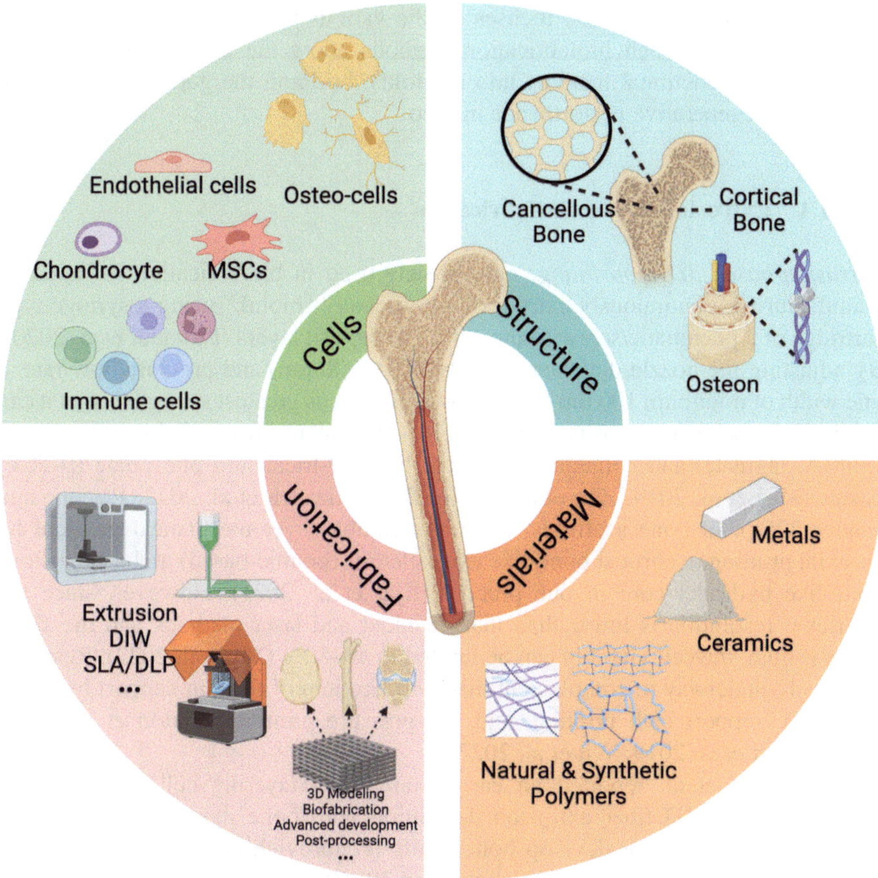

Fig. 11.1 Illustration showing things to consider when doing biofabrication for bone tissue engineering. (Created in BioRender. Hwang, N. 2025 https://BioRender.com/4yss1ke)

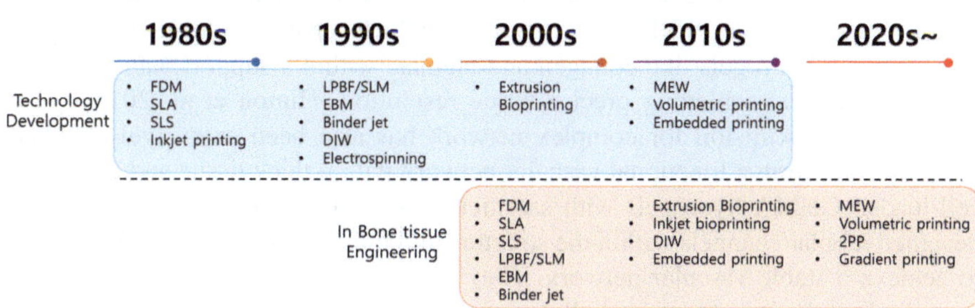

Fig. 11.2 Flow chart of major biofabrication technology development and use in bone tissue engineering by decade

as CT and MRI. This section focuses on the various biofabrication techniques to achieve this goal. Such biofabrication methods allow the precise integration of structural and functional features into scaffolds, bridging the gap between digital design and regenerative performance in vivo.

11.3.1.1 Extrusion-Based Biofabrication

Extrusion-based 3D bioprinting, most widely used in biofabrication for additive manufacturing, continuously extrudes high-viscosity "bioink" using a syringe-type cartridge or a pneumatic/screw (motor) head to deposit layers (Davoodi et al. 2020). By adjusting the nozzle diameter (usually 200–1000 μm) and pressure/flow rate, a line width of minimum 100 μm can be achieved, and its greatest strength is that it can handle inks with a viscosity range of 10^2–10^8 mPa·s, from hydrogels such as GelMA, alginate, and collagen to ceramic based β-tricalcium phosphate (β-TCP) pastes (Miri et al. 2019; Zhu et al. 2024b; Beheshtizadeh et al. 2022; Placone and Engler 2018). In bone scaffolds, to form a double-layer mechanical gradient by co-axial printing, a cortical bone-like exoskeleton (ceramic-based) and a cancellous bone-like hydrogel core in one process (Kjar et al. 2021). However, since the interlayer resolution is lower than that of inkjet and laser methods and the shear stress is high, the cell viability can be limited to 40–80% (Xu et al. 2022). Research is actively underway to complement this with freedom of form in support hydrogel (FRESH), support bath printing, and low-pressure printing (Hinton et al. 2015; Skylar-Scott et al. 2019; Wu et al. 2022).

Fedorovich et al. reported an early example of layering cell-laden alginate hydrogels using 3D fiber extrusion deposition with bone marrow mesenchymal stem cells (BMSCs) for develop bone grafts (Fedorovich et al. 2008). J, Franco et al. prepared a pseudoplastic ink containing 30–50 vol.% of solid hydroxyapatite, (β-TCP) using a F-127 solution, achieving a resolution of 100 μm and low printing pressure (Franco et al. 2010). In addition to this, there are many extrusion-based studies on bone tissue engineering using various combinations of materials and bioink. In 2015, the FRESH technology, which enabled stable printing of low-elasticity hydrogels like collagen and alginate within a support bath, launched research aimed at achieving precise tissue resolution (Hinton et al. 2015). Also, multi-material extrusion for complex network has also been extensively studied. Kolesky et al. form a functional vascular network within thick tissue and co-printed cell-loaded GelMA hydrogels with sacrificial ink (Pluronic F127), creating freely designed tubular channels within the structure and lining these with endothelial cells to achieve a stable vascular network. They attempted to regenerate bone tissue in areas such as the jaw, ear, and skull demonstrating integrated vascular strategies for bone tissue regeneration (Kang et al. 2016). Recently, advanced 3D printing strategies have increasingly focused on the fabrication of highly functionalized scaffolds that combine precise architectural resolution with bioactivity (Xie et al. 2022; Yang et al. 2024; Fig. 11.3).

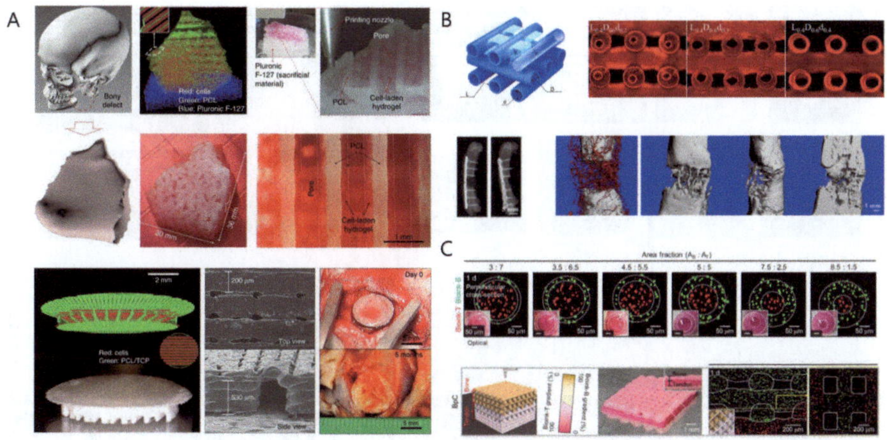

Fig. 11.3 Representative extrusion printing for bone tissue engineering examples (edited from each reference) (*a*) 3D modeling and reconstruction of mandible bony defect from human CT image data and 3D architecture of calvarial bone construct (Kang et al. 2016) (*b*) Hollow structure and grid of hydrogel-based scaffolds and large-sized segmental bone defect repair (Yang et al. 2024) (*c*) Development of the core-shell/multilayer bioprinting for tendon-to-bone structure (Kim et al. 2025)

Inkjet printing in tissue engineering refers to the precise deposition of low-viscosity liquid droplets—often containing bioactive molecules, proteins, or even living cells—onto a substrate with high spatial resolution (Wu et al. 2023; Negro et al. 2018). Using drop-on-demand or continuous flow nozzles, the technology enables accurate control over the location and dosage of growth factors such as BMP-2 (Cooper et al. 2010) and SDF-1β (Herberg et al. 2014), making it particularly suited for creating spatially defined biochemical cues within scaffolds or on cell culture surfaces. Because inkjet printing operates under relatively low shear stress and ambient temperature, it can preserve the bioactivity of delicate biomolecules (Xu et al. 2022). However, the technique is restricted to low-viscosity inks, which limits its applicability for high-strength or highly viscous formulations. Most bone regeneration bioinks, such as hydrogels or ceramic slurries, are inherently viscous to be directly print; therefore, inkjet is less used than extrusion-based printing in most studies (Derakhshanfar et al. 2018).

Direct ink writing (DIW) is an extrusion-based additive manufacturing in which viscoelastic, shear-thinning "inks" (ceramics, polymers/composites, glasses, metals, functional nanomaterials) are deposited along programmed toolpaths and immediately self-support (Saadi et al. 2022). DIW, sometimes confused with extrusion bioprinting, is a more broad concept of a materials-centric printing focused largely on non-living inks, especially ceramics in bone tissue engineering, and is comfortable with harsh post-processing (drying, high-temperature sintering, thermal/UV cures), higher solids loading, and higher extrusion pressures whereas extrusion bioprinting prioritizes cell health and biofunction during and after printing (Lewis 2006; Lewis et al. 2006).

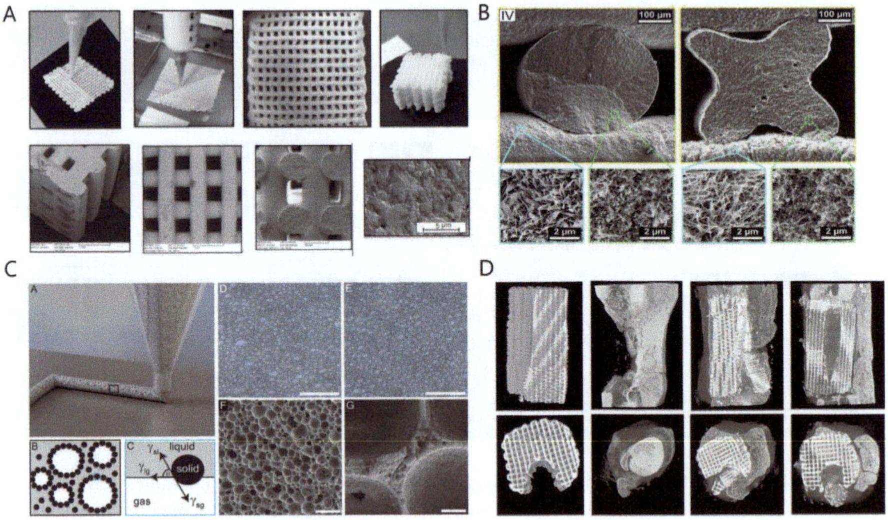

Fig. 11.4 Using various DIW techniques for bone tissue engineering (edited from each references) (*a*) Biphasic calcium phosphates 3D printing scaffold (Beheshtizadeh et al. 2022) (*b*) Star-shaped modification geometry of the 3D-printed calcium phosphate scaffold (Raymond et al. 2022) (*c*) Direct foam writing of architected ceramics (Muth et al. 2017) (*d*) Micro-CT images of printed scaffold to segmental defects (Vidal et al. 2020)

Recently, Raymond et al. studied using a nozzle that prints star-shaped strands, creating abundant concave microtopographies on the filament surface. In a rabbit distal femur defect, star strands improved osteoconduction/osteogenic ingrowth particularly guiding bone formation toward the scaffold center (Raymond et al. 2022). Wu et al. introduce a hexagonal close-packed (HCP) pore architecture in 3D-printed CaP ceramics to boost osteoinductivity via structural design alone (Wu et al. 2024a). Guo et al. combined 3D printing with online mixing of zirconia/alumina ceramic foams to fabricate scaffolds with simultaneous compositional and porosity gradients, mimicking bone's hierarchical porosity (macro to micro) and multiple gradients in a single process (Guo et al. 2025). Moreover, Daneshmandi et al. used an ultra-low binder CaP–graphene formulation, the team 3D-printed scaffolds with very high solids content (~90%) and high porosity (~95%) yielding resorbable, osteoinductive matrices. The constructs promoted osteogenic differentiation of hMSCs in vitro and supported significant bone formation in a mouse calvarial defect in vivo (Daneshmandi et al. 2022; Fig. 11.4).

Fused deposition modeling (FDM) is a common method for manufacturing 3D structures which melt and extrude thermoplastic filaments through a heated nozzle to build parts layer by layer. Because the extrusion temperature depends on the polymer (≈70–120 °C for PCL, ≈175–195 °C for PLA, and ≈360 °C for PEEK), FDM is not suitable for directly printing cell-laden bioinks, but it precisely handles load-bearing polymers and polymer–ceramic composites (e.g., PLA/PEEK with HA or β-TCP) to make cortical-bone-like frames (Winarso et al. 2022; Dua et al. 2021). Typical FDM nozzles are 200–400 μm, giving line widths on the order of the nozzle diameter and layer heights of ~100–400 μm. For PLA bone scaffolds, reported compressive strength is commonly 2–10 MPa (modulus 50–200 MPa), and porosity can be tuned broadly (≈40–80%). Higher strengths generally require stiffer polymers (e.g., PEEK), ceramic reinforcement, or denser architectures rather than plain lattices. FDM's additional advantages are large build volumes and relatively low equipment cost compared with many additive manufacturing modalities.

In FDM-based bone tissue engineering, PCL and PLA are the two most commonly used polymers. PCL has a low melting point (~60 °C) and good printability, degrades slowly over years, and has become a mainstay for bone scaffolds; early studies by Hutmacher et al. and Zein et al. showed that FDM can produce reproducible, interconnected PCL scaffolds with controllable porosity and support osteoblastic responses (Hutmacher et al. 2001; Zein et al. 2002). Subsequent work established that pore size and toolpath can be tuned as design parameters to balance mechanics and infiltration, and that PCL–ceramic composites (e.g., PCL/β-TCP or PCL/HA) improve surface bioactivity and stiffness relative to neat PCL. Lee et al. demonstrated the feasibility of 3D-printed PCL/β-TCP scaffolds for canine mandibular critical-size defects (Lee et al. 2020a), while Jeong et al. reported patient-specific PCL/β-TCP scaffolds for complex zygomatico-maxillary reconstruction in humans. Recently (Jeong et al. 2022), Ghezzi et al. pushed ceramic loading to ~70 wt% β-TCP in PCL via FDM, exploring the mechanics–biology trade-off at high filler contents (Ghezzi et al. 2024). PLA is also widely used in FDM because of its availability and higher stiffness than PCL, although it degrades faster and can be more brittle; nevertheless, optimized geometries and PLA/HA composites have shown enhanced mechanics and osteogenic performance in vitro and in vivo (Wasti and Adhikari 2020). Recent studies include high-strength porous PLA gyroid scaffolds (FDM) and PLA/n-HA composite scaffolds with customized mechanical properties and in vivo efficacy (Wang et al. 2021). Beyond PCL and PLA, PEEK provides higher strength and temperature resistance but is biologically inert. FDM/FFF-printed PEEK/HA composites and related strategies have improved bioactivity while retaining mechanical robustness, underscoring the role of polymer–ceramic hybridization (Dua et al. 2021; Fig. 11.5).

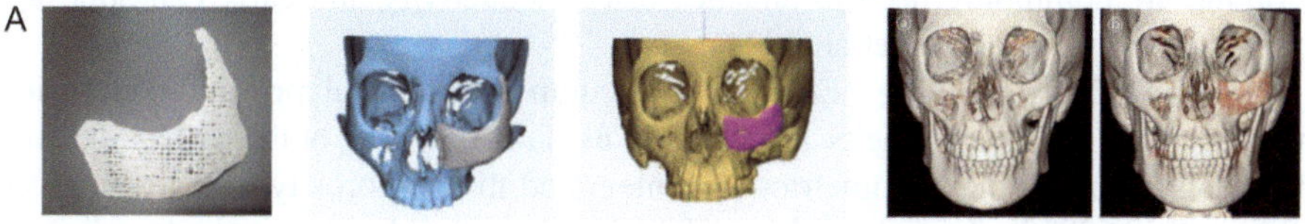

Fig. 11.5 Clinical application of FDM Printed patient specific PCL/TCP scaffolds (Jeong et al. 2022)

11.3.1.2 Laser-Based Technologies

Stereolithography (SLA) and digital light processing (DLP or DLP-SLA) selectively photopolymerizes photocurable resins or hydrogel precursors using a laser beam to point by point-SLA or cures the entire layer at once-DLP. With a pixel/laser spot size of ~25–100 μm, it can achieve sub-100 μm microchannels and surface pores (Li et al. 2023; Luo et al. 2023). Biocompatible hydrogels such as GelMA and PEGDA enable direct cell-laden DLP with ~80–90% viability (Zheng et al. 2021). By contrast, ceramic-rich DLP resins (e.g., HA slurries) are typically printed acellularly and later sintered, with cells seeded post-fabrication (Liang et al. 2022; Kim et al. 2019). DLP, which cures a single layer at a time, offers high throughput, making it advantageous for the fabrication of complex cancellous bone structures. It can also create mechanical and biochemical gradients through multiple resin exchange modules (Mo et al. 2025). However, cleaning and post-curing processes are essential to minimize cytotoxicity from UV exposure and residual photoinitiators (Quan et al. 2020).

Selective laser sintering (SLS) is a powder-bed process that uses a scanning laser to fuse thermoplastic polymer powders layer by layer, with the unfused powder serving as a self-supporting medium. Typical SLS systems use CO_2 lasers and polymer powders in the ~20–150 μm size range and use polymer like polyamide, PCL, PEEK, and ceramics for bone tissue engineering (DiNoro et al. 2022). In recent SLS work in bone tissue engineering, PLA/$CaCO_3$ composite was formulated to print interconnected-porosity scaffolds without any solvent steps, demonstrated cytocompatibility, and argued suitability for patient-specific implants (Gayer et al. 2019). In parallel, borate bioactive glass (BBG)/PCL composites have been SLS-printed as case-specific lattices and then improved regeneration in a rabbit radius defect in vivo (Han et al. 2023).

Laser powder bed fusion (LPBF/SLM) is a powder bed fusion process that uses a high-power fiber laser to fully melt metal or metal–ceramic composite powders layer by layer, producing near fully dense structures with fine feature resolution (Cao et al. 2021). In bone regeneration, LPBF is widely applied to fabricate load-bearing metallic implants, such as Ti-6Al-4 V or TiNb alloys, with precisely tailored lattice architectures to match the compressive strength of cortical and reduce stress shielding (Carluccio et al. 2020). By adjusting unit cell geometry and strut thickness, LPBF can produce interconnected porosity in the range of 50–80% with pore sizes of 300–800 μm, promoting vascular ingrowth and osseointegration (Pattanayak et al. 2011). Post-printing surface modifications, e.g., hydroxyapatite coatings, or ion doping, are commonly used to enhance osteoconductivity and early cell adhesion (Biemond et al. 2013; Xu et al. 2024).

Electron Beam Melting (EBM) is a vacuum-based metal powder bed fusion process that selectively melts alloys such as Ti-6Al-4V to build patient-specific implants with complex geometries and integrated macro-porosity in a single piece (Murr et al. 2012). In orthopedics, EBM has been used extensively to fabricate clinical components, including hip and knee joint implants, and various porous implant designs have already been proposed. Recent reviews summarized the widespread use of EBM in patient-specific implants across multiple orthopedic areas (Palmquist et al. 2023). In short, EBM-based bone applications represent a largely established technology, with current research focused more on polishing and validating what is already in routine clinical use rather than reinventing the process itself.

Direct energy deposition (DED) employs a coaxial nozzle to simultaneously feed powder or wire and a high-energy laser or electron beam to melt the material directly at the deposition point. Unlike powder bed methods, DED allows the fabrication of large structures (>30 cm) and the repair or augmentation of existing implants, making it suitable for custom-fit segmental bone defect reconstruction (Svetlizky et al. 2021). DED is used predominantly as a coating/surface modification laser-cladding technique. It deposits metallurgically bonded layers, hundreds of micrometers to millimeters thick, on new or existing implants to add wear/corrosion resistance and bioactivity (Ke et al. 2019; Avila et al. 2021). In addition, DED coatings and follow-on surface modifications can deliberately introduce controlled porosity, increase surface area and mechanical interlocking, and thereby enhance early cell attachment and long-term osseointegration (Ryu et al. 2021; Ryu et al. 2020). Because processing temperatures exceed ~1000 °C, living cells and proteins cannot be incorporated directly.

11.3.1.3 Binder Jetting

Binder jetting is a manufacturing technique in which a liquid binder is selectively deposited onto successive layers of powder materials such as calcium phosphate (CPC), β-TCP, or bioactive glass. The binder locally fuses powder particles together, gradually building a three-dimensional structure layer by layer (Du et al. 2020). After printing, the part may undergo curing and sintering, to achieve the desired mechanical and biological properties (Ke and Bose 2018). In bone tissue engineering, binder jetting enables the fabrication of complex, mechanically stable ceramic scaffolds with tailored porosity, which can later be functionalized with topographical surface modification or cell infiltration (Ahn et al. 2021; Fig. 11.6).

11.3.1.4 Electrospinning

Electrospinning uses high-voltage electric fields to spin polymer solutions/melts into continuous fibers with nano- to micro-diameters, creating highly porous mats. Its fibrous topography, large surface area, and ability to design components, alignments, and multilayers (including coaxial) similar to the ECM make it widely used in tissue engineering (Zulkifli et al. 2023). In bone tissue engineering, strategies typically reported include the use of composite nanofibers blended with calcium phosphates such as HA/β-TCP, surface mineralization/coating, and the controlled release of

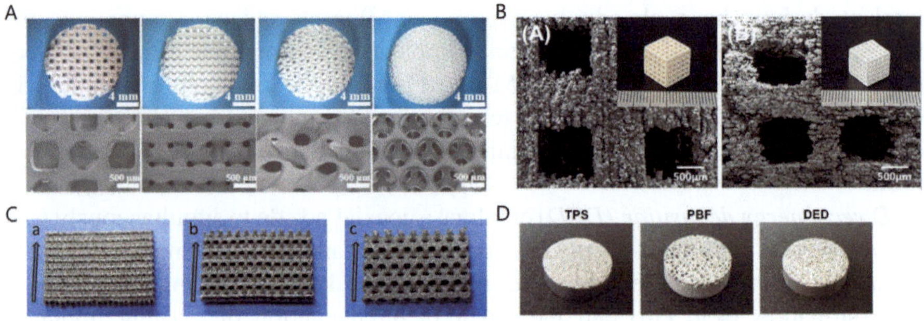

Fig. 11.6 Various laser-based or binder jet 3D-printed scaffold for bone tissue engineering (**a**) DLP printed CaP ceramic composites (Wu et al. 2024a) (**b**) Internal microstructures of binder jet fabricated calcium phosphate scaffolds (Ahn et al. 2021) (**c**) Porous titanium plates manufactured by SLM[96] (**d**) Comparison various Titanium pore structures prepared by titanium plasma spray (TPS), powder bed fusion (PBF), and DED methods (Ryu et al. 2021)

BMP-2, RGD, and antibiotics to promote osteoblast attachment, proliferation, differentiation, and mineralization (Shin et al. 2012). However, the jets are randomly curved, and they are fundamentally limited to 2.5-D sheets or patch-like scaffold.

Melt electrospinning writing (MEW) is a high-resolution, fiber-based additive process that "direct-writes" a molten polymer jet under an electric field, enabling precise control of fiber diameters on the order of a few micrometers and pitches from tens to hundreds of micrometers. Using polymers such as PCL and PLA (and their composites), it can produce regular lattices and even conformal builds on curved surfaces (Kade and Dalton 2021). On the materials side, composite and post-processing strategies using nanofillers, inorganic particles (e.g., calcium phosphates), and ion doping have been proposed to improve both mechanical/biological performance and printing stability (Saiz et al. 2024). In bone tissue engineering, MEW-fabricated microfiber lattices support the adhesion, proliferation, and differentiation of osteogenic stem cells and chondrocytes, and by tuning pore size, studies have leveraged sensitive changes in cell behavior (infiltration, morphology, phenotype) to regulate osteoconductivity and tissue ingrowth (Loewner et al. 2022; Han et al. 2021).

11.3.1.5 Recent Approaches

Volumetric bioprinting, without stacking layers, the entire 3D structure is cured at once by projecting multi-angle (tomographic) light patterns for a few seconds into a hydrogel contained in a rotating vial. Visible light is mainly used (typically 405 or 455 nm); centimeter-scale structures can be printed in tens of seconds, with resolutions of 50–80 μm under optimized conditions. High cell viability (generally ≥85–90%) has been reported even in cell-dense bioresins. Optical absorption and scattering, particularly cell-induced scattering, must be controlled, and refractive-index matching or photoinitiator design is used to maintain resolution. Dual wavelengths and tailored chemistry can also be used to impart internal mechanical gradients (Alvarez-Castano et al. 2025; Bernal et al. 2019; Gehlen et al. 2023).

Two photon polymerization (2PP) printing method using a Ti sapphire femtosecond laser, nonlinear two-photon absorption is confined to the focal volume to directly write submicron features (down to ~100–200 nm). 2PP technology is primarily used to fabricate complex microneedle geometries due to its excellent flexibility and high resolution. Ceramic particles such as hydroxyapatite are unsuitable for direct template design studies due to their light scattering in solvents. Recently, a study presented a novel approach for 3D printing calcium phosphate structures with a precision of approximately 300 nm using nanoclusters (Rad et al. 2021; Roohani et al. 2025).

Using ultrasound in the MHz range, droplets can be ejected without contact or cells/structures can be patterned within a gel. Droplet frequencies can reach the kHz range, the method accommodates high-viscosity fluids and cell spheroids, and cell viability is greater than extrusion method. Positional resolution is generally on the order of tens of micrometers, depending on the setup. Because the printed structures have limited self-support, hybrid operation with a support bath or a frame is practical (Wu et al. 2024b).

In embedded (supported-bath) printing such as FRESH or SWIFT, low-viscosity inks are extruded and solidified within a support bath, such as a gelatin microparticle slurry (FRESH) or a dense cellular matrix (SWIFT). In FRESH, the bath is melted at 37 °C to leave only the printed construct; typical filament diameters are ~200 μm and reported with high cell viabilities. Using a coaxial nozzle enables continuous tubular hydrogels with inner diameters of 100–600 μm, allowing the fabrication of perfusable channels (Hinton et al. 2015; Skylar-Scott et al. 2019).

Gradient biofabrication refers in this section to advanced biofabrication strategies that deliberately build spatial variation in material composition, mechanical properties, porosity, and biological cues within one construct. This is well suited to mimicking graded native interfaces—e.g., cortical-to-cancellous bone or osteochondral/tendon–bone junctions—where abrupt transitions can concentrate stress and impair integration (Liu et al. 2025). Functionally graded designs can impose continuous or stepwise changes in stiffness, bioactive content, or degradation, while multilayer or multiphase architectures enable precise placement of distinct cell populations and signaling factors (Niu et al. 2023). To realize these patterns, multiple processes can be combined with spatially controlled materials, and bio-signals can optimize both mechanical and biological performance at complex junctions. However, most research is still at the multiphasic level, and many challenges remain in producing gradient-integrated biofabricated scaffolds.

Several studies have demonstrated the potential of gradient biofabrication in bone tissue engineering. Kilian et al. loaded cells into an alginate–methylcellulose bioink and, using calcium phosphate cement with multichannel co-extrusion, and fabricated a multilayer mineralized construct consisting of cartilage-calcified layer bone in vitro (Kilian et al. 2020). Guo et al. achieved composition gradients and a hierarchical

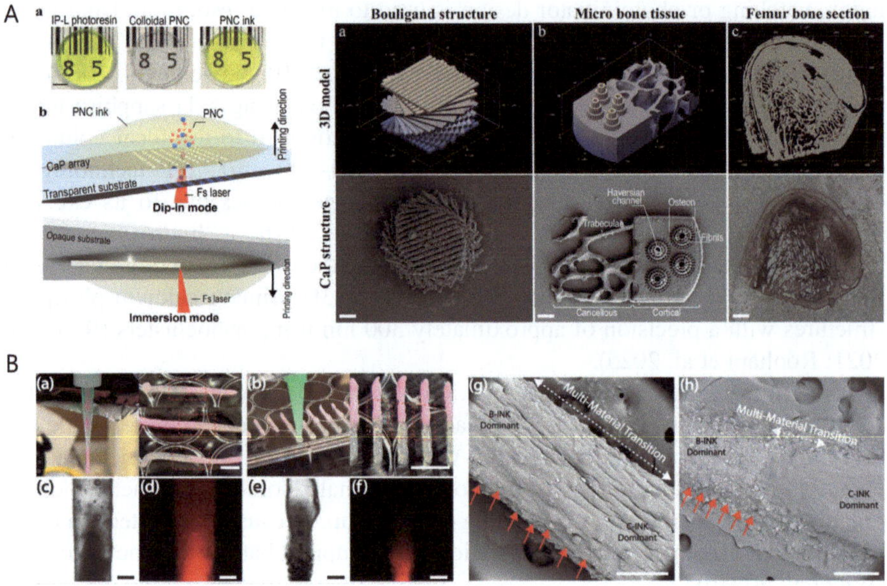

Fig. 11.7 Recent biofabrication approaches (**a**) 2PP-structured CaP biomimetic lattices (Roohani et al. 2025) (**b**) Gradient multi-material fiber architectures for osteochondral healing (Bedell et al. 2023)

pore architecture in a single process by combining extrusion 3D printing with alumina slurry and ZrO_2 foam templating and using a static mixer for continuous multicomponent blending (Guo et al. 2023). Wu et al. manufactured calcified interfacial layer composed of PCL/nHA plus tasquinimod (TA) was inserted between a cartilage layer (GelMA + chondrocytes) and a porous PCL bone layer to block vascular ingrowth and prevent cartilage calcification (Wu et al. 2024c). Also, Kim et al. bioprinted a multilayer construct and engineered a gradient core–shell interface at the boundary to mimic enthesis characteristics using tendon- and bone-derived dECM bioinks (Kim et al. 2025; Fig. 11.7).

11.3.2 Bioinks and Biomaterials for Bone Biofabrication

The key to biofabrication technology lies in the selection and combination of appropriate bioinks and biomaterials. Bioinks for bone tissue regeneration must ensure cell viability while simultaneously providing structural stability, bioactivity, and differentiation—inducing capabilities. Typically, Table 11.1 shows the type of materials that are mainly used depending on the biofabrication method. Therefore, this section briefly introduces materials and characteristics commonly used in biofabrication of bone regeneration.

Table 11.1 Summary table of biofabrication methods and material used in recent studies

Method	Material	Year	Reference
Extrusion bioprinting	Hydrogel (alginate/fibrin/F-127)	2016	Kang et al. (2016)
	Hydrogel (alginate/methylcellu-lose/CaP)	2020	Kilian et al. (2020)
	Hydrogel (fibrinogen/gelatin)	2023	Pitacco et al. (2023)
	Hydrogel (GelMA/Laponite)	2024	Yang et al. (2024)
	Hydrogel (GelMA/CaP)	2022	Xie et al. (2022)
	Hydrogel (GelMA)	2020	Freeman et al. (2020)
	Hydrogel (dECM/CaP/PVA)	2025	Kim et al. (2025)
	Hydrogel (dECM)	2014	Pati et al. (2014)
	Hydrogel (dECM-MA/alginate)	2020	Lee et al. (2020b)
DIW/robocasting	Ceramic (CaP composite)	2022	Beheshtizadeh et al. (2022)
	Ceramic (CaP composite)	2022	Raymond et al. (2022)
	Ceramic (CaP composite)	2021	Kim et al. (2021a)
	Ceramic (CaP composite)	2020	Vidal et al. (2020)
	Ceramic (CaP composite)	2021	Raymond et al. (2021)
	Ceramic (ZrO2/Al2O3)	2025	Guo et al. (2025)
	Ceramic (CaP/graphene)	2022	Daneshmandi et al. (2022)
	Ceramic (HAP/PLGA)	2016	Jakus et al. (2016)
FDM/FFF	Polymer (PCL/β-TCP)	2020	Lee et al. (2020a)
	Polymer (PCL/β-TCP)	2022	Jeong et al. (2022)
	Polymer (PCL/β-TCP)	2024	Ghezzi et al. (2024)
	Polymer (PCL/SrHA)	2019	Liu et al. (2019)
	Polymer (PCL/Mg)	2021	Dong et al. (2021)
	Polymer (PLA/n-HA)	2021	Wang et al. (2021)
	Polymer (PEEK/HAP)	2022	Zheng et al. (2022)
SLA/DLP	Ceramic (CaP composite)	2024	Wu et al. (2024a)
	Ceramic (CaP composite)	2019	Kim et al. (2019)
	Ceramic (HAP slurry)	2022	Liang et al. (2022)
	Ceramic (HAP/resin)	2023	Xiong et al. (2024)
	Hydrogel (GelMA/PEGDA/F127DA)	2023	Gao et al. (2023)
	Hydrogel (GelMA/HAP)	2022	Song et al. (2022)
SLS	Polymer (PLA/CaCO3)	2019	Gayer et al. (2019)
	Polymer (PCL/bioactive glass)	2023	Han et al. (2023)
	Ceramic (bioactive glass)	2020	Kolan et al. (2020)
LPBF/SLM	Metal (Tantalium)	2024	Xu et al. (2024)
	Metal (Ti6Al4V)	2023	Kovacs et al. (2023)
	Metal (titanium)	2016	Taniguchi et al. (2016)
DED	Coating (HAP on Ti6Al4V)	2019	Ke et al. (2019)
	Coating (Ti pore)	2021	Ryu et al. (2021)
	Coating (Ti pore)	2020	Ryu et al. (2020)

(continued)

Table 11.1 (continued)

Method	Material	Year	Reference
Binder jetting	Ceramic (TCP)	2018	Ke and Bose (2018)
	Ceramic (TCP)	2018	Nandi et al. (2018)
	Polymer (PCL/CaP)	2021	Ahn et al. (2021)
Volumetric bioprinting	Hydrogel (GelMA)	2023	Gehlen et al. (2023)
Nanoscale printing (2PP-like)	Ceramic (CaP)	2025	Roohani et al. (2025)

11.3.2.1 Natural and Synthetic Polymers

Natural polymers such as alginate, gelatin, collagen, and hyaluronic acid are widely used as basic materials for bioinks due to their excellent cell affinity and biodegradability and their ability to mimic tissue-specific ECM environments (Malda et al. 2013). However, when used alone, they lack mechanical strength, so they are often combined with modified natural polymers such as photocurable GelMA (Yue et al. 2015). This combination offers a balance between cell viability and printability, allowing for simultaneous control of mechanical properties and biological function. These materials are most commonly processed through extrusion-based bioprinting for cell-laden constructs, while photocurable variants like GelMA are widely used in light-based techniques such as SLA and DLP for high-resolution scaffold fabrication (Gao et al. 2023; Song et al. 2022; Alparslan and Bayraktar 2025).

Synthetic polymers provide the structural backbone of many bone biofabrication strategies because their properties and processing can be tightly engineered (Malda et al. 2013). Thermoplastics such as PCL, PLA, PLGA, and PEEK are readily shaped by extrusion/FDM to form load-bearing lattices with porous architectures, while photocurable PEG-based systems (e.g., PEGDA or PEG-copolymers) enable high-resolution light-based printing (SLA/DLP) of hydrogel networks. Because most synthetic polymers are bioinert, bioactivity is introduced through surface activation (plasma/alkali) or by compounding with osteoconductive fillers such as hydroxyapatite or β-tricalcium phosphate to improve cell attachment and mechanical performance. Thermal processing inhibits direct cell-laden FDM with these polymers, so cells are typically seeded post-fabrication or incorporated via hybrid designs (Kang et al. 2016; Wang et al. 2021; Liu et al. 2019; Zheng et al. 2022; Gao et al. 2023).

11.3.2.2 Bioceramics and Bioactive Glass

Inorganic-based bioceramics, such as hydroxyapatite (HA), β-tricalcium phosphate (β-TCP), and bioactive glass, resemble the inorganic components of bone tissue and possess excellent osteoconductive properties, making them essential components of bone regeneration scaffolds (Hou et al. 2022). These materials are used as stand-alone scaffolds or as composite bioinks mixed with hydrogels to enhance mechanical stability and promote osteogenic differentiation. Bioceramics are most frequently processed through techniques such as extrusion-based 3D printing and DIW for hydrogel–ceramic composites, binder jetting for powder-based constructs, and light-based methods like SLA/DLP when formulated as photocurable ceramic slurries for high-resolution scaffold fabrication (Vidal et al. 2020; Wang et al. 2021; Kim et al. 2021a; Raymond et al. 2021; Liu et al. 2019; Song et al. 2022; Kolan et al. 2020; Nandi et al. 2018).

11.3.2.3 Metal and Metal Ion Modulation

Metal ions such as magnesium (Mg), strontium (Sr), and zinc (Zn) have been reported to have positive effects on bone tissue remodeling, immune regulation, and angiogenesis. Magnesium-based alloys, in particular, are attracting attention as scaffold materials due to their excellent biodegradability and mechanical strength. Hydrogels doped with metal nanoparticles or ions are being utilized as bioinks that impart osteo-immunomodulation functions, emerging as a strategy for simultaneously targeting bone regeneration and inflammation control (Zhou et al. 2021; Li et al. 2022). These materials are commonly incorporated into extrusion-based printing when used in hydrogel as an ion form, while bulk metallic scaffolds or porous metal structures are often fabricated via LPBF, SLM, and EBM to achieve the required mechanical strength and tailored degradation profiles (Taniguchi et al. 2016; Liu et al. 2019; Dong et al. 2021; Kovacs et al. 2023; Ran et al. 2023).

11.3.2.4 Decellularized Extracellular Matrix

The native extracellular matrix (ECM) delivers complex biochemical and mechanical cues to cells, forming the foundation for tissue regeneration. Bone ECM, a composite of inorganic apatite and organic components (primarily type I collagen and non-collagenous proteins), exhibits osteoconductive properties and, in certain contexts, osteoinductive behavior (Frantz et al. 2010; Lin et al. 2020). From this standpoint, tissue-derived decellularized bone matrix (dBM; a form of bone-derived dECM) has emerged as a natural scaffold for bone repair. Cellular and nuclear materials are removed to reduce immunogenicity while preserving ECM proteins, glycosaminoglycans, and mineral architecture, thereby providing intrinsic biological signals and microstructural features that promote progenitor-cell adhesion and differentiation as well as angiogenesis. Decellularization typically combines chemical, enzymatic, and physical steps, with the central goal of maintaining ECM function while minimizing immune responses. In contemporary biofabrication, dECM is actively deployed as a bioink or functional filler (Pati et al. 2014). dECM is blended with polymers formulate cell-laden inks, or methacrylated dECM hydrogels enable extrusion bioprinting with clinically relevant thickness and cell viability (Lee et al. 2020b; Yun et al. 2021). Currently, research directly utilizing dECM for bone biofabrication is still in its infancy, with few reported cases. Therefore, future research is expected to expand into hybrid/composite combinations of dECM with synthetic polymers such as PCL, PLA, PLGA, and PEEK, as well as bioceramics such as HA, β-TCP, and bioactive glass.

11.3.3 Biofabrication Post-process

Biofabrication techniques provide a versatile platform for generating biomimetic scaffolds tailored for bone regeneration. However, the initial fabrication process alone is often insufficient to meet the complex biological and mechanical requirements of the in vivo environment. The highly dynamic nature of bone, characterized by continuous remodeling and structural complexity, further complicates efforts to fully recapitulate its native architecture (Alaribe et al. 2016). To this end, post-processing strategies are crucial for modifying scaffold characteristics, enhancing mechanical strength, and improving bioactivity. These strategies can be broadly categorized into structural modification for mechanical reinforcement and surface biofunctionalization with growth factors, cells, and extracellular matrix components.

11.3.3.1 Crosslinking

Post-fabrication surface modification plays a critical role in reinforcing the mechanical stability and durability of biofabricated scaffolds, particularly when they are intended for load-bearing applications. Natural and synthetic polymers commonly used in bone tissue engineering—such as collagen, hyaluronic acid, alginate, gelatin methacrylate (GelMA), and polycaprolactone (PCL)—generally exhibit relatively poor mechanical strength and limited structural integrity when compared to native bone tissue (Koons et al. 2020). To address these limitations, post-fabrication crosslinking is commonly employed to enhance the stiffness, elasticity, and structural stability of polymer-based scaffolds. Crosslinking is a widely used strategy to improve the stiffness, elasticity, and long-term stability of these polymer-based scaffolds. In particular, photo-crosslinking using ultraviolet (UV) light or chemical crosslinking agents such as 1-ethyl-3-(3-dimethylaminopropyl) carbodiimide (EDC) and N-hydroxysuccinimide (NHS) enables the formation of covalent bonds between polymer chains, thereby increasing network density and resistance to degradation (Yang 2012). The degree of crosslinking can be precisely controlled by adjusting reaction time, crosslinker concentration, or light exposure parameters, allowing for fine-tuning of mechanical properties to closely resemble those of native bone. Moreover, appropriate crosslinking not only enhances mechanical performance but also improves scaffold handling during surgical implantation, maintains dimensional stability during cell culture, and prolongs scaffold lifespan in vivo. However, excessive crosslinking should be avoided, as it may reduce porosity, hinder cell infiltration, and alter the presentation of biological cues, ultimately compromising the scaffold's regenerative potential. Therefore, careful optimization of crosslinking conditions is essential to balance mechanical reinforcement with biological functionality in bone tissue applications.

11.3.3.2 Surface Modification

Surface coating with inorganic nanoparticles represents an alternative strategy for enhancing the mechanical properties of biofabricated scaffolds. The deposition of inorganic nanoparticles such as hydroxyapatite (HAP), whitlockite (WH), tri-calcium phosphate (β-TCP), and bioactive glass nanoparticles onto the surfaces of biofabricated scaffolds has emerged as a promising post-processing strategy to mimic the mineralized composition of native bone extracellular matrix. These inorganic coatings introduce bioinspired mineral phases that not only increase surface roughness and mechanical hardness but also enhance the scaffold's osteoconductive and osteo-integrative properties (Zhang et al. 2014; Liu et al. 2023). In addition to inorganic coatings, the incorporation of growth factor proteins onto the scaffold surface offers a potent biological strategy to promote cellular activities essential for bone regeneration. Proteins such as bone morphogenetic protein-2 (BMP-2), vascular endothelial growth factor (VEGF), and platelet-derived growth factor (PDGF) can be immobilized or loaded onto the scaffold using covalent binding, heparin-mediated affinity interactions, or encapsulation in microgels for sustained release. These growth factors actively stimulate osteogenesis, angiogenesis, and the recruitment of progenitor cells, thereby accelerating tissue integration and functional recovery. Furthermore, plasma surface modification, including oxygen or nitrogen plasma treatment, can be used to activate the surface of the scaffold by introducing polar functional groups (–OH, –COOH, $–NH_2$). This enhances surface wettability and facilitates subsequent coating with proteins or biomolecules. Plasma treatment also improves cell adhesion and spreading by modifying the surface chemistry without altering the scaffold's bulk mechanical properties. Finally, topographical modification of the scaffold surface at the micro- and nanoscale level—such as grooves, ridges, or nanopillars—has been shown to influence cellular behavior through contact guidance. Techniques such as laser ablation, electrospinning, or lithography can be employed to engineer-specific surface patterns. These features modulate cytoskeletal organization, focal adhesion dynamics, and stem cell lineage commitment, providing a powerful tool to direct osteogenic differentiation and promote tissue organization in a spatially controlled manner.

11.4 Pre-/Clinical Evaluation

The translation of biofabricated materials from bench to bedside requires rigorous preclinical and clinical assessment to ensure safety, efficacy, and reproducibility. Although biofabrication techniques have enabled the generation of highly customized and biomimetic scaffolds for bone tissue engineering, regulatory approval for

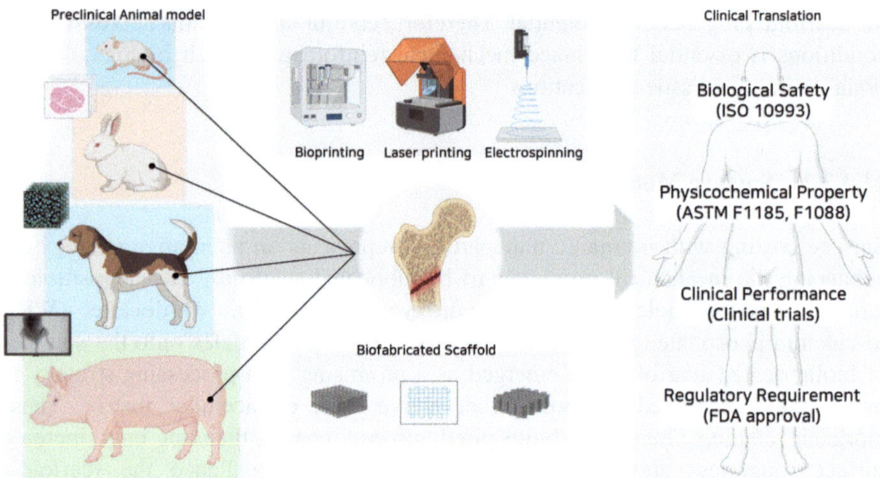

Fig. 11.8 Schematic illustration of preclinical model to clinical translation. (Created in BioRender. Hwang, N. 2025. https://BioRender.com/yyce1bq)

clinical use depends on comprehensive testing that addresses both the mechanical properties and biological functionality of the scaffolds (Martin et al. 2014). This section summarizes the key evaluation strategies employed during preclinical and clinical studies, as well as the challenges that must be addressed to achieve successful clinical translation (Fig. 11.8).

11.4.1 Animal Models

The selection of appropriate animal models is essential for bridging the gap between preclinical and clinical studies. Calvarial defect models in rodents are widely used as critical-sized defects due to their reproducibility and ease of surgical access. These models are ideal for initial proof-of-concept studies focusing on osteoconduction and early bone formation (Spicer et al. 2012). Other bone defect models (long bone, femoral head) provide more clinically relevant load-bearing environments (Kim et al. 2023; Xavier et al. 2022). They allow the evaluation of mechanical performance under physiological stress, as well as endochondral ossification processes. In addition to these models, regenerative models associated with diseases such as spinal fusion, avascular necrosis, and osteoporosis have also been established. Likewise, large-animal models such as sheep, dogs, and pigs are necessary for scaling up to human-sized defects. These models provide more accurate predictions of clinical performance in terms of mechanical stability, immune response, and vascularization.

11.4.2 Parameters

Mechanical and microstructural evaluations can be conducted using regenerated bone harvested from the created defect sites. Micro-computed tomography (μCT) and nano-computed tomography (nanoCT) are widely used to quantify scaffold architecture, bone volume fraction (BV/TV), mineral density, and trabecular microstructure. These imaging modalities also enable longitudinal monitoring of scaffold degradation and bone regeneration over time (Kim et al. 2021b; Peyrin et al. 2014). Mechanical testing is performed using techniques such as compressive strength testing, three-point bending, and push-out tests to evaluate the load-bearing capacity and degree of osseointegration of the regenerated tissue (Bailey and Vashishth 2018).

In parallel with mechanical and structural analyses, immunological and angiogenic assessments are essential to fully understand the host response and regenerative potential of the scaffold. The regenerated tissues and peri-implant regions harvested from animal models can be analyzed using single-cell RNA sequencing (scRNA-seq), flow cytometry, and immunohistochemistry to map the phenotypic and functional states of immune cells. Particular attention is paid to macrophage polarization (e.g., M1 vs. M2) and T-cell responses, which play pivotal roles in orchestrating tissue repair (Moon et al. 2023). Angiogenic response is typically evaluated using immunofluorescent staining for endothelial markers (e.g., CD31, VEGFR2) and pericyte markers, in addition to quantifying vascular density and maturity through μCT angiography or Doppler ultrasound. These analyses reveal how the scaffold influences neovascularization, which is critical for nutrient delivery and long-term integration.

11.4.3 Clinical Translation

For clinical translation, scaffolds must comply with rigorous safety and regulatory requirements defined by international standards and governing bodies. Currently, for example, bone graft substitutes for dental materials and pre−/clinical testing guidelines are well-defined. Specifically, there is the guideline for biological evaluation of medical devices (ISO 10993). It provides detailed procedures for the biological evaluation of medical devices and their constituent materials, including tests for irritation. Representative examples include tests for genotoxicity, carcinogenicity, and reproductive toxicity (ISO 10993-3); tests for interactions with blood (ISO 10993-4); tests for in vitro cytotoxicity (ISO 10993-5); tests for irritation and skin sensitization (ISO 10993-10); tests for systemic toxicity (ISO 10993-11); identification and quantification of degradation products from polymeric, ceramics, metals, and alloys medical devices (ISO 10993-13,14,15); etc. Beyond these safety evaluations, physicochemical characterization of the bone graft material is also required to demonstrate product consistency and performance. Such evaluations typically include (1) porosity and pore size analysis, which are critical for ensuring cell infiltration and vascular ingrowth; (2) compressive strength testing, which verifies the mechanical integrity of the scaffold, particularly for load-bearing applications; and (3) additional structural and compositional assessments, such as phase composition, Ca/P ratio, and degradation kinetics (ASTM F1185, F1088, and related standards).

While these pre-/clinical evaluation frameworks are well established for conventional bone graft substitutes, it should be noted that the field of biofabricated scaffolds is rapidly evolving. Novel designs incorporating living cells, growth factors, or dynamic architectures may not be fully addressed by current guidelines. Therefore, future regulatory frameworks must be adapted to accommodate the unique characteristics of next-generation biofabricated constructs, with particular emphasis on long-term safety, immunological compatibility, and clinical efficacy.

11.5 Future Perspectives

Recent advances in artificial intelligence (AI) are fundamentally reshaping the landscape of bone tissue engineering, particularly through the usage of machine learning and digital twin technologies into biofabrication workflows. With the growing availability of high-resolution imaging, patient-specific omics data, and digitally integrated fabrication platforms, machine learning models such as deep/convolutional neural networks, gradient boosting, and reinforcement learning are expected to evolve from passive predictors into active design partners—guiding the generation of optimal scaffold architectures, bioink formulations, and even dynamic culture conditions in real time (Kolomenskaya et al. 2024; Fang et al. 2021; Hsieh et al. 2021; Wu et al. 2024d; Peng et al. 2023). Among the most promising embodiments of AI in biofabrication is the concept of digital twin—a dynamic, data-driven virtual replica of patient-specific biological environments that integrates real-time monitoring, machine learning-based predictive modeling, and iterative adaptation of design and function throughout the regeneration timeline (Ahmed et al. 2024; Zhou et al. 2025; Diniz et al. 2025). By linking in silico simulations with empirical data, digital twins offer a platform for optimizing fabrication parameters and conducting personalized preclinical trials (Ahmadian et al. 2022; Sun et al. 2023). The synergistic convergence of AI and biofabrication offers a compelling vision: a precise, efficient, and personalized solution for bone regeneration.

The evolution of biofabrication technologies has also facilitated the development of scaffold systems tailored to individual patient needs in bone tissue engineering. Enabled by advances in medical imaging, computer-aided design (CAD), and additive manufacturing, anatomically customized scaffolds can be fabricated with high fidelity to conform precisely to the geometry of individual bone defects, offering enhanced fit and surgical predictability (Mekhileri et al. 2018; Costa et al. 2014; Koc et al. 2019). Personalized implant scaffolds—predominantly composed

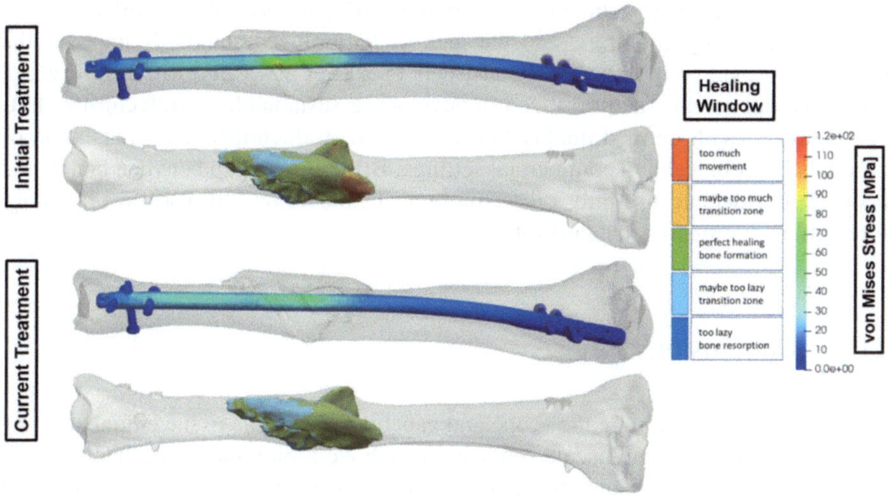

Fig. 11.9 Utilization of digital twin technology in orthopedics: FEA analysis of a patient's femur fracture treated with an intramedullary nail (Andres et al. 2025)

of PCL and TCP—have already been investigated in several clinical trials, highlighting their translational potential in patient-specific bone regeneration (Xu and Ivanovski 2025). While anatomical personalization has become increasingly feasible, there has been growing interest in integrating immunomodulatory strategies into patient-specific scaffold design. Several preclinical studies have begun to explore how scaffold properties can be tailored to modulate host immune responses, with the goal of improving tissue regeneration outcomes in a personalized manner (Chen et al. 2020; Biglari et al. 2025; Raheem et al. 2025). These efforts reflect a shift toward immunologically responsive scaffolds that not only match the anatomical defect but also actively engage with the patient's immune microenvironment. Despite this progress, several challenges remain in the clinical translation of such complex scaffolds—including the need for scalable and standardized immuno-characterization methods, regulatory pathways for personalized biomaterials, and effective prediction of patient-specific immune outcomes. To address these challenges, optimal digital twin technologies—integrating patient-derived anatomical, physiological, and immunological data—will be essential for the rational design and real-time adaptation of truly personalized scaffolds (Fig. 11.9).

As biofabrication technologies mature, the future of biofabrication hinges on the successful integration of sustainable scale-up strategies with robust standardization frameworks. Emerging innovations such as automated multi-material bioprinters, AI-driven quality control, and modular bioreactor systems promise to unlock new possibilities for high-throughput, clinically viable constructs (Sears et al. 2017; Filippi et al. 2025; Kazimierczak and Przekora 2022). Concurrently, there is a growing urgency to establish standardized protocols for bioink formulation, scaffold characterization, and functional validation. Regulatory frameworks remain fragmented among countries, and the lack of harmonized standards impedes the clinical approval of biofabricated constructs (Sekar et al. 2021). Moving forward, future directions must be prioritized in developing sustainable manufacturing strategies aligned with defined quality benchmarks, reproducibility, and translation of products into clinical and commercial settings. Bridging the gap between bench and bedside will depend not only on technological innovation but also on regulatory foresight and systemic standardization.

11.6 Conclusion

Biofabrication is redefining the scope and capabilities of bone tissue engineering by enabling the precise, multiscale replication of bone's biological, mechanical, and spatial complexity. Through the integration of advanced additive manufacturing platforms, bioactive biomaterials, vascularization strategies, and gradient architectures, it is now possible to engineer constructs that not only restore bone morphology but also recapitulate its functional microenvironment. As standardized evaluation protocols, clinical translation frameworks, and ethical guidelines mature, the incorporation of artificial intelligence and digital twin systems will further accelerate the optimization and personalization of biofabricated bone constructs. Collectively, these developments position biofabrication as a transformative driver for the next generation of patient-specific, functional bone regeneration therapies.

Competing Interests The author(s) has no competing interests to declare that are relevant to the content of this manuscript.

References

Ahmadian H et al (2022) Toward an artificial intelligence-assisted framework for reconstructing the digital twin of vertebra and predicting its fracture response. Int J Numer Meth Bio 38:e3601. https://doi.org/10.1002/cnm.3601

Ahmed N, Narayanan LK, Shirwaiker R (2024) A framework for digital twin integration in biofabrication and a scaffold 3D bioplotting case study. Manuf Lett 41:1182–1191. https://doi.org/10.1016/j.mfglet.2024.09.144

Ahn JH et al (2021) 3D-printed biodegradable composite scaffolds with significantly enhanced mechanical properties via the combination of binder jetting and capillary rise infiltration process. Addit Manuf 41:101988. https://doi.org/10.1016/j.addma.2021.101988

Alaribe FN, Manoto SL, Motaung SCKM (2016) Scaffolds from biomaterials: advantages and limitations in bone and tissue engineering. Biologia 71:353–366. https://doi.org/10.1515/biolog-2016-0056

Alparslan C, Bayraktar S (2025) Advances in digital light processing (DLP) bioprinting: a review of biomaterials and its applications, innovations, challenges, and future perspectives. Polymers (Basel) 17. https://doi.org/10.3390/polym17091287

Alvarez-Castano MI et al (2025) Holographic tomographic volumetric additive manufacturing. Nat Commun 16:1551. https://doi.org/10.1038/s41467-025-56852-4

Andres A et al (2025) Advantages of digital twin technology in orthopedic trauma surgery—exploring different clinical use cases. Sci Rep 15:19987. https://doi.org/10.1038/s41598-025-04792-w

Avila JD, Stenberg K, Bose S, Bandyopadhyay A (2021) Hydroxyapatite reinforced Ti6Al4V composites for load-bearing implants. Acta Biomater 123:379–392. https://doi.org/10.1016/j.actbio.2020.12.060

Baht GS, Vi L, Alman BA (2018) The role of the immune cells in fracture healing. Curr Osteoporos Rep 16:138–145. https://doi.org/10.1007/s11914-018-0423-2

Bailey S, Vashishth D (2018) Mechanical characterization of bone: state of the art in experimental approaches-what types of experiments do people do and how does one interpret the results? Curr Osteoporos Rep 16:423–433. https://doi.org/10.1007/s11914-018-0454-8

Bedell ML et al (2023) The effect of multi-material architecture on the ex vivo osteochondral integration of bioprinted constructs. Acta Biomater 155:99–112. https://doi.org/10.1016/j.actbio.2022.11.014

Beheshtizadeh N, Azami M, Abbasi H, Farzin A (2022) Applying extrusion-based 3D printing technique accelerates fabricating complex biphasic calcium phosphate-based scaffolds for bone tissue regeneration. J Adv Res 40:69–94. https://doi.org/10.1016/j.jare.2021.12.012

Beisekenov N, Sadenova M, Azamatov B, Syrnev B (2025) Analysis of biomechanical characteristics of bone tissues using a Bayesian neural network: a narrative review. J Funct Biomater 16. https://doi.org/10.3390/jfb16050168

Bernal PN et al (2019) Volumetric bioprinting of complex living-tissue constructs within seconds. Adv Mater 31:1904209. https://doi.org/10.1002/adma.201904209

Biemond JE, Hannink G, Verdonschot N, Buma P (2013) Bone ingrowth potential of electron beam and selective laser melting produced trabecular-like implant surfaces with and without a biomimetic coating. J Mater Sci-Mater M 24:745–753. https://doi.org/10.1007/s10856-012-4836-7

Biglari N et al (2025) Advanced biomaterials in immune modulation: The future of regenerative therapies. Int J Pharm 682:125972. https://doi.org/10.1016/j.ijpharm.2025.125972

Bolamperti S, Villa I, Rubinacci A (2022) Bone remodeling: an operational process ensuring survival and bone mechanical competence. Bone Res 10:48. https://doi.org/10.1038/s41413-022-00219-8

Cao S, Zou YC, Lim CVS, Wu XH (2021) Review of laser powder bed fusion (LPBF) fabricated Ti-6Al-4V: process, post-process treatment, microstructure, and property. Light-Adv Manuf 2: 20. https://doi.org/10.37188/lam.2021.020

Carluccio D, Demir AG, Bermingham MJ, Dargusch MS (2020) Challenges and opportunities in the selective laser melting of biodegradable metals for load-bearing bone scaffold applications. Metall Mater Trans A 51:3311–3334. https://doi.org/10.1007/s11661-020-05796-z

Chen SX et al (2020) Mesenchymal stem cell-laden, personalized 3D scaffolds with controlled structure and fiber alignment promote diabetic wound healing. Acta Biomater 108:153–167. https://doi.org/10.1016/j.actbio.2020.03.035

Cooper GM et al (2010) Inkjet-based biopatterning of bone morphogenetic protein-2 to spatially control calvarial bone formation. Tissue Eng Part A 16:1749–1759. https://doi.org/10.1089/ten.TEA.2009.0650

Costa PF et al (2014) Biofabrication of customized bone grafts by combination of additive manufacturing and bioreactor knowhow. Biofabrication 6:035006. https://doi.org/10.1088/1758-5082/6/3/035006

Daneshmandi L, Holt BD, Arnold AM, Laurencin CT, Sydlik SA (2022) Ultra-low binder content 3D printed calcium phosphate graphene scaffolds as resorbable, osteoinductive matrices that support bone formation in vivo. Sci Rep 12:6960. https://doi.org/10.1038/s41598-022-10603-3

Davoodi E et al (2020) Extrusion and microfluidic-based bioprinting to fabricate biomimetic tissues and organs. Adv Mater Technol 5. https://doi.org/10.1002/admt.201901044

Derakhshanfar S et al (2018) 3D bioprinting for biomedical devices and tissue engineering: a review of recent trends and advances. Bioact Mater 3:144–156. https://doi.org/10.1016/j.bioactmat.2017.11.008

Diniz P et al (2025) Digital twin systems for musculoskeletal applications: a current concepts review. Knee Surg Sport Tr A 33:1892–1910. https://doi.org/10.1002/ksa.12627

DiNoro JN et al (2022) Laser sintering approaches for bone tissue engineering. Polymers (Basel) 14. https://doi.org/10.3390/polym14122336

Dong Q et al (2021) 3D-printed Mg-incorporated PCL-based scaffolds: a promising approach for bone healing. Mater Sci Eng C Mater Biol Appl 129:112372. https://doi.org/10.1016/j.msec.2021.112372

Du WC, Ren XR, Pei ZJ, Ma C (2020) Ceramic binder jetting additive manufacturing: a literature review on density. J Manuf Sci E-T Asme 142:040801. https://doi.org/10.1115/1.4046248

Dua R, Rashad Z, Spears J, Dunn G, Maxwell M (2021) Applications of 3D-printed PEEK via fused filament fabrication: a systematic review. Polymers (Basel) 13. https://doi.org/10.3390/polym13224046

Einhorn TA, Gerstenfeld LC (2015) Fracture healing: mechanisms and interventions. Nat Rev Rheumatol 11:45–54. https://doi.org/10.1038/nrrheum.2014.164

Fakhry M, Hamade E, Badran B, Buchet R, Magne D (2013) Molecular mechanisms of mesenchymal stem cell differentiation towards osteoblasts. World J Stem Cells 5:136–148. https://doi.org/10.4252/wjsc.v5.i4.136

Fang YJ et al (2021) Opportunistic osteoporosis screening in multi-detector CT images using deep convolutional neural networks. Eur Radiol 31:1831–1842. https://doi.org/10.1007/s00330-020-07312-8

Fedorovich NE, De Wijn JR, Verbout AJ, Alblas J, Dhert WJ (2008) Three-dimensional fiber deposition of cell-laden, viable, patterned constructs for bone tissue printing. Tissue Eng Part A 14:127–133. https://doi.org/10.1089/ten.a.2007.0158

Filippi M, Mekkattu M, Katzschmann RK (2025) Sustainable biofabrication: from bioprinting to AI-driven predictive methods. Trends Biotechnol 43:290–303. https://doi.org/10.1016/j.tibtech.2024.07.002

Frade BB, Dias RB, Gemini Piperni S, Bonfim DC (2023) The role of macrophages in fracture healing: a narrative review of the recent updates and therapeutic perspectives. Stem Cell Investig 10:4. https://doi.org/10.21037/sci-2022-038

Franco J, Hunger P, Launey ME, Tomsia AP, Saiz E (2010) Direct write assembly of calcium phosphate scaffolds using a water-based hydrogel. Acta Biomater 6:218–228. https://doi.org/10.1016/j.actbio.2009.06.031

Frantz C, Stewart KM, Weaver VM (2010) The extracellular matrix at a glance. J Cell Sci 123: 4195–4200. https://doi.org/10.1242/jcs.023820

Freeman FE et al (2020) 3D bioprinting spatiotemporally defined patterns of growth factors to tightly control tissue regeneration. Sci Adv 6:eabb5093. https://doi.org/10.1126/sciadv.abb5093

Gao J et al (2023) 3D-printed GelMA/PEGDA/F127DA scaffolds for bone regeneration. J Funct Biomater 14. https://doi.org/10.3390/jfb14020096

Gayer C et al (2019) Development of a solvent-free polylactide/calcium carbonate composite for selective laser sintering of bone tissue engineering scaffolds. Mater Sci Eng C Mater Biol Appl 101:660–673. https://doi.org/10.1016/j.msec.2019.03.101

Gehlen J, Qiu WW, Schädli GN, Müller R, Qin XH (2023) Tomographic volumetric bioprinting of heterocellular bone-like tissues in seconds. Acta Biomater 156:49–60. https://doi.org/10.1016/j.actbio.2022.06.020

Ghezzi B et al (2024) Composite PCL scaffold with 70% beta-TCP as suitable structure for bone replacement. Int Dent J 74:1220–1232. https://doi.org/10.1016/j.identj.2024.02.013

Guo WW et al (2023) 3D printing of multifunctional gradient bone scaffolds with programmable component distribution and hierarchical pore structure. Compos Part A-Appl S 166:107361. https://doi.org/10.1016/j.compositesa.2022.107361

Guo WW et al (2025) Direct ink writing of functionally graded bone scaffolds using ceramic foams to mimic natural bone hierarchical porosity and multiple gradients. Compos Part B Eng 300: 112465. https://doi.org/10.1016/j.compositesb.2025.112465

Hadjidakis DJ, Androulakis II (2006) Bone remodeling. Ann N Y Acad Sci 1092:385–396. https://doi.org/10.1196/annals.1365.035

Han Y et al (2021) Effect of pore size on cell behavior using melt Electrowritten scaffolds. Front Bioeng Biotechnol 9:629270. https://doi.org/10.3389/fbioe.2021.629270

Han Y et al (2022) The secretion profile of mesenchymal stem cells and potential applications in treating human diseases. Signal Transduct Target Ther 7:92. https://doi.org/10.1038/s41392-022-00932-0

Han J et al (2023) Biodegradable BBG/PCL composite scaffolds fabricated by selective laser sintering for directed regeneration of critical-sized bone defects. Mater Design 225:111543. https://doi.org/10.1016/j.matdes.2022.111543

Hench LL, Polak JM (2002) Third-generation biomedical materials. Science 295:1014–1017. https://doi.org/10.1126/science.1067404

Herberg S et al (2014) Inkjet-based biopatterning of SDF-1beta augments BMP-2-induced repair of critical size calvarial bone defects in mice. Bone 67:95–103. https://doi.org/10.1016/j.bone.2014.07.007

Hersel U, Dahmen C, Kessler H (2003) RGD modified polymers: biomaterials for stimulated cell adhesion and beyond. Biomaterials 24:4385–4415. https://doi.org/10.1016/s0142-9612(03)00343-0

Hinton TJ et al (2015) Three-dimensional printing of complex biological structures by freeform reversible embedding of suspended hydrogels. Sci Adv 1:e1500758. https://doi.org/10.1126/sciadv.1500758

Hou X et al (2022) Calcium phosphate-based biomaterials for bone repair. J Funct Biomater 13. https://doi.org/10.3390/jfb13040187

Hsieh CI et al (2021) Automated bone mineral density prediction and fracture risk assessment using plain radiographs via deep learning. Nat Commun 12:5472. https://doi.org/10.1038/s41467-021-25779-x

Hutmacher DW et al (2001) Mechanical properties and cell cultural response of polycaprolactone scaffolds designed and fabricated via fused deposition modeling. J Biomed Mater Res 55:203–216. https://doi.org/10.1002/1097-4636(200105)55:2<203::aid-jbm1007>3.0.co;2-7

Jakus AE et al (2016) Hyperelastic "bone": a highly versatile, growth factor-free, osteoregenerative, scalable, and surgically friendly biomaterial. Sci Transl Med 8:358ra127. https://doi.org/10.1126/scitranslmed.aaf7704

Jeong J, Kim JH, Shim JH, Hwang NS, Heo CY (2019) Bioactive calcium phosphate materials and applications in bone regeneration. Biomater Res 23:4. https://doi.org/10.1186/s40824-018-0149-3

Jeong WS et al (2022) Clinical application of 3D-printed patient-specific Polycaprolactone/Beta Tricalcium phosphate scaffold for complex Zygomatico-maxillary defects. Polymers (Basel) 14. https://doi.org/10.3390/polym14040740

Kade JC, Dalton PD (2021) Polymers for melt electrowriting. Adv Healthc Mater 10:2001232. https://doi.org/10.1002/adhm.202001232

Kang HW et al (2016) A 3D bioprinting system to produce human-scale tissue constructs with structural integrity. Nat Biotechnol 34:312–319. https://doi.org/10.1038/nbt.3413

Kazimierczak P, Przekora A (2022) Bioengineered living bone grafts-a concise review on bioreactors and production techniques in vitro. Int J Mol Sci 23:1765. https://doi.org/10.3390/ijms23031765

Ke DX, Bose S (2018) Effects of pore distribution and chemistry on physical, mechanical, and biological properties of tricalcium phosphate scaffolds by binder-jet 3D printing. Addit Manuf 22:111–117. https://doi.org/10.1016/j.addma.2018.04.020

Ke D, Vu AA, Bandyopadhyay A, Bose S (2019) Compositionally graded doped hydroxyapatite coating on titanium using laser and plasma spray deposition for bone implants. Acta Biomater 84:414–423. https://doi.org/10.1016/j.actbio.2018.11.041

Kilian D et al (2020) 3D Bioprinting of osteochondral tissue substitutes - -chondrogenesis in multi-layered mineralized constructs. Sci Rep-Uk 10:8277. https://doi.org/10.1038/s41598-020-65050-9

Kim JW, Lee JB, Koh YH, Kim HE (2019) Digital light processing of freeze-cast ceramic layers for macroporous calcium phosphate scaffolds with tailored microporous frameworks. Materials (Basel) 12. https://doi.org/10.3390/ma12182893

Kim Y et al (2021a) Biofabrication of 3D printed hydroxyapatite composite scaffolds for bone regeneration. Biomed Mater 16. https://doi.org/10.1088/1748-605X/abcf03

Kim Y, Brodt MD, Tang SY, Silva MJ (2021b) MicroCT for scanning and analysis of mouse bones. Methods Mol Biol 2230:169–198. https://doi.org/10.1007/978-1-0716-1028-2_11

Kim JH et al (2023) Antioxidant-Coated multifunctional whitlockite scaffold for the treatment of Steroid-Induced osteonecrosis of the femoral head. Chem Eng J 474:145362. https://doi.org/10.1016/j.cej.2023.145362

Kim W et al (2025) 3D bioprinted multi-layered cell constructs with gradient core-shell interface for tendon-to-bone tissue regeneration. Bioact Mater 43:471–490. https://doi.org/10.1016/j.bioactmat.2024.10.002

Kjar A, McFarland B, Mecham K, Harward N, Huang Y (2021) Engineering of tissue constructs using coaxial bioprinting. Bioact Mater 6:460–471. https://doi.org/10.1016/j.bioactmat.2020.08.020

Koc B et al (2019) Biomanufacturing of customized modular scaffolds for critical bone defects. Cirp Ann-Manuf Techn 68:209–212. https://doi.org/10.1016/j.cirp.2019.04.106

Kolan KCR, Huang YW, Semon JA, Leu MC (2020) 3D-printed biomimetic bioactive glass scaffolds for bone regeneration in rat calvarial defects. Int J Bioprint 6:274. https://doi.org/10.18063/ijb.v6i2.274

Kolomenskaya E, Butova V, Poltavskiy A, Soldatov A, Butakova M (2024) Application of artificial intelligence at all stages of bone tissue engineering. Biomedicines 12:76. https://doi.org/10.3390/biomedicines12010076

Koons GL, Diba M, Mikos AG (2020) Materials design for bone-tissue engineering. Nat Rev Mater 5:584–603. https://doi.org/10.1038/s41578-020-0204-2

Kovacs AE et al (2023) Comparative analysis of bone ingrowth in 3D-printed titanium lattice structures with different patterns. Materials (Basel) 16. https://doi.org/10.3390/ma16103861

Kuang X et al (2019) Grayscale digital light processing 3D printing for highly functionally graded materials. Sci Adv 5:eaav5790. https://doi.org/10.1126/sciadv.aav5790

Kusumbe AP, Ramasamy SK, Adams RH (2014) Coupling of angiogenesis and osteogenesis by a specific vessel subtype in bone. Nature 507:323–328. https://doi.org/10.1038/nature13145

Lee S, Choi D, Shim JH, Nam W (2020a) Efficacy of three-dimensionally printed polycaprolactone/beta tricalcium phosphate scaffold on mandibular reconstruction. Sci Rep 10:4979. https://doi.org/10.1038/s41598-020-61944-w

Lee J, Hong J, Kim W, Kim GH (2020b) Bone-derived dECM/alginate bioink for fabricating a 3D cell-laden mesh structure for bone tissue engineering. Carbohydr Polym 250:116914. https://doi.org/10.1016/j.carbpol.2020.116914

Lewis JA (2006) Direct ink writing of 3D functional materials. Adv Funct Mater 16:2193–2204. https://doi.org/10.1002/adfm.200600434

Lewis JA, Smay JE, Stuecker J, Cesarano J (2006) Direct ink writing of three-dimensional ceramic structures. J Am Ceram Soc 89:3599–3609. https://doi.org/10.1111/j.1551-2916.2006.01382.x

Li S et al (2022) Application of bioactive metal ions in the treatment of bone defects. J Mater Chem B 10:9369–9388. https://doi.org/10.1039/d2tb01684b

Li W et al (2023) Stereolithography apparatus and digital light processing-based 3D bioprinting for tissue fabrication. Iscience 26:106039. https://doi.org/10.1016/j.isci.2023.106039

Liang H et al (2022) Nano-hydroxyapatite bone scaffolds with different porous structures processed by digital light processing 3D printing. Int J Bioprint 8:502. https://doi.org/10.18063/ijb.v8i1.502

Lin X, Patil S, Gao YG, Qian A (2020) The bone extracellular matrix in bone formation and regeneration. Front Pharmacol 11:757. https://doi.org/10.3389/fphar.2020.00757

Liu DH et al (2019) 3D printed PCL/SrHA scaffold for enhanced bone regeneration. Chem Eng J 362:269–279. https://doi.org/10.1016/j.cej.2019.01.015

Liu QZ et al (2023) Bioactive magnesium-based whitlockite ceramic as bone cement additives for enhancing osseointegration and bone regeneration. Mater Design 229:111914. https://doi.org/10.1016/j.matdes.2023.111914

Liu Y et al (2025) Gradient scaffolds in bone-soft tissue interface engineering: structural characteristics, fabrication techniques, and emerging trends. J Orthop Translat 50:333–353. https://doi.org/10.1016/j.jot.2024.10.015

Loewner S et al (2022) Recent advances in melt electro writing for tissue engineering for 3D printing of microporous scaffolds for tissue engineering. Front Bioeng Biotech 10:896719. https://doi.org/10.3389/fbioe.2022.896719

Luo Z et al (2023) Digital light processing 3D printing for microfluidic chips with enhanced resolution via dosing- and zoning-controlled vat photopolymerization. Microsyst Nanoeng 9: 103. https://doi.org/10.1038/s41378-023-00542-y

Malda J et al (2013) 25th anniversary article: engineering hydrogels for biofabrication. Adv Mater 25:5011–5028. https://doi.org/10.1002/adma.201302042

Marsell R, Einhorn TA (2011) The biology of fracture healing. Injury 42:551–555. https://doi.org/10.1016/j.injury.2011.03.031

Martin I, Simmons PJ, Williams DF (2014) Manufacturing challenges in regenerative medicine. Sci Transl Med 6:232fs16. https://doi.org/10.1126/scitranslmed.3008558

Mccauley PJ, Bayles AV (2024) Nozzle innovations that improve capacity and capabilities of multimaterial additive manufacturing. ACS Eng Au 4:368–380. https://doi.org/10.1021/acsengineeringau.4c00001

Mekhileri NV et al (2018) Automated 3D bioassembly of micro-tissues for biofabrication of hybrid tissue engineered constructs. Biofabrication 10:024103. https://doi.org/10.1088/1758-5090/aa9ef1

Miri AK et al (2019) Effective bioprinting resolution in tissue model fabrication. Lab Chip 19: 2019–2037. https://doi.org/10.1039/c8lc01037d

Mo Y et al (2025) Multi-material DLP printing: enhanced layer stacking precision with common flexible interface support. J Manuf Process 141:1011–1019. https://doi.org/10.1016/j.jmapro.2025.03.040

Moon S, Hong J, Go S, Kim BS (2023) Immunomodulation for tissue repair and regeneration. Tissue Eng Regen Med 20:389–409. https://doi.org/10.1007/s13770-023-00525-0

Morgan EF, Unnikrisnan GU, Hussein AI (2018) Bone mechanical properties in healthy and diseased states. Annu Rev Biomed Eng 20:119–143. https://doi.org/10.1146/annurev-bioeng-062117-121139

Murr LE, Gaytan SM, Martinez E, Medina F, Wicker RB (2012) Next generation orthopaedic implants by additive manufacturing using electron beam melting. Int J Biomater 2012:245727. https://doi.org/10.1155/2012/245727

Muth JT, Dixon PG, Woish L, Gibson LJ, Lewis JA (2017) Architected cellular ceramics with tailored stiffness via direct foam writing. Proc Natl Acad Sci USA 114:1832–1837. https://doi.org/10.1073/pnas.1616769114

Nandi SK, Fielding G, Banerjee D, Bandyopadhyay A, Bose S (2018) 3D printed beta-TCP bone tissue engineering scaffolds: effects of chemistry on in vivo biological properties in a rabbit tibia model. J Mater Res 33:1939–1947. https://doi.org/10.1557/jmr.2018.233

Negro A, Cherbuin T, Lutolf MP (2018) 3D inkjet printing of complex, cell-laden hydrogel structures. Sci Rep 8:17099. https://doi.org/10.1038/s41598-018-35504-2

Niu X, Li N, Du Z, Li X (2023) Integrated gradient tissue-engineered osteochondral scaffolds: challenges, current efforts and future perspectives. Bioact Mater 20:574–597. https://doi.org/10.1016/j.bioactmat.2022.06.011

O'Brien FJ (2011) Biomaterials & scaffolds for tissue engineering. Mater Today 14:88–95. https://doi.org/10.1016/S1369-7021(11)70058-X

Palmquist A, Jolic M, Hryha E, Shah FA (2023) Complex geometry and integrated macro-porosity: clinical applications of electron beam melting to fabricate bespoke bone-anchored implants. Acta Biomater 156:125–145. https://doi.org/10.1016/j.actbio.2022.06.002

Pati F et al (2014) Printing three-dimensional tissue analogues with decellularized extracellular matrix bioink. Nat Commun 5:3935. https://doi.org/10.1038/ncomms4935

Pattanayak DK et al (2011) Bioactive Ti metal analogous to human cancellous bone: fabrication by selective laser melting and chemical treatments. Acta Biomater 7:1398–1406. https://doi.org/10.1016/j.actbio.2010.09.034
Peng B et al (2023) Machine learning-enabled constrained multi-objective design of architected materials. Nat Commun 14:6630. https://doi.org/10.1038/s41467-023-42415-y
Peyrin F, Dong P, Pacureanu A, Langer M (2014) Micro- and nano-CT for the study of bone ultrastructure. Curr Osteoporos Rep 12:465–474. https://doi.org/10.1007/s11914-014-0233-0
Pitacco P, Sadowska JM, O'Brien FJ, Kelly DJ (2023) 3D bioprinting of cartilaginous templates for large bone defect healing. Acta Biomater 156:61–74. https://doi.org/10.1016/j.actbio.2022.07.037
Placone JK, Engler AJ (2018) Recent advances in extrusion-based 3D printing for biomedical applications. Adv Healthc Mater 7:e1701161. https://doi.org/10.1002/adhm.201701161
Qin L, Liu W, Cao H, Xiao G (2020) Molecular mechanosensors in osteocytes. Bone Res 8:23. https://doi.org/10.1038/s41413-020-0099-y
Quan H et al (2020) Photo-curing 3D printing technique and its challenges. Bioact Mater 5:110–115. https://doi.org/10.1016/j.bioactmat.2019.12.003
Rad ZF, Prewett PD, Davies GJ (2021) High-resolution two-photon polymerization: the most versatile technique for the fabrication of microneedle arrays. Microsyst Nanoeng 7:71. https://doi.org/10.1038/s41378-021-00298-3
Raggatt LJ, Partridge NC (2010) Cellular and molecular mechanisms of bone remodeling. J Biol Chem 285:25103–25108. https://doi.org/10.1074/jbc.R109.041087
Raheem A et al (2025) Smart biomaterials in healthcare: breakthroughs in tissue engineering, immunomodulation, patient-specific therapies, and biosensor applications. Appl Phys Rev 12: 011333. https://doi.org/10.1063/5.0238817
Ran Z et al (2023) 3D-printed biodegradable magnesium alloy scaffolds with zoledronic acid-loaded ceramic composite coating promote osteoporotic bone defect repair. Int J Bioprint 9:769. https://doi.org/10.18063/ijb.769
Raymond Y et al (2021) Hydrothermal processing of 3D-printed calcium phosphate scaffolds enhances bone formation in vivo: a comparison with biomimetic treatment. Acta Biomater 135:671–688. https://doi.org/10.1016/j.actbio.2021.09.001
Raymond Y et al (2022) 3D printing with star-shaped strands: a new approach to enhance in vivo bone regeneration. Biomater Adv 137:212807. https://doi.org/10.1016/j.bioadv.2022.212807
Roohani I et al (2025) Bioinspired nanoscale 3D printing of calcium phosphates using bone prenucleation clusters. Adv Mater 37. https://doi.org/10.1002/adma.202413626
Roseti L et al (2017) Scaffolds for bone tissue engineering: state of the art and new perspectives. Mater Sci Eng C Mater Biol Appl 78:1246–1262. https://doi.org/10.1016/j.msec.2017.05.017
Ryu DJ et al (2020) Osteo-compatibility of 3D titanium porous coating applied by direct energy deposition (DED) for a Cementless Total knee arthroplasty implant: in vitro and in vivo study. J Clin Med 9. https://doi.org/10.3390/jcm9020478
Ryu DJ et al (2021) Enhanced osseointegration through direct energy deposition porous coating for cementless orthopedic implant fixation. Sci Rep-Uk 11:22317. https://doi.org/10.1038/s41598-021-01739-9
Saadi MASR et al (2022) Direct ink writing: a 3D printing technology for diverse materials. Adv Mater 34:2108855. https://doi.org/10.1002/adma.202108855
Saiz PG, Reizabal A, Vilas-Vilela JL, Dalton PD, Lanceros-Mendez S (2024) Materials and strategies to enhance melt Electrowriting potential. Adv Mater 36. https://doi.org/10.1002/adma.202312084
Schaffler MB, Kennedy OD (2012) Osteocyte signaling in bone. Curr Osteoporos Rep 10:118–125. https://doi.org/10.1007/s11914-012-0105-4
Schindeler A, McDonald MM, Bokko P, Little DG (2008) Bone remodeling during fracture repair: the cellular picture. Semin Cell Dev Biol 19:459–466. https://doi.org/10.1016/j.semcdb.2008.07.004
Sears N, Dhavalikar P, Whitely M, Cosgriff-Hernandez E (2017) Fabrication of biomimetic bone grafts with multi-material 3D printing. Biofabrication 9:025020. https://doi.org/10.1088/1758-5090/aa7077

Sekar MP et al (2021) Current standards and ethical landscape of engineered tissues-3D bioprinting perspective. J Tissue Eng 12:20417314211027677. https://doi.org/10.1177/20417314211027677

Shin SH, Purevdorj O, Castano O, Planell JA, Kim HW (2012) A short review: recent advances in electrospinning for bone tissue regeneration. J Tissue Eng 3:2041731412443530. https://doi.org/10.1177/2041731412443530

Sivaraj KK, Adams RH (2016) Blood vessel formation and function in bone. Development 143:2706–2715. https://doi.org/10.1242/dev.136861

Skylar-Scott MA et al (2019) Biomanufacturing of organ-specific tissues with high cellular density and embedded vascular channels. Sci Adv 5:eaaw2459. https://doi.org/10.1126/sciadv.aaw2459

Song N, Scholtemeijer M, Shah K (2020) Mesenchymal stem cell immunomodulation: mechanisms and therapeutic potential. Trends Pharmacol Sci 41:653–664. https://doi.org/10.1016/j.tips.2020.06.009

Song P et al (2022) DLP fabricating of precision GelMA/HAp porous composite scaffold for bone tissue engineering application. Compos Part B-Eng 244:110163. https://doi.org/10.1016/j.compositesb.2022.110163

Spicer PP et al (2012) Evaluation of bone regeneration using the rat critical size calvarial defect. Nat Protoc 7:1918–1929. https://doi.org/10.1038/nprot.2012.113

Sun T, He X, Li Z (2023) Digital twin in healthcare: recent updates and challenges. Digit Health 9:20552076221149651. https://doi.org/10.1177/20552076221149651

Svetlizky D et al (2021) Directed energy deposition (DED) additive manufacturing: physical characteristics, defects, challenges and applications. Mater Today 49:271–295. https://doi.org/10.1016/j.mattod.2021.03.020

Takayanagi H (2007) Osteoimmunology: shared mechanisms and crosstalk between the immune and bone systems. Nat Rev Immunol 7:292–304. https://doi.org/10.1038/nri2062

Taniguchi N et al (2016) Effect of pore size on bone ingrowth into porous titanium implants fabricated by additive manufacturing: an experiment. Mat Sci Eng C-Mater 59:690–701. https://doi.org/10.1016/j.msec.2015.10.069

Teitelbaum SL (2000) Bone resorption by osteoclasts. Science 289:1504–1508. https://doi.org/10.1126/science.289.5484.1504

Vidal L et al (2020) Regeneration of segmental defects in metatarsus of sheep with vascularized and customized 3D-printed calcium phosphate scaffolds. Sci Rep 10:7068. https://doi.org/10.1038/s41598-020-63742-w

Wang WZ et al (2021) 3D printing of PLA/n-HA composite scaffolds with customized mechanical properties and biological functions for bone tissue engineering. Compos Part B-Eng 224:109192. https://doi.org/10.1016/j.compositesb.2021.109192

Wasti S, Adhikari S (2020) Use of biomaterials for 3D printing by fused deposition modeling technique: a review. Front Chem 8:315. https://doi.org/10.3389/fchem.2020.00315

Winarso R, Anggoro PW, Ismail R, Jamari J, Bayuseno AP (2022) Application of fused deposition modeling (FDM) on bone scaffold manufacturing process: a review. Heliyon 8:e11701. https://doi.org/10.1016/j.heliyon.2022.e11701

Winkler DG et al (2003) Osteocyte control of bone formation via sclerostin, a novel BMP antagonist. EMBO J 22:6267–6276. https://doi.org/10.1093/emboj/cdg599

Wu Q et al (2022) Embedded extrusion printing in yield-stress-fluid baths. Matter-Us 5:3775–3806. https://doi.org/10.1016/j.matt.2022.09.003

Wu CS, Zhu YJ, Woo YJ (2023) Advances in 3D bioprinting: techniques, applications, and future directions for cardiac tissue engineering. Bioengineering-Basel 10:842. https://doi.org/10.3390/bioengineering10070842

Wu YH et al (2024a) 3D printing calcium phosphate ceramics with high osteoinductivity through pore architecture optimization. Acta Biomater 185:111–125. https://doi.org/10.1016/j.actbio.2024.07.008

Wu MX et al (2024b) Sound innovations for biofabrication and tissue engineering. Microsyst Nanoeng 10:170. https://doi.org/10.1038/s41378-024-00759-5

Wu D et al (2024c) Enhanced osteochondral regeneration with a 3D-printed biomimetic scaffold featuring a calcified interfacial layer. Bioact Mater 36:317–329. https://doi.org/10.1016/j.bioactmat.2024.03.004

Wu C, Xu YA, Fang JG, Li Q (2024d) Machine learning in biomaterials, biomechanics/Mechanobiology, and biofabrication: state of the art and perspective. Arch Comput Method E 31:3699–3765. https://doi.org/10.1007/s11831-024-10100-y

Xavier A, Toumi H, Lespessailles E (2022) Animal model for glucocorticoid induced osteoporosis: a systematic review from 2011 to 2021. Int J Mol Sci 23:377. https://doi.org/10.3390/ijms23010377

Xie M et al (2022) In situ 3D bioprinting with bioconcrete bioink. Nat Commun 13:3597. https://doi.org/10.1038/s41467-022-30997-y

Xiong S et al (2024) DLP fabrication of HA scaffold with customized porous structures to regulate immune microenvironment and macrophage polarization for enhancing bone regeneration. Mater Today Bio 24:100929. https://doi.org/10.1016/j.mtbio.2023.100929

Xu C, Ivanovski S (2025) Clinical translation of personalized bioengineered implant scaffolds. Nat Rev Bioeng 3:390–407. https://doi.org/10.1038/s44222-024-00269-z

Xu HQ, Liu JC, Zhang ZY, Xu CX (2022) A review on cell damage, viability, and functionality during 3D bioprinting. Mil Med Res 9:70. https://doi.org/10.1186/s40779-022-00429-5

Xu JF et al (2024) Selective laser melting of the porous ta scaffold with Mg-doped calcium phosphate coating for orthopedic applications. ACS Biomater Sci Eng 10:1435–1447. https://doi.org/10.1021/acsbiomaterials.3c01503

Yang CR (2012) Enhanced physicochemical properties of collagen by using EDC/NHS-crosslinking. B Mater Sci 35:913–918. https://doi.org/10.1007/s12034-012-0376-5

Yang J et al (2024) A mechanical-assisted post-bioprinting strategy for challenging bone defects repair. Nat Commun 15:3565. https://doi.org/10.1038/s41467-024-48023-8

Yue K et al (2015) Synthesis, properties, and biomedical applications of gelatin methacryloyl (GelMA) hydrogels. Biomaterials 73:254–271. https://doi.org/10.1016/j.biomaterials.2015.08.045

Yun S et al (2021) Bone fracture-treatment method: fixing 3D-printed polycaprolactone scaffolds with hydrogel type bone-derived extracellular matrix and β-tricalcium phosphate as an osteogenic promoter. Int J Mol Sci 22:9084. https://doi.org/10.3390/ijms22169084

Zein I, Hutmacher DW, Tan KC, Teoh SH (2002) Fused deposition modeling of novel scaffold architectures for tissue engineering applications. Biomaterials 23:1169–1185. https://doi.org/10.1016/s0142-9612(01)00232-0

Zhang BGX, Myers DE, Wallace GG, Brandt M, Choong PFM (2014) Bioactive coatings for orthopaedic implants-recent trends in development of implant coatings. Int J Mol Sci 15:11878–11921. https://doi.org/10.3390/ijms150711878

Zheng ZZ et al (2021) Visible light-induced 3D bioprinting technologies and corresponding bioink materials for tissue engineering: a review. Eng Proc 7:966–978. https://doi.org/10.1016/j.eng.2020.05.021

Zheng JB et al (2022) Additively-manufactured PEEK/HA porous scaffolds with excellent osteogenesis for bone tissue repairing. Compos Part B-Eng 232:109508. https://doi.org/10.1016/j.compositesb.2021.109508

Zhou H, Liang B, Jiang HT, Deng ZL, Yu KX (2021) Magnesium-based biomaterials as emerging agents for bone repair and regeneration: from mechanism to application. J Magnes Alloy 9:779–804. https://doi.org/10.1016/j.jma.2021.03.004

Zhou C, Liu CR, Liao ZD, Pang Y, Sun W (2025) AI for biofabrication. Biofabrication 17:012004. https://doi.org/10.1088/1758-5090/ad8966

Zhu S, Chen W, Masson A, Li YP (2024a) Cell signaling and transcriptional regulation of osteoblast lineage commitment, differentiation, bone formation, and homeostasis. Cell Discov 10:71. https://doi.org/10.1038/s41421-024-00689-6

Zhu Y et al (2024b) Strategies of functionalized GelMA-based bioinks for bone regeneration: recent advances and future perspectives. Bioact Mater 38:346–373. https://doi.org/10.1016/j.bioactmat.2024.04.032

Zulkifli MZA, Nordin D, Shaari N, Kamarudin SK (2023) Overview of electrospinning for tissue engineering applications. Polymers (Basel) 15. https://doi.org/10.3390/polym15112418

Chapter 12
Biofabrication of Skeletal Muscle Tissue and Its Interfaces

Maria Celeste Tirelli, Fabio Maiullari, Marina Volpi, Nicole Fratini, Nehar Celikkin, Yurii Promovych, Cesare Gargioli, Wojciech Święszkowski, and Marco Costantini

Abstract Skeletal muscle tissue engineering has emerged as a critical field in regenerative medicine due to the limited capacity of large or chronically damaged muscles to self-repair. Native skeletal muscle displays a highly organized, vascularized, and mechanically integrated architecture that is essential for force generation and transmission; however, conventional scaffold-based approaches have failed to reproduce this level of complexity, resulting in constructs with limited functional performance. Recent advances in biofabrication have enabled the recreation of aligned myofiber architectures, biomimetic tissue interfaces, and biomimetic vascular networks, offering new opportunities for functional muscle regeneration and in vitro modeling. This chapter reviews the state of the art in skeletal muscle biofabrication with a particular emphasis on fiber-based, microfluidic-assisted rotary wet-spinning (RoWS). We analyze how this biofabrication strategy has been employed to engineer structurally and functionally relevant skeletal muscle tissues and to recreate complex interfaces such as the myotendinous junction. Particular emphasis is placed on their ability to generate spatially organized constructs that support the formation of physiologically relevant muscle-tendon transitions and enable the integration of biomimetic microvascular networks, thereby enhancing tissue maturation, viability, and functional performance. Collectively, these

M. C. Tirelli · F. Maiullari · N. Celikkin · Y. Promovych · M. Costantini (✉)
Institute of Physical Chemistry, Polish Academy of Sciences, Warsaw, Poland
e-mail: mcostantini@ichf.edu.pl

M. Volpi · W. Święszkowski
Faculty of Materials Science and Engineering, Warsaw University of Technology, Warsaw, Poland

N. Fratini
Department of Molecular Medicine, Sapienza University, Rome, Italy

National Research Council–Institute for Biomedical Technologies (CNR-ITB), Milan, Italy

C. Gargioli
Department of Biology, University of Rome Tor Vergata, Rome, Italy

Y. M. Elçin (ed.), *Biofabrication in Regenerative Medicine*, Stem Cell Biology and Regenerative Medicine 1519, https://doi.org/10.1007/978-3-032-30294-6_12

approaches demonstrate that the convergence of structural guidance, biochemical signaling, and dynamic biofabrication technologies is redefining skeletal muscle tissue engineering and accelerating the development of clinically relevant muscle substitutes and physiologically faithful in vitro models.

Keywords Skeletal muscle · Biofabrication · Rotary Wet-spinning (RoWS) · Myotendinous junction · Vascularization · 3D bioprinting

Abbreviations

1D	One-dimensional
2D	Two-dimensional
3D	Three-dimensional
ACA	ε-aminocaproic acid.
BTX	α-bungarotoxin.
CD31	Cluster of differentiation 31/PECAM-1
COLI	Collagen type I
COL6	Collagen type VI
COL22A1	Collagen type XXII alpha 1 chain
DAPI	4′,6-diamidino-2-phenylindole
DLP	Digital light processing
DRAQ5	Far-red DNA dye (DRAQ5 nuclear stain)
ECM	Extracellular matrix
EGFR	Epidermal growth factor receptor
eSM	Engineered skeletal muscle
FBN1	Fibrillin 1
FDR	False discovery rate
GelMA	Gelatin methacryloyl
GMHA	Glycidyl methacrylated hyaluronic acid
GMP	Good manufacturing practice
GO	Gene ontology
hMPC	Human muscle progenitor cells
hPeri	Human pericytes
hiPSC	Human induced pluripotent stem cells
HSPG2	Heparan sulfate proteoglycan 2
HUVEC	Human umbilical vein endothelial cells
ITGB1/3	Integrin beta 1/integrin beta 3
ITOP	Integrated tissue-organ printer/integrated tissue-organ printing
LC–MS/MS	Liquid chromatography-tandem mass spectrometry
LAM/LAM-1	Laminin/laminin-1 complex
LMW	Low molecular weight
MAPK	Mitogen-activated protein kinase
Mabs	Mesoangioblasts

MHC/MyHC	Myosin heavy chain
MPH	Microfluidic printing head
MRFs	Myogenic regulatory factors
MSC	Mesenchymal stromal/stem cells
MTJ	Myotendinous junction
MTU	Muscle–tendon unit
NCAM1	Neural cell adhesion molecule 1
NeuF	Neurofilament
NID1/2	Nidogen 1/nidogen 2
NMPs	Neuromesodermal progenitors
NMJ	Neuromuscular junction
OCT	Optical coherence tomography
PCA	Principal component analysis
PDGFRA/B	Platelet-derived growth factor receptor alpha/beta
PECAM-1	Platelet endothelial cell adhesion molecule-1
PF	Polyethylene glycol–fibrinogen (PEG–fibrinogen)
PTK2	Protein tyrosine kinase 2 (FAK)
PXN	Paxillin
qPCR	Quantitative polymerase chain reaction
RAS-RAF-MAPK	RAS-RAF-mitogen-activated protein kinase pathway
RHOA/RAC1	Ras homolog family member A/Rac family small GTPase 1
ROCK1	Rho-associated coiled-coil containing protein kinase 1
RoWS	Rotary wet-spinning
SMA	Smooth muscle actin
SM	Skeletal muscle
SMTE	Skeletal muscle tissue engineering
Syn	Synaptophysin
TA	Tibialis anterior
TF	Transcription factor
THBS4	Thrombospondin 4
vWF	von Willebrand factor
VML	Volumetric muscle loss

12.1 Introduction

Skeletal muscle tissue represents nearly 40% of total human body mass and plays a fundamental role in locomotion, posture, respiration, thermoregulation, and metabolic homeostasis (Sabetkish et al. 2024; Pillai Babu et al. 2026). Beyond its contractile function, skeletal muscle is a highly dynamic and metabolically active tissue that participates in glucose uptake, amino acid storage, and endocrine signaling via myokines, which regulate systemic physiology (Pillai Babu et al. 2026). Skeletal muscle possesses a remarkable regenerative capacity mediated by satellite cells, a population of muscle-resident stem cells located between the basal lamina and the sarcolemma of muscle fibers, which are activated in response to injury to restore tissue structure and function (Liu et al. 2025). However, this regenerative potential is limited in cases of severe trauma, volumetric muscle loss (VML), genetic diseases such as muscular dystrophies, cancer cachexia, aging-related sarcopenia, or metabolic disorders, where the extent of tissue damage exceeds the intrinsic repair capacity (Sabetkish et al. 2024; Lee et al. 2023). In these conditions, muscle regeneration is often incomplete and characterized by fibrotic scar formation, impaired vascularization, and permanent functional deficits. Current clinical treatments, including autologous muscle grafts and flap transplantation, remain constrained by donor site morbidity, limited tissue availability, and incomplete functional recovery (Lee et al. 2023). These limitations have driven the rapid development of skeletal muscle tissue engineering (SMTE), a multidisciplinary field combining biomaterials science, biofabrication, stem cell biology, and biophysical stimulation to develop functional muscle substitutes for regenerative medicine, disease modeling, and biohybrid systems (Filippi et al. 2023).

Native skeletal muscle exhibits a highly organized and hierarchical architecture spanning multiple length scales. At the molecular level, sarcomeres form the fundamental contractile units composed of actin and myosin filaments. These sarcomeres assemble into myofibrils, which in turn form multinucleated myofibers aligned in parallel bundles known as fascicles, ultimately creating whole muscles connected to tendons and bone through specialized interfaces such as the myotendinous junction (MTJ) (Pillai Babu et al. 2026; Fornetti et al. 2023). This hierarchical organization is essential for efficient force generation and transmission, as the anisotropic alignment of myofibers ensures coordinated contraction and mechanical stability. In addition to its structural organization, skeletal muscle function relies on the integration of vascular, neural, and extracellular matrix (ECM) components, which provide metabolic (Lee et al. 2023; Kim et al. 2018) support, electrical signaling, and biochemical cues that regulate cell behavior and tissue homeostasis (Filippi et al. 2023). Therefore, recreating the structural, cellular, and biochemical complexity of native skeletal muscle remains a central challenge in tissue engineering.

Early skeletal muscle engineering strategies primarily relied on scaffold-based approaches, including porous biomaterials fabricated via techniques such as electrospinning, solvent casting, freeze-drying, and phase separation. Electrospun fibrous scaffolds can provide anisotropic topographical cues that promote myoblast alignment and myotube formation; however, their dense fiber networks often limit cell infiltration and vascularization, restricting tissue maturation and integration (Lee et al. 2023; Kim et al. 2018). Similarly, porous scaffolds fabricated by solvent casting or freeze-drying typically exhibit limited pore interconnectivity and inadequate spatial control over cell organization, leading to heterogeneous cell distribution and suboptimal functional outcomes (Lee et al. 2023). Microfabrication approaches, including micropatterning and microgrooved substrates, have also been explored to guide cellular alignment and promote anisotropic tissue formation, although these strategies are generally limited to two-dimensional or thin tissue constructs and cannot easily be scaled to clinically relevant volumes (Kim et al. 2018).

To overcome these limitations, three-dimensional bioprinting has emerged as a powerful tool for skeletal muscle biofabrication, enabling precise control over the spatial deposition of cells and biomaterials. Extrusion-based bioprinting enables the fabrication of aligned hydrogel filaments containing muscle progenitor cells, which can recapitulate the parallel organization of native muscle fibers and support functional maturation (Lee et al. 2023; Fornetti et al. 2023). Coaxial and multi-material bioprinting approaches have further enabled the fabrication of artificial muscle fascicles composed of cell-dense cores surrounded by supportive hydrogel shells, promoting enhanced myotube formation, spontaneous contractility, and improved tissue regeneration following implantation (Lee et al. 2023). Similarly, multi-material bioprinting strategies incorporating perfusable microchannel networks have enabled the fabrication of centimeter-scale skeletal muscle constructs with improved cell survival, structural stability, and mechanical function by facilitating nutrient diffusion and waste removal throughout the tissue volume (Filippi et al. 2023). These advances demonstrate the potential of bioprinting technologies to recreate complex tissue architectures and improve the physiological relevance of engineered muscle constructs.

More recently, advanced biofabrication approaches have focused on improving cellular alignment and tissue anisotropy by incorporating structural guidance cues into bioinks and scaffolds. The integration of anisotropic fibrillar structures within bioinks has been shown to promote directional cell growth and enhance myotube alignment during extrusion-based bioprinting, enabling the generation of structurally organized muscle tissues (Heilig et al. 2025). Similarly, composite hydrogels containing aligned fillers or ECM-derived components have been developed to mimic the anisotropic microenvironment of native skeletal muscle and improve myogenic differentiation and tissue organization (Heilig et al. 2025; Sprenger et al. 2024). Alternative biofabrication strategies, including magnetic bioprinting and scaffold-free tissue assembly, have enabled the generation of muscle tissues with controlled geometry and enhanced maturation by applying external physical cues to guide cellular organization and differentiation (Demri et al. 2025; Nie et al. 2023). Light-based and microfluidic bioprinting techniques have also demonstrated the ability to produce highly organized muscle constructs with aligned myotubes, preserved stem cell niches, and functional contractile properties, enabling physiologically relevant in vitro muscle models (Liu et al. 2025; Nie et al. 2023).

Microfluidic-assisted biofabrication has also emerged as a promising strategy for generating highly cellularized, structurally organized muscle constructs. Core-shell microfiber fabrication techniques enable the encapsulation of cells within biomimetic ECM environments, maintaining high cell viability and promoting tissue maturation, thereby allowing the generation of thick, multicellular constructs with tissue-like cellular density and organization (Nie et al. 2023). These fiber-based approaches provide superior control over cell distribution, structural anisotropy, and tissue architecture compared to conventional scaffold fabrication techniques, making them particularly suitable for recreating the hierarchical organization of skeletal muscle.

In addition to structural organization, recreating physiologically relevant tissue interfaces is critical for functional muscle engineering. Native skeletal muscle operates within the muscle-tendon unit, where the myotendinous junction enables efficient force transmission between the muscle fibers and the tendon. Biofabrication strategies incorporating tendon-mimicking anchors and biomimetic interfaces have demonstrated improved force transmission, structural stability, and tissue maturation in engineered muscle constructs, highlighting the importance of recreating functional interfaces in engineered musculoskeletal systems (Lee et al. 2023; Filippi et al. 2025). Similarly, integrating perfusable vascular networks and biomimetic ECM components has been shown to significantly enhance tissue viability, maturation, and functional performance, thereby addressing key limitations associated with diffusion-limited nutrient transport in thick engineered tissues (Filippi et al. 2023; Nie et al. 2023).

Despite these significant advances, recreating functional skeletal muscle tissue with physiologically relevant architecture, vascularization, and tissue interfaces remains a major challenge. In particular, achieving precise control over cellular alignment and hierarchical organization at clinically relevant scales remains difficult using conventional bioprinting and scaffold-based approaches. To address these limitations, fiber-based biofabrication strategies, including wet-spinning and microfluidic-assisted spinning techniques, have emerged as powerful tools for generating aligned hydrogel fibers that closely mimic the structural organization of native muscle tissue. Among these approaches, rotary wet-spinning (RoWS) is particularly promising for producing continuous, highly aligned, and densely cellularized hydrogel fibers with controlled architecture and mechanical properties. These fiber-based constructs provide a biomimetic platform for recreating skeletal muscle tissue and its interfaces, offering new opportunities for regenerative medicine, disease modeling, and biohybrid actuator applications.

12.2 Rotary Wet-Spinning (RoWS) Biofabrication Strategies for Skeletal Muscle

RoWS has emerged as a powerful fiber-based biofabrication strategy for engineering anisotropic skeletal muscle tissues with biomimetic structural and functional properties. In contrast to conventional extrusion-based bioprinting, which deposits discrete filaments layer-by-layer, RoWS enables the continuous generation of highly aligned hydrogel microfibers by extruding bioinks into a rotating crosslinking bath (Fig. 12.1a, b), where controlled rotational flow and shear forces promote uniaxial alignment of encapsulated cells and extracellular matrix components. This process enables the fabrication of long, continuous, and densely cellularized fibers that closely recapitulate the fascicular organization of native skeletal muscle (Fig. 12.1c, h). By providing microscale structural guidance cues, RoWS directly

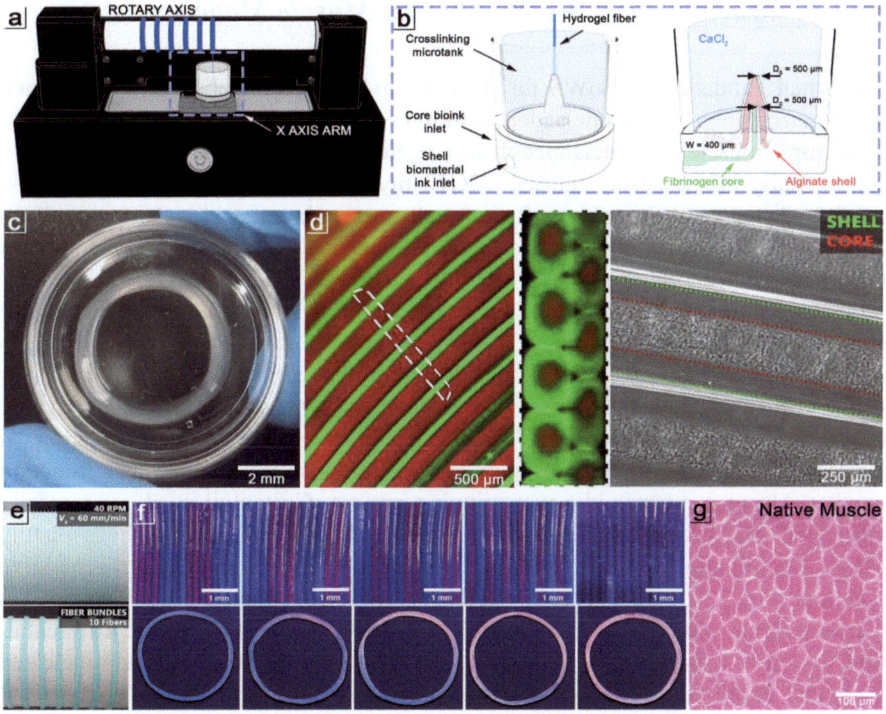

Fig. 12.1 (**a**) 3D rendering model of the 3D RoWS highlighting its three main components: (i) the microfluidic printing head, (ii) the rotating drum collector, and (iii) the x-axis motion arm. (**b**) (left) Schematic representation of the microfluidic printing head (MPH) and its core/shell inlet channels, (right) cross-section view of the microfluidic printing head showing fluidic paths within the MPH. (**c**) Hydrogel core/shell fiber bundle composed of parallel aligned fibers. (**d**) Fluorescence and bright field image of the bundle, demonstrating the precise fiber organization and well-defined core/shell architecture. (**e**) Representative spiral fiber patterns obtained at different translation speeds and assembly of fiber bundles with a defined number of fibers. (Reprinted from Reggio et al. (2025), Copyright 2025, with permission from WILEY-VCH Verlag GmbH & Co. CC BY-NC-ND 4.0). (**f**) (top) Single-layer scaffold with varying ratios of the two inks, generating core-shell microfibers by tuning the ink delivery time. (Reprinted from Volpi et al. (2024), Copyright 2024, with permission from WILEY-VCH Verlag GmbH & Co. CC BY-NC-ND 4.0). (**g**) Representative cross-section of native skeletal muscle tissue. (Reprinted from (Grunow et al. 2021), Copyright 2021, with permission from PLoS One. CC BY-NC-ND 4.0)

influences cell morphology, cytoskeletal organization, and myogenic differentiation, highlighting the central role of biofabrication-induced anisotropy in skeletal muscle tissue engineering (Pillai Babu et al. 2026; Costantini et al. 2017; Celikkin et al. 2023).

12.2.1 Murine-Based RoWS Skeletal Muscle Models

The initial validation of RoWS for skeletal muscle biofabrication was established using murine myogenic models, demonstrating its ability to generate highly aligned, anisotropic muscle constructs that closely replicate native muscle fascicular organization. Early studies using murine C2C12 myoblasts or mesoangioblasts (Mabs) confirmed that RoWS enables efficient cell encapsulation within hydrogel fibers composed of biomimetic matrices such as alginate and PEG-fibrinogen, resulting in highly aligned myotubes oriented along the fiber axis (Fig. 12.2a) (Celikkin et al. 2023; Costantini et al. 2021). This anisotropic microenvironment promoted cellular elongation, cytoskeletal alignment, and fusion into multinucleated myotubes, demonstrating that structural cues imposed during biofabrication directly regulate myogenic differentiation and tissue organization. A major advancement in the translational application of RoWS was demonstrated by the biofabrication of implantable murine myo-substitutes that restored muscle mass and function in vivo. Using a microfluidic wet-spinning system, Costantini et al. successfully fabricated macroscopic bundles of aligned hydrogel microfibers encapsulating Mabs, a population of perivascular myogenic progenitors with strong regenerative potential (Fig. 12.2b) (Costantini et al. 2021). These constructs closely recapitulated native skeletal muscle histoarchitecture and supported robust myogenic differentiation in vitro, characterized by extensive formation of aligned multinucleated myotubes expressing muscle-specific markers, including myosin heavy chain and laminin. Importantly, the wet-spinning system enabled rapid fiber production at extrusion velocities approaching 4 m min^{-1}, allowing the generation of clinically relevant construct volumes with controlled architecture and high cellular density (Costantini et al. 2021).

The therapeutic potential of RoWS-fabricated muscle constructs was further demonstrated in a murine model of volumetric muscle loss (VML), where approximately 90% of the tibialis anterior muscle was surgically ablated. Implantation of RoWS-engineered myo-substitutes led to rapid and extensive muscle regeneration within 20 days, restoring muscle mass, architecture, and functionality. Histological analysis confirmed the formation of organized, parallel myofibers expressing muscle-specific proteins and surrounded by laminin-rich basal lamina, closely resembling native muscle tissue (Fig. 12.2c). Notably, the engineered constructs supported the formation of functional vascular networks and neuromuscular junctions, as evidenced by the presence of endothelial markers, such as von Willebrand factor, and neuromuscular synapse markers, including synaptophysin and acetylcholine receptor clusters (Fig. 12.2d, e). These findings demonstrated that RoWS constructs support not only muscle regeneration but also the formation of critical supporting structures required for long-term tissue survival and functionality. Functional analysis further confirmed the physiological integration of RoWS-engineered muscle constructs. Electrophysiological measurements demonstrated significant recovery of contractile force, with reconstructed muscles achieving substantially higher tetanic force compared to untreated controls. Additionally, the presence of

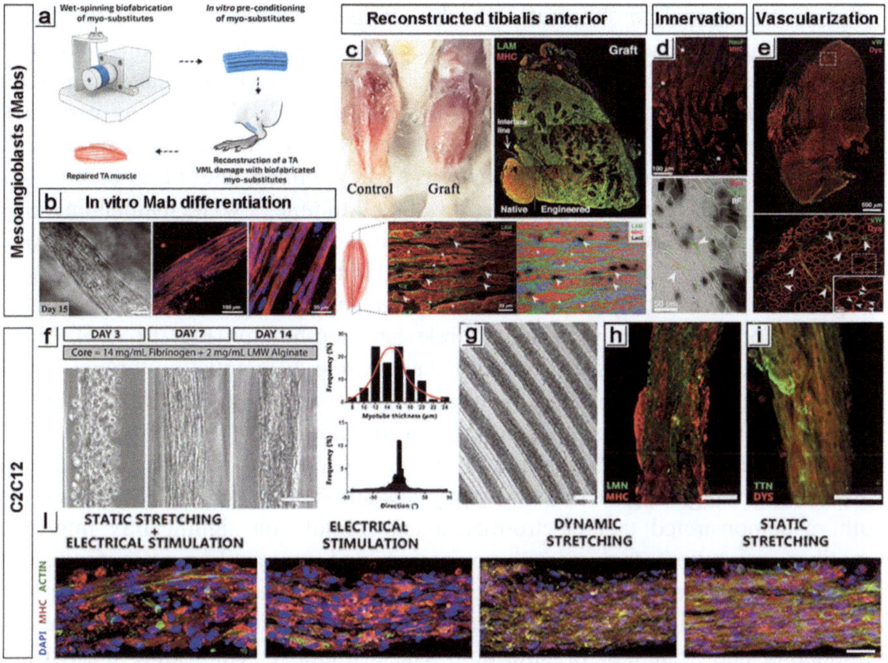

Fig. 12.2 (**a**) Schematic representation of the wet-spinning setup used for the biofabrication of aligned myo-substitutes. (**b**) Immunofluorescence staining for myosin heavy chain (MHC, red) performed on 3D biofabricated constructs loaded with mesoangioblasts (Mabs) after 15 days of in vitro culture. (**c**) Macroscopic view of the implanted myo-substitute 20 days after grafting into the tibialis anterior (TA) muscle. Cross-sections of explanted grafted TA were LacZ-labeled and immunostained for MHC (red) and laminin (LAM, green). (**d**) Immunofluorescence analysis of neuromuscular integration. Sections stained for neurofilament (NeuF, green) and MHC (red) reveal reconstructed muscle innervation (asterisks). Synaptophysin (Syn) and α-bungarotoxin (BTX) immunolabeling identify neuromuscular junction formation (arrowheads). (**e**) Vascularization of implanted constructs. Enlarged view of the dashed area and white arrows indicate newly formed vessels. Inset: higher magnification showing vWF-positive capillaries (arrows). (Reprinted from Costantini et al. (2021), Copyright 2021, with permission from Springer Nature. CC BY-NC-ND 4.0). (**f**) Bright-field micrographs of C2C12 cells during maturation within core-shell fibers at different time points. The core bioink consisted of 14 mg mL^{-1} fibrinogen and 2 mg mL^{-1} low-molecular-weight (LMW) alginate (scale bar: 150 μm). Quantification of myotube thickness and directionality (0° corresponding to the fiber longitudinal axis). (**g**) Bright-field micrographs showing the volumetric fraction of mature bundles at day 14 (scale bar: 500 μm). (**h**) Confocal images of engineered skeletal muscle (eSM) constructs stained for laminin (green) and MHC (red), and (**i**) for titin (green) and dystrophin (red). (**l**) Confocal images of physically stimulated myo-substitutes after 14 days of culture, stained for actin (green), MHC (red), and DAPI (blue) (magnification 20×; scale bar: 50 μm). (Reprinted from Celikkin et al. (2023), Copyright 2023, with permission from IOP Science. CC BY-NC-ND 4.0 (Celikkin et al. 2023; Costantini et al. 2021))

satellite cells within the regenerated tissue indicated the establishment of a functional stem cell niche, suggesting the potential for long-term regenerative capacity and physiological remodeling. These findings underscore RoWS's ability to generate fully functional muscle substitutes capable of restoring structural and functional properties following severe muscle injury (Costantini et al. 2021). Further improvements in RoWS technology have been achieved through the development of advanced microfluidic-assisted spinning systems capable of generating core-shell fiber architectures and improving fabrication scalability. Celikkin et al. demonstrated that RoWS systems can produce continuous hydrogel fibers with fibrin-based cores and alginate shells at production rates exceeding 4 m min^{-1}, while maintaining high cell viability and promoting robust myogenic differentiation (Fig. 12.2f, l) (Celikkin et al. 2023). Encapsulated murine myoblasts exhibited strong expression of contractile proteins, including myosin heavy chain, titin, and dystrophin, and formed highly aligned myotubes with physiologically relevant morphology (Fig. 12.2f, i). These findings highlight RoWS's ability to regulate muscle differentiation through structural confinement and matrix organization, demonstrating the critical role of biofabrication-induced anisotropy in skeletal muscle tissue engineering. The functional maturation of RoWS-engineered murine muscle constructs has been further enhanced by integrating them with biophysical stimulation systems. Moreover, the authors demonstrated that electro-mechanical stimulation significantly improves myofiber maturation, sarcomeric organization, and contractile protein expression in RoWS-fabricated constructs (Fig. 12.2l). Electrical stimulation promoted excitation-contraction coupling, while mechanical stimulation enhanced cytoskeletal remodeling and structural organization. These findings demonstrate that RoWS provides a structurally optimized platform that can be further enhanced through biophysical conditioning to generate functional muscle tissue analogs with physiologically relevant properties (Celikkin et al. 2023).

Collectively, murine-based studies have established RoWS as a highly effective and scalable biofabrication strategy for skeletal muscle tissue engineering. The ability to generate continuous, anisotropic, and densely cellularized fibers enables precise control over tissue architecture, promotes functional maturation, and supports vascularization, innervation, and long-term integration in vivo. These findings position RoWS as a promising platform for developing clinically relevant skeletal muscle substitutes for regenerative medicine and for the treatment of volumetric muscle loss.

12.2.2 Human-Based RoWS Skeletal Muscle Models

Building on the success of murine models, RoWS has been successfully translated to human skeletal muscle biofabrication using clinically relevant cell sources, including human primary myoblasts and stem cell-derived myogenic progenitors (Fig. 12.3) (Reggio et al. 2025; Costantini et al. 2021). Recently, the mechanistic impact of RoWS on human myogenic progenitors was elucidated through state-of-the-art label-free LC–MS/MS high-resolution proteomics (Fig. 12.3c, e) (Reggio et al. 2025). Notably, pericyte-derived myo-substitutes generated via RoWS using PEG-fibrinogen (PF) hydrogel exhibited a highly organized anisotropic architecture

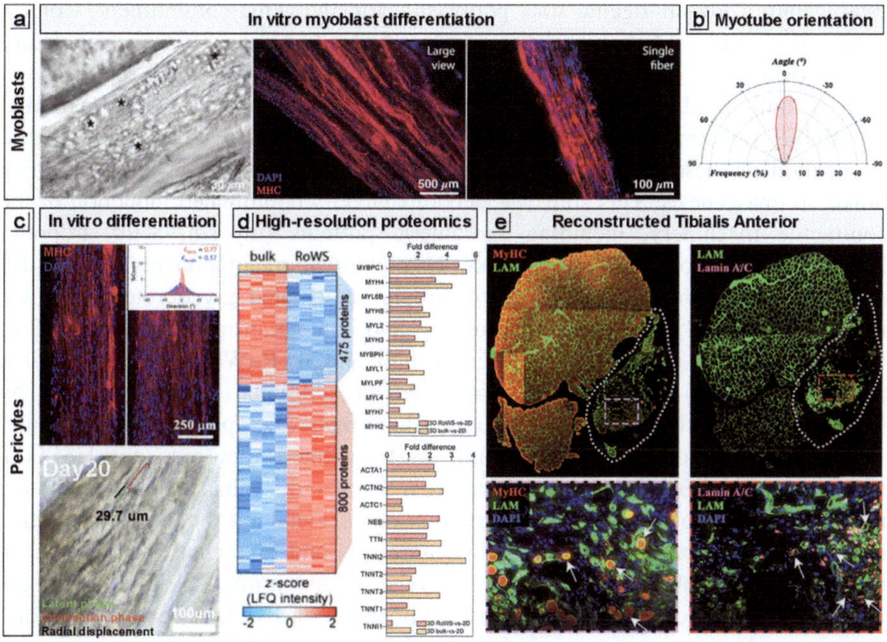

Fig. 12.3 (**a**) Wet-spun microfiber yarns containing human myogenic precursors after 15 days of in vitro culture. Immunofluorescence staining for myosin heavy chain (MHC, red) demonstrates myogenic differentiation within aligned fiber constructs. (**b**) Polar plot analysis showing significant alignment of myotubes along the longitudinal axis of the spun fibers, confirming anisotropic structural organization. (Reprinted from Costantini et al. (2021), Copyright 2021, with permission from Springer Nature. CC BY-NC-ND 4.0). (**c**) In vitro myogenic organization of human pericytes (hPeri) within 3D-biofabricated core-shell fibers. Immunostaining for MHC (red) and DAPI (blue) highlights multinucleated myotube formation within aligned constructs. In the lower panel, representative bright-field images from spontaneous twitching recordings at day 20 show displacement of a reference segment during fiber contraction, indicating functional activity. (**d**) Heatmap illustrating significantly modulated proteins in the comparison between 3D RoWS-biofabricated and 3D bulk constructs. Bar plots report fold changes (3D biofabricated vs 2D culture and 3D bulk vs 2D culture) of proteins annotated as sarcomeric components. (**e**) Engraftment of hPeri-derived 3D-biofabricated myo-substitutes in mouse tibialis anterior (TA) volumetric muscle loss model. Immunofluorescence staining for myosin heavy chain (MyHC), laminin (LAM), and human lamin A/C confirms donor-derived muscle regeneration. Enlarged views of selected regions are shown. (Reprinted from Reggio et al. (2025), Copyright 2025, with permission from WILEY-VCH Verlag GmbH & Co. CC BY-NC-ND 4.0 (Reggio et al. 2025; Costantini et al. 2021))

and spontaneous contractile activity along the longitudinal axis, indicative of advanced structural and functional maturation (Fig. 12.3c). Principal component analysis clearly segregated samples by culture condition, demonstrating that the 3D PF environment profoundly reshapes the proteomic landscape of differentiating pericytes. Compared with 2D cultures, PF-based differentiation induced extensive proteome remodeling, with ~61% of proteins significantly modulated in 3D bulk cultures and ~ 66% in 3D RoWS constructs (FDR < 0.01). Network analysis revealed suppression of mitogenic pathways (RAS, EGFR, PDGFRA/B) and focal adhesion/cytoskeletal regulators (ITGB1/3, PTK2, ROCK1, RHOA, RAC1), establishing a low-mitogenic state permissive for myogenic commitment. Consistently, transcription factor enrichment identified all major myogenic regulatory factors (MYOD1, MYOG, MYF5, MYF6) among the top-enriched regulators in both 3D bulk-vs-2D and RoWS-vs-2D comparisons. Given that RAS-RAF-MAPK and EGFR signaling repress MYOD and MYOG to maintain proliferative states, attenuation of these axes in PF constructs effectively releases the transcriptional brake on myogenesis. This shift was accompanied by coordinated induction of the contractile machinery, including sarcomeric proteins (myosin, actin, troponin isoforms), late myogenic markers, sarcoplasmic reticulum components required for excitation-contraction coupling, and dystrophin-associated glycoprotein complex members essential for membrane stability and force transmission (Fig. 12.3d). Importantly, direct comparison between 3D bulk and 3D RoWS constructs revealed that biofabrication-induced anisotropy adds an additional regulatory layer by strongly enriching basal lamina and extracellular matrix components such as collagen and fibrillar proteins, laminin complexes, ECM interactors (nidogens, HSPG2), and stabilizers (FBN1) indicating that RoWS not only enhances alignment and maturation but also stimulates reconstruction of a skeletal muscle niche-like microenvironment that reinforces structural organization and functional competence. In this context, the enhanced maturation observed in human myo-substitutes emerges from the synergistic interplay between biomimetic, bioactive hydrogel matrices and the structural anisotropy imposed by the RoWS process. While the bioactive matrix provides a permissive biochemical niche, the controlled architectural alignment introduced by RoWS translates these cues into higher-order tissue organization driving the coordinated molecular maturation and tissue-level functionality in human constructs. Crucially, in vivo implantation in a mouse tibialis anterior volumetric muscle loss model demonstrated that hPeri-derived 3D RoWS myo-substitutes successfully engrafted, generated human-specific regenerating myofibers, and promoted robust neo-vascularization and neuromuscular integration within the host tissue (Fig. 12.3e) (Reggio et al. 2025). Another key advantage of RoWS for human skeletal muscle biofabrication is its scalability and ability to produce long, continuous fibers that can be assembled into larger tissue constructs. This capability is particularly relevant for translational applications, as clinically meaningful muscle grafts require centimeter-scale tissue dimensions and functional integration.

Unlike conventional extrusion bioprinting approaches, which may be limited by printing speed and structural resolution, RoWS enables rapid and reproducible fabrication of aligned muscle fibers while maintaining high cellular density and viability. These advances position RoWS as a highly promising platform for engineering clinically relevant skeletal muscle tissues. Collectively, the translation of RoWS from murine to human models demonstrates its versatility and robustness as a skeletal muscle biofabrication strategy. The ability to generate aligned, functional human muscle tissue highlights its potential for developing implantable muscle grafts and physiologically relevant in vitro models. Continued advancements in biomaterials, bioreactor integration, and interface engineering are expected to further enhance the performance and translational potential of RoWS-engineered skeletal muscle constructs (Table 12.1).

Table 12.1 Summary of biofabrication strategies for skeletal muscle tissue. The table compares RoWS and other advanced biofabrication approaches across bioink composition, cellular models, structural organization, scalability, and functional maturation outcomes

Biofabrication technique	Bioink	Cell model	Structural organization achieved	Construct dimensions	System scalability	Maturation/functional tests	References
Microfluidic-enhanced rotary wet-spinning (RoWS)	Alginat/fibrinogen	Murine C2C12 myoblasts	Highly aligned myofibers and fascicle-like bundles	Continuous fibers, meters long; 100–300 μm diameter	Continuous production, high-throughput fiber spinning	Myotube formation, MyHC expression, anisotropic alignment	Celikkin et al. (2023)
RoWS	Alginat/PEG-fibrinogen	Murine and human myoblasts	Aligned muscle bundles with enhanced sarcomere organization	Cm-scale constructs assembled from fibers	Scalable fiber assembly into large bundles	Contractility and force measurements, gene expression, VML model	Costantini et al. (2021)
RoWS	Alginat/PEG-fibrinogen	Human pericytes	Highly aligned myo-bundles	Cm-scale constructs assembled from fibers	Scalable fiber assembly into large bundles	Spontaneous myofiber contraction, high-resolution proteomics	Reggio et al. (2025)
Coaxial extrusion bioprinting	GelMA/GMHA	Human skeletal muscle cells	Muscle fascicle-like structures	Cm-scale constructs	Moderate throughput layer-by-layer printing	Functional regeneration in vivo, muscle maturation	Liu et al. (2025) and Lee et al. (2023)
FLight light-based bioprinting	Photopolymerizable ECM-derived hydrogels, GelNB-GelSH	Mouse primary myoblasts	Aligned mini-muscles with the potential to preserve in vivo the stem cell niche	Mm-scale muscle units	High-speed parallel light patterning	Functional contraction, stem cell self-renewal	Liu et al. (2025)
Magnetic bioprinting	Magnetized cell aggregates	hiPSC, C2C12	Aligned muscle tissue via magnetic actuation	Mm-cm constructs	Rapid scalable assembly	Force generation, contraction analysis	Filippi et al. (2023) and Demri et al. (2025)
Perfusable extrusion bioprinting	GelMA/alginate and sacrificial inks	C2C12	Perfusable muscle tissue	Cm-scale constructs	Moderate throughput extrusion	Perfusion testing, secretome analysis	Filippi et al. (2023)

(continued)

Table 12.1 (continued)

Biofabrication technique	Bioink	Cell model	Structural organization achieved	Construct dimensions	System scalability	Maturation/functional tests	References
Extrusion bioprinting with fibrillar bioinks	GelMA/PCL bundles	C2C12	Enhanced anisotropic alignment	Cm-scale constructs	Scalable extrusion process	Improved myotube alignment and maturation	Heilig et al. (2025)
Microfluidic-assisted extrusion bioprinting	Alginate/PEG-fibrinogen	Murine C2C12 myoblasts	Highly aligned myofibers and fascicle-like bundles	Continuous fibers, meters long; 100–300 μm diameter	Continuous production, high-throughput fiber spinning	Myotube formation, MyHC expression, anisotropic alignment	Costantini et al. (2017)
ITOP technology	PCL/fibrin/gelatin	Human muscle progenitor cell (hMPC)	Highly aligned myofibers	Cm-scale constructs	Moderate throughput extrusion	TA repair in vivo, force measurement, MyHC expression, neural integration	Kim et al. (2018)

12.3 Biofabrication of the Myotendinous Junction Using RoWS Strategies

The myotendinous junction (MTJ) is a highly specialized interface that enables the efficient transmission of contractile forces from skeletal muscle to tendons and, ultimately, to bone. Structurally, the MTJ is characterized by extensive folding of muscle fiber membranes into the tendon extracellular matrix, forming interdigitated projections that increase the contact surface area and reduce mechanical stress concentration. This structural complexity is supported by specialized molecular adhesion complexes, including integrins and cytoskeletal linker proteins, which anchor muscle fibers to the collagen-rich tendon matrix and ensure mechanical continuity between tissues. The graded transition in cellular composition, extracellular matrix organization, and mechanical properties across the MTJ is essential for maintaining musculoskeletal function and preventing tissue failure under repeated mechanical loading (Volpi et al. 2024; De Paolis et al. 2026).

Despite its physiological importance, the MTJ exhibits limited regenerative capacity after injury, often leading to fibrotic scar formation and incomplete functional recovery. The complexity of this interface presents significant challenges for tissue engineering, as conventional scaffold-based and bioprinting approaches often fail to recreate the continuous structural and compositional gradients required for proper muscle-tendon integration. RoWS and microfluidic-assisted wet-spinning have emerged as promising biofabrication strategies for MTJ engineering, enabling the generation of continuous hydrogel fibers with spatially controlled cellular composition and anisotropic organization (Volpi et al. 2024; De Paolis et al. 2026).

12.3.1 Murine-Based MTJ Biofabrication Models

Murine cell-based models have provided essential proof-of-concept evidence for MTJ biofabrication using RoWS technologies. Using murine C2C12 myoblasts and NIH 3 T3 fibroblasts to represent the muscle and tendon compartments, respectively, microfluidic-assisted wet-spinning enabled the fabrication of continuous hydrogel fibers with a precisely controlled spatial distribution of myogenic and tenogenic cell populations. This approach employed programmable syringe pumps and a coaxial extrusion system integrated with a rotating collection drum, enabling sequential deposition of distinct bioinks and the formation of tri-compartmentalized constructs comprising muscle-like, tendon-like, and transitional MTJ regions (Fig. 12.4a–c).

Structural analysis revealed that both myogenic and tenogenic cells exhibited pronounced alignment along the fiber axis, reflecting the anisotropic microenvironment generated during wet-spinning (Volpi et al. 2024). This alignment promoted directional cytoskeletal organization and facilitated tissue-specific differentiation. Myogenic regions exhibited the formation of aligned multinucleated myotubes expressing myosin heavy chain, while tendon-like regions demonstrated abundant

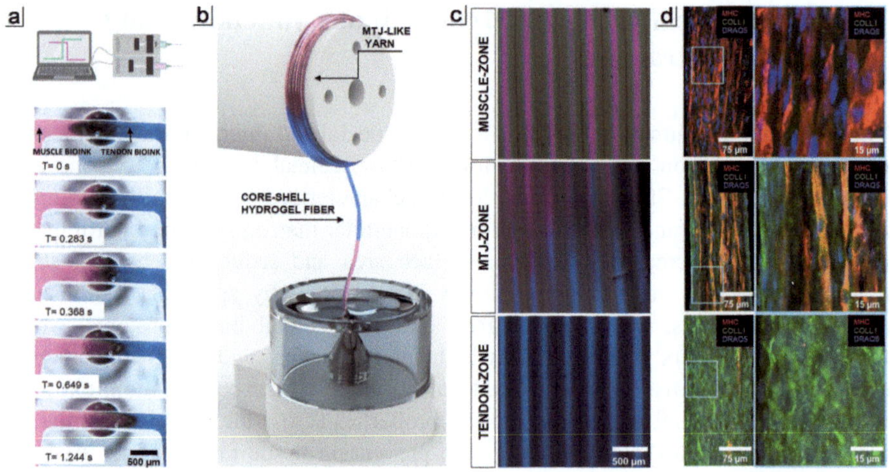

Fig. 12.4 3D RoWS technique for the biofabrication of mouse-derived myotendinous junction (MTJ)-like scaffolds. (**a**) Schematics of programmable syringe pumps set and representative time-lapse optical images of the T-junction during the sequential delivery of muscle and tendon ink. (**b**) Schematic of the microfluidic-assisted wet-spinning process of MTJ-like yarns. (**c**) Fluorescence images of core-shell fibers with graded core composition to generate three different scaffold regions: muscle, MTJ, and tendon. (**d**) Representative confocal images of tissue-specific regions, i.e., muscle, MTJ, and tendon, stained for myosin heavy chain (MHC), collagen type I (COLI), and DRAQ5 at day 14 of culture. (Reprinted from Volpi et al. (2024), Copyright 2024, with permission from WILEY-VCH Verlag GmbH & Co. CC BY-NC-ND 4.0 (Volpi et al. 2024))

deposition of collagen type I and type III, key structural components of tendon extracellular matrix. Importantly, the transitional MTJ region exhibited intermediate structural characteristics, including collagen-rich extracellular matrix embedding developing myotubes, closely resembling the graded morphology of native MTJs (Fig. 12.4d) (Volpi et al. 2024). The spatial control achieved through RoWS enabled a continuous transition between the muscle and tendon compartments. Quantitative analysis confirmed gradient-like transitions in marker expression, with myogenic markers decreasing and tenogenic markers increasing across the junction region. Furthermore, differentiated myotubes extended into the tendon-like matrix, forming interdigitated muscle-tendon structures analogous to the finger-like projections observed in native MTJs. These findings demonstrate that microfluidic-assisted RoWS enables the recreation of both structural and functional features of the muscle-tendon interface (Volpi et al. 2024).

12.3.2 Human-Based MTJ Biofabrication Models

The successful translation of MTJ biofabrication strategies to human cell systems represents a critical step toward clinical and translational applications. Using human pericytes and tendon-derived stem cells, RoWS enabled the fabrication of continuous hydrogel constructs containing spatially organized muscle, tendon, and junctional regions (Fig. 12.5a) (De Paolis et al. 2026). Following in vitro maturation, engineered muscle compartments exhibited aligned multinucleated myotubes expressing contractile proteins, such as myosin heavy chain, while tendon compartments exhibited abundant extracellular matrix deposition, including collagen types I and III, tenomodulin, and tenascin C, which are characteristic markers of tendon differentiation (De Paolis et al. 2026).

Importantly, the junction region exhibited a progressive transition in cellular phenotype and extracellular matrix composition, recapitulating key features of the native MTJ. Engineered muscle fibers extended projections into the tendon-like matrix, forming interdigitated structures that closely resembled the morphology of physiological muscle-tendon interfaces. In addition, the junction region expressed MTJ-specific extracellular matrix proteins, including collagen types XXII and VI and thrombospondin-4, which play essential roles in stabilizing the muscle-tendon interface and facilitating force transmission (Fig. 12.5b, c) (De Paolis et al. 2026). Proteomic and molecular analyses further confirmed the formation of a specialized junctional microenvironment characterized by the coexistence of muscle-specific and tendon-specific molecular signatures. The polarized localization of adhesion-related proteins, including paxillin and neural cell adhesion molecule-1, demonstrated the establishment of functional cell-matrix interactions and structural

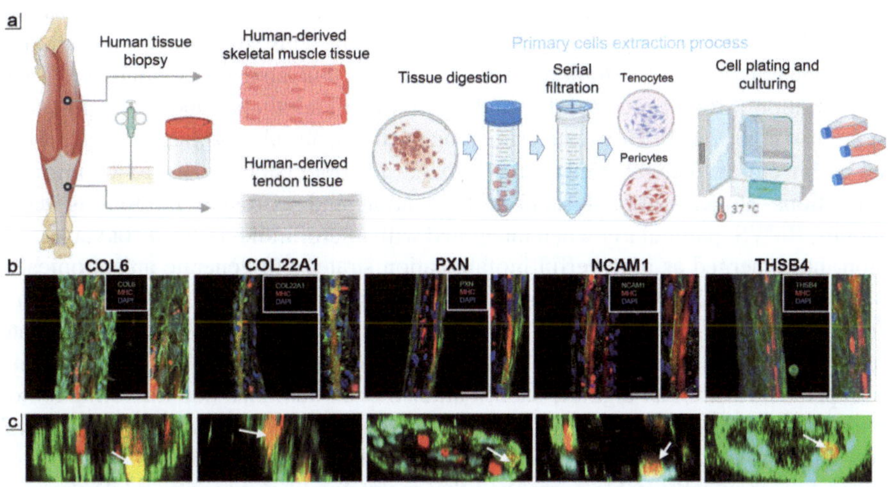

Fig. 12.5 Biofabrication of human-derived MTJ using 3D RoWS technology. (**a**) Schematic representation of the cell isolation protocol. Two primary cell populations were obtained and cultured: human pericytes (hPeri) and human tendon-derived stem cells (hTDSCs). (**b**) Representative confocal images of 3D bioprinted MTJ-like constructs stained against MTJ-specific markers (i.e., collagen type VI (COL6), collagen type XXII (COL22A1), paxillin (PXN), neural cell adhesion molecule 1 (NCAM1), and thrombospondin 4 (THBS4)). (**c**) Orthogonal view of MTJ-mimicking constructs stained against MTJ-specific markers. Scale bar magnification: 50 μm–20 μm. (Reprinted from De Paolis et al. (2026), Copyright 2026, with permission from IOP Science. CC BY-NC-ND 4.0)

integration between muscle and tendon compartments (De Paolis et al. 2026). These findings confirm that RoWS enables the recreation of physiologically relevant muscle-tendon interfaces at structural, cellular, and molecular levels. Collectively, murine and human studies demonstrate that RoWS provides a powerful platform for engineering biomimetic myotendinous junctions. By enabling precise spatial control over cellular organization, extracellular matrix composition, and structural alignment, this technology allows the recreation of the graded architecture and functional characteristics of native MTJs. The ability to engineer structurally integrated muscle-tendon constructs using clinically relevant human cells represents an important step toward the development of regenerative therapies for musculoskeletal injuries and the creation of physiologically relevant in vitro models (Table 12.2).

12.4 Engineering Anisotropic Vasculature Networks Using RoWS

The successful engineering of functional skeletal muscle substitutes critically depends on integrating a biomimetic vascular network capable of supporting the high metabolic demands of contractile tissue. In native skeletal muscle, capillaries are not randomly distributed but instead form highly organized, anisotropically aligned networks that run parallel to myofibers, ensuring efficient oxygen delivery, metabolic exchange, and coordinated tissue function. This structural organization is essential not only for sustaining muscle viability but also for regulating muscle regeneration through reciprocal signaling between endothelial and myogenic cells (Paradiso et al. 2024). However, recreating such anisotropic and hierarchical vascular architectures in engineered tissues remains a major challenge due to the intrinsic limitations of conventional scaffold fabrication and extrusion bioprinting techniques. RoWS, particularly when integrated with microfluidic-assisted coaxial extrusion, has emerged as a powerful biofabrication strategy to generate anisotropically aligned, branched, and lumenized vascular networks within fibrous hydrogel scaffolds (Fig. 12.6). A key advantage of this approach lies in its ability to create lumenized vascular structures within the fiber core. Using a fibrin-based core bioink encapsulated within an alginate shell, Paradiso et al. demonstrated the formation of endothelialized microvascular networks through microfluidic-assisted coaxial wet-spinning (Fig. 12.6a–d) (Paradiso et al. 2024). The core-shell architecture provides a mechanically stable outer shell that maintains fiber integrity, while the soft, biomimetic fibrin core supports endothelial cell migration, proliferation, and vascular morphogenesis. Importantly, the coaxial geometry enables the formation of continuous tubular compartments that serve as templates for lumen formation and endothelialization. Over time, encapsulated endothelial cells reorganize along the fiber axis, forming continuous CD31-positive vascular structures with clearly defined lumens and endothelial monolayers, indicative of functional vessel-like architectures (Fig. 12.6d). The rotary collection process plays a critical role in

Table 12.2 Summary of biofabrication strategies for muscle-tendon units and myotendinous junctions

Biofabrication technique	Bioink composition (s)	Cell model	Structural organization achieved	Construct dimensions	Scalability/ max throughput	Maturation/ functionality tests	References
Microfluidic-assisted rotary wet-spinning (RoWS)	Alginate shell, fibrin/alginate core	C2C12 + NIH/3 T3	Gradient MTJ fibers with aligned muscle and tendon compartments	Continuous fibers, cm-scale bundles	Continuous spinning, high throughput	Myosin heavy chain, collagen I/III expression, MTJ interface formation	Volpi et al. (2024)
RoWS	Alginate/fibrin	Human pericytes, tendon stem cells	Human MTJ with interdigitated architecture and biomimetic interface	Cm-scale constructs	High-throughput continuous fiber fabrication	Collagen type I, collagen type III, tenascin, tenomodulin, myosin heavy chain, proteomic analysis	De Paolis et al. (2026)
Multi-material extrusion bioprinting (integrated organ printing)	Gelatin, fibrinogen, hyaluronic acid bioinks; PU and PCL	C2C12, NIH/3 T3	Region-specific muscle, tendon, and MTJ compartments with stiffness gradient	20 mm × 5 mm × 1 mm constructs	Layer-by-layer fabrication (~30 min per construct)	Myotube formation, collagen deposition, MTJ marker expression: Paxillin, Talin, vinculin, integrin β1	Merceron et al. (2015)
Multi-material extrusion bioprinting	GelMA, fibrinogen, gelatin, Matrigel	C2C12, NIH/3 T3	Integrated MTU with a mechanically	Cm-scale constructs	Scalable extrusion printing	Contractile force generation up to ~350 μN	Filippi et al. (2025)

(continued)

Table 12.2 (continued)

Biofabrication technique	Bioink composition (s)	Cell model	Structural organization achieved	Construct dimensions	Scalability/ max throughput	Maturation/ functionality tests	References
			optimized interface				
Extrusion bioprinting	Muscle dECM, tendon dECM, collagen	Human adipose-derived stem cells	Muscle, tendon, and MTJ regions with biochemical gradients	Mm-scale constructs	Moderate throughput extrusion	Myogenic and tenogenic differentiation, MTJ gene expression	Kim et al. (2018)
Light-based DLP bioprinting with stiffness gradients	Photopolymerizable elastomeric scaffold	C2C12, NIH/3 T3	Mechanical stiffness gradient mimicking MTJ transition	Mm-scale constructs	High-resolution rapid printing	Enhanced MTJ differentiation markers	Kiratitanaporn et al. (2024)

establishing vascular anisotropy. As hydrogel fibers are continuously deposited onto the rotating drum collector, they form tightly packed, parallel fiber bundles characterized by highly aligned cellular and extracellular matrix organization. This mechanical guidance promotes directional endothelial cell migration and cytoskeletal alignment along the longitudinal fiber axis, resulting in the formation of oriented capillary-like networks that closely resemble native muscle microvasculature. Confocal imaging and morphological analysis revealed that endothelial cells exhibited elongated morphology and a preferential orientation parallel to the fiber direction, confirming RoWS's ability to guide vascular alignment at both cellular and tissue levels (Paradiso et al. 2024). Importantly, this biofabrication strategy also supports the formation of complex branched vascular networks within the engineered fibers. During in vitro maturation, endothelial cells within the fibrin core undergo spontaneous angiogenic remodeling, forming interconnected and extensively branched capillary-like structures distributed throughout the fiber volume. These networks exhibit continuous CD31 expression and endothelial-specific morphology, confirming successful endothelial differentiation and vascular network formation (Fig. 12.6d) (Paradiso et al. 2024). The confined cylindrical geometry of the fiber core facilitates controlled endothelial self-organization while maintaining overall structural alignment, enabling the development of anisotropic vascular networks that combine both directional organization and microvascular complexity.

Beyond supporting capillary-like network formation, RoWS enables the fabrication of larger lumenized vascular structures with physiologically relevant diameters. In a modular biofabrication strategy, pre-endothelialized microvascular seeds were embedded within fibrin-based bioinks and processed using the RoWS platform to generate tubular vascular fibers containing continuous endothelial linings and uniformly developed lumens ranging from 100 to 200 μm in diameter (results not yet

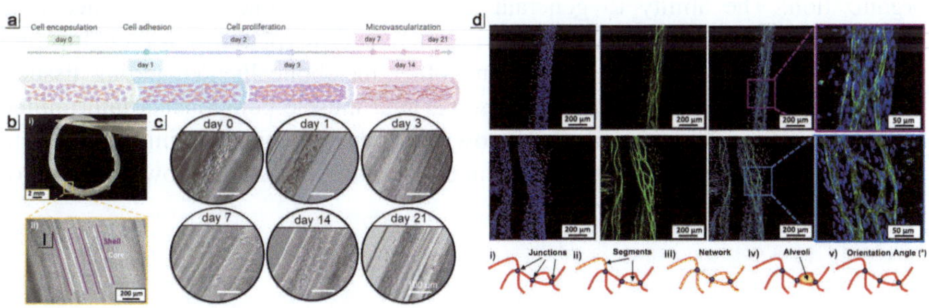

Fig. 12.6 (**a**) Schematics of the cell-material interaction occurring within the fibrin core upon cell encapsulation. (**b**) Wet-spun hydrogel bundle visualized as a macroscopic image of the overall fibrous cell-laden scaffold and optical zoom-in of the highly aligned core-shell cellularized fibers. (**c**) Representative optical images of the MSC/HUVEC population dynamics within the hydrogel fibers. (**d**) Representative confocal images of DRAQ5 (blue, cell nuclei) and CD31 (green, endothelial-like cell features) immunostained at days 7, 14, and 21, showing an interconnected capillary-like network oriented along the fiber axis and branching over the 3-week culture period. Scale bar: 200 μm (zoom-in: 50 μm). (Reprinted from Paradiso et al. (2024), Copyright 2024, with permission from American Chemical Society. CC BY-NC-ND 4.0)

published). These engineered vascular fibers exhibited homogeneous CD31 expression and formed stable, lumenized vessel-like structures that supported endothelial maturation and vascular network integration. The ability to produce stable lumenized vascular conduits represents a major advancement over traditional hydrogel encapsulation methods, which often fail to maintain open luminal architectures due to hydrogel collapse or insufficient mechanical support. Furthermore, the modularity of the RoWS approach enables the independent fabrication and subsequent assembly of vascular and muscle components, allowing the generation of integrated, hierarchically organized vascularized muscle tissues. By combining independently matured vascular fibers and skeletal muscle constructs, it is possible to recreate the spatial organization of native muscle, where vascular networks run parallel to aligned myofibers. This compartmentalized biofabrication strategy preserves the structural and functional integrity of both tissue components while enabling their integration into a cohesive, anisotropically organized construct. In addition to promoting vascular alignment and lumen formation, the RoWS platform provides precise control over fiber geometry, core diameter, and shell thickness, enabling the tuning of vascular structure and function (results not yet published). By modulating extrusion flow rates, bioink composition, and rotational speed, one can generate vascular fibers with controlled lumen size, wall thickness, and spatial organization. This level of control allows the recreation of vascular structures ranging from capillary-scale microvessels to larger vascular conduits, supporting the development of multi-scale vascular networks within engineered tissues. Collectively, these studies demonstrate that RoWS represents a highly versatile and effective strategy for engineering anisotropic, branched, and lumenized vascular networks. By combining microfluidic coaxial extrusion with rotational fiber deposition, RoWS enables the fabrication of vascular structures that recapitulate key features of native vasculature, including lumen formation, endothelial alignment, and hierarchical network organization. The ability to generate anisotropically aligned vascular networks within scalable fibrous scaffolds provides a powerful platform for engineering vascularized skeletal muscle tissues and other metabolically demanding tissues. Moreover, the capacity to integrate vascular and muscle components into unified constructs represents an important step toward the development of clinically relevant tissue substitutes capable of restoring functional muscle tissue following injury or disease (Table 12.3).

12.4.1 Future Perspectives of In Vitro Modeling and Clinical Translation

The continued evolution of biofabrication technologies, particularly RoWS and microfluidic-assisted fiber engineering, is transforming skeletal muscle tissue engineering by enabling the generation of structurally organized, vascularized, and multi-tissue constructs that increasingly recapitulate native muscle physiology.

Table 12.3 Summary of biofabrication approaches for engineered vascularized skeletal muscle tissues

Biofabrication technique	Bioink	Cell model	Structural organization achieved	Construct dimensions	System scalability	Maturation/ functional tests	References
Microfluidic-enhanced rotary wet-spinning (RoWS)	Alginate shell, fibrin core	HUVEC, MSC	Anisotropic, branched, and lumenized microvascular networks aligned along fiber axis	Continuous fibers, cm-scale bundles	Continuous spinning, high throughput	CD31+ endothelial networks, lumen formation, perfusable microvascular structures	Paradiso et al. (2024)
Extrusion-based 3D bioprinting with integrated perfusable channels	Fibrin-based bioink	Human myoblast, HUVEC, human pericytes	Spatially organized, perfusable vascular channels embedded within aligned skeletal muscle constructs	Clinically relevant, cm-scale muscle flaps	Layer-by-layer extrusion; scalable to clinically relevant flap dimensions	Perfusion capability; $CD31^+$ endothelial lining; muscle maturation markers; functional recovery in volumetric muscle loss model	Fischer et al. (2025)
Embedded multi-material bioprinting	Nanofibrous ECM-based hydrogels	hiPSC-derived myofibers	Vessel-integrated muscle-like lattices; dense aligned mm-long myofibers + passively perfusable vessel-like microchannels in endomysium-like matrix	Cm-scale constructs	Modular bioprinting enables scaling to cm-scale with custom geometries	Enhanced in vitro myofiber maturation; host vessel invasion and paracrine factors boost new muscle formation and functional recovery in volumetric muscle loss models	Lee et al. (2024)
3D bioprinting + PDMS demolding + hydrogel wrapping	Gelatin-fibrinogen/ fibrinogen-thrombin/ HFG hydrogel	C2C12, HUVEC	Oriented myotubes; external HUVEC network; timing-dependent vascular integration	14 mm × 1 mm × 2 mm bundles; ~100 μm vascular hydrogel layer	PDMS mold enables reproducible wrapping; scalable to multi-bundle constructs	Myogenic marker upregulation; high HUVEC viability; $CD31^+$/VE-cadherin$^+$ structures; improved myotube maturation, late vascularization	Jia et al. (2024)

These advances position engineered skeletal muscle tissues not only as promising candidates for regenerative therapies but also as powerful in vitro platforms for modeling human neuromuscular development, disease progression, and therapeutic responses. The ability to reproduce key structural and functional features of native muscle—including anisotropic fiber alignment, functional vascular networks, and physiologically relevant muscle-tendon interfaces—represents a major step toward bridging the gap between in vitro models and clinical applications (Celikkin et al. 2023; Volpi et al. 2024; De Paolis et al. 2026; Paradiso et al. 2024).

12.4.2 Neuromesodermal Progenitors as a Unique Cell Source for Engineering Integrated Neuromuscular and Vascular Systems

A major emerging frontier in skeletal muscle bioengineering is the identification of appropriate cell sources capable of generating not only skeletal muscle tissue but also its associated neural and vascular components. Neuromesodermal progenitors (NMPs), a transient embryonic progenitor population, represent a particularly promising and unique cell source for engineering fully integrated neuromuscular tissues. NMPs are bipotent progenitors that can differentiate into both neural and mesodermal lineages, giving rise to spinal motor neurons, skeletal muscle, and associated supporting cell populations during embryonic development (Gouti et al. 2014; Tsakiridis et al. 2014). This intrinsic developmental potential allows NMPs to simultaneously generate multiple functionally interconnected tissue types within a single differentiation framework, closely recapitulating coordinated neuromuscular development.

Recent studies have demonstrated that human pluripotent stem cell-derived NMPs can self-organize into complex neuromuscular organoids containing spinal motor neurons, skeletal muscle fibers, and supporting glial cells that establish functional neuromuscular junctions capable of driving spontaneous muscle contraction (Gouti et al. 2014; Moysidou et al. 2025). These systems recapitulate key developmental processes, including motor neuron differentiation, muscle fiber maturation, and synaptic connectivity. Motor neuron projections extend into developing muscle tissues, forming neuromuscular junctions that enable functional excitation-contraction coupling. This integrated development represents a major advantage over traditional muscle-only differentiation approaches, which lack functional neural integration.

Beyond neuromuscular integration, mesodermal progenitors derived from NMP populations provide a developmental link to vascular formation. During embryonic development, endothelial and mesenchymal progenitors arise from mesodermal lineages closely related to skeletal muscle progenitors. This shared developmental origin supports coordinated formation of muscle and vascular systems, highlighting the potential of NMP-derived mesodermal populations to contribute to vascularized skeletal muscle constructs (Moysidou et al. 2025). The use of such developmentally relevant progenitor populations may improve vascular integration and functional maturation of engineered muscle tissues.

The integration of NMP-derived progenitors with biofabrication platforms such as RoWS offers a particularly promising strategy for engineering innervated and vascularized skeletal muscle tissues. The anisotropic microarchitecture generated by RoWS supports directional neurite outgrowth and vascular alignment, facilitating the formation of organized neuromuscular and vascular networks within engineered constructs. The combination of developmentally relevant progenitors and structurally guided biofabrication provides a powerful platform for recreating physiologically integrated musculoskeletal tissues.

Importantly, NMP-derived neuromuscular systems also provide valuable platforms for modeling neuromuscular diseases and evaluating therapeutic interventions. Human NMP-derived neuromuscular models have been shown to recapitulate key pathological features of neuromuscular disorders, including impaired neuromuscular junction formation and reduced muscle contractility. These models provide physiologically relevant platforms for studying disease mechanisms and testing therapeutic strategies in human-derived tissues.

12.4.3 Toward Fully Integrated, Functional Skeletal Muscle Tissues

The integration of NMP-derived progenitors into RoWS biofabrication platforms represents a promising strategy to overcome key limitations in skeletal muscle tissue engineering. The ability of NMPs to generate neural, muscular, and supporting mesodermal cell populations within a unified developmental framework offers significant advantages for recreating the structural and functional complexity of native skeletal muscle tissue.

Future biofabrication strategies may leverage NMP-derived progenitors to generate fully integrated neuromuscular constructs containing aligned muscle fibers, functional motor neuron innervation, vascular networks, and tendon interfaces. The combination of developmentally relevant progenitor populations with advanced biofabrication techniques provides a powerful platform for engineering physiologically relevant tissue constructs that support functional muscle regeneration.

In addition to regenerative medicine applications, these integrated systems hold significant promise for in vitro modeling of neuromuscular development, disease progression, and therapeutic response. Patient-specific induced pluripotent stem cell-derived NMPs can be used to generate personalized neuromuscular tissue models, enabling the study of disease mechanisms and evaluation of therapeutic interventions in a patient-specific context. Such personalized tissue models represent a major step toward precision medicine and may significantly improve the development of effective treatments for neuromuscular diseases.

12.4.4 *Clinical Translation and Future Outlook*

The convergence of stem cell biology, developmental biology, and advanced biofabrication technologies is creating unprecedented opportunities for engineering functional skeletal muscle tissues for clinical applications. RoWS provides scalable, reproducible methods for generating aligned muscle constructs with physiologically relevant architecture, while NMP-derived progenitors offer a powerful cell source for integrated neuromuscular and vascular systems. Future research efforts will focus on improving tissue maturation, functional integration, and scalability, as well as achieving full neuromuscular and vascular integration within engineered constructs. The integration of engineered muscle constructs with host vasculature and nervous system following implantation represents a critical step toward achieving functional tissue regeneration.

Collectively, the combination of NMP-derived progenitors and RoWS biofabrication strategies represents a transformative approach for engineering complex skeletal muscle tissues with integrated neural and vascular components. These advances hold significant promise for advancing both in vitro modeling and clinical translation, bringing engineered skeletal muscle tissues closer to clinical application in regenerative medicine.

12.5 Conclusion

The field of skeletal muscle biofabrication has undergone a profound transformation over the past decade, shifting from scaffold-based approximations of muscle tissue toward highly organized, multi-scale, and functionally integrated constructs that increasingly recapitulate native musculoskeletal architecture. As highlighted throughout this chapter, the convergence of advanced biomaterials, stem cell biology, microfluidics, and biofabrication technologies has enabled the engineering of aligned myofiber bundles, biomimetic myotendinous junctions (MTJs), and anisotropic vascular networks—three essential structural pillars required for functional skeletal muscle regeneration.

Among the various strategies available, rotary wet-spinning (RoWS) has emerged as a particularly powerful and versatile fiber-based biofabrication platform. By enabling the continuous production of highly aligned, densely cellularized hydrogel fibers, RoWS directly addresses one of the most critical challenges in skeletal muscle tissue engineering: recreating anisotropic architecture at clinically relevant scales. Beyond merely providing geometric alignment, RoWS-induced structural anisotropy has been shown to modulate cellular phenotype, cytoskeletal organization, and proteomic remodeling, demonstrating that biofabrication parameters themselves act as active regulators of tissue maturation. The ability to translate RoWS from murine to human cell systems, including pericyte-derived myo-substitutes with advanced proteomic maturation signatures, underscores its robustness and translational potential.

Importantly, this chapter emphasizes that functional skeletal muscle engineering cannot be reduced to myofiber generation alone. Native muscle operates within an integrated continuum of muscle-tendon-vascular-neural structures. The successful recreation of graded MTJ interfaces using microfluidic-assisted RoWS demonstrates that spatially controlled fiber fabrication can generate transitional regions with biomimetic structural and molecular characteristics. Likewise, integrating anisotropically aligned and lumenized vascular networks into fibrous scaffolds addresses the long-standing limitation of diffusion-constrained engineered tissues. The capacity to fabricate branched, endothelialized, and hierarchically organized vascular architectures within aligned muscle constructs represents a major advancement toward metabolically competent and implantable muscle substitutes.

The integration of developmentally relevant progenitor populations, particularly neuromesodermal progenitors (NMPs), further expands the horizon of skeletal muscle bioengineering. By leveraging their intrinsic capacity to generate both neural and mesodermal derivatives, NMP-based approaches may offer in the future a biologically coherent framework for engineering innervated, vascularized, and mechanically integrated muscle tissues. When combined with anisotropic biofabrication platforms such as RoWS, these progenitor systems may enable the recreation of fully integrated neuromuscular units that more faithfully mirror embryonic development and adult tissue organization.

Despite these advances, several challenges remain before fully functional skeletal muscle substitutes can be routinely translated into clinical practice. Long-term functional integration with host vasculature and innervation, immune compatibility, scalability under good manufacturing practice (GMP) conditions, and reproducible maturation of centimeter-scale constructs remain active areas of investigation. Moreover, standardized functional assessment metrics—ranging from contractile force measurements to vascular perfusion capacity and neuromuscular integration—will be essential to enable meaningful cross-platform comparison and regulatory evaluation. Nevertheless, the field's trajectory is clear. The transition from isotropic hydrogel constructs to anisotropic, multi-compartmentalized, and vascularized muscle systems marks a paradigm shift in skeletal muscle tissue engineering. RoWS and related fiber-based biofabrication strategies provide a structurally instructive framework that guides cellular organization across scales, while advances in stem cell biology and developmental modeling introduce new possibilities for engineering fully integrated musculoskeletal units.

Collectively, the studies presented in this chapter demonstrate that the future of skeletal muscle biofabrication lies in the deliberate integration of structural anisotropy, biochemical signaling, vascularization, and neural connectivity within scalable and reproducible manufacturing platforms. By combining engineering precision with developmental biology principles, the field is moving closer to the realization of clinically relevant muscle grafts and physiologically faithful in vitro models for regenerative medicine, disease modeling, and biohybrid systems. The continued convergence of these disciplines is poised to redefine the boundaries of skeletal muscle regeneration and functional tissue replacement.

Disclosure of Interests All authors declare they have no conflict of interest.

Funding This work was supported by the National Science Centre, Poland (NCN) within SONATA BIS 12 (project no. 2022/46/E/ST8/00284 to M.C.).

References

Celikkin N, Presutti D, Maiullari F, Volpi M, Promovych Y, Gizynski K et al (2023) Combining rotary wet-spinning biofabrication and electro-mechanical stimulation for the in vitro production of functional myo-substitutes. Biofabrication 15. https://doi.org/10.1088/1758-5090/ace934

Costantini M, Testa S, Mozetic P, Barbetta A, Fuoco C, Fornetti E et al (2017) Microfluidic-enhanced 3D bioprinting of aligned myoblast-laden hydrogels leads to functionally organized myofibers in vitro and in vivo. Biomaterials 131:98–110. https://doi.org/10.1016/j.biomaterials.2017.03.026

Costantini M, Testa S, Fornetti E, Fuoco C, Sanchez Riera C, Nie M et al (2021) Biofabricating murine and human myo-substitutes for rapid volumetric muscle loss restoration. EMBO Mol Med 13. https://doi.org/10.15252/emmm.202012778

De Paolis F, Volpi M, Fuoco C, Reggio A, Deodati R, Bernardini S et al (2026) Recapitulating the human myotendinous junction *in vitro* using a 3D bioprinted model. Biofabrication 18:015035. https://doi.org/10.1088/1758-5090/ae3d86

Demri N, Morizur L, Dumas S, Gropplero G, Martinat C, Descroix S et al (2025) Magnetic bioprinting and actuation of stretchable muscle tissue. Adv Healthc Mater. https://doi.org/10.1002/adhm.202503035

Filippi M, Yasa O, Giachino J, Graf R, Balciunaite A, Stefani L et al (2023) Perfusable biohybrid designs for bioprinted skeletal muscle tissue. Adv Healthc Mater 12. https://doi.org/10.1002/adhm.202300151

Filippi M, Mock D, Fuentes J, Michelis MY, Balciunaite A, Paniagua P et al (2025) Multicellular muscle-tendon bioprinting of mechanically optimized musculoskeletal bioactuators with enhanced force transmission. Sci Adv 11(29):eadv2628

Fischer EO, Tsukerman A, Machour M, Shuhmaher M, Silverstein A, Yaakov M et al (2025) Bioprinting Perfusable and vascularized skeletal muscle flaps for the treatment of volumetric muscle loss. Adv Healthc Mater 14. https://doi.org/10.1002/adhm.202404542

Fornetti E, De Paolis F, Fuoco C, Bernardini S, Giannitelli SM, Rainer A et al (2023) A novel extrusion-based 3D bioprinting system for skeletal muscle tissue engineering. Biofabrication 15. https://doi.org/10.1088/1758-5090/acb573

Gouti M, Tsakiridis A, Wymeersch FJ, Huang Y, Kleinjung J, Wilson V et al (2014) In vitro generation of neuromesodermal progenitors reveals distinct roles for wnt signalling in the specification of spinal cord and paraxial mesoderm identity. PLoS Biol 12. https://doi.org/10.1371/journal.pbio.1001937

Grunow B, Stange K, Bochert R, Tönißen K (2021) Histological and biochemical evaluation of skeletal muscle in the two salmonid species Coregonus maraena and Oncorhynchus mykiss. PLoS One 16. https://doi.org/10.1371/journal.pone.0255062

Heilig S, Lamberger Z, Sprenger L, Priebe V, Mussoni C, Docheva D et al (2025) Fibrillar bundles as fibrous filler materials for attaining cell anisotropy in bioprinting. Adv Healthc Mater. https://doi.org/10.1002/adhm.202503767

Jia M, Fan T, Jia T, Liu X, Liu H, Gu Q (2024) Temporal and spatial regulation of biomimetic vascularization in 3D-printed skeletal muscles. Biodes Manuf 7:597–610. https://doi.org/10.1007/s42242-024-00315-0

Kim JH, Seol YJ, Ko IK, Kang HW, Lee YK, Yoo JJ et al (2018) 3D bioprinted human skeletal muscle constructs for muscle function restoration. Sci Rep:8. https://doi.org/10.1038/s41598-018-29968-5

Kiratitanaporn W, Guan J, Tang M, Xiang Y, Lu TY, Balayan A et al (2024) 3D printing of a biomimetic Myotendinous junction assisted by artificial intelligence. Biomater Sci 12:6047–6062. https://doi.org/10.1039/d4bm00892h

Lee H, Kim SH, Lee JS, Lee YJ, Lee OJ, Ajiteru O et al (2023) Functional skeletal muscle regeneration using muscle mimetic tissue fabricated by microvalve-assisted coaxial 3D bioprinting. Adv Healthc Mater 12. https://doi.org/10.1002/adhm.202202664

Lee MC, Jodat YA, Endo Y, Rodríguez-delaRosa A, Zhang T, Karvar M et al (2024) Engineering large-scale hiPSC-derived vessel-integrated muscle-like lattices for enhanced volumetric muscle regeneration. Trends Biotechnol 42:1715–1744. https://doi.org/10.1016/j.tibtech.2024.08.001

Liu H, Winkelbauer M, Janiak J, Weber P, Kalkan AK, Kim I et al (2025) Filamented light (FLight) bioprinting of mini-muscles with self-renewal potential. Adv Mater 37. https://doi.org/10.1002/adma.202501147

Merceron TK, Burt M, Seol YJ, Kang HW, Lee SJ, Yoo JJ et al (2015) A 3D bioprinted complex structure for engineering the muscle-tendon unit. Biofabrication 7. https://doi.org/10.1088/1758-5090/7/3/035003

Moysidou C-M, Martins IA, El-Shimy IA, Cea D, Bukas C, Mekki I et al (2025) Guided maturation of human neuromuscular organoids via electrical stimulation. https://doi.org/10.1101/2025.10.30.685366

Nie M, Nagata S, Oda H, Takeuchi S (2023) Millimeter-thick 3D tissues constructed by densely cellularized core-shell microfluidic bioprinting. Biofabrication 15. https://doi.org/10.1088/1758-5090/accd23

Paradiso A, Volpi M, Martinez DC, Jaroszewicz J, Costantini M, Swieszkowski W (2024) Engineering biomimetic microvascular capillary networks in hydrogel fibrous scaffolds via microfluidics-assisted co-axial wet-spinning. ACS Appl Mater Interfaces 16:65927–65941. https://doi.org/10.1021/acsami.4c15221

Pillai Babu D, Sreena R, Brenner K, Nathanael AJ, Kishore V (2026) Progress in skeletal muscle tissue engineering: advancing from 3D to 4D bioprinting. Progress in Biomed Eng 8. https://doi.org/10.1088/2516-1091/ae1e47

Reggio A, Fuoco C, De Paolis F, Deodati R, Testa S, Celikkin N et al (2025) 3D Rotary Wet-Spinning (RoWS) biofabrication directly affects proteomic signature and myogenic maturation in muscle pericyte–derived human myo-substitute. Aggregate 6. https://doi.org/10.1002/agt2.727

Sabetkish S, Currie P, Meagher L (2024) Recent trends in 3D bioprinting technology for skeletal muscle regeneration. Acta Biomater 181:46–66. https://doi.org/10.1016/j.actbio.2024.04.038

Sprenger L, Lu HH, Trippmacher S, Mansfeld U, Milkin P, Ionov L et al (2024) Composite alginate Dialdehyde-gelatin (ADA-GEL) hydrogel containing short ribbon-shaped fillers for skeletal muscle tissue biofabrication. ACS Appl Mater Interfaces 16:44605–44622. https://doi.org/10.1021/acsami.4c10751

Tsakiridis A, Huang Y, Blin G, Skylaki S, Wymeersch F, Osorno R et al (2014) Distinct Wnt-driven primitive streak-like populations reflect in vivo lineage precursors. Development (Cambridge) 141:1209–1221. https://doi.org/10.1242/dev.101014

Volpi M, Paradiso A, Walejewska E, Gargioli C, Costantini M, Swieszkowski W (2024) Automated microfluidics-assisted hydrogel-based wet-spinning for the biofabrication of biomimetic engineered Myotendinous junction. Adv Healthc Mater 13. https://doi.org/10.1002/adhm.202402075

Chapter 13
Collagen-Based Vascular Tissue Engineering: Deconstructing the Step-by-Step Fabrication of Biocast-Vascular Models

Silvia Rodriguez-Fernandez, Rafaelle Vinturelle, Francesco Copes, and Diego Mantovani

Abstract New therapeutic strategies rely on preclinical models that accurately predict human physiological and pathological responses. Conventional two-dimensional cell cultures and animal models present major limitations when studying vascular biology, motivating the development of human-relevant three-dimensional alternatives. Vascular tissue engineering (VTE) has emerged as a promising approach to create in vitro artery models that recapitulate native structure, function, and mechanics. This chapter focuses on collagen type I (Coll-I)–based artery constructs fabricated using casting strategies to generate small-caliber tubular geometries. The main vascular cell sources suitable for these models are first reviewed, followed by a discussion of scaffold design, highlighting Coll-I for its abundance in arterial extracellular matrix, intrinsic bioactivity, and ability to form cell-laden hydrogels. Principles of collagen biocasting and device designs enabling tubular artery formation are described. The chapter then addresses construct maturation, emphasizing cell-mediated remodeling, biochemical cues, and mechanical stimulation required to achieve native-like properties. Finally, current limitations and future perspectives of collagen-based in vitro artery models are discussed, including their application in disease modeling, drug testing, and medical device evaluation.

Keywords Vascular tissue engineering (VTE) · Collagen type I · Collagen hydrogel · Casting · Bioreactor · In vitro model · Small caliber artery

---

S. Rodriguez-Fernandez · R. Vinturelle · F. Copes · D. Mantovani (✉)
Laboratory for Biomaterials and Bioengineering, Canada Research Chair Tier I for the Innovation in Surgery, Department of Min-Met-Materials Engineering and Regenerative Medicine, CHU de Quebec Research Center, Laval University, Quebec City, QC, Canada
e-mail: diego.mantovani@gmn.ulaval.ca

Y. M. Elçin (ed.), *Biofabrication in Regenerative Medicine*, Stem Cell Biology and Regenerative Medicine 1519, https://doi.org/10.1007/978-3-032-30294-6_13

Abbreviations

2D	Two-dimensional
3D	Three-dimensional
Coll-I	Collagen type I
dECM	Decellularized extracellular matrix
EC	Endothelial cell
ECM	Extracellular matrix
FB	Fibroblast
hEC	Human endothelial cell
hFB	Human fibroblast
HDL	High-density lipoprotein
hSMC	Human smooth muscle cell
hTERT	Human telomerase reverse transcriptase
ID	Inner diameter
iPSC	Induced pluripotent stem cell
LDL	Low-density lipoprotein
MSC	Mesenchymal stem cell
MMP-2	Matrix metalloproteinase-2
MMP-9	Matrix metalloproteinase-9
PCL	Polycaprolactone
PDGF	Platelet-derived growth factor
rSMC	Rat smooth muscle cell
SMC	Smooth muscle cell
TGF-β1	Transforming growth factor-β1
VTE	Vascular tissue engineering

13.1 Introduction

New therapies to treat diseases are developed through a process that begins with in vitro experiments and progresses to in vivo testing using animal models. In vitro two-dimensional (2D) cell culture models are a cost-efficient approach to study diseases at the cellular level, but they do not provide information at the systemic level, a limitation that is particularly problematic when studying blood vessels. Moreover, their cell–cell and cell–extracellular matrix (ECM) interactions differ from those in native tissues, leading to altered phenotypes, changes in gene and protein expression, and ultimately modified cellular responses to drugs (Kapałczyńska et al. 2018).

Animal models are used to reproduce pathophysiological conditions in complex biological environments that mimic the human body, or to assess the efficacy and safety of novel treatments before clinical trials (Andrade et al. 2016). However, animal models are highlighted by the poor predictive accuracy, illustrated by high drug failure rates in human trials due to the inherent physiological differences from humans (Robinson et al. 2019; Norman 2019). Furthermore, the use of animals in research increasingly conflicts with ethical principles (Akhtar 2015). These observations emphasize the need for alternative, human-relevant models.

Over the past decades, tissue engineering products have gained considerable attention as a human-based alternative to conventional preclinical methods (Joyce et al. 2023). In particular, vascular tissue engineering (VTE) has emerged as a promising strategy for developing functional blood vessel constructs. VTE involves the use of cells seeded within three-dimensional (3D) scaffolds that mimic the native ECM and aim to reproduce both the biological and mechanical properties of natural vessels, either as vascular substitutes or as advanced in vitro models (Marei et al. 2022). Numerous studies have explored different biomaterials, biofabrication techniques, and cultured conditions to create engineered blood vessels, promote their maturation, and expose them to controlled mechanical stimulation to maturate the construct (Bosch-Rué et al. 2025; Song et al. 2018).

Among vascular targets, small-caliber arteries (<6 mm diameter), such as coronary arteries, are the most widely studied in VTE research for both implantable grafts and in vitro models. The reason is they are highly susceptible to narrowing and occlusion, which can severely restrict or block blood flow through the vessel. The limited success of current clinical interventions to treat these disease-related conditions, such as balloon angioplasty, stenting, and bypass grafting with autologous or synthetic grafts, often fail due to thrombosis, mechanical properties mismatch, and poor long-term patency (Pashneh-Tala et al. 2016). Consequently, the engineering of in vitro human-relevant small caliber artery constructs that accurately reproduce the native artery's size, multilayered wall architecture, and mechanical properties and that can withstand or be exposed to physiological hemodynamic conditions is essential. Such constructs can serve not only as potential implantable grafts but also as advanced platforms to investigate occlusive disease mechanisms, such as those involved in atherosclerosis, and to evaluate novel drugs or devices before preclinical or clinical testing (Marei et al. 2022). In this chapter, small-caliber arteries are therefore used as the main example to illustrate the step-by-step development of VTE models. The discussion first introduces the type of cells that can serve or differentiate into the vascular cell protagonists of these constructs. It then turns to scaffold design, focusing on the selection of a polymeric matrix. Collagen type I (Coll-I) is chosen as the reference biomaterial, not only because it was used in some of the earliest tissue-engineered vascular grafts (Weinberg and Bell 1986) and has been extensively characterized over nearly four decades (Amirrah et al. 2022) but also because it remains a highly effective polymer for tissue engineering due to its prevalence in the native arterial extracellular matrix, intrinsic bioactivity, and capacity to support cell adhesion, proliferation, and matrix remodeling (Figueiredo et al. 2025).

A particular strength of collagen is its ability to form hydrogels in which cells can be directly embedded, greatly simplifying the fabrication of tubular constructs (Weinberg and Bell 1986). This feature makes collagen especially compatible with casting approaches, which enable the rapid formation of a macroscale tubular structure of arteries. Given that printing collagen in a robust, macroscale format remains technically challenging, casting currently offers the most practical route for generating collagen-based vascular models at this scale (Marei et al. 2022). The chapter therefore presents several examples of casting devices and workflows, illustrating different strategies used by researchers to produce a VTE artery model.

A key challenge addressed in the chapter is the maturation phase, during which the initially cast collagen scaffold is remodeled by cells into a tissue with more native-like mechanical and histological properties (Pineda-Castillo et al. 2023; Stegemann and Nerem 2003a). Several examples of how parameters such as cell source, casting platforms, and biochemical and mechanical stimulation modulate this process and ultimately determine construct performance are exposed.

Finally, the chapter briefly surveys the development of collagen-based pathological models of small-caliber arteries, particularly atherosclerotic models, summarizing the current state of collagen-cast vascular models, their limitations, and how emerging technologies could further advance collagen-based VTE while maintaining collagen in its hydrogel form as a central material platform.

13.2 The Workforce in Tissue-Engineered Models: Cells

For the development of an in vitro arterial wall model, it is essential to use the relevant cell types found in the native tissue. Arteries present a tri-layered structure composed of three principal vascular cell types: endothelial cells (ECs) in the tunica intima (intima layer), forming a monolayer barrier; smooth muscle cells (SMCs) in the tunica media (media layer), arranged circumferentially; and fibroblast (FBs) in the tunica adventitia (adventitia layer), more dispersed in the matrix (Fig. 13.1).

In addition to their type, cells can be modified to fit specific needs and counteract innate limitation of their native equivalent. The choice of cell source ultimately depends on the specific objectives of the model and the research questions being addressed. Thus, cells used can be divided into four categories: (1) primary adult vascular cells harvested directly from donor tissues; (2) primary mesenchymal stem cells (MSCs), also isolated from donor tissues, which can differentiate into vascular cells; (3) vascular cells differentiated from induced pluripotent stem cells (iPSCs); and (4) immortalized vascular cell lines. Below, we describe the advantages and limitations of each of these cell sources.

13.2.1 Primary Adult Cells

Primary adult cells are isolated from donor tissues and are commonly employed in VTE (Song et al. 2018). They tend to better preserve native gene and protein expression patterns compared to immortalized or stem cell–derived lines (Richter et al. 2021). Nevertheless, primary cells have notable limitations. Their extraction

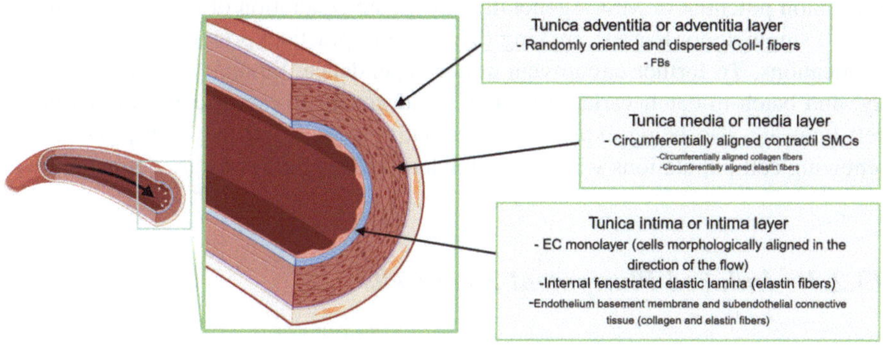

Fig. 13.1 Schematic representation of the structural organization of a healthy small-caliber artery wall, highlighting the three main layers (tunica intima, tunica media, and tunica adventitia) and their predominant cellular and extracellular matrix components; smaller font sizes indicate components that are less abundant in the corresponding layer (Hsieh et al. 2014; Chia et al. 2020; Basatemur et al. 2019; Cao et al. 2022; Xu and Shi 2014; Milutinović et al. 2020; Krüger-Genge et al. 2019). *Coll-I* collagen type I, *ECs* endothelial cells, *FBs* fibroblasts, *SMCs* small muscle cells. (Created in https://BioRender.com)

usually involves invasive procedures, such as blood vessel biopsies. Additionally, the yield of cells is often low, and their capacity to proliferate is limited, particularly when sourced from older donors. These parameters are also strongly donor dependent, leading to considerable variability in cell yield, phenotype, and functional performance between isolates from different individuals. Moreover, the isolation and maintenance of primary cells are labor-intensive and costly (Song et al. 2018; Jouda et al. 2022). Given these limitations, primary multipotent stem cells such as MSCs and pluripotent stem cells such as iPSCs have emerged as attractive alternatives capable of generating vascular-specific lineages (Au et al. 2008; Collado et al. 2017).

13.2.2 Primary Mesenchymal Stem Cells

MSCs are multipotent cells that can be differentiated into SMCs and ECs using biochemical or mechanical cues, such as transforming growth factor -β1 (TGF- β1) and mechanical shear stress (Au et al. 2008; Dong et al. 2009). MSCs are isolated from diverse sources, including bone marrow, adipose tissue, peripheral blood, and vessel walls. They exhibit paracrine activity through secretion of extracellular vesicles and soluble factors such as angiogenic cytokines. This paracrine-mediated angiogenic response supports capillary-like network formation, endothelial cell migration, and tissue recovery in ischemic models. However, donor variability, limited self-renewal, and a decline in functional capacity with donor age limit reproducibility and scale-up (Kuchroo et al. 2015; Maacha et al. 2020). Despite sharing many of these constraints with primary adult vascular cells, the higher expansion potential of MSCs generally allows the generation of larger cell numbers from a single donor harvest, making them a more practical primary source for VTE applications. To further circumvent donor dependence, limited proliferative capacity, and batch-to-batch variability, iPSCs and genetically engineered immortalized cell lines are also being explored as alternative sources, as they can provide self-renewing cell populations with more standardized properties for model generation.

13.2.3 Induced Pluripotent Stem Cells

iPSCs are somatic (typically adult) cells that have been reprogrammed back to a pluripotent state by forced expression of specific transcription factors, thereby regaining the capacity to self-renew indefinitely and to differentiate into virtually any cell type, including vascular cells. iPSCs thus provide an almost unlimited, renewable source of patient-specific cells that can, in principle, generate vascular lineages with defined genetic backgrounds for disease modeling and regenerative applications (Shi et al. 2017). However, current iPSCs present certain limitations. The functional maturity of iPSC-derived vascular cells is a challenge. Although many protocols yield cells expressing physiologically relevant markers, differences in phenotype and behavior compared to primary vascular cells persist, especially regarding functional integration and response to hemodynamic forces when compared to primary vascular cells (Collado et al. 2017). Moreover, differentiation protocols for generating vascular cells from iPSCs vary widely in efficiency, purity, and functional output between laboratories. In addition, the differentiation of iPSCs into ECs and SMCs generally relies on multi-step, cytokine-intensive protocols that are technically demanding, time-consuming, and costly, which further complicates their routine use in VTE models (Jiao et al. 2024). This can be addressed by establishing standardized protocols and by better understanding how each step influences the functional properties of the cells (Jouda et al. 2022).

In applications where ease of culture, rapid expansion, and high experimental reproducibility are prioritized, researchers frequently turn to immortalized cell lines, thereby circumventing the lengthy reprogramming and differentiation steps required for iPSC-derived vascular cells (Obinata 2007).

13.2.4 Immortalized Cells

Immortalized cell lines are populations of cells that have acquired the ability to proliferate indefinitely, typically through the introduction of viral oncogenes, ectopic expression of telomerase (hTERT), or other genetic modifications that prevent cellular senescence (Obinata 2007; Shitova et al. 2024). These cell lines are well-established, easier to work with, and cost-effective, offering a long lifespan and consistent growth. However, immortalized cells may produce outcomes that differ from those observed in vivo, due to their altered genetic (Richter et al. 2021; Shitova et al. 2024). Despite the drawbacks, immortalized cell lines could be used in the initial stages of arterial model engineering to design and optimize new assays, methodologies, and in vitro platforms for vascular model generation. Once the platform and culture conditions have been established and validated using these robust cell sources, key experiments can then be repeated with primary or stem cell–derived vascular cells to ensure that the final arterial constructs exhibit physiologically relevant structure and function.

13.2.5 Co-culture

Interactions between vascular cells, especially ECs and SMCs, influence cellular adhesion, migration, proliferation, and phenotypic modulation within vascular tissue (Lust et al. 2021). To reproduce these cell-cell dynamics, researchers have developed co-culture models that mimic physiological cellular communication in vitro (Powell et al. 1998; Williams and Wick 2005; Ganesan et al. 2017). Co-culture systems can be categorized as direct or indirect. In direct co-culture, different cell types are placed in direct physical contact, either layered on top of one another or positioned side by side. In contrast, indirect co-culture uses permeable membranes, such as Transwell inserts, to spatially separate cell populations. Soluble paracrine factors are exchanged without direct contact. Both approaches alone do not fully emulate the complexity of the native ECM, which plays a decisive role in influencing cell function and behavior. To address this limitation, advanced scaffolding strategies, incorporating varied materials and architectures, have been introduced, facilitating the creation of 3D culture environments that provide more physiologically relevant cues for vascular cell co-culture (Lust et al. 2021).

13.3 The Framework of the Cells: Polymeric Scaffolds

In tissue engineering, a scaffold is a cytocompatible 3D structure that temporarily replaces or mimics the native ECM. It provides a physical structure for cells to attach, migrate, proliferate, establish cell–cell communication, and organize into new tissue. It supports nutrient and oxygen transport and gives mechanical stability to the cells, and it can provide biochemical and biophysical factors that regulate cell behavior. As the new tissue forms, the scaffold, designed to degrade or remodel, will allow the regenerated tissue to progressively assume the structural support and functional properties of the native tissue (Di Francesco et al. 2023).

Scaffold materials used to engineer a VTE model can be classified into two main categories: synthetic and natural polymers (Pashneh-Tala et al. 2016; Di Francesco et al. 2023; Li et al. 2023). Synthetic polymers, such as polycaprolactone, are easily tunable and processable, facilitating reproducible scaffold fabrication (Li et al. 2023;

Leal et al. 2021). However, they do not present cell-binding motives required for optimal cell adhesion and proliferation and are frequently hydrophobic. Therefore, surface modifications or blending with bioactive molecules (e.g., RGD peptides, collagen) are often necessary to improve cell adhesion (Mohan et al. 2025; Zheng et al. 2012).

By contrast, natural polymers such as collagen, gelatin, elastin, or fibrin can be derived from the ECM of different organisms and tissues. These materials offer significant advantages, including bioactivity and cell-recognition and adhesion motifs that facilitate cell attachment and promote tissue-specific remodeling by cells. However, natural materials generally exhibit inferior mechanical properties and higher batch-to-batch variability compared to synthetics; they frequently require cross-linking or combination with other polymers to tune mechanical properties (Di Francesco et al. 2023; Li et al. 2023).

In VTE, Coll-I is the most used natural polymer (Leal et al. 2021), not only because of its inherit biological properties that support cell behavior, but also due to its structural and mechanical roles in native arterial ECM (Rhodes and Simons 2007). Thus, collagen and elastin collaborate to generate the nonlinear, anisotropic, and viscoelastic behavior of arteries. At low strain, elastin of the arterial elastic lamellae accommodates vessel deformation, providing compliance and elastic recoil. As pressure increases, collagen fibers are progressively recruited, increasing stiffness and limiting vessel expansion, shifting load to the tunica adventitia where Coll-I predominates (Camasão and Mantovani 2021; Bartolf-Kopp and Jungst 2024). These properties make Coll-I particularly advantageous for VTE models designed to mimic physiological function and cell-matrix interactions, reflecting its structural and functional role on native vessels (Di Francesco et al. 2023).

13.3.1 From Isolated Collagen I to Cell-Laden Collagen I Scaffolds

Coll-I is the most abundant type of collagen in connective tissues where structural and mechanical support are required. This protein can be isolated from different animal tissues, such as rat tail tendon (Rajan et al. 2006; Habermehl et al. 2005), porcine skin (He et al. 2020), or fish scales (Pati et al. 2010), and processed into reconstituted fibrillar scaffold without loss of bioactivity when handled under mild conditions (Amirrah et al. 2022; Figueiredo et al. 2025). The Coll-I isolation process and characterization were extensively reviewed by Pires et al. (2025) and Amirrah et al. (2022). After isolation, Coll-I is commonly solubilized in acidic solutions and subsequently processed to obtain collagen scaffolds (Walters and Stegemann 2013).

Two strategies are used to engineer a collagen fibrillar scaffold from an acidic solution, depending on when cells are added. In the first approach, collagen is processed into a cell-free scaffold, using techniques such as electrospinning, circular knitting (Zhang et al. 2019), or freeze-drying (Kim et al. 1999), and cells are seeded afterward onto the structure. After seeding, cells must adhere to the surface and colonize the scaffold before they can exert substantial remodeling, which makes this strategy a relatively time-consuming route to produce a VTE model.

The second processing strategy integrates cells during the formation of the collagen scaffold through gelation, resulting in a cell-laden collagen hydrogel in a single step. Hydrogels are 3D cross-linked networks of hydrophilic polymers that imbibe and retain large amounts of water. They can mimic ECM in terms of porosity and solute diffusion transport, and mechanics can be tuned to approximate native ECM, while supporting cell encapsulation (Pien et al. 2021). A cell-laden collagen hydrogel is prepared by neutralizing the acidic Coll-I solution, mixing it with a cell suspension, and allowing collagen to physical self-assemble into a fibrillar hydrogel at 37 °C within minutes (Figueiredo et al. 2025; Rajan et al. 2006; Boccafoschi et al. 2005). The resulting construct contains cells uniformly distributed and adhered throughout the matrix, enabling immediate cell–matrix interactions, rapid remodeling, and faster maturation.

Although other natural and synthetic polymers have been explored to produce hydrogel scaffolds for tissue engineering (Pien et al. 2021), even for VTE (Jin et al. 2022), most of them do not easily form cell-compatible fibrillar scaffolds under physiological conditions such as collagen alone. Therefore, it is required additional chemical or physical cross-linking to achieve stable gels that can encapsulate cells at physiological pH and temperature (Pien et al. 2021). These extra steps introduce formulation complexity and can induce cytotoxicity or diffusional constraints during gelation. This makes the process development more demanding than the straightforward temperature and pH-triggered assembly of collagen fibers, in addition to the cell encapsulation, reinforcing the practical advantage of Coll-I hydrogels as an efficient and relevant scaffold for tissue engineering.

13.3.1.1 Vascular Cells-Collagen Interaction in Hydrogels: Living in Tension

As stated, vascular cells exhibit distinct phenotypes in 2D versus 3D cultures. The polymer used in 3D systems further influences intercellular crosstalk and cell behavior. In the specific case of Coll-I hydrogels, a key aspect of cell-matrix interaction is the ability of SMCs and FBs, when encapsulated into the hydrogel, to exert tensile forces that compact and reorganize the collagen fibers, producing a cell-populated collagen lattice (Weinberg and Bell 1985; Kural and Billiar 2013). This contraction depends on factors such as initial cell density, collagen concentration, and culture time (Weinberg and Bell 1985; Camasão et al. 2019). Collagen gel contraction assays show substantial reductions in gel size within 24–48 h, with SMCs and FBs often contracting the Coll-I hydrogels by half their initial diameter (Camasão et al. 2019; L'Heureux et al. 1993). From an engineering perspective, this property can be challenging to control, but it also offers a powerful tool. Cell-mediated compaction and fiber reorganization can guide the formation and maturation of multilayered vascular tissue constructs, making SMC and FB behavior a key factor in designing functional VTE models.

13.4 Giving Shape to Coll-I-Based VTE Models: Biocasting

To translate the described cell-laden hydrogel-based approach into VTE, each relevant vascular cell type can be incorporated into a dedicated Coll-I hydrogel. Thus, FBs and SMCs can be embedded in separate hydrogels to form the adventitia-like layer and the media-like layer, respectively. ECs can be seeded on top of the media-like layer to form the intima-like layer.

The simplest and most widely used method to shape a cell-laden Coll-I hydrogel is casting, in which a pre-gel solution of collagen, medium, and cells is poured into a mold and allowed to jellify. Using this technique, planar Coll-I-based VTE models that recapitulate arterial wall layers can be produced, using culture plates or custom molds like casting devices. Anchoring systems, such as glued cotton gauzes, are added to the molds to minimize dimensional changes driven by SMCs and/or FBs embedded in the hydrogels (Fig. 13.2a) (Loy et al. 2017; Bono et al. 2016; Lévesque et al. 2018).

In literature, planar constructs range from single media-like layers (Wang and Tarbell 2000) to bilayer models combining media-like and intima-like (Liu et al. 2023), whereas tri-layer flat models remain less common (Loy et al. 2017). These planar models are well-suited to investigate cell–matrix and cell–cell interactions and to study mechanotransduction under well-controlled and simple conditions (Loy et al. 2017; Bono et al. 2016). Furthermore, planar models are accessible for imaging and biochemical assays, being a powerful platform to test drugs and to study physiological process and the onset of pathologies (Loy et al. 2017). However, their planar geometry limits the precise reproduction of physiological hemodynamic forces, so applying realistic combinations of lumen-confined flow and pressure remains more challenging than in tubular models.

13.4.1 Mimicking the Tubular Geometry

The first tubular Coll-I-based artery model was produced using a casting approach 40 years ago, successfully imitating the native geometry of a blood vessel (Fig. 13.2b) (Weinberg and Bell 1986). Using a cylindrical mold with a central mandrel, they exploited the described intrinsic ability of SMCs and FBs to compact a Coll-I hydrogel, thereby forming a tubular lattice around the mandrel. Specifically, once the media-like layer was cast in the mold around the central mandrel and stabilized, the external adventitia-like layer was formed around the media-like layer. To complete the model, the mandrel was removed, and ECs were seeded onto the

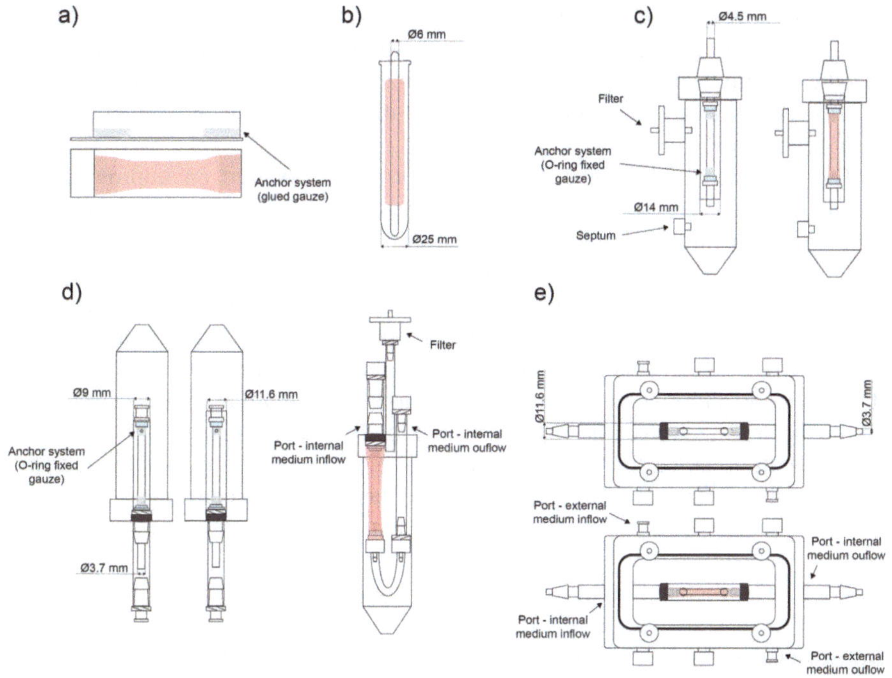

Fig. 13.2 Representative casting devices used for arterial wall modeling, indicating inner diameter (ID) of the molds and external diameter of the mandrels. (**a**) Planar model: culture-chamber slide used as a mold, with cotton gauze glued to the base to anchor the collagen gel (Loy et al. 2017). (**b**) Pioneering Weinberg–Bell casting device using a test tube as the mold and a central removable glass mandrel (Weinberg and Bell 1986). (**c**) Static tubular casting device, in which a syringe barrel mold is inserted into a silicone stopper fixed to a 50-mL tube lid; two gauze grips mounted on the mandrel prevent longitudinal compaction of the cell-laden gel during gelation, and the 50-mL tube serves as a closed chamber for static culture (Meghezi et al. 2015). (**d**) Dynamic system with a similar stopper–syringe configuration, but integrated into a flow circuit that enables perfusion culture to mimic blood flow; two interchangeable syringe barrel molds with different IDs are used to form media-like and adventitia-like layers (Loy et al. 2018). (**e**) Modified TGT DynaGen system, featuring a custom pre-formed syringe mold held between anchors, which allows medium exchange through internal and external chamber ports and support dynamic culture condition (Camasão et al. 2022)

luminal surface of the media-like layer, resulting in a tri-layered construct resembling the native vessel organization.

Since this pioneering work that established the foundation for the field of VTE, multiple variations of tubular hydrogel casting devices have been developed, some of which are illustrated in Fig. 13.2. These devices have been designed not only for the fabrication of in vitro vascular models but also to the production of potentially implantable engineered vessels, since the underlying casting principles are largely the same. Some of them are lab-built and rely on readily available laboratory materials (Weinberg and Bell 1986; Camasão et al. 2019; L'Heureux et al. 1993; Meghezi et al. 2015; Loy et al. 2018; Camasão et al. 2022; Berglund et al. 2003;

Boccafoschi et al. 2007). While simple and cost-effective, they could be less reproducible due to variations in manual assembly. Other approaches introduced specific custom-designed hardware, which enhances reproducibility and control but increases casting device complexity and manufacturing cost (Camasão et al. 2022; Tranquillo et al. 1996).

The evolution of hydrogel casting platforms has focused on improving both casting hardware design and construct fabrication workflow. Taken together, those developments allow hydrogel casting platforms to be analyzed according to three design aspects that can determine the structural and functional performance of engineered constructs. The first relates to geometric fidelity, including lumen diameter and wall thickness relative to native arterial dimensions, as well as construct length, which researchers adjust according to the intended application of the construct. The second involves strategies for constructing multilayered constructs that mimic the organization of the vascular wall. Finally, the third design aspect concerns the integration of casting and culture on the same platform, thereby reducing handling, contamination risk, and mechanical damage of the construct.

13.4.1.1 Geometric Fidelity

Dimensional control is important for reproducing the geometry of arteries, where both lumen diameter and wall thickness must closely mimic the native vessel. To recreate small-caliber arteries, non-adherent mandrels with diameters of 6 mm or less are typically used to define the lumen. Mandrels can be made of glass (L'Heureux et al. 1993; Berglund et al. 2003; He and Matsuda 2002) or polymeric materials such as polystyrene (Meghezi et al. 2015; Loy et al. 2018; Boccafoschi et al. 2007), polyetheretherketone (Pien et al. 2023), or Teflon (Girton et al. 2000). To prevent adhesion of collagen or cells, mandrel surfaces are commonly treated with non-stick coatings, including Pluronic F127 (Syedain et al. 2011) or Vaseline (Barocas et al. 1998).

The initial wall thickness of the construct depends first on the initial pre-gel volume relative to the mold cross-sectional area. In tubular molds, this cross-section is defined by the outer mandrel diameter (or the media-like diameter) and the inner mold diameter, which set the initial wall thickness. Reported tubular mold configurations span from a 5 mm annular wall (mandrel 5 mm, mold 15 mm; (He and Matsuda 2002) to a 2.6 mm annular wall (mandrel 3.8 mm, mold 9 mm; (Pezzoli et al. 2018). SMC and FB cell density (Camasão et al. 2019) and collagen concentration (Cummings et al. 2004) also influence wall thickness, because cells compact collagen during maturation, therefore, reducing initial thickness. To achieve a target wall thickness of, for example, less than 1 mm in small-caliber arteries (Harteveld et al. 2018; Zhu and Friedman 2003), mold and mandrel diameters, pre-gel volume, and cell-dependent remodeling parameters must be selected and controlled accordingly.

Construct length is another design parameter and is often initially set by the mold length. To produce long hydrogels that are easy to handle, larger molds have been used, including glass tubes (Berglund et al. 2003; He and Matsuda 2002), 15-mL polypropylene tubes (L'Heureux et al. 1993; Boccafoschi et al. 2007), and modified syringe barrels (Fig. 13.2c–e) (Meghezi et al. 2015; Loy et al. 2018; Camasão et al. 2022). Shorter constructs can be produced using a simple casting device, such as by fixing the mandrel inside the well of a 48-multi-well plate (Pien et al. 2023; Camasão et al. 2020; González-Pérez et al. 2021), or by using specific-custom casting devices (Tranquillo et al. 1996). However, after gelation, cell-mediated collagen compaction can distort construct length during maturation. Several strategies have been implemented to mitigate this effect. Acellular collagen coatings applied to mandrels (Berglund et al. 2003; Boccafoschi et al. 2007), and physical anchoring supports similar to those used for flat models (Meghezi et al. 2015; Loy et al. 2018; Camasão et al. 2022; Pezzoli et al. 2018) help prevent undesired shortening and preserve length integrity.

13.4.1.2 Strategies for Multilayer Construction

To develop multilayer constructs that mimic the three-layer organization of the arterial wall, most casting platforms rely on sequential casting workflows to build media- and adventitia-like layers. In the approach described by L'Heureux et al., the media-like layer is cast in a tube around a removable glass mandrel. After compaction, the mandrel with the media-like layer is reinserted in a tube to cast the adventitia-like layer (L'Heureux et al. 1993). Loy et al. designed a casting platform that relies on a sequential two-mold setup: the media-like layer is first cast inside a small syringe barrel; this mold is then removed, and the cell-laden collagen construct is then densified for 1 h, after which a larger barrel is mounted onto the same casting device to fabricate the adventitia-like layer concentrically around the media (Loy et al. 2018). This workflow shortens the layering step compared with approaches in which the media-like layer must compact for several days before the adventitia-like layer can be cast (Weinberg and Bell 1986). Camasão et al. proposed an alternative platform in which the mold is fixed in the casting device. The mold consists of a syringe barrel with two ports for pre-gel solution injection. In this casting platform, both layers are cast within the same mold, allowing overnight compaction of the media-like layer prior to casting the adventitia-like layer (Camasão et al. 2022).

In most published casting platforms, an intima-like layer is formed by endothelialization, which is performed by injecting an ECs suspension into cannulated or anchored tubular constructs, followed by controlled rotation to promote homogeneous luminal cell adhesion (Weinberg and Bell 1986; Camasão and Mantovani 2021; Walters and Stegemann 2013; Zhang et al. 2019; Kim et al. 1999; Boccafoschi et al. 2005). Rotation is implemented manually, by intermittent manual turning of the construct (L'Heureux et al. 1993), or using a dedicated rotational bioreactor (Meghezi et al. 2015; Loy et al. 2018; Camasão et al. 2020).

13.4.1.3 Integration of Casting and Culture

In the early casting platforms, constructs had to be transferred into Petri dishes for cell-mediated compaction and/or subsequent maturation (Weinberg and Bell 1986; L'Heureux et al. 1993). This step often increased the risk of contamination and mechanical damage. To overcome these limitations, later designs integrated the casting process directly within dedicated culture chambers, which significantly improved sterility and handling efficiency.

An example of this evolution was presented by Meghezi et al., who developed a configuration in which the casting platform was anchored to the lid of a 50 mL tube, using the tube itself as the culture chamber. This enclosed system included a gas-exchange filter and a port for medium injection and removal, allowing it to work as a static bioreactor while maintaining a sterile environment throughout construct maturation (Fig. 13.2c) (Meghezi et al. 2015).

The most advanced systems incorporated an integrated casting platform within culture chambers equipped with multiple ports (at least two) to allow dynamic culture conditions and/or hemodynamic-like mechanical stimuli. For example, Loy et al. (2018) developed a bioreactor culture chamber in which a luminal flow stimulus could be applied within the construct (Fig. 13.2d), while Camasão et al. (2022) modified a commercial bioreactor chamber to provide external medium flow and internal pulsatile flow within the construct (Fig. 13.2e).

13.5 Maturation: A Matter of Time

It is widely known that cells can actively modify their extracellular environment to better suit their functional requirements both in vivo and in vitro. This capacity is taken advantage of by tissue engineering in a process known as maturation. Maturation is a time-gated multifactorial process in which cells remodel the scaffold to desired histological organization and mechanical properties. It is an essential step to engineer tissue mimicking native vessels (Bosch-Rué et al. 2025).

In the case of collagen-based VTE models produced as described above, the outcomes of maturation depend on multiple variables, including the cell type and density, the scaffold composition, the casting platform, and culture conditions such as whether they are static or dynamic and whether external biochemical or mechanical stimuli are applied. Table 13.1 illustrates how even subtle variations in these parameters can modify the properties and performances of the collagen-based constructs.

Coll-I constructs maturation begins after casting and may overlap with sequential layer deposition, depending on the workflow. Early maturation begins with layer compaction and fusion which prevents delamination (L'Heureux et al. 1993), while embedded cells exert tensile forces on the scaffold, gradually generating sufficient stiffness for subsequent handling (L'Heureux et al. 1993; Boccafoschi et al. 2007).

Table 13.1 Examples illustrating how small details in the fabrication and culture of collagen type I–based vascular tissue-engineered model

Variables	Experimental condition	Outcomes	References
Type of vascular cells	Tri-layered planar constructs (hFBs, hSMCs and hECs) vs. mono/bilayered planar constructs (hSMC, or hSMC and hECs)	The presence of an adventitia like layers (then, hFBs), increased elastin-related protein deposition, especially in the media-like layer (i.e., by hSMCs) and higher elasticity compared with bi and mono-later constructs	Loy et al. (2017)
Cell density	Comparation of three hSMC densities: (0.5, 1.5, and 4.5 × 10^6 hSMCs/mL) in a tubular media-like construct	Higher densities (>1.5 × 10^6 cell/mL) of hSMCs produced a media-like layer with more elastin-related proteins, increased the collagen contraction velocity, and improved viscoelasticity and stiffness	Camasão et al. (2022)
Concentration of Coll-I	2 mg/mL vs. 4 mg/mL Coll-I gels, in a tubular media-like layer (hSMCs)	Higher compaction, toughness and ultimate tensile stress for 2 mg/ml media-like layers; higher stiffness for 4 mg/mL media-like layers	Cummings et al. (2004)
No anchor system in the casting system device	Casting device consisted of a removable mandrel inside a test tube; construct culture was done with the mandrel	Construct longitudinally compacted; if construct was periodically manually detached from the mandrel, circumferential hSMC alignment was promoted	L'Heureux et al. (1993)
Anchor systems in the casting system device	Casting device incorporated anchor systems; construct culture was done without mandrel	Longitudinally compaction of the construct was prevented; SMC and collagen were longitudinally aligned, in the direction of the anchor systems	Loy et al. (2018)
Addition of a "alignment" step during casting workflow	Magnetic-field alignment during gelation of the media-like layer	Accelerated circumferential alignment of collagen and SMC	Barocas et al. (1998)
Biochemical factors during culture	(PDGF, heparin, TGF-β1 supplementation in Coll-I-based media-like layers (rSMCs) vs. culture plastic 2D rSMCs culture	PDGF markedly increased proliferation in 2D and modestly in 3D; TGF-β1 and heparin inhibited proliferation in 2D culture and had minimal further effect in 3D	Stegemann and Nerem (2003b)

(continued)

Table 13.1 (continued)

Variables	Experimental condition	Outcomes	References
		where growth was already low; PDGF and TGF-β1 both increased gel compaction, whereas heparin reduced compaction	
Culture conditions: Biochemical factors and mechanical stimuli during culture	Culture of tubular media-like model (rSMCs) in static and dynamic conditions (10% cyclic strain), with media supplemented with PDGF or TGF-β1	PDGF increased compaction of the media-like layer in static conditions, while dynamic conditions inhibit the effect of PDGF; the opposite is observed with TGF-β1 supplementation; PDGF stimulation resulted in a more open matrix, while TGF-b caused a denser matrix in both static and dynamic. Mechanical stimuli aligned circumferential SMC	Stegemann and Nerem (2003a)
Culture conditions: Biochemical factors and dynamic culture with mechanical stimuli	Media-like layer (hSMCs) dynamic culture supplemented with TGF-β1 and hyaluronic acid oligomers under 2.5% cyclic strain and frequencies of 0.5, 1.5, and 3 Hz	Maximal elastogenic markers observed at 1.5 Hz; higher frequencies increase the expression of MMP-9; no circumferential SMC alignment	Venkataraman et al. (2014)
Culture conditions: Dynamic culture conditions with mechanical stimuli	Planar media-like construct (hSMCs) culture in dynamic static vs. dynamic conditions (5% cyclic strain, frequency of 1 Hz or gradually increasing frequency from 0.1 to 1 Hz)	Static constructs had higher gene expression of collagen, elastin, and MMP-2 than dynamic constructs; SMC and collagen alignment in the direction of the strain, while collagen remains isotropic in static conditions; gradual increasing frequency improved viscoelastic properties of the medial-like layer	Lévesque et al. (2018)
Culture conditions: Dynamic culture conditions and mechanical stimuli	Tubular media-like constructs (hSMCs) culture in static vs. dynamic conditions (10% cyclic strain)	Dynamic conditions promoted circumferential alignment of SMCs and collagen fibers, more homogeneous cell distribution and more compaction vs. static	Bono et al. (2017)

(continued)

Table 13.1 (continued)

Variables	Experimental condition	Outcomes	References
		cultured constructs; viscoelasticity and stiffness were also improved under dynamic conditions	
Culture conditions: Dynamic culture conditions with mechanical stimuli	Tri-layered model cultured (hFBs, hSMCs and hECs) in static vs. dynamic conditions: Combined pulsatile flow (100 mL/min, 1 Hz + cyclic stretch (80–120 mmH); blood-like viscosity	Dynamic conditions promoted circumferential alignment of SMCs and collagen fibers, more homogeneous cell distribution, more proliferation of SMCs, collagen and elastin-related protein deposition, and more compaction; viscoelasticity and stiffness were also improved under dynamic conditions	Camasão et al. (2022)
Different days of culturing in dynamic conditions with mechanical stimuli; cell type	4 and 8 days of culture in dynamic conditions (10% cyclic strain, 0.5 Hz) of a media-like layer (hSMCs) and adventitia-like layer (hFBs)	For media-like layer and adventitia-like layer, 4 days of dynamic culture increased collagen/elastin expression and stiffness; 8 days induced MMP-2 activation and mechanical weakening of the media-like layer, while for the adventitia-like layer, there is not deterioration	Seliktar et al. (2003)

hECs human endothelial cells, *hFBs* human fibroblasts, *hSMCs* human smooth muscle cells, *MMP-2* matrix metalloproteinase-2, *MMP-9* matrix metalloproteinase-9, *PDGF* platelet-derived growth factor, *rSMCs* rat smooth muscle cells, *TGF-β1* transforming growth factor-β1

Over the following days to weeks, Coll-I-based constructs undergo extensive remodeling to modify and develop a mature ECM (Stegemann et al. 2007). For example, ECs form stable junctions and a functional endothelium within approximately 5–7 days (Akther et al. 2024), while SMCs contribute to the ECM medial layer modifications by degrading the Coll-I scaffold and depositing new collagen and elastin over a longer period. SMCs are particularly important due to their phenotypic plasticity that could be regulated by researchers to guide the maturation process (Beamish et al. 2010). For example, initially promoting a synthetic phenotype on SMCs could enhance ECM production and populate the medial layer, whereas transitioning to a contractile phenotype later would restore the mechanical functionality. Biochemical stimuli, such as platelet-derived growth factor, transforming growth factor-β1, or heparin, as well as mechanical stimuli, can be applied during culture to modulate SMC phenotype and ECM production (Ogle and Mooradian 2002).

Maturation can occur under static conditions, such as in Petri dishes or static bioreactors, but dynamic culture generally accelerates tissue remodeling and enhances construct functionality (Loy et al. 2018; Camasão et al. 2022; Seliktar et al. 2000; Chang and Niklason 2017). Dynamic culture ranges from simple medium movement which improves nutrient and oxygen transport, to the application of physiologically relevant mechanical stimuli, such as shear stress and cyclic strain, which are key regulators of vascular cell behavior. In vivo, hemodynamic forces, such as radial stress from pulsatile pressure and longitudinal shear from laminar flow, activate mechanotransduction pathways that govern ECM remodeling, SMC phenotype, and endothelial function (Hsieh et al. 2014; Lu and Kassab 2011; García-Cardeña and Slegtenhorst 2016). Reproducing these forces in vitro in different grades, isolated or combined, guides cellular alignment, promotes anisotropic collagen organization, and enhances ECM deposition, resulting in constructs with improved mechanical integrity (Camasão et al. 2022; Venkataraman et al. 2014; Chistiakov et al. 2017).

Bioreactors are central to dynamic culture of VTE constructs, providing controlled environments that regulate pH, oxygen tension, nutrient supply, and waste removal, while delivering reproducible mechanical and biochemical stimuli (Chen and Hu 2006). Perfusion bioreactors enable luminal perfusion of constructs, generating shear stress for ECs and cyclic strain for SMCs. These systems may range from simple setups using external pumps to advanced computer-controlled devices that integrate casting and culture chambers and monitor pressure and flow in real time (Camasão et al. 2022; Zhao et al. 2016). By controlling the timing, magnitude, and type of stimuli, bioreactors facilitate coordinated maturation, balancing ECM production, degradation, and cellular organization. In practice, bioreactors used for VTE vary widely in complexity, and their application dates back several decades (Niklason et al. 1999). In Table 13.1, there are several examples of studies that used bioreactors for the dynamic maturation of collagen-based VTE models.

Ultimately, understanding how the variables affecting maturation of Coll-I constructs, and properly orchestrating them, would allow the generation of vascular constructs that faithfully replicate the structural, mechanical, and functional properties of native arteries. This approach would provide constructs capable of withstanding physiological pressures and flows, with histological and mechanical properties closely resembling native arteries, providing a robust platform for both fundamental research and translational applications.

13.6 Development of Collagen-Based Pathological Models

One of the major consequences of cardiovascular diseases is vascular tissue remodeling, which can result in aneurysms, myocardial infarction, ischemia, and stroke. A primary cause of this remodeling is atherosclerosis, a condition that progressively narrows the vessels' lumen. Atherosclerosis is driven by both biochemical and mechanical factors (Hurtubise et al. 2016).

Biochemical factors include systemic conditions such as dyslipidemia (high low-density lipoprotein (LDL), low high-density lipoprotein (HDL)), oxidative stress, chronic inflammation, hyperglycemia, and endothelial activation induced by circulating cytokines or modified lipoproteins. Mechanical factors, likewise, involve hemodynamic disturbances, particularly disturbed or oscillatory shear stress, low shear regions found at arterial bifurcations and curvatures, and increased circumferential stretch or pressure (e.g., hypertension). These mechanical cues disrupt endothelial cell alignment and compromise endothelial barrier function (Hurtubise et al. 2016; Chen et al. 2024).

Atherosclerosis primarily affects the tunica intima of arteries. It is characterized by lipid accumulation within the vascular wall, triggering chronic inflammation and promoting the formation of atheromatous plaques. Endothelial dysfunction is an early hallmark of the disease and is followed by a sustained inflammatory response that recruits immune cells to the developing lesion (Van Varik et al. 2012; Libby 2021). Lipoproteins trapped in the vessel wall are phagocytosed by differentiated monocytes (macrophages), which subsequently transform into foam cells. In parallel, endothelial dysfunction contributes to the dysregulation of SMC behavior, leading to their proliferation and migration into the subendothelial space. Together, these processes drive the progression and maturation of the atherosclerotic plaque (Libby 2021).

Despite extensive research, atherosclerosis remains neither fully understood nor effectively diagnosed or treated. Moreover, as mentioned previously, current vascular models, such as 2D in vitro systems and animal models, have significant limitations, underscoring the need for intermediate approaches that more accurately recapitulate human vascular physiology. VTE offers an alternative to recreating vascular pathologies in vitro by combining cells, scaffolds, and perfusion bioreactors. Some reviews share the idea that the development of a relevant pathological model should rely on several key factors, some of them shared with the general requirements of a physiological model (Lust et al. 2021; Chen et al. 2022; Hosseini et al. 2021):

- Reproducibility.
  - The model should be simple to produce and scalable for testing different conditions.
- Relevant cellular components.
  - Incorporation of ECs, SMCs, FBs, and immune cells to recreate the multicellular vessel wall environment.
  - Establishment of a homogeneous endothelial barrier and appropriate cellular behavior under physiological and pathological conditions.
- Scaffold composition and properties.

Table 13.2 In vitro pathological collagen-based models

Cell types	Shape	Mechanical stimuli	Disease factor	References
ECs, SMCs, FBs Bone marrow primary cells	Tubular	Yes	Vascular stenosis by scaffold molding	Jones et al. (2017)
ECs, SMCs Monocyte cells	Flat	Yes, some models	Lipoprotein accumulation and oxidation; low shear stress; inflammation; transmigration of monocytes; foam cell formation; intimal thickening by incorporation of multilayers of SMCs	Liu et al. (2023)
ECs, SMCs Monocyte cells (murine)	Flat	No	Monocyte cells adhesion and transmigration; inflammation; foam cell formation	Akther et al. (2024)

ECs endothelial cells, *FBs* fibroblasts, *SMCs* smooth muscle cells

  - Use of materials with suitable biochemical and biomechanical properties to support proper cell–cell communication and diffusion of soluble factors.
- Mechanical stimulation.
  - Application of mechanical cues to mimic the native hemodynamic environment.
- Disease-specific factors.
  - Inclusion of pathological stimuli such as LDL-cholesterol, calcification, or altered shear stress to reproduce disease-relevant conditions.

Despite significant progress in vascular tissue engineering, no single collagen-based model from casting has yet integrated all the requirements for a fully biomimetic pathological arterial wall (Hosseini et al. 2021). Table 13.2 summarizes existing collagen-based models and highlights the specific features addressed by each.

13.7 Challenges and Future Directions of Coll-Based VTE Models

Despite advancements in the field, no collagen-based VTE model produced via casting fully reproduces the structural, mechanical, and functional properties of native small-caliber arteries (Shakeel and Corridon 2023). Several models still rely on simplified or flat geometries, lack adventitial fibroblasts, or operate under static conditions that fail to reproduce physiological shear stress, cyclic strain, and pressure. Moreover, pathological models often do not capture essential features of vascular diseases, such as SMC over-proliferation, ECM modifications, or calcification. In addition, maturation is a chronophagic process, taking several weeks for cells to remodel the ECM and transition toward native-like phenotypes (Stegemann et al. 2007).

Nevertheless, Coll-I remains one of the most promising biomaterials for vascular modeling due to its biological identity as a native ECM protein and its capacity for cell-driven remodeling when presented as a hydrogel. These properties are advantageous in disease-oriented systems, where tracking cell migration and ECM turnover is essential. Collagen also enables dynamic studies that are difficult to achieve with nondegradable synthetic scaffolds, which often act as passive barriers to cell-matrix interactions. Decellularized native ECM (dECM), rich in Coll-I, could be proposed as an alternative biomaterial. dECM hydrogels could provide tissue-specific bioactive components and improved cell adhesion, survival, and phenotype maturation over single-component collagen systems (Di Francesco et al. 2024).

The mechanical properties of cell-laden collagen hydrogels alone do not generally compare to native tissue. To address this, researchers commonly mix collagen with other natural polymers (e.g., recombinant elastin, fibronectin, fibrin) or introduce layers to mimic elastic lamellae, enhancing elasticity and mechanical stiffness (Pezzoli et al. 2018; Cummings et al. 2004; Camasão et al. 2020; González-Pérez et al. 2021). Meanwhile, synthetic reinforcements, such as Dacron, polycaprolactone, polyester, and polyurethane-nylon, can be integrated into the model to increase tensile strength and burst pressure while remaining compatible with hydrogel-based approaches (Weinberg and Bell 1986; Pien et al. 2023; Kobashi and Matsuda 1999). While these strategies improve mechanical performance, the introduction of additional polymers or structural components also increases model's complexity. Fundamental studies are needed to clarify how these additional materials interact with cells and affect matrix remodeling and tissue maturation.

Advanced fabrication technologies, most notably 3D bioprinting, have attracted considerable interest in their potential to automate and precisely customize complex vascular structures. While pilot studies have demonstrated the feasibility of bioprinting multilayered, cell-laden collagen-based constructs, important technical limitations persist (Kim et al. 2023). The rheological properties of collagen are not fully compatible with most current printing platforms, which constrains the ability to print high-fidelity, cell-dense, small-diameter tubular structures on the scale of native small-caliber arteries (Muthusamy et al. 2021; Debnath et al. 2025). Thus, casting remains, for now, the gold standard for producing cell-laden collagen hydrogels in vascular applications.

Better understanding of what impact maturation could guide and support targeted interventions and improve maturation (Chang and Niklason 2017). Progress in maturation will depend on the systematic integration of knowledge about biochemical and mechanical stimuli, and on the development of controlled, stepwise protocols using bioreactors. The development of collagen hydrogels capable of delivering regulatory molecules, thus functioning as delivery systems, may represent a next step toward accelerating maturation, while also minimizing the need for manual medium supplementation in VTE model cultures (Song and Gerecht 2023; Copes et al. 2019).

Over the past four decades, numerous collagen-based VTE models have been established using casting-based fabrication strategies. These efforts have yielded substantial advances in mechanistic understanding of tissue maturation and in the development of increasingly sophisticated casting and bioreactor systems. Although no current approach fully reproduces the structure and function of native small-caliber arteries, the field now benefits from a better understanding of the challenges ahead. The challenge of replicating native vascular structures is fundamentally multidisciplinary. Progress depends on collaborative contributions from biology, materials science, and engineering, integrating their expertise into models that address clinical and research needs. A fully functional vascular tissue construct will require advances across all these domains to converge toward solutions that meet practical and translational expectations.

Competing Interests The author(s) has no competing interests to declare that are relevant to the content of this manuscript.

References

Akhtar A (2015) The flaws and human harms of animal experimentation. Camb Q Healthc Ethics 24(4):407–419. https://doi.org/10.1017/S0963180115000079

Akther F, Sajin D, Moonshi SS, Wu Y, Vazquez-Prada KX, Ta HT, Akther F, Sajin D, Moonshi SS, Wu Y, Vazquez-Prada KX, Ta HT (2024) Modeling foam cell formation in a hydrogel-based 3D-intimal model: a study of the role of multi-diseases during early atherosclerosis. Adv Biol 8(4):2300463. https://doi.org/10.1002/ADBI.202300463

Amirrah IN, Lokanathan Y, Zulkiflee I, Wee MFMR, Motta A, Fauzi MB (2022) A comprehensive review on collagen type I development of biomaterials for tissue engineering: from biosynthesis to bioscaffold. Biomedicine 10(9):2307. https://doi.org/10.3390/BIOMEDICINES10092307

Andrade EL, Bento AF, Cavalli J, Oliveira SK, Freitas CS, Marcon R, Schwanke RC, Siqueira JM, Calixto JB (2016) Non-clinical studies required for new drug development—part I: early in silico and in vitro studies, new target discovery and validation, proof of principles and robustness of animal studies. Braz J Med Biol Res 49(11):e5644. https://doi.org/10.1590/1414-431X20165644

Au P, Tam J, Fukumura D, Jain RK (2008) Bone marrow-derived mesenchymal stem cells facilitate engineering of long-lasting functional vasculature. Blood 111(9):4551–4558. https://doi.org/10.1182/blood-2007-10

Barocas VH, Girton TS, Tranquillo RT (1998) Engineered alignment in media equivalents: magnetic prealignment and mandrel compaction. J Biomech Eng 120(5):660–666. https://doi.org/10.1115/1.2834759

Bartolf-Kopp M, Jungst T (2024) The past, present, and future of tubular melt electrowritten constructs to mimic small diameter blood vessels—a stable process? Adv Healthc Mater 13(19):e2400426. https://doi.org/10.1002/adhm.202400426

Basatemur GL, Jørgensen HF, Clarke MCH, Bennett MR, Mallat Z (2019) Vascular smooth muscle cells in atherosclerosis. Nat Rev Cardiol 16(12):727–744. https://doi.org/10.1038/s41569-019-0227-9

Beamish JA, He P, Kottke-Marchant K, Marchant RE (2010) Molecular regulation of contractile smooth muscle cell phenotype: implications for vascular tissue engineering. Tissue Eng Part B Rev 16(5):467–491. https://doi.org/10.1089/TEN.TEB.2009.0630

Berglund JD, Mohseni MM, Nerem RM, Sambanis A (2003) A biological hybrid model for collagen-based tissue engineered vascular constructs. Biomaterials 24(7):1241–1254. https://doi.org/10.1016/S0142-9612(02)00506-9

Boccafoschi F, Habermehl J, Vesentini S, Mantovani D (2005) Biological performances of collagen-based scaffolds for vascular tissue engineering. Biomaterials 26(35):7410–7417. https://doi.org/10.1016/J.BIOMATERIALS.2005.05.052

Boccafoschi F, Rajan N, Habermehl J, Mantovani D (2007) Preparation and characterization of a scaffold for vascular tissue engineering by direct-assembling of collagen and cells in a cylindrical geometry. Macromol Biosci 7(5):719–726. https://doi.org/10.1002/MABI.200600242

Bono N, Pezzoli D, Levesque L, Loy C, Candiani G, Fiore GB, Mantovani D (2016) Unraveling the role of mechanical stimulation on smooth muscle cells: a comparative study between 2D and 3D models. Biotechnol Bioeng 113(10):2254–2263. https://doi.org/10.1002/BIT.25979

Bono N, Meghezi S, Soncini M, Piola M, Mantovani D, Fiore GB (2017) A dual-mode bioreactor system for tissue engineered vascular models. Ann Biomed Eng 45(6):1496–1510. https://doi.org/10.1007/s10439-017-1813-9

Bosch-Rué E, Zhang Q, Truskey GA, Buitrago JO, Bosch BM, Pérez RA (2025) Development of small tissue engineered blood vessels and their clinical and research applications. Biofabrication 17(3):032005. https://doi.org/10.1088/1758-5090/ADD626

Camasão DB, Mantovani D (2021) The mechanical characterization of blood vessels and their substitutes in the continuous quest for physiological-relevant performances. a critical review. Mater Today Bio 10:100106. https://doi.org/10.1016/J.MTBIO.2021.100106

Camasão DB, Pezzoli D, Loy C, Kumra H, Levesque L, Reinhardt DP, Candiani G, Mantovani D (2019) Increasing cell seeding density improves elastin expression and mechanical properties in collagen gel-based scaffolds cellularized with smooth muscle cells. Biotechnol J 14(3): e1700768. https://doi.org/10.1002/BIOT.201700768

Camasão DB, González-Pérez M, Palladino S, Alonso M, Rodríguez-Cabello JC, Mantovani D (2020) Elastin-like recombinamers in collagen-based tubular gels improve cell-mediated remodeling and viscoelastic properties. Biomater Sci 8(12):3536–3548. https://doi.org/10.1039/D0BM00292E

Camasão DB, Li L, Drouin B, Lau C, Reinhardt DP, Mantovani D (2022) Physiologically relevant platform for an advanced in vitro model of the vascular wall: focus on in situ fabrication and mechanical maturation. In vitro models 1(2):179–195. https://doi.org/10.1007/S44164-022-00012-1

Cao G, Xuan X, Hu J, Zhang R, Jin H, Dong H (2022) How vascular smooth muscle cell phenotype switching contributes to vascular disease. Cell Commun Signal 20(1):180. https://doi.org/10.1186/s12964-022-00993-2

Chang WG, Niklason LE (2017) A short discourse on vascular tissue engineering. Npj Regener Med *2(1)*:7. https://doi.org/10.1038/s41536-017-0011-6

Chen HC, Hu YC (2006) Bioreactors for tissue engineering. Biotechnol Lett 28(18):1415–1423. https://doi.org/10.1007/s10529-006-9111-x

Chen J, Zhang X, Millican R, Lynd T, Gangasani M, Malhotra S, Sherwood J, Hwang PT, Cho Y, Brott BC, Qin G, Jo H, Yoon Y, Jun H-W (2022) Recent progress in vitro models for atherosclerosis studies. Front Cardiovasc Med 1:790529. https://doi.org/10.3389/fcvm.2021.790529

Chen L, Qu H, Liu B, Chen BC, Yang Z, Shi DZ, Zhang Y (2024) Low or oscillatory shear stress and endothelial permeability in atherosclerosis. Front Physiol 15:1432719. https://doi.org/10.3389/fphys.2024.1432719

Chia PY, Teo A, Yeo TW (2020) Overview of the assessment of endothelial function in humans. Front Med (Lausanne) 7:542567. https://doi.org/10.3389/fmed.2020.542567

Chistiakov DA, Orekhov AN, Bobryshev YV (2017) Effects of shear stress on endothelial cells: go with the flow. Acta Physiol (Oxf) 219(2):382–408. https://doi.org/10.1111/APHA.12725

Collado MS, Cole BK, Figler RA, Lawson M, Manka D, Simmers MB, Hoang S, Serrano F, Blackman BR, Sinha S, Wamhoff BR (2017) Exposure of induced pluripotent stem cell-derived vascular endothelial and smooth muscle cells in coculture to hemodynamics induces primary vascular cell-like phenotypes. Stem Cells Transl Med 6(8):1673. https://doi.org/10.1002/SCTM.17-0004

Copes F, Chevallier P, Loy C, Pezzoli D, Boccafoschi F, Mantovani D (2019) Heparin-modified collagen gels for controlled release of pleiotrophin: potential for vascular applications. Front Bioeng Biotechnol 7:74. https://doi.org/10.3389/FBIOE.2019.00074

Cummings CL, Gawlitta D, Nerem RM, Stegemann JP (2004) Properties of engineered vascular constructs made from collagen, fibrin, and collagen-fibrin mixtures. Biomaterials 25(17):3699–3706. https://doi.org/10.1016/j.biomaterials.2003.10.073

Debnath S, Agrawal A, Jain N, Chatterjee K, Player DJ (2025) Collagen as a bio-ink for 3D printing: a critical review. J Mater Chem B 13(6):1890–1919. https://doi.org/10.1039/D4TB01060D

Di Francesco D, Pigliafreddo A, Casarella S, Di Nunno L, Mantovani D, Boccafoschi F (2023) Biological materials for tissue-engineered vascular grafts: overview of recent advancements. Biomolecules 13(9):1389. https://doi.org/10.3390/BIOM13091389

Di Francesco D, Marcello E, Casarella S, Copes F, Chevallier P, Carmagnola I, Mantovani D, Boccafoschi F (2024) Characterization of a decellularized pericardium extracellular matrix hydrogel for regenerative medicine: insights on animal-to-animal variability. Front Bioeng Biotechnol 12:1452965. https://doi.org/10.3389/FBIOE.2024.1452965

Dong JD, Gu YQ, Li CM, Wang CR, Feng ZG, Qiu RX, Chen B, Li JX, Zhang SW, Wang ZG, Zhang J (2009) Response of mesenchymal stem cells to shear stress in tissue-engineered vascular grafts. Acta Pharmacol Sin 30(5):530–536. https://doi.org/10.1038/aps.2009.40

Ganesan MK, Finsterwalder R, Leb H, Resch U, Neumüller K, Martin RD, Petzelbauer P (2017) Three-dimensional coculture model to analyze the cross talk between endothelial and smooth muscle cells. Tissue Eng Part C Methods 23(1):38–49. https://doi.org/10.1089/ten.tec.2016.0299

García-Cardeña G, Slegtenhorst BR (2016) Hemodynamic control of endothelial cell fates in development. Annu Rev Cell Dev Biol 32:633–648. https://doi.org/10.1146/annurev-cellbio-100814-125610

Girton TS, Oegema TR, Grassl ED, Isenberg BC, Tranquillo RT (2000) Mechanisms of stiffening and strengthening in media-equivalents fabricated using glycation. J Biomech Eng 122(3):216–223. https://doi.org/10.1115/1.429652

González-Pérez M, Camasão DB, Mantovani D, Alonso M, Rodríguez-Cabello JC (2021) Biocasting of an elastin-like recombinamer and collagen bi-layered model of the tunica adventitia and external elastic lamina of the vascular wall. Biomater Sci 9(10):3860–3874. https://doi.org/10.1039/D0BM02197K

Habermehl J, Skopinska J, Boccafoschi F, Sionkowska A, Kaczmarek H, Laroche G, Mantovani D (2005) Preparation of ready-to-use, stockable and reconstituted collagen. Macromol Biosci 5(9):821–828. https://doi.org/10.1002/MABI.200500102

Harteveld AA, Denswil NP, Hecke WV, Kuijf HJ, Vink A, Spliet WGM, Daemen MJ, Luijten PR, Zwanenburg JJM, Hendrikse J, van der Kolk AG (2018) Ex vivo vessel wall thickness measurements of the human circle of Willis using 7T MRI. Atherosclerosis 273:106–114. https://doi.org/10.1016/J.ATHEROSCLEROSIS.2018.04.023

He H, Matsuda T (2002) Newly designed compliant hierarchic hybrid vascular graft wrapped with microprocessed elastomeric film—I: morphogenesis and compliance change upon implantation. Cell Transplant 11(1):75–87

He L, Lan W, Zhao Y, Chen S, Liu S, Cen L, Cao S, Dong L, Jin R, Liu Y (2020) Characterization of biocompatible pig skin collagen and application of collagen-based films for enzyme immobilization. RSC Adv 10(12):7170–7180. https://doi.org/10.1039/C9RA10794K

Hosseini V, Mallone A, Nasrollahi F, Ostrovidov S, Nasiri R, Mahmoodi M, Haghniaz R, Baidya A, Salek MM, Darabi MA, Orive G, Shamloo A, Dokmeci MR, Ahadian S, Khademhosseini A (2021) Healthy and diseased in vitro models of vascular systems. Lab Chip 21(4):641–659. https://doi.org/10.1039/d0lc00464b

Hsieh HJ, Liu CA, Huang B, Tseng AH, Wang DL (2014) Shear-induced endothelial mechanotransduction: the interplay between reactive oxygen species (ROS) and nitric oxide (NO) and the pathophysiological implications. J Biomed Sci 21(1):3. https://doi.org/10.1186/1423-0127-21-3

Hurtubise J, McLellan K, Durr K, Onasanya O, Nwabuko D, Ndisang JF (2016) The different facets of dyslipidemia and hypertension in atherosclerosis. Curr Atheroscler Rep 18(12):82. https://doi.org/10.1007/s11883-016-0632-z

Jiao Y-C, Wang Y-X, Liu W-Z, Xu J-W, Zhao Y-Y, Yan C-Z, Liu F-C (2024) Advances in the differentiation of pluripotent stem cells into vascular cells. World J Stem Cells 16(2):137–150. https://doi.org/10.4252/wjsc.v16.i2.137

Jin Q, Jin G, Ju J, Xu L, Tang L, Fu Y, Hou R, Atala A, Zhao W (2022) Bioprinting small-diameter vascular vessel with endothelium and smooth muscle by the approach of two-step crosslinking process. Biotechnol Bioeng 119(6):1673–1684. https://doi.org/10.1002/BIT.28075

Jones RS, Chang PH, Perahia T, Harmon KA, Junor L, Yost MJ, Fan D, Eberth JF, Goodwin RL (2017) Design and fabrication of a three-dimensional in vitro system for modeling vascular stenosis. Microsc Microanal 23(4):859–871. https://doi.org/10.1017/S1431927617012302

Jouda H, Murillo LL, Wang T (2022) Current progress in vascular engineering and its clinical applications. Cells 11(3):493. https://doi.org/10.3390/cells11030493

Joyce K, Buljovcic Z, Rosic G, Kaszkin-Bettag M, Pandit A (2023) Issues with tissues: trends in tissue-engineered products in clinical trials in the European Union. Tissue Eng Part B Rev 29(1): 78–88. https://doi.org/10.1089/ten.TEB.2022.0094

Kapałczyńska M, Kolenda T, Przybyła W, Zajączkowska M, Teresiak A, Filas V, Ibbs M, Bliźniak R, Łuczewski Ł, Lamperska K (2018) 2D and 3D cell cultures—a comparison of different types of cancer cell cultures. Arch Med Sci 14(4):910–919. https://doi.org/10.5114/AOMS.2016.63743

Kim BS, Nikolovski J, Bonadio J, Smiley E, Mooney DJ (1999) Engineered smooth muscle tissues: regulating cell phenotype with the scaffold. Exp Cell Res 251(2):318–328. https://doi.org/10.1006/EXCR.1999.4595

Kim SJ, Kim MG, Kim J, Jeon JS, Park J, Yi HG (2023) Bioprinting methods for fabricating in vitro tubular blood vessel models. Cyborg Bionic Syst 4:0043. https://doi.org/10.34133/CBSYSTEMS.0043

Kobashi T, Matsuda T (1999) Fabrication of compliant hybrid grafts supported with elastomeric meshes. Cell Transplant 8(5):477–488. https://doi.org/10.1177/096368979900800503

Krüger-Genge A, Blocki A, Franke RP, Jung F (2019) Vascular endothelial cell biology: an update. Int J Mol Sci 20(18):4411. https://doi.org/10.3390/ijms20184411

Kuchroo P, Dave V, Vijayan A, Viswanathan C, Ghosh D (2015) Paracrine factors secreted by umbilical cord-derived mesenchymal stem cells induce angiogenesis in vitro by a vegf-independent pathway. Stem Cells Dev 24(4):437–450. https://doi.org/10.1089/scd.2014.0184

Kural MH, Billiar KL (2013) Regulating tension in three-dimensional culture environments. Exp Cell Res 319(16):2447–2459. https://doi.org/10.1016/J.YEXCR.2013.06.019

L'Heureux NS, Germain LS, Labbé R, Auger FA (1993) In vitro construction of a human blood vessel from cultured vascular cells: a morphologic study. J Vasc Surg 17(3):499–509. https://doi.org/10.1067/MVA.1993.38251

Leal BBJ, Wakabayashi N, Oyama K, Kamiya H, Braghirolli DI, Pranke P (2021) Vascular tissue engineering: polymers and methodologies for small caliber vascular grafts. Front Cardiovasc Med 7:592361. https://doi.org/10.3389/FCVM.2020.592361

Lévesque L, Loy C, Lainé A, Drouin B, Chevallier P, Mantovani D (2018) Incrementing the frequency of dynamic strain on SMC-cellularised collagen-based scaffolds affects extracellular matrix remodeling and mechanical properties. ACS Biomater Sci Eng 4(11):3759–3767. https://doi.org/10.1021/ACSBIOMATERIALS.7B00395

Li MX, Wei QQ, Mo HL, Ren Y, Zhang W, Lu HJ, Joung YK (2023) Challenges and advances in materials and fabrication technologies of small-diameter vascular grafts. Biomater Res 27(1):58. https://doi.org/10.1186/S40824-023-00399-2

Libby P (2021) The changing landscape of atherosclerosis. Nature 592(7855):524–533. https://doi.org/10.1038/s41586-021-03392-8

Liu M, Samant S, Vasa CH, Pedrigi RM, Oguz UM, Ryu S, Wei T, Anderson DR, Agrawal DK, Chatzizisis YS (2023) Co-culture models of endothelial cells, macrophages, and vascular smooth muscle cells for the study of the natural history of atherosclerosis. PLoS One 18(1): e0280385. https://doi.org/10.1371/journal.pone.0280385

Loy C, Meghezi S, Lévesque L, Pezzoli D, Kumra H, Reinhardt D, Kizhakkedathu JN, Mantovani D (2017) A planar model of the vessel wall from cellularized-collagen scaffolds: focus on cell-matrix interactions in mono-, bi- and tri-culture models. Biomater Sci 5(1):153–162. https://doi.org/10.1039/C6BM00643D

Loy C, Pezzoli D, Candiani G, Mantovani D (2018) A cost-effective culture system for the in vitro assembly, maturation, and stimulation of advanced multilayered multiculture tubular tissue models. Biotechnol J 13(1). https://doi.org/10.1002/BIOT.201700359

Lu D, Kassab GS (2011) Role of shear stress and stretch in vascular mechanobiology. J R Soc Interface 8(63):1379–1385. https://doi.org/10.1098/rsif.2011.0177

Lust ST, Shanahan CM, Shipley RJ, Lamata P, Gentleman E (2021) Design considerations for engineering 3D models to study vascular pathologies in vitro. Acta Biomater 132:114–128. https://doi.org/10.1016/J.ACTBIO.2021.02.031

Maacha S, Sidahmed H, Jacob S, Gentilcore G, Calzone R, Grivel JC, Cugno C (2020) Paracrine mechanisms of mesenchymal stromal cells in angiogenesis. Stem Cells Int 2020:4356359. https://doi.org/10.1155/2020/4356359

Marei I, Samaan TA, Al-Quradaghi MA, Farah AA, Mahmud SH, Ding H, Triggle CR (2022) 3D tissue-engineered vascular drug screening platforms: promise and considerations. Front Cardiovasc Med 9:847554. https://doi.org/10.3389/FCVM.2022.847554/XML

Meghezi S, Seifu DG, Bono N, Unsworth L, Mequanint K, Mantovani D (2015) Engineering 3D cellularized collagen gels for vascular tissue regeneration. J Vis Exp 2015(100):e52812. https://doi.org/10.3791/52812

Milutinović A, Šuput D, Zorc-Pleskovič R (2020) Pathogenesis of atherosclerosis in the tunica intima, media, and adventitia of coronary arteries: an updated review. Bosn J Basic Med Sci 20(1):21–30. https://doi.org/10.17305/bjbms.2019.4320

Mohan T, Gürer F, Bračič D, Lackner F, Nagaraj C, Maver U, Gradišnik L, Finšgar M, Kargl R, Kleinschek KS (2025) Functionalization of polycaprolactone 3D scaffolds with hyaluronic acid glycine-peptide conjugates and endothelial cell adhesion. Biomacromolecules 26(3): 1771–1787. https://doi.org/10.1021/ACS.BIOMAC.4C01559/SUPPL_FILE/BM4C01559_SI_001.PDF

Muthusamy S, Kannan S, Lee M, Sanjairaj V, Lu WF, Fuh JYH, Sriram G, Cao T (2021) 3D bioprinting and microscale organization of vascularized tissue constructs using collagen-based bioink. Biotechnol Bioeng 118(8):3150–3163. https://doi.org/10.1002/BIT.27838

Niklason LE, Gao J, Abbott WM, Hirschi KK, Houser S, Marini R, Langer R (1999) Functional arteries grown in vitro. Science 284(5413):489–493. https://doi.org/10.1126/SCIENCE.284.5413.489

Norman GAV (2019) Limitations of animal studies for predicting toxicity in clinical trials: is it time to rethink our current approach? JACC: Basic Transl Sci 4(7):845–854. https://doi.org/10.1016/j.jacbts.2019.10.008

Obinata M (2007) The immortalized cell lines with differentiation potentials: their establishment and possible application. Cancer Sci 98(3):275–283. https://doi.org/10.1111/j.1349-7006.2007.00399.x

Ogle BM, Mooradian DL (2002) Manipulation of remodeling pathways to enhance the mechanical properties of a tissue engineered blood vessel. J Biomech Eng 124(6):724–733. https://doi.org/10.1115/1.1519278

Pashneh-Tala S, MacNeil S, Claeyssens F (2016) The tissue-engineered vascular graft-past, present, and future. Tissue Eng Part B Rev 22(1):68–100. https://doi.org/10.1089/ten.teb.2015.0100

Pati F, Adhikari B, Dhara S (2010) Isolation and characterization of fish scale collagen of higher thermal stability. Bioresour Technol 101(10):3737–3742. https://doi.org/10.1016/J.BIORTECH.2009.12.133

Pezzoli D, Paolo JD, Kumra H, Fois G, Candiani G, Reinhardt DP, Mantovani D (2018) Fibronectin promotes elastin deposition, elasticity and mechanical strength in cellularised collagen-based scaffolds. Biomaterials 180:130–142. https://doi.org/10.1016/J.BIOMATERIALS.2018.07.013

Pien N, Vlierberghe SV, Dubruel P, Mantovani D (2021) Hydrogel processing techniques and vascular tissue engineering. In: I N, X W, S v V (eds) Injectable hydrogels for 3D bioprinting. Royal Society of Chemistry, pp 201–206. https://doi.org/10.1039/9781839163975-00201

Pien N, Francesco DD, Copes F, Bartolf-Kopp M, Chausse V, Meeremans M, Pegueroles M, Jüngst T, Schauwer CD, Boccafoschi F, Dubruel P, Vlierberghe SV, Mantovani D (2023) Polymeric reinforcements for cellularized collagen-based vascular wall models: influence of the scaffold architecture on the mechanical and biological properties. Front Bioeng Biotechnol 11: 1285565. https://doi.org/10.3389/FBIOE.2023.1285565

Pineda-Castillo SA, Acar H, Detamore MS, Holzapfel GA, Lee CH (2023) Modulation of smooth muscle cell phenotype for translation of tissue-engineered vascular grafts. Tissue Eng Part B Rev 29(5):574–588. https://doi.org/10.1089/ten.teb.2023.0006

Pires Figueiredo M, Rodríguez-Fernández S, Copes F, Mantovani D (2025) Review of collagen type I-based hydrogels: focus on composition-structure-properties relationships. NPJ Biomed Innov 2(1):16. https://doi.org/10.1038/S44385-025-00018-W

Powell RJ, Bhargava J, Basson MD, Sumpio BE (1998) Coculture conditions alter endothelial modulation of TGF-β1 activation and smooth muscle growth morphology. Am J Phys Heart Circ Phys 274(2):H642–H649. https://doi.org/10.1152/ajpheart.1998.274.2.H642

Rajan N, Habermehl J, Coté MF, Doillon CJ, Mantovani D (2006) Preparation of ready-to-use, storable and reconstituted type I collagen from rat tail tendon for tissue engineering applications. Nat Protoc 1(6):2753–2758. https://doi.org/10.1038/NPROT.2006.430

Rhodes JM, Simons M (2007) The extracellular matrix and blood vessel formation: not just a scaffold. J Cell Mol Med 11(2):176–205. https://doi.org/10.1111/J.1582-4934.2007.00031.X

Richter M, Piwocka O, Musielak M, Piotrowski I, Suchorska WM, Trzeciak T (2021) From donor to the lab: a fascinating journey of primary cell lines. Front Cell Dev Biol 9:711381. https://doi.org/10.3389/fcell.2021.711381

Robinson NB, Krieger K, Khan F, Huffman W, Chang M, Naik A, Yongle R, Hameed I, Krieger K, Girardi LN, Gaudino M (2019) The current state of animal models in research: a review. Int J Surg 72:9–13. https://doi.org/10.1016/j.ijsu.2019.10.015

Seliktar D, Black RA, Vito RP, Nerem RM (2000) Dynamic mechanical conditioning of collagen-gel blood vessel constructs induces remodeling in vitro:351–362. https://doi.org/10.1114/1.275

Seliktar D, Nerem RM, Galis ZS (2003) Mechanical strain-stimulated remodeling of tissue-engineered blood vessel constructs. Tissue Eng 9(4):657–666. https://doi.org/10.1089/107632703768247359

Shakeel A, Corridon PR (2023) Mitigating challenges and expanding the future of vascular tissue engineering—are we there yet? Front Physiol 13:1079421. https://doi.org/10.3389/FPHYS.2022.1079421

Shi Y, Inoue H, Wu JC, Yamanaka S (2017) Induced pluripotent stem cell technology: a decade of progress. Nat Rev Drug Discov 16(2):115–130. https://doi.org/10.1038/nrd.2016.245

Shitova M, Alpeeva E, Vorotelyak E (2024) Review of hTERT-immortalized cells: how to assess immortality and confirm identity. Int J Mol Sci 25(23):13054. https://doi.org/10.3390/ijms252313054

Song J, Gerecht S (2023) Hydrogels to recapture extracellular matrix cues that regulate vascularization. Arterioscler Thromb Vasc Biol 43(8):E291–E302. https://doi.org/10.1161/ATVBAHA.122.318235

Song HHG, Rumma RT, Ozaki CK, Edelman ER, Chen CS (2018) Vascular tissue engineering: progress, challenges, and clinical promise. Cell Stem Cell 22(3):340–354. https://doi.org/10.1016/J.STEM.2018.02.009

Stegemann JP, Nerem RM (2003a) Phenotype modulation in vascular tissue engineering using biochemical and mechanical stimulation. Ann Biomed Eng 31(4):391–402. https://doi.org/10.1114/1.1558031/METRICS

Stegemann JP, Nerem RM (2003b) Altered response of vascular smooth muscle cells to exogenous biochemical stimulation in two- and three-dimensional culture. Exp Cell Res 283(2):146–155. https://doi.org/10.1016/s0014-4827(02)00041-1

Stegemann JP, Kaszuba SN, Rowe SL (2007) Review: advances in vascular tissue engineering using protein-based biomaterials. Tissue Eng 13(11):2601–2613. https://doi.org/10.1089/TEN.2007.0196

Syedain ZH, Meier LA, Bjork JW, Lee A, Tranquillo RT (2011) Implantable arterial grafts from human fibroblasts and fibrin using a multi-graft pulsed flow-stretch bioreactor with noninvasive strength monitoring. Biomaterials 32(3):714–722. https://doi.org/10.1016/j.biomaterials.2010.09.019

Tranquillo RT, Girton TS, Bromberek BA, Triebes TG, Mooradian DL (1996) Magnetically orientated tissue-equivalent tubes: application to a circumferentially orientated media-equivalent. Biomaterials 17(3):349–357. https://doi.org/10.1016/0142-9612(96)85573-6

Van Varik BJ, Rennenberg RJMW, Reutelingsperger CP, Kroon AA, De Leeuw PW, Schurgers LJ (2012) Mechanisms of arterial remodeling: lessons from genetic diseases. Front Genet 3:290. https://doi.org/10.3389/fgene.2012.00290

Venkataraman L, Bashur CA, Ramamurthi A (2014) Impact of cyclic stretch on induced elastogenesis within collagenous conduits. Tissue Eng Part A 20(9–10):1403–1415. https://doi.org/10.1089/ten.TEA.2013.0294

Walters BD, Stegemann JP (2013) Strategies for directing the structure and function of 3D collagen biomaterials across length scales. Acta Biomater 10(4):1488. https://doi.org/10.1016/J.ACTBIO.2013.08.038

Wang S, Tarbell JM (2000) Effect of fluid flow on smooth muscle cells in a 3-dimensional collagen gel model. Arterioscler Thromb Vasc Biol 20(10):2220–2225. https://doi.org/10.1161/01.ATV.20.10.2220/ASSET/9E27FAE8-B031-44A4-A2B5-D12DEBAB2A64/ASSETS/GRAPHIC/HQ1001448006.JPEG

Weinberg CB, Bell E (1985) Regulation of proliferation of bovine aortic endothelial cells, smooth muscle cells, and adventitial fibroblasts in collagen lattices. J Cell Physiol 122(3):410–414. https://doi.org/10.1002/JCP.1041220311

Weinberg CB, Bell E (1986) A blood vessel model constructed from collagen and cultured vascular cells. Science 231(4736):397–400. https://doi.org/10.1126/SCIENCE.2934816

Williams C, Wick TM (2005) Endothelial cell-smooth muscle cell co-culture in a perfusion bioreactor system. Ann Biomed Eng 33(7):920–928. https://doi.org/10.1007/s10439-005-3238-0

Xu J, Shi GP (2014) Vascular wall extracellular matrix proteins and vascular diseases. Biochim Biophys Acta 1842(11):2106. https://doi.org/10.1016/J.BBADIS.2014.07.008

Zhang F, Xie Y, Celik H, Akkus O, Bernacki SH, King MW (2019) Engineering small-caliber vascular grafts from collagen filaments and nanofibers with comparable mechanical properties to native vessels. Biofabrication 11(3):035020. https://doi.org/10.1088/1758-5090/AB15CE

Zhao J, Griffin M, Cai J, Li S, Bulter PEM, Kalaskar DM (2016) Bioreactors for tissue engineering: an update. Biochem Eng J 109:268–281. https://doi.org/10.1016/j.bej.2016.01.018

Zheng W, Wang Z, Song L, Zhao Q, Zhang J, Li D, Wang S, Han J, Zheng XL, Yang Z, Kong D (2012) Endothelialization and patency of RGD-functionalized vascular grafts in a rabbit carotid artery model. Biomaterials 33(10):2880–2891. https://doi.org/10.1016/J.BIOMATERIALS.2011.12.047

Zhu H, Friedman MH (2003) Relationship between the dynamic geometry and wall thickness of a human coronary artery. Arterioscler Thromb Vasc Biol 23(12):2260–2265. https://doi.org/10.1161/01.ATV.0000095976.40874.E0/ASSET/8D3C9097-5680-4177-9128-96BCF38273FB/ASSETS/GRAPHIC/28FF3.JPEG

Chapter 14
Biofabrication for Ocular Disorders

Anas Abu-Dieh, Grace Lin, Amrit Das, Myriam Belaiche, Marie-Claude Robert, and May Griffith

Abstract Vision loss from disease, injury, or aging remains one of the most devastating impairments worldwide, driving rapid advances in regenerative ophthalmology. Here, we provide an integrative overview of biofabrication strategies for ocular tissues, highlighting how engineering, material sciences, and stem cell

---

Authors Ana Abu-Dieh and Grace Lin have equally contributed to this chapter.

A. Abu-Dieh
Department of Ophthalmology, CHU de Québec-Université Laval, Quebec City, QC, Canada

Hôpital Maisonneuve-Rosemont Research Center, Université de Montréal, Montreal, QC, Canada

G. Lin
Hôpital Maisonneuve-Rosemont Research Center, Université de Montréal, Montreal, QC, Canada

Centre de recherche du Centre hospitalier de l'Université de Montréal, Montreal, QC, Canada

A. Das
Department of Ophthalmology, Université de Montréal, Montreal, QC, Canada

M. Belaiche
Institute of Biomedical Engineering, Université de Montréal, Montreal, QC, Canada

M.-C. Robert
Hôpital Maisonneuve-Rosemont Research Center, Université de Montréal, Montreal, QC, Canada

Centre de recherche du Centre hospitalier de l'Université de Montréal, Montreal, QC, Canada

Department of Ophthalmology, Université de Montréal, Montreal, QC, Canada

M. Griffith (✉)
Hôpital Maisonneuve-Rosemont Research Center, Université de Montréal, Montreal, QC, Canada

Centre de recherche du Centre hospitalier de l'Université de Montréal, Montreal, QC, Canada

Department of Ophthalmology, Université de Montréal, Montreal, QC, Canada

Institute of Biomedical Engineering, Université de Montréal, Montreal, QC, Canada
e-mail: may.griffith@umontreal.ca

Y. M. Elçin (ed.), *Biofabrication in Regenerative Medicine*, Stem Cell Biology and Regenerative Medicine 1519, https://doi.org/10.1007/978-3-032-30294-6_14

biology are converging to restore the structure and function of the eye. Following a brief overview of ocular anatomy, the chapter surveys progress across the cornea, lens, retina, optic nerve, and adnexal tissues. In the cornea, clinical translation is most advanced, with recombinant collagen hydrogels, decellularized matrices, and stem cell–based constructs supporting epithelial, stromal, and endothelial regeneration. For the lens, biofabrication research spans synthetic intraocular lenses and regenerative approaches using endogenous epithelial cells or stem-cell-derived lentoid bodies. Retinal biofabrication focuses on scaffold-guided replacement of retinal pigment epithelium and photoreceptors (RPE), with promising outcomes from pluripotent stem cell–derived RPE monolayers and emerging 3D-bioprinted retinal tissues. The optic nerve presents one of the greatest challenges due to its limited intrinsic regeneration. However, multi-therapeutic strategies are redefining possibilities for axonal repair. Parallel efforts around the world address conjunctival, lacrimal, and eyelid reconstruction, underscoring the systemic potential of biomaterials across the ocular system. Together, these developments illustrate a paradigm shift from more prosthetic replacement toward biologically integrated, regenerative solutions, establishing biofabrication as a transformative platform for restoring vision. This chapter is not meant to be comprehensive but to provide a synopsis of the developments in regenerative ophthalmology.

Keywords Regenerative ophthalmology · Vision restoration · Ocular biofabrication · Stem cell biology · Cornea · Lens · Lentoid bodies · Retinal biofabrication · 3D-bioprinted retinal tissues · Axonal repair · Clinical translation

Abbreviations

ADDE	Aqueous-deficient Dry Eye
ADMSC	Adipose Tissue-derived Mesenchymal Stem Cells
AM	Amniotic Membrane
AMD	Age-related Macular Degeneration
APCS	Acellular Porcine Corneal Stroma
ASTM	American Society for Testing and Materials
BCVA	Best Corrected Visual Acuity
BM	Bone Marrow
BMJ	British Medical Journal
BMP	Bone Morphogenetic Protein
BMSC	Bone Marrow-derived Mesenchymal Stem Cells
BPCDX	Bioengineered Porcine Construct, Double-cross-linked
BSI	British Standards Institution.
CALEC	Cultivated Autologous Limbal Epithelial Cells
CjSC	Conjunctival Stem Cells
CLP	Collagen-like Peptide
CMHA-S	Thiolated Carboxymethyl Hyaluronic Acid

CNS	Central Nervous System
COMET	Cultivated Oral Mucosal Epithelial Transplantation
CPCB-RPE1	California Project to Cure Blindness Retinal Pigment Epithelium-1
CLET	Cultivated Limbal Stem Cell Transplantation
CXCR-4	Chemokine Receptor Type 4
DED	Dry Eye Disease
DLP	Digital Light Processing
DPSC	Dental Pulp Stem Cells.
ECM	Extracellular Matrix
EDC	1-ethyl-3-(3-dimethylaminopropyl)carbodiimide
EDTRS	Early Treatment Diabetic Retinopathy Study
EHS	Engelbreth-Holm-Swarm
EU	European Union
FDA	Food and Drug Administration
FCSC	Fetal Cartilage Stem Cells
FGF	Fibroblast Growth Factor
HFSC	Hair Follicle Stem Cells
hESC	Human Embryonic Stem Cells
HSK	Herpes Simplex Keratitis
HSC	Hematopoietic Stem Cells
IGF	Insulin-like Growth Factor
IMDRF	International Medical Device Regulators Forum
IOL	Intraocular Lens
iCEP	iPSC-derived Corneal Epithelial Cell Sheets
iPSC	Induced Pluripotent Stem Cells
ISO	International Organization for Standardization
KPro	Keratoprosthesis
LAP	Laser-assisted Printing
LEC	Lens Epithelial Cells
LG	Lacrimal Glands
LGN	Lateral Geniculate Nucleus
LSC	Limbal Stem Cells
LSCD	Limbal Stem Cell Deficiency
MEA	Microelectrode Arrays
MHC	Major Histocompatibility Complexes
MMC	Macromolecular Crowding
MPC	2-methacryloyloxyethyl phosphorylcholine
MSC	Mesenchymal Stem Cells
NHS	N-hydroxysuccinimide
OCT	Optical Coherence Tomography
OMSC	Oral Mucosa Stem Cells
PCO	Posterior Capsule Opacification
PCL	poly(ε-caprolactone)
PDMS	Polydimethylsiloxane

PE	Polyethylene
PECD	Persistent Corneal Epithelial Defect
PEDF	Pigment Epithelium-derived Factor
PEG	Polyethylene Glycol
PEGDMA	Poly(ethylene glycol) dimethacrylate
PEMA	Poly(ethyl methacrylate)
PHEMA	Poly(2-hydroxyethyl methacrylate)
PHBHHx	Poly(3-hydroxybutyrate-co-3-hydroxyhexanoate)
PLGA	Poly(lactic-co-glycolic acid)
PMA	Polymethyl acrylate
PMMA	Polymethyl Methacrylate
PTFE	Polytetrafluoroethylene
PUK	Penetrating Ulcerative Keratitis
RGC	Retinal Ganglion Cells
RHCIII	Recombinant Human Collagen Type III
rGO	Reduced Graphene Oxide
RPE	Retinal Pigment Epithelium
RReSTORe	Retinal Ganglion Cell Repopulation, Stem Cell Transplantation, and Optic Nerve Regeneration Consortium
SCET	Simple Conjunctival Epithelial Transplantation
SCOTS	Stem Cell Ophthalmology Treatment Study
SLA	Stereolithography
SS	Sjögren's Syndrome
TGF-β	Transforming Growth Factor Beta
TON	Traumatic Optic Neuropathy
UMSC	Umbilical Cord-derived Mesenchymal Stem Cells
VEGF	Vascular Endothelial Growth Factor
WJSC	Wharton's Jelly Stem Cells

14.1 Introduction: The Human Eye and Biofabrication

The human eye is a specialized sensory organ that converts incoming light into electrical signals interpreted by the brain as vision (Fig. 14.1). Light enters through the transparent cornea, passes through the lens, and is focused onto the retina, where photoreceptors transduce it into neural signals. These signals are then transmitted via the optic nerve to the visual cortex, where they are processed into visual perception.

Ocular tissues can be compromised by congenital or genetic disorders, infection, trauma, or aging, and vision loss is consequently among the most feared causes of reduced quality of life worldwide (Ying 2025). The main parts of the eye being explored in regenerative medicine include the cornea, lens, retina, and optic nerve. Technologies tested include gene therapy, stem cell therapy, and use of bioengineered materials.

Biofabrication can broadly be described as "a process that results in a defined product with biological function" (Groll et al. 2016). It refers to the use of living cells, biomaterials, and bioactive molecules to engineer tissues, scaffold, or organs/

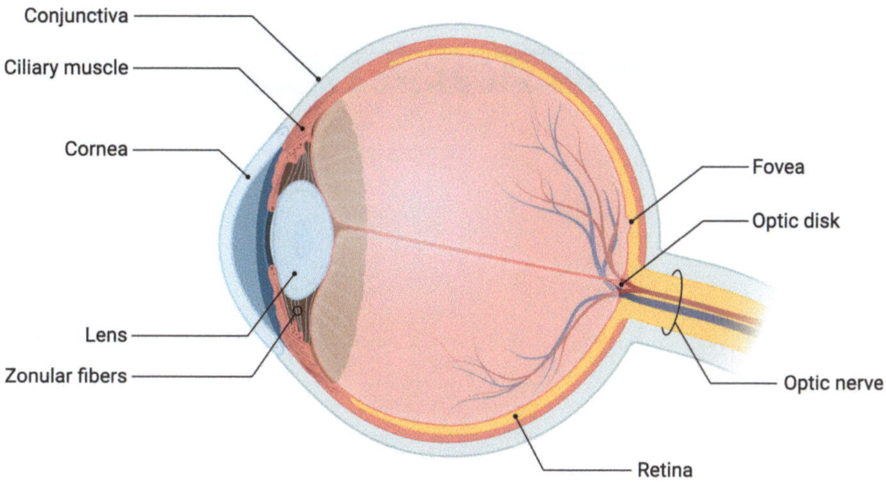

Fig. 14.1 The main parts of the human eye. (Created in BioRender (license number: DV293S1NCQ))

organoids for biomedical applications. The main technologies that are identified with biofabrication in recent years are bioprinting and bioassembly. Automation and precision aided by computers and even more recently machine learning and artificial intelligence are the further hallmarks of biofabrication. In this chapter, we will examine efforts for biofabricating or recreating engineered constructs to regenerate different parts of the eye, with examples from the cornea, lens, retina, and optic nerves. It is not intended to be comprehensive, and as such, we will attempt to reference reviews or articles where further information can be obtained.

14.1.1 Structure and Function of the Cornea

The cornea is the transparent, avascular outermost tissue of the eye. It serves as both a protective barrier and the primary refractive surface, contributing approximately two-thirds of the eye's total optical power. It is composed of five specialized histological layers: epithelium, Bowman's layer, stroma, Descemet's membrane, and endothelium (Fig. 14.2). The cornea is densely innervated, with sensory nerve endings arising from the trigeminal ganglia in the brain providing neurotrophic support for overall corneal health. Collectively, the corneal structure and avascularity maintain corneal transparency and structural integrity. Despite the cornea's remarkable capacity for self-repair, traditional therapeutic strategies such as corneal transplantation or long-term pharmacologic interventions remain limited by donor shortages, immune rejection, and potential long-term complications (Ljubimov and Saghizadeh 2015).

The epithelium, continuously renewed by limbal stem cells at its periphery, the corneoscleral junction, serves as the first line of defense against mechanical,

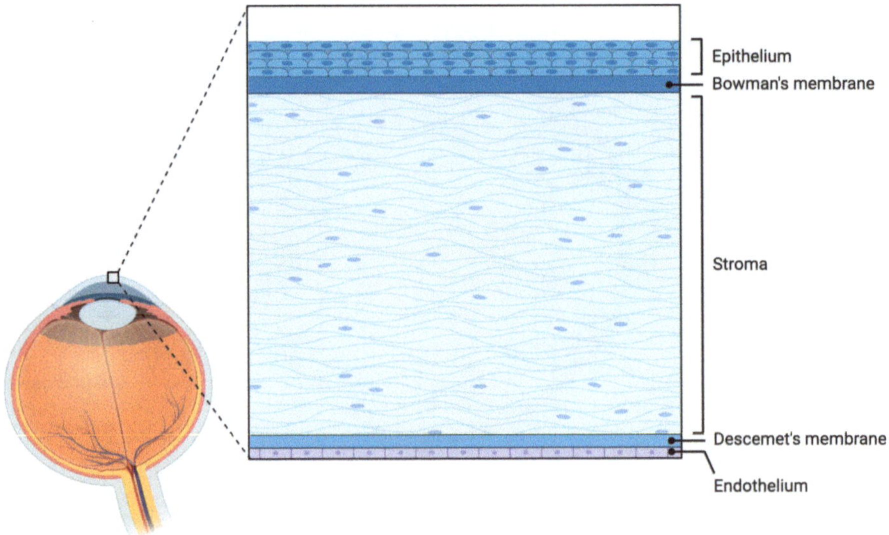

Fig. 14.2 Corneal layers. (Created in BioRender (license number: TL293SFU8X))

chemical, and microbial insults. Damage to the limbal stem cell niche disrupts epithelial regeneration, leading to persistent epithelial defects, marked surface irregularities, conjunctivalization, and vision impairment (Suanno et al. 2024). Between the epithelium and stroma, the Bowman's layer is an acellular condensation of collagen (types I and V) and proteoglycans that forms the smooth anterior surface of the corneal stroma. This layer supports corneal shape but cannot regenerate so injury to this layer can result in scarring (Sridhar 2018). The stroma constitutes close to 85% of the corneal thickness and is a transparent arrangement of collagen and extracellular matrix (ECM) in lamellae (Meek and Knupp 2015). Keratocytes located between lamellae form a network, surrounded by ECM containing collagens I, III, V, and VI and glycosaminoglycans (e.g., keratan, dermatan, chondroitin sulfate). Keratocytes maintain ECM homeostasis through synthesis of collagen, glycosaminoglycans, and matrix metalloproteinases. Inferiorly, the Descemet's membrane is an elastic layer composed mainly of type IV collagen and laminin, continually produced by endothelial cells. The endothelium, a monolayer of hexagonal cells on the posterior surface, maintains corneal dehydration through its ion pump activity, a critical mechanism for transparency. The most important pump is the Na + K+ ATPase ion pump. Loss or dysfunction of these endothelial cells, as well as their pumps, leads to stromal and epithelial edema, subepithelial fibrosis, and ultimately loss of vision (Ljubimov and Saghizadeh 2015).

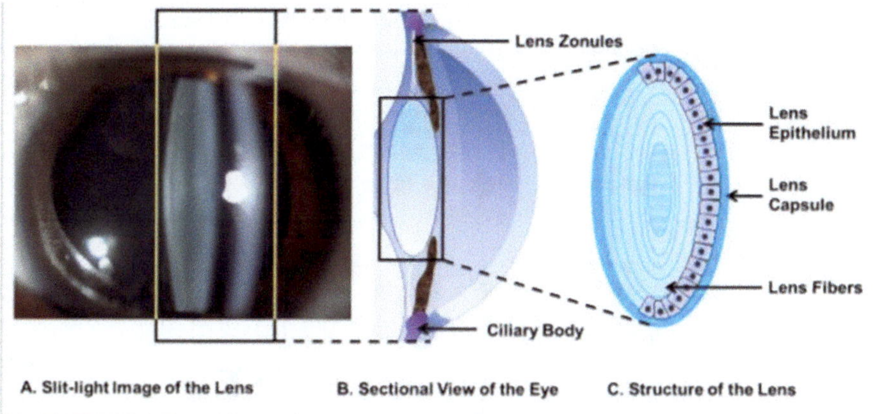

Fig. 14.3 Anatomy of the crystalline lens. Reprinted from Ruan et al. (2020), licensed under CC BY-NC 4.0. (This figure is reproduced under the Creative Commons Attribution Non-Commercial (CC BY-NC 4.0) license from BMJ Open Ophthalmology)

14.1.2 Structure and Function of the Lens

The lens (Fig. 14.3) is a transparent, avascular, and biconvex structure that sits posterior to the iris and anterior to the vitreous body (Ruan et al. 2020).

The lens provides the remaining one third of the eye's dioptric power and enables accommodation by dynamically altering its curvature to focus light at varying distances (Smith 1997). This process is mediated by contraction and relaxation of the ciliary muscle, which modulates tension in the zonular fibers: reduced zonular tension increases lens curvature for near vision, whereas increased tension flattens the lens for distance focus (Dubbelman and Van der Heijde 2001; Donaldson et al. 2017). It is enclosed by an elastic capsule composed primarily of type IV collagen and laminin, which serves both as a basement membrane for the anterior lens epithelial cells (LECs) and as an anchoring structure for the zonules of Zinn (Dubbelman and Van der Heijde 2001; Donaldson et al. 2017; Wederell and de Iongh 2006). The LECs form a metabolically active monolayer responsible for maintaining ionic and water homeostasis, nutrient transport, and waste clearance, thereby preserving lens transparency (Liu et al. 2023). Lens transparency is further ensured by the highly ordered organization of fiber cells enriched in α-, β-, and γ-crystallins, which together account for approximately 90% of the lens dry mass. These proteins are long-lived and nonrenewable; cumulative damage and aggregation over time, despite the chaperone function of α-crystallins, disrupt optical homogeneity and underlie increasing stiffness of the lens (presbyopia) and cataract formation (Donaldson et al. 2017; Hejtmancik and Shiels 2015).

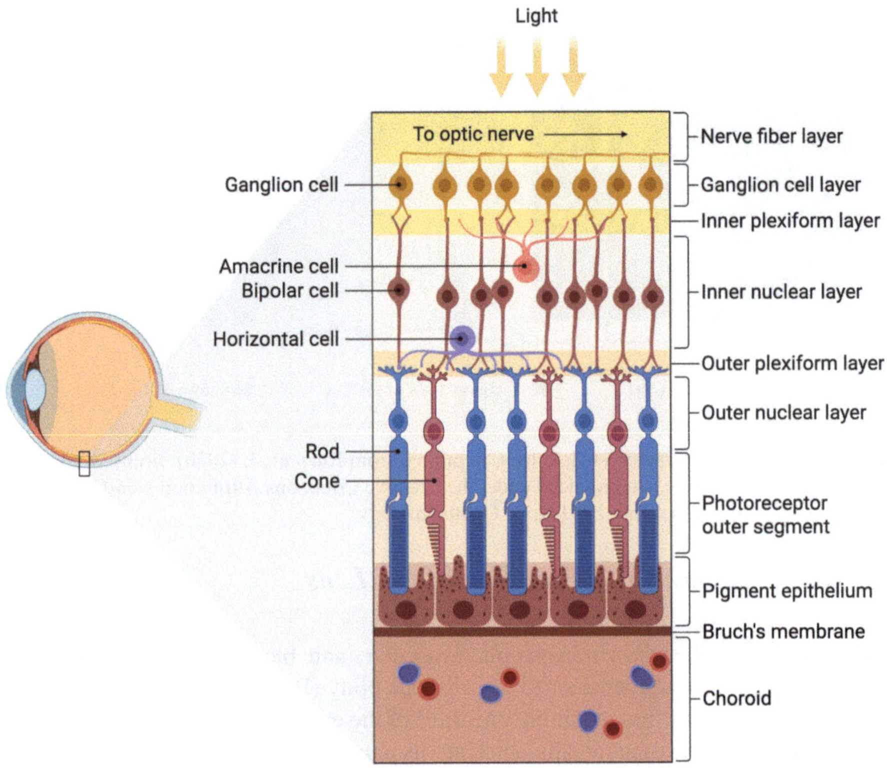

Fig. 14.4 Anatomy of the retina. (Created in BioRender (license number: FQ293SGJKJ))

14.1.3 Structure and Function of the Retina

The retina is a thin multilayered neural tissue that lines the posterior cavity of the eye and performs the transduction of light stimuli to electric impulses (Mahabadi and Al Khalili 2025). The retina itself can be further divided into a neurosensory retina and a retinal pigment epithelium (RPE) (Pollreisz et al. 2020). The neurosensory retina contains two classes of specialized photoreceptors, rods and cones. Rods are highly sensitive to low light levels and support scotopic vision while cones support color vision in brighter light conditions (Mahabadi and Al Khalili 2025). Photoreceptors synapse with bipolar, horizontal, and amacrine interneurons (Mahabadi and Al Khalili 2025). The ganglion cell layer, whose axons converge at the optic disc to form the optic nerve, receives inputs from the amacrine and bipolar cells (Mahabadi and Al Khalili 2025).

The RPE is a monolayer of pigmented epithelial cells found between the neuro-sensory retina and the choroid (Simó et al. 2010). It provides essential support to the photoreceptors by phagocytosing their shed outer segments, shuttling nutrients and waste products, absorbing scattered light, and secreting growth factors, such as vascular endothelial growth factor (VEGF) and pigment epithelium-derived factor

(PEDF), to maintain the choriocapillaris (Simó et al. 2010). Disturbance of RPE–photoreceptor interaction can result in a spectrum of numerous degenerative retinal disorders, including age-related macular degeneration and retinitis pigmentosa, among others (Zhang et al. 2025a).

The retina is organized into ten histological layers (Fig. 14.4), from the inner limiting membrane to the photoreceptor outer segments, with neurons, synapses, and graded potentials arranged in a precise manner to support the laminar and retinotopic flow of spatially and temporally resolved visual information (Mahabadi and Al Khalili 2025). The macula is the retinal area near the posterior pole that is specialized for high-resolution central vision, with the remainder of the retina supporting motion detection and peripheral awareness (Koksaldi et al. 2025). The retina itself is one of the most metabolically active tissues in the body. Retinal damage from ischemia, inflammation, or degeneration is typically permanent due to its complex and well-ordered structure and fragility of cellular components, making it a primary target for regenerative and biofabrication approaches (Joyal et al. 2018).

14.1.4 Structure and Function of the Optic Nerve

The optic nerve, or cranial nerve II, is the primary conduit responsible for vision. The optic nerve contains the fibers of the retinal ganglion cells (Smith and Czyz 2025; Smith and Czyz 2025). Structurally, the optic nerve is one of the two white matter tracts of the central nervous system (CNS); the other being the optic chiasm, rather than a peripheral nerve, as it is derived from the diencephalon embryologically and is

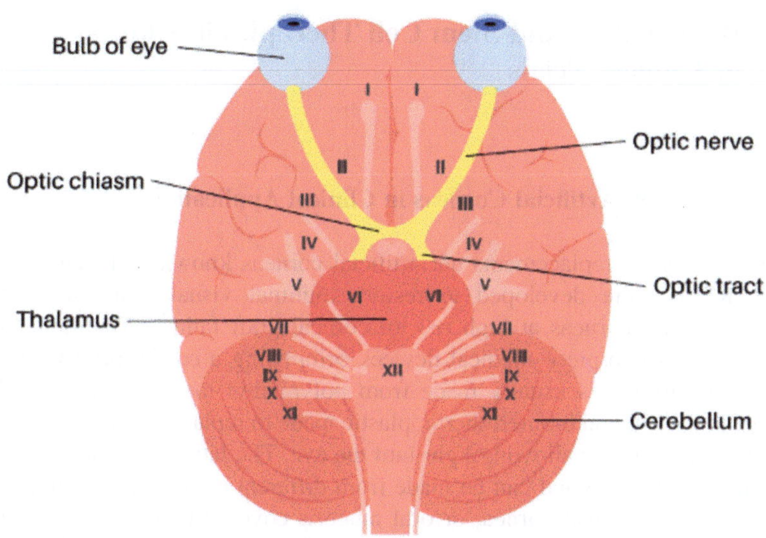

Fig. 14.5 Anatomy of the optic nerve and optic chiasm. (Reproduced from Shutterstock ID: 2490326819-1 image, Standard License)

myelinated by oligodendrocytes rather than Schwann cells (Smith and Czyz 2025) (Fig. 14.5). The optic nerve is classically divided into four portions: intraocular (optic nerve head), intraorbital, intracanalicular, and intracranial (Hayreh 2006). The intraocular segment can be seen as a rounded elevation of the eye wall and is known as the optic disc (Bourne 2012) and is also the physiological blind spot due to the absence of rods or cones (Urale et al. 2022). The intraorbital segment of the optic nerve consists of an S-shaped and can accommodate ocular movements, while the intracanalicular segment runs through the optic canal of the sphenoid bone and then the intracranial portion, which connects to the optic chiasm (Salazar et al. 2018). Fibers of the optic nerve from the nasal retina cross over at the optic chiasm to the contralateral hemisphere to process binocular vision (Mahabadi and Al Khalili 2025).

Functionally, the optic nerve transmits visual information as electrical impulses (Gupta et al. 2025). These impulses generated from the retina to the brain are carried through the optic nerve and optic tract to the lateral geniculate nucleus (LGN) in the thalamus and toward the primary visual cortex in the occipital lobe (Gupta et al. 2025). Like all white matter tracts of the central nervous system, the optic nerve has no regenerative ability. If damaged through glaucoma, optic neuritis, ischemic optic neuropathy, or trauma, the resulting loss of retinal ganglion cells and blindness is permanent (Weber et al. 2008). For this reason, biofabrication of the optic nerve is an active area of research, including the examination of stem cell–derived retinal ganglion cells, axonal guidance scaffolds, and neuroprotective biomaterials to support remyelination and functional reconnection between the retina and the brain (Obeng et al. 2025; Liu et al. 2024).

14.2 Biomaterials and Stem Cell Therapies in Clinics or Clinical Trials

14.2.1 Cornea

14.2.1.1 Current Artificial Corneas in Clinical Application

The earliest cornea replacements are artificial corneas known as keratoprostheses (KPro). KPros were developed to restore minimal visual function in mainly end-stage disease corneas at high risk of corneal graft failure. Traditional KPros are produced as two-piece medical devices comprising a core (optic) with a skirt (haptic). The former is usually made from polymethyl methacrylate (PMMA), a transparent, robust, and bioinert thermoplastic made to replace the optical properties of the corneal tissue by allowing light into the eye. The latter functions to integrate the device into the eye and can be made from different materials including plastic, metal, a piece of human cornea, or oral mucosa–covered tooth. Two of the best-known KPro designs to date are the Boston Keratoprosthesis (Dohlman 2022) and the Osteo-OdontoKeratoprosthesis (Avadhanam et al. 2015; Kaur 2018). Both require irreversible and invasive surgeries for installation. While the innovation of KPros has proven useful in clinical settings in recent years, there are possible shortcomings inherent to its rigidity and poor biointegration, such as aberrant healing and abnormal fibrosis at the KPro-host junction, resulting in poor long-term clinical outcomes (Wilson 2020; Bamashmus et al. 2020).

Key future directions for development of the KPro, therefore, center around optimizing biocompatibility and biointegration to minimize inflammatory reactions and foreign body responses, while ensuring cell adhesion and extracellular matrix formation. One potential avenue is coating with hydroxyapatite (Hap) to improve adhesion of keratocytes, which has shown induction of larger fibroblast morphology parallel to the implant (Li et al. 2018; Dong et al. 2014; Wang et al. 2011). The CorNeat is a more recently developed KPro. This KPro is made up of electrospun carbonated polyurethane fiber skirt and a large 10 mm PMMA optical element and is secured under the conjunctiva to serve as a scaffold for migration of host fibroblasts (Litvin et al. 2021). In an early clinical trial, the CorNeat KPro was implanted in the right eye of a patient with bilateral corneal opacification and neovascularization secondary to multiple failed grafts, with improvement of vision from hand movement to 1/16 at 12 months (Bahar et al. 2023). A single-arm, open-label, prospective, multicenter trial in Canada, France, Israel, and the Netherlands is recruiting participants with corneal blindness who are not candidates for traditional transplantation for further studies, with expected results in 2026 (CorNeat Vision Ltd 2024).

14.2.1.2 Emerging Therapies: Natural or Biomimetic Corneal Constructs

Regenerating corneal tissues is the approach for non-end-stage corneas, leveraging the use of biomaterials and novel bioengineering techniques. Natural or biomimetic constructs have been developed to mimic the corneal extracellular matrix (ECM) to support regeneration. Novel bioengineering approaches to natural constructs include self-assembled corneal equivalents, decellularized corneal implants, artificial corneas with regenerative potential, and hydrogel implants. Self-assembled corneal equivalents designate the stimulation of production of collagen and other ECM molecules by addition of chemicals to cells in culture. The resulting sheets of scaffold are then air-lifted to form a stack that imitates the natural structure of the stroma (Proulx et al. 2010), and corneal epithelial and endothelial cells can be added to the end surfaces to further simulate the natural corneal structure. Macromolecular crowding (MMC) is a form of self-assembly, where inert, high-molecular-weight polymers are added to the culture media of corneal fibroblasts (Gurdal and Zeugolis 2025). By recreating the dense environment as seen in living tissue, the cells are driven to accelerate their production and deposition of their ECM components, which include several collagens and fibronectin. Studies with self-assembly are largely in vitro, though a preclinical in vivo study was conducted in 2014 on healthy feline eyes. At 4 months, the grafts were healthy, transparent, and avascular, with corneal innervation returning to baseline levels (Boulze Pankert et al. 2014).

Table 14.1 Descriptions of completed clinical trials evaluating bioengineered corneal therapies, divided by cellular layer of the cornea

Corneal construct	Components	Description of study	Findings	References
Biomaterials targeting the epithelium				
KIO-201 (Graue-Hernandez et al. 2023)	Cross-linked thiolated carboxymethyl hyaluronic acid 0.75% (CMHA-S)	Prospective, open-label, single center study of 9 eyes in 8 subjects diagnosed with stage 1 and stage 2 persistent corneal epithelial defect (PCED), receiving KIO-201 with a dosing regimen of 6 times per day over 4 weeks	5/8 participants showed an appreciable reduction in the lesion area by the end of the 4-week treatment period	Graue-Hernandez et al. (2023)
Biomaterials targeting the stroma				
Decellularized xenogeneic corneal implant (Zhang et al. 2015)	Acellular porcine corneal stroma (APCS)	Anterior lamellar keratoplasty grafts in 47 patients with fungal corneal ulcers	Successful epithelialization in all grafts but four (dissolution of graft) Transparency and no rejection in 87% ($n = 41$) Improvement in best corrected visual acuity (BCVA) by 2 lines in 72%	Zhang et al. (2015)
Decellularized xenogeneic corneal implant (Zheng et al. 2019)	Acellular porcine corneal stroma (APCS)	Deep anterior lamellar keratoplasty and double lamellar keratoplasty in 9 and 5 patients with herpes simplex keratitis (HSK)	Transparent/minimal opacities in 7 patients (53.8%) Neovascularization in 11 patients (84.6%), with stabilization 3 patients (23.1%) had graft dissolution	Zheng et al. (2019)
Decellularized xenogeneic corneal implants (Li et al. 2019)	Acellular porcine corneal stroma (APCS)	Deep anterior lamellar keratoplasty in 39 patients with infectious keratitis	Graft failure in 12 patients (noninfectious graft melting, extensive neovascularization, recurring infection) Significant and higher relative risk of graft rejection in HSK and large grafts (>8 mm) 40% increase in patients with visual acuity of 20/40 or better	Li et al. (2019)

Decellularized xenogeneic corneal implants (Chen et al. 2025)	Acellular porcine corneal stroma (APCS)	Lamellar keratoplasty in 58 patients with penetrating ulcerative keratitis (PUK), receiving human cornea ($n = 27$) and APCS ($n = 31$)	No significant difference in best corrected visual acuity (BCVA) at 1 and 12 months, with a comparable number of transparent corneas at 12 months Significantly better results (BCVA and transparency) in human cornea at earlier time points (3, 6 months) Prolonged epithelial healing time with APCS in patients with autoimmune diseases	Chen et al. (2025)
Cell-free biosynthetic RHC III hydrogel (Fagerholm et al. 2014; Fagerholm et al. 2010)	Recombinant human collagen III (RHCIII), cross-linked with EDC and NHS	Anterior lamellar keratoplasty, hydrogel implanted in 10 patients with keratoconus ($n = 9$) and central scarring ($n = 1$), vs control ($n = 9$) by allograft full-thickness keratoplasty	No rejections nor adverse immune reactions at 4 years post-operation in the 10 patients Minimal immune reaction in hydrogel group compared to control Regeneration of nerves in hydrogel group	Fagerholm et al. (2014 and Fagerholm et al. (2010)
RHCIII-MPC (Islam et al. 2018)	RHCIII base formulation (Fagerholm et al. 2010), with the incorporation of 2-methacryloyloxyethyl phosphorylcholine (MPC)	Anterior lamellar keratoplasty in 7 unilaterally blind patients at high risk of conventional corneal allograft rejection	Greatest improvement in patients with scarring or ulcers due to infection ($n = 3$); worst in immune and degenerative disorders Near restoration of corneal sensitivity	Islam et al. (2018)
Bioengineered porcine construct, double cross-linked (BPCDX) (Rafat et al. 2023)	Type I porcine dermal collagen, dual chemical and photochemical cross-linking	Implantation into stromal pockets created with femtosecond lasers in 20 advanced keratoconus patients	Fourteen of 14 initially blind subjects achieved a best-corrected vision (spectacle or contact lens) of 20/36	Rafat et al. (2023)

(continued)

Table 14.1 (continued)

Corneal construct	Components	Description of study	Findings	References
NANOULCOR (González-Gallardo et al. 2023)	Nanostructured fibrin-agarose biocompatible scaffold, combined with allogeneic corneal epithelial and stromal cells	Anterior corneal substitute in 5 patients with severe trophic ulcers refractory to conventional treatment	No signs of graft rejection, local infection, or corneal neovascularization after 2 years of follow-up	González-Gallardo et al. (2023)
Biomaterials targeting the endothelium				
EndoArt implant (Daphna et al. 2024)	Transparent, foldable, and hydrophilic device composed of a copolymer of hydroxyethyl methacrylate and methyl methacrylate	Implantation through peripheral corneal incision in 24 eyes of 24 patients with low-to-normal visual potential with chronic corneal edema, 12-month follow-up	Best-corrected distance visual acuity improved 60% gained at least 3 early treatment diabetic retinopathy study (ETDRS) lines Implants remained transparent	Daphna et al. (2024)

Decellularized corneal implants refer to the removal of cells from tissues and organs. The remaining ECM can be pre-seeded with exogenous therapeutic cells before implantation (Gonzalez-Andrades et al. 2011; Fernández-Pérez et al. 2021) or recolonized by healthy cells (Hashimoto et al. 2015; Lin et al. 2017). The inherent lack of major histocompatibility complexes (MHC) on decellularized implants allows for the circumvention of risks of graft rejection (Fernández-Pérez et al. 2021; Ahearne et al. 2020). They have been studied in clinical trials with promising results, as can be seen in Table 14.1.

Most notably, collagen has been studied extensively as a biomaterial, given its predominance in the corneal stromal ECM and biocompatibility. The Griffith and Fagerholm team conducted the first clinical study using cell-free biosynthetic hydrogels, produced from recombinant human collagen type III (RHCIII), cross-linking with 1-ethyl-3-(3-dimethylaminopropyl) carbodiimide (EDC) and its co-reactant, N-hydroxysuccinimide (NHS), to promote in situ corneal tissue and nerve regeneration (Fagerholm et al. 2014; Fagerholm et al. 2010). Details on the clinical results are summarized in Table 14.1.

Preclinical in vivo animal studies have demonstrated success with various bioengineered implants in both solid and liquid form, the latter offering a more resilient and biocompatible alternative to clinical glue (e.g., cyanoacrylate) application in the case of corneal ulcers, thinning, or perforations (Yin et al. 2019). Short-strand collagen-like peptide (CLP) conjugated to polyethylene glycol (PEG) has shown successful tissue and nerve regeneration both as solid implants (Jangamreddy et al. 2018; Buznyk et al. 2025) and injectable self-gelling liquid hydrogels (McTiernan et al. 2020). These CLP-based hydrogels could be modified by the addition of 2-methacryloyloxyethyl phosphorylcholine (MPC) to confer further anti-inflammatory effects, reduced corneal swelling, haze, and neovascularization (Simpson et al. 2021; Simoliunas et al. 2024). With the introduction of nanoparticles delivering drugs or bioactives, Simoliunas et al. (2024) also showed that CLP-MPC-based injectable hydrogels blocked Herpes Simplex Virus serotype-1 (HSV-1) activity in infected, perforated rabbit corneas. Implants using gelatin methacrylate (GelMA) (Wang et al. 2023; Kong et al. 2020), thiolated gelatin (Agrawal et al. 2024; Rosenquist et al. 2023), and gelatin derived from porcine collagen (Soltani Sharif Abadi et al. 2023) have similarly demonstrated successful regeneration in animal studies. Biomaterials supplemented with exogenous therapeutic cells, as in the cases of silk fibroin with human corneal stromal cells (Bhattacharjee and Ahearne 2022; Ghezzi et al. 2017) and alginate-chitosan with rabbit limbal stem cells (Xu et al. 2019), have also been studied.

14.2.1.3 Stem Cell-Based Therapies

Stem cell therapies, along with their associated secretome, are also a promising avenue for corneal medicine, due to their pluripotency and anti-inflammatory properties (Lin et al. 2025), which are advantageous in corneal regeneration. Various methods of stem cell delivery are described in literature, including seeding onto

Table 14.2 Preclinical findings for therapeutic use of stem cells and their secretome

Nature of stem cell therapy	Pathologies studied	Proposed mechanisms	Effects of secretome	References
Bone marrow-derived mesenchymal stem cells (BMSC) (Galindo et al. 2025; Dinç et al. 2021; Shukla et al. 2019)	Limbal stem cell deficiency (LSCD), corneal alkali burns, dry eye disease (DED), corneal epithelial defects	Reversal of miRNA profile changes	miR-204 as primary immunomodulatory cargo, exerting an effect on IL-6R to induce a phenotypic switch in the macrophage population	Galindo et al. (2025), Dinç et al. (2021) and Shukla et al. (2019)
Adipose tissue-derived mesenchymal stem cells (ADMSC) (Galindo et al. 2025; Ryu et al. 2023; Li and Zhang 2020; Wang et al. 2021a; Shang et al. 2020)	LSCD, DED, endothelial cell senescence, corneal epithelial defect	Promote clearance of neutrophils, increasing the reverse transendothelial cell migration of CXCR4^{high} neutrophils	Suppression of NLRP3 inflammasome activation Induce endothelial cell proliferation and suppress TGF-β- or H2O2-induced oxidative stress and senescence	`
Umbilical cord-derived mesenchymal stem cells (UMSC) (Call et al. 2019; Liu et al. 2022; Zhou et al. 2023; Kacham et al. 2021)	Congenital and acquired stromal opacities, graft-vs-host dry eye disease, Sjogren's syndrome, corneal epithelial defects	Production of collagen V and rearrangement of collagen fibrils	Expression of miR-21, inhibiting PTEN/PI3K/AKT pathway Activation of p44/42 MAPK pathway miR-204 cargo	Call et al. (2019), Liu et al. (2022), Zhou et al. (2023) and Kacham et al. (2021)

amniotic membranes (López et al. 2021; Galindo et al. 2025), subconjunctival injection (Dinç et al. 2021), topical application (Call et al. 2019), and intrastromal injection (Soleimani et al. 2023). Furthermore, various stem cell sources and secretomes have been therapeutically studied for different corneal pathologies, with promising preclinical results. Some recent findings from commonly studied stem cells have been summarized in Table 14.2. Other types of stem cells in literature include Wharton's jelly stem cells (WJSC) (Feiertag et al. 2020), oral mucosal stem cells (OMSC) (López et al. 2021), fetal cartilage stem cells (FCSC) (Park et al. 2021), and hair follicle stem cells (HFSC) (Olszewski et al. 2022).

A recent single-arm, open-label prospective clinical study on 16 patients with both non-Sjogren and Sjogren's syndrome dry eye evaluated the efficacy of topical eye drops of umbilical cord-derived mesenchymal stem cells (UMSC), administered twice daily. They found significant improvements in symptoms, tear production, meibomian gland blockage, and conjunctival redness (Zhang et al. 2025b).

Multiple advancements in the field of stem cell therapy have been made for treatment of limbal stem cell deficiency (LSCD), which is currently treated with autologous limbal stem cell transplantation, though this requires unilateral or partial LSCD and raises the risk of donor eye destabilization. Allogeneic limbal stem cell transplantation, despite the use of systemic immunosuppression, is reported to be limited to 50% success at 5 years (Kacham et al. 2021). Of the most promising approaches, there are cultivated limbal stem cell transplantation (CLET) and cultivated autologous limbal epithelial cell (CALEC) transplants. CLET was developed in 1997 by Pellegrini, and ex vivo expanded human corneal epithelial cells with stem cells were the first approved CLET in the EU in 2015 (Pellegrini et al. 2016). CALEC is a construct developed through successful expansion of autologous limbal stem cell (LSC) on human amniotic membrane. In phase I/II trials, 14/16 limbal biopsies resulted in successful CALEC grafts, and 92% of grafts showed partial or complete success at 18 months, with no safety issues. Cultivated oral mucosal epithelial transplantation (COMET) has also shown viability and safety as a clinical alternative (Satake et al. 2011; Gopakumar et al. 2019; Toshida et al. 2023). Allogeneic human iPSC-derived corneal epithelial cell sheets (iCEPSs) were transplanted onto four eyes in the context of a single-arm, non-randomized clinical trial. No serious adverse events were reported, and disease stage had improved, corrected distance visual acuity was enhanced, and corneal opacification had diminished in all treated eyes at the end of 52 weeks (Soma et al. 2024). A larger clinical trial is planned to further evaluate the efficacy.

Adipose-derived mesenchymal stem cells (ADMSC) injected intrastromally via femtosecond laser has been evaluated in a clinical trial involving eight patients with severe keratoconus, and visual acuity improved moderately, corneal ectasia parameters reduced slightly, and stromal keratocytes density increased after 6 months (Ramin et al. 2023).

A first-in-human clinical trial evaluated allogenic iPSC-derived corneal endothelial cell substitutes in the treatment of bullous keratopathy, with improvement of visual acuity and corneal stromal edema, with no adverse events for up to 1 year after surgery (Hirayama et al. 2025).

14.2.2 Conjunctiva

A wide range of insults can damage the conjunctiva. This includes but is not limited to severe inflammation, immune-mediated diseases such as Stevens–Johnson syndrome and cicatricial pemphigoid, chemical and thermal burns, trauma, surgical complications, chronic infections, radiotherapy, prolonged use of topical mitomycin C or 5-fluorouracil, conjunctival fibrosis, and dry eye disease.

14.2.2.1 Currently Available Treatments for Conjunctival Defects

Current treatments of conjunctival defects are mostly non-regenerative substitutive approaches that aim to replace damaged tissue. Substitutes that have been successful in restoring the cornea include conjunctival grafts (Thoft 1977; Vastine et al. 1982), amniotic membrane transplantation (Solomon et al. 2003; Tseng et al. 1997), as well as oral (Hosni 1974; Shore et al. 1992) or nasal turbinate (Kuckelkorn et al. 1996; Wenkel et al. 2000) mucosal grafts that are used in more select cases. However, limited donor tissue availability, the complexity of these surgeries, and the risks they entail, as well as the variability of results that arise from such treatments, have encouraged many researchers to turn to regenerative approaches for conjunctival disease treatment.

14.2.2.2 Stem Cell-Based Therapies for the Conjunctiva

Among recent advances in alternatives for biological regeneration of native conjunctiva are stem cell–based therapies. For instance, Zhong and Chen 2022 described a promising isolation and expansion technique of conjunctival stem cells (Zhong and Chen 2022). They used collagenase to release the cells from human or rabbit conjunctival tissue, which were then expanded in a feeder-free medium. Under these conditions, cells had a high proliferation rate, expressed stem cell markers, and demonstrated differentiation potency. This expansion protocol was used by the same research team to develop injectable GelMA hydrogels containing conjunctival stem cells (CjSCs) using digital light processing (DLP)-based bioprinting. In vitro, the cells once again showed strong viability, maintained their stemness, and were able to differentiate into goblet cells. The micro-constructs were subsequently injected to the bulbar conjunctival epithelium in an ex vivo rabbit model. After delivery, the cells survived and were densely localized within the subconjunctival region, which shows that the hydrogel effectively retained the cells at their target site (Zhong et al. 2021). In parallel, human embryonic stem cells have successfully been differentiated into conjunctival epithelial cells and goblet cells using a three-step induction protocol by Hu et al. 2024). These studies all mark important steps in building efficient in vitro expansion strategies of endogenous conjunctival stem cells, which have become a potential strategy to treat conjunctival disorders, although there hasn't been any in vivo study so far.

14.2.2.3 Tissue-Engineering Advances for Conjunctival Defects

Tissue-engineering has also risen as a promising alternative for ocular surface disorders. Conjunctival epithelial cell sheets grown on amniotic membrane is a therapy that has already been successfully implanted in humans for the treatment of primary pterygium, with epithelialization and recovery shown to be faster compared to denuded AM alone (Ang et al. 2005). Several earlier-stage tissue-engineered constructs have also shown promising results in preclinical models. Notably, Kobayashi et al. (2015) engineered ex vivo nasal mucosal epithelial cell sheets containing a high density of goblet cells. After transplantation in rabbits, the micro-constructs showed stratified layers of differentiated epithelial cells and adhered well to host tissue. This study represents an important step in tissue-engineered goblet cell transplantation to treat severe ocular surface diseases (Kobayashi et al. 2015). Similarly, transplantation of progenitor cell-derived epidermal sheets expanded on denuded amniotic membrane has shown to successfully reconstruct the conjunctiva of injured rhesus monkeys. Histological and electron microscopy evaluation after the procedure showed that the cell sheets were healthy, multilayered, adherent to the amniotic membrane, and similar in appearance to normal conjunctival epithelium, thus confirming the translational potential of this approach (Lu et al. 2011a).

More recently, organoid-based therapies have been explored as an alternative strategy for conjunctival regeneration. van Velthoven et al. (2024) grew human conjunctival organoids derived from conjunctival biopsies, dissociated them into single cells, and subsequently cultured them on fibrin scaffolds to form transplantable epithelial sheets (van Velthoven et al. 2024). They were applied on 34 rabbits with induced conjunctival defects. Histologic examinations showed complete epithelial regeneration by days 7 and 21, normal distribution of goblet cells, and the presence of human CK14 cells, which confirmed that the transplanted human cells were the ones to restore the defects. This breakthrough shows that conjunctival organoid–derived cell sheets may hold promise for the treatment of ocular surface disorders.

In parallel, synthetic conjunctival substitutes have also been investigated. For example, Xie et al. (2023) used melt electrowritten PCL scaffolds combined with a two-step co-culture of human conjunctival stromal and epithelial cells to generate a bilayer construct that replicates key features of native conjunctiva, although this work remains at the in vitro stage (Xie et al. 2023).

In addition to the ex vivo cell-based approaches previously mentioned, in vivo epithelial expansion techniques have recently been explored, namely, simple conjunctival epithelial transplantation (SCET), which uses small autologous conjunctival tissue fragments glued onto an amniotic membrane patch placed over the scleral defect. In a recent clinical study of six patients undergoing pterygium excision, these fragments expanded over the amniotic membrane and regenerated a conjunctival epithelium expressing appropriate molecular markers, with no recurrence at 12 months (Bertolin et al. 2022). This strategy provides an alternative method for promoting conjunctival renewal without the need for ex vivo cell culture.

14.2.2.4 Biomaterials for the Conjunctiva

Progress in the use of biomaterials that support host-driven conjunctival regeneration has also been made (Makuloluwa et al. 2021; Mousavi et al. 2024). This includes decellularized conjunctival matrices, which have risen as favorable substrates. Decellularized rabbit conjunctival ECM (Wen et al. 2014), porcine decellularized conjunctival ECM (https://europepmc.org/article/med/32860970; Zhao et al. 2019), and human decellularized conjunctival ECM (Kasbekar et al. 2018; Witt et al. 2018) have all shown to support the growth of a stratified conjunctival epithelium containing goblet cells in vivo. Decellularized porcine conjunctiva has even been tested in humans. It has been used to treat severe symblepharon in 16 patients in an interventional case series published in 2024 (Shan et al. 2023). Despite their success, decellularized extracellular matrices derived from animal or human tissues have different limitations, such as limited donor tissue availability, risk of pathogen transfer and immunological reactions, and the variability of ECM composition and architecture across donor tissues (Hoshiba et al. 2010; Lu et al. 2011b).

Other acellular scaffolds that are available clinically to treat conjunctival defects are decellularized dermal substrates, namely AlloDerm and OloGen. We explore these biomaterial options into more detail in Sect. 2.5.1.

Collagen-based substrates have also been evaluated in vivo with successful reepithelialization, repopulation with goblet cells, and reduction of fibrosis, namely, plastic compressed collagen gels (Witt et al. 2019) and vitrified recombinant human collagen scaffolds (Zhou et al. 2014).

There has also been progress in biomaterials that prevent conjunctival scarring. For instance, collagen-glycosaminoglycan (Hsu et al. 2000) and PLGA acellular porous scaffolds (Lee et al. 2003) were placed onto full-thickness conjunctival wounds of rabbit eyes in vivo and were shown to reduce fibrosis and fornix shortening and reorient collagen fibers in an arrangement normally found healthy conjunctivas. While these scaffolds can be useful to cover small epithelial defects, epithelialization took a long time, they were not elastic enough for fornix reconstruction, and their behavior under chronic inflammation is unknown. That is why their use is not recommended in situations where donor epithelium is needed (Schrader et al. 2009).

Other emerging biomaterials for conjunctival restoration are fibrin, silk fibroin, PCL, PGLA, titaminates, and surface-modified PTFE, which currently remain at preclinical stages (Makuloluwa et al. 2021).

14.2.2.5 Pharmacologic Agents Used in Biofabrication for the Conjunctiva

As far as pharmacologic agents, topical application of retinoic acid has recently shown to promote conjunctival epithelium differentiation and goblet cells regeneration in 2D culture, 3D conjunctival organoids, as well as in a murine model in a study by Shi et al. 2025). While technologies aimed to regenerate the conjunctiva are an important focus of ongoing research, most remain at preclinical stages. As a consequence, autografts or allogenic grafts remain the gold standard for ocular surface disorder treatment. This highlights the need for continued efforts to develop new treatments and to increase the translational rate of existing preclinical therapies.

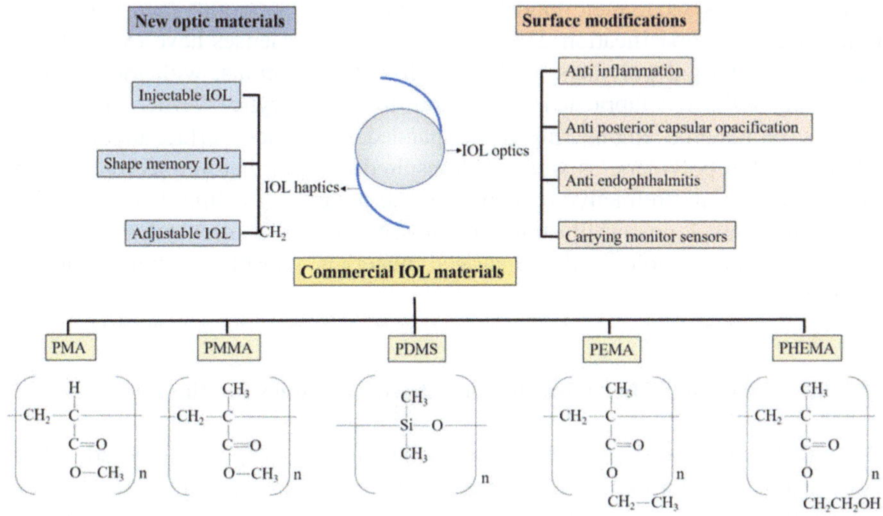

Fig. 14.6 Evolution of intraocular lens materials used in commercial IOLs. *PMA* polymethylacrylate, *PMMA* polymethylmethacrylate, *PDMS* polydimethylsiloxane, *PEMA* polyethyl methacrylate, *PHEMA* poly2-hydroxyethylmethacrylate. (Reproduced from Luo et al. (2022) under the Creative Commons Attribution License (CC BY))

14.2.3 Lens

14.2.3.1 The Evolution of Intraocular Lens

The earliest attempts to reproduce the function of part of the eye was development of the intraocular lens (IOL) by Harold Ridley and the first implantation on 29 November 1949 (Apple and Sims 1996). This IOL was made from polymethyl methacrylate (PMMA) from a pre-cast sheet of PMMA, the same shape and size of the human lens. PMMA is a rigid, transparent polymer previously used in aircraft canopies during World War II and later found to be well tolerated in the eye (Apple and Sims 1996). Since 1949, the IOL has gone through more than 75 years of development (Luo et al. 2022). In fact, subsequent IOLs evolved significantly in both design and material composition, incorporating advances that enhanced biocompatibility, optical performance, and surgical handling (Fig. 14.6). During the 1960s and 1970s, improvements in PMMA purity and surface finishing enhanced biocompatibility and reduced postoperative inflammation. In 1976, the very first foldable (soft) IOL was introduced (Allarakhia et al. 1987). Foldable silicone and hydrogel polymers enabled implantation through smaller incisions and accelerated the adoption of phacoemulsification techniques. Polydimethylsiloxane (PDMS) and other silicone-based materials exhibit refractive indices which are higher than those of PMMA (Kapoor et al. 2020). Consequently, silicone IOLs achieved the same refractive power as PMMA lenses while maintaining a thinner profile (Čanović et al. 2019). By the 1990s, hydrophobic and hydrophilic acrylic materials emerged as dominant choices due to their optical clarity, mechanical flexibility, and low rates of posterior capsule opacification. In summary, intraocular lenses have evolved from being made of rigid polymers to flexible, foldable materials, with most modern commercial IOLs now fabricated from various forms of acrylic (Werner 2021). More recently, biomaterial engineering has expanded to include surface-modified and light-adjustable polymers, as well as bioinspired designs that aim to replicate the accommodative and refractive dynamics of the natural crystalline lens (Luo et al. 2022). These developments illustrate a progressive shift from inert optical substitutes toward advanced, biologically integrated materials capable of functional lens restoration.

14.2.3.2 Emerging Therapies: Regenerative Therapies for the Lens

In parallel with these advances in synthetic biomaterials, recent decades have witnessed a growing interest in regenerative strategies aimed at restoring or regenerating the native crystalline lens rather than replacing it. Building on discoveries in developmental biology and stem cell research, investigators have identified populations of lens epithelial progenitor cells capable of self-renewal and differentiation into transparent fiber cells under appropriate biochemical and biomechanical cues, providing an endogenous source for lens tissue regrowth (Lin et al. 2016; Yang et al. 2010).

Early animal studies demonstrated that preservation of the lens capsule after cataract extraction can provide a natural scaffold for endogenous lens regeneration, particularly when coupled with modulation of growth factors. Indeed, maintenance of the capsular integrity enhanced the shape and growth of regenerated lenses in rabbits and cats following endocapsular extraction (Gwon et al. 1993). In rats, longitudinal imaging confirmed regrowth of lens tissue from residual lens epithelial cells within an intact capsular bag (Zhou et al. 2016). Concurrently, advances in stem cell biology have enabled protocols to derive lens progenitor cells and three-dimensional lentoid bodies from pluripotent stem cells. Human embryonic stem cells (hESCs) can be differentiated into lens progenitor-like cells and lentoid bodies using defined sequential cues involving FGF and BMP signaling, demonstrating roles for these pathways in lens lineage specification (Lin et al. 2016; Yang et al. 2010; Gwon et al. 1993; Zhou et al. 2016; Mengarelli and Barberi 2013).

Complementary work has generated functional lentoid bodies from human-induced pluripotent stem cells (iPSCs) derived from somatic sources, establishing organoid-like systems that express lens-specific markers and exhibit refractive properties (Fu et al. 2017; Anand et al. 2016). Building on these approaches, human pluripotent stem cells have also been used to create light-focusing human micro-lenses in vitro that recapitulate features of lens development and can model drug-induced cataract changes (Murphy et al. 2018). Together, these efforts represent a paradigm shift from purely prosthetic replacement toward biologically driven lens regeneration, integrating principles of developmental signaling, stem cell biology, and biomaterial design to achieve functional visual restoration.

14.2.4 Retina

14.2.4.1 Clinical Advances in Retinal Biofabrication and Cell Therapy

Retinal degenerative diseases, including age-related macular degeneration (AMD), Stargardt's macular dystrophy, and retinitis pigmentosa, continue to be among the most common causes of irreversible blindness. Degeneration of the retinal pigment epithelium (RPE) is a fundamental pathogenic feature in both AMD and inherited macular dystrophies, and it culminates in secondary loss of the photoreceptor cell layer, leading to progressive and irreversible vision loss. Although treatments such as anti-VEGF injections, laser photocoagulation, or prosthetic implants can slow disease progression, none can fully reverse the loss of cellular architecture after the RPE–photoreceptor complex has been irreversibly compromised. There have been promising studies in which retinal glial cells have been reprogrammed into neuronal cells but such studies are beyond the scope of this chapter. Here, we discuss biofabrication and stem cell–based RPE replacements that have emerged as essential strategies to restore both structure and function of the retina (Duncan et al. 2024).

14.2.4.2 Human Embryonic Stem Cell–Derived RPE: First-in-Human Trials

Schwartz et al. (2015) demonstrated the initial clinical proof of concept for pluripotent cell–based retinal regeneration. In this study, he reported 2 open-label phase 1/2 studies of subretinal transplantation of hESC-derived RPE in 18 patients: 9 with dry AMD and 9 with Stargardt's macular dystrophy. At a median follow-up of 22 months, there was no sign of tumorigenesis, ectopic growth or immune rejection, demonstrating moderate-to long-term safety. Thirteen (72%) eyes had subretinal pigmentation consistent with surviving grafts, and 10 eyes had an improvement in best-corrected visual acuity (BCVA) of ≥15 letters, whereas untreated fellow eyes did not have similar improvements. Near and far activity-related quality-of-life indices improved by 8–25 points. Optical coherence tomography (OCT) imaging revealed an ordered pigmented cell layer sitting on Bruch's membrane, which is consistent with anatomical integration of the transplanted RPE monolayer. These findings provided the first demonstration that hESC-derived cells can survive, integrate, and potentially restore vision in humans with retinal degeneration (Schwartz et al. 2015).

14.2.4.3 Autologous iPSC-Derived RPE Sheet Transplantation

To avoid ethical and immunologic issues associated with allogeneic hESC therapy, Mandai et al. (2017) performed the world's first autologous induced pluripotent stem cell (iPSC)–derived RPE sheet transplantation in a 77-year-old patient with neovascular AMD.

A 1.3 × 3.0 mm iPSC–RPE sheet, derived from the patient's skin fibroblasts, was implanted under the macula following surgical excision of the neovascular membrane. At 1-year follow-up, the graft remained intact, without evidence of rejection or tumorigenesis, and choroidal vasculature demonstrated a normalized pattern with no evidence of recurrent neovascularization. Despite stable visual acuity, the study demonstrated the feasibility and genomic safety of autologous iPSC therapy and opens the door to future personalized retinal regeneration clinical trials (Mandai et al. 2017).

14.2.4.4 Bioengineered RPE Monolayers on Scaffolds

Building on these studies, additional work shifted toward tissue-engineered composite implants more representative of native retinal structure. Kashani et al., leading a phase 1/2a study in the USA, described the California Project to Cure Blindness Retinal Pigment Epithelium-1 (CPCB–RPE1) implant, an hESC–RPE monolayer cultured on a 6 μm parylene substrate which more closely recapitulates the underlying Bruch's membrane (Kashani et al. 2018).

In five eyes of five patients with advanced stage dry AMD, the implant was successfully placed in four. After 12 months of follow-up, OCT assessment demonstrated maintenance of graft location and polarized RPE structure, with reconstitution of external limiting membrane superimposed on the implant. Functionally, one patient gained 17 letters on the standardized Early Treatment Diabetic Retinopathy Study (ETDRS) chart and two others showed increased fixation stability on the implant. No ocular or systemic serious adverse events were noted. Thus, this study shows that a bioengineered, scaffold-based RPE tissue construct can result in anatomic and functional repair in advanced AMD (Kashani et al. 2021).

14.2.4.5 Bioengineered Retinal Sheets from iPS Cells for Macular Regeneration

In a preclinical study in mini-pigs, Barabino et al. used a hypoimmunogenic iPS cell line to generate spontaneously polarized retinal sheets for replacement of damaged maculas. These retinal sheets were enriched in retinal progenitor and cone precursor cells that differentiated into mature S and M/L cones in long-term cultures. In a mini-pig model of chemically induced retinal degeneration, implanted retinal sheets were able to integrate into the host retina and formed a new, yet immature, photoreceptor layer. In one eye, functional and immunohistochemical assays showed that the implanted sheets were responsive to light stimuli and established putative synaptic connections with host bipolar neurons (Barabino et al. 2024).

14.2.5 *Eyelid and the Lacrimal System*

14.2.5.1 Biomaterials Used for Eyelid Reconstruction

Emerging biomaterials in eyelid reconstruction include amniotic membrane grafts, decellularized grafts, human and porcine acellular dermal matrices (Vahdani et al. 2018; Eah and Sa 2021; Custer and Maamari 2021), natural polymers, and synthetic polymers. Natural polymers are typically derived from ECM components, such as collagen type I, chitosan, and keratin. Electrospinning, freeze-drying, and 3D printing have all been utilized as biofabrication techniques to produce scaffolds from natural polymers. Synthetic polymers for tarsal plate reconstruction include materials such as polyethylene (PE), poly(3-hydroxybutyrate-co-3-hydroxyhexanoate) (PHBHHx), poly(lactic-co-glycolic) acid (PLGA), and poly(ε-caprolactone) (PCL), though are limited by poor tissue compatibility and implant-related inflammation (Wu et al. 2024a; Zhou et al. 2010; Gao et al. 2015). Three-layer constructs derived from palmaris longus tendon with superiorly based nasolabial skin flap and palatal mucosal graft (Wang et al. 2021b) have also been studied.

Cellular approaches have been investigated in preclinical models, with biomaterials serving as scaffolds. For instance, ADSC embedded in 3D-printed collagen/alginate scaffolds for tarsal plate reconstruction enhanced meibocyte-like cells in their treated group (Lee et al. 2024). As ADSC can be sourced from orbital fat, which is embryologically related to structures of the eyelid, these are an appealing source of therapeutic cells, as they may more readily differentiate into cells specific to the eyelid (Wu et al. 2024a).

Another technology used in eyelid and conjunctiva reconstruction is AlloDerm. AlloDerm is an acellular human dermal allograft that has been used to treat patients undergoing evisceration and orbital implant insertion (Jung et al. 2013; Park et al. 2018) as well as in posterior lamellar reconstruction of eyelid defects, where complete resurfacing occurred within 6–18 weeks (Pushpoth et al. 2008). OloGen, another dermal substitute, is a collagen-glycosaminoglycan scaffold that has proven effective in the treatment of eyelid reconstruction and scleral necrosis after pterygium excision (Yuan 2018; Cho and Lee 2015). Beyond promoting eyelid and conjunctival regeneration, another benefit of acellular matrices is the absence of antigenic cells, which theoretically reduces the risk of rejection compared to fresh tissue (Makuloluwa et al. 2021).

14.2.5.2 Tissue Engineering for Lacrimal Gland Pathologies

The lacrimal glands (LG) are important exocrine glands within the orbit that secrete the aqueous tear film that protects the surface of the eye. Disruption in this function can have several causes and is characteristic of the autoimmune Sjogren's syndrome (SS) and can lead to dry eye syndrome, causing ocular discomfort and potential surface damage.

Nasolacrimal duct obstruction and stenosis have long utilized silicone for stents and tubes, though success rates for these procedures have widely varied. Polypropylene has been studied as an alternative to silicone, particularly appealing for resource-constrained areas (Baruah et al. 2018), though the success rates were lower than with silicone (https://bmfj.journals.ekb.eg/article_254383.html). While PLLA, PCL, and polyethylene glycol (PEG) are FDA-approved materials, they have been less appealing for nasolacrimal use because of degradation, strength, and remodeling issues (Wu et al. 2024a). Novel PLLA–PCL–PEG complexes in varying ratios were studied in rabbit lacrimal ducts, with the PLLA: PCL6: 4 + 5% PEG composition demonstrating superior biodegradability, reduced irritation, and quicker tissue recovery when compared to the silica gel control group (Zhan et al. 2017).

Natural biomaterials for lacrimal gland tissue engineering have been evaluated, although degradation and loss of function over time of the models remain issues (Anguiano et al. 2020). Matrigel is a gelatinous basement membrane matrix extracted from the Engelbreth–Holm–Swarm (EHS) mouse sarcoma. It contains structural proteins, such as laminin, collagen IV, entactin, and heparin sulfate proteoglycans, as well as growth factors, such as epidermal growth factor (EGF), fibroblast growth factor (FGF), and insulin-like growth factor 1 (IGF-1). It has been used as a 3D matrix for organoid growth and simulates the lacrimal gland microenvironment for growth of acinar cells (Schechter et al. 2002). Other natural biomaterials studied include decellularized LG hydrogels derived from porcine decellularized LG (Wiebe-Ben Zakour et al. 2024), chitosan (Hsiao and Yang 2017), silk fibroin (Dai et al. 2022), human amniotic membrane (Singh et al. 2022), collagen (Rusch et al. 2021), and fibrin (Li et al. 2024).

Systemic and local administrations of stem cells have demonstrated preclinical success in vivo in increasing lacrimal gland tear production. Systemic BMSC (Lu et al. 2020) and UMSC (Yao et al. 2019) in mouse models of SS are hypothesized to upregulate water channel aquaporin five gene expression, reduce lymphocytic infiltration, and upregulate IL-27. Topical (Beyazyıldız et al. 2014), intralacrimal (Bittencourt et al. 2016), and subconjunctival (Shin et al. 2023) administration have also successfully increased goblet cell count, tear production, and decreased inflammation. Human-induced pluripotent stem cells (iPSC) have been used to differentiate into lacrimal gland organoids (Hayashi et al. 2022; Utine et al. 2020), and Matrigel, mentioned above, has been shown to support acinar differentiation for organoid development (Asal et al. 2023).

Møller-Hansen et al. (2021) demonstrated safety, feasibility, and clinical potential of intralacrimal injection of ADSC (22 million ADSC/mL) at 50% glandular capacity for the treatment of aqueous-deficient dry eye (ADDE) (Møller-Hansen et al. 2021). In 2024, they completed a double-blind randomized prospective trial in 54 patients with dry eye disease secondary to SS. Findings from this study reported significant reductions in both objective and subjective signs and symptoms of dry eye (Møller-Hansen et al. 2024).

14.2.6 *Optic Nerve*

The therapeutic aim of optic nerve biofabrication is to restore axonal continuity between the retina and the brain's visual centers through stem cell–based replacement, biomaterial scaffolds and biohybrid neurointerfaces. Recent translational studies are beginning to move from preclinical discoveries to early clinical evaluation with an increased focus on safety, integration, and preservation of residual vision (Liu et al. 2025).

14.2.6.1 Stem Cell–Based and Biofabrication-Oriented Strategies for Optic Nerve Regeneration

Optic neuropathies, a diverse class of diseases, ischemic, inflammatory, traumatic, hereditary, toxic, or glaucomatous, share a common mechanism of disease: death of retinal ganglion cells (RGCs) and degeneration of their axons, the optic nerve, and a very limited intrinsic regenerative capacity in the adult mammalian CNS (Tan et al. 2022). In this regard, the optic nerve represents an especially daunting, and simultaneously, fascinating target for the regeneration medicine and biofabrication efforts. Strategies along three complementary lines of investigation have been recently pursued: RGC repopulation, adult stem cell–based neuroprotection, and cell-based therapy for traumatic optic neuropathy (TON), the latter effort gaining an increasing degree of international coordination.

14.2.6.2 RGC Repopulation and the RReSTORe Roadmap

To tackle the challenges to optic nerve rebuilding in an organized fashion, the Retinal Ganglion Cell Repopulation, Stem Cell Transplantation, and Optic Nerve Regeneration (RReSTORe) consortium was launched in 2021. RReSTORe is an international group of more than 220 members in basic, translational, and clinical science that aims to set "audacious goals" for optic nerve regeneration, including (Ying 2025) identifying and prioritizing key challenges in RGC regeneration, (Groll et al. 2016) generating novel tools and experimental paradigms, and (Ljubimov and Saghizadeh 2015) initiating collaborative research projects (Johnson et al. 2023).

RReSTORe points out that strategies like pluripotent stem cell–derived RGC transplantation and endogenous RGC regeneration (glial trans-differentiation) have significant conceptual overlap and have now become priority research areas for the major funding agencies. The consortium is organized into subtopic discussion groups on RGC specification, axon guidance, synaptic integration, and clinical translation and provides a conceptual roadmap for future biofabrication strategies that will most likely be a hybrid of cell replacement, guidance scaffolds, and circuit-level reconstruction (Johnson et al. 2023).

14.2.6.3 Adult Stem Cell Therapies for Optic Neuropathies

One area of research involves adult stem cells, specifically mesenchymal stem cells (MSCs) and hematopoietic stem cells (HSCs), as neuroprotective and immunomodulatory therapies for a range of optic neuropathies. Tan et al. discuss the current state of adult stem cell therapeutics for inflammatory, ischemic, hereditary, and toxic and nutritional optic neuropathies, although in almost all cases, stem cells act via paracrine mechanisms and do not actually replace lost RGCs (Liu et al. 2025). Adult stem cells of multiple etiologies have led to improvement in visual acuity and fields on the clinical level during early phase clinical trials and case series. Autologous peripheral HSCs and umbilical cord–derived MSCs have both been linked to functional improvement in neuromyelitis optica spectrum disorder–associated optic neuritis, and bone marrow–derived MSCs have been shown to promote functional improvement in idiopathic, recurrent, and autoimmune optic neuritis. In the same manner, autologous bone marrow–derived stem cells have been utilized in cases of hereditary optic neuropathies, such as Leber hereditary optic neuropathy (LHON), in which case series have been shown to improve visual acuity and peripheral vision. Mechanistically, this could be mediated by neurotrophic factor secretion (BDNF, CNTF, NGF), modulation of the inflammatory response, and/or endogenous repair by optic nerve microenvironment remodeling (Liu et al. 2025)

While adult stem cells do not recapitulate the full architecture of the optic nerve, they may be a readily available first step toward clinically relevant bioengineered neuroprotection in combination with controlled-release biomaterials in future iterations (Liu et al. 2025)

14.2.6.4 SCOTS: Autologous BMSC Therapy in Optic Neuropathy

The Stem Cell Ophthalmology Treatment Study (SCOTS) is the largest registered ophthalmic stem cell trial, and the first being prospectively conducted to treat retinal and optic nerve diseases using autologous bone marrow–derived stem cells (BMSCs). Bone marrow is aspirated from the iliac crest of SCOTS patients and concentrated to produce a BMSC-rich fraction. BMSCs are infused by multiple routes (retrobulbar, subtenon, intravitreal, intra-optic nerve, subretinal, and intravenous) dependent on the severity of disease and arm allocation (Weiss et al. 2015).

One case report from the SCOTS cohort described a 54-year-old woman with relapsing autoimmune optic neuropathy who presented with severe bilateral visual loss with marked visual field constriction (20/350–20/400 OD, 20/70 OS). The patient lived with 20/400 vision in her right eye for more than 2.5 years prior to the intervention. Pars plana vitrectomy with injection of intra-optic nerve BMSCs in the more affected eye and periocular/intravitreal BMSCs in the fellow eye was performed and visual acuity at 15 months post-op was 20/150 OD and 20/20 OS with robust bilateral visual field recovery and increased macular and retinal nerve fiber layer thickness on OCT. The patient, although living with relapsing optic neuritis, was able to taper systemic immunosuppression and did not require further steroid pulses during follow-up.

While the SCOTS trial is open-label and non-randomized, thus precluding definitive conclusions about efficacy, it serves as a model of a pragmatic, patient-funded stem cell platform for the treatment of optic nerve and retinal disorders, and demonstrates that this intensive, multimodal delivery of BMSCs can be safely performed with encouraging functional signals in selected optic neuropathies (Weiss et al. 2015).

14.2.6.5 Cell-Based Therapies for Traumatic Optic Neuropathy

Traumatic optic neuropathy (TON) represents another well-characterized and therefore highly instructive model of optic nerve injury, in which primary mechanical damage is followed by secondary cascades of oxidative stress, neuroinflammation, glial scarring, and delayed, progressive RGC loss (Wang et al. 2026). Wang et al. focus on TON as a therapeutic target and discuss cell-based therapies for both RGC replacement and rescue.

In preclinical models, ESC- and iPSC-derived RGC-like cells can integrate into the host retina and survive for weeks to months, with a limited potential to improve visual function via long-range axonal reconnection. In addition, adult stem cells, particularly MSCs derived from bone marrow, umbilical cord, placenta, and adipose tissue, can promote RGC survival, stimulate axonal regeneration, and mediate partial functional recovery in a trophic support– and immune modulation–dependent manner. NSPCs may also serve as "neuronal relays" that bridge damaged segments of the optic pathway (Wang et al. 2026).

In the review by Wang et al. (2026), it was noted that two phase I clinical trials for TON in humans were completed in which the cell-based therapies were safe and well-tolerated, showing visual acuity improvements, although further long-term and larger-scale studies are still required to establish whether a durable benefit can be achieved. They also discussed the potential of cell-derived products such as extracellular vesicles and cell extracts and predicts scaffold-based transplantation as a likely future direction to improve cell survival, axonal guidance, and functional integration (Wang et al. 2026).

14.3 Biofabricated Parts of the Eye

14.3.1 Biofabrication Strategies for the Cornea

Given the avascular nature of the cornea, various biofabrication techniques, including 3D printing, are appealing and have been explored in recent years for the development of functional artificial corneal constructs (Balters and Reichl 2023). Extrusion-based and light-based bioprinting are the most commonly employed approaches, though combining biofabrication approaches may yield optimal results (Thomas et al. 2022).

Extrusion-based printing, the most common technique for patterning injectable hydrogel systems, involves the extrusion of pre-polymerized bioinks onto a printing platform, in a coordinated layer-by-layer pattern using a pressurized air system. Recent advancements have also allowed for printing of acellular constructs of ECM for corneal stromal regeneration (Park et al. 2021; Ulag et al. 2020; Kim et al. 2019; Characterization of cornea-specific bioink 2025) and transplantable corneal endothelial transplants (Kim et al. 2018).

Light-based printing polymerizes materials with precise projections of light, allowing for high resolution, accuracy, and speed (Zhang et al. 2024). Primary subtypes of light-based printing include DLP-based printing, which has been employed for limbal stem/progenitor cell (LSC) hydrogel grafts (Zhong et al. 2021); SLA-based printing, which has been used to produce corneal stromal constructs encapsulating viable fibroblasts and exhibiting good mechanical and light properties (Mahdavi et al. 2020); and laser-assisted printing (LAP). In LAP, a laser beam focuses energy to produce bioink onto a biocompatible surface, and this technique has been able to successfully print viable stem cells for corneal epithelial and stromal constructs (He et al. 2022).

Biofabrication techniques continue to be explored, with studies producing corneal constructs through other approaches such as electrospinning to produce controlled shapes (Zhang et al. 2024), multi-material bioprinting (Puistola et al. 2025), and aerosol jet printing (Gibney et al. 2021).

14.3.2 Biofabrication Strategies for the Lens

14.3.2.1 Current Biofabrication Strategies and the Associated Challenges

Current biofabrication research for the crystalline lens is converging on two complementary directions: in situ regeneration inside the native capsular bag and bioengineered replacement optics that better emulate native lens biology and mechanics.

For regeneration, a landmark strategy is "regenerative cataract surgery" or minimally invasive lens-content removal that preserves the lens capsule and residual lens epithelial stem/progenitor cells (LECs). In theory, this strategy enables these cells to repopulate the capsule and rebuild a transparent, functional lens in animal models and (in early work) pediatric patients (Lin et al. 2016). More recent regenerative work is also exploring cell delivery into the capsule, for example, implanting hESC-derived lens-fated cells in a hyaluronate-based gel to drive lens-like tissue formation in vivo with reported restoration of lens-like geometry and transparency in rabbit models (Chen et al. 2023). In parallel, biofabrication is advancing through stem cell–derived "micro-lens" and lentoid platforms that generate transparent, light-focusing lens-like tissues in vitro. This is useful both as scalable human models for lens development and as a test bed for future engineered-lens design rules (Murphy et al. 2018). On the implant side, biomaterials research is moving beyond conventional rigid IOL paradigms toward hydrogel-based and interface-engineered implants that aim to match the native lens' optical index and softness (for dynamic focusing) while controlling cell and material interactions within the capsular bag (Cui et al. 2024).

The central challenges in biofabricating a lens are that optical, mechanical, and biological integration problems that are tightly coupled. Transparency is not just "clear material"; it is an emergent property of extremely high crystallin packing and short-range order that minimizes refractive-index fluctuations and scatter, highly aligned fiber-cell architecture, and a developmental program that eliminates organelles to create an organelle-free zone, because nuclei and mitochondria, among other structures, are potent scatterers (Murphy et al. 2018; Brennan et al. 2023; Bassnett et al. 2011). Maintaining that transparent state over time is further complicated by the lens' avascularity and reliance on specialized internal transport and microcirculation for ion, water, and nutrient homeostasis rather than vascular perfusion. This means that engineered constructs must still solve long-range homeostasis without introducing haze-inducing gradients or swelling (Giannone et al. 2021). Accommodation adds a second layer of difficulty: the natural lens focuses dynamically because its biomechanical properties (stiffness and elasticity) and optical gradients govern how it deforms under zonular and ciliary forces (Cheng 2024; Kling et al. 2024). Replicating both the magnitude and spatial distribution of stiffness and refractive index in a stable, implantable or regenerating construct remains a major barrier, even when hydrogels can be tuned toward native-like refractive index and modulus (Cui et al. 2024; Kling et al. 2024).

Finally, cellular integration is uniquely challenging because the "integration site" is the capsular bag: residual LECs can undergo wound-healing responses (hyperproliferation/EMT/migration) that drive posterior capsule opacification (PCO), the most common long-term complication after lens replacement. Hence, biofabricated lenses must either orchestrate orderly epithelial-to-fiber differentiation without fibrosis (regeneration route) or actively control cell adhesion, migration, and capsule interactions through antifouling/adhesive or drug-responsive interfaces (implant route) (Lin et al. 2016; Cooksley et al. 2021).

14.3.2.2 Biofabrication Techniques for Intraocular Lens

Recent advances in biofabrication of intraocular lenses (IOLs) increasingly exploit additive manufacturing (3D printing) to enable rapid prototyping, geometric customization, and material innovation beyond conventional molded optics (Brighesh et al. 2025; https://www-tandfonline-com.proxy3.library.mcgill.ca/doi/full/10.1080/02713683.2024.2344164). Proof-of-concept studies have demonstrated that stereolithography (SLA/DLP) printing can generate optically transparent, foldable IOL-like constructs using photopolymerizable synthetic resins with clinically relevant geometries (approximately 6 mm optic, looped haptics). In a recent study, clear one-piece IOL prototypes were printed from a resin composed primarily of 2phenoxyethyl acrylate and poly(-ethylene glycol) dimethacrylate (PEGDMA), showing high optical transmittance, foldability, shape recovery, and cytocompatibility with human lens epithelial cells in vitro, as well as feasibility within an ex vivo human capsular bag model. Such approaches highlight how 3D printing can decouple IOL fabrication from traditional lathe cutting or injection molding, opening the possibility of patient-specific optics (e.g., customized curvature, thickness, or haptic design) and accelerated material screening at the research stage (Brighesh et al. 2025; https://www-tandfonline-com.proxy3.library.mcgill.ca/doi/full/10.1080/02713683.2024.2344164).

In parallel, hydrogel-based and biosynthetically modified IOL materials are being explored to better emulate the native lens microenvironment and improve biological integration (Luo et al. 2022; Vacalebre et al. 2023). Hydrogels such as poly (2hydroxyethyl methacrylate) (PHEMA), PEG-based networks, and injectable or photo-cross-linkable polymer systems have long been investigated for artificial lens applications due to their optical clarity and mechanical compliance compatible with minimally invasive implantation (Percival and Jafree 1994). Building on this, bioactive strategies incorporate extracellular matrix (ECM) components or motifs, particularly collagen type IV, the principal structural collagen of the native lens capsule basement membrane (Danysh and Duncan 2009; West-Mays and Korol 2014). Collagen IV forms a supramolecular basement membrane network with laminin and nidogen and is closely associated with proteoglycans such as perlecan, features that regulate lens epithelial cell adhesion and differentiation, as well as capsule integrity. This makes collagen IV–informed coatings or composites attractive for the next-generation IOL interfaces (Cheng 2024; Danysh and Duncan 2009). Experimental models have used collagen IV substrates and membranes to study lens epithelial cell behavior and posterior capsule opacification (PCO), underscoring its relevance for directing cell–material interactions at the IOL–capsule interface (Mencucci et al. 2015). Beyond collagen-based systems, a wide range of synthetic and hybrid materials, including hydrophobic and hydrophilic acrylics, silicones, PEG-derived hydrogels, and surface-functionalized polymers, are under investigation to create a product uniting optical performance, mechanical stability, foldability, and long-term biocompatibility (Luo et al. 2022; Werner 2021; Vacalebre et al. 2023). Collectively, these strategies illustrate how modern IOL biofabrication is evolving toward multi-material, bioactive, and potentially printable lens substitutes that better recapitulate both the physical and biological functions of the native crystalline lens (Brighesh et al. 2025; Vacalebre et al. 2023).

14.3.3 Biofabrication Strategies for the Retina

14.3.3.1 Biofabrication and Biomaterials for Retinal Regeneration

Successful restoration of the RPE and other photoreceptor supporting layers will demand constructs that integrate into the subretinal space and can provide structural, metabolic, and trophic support to photoreceptors and other retinal neurons. Three main categories of retinal biofabrication efforts have evolved to date: (Ying 2025) engineered RPE monolayer implants, (Groll et al. 2016) natural polymer hydrogels for engineering Bruch's membrane (BM)-mimetic scaffolds, and (Ljubimov and Saghizadeh 2015) high-resolution electronic interfaces and 3D-bioprinted retinal tissues.

14.3.3.2 Bioengineered RPE Monolayers on Synthetic Scaffolds

One breakthrough in the field was the first successful preclinical and clinical tests of engineered RPE monolayers cultured on ultrathin (less than 10 μm) biostable scaffolds intended to substitute for atrophic RPE in geographic atrophy (GA) or advanced dry age-related macular degeneration (AMD). The most compelling line of evidence has come from CPCB-RPE1, a composite of human embryonic stem cell–derived RPE (hESC–RPE) cells grown on a 6-μm-thick parylene membrane engineered to recapitulate BM structure and mechanical properties (Kashani et al. 2018).

In their first in human Phase 1/IIa proof-of-concept study published in Science Translational Medicine, Kashani et al. (2018) implanted CPCB-RPE1 in patients with late-stage dry AMD. The parylene scaffold supported RPE polarization, diffusion of nutrients, and stable positioning in the subretinal space. Structural integration and stabilization of vision were seen in 4/5 implanted patients, with one patient gaining 17 ETDRS letters. In a subsequent Phase 1/2a multicenter clinical trial with 16 patients, safety, surgical feasibility, and functional gain were further demonstrated: 27% of treated eyes improved >5 ETDRS letters, vs. 7% of fellow eyes, and no unexpected serious adverse events occurred at 1 year (Kashani et al. 2021).

Collectively, these clinical studies present the strongest evidence to date that RPE monolayers on engineered scaffolds outperform RPE cell suspensions by surviving longer, localizing better, and having the potential to provide functional benefit.

14.3.3.3 Natural Polymer–Based Hydrogels for RPE Regeneration

Parallel approaches have investigated natural biomaterials as an alternate source of biodegradable and cell-friendly substrates for transplantation of RPE. A particularly promising example is the silk fibroin/PEG (SF/PEG) hydrogel platform which leverages the natural biocompatibility of silk with the tunable mechanics of PEG. Jeong et al. (2020) showed that in vitro the 20-second sonicated SF/PEG hydrogel demonstrated improved porosity, cell adhesion and proliferation, and upregulation of RPE-specific genes (RPE65, CRALBP) compared with silk alone. Resulting bioinks support robust RPE survival and matrix production and hold promise for RPE replacement via injectable or sheet-based strategies in retinal degeneration. Hydrogels such as SF/PEG may eventually serve as biodegradable BM substitutes with long-term integration potential and nutrient exchange without permanent synthetic scaffolds (Jeong et al. 2020).

14.3.3.4 3D Bioprinting for Retinal Tissue Engineering

Three-dimensional (3D) bioprinting of retinal cells and biomaterials enables recreation of the laminated cellular architecture of the retina. As summarized in the review by Wu et al., extrusion, droplet-based, and laser bioprinting have all been used to assemble retinal constructs using multiple cell types, biomimetic mechanics, and micro-architectures that resemble the outer retina. Current limitations are related to cell viability, polarity, vascularization, and maturation. However, 3D-printed retinal models have already shown great promise as drug testing and disease modeling platforms and may be useful for transplantation in the future (Wu et al. 2024b).

Bioinks containing extracellular matrix (ECM) components like hyaluronic acid and collagen have been particularly successful in promoting photoreceptor precursor survival and differentiation. As printing resolution improves, microfluidic co-culture systems advance, and printing technology becomes more accessible, completely bioprinted retinal tissue may become clinically feasible (Wu et al. 2024b).

14.3.3.5 Graphene-Based Microelectrode Arrays for Retinal Biointerfaces

Beyond cellular constructs, graphene-based microelectrode arrays (MEAs) represent another frontier for engineering electronics to interface with regenerated or residual retinal tissue. Reduced graphene oxide (rGO) electrodes have a high charge injection limit and low impedance and can be used for both recording and stimulating retinal neurons. Duvan et al. demonstrated in a promising animal model that rGO microelectrodes (25–100 μm) enable bidirectional interfacing that can stimulate retinal ganglion cells (RGCs) and record spontaneous and light-evoked activity at high fidelity. The high transparency and subcellular resolution make it possible to excite RGCs with fewer and more precisely defined electrical pulses, minimizing collateral activation of unintended axons, a significant limitation of prior prostheses. Graphene may thus enable high-acuity artificial vision when combined with biological reconstruction of the outer retina. While this approach is primarily targeted at advanced photoreceptor loss, such interfaces may eventually be hybridized with stem cell- or scaffold-based implants to comprehensively restore the retina (Duvan et al. 2024).

14.3.4 Optic Nerve

14.3.4.1 Biofabrication and Biomaterials for Optic Nerve Regeneration

The existing landscape of human clinical studies for optic nerve regeneration is extremely limited. To our knowledge, the optic nerve is the only major component of the visual system for which no biomaterial implant has been trialed in humans. This is not surprising given that the optic nerve is part of the central nervous system, a location that is characterized by an innate lack of regeneration. Scaffold-supported cellular therapies for the cornea and retina have both made it to early-phase clinical trials, but a lack of basic regenerative capacity and suitable materials for long-distance guidance has limited optic nerve regeneration in humans to date. However, as described above, recent preclinical studies have developed a wide variety of promising biofabrication strategies to support optic nerve regeneration, establishing the basis for future clinical translation. The data highlight how various engineered material approaches can be designed to modify the inhibitory CNS environment, support RGC survival, and promote directed axonal regrowth.

14.3.4.2 Conductive Injectable Hydrogels

A particularly compelling, recent study is an injectable conductive hydrogel that has been shown to restore optic nerve function after injury. The material is injected at the site of lesion, where it polymerizes in situ to form a soft, electrically conductive hydrogel that promotes axonal elongation and restores electrophysiological continuity across the injury. Optic nerve crush models showed that this conductive biomaterial can significantly improve visual evoked potentials, restore electroretinographic response, promote RGC survival, and attenuate secondary degeneration. This work represents a proof-of-concept that a biomaterial alone can be designed to provide structural and electrical support that has a meaningful impact on structural and functional outcomes after optic nerve injury (Yu et al. 2025).

14.3.4.3 Cell-Laden Hydrogels for Microenvironment Modulation

Injectable hydrogels are also being developed as platforms that are capable of supporting therapeutic cells at the site of injury. One such GelMA-based hydrogel is an encapsulation system for dental pulp stem cells (DPSCs) with strong potential for optic nerve regeneration. DPSCs, which can be readily obtained from the oral cavity, are known to support endogenous RGC survival and outgrowth, with observed benefits for retinal preservation and secondary degeneration. This system was designed to use a GelMA hydrogel to inject the DPSCs at the site of injury, where the cell-laden matrix then serves as a supportive and degradable environment in which the transplanted cells can survive over time and release their trophic signals. The resulting bioink showed improved ability to remodel the environment of the injured optic nerve in experimental models. It was able to increase RGC survival, reduce apoptosis, support organized axonal regrowth, and attenuate glial scarring, showing the potential for a biomaterial to serve as a dynamic, bioactive microenvironment for transplanted cells, which promotes regeneration beyond the abilities of cell therapy alone (Luo et al. 2025).

14.3.4.4 Nerve Guidance Conduits

One recent area of work is the translation of nerve guidance conduits for application to optic nerve regeneration. Nerve guidance conduits have a long history of peripheral nerve regeneration and have been adapted to mimic many of the architectural and biochemical characteristics of native nerve tissue. In their traditional form, they are solid tubular devices that provide aligned internal architecture and/or biochemical cues to guide axonal growth within their lumen. In the context of CNS injury, this design can be beneficial in counteracting the disorganized and inhibitory milieu that characterizes injury, promoting organized and directed regrowth. In analyzing a wide variety of biomaterials including collagen, PLGA, silk fibroin, and chitosan, a recent work concluded that nerve guidance conduits combining micro- and nanoscale topographical features, as well as incorporation of neurotrophic factors, represent a promising candidate approach to provide anatomically relevant guidance of axons from the retina toward central visual targets. Although this work and others like it have not yet been tested in the optic nerve, they set out a general architectural strategy for future, anatomically aligned optic nerve scaffolds (Obeng et al. 2025).

A more organized version of the above concept is represented by a hybrid nerve guidance conduit that is composed of a bundle of aligned PLGA microfibers that are then enveloped in a micro−/nanopatterned membrane. This more complex design attempts to recapitulate aspects of native nerve fascicle organization. Importantly, it was shown to provide strong directional cues that can support and orient migration of neurons as well as glial cells. In vitro studies report that nearly all cells migrate along the patterned surface of the material, and the conduit is rapidly colonized with cells after implantation within days, showing that it supports and orients regenerating axons. Scaffolds of this type are highly relevant to the problem of segmental optic nerve injury, in which directional regrowth over long distances is required (Peng et al. 2017).

14.3.4.5 Multi-therapeutic Biofabrication Strategies for Long-Distance Regeneration

One of the greatest challenges for long-term restoration of vision is the regeneration of optic nerve axons over long distances, as many of the strategies described above struggle to provide control over axon regrowth or guidance for more than a few millimeters. Recent work points out that biomaterials alone will not be sufficient and instead must be used in conjunction with a range of complementary modalities, including molecular pathway modulation, growth-factor delivery, genetic reprogramming, and electrical stimulation. A number of multi-therapeutic frameworks have been proposed that suggest that scaffolds for optic nerve regeneration should be designed to actively guide regenerating axons beyond the optic nerve head through the optic chiasm and toward central targets. This sets up a complex but realistic regenerative strategy in which biomaterials are centrally important to a concerted regeneration approach that has the potential to overcome inhibitory mechanisms both locally and over long distances within the CNS (Liu et al. 2025).

Developed in a peripheral nerve injury model, a family of adaptable hydrogels enriched with magnesium ions and silk fibroin is an interesting example of how some key principles of biomaterial design that have been developed in other nerve injury models may be highly relevant to future optic nerve regeneration studies. Briefly, these hydrogels exhibit highly dynamic reorganization in response to cellular forces, promote infiltration of endogenous cells, and repolarize macrophages toward a pro-regenerative phenotype. The dual immunomodulatory and mechanoresponsive capabilities of this system address two key limitations to optic nerve regeneration: glial scarring and lack of structural support for axons. As such, the key mechanisms of action of this system, both direct modulation of inflammation and cellular repolarization, as well as structural adaptability and support for neurite outgrowth, are of high relevance (Gao et al. 2024).

14.4 Regulatory Landscape for Biofabricated Eye Structures

In general, technologies for replacing functional tissues or parts of the eye can be divided into medical devices and medicinal products. The former general comprises cell-free technologies that facilitate regeneration of eye structures by allowing endogenous progenitor or stem cells to affect the regeneration through non-pharmaceutical means (Canada 2025). Medicinal products, on the other hand, include cell-therapies or cellular derivatives, small molecules given to promote an effect through pharmacological, immunological or metabolic means (Medicinal products in the European Union 2025). However, there are products as shown above that straddle both definitions and these are regulated as combination products. Combinations of medical devices delivering genes, drugs, or cells, however, are regulated as combination products.

The regulation of medical devices and medicinal products are now harmonized as much as possible globally. The harmonization of medical devices has occurred through forums like the International Medical Device Regulators Forum (IMDRF). The IMDRF aims to promote convergence, support innovation, and reduce regulatory barriers, allowing for regulations that standardize procedures across countries to ensure the safety and effectiveness of devices while making it easier for manufacturers to sell them globally. The international harmonization of regulatory requirements for medicinal products was pioneered by the European community in the 1980s, Europe moved toward the development of a single market for pharmaceuticals.

Researchers will need to note the various standards that their products will be judged by harmonized regulatory requirements. These standards include ASTM (USA), BSI (UK), and ISO (international, various countries). While the standards are voluntary, the requirement for compliance is not. Examples of standards for medical devices include ISO 10993 (Huateng 2025) and ISO 13485 (ISO [Internet] 2025). These standards are often coupled with requirements for other standards such as ISO 14971 for risk management in medical devices, which focuses on ensuring patient safety by balancing risks against benefits and is crucial for regulatory compliance.

14.5 Conclusions

The purpose of this chapter was to provide an integrated overview of how biofabrication principles are being applied across the major anatomical components of the eye, from transparent anterior tissues to highly specialized neural structures and to clinically assess their translational progress.

Beginning with foundational descriptions of anatomy and physiology, the chapter established the unique biological and functional constraints that make the eye both an attractive and demanding target for regenerative medicine. The cornea emerged as the most clinically advanced example, with multiple bioengineered and cell-based constructs already in clinical trials. In contrast, lens biofabrication illustrates a field in transition, spanning mature intraocular lens technologies, emerging additive manufacturing approaches, and ambitious regenerative strategies aimed at endogenous lens regeneration or stem cell-derived lentoid constructs. Retinal biofabrication was presented as a paradigm of scaffold-guided cell replacement, with strong clinical proof-of-concept for stem cell–derived retinal pigment epithelium monolayers and growing interest in bioprinted tissues and bioelectronic interfaces. The optic nerve, while remaining the most challenging target, exemplifies how biofabrication may enable future breakthroughs through combinatorial strategies integrating biomaterials, cells, and surgical approach.

Across all tissues, common themes emerged: the importance of recapitulating native microenvironments, the need for precise control of cell–material interactions, and the growing convergence of biofabrication with regulatory science. Together, these advances underscore a shift from purely substitutive therapies toward biologically integrated, regenerative solutions. As highlighted throughout this chapter, continued interdisciplinary collaboration and rigorous translational pathways will be essential to realize the full clinical potential of ocular biofabrication.

Competing Interests The author(s) has no competing interests to declare that are relevant to the content of this manuscript. MG acknowledges support from her Tier 1 Canada Research Chair and the Caroline Durand Foundation Research Chair.

References

Agrawal P, Tiwari A, Chowdhury SK, Vohra M, Gour A, Waghmare N et al (2024) Kuragel: a biomimetic hydrogel scaffold designed to promote corneal regeneration. iScience [Internet] 27(5):109641. [cited 2025 Aug 28]. Available from: https://www.ncbi.nlm.nih.gov/pmc/articles/PMC11031829/

Ahearne M, Fernández-Pérez J, Masterton S, Madden PW, Bhattacharjee P (2020) Designing scaffolds for corneal regeneration. Adv. Funct. Mater. [Internet] 30(44):1908996. [cited 2025 Dec 12]. Available from: https://onlinelibrary.wiley.com/doi/abs/10.1002/adfm.201908996

Allarakhia L, Knoll RL, Lindstrom RL (1987 Nov) Soft intraocular lenses. J Cataract Refract Surg 13(6):607–620

Anand T, Talluri TR, Kumar D, Garrels W, Mukherjee A, Debowski K et al (2016) Differentiation of Induced Pluripotent Stem Cells to Lentoid Bodies Expressing a Lens Cell-Specific Fluorescent Reporter. Plos One [Internet] 11(6):e0157570. [cited 2025 Dec 14]. Available from: https://journals.plos.org/plosone/article?id=10.1371/journal.pone.0157570

Ang LPK, Tan DTH, Cajucom-Uy H, Beuerman RW (2005) Autologous cultivated conjunctival transplantation for pterygium surgery. Am. J. Ophthalmol. [Internet] 139(4):611–619. [cited 2025 Dec 12]. Available from: https://www.sciencedirect.com/science/article/pii/S0002939404013340

Anguiano M, Morales X, Castilla C, Pena AR, Ederra C, Martínez M et al (2020) The use of mixed collagen-Matrigel matrices of increasing complexity recapitulates the biphasic role of cell adhesion in cancer cell migration: ECM sensing, remodeling and forces at the leading edge of cancer invasion. PLoS One 15(1):e0220019

Apple DJ, Sims J (1996) Harold Ridley and the invention of the intraocular lens. Surv Ophthalmol 40(4):279–292

Asal M, Koçak G, Sarı V, Reçber T, Nemutlu E, Utine CA et al (2023) Development of lacrimal gland organoids from iPSC derived multizonal ocular cells. Front Cell Dev Biol [Internet] 10: 1058846. [cited 2025 Nov 12]. Available from: https://pmc.ncbi.nlm.nih.gov/articles/PMC9846036/

Avadhanam VS, Smith HE, Liu C (2015) Keratoprostheses for corneal blindness: a review of contemporary devices. Clin Ophthalmol [Internet] 9:697–720. [cited 2025 Oct 27]. Available from: https://pmc.ncbi.nlm.nih.gov/articles/PMC4406263/

Bahar I, Reitblat O, Livny E, Litvin G (2023) The first-in-human implantation of the CorNeat keratoprosthesis. Eye (Lond) 37(7):1331–1335

Balters L, Reichl S (2023) 3D bioprinting of corneal models: A review of the current state and future outlook. J Tissue Eng 14:20417314231197793

Bamashmus MA, Al-Shekeil MA, Mukred FA, Al-Akhlee HA (2020) Traumatic wound dehiscence after penetrating keratoplasty: Clinical features and outcome in 53 cases in Yemen. Taiwan J Ophthalmol 10(1):32–36

Barabino A, Mellal K, Hamam R, Polosa A, Griffith M, Bouchard JF et al (2024) Molecular characterization and sub-retinal transplantation of hypoimmunogenic human retinal sheets in a minipig model of severe photoreceptor degeneration. Development [Internet] 151(23): dev203071. [cited 2025 Dec 14]. Available from: https://doi.org/10.1242/dev.203071

Baruah B, Sarawgi M, Sahu P, Dubey KP, Gupta A, Kumar A (2018) Polypropylene in endoscopic dacryocystorhinostomy: a novel stent. Indian J Otolaryngol Head Neck Surg 70(2):240–243

Bassnett S, Shi Y, Vrensen GFJM (2011) Biological glass: structural determinants of eye lens transparency. Philos Trans R Soc Lond Ser B Biol Sci 366(1568):1250–1264

Bertolin M, Pedrotti E, Bonacci E, Bosello F, Barbaro V, Breda C et al (2022) 22 Renewal of conjunctival epithelium over amniotic membrane to perform autologous simple conjunctival epithelial transplantation (SCET): in vitro validation and results of clinical application for primary pterygium. BMJ Open Ophthalmol [Internet] 7(Suppl 2):A9–10. [cited 2025 Dec 12]. Available from: https://pmc.ncbi.nlm.nih.gov/articles/PMC11366821/

Beyazyıldız E, Pınarlı FA, Beyazyıldız O, Hekimoğlu ER, Acar U, Demir MN et al (2014) Efficacy of topical mesenchymal stem cell therapy in the treatment of experimental dry eye syndrome model. Stem Cells Int 2014:250230

Bhattacharjee P, Ahearne M (2022) Silk fibroin based interpenetrating network hydrogel for corneal stromal regeneration. Int. J. Biol. Macromol. [Internet] 223:583–594. [cited 2025 Nov 11]. Available from: https://www.sciencedirect.com/science/article/pii/S0141813022025697

Bittencourt MKW, Barros MA, Martins JFP, Vasconcellos JPC, Morais BP, Pompeia C et al (2016) Allogeneic Mesenchymal Stem Cell Transplantation in Dogs With Keratoconjunctivitis Sicca. Cell Med 8(3):63–77

Boulze Pankert M, Goyer B, Zaguia F, Bareille M, Perron MC, Liu X et al (2014) Biocompatibility and functionality of a tissue-engineered living corneal stroma transplanted in the feline eye. Invest Ophthalmol Vis Sci 55(10):6908–6920

Bourne RR (2012) The optic nerve head in glaucoma. Commun Eye Health [Internet] 25(79–80): 55–57. [cited 2025 Dec 12]. Available from: https://pmc.ncbi.nlm.nih.gov/articles/PMC3588134/

Brennan L, Costello MJ, Hejtmancik JF, Menko AS, Riazuddin SA, Shiels A et al (2023) Autophagy requirements for eye lens differentiation and transparency. Cells 12(3):475

Brighesh B, Alsuliman N, Nimer A, Albosaad O, Alokosh B, Alnaili T et al (2025) Optical properties of artificial intraocular lenses and considerations for additive manufacturing. Front Med (Lausanne) [Internet] 12:1563766. [cited 2025 Dec 14]. Available from: https://pmc.ncbi.nlm.nih.gov/articles/PMC12034678/

Buznyk O, Goodarzi H, Gómez Laguna J, Reddy J, Liszka A, Edin E et al (2025) Collagen analogs promote tissue regeneration in HSV-1-infected corneas in animal models. J Func Biomater [Internet] 16(10):377. [cited 2025 Nov 3]. Available from: https://www.mdpi.com/2079-4983/16/10/377

Call M, Elzarka M, Kunesh M, Hura N, Birk DE, Kao WW (2019) Therapeutic efficacy of mesenchymal stem cells for the treatment of congenital and acquired corneal opacity. Mol Vis 25:415–426

Canada.ca-Health Canada (2020) About medical devices [Internet] [cited 2025 Dec 14]. Available from: https://www.canada.ca/en/health-canada/services/drugs-health-products/medical-devices/about-medical-devices.html

Čanović S, Konjevoda S, Pavičić AD, Stanić R, Čanović S, Konjevoda S et al (2019) Intraocular Lens (IOL) materials. In: Intraocular lens [Internet]. IntechOpen. [cited 2025 Dec 14]. Available from: https://www.intechopen.com/chapters/70120

Characterization of cornea-specific bioink: high transparency, improved in vivo safety [Internet]. [cited 2025 Nov 12]. Available from: https://journals.sagepub.com/doi/epdf/10.1177/2041731418823382?src=getftr&utm_source=sciencedirect_contenthosting&getft_integrator=sciencedirect_contenthosting

Chen X, Wang H, Chen H, Ren L, Wang W, Xu J et al (2023) Lens regeneration in situ using hESCs-derived cells -similar to natural lens. iScience 26(6):106921

Chen Y, Liu X, Cao L, Gao R, You Z (2025) Comparison of transplantation outcomes of human cornea vs. acellular porcine corneal stroma in noninfectious peripheral ulcerative keratitis: a single-center retrospective cohort study. Xenotransplantation [Internet] 32(6):e70085. [cited 2025 Nov 10]. Available from: https://onlinelibrary.wiley.com/doi/abs/10.1111/xen.70085

Cheng C (2024) Tissue, cellular, and molecular level determinants for eye lens stiffness and elasticity. Front Ophthalmol [Internet]. [cited 2025 Dec 14]. 4. Available from: https://www.frontiersin.org/journals/ophthalmology/articles/10.3389/fopht.2024.1456474/full

Cho CH, Lee SB (2015) Biodegradable collagen matrix (Ologen™) implant and conjunctival autograft for scleral necrosis after pterygium excision: two case reports. BMC Ophthalmol 24(15):140

Comparative study of Endonasal Dacryocystorhinostomy with Silicone or polypropylene stents using Mitomycin-C [Internet]. [cited 2025 Nov 15]. Available from: https://bmfj.journals.ekb.eg/article_254383.html

Cooksley G, Lacey J, Dymond MK, Sandeman S (2021) Factors affecting posterior capsule opacification in the development of intraocular lens materials. Pharmaceutics [Internet] 13(6): 860. [cited 2025 Dec 14]. Available from: https://pmc.ncbi.nlm.nih.gov/articles/PMC8230425/

CorNeat Vision Ltd. (2024) A Single Arm, Open Label, Multicenter Clinical Investigation to Evaluate the Clinical Safety and Performance of the CorNeat Keratoprosthesis, for Treatment of Corneal Blindness [Internet]. clinicaltrials.gov; [cited 2025 Dec 11]. Report No.: NCT05694247. Available from: https://clinicaltrials.gov/study/NCT05694247

Cui H, Li P, Su Z, Shiqiang G, Dong H, Dong X (2024) Preparation and stability study of an injectable hydrogel for artificial intraocular lenses. Polymers 10(16):2562

Custer PL, Maamari RN (2021) Porcine dermal matrix sandwich graft for lower eyelid reconstruction. Orbit 40(2):138–144

Dai M, Xu K, Xiao D, Zheng Y, Zheng Q, Shen J et al (2022) In situ forming hydrogel as a tracer and degradable lacrimal plug for dry eye treatment. Adv Healthc Mater 11(19):e2200678
Danysh BP, Duncan MK (2009) The lens capsule. Exp Eye Res [Internet] 88(2):151–164. [cited 2025 Dec 15]. Available from: https://pmc.ncbi.nlm.nih.gov/articles/PMC2674021/
Daphna O, Auffarth GU, Lapid-Gortzak R, Chaurasia S, Gilboa E, Lemze A et al (2024) A novel artificial endothelial replacement membrane for the treatment of chronic corneal edema. Cornea 44(10):1240–1247
Decellularized porcine conjunctiva as an alternative substrate for tissue-engineered epithelialized conjunctiva. – Abstract-Europe PMC [Internet]. [cited 2025 Dec 12]. Available from: https://europepmc.org/article/med/32860970
Dinç E, Ayaz L, Kurt AH, Dursun Ö, Yılmaz G, Vatansever M et al (2021) Effects of bone marrow and adipose-derived mesenchymal stem cells on microRNA expressions in acute alkaline corneal burn. J Ocul Pharmacol Ther 37(4):200–208
Dohlman C (2022) The boston keratoprosthesis-the first 50 years: some reminiscences. Annu Rev Vis Sci 8:1–32
Donaldson PJ, Grey AC, Maceo Heilman B, Lim JC, Vaghefi E (2017) The physiological optics of the lens. Prog Retin Eye Res 56:e1–24
Dong Y, Yang J, Wang L, Ma X, Huang Y, Qiu Z et al (2014) An improved biofunction of titanium for keratoprosthesis by hydroxyapatite-coating. J Biomater Appl 28(7):990–997
Dubbelman M, Van der Heijde GL (2001) The shape of the aging human lens: curvature, equivalent refractive index and the lens paradox. Vis Res 41(14):1867–1877
Duncan JL, Bowman A, Laster A, Gelfman C, Birch DG, Boye SE et al (2024) Inherited retinal degenerations and non-neovascular age-related macular degeneration: progress and unmet needs. Transl Vis Sci Technol [Internet] 13(12):28. [cited 2025 Dec 14]. Available from: https://pmc.ncbi.nlm.nih.gov/articles/PMC11654773/
Duvan FT, Cunquero M, Masvidal-Codina E, Walston ST, Marsal M, de la Cruz JM et al (2024) Graphene-based microelectrodes with bidirectional functionality for next-generation retinal electronic interfaces. Nanoscale Horiz 9(11):1948–1961
Eah KS, Sa HS (2021) Reconstruction of large upper eyelid defects using the reverse hughes flap combined with a sandwich graft of an acellular dermal matrix. Ophthalmic Plast Reconstr Surg 37(3S):S27–S30
Fagerholm P, Lagali NS, Merrett K, Jackson WB, Munger R, Liu Y, et al. A biosynthetic alternative to human donor tissue for inducing corneal regeneration: 24-month follow-up of a phase 1 clinical study. Sci Transl Med 2010;2(46):46ra61.
Fagerholm P, Lagali NS, Ong JA, Merrett K, Jackson WB, Polarek JW et al (2014) Stable corneal regeneration four years after implantation of a cell-free recombinant human collagen scaffold. Biomaterials 35(8):2420–2427
Feiertag E, Maassen J, Mueller A, Harnisch F, Skazik-Voogt C, Engelmann K et al (2020) From cord to eye: wharton jelly-derived stem cells differentiate into corneal endothelial-like cells. Cornea 39(7):877–885
Fernández-Pérez J, Madden PW, Brady RT, Nowlan PF, Ahearne M (2021) The effect of prior long-term recellularization with keratocytes of decellularized porcine corneas implanted in a rabbit anterior lamellar keratoplasty model. Plos One [Internet] 16(6):e0245406. [cited 2025 Oct 27]. Available from: https://journals.plos.org/plosone/article?id=10.1371/journal.pone.0245406
Fu Q, Qin Z, Jin X, Zhang L, Chen Z, He J et al (2017) Generation of functional lentoid bodies from human induced pluripotent stem cells derived from urinary cells. Invest Ophthalmol Vis Sci 58(1):517–527
Full article: stereolithographic rapid prototyping of clear, foldable, non-refractive intraocular lens designs: a proof-of-concept study [Internet]. [cited 2025 Dec 14]. Available from: https://www-tandfonline-com.proxy3.library.mcgill.ca/doi/full/10.1080/02713683.2024.2344164
Galindo S, López-Paniagua M, de la Mata A, Herreras JM, García-Vázquez C, Marceñido B et al (2025) Bone marrow- *versus* adipose tissue-derived mesenchymal stem cells for corneal failure

in an experimental model of limbal stem cell deficiency. Exp Eye Res [Internet]:110737. [cited 2025 Nov 10]. Available from: https://www.sciencedirect.com/science/article/pii/S001448352500510X

Gao Q, Hu B, Ning Q, Ye C, Xie J, Ye J et al (2015) A primary study of poly(propylene fumarate)–2-hydroxyethyl methacrylate copolymer scaffolds for tarsal plate repair and reconstruction in rabbit eyelids. J Mater Chem B [Internet] 3(19):4052–4062. [cited 2025 Dec 15]. Available from: https://pubs.rsc.org/en/content/articlelanding/2015/tb/c5tb00285k

Gao Y, Wang Y, Zhang J, Zhang M, Dai C, Zhang Y et al (2024) Advancing neural regeneration via adaptable hydrogels: Enriched with Mg2+ and silk fibroin to facilitate endogenous cell infiltration and macrophage polarization. Bioact Mater 33:100–113

Ghezzi CE, Marelli B, Omenetto FG, Funderburgh JL, Kaplan DL (2017) 3D functional corneal stromal tissue equivalent based on corneal stromal stem cells and multi-layered silk film architecture. Plos One [Internet] 12(1):e0169504. [cited 2025 Nov 11]. Available from: https://journals.plos.org/plosone/article?id=10.1371/journal.pone.0169504

Giannone AA, Li L, Sellitto C, White TW (2021) Physiological mechanisms regulating lens transport. Front Physiol [Internet] 12. [cited 2025 Dec 14]. Available from: https://www.frontiersin.org/journals/physiology/articles/10.3389/fphys.2021.818649/full

Gibney R, Patterson J, Ferraris E (2021) High-resolution bioprinting of recombinant human collagen type III. Polymers [Internet] 13(17):2973. [cited 2025 Nov 12]. Available from: https://www.mdpi.com/2073–4360/13/17/2973

Gonzalez-Andrades M, de la Cruz Cardona J, Ionescu AM, Campos A, del Mar Perez M, Alaminos M (2011) Generation of bioengineered corneas with decellularized xenografts and human keratocytes. Invest Ophthalmol Vis Sci [Internet] 52(1):215–222. [cited 2025 Oct 27]. Available from: https://doi.org/10.1167/iovs.09-4773

González-Gallardo C, Martínez-Atienza J, Mataix B, Muñoz-Ávila JI, Daniel Martínez-Rodríguez J, Medialdea S et al (2023) Successful restoration of corneal surface integrity with a tissue-engineered allogeneic implant in severe keratitis patients. Biomed Pharmacother 162: 114612

Gopakumar V, Agarwal S, Srinivasan B, Krishnakumar S, Krishnan UM, Iyer G (2019) Clinical outcome of autologous cultivated oral mucosal epithelial transplantation in ocular surface reconstruction. Cornea 38(10):1273–1279

Graue-Hernandez EO, Daniels E, Dentiste A, Garfias Y, Jimenez-Collado D, Navas A et al (2023) KIO-201, a crosslinked, chemically modified form of hyaluronic acid, improves wound healing in patients with persistent corneal epithelial defects. Invest Ophthalmol Vis Sci 64(8):3123

Groll J, Boland T, Blunk T, Burdick JA, Cho DW, Dalton PD et al (2016) Biofabrication: reappraising the definition of an evolving field. Biofabrication 8(1):013001

Gupta M, Ireland AC, Bordoni B (2025) Neuroanatomy, visual pathway. In: StatPearls [Internet]. StatPearls Publishing, Treasure Island (FL). [cited 2025 Dec 12]. Available from: http://www.ncbi.nlm.nih.gov/books/NBK553189/

Gurdal M, Zeugolis DI (2025) Macromolecular crowding agent dependent extracellular matrix deposition and growth factor retention in human corneal fibroblast cultures. Exp Eye Res 250: 110162

Gwon A, Gruber LJ, Mantras C (1993 Nov) Restoring lens capsule integrity enhances lens regeneration in New Zealand albino rabbits and cats. J Cataract Refract Surg 19(6):735–746

Hashimoto Y, Funamoto S, Sasaki S, Negishi J, Honda T, Hattori S et al (2015) Corneal regeneration by Deep Anterior Lamellar Keratoplasty (DALK) using decellularized corneal matrix. PLoS One [Internet] 10(7):e0131989. [cited 2025 Oct 27]. Available from: https://pmc.ncbi.nlm.nih.gov/articles/PMC4498638/

Hayashi R, Okubo T, Kudo Y, Ishikawa Y, Imaizumi T, Suzuki K et al (2022) Generation of 3D lacrimal gland organoids from human pluripotent stem cells. Nature [Internet] 605(7908): 126–131. [cited 2025 Nov 12]. Available from: https://www.nature.com/articles/s41586-022-04613-4

Hayreh SS (2006) Orbital vascular anatomy. Eye (Lond) 20(10):1130–1144

He B, Wang J, Xie M, Xu M, Zhang Y, Hao H et al (2022 Nov) 3D printed biomimetic epithelium/stroma bilayer hydrogel implant for corneal regeneration. Bioact Mater 17:234–247

Hejtmancik JF, Shiels A (2015) Overview of the lens. Prog Mol Biol Transl Sci 134:119–127

Hirayama M, Hatou S, Nomura M, Hokama R, Hirayama OI, Inagaki E et al (2025) A first-in-human clinical study of an allogenic iPSC-derived corneal endothelial cell substitute transplantation for bullous keratopathy. Cell Rep Med 6(1):101847

Hoshiba T, Lu H, Kawazoe N, Chen G (2010) Decellularized matrices for tissue engineering. Expert Opin Biol Ther 10(12):1717–1728

Hosni FA (1974) Repair of trachomatous cicatricial entropion using mucous membrane graft. Arch Ophthalmol 91(1):49–51

Hsiao YC, Yang TL (2017) Regulating temporospatial dynamics of morphogen for structure formation of the lacrimal gland by chitosan biomaterials. Biomaterials 113:42–55

Hsu WC, Spilker MH, Yannas IV, Rubin PA (2000) Inhibition of conjunctival scarring and contraction by a porous collagen-glycosaminoglycan implant. Invest Ophthalmol Vis Sci 41(9):2404–2411

Hu X, Dong C, Zou D, Wei C, Wang Y, Li Z et al (2024) Directed differentiation of human embryonic stem cells into conjunctival epithelial cells. Exp Cell Res [Internet] 442(2):114227. [cited 2025 Dec 12]. Available from: https://www.sciencedirect.com/science/article/pii/S0014482724003185

Huateng. HuaTeng|Professional Medical Research Services [Internet]. [cited 2025 Dec 14]. Available from: https://en.htscience.com/

Islam MM, Buznyk O, Reddy JC, Pasyechnikova N, Alarcon EI, Hayes S et al (2018) Biomaterials-enabled cornea regeneration in patients at high risk for rejection of donor tissue transplantation. npj Regener Med 3:2

ISO [Internet]. [cited 2025 Dec 14]. ISO 13485:2016. Available from: https://www.iso.org/standard/59752.html

Jangamreddy JR, Haagdorens MKC, Mirazul Islam M, Lewis P, Samanta A, Fagerholm P et al (2018) Short peptide analogs as alternatives to collagen in pro-regenerative corneal implants. Acta Biomater 69:120–130

Jeong YW, Kim HS, Thangavelu M, Choi MJ, Lee GW, Song CU et al (2020) Progress in silk fibroin based composite scaffold/hydrogel: silk fibroin/PEG hydrogel for the RPE regeneration a promising biomaterial for clinical application. Front Mater [Internet]. [cited 2025 Dec 12]; 7. Available from: https://www.frontiersin.org/journals/materials/articles/10.3389/fmats.2020.504642/full

Johnson TV, Baranov P, Di Polo A, Fortune B, Gokoffski KK, Goldberg JL et al (2023) The retinal ganglion cell repopulation, stem cell transplantation, and optic nerve regeneration consortium. Ophthalmol Sci [Internet] 3(4):100390. [cited 2025 Dec 12]. Available from: https://pmc.ncbi.nlm.nih.gov/articles/PMC10630665/

Joyal JS, Gantner ML, LEH S (2018) Retinal energy demands control vascular supply of the retina in development and disease: The role of neuronal lipid and glucose metabolism. Prog Retin Eye Res [Internet] 64:131–156. [cited 2025 Dec 12]. Available from: https://pmc.ncbi.nlm.nih.gov/articles/PMC5963988/

Jung SK, Paik JS, Sonn UH, Yang SW (2013) Surgical outcomes of acellular human dermal grafts for large conjunctiva defects in orbital implant insertion. Graefes Arch Clin Exp Ophthalmol 251(7):1849–1854

Kacham S, Bhure TS, Eswaramoorthy SD, Naik G, Rath SN, Parcha SR et al (2021) Human umbilical cord-derived mesenchymal stem cells promote corneal epithelial repair in vitro. Cells 10(5):1254

Kapoor S, Gupta S, Kapoor S, Gupta S (2020) Basic science of intraocular lens materials. In: Intraocular lens [Internet]. IntechOpen. [cited 2025 Dec 14]. Available from: https://www.intechopen.com/chapters/72219

Kasbekar S, Kaye SB, Williams RL, Stewart RMK, Leow-Dyke S, Rooney P (2018) Development of decellularized conjunctiva as a substrate for the ex vivo expansion of conjunctival epithelium. J Tissue Eng Regen Med 12(2):e973–82

Kashani AH, Lebkowski JS, Rahhal FM, Avery RL, Salehi-Had H, Dang W et al (2018) A bioengineered retinal pigment epithelial monolayer for advanced, dry age-related macular degeneration. Sci Transl Med. 10(435):eaao4097

Kashani AH, Lebkowski JS, Rahhal FM, Avery RL, Salehi-Had H, Chen S et al (2021) One-year follow-up in a phase 1/2a clinical trial of an allogeneic RPE cell bioengineered implant for advanced dry age-related macular degeneration. Transl Vis Sci Technol 10(10):13

Kaur J (2018) Osteo-odonto keratoprosthesis: Innovative dental and ophthalmic blending. J Indian Prosthodont Soc 18(2):89–95

Kim KW, Lee SJ, Park SH, Kim JC (2018) Ex vivo functionality of 3D bioprinted corneal endothelium engineered with ribonuclease 5-overexpressing human corneal endothelial cells. Adv. Healthc. Mater. [Internet] 7(18):1800398. [cited 2025 Nov 12]. Available from: https://onlinelibrary.wiley.com/doi/abs/10.1002/adhm.201800398

Kim H, Jang J, Park J, Lee KP, Lee S, Lee DM et al (2019) Shear-induced alignment of collagen fibrils using 3D cell printing for corneal stroma tissue engineering. Biofabrication [Internet] 11(3):035017. [cited 2025 Nov 12]. Available from: https://doi.org/10.1088/1758-5090/ab1a8b

Kling S, Frigelli M, Aydemir ME, Tahsini V, Torres-Netto EA, Kollros L et al (2024) Optical coherence tomography quantifies gradient refractive index and mechanical stiffness gradient across the human lens. Commun Med (Lond) 4(1):162

Kobayashi M, Nakamura T, Yasuda M, Hata Y, Okura S, Iwamoto M et al (2015) Ocular surface reconstruction with a tissue-engineered nasal mucosal epithelial cell sheet for the treatment of severe ocular surface diseases. Stem Cells Transl Med 4(1):99–109

Koksaldi S, Kayabasi M, Karti O, Saatci AO. Clinical anatomy of the macula Med Hypothesis Discov Innov Ophthalmol [Internet] 2025;14(2):17–27. [cited 2025 Dec 12]. Available from: https://pmc.ncbi.nlm.nih.gov/articles/PMC12330045/

Kong B, Chen Y, Liu R, Liu X, Liu C, Shao Z et al (2020) Fiber reinforced GelMA hydrogel to induce the regeneration of corneal stroma. Nat Commun [Internet] 11(1):1435. [cited 2025 Aug 28]. Available from: https://www.nature.com/articles/s41467-020-14887-9

Kuckelkorn R, Schrage N, Redbrake C, Kottek A, Reim M (1996) Autologous transplantation of nasal mucosa after severe chemical and thermal eye burns. Acta Ophthalmol Scand 74(5): 442–448

Lee SY, Oh JH, Kim JC, Kim YH, Kim SH, Choi JW (2003) In vivo conjunctival reconstruction using modified PLGA grafts for decreased scar formation and contraction. Biomaterials 24(27): 5049–5059

Lee H, Park YH, Kang HJ, Lee H (2024) Three-dimensional bioprinting of tarsal plates with adipose-derived mesenchymal stem cells: evaluation of meibomian gland reconstruction in a rat model. Biomedicines [Internet] 12(11):2567. [cited 2025 Nov 16]. Available from: https://www.mdpi.com/2227–9059/12/11/2567

Yu B, Li XR, Zhang XM. Mesenchymal stem cell-derived extracellular vesicles as a new therapeutic strategy for ocular diseases. World J Stem Cells [Internet]. 2020;12(3):178–187. [cited 2023 Sept 3]. Available from: https://www.ncbi.nlm.nih.gov/pmc/articles/PMC7118288/

Li L, Jiang H, Wang LQ, Huang YF (2018) Experimental study on the biocompatibility of keratoprosthesis with improved titanium implant. Int J Ophthalmol [Internet] 11(11): 1741–1745. [cited 2025 Dec 11]. Available from: https://pmc.ncbi.nlm.nih.gov/articles/PMC6232317/

Li S, Li M, Gu L, Peng L, Deng Y, Zhong J et al (2019) Risk factors influencing survival of acellular porcine corneal stroma in infectious keratitis: a prospective clinical study. J Transl Med [Internet] 17:434. [cited 2025 Aug 28]. Available from: https://www.ncbi.nlm.nih.gov/pmc/articles/PMC6941327/

Li S, Dan X, Chen H, Li T, Liu B, Ju Y et al (2024) Developing fibrin-based biomaterials/scaffolds in tissue engineering. Bioact Mater 40:597–623

Lin H, Ouyang H, Zhu J, Huang S, Liu Z, Chen S et al (2016) Lens regeneration using endogenous stem cells with gain of visual function. Nature 531(7594):323–328

Lin Y, Zheng Q, Hua S, Meng Y, Chen W, Wang Y (2017) Cross-linked decellularized porcine corneal graft for treating fungal keratitis. Sci Rep [Internet] 7(1):9955. [cited 2025 Oct 27]. Available from: https://www.nature.com/articles/s41598-017-08207-3

Lin G, Kulbay M, Wu KY, Tran SD, Marchand M (2025) Regenerative medicine in ophthalmology. In: Handbook of regenerative medicine. CRC Press

Litvin G, Klein I, Litvin Y, Klaiman G, Nyska A (2021) CorNeat KPro: ocular implantation study in rabbits. Cornea 40(9):1165–1174

Liu X, Li X, Wu G, Qi P, Zhang Y, Liu Z et al (2022) Umbilical cord mesenchymal stem cell-derived small extracellular vesicles deliver miR-21 to promote corneal epithelial wound healing through PTEN/PI3K/Akt pathway. Stem Cells Int [Internet] 2022(1):1252557. [cited 2025 Nov 11]. Available from: https://onlinelibrary.wiley.com/doi/abs/10.1155/2022/1252557

Liu Z, Huang S, Zheng Y, Zhou T, Hu L, Xiong L et al (2023) The lens epithelium as a major determinant in the development, maintenance, and regeneration of the crystalline lens. Prog Retin Eye Res 92:101112

Liu ZG, Zhou LY, Sun YQ, Ma YH, Liu CM, Zhang BY (2024) Unlocking the potential for optic nerve regeneration over long distances: a multi-therapeutic intervention. Front Neurol 15: 1526973

Liu ZG, Zhou LY, Sun YQ, Ma YH, Liu CM, Zhang BY (2025) Unlocking the potential for optic nerve regeneration over long distances: a multi-therapeutic intervention. Front Neurol [Internet] 15:1526973. [cited 2025 Dec 14]. Available from: https://pmc.ncbi.nlm.nih.gov/articles/PMC11754882/

Ljubimov AV, Saghizadeh M (2015 Nov) Progress in corneal wound healing. Prog Retin Eye Res 49:17–45

López S, Hoz L, Tenorio EP, Buentello B, Magaña FS, Wintergerst A et al (2021) Can human oral mucosa stem cells differentiate to corneal epithelia? Int J Mol Sci [Internet] 22(11):5976. [cited 2023 Aug 28]. Available from: https://www.mdpi.com/1422–0067/22/11/5976

Lu R, Zhang X, Huang D, Huang B, Gao N, Wang Z et al (2011a) Conjunctival reconstruction with progenitor cell-derived autologous epidermal sheets in rhesus monkey. Plos One [Internet] 6(11):e25713. [cited 2025 Dec 12]. Available from: https://journals.plos.org/plosone/article?id=10.1371/journal.pone.0025713

Lu H, Hoshiba T, Kawazoe N, Koda I, Song M, Chen G (2011b) Cultured cell-derived extracellular matrix scaffolds for tissue engineering. Biomaterials 32(36):9658–9666

Lu X, Li N, Zhao L, Guo D, Yi H, Yang L et al (2020) Human umbilical cord mesenchymal stem cells alleviate ongoing autoimmune dacryoadenitis in rabbits via polarizing macrophages into an anti-inflammatory phenotype. Exp Eye Res 191:107905

Luo C, Wang H, Chen X, Xu J, Yin H, Yao K (2022) Recent advances of intraocular lens materials and surface modification in cataract surgery. Front Bioeng Biotechnol 10:913383

Luo L, Xing Z, Li Y, Wang B, Dong N, Sun J et al (2025) Injective hydrogel encapsulating dental pulp stem cells for the treatment of traumatic optic nerve injury. Front Bioeng Biotechnol 13: 1528749

Mahabadi N, Al Khalili Y (2025) Neuroanatomy, retina. In: StatPearls. StatPearls Publishing, Treasure Island. [cited 2025 Dec 12]. Available from: http://www.ncbi.nlm.nih.gov/books/NBK545310/

Mahdavi SS, Abdekhodaie MJ, Kumar H, Mashayekhan S, Baradaran-Rafii A, Kim K (2020) Stereolithography 3D bioprinting method for fabrication of human corneal stroma equivalent. Ann Biomed Eng [Internet] 48(7):1955–1970. [cited 2025 Nov 12]. Available from: https://doi.org/10.1007/s10439-020-02537-6

Makuloluwa AK, Hamill KJ, Rauz S, Bosworth L, Haneef A, Romano V et al (2021) Biological tissues and components, and synthetic substrates for conjunctival cell transplantation. Ocul Surf 22:15–26

Mandai M, Watanabe A, Kurimoto Y, Hirami Y, Morinaga C, Daimon T et al (2017) Autologous induced stem-cell-derived retinal cells for macular degeneration. N Engl J Med 376(11): 1038–1046

McTiernan CD, Simpson FC, Haagdorens M, Samarawickrama C, Hunter D, Buznyk O et al (2020) LiQD cornea: pro-regeneration collagen mimetics as patches and alternatives to corneal transplantation. Sci Adv 6(25):eaba2187

Medicinal products in the European Union: The legal framework for medicines for human use| Think Tank|European Parliament [Internet]. [cited 2025 Dec 14]. Available from: https://www.europarl.europa.eu/thinktank/en/document/EPRS_IDA(2015)554174

Meek KM, Knupp C (2015 Nov) Corneal structure and transparency. Prog Retin Eye Res 49:1–16

Mencucci R, Favuzza E, Boccalini C, Gicquel JJ, Raimondi L (2015) Square-edge intraocular lenses and epithelial lens cell proliferation: implications on posterior capsule opacification in an in vitro model. BMC Ophthalmol 19(15):5

Mengarelli I, Barberi T (2013) Derivation of multiple cranial tissues and isolation of lens epithelium-like cells from human embryonic stem cells. Stem Cells Transl Med [Internet] 2(2):94–106. [cited 2025 Dec 14]. Available from: https://pmc.ncbi.nlm.nih.gov/articles/PMC3659756/

Møller-Hansen M, Larsen AC, Toft PB, Lynggaard CD, Schwartz C, Bruunsgaard H et al (2021) Safety and feasibility of mesenchymal stem cell therapy in patients with aqueous deficient dry eye disease. Ocul Surf 19:43–52

Møller-Hansen M, Larsen AC, Wiencke AK, Terslev L, Siersma V, Andersen TT et al (2024) Allogeneic mesenchymal stem cell therapy for dry eye disease in patients with Sjögren's syndrome: A randomized clinical trial. Ocul Surf 31:1–8

Mousavi Z, Bagheri M, Rostaminasab G, Mikaeili A, Djalilian AR, Rezakhani L (2024) Tissue engineering strategies for ocular regeneration; from bench to the bedside. Heliyon [Internet] 10(20):e39398. [cited 2025 Dec 12]. Available from: https://www.sciencedirect.com/science/article/pii/S2405844024154291

Murphy P, Kabir MH, Srivastava T, Mason ME, Dewi CU, Lim S et al (2018) Light-focusing human micro-lenses generated from pluripotent stem cells model lens development and drug-induced cataract in vitro. Development 145(1):dev155838

Obeng E, Shen B, Wang W, Xie Z, Zhang W, Li Z et al (2025) Engineered bio-functional material-based nerve guide conduits for optic nerve regeneration: a view from the cellular perspective, challenges and the future outlook. Regener Biomater 12:rbae133

Olszewski C, Maassen J, Guenther R, Skazik-Voogt C, Gutermuth A (2022) Mechanotransductive differentiation of hair follicle stem cells derived from aged eyelid skin into corneal endothelial-like cells. Stem Cell Rev Rep 18(5):1668–1685

Park SJ, Kim Y, Jang SY (2018) The application of an acellular dermal allograft (AlloDerm) for patients with insufficient conjunctiva during evisceration and implantation surgery. Eye (Lond) 32(1):136–141

Park IS, Kim BK, Truong MD, Yang HS, Park SH, Park HS et al (2021) Corneal repair with adhesive cell sheets of fetal cartilage-derived stem cells. Tissue Eng Regen Med 18(1):187–198

Pellegrini G, Lambiase A, Macaluso C, Pocobelli A, Deng S, Cavallini GM et al (2016) From discovery to approval of an advanced therapy medicinal product-containing stem cells, in the EU. Regen Med 11(4):407–420

Peng SW, Li CW, Chiu IM, Wang GJ (2017) Nerve guidance conduit with a hybrid structure of a PLGA microfibrous bundle wrapped in a micro/nanostructured membrane. Int J Nanomedicine 12:421–432

Percival SP, Jafree AJ (1994) Preliminary results with a new hydrogel intraocular lens. Eye (Lond) 8(Pt 6):672–675

Pollreisz A, Neschi M, Sloan KR, Pircher M, Mittermueller T, Dacey DM et al (2020) Atlas of human retinal pigment epithelium organelles significant for clinical imaging. Invest Ophthalmol Vis Sci 61(8):13

Proulx S, Uwamaliya J d'A, Carrier P, Deschambeault A, Audet C, Giasson CJ et al (2010) Reconstruction of a human cornea by the self-assembly approach of tissue engineering using the three native cell types. Mol Vis [Internet] 16:2192–2201. [cited 2025 Aug 27]. Available from: https://www.ncbi.nlm.nih.gov/pmc/articles/PMC2994343/

Puistola P, Huhtanen S, Hopia K, Miettinen S, Mörö A, Skottman H (2025) Multi-material 3D bioprinting of human stem cells to engineer complex human corneal structures with stroma and epithelium. Bioprinting [Internet] 46:e00391. [cited 2025 Nov 12]. Available from: https://www.sciencedirect.com/science/article/pii/S2405886625000077

Pushpoth S, Tambe K, Sandramouli S (2008) The use of AlloDerm in the reconstruction of full-thickness eyelid defects. Orbit 27(5):337–340

Rafat M, Jabbarvand M, Sharma N, Xeroudaki M, Tabe S, Omrani R et al (2023) Bioengineered corneal tissue for minimally invasive vision restoration in advanced keratoconus in two clinical cohorts. Nat Biotechnol [Internet] 41(1):70–81. [cited 2025 Nov 10]. Available from: https://www.nature.com/articles/s41587-022-01408-w

Ramin S, Abbasi A, Ahadi M, Moallemi Rad L, Kobarfad F (2023) Assessment of the effects of intrastromal injection of adipose-derived stem cells in keratoconus patients. Int J Ophthalmol 16(6):863–870

Rosenquist J, Folkesson M, Höglund L, Pupkaite J, Hilborn J, Samanta A (2023) An injectable, shape-retaining collagen hydrogel cross-linked using thiol-maleimide click chemistry for sealing corneal perforations. ACS Appl Mater Interfaces 15(29):34407–34418

Ruan X, Liu Z, Luo L, Liu Y (2020) Structure of the lens and its associations with the visual quality. BMJ Open Ophth 5(1) [cited 2025 Dec 11]. Available from: https://bmjophth.bmj.com/content/5/1/e000459

Rusch RM, Ogawa Y, Sato S, Morikawa S, Inagaki E, Shimizu E et al (2021) MSCs become collagen-type I producing cells with different phenotype in allogeneic and syngeneic bone marrow transplantation. Int J Mol Sci 22(9):4895

Ryu Y, Hwang JS, Bo Noh K, Park SH, Seo JH, Shin YJ (2023) Adipose mesenchymal stem cell-derived exosomes promote the regeneration of corneal endothelium through ameliorating senescence. Invest Ophthalmol Vis Sci 64(13):29

Salazar JJ, Ramírez AI, Hoz RD, Salobrar-Garcia E, Rojas P, Fernández-Albarral JA et al (2018) Anatomy of the human optic nerve: structure and function. In: Optic nerve [Internet]. IntechOpen. [cited 2025 Dec 12]. Available from: https://www.intechopen.com/chapters/62850

Satake Y, Higa K, Tsubota K, Shimazaki J (2011) Long-term outcome of cultivated oral mucosal epithelial sheet transplantation in treatment of total limbal stem cell deficiency. Ophthalmology 118(8):1524–1530

Schechter J, Stevenson D, Chang D, Chang N, Pidgeon M, Nakamura T et al (2002) Growth of purified lacrimal acinar cells in Matrigel raft cultures. Exp Eye Res 74(3):349–360

Schrader S, Notara M, Beaconsfield M, Tuft SJ, Daniels JT, Geerling G (2009) Tissue engineering for conjunctival reconstruction: established methods and future outlooks. Curr. Eye Res. [Internet] 34(11):913–924. [cited 2025 Dec 12]. Available from: https://doi.org/10.3109/02713680903198045

Schwartz SD, Regillo CD, Lam BL, Eliott D, Rosenfeld PJ, Gregori NZ et al (2015) Human embryonic stem cell-derived retinal pigment epithelium in patients with age-related macular degeneration and Stargardt's macular dystrophy: follow-up of two open-label phase 1/2 studies. Lancet 385(9967):509–516

Shan F, Feng X, Li J, Yang S, Wang F, Shi W et al (2023) Decellularized porcine conjunctiva in treating severe symblepharon. J Funct Biomater [Internet] 14(6):318. [cited 2025 Dec 12]. Available from: https://pmc.ncbi.nlm.nih.gov/articles/PMC10299224/

Shang Q, Chu Y, Li Y, Han Y, Yu D, Liu R et al (2020) Adipose-derived mesenchymal stromal cells promote corneal wound healing by accelerating the clearance of neutrophils in cornea. Cell Death Dis [Internet] 11(8):707. [cited 2025 Nov 16]. Available from: https://www.nature.com/articles/s41419-020-02914-y

Shi R, Jin M, Jin J, Xu L, Liu Z, Zheng L et al (2025) Retinoic acid promotes conjunctival epithelium differentiation and goblet cell regeneration: evidence from novel 3D conjunctival organoids and whole-mount PAS staining. Ocul Surf [Internet] 37:301–313. [cited 2025 Dec 12]. Available from: https://www.sciencedirect.com/science/article/pii/S1542012425000679

Shin S, Yoon SG, Kim M, Cheon EJ, Jeon Y, Lee HJ et al (2023) The effect of mesenchymal stem cells on dry eye in sjogren syndrome mouse model. Int J Mol Sci [Internet]. 24(2):1039. [cited 2025 Nov 12]. Available from: https://www.mdpi.com/1422–0067/24/2/1039

Shore JW, Foster CS, Westfall CT, Rubin PA (1992) Results of buccal mucosal grafting for patients with medically controlled ocular cicatricial pemphigoid. Ophthalmology 99(3):383–395

Shukla S, Mittal SK, Foulsham W, Elbasiony E, Singhania D, Sahu SK et al (2019) Therapeutic efficacy of different routes of mesenchymal stem cell administration in corneal injury. Ocul Surf 17(4):729–736

Simó R, Villarroel M, Corraliza L, Hernández C, Garcia-Ramírez M (2010) The retinal pigment epithelium: something more than a constituent of the blood-retinal barrier--implications for the pathogenesis of diabetic retinopathy. J Biomed Biotechnol 2010:190724

Simoliunas E, Ruedas-Torres I, Jiménez-Gómez Y, Edin E, Aghajanzadeh-Kiyaseh M, et al (2024) Inflammation-suppressing cornea-in-a-syringe with anti-viral GF19 peptide promotes regeneration in HSV-1 infected rabbit corneas. NPJ Regen Med. 9(1):11. Available from: https://www.nature.com/articles/s41536-024-00355-1

Simpson FC, McTiernan CD, Islam MM, Buznyk O, Lewis PN, Meek KM et al (2021) Collagen analogs with phosphorylcholine are inflammation-suppressing scaffolds for corneal regeneration from alkali burns in mini-pigs. Commun Biol 4(1):608

Singh VK, Sharma P, Vaksh UKS, Chandra R (2022) Current approaches for the regeneration and reconstruction of ocular surface in dry eye. Front Med (Lausanne) 9:885780

Smith G. The eye and visual optical instruments. Cambridge: Cambridge University Press; 1997.828 p.

Smith AM, Czyz CN (2025) Neuroanatomy, cranial nerve 2 (optic). In: StatPearls [Internet]. StatPearls Publishing, Treasure Island (FL). [cited 2025 Dec 12]. Available from: http://www.ncbi.nlm.nih.gov/books/NBK507907/

Soleimani M, Mirshahi R, Cheraqpour K, Baharnoori SM, Massoumi H, Chow C et al (2023) Intrastromal versus subconjunctival injection of mesenchymal stem/stromal cells for promoting corneal repair. Ocul Surf 30:187–195

Solomon A, Espana EM, Tseng SCG (2003) Amniotic membrane transplantation for reconstruction of the conjunctival fornices. Ophthalmology 110(1):93–100

Soltani Sharif Abadi A, Ordys A, Kukielka K, Pierscionek B (2023) Review on challenges for robotic eye surgery; surgical systems, technologies, cost-effectiveness, and controllers. Int J Med Robot 19(4):e2524

Soma T, Oie Y, Takayanagi H, Matsubara S, Yamada T, Nomura M et al (2024) Induced pluripotent stem-cell-derived corneal epithelium for transplant surgery: a single-arm, open-label, first-in-human interventional study in Japan. The Lancet [Internet] 404(10466): 1929–1939. [cited 2025 Nov 16]. Available from: https://www.thelancet.com/journals/lancet/article/PIIS0140-6736%2824%2901764–1/fulltext?utm_source=chatgpt.com

Sridhar MS (2018) Anatomy of cornea and ocular surface. Indian J Ophthalmol 66(2):190–194

Suanno G, Genna VG, Maurizi E, Dieh AA, Griffith M, Ferrari G (2024) Cell therapy in the cornea: the emerging role of microenvironment. Prog Retin Eye Res 102:101275

Tan S, Yao Y, Yang Q, Yuan XL, Cen LP, Ng TK (2022) Diversified treatment options of adult stem cells for optic neuropathies. Cell Transplant 31:9636897221123512

Thoft RA (1977) Conjunctival transplantation. Arch Ophthalmol 95(8):1425–1427

Thomas MB, Selvam S, Agrawal P, Bellur P, Waghmare N, Chowdhury SK et al (2022) Print me a cornea – are we there yet? Bioprinting [Internet] 28:e00227. [cited 2025 Nov 11]. Available from: https://www.sciencedirect.com/science/article/pii/S2405886622000379

Toshida H, Kasahara T, Kiriyama M, Iwasaki Y, Sugita J, Ichikawa K et al (2023) Early clinical outcomes of the first commercialized human autologous ex vivo cultivated oral mucosal epithelial cell transplantation for limbal stem cell deficiency: two case reports and literature review. Int J Mol Sci [Internet] 24(10):8926. [cited 2025 Nov 16]. Available from: https://www.mdpi.com/1422–0067/24/10/8926

Tseng SC, Prabhasawat P, Lee SH (1997) Amniotic membrane transplantation for conjunctival surface reconstruction. Am J Ophthalmol 124(6):765–774

Ulag S, Ilhan E, Sahin A, Karademir Yilmaz B, kalaskar DM, Ekren N et al (2020) 3D printed artificial cornea for corneal stromal transplantation. Eur Polym J [Internet] 133:109744. [cited 2025 Nov 12]. Available from: https://www.sciencedirect.com/science/article/pii/S0014305720301518

Urale PWB, Puckett AM, York A, Arnold D, Schwarzkopf DS (2022) Highly accurate retinotopic maps of the physiological blind spot in human visual cortex. Hum Brain Mapp [Internet] 43(17): 5111–5125. [cited 2025 Dec 12]. Available from: https://pmc.ncbi.nlm.nih.gov/articles/PMC9812231/

Utine AC, Asal M, Guven S (2020) Induced pluripotent stem cells derived lacrimal gland. Investig Ophthalmol Vis Sci 61(7)

Vacalebre M, Frison R, Corsaro C, Neri F, Santoro A, Conoci S et al (2023) Current state of the art and next generation of materials for a customized intraocular lens according to a patient-specific eye power. Polymers (Basel) 15(6):1590

Vahdani K, Siapno DL, Lee JH, Woo KI, Kim YD (2018) Long-term outcomes of acellular dermal allograft as a tarsal substitute in the reconstruction of extensive eyelid defects. J. Craniofac. Surg. [Internet] 29(5):1327. [cited 2025 Nov 15]. Available from: https://journals.lww.com/jcraniofacialsurgery/abstract/2018/07000/long_term_outcomes_of_acellular_dermal_allograft.49.aspx

van Velthoven A, Schaafsma MJS, Bannier-Hélaouët M, Clevers H, LaPointe VLS, Dickman MM (2024) In vivo conjunctival regeneration using an organoid-based therapy: a pre-clinical study. Invest Ophthalmol Vis Sci [Internet] 65(7):5347–5347. [cited 2025 Dec 12]. Available from: https://iovs.arvojournals.org/article.aspx?articleid=2799418

Vastine DW, Stewart WB, Schwab IR (1982) Reconstruction of the periocular mucous membrane by autologous conjunctival transplantation. Ophthalmology 89(9):1072–1081

Wang L, Jeong KJ, Chiang HH, Zurakowski D, Behlau I, Chodosh J et al (2011) Hydroxyapatite for keratoprosthesis biointegration. Invest Ophthalmol Vis Sci 52(10):7392–7399

Wang G, Li H, Long H, Gong X, Hu S, Gong C (2021a) Exosomes derived from mouse adipose-derived mesenchymal stem cells alleviate benzalkonium chloride-induced mouse dry eye model via inhibiting NLRP3 inflammasome. Ophthalmic Res [Internet] 65(1):40–51. [cited 2023 Aug 25]. Available from: https://doi.org/10.1159/000519458

Wang W, Meng H, Yu S, Liu T, Shao Y (2021b) Reconstruction of giant full-thickness lower eyelid defects using a combination of palmaris longus tendon with superiorly based nasolabial skin flap and palatal mucosal graft. J Plast Surg Hand Surg 55(3):147–152

Wang F, Zhang W, Qiao Y, Shi D, Hu L, Cheng J et al (2023) ECM-like adhesive hydrogel for the regeneration of large corneal stromal defects. Adv. Healthc. Mater. [Internet] 12(21):2300192. [cited 2025 Aug 28]. Available from: https://onlinelibrary.wiley.com/doi/abs/10.1002/adhm.202300192

Wang Y, Chen M, Tang Z, Gu P (2026) Cell-based therapies for traumatic optic neuropathy: recent advances, challenges, and perspectives. Neural Regen Res 21(5):1961–1980

Weber AJ, Harman CD, Viswanathan S (2008) Effects of optic nerve injury, glaucoma, and neuroprotection on the survival, structure, and function of ganglion cells in the mammalian retina. J Physiol [Internet] 586(Pt 18):4393–4400. [cited 2025 Dec 12]. Available from: https://pmc.ncbi.nlm.nih.gov/articles/PMC2614024/

Wederell ED, de Iongh RU (2006) Extracellular matrix and integrin signaling in lens development and cataract. Semin Cell Dev Biol 17(6):759–776

Weiss JN, Levy S, Benes SC (2015) Stem Cell Ophthalmology Treatment Study (SCOTS) for retinal and optic nerve diseases: a case report of improvement in relapsing auto-immune optic neuropathy. Neural Regen Res 10(9):1507–1515

Wen D, Wang H, Liu H (2014) Transplantation of the allogeneic conjunctiva and conjunctival extracellular matrix. Bratisl Lek Listy 115(3):136–139

Wenkel H, Rummelt V, Naumann GOH (2000) Long term results after autologous nasal mucosal transplantation in severe mucus deficiency syndromes. Br. J. Ophthalmol. [Internet] 84(3): 279–284. [cited 2025 Dec 12]. Available from: https://bjo.bmj.com/content/84/3/279

Werner L (2021 Nov) Intraocular lenses: overview of designs, materials, and pathophysiologic features. Ophthalmology 128(11):e74–93

West-Mays JA, Korol A (2014) The lens capsule: synthesis, remodeling, and MMPs. In: Saika S, Werner L, Lovicu FJ (eds). Springer Japan, Tokyo, pp 39–57. [cited 2025 Dec 15]. Available from: http://link.springer.com/10.1007/978-4-431-54300-8_3

Wiebe-Ben Zakour KE, Kaya S, Grumm L, Matros J, Hacker MC, Geerling G et al (2024) Modulation of decellularized lacrimal gland hydrogel biodegradation by genipin crosslinking. Invest Ophthalmol Vis Sci 65(5):24

Wilson SE (2020) Corneal wound healing. Exp Eye Res 197:108089

Witt J, Mertsch S, Borrelli M, Dietrich J, Geerling G, Schrader S et al (2018) Decellularised conjunctiva for ocular surface reconstruction. Acta Biomater 67:259–269

Witt J, Borrelli M, Mertsch S, Geerling G, Spaniol K, Schrader S (2019) Evaluation of plastic-compressed collagen for conjunctival repair in a rabbit model. Tissue Eng Part A 25(15–16): 1084–1095

Wu KY, Fujioka JK, Goodyear E, Tran SD (2024a) Polymers and biomaterials for posterior lamella of the eyelid and the lacrimal system. Polymers (Basel) [Internet] 16(3):352. [cited 2025 Nov 15]. Available from: https://pmc.ncbi.nlm.nih.gov/articles/PMC10857064/

Wu KY, Osman R, Kearn N, Kalevar A (2024b) Three-dimensional bioprinting for retinal tissue engineering. Biomimetics (Basel) 9(12):733

Xie J, Gao Q, del Prado ZN, Venkateswaran N, Mousa HM, Salero E et al (2023) Establishment of a bi-layered tissue engineered conjunctiva using a 3D-printed melt electrowritten poly-(-ε-caprolactone) scaffold. Int Ophthalmol [Internet] 43(1):215–232. [cited 2025 Dec 12]. Available from: https://pmc.ncbi.nlm.nih.gov/articles/PMC9902434/

Xu W, Liu K, Li T, Zhang W, Dong Y, Lv J et al (2019) An in situ hydrogel based on carboxymethyl chitosan and sodium alginate dialdehyde for corneal wound healing after alkali burn. J Biomed Mater Res A 107(4):742–754

Yang C, Yang Y, Brennan L, Bouhassira EE, Kantorow M, Cvekl A (2010) Efficient generation of lens progenitor cells and lentoid bodies from human embryonic stem cells in chemically defined conditions. FASEB J 24(9):3274–3283

Yao G, Qi J, Liang J, Shi B, Chen W, Li W et al (2019) Mesenchymal stem cell transplantation alleviates experimental Sjögren's syndrome through IFN-β/IL-27 signaling axis. Theranostics 9(26):8253–8265

Yin J, Singh RB, Al Karmi R, Yung A, Yu M, Dana R (2019) Outcomes of cyanoacrylate tissue adhesive application in corneal thinning and perforation. Cornea 38(6):668–673

Ying GS (2025) The global burden of blindness and visual impairment: progress and challenges. Ophthalmic Epidemiol 26:1–3

Yu C, Zhou Y, Yao S, Wang Z, Ye S, Qi R et al (2025) A facile strategy to restore the optic nerve functionality using an injectable conducting hydrogel. Adv Sci (Weinh) 12(21):e2415601

Chen X, Yuan F. Ologen implantation versus conjunctival autograft transplantation for treatment of pterygium. J Ophthalmol [Internet] 2018;2018:1617520. [cited 2025 Dec 12]. Available from: https://pmc.ncbi.nlm.nih.gov/articles/PMC6142751/

Zhan X, Guo X, Liu R, Hu W, Zhang L, Xiang N (2017) Intervention using a novel biodegradable hollow stent containing polylactic acid-polyprolactone-polyethylene glycol complexes against lacrimal duct obstruction disease. Plos One [Internet] 12(6):e0178679. [cited 2025 Dec 15]. Available from: https://journals.plos.org/plosone/article?id=10.1371/journal.pone.0178679

Zhang MC, Liu X, Jin Y, Jiang DL, Wei XS, Xie HT (2015) Lamellar keratoplasty treatment of fungal corneal ulcers with acellular porcine corneal stroma. Am. J. Transplant. [Internet] 15(4): 1068–1075. [cited 2025 Aug 27]. Available from: https://www.sciencedirect.com/science/article/pii/S1600613522001812

Zhang SY, Zhang M, Li XY, Huang S, Han D, Chang L et al (2024) Development of a novel bioartificial cornea using 3D bioprinting based on electrospun micro nanofibrous decellularized extracellular matrix. Biofabrication 16(2):025039

Zhang Q, Xie B, Ding L, Xiang L, Wang J, Lv J et al (2025a) Amino acid metabolism and photoreceptor degenerative diseases: mechanisms, early diagnosis, and therapeutic prospects. Exp Eye Res 259:110563

Zhang D, Chen T, Liang Q, Feng X, Jiang J, Chen Z et al (2025b) A first-in-human, prospective pilot trial of umbilical cord-derived mesenchymal stem cell eye drops therapy for patients with refractory non-Sjögren's and Sjögren's syndrome dry eye disease. Stem Cell Res Ther [Internet] 16(1):202. [cited 2025 Nov 16]. Available from: https://doi.org/10.1186/s13287-025-04292-8

Zhao L, Jia Y, Zhao C, Liu T, Zhang S, Dong M et al (2019) Ocular surface repair using decellularized porcine conjunctiva [Internet]. Soc Sci Res Netw. [cited 2025 Dec 12]. Rochester. Available from: https://papers.ssrn.com/abstract=3415230

Zheng J, Huang X, Zhang Y, Wang Y, Qin Q, Lin L et al (2019) Short-term results of acellular porcine corneal stroma keratoplasty for herpes simplex keratitis. Xenotransplantation [Internet] 26(4):e12509. [cited 2025 Aug 27]. Available from: https://onlinelibrary.wiley.com/doi/abs/10.1111/xen.12509

Zhong Z, Chen S (2022) Isolation and expansion of primary Conjunctival Stem Cells (CjSCs) from human and rabbit tissues. Bio-protocol [Internet] 12(24) [cited 2025 Dec 12]. Available from: https://bio-protocol.org/en/bpdetail?id=4569&type=0

Zhong Z, Deng X, Wang P, Yu C, Kiratitanaporn W, Wu X et al (2021) Rapid bioprinting of conjunctival stem cell micro-constructs for subconjunctival ocular injection. Biomaterials [Internet] 267:120462. [cited 2025 Dec 12]. Available from: https://www.sciencedirect.com/science/article/pii/S0142961220307080

Zhou J, Peng SW, Wang YY, Zheng SB, Wang Y, Chen GQ (2010) The use of poly (3-hydroxybutyrate-co-3-hydroxyhexanoate) scaffolds for tarsal repair in eyelid reconstruction in the rat. Biomaterials 31(29):7512–7518

Zhou H, Lu Q, Guo Q, Chae J, Fan X, Elisseeff JH et al (2014) Vitrified collagen-based conjunctival equivalent for ocular surface reconstruction. Biomaterials 35(26):7398–7406

Zhou KJ, Li YN, Huang FR, Wang QM, Yu AY (2016) In vivo observation of lens regeneration in rat using ultra-long scan depth optical coherence tomography. Invest Ophthalmol Vis Sci 57(15):6615–6623

Zhou J, Ding Y, Zhang Y, Zheng D, Yan L, Guo M et al (2023) Exosomes from bone marrow-derived mesenchymal stem cells facilitate corneal wound healing via regulating the p44/42 MAPK pathway. Graefes Arch Clin Exp Ophthalmol [Internet] 261(3):723–734. [cited 2023 Aug 25]. Available from: https://doi.org/10.1007/s00417-022-05956-4

Chapter 15
Three-Dimensional Engineered Platforms for Disease Modeling

Thi Thai Thanh Hoang, David H. Ramos-Rodriguez, and J. Kent Leach

Abstract Three-dimensional (3D) platforms, especially microphysiological systems (MPS), have become transformative tools for modeling human diseases with greater physiological relevance than traditional 2D cultures. Moreover, MPS technologies are being developed to complement animal models, accelerating translational success while mitigating ethical concerns. In this chapter, we summarize recent advances in the development of MPS for modeling muscle disorders, bone diseases, cartilage degeneration, gut physiology and microbiome interactions, and skin pathologies, as well as their applications in drug screening. These platforms integrate engineered hydrogels, microfluidic systems, organoids, and mechanical or biochemical cues to recapitulate native tissue architecture, cellular heterogeneity, immune interactions, and multicellular crosstalk. Finally, we discuss future directions for applying MPS in aging and age-related disease research, personalized medicine, and biomarker discovery.

Keywords Microphysiological system · Bone · Cartilage · Muscle · Skin · Gut

Abbreviations

3D	Three-dimensional
3D CAD	Three-dimensional computer-aided design
AC	Astrocyte
ALS	Amyotrophic lateral sclerosis
BBB	Blood-brain barrier
BDNF	Brain-derived neurotrophic factor

T. T. T. Hoang · D. H. Ramos-Rodriguez
Department of Orthopaedic Surgery, UC Davis Health, Sacramento, CA, USA

J. K. Leach (✉)
Department of Orthopaedic Surgery, UC Davis Health, Sacramento, CA, USA

Department of Biomedical Engineering, University of California, Davis, CA, USA
e-mail: jkleach@ucdavis.edu

Y. M. Elçin (ed.), *Biofabrication in Regenerative Medicine*, Stem Cell Biology and Regenerative Medicine 1519, https://doi.org/10.1007/978-3-032-30294-6_15

BMAC	Bone marrow aspirate concentrate
BM-MSCs	Bone marrow-derived mesenchymal stem cells
ChAT	Choline acetyltransferase
CKD	Chronic kidney disease
CMC	Chondrometabolic cartilage
CM	Conditioned medium
Col I/IV	Collagen I and collagen IV
COPD	Chronic obstructive pulmonary disease
CORR	CRISPR-corrected isogenic controls
DEJ	Dermal-epidermal junction
DMEM	Dulbecco's Modified Eagle Medium
DMD	Duchenne muscular dystrophy
DTT	Dithiothreitol
ECM	Extracellular matrix
ESCs	Embryonic stem cells
EVs	Extracellular vesicles
FN	Fibronectin
GDF15	Growth differentiation factor 15
GDNF	Glial cell-derived neurotrophic factor
GelMA	Methacrylated gelatin
HB9	Homeobox HB9
HAMA	Methacrylated hyaluronic acid
hASCs	Human adipose tissue-derived stem cells
hMMTs	Human skeletal muscle microtissues
hMSCs	Human mesenchymal stromal cells
HSPC	Hematopoietic stem and progenitor cell
HUVECs	Human umbilical vein endothelial cells
IBD	Inflammatory bowel disease
IFN-γ	Interferon-gamma
IGF-1	Insulin-like growth factor 1
IO	Intestinal organoids
iPSC	Induced pluripotent stem cell
Islet1	Islet LIM homeobox 1
Jag-1	Jagged 1
LN	Laminin
LPS	Lipopolysaccharide
MACS	Magnetic-activated cell sorting
MAP 2	Microtubule-associated protein 2
MM	Multiple myeloma
MN	Motor neuron
MPCs	Myogenic progenitor cells
MPS	Microphysiological systems
MRF4	Myogenic regulatory factor 4
MTJ	Myotendinous junction

MyoD	Myogenic differentiation 1
NAMs	New approach methodologies
NMDs	Neuromuscular diseases
NMJ	Neuromuscular junction
NSAIDs	Non-steroidal anti-inflammatory drugs
OA	Osteoarthritis
OBs	Osteoblasts
OoC	Organ-on-a-chip
PDMS	Polydimethylsiloxane
PEG-4MAL	Maleimide-functionalized poly(ethylene glycol)
PEGASO	Personalisation of induced pluripotent stem cell–based body-on-chips for in vitro testing of therapeutic agents against brain disorders
PIV	Particle image velocimetry
RT-PCR	Reverse transcription polymerase chain reaction
SAA	Sarcomeric α-actinin
SCFAs	Short-chain fatty acids
SoCE	Skin-on-chip equivalent
SV2	Synaptic vesicle glycoprotein 2A
TEER	Trans-epithelial electrical resistance
TNF-α	Tumor necrosis factor-alpha
TUBB3	tubulin β3
TUJ1	βIII-tubulin antibody
WAPs	White adipocyte progenitor cells
YFP	Yellow fluorescent protein

15.1 Introduction

Animal studies remain the gold standard for understanding disease mechanisms and testing therapeutics. However, ethical concerns and the need to reduce animal use have driven scientists to seek alternative approaches. Moreover, the high failure rate in translating successful animal results to clinical outcomes reflects fundamental species differences in molecular, cellular, and immune responses, even in immune-deficient or semi-humanized models (Van Norman 2019; Ingber 2022). Therefore, there is an urgent need for new approach methodologies (NAMs) to accelerate translational research.

To bridge fundamental research and clinical application, advanced in vitro platforms that more closely mimic human tissues and disease states are essential. These models should more accurately emulate human physiology and yield intervention outcomes in a significantly shorter timeframe. They should also possess scalable screening capacity and accuracy (Holtze et al. 2021; Leung et al. 2022). Microphysiological systems (MPS) address these requirements by offering precise spatial and temporal control for studying biological processes at molecular, cellular, tissue, and organ levels under dynamic culture. These systems enable investigations into physiological and pathological mechanisms as well as the effects of mechanical, electrical, and biochemical stimuli. By incorporating patient-derived cells, MPS also facilitate the development of personalized therapeutic strategies (Roth and Berlin 2021), advancing both in vitro and in vivo studies toward more predictive and human-relevant outcomes.

Herein, we highlight the recent development of MPS systems for disease modeling of musculoskeletal tissues and related systems, such as the skin and gut. The musculoskeletal system consists of muscles, bones, tendons, ligaments, cartilage, and menisci, which work together to provide structural support, stability, protection of internal organs, and locomotion. Many musculoskeletal diseases cause pain and inflammation, leading to systemic effects and significant disability. Based on their causes, these diseases can be classified as immunological disorders (e.g., rheumatoid arthritis, spondyloarthropathies), genetic disorders (e.g., Duchenne muscular dystrophy, osteogenesis imperfecta), or conditional disorders (e.g., osteoarthritis, osteoporosis, tendinitis, traumatic injuries, sarcopenia, and cachexia) associated with aging, as well as social, behavioral, and environmental factors (Li et al. 2025; Song et al. 2025). These conditions often lack effective curative interventions and are exacerbated by aging and obesity (Li et al. 2025). Therefore, there is an urgent need to accelerate the development of interventions for these incurable diseases. The skin serves as a protective barrier for the musculoskeletal system and plays essential roles in force transmission, temperature regulation, and vitamin D synthesis, which supports bone health. Its elasticity enables the full range of joint motion. Consequently, skin disorders can also adversely affect musculoskeletal health. In addition to the skin, the gut is an important organ influencing musculoskeletal health. Growing evidence has underscored the significance of the gut-musculoskeletal axis, including the "gut-muscle axis" and "gut–bone axis," in maintaining systemic homeostasis. The composition of the intestinal microbiota is dynamic and changes with age (Ozkan et al. 2024). Age-related alterations often disturb microbial balance, increasing opportunistic pathogens while reducing beneficial probiotic species. Dysbiosis of the gut microbiota can influence energy metabolism, immune and endocrine regulation, and the production of bioactive metabolites, thereby impairing musculoskeletal integrity. These insights have motivated researchers to develop MPSs that model individual organs and organ crosstalk that influence musculoskeletal tissue development, function, and repair.

15.2 Three-Dimensional Platform in Modeling Muscle Diseases

15.2.1 Three-Dimensional Platform in Modeling Cachexia

Cachexia is a complex and multifactorial syndrome that extends beyond simple weight loss. It involves a systemic inflammatory response, metabolic disturbances, and alterations in immune function. In addition to muscle wasting, cachexia often leads to adipose tissue depletion, weakness, fatigue, and diminished quality of life.

This condition is commonly seen in patients with advanced stages of chronic diseases, including cancer, heart failure, chronic obstructive pulmonary disease (COPD), and chronic kidney disease (CKD). Cachexia affects up to 70% of cancer patients and accounts for approximately 22% of cancer-related deaths (Ni and Zhang 2020). The mechanisms underlying cachexia are not fully understood but involve a combination of factors such as tumor-derived factors, cytokine dysregulation, metabolic abnormalities, and nutritional deficiencies. Effective management of cachexia requires a multidisciplinary approach that addresses both the underlying disease and the associated symptoms, focusing on strategies to preserve muscle mass, improve nutritional status, and enhance the overall quality of life (Ni and Zhang 2020). Despite the serious effects of cachexia, there are still no approved drugs for its treatment, creating an urgent need to accelerate research. In this context, methodological approaches for drug testing play a crucial role.

The use of patient-derived tumor organoids is a promising tool to study cancer-induced cachexia. Pancreatic tumor organoids, for example, have been developed to study pancreatic cancer-induced cachexia. These organoids closely mimic the characteristics of the primary tumor and exhibit typical features of malignancy. Importantly, they express several genes characteristic of cachexia, including IL-6, tumor necrosis factor-alpha (TNF-α), and growth differentiation factor 15 (GDF15) (Vaes et al. 2020). Using such organoids, researchers can investigate the tumor-derived factors that contribute to the development and progression of the disease. This approach allows for the identification of specific molecular pathways and signaling cascades involved in cachexia induction, providing valuable insights into potential therapeutic targets for combating this syndrome. Additionally, studying cachexia within the context of tumor organoids allows for personalized medicine approaches, as the organoids can be derived from individual patient tumors that reflect the unique molecular characteristics of each patient's disease. Overall, patient-derived tumor organoids represent a powerful tool for advancing our understanding of cachexia and developing targeted therapies to improve patient outcomes.

Cachexia has also been modeled using advances in 3D bioprinting (Xue et al. 2022). Human white adipocyte progenitor cells (WAPs) were encapsulated in a bioink composed of methacrylated gelatin (GelMA) and methacrylated hyaluronic acid (HAMA) for printing (Fig. 15.1a). This bioprinted scaffold successfully supported the differentiation of adipocytes from progenitor cells. Pancreatic cancer cell-conditioned media are introduced to the system to mimic cancer-induced cachexia in vitro. The addition of the conditioned medium stimulates the formation of a vascularized structure within the bioprinted scaffold, as occurs in the tumor microenvironment. This vascularization facilitates nutrient and oxygen exchange, supporting the growth and function of both adipocytes and cancer cells within the system. The effects of cancer-induced cachexia are observed in this model through increased lipolysis, which leads to the breakdown of fat tissue and the accumulation of extracellular matrix (ECM) components. These changes reflect the pathological alterations observed in cachexia patients, providing a valuable platform for studying the mechanisms underlying cancer-associated cachexia and for screening potential therapeutic interventions.

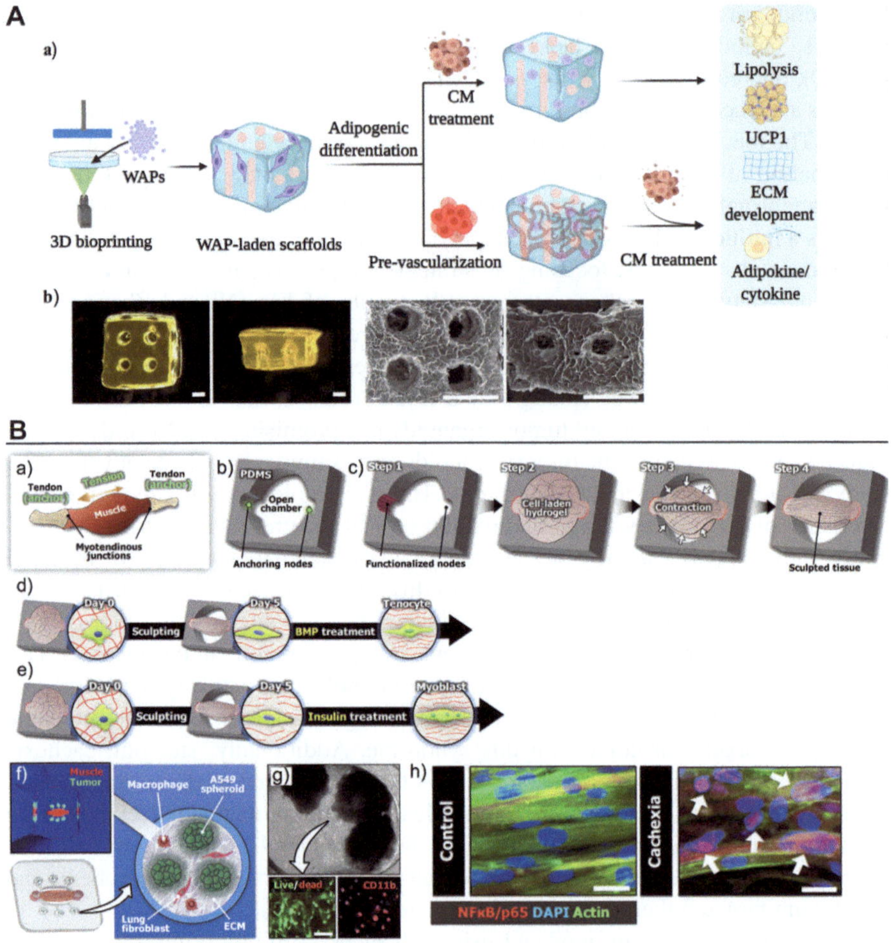

Fig. 15.1 (**A**) Schematic of human white adipocyte progenitor (WAP)-laden scaffold 3D printing: (**a**) Experimental design for adipogenic differentiation, pre-vascularization, and conditioned medium (CM) induction. Adipose remodeling was assessed by lipolysis, browning gene expression, ECM development, and cytokine/adipokine profiles. (**b**) Left: microscopic images of 3D-printed acellular scaffolds (scale bar = 1 mm). Right: SEM images of 3D-printed acellular scaffolds (scale bar = 2 mm). (Reproduced with permission from Xue et al. (2022)). (**B**) Surface-directed sculpting of engineered tissue shape and microphysiological model of human cancer-cachexia: (**a**) muscle anchorage at the myotendinous junctions. (**b**) Sculpting device with tissue chamber and two anchorage nodes (green dots). (**c**) Sequential steps of surface-directed tissue sculpting. (**d**) Tenogenic differentiation scheme. (**e**) Myogenic differentiation scheme. (**f**) Microdevice for modeling cancer cachexia. (**g**) Tumor compartment containing A549 spheroids (top). Lower images show live/dead (green/red, left) and CD11b (red) staining (right). Scale bars, 100 μm. (**h**) p65/NFκB (p65, red) and F-actin (green) staining at day 4. Scale bars represent 50 μm. Arrows indicate p65-stained nuclei of control and cachexia myotubes. (Reproduced with permission from Mondrinos et al. (2021))

Organ-on-a-chip (OoC) models offer a more physiologically relevant environment compared to traditional cell culture models, allowing researchers to better mimic the complex interactions between different cell types and tissues involved in the development and progression of cachexia. For example, the liver OoC has been instrumental in studying liver-specific functions, such as the expression of phase I or phase II metabolizing enzymes. This enables researchers to investigate how alterations in liver metabolism contribute to the metabolic dysregulation observed in cachexia, offering insights into potential therapeutic targets and interventions for this debilitating syndrome (Ni and Zhang 2020). Other OoC models aim to replicate the complex interplay between different organs and tissues involved in the pathogenesis of cachexia, providing a more comprehensive understanding of the syndrome. For instance, skeletal muscles-on-a-chip allow researchers to investigate the mechanisms underlying muscle wasting and dysfunction in cachexia. By culturing primary skeletal muscle cells in a microfluidic system that mimics the mechanical and biochemical cues present in vivo, researchers can study how factors such as inflammation, oxidative stress, and altered signaling pathways contribute to muscle atrophy and weakness in cachexia. Similarly, adipose tissue-on-a-chip enable the study of adipose tissue dysfunction and its role in cachexia-associated weight loss. These models facilitate examination of how changes in adipokine secretion, lipid metabolism, and adipose tissue inflammation contribute to the wasting of adipose tissue and the development of cachexia. Moreover, multi-organ-on-a-chip platforms have been developed to simulate the crosstalk between different organs involved in the disease, such as the liver, skeletal muscle, adipose tissue, and immune system. These models allow researchers to investigate how systemic factors, such as circulating cytokines, hormones, and metabolites, mediate the progression of cachexia and its impact on multiple organ systems. Hence, OoC models offer a powerful tool for studying cachexia by providing a physiologically relevant platform to investigate the complex interactions between different organs and tissues involved in the syndrome. These models have the potential to uncover novel insights into the pathophysiology of cachexia and identify new therapeutic targets for its treatment.

Another cachexia MPS was created based on the mechanical regulation of contractile cells (Mondrinos et al. 2021). This innovative system regulated mechanical forces through its design, which consisted of an open circular cavity in a polydimethylsiloxane (PDMS) mold with notches on either end to allow for cell anchoring (Mondrinos et al. 2021). The backbone of this MPS was functionalized through a two-step process. First, the anchor point surface was introduced to a heterobifunctional cross-linker, which promoted cell adhesion and proliferation. Then, a cell-ECM mixture was deposited into the cavity of the PDMS mold. Over time, areas outside the anchor points experienced poor cell adhesion, leading to detachment of the cell matrix from the rest of the PDMS mold. This resulted in tethering only at the anchor points, creating linearly aligned tissues (Fig. 15.1b) that exhibited enhanced tenogenic and myogenic differentiation of mesenchymal stem cells in the presence of soluble factors. This suggests that the mechanical regulation provided by the MPS promotes specific cell differentiation pathways. The result is an in vitro sculpted tissue with high potential to be used as a small-scale translatable tool for muscle drug screening and disease study. This system offers a novel approach to mimic the mechanical cues present in the native muscle tissue microenvironment, providing a valuable platform for studying the molecular mechanisms underlying cachexia and for developing targeted therapeutic interventions.

15.2.2 Three-Dimensional Platform in Modeling Neuromuscular Disease

Neuromuscular diseases (NMDs) are severe and often life-threatening disorders characterized by impaired communication between nerves and muscles. Amyotrophic lateral sclerosis (ALS) is a prominent and particularly aggressive form of NMD, with most patients surviving only 2–5 years after diagnosis (Osaki et al. 2018). The absence of curative treatments underscores the urgent need for reliable, physiologically relevant drug screening models to improve the likelihood of success in clinical trials.

Developing a 3D human neuromuscular model that recapitulates both healthy and ALS disease states provides a valuable platform for therapeutic discovery (Osaki et al. 2020). Human-induced pluripotent stem cell (iPSC)–derived skeletal muscle cells were encapsulated in a gel mixture composed of porcine type I collagen and 10% Matrigel into one compartment of chip system. This setup promoted the self-assembly of muscle cell bundles anchored at both ends to micropillars within 24 h (Fig. 15.2). The bundles were then cultured in differentiation media to induce myotube formation and maturation. In a separate chamber of the chip, predifferentiated motor neuron spheroids were embedded within type I collagen hydrogels. To sustain co-culture, the compartment housing motor neurons was maintained in commercially sourced human ESC (hESC) medium supplemented with retinoic acid (RA), brain-derived neurotrophic factor (BDNF), and glial cell-derived neurotrophic factor (GDNF). The muscle compartment was supplied with DMEM containing 10% horse serum, recombinant human IGF-1, and penicillin–streptomycin. Cell maturation and phenotype were assessed through both myogenic markers (MyoD, myogenin, sarcomeric α-actinin, MRF4, myosin heavy chain) and motor neurogenic markers (TUJ1, MAP 2, synaptophysin, HB9, Islet1, choline acetyltransferase (ChAT)) using flow cytometry and RT-PCR. This integrated system enabled the study of neuromuscular physiology, disease mechanisms, and potential interventions for ALS in a controlled in vitro environment.

15.2.3 Three-Dimensional Platform in Modeling Duchenne Muscular Dystrophy (DMD)

Duchenne muscular dystrophy (DMD) is a fatal, progressive disorder characterized by muscle degeneration resulting from mutations in the dystrophin gene. While the molecular mechanisms underlying DMD are not yet fully understood, no curative

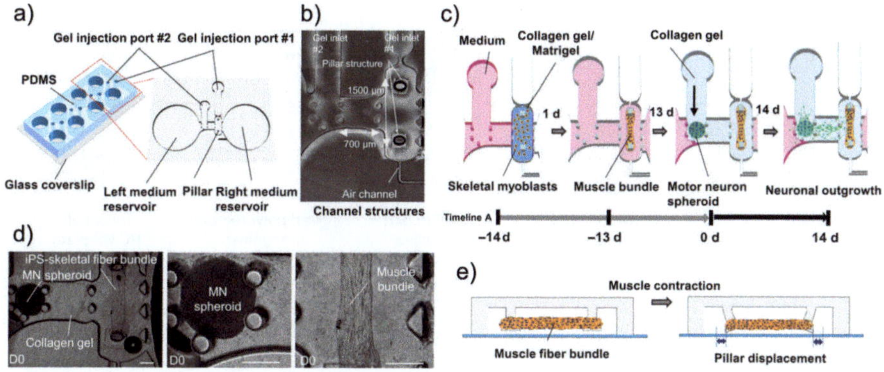

Fig. 15.2 Schematic illustrating device coating and injection of skeletal muscle cells and the motor neuron (MN) spheroid into a neuromuscular junction (NMJ) chip: (**a**) illustration of an NMJ chip and the microfluidic structure in the NMJ chip, (**b**) pillar structures and air channels in an NMJ chip, (**c**) injection of iPSC-derived skeletal myoblasts suspended in a collagen/Matrigel mixture into gel injection port 1. After 13 days, MN spheroids are injected into gel injection port 2 with collagen solution. After gelation, both types of culture medium were added into the two medium reservoirs. (**d**) Image of the spheroid and the muscle strip just after spheroid and gel addition. Scale bars are 200 μm. (**e**) After culturing for the desired period or formation of the NMJ, muscle contraction is produced by electrical, chemical, or optical stimulation, and force is measured by the deflection of the pillar head. Scale bars, 100 μm. (Reproduced from Osaki et al. (2018) with permission)

treatment currently exists. Ebrahimi et al. presented a strategy to generate 3D human skeletal muscle microtissues (hMMTs) from immortalized myoblasts derived from both DMD patients and healthy donors (Ebrahimi et al. 2021). They engineered three-dimensional (3D) human muscle microtissues (hMMTs) using the MyoTACTIC culture device, a custom-designed elastomeric 96-well plate (Fig. 15.3) (Afshar et al. 2020). Each well consists of an elliptical inner chamber containing two vertical posts with micro-posts that serve as tendon-like anchor points to establish uniaxial tension and guide tissue remodeling. The hook feature at the top of each post is a critical design element, as hMMTs detach and migrate off hook-less posts within 2 days of cell seeding. During remodeling, hMMTs consistently migrate to the position just below the slanted tips of the micro-posts, where they remain stably anchored for at least 1 week in differentiation-inducing media. The MyoTACTIC platform was iteratively optimized in terms of post geometry, chamber design, and material stiffness to enable reliable formation of hMMT arrays suitable for high-throughput functional analyses (Afshar et al. 2020). These engineered tissues replicate key pathological features of DMD, including abnormal calcium regulation and the spontaneous emergence of dystrophin-positive revertant fibers in DMD hMMTs carrying an exon 2 duplication, a mutation found in many patients but not previously modeled in vitro 2D culture. Additionally, they demonstrated the utility of this "DMD in a dish" model as a preclinical platform for evaluating candidate therapeutics and elucidating their mechanisms of action.

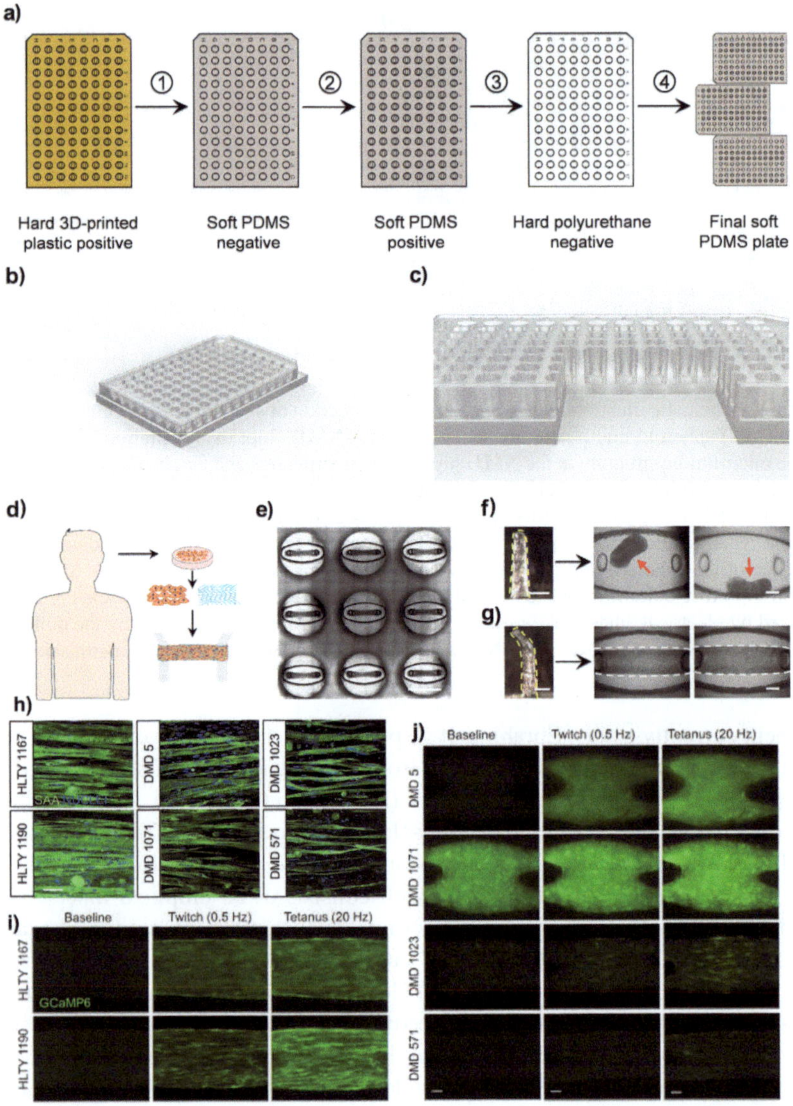

Fig. 15.3 The MyoTACTIC platform for modeling Duchenne muscular dystrophy. (**a**) Production steps for the MyoTACTIC platform: three-dimensional computer-aided design (3D CAD), fabrication of a negative PDMS mold, casting of a positive PDMS replica, and generation of a rigid negative polyurethane mold used to fabricate multiple PDMS plates. (**b**) 3D rendering of the MyoTACTIC 96-well plate design. (**c**) Cross-section of a well showing the location of the micro-posts. (**d**) Schematic overview of human cell isolation and subsequent generation of 3D human skeletal muscle microtissues (hMMTs) in MyoTACTIC. (**e**) Stitched phase-contrast image of nine wells of MyoTACTIC containing remodeled hMMTs 10 days post-seeding. Scale bar, 5 mm. (**f**) Representative image of collapsed hMMTs (red arrows) seeded in wells with hook-less posts. (**g**) Representative image of successfully remodeled hMMTs (white dashed lines) seeded in wells with hook-featured posts. Micro-posts are outlined with yellow dashed lines. Scale bars, 500 μm. (Reproduced with permission from Afshar et al. (2020)). (**h**) Myotube formation from immortalized healthy (HLTY) and DMD myoblast lines after 10 days of differentiation. hMMTs were

Although dystrophin is highly concentrated at the neuromuscular junction (NMJ), its precise role in DMD-related NMJ dysfunction is not fully understood. Paredes-Redondo et al. integrated transcriptomic profiling with patient-derived DMD neuromuscular circuit models and CRISPR-corrected isogenic controls (CORR) within compartmentalized microdevices (Paredes-Redondo et al. 2021). These microdevices (Fig. 15.4a) were based on the design described by Machado et al. (Machado et al. 2019). Each device (5 mm^2) contained a central compartment (myofibers) connected to two outer compartments (motor neuron/astrocyte aggregates, 2 mm long and 500 μm wide) via microchannels that were 500 μm long and 10 μm in width and height, respectively. The channels enabled motor axons to project through while maintaining physical separation of motor neuron and myofiber cell bodies. The small size of the device allowed arrays of multiple devices to be mounted on a single plate, enabling parallel replicates within one culture. The presence of two outer compartments further allowed direct comparison of motor neuron (MN)/astrocyte aggregates with different genotypes projecting axons onto the same myofiber target within a single device. The devices had an open design, as neurons cultured in closed devices exhibited reduced survival. The generated spinal-type MNs expressing photosensor channelrhodopsin-2^{H134R} (ChR2-MNs) and CAG::Gdnf transgenic astrocytes (ACs) from mouse embryonic stem cells (ESCs) in separate cultures, followed by enrichment using magnetic-activated cell sorting (MACS) of both cell types and aggregation into neural spheroids (Fig. 15.4b). On day −2, three spheroids of MACS-enriched ChR2-MNs and ACs were seeded into both outer compartments of the microdevice in a fibrin/Matrigel hydrogel (Fig. 15.4c, d). On day −1, the isogenic pair of human DMD-R3381X and CORR-R3381X MPCs (myogenic progenitor cells) were loaded separately into the central compartment of the microdevice and then sealed in a fibrin/Matrigel hydrogel. The motor axons of mouse ESC–derived ChR2-MNs [labeled by yellow fluorescent protein (YFP)] grew through the microchannels from the outer compartments to the central compartment of the microdevice. On day 0, the initial distribution of ChR2-MN axons was similar in the microdevices containing DMD-R3381X and CORR-R3381X MPCs (Fig. 15.4e), as demonstrated by the quantification of YFP-positive area representing motor axons in the central compartment (Fig. 15.4f). They entrained the light-responsive ChR2-MNs on days 4 and 5 for 1 h/day (Blue light (470 nm)) after initiation of secondary differentiation (Fig. 15.4c). The stimulation increased neural activity and helped promote NMJ formation in vitro. In response to light stimulation, myofiber contraction and relaxation were visualized as velocity vectors with different sizes proportional to the local displacement

Fig. 15.3 (continued) immunostained for sarcomeric α-actinin (SAA, green), and nuclei (Hoechst 33342, blue). Scale bar, 50 μm. (**i–j**) In situ measurement of intracellular calcium transients in healthy (**i**) and DMD (**j**) hMMTs. Shown are representative epi-fluorescence images of baseline and peak GCaMP6 signals (green) in response to low-frequency (0.5 Hz, twitch contractions) and high-frequency (20 Hz, tetanic contractions) electrical stimulation at day 10 of differentiation. Scale bars represent 200 μm. (Reproduced with permission from Ebrahimi et al. (2021))

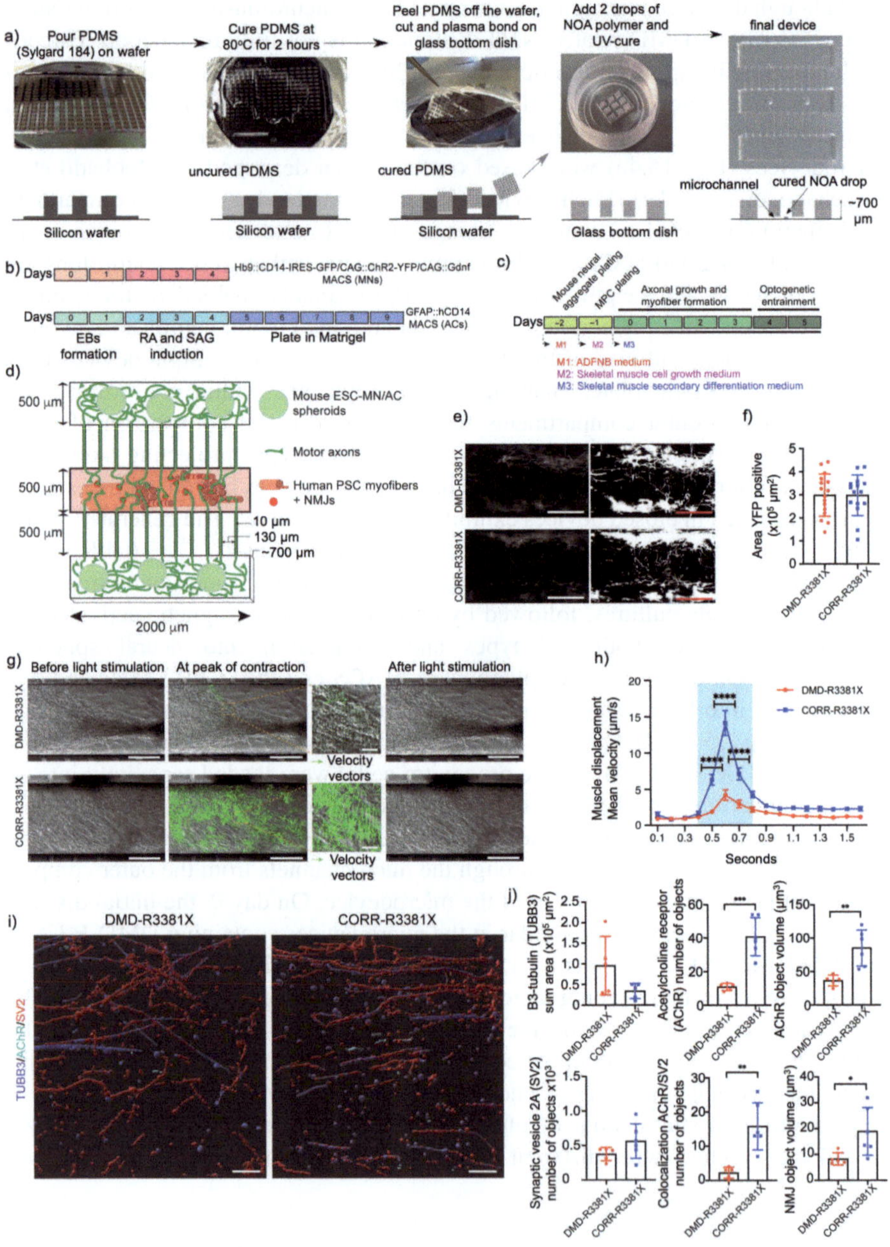

Fig. 15.4 Optogenetic modeling of neuromuscular circuits in Duchenne muscular dystrophy (DMD) with CRISPR-corrected isogenic controls. (**a**) Microdevice fabrication. Reproduced with permission from Machado et al. (2019). (**b**) Timeline of mouse embryonic stem cells–motor neuron (ESC–MN) and ESC–astrocyte (ESC–AC) differentiation. RA, retinoic acid; SAG, smoothened agonist. (**c**) Timeline of the neuromuscular circuit assembly and medium changes in the microdevices. (**d**) Schematic of the microdevice: myogenic progenitor cells (MPCs) in the central compartment, the two outer compartments culturing MN/AC spheroids, motor axons projecting through microchannels and innervating myofibers. (**e**) Representative images of YFP-positive

(Fig. 15.4g). Compared to CORR-R3381X myofibers in microdevices, DMD-R3381X myofibers had fewer and smaller velocity vectors when stimulated by optogenetic activation of ChR2-MNs, indicating limited displacement in DMD conditions. Quantification of myofiber contraction velocity revealed a significantly reduced maximum contraction velocity in DMD-R3381X myofibers (~5 μm/s), compared with CORR-R3381X myofibers (~15 μm/s) (Fig. 15.4h). Immunocytochemistry of the presynaptic marker synaptic vesicle glycoprotein 2A (SV2) and β3-tubulin (TUBB3) in the myofiber compartments did not show statistically significant differences in the number of SV2 objects and motor axon distribution between DMD-R3381X and CORR-R3381X conditions (Fig. 15.4i, j). Quantification of the postsynaptic marker nicotinic AChR revealed a significantly reduced number of AChR objects in DMD-R3381X myofiber compartments compared to CORR-R3381X myofiber compartment. Accordingly, the number of NMJs, as determined by the colocalization of presynaptic and postsynaptic markers (SV2 and AChR), was significantly lower in DMD-R3381X than in CORR-R3381X conditions. We also found that AChR and NMJ volumes were significantly reduced in DMD-R3381X myofiber compartments. Together, these results suggest that NMJ defects in DMD may contribute to compromised myofiber contraction, thereby reflecting muscle weakness in patients with DMD. Their findings revealed reduced NMJ size and impaired optogenetically induced myofiber contractions in DMD models, both of which were restored by inhibiting TGFβ signaling. This rescue effect was confirmed using a high-throughput 96-well human neuromuscular co-culture platform. Mechanistically, the improvement corresponded with the normalization of disrupted gene programs in DMD muscle cells, particularly those governing NMJ formation (e.g., *MUSK*) and axon guidance (e.g., *SLIT2*, *SLIT3*). This study introduced a human-relevant MPS for dissecting NMJ defects in DMD and testing potential therapies, highlighting neuromuscular connectivity enhancement as a promising treatment avenue.

Fig. 15.4 (continued) motor axons in central compartments of microdevices containing MPCs at 0 h and converted grayscale images. Scale bars represent 250 μm. (**f**) Quantification of YFP-positive area in central compartments. $n = 16$. Values are means ± SEM; unpaired *t* test. (**g**) Particle image velocimetry (PIV) analysis in central compartments containing DMD- and CORR-R3381X neuromuscular circuits following optogenetic stimulation on day 5. Representative images show before, during, and after optogenetic stimulation. Green arrows represent velocity vectors. Scale bars represent 250 μm. (**h**) Quantification of mean velocity in the central compartments containing DMD- and CORR-R3381X myofibers in response to optogenetic stimulation. Blue shading indicates the time during optogenetic stimulation. $n = 24$. Values are means ± SEM; two-way ANOVA and Sidak's multiple comparisons test, $^{****}P < 0.0001$. (**i**) Representative 3D reconstruction images of immunocytochemistry of TUBB3 (blue), SV2 (red), and acetylcholine receptor (AChR; turquoise) in central compartments containing innervated DMD- and CORR-R3381X myofibers. Scale bars represent 50 μm. (**j**) Quantification of TUBB3, SV2, AChR, and NMJs in central compartments containing DMD- and CORR-R3381X neuromuscular circuits. $n = 5$ for DMD-R3381X and $n = 6$ for CORR-R3381X. Values are means ± SD; unpaired *t* test, $^{*}P < 0.05$, $^{**}P < 0.01$, and $^{***}P < 0.001$. (Reproduced with permission from Paredes-Redondo et al. (2021))

15.3 Three-Dimensional Platform in Modeling Tendon-Related Disease

Muscle is directly connected to tendon at a specialized junction that efficiently converts muscular contraction into controlled skeletal movement. Damage to this junction, often caused by traumatic injury, compromises mechanical load distribution, resulting in reduced mobility and diminished quality of life. Such injuries are common in high-impact athletic activities and can also occur from habitual overuse, particularly in older adults.

Volpi et al. developed an automated, microfluidics-assisted, hydrogel-based wet-spinning technique for the biofabrication of biomimetic engineered myotendinous junctions (Volpi et al. 2024). They used 3D printing wet-spinning technique combined with programmable syringe pumps to rapidly switch m-ink (muscle bioink) and t-ink (tendon bioink). By fine-tuning the wet-spinning parameters, they obtained biomimetic, highly compartmentalized scaffolds that promoted anisotropic alignment of both muscle and tendon precursor cells (Fig. 15.5).

15.4 Three-Dimensional Platform in Modeling Bone Diseases

Osteoporosis, a silent disease of the twenty-first century (Wei et al. 2025), is characterized by loss of bone mass, deterioration of bone microarchitecture, and increased risk of fractures (Duan et al. 2025), which leads to compromised bone regeneration (von Rüden and Augat 2016). Its prevalence rises annually in parallel with the growing older population. Osteoporosis-related fractures are associated with mortality rates of approximately 9% in women and 24% in men within one year after the fracture (Li et al. 2025). Current treatments for osteoporosis rely on long-term medication, with no definitive cure available. This highlights the urgent need for ongoing drug discovery and development. Advanced methodological approaches for drug testing are critically needed to accelerate the drug testing process and increase high possibility of clinical success. Organoids are self-organized three-dimensional structures derived from pluripotent or tissue-specific progenitor cells that recapitulate key aspects of native tissue architecture and function. Bone organoids have been developed as physiologically relevant models that mimic native tissue development and remodeling, providing powerful platforms for studying disease mechanisms, drug screening, and regenerative therapies (Zhao et al. 2024).

Lee et al. developed a bone-on-a-chip by co-culturing osteoblasts, osteocytes, and osteoclasts in an extracellular matrix environment that can represent normal bone, osteopenia, and osteoporotic conditions (Lee et al. 2024). In this system, the microarchitecture is carefully engineered using PDMS microfabrication to create adjacent vascular and bone compartments separated by micro-scale pillars, allowing

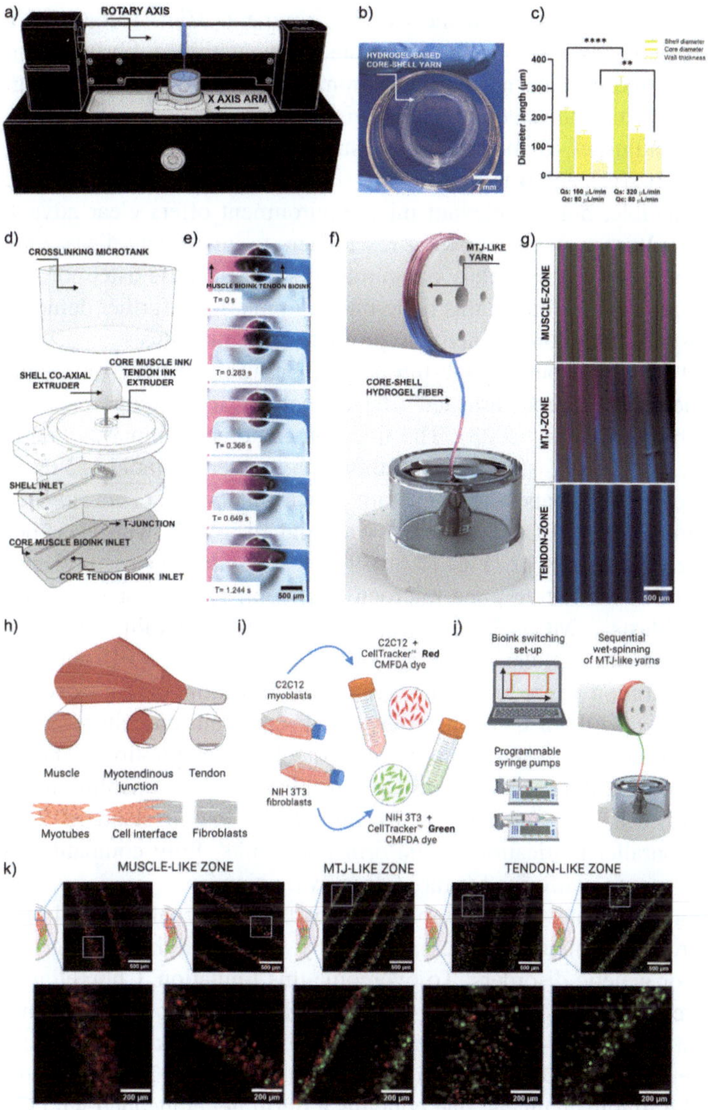

Fig. 15.5 The biofabrication of myotendinous junction (MTJ)-like scaffolds: (**a**) Rotatory microfluidic-assisted 3D printer for the wet-spinning of hydrogel core–shell bundles. (**b**) Macroscopic image of a core–shell hydrogel bundle. Shell composition: 3% (w/v) alginate, core composition: 1.4% (w/v) fibrinogen +0.2% (w/v) alginate. (**c**) Fiber diameter, core diameter, and shell thickness for the selected shell flow rate (Q_s) and core flow rate (Q_c). (**d**) Design of the microfluidic head used to fabricate MTJ-like yarns. The core ink channels are equipped with a T-junction to guarantee the sequential delivery of muscle-like ink (m-ink) and tendon-like ink (t-ink). (**e**) Time-lapse optical images of the T-junction during the sequential delivery of m-ink and t-ink. (**f**) Schematic of the microfluidic-assisted wet-spinning process of MTJ-like yarns. (**g**) Fluorescence images of core–shell fibers with graded core composition to generate three different scaffold regions: muscle, MTJ, and tendon. $n = 5$; significant differences: $^{*}p < 0.05$, $^{**}p < 0.01$, $^{***}p < 0.001$, and $^{****}p < 0.0001$. Schematics of the wet-spinning process for the biofabrication of multicellular myotendinous junction (MTJ)-like scaffolds. (**h**) Native anatomy of the muscle-

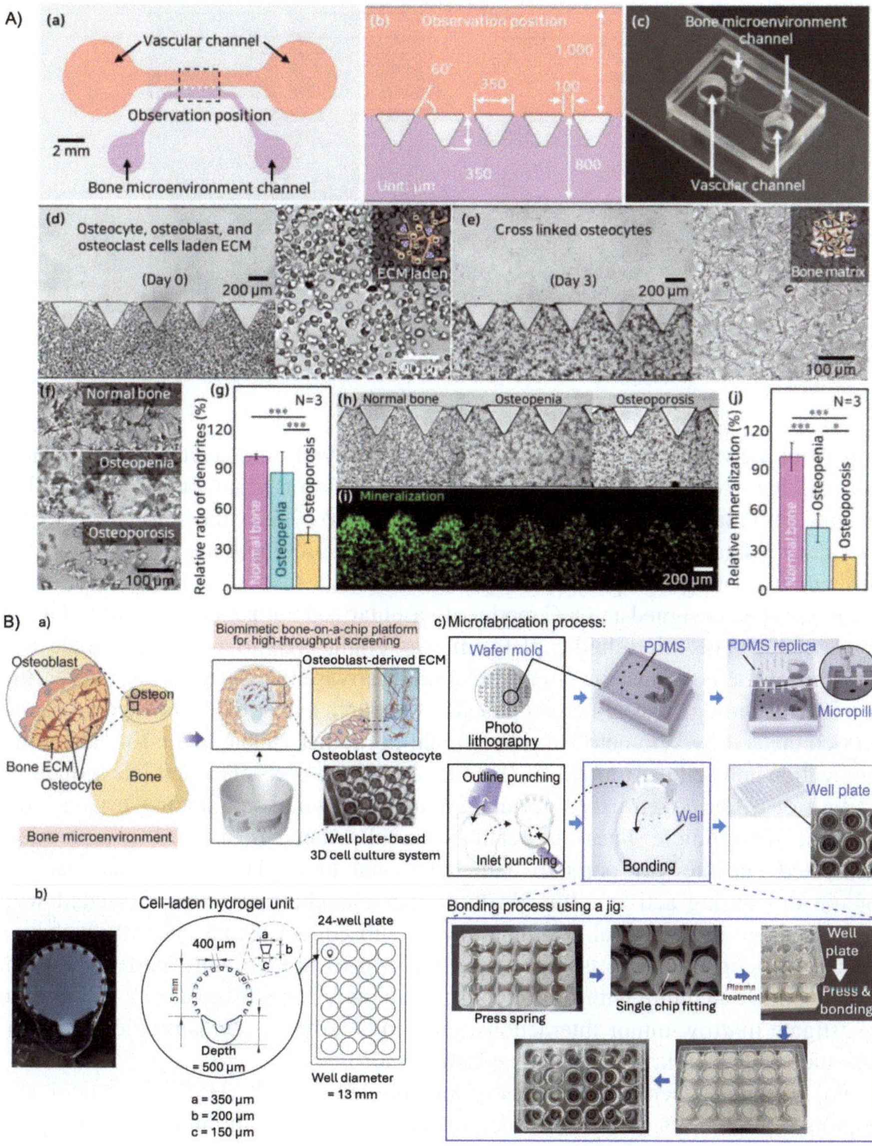

Fig. 15.6 (**A**) A bone-on-a-chip co-culturing osteoblasts, osteocytes, and osteoclasts. (**a**) Top view; (**b**) detailed dimensions; and (**c**) optical image of the bone-on-a-chip. (**d**) Three types of bone cells in fibrin gel (cell laden ECM) on day 0. (**e**) Bone microenvironment on day 3. (**f**) Images of bone microenvironment under normal, osteopenia, and osteoporotic conditions. (**g**) Relative ratio of dendrites in these conditions. (**h**) Bone microenvironment of each bone conditions; and (**i**) calcein fluorescence staining. (**j**) Difference in mineralization level. (*$p < 0.05$, **$p < 0.01$, ***$p < 0.001$). Reused with permission from Lee et al. (2024). (**B**) A high-throughput biomimetic bone-on-a-chip platform. (**a**) 3D osteon niche in vivo and the configurational mimicking of bone in the bone-on-a-chip platform. (**b**) Design of bone-on-a-chip unit integrated in a single well within a 24-well plate. (**c**) The overall fabrication process of the bone-on-a-chip. (Reused with permission from (Paek et al. 2023))

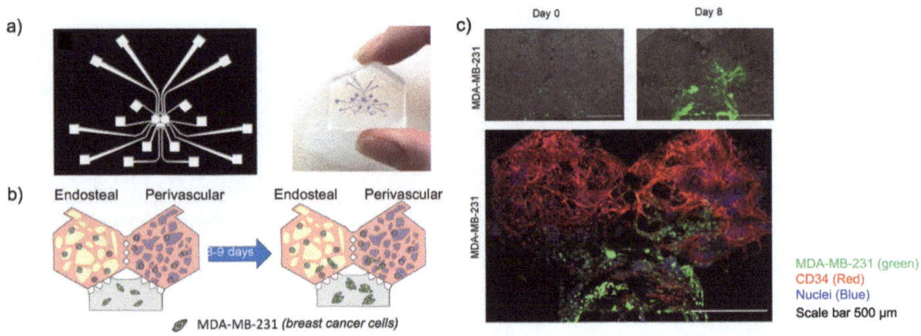

Fig. 15.7 An organ-on-a-chip recreating the bone marrow's endosteal and perivascular niches. (Reused with permission from Glaser et al. (2022))

cells from individuals with Shwachman–Diamond syndrome, the chip recapitulated hallmark hematopoietic defects and uncovered a previously unreported abnormality in neutrophil maturation. As a human-specific in vitro system, the bone marrow chip provides a valuable alternative to animal models for probing bone marrow dysfunction and evaluating therapeutic strategies.

Glaser et al. designed an OoC model of vascularized human bone marrow (Glaser et al. 2022). The microfluidic platform was engineered to mimic the scale and function of the bone marrow's endosteal and perivascular niches while preserving its essential biological role-hematopoiesis. It features two adjacent hexagonal chambers connected by symmetrical bidirectional ports that enable niche-to-niche communication and cellular trafficking (Fig. 15.7a). These ports also facilitate sequential loading of a fibrinogen-based gel containing cells while minimizing leakage into adjacent microfluidic lines. Beneath these chambers is a third compartment connected via one-way ports to both hexagonal units. This lower chamber can remain dry during active culture in the upper chambers and can be seeded with tissue at later experimental stages, allowing subsequent media and cell exchange through the connecting ports. The model reproduces in vivo bone marrow function and supports co-culture with cancer cells in the lower compartment (Fig. 15.7b, c) to investigate marrow-tumor interactions, enabling studies of hematologic malignancies such as leukemia and myelodysplastic syndromes.

To investigate hematopoietic stem and progenitor cell (HSPC) behavior and responses to pathological stimuli such as radiation, a high-throughput, multi-niche human bone marrow-on-a-chip was developed in a 96-well plate format (Fig. 15.8a) (Nelson et al. 2021). The device enables parallel experiments for modeling bone marrow physiology, pathology, and therapeutic testing, with each plate containing eight independent devices. Each device comprises five channels: one central gel channel, two media channels, and two outer gel channels. The channel height was set to 150 μm, and the communication pores between the gel channels were narrowed to 50 μm in width. The number of communication pores was limited to reduce media leakage from the central channel during osteogenesis. The design incorporates a

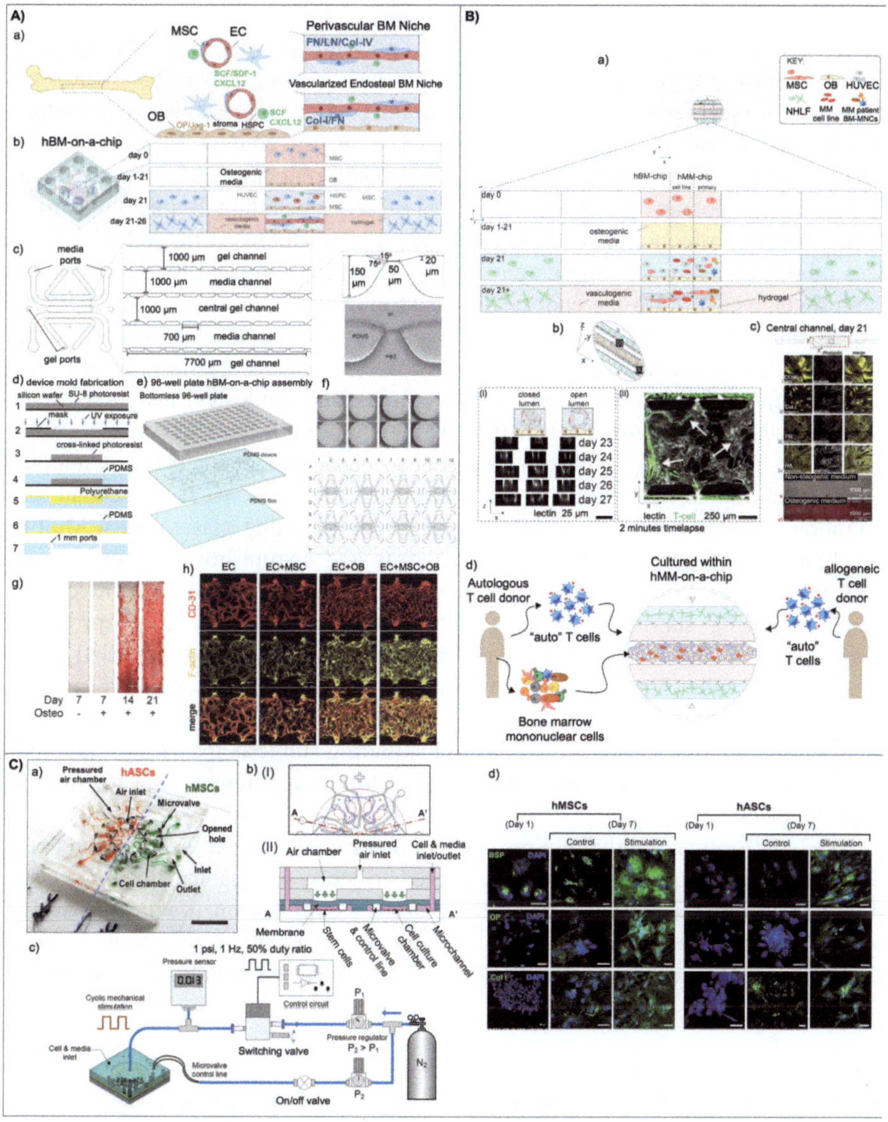

(**A**) Multi-niche human bone marrow-on-a-chip in a 96-well plate format. (**a**) Central perivascular (without osteoblasts, OBs) and vascularized endosteal niches (with OBs). MSC = mesenchymal or marrow stromal cells, including pericytes; OB = osteoblasts and mineralized bone-like tissue layer; other components of the BM stroma, including CXCL12-abundant reticular (CAR) cells, mature hematopoietic cells, and adipocytes. FN = fibronectin; LN = laminin; Col I and IV = collagen I and collagen IV; OP = osteopontin; Jag-1 = Jagged 1. (**b**) Five-channel PDMS device: MSCs differentiated 21 days to form an endosteal layer, followed by HUVEC/MSC/HSPC seeding for 5-day vasculogenesis. (**c–f**) Device design, mold fabrication, and 3D plate assembly. (**g**) Alizarin red staining of differentiated MSCs (day 21) within the central channel. (**h**) CD31 (red) and F-actin (yellow) staining showing vasculogenesis. Reused and permission from Nelson et al. (2021). (**B**) Multi-niche human bone marrow-on-a-chip (hMM-on-a-chip) incorporating multiple myeloma (MM) to study CAR-T cell interactions. (**a, b**) Top view of a single device over the culture period.

human MSC-derived endosteal surface overlaid with a 3D microvascular hydrogel network representing the central marrow and perivascular niches. The human bone marrow-on-a-chip recapitulates both the vascularized endosteal niche (with osteoblasts and mineralized bone-like tissue) and the central perivascular niche (without osteoblasts) found in long bone cavities. The niches contain MSCs (including pericytes), stromal cells such as CXCL12-abundant reticular cells, adipocytes, and mature hematopoietic cells, along with ECM proteins including fibronectin, laminin, collagens I/IV, osteopontin, and Jagged 1. The 5-channel PDMS microfluidic device was fabricated using soft lithography. MSCs were differentiated for 21 days in the central channel to form the endosteal layer, followed by the seeding of HUVECs, MSCs, and HSPCs. Over 5 days, vasculogenesis occurred, establishing the human bone marrow-on-a-chip.

This human bone marrow-on-a-chip contains only endosteal and perivascular stromal cells. Next, Ghoshal et al. extended the multi-niche human bone marrow on-a-chip by incorporating multiple myeloma to study the interactions of adoptive CAR-T cell therapies (Ghoshal et al. 2025). Multiple myeloma is the second most common hematological cancer, affecting antibody-secreting plasma cells. Multiple myeloma cells accumulate in the bone marrow and disrupt normal hematopoiesis and immune function. Multiple myeloma cells interact with bone marrow components, receiving survival signals, growth factors, and chemotherapy protection (Ghoshal et al. 2025). The human multiple myeloma-on-a-chip was used to test therapeutic T cells (Fig. 15.8b). Both healthy and patient T cells caused measurable target myeloma cytotoxicity. Importantly, several key memory T cell subpopulations were preserved after prolonged culture. This finding suggests the device can model effector cell durability in vivo and aid in developing a potential cure for multiple myeloma.

OoC platforms not only help researchers investigate biochemical cues and cell–cell interactions but can also be engineered to study mechanical loading. Using microfabrication technology, Park et al. created a chip equipped with microvalves and microscale culture chambers, separated from an air-pressure chamber (Fig. 15.8c) (Park et al. 2012). This design supported the simultaneous culture of

(continued) (**b**) Rotated view showing the five channels of a single hMM-on-a-chip device, with immature versus mature lumens (white arrows: perfused cells). (**c**) Endosteal and MSC markers: (i) CD90, (ii) type I collagen, (iii) fibronectin, and (iv) hyaluronan. Scale bars represent 100 μm. Alizarin red staining of devices cultured with (v) non-osteogenic and (vi) osteogenic media. (**d**) Experimental schematic showing the primary cell sources used to culture the hMM-on-a-chip devices. Graft-versus-host effects of CAR-T cells within the hMM-on-a-chip microenvironment. (Reused with permission from Ghoshal et al. (2025)). (**C**) The mechanical stimulation microchip comprised of a cover, an air chamber, looped microvalves, and 12 cell culture chambers. (**a**) The microchip consists of a cover, an air chamber, looped microvalves, and 12 paired cell culture chambers sharing a common inlet/outlet channel. hMSCs and hASCs were individually loaded into opposite halves of the chip. Scale bar = 1 cm. (**b**) Schematic top (I) and cross-sectional (II) views of the device designed for simultaneous dual-stem-cell culture and cyclic pneumatic stimulation. (**c**) Experimental setup for mechanical stimulation using a nitrogen-pressurized air chamber. (**d**) Osteogenic markers (BSP, OP, Col I—green) and nuclei—blue—after 1 and 7 days. Scale bar represents 100 μm. (Reused with permission from Park et al. (2012))

two different stem cell types (e.g., human bone marrow-derived mesenchymal stem cells (hMSCs) and adipose tissues-derived stem cells (hASCs)) in dedicated chambers, while dynamic compressive forces were applied evenly to each. The device delivered dynamic hydraulic compression at 1 Hz and 1 psi, which enhanced the production of osteogenic matrix proteins bone sialoprotein, osteopontin, and type I collagen, as well as integrin markers CD11b and CD31 in both stem cell types. In hMSCs, stimulation resulted in strong alkaline phosphatase activity and positive Alizarin Red staining, whereas hASCs did not exhibit a notable increase in these staining results under the same conditions. Mechanical stimulation upregulated β1 integrin and osteogenic gene expression in both hMSCs and hASCs. Overall, both stem cell types demonstrated increased osteogenic gene expression compared with their non-stimulated controls.

Recently, scientists have recognized that crosstalk between the kidney and bone (Duan et al. 2025), the gut and bone (Wei et al. 2025), and other bone–organ axes (Deng et al. 2024) plays a crucial role in understanding and modulating osteoporosis. This underscores the importance of OoC systems that enable studies of inter-organ communication using human-derived cells.

15.4.1 Three-Dimensional Platform in Modeling Cartilage Diseases

Two major cartilage-related diseases include osteoarthritis (OA) and rheumatoid arthritis (RA). OA is characterized by progressive deterioration of articular cartilage, osteophyte formation, degeneration of ligaments, synovial inflammation, meniscus degradation, and hypertrophy of the joint capsule (Nogueira-Recalde et al. 2025). The pathophysiology of OA is multifactorial, involving a complex interplay of mechanical, biochemical, and genetic factors that ultimately damage joint structures, causing pain and functional impairment. OA can develop from cartilage degradation due to overuse, injury, or long-term load-bearing, as well as from prolonged inactivity. OA often results in reduced mobility, leading to loss of independence and increased frailty in affected individuals (Nogueira-Recalde et al. 2025). Osteoarthritis (OA) is the most common degenerative joint disease, with a prevalence of approximately 5%, whereas rheumatoid arthritis (RA) is the most common autoimmune-mediated joint disease, affecting 0.5–1% of the population (Damerau et al. 2025). Like OA, RA is characterized by cartilage degradation, but it is also driven by systemic autoimmune inflammation that targets synovial joints. RA pathogenesis involves aberrant immune activation, with infiltration of T cells, B cells, and macrophages into the synovium, leading to synovial hyperplasia (pannus formation), overproduction of pro-inflammatory cytokines (e.g., TNF-α, IL-1β, IL-6), and activation of osteoclasts. This chronic inflammatory process not only erodes cartilage and bone but can also cause extra-articular manifestations, including cardiovascular, pulmonary, and ocular complications. Without timely treatment, RA can result in irreversible joint deformities, severe pain, and long-term disability. Despite detailed insights into the pathogenesis of OA and RA, current treatments primarily focus on symptom management rather than disease modification. Recommended clinical approaches include moderate exercise, physiotherapy, and, in advanced cases, surgical joint replacement. However, no pharmacological agents effectively cure OA or RA. Analgesics and non-steroidal anti-inflammatory drugs (NSAIDs) are prescribed to reduce pain and inflammation but do not reverse joint degeneration (Richard et al. 2023; Latourte et al. 2020). This underscores the urgent need for disease-modifying interventions for OA (Latourte et al. 2020). Achieving this goal requires physiologically relevant disease models that can accelerate the discovery and evaluation of novel pharmacological therapies.

Abnormally high shear stress often reflects irregular joint loading, such as when surface articulation is impaired following injury or due to excess body weight. In contrast, shear stress is one of the earliest mechanical forces to decline in individuals who are bedridden, making it a critical parameter for understanding cartilage behavior under both healthy and pathological states. To focus on mechanical theories, Damerau et al. designed a MPS with an incubation chamber tailored to deliver controlled shear stress, eliciting biological responses that closely mimic those seen during natural joint motion in vivo (Damerau et al. 2025). This platform also enables standardized in vitro culture of human chondrometabolic cartilage (CMC) tissues. Their results show that physiological shear stress shields CMCs from TNF-α-driven arthritic changes, replicating in vivo protective effects. Conversely, when mechanical loading is pathologically reduced, TNF exposure tips the balance toward matrix breakdown rather than synthesis, a shift that can be reversed by JAK pathway inhibition.

Focusing on the role of mechanical loading, Contentin et al. developed an in vitro model to mimic mechanically induced OA (Contentin et al. 2025). In their approach, hyaline-like cartilage constructs were generated by culturing equine bone marrow–derived mesenchymal stem cells (BM-MSCs) within collagen sponges in chondrogenic medium for 21 days. They first confirmed that the BM-MSC–derived chondrocytes expressed the mechanosensitive ion channel TRPV4, a key regulator in cartilage mechanobiology. Engineered cartilage was then subjected to cyclic compression (2.5 kPa at 0.2 Hz for 15 min every 36 h over 3 days) to assess mechanosensitivity and the impact of mechanical stimulation on cell viability, ECM composition, and cartilage marker expression. The study revealed that excessive mechanical stress can trigger osteoarthritic-like responses, including the production of inflammatory mediators, downregulation of ECM components, and increased expression of matrix-degrading enzymes. These findings highlight the importance of controlled loading in cartilage models and demonstrate the potential of MSC-derived cartilage constructs to recapitulate degenerative features of OA. This platform offers a promising foundation for studying OA pathogenesis and developing therapeutic strategies to preserve cartilage integrity, slow disease progression, and enhance repair outcomes.

Schneider et al. developed on-chip 3D potency assay with the objective to improve prediction of clinical outcomes better than 2D culture (Schneider et al.

2025; Schneider et al. 2022). This in vitro system would dramatically improve current efforts of therapeutic cell product development and translation. Regulatory agencies require potency metrics, i.e., quantitative measures of biologic function, as a measure of quality and consistency for product scale-up and release. However, the identification of such potency metrics and surrogates is particularly challenging for cellular products because of unclear and/or pleiotropic mechanisms. Most potency assays evaluate cell surface markers, secreted products, or transcriptomics for cells cultured on 2D supports that have lacked success in translation. An on-chip microfluidic potency assay for MSCs that maintains cells in 3D, within a soft hydrogel and exposed to fluid flow, recapitulated secretory activities of human MSCs implanted in immunodeficient mice better than conventional 2D assays. Microfluidic chips of PDMS were cast in an aluminum macro-mold with steel wire and bonded with oxygen plasma to glass slides. Small steel wires ($d = 0.02$ in) were used to create the fluidic channels, which were later removed to form open conduits. The assembled device was sealed with a thin PDMS layer and connected to tubing for media perfusion. Inside the chip, a soft hydrogel was formed from 20 kDa four-arm maleimide-functionalized poly(ethylene-glycol) (PEG-4MAL) mixed with adhesive peptides (such as RGD) and biodegradable cross-linkers VPM (GCRDVPMSMRGGDRCG) and nondegradable dithiothreitol (DTT). Human MSCs were encapsulated within the hydrogel, which provided a supportive 3D environment (Fig. 15.9). Secretome analysis of the media at day 4 revealed clear distinction between microfluidic and 2D cultures in response to defined inflammatory stimuli (interferon-gamma (IFN-γ)). This result emphasized the influence of culture system on hMSC secretory response and the need for precisely defined culture environments in potency assay development (Schneider et al. 2022).

Building on the same chip design, the system was next applied to test patient-derived bone marrow aspirate concentrate (BMAC) for predicting clinical outcomes (Fig. 15.9) (Schneider et al. 2025). Cells were entrapped in RGD-functionalized PEG-4MAL and cross-linked with both degradable and nondegradable linkers. This matrix was engineered to encapsulate BMAC cells, maintain their function, and permit perfusion, though it was not intended to fully mimic the joint cavity environment. The hydrogel containing BMAC cells was loaded into the chip and continuously perfused at 1.0 μL/min. Schneider et al. proposed that BMAC secretory activity might depend on the composition and viscosity of surrounding media, similar to synovial fluid (Schneider et al. 2025). To test this, they formulated an osteoarthritis-simulated synovial fluid (simSF) based on analyte profiles of patient samples. They mimic included abundant proteins and glycosaminoglycans to match viscosity and shear-thinning properties of OA synovial fluid. BMAC cultures were tested under both basal control media and simSF conditions, in parallel 2D and on-chip 3D platforms. Analysis across 22 donors after 24 h showed that the strongest differences came from the culture platform itself, with clear clustering between 2D and 3D conditions.

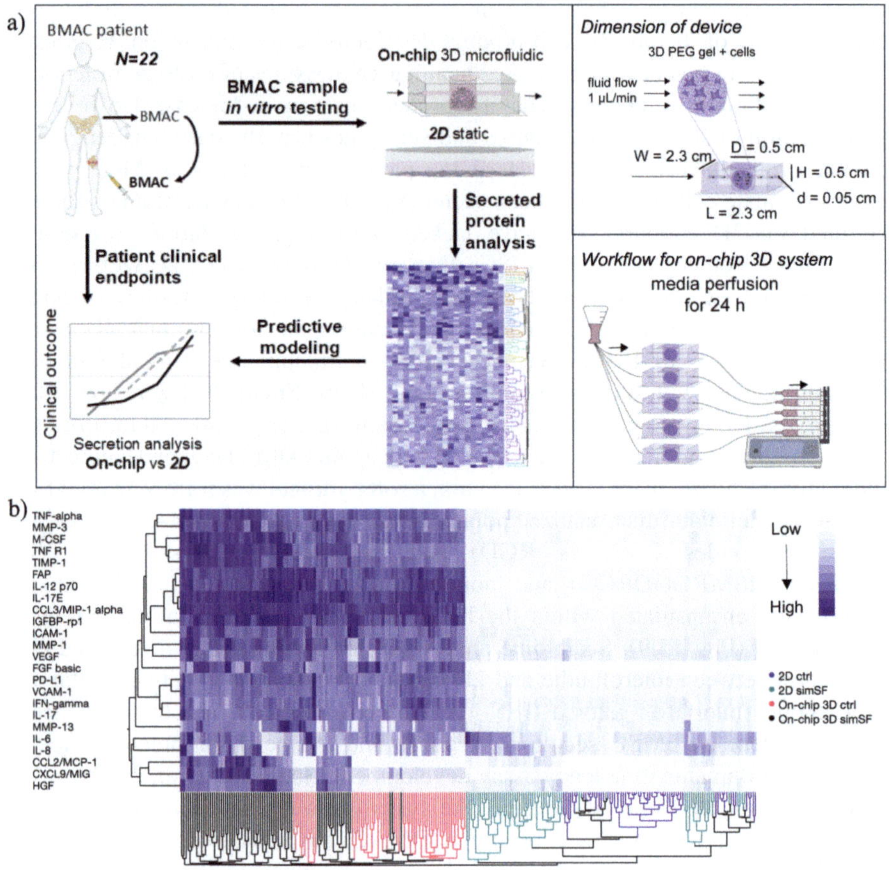

Fig. 15.9 A microfluidic on-chip 3D system. (**a**) Patient-derived bone marrow aspirate concentrate (BMAC) samples ($N = 22$) were evaluated for secretion profiles in on-chip 3D microfluidic and conventional 2D culture models. (**b**) Hierarchical clustering heatmap showing secretion profiles; darker purple indicates higher secretion levels. (Reused with permission from Schneider et al. (2025))

15.5 Three-Dimensional Models for Gut Function and Pathologies

The human gut and its microbiome present a unique challenge in disease modeling that is normally overlooked in other tissues and organs. Approximately 100 trillion microorganisms contribute to gut function and homeostasis, with a diversity that ranges from 160 to 1000 unique species (Ozkan et al. 2024). Characterizing each interaction and combination using conventional models is unrealistic, which, in addition to our lack of understanding of how microbiome species and their population numbers influence disease progression, hinders our conventional reductionist models. Aside from traditional rodent models that recapitulate monogastric

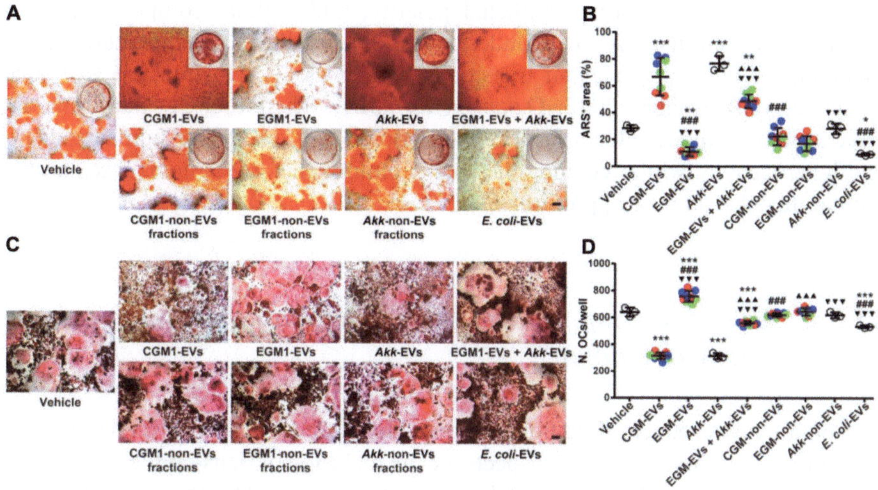

Fig. 15.10 Children's gut microbiota (CGM)-EVs and Akk-EVs can be transported to the mouse bone tissues and directly promote osteogenesis and inhibit osteoclastogenesis in vitro. (**a**) Representative ARS staining images of BMSCs receiving different treatments and (**b**) quantitation of the percentage of ARS-positive areas per well in a 48-well plate. Scale bar represents 100 μm; $n = 3$ per group. (**c**) Representative TRAP staining images of RAW264.7 cells receiving different treatments and (**d**) quantification of osteoclast number per well in a 48-well plate. Scale bar represents 100 μm; $n = 3$ per group. Data are presented as mean ± SD. For panels **B** and **D**, red dots indicate CGM1-EVs or EGM1-EVs, green dots indicate CGM2-EVs or EGM2-EVs, and blue dots indicate CGM3-EVs or EGM3-EVs. (Reused with permission from Liu et al. (2021))

physiology and can mimic some aspects of human gut immune response (Liu et al. 2021), larger animal models and non-mammalian models are suitable for study of specific aspects of gut function. Animal models such as pig and zebrafish are commonly used for their capacity to mimic human physiology and for enabling the study of gut motility, respectively (Lu et al. 2021).

Currently, animal models remain indispensable for studying systemic response, disease progression and aging. For example, Liu et al. showed that transplanting child gut microbiota, compared to elderly microbiota, preserves bone mass and strength in ovariectomized mice. They identified *Akkermansia muciniphila* as a key taxon and demonstrated that bacterial extracellular vesicles from child microbiota or *A. muciniphila* enhance osteogenesis revealing an EV-mediated gut–bone communication axis (Liu et al. 2021) (Fig. 15.10). However, these models are limited by species-specific differences in bile-acid pools, mucin glycosylation, immune repertoires, microbiota composition, epithelial turnover rates, and pathogen tropism.

Moreover, 2D models exhibit a simplified gut response due to flattened epithelium, lack of anatomical features such as crypt–villus, and loss of oxygen/mucus gradients and barrier defects that drive disease progression. In contrast, 3D human systems, organoids, assembloids, or gut-on-chip platforms aim to mimic one or more organ components including epithelial polarity, multicellular composition, ECM mechanics, or luminal flow/shear under physiologic gradients. These features enable modeling of clinically relevant transitions with readouts that translate to human tissue response (Ingber 2022; Ozkan et al. 2024). Therefore, 3D platforms and patient-derived models fill a critical translational gap to capture human genetics and heterogeneity while retaining the spatial biology that 2D systems lose and that animal models can only approximate.

15.5.1 Gut-on-a-Chip Models to Study Disease Progression and Microbiome

Gut-on-a-chip introduces fluid flow and pressure needed for mechanical deformation that controls gut function. Other aspects are the inclusion of trans-epithelial electrical resistance (TEER), pH changes, and metabolite tracking. The former is especially relevant to studying metabolite production and consumption in the human gut microbiome. Conditions such as inflammatory bowel disease (IBD), Crohn's disease, and ulcerative colitis have a key immunological component that is characterized by an abnormal and prolonged response. To model this aspect of gut pathologies, monocyte-derived macrophages and human intestinal organoids can be integrated into a microfluidic platform to exhibit an inflammatory phenotype and demonstrate feasibility to recreate the transcriptomic signature of IBD and utility as a drug screening tool to assess dose-dependent responses (Beaurivage et al. 2020).

Recent efforts to understand the effect of microbiome health on other organs have led to the development of a multi-organ-on-a-chip system that combines a human microbial-crosstalk gut component with a liver-on-a-chip component to model the bidirectional connection between gut and liver (Lucchetti et al. 2024). These platforms facilitate the introduction of bacterial culture into multi-organ models to study metabolite production under specific tissue conditions. 3D-printed models represent another approach for modeling intestinal pathologies that can replicate composition and architecture of the gut microenvironment. In some cases, researchers have studied the dynamics of co-cultured bacteria populations under anaerobic and aerobic conditions using an intestine-on-a-chip platform (Jalili-Firoozinezhad et al. 2019). A growing area of research is the use of 3D intestinal organoids (IO) and their extracellular vesicles (IOEVs) to study disease progression. Wang et al. showed that IOEVs can repair epithelial injury early enough to slow the cascade that drives mucosal inflammation into systemic bone loss. In a dextran sulfate sodium-induced model of IBD with osteoporosis, combined IO + IOEV therapy restored barrier integrity by upregulating ZO-1 and Ki67 and downregulating Caspase-3. This response dampened pro-inflammatory cytokines and improved bone metrics such as BMD, BV/TV, consistent with miRNA-mediated signals carried by IOEVs that both resolve gut inflammation and rebalance osteoclast/osteoblast activity (Wang et al. 2025).

Another important aspect of the human gut that cannot be studied using animal models is the innate immune response relevant to infection or inflammatory bowel disease. Tsuruta et al. created human iPSC-derived intestinal organoids populated with iPSC-derived monocytes that mature into tissue-resident macrophages dispersed throughout the epithelium. These macrophage-competent organoids phagocytose *Escherichia coli* bioparticles and produced stronger cytokine responses to LPS, yielding a tractable human model to study epithelial–innate immune crosstalk in gut inflammation (Tsuruta et al. 2022).

15.5.2 Modeling Gut Crosstalk and Metabolomics

Gut-derived metabolites including short-chain fatty acids (SCFAs), bile acid derivatives, and tryptophan metabolites signal through endocrine pathways to coordinate homeostasis across major organs. In the context of musculoskeletal health, several studies have demonstrated the role of gut microbiome on intraosseous tumor growth (Pal et al. 2022), bone metabolism (Ko et al. 2023), and osteoarthritis (Wu et al. 2024). Yet much of our mechanistic insight comes from reductionist 2D in vitro assays exposing cells to single microbial metabolites. Recent work has shifted toward in vivo interrogation of the gut–bone axis, employing germ-free or antibiotic-perturbed models, fecal microbiota transfer, or probiotic supplementation (Ballerini et al. 2025; Liu et al. 2022) (Fig. 15.11). These studies typically test defined probiotic taxa (e.g., *Lactobacillus*, *Clostridium*) and their metabolites to assess effects on systemic inflammation, osteoblast/osteoclast activity, and disease progression (Zhang et al. 2024; Chen et al. 2024).

Beyond MSK health, gut-organ crosstalk is a system-level regulator of physiology, with microbial metabolites and endocrine signaling hepatic, cardiovascular, renal, and neuroimmune function. For example, Fanizza et al. introduced PEGASO (PErsonalisation of induced pluripotent stem cell-based body-on-chips for in vitro testinG of therApeutic agentS against brain disOrders), a multi-organ microphysiological system that models the gut–liver–immune–BBB–brain axis to study drug absorption, metabolism, and neuroactivity within a single recirculating platform (Fanizza et al. 2025). Each compartment was populated with human iPSC-derived cell types, intestinal, hepatic, endothelial, astrocytic, and neuronal, each of them maintained under physiologically relevant flow and oxygenation. As proof of concept, donepezil, an acetylcholinesterase inhibitor used for Alzheimer's disease, was administered through the gut module, and investigators tracked its passage and bioactivity across the connected tissues. The drug successfully traversed the gut, underwent partial hepatic metabolism, crossed the BBB, and reached the brain module, where it significantly reduced acetylcholinesterase activity without compromising cell viability or barrier integrity. This study highlights the potential of integrated organ-on-chip systems to replicate pharmacokinetic and pharmacodynamic processes along the gut–brain axis.

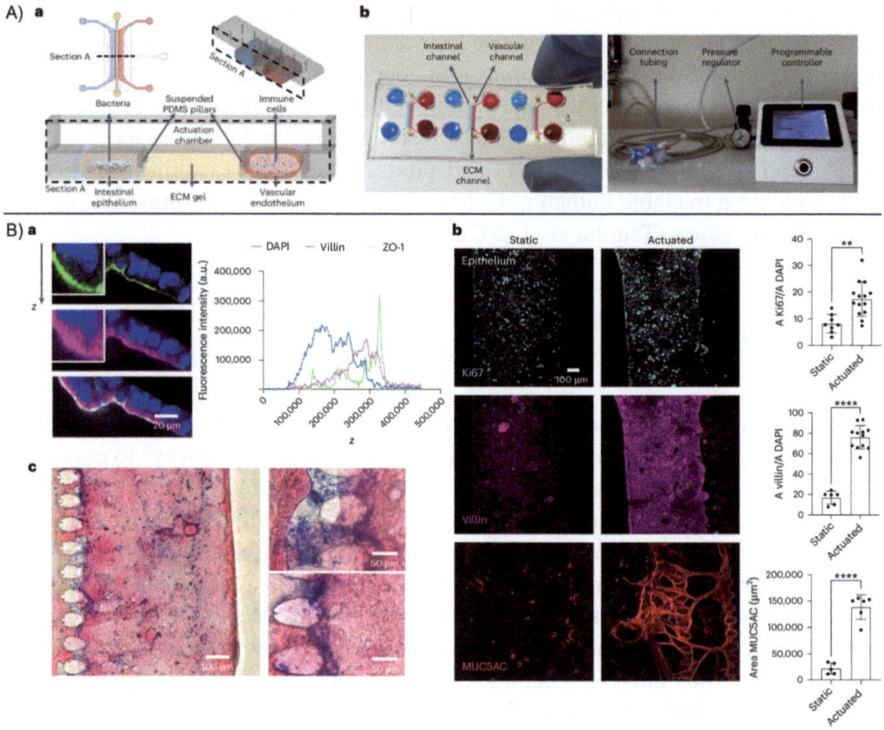

Fig. 15.11 (**A**) The hiPSCs-derived gut-on-a-chip model. (**a**) The device is composed of an intestinal epithelial channel and a vascular endothelial channel separated by ECM-like gel; a superimposed actuation chamber allows cyclic controlled deformation of the construct that mimics peristalsis. PDMS, polydimethylsiloxane. (**b**) Microfluidic device and external actuation system. (**B**) A gut-on-a-chip incorporating human fecal samples and peristalsis. (**a**) Representative confocal image and corresponding z-axis fluorescence intensity profiles showing nuclei (DAPI, blue), apical tight junction protein ZO-1 (green), and villin (magenta), illustrating epithelial cell polarization. (**b**) Fluorescence microscopy images and quantification of Ki67 (cyan), villin (magenta), and MUC5AC (red) expression in static and mechanically actuated chips. Mechanical actuation increased cell proliferation (Ki67; n_static = 8, n_actuated = 14, $P = 0.0013$), epithelial maturation (villin; n_static = 6, n_actuated = 12, $P = 3.3 \times 10^{-9}$), and mucus secretion (MUC5AC; n_static = 5, n_actuated = 6, $P = 2.91 \times 10^{-6}$). Data are mean ± SD; two-tailed unpaired t-test (**$P \leq 0.01$, ****$P \leq 0.0001$). (**c**) Representative histological images ($n = 4$, two independent experiments) showing epithelial cells stained with eosin (magenta) and mucus with Alcian blue (blue). (Reused with permission from Ballerini et al. (2025))

Silva et al. generated human iPSC-derived multilineage organoids in which cardiac mesoderm and gut endoderm co-emerge, enabling paracrine crosstalk during development. This work showed that the presence of gut/endodermal tissue drives more advanced cardiac features, cardiomyocyte expansion, enrichment of atrial/nodal cells, myocardial compaction, and fetal-like functional maturation, providing a tractable model for multi-tissue interactions in organogenesis (Silva et al. 2021).

The future of gut disease modeling is converging on intestinal organoids and gut-on-a-chip platforms to overcome key limitations of current in vitro systems. Progress will depend on improving scalability, reproducibility, and standardization, as well as incorporating vascular, neural, and immune elements to better capture intestinal complexity. Advances in biomaterials and microfabrication will enhance control of biomechanical cues, fluid flow, and nutrient gradients. Integrating patient-derived organoids and microbiome components will further enable precision medicine by supporting individualized drug screening and mechanistic insight into patient-specific disease phenotypes.

15.6 Three-Dimensional Models to Study Skin Diseases

The onset of biomaterials and fabrication techniques has made skin disease models a common tool for researchers and clinicians alike. These models range from simple, co-cultured, collagen-based hydrogels to complex multiphase structures that recapitulate specific aspects of skin anatomy, extracellular environment, and introduce specific physiological elements such as neurons or relevant cytokines. Furthermore, the ready availability of skin cells without the need for surgical intervention has led to the development of models that allow for personalized medicine by using patient cells. Commercially available products such as MelanoDerm, NativeSkin, and ZEVASKYN are highly specialized models that enable studies on skin pigmentation, short-term overall behavior, and dermal-epidermal junction (DEJ) anchoring fibrils, respectively.

However, two critical limitations of in vitro skin models are short lifespan and the lack of an immune system component. The latter is a master regulator of several common conditions, such as psoriasis, vitiligo, atopic dermatitis, and cutaneous lupus. To this end, skin-on-a-chip biomimetic models can recreate the dermal, DEJ, and epidermal layers, complete with a fibroblast and keratinocyte population and build upon traditional human skin equivalent models containing only fibroblasts and keratinocytes (Murphy et al. 2017a; Murphy et al. 2017b). These full-thickness skin-on-a-chip platforms have been used to study skin permeability, toxicity, and diseases related to keratinocyte differentiation (Sriram et al. 2018) (Fig. 15.12). In these cases, the most common approach is to create individual microfluidic devices with monolayer cultures to represent each skin stratum, using porous membranes and an air-liquid interface to enable keratinocyte stratification (Wufuer et al. 2016).

Skin function is deeply connected to microbial balance. Skin dysbiosis is a poorly understood condition that increases the likelihood of chronic inflammatory skin diseases. Moreover, understanding the interplay between gut and skin microbiomes has become a key aspect of modeling the systemic effects of microbial imbalance (Gorini et al. 2025). Unfortunately, the complex microbiome interactions are yet to be translated into in vitro or ex vivo disease models, and most of our understanding comes from traditional animal models (Dokoshi et al. 2024).

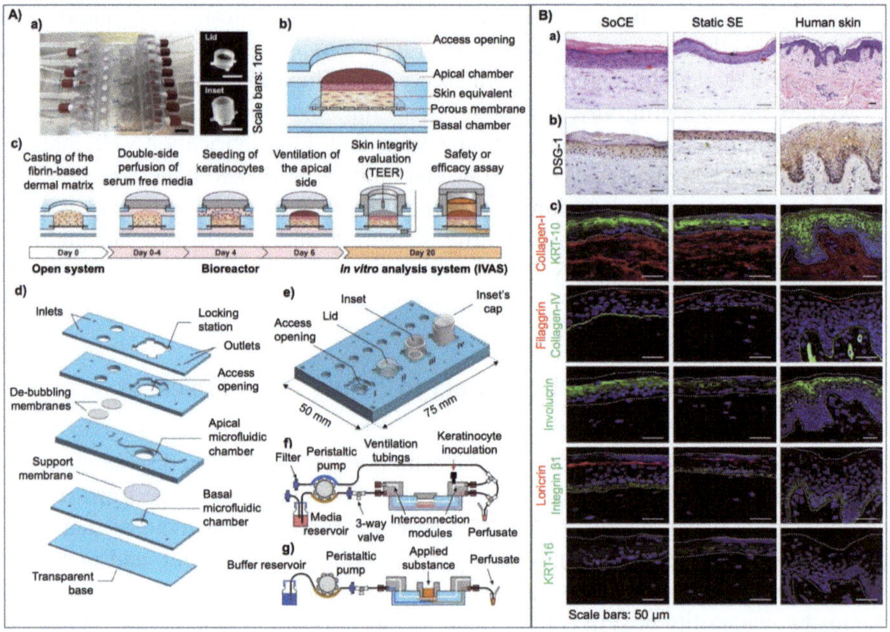

Fig. 15.12 (**A**) Skin-on-chip equivalent (SoCE). (**a**) Photographs of a multi-chamber microfluidic chip in its bioreactor setup, along with a set of interchangeable lids and insets. (**b**) Schematic structure of the full-thickness skin-on-a-chip. (**c**) Timeline of the skin-on-a-chip culture and in vitro assay protocol. (**d**) Detailed overview of one device unit composed of five microstructured layers assembled and thermally bonded together. (**f**) Overview of the four-chamber organ-on-a-chip device. (**g**) Diagram of the experimental setup during a permeation test. (**B**) Epidermal structure and differentiation marker expression in skin-on-chip (SoCE) and static skin equivalents (Static SE) after 2 weeks of air-liquid interface culture, compared with normal human skin. (**a**) Histological images show enhanced epidermal morphogenesis in SoCEs compared with static SEs, characterized by polarized columnar basal keratinocytes (red arrow), prominent keratohyalin granules (black arrow), a thicker viable epidermis, and an orthokeratinized stratum corneum. (**b**) Expression of desmoglein-1 (DSG-1) in differentiated layers. (**c**) Immunofluorescence staining demonstrates expression of keratinocyte differentiation markers KRT-10 (green), filaggrin (red), involucrin (green), and loricrin (red); basement membrane components collagen type IV (green) and integrin-β1 (green); proliferation-associated marker KRT-16 (green); and dermal matrix protein collagen type I (red). Nuclei are stained with DAPI (blue). Dashed lines indicate the surface of the stratum corneum (white) and the dermo-epidermal junction (yellow). Green arrows indicate artifactual separation between the epidermis and dermis. (Reused with permission from Sriram et al. (2018))

Future developments in skin disease modeling will be driven by the integration of advanced 3D skin equivalents, patient-derived organoids, and skin-on-a-chip systems. A major challenge remains the faithful recapitulation of native skin complexity, including innervation, vascular and lymphatic networks, immune populations, and appendages such as hair follicles and sebaceous glands. Incorporating these elements will be essential to accurately model inflammatory disorders, wound healing, fibrosis, and tumor progression. Emerging biomaterial strategies will improve control over mechanical stiffness, ECM composition, and biochemical signaling, enabling more disease-relevant platforms. Advances in microfluidic perfusion will further support studies of dynamic processes such as immune infiltration, angiogenesis, and pathogen colonization. Finally, integrating patient-derived cells with high-throughput omics and genome-editing tools will advance personalized dermatological research and reduce reliance on animal models.

15.7 Conclusion and Future Outlook

In this chapter, we summarized recently reported 3D disease models spanning musculoskeletal, gut, and skin pathologies. These representative systems have been developed by integrating hydrogels, microfluidic devices, mechanical loading, and organoid constructs with diverse cell types. Collectively, these approaches aim to recreate the interactions between the primary tissue-specific cells (musculoskeletal, skin, or gut cells) and surrounding cell populations such as macrophages, vascular cells, and neurons. Through these strategies, they more accurately recapitulate systemic cellular crosstalk, dynamic interactions, and three-dimensional architecture under physiological conditions.

Looking ahead, MPS models offer powerful opportunities for areas of significant societal impact that are difficult to study in vivo, such as aging. They can help elucidate the underlying mechanisms of aging and age-related diseases and identify new therapeutic targets without requiring many years to observe the effects. For drug discovery, MPS platforms support high-throughput screening and more predictive evaluation of efficacy, safety, and mechanisms of action. Although MPS technologies cannot yet fully replace animal models, they can markedly reduce animal use, mitigate ethical issues, and improve the success of drug candidates entering clinical trials. For personalized medicine, MPS can be tailored to individual patients by incorporating patient-derived cells or tissues. By studying how different individuals respond to drugs or disease treatments in these personalized models, researchers can identify factors that influence treatment outcomes and optimize therapeutic strategies for each patient. To understand environmental and lifestyle factors, MPS can be exploited to study the effects of environmental factors, such as pollutants or dietary components, on human health. By exposing these systems to various environmental stimuli, we can identify factors that contribute to disease development or progression. Similarly, lifestyle factors such as exercise or stress can be studied in MPS to understand their impact on human health. For biomarker discovery, MPS can be used to identify biomarkers (indicators of normal or pathological biological processes) that can be used for disease diagnosis, prognosis, or monitoring. By analyzing cellular responses and molecular changes in these systems, researchers can identify novel biomarkers associated with specific diseases or treatment responses, providing valuable diagnostic and prognostic tools for clinicians. Scientists will gain deeper insights into human biology and develop innovative approaches to improve health outcomes by leveraging these advanced technologies.

Acknowledgments TTTH received support from the California Institute for Regenerative Medicine (CIRM) Stem Cell and Gene Therapy Training Grant (# EDUC4–12792). The contents of this publication are solely the responsibility of the authors and do not necessarily represent the official views of CIRM or any other agency of the State of California. JKL also acknowledges financial support from the Lawrence J. Ellison Endowed Chair of Musculoskeletal Research.

Competing Interests The author(s) has no competing interests to declare that are relevant to the content of this manuscript.

References

1. Afshar ME et al (2020) A 96-well culture platform enables longitudinal analyses of engineered human skeletal muscle microtissue strength. Sci Rep 10(1):6918
2. Ballerini M et al (2025) A gut-on-a-chip incorporating human faecal samples and peristalsis predicts responses to immune checkpoint inhibitors for melanoma. Nat. Biomed. Eng. 9(6): 967–984
3. Beaurivage C et al (2020) Development of a human primary gut-on-a-chip to model inflammatory processes. Sci Rep 10(1):21475
4. Chen C et al (2024) Microbial tryptophan metabolites ameliorate ovariectomy-induced bone loss by repairing intestinal AhR-mediated gut-bone signaling pathway. Adv Sci 11(36): 2404545
5. Chou DB et al (2020) On-chip recapitulation of clinical bone marrow toxicities and patient-specific pathophysiology. Nat Biomed Eng 4(4):394–406
6. Contentin R et al (2025) Mechanical stimulation of equine bone marrow mesenchymal stromal cell-derived cartilage-like in vitro model triggers osteoarthritis features. ACS Biomater Sci Eng 11(7):4153–4165
7. Damerau A et al (2025) Microphysiological system-generated physiological shear forces reduce TNF-alpha-mediated cartilage damage in a 3D model of arthritis. Adv Sci (Weinh) 12(7): e2412010
8. Deng AF et al (2024) Bone-organ axes: bidirectional crosstalk. Mil Med Res 11(1):37
9. Dokoshi T et al (2024) Dermal injury drives a skin to gut axis that disrupts the intestinal microbiome and intestinal immune homeostasis in mice. Nat Commun 15(1):3009
10. Duan Y et al (2025) Crosstalk between kidney and bones: new perspective for modulating osteoporosis. Ageing Res Rev 109:102776
11. Ebrahimi M et al (2021) De novo revertant fiber formation and therapy testing in a 3D culture model of Duchenne muscular dystrophy skeletal muscle. Acta Biomater 132:227–244
12. Fanizza F et al (2025) A gut–brain axis on-a-chip platform for drug testing challenged with donepezil. Lab Chip 25(7):1854–1874
13. Ghoshal D et al (2025) Multi-niche human bone marrow on-a-chip for studying the interactions of adoptive CAR-T cell therapies with multiple myeloma. Biomaterials 316:123016
14. Glaser DE et al (2022) Organ-on-a-chip model of vascularized human bone marrow niches. Biomaterials 280:121245
15. Gorini F et al. (2025) The role of microbiota in the pathogenesis of bullous pemphigoid and pemphigus vulgaris: evidence, controversies, and perspectives. Int J Mol Sci 26(13):6076
16. Holtze S et al (2021) Alternative animal models of aging research. Front Mol Biosci 8:660959

17. Ingber DE (2022) Human organs-on-chips for disease modelling, drug development and personalized medicine. Nat Rev Genet 23(8):467–491
18. Jalili-Firoozinezhad S et al (2019) A complex human gut microbiome cultured in an anaerobic intestine-on-a-chip. Nat Biomed Eng 3(7):520–531
19. Ko FC et al (2023) Colon epithelial cell-specific Bmal1 deletion impairs bone formation in mice. Bone 168:116650
20. Latourte A, Kloppenburg M, Richette P (2020) Emerging pharmaceutical therapies for osteoarthritis. Nat Rev Rheumatol 16(12):673–688
21. Lee S et al (2024) Bone-on-a-chip simulating bone metastasis in osteoporosis. Biofabrication 16(4):045025
22. Leung CM et al. (2022) A guide to the organ-on-a-chip. Nat Rev Methods Primers 2(1):33
23. Li X et al (2025) Current cutting-edge omics techniques on musculoskeletal tissues and diseases. Bone Res 13(1):59
24. Liu JH et al (2021) Extracellular vesicles from child gut microbiota enter into bone to preserve bone mass and strength. Adv Sci 8(9):2004831
25. Liu Z et al (2022) Altered gut microbiota and metabolites profile are associated with reduced bone metabolism in ethanol-induced osteoporosis. Cell Prolif 55(7):e13245
26. Lu H et al (2021) Zebrafish model for human gut microbiome-related studies: advantages and limitations. Med Microecol 8:100042
27. Lucchetti M et al (2024) An organ-on-chip platform for simulating drug metabolism along the gut–liver axis. Adv Healthc Mater 13(20):2303943
28. Machado CB et al (2019) In vitro modelling of nerve-muscle connectivity in a compartmentalised tissue culture device. Adv Biosyst 3(7):1800307
29. Mondrinos MJ et al (2021) Surface-directed engineering of tissue anisotropy in microphysiological models of musculoskeletal tissue. Sci Adv 7(11):eabe9446
30. Murphy KC et al (2017a) Engineering fibrin hydrogels to promote the wound healing potential of mesenchymal stem cell spheroids. Acta Biomater 64:176–186
31. Murphy KC et al (2017b) Multifactorial experimental design to optimize the anti-inflammatory and proangiogenic potential of mesenchymal stem cell spheroids. Stem Cells 35(6):1493–1504
32. Nelson MR et al (2021) A multi-niche microvascularized human bone marrow (hBM) on-a-chip elucidates key roles of the endosteal niche in hBM physiology. Biomaterials 270:120683
33. Ni J, Zhang L (2020) Cancer cachexia: definition, staging, and emerging treatments. Cancer Manag Res 12:5597–5605
34. Nogueira-Recalde U et al (2025) Neutralization of acyl CoA binding protein (ACBP) for the experimental treatment of osteoarthritis. Cell Death Differ 32(8):1484–1498
35. Osaki T, Uzel SGM, Kamm RD (2018) Microphysiological 3D model of amyotrophic lateral sclerosis (ALS) from human iPS-derived muscle cells and optogenetic motor neurons. Sci Adv 4(10):eaat5847
36. Osaki T, Uzel SGM, Kamm RD (2020) On-chip 3D neuromuscular model for drug screening and precision medicine in neuromuscular disease. Nat Protoc 15(2):421–449
37. Ozkan A et al (2024) Intestinal organ chips for disease modelling and personalized medicine. Nat Rev Gastroenterol Hepatol 21(11):751–773
38. Paek K et al (2023) A high-throughput biomimetic bone-on-a-chip platform with artificial intelligence-assisted image analysis for osteoporosis drug testing. Bioeng Transl Med 8(1): e10313
39. Pal S et al (2022) The microbiome restrains melanoma bone growth by promoting intestinal NK and Th1 cell homing to bone. J Clin Invest 132(12):e157340
40. Paredes-Redondo A et al (2021) Optogenetic modeling of human neuromuscular circuits in Duchenne muscular dystrophy with CRISPR and pharmacological corrections. Sci Adv 7(37): eabi8787
41. Park SH et al (2012) Chip-based comparison of the osteogenesis of human bone marrow- and adipose tissue-derived mesenchymal stem cells under mechanical stimulation. PLoS One 7(9): e46689

42. Richard MJ, Driban JB, McAlindon TE (2023) Pharmaceutical treatment of osteoarthritis. Osteoarthr Cartil 31(4):458–466
43. Roth A, Berlin M-W (2021) Human microphysiological systems for drug development. Science 373(6561):1304–1306
44. Schneider RS et al (2022) High-throughput on-chip human mesenchymal stromal cell potency prediction. Adv Healthc Mater 11(2):e2101995
45. Schneider RS et al (2025) On-chip 3D potency assay for prediction of clinical outcomes for cell therapy candidates for osteoarthritis. Nat Commun 16(1):4915
46. Silva AC et al (2021) Co-emergence of cardiac and gut tissues promotes cardiomyocyte maturation within human iPSC-derived organoids. Cell Stem Cell 28(12):2137–2152. e6
47. Song C, Yang J, Gu Z (2025) Latest developments of microphysiological systems (MPS) in aging-related and geriatric diseases research: a review. Ageing Res Rev 107:102728
48. Sriram G et al (2018) Full-thickness human skin-on-chip with enhanced epidermal morphogenesis and barrier function. Mater Today 21(4):326–340
49. Tsuruta S et al (2022) Development of human gut organoids with resident tissue macrophages as a model of intestinal immune responses. Cell. Mol. Gastroenterol. Hepatol 14(3):726–729. e5
50. Vaes RDW et al (2020) Generation and initial characterization of novel tumour organoid models to study human pancreatic cancer-induced cachexia. J Cachexia Sarcopenia Muscle 11(6):1509–1524
51. Van Norman GA (2019) Limitations of animal studies for predicting toxicity in clinical trials: is it time to rethink our current approach? JACC Basic Transl Sci 4(7):845–854
52. Volpi M et al (2024) Automated microfluidics-assisted hydrogel-based wet-spinning for the biofabrication of biomimetic engineered myotendinous junction. Adv Healthc Mater 13(32): e2402075
53. von Rüden C, Augat P (2016) Failure of fracture fixation in osteoporotic bone. Injury 47(Suppl 2):S3–s10
54. Wang M et al (2025) Combination therapy using intestinal organoids and their extracellular vesicles for inflammatory bowel disease complicated with osteoporosis. J. Orthop. Trauma 53: 26–36
55. Wei J et al (2025) Gut-bone axis perturbation: Mechanisms and interventions via gut microbiota as a primary driver of osteoporosis. J Orthop Translat 50:373–387
56. Wu M et al (2024) The roles and regulatory mechanisms of TGF-β and BMP signaling in bone and cartilage development, homeostasis and disease. Cell Res 34(2):101–123
57. Wufuer M et al (2016) Skin-on-a-chip model simulating inflammation, edema and drug-based treatment. Sci Rep 6(1):37471
58. Xue W et al (2022) 3D bioprinted white adipose model for in vitro study of cancer-associated cachexia induced adipose tissue remodeling. Biofabrication 14(3):034106
59. Zhang Y-W et al (2024) Targeting the gut microbiota-related metabolites for osteoporosis: the inextricable connection of gut-bone axis. Ageing Res Rev 94:102196
60. Zhao D et al (2024) Bone organoids: recent advances and future challenges. Adv Healthc Mater 13(5):e2302088

Chapter 16
Use of Artificial Intelligence in Biofabrication

Gökçe Uysal, Ayşe Eser Elçin, and Yaşar Murat Elçin

Abstract Artificial intelligence is a central technological component that transforms biofabrication from traditional experimental applications into an engineering field based on high accuracy, predictability, and automation. Machine learning and deep learning algorithms play critical roles in modeling biological processes that are difficult to observe directly, highly variable, and nonlinear, such as bioink rheology, cell behavior, tissue maturation, and printing parameters. These algorithms deliver high performance in tasks such as real-time error detection during printing, filament stability prediction, microstructure topology generation, and mechanical-biological output estimation in terms of process optimization and product quality improvement. Therefore, artificial intelligence has evolved beyond being a technology that merely increases the operational efficiency of biofabrication. It has become a fundamental framework that shapes the future direction of the field, transforming biofabrication into an interdisciplinary, computational, and autonomous biomedical engineering paradigm by modeling process–design–material interactions holistically.

Keywords Biofabrication · Artificial intelligence · Machine learning · Deep learning · Digital twin

---

G. Uysal
Stem Cell Institute, Ankara University, Ankara, Türkiye

A. E. Elçin
Tissue Engineering, Biomaterials and Nanobiotechnology Laboratory, Ankara University, Ankara, Türkiye

Stem Cell Institute, Ankara University, Ankara, Türkiye

Y. M. Elçin (✉)
Tissue Engineering, Biomaterials and Nanobiotechnology Laboratory, Ankara University, Ankara, Türkiye

Department of Chemistry, Faculty of Science, Ankara University, Ankara, Türkiye
e-mail: elcin@ankara.edu.tr

Y. M. Elçin (ed.), *Biofabrication in Regenerative Medicine*, Stem Cell Biology and Regenerative Medicine 1519, https://doi.org/10.1007/978-3-032-30294-6_16

Abbreviations

3D	Three-dimensional
AE	Autoencoder
AI	Artificial intelligence
ANN	Artificial neural networks
BO	Bayesian optimization
CNN	Convolutional neural network
CT	Computed tomography
DL	Deep learning
DT	Digital twin
DNN	Deep neural network
ECM	Extracellular matrix
GAN	Generative adversarial network
GRACE	Generative, adaptive, context-aware 3D printing
GPU	Graphics processing unit
GPR	Gaussian process regression
LSTM	Long short-term memory
ML	Machine learning
MLP	Multilayer Perceptrons
MRI	Magnetic resonance imaging
PCA	Principal component analysis
PET	Positron emission tomography
RNN	Recurrent neural network
RL	Reinforcement learning
RF	Random Forest
SVM	Support vector machine
UV	Ultraviolet
XAI	Explainable artificial intelligence
XGBoost	eXtreme gradient boosting

16.1 Introduction

In the first quarter of the twenty-first century, biofabrication studies underwent a major transformation, shifting from a bioengineering approach involving the production of biological tissues and organ-like systems to a new epistemological ground based on data science, automation, and artificial intelligence(AI)-based methods (Zhou et al. 2025; Chen et al. 2024; Kim et al. 2020).

The essence of biofabrication lies in the controlled assembly of components, such as biopolymers, biomolecules, and living cells, using advanced production technologies to create functional biomimetic structures (Zhou et al. 2025; Mironov et al. 2009). However, this process is inherently highly variable and uncertain, and the heterogeneous data involved, such as cell behavior, material rheology, culture medium conditions, and printing parameters, and their complex nonlinear relationships further complicate the process (Ogunsanya and Desai 2023; Xu et al. 2024). Optimizing these relationships using traditional methods often relies on a trial-and-error approach, making the process costly and time-consuming (Elnemr et al. 2025). At this point, artificial intelligence-based learning systems have begun to transform the information processing and decision-making processes of biofabrication (Zhou et al. 2025). Today, biofabrication processes consist of multilayered stages that generate high-volume and heterogeneous data, including medical imaging, computational tissue design, material characterization, 3D bioprinting, and automation workflows (Bardini and Di Carlo 2024; Allenby and Woodruff 2022; Pavlovich et al. 2016). The inability of statistical methods to process the volume of data at these stages has brought AI technologies to the forefront of biofabrication (Wu et al. 2024). This transition means that biofabrication now uses data as a biomaterial, not just cells, and is defined as "the shift from biological production to digital biosynthesis" (Zhou et al. 2025; Bardini and Di Carlo 2024; Ahmed et al. 2024).

As outlined in Table 16.1, AI algorithms are prominent in the four fundamental stages of biofabrication. This framework represents the fundamental structural transformation that differentiates biofabrication from traditional production technologies. In the manufacturing of living biomaterials, an algorithmic feedback loop is established that enables the system to train and update itself based on its real-time behavior. Throughout the production process, critical parameters such as material viscosity, temperature fluctuations, and cell density are continuously monitored, and these data streams are processed by artificial intelligence algorithms to ensure that the system re-optimizes itself at every deviation. In other words, process parameters are automatically recalibrated whenever an error is detected, allowing production accuracy to be continuously refined. As a result, biofabrication is no longer a static production line but a dynamic, self-updating learning system capable of improving its performance over time.

Table 16.1 Stages of AI algorithm involvement in the biofabrication process

Stage	Function
Data acquisition and preprocessing	Classification and cleaning of high-volume heterogeneous data obtained from cell images, microscopic morphology, sensor signals, and environmental parameters (Chen et al. 2025; Rafieyan et al. 2024; Freeman et al. 2022)
Modeling and simulation	Integration of live tissue behavior, rheological properties, and pressure parameters using statistical or physics-based models (Chen et al. 2024; Ramesh et al. 2024)
Real-time control	Autonomous detection of errors or live cell stress during the bioprinting process and real-time correction of printing parameters by artificial intelligence algorithms (Florczak et al. 2025; Kelly et al. 2025; Matavosian and Bonassar 2025)
Predictive optimization	Generation of optimal design geometries by predicting the mechanical, electrical, or biochemical performance of the bio-structure in advance (Zhou et al. 2025; Rajitha et al. 2024; Barrera et al. 2021)

The role of AI in this context is not limited to technical optimization. These algorithms also change the conceptual representation of the complexity of biological data. Traditional biotechnological approaches typically use deterministic models (Gernaey et al. 2010; Wilkinson 2009). However, AI, by offering a probabilistic and adaptive framework, treats uncertainties in biological systems not as problems but as sources of information. Thus, the behavior of the system is not only predicted but also continuously learned and redefined. This new paradigm is embodied in the concept of "computational biofabrication" proposed by Bardini and Di Carlo, which interprets biofabrication not merely as a production technology but as a process of cognitive mapping of biological data (Bardini and Di Carlo 2024). Accordingly, AI algorithms extract a "digital model of life"; thus, the functioning of biological systems is not merely imitated but can be learned, simulated, and developed.

These developments, as highlighted in Fig. 16.1, have paved the way for biofabrication to move beyond the classical "wet lab" boundaries and transition into the "dry lab" environment. In this digital paradigm, deep learning (DL) models can predict cell behavior without the need for physical experimentation. In a complementary role, generative adversarial networks (GANs) compensate for data

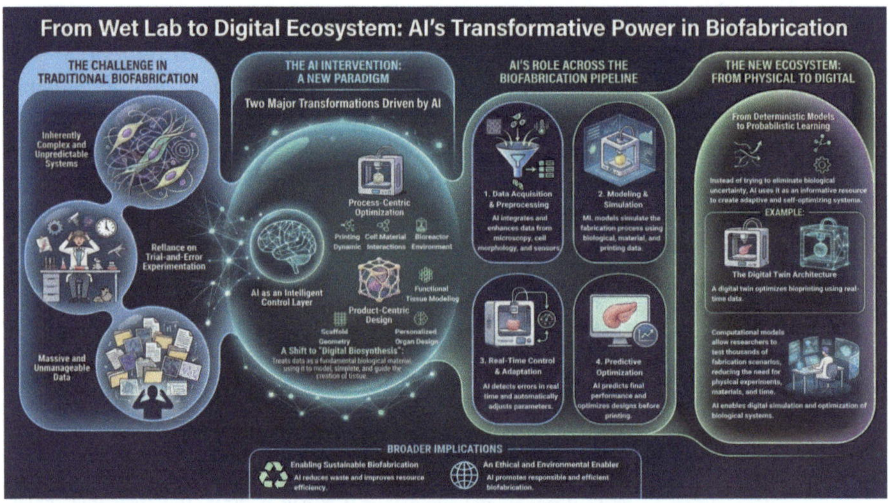

Fig. 16.1 From wet lab to digital ecosystem: AI's transformative role in biofabrication. The figure illustrates how artificial intelligence reshapes the biofabrication landscape by enabling a transition from conventional wet-lab workflows to a digital, data-driven ecosystem. The left panel highlights major challenges in traditional biofabrication, including the inherent complexity of biological systems, reliance on trial-and-error experimentation, and the generation of massive and unmanageable datasets. The central panel presents two major AI-driven transformations: process-centric optimization of printing dynamics, cell–material interactions, and bioreactor environments, and product-centric design of scaffold geometry, functional tissues, and personalized organ constructs. The right panel depicts the emergence of a new ecosystem enabled by probabilistic learning, digital twin architectures, and computational "dry-lab" biofabrication, where AI supports real-time adaptation, predictive optimization, and simulation-driven tissue engineering. Broader implications include sustainable biofabrication strategies and AI's role as an ethical and environmental enabler for future biomedical manufacturing

scarcity by creating synthetic variants of biological images (Baniukiewicz et al. 2019; Osokin et al. 2017). As a result, researchers can now test thousands of variations in a virtual environment without experimenting in the complex parameter space of biofabrication techniques.

From a broader perspective, this digitalization process is transforming the ethical, sustainability, and industrial scalability dimensions of biofabrication. Within this context, the concept of "sustainable biofabrication" has been discussed in the literature as a framework for reducing experimental waste, optimizing energy consumption, and enabling material recycling through AI-supported computational models, as exemplified by the work of Filippi et al. (2025). In this framework, AI is positioned not merely as a technical tool but as an integral component of biofabrication workflows that embeds environmental and social responsibility considerations into the design and decision-making processes.

Consequently, the use of AI in biofabrication is redefining every stage of the production process: biological systems are no longer observed but learned; they are no longer produced but simulated and optimized. This transformation is turning biofabrication into a scientific discipline that will shape its future, not only in laboratories but also in digital ecosystems.

16.2 The Evolution of Biofabrication

The intelligent and autonomous architecture achieved by biofabrication was initially based on deterministic physical models, with methods such as finite element analysis, computational fluid dynamics, and topology optimization determining skeletal stability and pore distribution taking center stage (Carter et al. 1988; Hendrikson et al. 2017; Badali et al. 2024). Computational design, which emerged in the late 1990s, enables the mathematical modeling of complex geometries, their reshaping with optimization algorithms, and their production in a digital environment (Arjoca et al. 2023; Chansoria et al. 2023).

The early 2000s marked the emergence of computer aided tissue engineering, representing a critical intersection where multivariate mathematical models were extensively applied to understand and predict cell behavior within engineered constructs (Post et al. 2022; Sun et al. 2004). However, the systems were still experiment-centric; computers were not decision-makers but merely prediction partners.

After 2015, the increasing volume of data accelerated the introduction of classical machine learning (ML) approaches in biofabrication. During this period, support vector machines, random forests, regression models, and clustering methods revealed strong relationships in multidimensional data, such as cell adhesion, proliferation, material composition, rheological behavior, and print quality (Wu et al. 2024; Ahmed et al. 2024; Jin et al. 2023). It is possible to say that the advent of DL has ushered in a new era in biofabrication. While convolutional neural networks (CNNs) represent tissue morphology in high-resolution latent spaces, autoencoders convert scaffold microarchitectures into compressed mathematical forms (Barrera et al. 2021; Sun et al. 2025; Ng et al. 2020). Transformer-based models have begun to capture the multidimensional structure of biofabrication by solving multimodal data (images, sensor outputs, rheology measurements, omic sequences) using a single algorithm (Zhou et al. 2025; Wu et al. 2024; Aarthi et al. 2025).

Currently, a process is ongoing that evolves from the deterministic geometries of computational design to sensor-fed smart production lines and from static simulations to continuously learning digital twin (DT) ecosystems. AI-based digital twins can now predict the entire cycle, from the rheological profile of the raw material to cell behavior, and from the thermal equilibrium of the printing process to the post-processing stages (Zhou et al. 2025; Chen et al. 2024; Bonatti et al. 2022).

16.3 Algorithmic Foundations of AI-Driven Modeling

Biofabrication processes require an understanding of the complex nonlinear relationships between physical parameters, such as temperature and viscosity, and biological outputs, such as cell viability. AI algorithms have enabled the analysis of these relationships far more efficiently and rapidly than traditional trial-and-error approaches (Yu et al. 2025). This conceptual progression from data-driven analysis to generative modeling is schematically summarized in Fig. 16.2, which presents the hierarchical organization of AI architectures.

16.3.1 Machine Learning Algorithms

LeCun, Bengio, and Hinton, known as the architects of AI, defined machine learning in their 2015 paper as "a set of methods that enable computers to extract patterns from data and make predictions." They analyzed in detail the transition from "shallow" to "deep" models using multilayer artificial neural networks, which enable the automatic learning of hierarchical representations of data during the learning process. This led to the emergence of "deep learning" models, which form the methodological foundation of "machine learning." Machine learning, whose classic goal is to create models capable of generalizing from data, has been developed into a layered representation learning model in which the system directly extracts hierarchical representations (features) of the data. This perspective is defined as a conceptual leap by the creators of the algorithm (LeCun et al. 2015).

Machine learning is a subfield of AI that aims to enable computer systems to learn patterns from data and make decisions or predictions based on these patterns without the need for explicit programming. The fundamental principle of the field is that learning can be modeled as a *computational process*: the system discovers statistical regularities in the data, represents these regularities as a mathematical function, and generalizes using this function when encountering new data (Mitchell 1997). Unlike

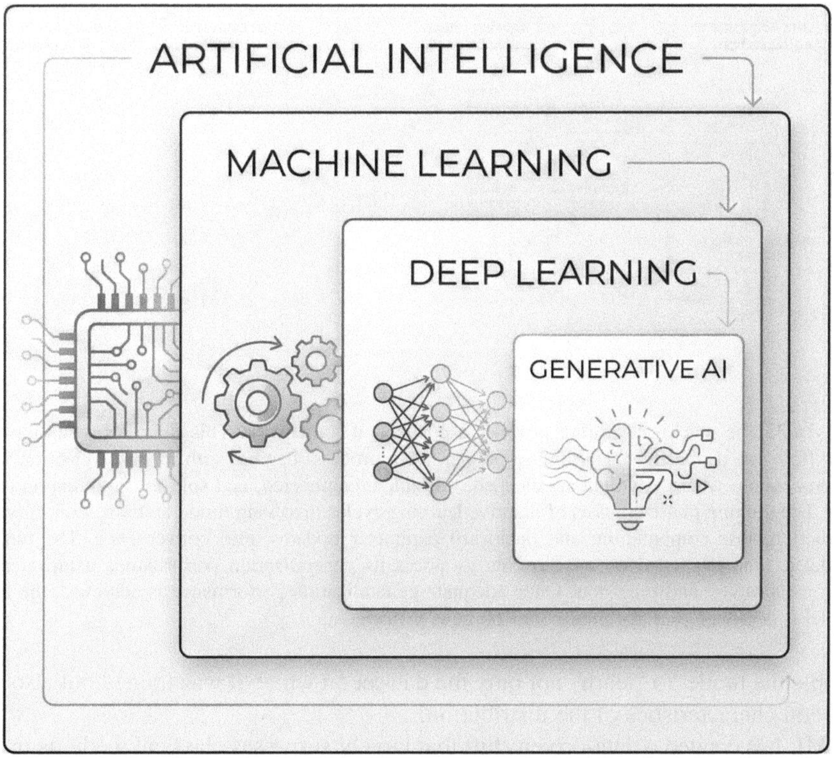

Fig. 16.2 The hierarchical structure of AI architectures. AI occupies the outermost layer as a broad field aimed at mimicking human-like cognitive abilities, while machine learning, which learns statistical relationships from data, is located within it (Hinton 2007). Deep learning, a subset of machine learning, can represent complex patterns at an abstract level using multilayered neural networks (Ullman 2019). Generative AI, occupying the innermost layer, is a specialized subfield of deep learning that not only classifies or predicts but also generates new data (Zhang et al. 2025)

classical programming, this approach is based on the idea of "deriving rules from data" rather than "writing rules."

Modern machine learning essentially consists of three components: data, models, and learning algorithms (Murphy 2012). Data refer to the observations used for training the model. A model is a mathematical relationship that represents the underlying structure of the data and can range from simple functions, such as linear regression, to deep neural networks with millions of parameters (Goodfellow et al. 2016). A learning algorithm is a set of methods that aims to reduce errors by optimizing model parameters, as illustrated in Fig. 16.3.

The logic of machine learning also revolves around the concept of generalization. The performance of a model is evaluated not only on the data it was trained on but also on how it behaves with examples it has never seen before. Therefore, techniques such as regularization, cross-validation, and early stopping ensure that the learning process is balanced with respect to overfitting (Bishop 2006). These mechanisms

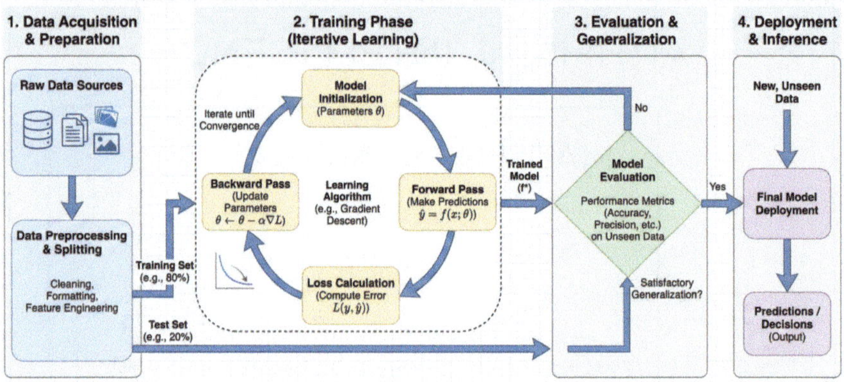

Fig. 16.3 The machine learning process: a conceptual framework. This figure presents the full workflow of a machine learning pipeline. The process begins with data acquisition and preprocessing, where raw data are cleaned, formatted, engineered, and split into training and test sets. The training phase consists of iterative learning cycles involving model initialization, forward prediction, loss computation, and backward parameter updates until convergence. The trained model is then evaluated on unseen data to assess its generalization performance using metrics such as accuracy and precision. Once adequate generalization performance is achieved, the final model is deployed to make predictions on new, unseen data

enable the model to “learn” not only the dataset on which it was trained but also the general characteristics of the distribution.

ML has created a data-driven shift that largely surpasses classical methods in the biofabrication process. This process requires high precision in the production of complex structures composed of cells, hydrogels, and biocomposites. However, optimizing parameters such as printing speed, pressure, temperature, viscosity, and cell density is quite time-consuming with classical methods. Machine learning transforms the production process into a predictable, adaptable, and self-improving system by analyzing the nonlinear relationships between these complex variables (Shin et al. 2022).

Currently, machine learning is divided into subcategories, such as supervised, unsupervised, and reinforcement learning. In supervised learning, data are labeled and provided as input-output pairs, and the model learns a mapping function; many applications, such as image classification, fall into this category (Jordan and Mitchell 2015). In contrast, unsupervised learning focuses on discovering hidden structures within the data, or more explicitly, the proximity of data points to each other, without labeled data; clustering and dimensionality reduction are examples of this type of learning. Reinforcement learning is based on an agent learning the optimal action strategy by interacting with its environment; it is common in decision-making, robotics, and autonomous systems (Sutton and Barto 2018).

16.3.1.1 Supervised Learning

Supervised learning is the most commonly used ML approach in biofabrication. In supervised learning, labeled data are used to model the complex relationship between inputs and desired outputs; that is, it is a fundamental approach that enables a machine learning model to statistically learn the relationships between input data and their corresponding output labels. The goal of this approach is for the model to generalize from labeled examples it has seen in the past and produce accurate predictions on new and unseen data (LeCun et al. 2015). The infographic in Fig. 16.4 shows the working logic and basic algorithms of the supervised learning approach. Supervised learning is commonly applied in classification and regression tasks. In classification, the model makes a categorical class prediction, whereas in regression, it predicts a continuous value (Goodfellow et al. 2016). The learning process is based on minimizing the error function, which measures the difference between the values predicted by the model and the actual labels, and parameter updates are performed to reduce this difference (Bishop 2006).

In biofabrication, the model learns the relationship between inputs, such as printing parameters, bioink composition, rheological indices, cell density, and temperature, and outputs, such as cell viability, filament width, mechanical strength, or printing error, using labeled data. Thus, functional relationships in the input-output space, which are often nonlinear, high-dimensional, and complex, are modeled in a data-driven manner (Wu et al. 2024; Freeman et al. 2022; Yu et al. 2025; Mohammadnabi et al. 2025). In classification problems, print quality classes or cell response categories (such as "high/medium/low viability") are predicted; in regression problems, continuous variables such as mechanical properties, filament thickness, porosity level, or cell viability percentage are predicted (Yang et al. 2021). Owing to the multivariable nature of biofabrication, most of these algorithms can be used in both classification and regression modes (Rafieyan et al. 2024; Piotrowska et al. 2025).

Random forest (RF) is one of the most frequently used methods in this context. RF is a powerful ensemble learning method developed to overcome the limitations of a single decision tree based on the collective decision of multiple trees (Noi and Kappas 2018). The algorithm first trains independent decision trees on hundreds of different subsets created by resampling the original dataset using bootstrap sampling (the computer repeatedly selects random samples from the original dataset, creating a slightly different dataset each time). This approach reduces overfitting by allowing the model to observe different data distributions (Breiman 2001). Each tree uses a randomly selected subset of variables, not all variables, in its split decisions; this mechanism reduces the similarity between trees and increases the overall accuracy of the ensemble structure (Zhou et al. 2025). The final prediction is obtained through the average or majority vote of the outputs of these trees. This ensemble structure reduces the risk of overfitting by lowering the model variance while allowing the interpretation of which process or material variable affects the output to what extent through feature importance scores (Lundberg et al. 2020). In biofabrication, RF has

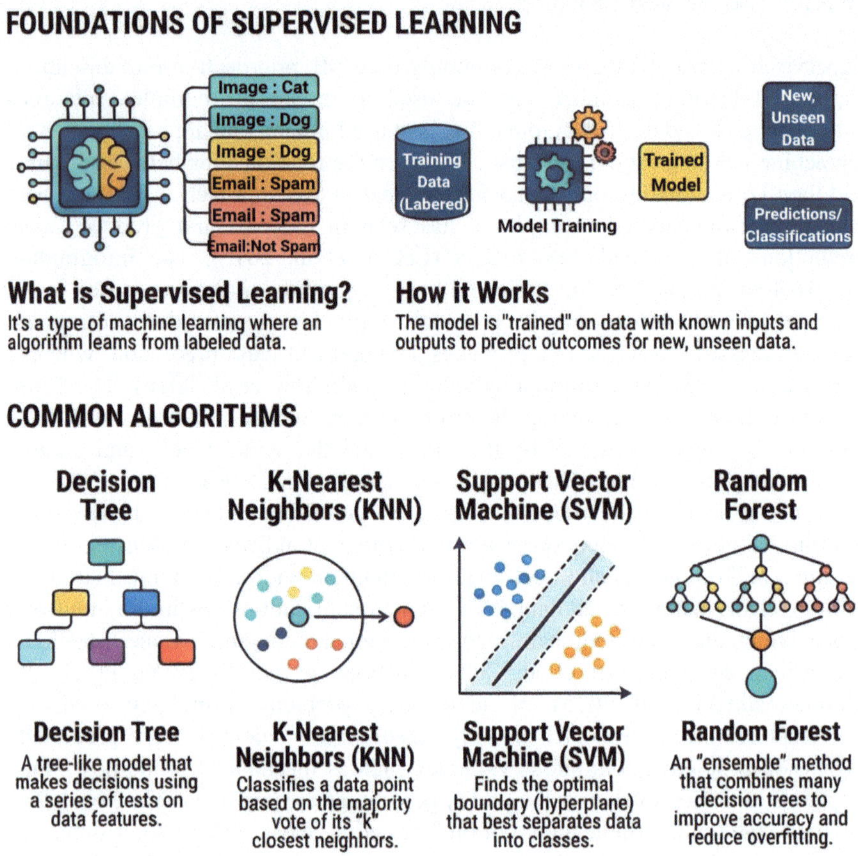

Fig. 16.4 Conceptual overview and representative algorithms of supervised learning. This figure presents a schematic overview of supervised learning, illustrating how models learn statistical mappings from labeled training data to predict outputs for previously unseen inputs. The upper panel depicts the supervised learning pipeline, including labeled data acquisition, model training, and inference on new data. The lower panel summarizes representative supervised learning algorithms—decision trees, K-nearest neighbors (KNN), support vector machines (SVM), and random forests—highlighting their distinct learning principles, including rule-based decision making, distance-based classification, margin maximization, and ensemble learning for classification and regression tasks

been used to predict the effects on printability, correlate printing parameters with cell viability, and model scaffold quality in a multidimensional parameter space (Zhou et al. 2025; Wu et al. 2024; Tian et al. 2021). As an illustrative study, Rafieyan et al. (2024) demonstrated that tree-based ensemble learning algorithms, such as random forest and XGBoost, can accurately predict printability, cellular responses, and overall scaffold quality in 3D bioprinted scaffold fabrication.

Support vector machines (SVM) are supervised learning algorithms that aim to construct a maximum-margin decision boundary between classes. While SVM learns a linear decision function in the feature space, the use of kernel functions enables the modeling of nonlinear relationships in the original input space, allowing SVM to be applied to both classification and regression problems (Cortes and Vapnik 1995). The fundamental objective of SVM is to identify a hyperplane that separates classes with the widest possible margin, as wider margins are theoretically associated with better generalization to unseen data. Vapnik's statistical learning theory demonstrates that decision boundaries with large margins tend to exhibit superior generalization performance. Rather than relying on all training samples, SVM bases its decision function solely on a small subset of critical data points, known as support vectors, which lie closest to the decision boundary. As explained by Burges, the decision function is entirely determined by the influence of these support vectors. Through the kernel trick, complex nonlinear decision boundaries in the input space can be represented as linear separators in a higher-dimensional feature space (Burges 1998). The strong generalization capability of SVM in high-dimensional settings, its effectiveness with limited training data, and its capacity to model nonlinear decision boundaries make it particularly suitable for biofabrication data. Accordingly, SVM has been successfully applied to tasks such as optimizing extrusion printing parameters and predicting print quality or filament width in Pluronic hydrogels, where different parameter combinations are classified into desirable and undesirable printing regimes (Wu et al. 2024).

The K-nearest neighbors (KNN) algorithm is an intuitive yet powerful supervised learning method that does not learn a complex model during the training phase and relies entirely on calculating the distances between examples. The basic principle is that the class of a new example is determined by looking at the class of the K nearest examples in the training set; this proximity is used for classification by majority voting and for regression by calculating the average or median (Zhang and Zhou 2007). The simple structure of KNN offers significant advantages, particularly when there is no prior knowledge of the shape of the data distribution, the decision boundaries exhibit nonlinear structures, or the assumptions of parametric models are not met. The literature indicates that two fundamental factors determine the performance of KNN: the distance metric used and the number of neighbors K selected. Therefore, optimizing the distance functions can significantly improve the accuracy of KNN (Weinberger and Saul 2009). In this context, KNN is positioned as a powerful basic algorithm preferred for small datasets, problems where class distributions are not distinct, and when a quick initial model is needed (Noi and Kappas 2018; Zhang et al. 2018). In biofabrication, KNN has been used to classify printing defects (delamination, filament breakage, and clumping) (Wu et al. 2024). Accordingly, KNN is commonly employed for classification and regression tasks in biofabrication studies.

XGBoost (eXtreme Gradient Boosting) is an optimized and regularized variant of gradient boosting methods based on decision trees, offering strong classification and regression modeling capabilities. The algorithm iteratively improves model performance by sequentially adding decision trees that learn from the prediction errors (residuals) of the existing ensemble (Chen and Guestrin 2016). In biofabrication, XGBoost has been applied to the optimization of printing parameters and process windows, as well as to the prediction of critical quality metrics derived from multidimensional material and cellular parameters. Recent biofabrication studies have demonstrated that XGBoost achieves high predictive accuracy in optimizing printing parameters affecting cell viability, predicting key quality indicators such as filament width and porosity, and efficiently exploring high-dimensional parameter spaces in 3D scaffold fabrication (Rafieyan et al. 2024; Yu et al. 2025; Mohammadnabi et al. 2025).

Artificial neural networks (ANNs) are computational models inspired by the information-processing principles of biological neural systems and consist of a large number of interconnected simple processing units, known as neurons (LeCun et al. 2015). Among ANN architectures, multilayer perceptrons (MLPs) have become a fundamental framework for modeling the high-dimensional and nonlinear relationships commonly encountered in biofabrication processes. The theoretical strength of ANNs as universal function approximators arises from their ability to transform complex dependencies in the input space into hierarchical, multi-scale representations across successive layers. As noted by Schmidhuber, deep architectures automatically extract hierarchical features from data, enabling the learning of highly complex relationships (Schmidhuber 2015). This representational capability is consistent with the framework proposed by Jordan and Mitchell, who conceptualize machine learning as a class of experience-driven function approximation mechanisms (Jordan and Mitchell 2015). According to the Universal Approximation Theorem, a feedforward artificial neural network with at least one hidden layer and suitable activation functions can approximate any continuous function on a compact domain to arbitrary accuracy, given sufficient model capacity (Schmidhuber 2015).

The learning capacity of deep neural networks becomes particularly evident when dealing with high-dimensional image data or complex process-related datasets. Mnih et al. demonstrated that deep neural networks are capable of abstracting meaningful representations directly from raw pixel inputs, highlighting their ability to learn complex processes through hierarchical feature representations (Mnih et al. 2015). However, the representational power of deep models also introduces a critical requirement for explainability, as emphasized by Barredo-Arrieta et al. (2020). As model complexity and parameter scale increase, the transparency of decision-making mechanisms decreases. In application domains with high clinical relevance, such as biofabrication, understanding how specific input variables influence model outputs therefore becomes essential. Accordingly, ANN architectures, including multilayer perceptrons (MLPs), serve as indispensable analytical tools for both forward design and inverse design tasks. In forward design, ANNs are employed for predicting mechanical properties and forecasting biological outcomes such as cell viability, whereas in inverse design, they are used to optimize input parameters to achieve targeted mechanical or biological outputs. ANNs learn complex relationships among multiple inputs—including bioink composition, viscoelastic rheology, temperature profiles, and cell viability—by optimizing model parameters across high-dimensional design spaces (Xu et al. 2024; Tian et al. 2021; Mohammadrezaei et al. 2024). Input variables such as bioink composition (e.g., polymer concentration, cross-linker ratio, temperature, and pH), extrusion parameters (pressure, printing speed, and nozzle diameter), thermal profiles, and output variables including mechanical properties (Young's modulus, compressive modulus, and yield strength) or biological indicators (cell viability and proliferation rate) have been successfully modeled using ANN frameworks in both forward and inverse design contexts (Quan et al. 2025). For instance, neural network models developed to predict the Young's modulus of cartilage scaffolds have been integrated as surrogate models in optimization studies investigating the effects of pressure-related parameters on scaffold compressive strength through variables such as layer thickness and dwell time (Wu et al. 2024).

Bayesian optimization (BO) is a sequential, model-based optimization framework that offers substantial advantages for identifying optimal solutions, particularly in scenarios where data acquisition is expensive, time-consuming, or limited. BO relies on a probabilistic surrogate model—most commonly Gaussian process regression or, in some cases, Bayesian neural networks—to approximate the objective function. Based on this surrogate, acquisition functions such as expected improvement are employed to systematically select the most informative next parameter configuration to evaluate (Shahriari et al. 2016). In recent years, next-generation implementations that integrate Bayesian optimization with high-dimensional material formulation, multi-objective optimization strategies, and robotic experimental automation have increasingly transformed biofabrication design into a data-driven and autonomous paradigm (Frazier 2018; Wang et al. 2023).

16.3.1.2 Unsupervised Learning

Unsupervised learning aims to identify hidden patterns, structures, and clusters within a dataset when prior knowledge or labeled data are unavailable. It constitutes a fundamental machine learning paradigm focused on discovering internal structures, statistical regularities, and latent representation spaces directly from unlabeled data. In this setting, models learn from the underlying data distribution without external supervision and reveal structural relationships by grouping similar samples, modeling data densities, or generating low-dimensional representations (Chen et al. 2024; Hastie et al. 2009).

Clustering techniques (e.g., K-means and Gaussian mixture models) and dimensionality reduction methods (e.g., principal component analysis and t-distributed stochastic neighbor embedding) are canonical examples of unsupervised learning approaches, as they aim to uncover natural groupings or dominant sources of variance within data (Bishop 2006). A key advantage of unsupervised learning lies in its ability to exploit large volumes of unlabeled data, thereby avoiding the cost and subjectivity associated with manual labeling. However, the interpretability of the learned representations and their suitability for downstream tasks often require additional validation and domain-specific evaluation (Murphy 2012).

In biofabrication, unsupervised learning methods have been employed to cluster heterogeneous bioink formulations based on printability, rheological characteristics, or biocompatibility; to partition high-dimensional printing parameter spaces into "successful," "marginal," and "unsuccessful" printing regimes; and to identify subpopulations in cellular phenotypes, gene expression profiles, or image-based response data (Wu et al. 2024; Rafieyan et al. 2024; Rives et al. 2021).

Within this context, the K-means algorithm relies on the concept of the cluster "mean," or centroid, as its fundamental statistical descriptor. Because no label information is available, K-means identifies structure in the data solely through similarity measures. At each iteration, samples are assigned to the nearest centroid, after which the centroids are updated as the arithmetic mean of all points within each cluster. This procedure minimizes the within-cluster sum of squared errors and positions each centroid as the best least-squares representative of its cluster (Lloyd 1982). Through this iterative process, centroids act as reference points that reveal the internal organization of the data, progressively sharpening cluster boundaries and partitioning the data distribution into geometrically meaningful subgroups. Consequently, the "mean" in K-means is not merely a technical parameter but a central statistical mechanism for data representation, pattern extraction, and the organization of unstructured data in unsupervised learning (MacQueen 1967).

K-means, hierarchical clustering, and density-based methods are therefore widely applied to separate samples exhibiting similar behaviors by jointly considering print quality, material composition, and process parameters in scaffold datasets. For example, Rafieyan et al. applied K-means clustering to a 3D bioprinted scaffold dataset comprising numerous material and process variables and identified five distinct scaffold clusters (Rafieyan et al. 2024). Each cluster was shown to correspond to a specific printing regime and characteristic cellular response profile.

Beyond classical methods, autoencoders (AEs) play a central role in unsupervised deep learning. AEs compress high-dimensional input data into a low-dimensional latent space and learn to reconstruct the original data from this representation, thereby enabling both data compression and high-level feature extraction. In biofabrication, AEs facilitate the representation of scaffold microstructures in latent space, support the discovery of novel structural topologies through latent-space exploration, enable inverse design for targeted mechanical properties, and allow the detection of printing defects or anomalous material behavior via anomaly detection frameworks (Wu et al. 2024).

16.4 Deep Learning Architectures and Network Models in Biofabrication

Deep learning (DL) represents an extension of artificial neural networks characterized by multilayered and highly complex architectures, encompassing both supervised and unsupervised learning paradigms. By applying successive nonlinear transformations across multiple hidden layers, DL models learn hierarchical feature representations from high-dimensional and complex datasets. In this framework, learning relies on the automatic extraction of representations through layered nonlinear transformations rather than on manually engineered, human-defined features. As a result, DL models can progressively uncover abstract patterns embedded in signals, images, text, or scientific measurements (LeCun et al. 2015).

Schmidhuber's concept of "credit assignment paths" highlights a fundamental distinction between deep learning models and shallow artificial neural networks. Deep architectures are capable of learning complex, multistage relationships by updating parameters along long causal chains composed of numerous sequential computational steps (Schmidhuber 2015). This capability is particularly critical for sequential data with temporal dependencies and for problems that require multi-level abstractions.

The rapid development of deep learning over the past decade has been driven not only by algorithmic advances but also by the maturation of hardware accelerators, such as graphics processing units (GPUs), and the widespread adoption of software frameworks including TensorFlow, PyTorch, and Caffe. As demonstrated by Wang et al., this technological ecosystem has enabled the scalable, efficient, and industrial-level deployment of deep learning models on large-scale datasets (Wang et al. 2019).

The impact of deep learning on scientific research extends well beyond conventional tasks such as classification and regression. Herrmann and Kollmannsberger show that DL spans a broad methodological spectrum in computational science, ranging from surrogate models that replace expensive numerical simulations to physics-informed learning approaches that explicitly incorporate governing physical laws into training, as well as generative design strategies and reinforcement learning–based decision-making systems (Herrmann and Kollmannsberger 2024).

Within this broader context, deep learning has emerged as a transformative epistemological tool in modern science and engineering, particularly in complex, multivariable domains such as computational biology, medical imaging, and biofabrication. By integrating representation learning, automatic feature extraction, high-dimensional function approximation, and data-driven modeling, DL provides a powerful framework for capturing the inherently multi-scale, nonlinear nature of biological systems. Consequently, deep learning approaches offer highly suitable tools for modeling both process dynamics and product functionality in biofabrication (Wu et al. 2024; Mohammadnabi et al. 2025). A schematic overview of this integrated deep learning pipeline for biofabrication applications is presented in Fig. 16.5.

The practical success of artificial neural networks has accelerated in parallel with advances in training algorithms and the proliferation of large-scale computing infrastructures. These developments have substantially improved the trainability of ANNs on large datasets. As demonstrated by Wang et al., modern deep learning frameworks have enabled the rapid and scalable integration of neural network models into both academic research and industrial applications (Wang et al. 2019). Consequently, ANN architectures now form the foundation not only of classical classification and regression tasks but also of more advanced model families, including convolutional neural networks, recurrent neural networks, graph neural networks, autoencoders, generative models, and reinforcement learning agents.

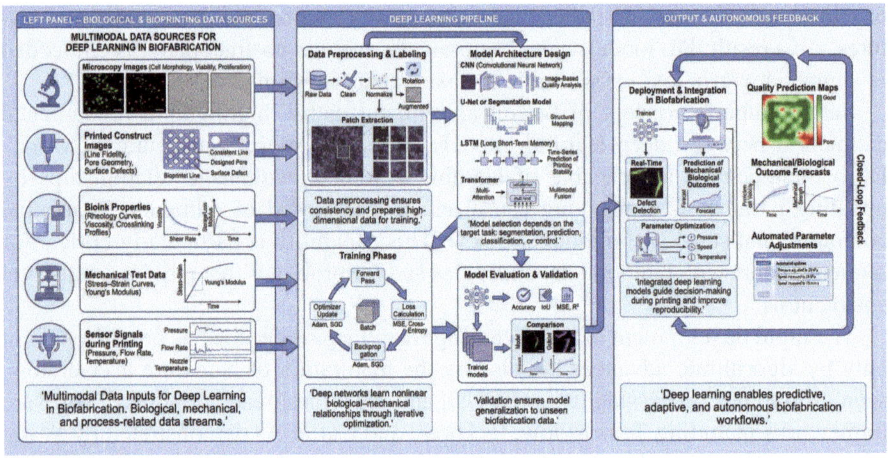

Fig. 16.5 Deep learning workflow for biofabrication applications. This figure presents an end-to-end deep learning pipeline integrating multimodal biofabrication data sources, including microscopy images, printed construct images, bioink rheological properties, mechanical testing data, and real-time process sensor signals. The workflow illustrates key stages of deep learning–based biofabrication, encompassing data preprocessing and augmentation, model architecture selection (e.g., CNNs, U-Net–based segmentation models, LSTM networks, and transformer architectures), training and validation, and deployment within closed-loop biofabrication systems. Through predictive modeling, real-time defect detection, parameter optimization, and autonomous feedback control, deep learning enables adaptive, reproducible, and data-driven biofabrication workflows

CNNs are deep learning architectures specifically designed for image-based data analysis and have become one of the core methodologies in biomedical imaging and biofabrication. The fundamental principle of CNNs is the automatic learning of hierarchical features—ranging from low-level edges to high-level semantic structures—through local receptive fields and shared convolutional filter weights (LeCun et al. 1998). While convolutional layers extract spatial patterns, pooling layers progressively downsample these representations to increase abstraction; fully connected layers subsequently map these learned features to classification or regression outputs (Goodfellow et al. 2016).

Modern CNNs architectures have revolutionized large-scale image recognition, primarily due to the high representational capacity afforded by deep hierarchical structures. In the biomedical domain, CNNs have been extensively applied to the automated detection and characterization of complex tissue morphologies in MRI, CT, PET, and microscopy data (Krizhevsky et al. 2012). As a result, CNNs now constitute the backbone of contemporary AI-based image analysis, overcoming the limitations of manual feature engineering while enabling the modeling of complex biological structures through hierarchical representations.

In biomanufacturing and biofabrication, CNNs play a central role in image-driven workflows owing to their ability to automatically learn features from both two-dimensional and three-dimensional data. CNNs can analyze image streams acquired from in situ cameras during extrusion-based bioprinting, enabling real-time anomaly detection and print quality monitoring. Defects such as filament breakage, nozzle clogging, delamination, and pore closure can be detected directly during the printing process. Furthermore, three-dimensional CNNs trained on virtual tomograms or micro-computed tomography (μCT) images derived from computer-aided design models can be used to directly estimate mechanical properties—including porosity, effective Young's modulus, and shear modulus—from image data. This approach provides substantially faster assessments than classical finite element simulations. In tumor microenvironment modeling, CNN-based methods are also employed to validate bioprinted tumor constructs and organoid models through automated tumor segmentation and characterization using CT and MRI data (Wu et al. 2024; Piotrowska et al. 2025).

Long short-term memory (LSTM) networks were developed to address the limitations of classical recurrent neural networks (RNNs) in learning long-term temporal dependencies. The gating mechanisms of LSTM cells—including the input gate, forget gate, and output gate—regulate the flow of information into, within, and out of the cell state, thereby substantially mitigating the vanishing gradient problem (Hochreiter and Schmidhuber 1997). In biofabrication, LSTM models are used to analyze time-series sensor data in order to predict the evolution of quality defects in extrusion processes, anticipate process drift and parameter deviations in multilayer printing, and support the simulation of functional loading scenarios in implant and prosthesis design by learning individualized motion patterns (Wu et al. 2024).

Beyond these specific architectures, deep learning contributes directly to quality by design objectives by reducing inefficiencies, improving product quality and repeatability, and enabling scalability. DL-based models minimize costly biological material waste by reducing the number of experimental iterations required for bioink formulation and process optimization. They further enable precise control of process variability by accurately modeling complex parameter–output relationships and provide the computational foundation for digital twin development and the advancement of "dark factory" paradigms through the integration of multimodal data sources, including imaging, mechanical testing, -omics data, and time-series signals (Bardini and Di Carlo 2024; Mohammadnabi et al. 2025).

16.5 Methodological Foundations of AI in Biofabrication

16.5.1 Learning-Based Bioink and Biomaterial Design

The success of biofabrication products critically depends on the accurate definition and optimization of the rheological, mechanical, and biochemical properties of bioinks. Bioinks provide the microenvironment required for cell survival while simultaneously governing the physical stability and fidelity of the printing process (Chen et al. 2023). These requirements are often conflicting: high cell viability typically favors soft, low-viscosity environments, whereas mechanical robustness relies on increased viscosity and cross-linking capacity. As a result, bioink design constitutes a highly complex, multivariable optimization problem involving hundreds of interacting parameters, including polymer concentration, temperature, pH, cross-linker ratio, cell density, nozzle speed, extrusion pressure, and curing conditions (Elango and Zamora-Ledezma 2025).

ML has fundamentally transformed this optimization process. ML algorithms can learn causal and nonlinear relationships between bioink compositions and printing outcomes by training on high-dimensional experimental datasets, enabling the prediction of performance for previously untested formulations (Wu et al. 2024; Rafieyan et al. 2024; Freeman et al. 2022). This shift has moved biomaterial research from heuristic trial-and-error strategies toward statistically grounded and predictive design paradigms.

The effectiveness of AI-driven optimization is strongly dependent on data quality and availability, motivating the development of autonomous data acquisition systems in biofabrication laboratories. The Aceman system introduced by Zhu et al. automatically extracts bioink viscosity and cellular distribution information from microscopy images and feeds these data into machine learning models for real-time optimization (Zhu et al. 2025). By employing active learning strategies, the system selectively guides new experiments toward regions of highest uncertainty, significantly reducing experimental burden while enabling continuous self-improvement.

Recent bioink optimization strategies increasingly rely on multimodal data fusion, integrating chemical, mechanical, optical, acoustic, and cellular measurements. Castilho et al. demonstrated that such multimodal integration in hybrid biofabrication systems enhances interlayer scaffold integrity (Castilho et al. 2020). By mapping multi-scale data into unified latent spaces, AI models can infer mechanical stiffness from cellular morphology or predict viscosity from optical signals, extending material characterization beyond conventional experimental measurements.

Collectively, these advances signal a paradigm shift in which bioinks evolve from passive carriers of cells into active, information-rich materials capable of learning from their own fabrication history. This concept aligns with the notion of "intelligent therapeutic platforms" described in Next-Generation Biomaterials, wherein biomaterials dynamically adapt, optimize, and respond to environmental conditions (Chakrapani et al. 2025). In this context, AI is not merely an auxiliary tool of materials science but constitutes a new epistemological framework through which biological complexity is interpreted directly from data rather than analytical equations.

Finally, AI-driven models are redefining tissue maturation and functional validation workflows. Deep learning architectures can predict key biological and biomechanical indicators—such as cell differentiation, metabolic activity, extracellular matrix production, vascularization, and mechanical integrity—using time-series and multimodal datasets, enabling early and accurate assessments of tissue functionality (Zhou et al. 2025). In tumor microenvironment models, AI-based high-throughput screening platforms are further transforming preclinical drug development by systematically evaluating combinatorial therapies. Altogether, these developments demonstrate that AI is not simply integrated into isolated stages of biofabrication but fundamentally reshapes its epistemology, experimental design, and production paradigms.

16.5.2 Digital Twins as Intelligent Biofabrication Models

A digital twin (DT) is defined as a dynamic virtual representation of a physical system that is continuously updated using sensor-derived data and functions as the computational memory of the production process (Tao et al. 2019; Jin et al. 2024; Katsoulakis et al. 2024). Originally developed for applications in aviation and Industry 4.0, the digital twin concept acquires a deeper and more complex meaning in the context of biofabrication, where the system being modeled is not purely mechanical but intrinsically biological. Ahmed et al. (2024) introduced a digital twin framework integrated into 3D bioprinting workflows, in which real-time data from sensors monitoring pressure, temperature, viscosity, and cell density are continuously acquired and processed to enable adaptive algorithmic decision-making. Through this mechanism, the bioprinting system learns from deviations accumulated in previous layers and dynamically optimizes subsequent printing cycles, marking a transition from conventional open-loop production toward closed-loop biofabrication systems. Within this architecture, artificial intelligence operates not merely as a control software layer but as a central computational component responsible for inference, prediction, and decision-making across both physical processes and data-driven learning modules. Figure 16.6 illustrates the architecture and workflow of an AI-enabled digital twin framework for biofabrication, highlighting the integration of physical systems, computational modeling, and closed-loop control.

One of the most impactful contributions of digital twin technology to biofabrication is the introduction of real-time feedback loops into the manufacturing process. These feedback-driven systems enable learning not only from historical datasets but also from the system's own behavior during ongoing production. Lindner and Blaeser describe such a framework within their scalable biofabrication model, where sensors embedded in the printing platform continuously monitor parameters such as layer height and density, while AI models dynamically adjust printing speed, extrusion pressure, and temperature (Lindner and Blaeser 2022). In this setting, each printed layer contributes to an evolving learning database. Reinforcement learning algorithms play a particularly prominent role by assigning reward or penalty signals based on structural quality, enabling the system to iteratively avoid suboptimal printing conditions and significantly reduce experimental inefficiencies.

Another defining characteristic of AI-enabled digital twins is their ability to operate across multiple spatial and temporal scales. Feng et al., through their shape–properties collaborative intelligence framework, established a multilevel modeling strategy linking cellular-scale micromechanical behavior to macroscopic

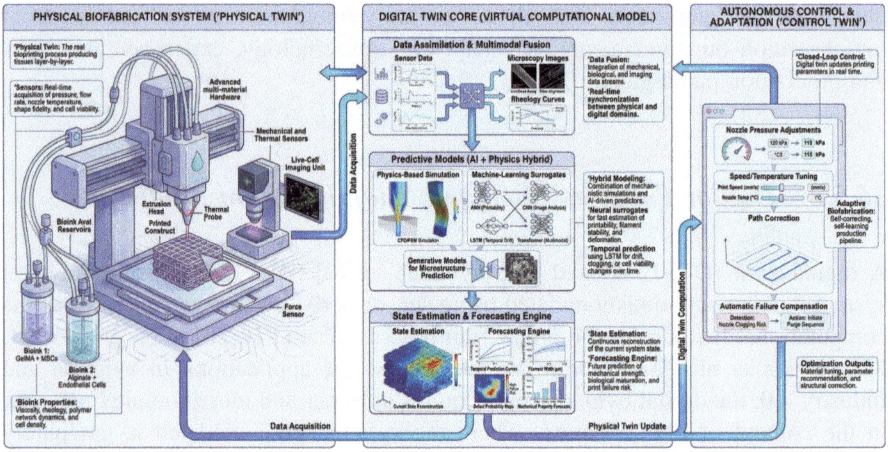

Fig. 16.6 Digital twin architecture and closed-loop workflow in biofabrication. The figure depicts an integrated digital twin framework comprising three interconnected layers: the physical biofabrication system (physical twin), the digital twin core (virtual computational model), and the autonomous control and adaptation layer (control twin). Multimodal data streams—including real-time sensor signals, microscopy images, and rheological measurements—are continuously acquired from the physical system and assimilated into the digital twin core through data fusion and state estimation. Hybrid predictive models combining physics-based simulations and machine learning surrogates enable real-time forecasting of printability, structural integrity, and biological outcomes. These predictions drive closed-loop control actions, such as adaptive adjustment of extrusion pressure, printing speed, temperature, and toolpath correction, enabling self-correcting, adaptive, and learning-driven biofabrication workflows

tissue geometry (Feng et al. 2025). A similar multi-scale philosophy underpins the multi-technology biofabrication approach proposed by Castilho et al., in which digitally reconstructed cellular microenvironments generated via microfluidic systems are integrated with macroscale printing parameters and organ-on-chip platforms (Castilho et al. 2020). This multi-scale coupling enables cellular-level phenomena—such as oxygen diffusion or cell proliferation—to directly inform and modify macroscopic production strategies, effectively transforming biofabrication into a hierarchically consistent modeling system.

More recently, digital twin technology has converged with generative artificial intelligence, extending its scope beyond replication toward exploration and hypothesis generation. While conventional digital twins are designed to emulate existing production processes, generative models enable the simulation of previously unobserved biological scenarios. As noted by Zhou et al., generative digital twins can propose novel tissue architectures and microstructural configurations that have not yet been realized experimentally (Zhou et al. 2025). For instance, generative adversarial network (GAN)–based models can infer plausible micro-morphologies arising from different bioink formulations, thereby guiding experimental design and expanding the accessible design space. In this sense, digital twins evolve from corrective control systems into exploratory computational platforms that support creative discovery within biofabrication.

Despite their transformative potential, the deployment of AI-driven digital twins in clinical biofabrication raises important ethical and regulatory challenges. Zhou et al. and Filippi et al. emphasize the necessity of explainable artificial intelligence (XAI) in this context, arguing that algorithmic decisions influencing biological production must be transparent, auditable, and clinically justifiable (Zhou et al. 2025; Filippi et al. 2025). XAI-enabled digital twins provide insight into which parameters are modified, how decisions are made, and why specific outcomes are produced, thereby establishing accountability and trust—key prerequisites for clinical translation.

Taken together, digital twins represent not merely a technical enhancement of biofabrication workflows but a conceptual expansion of the field itself. By enabling biological systems to be represented as adaptive, data-informed digital counterparts, artificial intelligence transforms biofabrication from a predominantly mechanical manufacturing process into a cognitively guided production paradigm. From this perspective, digital twins do not simply simulate biological fabrication; they provide a computational projection of biological complexity, positioning biofabrication as a technologically mediated reflection of nature's own adaptive processes.

16.5.3 Autonomous and Adaptive Bioprinting Systems

The evolution of artificial intelligence in biofabrication is characterized not only by increasing computational capacity but also by the emergence of autonomous biological production systems that learn from their own operational histories. In this paradigm, bioprinting platforms cease to function as passive mechanical instruments and instead operate as adaptive, self-improving production entities capable of continuous learning and optimization (Freeman et al. 2022). This transformation is driven by the convergence of machine learning, robotic automation, multimodal sensor fusion, closed-loop control, and reinforcement learning. Figure 16.7 provides a schematic overview of an AI-driven biofabrication pipeline, illustrating the transformation of multimodal biological and process data into autonomous control signals through integrated learning models and closed-loop feedback.

Historically, one of the principal limitations of biofabrication has been its reliance on human-in-the-loop procedures. Critical tasks such as pipetting, temperature regulation, layer alignment, and quality inspection have traditionally required direct human supervision, rendering the process susceptible to variability, operator-dependent bias, and limited reproducibility. As emphasized by Lindner and Blaeser in their *Scalable Biofabrication* framework, this human-centered workflow represents a major bottleneck for standardization and industrial translation (Lindner and Blaeser 2022). Their automated bioprinting architecture integrates robotic manipulators, multimodal sensor arrays, and AI-driven coordination strategies, enabling the system to autonomously detect deviations, predict performance degradation, and compensate for errors without interrupting production. In this setting, artificial intelligence functions not merely as a control layer but as a decision-making

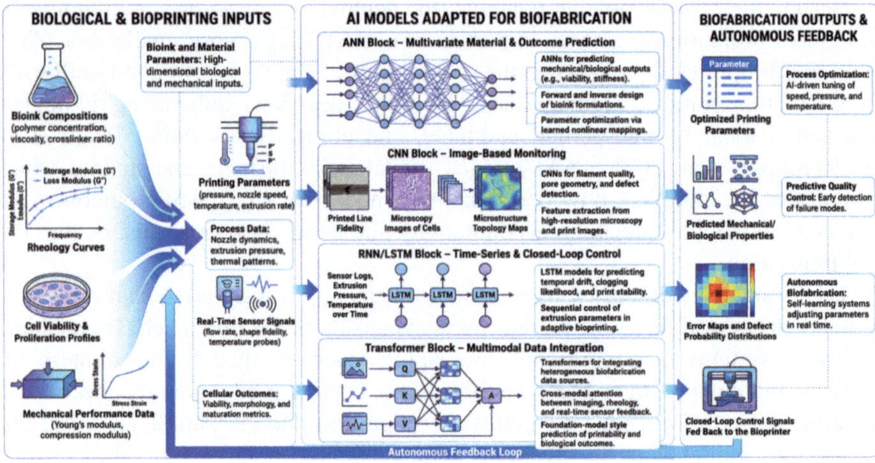

Fig. 16.7 AI-driven biofabrication pipeline from multimodal data acquisition to autonomous control. The figure illustrates an end-to-end artificial intelligence framework for biofabrication, integrating biological and bioprinting inputs, machine learning models, and closed-loop autonomous feedback. Multimodal inputs—including bioink composition, rheological profiles, printing parameters, real-time sensor signals, cellular outcomes, and mechanical performance data—are processed by specialized AI models adapted for biofabrication. Artificial neural networks (ANNs) enable multivariate material and outcome prediction, convolutional neural networks (CNNs) support image-based monitoring and defect detection, recurrent neural networks and long short-term memory (RNN/LSTM) architectures model temporal dynamics for closed-loop control, and transformer-based models integrate heterogeneous data streams through cross-modal attention. Model predictions are translated into optimized printing parameters, predictive quality control, and error probability maps, which are continuously fed back to the bioprinter to enable self-learning, adaptive, and autonomous biofabrication

authority governing production quality, thereby redefining Industry 4.0 principles within the biological manufacturing domain.

Conventional bioprinting workflows predominantly operate under open-loop control schemes, in which parameters such as extrusion pressure, printing speed, and temperature are predefined and remain fixed throughout the fabrication process. This static approach fails to account for dynamic variability arising from material heterogeneity, environmental fluctuations, and evolving cellular behavior. To overcome this limitation, Zhou et al. introduced closed-loop AI-driven biofabrication, in which real-time optical, thermal, and acoustic sensor data continuously inform adaptive parameter updates (Zhou et al. 2025). Reinforcement learning further enhances this framework by interpreting each printing outcome as a reward or penalty signal, enabling the system to refine its control policies iteratively. Defects such as filament breakage, layer delamination, or pore collapse generate negative reinforcement, whereas structurally and biologically optimal outcomes reinforce successful parameter configurations. Over time, the system develops a form of production memory, effectively encoding experiential knowledge within its control strategy.

A representative example of this paradigm is the Aceman system developed by Zhu et al., in which robotic cell culture modules autonomously analyze microscopy images, quantify cell density and spatial distribution, and determine optimal seeding densities and media exchange schedules (Zhu et al. 2025). By coupling active learning strategies with automated experimentation, such systems minimize experimental redundancy while continuously improving predictive performance. These approaches extend biofabrication beyond automation toward genuinely self-guided production.

A critical prerequisite for autonomous biofabrication is the ability to perceive and interpret the production environment through multichannel sensing. In this context, sensor fusion functions as the nervous system of intelligent bioprinting platforms. Optical, mechanical, thermal, and electrical data streams are integrated in real time to construct a unified state representation of the fabrication process. Feng et al. demonstrated this principle in the fabrication of piezoelectric scaffolds by simultaneously monitoring mechanical deformation and electrical output, allowing AI models to learn complex relationships among material composition, geometry, and functional performance (Feng et al. 2025). This multisensory integration forms the foundation of digital twin architectures, in which every physical measurement is instantaneously mirrored within a computational model capable of forecasting future system states.

Recent advances further extend this concept through the integration of context-aware and generative fabrication strategies. In a landmark study, Florczak et al. introduced Generative, Adaptive, Context-Aware 3D Printing (GRACE), a volumetric printing framework that combines real-time imaging, computer vision, and parametric modeling to enable printers to detect, interpret, and adapt to the biological and structural context of the printable material itself (Florczak et al. 2025). Unlike traditional printers that blindly execute predefined geometries, GRACE-equipped systems autonomously generate and modify printing paths based on spatial cues derived from living cell distributions, scaffold architecture, and environmental constraints. By integrating light-sheet imaging with volumetric printing, GRACE enables adaptive overprinting, precise alignment of sequential constructs, and the fabrication of biomimetic tissue architectures that conform to cellular organization across scales (Florczak et al. 2025). This approach exemplifies a new class of autonomous biofabrication systems in which fabrication becomes context-sensitive, generative, and responsive rather than prescriptive.

At the apex of AI-supported automation lie fully autonomous robotic bioprinting platforms. In these systems, robotic arms and mobile printheads operate with sub-millimeter precision, while computer vision modules continuously assess layer fidelity and structural integrity. As noted by Lindner and Blaeser, the role of the human operator shifts toward supervision and system-level oversight, while calibration, correction, and optimization are performed autonomously (Lindner and Blaeser 2022). Emerging concepts such as collective production intelligence, or swarm biofabrication, further extend this paradigm by enabling multiple printers to share experiential knowledge through cloud-based learning infrastructures, thereby facilitating distributed optimization and coordinated production.

Collectively, autonomous production systems mark a conceptual threshold at which biofabrication transitions from mechanized fabrication to computationally guided biological evolution. These platforms accumulate experiential knowledge, adapt to environmental variability, and transfer learned improvements across production cycles, digitally echoing evolutionary principles of selection, adaptation, and optimization. In this sense, autonomous bioprinting systems do not merely replicate biological structures; they operationalize aspects of biological intelligence itself. Cells embody life, while algorithms encode its evolving memory—together forming a cybernetic synthesis that redefines the future of biofabrication.

16.5.4 Integrated and Cognitive Biosystems

Biofabrication extends beyond linear workflows that rely on a single production modality. Artificial intelligence, once primarily employed for optimizing individual printing parameters, has evolved into a high-level decision architecture capable of coordinating multiple fabrication technologies simultaneously. In this emerging paradigm, optical photopolymerization, electrospinning, magnetic guidance, microfluidic tissue construction, piezoelectric stimulation, and real-time biosensor feedback converge into a unified production intelligence. This convergence underpins the concept of multi-technological biofabrication, in which AI functions as an integrative control layer that harmonizes heterogeneous fabrication platforms into a coherent system (Castilho et al. 2020).

The necessity of synchronizing multiple fabrication technologies has become a central principle in contemporary biofabrication research. As articulated by Castilho et al., "the functional production of a tissue or organ requires not a single bioprinting method, but the synchronized operation of multiple fabrication technologies." Increasingly, this synchronization is achieved through algorithmic coordination rather than manual intervention (Castilho et al. 2020). AI systems regulate not only the timing and intensity of each fabrication modality but also continuously recalibrate process parameters in response to sensor-derived biological and mechanical feedback. As a result, biofabrication workflows become adaptive, self-correcting, and dynamically optimized.

A major consequence of this integrative approach is the transformation of biomaterials from passive structural components into active information carriers. As highlighted in the Next-Generation Biomaterials report, contemporary biomaterials are no longer designed solely to provide mechanical support or biocompatibility; instead, they are engineered to sense, record, and respond to environmental stimuli in conjunction with computational control systems (Chakrapani et al. 2025). This capability positions biomaterials as functional participants within an intelligent production ecosystem rather than inert substrates.

Among the most illustrative examples of AI-enabled intelligent biosystems are advanced organ-on-chip platforms, which integrate biological realism with computational control strategies (Vijayaragavan, and M, V., Dharshini, P., Karunakaran,

K., Kesavan, K.,, and Raj, R.D. 2025; Li et al. 2023; Monga et al. 2025). In these systems, AI-powered control facilitates the coordinated regulation of multiple biological and physical processes, enabling dynamic modulation of cellular microenvironments and improving physiological fidelity. At the core of many organ-on-chip architectures lies microfluidic flow control, which governs nutrient transport, oxygen delivery, and waste removal at the cellular scale. Recent studies show that AI-based models can optimize flow dynamics in microfluidic systems by learning the complex, nonlinear relationships between fluid pressure, flow velocity, and local cell density (Manekar et al. 2025; Tsai et al. 2023; Galan et al. 2020). Together, these developments position organ-on-chip platforms as prototypical AI-regulated biosystems in which microfluidic control and data-driven learning jointly enable proactive, adaptive, and physiologically relevant biofabrication environments. While microfluidic control enables fine-grained regulation of cellular microenvironments, AI-driven biofabrication increasingly extends beyond fluid dynamics to coordinate structural geometry and material behavior across multiple fabrication modalities.

Beyond microfluidic control, AI has also enabled the joint optimization of geometric complexity and material behavior in multi-technological biofabrication. Feng et al. developed an AI framework that models and optimizes the interplay between geometric features—such as pore shape, orientation, and filament curvature—and material properties, including elasticity, viscosity, and degradation kinetics (Feng et al. 2025). With each fabrication cycle, the system updates its internal representations of shape–material–function relationships. The resulting constructs are therefore not only geometrically accurate but also exhibit mechanical and biological performance aligned with targeted tissue functionalities.

The growing complexity, energy demands, and material consumption of multi-technological biofabrication systems necessitate a redefinition of sustainability principles. Filippi et al. highlighted the role of AI in reducing energy consumption and minimizing material waste through predictive optimization of motor temperatures, UV irradiation dosage, and fabrication time. Their analysis demonstrated that such strategies can reduce total energy expenditure by up to 20%. Moreover, data-driven production analysis enables the identification of opportunities for recycling unused bioinks and repurposing discarded materials (Filippi et al. 2025). In this context, AI operates not only as a production optimization tool but also as a governance mechanism that embeds sustainability considerations directly into the design and operation of biofabrication platforms.

16.6 Future Perspectives and Ethical Implications

When integrated with artificial intelligence, biofabrication moves beyond the boundaries of classical engineering and increasingly enters the domain of computational biology. In this expanded paradigm, sensor outputs, data streams, and algorithmic decisions function as digital representations of underlying biological events. The implications of this shift are substantial: AI no longer merely imitates biological processes but actively participates in modeling, interpreting, and reproducing the causal logic through which biological functions are understood. Zhou et al. characterize this transformation by emphasizing that the future of biofabrication depends on AI systems that can operate in synchrony with biological dynamics (Zhou et al. 2025). This alignment transforms the laboratory from a production-oriented workspace into a dynamic information ecosystem, in which biological systems generate data, computational models learn from these data, and iterative feedback cycles guide both fabrication and biological design. Consequently, biofabrication evolves from a human-centered activity into a collaborative process shaped by the interaction between natural and artificial intelligence.

Generative artificial intelligence further extends this transformation by shifting biofabrication from a predominantly technical practice toward a creative and predictive discipline. As discussed by Filippi et al., while conventional digital twins primarily replicate existing biological processes, generative models can propose novel tissue morphologies, bioink formulations, and cellular architectures (Filippi et al. 2025). These outputs do not represent direct extrapolations from existing datasets but emerge from the model's capacity to construct biologically plausible scenarios based on learned abstractions. In this sense, AI facilitates algorithmic discovery cycles that parallel—and in some cases accelerate—natural evolutionary processes. Biofabrication therefore transitions toward a hybrid framework in which hypothesis generation, simulation, and biological prototyping are tightly coupled within computational environments.

As AI systems increasingly influence not only technical parameters but also the conceptual boundaries of living matter, ethical frameworks must evolve accordingly. Both Zhou et al. and Filippi et al. underscore the central role of XAI in this context. XAI mechanisms clarify why specific fabrication pathways are selected, which parameters are modified, and how these changes affect biological outcomes (Zhou et al. 2025; Filippi et al. 2025). Such transparency is essential for clinical safety, regulatory compliance, and ethical accountability, particularly as AI-assisted biofabrication engages with constructs that approach the characteristics of synthetic or semiautonomous biological systems. Under these conditions, each fabrication step becomes not only a technical operation but also an ethically significant decision requiring traceability and justification.

In AI-driven biofabrication, data increasingly assume the role of biological elements. Cellular behavior profiles, gene expression patterns, and bioink compositional parameters constitute the raw material for algorithmic modeling and optimization. This development raises fundamental questions regarding data stewardship, ownership, and responsibility: who controls biological data, and who is accountable for the digital twins derived from living systems? As emphasized in the *Next-Generation Biomaterials* report, biofabrication now involves the creation and governance of "living data," giving rise to the concept of bio-data sovereignty—the regulation of biological information within digital infrastructures (Chakrapani et al. 2025). In future clinical and personalized applications, engineered tissues derived from individual donors may be linked to digital identities, creating complex ethical intersections between data governance and biological autonomy.

AI-enabled management of biofabrication workflows also contributes directly to environmental sustainability. Filippi et al. demonstrated that predictive optimization frameworks can reduce energy consumption by up to 20% while minimizing material waste (Filippi et al. 2025). By incorporating metrics such as energy efficiency, carbon footprint, and material reuse into algorithmic decision-making, AI enables biofabrication systems to align more closely with sustainability objectives. In this respect, computational optimization evolves beyond efficiency enhancement to support environmentally responsible manufacturing practices.

Perhaps the most profound consequence of these developments is the gradual reconfiguration of the relationship between biological systems and artificial intelligence. Biofabrication increasingly functions as a platform through which biological complexity is extended, interpreted, and shaped by computational reasoning. AI-assisted fabrication of tissues and organoids enables not only structural replication but also the modeling of adaptive biological behaviors. As noted by Zhou et al., AI-supported biofabrication introduces new modes of biological understanding by translating aspects of natural intelligence into computational representations (Zhou et al. 2025). Within this emerging landscape, biofabrication artifacts encompass not only physical tissues but also systems capable of adaptive information processing.

Ultimately, the future of AI-supported biomanufacturing resides at the intersection of science, ethics, law, and philosophy. Each engineered construct embodies a combination of biological design choices, algorithmic decisions, and ethical considerations. Engineering thus progresses from imitating nature toward reasoning alongside it—participating in biological logic while reshaping it through computational abstraction. In this evolving epistemic framework, AI represents not merely a technological advancement but a catalyst for redefining concepts of life, knowledge, and human responsibility.

16.7 Conclusion and General Evaluation

Artificial intelligence has substantially accelerated biofabrication workflows while simultaneously redefining the conceptual and methodological boundaries of the field. What initially emerged as an engineering discipline focused on mimicking biological structure and function has evolved into a data-driven paradigm that integrates elements of computational biology, automation, and predictive modeling. Central to this transformation are learning-based architectures capable of extracting information from high-dimensional biological data, adapting through iterative feedback, and continuously improving performance via systematic error correction. As a result, biofabrication laboratories increasingly function as hybrid environments in which biological processes and computational intelligence operate in close coordination.

AI-enabled biofabrication introduces a new operational framework in which biological behavior is represented, analyzed, and optimized through mathematical models and algorithmic reasoning. Sensor networks act as continuous information sources, machine learning models perform hierarchical feature extraction, and data accumulated across fabrication cycles contribute to progressively refined production strategies. These mechanisms enable rapid design–test–redesign loops, reducing experimental inefficiencies and facilitating optimization at temporal scales that are difficult to achieve through conventional experimental approaches. Consequently, biofabrication is transitioning from a predominantly physical manufacturing process toward an iterative, data-guided optimization framework.

Within this context, decision-making in biofabrication is no longer defined solely by human intervention but by the processes through which decisions are generated, evaluated, and validated. Manufacturing quality is increasingly assessed not only through biological and mechanical performance metrics but also through the transparency, traceability, and accountability of algorithmic decision pathways. XAI plays a critical role in maintaining interpretability and enabling effective human oversight, particularly in applications with clinical or regulatory relevance. At the same time, challenges related to biological data governance, the autonomy of digital twins, and the distribution of responsibility between human operators and algorithmic systems highlight the need for robust ethical and regulatory frameworks.

Overall, AI-assisted biofabrication represents a significant synthesis in the evolution of science and engineering. By integrating biological knowledge with computational modeling and automated decision-making, the field enables new modes of fabrication, analysis, and understanding. Each engineered construct reflects not only biological design principles but also the computational logic and ethical considerations embedded in the systems that guide its production. As data, materials, energy, and decision-making processes become increasingly interconnected, biofabrication is positioned to evolve through a co-adaptive relationship between biological innovation and computational reasoning, shaping future research and translational applications in a responsible and systematic manner.

Statement Regarding Preparation of Figures

All figures in this chapter were generated by the authors using AI-assisted tools, including Google Gemini and Google NotebookLM, as supportive visualization and content-organization instruments. These tools were employed solely to facilitate the graphical representation of complex scientific concepts. The conceptual framework, scientific interpretation, figure design logic, and final validation of all visual materials were entirely conducted by the authors, based on their subject-matter expertise.

Competing Interests Y.M.E. is the founder and shareholder of Biovalda Health Technologies, Inc. (Ankara, Turkey). The authors declare no competing financial interests in relation to this particular article. The authors are alone responsible for the content and writing of the paper.

References

Aarthi S, Raja S, Rusho MA, Yishak S (2025) Bridging plant biotechnology and additive manufacturing: a multicriteria decision approach for biopolymer development. Adv Polym Technol 2025:Art 9685300. https://doi.org/10.1155/adv/9685300

Ahmed N, Narayanan LK, Shirwaiker R (2024) A framework for digital twin integration in biofabrication and a scaffold 3D bioplotting case study. Manuf Lett 41:1182–1191. https://doi.org/10.1016/J.MFGLET.2024.09.144

Allenby MC, Woodruff MA (2022) Image analyses for engineering advanced tissue biomanufacturing processes. Biomaterials 284:121514. https://doi.org/10.1016/j.biomaterials.2022.121514

Arjoca S, Robu A, Neagu M, Neagu A (2023) Mathematical and computational models in spheroid-based biofabrication. Acta Biomater 165:125–139. https://doi.org/10.1016/j.actbio.2022.07.024

Badali V, Checa S, Zehn MM, Marinkovic D, Mohammadkhah M (2024) Computational design and evaluation of the mechanical and electrical behavior of a piezoelectric scaffold: a preclinical study. Front Bioeng Biotechnol 11:1261108. https://doi.org/10.3389/fbioe.2023.1261108

Baniukiewicz P, Lutton EJ, Collier S, Bretschneider T (2019) Generative adversarial networks for augmenting training data of microscopic cell ımages. Front Comput Sci 1:10. https://doi.org/10.3389/fcomp.2019.00010

Bardini R, Di Carlo S (2024) Computational methods for biofabrication in tissue engineering and regenerative medicine—a literature review. Comput Struct Biotechnol J 23:601–616. https://doi.org/10.1016/j.csbj.2023.12.035

Barredo-Arrieta A, Díaz-Rodríguez N, Del Ser J, Bennetot A, Tabik S, Barbado A, García S, Gil-Lopez S, Molina D, Benjamins R, Chatila R, Herrera F (2020) Explainable artificial intelligence (XAI): concepts, taxonomies, opportunities and challenges toward responsible AI. Inf Fusion 58:82–115. https://doi.org/10.1016/j.inffus.2019.12.012

Barrera MDB, Franco-Martínez F, Lantada AD (2021) Artificial intelligence aided design of tissue engineering scaffolds employing virtual tomography and 3d convolutional neural networks. Materials 14(18):5278. https://doi.org/10.3390/ma14185278

Bishop CM (2006) Pattern recognition and machine learning. Springer, New York

Bonatti AF, Vozzi G, Chua CK et al (2022) A deep learning quality control loop of the extrusion-based bioprinting process. Int J Bioprint 8(4):620. https://doi.org/10.18063/ijb.v8i4.620

Breiman L (2001) Random forests. Mach Learn 45(1):5–32. https://doi.org/10.1023/A:1010933404324

Burges CJC (1998) A tutorial on support vector machines for pattern recognition. Data Min Knowl Disc 2(2):121–167. https://doi.org/10.1023/A:1009715923555

Carter DR, Blenman PR, Beaupré GS (1988) Correlations between mechanical stress history and tissue differentiation in initial fracture healing. J Orthop Res 6:736–748. https://doi.org/10.1002/jor.1100060517

Castilho M, Feyen D, Malda J (2020) Multitechnology biofabrication: a new approach for the manufacturing of functional tissue structures. Biofabrication 12(2):022002. https://doi.org/10.1016/j.tibtech.2020.04.014

Chakrapani G, Kumar VV, Zare M (2025) Next-generation biomaterials: design strategies, clinical translation, and the rise of intelligent therapeutic platforms. ACS Omega 10:46272–46293. https://doi.org/10.1021/acsomega.5c06034

Chansoria P, Rütsche D, Wang A, Liu H, D'Angella D, Rizzo R, Hasenauer A, Weber P, Qiu W, Ibrahim NBM, Korshunova N, Qin XH, Zenobi-Wong M (2023) Synergizing algorithmic design, photoclick chemistry and multi-material volumetric printing for accelerating complex shape engineering. Adv Sci 10(26):e2300912. https://doi.org/10.1002/advs.202300912

Chen T, Guestrin C (2016) XGBoost: a scalable tree boosting system. In: Proceedings of the 22nd ACM SIGKDD international conference on knowledge discovery and data mining, pp 785–794. https://doi.org/10.1145/2939672.2939785

Chen X, Fazel Anvari-Yazdi A, Duan X, Zimmerling A, Gharraei R, Sharma NK, Sweilem SM, Ning L (2023) Biomaterials/bioinks and extrusion bioprinting. Bioact Mater 28:511–536. https://doi.org/10.1016/j.bioactmat.2023.06.006

Chen H, Zhang B, Huang J (2024) Recent advances and applications of artificial intelligence in 3D bioprinting. Biophys Rev 5(3):031301. https://doi.org/10.1063/5.0190208

Chen J, Fu L, Xiang R, Luo S, Huang X, Yu H, Sun L (2025) Artificial intelligence-assisted microfluidic bio-imaging—from sensors to applications: a review. IEEE Sensors J 25(2): 2056–2070. https://doi.org/10.1109/JSEN.2024.3507081

Cortes C, Vapnik V (1995) Support-vector networks. Mach Learn 20:273–297. https://doi.org/10.1007/BF00994018

Elango J, Zamora-Ledezma C (2025) Rheological, structural, and biological trade-offs in bioink design for 3D bioprinting. Gels 11(8):659. https://doi.org/10.3390/gels11080659

Elnemr M, Zheng L, Butt H (2025) A comparative bibliometric analysis of artificial ıntelligence in 3D hydrogel printing: insights from Scopus and web of science (2015–2025). ACS Omega 10(36):40726–40739. https://doi.org/10.1021/acsomega.5c04479

Feng P, Liu L, Yang F, Min R, Wu P, Shuai C (2025) Shape/properties collaborative intelligent manufacturing of artificial bone scaffold: structural design and additive manufacturing process. Biofabrication 17(1):012025. https://doi.org/10.1088/1758-5090/ad905f

Filippi M, Mekkattu M, Katzschmann RK (2025) Sustainable biofabrication: from bioprinting to AI-driven predictive methods. Trends Biotechnol 43(2):290–303. https://doi.org/10.1016/J.TIBTECH.2024.07.002

Florczak S, Größbacher G, Ribezzi D, Longoni A, Gueye M, Grandidier E, Malda J, Levato R (2025) Adaptive and context-aware volumetric printing. Nature 645(8079):108–114. https://doi.org/10.1038/s41586-025-09436-7

Frazier PI (2018) A tutorial on Bayesian optimization. arXiv: https://doi.org/10.48550/arXiv.1807.02811

Freeman S, Calabro S, Williams R, Jin S, Ye K (2022) Bioink formulation and machine learning-empowered bioprinting optimization. Front Bioeng Biotechnol 10:913579. https://doi.org/10.3389/fbioe.2022.913579

Galan EA, Zhao H, Wang X, Dai Q, Huck WTS, Ma S (2020) Intelligent microfluidics: the convergence of machine learning and microfluidics in materials science and biomedicine. Matter 3(6):1893–1922. https://doi.org/10.1016/j.matt.2020.08.034

Gernaey KV, Lantz AE, Tufvesson P, Woodley JM, Sin G (2010) Application of mechanistic models to fermentation and biocatalysis for next-generation processes. Trends Biotechnol 28(7): 346–354. https://doi.org/10.1016/j.tibtech.2010.03.006

Goodfellow I, Bengio Y, Courville A (2016) Deep learning. MIT Press, Cambridge

Hastie T, Tibshirani R, Friedman J (2009) The elements of statistical learning, 2nd edn. Springer, New York. https://doi.org/10.1007/978-0-387-84858-7

Hendrikson WJ, van Blitterswijk CA, Rouwkema J, Moroni L (2017) The use of finite element analyses to design and fabricate three-dimensional scaffolds for skeletal tissue engineering. Front Bioeng Biotechnol 5:30. https://doi.org/10.3389/fbioe.2017.00030

Herrmann L, Kollmannsberger S (2024) Deep learning in computational mechanics: a review. Comput Mech 74:281–331. https://doi.org/10.1007/s00466-023-02434-4

Hinton GE (2007) Learning multiple layers of representation. Trends Cogn Sci 11(10):428–434. https://doi.org/10.1016/j.tics.2007.09.004

Hochreiter S, Schmidhuber J (1997) Long short-term memory. Neural Comput 9(8):1735–1780. https://doi.org/10.1162/neco.1997.9.8.1735

Jin Z, Zhang Z, Shao X, Gu GX (2023) Monitoring anomalies in 3D bioprinting with deep neural networks. ACS Biomater Sci Eng 9(7):3945–3952. https://doi.org/10.1021/acsbiomaterials.0c01761

Jin L, Zhai X, Wang K, Zhang K, Wu D, Nazir A, Jiang J, Liao WH (2024) Big data, machine learning, and digital twin assisted additive manufacturing: a review. Mater Des 244:113086. https://doi.org/10.1016/J.MATDES.2024.113086

Jordan MI, Mitchell TM (2015) Machine learning: trends, perspectives, and prospects. Science 349(6245):255–260. https://doi.org/10.1126/science.aaa8415

Katsoulakis E, Wang Q, Wu H, Shahriyari L, Fletcher R, Liu J, Achenie L, Liu H, Jackson P, Xiao Y, Syeda-Mahmood T, Tuli R, Deng J (2024) Digital twins for health: a scoping review. NPJ Digit Med 7(1):77. https://doi.org/10.1038/s41746-024-01073-0

Kelly D, Sergis V, Ventura i Blanco L, Mason K, Daly AC (2025) Autonomous control of extrusion bioprinting using convolutional neural networks. Adv Funct Mater 35:2424553. https://doi.org/10.1002/adfm.202424553

Kim J, McKee JA, Fontenot JJ, Jung JP (2020) Engineering tissue fabrication with machine intelligence: generating a blueprint for regeneration. Front Bioeng Biotechnol 7:443. https://doi.org/10.3389/fbioe.2019.00443

Krizhevsky A, Sutskever I, Hinton GE (2012) ImageNet classification with deep convolutional neural networks. Adv Neural Inf Proces Syst 25:1097–1105. https://doi.org/10.1145/3065386

LeCun Y, Bottou L, Bengio Y, Haffner P (1998) Gradient-based learning applied to document recognition. Proc IEEE 86(11):2278–2324. https://doi.org/10.1109/5.726791

LeCun Y, Bengio Y, Hinton G (2015) Deep learning. Nature 521:436–444. https://doi.org/10.1038/nature14539

Li X, Zhu H, Gu B, Yao C, Gu Y, Xu W, Zhang J, He J, Liu X, Li D (2023) Advancing intelligent organ-on-a-chip systems with comprehensive in situ bioanalysis. Adv Mater 36:2305268. https://doi.org/10.1002/adma.202305268

Lindner M, Blaeser A (2022) Scalable biofabrication: a perspective on the current state and future potentials of process automation in 3D bioprinting applications. Biofabrication 14(4):045008. https://doi.org/10.3389/fbioe.2022.855042

Lloyd SP (1982) Least squares quantization in PCM. IEEE Trans Inf Theory 28(2):129–137. https://doi.org/10.1109/TIT.1982.1056489

Lundberg SM, Erion G, Chen H, DeGrave A, Prutkin JM, Nair B, Katz R, Himmelfarb J, Bansal N, Lee S-I (2020) Explainable AI for trees: from local explanations to global understanding. Nat Mach Intell 2(1):56–67. https://doi.org/10.1038/s42256-019-0138-9

MacQueen J (1967) Some methods for classification and analysis of multivariate observations. In: Le Cam LM, Neyman J (eds) Proceedings of the fifth Berkeley symposium on mathematical statistics and probability, vol 1. University of California Press, Berkeley, pp 281–297

Manekar K, Bhaiyya ML, Hasamnis MA, Kulkarni MB (2025) Intelligent microfluidics for plasma separation: integrating computational fluid dynamics and machine learning for optimized microchannel design. Biosensors 15(2):94. https://doi.org/10.3390/bios15020094

Matavosian AA, Bonassar LJ (2025) Reimagining bioprinters: real-time monitoring for quality control of bioprinted constructs and future vision. Biofabrication 17(4):042008. https://doi.org/10.1088/1758-5090/ae11d4

Mironov V, Trusk T, Kasyanov V, Little S, Swaja R, Markwald R (2009) Biofabrication: a 21st century manufacturing paradigm. Biofabrication 1(2):022001. https://doi.org/10.1088/1758-5082/1/2/022001

Mitchell TM (1997) Machine learning. McGraw-Hill, New York

Mnih V, Kavukcuoglu K, Silver D, Rusu AA, Veness J, Bellemare MG et al (2015) Human-level control through deep reinforcement learning. Nature 518:529–533. https://doi.org/10.1038/nature14236

Mohammadnabi S, Moslemy N, Taghvaei H, Zia AW, Askarinejad S, Shalchy F (2025) Role of artificial intelligence in data-centric additive manufacturing processes for biomedical applications. J Mech Behav Biomed Mater 166:106949. https://doi.org/10.1016/j.jmbbm.2025.106949

Mohammadrezaei D, Podina L, de Silva J, Kohandel M (2024) Cell viability prediction and optimization in extrusion-based bioprinting via neural network-based Bayesian optimization models. Biofabrication 16(2):025016. https://doi.org/10.1088/1758-5090/ad17cf

Monga A, Jain K, Popli H, Telgote P, Kaur G, Rizwani F, Chauhan R, Kaur D, Chauhan A, Tuli HS (2025) Organs-on-chips: revolutionizing biomedical research. Biophysica 5(3):38. https://doi.org/10.3390/biophysica5030038

Murphy KP (2012) Machine learning: a probabilistic perspective. MIT Press, Cambridge

Ng WL, Chan A, Ong YS, Chua CK (2020) Deep learning for fabrication and maturation of 3D bioprinted tissues and organs. Virtual Phys Prototyp 15:340–358. https://doi.org/10.1080/17452759.2020.1771741

Noi PT, Kappas M (2018) Comparison of random Forest, k-nearest neighbor, and support vector machine classifiers for land cover classification using Sentinel-2 imagery. Sensors 18(1):18. https://doi.org/10.3390/s18010018

Ogunsanya M, Desai S (2023) Physics-based and data-driven modeling for biomanufacturing 4.0. Manuf Lett 36:91–95. https://doi.org/10.1016/j.mfglet.2023.04.003

Osokin A, Chessel A, Carazo-Salas RE, Vaggi F (2017) GANs for biological image synthesis. In: 2017 IEEE international conference on computer vision (ICCV), pp 2252–2261. http://arxiv.org/abs/1708.04692

Pavlovich MJ, Hunsberger J, Atala A (2016) Biofabrication: a secret weapon to advance manufacturing, economies, and healthcare. Trends Biotechnol 34(9):679–680. https://doi.org/10.1016/j.tibtech.2016.07.002

Piotrowska U, Tsoi J, Singh P, Banerjee A, Sobczak M (2025) 3D bioprinting and artificial intelligence for tumor microenvironment modeling: a scoping review of models, methods, and integration pathways. Mol Pharm 22:5801–5823. https://doi.org/10.1021/acs.molpharmaceut.5c01062

Post JN, Loerakker S, Merks RM, Carlier A (2022) Implementing computational modeling in tissue engineering: where disciplines meet. Tissue Eng A 28:542–554. https://doi.org/10.1089/ten.tea.2021.0215

Quan R, Cantero Chinchilla S, Liu F (2025) Investigation of the effects of 3D printing parameters on the mechanical properties of bone scaffolds: experimental study integrated with artificial neural networks. Bioengineering 12(3):315. https://doi.org/10.3390/bioengineering12030315

Rafieyan S, Ansari E, Vasheghani-Farahani E (2024) A practical machine learning approach for predicting the quality of 3D (bio) printed scaffolds. Biofabrication 16:045014. https://doi.org/10.1088/1758-5090/ad6374

Rajitha A, Kansal L, Raj G, Kalra R, Dhamija K, Abdul-Zahra DS (2024) Biomaterials and artificial intelligence: predictive modeling and design. In: E3S web of conferences, vol 505. https://doi.org/10.1051/e3sconf/202450501003

Ramesh S, Deep A, Tamayol A, Kamaraj A, Mahajan C, Madihally S (2024) Advancing 3D bioprinting through machine learning and artificial intelligence. Bioprinting 38:e00331. https://doi.org/10.1016/J.BPRINT.2024.E00331

Rives A, Meier J, Sercu T, Goyal S, Lin Z, Liu J, Guo D, Ott M, Zitnick CL, Ma J, Fergus R (2021) Biological structure and function emerge from scaling unsupervised learning to 250 million protein sequences. Proc Natl Acad Sci 118(15):e2016239118. https://doi.org/10.1073/pnas.2016239118

Schmidhuber J (2015) Deep learning in neural networks: an overview. Neural Netw 61:85–117. https://doi.org/10.1016/j.neunet.2014.09.003

Shahriari B, Swersky K, Wang Z, Adams RP, de Freitas N (2016) Taking the human out of the loop: a review of Bayesian optimization. Proc IEEE 104(1):148–175. https://doi.org/10.1109/JPROC.2015.2494218

Shin J, Lee Y, Li Z, Hu J, Park SS, Kim K (2022) Optimized 3D bioprinting technology based on machine learning: A review of recent trends and advances. Micromachines 13(3):363. https://doi.org/10.3390/mi13030363

Sun W, Darling A, Starly B, Nam J (2004) Computer-aided tissue engineering: overview, scope and challenges. Biotechnol Appl Biochem 39(Pt 1):29–47. https://doi.org/10.1042/BA20030108

Sun J, Yao K, Zhu H, Huang K, Huang D (2025) Deep learning for polymer scaffold bioimage analysis: opportunities and challenges. Int J Bioprint 11(2):16–33. https://doi.org/10.36922/ijb.4035

Sutton RS, Barto AG (2018) Reinforcement learning: an introduction. MIT Press, Cambridge

Tao F, Zhang H, Liu A, Nee AYC (2019) Digital twin in industry: state-of-the-art. IEEE Trans Industr Inform 15(4):2405–2415. https://doi.org/10.1109/tii.2018.2873186

Tian S, Stevens R, McInnes BT, Lewinski NA (2021) Machine assisted experimentation of extrusion-based bioprinting systems. Micromachines 12(7). https://doi.org/10.3390/mi12070780

Tsai HF, Podder S, Chen PY (2023) Microsystem advances through integration with artificial intelligence. Micromachines 14(4):826. https://doi.org/10.3390/mi14040826

Ullman S (2019) Using neuroscience to develop artificial intelligence. Science 363(6428):692–693. https://doi.org/10.1126/science.aau6595

Vijayaragavan V, Vijayakumar M, Dharshini P, Karunakaran K, Kesavan K, Raj RD (2025) AI and automation in organ-on-a-chip technology: advancing personalized medicine and disease modeling. In: 2025 IEEE 6th international conference in robotics and manufacturing automation (ROMA), pp 40–45

Wang Z, Liu K, Li J, Zhu Y, Zhang Y (2019) Various frameworks and libraries of machine learning and deep learning: a survey. Arch Comput Methods Eng 31:1–24. https://doi.org/10.1007/s11831-018-09312-w

Wang X, Jin Y, Schmitt S, Olhofer M (2023) Recent advances in Bayesian optimization. ACM Comput Surv 55(13s):1–36. https://doi.org/10.1145/3582078

Weinberger KQ, Saul LK (2009) Distance metric learning for large margin nearest neighbor classification. J Mach Learn Res 10:207–244. https://dl.acm.org/doi/10.5555/1577069.1577078

Wilkinson DJ (2009) Stochastic modelling for quantitative description of heterogeneous biological systems. Nat Rev Genet 10:122–133. https://doi.org/10.1038/nrg2509

Wu C, Xu Y, Fang J, Li Q (2024) Machine learning in biomaterials, biomechanics/mechanobiology, and biofabrication: state of the art and perspective. Arch Comput Methods Eng 31:3699–3765. https://doi.org/10.1007/s11831-024-10100-y

Xu Y, Sarah R, Habib A, Liu Y, Khoda B (2024) Constraint based Bayesian optimization of bioink precursor: a machine learning framework. Biofabrication 16(4):045031. https://doi.org/10.1088/1758-5090/ad716e

Yang Y, Ji Z, Miao J, Qian X, Chen Y, Wang M (2021) A survey on deep semi-supervised learning. https://doi.org/10.48550/arXiv.2103.00550

Yu J, Yao D, Wang L, Xu M (2025) Machine learning in predicting and optimizing polymer printability for 3D bioprinting. Polymers 17(13):1873. https://doi.org/10.3390/polym17131873

Zhang ML, Zhou ZH (2007) ML-KNN: A lazy learning approach to multi-label learning. Pattern Recogn 40(7):2038–2048. https://doi.org/10.1016/j.patcog.2006.12.019

Zhang S, Li X, Zong M, Zhu X, Wang R (2018) Efficient kNN classification with different numbers of nearest neighbors. IEEE Trans Neural Netw Learn Syst 29(5):1774–1785. https://doi.org/10.1109/TNNLS.2017.2673241

Zhang Z, Chakraborty S, Bedi A S, Mathew E, Saravanan V, Cong L, Velasquez A, Lin-Gibson S, Blewett M, Hendrycs D, London AJ, Zhong E, Raphael B, Ma J, Xing E, Altman R, Church G, Wang M (2025) Generative AI for biosciences: emerging threats and roadmap to biosecurity. arXXiv. https://arxiv.org/abs/2510.15975.

Zhou C, Liu C, Liao Z, Pang Y, Sun W (2025) AI for biofabrication. Biofabrication 17(1):012004. https://doi.org/10.1088/1758-5090/ad8966

Zhu K, Ding Y, Chen Y, Su K, Zheng J, Zhang Y, Hu Y, Wei J, Wang Z (2025) Advancing regenerative medicine: the Aceman system's pioneering automation and machine learning in mesenchymal stem cell biofabrication. Biofabrication 17(2):025021. https://doi.org/10.1088/1758-5090/adb803

A GLOBAL PERSPECTIVE ON REAL ESTATE CYCLES

THE NEW YORK UNIVERSITY SALOMON CENTER SERIES ON FINANCIAL MARKETS AND INSTITUTIONS

VOLUME 6

1. I.T. Vanderhoof and E. Altman (eds.): *The Fair Value of Insurance Liabilities*. 1997 ISBN 0-7923-9941-2
2. R. Levich (ed.): *Emerging Market Capital Flows*. 1997 ISBN 0-7923-9976-5
3. Y. Amihud and G. Miller (eds.): Bank Mergers & Acquisitions: *An Introduction and an Overview*. 1997 ISBN 0-7923-9975-7
4. J.F. Carpenter and D.L. Yermack (eds.): *Executive Compensation and Shareholder Value*. 1998 ISBN 0-7923-8179-3
5. I.T. Vanderhoof and E. Altman (eds.): *The Fair Value of Insurance Business* 2000 ISBN 0-7923-8634-5

A GLOBAL PERSPECTIVE ON REAL ESTATE CYCLES

Edited by
STEPHEN J. BROWN
David S. Loeb Professor of Finance
Stern School of Business
New York University

CROCKER H. LIU
Stern School of Business
New York University

KLUWER ACADEMIC PUBLISHERS
BOSTON / DORDRECHT / LONDON

Distributors for North, Central and South America:
Kluwer Academic Publishers
101 Philip Drive
Assinippi Park
Norwell, Massachusetts 02061 USA
Telephone (781) 871-6600
Fax (781) 681-9045
E-Mail <kluwer@wkap.com>

Distributors for all other countries:
Kluwer Academic Publishers Group
Distribution Centre
Post Office Box 322
3300 AH Dordrecht, THE NETHERLANDS
Telephone 31 78 6392 392
Fax 31 78 6546 474
E-Mail <services@wkap.nl>

Electronic Services <http://www.wkap.nl>

Library of Congress Cataloging-in-Publication Data

A global perspective on real estate cycles / edited by Stephen J. Brown, Crocker H. Liu.
p. cm.—(The New York University Salomon Center series on financial markets and institutions; v.6)
Rev. papers from a conference hosted by New York University's Salomon Center in March, 1999.
Includes bibliographical references.
ISBN 0-7923-7808-3 (alk. paper)
1. Real estate investment—Congresses. 2. Real estate development—Congresses. 3. Real estate business—Congresses. 4. Real estate investment trusts—Congresses. I. Brown, Stephen J. II. Liu, Crocker H. III. Series.
HD1382.5.G576 2000
333.33—dc21 00-025876

Printed on acid-free paper.

Printed in the United States of America

CONTENTS

LIST OF CONTRIBUTORS

Andrew Baum, *Henderson Investors, London and The University of Reading, UK*
Stephen Brown, *Stern School of Business, New York University*
Yoon Dokko, *School of Business Administration, Ajou University, Korea*
Robert Edelstein, *Haas School of Business, University of California, Berkeley*
Piet Eichholtz, *Limburg Institute of Financial Economics (LIFE), Maastricht University*
William Goetzmann, *Yale School of Management*
Ronald Huisman, *Rotterdam School of Management, Erasmus University and FinEdge Rotterdam*
Stefan Koeberle, *The World Bank, Washington DC*
Allan Lacayo, *Haas School of Business, University of California, Berkeley*
Daniel Lee, *Haas School of Business, University of California, Berkeley*
Crocker Liu, *Stern School of Business, New York University*
Bertrand Renaud, *The World Bank, Washington DC*
Susan Wachter, *The Wharton School, University of Pennsylvania*
Ming Zhang, *The World Bank, Washington DC*

FOREWORD

In March 1999, New York University Salomon Center in association with the Department of Finance at NYU Stern held a one-day conference on the impact of real estate cycles on the real estate industry both from a domestic as well as an international perspective. The conference featured the leading research on this topic in the United States, Europe and Asia. Currently, the real estate industry is at a critical point. New development projects around the world are being put on hold given recent developments in the international capital markets. The industry is hard hit by the decline in real estate investment trust (REIT) share prices and a shrinking pool of capital for real estate ventures. This has unfortunately coincided with serious financial problems of very large hedge funds and other institutional investors in the market for commercial mortgage backed securities. There is need for new insights into the implications of U.S. and global real estate cycles on real estate securities including REITs and mortgage-backed securities as well as direct real estate investment.

This global orientation is important given the high mobility of capital into the real estate, the increasing integration of real estate markets, and the proposed expansion of real estate investment trusts (REIT) into international real estate. The process of globalization has resulted in increased competition between cities for the attraction of investment. In response to the globalization of investment markets, local property cultures throughout the world are being transformed to accommodate the practices and requirements of institutional property markets. At the same time, a dearth of serious academic research currently exists on these markets. For example, the lack of attention paid to the real estate sector in Asia is surprising when one considers that thirty of forty percent of short term capital was advanced to countries in the region prior to the recent crisis. In fat, a commonly reported driver of this crisis was the exposure of major Asian banks to real estate. Allegedly, as real estate markets plummeted, banks suffered enormous losses due to their exposures to real estate developers, these problems then spread to the rest of the financial sector. An interesting observation comes from Paul Krugman's recent book, *The Return of Depression Economics*[1]:

"How did a few bad real estate loans and a botched devaluation in Thailand—a small, faraway country of which most people knew little—sent dominoes toppling from Indonesia to South Korea?"

Towards this end, our conference offered new insights into the implications of U.S. and global real estate cycles on real estate securities including REITs and mortgage-backed securities as well as direct real estate investment. The most important insight is that the amplitude and frequency of the cycles differ from place to place and time to time. To the extent that this implies that real estate markets around the world are not yet fully integrated, there are opportunities for global investors. There are also risks. The markets are becoming more correlated, most particularly in periods of crisis. Indeed, the relative immaturity of the Thai real estate market contributed significantly to the extent and severity of the Asian financial crisis of 1997. To exploit these opportunities and to manage the resulting risk, portfolio managers need to develop new data sources and empirical procedures designed to maximize the information content of the data that is available. The lack of high quality data emerges as the central and most pressing issue, not only from a portfolio management context, but also from the standpoint of public policy.

We thank Ingo Walter, the Director of the NYU Salomon Center, who greatly contributed to the planning of this conference, and we acknowledge with gratitude the Center for its very generous financial support. We also thank Mary Jaffier for her very professional handling of the administrative arrangements. We would like to thank the authors of the papers individually for contributing their research and ideas to this collection of papers. Finally, we would like to thank the following discussants and roundtable participants who contributed so much to the success of our conference: Kenneth Campbell, *CRA Real Estate Securities*, William Goetzmann, *Yale School of Management*, Samuel A. Lieber, *Alpine Management*, David Ling, *University of Florida*, Jianping Mei, *Stern School of Business, New York University*, Jay Sa-Aadu, *University of Iowa*, and Joseph Williams, *Professor's Capital.*

NOTE

1. Krugman, Paul, 1999, The Return of Depression Economics, Norton, New York.

A GLOBAL PERSPECTIVE ON REAL ESTATE CYCLES

1. INTRODUCTION

STEPHEN J. BROWN

NYU Stern School of Business

CROCKER H. LIU

NYU Stern School of Business

The real estate industry is cyclical by nature. However, the cycles are neither regular nor predictable. Furthermore, the amplitude and frequency of the cycles differ from place to place and from time to time. The paper by Yoon Dokko, Robert Edelstein, Allan Lacayo and Daniel Lee shows that this is true across cities in the United States, and Andrew Baum argues that this is the case in the United Kingdom and for Europe as a whole. Eichholtz and Huisman present evidence that suggests that the real estate markets are not yet fully integrated, consistent with the observation that institutional real estate investors have only just begun to look beyond national borders, though evidence presented by Goetzmann and Wachter suggests that the markets are becoming more highly correlated, particularly in crisis periods. Another explanation for the relative lack of integration is the immaturity of real estate markets, particularly in Asia. Renaud Zhang and Koeberle document how the immaturity of the Thai real estate market contributed to the extent and severity of the financial crisis in Thailand in 1997. Despite the importance of these issues from both a public policy standpoint, as well as from the standpoint of institutional portfolio management, there is very little high quality data available on a consistent basis across countries on a reasonable frequency. Goetzmann and Wachter propose empirical methods designed to maximize the information content of available data, while other authors describe efforts underway to develop new high quality data for these kinds of studies. Clearly, the data issue is the central and most pressing item on this particular research agenda.

In *The Global Real Estate Crash: Evidence from an International Database*, Goetzmann and Wachter analyse the problem of international real estate diversification by examining the cross-sectional behavior of the international office market. In so doing, it finds evidence of a global market "crash" in 1992 following a period of declining property values. It advocates a clustering procedure designed to identify groups of office markets that have moved together in the past, and to use these robust groups to estimate the reduction in risk that comes from international diversification. The study uses an international database of rents and yields constructed by the International Commercial Property Associates (ICPA) to analyse world office markets from the mid 1980's through the 1990's. The rents and yield numbers are used to infer total returns on an annual basis for 24 countries and a quarterly basis for some. The evidence strongly suggests that global office markets rise and fall with global business cycles, rather than in response to specific real estate factors such as tax law changes or specific institutional arrangements. This suggests an important role for global diversification. However, standard analysis is hampered by inadequate high quality data. For this reason, the paper argues for k-means clustering algorithms to be used as a form of data reduction (the properties of which are described in detail in Brown and Goetzmann 1997), that reduces uncertainty by aggregating like assets into clusters. Applying this analysis yields conservative portfolios that are tilted towards Continental Europe and the U.S., while more aggressive portfolios are tilted towards Asia and the Iberian countries.

A close study of the case of Thailand brings some understanding of the recent Asian crisis and the role of the Thai real estate cycle in precipitating a financial crisis both in Thailand and in global financial markets. Was the real estate cycle a cause or rather a response to the global financial "panic" that occurred at that time? The evidence presented in *Real Estate and the Asian Crisis: Lessons of the Thailand Experience* by Renaud, Zhang and Koeberle suggests that the real estate crisis in that country contributed heavily to a domestic financial crisis whose large cost was further amplified by a currency crisis. Despite the remarkable growth of the Thai economy over the three decades 1965–95, the real estate sector remained relatively immature. By 1995 poor credit risk management and excessive lending to the real estate sector had already contributed to the distress of Thai financial institutions. Therefore, when certain monetary policy mistakes led to a currency crisis in 1997, both the real estate and finance sectors were ill prepared to deal with the consequences. The paper suggests the need for structural improvements to prevent the recurrence of the real estate boom and bust and the extreme severity of the economic consequences both in Thailand and elsewhere. Reforms must include improvements in real estate market infrastructure and sector transparancy, restructuring of financial institutions and the strengthening of capital markets to encourage private sector monitoring and improving the links between the real estate industry and capital markets.

Real Estate Income and Value Cycles: A Model of Market Dynamics by Dokko, Edelstein, Lacayo and Lee develops a model of real estate cycles that links economic fundamentals to real estate income and value. Both the challenge and the incentive to develop such a model arises from the fact that cyclical behavior in various geographic real estate markets is asynchronous, and because the severity of the cycles vary across different real estate sectors. Prior research has attempted to relate real estate cycles to the general macroeconomic cycle, despite the fact that residential cycles are counter-cyclical and commercial construction cycles are coincident with the macroeconomic cycle. Work that links cycles to construction delays is unsatisfactory. This paper instead abstracts from the economic trend, recognizing that the property value is the capitalized value of future expected income and thus infers cycles in real estate values from the cyclical patterns of real estate income. The model is estimated on the basis of quarterly data on domestic product and employment growth, real interest rates and inflation, along with NOI, vacancy rates, absorbton rates and construction permits for 20 metropolitan statistical areas (MSAs). The results of this exercise show that the characteristics of the real estate cycle differ significantly from city to city.

What factors explain the cross-sectional differences between expected returns on international property shares? *The Cross Section of Global Property Share Returns* by Eichholtz and Huisman present evidence that the observed return on real estate is less compensation for adequately diversified international risk exposure than it is a reflection of circumstances within each country. This is consistent with the observed fact that pension funds and other institutional real estate investors have traditionally looked only at their own real estate markets and have only begun to look beyond national borders. Smaller property companies offer a significantly higher expected return than larger companies, and returns are highest where interest rates are lowest and declining and where the term structure of interest rates is upwardly sloped. The data for the study comes from Global Property Research (GPR) that covers 30 global markets. This study concentrates on the six largest national property share markets. Annual returns are cross-sectionally correlated with fund characteristics, including systematic risk measured both against GPR global property returns and against other indices. Systematic risk measures do not explain the cross sectional distribution of returns, while size is significant. Country specific interest rate variables are also significant. This offers opportunities and a caution for global investors. High beta risk strategies will not be rewarded, although strategies that focus on interest rate differentials will yield a higher return. These results suggest that opportunities will be enhanced by the development of the global property share market that allows investors to build up exposure to foreign property markets in a relatively liquid and cost-effective way.

While there may be no universally recognized definition of what constitutes cycles, particularly in the real estate area, the notion that there are predictable patterns in European real estate is widely accepted by practitioners. Cycles are simple, symmetric and highly predictable. Using data from the Investment Property Databank (IPD), *Evidence of cycles in European commercial real estate markets, and some hypotheses* by Baum studies the relative performance of real estate, stocks and bonds. In the context of the United Kingdom researchers have indicated the existence of different cycles of different durations. In particular, the development cycle is not coincident with the identifiable rent cycle but is rather pro-cyclical with GDP growth and property values. The IPD data shows that the cycles range in length from 4 to 12 years, and that the recurrent but irregular patterns may be the product of overlapping cycles of different lengths (5 to 9 years). While the property cycle is linked to the economic cycle, the precise nature of the relationship varies from one cycle to the next. The relationships are different in the non UK European markets, where there is neither ready substitution nor a price-elastic supply response. As a consequence, cycles are elongated and exaggerated. However, we would expect that with increased globalization these markets will be brought into line. This is illustrated by the case of the property market in the City of London, and in the context of the introduction of a single European currency which will facilitate the development of a securitised market. This globalization will promote both a more efficient flow of capital and a less pronounced real estate cycle.

2. THE GLOBAL REAL ESTATE CRASH: EVIDENCE FROM AN INTERNATIONAL DATABASE

WILLIAM N. GOETZMANN

Yale School of Management

SUSAN M. WACHTER

The Wharton School

INTRODUCTION

The past decade has been a period of globalization in the world's investment markets. Access to international investment has broadened dramatically as barriers to cross-border investment have lifted. During the 1980's many equity and debt markets around the world performed well, and none more so than those in emerging markets. Willingness by U.S. investors to diversify beyond their borders was based, in part, upon the availability of statistical information about the risk and return characteristics of these markets, as well as upon the increasing use of optimization models to manage portfolio risk and return.

All of these trends are true for real estate as well. A decade ago it was virtually impossible to obtain performance information about international real estate investments. Today, such data are available for established as well as emerging real estate markets. In the 1980's and 1990's international real estate investors actively pursued a global development strategy, and investment portfolio managers sought high returns and diversification in cross-border real estate deals. In a fashion similar to the world's stock markets, the highest returns to real estate investment over the recent period have been in emerging real estate markets, most notably the Far East. While international investment in real estate has yielded high returns for some investors, it engenders significant risk. For example, investors who sought the safety of international real estate markets in the 1990's experienced shocking declines in both U.K. and Japan and lackluster performance in most continental European

S.J. Brown and C.H. Liu (eds.). A GLOBAL PERSPECTIVE ON REAL ESTATE CYCLES.

markets as well. In theory, international diversification lowers investor risk. In practice, this diversification has some serious pitfalls.

In this paper, we focus on the problem of international real estate diversification by examining the cross-sectional behavior of the international office market. We find clear evidence of a global market "crash" in 1992, which was preceded in most cases by declining property values since the end of the 1980's. We explore the role of international real estate investments in the portfolio. We address some of the pitfalls of international diversification through the use of a statistical method, "cluster analysis" to identify meaningful groups of office markets that moved together over the last eight years. The clustering method identifies three major "families" of commercial property markets, and shows them to be relatively robust groups. These groups are then used in a mean-variance optimization framework to estimate the potential reduction in risk, if any, that a U.S. investor might have achieved through international diversification.

Our analysis suggests that the use of raw historical data for the construction of international portfolios is likely to be dangerously misleading, due to uncertainty regarding inputs to the mean-variance optimization. The aggregation procedures we use reduce this uncertainty, and provide guidelines for prudent cross-border diversification. One approach to the data problem taken by Liu and Mei (1994) is to gather higher quality data. They use returns to investable property trusts in a number of other countries to examine the benefits of diversification. Where property trusts exist and data are available, this is obviously an attractive alternative to the use of appraisal data. However many cross-border real estate investment decisions must be made on the basis of different information.

THE ICPA DATA

For ten years, International Commercial Property Associates has maintained a database of commercial rents and yields for a number of countries around the world. The rent data is gathered by Hillier-Parker in the U.K. and affiliates in Southeast Asia and Australia and Landauer in the U.S. Other real estate research firms report information to ICPA for rents in Europe, Canada and Scandinavia. These data, despite certain limitations, provide a fascinating glimpse of the world real estate crash over the late 1980's and late 1990's.

In our analysis of the International Commercial Property Associates [ICPA] data, we focus on world office markets. These are defined by ICPA as first class, or class A office spaces in excess of 5,000 square feet in prime locations in principal cities. These are total returns, i.e. income and appreciation, however the appreciation is *not* based upon appraisals, but upon changes in capitalized rents. The rents are asking rents. This may make it difficult to exactly identify crashes in the office market, since effective rents typically lead asking rents in declining markets. In addition, it is difficult to determine from the ICPA data sources the extent to which the rents could be considered "net." Without clear evidence on this, we make the assumption that they are not. Thus, while effective rents are desirable, they are not easily

Table 1. Summary Statistics For ICPA Total Returns

	Local Currency		Dollar Denominated	
	Arith. Mean	Stand. Dev.	Arith. Mean	Stand. Dev.
Australia	9.35	31.33	7.63	21.05
Belgium	19.36	23.90	13.25	14.27
Canada	11.29	17.34	10.00	12.69
Denmark	0.82	15.62	−3.13	10.04
Finland	9.08	34.31	7.38	24.77
France	17.07	30.55	11.75	20.62
Germany	20.43	19.95	14.63	13.80
Holland	20.01	21.61	13.88	14.18
HongKong	35.25	38.89	35.13	39.19
Ireland	12.86	17.59	10.25	9.07
Italy	21.51	41.91	18.25	30.17
Malaysia	11.13	37.10	NA	NA
Norway	1.68	16.41	1.13	13.25
Singapore	27.70	44.52	36.75	23.24
Portugal	36.75	23.24	22.50	38.93
Spain	23.93	51.64	18.25	39.07
Sweden	07.70	44.11	05.75	33.28
Switzerl.	10.95	61.81	3.50	47.08
Taiwan	39.47	42.96	32.25	41.80
UK	07.96	33.31	5.75	24.84
USA	07.75	9.10	7.75	09.10
Averages	16.76	31.29	13.55	24.57

obtained. Yields are implicitly a function of appraised property values and net operating income in each market. Thus, the estimated total return $T_{i,t}$ for country I at time t is:

$$T_{i,t} = Y_{i,t-1} + [R_{i,t}/Y_{i,t-1}][Y_{i,t-2}/R_{i,t-1}] - 1$$

Where rents $[R_{i,t}]$ and yields $[Y_{i,t}]$ are collected on an annual basis for 24 countries, and a quarterly basis for some countries. Returns provided by ICPA are nominal, and denominated in each country's own currency.

Summary statistics about these return series are instructive. The equally-weighted global average returns to investment in office markets was 13.5% in dollar-denominated terms over the period. This return compares favorably with the total return to investment in the S&P 500 over the 1986 through 1993 period (14.1%), however the risk of global office market investment was considerably greater. Whether calculated in dollar terms, or in terms of local currency, the volatility of most office markets around the world far exceeded that of the U.S. The average standard deviation was higher than 25% per year. The volatility of dollar-denominated returns in certain markets was extraordinary over the period. Hong Kong, Malaysia, Portugal, Spain, Switzerland and Taiwan all had standard deviations exceeding 35% per year. The volatility is largely due to changes in the capitalized

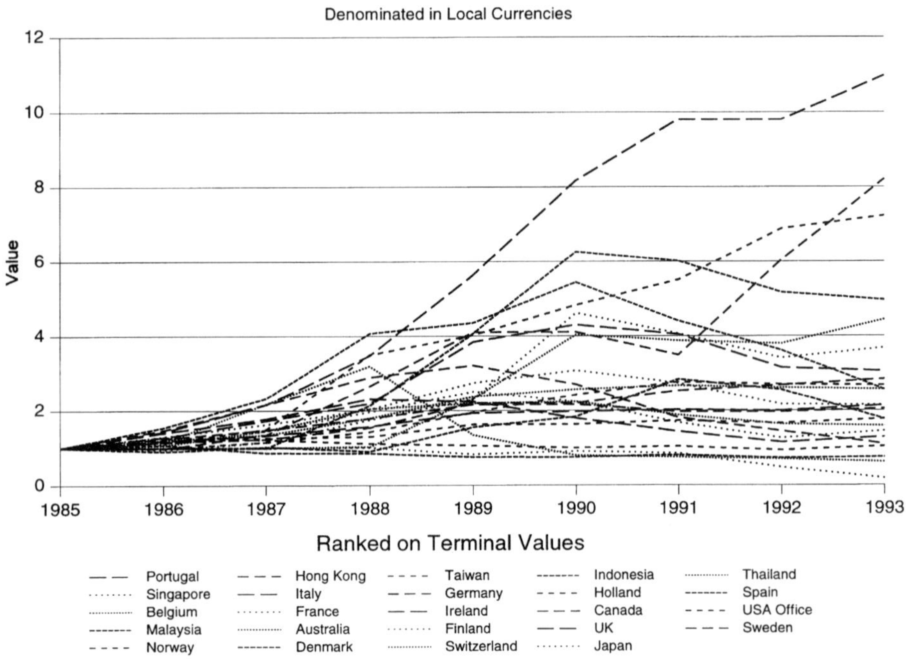

Figure 2.1. Global Office Markets Wealth Indices

rents. This method of estimating values implicitly assumes that new asking rents are good proxies for the expected future rents. Sometimes this is a reasonable assumption, and sometimes it is not. Property managers are often able to diversify their exposure to shocks in rents by diversification across lease maturities. The simplicity of the capitalized rent series does not account for this. Despite the limitations of the dataset, it provides a useful basis for comparison of the performance of office markets around the world. While estimates risk and return are approximate, they clearly suggest that overseas markets have been more volatile than those in the U.S.

THE GLOBAL REAL ESTATE CRASH

Figure 1 shows the cumulative wealth indices for all of the countries. Note that most markets were flat or down over the second half of the sample period. In particular, we find that the 1992 downturn in rents and property values in the United States was a world-wide phenomenon, experienced by twenty-one of the twenty-four markets studied. In addition, the drop in office building values was as severe as it was broad. In several countries, property values decreased by more than thirty percent. Figure 2 shows the wealth indices converted to U.S. dollar returns, and the

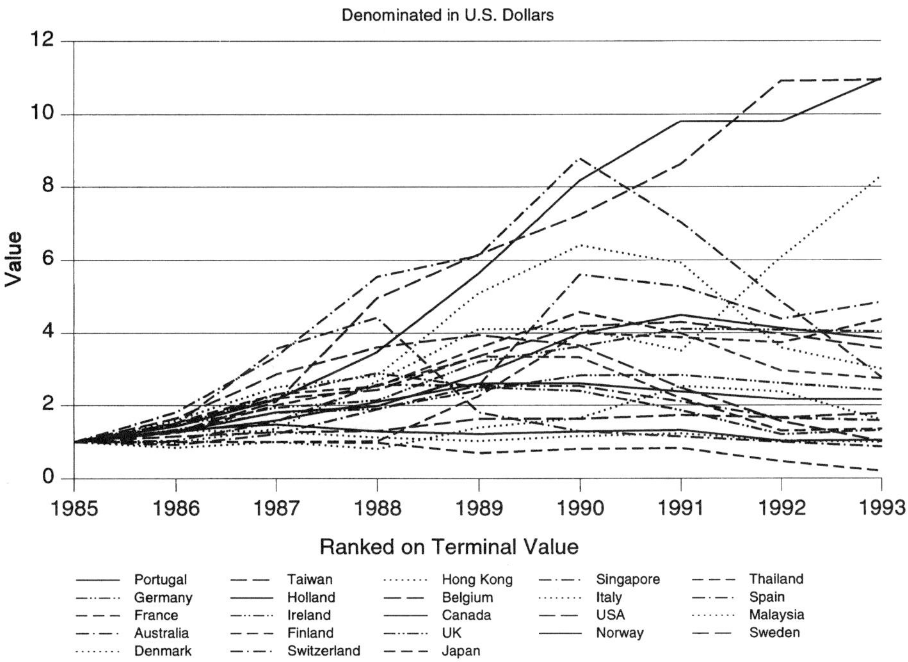

Figure 2.2. Global Office Markets Wealth Indices

basic trends are unaffected. The message of this cross-sectional analysis of the ICPA data is clear. The recent U.S. crash was a global crash. There were few safe havens in the early 1990's for investors in global office markets. Figures 3 and 4 plot the average annual return for each index in local currency and dollar terms. From 1986 through 1990, a negative return for any country was rare. 1991 and 1993 were mixed years, but in 1992, the year of the global real estate crash, only three of the twenty-four countries had positive returns.

WHY DID IT HAPPEN?

From the perspective of the United States market, it is tempting to explore domestic reasons for the real estate downturn. Potential causes include the 1986 tax law change, shifting bank and insurance regulation and evolving U.S. pension policy. Fergus and Goodman (1994) among others suggest that the magnitude of the U.S. crisis was due to the rapid constriction in bank credit. None of these is sufficient to explain such a widespread global downturn, however. While the U.S. is one of the world's most important economies, direct U.S. real estate investment across the globe is unlikely to have caused the crash. Current research suggests a number of

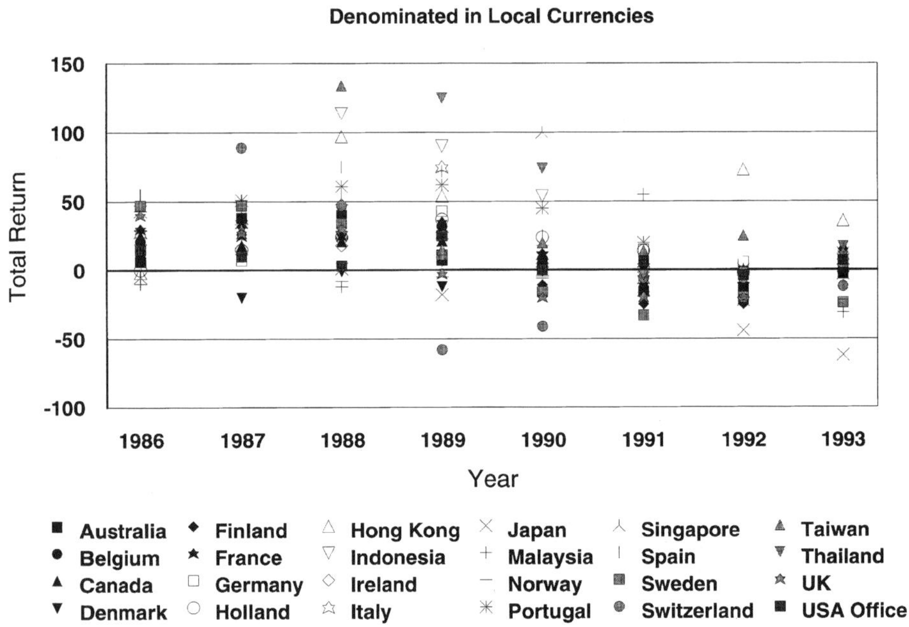

Figure 2.3. Returns in Global Office Markets

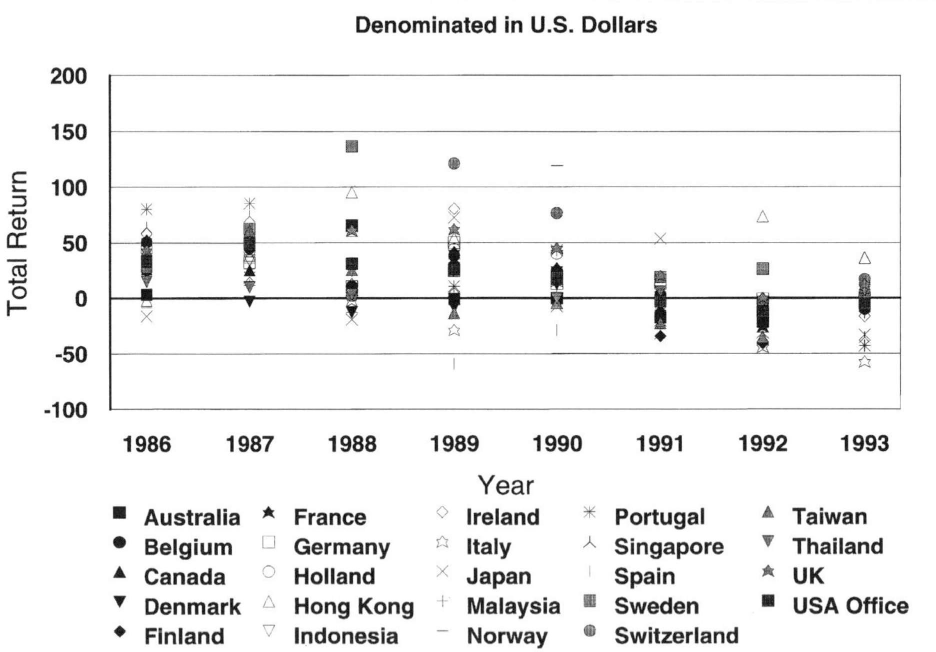

Figure 2.4. Returns in Global Office Markets

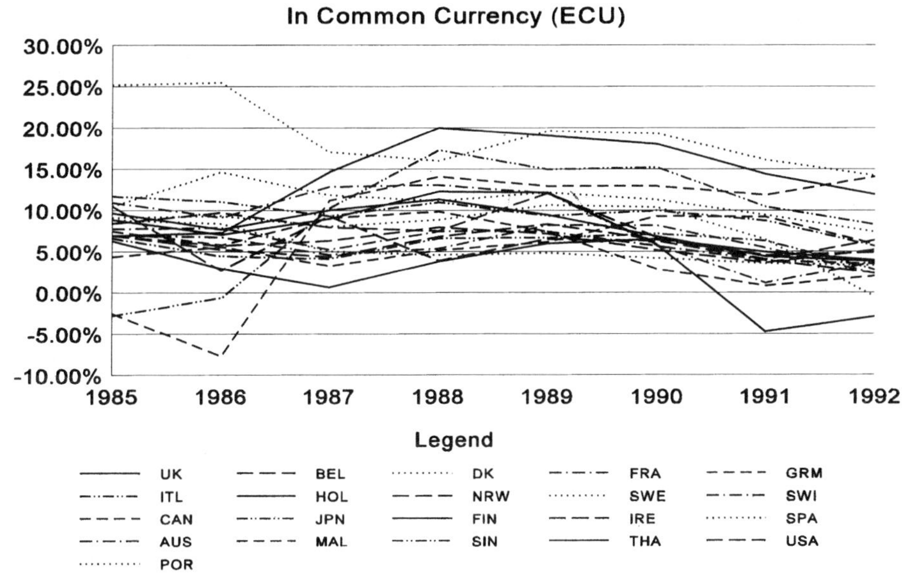

Figure 2.5. Percent Change in GDP

contributing international factors. Renaud (1994), for instance, attributes the crash to a massive surge of Japanese international investment capital in the 1980's. He traces a cascade of international property investment that may have led to price disequilibrium in office markets. In addition, Renaud (1994) and Hendershott and Kane (1992) have linked the 1980's building frenzy to easy credit and lax regulation in the U.S., Japan and elsewhere.

While Japanese capital increases and global institutional changes certainly provided the context for the global crash, there is some evidence for an underlying economic basis for the crisis. Figure 5 shows the percentage change in gross domestic product [GDP] for each of the countries in the database over the period. Note that a global contraction in production began in 1988 and 1989. Virtually all GDP growth rates in the sample were lower in 1991 and 1992 than in the 1987–1990 period. While insufficient time-series data exist to test for causality between the two variables, it is doubtful that the real estate crash precipitated the global contraction in production, but the reverse is certainly plausible. In fact, it is likely that the demand for office real estate values respond to fluctuations in demand from the production sector. The story told by these figures is a simple one. Global office markets move up and down with global business cycles. Such movements may have occurred regardless of credit expansions or constrictions, bank regulatory changes, or the Japanese financial crisis. None-the-less, each of these could have been exacerbating factors, since none is properly exogenous.

It is appealing to look for fluctuations in demand for office space as a possible explanation for the office market slump, if only for purposes of parsimony. The co-incidence of the global recession and the real estate crash alone is insufficient to explain why the decrease in demand for office space was unanticipated. Figure 5 suggests that trends in GDP growth might have been forecastable by developers, bankers and mortgage lenders, however this conjecture is 20/20 hindsight. A test of the rationality of developers and lenders during the 1980's awaits future analysis that takes into account the forecasts of GDP at that time, as well as anticipated future office space.

Regardless of the root causes for the global crash, it is valuable to know the degree to which exposure to a common set of economic variables drives returns in the world's office markets. One empirical approach to this question is to extract latent variables from historical data. To this end, we calculated the principal components from the matrix of total returns. Since we have more countries than time periods, the maximum number of orthogonal principal components is limited to eight. The variance explained by these factors (in order of importance) is: .44, .21, .13, .09, .06, .04, .015, 0, 0. In other words, 44% of the variation in global office market returns is captured by a single factor. Whether this factor is global inflation, global production or some unidentified source of risk is an open empirical question. An examination of the weights comprising the first principal component suggest that it is close to being and equal-weighted index formed from the individual series. Thus there appears to be at least one, strong, common factor that drove international office markets in the recent past. While diversification might help to reduce some of the extraordinary non-systematic risk implied by the high volatility of many of the markets, there is undoubtedly a high lower bound on the benefits of spreading risks internationally. In the next section, we address some major issues confronting the creation of a global real estate portfolio, and provide a method for reducing errors associated with portfolio creation.

INTERNATIONAL DIVERSIFICATION: APPLYING MEAN-VARIANCE ANALYSIS

Asset allocation using mean-variance analysis has become increasingly popular among institutional investors over the past decade. In fact, it has been a major impetus towards global investment because it typically indicates that international diversification reduces risk. In theory, mean-variance analysis identifies a set of portfolios that maximize the investor's expected return for each level of risk. This set of portfolios is called the *efficient frontier* since it represents all of the undominated portfolios in risk and return space. In practice, the identification of the efficient frontier is hampered by problems of estimation. An exact identification of the efficient frontier is only possible when the future means, standard deviations and correlations of each asset in the choice set are known with certainty. Typically, these inputs are estimated from historical time-series data. Thus, errors are large when only a short historical period is available for analysis. The effect of these errors on the investment decision can be dramatic. Assets with high means tend to dominate the portfolios on the efficient frontier. This is the case even when the high means are due to estimation error. For example, when the number of assets included in the choice set grows large, the chance that one will have an unusually high mean *due entirely to chance* also increases. One approach to reducing estimation error is to optimize over a few sub-indices for which means, standard deviations and correlation's can be well estimated. Elton and Gruber (1971) suggest that a useful first step towards mean-variance optimization is to aggregate individual assets into asset classes. If assets within classes can be expected to move together, and have similar risk and return characteristics, this will greatly improve the results of the mean-variance analysis. For instance, consider a simple case in which there are three asset classes. These classes can be treated as separate populations, and the individual asset return histories can be regarded as samples from the population. Each asset within a class shares the same mean, standard deviation and correlation with respect to the other two classes. Suppose one wished to estimate statistics about the asset class, rather than the individual assets comprising it. In this case, the standard error of the mean estimate will decrease in the square root of the number of included assets. In practice, since assets are *not* drawn from identical populations, there is a tradeoff between errors due to assignment to the wrong group versus errors due to estimation uncertainty.

Because the time-series data from IPCA is so short, and the appreciation is estimated via capitalization of rents, rather than appraisals or transactions, the estimation error in the means is likely to be dramatic. For this reason, we selected a relatively high level of aggregation i.e. three "families." To estimate these families, we apply a commonly-used clustering algorithm, k-means, so the time-series of returns. The procedure is described in more detail in the next section.

K-MEANS CLUSTER ANALYSIS

A useful first step to forming a diversified portfolio is to identify a few groups of assets that behave differently across groups and similarly within groups. There are a number of different approaches to grouping assets. Following Elton and Gruber (1971) and our own recent work, Abraham, Goetzmann and Wachter (1994) and Goetzmann and Wachter (1994) on residential housing indices and commercial rent indices, we apply the k-means clustering algorithm to country returns in order to identify meaningful clusters of countries which moved together in the past, and which are likely to move together in the future.

The procedure, developed by Hartigan (1975), assumes a fixed number of groups within the sample of observations and chooses an allocation of observations to groups to minimize within-group sums of squared deviations from the mean. For the global office markets, we assume that there are $J = 1 \ldots k$ distinct groups of office markets in the world, where a group is defined as more than one of the $j = 1 \ldots N$ office markets whose time-series of returns resemble each others. The clustering procedure allocates market j to group J in order to minimize the within-group sum of squared deviations from the group average. That is, we assume that the returns for any member of group J can be expressed as:

$$R_{J,t} = R_{J,t} + e_{J,t} \quad \text{where} \quad R_{J,t} = (1/n_J)\text{SUM}_{\text{over } I \text{ in } J}(R_{i,t})$$

And the algorithm seeks assignments of countries to groups in order to minimize the sum of squared errors:

$$\text{SSE} = \text{SUM}_{\text{from } J=1\ldots k}\text{SUM}_{\textit{from } t=1\ldots T}[R_{j,t} - (1/n_J)\text{SUM}_{\text{over } I \text{ in } J}(R_{i,t})]^2$$

To find a global minimum requires calculation of the SSE for every possible combination of countries to groups—a huge problem. Local optima may be found by beginning with a set of means in T space, corresponding to a set of k existing observations, and then seeking switches that reduce the SSE.

One problem is that the k-means procedure requires pre-specification of the number of groups. While it is natural to think of a North American group, a European group and an Asian Pacific group, perhaps the global markets are more naturally represented by a simple division into two markets, or a more complex division into five or ten independent clusters. To address this issue empirically, we use a bootstrapping procedure.

The bootstrap can be used to estimate confidence bands about the clusters, and also to estimate how many clusters appear in the data. Let $R_{i,t}$ represent the percent return for country I at time t, where t ranges from 1986 through 1993, and I includes twenty-four countries. $R_{i,t}$ is the vector of t returns for all countries in the sample at time t. For the bootstrap, we create a pseudo-history of returns by randomizing with replacement over the dimension of time, to generate t★, a vector of length eight, for which dates between 1986 through 1993 have been drawn with replacement with equal probability. We then create a pseudo-history R★ by selecting the cross-section of returns that correspond to the bootstrapped dates: $R_{i,t\star}$ corresponding to each new date in the pseudo-history. That is:

$$R^{\star}_{i,t} = R_{i,t^{\star}}$$

and t★ is a random element of {1986 . . . 1993}

Where random refers to random draws with replacement from the set. We apply k-means to this new matrix of data, and save the resulting clusters. When this procedure is repeated many times over, it provides a range of possible outcomes that differ from the original clustering result. Each of these draws has been generated by the same underlying multivariate distribution of the data, however it corresponds to a different historical pattern. We can summarize the results of the bootstrap in frequency of association tables that indicate how often, out of 1,000 simulations, two countries grouped together.

In order to determine whether the frequency of association is high or low, and in order to test whether it is significantly different from the null hypothesis of no association, we need benchmark frequencies. These are calculated by bootstrapping the data under the null hypothesis. To reproduce the distribution of the pairwise associations under the null hypothesis that there are no relationships among the countries and there are no differences in means, we created a pseudo-history by drawing with replacement from the entire sample, mixing across countries as well as time. That is, we do not preserve differences across rows or columns.

$$R^{\star NULL}_{i,t} = R_{i,t^\star}$$

where t★ is a random element of {1 . . . T}

I★ is a random element of {1 . . . N}

This reproduces the marginal distributional characteristics of the data, while destroying the country-specific and time-specific relations. We then apply the k-means algorithm to the pseudo-data, and save the results, as before. A thousand iterations of the procedure yields empirical quantiles of the frequency of association under the null hypothesis. Without these quantiles we would have no way to judge whether a frequency implies association or dissociation.

HOW MANY GROUPS?

To estimate the number of clusters in the data, we calculate the mean squared error difference between the cells in the association frequency table, and the median association frequency under the null. The number of clusters for which this value is maximized provides the greatest level of rejection of the null. We found that the mean squared deviation from the null hypothesis for each pre-specified cluster number grows quickly after two groups, and then drops after seven (see Figure 6). Three groups is near the maximum. Four through seven groups do almost as good a job at rejection of the null as does three, however. Figure 7 shows the geographical relationships among the clusters. Cluster one contains Belgium, Canada, Denmark, France, Germany, Holland, Ireland, Italy, Malaysia, Portugal, Singapore and the U.S.. Cluster two contains Australia, Finland, Spain, Sweden, Switzerland and the U.K. Cluster three contains Hong Kong and Taiwan. Figure 8 shows the clustering when seven groups are specified. With greater freedom to split countries into more groups, all four of the southeast Asian markets separate into groups. European countries separate from the U.S. and Canada and the group containing U.K. and Australia remains nearly unchanged.

TESTS OF ROBUSTNESS

How robust are these clusters? Could they simply be a result of chance similarities among a set of independent random variables? In Table 2, we show the result of robustness studies of the clusters. The table provides a frequency of association table for all countries when three groups are specified, as well as the 5%, 50% and 95% frequency quantiles from the bootstrap under the null. Without these intervals, one could not tell whether an association frequency of .4 was suggestive of association or of dissociation. Given three clusters, an association frequency between 37% and

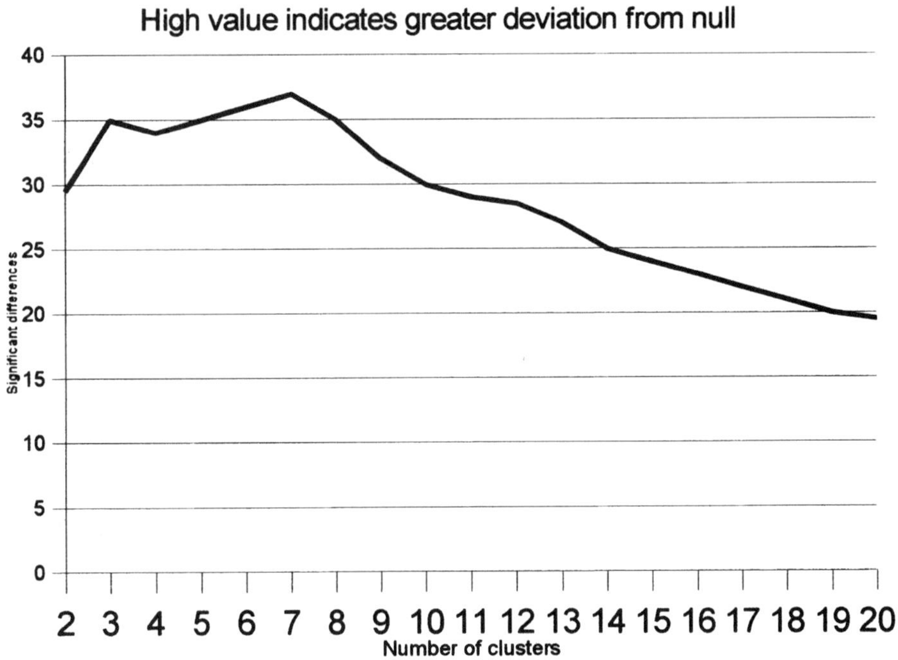

Figure 2.6. Test Statistic For Number of Clusters

Figure 2.7. K-Means With Three Groups

Figure 2.8. K-Means With Seven Groups

48% is suggestive, but not convincing evidence of association. The table suggests that ambiguous relationships between countries are relatively infrequent. Canada has the most association frequencies falling between the 5% and 95% thresholds, with seven. For instance, we cannot reject the hypothesis that Canada clusters with U.K. as well as Sweden, Belgium, France, Holland, Denmark, Malaysia and Norway. On the other hand, Australia, Sweden, Hong Kong and Taiwan are all relatively unambiguous in their relationships with other countries. In certain cases, these ambiguities are telling. For instance, even though they typically cluster in different groups, we cannot reject the hypothesis that Singapore and Australia belong in the same group, or that Singapore and Hong Kong belong in the same group. In other words, we cannot reject the hypothesis that the southeast Asian cluster extends beyond Hong Kong and Taiwan to include Singapore, and perhaps even Australia.

Figure 9 plots the association frequencies for four selected countries, U.S., U.K., Hong Kong and Taiwan. A bar over .48 high indicates a significant association between cities, and a bar less than .28 high indicates a significant dissociation. Notice that U.S. is strongly associated with the greatest number of other countries including much of Europe, while the U.K. has its own distinct group, including Australia. Oddly enough, although k-means groups Singapore with the U.S. using the avail-

Table 2. Association Frequencies

Each table entry represents the frequency with which two countries appeared in the same cluster, given 1,000 bootstraps. To evaluate the significance of association and dissociation between two countries, the frequency may be compared to the distribution of association frequencies expected under the null hypothesis of no associations. These are: 5% quantile = .28, 50% quantile = .37, 95% quantile = .48

	AUS	SPA	SWE	SWI	UK	BEL	CAN	FIN	FRA	GER	HOL	IRE	ITA	HK	POR	SIN	TAI	DEN	MAL	NOR	US
AUS	1.00	0.36	0.45	0.39	0.55	0.07	0.45	0.59	0.13	0.08	0.09	0.19	0.12	0.27	0.24	0.31	0.25	0.21	0.06	0.22	0.21
SPA	0.36	1.00	0.78	0.57	0.47	0.15	0.13	0.37	0.33	0.08	0.10	0.06	0.35	0.04	0.26	0.19	0.06	0.02	0.03	0.02	0.04
SWE	0.45	0.78	1.00	0.76	0.69	0.08	0.22	0.54	0.24	0.04	0.01	0.06	0.26	0.02	0.05	0.03	0.02	0.06	0.00	0.07	0.06
SWI	0.39	0.57	0.76	1.00	0.75	0.03	0.14	0.42	0.12	0.01	0.00	0.01	0.14	0.01	0.01	0.01	0.01	0.18	0.00	0.19	0.02
UK	0.55	0.47	0.69	0.75	1.00	0.12	0.31	0.66	0.25	0.10	0.10	0.12	0.26	0.04	0.08	0.06	0.04	0.24	0.01	0.25	0.07
BEL	0.07	0.15	0.08	0.03	0.12	1.00	0.39	0.28	0.80	0.85	0.88	0.67	0.76	0.05	0.56	0.30	0.19	0.26	0.54	0.25	0.34
CAN	0.45	0.13	0.22	0.14	0.31	0.39	1.00	0.57	0.34	0.46	0.41	0.66	0.29	0.09	0.22	0.22	0.11	0.46	0.33	0.46	0.55
FIN	0.59	0.37	0.54	0.42	0.66	0.28	0.57	1.00	0.42	0.26	0.28	0.37	0.40	0.10	0.17	0.16	0.11	0.15	0.13	0.16	0.22
FRA	0.13	0.33	0.24	0.12	0.25	0.80	0.34	0.42	1.00	0.66	0.73	0.50	0.93	0.03	0.48	0.29	0.11	0.12	0.37	0.12	0.18
GER	0.08	0.08	0.04	0.01	0.10	0.85	0.46	0.26	0.66	1.00	0.84	0.78	0.65	0.07	0.50	0.22	0.19	0.26	0.68	0.36	0.45
HOL	0.09	0.10	0.01	0.00	0.10	0.88	0.41	0.28	0.73	0.84	1.00	0.71	0.71	0.06	0.57	0.34	0.20	0.28	0.61	0.27	0.39
IRE	0.19	0.06	0.06	0.01	0.12	0.67	0.66	0.37	0.50	0.78	0.71	1.00	0.45	0.10	0.31	0.16	0.21	0.49	0.58	0.48	0.66
ITA	0.12	0.35	0.26	0.14	0.26	0.76	0.29	0.40	0.93	0.65	0.71	0.45	1.00	0.03	0.49	0.28	0.09	0.09	0.38	0.09	0.15
HK	0.27	0.04	0.02	0.01	0.04	0.05	0.09	0.10	0.03	0.07	0.06	0.10	0.03	1.00	0.28	0.31	0.84	0.04	0.12	0.04	0.10
POR	0.24	0.26	0.05	0.01	0.08	0.56	0.22	0.17	0.48	0.50	0.57	0.31	0.49	0.28	1.00	0.67	0.40	0.09	0.32	0.08	0.12
SIN	0.31	0.19	0.03	0.01	0.06	0.30	0.22	0.16	0.29	0.22	0.34	0.16	0.28	0.31	0.67	1.00	0.31	0.04	0.22	0.04	0.10
TAI	0.25	0.06	0.02	0.01	0.04	0.19	0.11	0.11	0.11	0.19	0.20	0.21	0.09	0.84	0.40	0.31	1.00	0.06	0.15	0.06	0.12
DEN	0.21	0.02	0.06	0.18	0.24	0.26	0.46	0.15	0.12	0.36	0.28	0.49	0.09	0.04	0.09	0.04	0.06	1.00	0.55	0.99	0.80
MAL	0.06	0.03	0.00	0.00	0.01	0.54	0.33	0.13	0.37	0.68	0.61	0.58	0.38	0.12	0.32	0.22	0.15	0.55	1.00	0.54	0.67
NOR	0.22	0.02	0.07	0.19	0.25	0.25	0.46	0.16	0.12	0.36	0.27	0.48	0.09	0.04	0.08	0.04	0.06	0.99	0.54	1.00	0.80
US	0.21	0.04	0.06	0.02	0.07	0.34	0.55	0.22	0.18	0.45	0.39	0.66	0.15	0.10	0.12	0.10	0.12	0.80	0.67	0.80	1.00

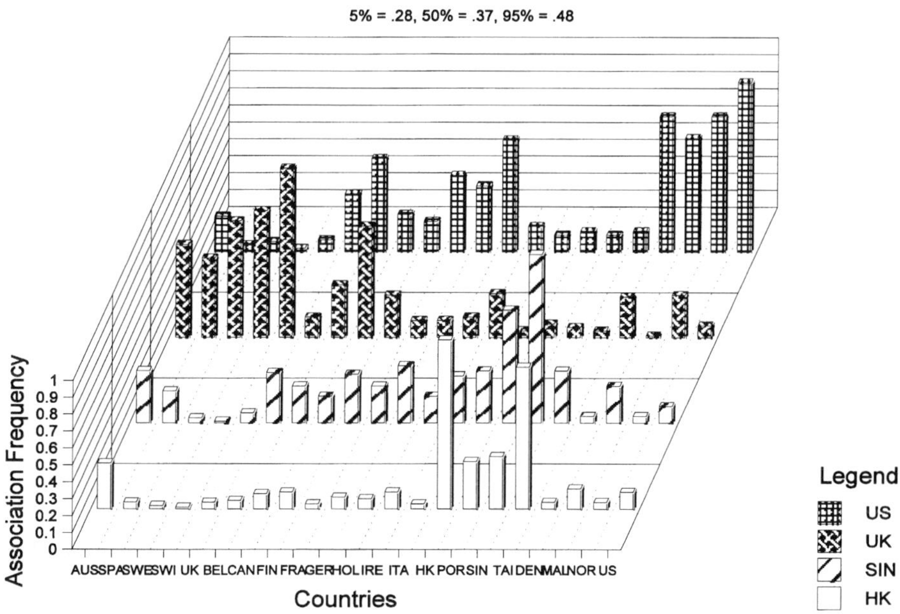

Figure 2.9. Association Freq. For US, UK, Sin, HK

able data, the association frequencies indicate that this is a low probability event. Singapore does not typically group with the U.S., the U.K. or with China. Its only constant partner is Portugal.

In sum, the cluster analysis indicates a few features of the global office market that may be useful for investment decisions. First, the U.S. and the U.K. separate into different clusters at both high and low levels of aggregation. Most countries on the continent separate from the U.K., and from the U.S. when seven groups are specified. While we cannot reject the hypothesis that the southeast Asian countries (excluding Australia) group together, it appears that their differences become important as more groups are specified. These clusters provide some general guidelines for international real estate diversification. First, it is clear that North America is *not* a separate group. At high levels of aggregation, it clusters with both European and Asian markets. In fact, it appears to be the dominant country in the largest cluster when three groups are specified. This is not surprising considering the role of the U.S. in the global economy. Even at lower levels of aggregation it still groups with Scandinavian and European countries. Given the relative comfort with which U.S. real estate investors have with investing in other English-speaking countries, it is encouraging to find that the U.S. clustere *apart* from U.K. and Australia. The bad news is that neither country served as a safe haven during the recent crash. Indeed the performance of portfolios based upon the three major clusters. Indicates that cluster 2, containing UK peaked in 1988.

EX POST SELECTION BIAS, AND REGRESSION TOWARDS THE MEAN

Although cluster analysis may reduce input uncertainty by aggregating like assets into classes, it cannot completely eliminate biases inherent in using historical data for mean-variance inputs. Since the procedure clusters in the space of historical returns, it will tend to group assets with high past returns together, even when these past returns are due to chance. While we may see *ex post* that the Portuguese market was a big winner, and the Asian markets formed a cluster that provided valuable diversification, it may have been difficult, if not impossible to discover this *ex ante*. These markets tend to group together, precisely because they are outliers. Thus, as a group, they are likely to regress toward the mean in future years. This is equally true for the big losers. Portfolio two is nearly unrepresented among efficient portfolios, due to its low return. Thus, the optimizer makes a useful recommendation that an investor avoid what appears to be a dominated asset. In other words, the optimizer tells us to stay away from U.K., Australian, Spanish and Scandinavian office markets. This is not surprising, given the magnitude of the 1992 crash in some of these countries, but it ignores the possibility that these markets have "bottomed out." It is straightforward to explore the implications of such a forecast. If we wish to assume that the Asian markets have peaked and the U.K. market has bottomed out, we simply decrease the mean for group three and increase the mean for group two. In other words, we "shrink" the mean estimates toward the average. This shrinkage presumes some future regression towards the mean.

While such shrinkage may appear *ad hoc*, there is a broad statistical literature offering guidelines for the magnitude of shrinkage desired. Most of it is based upon a simple intuition. Suppose for a moment that one had no economic information at all to distinguish among the different real estate markets. This state of ignorance corresponds to a "diffuse prior" with regard to the risk, return and correlation structure of the asset classes. In this circumstance, all means and standard deviations and off-diagonal elements of the correlation matrix would be set equal to each other. When these diffuse prior inputs are used in the mean-variance optimizer, they result in a minimum-variance portfolio that is equally weighted across all asset classes. This diffuse prior portfolio is useful, since the level of precision with which the optimization inputs are measured lays somewhere between a diffuse prior and the point estimates based upon historical data. Given the short history of returns collected by ICPA, it seems logical to strongly shrink the inputs towards each other, even for high levels of investor risk tolerance. The shrinkage thus builds in the anticipated regression towards the mean that is a likely result of clustering on historical returns.

CONCLUSION

The analysis of the ICPA data reveals some interesting features of the world real estate returns, and provides some guidance to global investors in the office market.

The ICPA data clearly indicates that the U.S. real estate crash was part of a global trend. This is useful information for policy makers, but disappointing for investors seeking international diversification.

While the plethora of new return data about international markets is tempting to institutional investors who seek to improve portfolio risk-return profiles, we recommend using the data judiciously. Simply using historical statistical inputs steers investors towards a risky strategy of chasing past winners. Cluster analysis represents an important intermediate stage of aggregation. Our application of k-means results in a set of three groups that capture differences among European, Scandinavian, Iberian and Asian markets. Statistics from these sub-groups result in a mean-variance analysis that appear to be well diversified across global real estate markets for most portions of the efficient frontier. More conservative portfolios are tilted towards Continental Europe and the U.S., while more aggressive portfolios are tilted towards Asia and the Iberian countries. We recommend a further precautionary step for institutional investors, that is, shrinking portfolio weights towards the "diffuse prior" portfolio.

Mean-variance optimization is a useful tool for evaluating the effect of cross-sectional asset relationships upon portfolio risk. But when long-term equilibrium expected returns cannot be reliably estimated from the data, mean variance optimization can be misleading. This is precisely the circumstance confronting international real estate investors. There is just enough information available to run an optimizer and to identify an efficient frontier, however there are serious pitfalls inherent in equating differences among historical returns with differences in expected returns.

ACKNOWLEDGMENT

The authors wish to thank the International Commercial Property Associates for use of their data. We also thank Crocker Liu, Matthew Spiegel as well as participants in the Berkeley Real Estate Workshop and the 1995 AREUEA meetings for helpful comments.

NOTES

1. The data for analysis was generously provided by International Commercial Property Associates. We thank Roger Ibbotson, Patric Hendershott, Bob Edelstein, the participants in the AREUEA 1995 conference and the Berkeley Real Estate Workshop for helpful suggestions. All errors are the sole responsibility of the authors. We thank Ibbotson Associates for making the EnCorr software available for our use.
2. See, for example, Harvey (1994).
3. See, for example, Jorion (1989).
4. These include Deutsche Immobilien Partner in Germany, Huoneistomarkkinoiti in Finland, Jan Henning Hansen Eindomstaksering in Norway and the Regional Group of Companies in Canada.
5. Countries are: Australia, Belgium, Canada, Denmark, Finland, France, Germany, Holland, Hong Kong, Indonesia, Ireland, Italy, Japan, Malaysia, Norway, Portugal, Singapore, Spain, Sweden, Switzerland, Taiwan, Thailand, UK and USA. Japan, Indonesia and Thailand lack data for the early years, and thus are not included in the cluster analysis.

6. We provide summary statistics only for countries with data beginning in 1986.

7. See Capozza (1994), for a discussion of domestic explanations for the U.S. real estate crisis.

8. We found little difference in results depending upon whether factors were extracted from local currency returns or dollar-based returns.

9. Although the small-sample distribution of the variance explained by the first principal component is difficult to calculate analytically, we bootstrapped it by repeatedly scrambling the time dimension for each series, so that the years no longer lined up, and then extracted the principal components. For i.i.d. returns, this simulates a null hypothesis of no common factor structure. We rejected the null hypothesis for the first principal component at the .002 probability level, based upon 1,000 bootstraps. The median bootstrap value was 32%, however, suggesting that random alignments of the series' could produce seemingly important principal components. None of the other principal components were unusual, however. This would seem to provide support for a single factor structure to global office market returns, however Brown (1989) shows that a multiple factor return generating process can give rise to a variance-covariance matrix with a single, large principal component such as the one identified here.

10. See Brown and Chen (1983) and Jorion (1986).

11. See Best and Grauer (1989) and Broadie (1993) for results on the effect of estimation error in the means.

12. Since there are more assets than time periods used to estimate the correlation matrix for the program, without a positivity constraint it would be possible to identify a portfolio with zero variance.

13. Panton, Lessia and Joy (1976) apply the algorithm to the world's equity markets.

14. The rejection function does *not* simply plot variance explained by grouping. If it did, then the explained variance would be maximized by the number of groups equal to the number of observations, irrespective of structure in the data.

15. These frequencies are 28%, 37% and 48% respectively.

16. Note that the diffuse prior portfolio is still comprised of sub-indices, since each country is a portfolio of the office buildings within it. A proper specification would weight each officer building equally, resulting in a "space-weighted" portfolio—something akin to a capital-weighted security portfolio.

REFERENCES

Abraham, J., Goetzmann, W. and Wachter, S., 1994, "Homogeneous Groupings of Metropolitan Housing Markets," *Journal of Housing Economics*, 3, 186–206, 1994.

Best, Michael, J. and Robert, R. Grauer, "On the Sensitivity of Mean-Variance Efficient Portfolios to Changes in Asset Means: Some Analytical and Computational Results," *The Review of Financial Studies*, 4:2, 1991, pp. 315–342.

Broadie, Mark, "Computing Efficient Frontiers Using Estimated Parameters," Working Paper, Columbia Business School, 1991.

Brown, Stephen, J., 1989, "The Number of Factors in Security Returns," *Journal of Finance* 44(5), 1247–1262.

——and Son-Nan Chen, 1983, "Estimation Risk and Simple Rules for Optimal Portfolio Selection," *Journal of Finance* 38(4), 1087–1094.

Capozza, Dennis, R., 1994, "Editor's Introduction: Special Issue on Real Estate in the 1989–1992 Financial Crisis," *AREUEA Journal* 22(1), 1–4.

Elton, E. and Gruber, M., 1971, "Improved Forecasting Through the Design of Homogeneous Groups," *Journal of Business* 44:4(1971), 432–450.

Goetzmann, W. and Wachter, S., 1994, "Clustering Methods and Commercial Rents," forthcoming, *AREUEA Journal.*

Hartigan, John. *Clustering Algorithms* New York, 1975, John Wiley & Sons.

Harvey, Campbell, 1994, "Predictable Risk and Return in Emerging Markets," forthcoming, *Review of Financial Studies.*

Hendershott, Patric and Edward Kane, 1992, "Causes and Consequences of the 1980's Commercial Construction Boom," *Journal of Applied Corporate Finance*, 5(1) Spring, 61–70.

Jorion, Philippe, 1989, "Asset Allocation with Hedged and Unhedged Foreign Stocks and Bonds," *Journal of Portfolio Management* 15(4), 49–54.

Jorion, Philippe, 1986, "Bayes-Stein Estimation for Portfolio Analysis," *Journal of Financial and Quantitative Analysis* 21(3), 279–292.

Liu, Crocker and Jian-Ping Mei, 1994, "Evidence on International Real Estate Integration and Diversification Consequences," Working Paper, New York University, Leonard Stern School of Business.

Panton, Don B., Lessia V.P. and Joy, O.M. 1976, "Comovement of International Equity Markets: A Taxonomic Approach," *Journal of Financial and Quantitative Analysis*, 11:3(September) pp. 415–432.

Renaud, Bertrand, 1994, "The 1985–1994 Global Real Estate Cycle: Are There Lasting Behavioral and Regulatory Lessons?" *Paper Presented at a Joint Session of the American Real Estate and Urban Economic Association and the American Finance Association ASSA meetings, Washington, D.C., 1994.*

Fergus, James, T. and John, L. Goodman, Jr., 1994, "The 1989–92 Credit Crunch for Real Estate: A Retrospective," *AREUEA Journal* 22(1), 5–32.

3. REAL ESTATE AND THE ASIAN CRISIS: LESSONS OF THE THAILAND EXPERIENCE.[1]

BERTRAND RENAUD

Brenaud@worldbank.org, Capital Markets Development Dept., The World Bank, Room MC-9-705, 1818 H Street WW, Washington DC 20433

MING ZHANG

Mzhang1@worldbank.org, Capital Markets Development Dept., The World Bank, Room MC-8-353, 1818 H Street WW, Washington DC 20433

STEFAN KOEBERLE

Skoeberle@worldbank.org, Capital Markets Development Dept., The World Bank, Room MC-13-817, 1818 H Street WW, Washington DC 20433

I. INTRODUCTION: THE ASIAN CRISIS DEBATE AND THE ROLE OF REAL ESTATE

The objectives of this paper are twofold. First, and primarily, it analyses the role of the real estate boom and bust of Thailand in the context of the Asia crisis debate. Second, in the process, it explores the weaknesses in real estate investment processes that might often be present in the real estate cycles of emerging markets. The generic question addressed in this study of Thailand is therefore in what manner the real estate sector can become an important structural weakness and a contributor to financial fragility. This sector is typically overlooked by managers of the economy, but given its large relative weight it can create significant financial risks in a small, open, emerging economy.

After decades of truly remarkable and genuine development success, the suddenness and intensity of the Asia crisis came as a shock to about everyone. In addition to the on-going strenuous rescue and stabilization work on the ground, the crisis has also sparked an intense and voluminous international debate about the causes of the crisis, and about the proper actions needed to stabilize these economies, achieve recovery and reduce the risk of further financial instability.[2] This debate initially focused on two polarized views of the Asian crisis. Some argued that the crisis was caused by fundamental economic weaknesses compounded by policy mistakes. Equally vocally, others attributed the crisis to a financial panic. This panic they said,

S.J. Brown and C.H. Liu (eds.). A GLOBAL PERSPECTIVE ON REAL ESTATE CYCLES.

was triggered by speculative attacks by hedge funds and large international banks, and marked by the herd behavior of international investors racing to be first out passed the door, capital flight and domestic bank runs.

These two views of the crisis are more complementary than inconsistent with each other. As Corsetti *et al.* (1998) have recently summed up: "deterioration of fundamentals is a necessary condition preceding a panic." Then, at the onset of the crisis, "movements of assets prices . . . and capital flow reversals may be excessive and not warranted by fundamentals."

As the global crisis continues to unfold in different regions of the world, managers of emerging economies are confronted with three worrisome questions. Are there fundamental weaknesses in the economy? If so, what are the main forms of "moral hazard" that allowed such weaknesses to develop? And, even if the country is perceived to have sound fundamentals what might be channels of contagion? Aside from shared elements of rapid growth and financial liberalization, the causes of the Asia crisis do differ significantly across countries. For instance, the Korean crisis in Northeast Asia had little to do with asset inflation of the kind seen in Thailand and other parts of Southeast Asia, or Japan a decade earlier.

This paper focuses on the role of real estate in the Thai crisis. It therefore addresses only two of the three questions of the Asian crisis debate. To what extent and in what manner was the real estate sector one of the fundamental weaknesses of the Thai economy? What were the specific moral hazard factors that turned the original Thai real estate boom into a costly bubble? The analysis leaves aside the important international finance question of the channels of contagion for the currency and financial crisis that deepened further Thai real estate problems.[3]

The presentation has five main parts.

- Part II explains how a strong macroeconomic performance led to the emergence of a modern real estate industry in Thailand after 1987. A decade later, new real estate assets formed a major part of national wealth and were rising rapidly in value. However, beneath a strong macroeconomic performance, important weaknesses began to develop by the early 1990s.
- Information on a new real estate industry in an emerging economy is neither very transparent nor comprehensive. Nor are they long time series. Yet there is adequate information in Thailand to document the weight of the entire sector in the national economy. There is also information to document the dynamics of the different real estate sectors during the most volatile phases of the cycle after 1988. Part III also documents the resource misallocation that eventually contributed in a major way to the banking crisis that preceded the currency crisis of July 1997.
- Why did resource misallocation on such scale happen? What were the specific forms of moral hazard? How did they induce aggregate over-investment? Part IV shows how and why valuations, investment decisions and financing were seriously flawed. This section identifies processes that may be found in a large number of other emerging economies, but may not be operating on the same scale made possible by the rapid growth of Thailand.

- Part V of the paper documents the immediate aftermath of the triple real estate, banking and currency crisis that hit Thailand by July 1997. Households have been hit by large wealth and job losses affecting domestic demand. Property investors and the corporate sector now hold bad assets affecting investment demand. The banking system is loaded with high levels of non-performing loans causing a credit crunch. What could be done to restore some liquidity in the sector? This section identifies factors that have initially obstructed loss-recognition and restructuring.
- The conclusion identifies the reforms needed in Thailand to reduce the risk of an another extremely costly real estate bubble in the future. Such directions for reform and sector strengthening have equal relevance to real estate investment processes in other emerging markets.

II. MACROECONOMIC DIMENSIONS OF THAI GROWTH

Prior to the analysis of the Thai real estate cycle proper, it seems useful to present a short macroeconomic anatomy of the fundamental forces behind the Thai Boom and the present crisis. In the context of the Asia crisis debate, the Thai experience is presented here as a two-step crisis reminiscent in terms of dynamics and severity of the experience of Chile in 1983. First, there was the strong and healthy Thai growth marked by the emergence of a modern if immature real estate industry. Then a poorly designed external financial liberalization turned what might have been a much needed cyclical downturn into a real estate bubble. By 1996, that bubble had already burst and left the country with a costly domestic dual real estate and banking crisis before capital inflows stopped. Eventually, these first losses were compounded by further losses from the July 1997 currency crisis, the sharp reversal of capital flows and the ensuing massive contraction of the economy. The herd behavior of international lenders and investors is also apparent. Capital inflows driven by low US domestic rates and shrinking spreads ignored the corporate and financial evidence on the low efficiency of new investment that was available on Thailand. Then panic and contagion set in.

A. Decades of Successful Thai Development and High Growth Rates

The performance of Thailand's economy has been truly remarkable during the three decades 1965–95. During 1965–80, growth averaged 7.3 percent annually, and it accelerated to 7.8 percent in 1980–95—roughly twice the growth rates of other low- and middle-income developing countries. Per capita GDP more than tripled. The aggregate domestic saving rate was very high and stayed around 30%. The share of the population below the poverty line fell from 12 to 4 percent. From 1965 to 1997, infant mortality declined by two-thirds, to 27 per thousand live births. Thailand's macroeconomic management won international praise, giving it unfettered access to burgeoning international private capital inflows.

B. Rapid Capital Inflows

Surges in capital inflows tend to produce a predictable pattern of macroeconomic effects: an acceleration in domestic demand and activity, a deterioration in the exter-

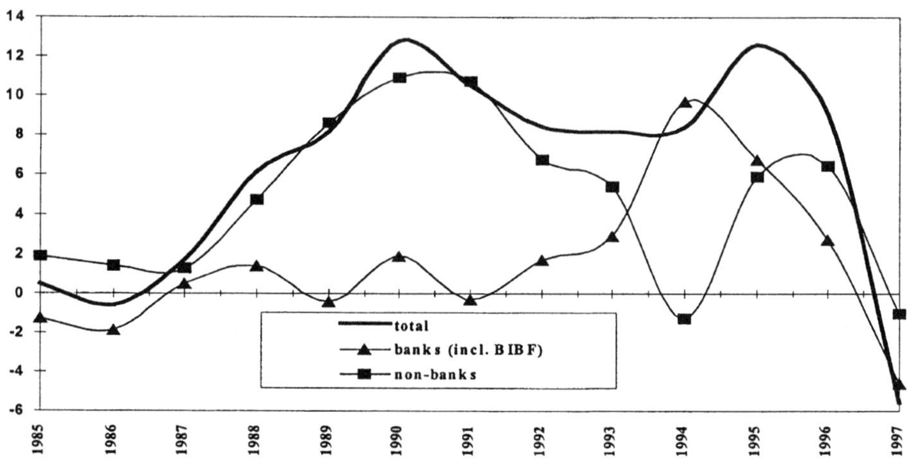

Figure 3.1. Private Capital Inflows as % of GDP

nal current account, *upward pressure on the prices of real estate* and financial assets and commodities. There are four basic causes of capital inflows: external developments, domestic policy changes affecting the real economy, changes in credit policy, and bandwagon effects. (Werner 1993, Schadler et al. 1993). Thailand is a small, open, rapidly emerging economy and it has experienced these four factors to a heightened degree.

In fact, Thailand stands out as one of the three countries that, together with Malaysia and China, have received the highest capital inflows relative to GDP in the world. Private capital inflows were already significant in the early 1980s, but declined as a result of the crisis in 1985–86. Initial capital inflows were led by Japan in the aftermath of the 1985 yen/dollar realignment. They surged in 1988, and ushered into the period when Thailand came to be regarded as one of the next Asian tiger economies. Between 1988 and 1996, Thailand received a cumulative total of US$ 100.3 billion. As a stock, this foreign capital is equivalent to 55% of Thailand's 1996 GDP. The flow amounts to 9.4% of GDP on an average annual basis. The year 1990 saw a peak of inflows of 13% of annual GDP. Associated with the domestic political crisis of 1992, annual inflows stabilized around an annual rate of 8% of GDP during a brief period in the early 1990s. Then inflows surged again to reach 12% of GDP in 1995. In 1997 they abruptly turned negative, as seen in Figure 1.

C. Composition of Capital Inflows and Impact on the Real Estate Boom

The composition of capital inflows, foreign direct investment (FDI), portfolio investment in equity, direct corporate private debt, bank inflows, and their intermediation by the domestic financial system, has had a significant impact on asset inflation.

Inflows triggered by resident banks borrowing abroad have played a key role in Thailand. There has been a significant difference between bank and non-bank capital inflows over two distinct periods. The first period is from 1988 to 1992 before capital controls were removed and bank-induced inflows were relatively small. Second, following financial liberalization there is the pre-crisis period of 1993 to 1996. With the establishment of the Bangkok International Banking Facilities (BIBF) regulations, resident banks used the BIBF channels to intermediate foreign funds into domestic currency. It can be seen from Figure 1 that after a first peak in 1990, capital inflows were moderating. Then there was a second massive surge just prior to the financial crash of 1997. Bank-induced inflows accounted for 37% of total inflows during 1988–96. After 1992, bank inflows increased sharply to 60% of total inflows during 1993–96.

Why were these BIBF structures created? The goal was that Bangkok compete with Hong Kong as South East Asia's financial center once the crown colony was handed over to the Chinese government in 1997. To encourage the growth of international banking business in Thailand, the Bangkok International Banking Facilities (BIBF) regulation was established in 1993 and granted significant tax advantages. Meanwhile, the Thai baht remained pegged to the US dollar. The 49 banks that had been granted BIBF licenses by 1996 included Thai commercial banks as well as foreign banks with and without local branches. On the liability side, BIBF banks took deposits or borrowings in foreign exchange from abroad; on the assets side, they were lending in foreign currency to Thai residents and non-residents. These BIBFs significantly increased the magnitude of short-term capital inflows by reducing the borrowing costs and easing access to foreign capital markets for smaller and less well known Thai firms. Between 1992 and 1995, the volume of short-term external debt more than doubled and grew from US$ 18.9 billion to US$ 41.1 billion.

The BIBFs contributed to extending a real estate boom that had already turned down and transformed it into a bubble. The BIBFs also raised foreign exchange risk in this non-traded sector. Part III focuses on the moral hazard elements and on the behavior of both bankers and developers that contributed to create a joint real estate and banking crisis whose high cost was soon compounded by the 1997 currency crisis.

D. Emergence of a Modern Real Estate Industry

During the decade 1987–97, a modern real estate industry emerged in Thailand. However, it was not a mature industry. It lacked depth and a modern regulatory and financial infrastructure as well as proper monitoring. Most of the industry's assets were and remain concentrated in the Bangkok Metropolitan Region (BMR), except for significant shares of the housing and hotel stocks. The large BMR dominates the Thai economy in a rather extreme way by international standards. At the time of the population census of 1994, the total population of Thailand was 58.3 million, with 8.7 million people or 15 percent living in Bangkok. 56% of the entire Thai urban population lives in the BMR. Yet only 36% of Thailand's population was urban in 1995. A very tentative breakdown in value by major market segment based on the available information is:

- Housing: 75% ± 8%
- Offices: 10% ± 4%
- Retail: 12% ± 5%
- Industrial: 3% ± 1%

These relative shares of the different types of real estate assets are orders of magnitudes. They are sensitive to the uneven fall in market prices after 1997.

One fundamental change in the housing industry during this period is the emergence and rapid growth of professional housing developers. Before 1984, house construction was mainly driven by individual owner-builders (Dowall 1989). The share of developer-built housing was only 12 percent in 1984. By 1996, this share had increased to 83%. In 1996, 2,540 developers applied for land subdivision permits around the country. 1,713 were registered as operating in the BMR in 1997. The residential market boom led to the rapid modernization of Bangkok's housing stock. New housing units were built not only for the city's rapidly increasing population, but also for households upgrading their housing conditions as they moved out of shop-houses—or even slums—to developer-constructed modern townhouses, condominiums and detached houses.

At the peak of the boom, 46 property companies and 35 construction firms were listed on the Stock Exchange of Thailand where their total capitalization grew very rapidly between 1990 and 1993. (See Figure 2 below)

E. Eroding Quality of Thai Growth After 1993

Forming beneath the robust performance of the economy, however, were weaknesses in the structural foundation of Thailand's success. They eventually undermined the economy's high growth momentum and are clear in retrospect:

- Fundamental weaknesses in the banking system operating under outdated regulatory rules and supervision—under-capitalization, insider lending, lack of disclosure, unsound practices, and protection from foreign competition—channeled savings into low-productivity investments.
- Economic competitiveness diminished as wage increases began to exceed productivity gains, and Thailand failed to progress to more technologically sophisticated exports.
- In the corporate sector, production plans and strategies overlooked the costs and riskiness of underlying projects. Weak policies regarding implicit guarantees, outdated lending practices, and poor banking supervision led to a very rapid and clearly excessive leverage that was the worst of the entire Asia region. The annual rate of growth of tangible assets of 29% between 1992 and 1996 was six times

Table 1. Thailand Erosion of Corporate Debt/Equity Ratios, 1992–1996

	1992	1993	1994	1995	1996
Thailand	80.5	88.0	90.6	107.0	114.6
Hong Kong	41.3	37.5	44.8	50.5	49.4
Singapore	38.1	27.8	25.5	31.3	39.3

Source: Michael Pomerleano, 1999 (sample of non-financial corporations).

that of OECD corporations and likely to be beyond the ability of local managerial skills. This capital investment was financed by external borrowings and not internal cash flows and corporate Thailand was a clear outlier among countries. Private growth had become a high debt, high leverage dynamics with limited capital and internal cash flow to buffer shocks. (See Pomerleano, 1998). Banks and finance companies were playing a central role in channeling funds toward projects that were increasingly marginal, and often unprofitable.

- In the public sector, the contribution of investments to total productivity growth began to shrink by the early 1990s.
- Yet under the pegged exchange rate, short-term unhedged funds continued to pour into Thailand. International lenders seemed satisfied with the unverified macroeconomic assumption that Thai borrowing to finance investment continued to be fine—and was not like the foreign financing of Mexican consumption prior to 1994.

By the end of 1994, some alarmed domestic and international observers were already reporting that overproduction in the real estate sector was serious and that lending to real estate should be curtailed, (Moody's, January 1995). The shares of real estate development companies listed on the SET were already falling sharply in mid-1995.

F. Asset Inflation and Real Estate Access to the Stock Market

Predictably, with high growth and massive capital inflows Thailand experienced a powerful asset price inflation both in real estate and financial equities. This inflation was shared by many Asian countries in the late 1980s and early 1990s. It was a misapprehended form of asset price inflation that coincided with essentially stable consumer prices. Channels of monetary policies were rapidly changing with liberalization, deregulation and financial innovation. Many other central banks around the world were caught by surprise. (see Renaud, 1997).[4]

The stock market boom itself played a role in fueling the real estate cycle. A Thai analysis of the 356 non-financial companies listed on the SET has shown that corporate over-investment was already apparent in 1993. Symptoms for that were declines in asset turnover, return on assets, profit margins, and return on equity. (See Pathra Securities Thailand, 1998). Real estate development companies listed on the Bangkok SET took advantage of the boom to expand their sources of funding.

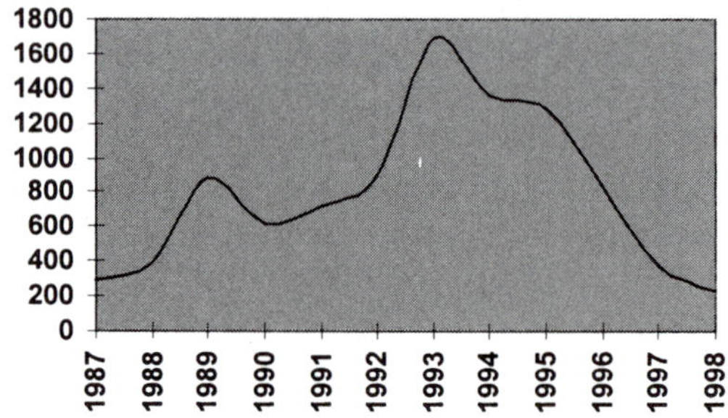

Figure 3.2. Thailand Stock Market Performance
Source: SET Index data base.

Taking Thai accounting practices at face value, the property companies as a group were highly leveraged. Security analysts reported high "gearing" or leverage ratios[5] of the order of 150% for most Thai property companies. By comparison, Hong Kong property companies, whose accounting practices are of much higher quality, had gearing ratios of the order of 40% to 50%.[6]

The share prices of Thai property companies had already started falling by the middle of 1995, some of them very steeply. This price behavior of the shares of listed property companies parallels the findings of analytical studies done on the UK and Hong Kong stock markets, where researchers find that the share price of listed property companies is a leading indicators of the performance of the property market. Property share prices were supporting other data indicating that, by 1995, the Thai real estate bust was on its way—and so was the stock market as a whole. (see Figure 2)

G. Early Warnings Prior to the 1997 Currency Crisis

The sharp fall in the Bangkok SET index reflected the rapid deterioration in corporate performance. Yet this fall was not heeded by many participants in the global markets. In addition to such corporate signal, there were also two early macroeconomic warning signs: capital investment productivity fell steadily, and Thailand's external terms of trade declined for a decade prior to the export slowdown of 1996. In 1995–96, policy mistakes combined with growing structural problems rendered the economy vulnerable to external shocks:

- A fixed exchange rate and public guarantees to creditors encouraged excessive private foreign borrowing, financed substantially by unhedged and progressively greater short-term foreign borrowing.
- The exchange rate peg to the US dollar aggravated the tendency to appreciation, as the dollar's rise against the yen increased the real value of the Baht.
- Inadequate supervision of financial institutions, loose private credit, and weak corporate governance created incentives to invest in speculative ventures, and led to a credit-driven boom in consumer spending and real estate.

These policies deepened the current account deficit over three years so that by July 1997, it had reached -8.0 percent of GDP. Despite speculative attacks on the fixed exchange rate early in 1997, the government failed to take corrective action in time. By the summer, private expectations about the sustainability of the exchange rate peg reversed abruptly. On July 2, 1997, a speculative attack on the baht finally forced the government to abandon the fixed exchange rate. This was followed by depositor runs on the finance companies and smaller banks that drove the financial sector into crisis and the economy into an instant deep recession. As the currency markets overshot, the value of the baht against the dollar depreciated by 85% between December 1996 and December 1997.

III. THE 1987–1997 THAI REAL ESTATE BOOM AND BUST

A. Total Weight of Real Estate in the Economy at the Onset of the 1997 Thai Crisis

Until very recently monetary authorities have ignored the potential impact of asset inflation on banking soundness (BIS, 1993). Yet, why did the real estate crisis have such a large impact on the Thai economy? What was the weight of real estate in the Thai economy at the start of the crisis? Why will the resolution costs of the Thai crisis be so large? The paradox of the Thai dual property and banking crisis is that the impact of the crisis on the economy is very large for two positive reasons. Thailand has a basic urban land and real estate infrastructure that makes these assets valuable and easily tradable: rapid asset appreciation can be broadly based (see Dowall, 1989). The level of bank intermediation is also high. In 1997, the outstanding claims of Thai deposit banks on the private sector were 105% of GDP. In 1994, the year of the Mexican crisis, the Mexican ratio was a mere 38%.

Valuing the total real estate stock is a very challenging task. Comprehensive, systematic and consistent information about the property sector is still lacking. Annex Table 1 presents an estimation of the total value of real estate stock in the BMR, based on stock, price and rental data compiled from various government departments and real estate consultancies such as Jones Lang Wootton and Richard Ellis. The estimated wealth held in the form of real estate in Bangkok amounted to baht 2,170 billion as of the end of 1997.[7] Approximately one-quarter of this value is non-residential, dominated by office and retail space. The rest is in various forms of residential buildings. This total value is more than the estimate Bangkok's gross provincial product in 1997, and is equivalent to 45% of the national GDP. Given that Bangkok property is only part—although a very significant part—of the total real estate stock of the country, it is safe to claim that *real estate is the largest component of Thailand's national wealth.*

B. Over-Investment and Resource Misallocation in the Residential Market

The residential stock forms over two-third of all real estate assets. It is estimated that 1.25 million new housing units have been completed in the BMR since 1988. By early 1998, the residential take-up rate was severely affected and the number of

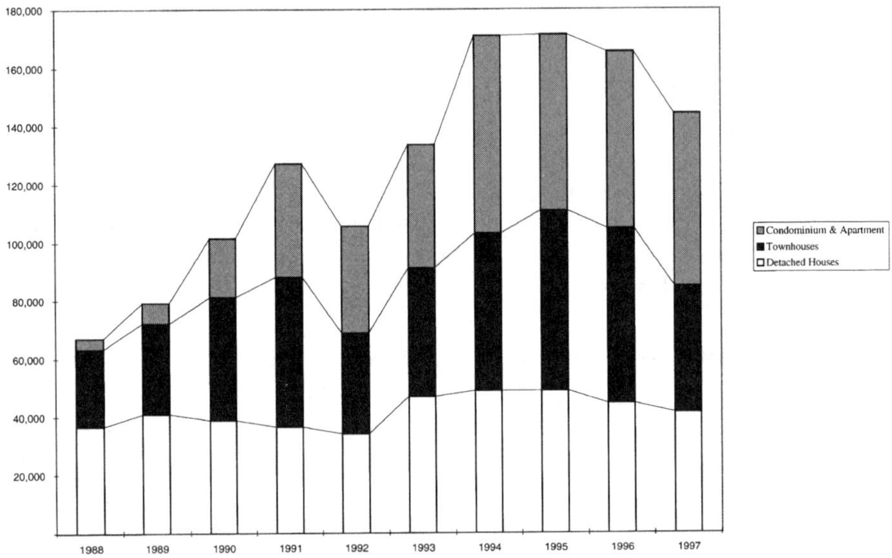

Figure 3.3. Annual Housing Completions by Types Bangkok Metropolitan Region
Source: Government Housing Bank, various issues.

new vacant units now stands at 350,000. This oversupply is enough to shelter about 1.225 million people.[8] The implied overall vacancy rate is an extraordinarily 28% for the new housing stock. Combining all pre-1988 and post-1988 housing units, the vacancy rate over the entire housing stock is estimated at 14%. Already in 1995 a government study found that approximately 300,000 residential units in the region were unoccupied (Richard Ellis 1998). This vacant stock was equivalent to twice the new housing supply at the peak of the boom in the market. What should have been seen as even more alarming is that more than half of these unoccupied units had already been transferred from developers to buyers. This implied that a significant group of buyers had purchased housing units during this period not for occupancy, but for speculation. Yet real estate lending by finance companies continued almost unabated. Over-investment and vacancy rates differ by types of housing unit. Figure 3 presents the annual housing output and its 9-fold increase between 1986 and 1996 under the combined pressures of very rapid income growth, high urban migration, and speculative building.

New residential production in Bangkok falls into three broad categories: (i) detached houses, (ii) townhouses, and (iii) condominiums and apartments. The composition of the new housing stock over time is shown in Figure 4. Of the three segments of housing supply, detached houses appear to be the most stable, with annual completion varying between 35,000 to 49,000 units. Townhouse supply has

Figure 3.4. Annual Housing Completion in Bangkok Metropolitan Region
Note: From 1993 onward, the data include five provinces instead of three.
Source: Government Housing Bank, various issues.

been more volatile along an upward trend. Townhouse output that serve middle and lower-middle class households was very responsive to change in overall demand for housing.

The most dramatic changes in Bangkok's residential development is the rapid expansion of *condominiums and apartments* in the market. Since 1988, annual supply of condominiums and apartments increased by more than 18 times from a mere 3,680 units to a peak of 68,000 units in 1994. Condominiums and apartments have now become the largest segment of annual housing supply in the BMR. A number of factors have contributed to the boom of the condominium and apartment market. The rising price of land and construction materials, the increasing difficulty of obtaining well-located land lots for new housing development, and wider recognition of the benefits of living in close proximity to the workplace or school, given Bangkok's notorious traffic congestion, have all played a role.

Not so easily observed from Figure 4, is the great volatility of the condominium and apartment segment. During the nine-year period, the greatest year-on-year increase of supply in this sector was 188%, while the greatest *decrease* was 11%. In 1994, the annual supply grew by 60%, but it *dropped* by 11% the next year. Until 1997, new supply in this sub-market had hardly responded to the current real estate slump. Resource misallocation was the greatest in the condominium and apartment

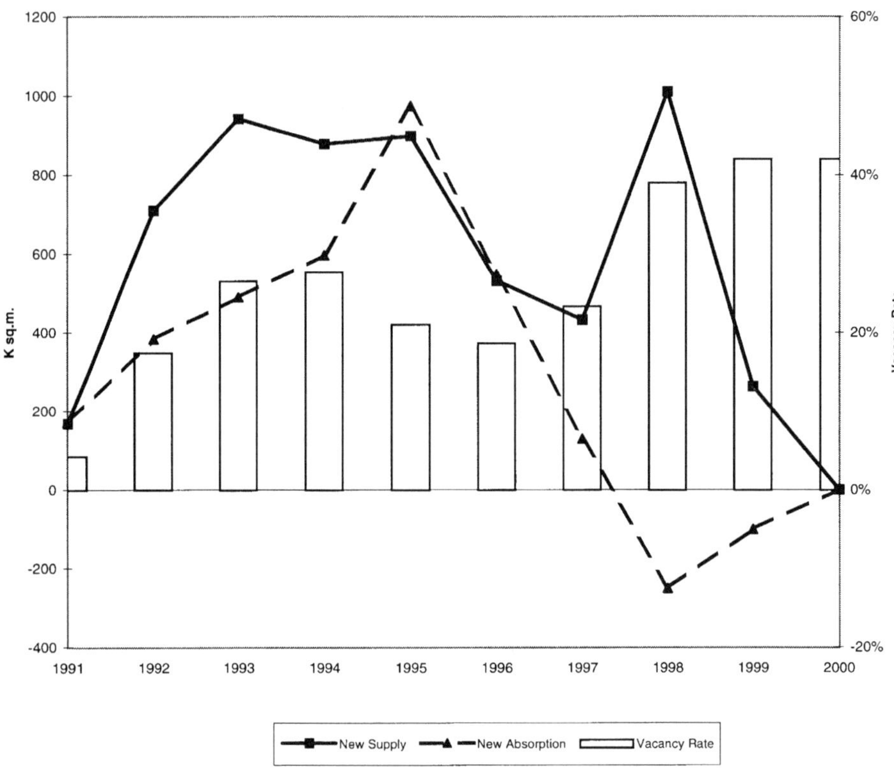

Figure 3.5. Bangkok Office Space Annual Supply and Demand
Source: Jones Lang Wootton (Jan 1998).

segment. By December 1997, vacancy rates had reached 50% in the downtown residential condominium sector, and were projected to deteriorate further. A much steeper drop was expected for both 1998 and 1999.

C. Over-Investment in The Office Market

Modern office buildings were only introduced to Bangkok rather recently, but the 1990s witnessed a boom of new office space across the city, exemplified in the most dramatic manner by the new Central Business District (CBD) along Sathorn Road that was a country road in the early 1980s. Total office space was less than 1.5 million square meters in 1991; by the end of 1997, total supply had quadrupled to 6 million square meters, with nearly 2 million sq.m. located in the CBD. Around 900,000 square meters of office space were added to the stock each year for three consecutive years up to 1995. JLW estimates of new supply, absorption and vacancy rates are presented in Figure 5. Rentals and capital values in Figure 6.

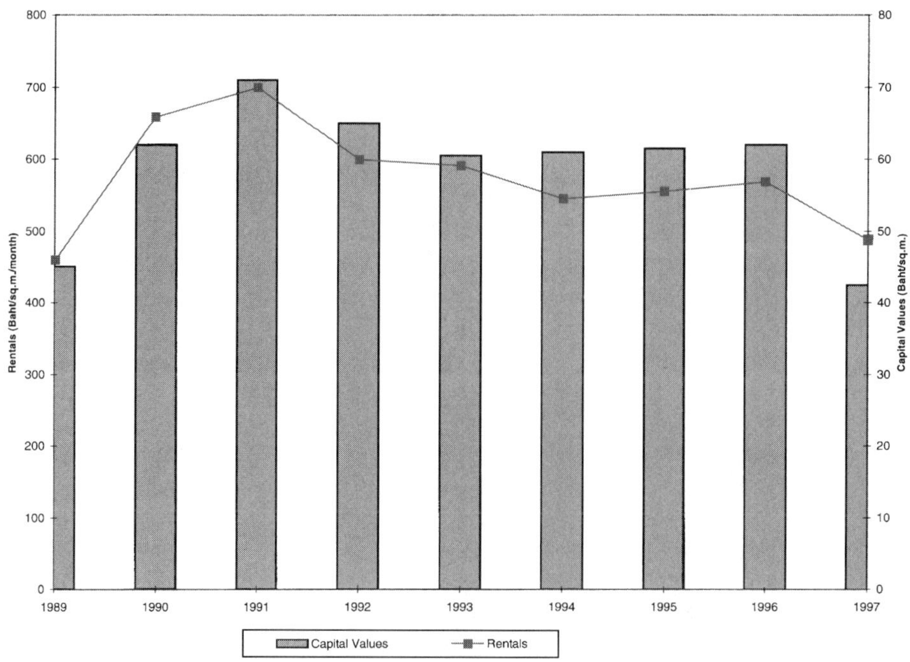

Figure 3.6. Average Rentals and Capital Values of Grade A Office Space in Bangkok CBD
Source: Jones Lang Wootton (Jan 1998).

Demand for new office space rose rapidly during the boom, but much more slowly than supply. New take up was able to keep pace with new supply only in years 1995 and 1996. In all other years the gap was wide. As a result, the office vacancy rate has stayed extremely high, hovering around 20% or higher most of the years.[9] Unfortunately, the worst was yet to come with a dramatic increase of new supply in the 1998 pipeline and a massive *decrease* in take-up resulting only from the closure of 63 finance companies expected to vacate about 200,000 m^2 of space, without considering other forms of corporate lay-off. Vacancy rates for the next two years are predicted to stay around 40%. Total unoccupied office space was projected at 2.8 million square meters at the end of 1998. 280,000 new office workers would need to be employed to absorb this amount of vacant space. In boom times, it had taken Bangkok five years under relative favorable economic environment (1993–1997) to accumulate a total take-up of this size.

D. An Immature Office Market

What is conspicuous in the Bangkok office market is that supply bore little relationship with rental values and capital values. As Figure 6 shows clearly, rental and capital values peaked as early as 1991. The business cycle and the real estate cycle diverged after 1992–1993, culminating in a real estate bust. The dramatic increase of Bangkok's office space therefore occurred under an environment of slowly decreasing values and vacancy rates that continued to be high. The movement in rental and capital value has been very small until 1997, which saw a 15% drop in gross rentals and a 30% fall in capital values which continued in 1998. As indicated in Part II, demand for office space has contracted sharply with the closure of the finance companies and layoffs elsewhere in the business sector. Some large purpose-built buildings have lost their financial anchor tenants in the process, thereby finding their worth reduced. New supply will outpace demand by a large margin for the next several years and most analysts project vacancy rates of the order of 40% for the next two years (see Figure 5).

It is difficult, though, to directly compare vacancy rates in an emerging market like Bangkok with those of a mature market. The office vacancy rates of the order of 20% experienced by the United States during the second half of the 1980s were considered then to be at 'extraordinarily high levels". Indeed, oversupply took almost seven to 10 years to be eliminated. (Hendershott and Kane, 1992). In an emerging market, annual additions will tend to be large as compared to the initial stock. As the base is small, vacancy rates can therefore climb rapidly. The issue remains whether new supply is grossly out of balance with future demand.[10]

Underlying the lack of link between supply and price movements is the fact that the majority of office buildings were built by companies whose core business was *not* office property development. Unlike the residential sector in Bangkok, where most of the properties were built by professional developers and sold to individual investors, investment and development in the office market was mostly undertaken by business companies who were not developers, and built for their own use, often their own land. As a result, over the past decade, there have been very few sales of whole buildings.[11]

The extraordinarily high BMR office vacancy rates reflect the fact that the Thai real estate industry is immature. As noted, the majority of office buildings in the BMR have not been built by specialized property companies who understand the specificity of real estate risks and the dynamics of cycles, but rather by a variety of business companies with very different core businesses. The management of these corporations has limited knowledge of—or interest in—the field of corporate real estate management. Their investment decisions were not driven by sustainable rents and yields, but by easy access to credit, tax considerations, a "trophy" mentality, and euphoria. Most office owners have only one building that carries their corporate name. These buildings have now turned into bad assets: interest rate on debt has risen sharply, occupancy rates and rentals have fallen. The misguided fall-back option of treating cash-flow losses on the building as temporary is not available, because core business profits are currently poor or negative. Any hope that capital gains will eventually make up for the currently negative interest coverage ratios and the indebtedness of these assets is misplaced (see below). Substantial restructuring of these assets and of the property industry will be needed within the industry during the next

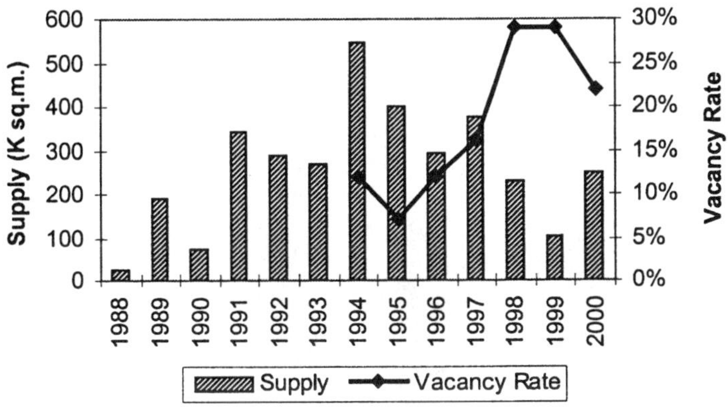

Figure 3.7. Annual Supply and Vacancy Rate of Retail Space in Bangkok Metropolitan Area
Source: Jones Lang Wootton (January 1998).

two to four years. The process is likely to go forward on a building by building basis.

E. The Retail Sector

Besides traditional stores and street vendors, a modern retail sector has very rapidly emerged in Bangkok after 1988. During the last five years, international retailers from Japan, Europe and the US have begun to play a major role in this sector. Retail space in the BMR is broken down into department stores (45%), malls (45%), and suburban superstores (10%).

At the end of 1997 there were around 3.5 million square meters of modern retail space in Bangkok Metropolitan Region. Most of this space was built during the last ten years, as the total retail stock before 1988 was only about 700,000 square meters. Figure 5 shows that commercial real estate development for retail use started to take off around 1991. Between 1991 and 1997, an annual average of 360,000 square meters of shopping areas was added to the city. New retail space supply saw a general downward trend since 1994, although 1997 saw an increase in both new supply and new take-up of stores. Vacancy rates, however, have been increasing since 1995, climbing steadily from 12% in 1994 to 16% in 1997. The situation has deteriorated sharply after September 1997 with the sharp fall of consumer purchases. Once again, there will be a sharp differentiation in asset performance across facilities: vacancies and losses will fall heavily on lower-grade space in weak locations. Unlike office properties, new supply of retail space was expected to decrease significantly in 1998 and 1999. But, demand was dropping even faster with the reduced purchasing power of customers. The retail vacancy rate, therefore, is expected to increase, possibly reaching 29% by the end of the year 1998. Rental and capital values of retail space, after increasing slightly but consistently from 1992 to 1997, experienced a 33% drop

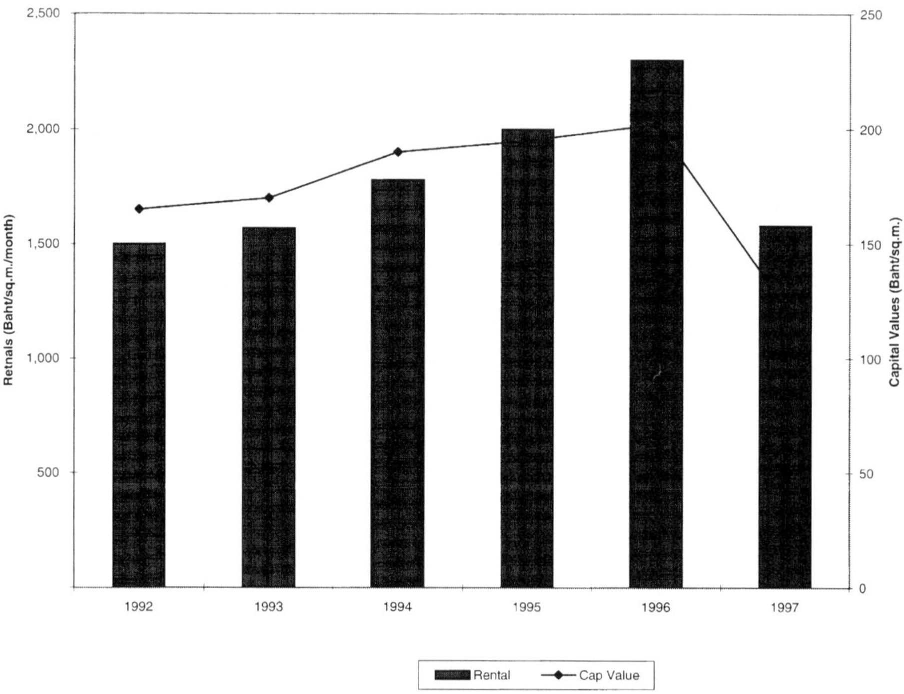

Figure 3.8. Average Retail Rentals and Capital Values, Prime Retail Space in Central Bangkok
Source: Jones Lang Wootton (January 1998).

in 1997 alone (see Figure 8). This fall was expected to continue through 1998 given the higher vacancy rate, and possibly level off afterwards.

IV. BEHAVIOR OF LENDERS AND DEVELOPERS IN AN IMMATURE MARKET

How could over-investment and resource misallocation in the various sectors of the real estate economy occur on such a scale? What were the factors that led lenders to such poor practices and developers to make such wasteful investment decisions? These questions are at the core of the Asian crisis debate about the main forms of "moral hazard' that allowed structural weaknesses to develop in Asian economies. Are there generic lessons for other immature real estate markets that can be gained from this examination of the Thai experience? Certainly, like the US in the aftermath of the Savings and Loans crisis, Thailand today is faced with the problems of regulating an "unholy" alliance between bankers and developers. (Litan, 1992). Part II has already shown that easy access to credit has been a central factor in resource misallocation in Thailand. We first look at lender behavior, conceptually and in the case of Thailand.

A. Thai Lenders' Behavior

1. A Conceptual Perspective: Four Paths to Banking Problems

The role of moral hazard should not be overemphasized. There can be other causes of banking problems. A recent review paper has argued that there have been four distinctive and often complementary ways for excessive and destabilizing lending to real estate; (Renaud, 1998). These four explanations are only outlined here before discussing specific features of the Thai market:

- *Disaster Myopia.* Building on Guttentag and Herring (1986), Herring and Wachter (1998) have shown that there is a built-in lender myopia that can affect real estate lending and may well be always present to some degree in markets experiencing a sustained real estate boom. Financial institutions are caught into over-lending to real estate markets and can thereby feed a severe boom and bust cycle if the cycle is not adequately monitored in terms of market trends and impact on financial returns. The reason behind disaster myopia is that lenders underestimate their *exposure to low-frequency shocks* when real estate prices have been climbing steadily for a sustained period of time. In Thailand, more than a decade of extremely rapid economic growth and sustained real estate appreciation have certainly lulled good bankers to underestimate the riskiness of their loans.
- *Moral Hazard.* In the aftermath of the Asia crisis, Paul Krugman (1998) has argued effectively that *over-guaranteed and under-regulated financial intermediaries* will cause moral hazard and overpricing of real estate assets until the boom collapses and then values will sharply reverse themselves.
- *Destructive Competition.* Financial liberalization and increased competition in the absence of an adequate legal an regulatory framework may lead to disruptive lending practices and loan under-pricing by *second-tier lenders* and weaker financial institutions with too much liquidity and no enough good borrowers. (Renaud, 1997). This problem was also clearly in evidence at the level of the global markets with the collapse of spreads on emerging market loans in 1995–96 below any reasonable risk markup.
- *Bad banking.* Finally, bad real estate lending practices can take various forms. The most forgivable forms of bad banking result from *outdated regulations and lending practices in a rapidly modernizing economy*. However, there is no excuse for delaying the necessary regulatory improvements. *Fraud and malpractice* are an additional story, but good bank supervisors are now familiar with most forms and are sharing their experience. (For a check list of typical forms from of bad banking see Annex 3. This annex offers a negative list of what good practice should be).

2. Flaws in Thai Financial Lending

The four causes of major banking problems were present in Thailand. The real estate boom has undone financial institutions in Thailand through various forms of inappropriate, outdated or just bad banking. Residential and commercial property lending practices in Thailand are now undergoing a complete overhaul. Unsatisfactory or bad practices point to the need for strict lending regulations focusing on sustainable yields rather that capital value. International experience shows that sound commercial credit risk management based on appropriate lending regulations can play a major positive role in avoiding serious property crises.

Outdated Forms of Secured Lending From an Earlier Agricultural Era. The banking practices in Thailand which developed during the earlier decades of growth were based on the very traditional mortgage lending practices of a large agricultural economy. These practices fell increasingly out of step with the new risk conditions associated with rapid urban growth under the boom. Most lending in Thailand is done on a secured basis. The collateral is generally fixed property. Thai law does not yet recognize floating liens on receivables and inventory. The loan advance is a percentage of the appraised value of the collateral. Valuation is generally done in-house. Some institutions rely on outside appraisal firms for the valuation of real estate property. While there are experienced appraisers in Thailand, there is no formal certification process and the incentives to produce high quality valuation are considered weak. As the boom progressed, overvaluation has facilitated excess lending to the sector. When the steep decline in property values started, this had negative effects on the capital position of banks and the remaining finance companies. Specific loan loss provisions cover non-performing loans (NPLs), while general reserves act as a dynamic cushion for the overall loan book. As property prices slump, Thailand's financial institutions face greater provisioning requirements against NPLs, because loan provision levels depend on the assessment of collateral values. The sharp real estate price decline is contributing heavily, if indirectly, to the 1997–98 liquidity crunch. The rapid recapitalization of banks is therefore essential to end the liquidity crunch.

Ineffectual Real Estate Credit Risk Management as well as the willingness of lenders to finance real estate during periods of euphoria are not unique to Thailand. Most forms of bad lending for real estate have also been experienced elsewhere during the global real estate boom of 1985–1994.

Connected lending (loans to directors and large shareholders) has been very extensive in Thailand. This bad practice has often been associated with *excessive loan concentration.* In Thailand, banking capital has been controlled by a limited group of about 16 corporate and family groups. During the boom, Thailand was a lender's market with high spreads. In spite of high domestic savings rates, foreign borrowings were needed to meet investment demand. This situation was reflected in high and rising loans-to-deposits ratios. Close inter-company links and related-company transactions in the real estate sector weakened a number of financial institutions in ways that could not be easily detected and anticipated—even by management.

Loan diversions hidden by misleading accounting and resulting from *weak internal controls and weak loan supervision by lenders* was common enough to be discussed frequently in both the Thai and the international press. (See *WJS*, September 1997).

For example, the management of listed companies borrowed against their core business and then redirected the funds to privately held companies heavily engaged in real estate projects and controlled by family members. Another more direct method was to borrow in the form of trade finance and then to use the funds for real estate transactions. In the latter case, proper internal controls and loan servicing and supervision should have been sufficient to control credit risk and prevent fraudulent behavior.

Impact of the BIFBs on the Loan Portfolios of Financial Institutions. With the additional capital inflows triggered by the BIBFs, significant amounts of lending went to non-tradable sectors, including real estate. During 1993–95, a reported 45% of net FDI and 15% net borrowing for BIBF respectively went to real estate and construction. In addition, some 5% of BIBF net lending went to the construction materials industry and 15% to financial institutions which in turn engaged in real estate financing. By the end of 1996, outstanding short-term and long-term loans by banks and finance companies to the real estate sector amounted to 800 billion Baht. Reported real estate loans in the total loan portfolio amounted to about 9% percent for banks and 26% for finance companies. However, these figures may be underestimated. Loans classified as real estate include only credit for real estate companies; loans used for property development by non-real estate developers were not treated as real estate loans. The actual portfolio for the real estate sector is therefore unclear. As already reported, indirect evidence also suggests that additional funds were diverted into real estate activities from business loans and funds raised on the stock market through equity issues.

By 1995, the Bank of Thailand alarmed by the developing real estate crisis instructed the deposit banks to refrain from further real estate lending. However, this instruction did not apply to finance companies. Similarly, international rating agencies had clearly identified the initial stages of a dual real estate and banking crises. (Moody's, January 1995). However, such outlook information had little or no impact on most international lenders from Japan, the rest of Asia and Europe who had the dominant share of the market in Thailand. The quarterly growth rate and level of outstanding real estate loans made by finance companies is presented in Figure 9 where both excessive growth rates in lending and excessive loan concentration by the Thai finance companies are in evidence.

By 1996, the real estate crisis had clearly burst into the open. Massive overproduction and the rising number of non-performing real estate loans for both housing and commercial property projects were rapidly undermining the financial sector. The government proposed a number of schemes, but they came too late for the currency crisis and were never implemented. First, there was a 20 billion baht lending scheme for civil servants and state enterprise employees. Then a 50 billion baht Resolution Trust Fund was proposed to take over problematic property-backed loans. The Secondary Mortgage Corporation (SMC) was created in June 1997 with the objective of securitizing mortgage loans and freeing the capital of commercial banks. However, the necessity of taking an up-front loss, technical issues regarding

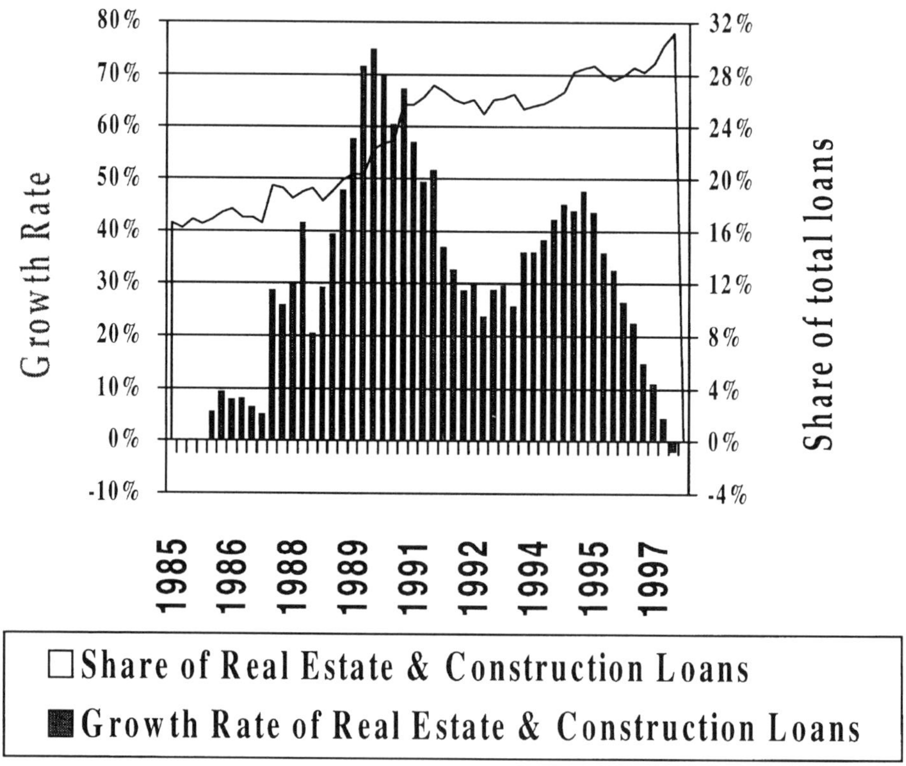

Figure 3.9.
Source: Bank of Thailand, various issues.

information on the quality of portfolios and their servicing, as well as the scarcity of potential investors make the SMC a medium term project, not a crisis management tool. In March 1997, the government set up the Property Loan Management Organization (PLMO) as a special vehicle to buy problem loans from financial institutions. As a result of the late 1997/early 1998 liquidity crisis which prevents its rapid funding and for technical reasons of loan evaluation, the PLMO did not work effectively. The July 7 currency crisis had the dual impact of stopping the rolling over of all short-term loans which funded finance companies and of raising the cost of dollar denominated debt by more than 30%. In August 1997, 56 finance companies were closed.

B. Thai Developers and Real Estate Investors Behavior

The behavior of Thai developers and investors can be examined in two steps in a manner similar to the preceding discussion of Thai lenders' behavior. Part II has examined the macroeconomic fundamentals that triggered the real estate boom. Part

III has documented the pattern of excess supply and overshooting across the various segments of the real estate market.

Real estate cycle analyses of advanced, high income, and mature urban economies have shown that there are intrinsic characteristics of real estate markets that tend to perpetuate or amplify the impacts of external forces on property values and overproduction. These endogenous factors would tend to generate cycles even if there were no strong external cyclical influences outside in the wider economy. Can we say that these impacts are amplified by the fact that Thailand's modern real estate industry is immature in terms of practices as well as in terms of the relatively small size of the stock compared with the volume of new output. Rapid incremental growth is an unavoidable feature of an emerging industry. The Thai experiences raises yet unanswered questions. In a shallow and immature industry, are the same factors that stimulated excessive growth and are also responsible for the steep bust difficult to avoid? Does this same shallowness of the real estate stock also offer easier prospects for recovery because the potential for continuing urban growth is very large? After all, Thailand is less than 40% urbanized and the scope for further urban growth is very large. But then, what kind of institutional and regulatory adjustments could turn an emerging real estate industry into a mature one and reduce its volatility?

1. Expected Cyclical Differences Across Sectors of Thai Real Estate

Analyses of real estate cycles in mature markets emphasize that the tendency to oversupply and output volatility in a specific segment of the real estate market is related to three main factors: development lags, stickiness of vacancy rates, inertia in rents. Differences in these three factors can help explain differences in the functioning of individual market segments such as offices versus housing.

Development Lag. One fundamental reason for the persistence of real estate cycles is the lag in supply adjustment in response to a change in demand. In addition to slow adjustment of the occupier market to changes in demand, the real estate industry is also characterized by development lag, i.e. the substantial time span between the initiation and completion of construction. The whole cycle of a development project, from the initial planning to the final completion, can take as short as several months and as long as several years. When the construction is completed, demand conditions may already have changed. This lag in construction, in combination with future demand uncertainty, results in wrong timing of project completion and *the tendency to overbuild. This tendency is compounded by the nature of asymmetric rewards from real estate development, biasing the risk assessment of the decision to build.* As Grenadier (1992) puts it, "If demand turns out to be high, the owner will gladly exercise the option to lease out all or most of the units at high rents, and benefit greatly. If demand instead turns out to be low, the owner will not exercise the option to lease all of the units immediately, but instead will wait for the market to turn around before paying the lump sum cost of leasing space. In this sense, the benefits of good outcomes outweigh the costs of poor outcomes". Two factors affect the probability of overbuilding: the longer the construction time, and the more volatile demand, the greater the probability of overbuilding. This also suggests that the commercial real estate properties are more likely to experience overbuilding than residential properties.

Stickiness of Vacancies. Two factors affect the stickiness of vacancies—demand volatility and adjustment cost. The more volatile the underlying demand and the higher the cost of space adjustment, the more sticky vacancy rates tend to be. Real estate cycles can be expected to be more persistent in an emerging market like Thailand because demand for real estate itself is more volatile, and because relocation is generally relatively more costly due to lack of a stock of readily available standardized space and high quality property management. We can also expect commercial real estate cycles to be more persistent than residential cycles as, generally, entry and exit costs are higher for commercial than for residential properties. Moreover, the underlying demand for commercial properties, especially for office space, is more volatile than that for residential properties.

Inertia of Rents in a Changing Economic Environment. As shown by Grenadier (1992), two types of lags can amplify and perpetuate real estate cycles triggered by external forces and economic fundamentals in the wider economy. Both are due to the considerable inertia of existing building owners in adjusting rents and occupancy levels to a changing economic environment, caused by the high transaction costs of moving in and out of space, incurred both by landlords and users. The moving cost of office relocation, for instance, is as high as one year's rent in many countries. In Bangkok, this cost is even higher: on average, the fitting cost of moving into new office space is as much as 5 years' rent (Richard-Ellis 1998). Grenadier has shown that these entry and exit costs can create a "band of inaction", i.e. a range of demand (or rent) over which exiting vacancy levels remain unchanged. In a booming market, this means space take-up can be slow to catch up with demand pressure, which in turn limits the total supply of rental space and drives up the marginal rental value. During the bust, the opposite occurs: tenants have the option to move to another place with much lower rent, but the high moving cost makes relocation unfeasible. Instead, tenants are more likely to choose to re-negotiate the leasing contract with the landlord, attempting to achieve a somewhat lower rent. Rent adjustment downward, therefore, is also sluggish.

2. Thai Factors That Have Amplified Local Cycles

As the evidence of Part III has show, Thai cyclical outcomes broadly conform to the prediction of existing analytical framework of real estate cycles. The office market has been the most volatile, and within the housing sector the central city high rise condominium segment has also been the most volatile. However, cyclical behavior is different from over-investment and resource misallocation. This section identifies the various factors specific to the Thailand market that account for such over-investment. Poor credit analyses on the lender side was matched by real estate investment decisions that often were not based on sound and objective financial and economic criteria.

Property Valuation in Thailand. As noted earlier, secured lending by Thai banks could only be based on land and real estate collateral, and thereby rested on property valuation. Valuation did not seem to pose severe problems in the housing market that was fluid and only based on new units. Elsewhere property valuation appears to face significant obstacles in the Thai real estate industry. Partly because there are no valuation standards and no formal certification process, the valuation profession is neither highly recognized nor valued in Thailand. Property valuation for project lending has often been done by in-house appraisers who were not separated from the loan operations in most cases; an internal arrangement that threatened the quality and independence of valuation. Underlying the limited professionalism and independence of real estate valuation in Thailand are difficulties with appraisal practices in this emerging real estate market where some critical elements toward an efficient market are still missing. Traditionally, three different property valuation approaches can be used. There are structural difficulties with each of these three traditional approaches to valuation (cost, sales comparison and the income capitalization approaches) in the Thai market, which can render appraisal results less reliable.

- *Weak Relationship between Rents and Vacancy Rates.* The rental market in Thailand is weak and small, except for some niches like the condominium market for foreigners. Partly as a result, there is no monitoring of either vacancy rates or rents. It is therefore hard to judge what would be a sustainable rent from a particular property. Without this notion of sustainable rent, it is difficult to apply the income capitalization approach to come up with reliable property valuation.
- *Lack of Trading and Absence of Comparable Assets.* There have been very few transactions in the office market. Even housing does not have a well functioning secondary market. In the absence of comparables, the sales comparison approach is not applicable. Construction costs, a possible proxy, are a very rough and inaccurate approximation of either value or replacement cost.
- *Construction Costs and Replacement Value.* While the construction costs of a property can be more reliably estimated, the replacement value is not equivalent to construction costs. In addition to construction costs, the replacement value is also affected by the value of the site, the valuation of which depends on market comparables, among other factors. After July 1997, replacement costs have risen by about 30% with the devaluation of the Baht. As a result, during the asset restructuring that has just begun most transactions can be expected to take place below replacement value, if the market is to be cleared at its deflated new putative "equilibrium" level.

Office Market Investment Decisions. Office development at the beginning of the boom showed signs of merely responding to pent-up demand, but over-exuberance in this sector became obvious by 1995 and 1996. The over-supply in 1998 was enormous and would take many years to be absorbed in a mature market. What characterizes Thailand is that most office buildings have been built by corporate owners that were not developers and office development was cost driven and not remotely a yield-driven behavior. The concepts of modern corporate real estate were also essentially unknown in Thailand until the advent of the triple crisis. Together with the momentum of office cycles, idiosyncratic investment behavior explains the paradox of continuing expansion in supply after 1995, when both values and rents began to erode even for grade-A office space. Office developers did not make a cautious estimate of cash flows. They did not build for sale nor did they consider that alternative as a benchmark. Why did Thai corporate businesses invest in offices then? Several reasons appear to stand out:

- *Land availability*. Decisions were often based on the availability of land owned by the company.
- *Easy access to loans*. As already discussed, easy money, the creation of the BIBF facilities, and the low comparative cost of capital all contributed to the Thai boom.
- With outdated lending practices and difficult credit evaluation, *real estate was the only acceptable collateral* that could be used for borrowing. This created an additional incentive to build properties in an appreciating market so that the firm could borrow more to expand.
- The possibility of *tax avoidance* made it more attractive to reinvest profits in real estate assets than distributing them as dividends.
- *A trophy mentality*. Symbolism, status, and value preservation converged to encourage businesses to build their own corporate centers.
- *Euphoria-based expectations* about the continuing rise of real estate values made building decisions easy to justify.

Housing Vacancy Rates. The different physical and economic characteristics of the three segments of the Thai residential market can explain heir comparative degree of volatility, as Part III has shown. However, what is very unexpected by international standards is the exceptionally high level of vacancy rates in the residential market, considerably above international levels. Vacancy rates reaching 28% of the new stock show that not only the whole housing sector in Bangkok was very much over-supplied, but they also suggest that investment decisions were deeply flawed for a sustained period of time. Certainly, the performance of the housing sector was very poorly monitored and analyzed. Some of the weaknesses affecting sector performance were:

- An over-accumulation of land banks by professional developers which was associated with speculation on land price. Land prices experienced an enormous appreciation during the late 1980s and early 1990s. The SET requirement for developers to have land banks for public listing on the exchange appears to have been a contributing factor. This requirement was rescinded too late in 1996 when the boom had started to turn into a bust.
- Absence of a secondary market for used housing, possibly for cultural reasons, but mostly attributable to the so-called "capital gains tax", which actually taxes sales proceeds rather than capital gains, thereby discouraging property trading.
- Under-developed rental markets.

- Easy financing for developers and lack of clear loan origination rules and appropriate financial requirements (see Annex III).
- A remarkable lack of coordinated, timely, and reliable market information made it hard for developers to evaluate demand.

V. MANAGING THE IMPACTS OF THE THAI TRIPLE CRISIS

Herring and Wachter (1998) state that a real estate crisis can happen without a banking crisis, and a banking crisis can happen without a real estate crisis. However, this proposition seems asymmetrical. It is easier to think of a country that has had a banking crisis without a real estate crisis, such as Korea in 1997, than of a country that has experienced a real estate crisis without a banking crisis. The costs of a real estate crisis that involves large resource misallocation can be high. The costs of dual real estate and banking crisis are higher still. Then there are the costs of a triple real estate, banking and currency crisis. Those have been devastating for Thailand. The losses associated with the US Savings & Loans crisis have had a strong political impact, yet they amounted only to 3% of the annual GNP level of the period and were readily absorbed. The expected losses in Thailand are at least 15 times larger. Based on the historical experience of Chile in 1983 and on current Thai estimates, the costs of cleaning up the finance and corporate sectors of Thailand will be above 45% of GNP.

Almost two years into the triple crisis, a difficult and costly banking and corporate restructuring is in progress in Thailand. Given the intensity of the crisis, these on-going reforms can be expected to have the same defining effect on the organization of the Thai economy and society as the Great Depression that reshaped the US. How long the Thai recovery will take is unpredictable. In that regard, it is noteworthy that in Chile more than 15 years after their crisis and in spite a superb decade of quality growth of about 7 percent per year clean-up costs have not been paid in full. Therefore, this part of paper examines the immediate impacts of the triple crisis on the various components of the real sector.

A. Scale of The Real Estate Asset Deflation and Potential Losses

Estimating the magnitude of real estate deflation for Thailand is very difficult given the quality and coverage of the information. To understand better the situation in Bangkok, Renaud, Zhang and Koeberle (1998) attempted to build *crude estimates* of the losses for all forms of commercial property on which they had data and for housing. (See Annex Table 2). They used the same analytical framework already used by Hendershott and Kane for the United States (1992) when they wanted to determine the impact of overbuilding on reduced future cash flows. The composition of such losses includes:

- The zero gross rents on vacant buildings;
- The reduced rents expected to be earned on the space in occupied buildings, as compared to a "normal rent" or to the return on alternative investments.
- Reduced cash flows also mean a decline in the value of commercial property. This reduction in rents applies to the *total* commercial stock. The value decline is related

	1991	1992	1993	1994	1995	1996	1997	1998	1999	2000
Real Interest Rate	8.60%	7.89%	6.75%	5.76%	8.07%	7.53%	7.23%	8.23%	8.23%	8.23%
Ex Post User Cost of Housing Ownership	-1.50%	1.50%	4.50%	7.00%	9.25%	8.88%	12.63%	21.63%	25.13%	19.13%

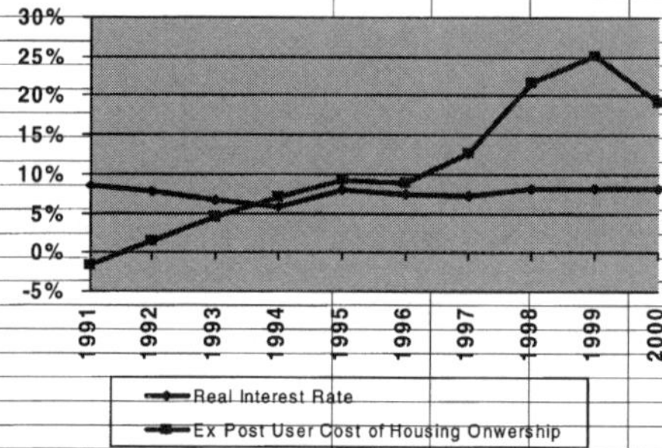

Figure 3.10.

to reduced future cash flows, and should be estimated relative to the stock's replacement cost.

The *minimum* estimated initial value of the 1997 residential stock is three times larger than the commercial stock (1,309 billion baht against 433 billion baht). The orders of magnitude of the *initial* wealth losses in each sector would appear comparable because of the greater amplitude of the losses on commercial properties: 430 billion baht of losses on housing compared to 371 billion baht of losses on commercial property.[12] These losses do not reflect the large fall in land prices.

B. Households: The Wealth Effect in Reverse

In term of asset value, housing is the largest component of the real estate stock. It is also likely to remain depressed for a number of years, for both demand and supply reasons. The demand for housing investment has declined sharply while the residential sector need will need to work out its very large stock of 28% vacant units that are moreover mistargeted to high income groups of limited size and growth potential. Prospects for reviving the economy through the household sector are not very good until well passed the year 2000. The magnitude of impact of the triple crisis on household sector and its investment activities in real estate is conjectural for lack of data. In the same manner that the asset inflation of the late 1980 and early 1990s contributed to the long Thai, asset deflation today is having a similar reverse on the economy via private consumption and investment.

On the consumption side, there are no readily available Thai data on the ratio of household net worth to household income and its evolution over the boom and bust for Thailand. International estimates for of the wealth effect on consumption is that the propensity to consume out incremental wealth is of the order of 3 percent out of total wealth and 6 percent out of financial wealth for the income deciles where wealth is concentrated. (Kähkönen in IMF, 1995).

On the household investment side there is every reason to expect that the demand housing investment has largely collapse because of three key negative factors: (1) the abrupt shift in the user cost of housing from a large negative value during the boom to a large and positive value with the bust; (2) the fall in household incomes; and (3) a drastic shift in expectations regarding the prospects for future income gains and the risk of unemployment. Figure 10 shows the sharp upswing in the user cost of capital after 1997.

C. Corporate Sector: Loss Recognition and Restructuring

A factor that is now bedeviling the loan portfolio restructuring of lenders comes from the past prevalence of leveraged speculation, often masked by inter-company transactions and the opaque structure of many Thailand corporations. Rapid loss recognition and portfolios restructuring in the real estate sector would be central to the critical return to liquidity in the market. This is happening very slowly for legal, managerial and economic reasons. This section discuss the problems of dealing with bad assets and the initial obstacles to restructuring in Thailand.

1. Dealing With Bad Assets: Rationale and Limits of Early Loss Recognition

Until new market expectations have been formed of what should be the new prices, the market will remain illiquid and balance-sheets will be very difficult to restructure. The central issue is the gap between the immediate liquidation value of a property at a time of great market instability and the perceived range of new "equilibrium" prices.

Falling demand, declines in rents, increases in vacancy rates and rising interest rates can turn even good real estate assets into bad ones. The immediate central issue are the spiraling losses associated with carrying bad assets. Who will bear theses losses? This is a key lesson learned in the US during the Savings & Loans crisis, in the Nordic countries during their banking crisis, by French banking regulators intervening failed specialist real estate lenders, and by others in the UK and Australia. The implicit carrying cost of a leveraged bad asset grows very quickly—almost explosively—greater than the loss would be in case of recognition of the loss through sale of the bad asset. This could be true even at its new and drastically lower value which was in fact lower that the replacement costs that had sharply risen with the large baht devaluation. It is all a matter of the allocation and sharing of losses. Potential buyers would come in under very different conditions. While the value of the property to heavily leveraged existing asset holders has fallen sharply, new buyers will have far smaller or no expected cash flow losses. The rate of growth of losses is directly linked to the degree of leverage. This point can be made clearer by the use of "T-accounts."[13]

T-ACCOUNT OF A GOOD ASSET PRIOR TO THE REAL ESTATE OVERSUPPLY. Consider a leveraged property in Bangkok in 1992. The market value of the asset is appreciating at rate of say 20% per annum. The new leasing rent rate is good at

12.5% of capital value and produces a positive cash flow after deduction of operation and maintenance costs and before financial costs of 7%. The property is financed with Baht 100 million of liability at an interest rate of 14%. Under such notional figures, we get the following t-account.

Good Real Estate Asset Account, 1992

Capital appreciation	+20%	Cost of liability to carry asset -14%
Rent	+7%	

This is an attractive asset. The leveraged owner is making a high return on his equity. As shown in Part II, corporate leverage in Bangkok was particularly high by regional standards.[14]

T-ACCOUNT OF A GOOD ASSET TURNED BAD IN EARLY 1998. With overbuilding, high interest rates on floating rate loans, increasing rates of delinquency among tenants and a doubling of the cost of foreign debt, a large majority of commercial real estate assets have turned bad. A bad asset account have looked as follows in early 1998.

Bad Real Estate Asset Account, Early 1998

Market value of assets:	-20% p.a.	cost of liability to carry asset -18 to -24%
Net Rent:	+3.5% p.a.	

The total impact of the bad asset is a negative rate of (-20 + 3.5 - 22) = -38.5% per annum. This 38.5% rate is the measure of the cost of continuing to carry the liability. If the liability initially was B100 million it will have spiraled to B192 in two years. Loss recognition is not a long-term option: the liabilities on this bad asset will practically double by the end of the second year. The higher the leverage on the asset and the size of the loss as a percentage of the liability, the faster losses will grow.

Early loss recognition would therefore appear to be a critical ingredient in shortening the crisis and hastening recovery. As typically happens at the beginning of a real estate bust, the real estate industry in early 1998 has remained in a state of suspended animation. Valuations and asking prices have been unrealistically high. It is important to keep in mind that the real estate bust started sometimes in late 1995 and preceded the currency crisis. The year of 1998 was therefore the third year of denial of losses in this real estate. The burden of a leverage asset was also moderating as interest rates fell with the return of some liquidity.

If it is so clearly in the self-interest of holders of bad assets to dispose of them to new investors, why don't they do it quickly? There are a variety of practical reasons why, until early 1998, this has not yet happened in Thailand, or at least on a meaningful scale. Meanwhile, rational domestic as well as international investors observing this self-defeating behavior will only buy when this behavior of holding onto bad assets stops. Why? Because the pressure to wait for even lower future prices does not stop until sales *without assistance* start.

2. Initial Obstacles to Restructuring in the Property Sector

Several interdependent factors are playing a major role in preventing the return to liquidity in the Thai economy, and in the real estate sector in particular. They include: the present structure and practices of corporate governance; the enactment of the new bankruptcy law; effective and pragmatic foreclosure rules; the results of market-based sales of real estate assets by the Financial Restructuring Authority (FRA). The successful creation and operations of property funds is not yet a factor at present.

Business Governance. Why does loss recognition by business companies take so much time? Upstream of all delays, one might place the governance structure of many Thai listed as well as private companies. This governance structure is usually ill adapted to making the rapid and painful decisions needed in times of crisis. Corporate boards have interlocking directorates across a variety of companies. These boards have external directors who may be bankers or other influential members of the community, but who may be lacking experience in the core sector in which the company operates. Some members may face conflict of interest and of fiduciary responsibilities due to their ownership of interests in related companies. Other directors may be family members who may not have the training and skills to evaluate the long-term impact of decisions taken by management. During the boom, such weak governance was not a problem: board members tended to be passive supporters and cheerleaders of rapid expansion without paying due attention to risks. However, during the present period of steep asset deflation and liquidity crunch, such board structures easily lead to gridlock.

Passage of a Functional New Bankruptcy Law. Reorganization, company restructuring and asset disposal will be essential to unlocking the capital that is currently locked into bad projects and redirecting it to better uses. Finally, the new bankruptcy law which gives creditors more power to force debtors to pay up was voted by the Thai Senate on March 12, 1999 by 162 votes to one and voted by the Chamber of Deputies by the end of March. The new law removes a variety of legal and practical operational obstacles that had been impeding the reorganization of all forms of corporate entities, including those in the real estate sector.

Foreclosure Rules. Most lending in Thailand is done on a secured basis, with the collateral being fixed property and with the loan advance being a percentage of the appraised value of the collateral. Loan foreclosure rules therefore will have a significant impact on restoring liquidity in the real estate market to permit various owners to restructure their position. Foreclosure laws were amended with a goal to speed up the process of creditors being able to foreclose on properties. The procedures contained in the Thai Civil and Commercial Code were quite slow and time consuming. In particular, in order to foreclose and enter into possession of a property, there had to be a failure to pay interest on the debt for a period of five years.

Liberalization of Rules for Foreign Property Ownership. Thai rules on foreign property ownership were very restrictive. They currently play against the return of stability and liquidity in the real estate sector. A politically acceptable solution has been found to allow foreign financing work in support of a faster recovery, and serve Thai interests in better asset values. The new arrangements permit foreign ownership for a fixed and long number of years. These new rules might still be judged inadequate by foreign investors. In view of the present severe liquidity crisis, foreign capital will play a critical role in preventing the first FRA sales from taking place at very low "liquidation" prices rather than at the new, more realistic "equilibrium prices"—or no sales at all. This foreign ownership constraint seriously affects the flow of funds into the sector and thereby its restructuring. Moreover, without clear and transparent improvements, the risk premium asked by foreign investors in return for accepting uncertain legal conditions will be higher.

A solution that could balance the demands of investors and Thai interests may include:

- use of long-term leasehold
- geographic restriction on foreign land ownership
- ownership forms varying by type of assets
- property funds.

FRA Sales. 30 percent of the assets of the 56 closed finance companies were held by the FRA are real estate assets. The first FRA auctions were important in setting the tone for the entire market and for price expectations. The proper selection of the real estate assets for the first sales an the lot size will affect the range of potential bidders—and whether any sales will take place at all. The auction held in December 1998 were far from successful in terms of participation, volume of assets sold, and prices obtained. As a result, the FRA resorted to tendering in order to move forward on asset disposition. The final FRA auction sale of the assets of closed finance companies took place in August 1999. In March 1999, the balance of other assets had been transferred for final disposition to the Asset Management Corporation.

Overhaul of the "Capital Gains Tax". In the case of housing the "capital gains tax" which is in effect a heavy transaction tax is a significant obstacle to the development of the secondary market for existing homes. The three main flaws of the tax have been identified. (1) This "capital gains tax" is actually an excise tax based on the value of the property. It is not based on whether the owner experienced a gain or a loss. Even if the owner disposes of his property at a loss, he will pay the excise tax. (2) The basis for the tax assessment is the "assessed value" as assessed by the Land Department not the transaction price. During the boom, assessed values were below market prices, now they are above. (3) Long-term asset holders are penalized. There is no specific timetable for the reform of this tax.

Property Funds. The Security and Exchange Commission (SEC) that supervises the SET began studying the establishment of property trusts in 1994. Proposals were finalized in late 1995. However, no action was taken in 1996. The SEC issued the regulations that govern property funds in February 1997. These funds are established under the mutual fund regulations and governed by the SEC Act B.E. 2535. There are two categories of funds—"Public Funds" for offering to the public and "Institutional Funds" for institutional investors. Public funds are listed, institutional funds are unlisted. The rules for institutional investor are less stringent than those for public funds. Given the domestic liquidity crunch, one of the important features of property funds is that restrictions on units held and minimum unit holders do not apply to foreign institutional investors. There are no restrictions on foreign ownership, which be up to 100%. Once established, a fund is a separate legal entity. The Thai SEC had approved a large number of property funds by the Fall of 1998.

D. Banking Sector Restructuring and Recapitalization

In Thailand, as well as in much of the countries of Asia in crisis it is expected that the banks will ultimately bear a significant portion of the cost of the property bubble and the stock market crash. In Thailand the property sector's problems will lead in many cases to total losses on some property related loans, and will lead to greatly diminished values of the collateral. As indicated earlier, this problem is exacerbated until now by the old bankruptcy law and the legal difficulty of foreclosing. It is generally estimated that the banking system of Thailand will ultimately have to charge off more than 30% of its loans. As already mentioned, the level of financial intermediation in Thailand is high. As a result, system-wide 30% of losses represent an enormous amount of the order of 45% of GDP and representing several times the total annual central budget, maybe 5–7 times. The allocation of these losses is therefore an extremely difficult task, technically and politically. For the strongest individual banks it would take as much as 25 years to charge off NPL loans even against the level of their pre-crisis, pre-tax, pre-provision profits. Raising such amounts is very difficult internationally as well as domestically. A successful government recapitalization program must therefore be put in place. This recapitalization program needs to be accompanied by strong regulatory reforms. Such a program will involve some form of exchange of government securities against equity. Passage of these two restructuring packages must go through the legislature and it has been a difficult process. As a result, the recapitalization program is not yet operational in Thailand.

Whether one considers the prospect for a real estate recovery from the demand side, the supply side or the financing side, it is readily apparent that a recovery will not take place in the immediate future.

VI. CONCLUSION: BEYOND THE CRISIS

Thailand's financial and economic crisis once again shows that, in the present environment of rapid financial globalization, liberalizing the financial sector and opening the capital account without strengthening the regulatory and supervisory system can have an strong destabilizing effects in a few short years. Domestic euphoria combined with the herd mentality of international "asset allocators" helped to produce a surge of cheap foreign capital inflows that unhinged the Thai economy from its previous path of solid growth. Sound banking was also undermined by the moral hazard of expected implicit guarantees of the dollar/baht exchange rate, as well as of deposit rates. These policies further fueled the credit boom and asset inflation on both the stock market and the real estate market. A rich research agenda emerges from this crisis.

Analytically, does the Thai experience raises a new dimension of analytical problems for the understanding of cycles in emerging real estate markets? Because immature real estate markets like Bangkok are by nature more shallow in terms of existing space inventories, does it mean that cycles will tend to be more volatile during booms and bust? Does a shallow market also offer the prospects for easier recovery after a crisis?

From the viewpoint of macroeconomic stability, the real estate sector in a middle income, open economy cannot be ignored. If there is a unambiguous lesson out of the Thai crisis it is that the performance of real estate matters because it is the largest wealth component of the economy. A modern regulation and monitoring system matters very much for the stability of the financial system and that of the economy. A very important element of new supervision in an era of rapid financial technological change is the development of complementary private sector monitoring.

Looking beyond the crisis, reforms must enhance and strengthen the real estate sector, reduce asset volatility and prevent large resource misallocation. Three avenues for change are already being traveled by Thailand and most other countries of the Asia region: (1) reforms to improve real estate market infrastructure and sector transparency, (2) extensive restructuring of financial institutions, and (3) the strengthening of capital markets where incentives for private sector monitoring of financial institutions as well as links between the real estate industry and capital markets have barely started developing.

Within the larger debate on the Asia crisis, this paper has only analyzed one major domestic weakness that triggered the crisis in the case of Thailand. The problems for international capital flows and stability raise a host of separate additional policy questions. Among those are capital controls (inflows versus outflows), the modification of BIS risk coefficients, the implications and realism of an international lender of last resort, and a host of other technical issues.[15]

NOTES

1. Bertrand Renaud is the lead author of this paper which is based on field work carried out in early 1998 with Ming Zhang and Stefan Koeberle of the World Bank. Our initial report was presented under the title "How the Thai Real Estate Boom Undid Financial Institutions: What Can Be Done Now?" The paper was presented at the NESDB-World Bank Conference on Thailand's Economic Recovery and Competitiveness, Bangkok, Thailand May 1998. We borrowed that title from Lynne Browne and Karl Case (1992) about the Northeast banking crisis in the US. By sharing titles we wanted to emphasize to a Thai audience that the interactions between the real estate sector and banking institutions observed in Thailand were common to a large number of countries in the 1980s and the 1990s. Two other directly related papers are Renaud (1997) and (1998). All errors of commission or omission in the present paper are the responsibility of the authors. The views presented are not necessarily those of the World Bank as an institution.

2. The Roubini Home Page at NYU has been the key internet portal during this debate; see the bibliography.

3. There are different definitions of contagion. A broad definition used for by rating agencies such as *Moody's* is that contagion occurs when a financial and currency crisis in one country suddenly affects financial and macroeconomic conditions in other countries with a significant degree of severity. Such financial contagion is marked by sudden and massive reversal of capital flows triggered by an abrupt change in investors' perception of risks. For an individual corporate issuer there can then be a rapid transition from a liquidity squeeze to a solvency problem regardless of the fundamentals. The three main channels of transmission of contagion that *Moody's* watches for possible problems are trade, portfolio shifts by residents and non-residents, and the willingness of external creditors to provide more funds. Net capital outflows can be massive such as Brazil's hemorrhage of $30 billion in fifty days in the summer 1998. Contagion can affect countries with perceived sound fundamentals.

4. Monitoring the microeconomic performance of asset markets—residential and commercial property markets in particular—emerged as a new and totally unanticipated requirement even in OECD economies (BIS 1993, Goldstein et al. 1993). An article in the *Economist* of London points out the difficulties that central banks have had in the 1980s and 1990s with inflation targeting, and in particular with asset price inflation in real estate and equities. The article elegantly summarizes today's central banking problems into three questions: "Over the past two decades of financial innovation, central bankers have struggled with the questions of "what is money?" and "what is a bank?" Now, at the pinnacle of their power, it is disconcerting that they need to ask "what is inflation?" *Economist*, November 14th, 1998, "*The Central Banker as God*." Pp. 23–25.

5. Ratio of debt to equity.

6. Not surprisingly, by September 1997, the liabilities of Thai property and construction companies represented the lion's share (53%) of the total liabilities of all distressed listed companies whose operating cash flow could not cover interest expenses. (Pathra, 1998).

7. This point estimate of total real estate value is clearly biased downward. The estimates include only the housing stock built after 1988. About 1 million housing units were built before that year and are not excluded for lack of price data. Similarly, the non-residential stock recorded is likely to be incomplete since private information tends to focus on grade-A properties and commercial properties in the peripheral areas is scarce. This estimate of the total value of the real estate stock does not include hotels and tourist facilities, housing and real estate outside the BMR. It also excludes industrial real estate that consists mostly of serviced industrial land in the periphery of Bangkok and along the Eastern Seaboard, and not structures.

8. Assuming 3.5 individuals per household.

9. In comparison, between 1992 and 1997, the office vacancy rate was 5 to 9% in Tokyo, 2 to 9% in Singapore, 3 to 6% in Hong Kong, 2 to 7% in Makati, Philippines, 2 to 8% in Kuala Lumpur, and 8 to 15% in Jakarta (JLW Regional Property Markets in 1998).

10. Simple physical magnitudes can throw light on the scale of oversupply. At the end of 1997, local analysts estimated that the total office stock in the BMR could reach 7,050,000 sq.m. by the end of 1998 and 7,224,000 sq.m. by the end of 1999 (Richard Ellis). This is a fourfold increment compared to the end of 1991, when the total office stock was only 1,540,000 sq.m. What does this mean in terms of implied office employment? Based on an emerging economy standard of 10 sq.m. per office worker, the Bangkok office supply was increasing fast enough to accommodate an almost four-fold employment expansion from 154,000 to 705,000 persons in just seven year, or the creation of an average of 79,000 new office worker jobs per year. The implied required annual growth rate of office employment is 22% compounded. The pre-crisis actual growth rate of service employment over the last decade was of the order 6–8 percent per year. Investors in office space clearly did not take into account such a basic parameter.

11. According to Richard-Ellis, only 10 such sales occurred, with the main reason behind the transactions being financial difficulties and owner occupancy requirements. None of these 10 transactions were yield driven—as was also the case for office developments in general. Local professionals stress that a frequent consequence of owner-built office space is the inefficient utilization of space and poor property management. Anecdotal observations suggest that a significant portion of owner-occupied office

space was apparently not being fully used. The implicit vacancy rate for office space could therefore be even higher than reported and competition for users even keener.

12. The value of the baht depreciated by 85.5% from 25.61 baht per US dollar at the end of 1996 to 47.25 at the end of 1997. It was back to 36.69 by end 1998. Any property loss funded in dollars is amplified.

13. This analysis is illustrative of the pressures for early loss recognition. However, in an over-leveraged environment, consideration must also be given to a possible over-shooting in falling asset prices. At the time when this paper was prepared there was no data on the time path of real estate prices. There is a significant difference in perception between Thais and investors about the auctions conducted by the Financial Restructuring Agency. The last FRA auction was completed on 11 August 1999. The FRA recovered only 25% of outstanding loan principal overall. In the case of residential mortgage loans it recovered only 47%. Both ratios were significantly below Thai expectations.

14. There were some 35 property companies listed on the SET. Investment analysts report that Thai developers had gearing ratios (net debt to equity) that were at least three times of those typical for Hong Kong; over 150% for Thailand against 40–60% for Hong Kong. A very large number of developers may even have had gearing ratios above the 150% mark making most of them deeply insolvent by 1997.

15. For a very productive analysis of this separate set of issues, see Barry Eichengreen, February 1999.

BIBLIOGRAPHY

A characteristics of an emerging real estate market is the lack of centralized and consistent information, hence the need to rely on numerous sources. For a bibliography on Thai sources refer to Renaud, Zhang, and Koeberle, 1998.

Bank of International Settlements (BIS). 1993. *Sixty-third Annual Report.*

Baumgartner, Ulrich and Guy Meredith (eds.) 1995. *Savings Behavior and the Asset Price "bubble" in Japan. Analytical Studies.* Washington DC: International Monetary Fund.

Browne, Lynne E. and Karl Case. September 1992. "How the Commercial Real Estate Boom Undid the Banks" in Browne and Rosengren ed. *Real Estate and the Credit Crunch*, Federal Reserve Bank of Boston, Conference Series No. 36.

——and Robert J. Schiller. 1998. "The Behavior of Home Buyers in Boom and Post-Boom Markets" Federal reserve Bank of Boston: *New England Economic Review*, November/December 1988, 29–46.

——. March 1989. "The Efficiency of the Market for Single-Family Homes" *American Economic Review, Vol. 79.*

Corsetti, Giancarlo, Paolo Pesenti, Nouriel Roubini, November 1998 "The Asian Crisis: An overview of the Empirical Evidence and Policy Debate", forthcoming in Agenor, Miller, Vines and Axel (eds.) *The Asian Financial Crisis: Causes, Contagion and Consequences*, Cambridge UK: Cambridge University Press.

Dowall, David E. 1989. "Bangkok: A Profile of an Efficiently Performing Housing Market", *Urban Studies*, Vol. 26, pp. 327–339.

Eichengreen, Barry. February 1999. *Toward A New International Financial Architecture: A Practical Post-Asia Agenda.* Washington DC: Institute for International Economics.

Financial Sector Restructuring Authority. February 1998. "*Sales Process. Terms of Reference for a Real Estate Strategic Survey of Thailand*".

Goldstein, Morris and David Folkerts-Landau. 1993. *International Capital Markets.* Part II. Systemic Issues in International Finance, IMF, August 1993.

Grenadier, Steven R. 1992. *Real Estate and Other Long-term Development Projects*, Cambridge, Mass: Ph.D. Thesis, Harvard, July 1992.

——. 1995a. "The Persistence of Real Estate Cycles". *Journal of Real Estate Finance and Economics*, Vol. 10, 1995, pp. 94–119.

Guttentag, Jack and Richard Herring. 1986. *Disaster Myopia in International Banking*, Princeton University Essays in International Finance, No. 164, September 1986.

Hendershott, Patric H. and Edward Kane. 1992. "Causes and Consequences of the 1980s Commercial Construction Boom, *Journal of Applied Corporate Finance*, pp. 61–70.

Herring, Richard and Susan Wachter. 1998. "Real Estate Cycles and Banking Crises: An International Perspective," paper presented at the Wharton School Conference on Asian Twin Financial Crises, Long Term Credit Bank of Japan, Tokyo, March 1998.

Litan, Robert E. September 1992. "Banks and Real Estate: Regulating the Unholy Alliance," in Browne and Rosengren ed. *Real Estate and the Credit Crunch*, Federal Reserve bank of Boston, Conference Series No. 36.

McLennan, Duncan, John Muellbauer, and Mark Stephens. 1998. "Asymmetries in Housing and Financial Markets and EMU." *Oxford Review of Economic Policy*, Vol. 18, No. 3, Autumn 1998.

Moody's Investors Services. January 1995. *Critical Issues and Outlook for the Thai Banking System.*

——. March 1998. *Asian Banking and the Dangers of Moral Hazard.*

——. February 1999. *What Will it Take to Upgrade Asia's Troubled Banks.*

Peek, Joe and Eric Rosengren. September 1992. "Crunching the Recovery: Bank Capital and the Role of Bank Credit" in Browne and Rosengren ed. *Real Estate and the Credit Crunch*, Federal Reserve Bank of Boston, Conference Series No. 36.

Phatra Securities Thailand. 1998. *Keeping a Bead on NPLs: From the Bottom Up*, Special Issue, January 1998. (Includes coverage of non performing loans in the property sector.)

Pomerleano, Michael, 1998. "The East Asia Crisis and Corporate Finances: The Untold Microeconomic Story" *Emerging Markets Quarterly*, Vol. 2, No. 4, Winter 1998.

Renaud, Bertrand. 1997a. "The 1985 to 1994 Global Real Estate Cycle: An Overview" *Journal of Real Estate Literature*, 5: 13–44.

Renaud, Bertrand, Frederik Pretorius and Barnabe O. Pasadilla. 1997b. *Markets at Work, The Dynamics of the Private Residential Real Estate Industry In Hong Kong*, University of Hong Kong, June 1997.

Renaud, Bertrand, Ming Zhang and Stefan Koeberle, 1998a. "How the Real Estate Boom Undid Financial Institutions. What Can be Done Now? Proceedings of the NESDB-World Bank Conference on Thailand's Dynamic Recovery and Competitiveness, 21–21 May 1998, Bangkok.

Renaud, Bertrand, 1998b. "Real Estate Cycles and Banking Crises: What Have We Learned?" paper presented at the 1998 IPD Investment Conference, Brighton, UK, November 26, 1998.

Roubini, Nouriel *Asian Crisis Homepage, www.stern.nyu.edu/~nroubini/asia/AsiaHomepage.html*

Salomon Smith Barney (Global Equity Research, Financial Institutions: Thailand). 1998. "*Thai Legal Issues and Financial Recovery*", 31 March 1998.

Schadler, Susan, Maria Carkovic, Adam Bennett, and Robert Khan. 1993. "Recent Experiences in Surges in Capital Inflows", *IMF Occasional Paper No. 108*, December. (1993)

Sheng, Andrew. 28 April 1998. The Crisis of Money in the 21rst Century", City University of Hong Kong Guest Lecture.

——. 1996. *Bank Restructuring: Lessons from the 1980s*, Washington DC: World Bank.

Siamwalla, Ammar. 1997a. "Can a Developing Democracy Manage its Macroeconomy? The Case of Thailand, J. Douglas Dillon Lecture, Queen's University, Ontario. As reprinted in Thailand's Boom and Bust, Bangkok: Thailand Development Research Institute.

——. 1997b. "What went wrong? Why are we in this mess?" Journalistic version of the J. Douglas Dillon Lecture, Queen's University, Ontario. *Bangkok Post*, 12 November 1997, internet *http://www.bkkpost.samart.co.th.*

Simister, David. February 1998. *The Thai Real Estate Market Crisis*, Presentation to the National Housing Authority, Bangkok, Richard Ellis (Thailand).

Wall Street Journal. September 8, 1997. "High Tech Trauma. A Company's Travails Shows Why The Economy Is Shot In Thailand. Few Controls Let Alphatec Get Away With Odd Accounting". See also, *Financial Times*, "Alphatec rescue points way for Thailand" Companies & Markets Section p. 1, February 3, 1999.

Werner, Richard A. 1993. "Japanese Capital Flows: Did the World Suffer from Yen Illusion? Toward a Quantity Theory of Disaggregated Credit". Paper presented at the Annual Conference of the Royal Economic Society, London.

Annex Table 1. Tentative Value of the Real Estate Stock in the BMR at the End of 1997

Sector	Space/Unit	Estimated Value (billion Baht)
Commercial Real Estate Properties		**563**
Office	6.2 m sqm	220
Retail	3.3 m sqm	270
Industrial*	16,127 rai	73
Residential Real Estate Properties**	**1,291,407 units**	**1,608**
Luxury condominium	29,212 units	123
Low income condominium	278,126 units	278
Detached house	407,384 units	839
Townhouse	476,265 units	316
Luxury apartment	7,711 units	31
Low income apartment	92,709 units	22
Total Estimated Value		**2,171**
Estimated value compared to GDP of Thailand		45%
Estimated value compared to GDP of Bangkok***		118%

* Industrial real estate refers here only to serviced land.
** Residential properties include housing built after 1988.
*** Bangkok 1997 GDP is extrapolated from 1996 data.
Source: Renaud-Zhang-Koeberle 1998 calculations based on stock, price and rent data from various Jones Lang Wootton and Richard-Ellis estimates.

Annex Table 2. Impact of Real Estate Slump: Asset Depreciation and Value Held in Vacant Units

Sector	Estimated Value at end of 1997 (billion Baht)	Vacancy Rate	Value held in vacant space	Value depreciation in 1997	Value lost from depreciation
Commercial Real Estate Properties				**130**	**241**
Office	220	23.7%	52	33%	108
Retail	270	28%	76	33%	133
Industrial	73	2.9%	2	0%	0
Residential Real Estate Properties*				**300**	**138**
Luxury condominium	123	17%	21	10%	14
Low income condominium	278	20%	56	10%	31
Detached housing	839	19%	159	10%	93
Townhouse	316	18%	57	10%	35
Luxury Apt	31	12%	4	10%	3
Low income Apt	22	15%	3	10%	2
Total Value in Vacant Units			**430**		**379**

Note: For lack of data, housing price depreciation in 1997 is conservatively assumed to be 10% across the board.
Source: authors calculation based on Table 1 and additional data from Jones Lang Wootton and Richard-Ellis, various issues.

Annex 3. Bad Banking During Financial Liberalization and Real Estate Booms

Financial liberalization has brought to light a wide range of important issues regarding debt, financial fragility and systemic risk. Financial innovation and deregulation during the 1980s have been accompanied by rapid credit expansion and a substantial increase in bank lending as a share of GNP in many countries. Not only did the relative volume of loans increase, but its composition changed significantly under the sharply increasing pressure of competition from non-bank lending institutions.

Lending errors were frequently made and they were more or less always the same. They tended to be systematically related to the type of financial institutions. Large commercial banks, specialized lenders, and small banks tend to take different types of risks determined by the clientele they serve. The nature of the risks and returns changes with the type of clientele. Major banks finance major "blue chip" operators; lesser banks take the rest of borrowers.

There is an important element of bad banking during the real estate boom in every country, for both real estate and other loans. Under financial deregulation, poor practices have tended to be the mark of finance companies, mutual and cooperative institutions with newly extended asset powers entering new lines of business for which they were poorly prepared and institutions with undiversified assets that were inadequately supervised. In case of intervention, bank supervisors typically found that principles of sound banking were breached in the following manner, besides cases of fraud:

- Lending had been exceedingly concentrated in a few activities, especially real estate.
- Rapidly growing real estate portfolios had not been monitored.
- Even within the real estate sector, lending had been concentrated onto a few business groups or individuals.
- Counterparty risk had been ignored. Such risk has been shown to be twice as high for real estate loans as of industrial or business loans. Yet, lenders have usually not charged a risk premium. They have been satisfied with the buildings as collateral.
- Cash flow had not been correctly analyzed. Loans could appear to be current because of the existence and use of interest cash reserves—funded by debt—hiding cash deficiencies to cover debt service.
- Assets and liabilities had been mismatched.
- Attention had been exclusively focused on short-run fees and on maintaining activity in a market with excess capacity.
- Because of asset inflation, little concern had been shown about the risk that both the borrower and the collateral could be subject to the same shock.
- As the real estate boom went past its peak, further real estate lending took place to assist large corporate clients in unloading some of their real estate assets.
- Bank supervision during the recent sharp asset price cycle remained dominated by pre-deregulation norms and skills. It tended to perform rather poorly and late. Guidelines lagged behind market trends and did not address the increased riskiness of new lending. In the case of real estate lending, a thorough review of prudential rules, lending regulations regarding loan underwriting, and property valuation is now in progress in most countries.

Source: Renaud (1997a)

4. REAL ESTATE INCOME AND VALUE CYCLES: A MODEL OF MARKET DYNAMICS[1]

YOON DOKKO

Dean and Professor, School of Business Administration, Ajou University, Korea

ROBERT H. EDELSTEIN

Real Estate Development Chair, Haas School of Business, University of California at Berkeley, E-mail edelstel@haas.berkeley.edu, Fax:510-643-7357

ALLAN J. LACAYO

Research Associate, Fisher Center for Real Estate and Urban Economics, Haas School of Business, University of California at Berkeley

DANIEL C. LEE

Visiting Professor, Haas School of Business, University of California at Berkeley

I. INTRODUCTION

There is growing recognition among academics and practitioners that volatile macro, regional and local economic factors exert important influences on the cyclic behavior of real estate markets. Even though the economy itself may have changed, real estate cycles remain. The most recent example of the commercial real estate cycle occurred in the late 1980's and early 1990's. The unusual and severely distressed state of the U.S. commercial real estate markets during this period has been followed with an upturn of these markets in the mid 1990's.

Commercial real estate markets across cities were not uniformly depressed from the late 1980's to the early 1990's, suggesting that cyclical behavior in various geographic real estate markets is asynchronous. For example, in 1987, data from Coldwell Banker (figure 1) show downtown office buildings in Denver and Houston had vacancy rates greater than 30% and 20%, respectively. Simultaneously, the vacancy rates in Philadelphia and Boston were less than 10%, while those in Los Angeles and San Francisco were approximately 15%. The same data suggest that, by early 1995, Denver vacancies had declined to nearly 10%, Houston's vacancy rates had stabilized and hovered at around 20%, and, Philadelphia and Boston vacancy rates

S.J. Brown and C.H. Liu (eds.). A GLOBAL PERSPECTIVE ON REAL ESTATE CYCLES.

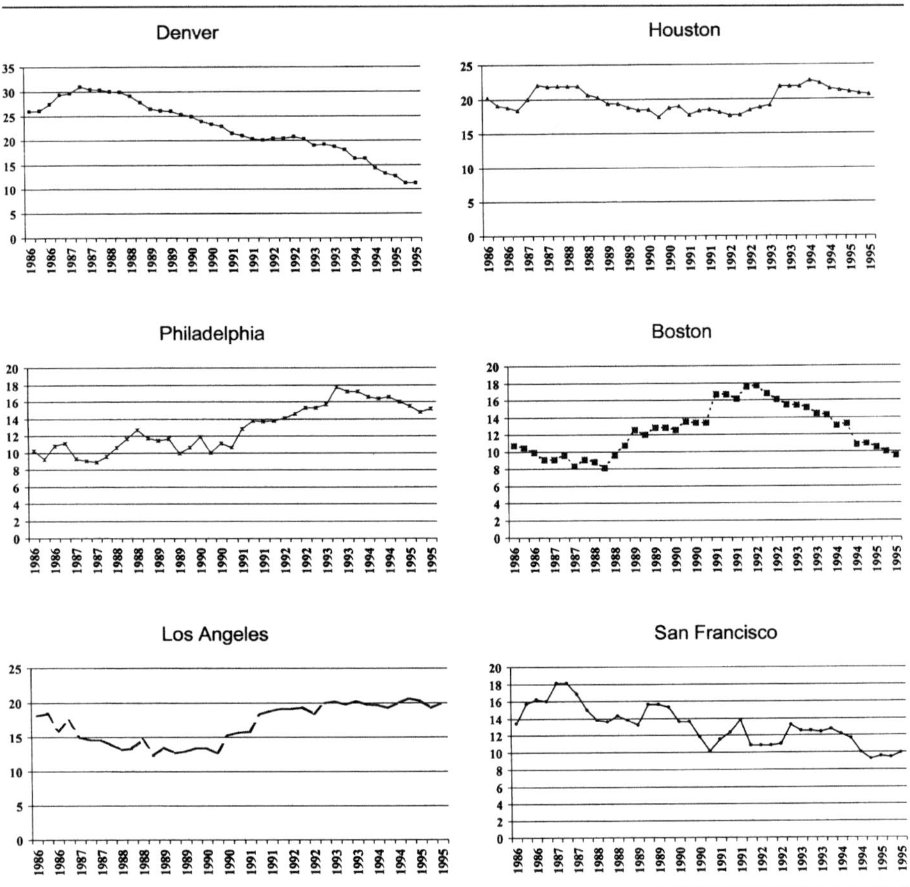

Figure 4.1. MSA office vacancy rates (percent) 1985:4–1995:4

had cycled up and then down to 15% and 10%, respectively. Concurrently, the office markets vacancy rate in Los Angeles was increasing and peaked at nearly 20%, while San Francisco's vacancy rate dropped to a low of 11%.[2]

In addition, real estate cycles are difficult to characterize because of varying severity across different real estate sectors. For example, the magnitude of the nationwide downturn in residential real estate markets during the late 1980's and early 1990's appears to be the worst since the great depression. But commercial real estate market episodes of the 1960's and 1970's are by no means dissimilar in direction or severity to those observed more recently in residential markets.[3]

The lack of uniformity in direction and magnitude of these cycles by sector, locale and over time has made it difficult to create a uniform explanation for real estate market cycles. It is not sufficient to merely observe upturns and downturns in value or rents in order to characterize the economic behavior of any market as "cyclical". Rather, one should devise a theoretical benchmark of the cycle that can be tested empirically.[4] A number of earlier research efforts develop behavioral models that examine the interrelationships between economic variables, real estate income and real estate values.[5] This paper confirms and furthers our understanding of the cyclical nature of real estate income and value.

The main objective of this paper is to extend earlier research efforts by developing a theory of real estate cycles that demonstrates the interrelationships among the economic cycle, real estate rental rates and property value cycles over time. Our theory is a continuous time dynamic model that is econometrically identifiable. This allows us to test our model specification using observed real estate office market data, and to establish the model's practical usefulness in understanding idiosyncrasies of some (office) real estate markets.

Our paper is subdivided into four subsequent sections. First, we introduce the reader to a selective review of the germane real estate cycle literature. We then proceed with the prime focus of this paper: we develop a theoretical model of real estate market cycles. We use this theoretical model in section IV to evaluate and statistically fit the model against actual market data. This enables us to ascertain if our real estate cycle theory is consistent with the observed market behavior. Finally, in the last section, we place our conclusions in perspective and suggest a strategy for future research in real estate cycles, as well as discuss the potential practical applications for our analysis.

II. A SELECTIVE REVIEW OF THE REAL ESTATE CYCLE LITERATURE

II.1 Real Estate Cycle Identification

Real estate cycle research has linked the real estate cycle to the general macroeconomic cycle. This relationship has been recognized and documented since World War II. Burns and Grebler (1982) uncovered six residential and four non-residential construction cycles in the United States between 1950 and 1978. Pritchett's (1984) analysis indicates that the magnitudes of the construction cycles for office, industrial and retail are different, with office the most volatile, industrial the least volatile and with retail somewhere in between the two.

The residential construction cycles tended to be counter-cyclical, while the commercial construction cycles tended to be co-incidental with the macroeconomic cycle. Guttentag (1960) explains the observed counter-cyclical residential construction activity as a function of credit and other resource availability to the residential building sector. Green (1997) performs tests for causality between economic and real estate investment cycles. Using Granger causality statistical tests for several alternative model specifications, Green's statistical analysis finds that while residential housing investment leads fluctuations in gross domestic product, the non-residential investment[6] series lags gross domestic product. Although Green does not provide us with an economic explanation of this result, his empirical work lends support to the hypothesis that structural economic factors cause commercial real estate value and income fluctuations.

Hekman (1985) finds that the office construction sector, for fourteen metropolitan statistical areas, is highly cyclical, following the national economic cycle. He also observes that local and regional economic conditions exert important forces on the MSA office market. Similarly, Crone and Voith (1988), for seventeen United States metropolitan statistical areas, uncover significant cyclical vacancy differences between major city office markets. These findings are reinforced by Dokko, et al. (1991), who demonstrate that local market conditions and macro-economic conditions, especially inflationary expectations, operate in concert to generate cyclical outcomes for local real estate markets.

For the national office market, Wheaton (1987) identifies a twelve-year recurring cycle in construction and vacancy. Torto and Wheaton (1988) find that the peaks and troughs of the office real rent cycle lag the vacancy rate troughs and peaks, respectively, by roughly one year. Rosen (1984) develops a natural vacancy rate model for the San Francisco office market that identifies rental rate adjustments used to predict local new construction, absorption, changes in vacancy and changes in rental rates. Although similar simultaneous equation model specifications are employed in all three works, one major difference in their results stands out. While Wheaton (1987) and Torto and Wheaton (1988) did not find prices or interest rates statistically significant in explaining rent adjustments in national aggregates of the office markets, Rosen (1984) finds financial variables are statistically significant using metropolitan statistical area—local market—data. These results are not necessarily contradictory; instead, they may confirm that local office markets respond to macro variables that may not be significant in the aggregate, when examining office markets nationally. The above research complements results by Crone and Voith (1988), Dokko, et al. (1991) and others.[7]

In sum, real estate construction, stock and rent-vacancy-value cycles have been identified and linked to both, local-regional and macroeconomic performance. However, cycle identification and theoretical explanations are not synonymous.

II.2 Explanations of Real Estate Cycles

Several commonly espoused explanations for the boom-bust real estate construction and asset stock cycles hone in on the alleged "inept" and/or "greedy" developer and/or the "bumbling" lender.[8] Using the logic of those views, the developer faces a long lag, from start to finish, in commercial real estate project construction. The developer is unable to forecast the future state of the marketplace accurately. Development commences when the market indicators appear to be favorable, only to have new construction space available under much less favorable market conditions. Hence, vacancy rates increase above, and rents decline below, what they might have been under favorable market conditions as a result of poorly timed additions to the inventory of leaseable office space. In contrast, when the real estate market is tight, the developer is unable to respond quickly to increased space demand because of the lags in construction; thereby, vacancies remain lower and rents higher than they might have been without the long lags in construction.

The construction lag explanation, while at most partially capable of explaining moderate fluctuations in some industrial markets, is unsatisfactory, by itself, as the prime cause of cycles in other property types and thus in general. One reason is that developers must recognize the existence of lags in construction as well as their own limited abilities to forecast uncertain market fundamentals. Therefore, it is not obvious that the real estate market automatically should exhibit recurring, persistent over-building and under-building cycles. Furthermore, while large office construction projects in many markets have significant production lags, for other types of real estate, such as tilt-up industrial space, lags for production are brief (less than a year). Thus the lag-forecast argument does not seem to explain the boom-bust cycle for this type of industrial real estate market.

An alternative explanation highlights lender behavior and nonrecourse financing as the culprits to cyclical real estate markets.[9] According to this view, the developer is "greedy" and if you provide nonrecourse project financing, or fees for construction, the developer will build. This argument depends upon lenders making recurrent bad lending decisions while failing to learn from prior history (i.e., past lending mistakes). A variant of this theme attributes lender behavior to regulatory or profitability constraints.[10] In turn, these constraints create real estate credit availability cycles that interplay with real estate market demand cycles to cause real estate booms and busts. These explanations, while perhaps contributing to observed cycles, inadequately explain the full extent of observed real estate cycles.

In Chinloy's (1996) cyclic real estate model, the key rental rate equation is a function of vacancies and space absorption expectations (i.e., excess supply and changes in *expected* excess supply). To the extent that disequilibrium occurs because of excess demand for space, the need for new space construction will be triggered. These actions move the market toward equilibrium, and generate a cycle of activity that is observed in market values and rent fluctuations over time—as the adjustment toward equilibrium continues. In Chinloy's model, the "indivisibility" of real estate space causes a "sluggish" response by the construction sector to increases in demand.

Born and Pyhrr (1994) incorporate cyclical economic factors—such as price cycles, inflation cycles, rent rate catch-up cycles and property life cycles—that impact cash flow variables and thus affect present value estimates of real estate assets. The model explains real estate value cycles as a convolution of fundamental, underlying economic, real estate supply and real estate demand cycles. The resulting model prescribes explicit incorporation of cyclical factors in appraiser cash flow models so as to produce superior present value estimates.

Other recent emerging explanations apply "real option" theory to real estate cycle analysis. These approaches give more weight to the impacts of the demand-side as a cause of the cycle than do other promulgated explanations. Grenadier (1995) develops a model that incorporates the significant costs of adjustment incurred by tenants when they move. These adjustment costs interplay with landlord, construction, and development behavior to create prolonged periods of vacancy for vacant space and prolonged periods of occupancy, once space is occupied—a model of "hysteresis".[11]

II.3 The Typical Regional Real Estate Cycle

Several research efforts have been devoted to examining the interrelationships among regional and economic factors and real estate market cycles. For examples, see, Pyhrr, et al. (1994, 1990, a, b), Pritchett (1977), Voith and Crone (1988), Chinloy (1996) and Green (1997). Three conclusions emerge from these studies. First, observed real estate cycles are a combination of several cycles produced by different underlying forces. Second, these forces are related to fundamental economic variables. Third, the typical real estate cycle usually follows a discernable pattern.

The cyclical pattern from this literature can be stylized as follows.[12] As the economic cycle declines to the trough, demand and supply forces result in an occupancy rate decline due to prior over-building and weakening subsequent demand caused by slackened economic activity. Occupancy rates are at the lowest level at the trough of the real estate cycle. Rental rates, simultaneously, are approaching the lowest point of their cycle. The rental rate cycle usually lags the occupancy rate cycle (Wheaton, 1987). Furthermore, over-building and other weakened general market demand lead to financial distress, insolvency, increased mortgage delinquency and foreclosures, especially for properties that are less desirable. Lower rental income collections, perceived higher risk, and depressed future property resale price expectations are factors placing downward pressure on current market values. Frequently, in such cycles, market values decline substantially below replacement costs. Consequently, significant increases in market occupancy and rental rate levels are necessary to justify subsequent new construction. In this risky environment, the overall market cap rate and/or the discount rate for present value computations will tend to rise. Finally, lenders with substantial real estate holdings through the foreclosure process are eager to dispose of their real estate because of economic and regulatory pressures. As a likely result of financial institution sales, market values may be depressed for a substantial period of time.

The nature of real estate performance shifts dramatically as the economic cycle turns toward its peak. As the cycle recovers and the economy, in general, becomes more buoyant, demand begins to grow, and at some point will exceed supply. The property space market has reversed itself. Occupancy rates improve as the typical first sign, followed by lagged rental rate increases. Subsequently, property market values begin to increase as real estate property NOI increases (because rents are rising and vacancies are falling). Real estate lenders may return to the market, providing new debt capital for an additional boost to market values. The cap rate (lagged) declines following this cyclical upturn.[13]

III. A MODEL OF REAL ESTATE VALUE CYCLES

Our strategy is to develop a model of real estate value cycles that depends upon and interplays with economic income cycles. The theory focuses on the cyclical analysis by abstracting from the economic trend. In order to do this, we recognize that the value of a property is the capitalized value of its future expected income. The key assumption for our analysis is that the present value relationship obtains.

Formally, borrowing from the appraisal literature, equation (1) represents the continuous-time relationship between the capital asset value of a real estate parcel and the assumed "true"—unobserved—expected stabilized net operating income at time t.[14]

$$\ln V = C_v + \delta(\ln Y^{\star}_S) \qquad (1)$$

Where, $\ln V$ = the natural logarithm of fair market value of a parcel at time t.
C_V = a constant.
$\ln Y^{\star}_S$ = the natural logarithm of "true" expected stabilized net operating income at time t.
δ = the point elasticity of fair market value, V, with respect to $Y^{\star}_S$. This is a continuous-time reformulation of the appraiser's cap rate and serves as the income capitalization variable.

δ is a measure of the sensitivity of value to changes in the true (unobserved) stabilized NOI of the overall cap rate used in property valuation. δ takes into account the state of the market, including the persistence of market disequilibrium caused by lags on both the supply and demand sides. Supply lags may arise because of the time required to assemble land, receive governmental reviews and approvals, secure financing and construct real projects. Demand lags are usually the resultant of unanticipated changes in market economic fundamentals. Hence, embedded in δ are the expected secular and cyclical effects of future vacancy and rent changes.

Equation (1) is a characterization of the income approach from appraisal theory. Since $Y^{\star}_S$, the "true" stabilized NOI is unobservable, we need to transform equation (1) for two reasons. First, in order to focus on the cycle effects, we remove the trend in $Y^{\star}_S$. Second, we assume an adjustment process between observable NOI and de-trended, stabilized NOI.

Abstracting from the trend for stabilized net operating income over time, we assume a secular growth rate of β. Equation (2) represents the de-trended stabilized NOI. β translates the trend for secular economic growth in the general economy into real estate property income.

$$\ln Y_S = \ln Y^{\star}_S - \beta t - C_Y \qquad (2)$$

Where $\ln Y_S$ = the natural logarithm of de-trended expected stabilized NOI, and C_Y = a logarithmic constant in stabilized NOI.

Substituting equation (2) into equation (1) we obtain yields equation (3):

$$\ln V = C^{\star} + \delta \ln Y_S + \delta\beta t \qquad (3)$$

where, in Equation (3), $C^{\star}$ is a generalized constant.

Taking the time derivative of equation (3), we obtain the instantaneous relationship between the rate of change of value and the rate of change in de-trended expected stabilized net operating income, equation (4):[15]

$$\frac{\dot{V}}{V} = \delta\left(\frac{\dot{Y}_S}{Y_S}\right) + \delta\beta \qquad (4)$$

As noted, we do not observe "true" de-trended stabilized net operating income. Instead, for a real estate parcel at each point in time, we observe the *actual* net operating income. Equation (5) represents our hypothesis that there is a rational economic partial adjustment process for the change in de-trended stabilized NOI, based upon the actual level of NOI, Y, and the expected de-trended stabilized NOI, Y_s:

$$\frac{\dot{Y}_S}{Y_S} = \omega(\ln Y - \ln Y_S) \tag{5}$$

Equation (5) indicates that differences between actual and de-trended, stabilized NOI lead to partial adjustments in expected, de-trended, stabilized NOI. These adjustments, in principle, move the market toward equilibrium. More precisely, changes between actual NOI and de-trended, stabilized NOI are deviations from expectations that require adjustments in our future expectations for changes in de-trended stabilized NOI growth. The partial adjustment coefficient, ω, needs to be less than unity in absolute value ($-1 \leq \omega \leq 1$), for the hypothesized adjustments in de-trended, stabilized NOI to converge. Values of ω reflect efforts by local office market players to adjust their expectations about stabilized NOI based on observed market NOI. Depending on the difference between actually observed and stabilized, unobserved, NOI, corrections in the growth rate of stabilized NOI may run counter ($\omega < 0$) or with ($\omega > 0$) the instantaneous difference between observed and stabilized NOI.

Equation (5) can be conveniently rearranged to solve for actual NOI as a function of de-trended, stabilized NOI:

$$\ln Y = \left(\frac{1}{\omega}\right)\left(\frac{\dot{Y}_S}{Y_S}\right) + \ln Y_S \tag{6}$$

Using equations (3) and (5), we can express expected de-trended stabilized NOI in terms of property values. Moreover, equation (4) allows us to express the rate of change in stabilized NOI in terms of a change in value. The outcome of these two transformations yields a relationship in value and actual income, denoted as equation (7). This equation is expressed solely in terms of observable market data:

$$\ln Y = \left(\frac{1}{\delta\omega}\right)\left(\frac{\dot{V}}{V}\right) + \left(\frac{1}{\delta}\right)\ln V - \beta t - \left(\frac{\beta}{\omega}\right) + C^{\star\star} \tag{7}$$

where $C^{\star\star} = -C^{\star}/\delta$, is a generalized constant.

In equation (7), the full relationship between observable NOI and value requires full identification of five coefficients. Three coefficients are parametric: trend, β, income capitalization, δ, and the partial adjustment coefficient, ω. And two of the coefficients are non-parametric constants: C_v and C_y, which are embedded in $C^{\star\star}$.

Since we are interested in understanding the real estate cycle relationship between observable NOI and V, we take the time derivative of equation (7). This yields equation (8), a full characterization of a local market real estate cycle in terms of β, δ, and ω:

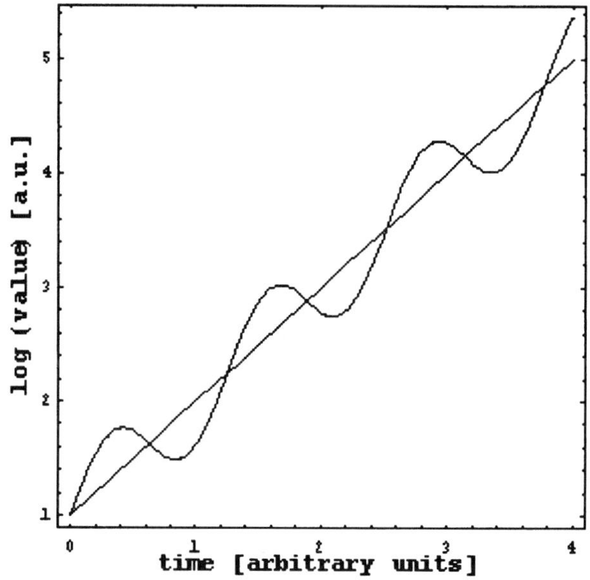

Figure 4.2. Log of Value over time

$$\left(\frac{\dot{Y}}{Y}\right)=\left(\frac{1}{\partial\omega}\right)(\dot{g}_V)+\left(\frac{1}{\partial}\right)g_V-\beta \qquad (8)$$

g_v is the instantaneous rate of change in fair market value, expressed in percent terms, $\dot{V}/V$. We define $\dot{g}_v$ in the following way: $\dot{g}_v$ is the time derivative of g_v and is the instantaneous rate of change for the percent change of fair market value.[16] Equation (8) has the trend removed, and is expressed in terms of "observable" market data for actual NOI and parcel market values. We can utilize equation (8) to trace out the dynamics of the cycles for observable net operating income, Y, and property fair market values, V. Equation (8) also permits us to examine the time sequencing of our expected real estate income and value cycles.

To examine the cyclical pattern of real estate income and real estate value, we subsume, for convenience and illustration purposes, a simple smooth de-trended sine function cycle for income and thus value growth—see figure 2. Under the assumed sine cycle with a constant trend rate for income growth, value will grow exponentially with a cycle around this trend. Figure 2, with the axes of time, t and log-value, V, show the expected exponential value growth with a cyclical fluctuation around this trend.

Figures 3 and 4 translate equation (8) and our cycle into a graphical presentation.[17] The axes for figure 3 are $\frac{\dot{V}}{V}$, defined as g_v, and $\frac{\dot{Y}}{Y}$, defined as g_Y. For figure 4, the axes measure g_v and $\dot{g}_v$. In figure 3, the second term of the right hand side of equa-

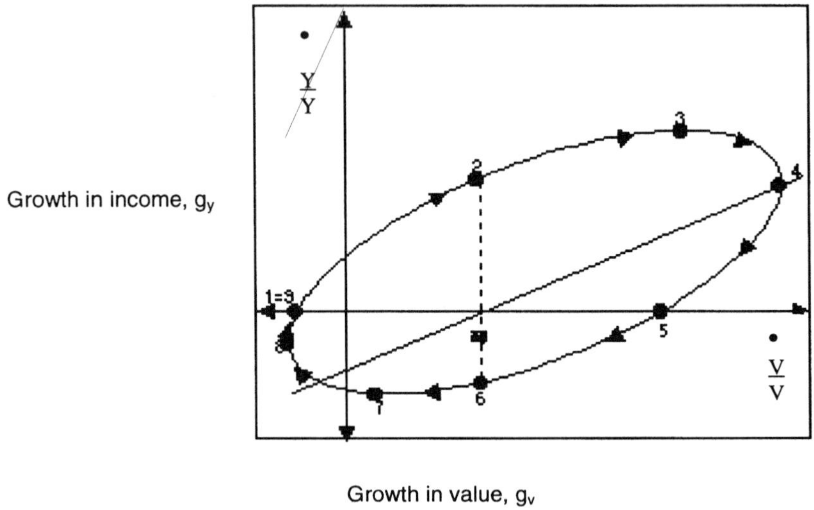

Figure 4.3. The Cyclical Relationship between NOI and Property Value

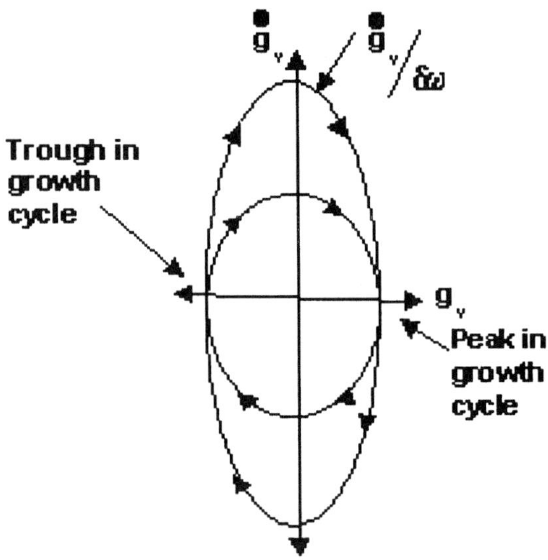

Figure 4.4. Cyclical Relationship between Value Growth Rate and the Change in the Rate of Change of Growth Value

tion (8) is shown as the oblique straight line intercepting the growth in value g_v, axis at $\delta\beta$. To understand why this is so, consider the case of observing a de-trended stabilized NOI growth rate of zero (i.e., $\dot{Y}/Y = 0$). In such a case, the change in the rate of growth in value (i.e., the acceleration) would be zero and the growth

Table 1. Expected Sequential Cyclical Patterns for NOI and Value

1	Trough of NOI
2	Trough of Value (less trend)
3	Peak of NOI Growth
4	Peak of Value Growth
5	Peak of NOI
6	Peak of Value (less trend)
7	Trough in Growth of NOI
8	Trough in Growth of Value
9	Trough in NOI

rate in property values would necessarily be constant at $\delta\beta$ in order to remove the trend parameter, β. As the cycle in NOI growth oscillates, the growth rate in value will oscillate along this line with slope of $1/\delta$, the reciprocal of the income capitalization rate from equation (1).

In figure 4, the inner circle is the relationship between the rate of growth of values and its time derivative (g_v and $\dot{g}_v$, respectively). To represent the first term on the right hand side, in equation (8), $\dot{g}_v$ is divided by $\delta\omega$, creating the elliptical path around the first circle. For each value of g_v, in figure 4, we add $\dot{g}_v/\delta\omega$ to the straight line—the second term on the right hand side in equation (8)—at the corresponding value of g_v to obtain the ellipsoid relationship between g_v and $\dot{g}_v$ in figure 4.

As can be seen from this schematic analysis of figures 3 and 4, NOI changes over the cycle are expected to occur in advance (lead) of value changes. This will be the result, in the up-turn, of a combination of both vacancies declining and rental rate increases.

In contrast, when the real estate market reaches the trough, vacancies are expected to peak (i.e., occupancy to be at its trough) before rents achieve the trough, leading to a declining NOI to its trough and a subsequent fall in property value toward its trough. The cyclical value for real estate income and parcel market value for the model is delineated in Table 1, with corresponding numbered positions in figure 3.

Because δ is anticipated to be greater than unity, using equation 1, a one percent decrease in NOI is accompanied by a greater than one percent decrease in market value, and vice versa. Hence, the cap rate derived from the model's cycle pattern would be counter-cyclical with cap rates rising as real estate markets decline, and vice versa. Therefore, as previously mentioned, our cycle theory generates an expected observable sequence of real estate income and value events that is consistent with earlier empirical research findings, and with the current understanding of the way real estate markets function.

IV. EMPIRICAL RESULTS

IV.1 The Statistical Model and Data Set

We employ equation (9) to estimate and test our model from section III[18]. Equation (9) is the statistical version of equation (7):

Actual versus Fitted NOI: Atlanta, Baltimore, Boston and Charlotte 1986:4 to 1995:2

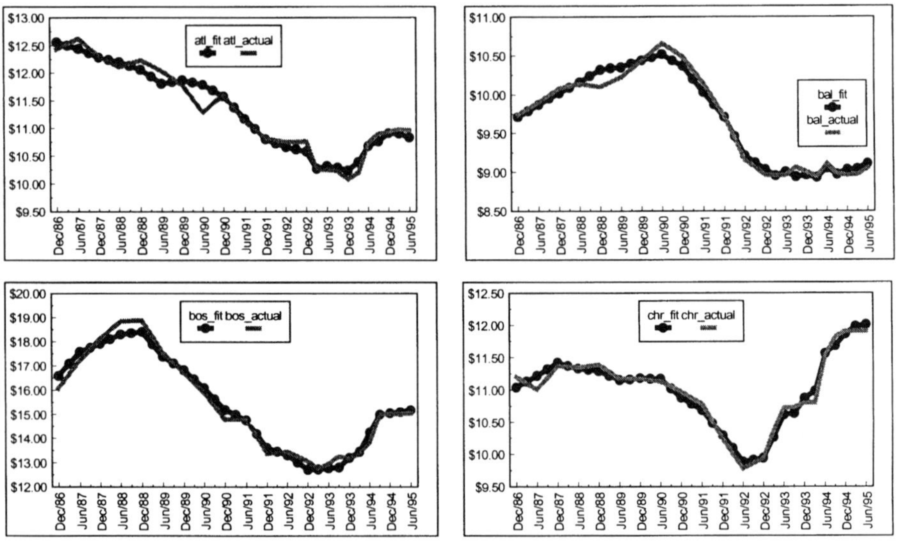

Actual versus Fitted NOI: Chicago, Dallas, Denver and Houston 1986:4 to 1995:2

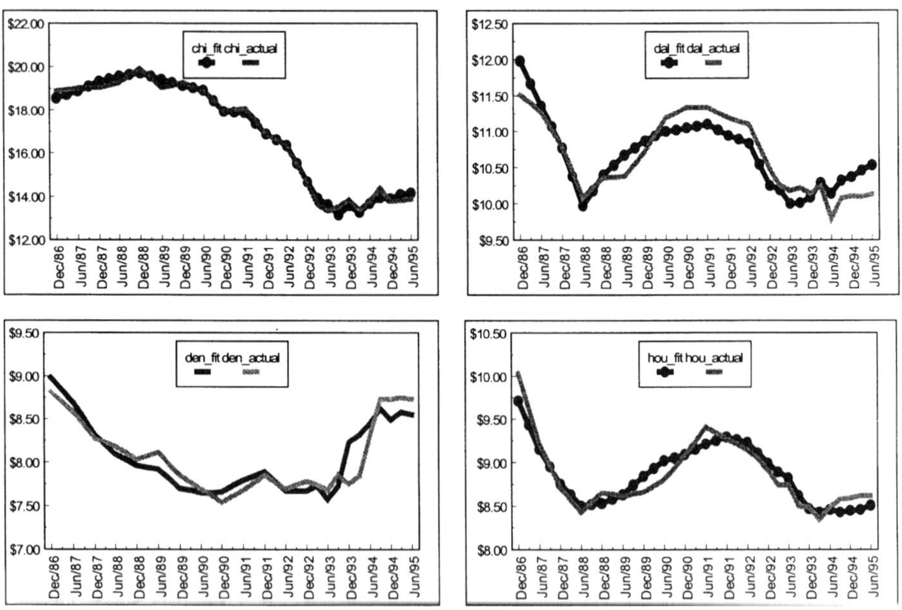

Figure 4.5. Actual vs. Fitted NOI for 20 Office Markets Used in Regression Estimation

Actual versus Fitted NOI: Los Angeles, Miami, Minneapolis and Orlando
1986:4 to 1995:2

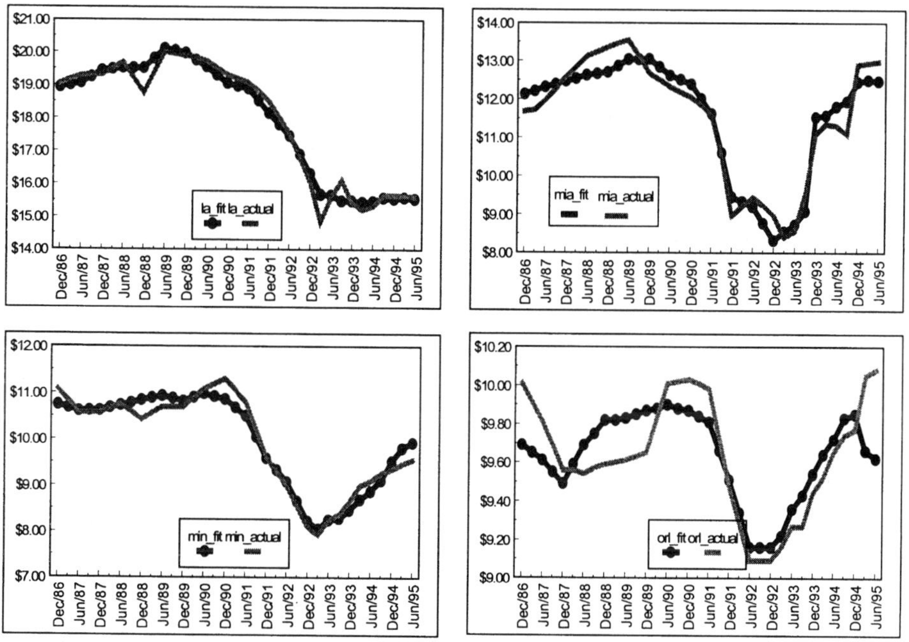

Actual versus Fitted NOI: Philadelphia, Phoenix, Sacramento and San Diego
1986:4 to 1995:2

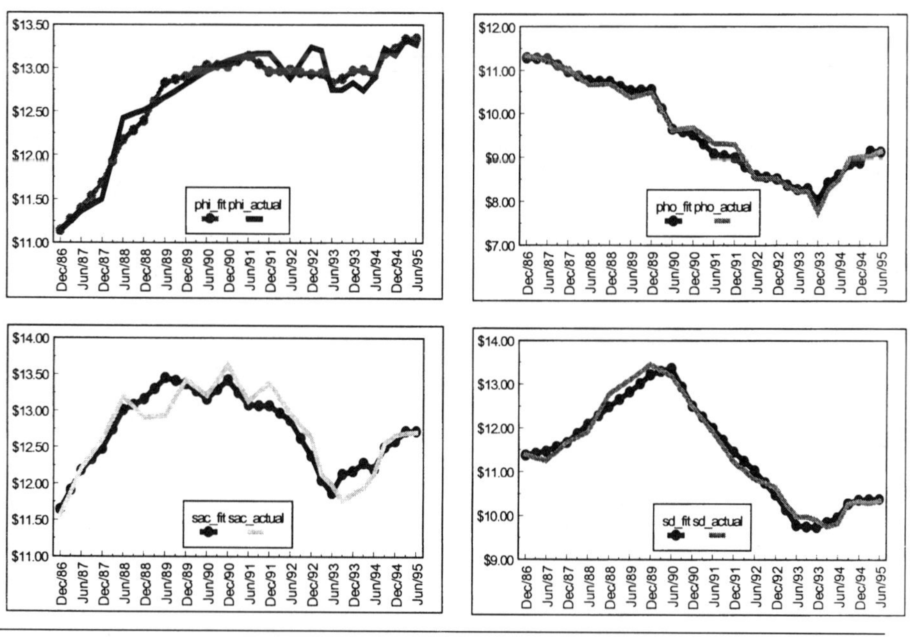

Figure 4.5. *Continued*

Actual versus Fitted NOI: San Francisco, Seattle, Tampa and D.C.
1986:4 to 1995:2

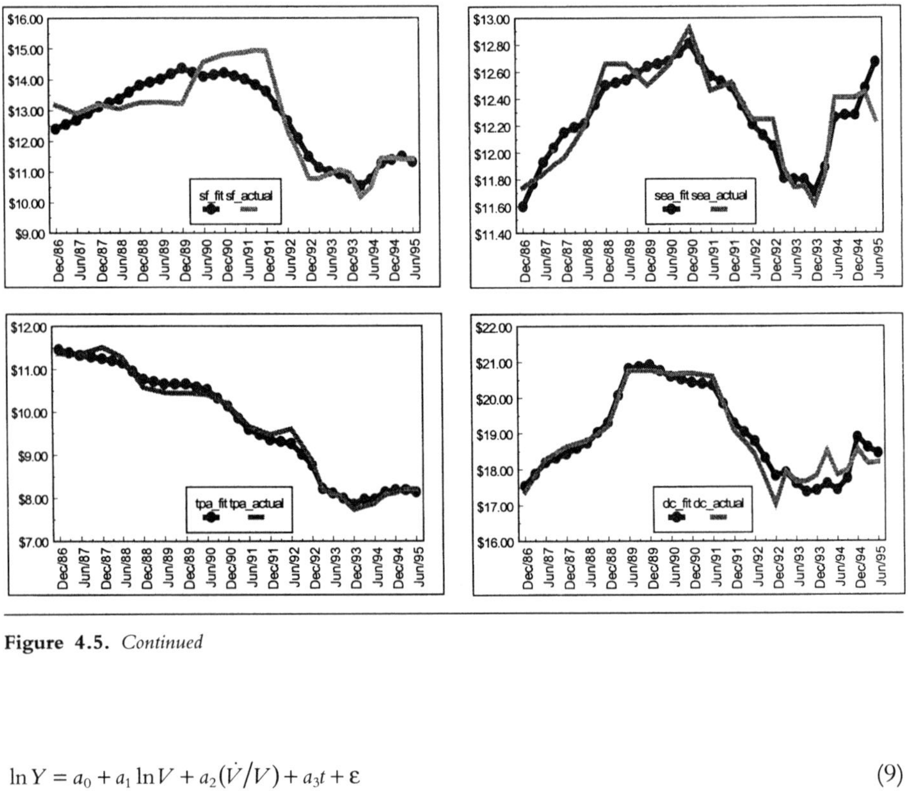

Figure 4.5. *Continued*

$$\ln Y = a_0 + a_1 \ln V + a_2(\dot{V}/V) + a_3 t + \varepsilon \qquad (9)$$

The coefficients to be estimated are functions of the cyclical parameters defined in the theory section. In particular, $a_0 = (C_v/\delta) - C_y - (\beta\omega/\delta)$, $a_1 = (1/\delta)$, $a_2 = (1/\delta\omega)$, and $a_3 = -\beta$. These four coefficients under-identify the cyclical model presented in section III; for every city, for the four coefficients, a_0, a_1, a_2,a_3, of equation (9), we are unable algebraically to unravel the five parameters needed to identity equation (7). However, the same four coefficients permit the identification of the cyclic parameters β, δ, and ω. In particular, we can solve for the following: $\beta = -a_3$, $\delta = (1/a_1)$, and $\omega = a_1/a_2$. Thus, a complete analysis of the income and value cycles is possible, even though full identification of equation (7) is not.

The econometric specification of our cyclical model is a system of twenty simultaneous equations, one for each of the twenty metropolitan office markets from our data set[19]. Using the method of three-stage least squares (3SLS), we estimate this system of equations to obtain the four coefficients of equation (9)[20,21]. The 3SLS procedure takes into account the impact of structural supply and demand instru-

Table 2. Primary and Instrumental Variables Used in 3SLS Estimation of a_0, a_1, a_2, a_3

Number of Variables	Primary and Instrumental Variables Employed in 3SLS Estimation	Source
1 per system	U.S. Gross Domestic Product Growth—used as an instrumental variable	Federal Reserve Economic Data
1 per system	U.S. Employment Growth—used as an instrumental variable	U.S. Bureau of Labor Statistics
1 per system	U.S. Real Interest Rate (10-yr. Treasury rate, adjusted for inflation)—used as an instrumental variable	Federal Reserve Economic Data
1 per system	U.S. Inflation Rate—used as instrumental variable	U.S. Bureau of Labor Statistics
20 per system	Office Vacancy Rates for 20 MSAs—used as instrumental variables	Coldwell Banker Commercial
20 per system	NOI/sf and Price/sf for 20 MSAs—are the primary variables used in the 3SLS procedure	National Real Estate Index
20 per system	Office Absorption Rates for 20 MSAs—used as instrumental variables	Fisher Center for Real Estate and Urban Economics
20 per system	Office Construction Permitted for 20 MSAs—used as instrumental variables	F.W. Dodge, MacGraw Hill construction data

ments upon the closed form system of 20. For example, Mueller (1995) suggests that macro-variables affect real estate through their impact on capital market variables (e.g., flow of funds, interest rates), while regional-city variables affect local real estate market supply-demand factors. Our analysis takes this dichotomy into account by utilizing macroeconomic instrumental variables, such as GDP, real interest rates, and inflation rates, and local instrumental variables such as absorption rates and construction permits. The use of these variables as instruments within the 3SLS procedure corrects for two classical statistical complications related to the structure of the error terms in the 20-equation simultaneous system, cross-equation correlations and simultaneity bias[22].

Table 2 summarizes the quarterly time series (1985:4 to 1995:2) for the 20 MSA's employed in the estimation of the model: NOI, Market Value and growth in Market Value. In addition, the table lists eighty-four instrumental variables utilized during the second stage of the 3SLS estimation of the twenty-equation system.

IV.2 Statistical Findings

Tables 3 and 4 contain two significant groups of results from our estimation; table 3 shows the consistent and unbiased estimates for the equation (9) coefficients a_0, a_1, a_2, a_3, with their respective t-Statistics. Table 4 reports the results of unit root tests performed on the time series vector of residuals for the system of twenty office

Table 3. Estimated Coefficients, t-Statistics and Implied Model Parameters

Model Coefficient	Coefficient		Model Coefficient	Coefficient	
	Estimate	t-statistic		Estimate	t-statistic
Atlanta a_0	−0.1829	−1.06354	Min. a_0	−2.2625	−26.3842
Atlanta a_1	0.5421	15.7656	Min. a_1	0.9498	55.5605
Atlanta a_2	0.0555	1.99469	Min. a_2	−0.21437	−15.9763
Atlanta a_3	−0.0022	−7.67128	Min. a_3	0.0027	6.00521
Baltimore a_0	−0.9120	−16.3742	New Orl. a_0	−0.0579	−0.293985
Baltimore a_1	0.6696	58.6961	New Orl. a_1	0.4890	11.9783
Baltimore a_2	−0.0570	−4.80172	New Orl. a_2	0.0440	1.15448
Baltimore a_3	0.0010	6.13632	New Orl. a_3	0.0012	2.56672
Boston a_0	−0.6224	−9.2551	Phil. a_0	−0.8455	−6.375
Boston a_1	0.6251	54.094	Phil. a_1	0.6608	25.1473
Boston a_2	−0.0296	−2.9642	Phil. a_2	−0.2374	−9.99967
Boston a_3	0.0020	5.17156	Phil. a_3	0.0046	27.5308
Charlotte a_0	−1.2846	−24.9461	Phoenix a_0	−0.9982	−8.26506
Charlotte a_1	0.7551	72.4133	Phoenix a_1	0.7050	28.7766
Charlotte a_2	−0.0162	−1.90713	Phoenix a_2	−0.2278	−9.22471
Charlotte a_3	0.0011	6.67683	Phoenix a_3	−0.0015	−4.17259
Chicago a_0	−0.2348	−2.81122	Sac a_0	−1.0489	−8.02781
Chicago a_1	0.5751	39.3674	Sac a_1	0.7178	27.3825
Chicago a_2	0.1001	6.51337	Sac a_2	−0.0782	−3.27488
Chicago a_3	−0.0007	−1.78006	Sac a_3	0.0001	0.289406
Dallas a_0	−1.0519	−6.30743	San Diegoa_0	−1.4669	−25.2181
Dallas a_1	0.7101	20.8407	San Diegoa_1	0.7771	69.1498
Dallas a_2	0.0885	3.67832	San Diegoa_2	0.0333	2.98036
Dallas a_3	0.0025	5.18547	San Diegoa_3	0.0041	17.2521
Denver a_0	−0.5750	−10.9154	S.F. a_0	−0.5621	−4.31211
Denver a_1	0.6301	53.8165	S.F. a_1	0.5652	24.3175
Denver a_2	0.2092	17.0463	S.F. a_2	−0.1963	−9.81186
Denver a_3	−0.0061	−16.2707	S.F. a_3	0.0060	8.83546
Houston a_0	−0.1426	−3.50898	Seattle a_0	−1.4207	−9.10457
Houston a_1	0.5146	59.2008	Seattle a_1	0.7786	25.3064
Houston a_2	−0.2908	−43.5298	Seattle a_2	−0.1792	−7.89092
Houston a_3	−0.0001	−0.36446	Seattle a_3	0.0019	7.81595
L.A. a_0	0.6420	6.48826	Tampa a_0	−0.1080	−0.688346
L.A. a_1	0.4165	24.1912	Tampa a_1	0.5262	16.51
L.A. a_2	0.0118	0.903302	Tampa a_2	0.0711	3.58404
L.A. a_3	−0.0020	−6.6413	Tampa a_3	−0.0050	−11.1527
Miami a_0	−0.1366	−1.50978	D.C. a_0	0.1629	2.04746
Miami a_1	0.5392	26.6061	D.C. a_1	0.4938	35.6114
Miami a_2	−0.0935	−6.71705	D.C. a_2	0.0184	2.16127
Miami a_3	−0.0020	−2.9009	D.C. a_3	0.0027	8.13106

markets we estimated using 3SLS[23]. Other summary regression statistics for the model are shown in Appendix 1.

The individual t-statistics in table 3 show that seventy of the eighty coefficients for equation (9) are significantly different from zero at the 95% confidence level. For convenience, we shade the coefficients that are statistically insignificant.

Table 4. Summary of Unit Root Tests Performed on the Regression Residuals for the 20 Office Markets Estimated jointly in the Model

Test Statistics					Vol. Lags					P-Values				
ATL	BAL	BOS	CHR	CHI	ATL	BAL	BOS	CHR	CHI	ATL	BAL	BOS	CHR	CHI
−4.2040	−3.9965	−2.2873	−4.1044	−2.7248	3	3	2	3	3	0.0025	0.0047	0.4388	0.0034	0.1745
−3.8409	−3.7863	−2.8617	−3.8302	−2.8824	3	3	2	3	3	0.0146	0.0173	0.1752	0.0151	0.1683
—	−9.9844	−11.0213	—	—	3	3	2	3	3	0.2452	0.4372	0.3712	0.1002	0.1551
13.4734			18.2277	15.9578										
DAL	DEN	HOU	LA	MIA	DAL	DEN	HOU	LA	MIA	DAL	DEN	HOU	LA	MIA
−1.3646	−3.1979	−2.8107	−2.7619	−3.4801	3	3	3	3	3	0.9249	0.0489	0.1405	0.1591	0.0216
−1.2187	−3.2628	−3.1705	−2.5901	−3.4533	2	3	3	3	3	0.9066	0.0726	0.0904	0.2845	0.0447
−4.5167	—	−11.6747	—	—	2	3	3	3	3	0.8546	0.2981	0.3337	0.1757	0.1465
	12.3466		15.2942	16.2589										
MIN	ORL	PHI	PHO	SAC	MIN	ORL	PHI	PHO	SAC	MIN	ORL	PHI	PHO	SAC
−2.7819	−2.4352	−3.4616	−2.4312	−2.6315	3	3	3	2	3	0.1513	0.3344	0.0228	0.3370	0.2184
−2.9002	−2.4676	−3.2667	−2.1132	−2.3285	3	3	3	2	3	0.1621	0.3444	0.0719	0.5387	0.4183
−9.8924	−4.9529	−13.6298	—	—	3	3	3	2	3	0.4434	0.8247	0.2384	0.3844	0.3529
			10.8046	11.3340										
SD	SF	SEA	TPA	DC	SD	SF	SEA	TPA	DC	SD	SF	SEA	TPA	DC
−3.6033	−2.6422	−4.6620	−3.0228	−3.8245	3	3	3	3	3	0.0151	0.2130	0.0006	0.0798	0.0078
−3.3574	−2.6521	−4.0416	−2.7458	−3.5533	3	3	3	3	3	0.0573	0.2565	0.0077	0.2176	0.0340
—	−9.4727	−14.2627	−8.7058	—	3	3	3	3	3	0.4100	0.4726	0.2125	0.5289	0.2899
10.3966				12.5109										

The estimated coefficients statistically differ from city to city[24]. This result is consistent with Crone and Voith (1988), and with Dokko, et al. (1991). It suggests that different cities experience cycles with either varying secular time trends, β, different elasticities for fair market value growth to changes in stabilized NOI, δ, or distinct rates of adjustments (i.e., cycle durations) to NOI perturbations, ω.[25]

With regards to the unit root tests in Table 4, they confirm the stationarity of our regression residuals and hence the unbiasedness and consistency of our estimated model coefficients[26]. In all Phillips and Perron, Augmented Dickey Fuller and Weighted Symmetric Test Statistics, for all twenty office markets, and for lags of at most 7 quarters, table 4 reports the closest statistics to the critical region for unit roots.

All the aforementioned statistics yield rejections of the hypothesis that (residuals are non-stationary) unit roots are present in the regression residuals for the MSAs in the regression specification for all 20 MSAs. Specifically, all p-values indicate the absence of unit roots for all office markets, at the 5% significance level, for lags of up to 3 quarters in most cases, except for the cases of Phoenix and Boston—where stationarity is still present for lags in variables of up to 2 quarters.

IV.3 Implied Real Estate Cycles

From our statistical results in Table 3, we compute the parameters, β, δ, and ω[27]. Fifty-four of the sixty coefficients used in the computations are statistically significant. We report the "implied" cyclic-parameters β, δ, and ω, for the 20 MSAs, in Table 5. Even the six statistically insignificant estimated coefficients used to produce implied model parameters, β, δ, and ω, result in statistical values well within the range of reasonable, expected cycle parameter values: β has no restrictions, $\delta > 1$, and $|\omega| \leq 1$. Thus all sixty cyclic parameters yield cyclic parameter values for our theoretical equation (7)—within theoretical model bounds.

Using the calculated cyclic parameters reported in table 5, inferences may be drawn about the nature of income cycles—and thus value cycles—in different cities. For example, our estimated parameter values indicate that eight of the twenty MSA's show an increasing secular growth rate of office market NOI. These MSAs are Atlanta, Phoenix, Chicago, Denver, Houston, Los Angeles, Tampa and Miami. The remaining 12 MSA's show a negative secular growth trend in office market NOI. These results coincide with the perceived downturn in commercial real estate during the late 1980's and early 1990's.

With respect to the implied partial adjustment coefficient, ω, all calculated coefficients are less than unity in absolute value, some are positive, and some are negative. While the sign is indicative of direction of adjustment between observed NOI and expected stabilized NOI, the magnitude of ω reflects the speed of adjustment of the partial adjustment process described by equation (5). For example, the estimated ω for Charlotte reflects relatively rapid adjustments to observed NOI in the opposite direction to that of the market change in NOI (with negative adjustment, $\omega < 0$). Whereas Los Angeles and San Diego exhibit comparably dramatic changes

Table 5. MSA-specific, Implied Model Parameters

Model Parameter	Parameter Value	Model Parameter	Parameter Value
Atlanta		Minneapolis	
β-trend	.22	β-trend	−.27
δ-cap	1.845	δ-cap	1.053
ω-expectations	.0977	ω-expectations	−.0887
Baltimore		Orlando	
β-trend	−.10	β-trend	−.12
δ-cap	1.493	δ-cap	2.045
ω-expectations	−.1175	ω-expectations	.1112
Boston		Philadelphia	
β-trend	−.20	β-trend	−.46
δ-cap	1.600	δ-cap	1.513
ω-expectations	−.2114	ω-expectations	−.0557
Charlotte		Phoenix	
β-trend	−.11	β-trend	.15
δ-cap	1.324	δ-cap	1.418
ω-expectations	−.4670	ω-expectations	−.0619
Chicago		Sacramento	
β-trend	.07	β-trend	−.01
δ-cap	1.739	δ-cap	1.393
ω-expectations	.0574	ω-expectations	−.0918
Dallas		San Diego	
β-trend	−.25	β-trend	−.41
δ-cap	1.408	δ-cap	1.287
ω-expectations	.0802	ω-expectations	.2335
Denver		San Francisco	
β-trend	.61	β-trend	−.60
δ-cap	1.587	δ-cap	1.769
ω-expectations	.0602	ω-expectations	−.0576
Houston		Seattle	
β-trend	.01	β-trend	−.19
δ-cap	1.943	δ-cap	1.284
ω-expectations	−.0354	ω-expectations	−.0869
Los Angeles		Tampa	
β-trend	.20	β-trend	.50
δ-cap	2.401	δ-cap	1.900
ω-expectations	.3544	ω-expectations	.0740
Miami		Washington D. C.	
β-trend	.20	β-trend	−.27
δ-cap	1.855	δ-cap	2.025
ω-expectations	−.0577	ω-expectations	.0672

in expectation about stabilized NOI that reinforce expectations about growth in NOI (i.e., positive coefficient of adjustment, $\omega > 0$). The reasons as to why these cities behave so differently may be found in market fundamentals. One explanation may be that absorption rates make the Southeast structurally different from Southern California. Southern California had a significantly slower rate of absorption than

Charlotte during much of the sample period. Thus, the pace at which expectations changed did not have to be so fast or dramatic in direction—reversing past expectations about NOI surprises.

All of the estimates of point elasticity of fair market value with respect to expected stabilized NOI, δ, are greater than unity in magnitude and with the appropriate sign. In all cases, increases in expected stabilized NOI result in a greater increase in fair market value. The observed range of point elasticities by MSA is quite broad, from a low of 1.053 for Minneapolis, to a high of 2.401 for Los Angeles. Put differently, the model closely replicate observed cycles in NOI. The empirical model fits the data extremely well. Second, office market cycles vary significantly across MSAs with respect to cycle phase, timing and amplitudes. The three-parameter model appears to be sufficiently flexible to adapt to such differences. The findings are consistent with the theoretical model as well as the findings of earlier studies. Put somewhat differently, the theory conforms to earlier cycle assessments, whether stylized facts or formal models, about the evolution of real estate cycles—with the added advantage that the structure is uniform across geographic locales. And third, the consistency, efficiency and unbiasedness of the estimated coefficients and the implied NOI and value cycle relationships make the model a potentially useful tool for understanding and predicting the dynamics of real estate markets.

CONCLUSION

In this article, we develop and test a real estate cycles theory that examines the interrelationships between economic activity and real estate income and value cycles. While the findings reinforce those of many earlier studies, the explicit link between theory and the empirical modeling improves our interpretive reliability and fundamental understanding of real estate income and value cycles. Further, the excellent overall fit of the statistical model and the associated structural explanations of cycles represent potentially useful knowledge advancements for both academics and practitioners. Understanding real estate price volatility, correlations and autocorrelations in market values and income, and identifying the timings of these peaks and troughs in real estate markets, allow practitioners to develop better value expectations and the ability to make more informed investment decisions.

The findings provide a simple way to characterize real estate cycles among and across MSAs. Each MSA's real estate cycle is described by three parameters: (1) a city specific cycle capitalization rate, δ, which captures the relative volatility of the city cycle; (2) a city trend growth rate, β, that synthesizes the citywide market value trend fundamentals; and (3) a city specific cyclical adjustment, ω, that reflects the dynamic duration of the city cycle.

By utilizing 3SLS, we are able to incorporate into the cyclical analyses the impacts of MSA (local) supply and demand variables, macroeconomic forces, simultaneity effects among value, income and other variables, as well as MSA auto-and-cross correlation effects.

For real estate professionals, such as lenders, developers or investors, a clear view of the dynamics of the real estate cycle should be an integral part of real estate investment analysis and decision making. At the property level, an improved understanding of the dynamics of the real estate cycle and its impact on parcel value and cash flow (income) should enhance practitioners ability to determine the locus of expected rewards and risks, leading to enhanced decision making. The model analyses could be adapted to link economic scenarios and MSA real estate cycles needed to create property specific financials that could be used for investment decision making.

NOTES

1. A special thanks to Samir Dutt, Steven J. Manson, David Howe and David Sapoznikow for their research assistance, and the participants of the Real Estate PhD seminar at the Haas School of Business Administration, University of California at Berkeley for their invaluable suggestions. We also have benefited from many suggestions and comments from our colleagues and anonymous referees. We acknowledge and thank the Fisher Center for Real Estate and Urban Economics at the Haas School of Business for its generous support of this project. Of course, any remaining errors of omissions and/or commissions are our responsibility.

2. Inter-city differences in real estate vacancy rates (as well as other real estate economic measures) are not unique for either our sample of cities or time set (1985–1995). For example, in September 1998, the national average for metropolitan vacancy rates had been 9.0%. Simultaneously, Albuquerque and Columbus had vacancy rates of 12.4% and 6.7% respectively, somewhere between the 14.1% vacancy of Los Angeles, and that of 3.0% in San Francisco.

3. As Smith and Tesarek (1991) note, the price deflation of the late 1980's for *residential* real estate was the worst since the great depression. However, *commercial* real estate price fluctuations of a similar magnitude as those observed during the late 1980' and early 1990's have been historically observed in the past. Burns and Grebler (1982) provides a time series comparison on public versus private sector real estate market activity—housing and non-housing. Hendershott and Kane (1995) also examine commercial market cycles using appraisal data.

4. Koopmans (1947) makes a compelling case for the necessity of integrating theory with empiricism in conducting cycles studies.

5. For example, see Grenadier (1995) and references contained therein. Also see Chinloy (1996), for a theory based study of rental housing markets cycles.

6. Green's results are robust in that they are consistent across many specifications. However, one should interpret these results with caution on two counts. First, when testing for causality, statistical correlations may appear to imply causality when in effect there is none present, if the underlying model specification is incorrect. And second, the identity relation between investment and gross domestic product in national income and product accounting data may be at the core of Green's results, not Granger causality.

7. For an excellent review of the fundamental issues in the office market real estate literature and some of the papers reviewed herein, please refer to Clapp (1993).

8. An excellent summary of explanations for the relationship between real estate cycles, developers and financial institutions is contained in "Origins and Causes of the S&L Debacle: A Blueprint for Reform" (1993)—especially, pp. 43–57.

9. Again refer to "Origins and Causes of the S&L Debacle: A Blueprint for Reform" (1993).

10. See, for example, Dokko, et al. (1990), Edelstein and Friend (1976) and Jaffee and Rosen (1979).

11. Consistent with Grenadier's (1995) analysis, Meese and Wallace (1993) show that fundamental economic variables determine long run residential values, but with a significant adjustment lag.

12. See Mueller (1995) for an excellent reference on this topic.

13. Obviously, this does not necessarily describe a market equilibrium adjustment. In fact, many analysts believe that real estate market equilibrium is the exception rather than the rule.

14. The continuous time present value model specifies fair market value as the following function

in true (unobserved) expected stabilized NOI: $V = c_V(Y_s^{\star})^{\delta}$. Upon taking the natural logarithm of this expression, we obtain equation (1).

15. By taking this time derivative we eliminate constants from the model structure in order to focus our attention on β, the cycle trend, and δ, the continuous time cap rate.

16. It is a term that enables us to quantify the relationship between fluctuations in the value and income cycles.

17. Our results are robust with respect to different underlying cycles. Our analysis can incorporate stochastic-cyclical NOI functions and can be solved for with respect to real estate value instead of real estate value growth. For example, consider the alternative structure for true NOI:

$dY = Y\mu[\cdot]dt + Y\sigma[\cdot]dz$, where $V = e^cY^{\delta}$, which implies that $V = g(Y)$. Then, by applying Ito's Lemma:

$$dV = g_Y\, dY + gtdt + (1/2)gvdY^2 = e^c\delta Y^{\delta-1}dY + (1/2)e^c\delta(\delta - 1)Y^{\delta-2}dY^2$$
$$= e^cY^{\delta}\{Y\mu[\cdot]dt + Y\sigma[\cdot]dz\} + (1/2)\ e^c\delta(\delta - 1)Y^{\delta-2}Y^2\sigma^2[\cdot]dt.$$

Thus, $dV = e^cdY^{\delta}\{\mu[\cdot] + (1/2)(\delta - 1)\sigma^2[\cdot]\}dt + e^cdY^{\delta}\sigma[\cdot]dz$
$= V^{\delta}\{\mu[\cdot] + (1/2)(\delta - 1)\sigma^2[\cdot]\} + V^{\delta}\sigma[\cdot]dz$, which can be written as
$(dV/V) = \delta\{\mu[\cdot] + (1/2)(\delta - 1)\sigma 2[\cdot]\}dt + \delta\sigma[\cdot]dz$. Since $(dY/Y) = \mu[\cdot]dt + \sigma[\cdot]dz$, we then obtain:
$(dV/V) = \delta(dY/Y) + (1/2)\delta(\delta - 1)dt$.

The first term in this last expression is identical to the first term in equation (4). But the second term is the stochastic contribution: ***as long as*** δ ***is constant and greater than unity***, the increased volatility of NOI will increase the value of the property. The analysis is otherwise similar to our non-stochastic case in the text. To proceed, we would put cycles from macroeconomic variables into the system by letting μ vary over time in some cyclic fashion. Likewise, taking the time derivative of equation (7) and expressing it in value terms we get that $\boxed{\ln V = C(V) + d\ln Y + A(\delta,\omega,\beta),}$ which is a second order partial differential equation. With the appropriate initial conditions for value and the instantaneous rate of change for value and NOI, this solution generates the non-linear, cyclical, interrelated path followed by Y and V.

18. Following our earlier discussion, in order to characterize the real estate value and income cycles it is sufficient to identify β, δ, and ω. Ideally, our econometric specification should mirror equation (8) of our model and not equation (7). However, equation (8) is impossible to estimate as we lack data that can reflect instantaneous changes in the rate of change of fair market value over time. If we were to difference the logarithm of our fair market value observations twice we would obtain incorrect "accelerators" for value and need to restructure our simultaneous equation system as one with an errors in variables problem. For simplicity, we use equation (7) as our model specification of choice as it is sufficient to yield identification of β, δ, and ω.

19. All necessary data is available, at the MSA level, for twenty selected cities: Atlanta, Baltimore, Boston, Charlotte, Chicago, Dallas, Denver, Houston, Los Angeles, Miami, Minneapolis, Orlando, Philadelphia, Phoenix, Sacramento, San Diego, San Francisco, Seattle, Tampa, and Washington D.C. The reason for specifying a separate equation for each city is our belief that each market is characterized by its own cycle in income and value. Thus it would be inappropriate to estimate data from different cities in the same equation.

20. Three stage least squares allows us to estimate the income cycles in twenty cities simultaneously, while enabling us the opportunity to incorporate the economic, supply and demand factors that are at the core of fluctuations in income and value for the twenty office markets employed in this study. Each of the three stages of least squares regression serves the purpose of yielding unbiased estimators for the coefficients a_0, a_1, a_2, a_3. Specifically, the first stage provides residuals valuable in calculating a variance-covariance matrix used in the third stage to enhance the efficiency of the final estimators for a_0, a_1, a_2, a_3, while correcting for sources of bias such as the presence of autocorrelation. In addition, the second stage of the procedure, allows for the introduction of instruments that corrects for residual autocorrelation and enhances the efficiency of the final estimators for a_0, a_1, a_2, a_3.

21. One year of data is lost in generating the log-differenced value data needed on the right hand side of equation (8) to obtain estimates of the four statistical coefficients a_0, a_1, a_2, a_3.

22. Applying 3SLS to a simultaneous equation system will result in statistically efficient and consistent estimates for the coefficients in the 20-equation system—a total of 80 estimates, presented in table

3. These estimators are also unbiased, implying real estate cycles that are similar to results obtained in earlier studies andto our own theoretical cycles model. For a technical discussion on the merits of our claims about our estimated coefficients please refer to Amemiya (1988).

23. Unit root tests are important to perform in any time series estimation because they provide evidence on stationarity of the series or lack thereof. Whenever time series are non-stationary, the resulting coefficient estimates are biased and inconsistent. Again refer to Amemiya (1988) or any other textbook on time series analysis for technical reference.

24. Although we do not formally test these hypotheses, visual inspection of the data and statistical findings suggest this conclusion.

25. Inspection of Appendix 1 reveals that most R^2, standard errors for the regressions, and variance of residuals suggest that the 3SLS procedure produced a good fit between observed Log-NOI from the National Real Estate Index data and estimated Log-NOI. 3SLS also produced very low Durbin Watson statistics—values statistically different from two—at 95% confidence level. In single equation models, the combination of good overall fits and low Durbin-Watson statistics typically implies biased coefficient estimates due to autocorrelation in the data. However, neither fit statistics nor autocorrelation statistics are very important in the estimation of simultaneous equation systems. 3SLS will correct for simultaneity bias, cross equation correlation as well as autocorrelation. Durbin-Watson statistics do not account for cross-correlation corrections that occur in this last stage of 3SLS, thus misdiagnosing the presence of autocorrelation, and bias in estimation. For these reasons we report in Appendix 1 other, less significant statistics, as opposed to placing these in the main body of our paper. These results lend support to our belief that our theoretical model explains observed real estate NOI cycles (and thus value cycles) very well.

26. For a formal treatment of the subject of testing for the presence of nonstationarity in our regression residuals please refer to Leybourne (1994).

27. As is evident from our earlier discussion, the estimated intercept coefficients are not necessary to identify β, δ, or ω.

REFERENCES

1. Ambrose, Brent and Hugh Nourse, "Factors Influencing Capitalization Rates," *The Journal of Real Estate Research*, Vol. 8, No. 2, (Spring, 1993), pp. 221–238.
2. Case, Karl and Robert Shiller, "Forecasting Prices and Excess Returns in the Housing Market," *Journal of the American Real Estate and Urban Economics Association*, Vol. 18, No. 3, (Fall, 1990), pp. 253–273.
3. Chinloy, Peter, "Real Estate Cycles and Empirical Evidence," *Journal of Housing Research*, vol. 7, Vol. 2, (1996), pp. 173–190.
4. Clapp, John M., *Dynamics of Office Markets: Empirical Findings and Research Issues*, AREUEA Monograph Series, Vol. 1, 1993.
5. Clayton Pritchett, "The Effect of Regional Growth Characteristics on Regional Housing Prices," *Journal of the American Real Estate and Urban Economics Association*, Vol. 5, (Summer, 1977) pp. 189–208.
6. Corgel, John and Gerald Gay, "Local Economic Base, Geographic Diversification, and Risk management of Mortgage Portfolios," *Journal of the American Real Estate and Urban Economic Association*, Vol. 15, (Fall, 1987) pp. 256–267.
7. Crone, Theodore and Richard Voith, "National Vacancy Rates and the Persistence of Shocks in U.S. Office Markets," *Journal of the American Real Estate and urban Economic Association*, (Winter, 1988), Vol. 16, No. 4, pp. 437–458.
8. Dokko, Yoon, Robert Edelstein and Scott Urdang, "Does Credit Rationing Affect Residential Construction? Déjà vu All over Again," *Journal of Real Estate Finance and Economics*, Vol. 3 (1990) pp. 357–371.
9. Dokko, Yoon, Robert Edelstein, Marshall Pomer and Scott Urdang, "Determinants of the Rate of Return for Nonresidential Real Estate: Inflation Expectations and Market Adjustment Lags," *Journal of the American Real Estate and Urban Economics Association*, Vol. 19, (Spring, 1991) pp. 52–69.
10. Edelstein, Robert H. and Irwin Friend, "Allocating Resources to Housing: the Private Sector," *Proceedings of the First Annual Conference on Housing*, Federal Home Loan Bank of San Francisco, (1976).

11. Froland, Charles, "What Determines Cap Rates on Real Estate?" *The Journal of Portfolio Management*, (Summer, 1987), pp. 55–60.
12. Gatzlaff, Dean and Dogan Tirtiroglu, "Real Estate Market Efficiency: Issues and Evidence," Working Paper, (June, 1993).
13. Grebler, Leo and Leland Burns, "Construction Cycles in the United States Since World War II," *Journal of the American Real Estate and Urban Economics Association*, Vol. 10 (Summer, 1982) pp. 123–151.
14. Green, Richard K. "Follow the Leader: How Changes in Residential and Non-residential Investment Predict Changes in GDP," *Real Estate Economics*, Vol. 25, No. 2, (1997) pp. 253–270.
15. Grenadier, Steven, "The Persistence of Real Estate Cycles," *Journal of Real Estate Finance and Economics*, Vol. 10, No. 2, (March 1995) pp. 95–119.
16. Harris, Jack and Waldo Born, "Timing Real Estate Acquisitions," *Real Estate Review*, (Summer, 1986) pp. 79–83.
17. Hartzell, David, John Hekman and Mike Miles, "Real Estate Returns and Inflation," *Journal of the American Real Estate and Urban Economics Association*, (Spring, 1987) pp. 617–637.
18. Hekman, John, "Rental Price Adjustment and Investment in the Office Market," *Journal of the American Real Estate and Urban Economics Association*, Vol. 13, No. 1, (Spring, 1985) pp. 32–47.
19. Hendershott, Patrick and Edward Kane, "US Office Market Value During the Past Decade: How Distorted Have Appraisals Been?" *Real Estate Economics*, Vol. 23, No. 2, (Summer 1995) pp. 101–116.
20. Jaffee, Dwight and Kenneth T. Rosen, "Mortgage Credit Availability and Residential Construction," *Brookings Papers on Economic Activity*, Vol. 2 (1979), pp. 333–386.
21. Kling, John and Thomas McCue, "Office Building Investment and the Macroeconomy: Empirical Evidence, 1973–1985," *Journal of the American Real Estate and Urban Economics Association*, Vol. 15, (Fall, 1987) pp. 234–255.
22. Koopmans, Tjalling C. "Measurement without Theory," *Review of Economics and Statistics*, Vol. 29, August, 1947.
23. Leybourne, S.J. "Testing for Unit Roots: A Simple Alternative to Dickey-Fuller," *Applied Economics*, Vol. 26, No. 7, July, 1994, pp. 721–729.
24. Meese, Richard and Nancy Wallace, "Testing the Present Value Relation for Housing Prices: Should I Leave my House in San Francisco?" *Journal of Urban Economics*, Vol. 35, (May 1994) pp. 245–266.
25. Meese, Richard and Nancy Wallace, "Determinants of Residential Housing Prices: Effects of Economic Factors or Speculative Bubbles?" Working Paper No. 91–193, *IBER*, U.C. Berkeley.
26. Mueller, Glenn, "Understanding Real Estate's Physical and Financial Market Cycles," *Real Estate Finance*, Vol. 12, No. 3, Fall 1995, pp. 47–52.
27. National Commission on Financial Institution Reform, Recovery and Enforcement, "Origins and Causes of the S&L Debacle: A Blueprint for Reform," *A Report to the President and Congress of the United States*, Washington, D.C., July 1993.
28. Peiser, Rick, "Capitalization Rates, Inflation and Investment Analysis in U.S. Real Estate," *Appraisal Review Journal*, (Spring/Summer, 1983) pp. 42–43.
29. Pritchett, Clayton, "Forecasting the Impact of Real Estate Cycles on Investment," *Real Estate Review*, Vol. 13, No. 4, (Winter, 1984) pp. 85–89.
30. Pyhrr, Stephen A., and Waldo L. Born, "Real Estate Valuation: The Effect of Market and Property Cycles," *The Journal of Real Estate Research*, Vol. 9, No. 4, (Fall, 1994), pp. 455–486.
31. Pyhrr, Stephen A., Waldo L. Born and James R. Webb, "Development of a Dynamic Investment Strategy under Alternative Inflation Cycle Scenarios," *The Journal of Real Estate Research*, Vol. 5, No. 2, (Summer, 1990), pp. 177–194.
32. Pyhrr, Stephen A., James R. Webb and Waldo L. Born, "Analyzing Real Estate Asset Performance During Periods of Market Disequilibrium Under Cyclical Economic Conditions: A Framework for Analysis," pp. 75–106 in Kappline, and Schwartz, editors, *Research in Real Estate*, Vol. 3, 1990.
33. Rayburn, William, Michael Devaney and Richard Evans, "A Test of Weak-Form Efficiency in Residential Real Estate Returns," *Journal of the American Real Estate and Urban Economics Association*. Vol. 15, (Fall, 1987) pp. 220–233.
34. Rosen, Kenneth, "Toward A Model of the Office Building Sector," *Journal of the American Real Estate and Urban Economics Association*. Vol. 12, (Fall, 1984) pp. 261–269.
35. Sagalyn, Lynne B., "Real Estate Risk and the Business Cycle: Evidence from Security Markets," *The Journal of Real Estate Research*, Vol. 5, No. 2, (Summer, 1990), pp. 203–220.
36. Wheaton, William, "Vacancy, Search, and Prices in a Housing Market Matcing Model," *Journal of Political Economy*, Vol. 98, No. 6, 1990.

37. Wheaton, William, "The Cyclical Behavior of the National Office Market," *Journal of the American Real Estate and Urban Economics Association* (Winter, 1987), pp. 281–299.
38. Wheaton, William and Ray Torto, "Vacancy Rates and The Future of Office Rents," *Journal of the American Real Estate and Urban Economics Association*, Vol. 16, No. 4, (Winter, 1988) pp. 430–436.

APPENDIX 1: Summary Regression Statistics

Dependent Variable: NOI				
MSA	**ATLANTA**	**MINNEAPOLIS**	**DALLAS**	**SAN DIEGO**
Mean of dependent variable	2.42811	2.29305	2.3671	2.43486
Std. de v. of dependent var.	0.068047	0.10621	0.047822	0.101372
Sum of squared residuals	5.92E-03	0.015562	0.015751	6.49E-03
Variance of residuals	1.69E-04	4.45E-04	4.50E-04	1.85E-04
Std. Error of regression	0.013005	0.021086	0.021214	0.013619
R-squared	*0.962402*	*0.959479*	*0.798321*	*0.981429*
Durbin-Watson statistic	0.683164	0.321424	0.224591	0.543682
MSA	**BALTIMORE**	**ORLANDO**	**DENVER**	**SAN FRANCISCO**
Mean of dependent variable	2.27216	2.2652	2.08533	2.54124
Std. de v. of dependent var.	0.062335	0.030979	0.048717	0.115402
Sum of squared residuals	2.64E-03	0.011751	0.013807	0.062531
Variance of residuals	7.53E-05	3.36E-04	3.94E-04	1.79E-03
Std. Error of regression	8.68E-03	0.018323	0.019862	0.042268
R-squared	**0.980194**	**0.640939**	**0.838615**	**0.863607**
Durbin-Watson statistic	0.441927	0.321564	0.720328	0.389168
MSA	**BOSTON**	**PHILADELPHIA**	**HOUSTON**	**SEATTLE**
Mean of dependent variable	2.73211	2.53859	2.18073	2.50798
Std. de v. of dependent var.	0.128009	0.051403	0.041645	0.029065
Sum of squared residuals	0.010644	3.65E-03	6.28E-03	3.53E-03
Variance of residuals	3.04E-04	1.04E-04	1.80E-04	1.01E-04
Std. error of regression	0.017439	0.01021	0.0134	0.010046
R-squared	*0.980904*	*0.95954*	*0.894243*	*0.877472*
Durbin-Watson statistic	0.604194	0.892301	0.444244	0.796101
MSA	**CHARLOTTE**	**PHOENIX**	**LOS ANGELES**	**TAMPA**
Mean of dependent variable	2.39623	2.25061	2.88504	2.26663
Std. de v. of dependent var.	0.052196	0.110327	0.10364	0.13422
Sum of squared residuals	2.30E-03	7.00E-03	9.34E-03	7.46E-03
Variance of residuals	6.58E-05	2.00E-04	2.67E-04	2.13E-04
Std. error of regression	8.11E-03	0.014137	0.016332	0.014596
R-squared	*0.975123*	*0.983122*	*0.974544*	*0.987832*
Durbin-Watson statistic	0.909326	0.635285	1.12291	0.320779
MSA	**CHICAGO**	**SACRAMENTO**	**MIAMI**	**WASHINGTON**
D.C.				
Mean of dependent variable	2.82315	2.54361	2.43745	2.94125
Std. de v. of dependent var.	0.146754	0.044523	0.145164	0.062695
Sum of squared residuals	5.98E-03	8.46E-03	0.046306	0.010019
Variance of residuals	1.71E-04	2.42E-04	1.32E-03	2.86E-04
Std. error of regression	0.013072	0.015548	0.036373	0.016919
R-squared	*0.991867*	*0.874834*	*0.936282*	*0.925867*
Durbin-Watson statistic	1.09463	0.580785	0.987515	0.601699

5. THE CROSS SECTION OF GLOBAL PROPERTY SHARE RETURNS

PIET EICHHOLTZ AND RONALD HUISMAN*

**Erasmus University, Rotterdam School of Management / Financial Management, P.O. Box 1738, 3000 DR The Netherlands, tel.: +31 10 4082428, e-mail: rhuisman@fac.fbk.eur.nl*

1. INTRODUCTION

International real estate investment is on the rise. Pension funds and other institutional real estate investors, who have traditionally looked only at their own real estate markets for investment opportunities, are increasingly looking across national borders. For investors based in countries like the Netherlands and the United Kingdom, this is just another step in a rather old tradition, but for United States investors, international property investment is really a rather new phenomenon.

This new international interest is helped considerably by the development of the global property share market, since this market allows investors to build up exposure to foreign property markets in a relatively liquid and cost-efficient way.

The increased investor interest in the international property share markets is accompanied by a growing academic literature in this area. This literature has devoted a lot of attention to the portfolio effects of international diversification through property shares. Early examples are Giliberto (1990) and Giliberto and Testa

Eichholtz is at the Limburg Institute of Financial Economics (LIFE) at Maastricht University, The University of Amsterdam and Global Property Research; all in the Netherlands. Huisman is at the Rotterdam School of Management at the Erasmus University Rotterdam and at FinEdge Financial Knowledge Centre in Rotterdam. The authors thank Dennis Capozza, David Geltner, Rachel Pownall, participants to the Homer Hoyt meeting in January 1999, the NYU Conference on The Dynamics of Real Estate Cycles in March 1999, the Real Estate Research Institute meeting in April 1999, and the Cutting Edge meeting in Cambridge in September 1999. Niels Hagemans, Hans Op 't Veld and Nils de Graaf of Global Property Research are thanked for their assistance in providing the data and the Real Estate Research Institute for funding. All errors remain to the authors.

(1990), who both use the stock returns of publicly traded property companies to demonstrate the risk-reduction potential of international diversification. They also calculate efficient international portfolios. Eichholtz (1996) compares the diversification benefits of international property share investments with international investments in stocks and bonds, and concludes that these benefits can be substantial. The nature of the risk premiums in international real estate returns has had less attention in the literature. Except for Eichholtz, Huisman, Koedijk and Schuin (1998), who show that continental factors are important drivers of international property share returns, this is still largely uncharted terrain.

This contrasts sharply with the availability of literature regarding the risk premia of United States Real Estate Investment Trusts (REITs). The first papers to study REIT returns using a multi index approach were Titman and Warga (1986) and Chan, Hendershott and Sanders (1990). The former paper uses a CAPM specification and a five-factor APT model to explain REIT returns and investigates whether the choice of either model has implications for REIT performance measurement. Since both models are unable to find significant risk adjusted abnormal returns, hard conclusions cannot be drawn regarding this issue. The paper does show, however, that a multi-index model has better explanatory power than the single index CAPM for US REITs. Chan, Hendershott and Sanders (1990) have found that REIT betas derived from a market model are 0.55 on average for the period 1980–1987, and that the explanatory power of the market returns depends to a large extent on the specification of the market index.

Taking a longer sample period, 1978–1996, Sanders (1997) confirms these results. To determine REIT betas, he uses the S&P 500 stock index and some small stock indices as independent variables in a single index model. He finds REIT betas of approximately 0.56, independent of the market index used. The R^2 of the market model varies from 0.39 when the S&P 500 is used to 0.52 for one of the Wilshire small stock indices. However, the explanatory power of the model is highly dependent on the time period chosen. Sanders also uses the Fama and French (1992) model, which is a multifactor model like the one used by Chan, Hendershott and Sanders (1990) but which also includes the book-to-market ratio for each company in the dataset. He found that the Fama French (1992) model generates an R^2 of 0.58 for the NAREIT Equity Index, while the standard CAPM specification generates an R^2 of 0.39. The better performance of the Fama French model in explaining REIT returns also holds relative to a CAPM specification using a small firm index. These findings are confirmed by Peterson and Hsieh (1997) and Eichholtz, Schweitzer and Op 't Veld (1999), who conclude that the risk factors in the returns of REITs are similar to those found for stocks by Fama and French (1992).

Ling and Naranjo (1997, 1998) also examine the determinants of United States commercial real estate returns. They use a multifactor model to investigate which systematic risk factors are priced in real estate markets, and they do that for real estate stocks as well as for directly held property. Their sample of real estate stocks includes not just REITs, but also stocks of other real estate related companies.

Relative to the previous studies, their main contribution is that they include the growth rate of per capita consumption as a systematic risk factor in their model. They find this factor to be priced, which confirms earlier research by Geltner (1989), who also showed that real estate returns are exposed to consumption risk. Besides consumption, they also find the treasury bill rate to be a systematic risk factor, and that also holds for unexpected inflation and the term structure of interest rates, but only when risk premia are allowed to vary over time.

The purpose of this paper is to extend the United States literature to the international arena, and to investigate the risk premia of international property share returns in more depth, using the methods previously employed for US stocks and REITs. Using an adjusted version of the Fama and French (1992) methodology, we shed more light on the risk factors in the returns of property shares in the six most important property share markets: Australia, France, Hong Kong, Japan, the United Kingdom, and the United States. In the next section, we describe the data and the data sources employed. Section 3 focuses on the methodology we use, and Section 4 provides results. The practical implications of these results are discussed in Section 5, while Section 6 gives conclusions.

2. DATA

The property share data we use are obtained from Global Property Research in the Netherlands.[1] The GPR global property share database contains information regarding listed property companies worldwide. In all, it covers approximately 30 countries. We analyze a sub-sample of this database, containing data obtained for the six largest national property share markets: Australia, France, Hong Kong, Japan, the United Kingdom, and the United States. The sample consists of 93 property companies in January 1984, and increasing to 283 companies in December 1998, whereby the total market value in December 1998 was 262.8 billion US Dollars. Further information about the sample of property companies is provided in Table 1. Currently the United States has by far the largest market for equity property companies, but in the mid-eighties, the United Kingdom property company market was the biggest. We analyze 123 United States property companies with a combined market value of $122.5 billion at December 1998, which amounts to nearly 50% of the sample's market value. France has the smallest market with 32 companies and a market value of $17 billion in December 1998. On average, the largest property companies can be found in Hong Kong and Japan. The dispersion around the average market capitalization is large for all countries considered here, but especially large for Hong Kong.

Table 1 also shows that property companies are treated differently by the tax authorities in different countries. In Australia and the United States, and in France until 1996, property companies are trusts, and not taxed at the corporate level. In Australia and the United States, a prerequisite for this is that they distribute 95% of their earnings as dividends to the shareholders each year. Besides that, property development by these trusts is only allowed to a very limited extent. That means an investment in such a company is really an indirect investment in a property port-

Table 1. Property Share Characteristics

	Australia	France	Hong Kong	Japan	United Kingdom	United States
Number of Companies in Index						
1984/1	4	10	15	7	31	26
1998/12	26	32	29	20	53	123
Total Market Capitalization (98/12)						
Local Currency (*1,000)	26,196	95,151	392,656	2,764,056	19,457	122,537
US Dollars (*1,000)	15,987	16,997	50,691	24,331	32,298	122,537
Market Capitalization at 98/12 in US$						
Average per Company (*1,000)	615	531	1,748	1,217	609	996
Minimum per Company (*1,000)	87	20	13	61	33	42
Maximum per Company (*1,000)	2,774	1,734	17,443	11,585	7,118	6,239
Corporate Taxation (%) Earnings	No	Yes, from '96	Yes	Yes	Yes	No
Distribution Requirement	Yes (95%)	No	No	No	No	Yes (95%)
Other Characteristics	Portfolios are diversified across the main urban areas, and usually strongly specialized by sector. International investment is rare.	Portfolios are usually diversified across property types. Office holdings are concentrated in the Paris region, while retail holdings are usually regionally diversified. International investment is very rare.	Portfolios are usually diversified across property types, and located in Hong Kong, although investment in mainland China often occurs.	Japanese companies usually invest in office properties in Tokyo. Other investments are rare. That also holds for international property investments	Portfolios are usually diversified across property types, with a focus on the London area, especially for offices. The sample contains a few international property companies.	Portfolios are usually specialized by sector, and diversified across regions. International investment by property companies is very rare.

Source: Global Property Research database.

Table 2. GPR US Dollar Market Weighted Total Return Index Statistics (January 1984 = 100)

	Index Value (6/98)	Mean Return	Standard Deviation	Skewness	Kurtosis
Australia	690.40	1.25%	5.16%	−0.85	4.92
France	461.54	1.01%	5.03%	0.03	0.30
Hong Kong	1,326.01	2.15%	11.35%	0.05	4.16
Japan	385.04	1.39%	11.55%	1.53	7.73
United Kingdom	538.18	1.20%	6.72%	−0.15	0.39
United States	578.39	1.11%	4.31%	0.60	2.91

The summary statistics represent monthly returns in US Dollars.

folio. In France, these prerequisites do not exist. In Hong Kong, Japan and the United Kingdom, property companies are treated as ordinary companies, which implies that they have to pay corporate taxes and are not required to distribute their earnings. This means that property companies in these countries can and do develop properties for their own portfolios and for those of third parties. To make the comparison between the two groups useful, we have excluded the pure developers from the sample.

For each property company we have monthly ex dividend prices, dividends, and the stock market capitalization. All these data are obtained on the last trading day of each month. The data spans the period January 1984 through June 1998. Table 2 provides total return index statistics to give insight into the performance of the property share markets under consideration. The first column gives the level at June 1998 of an investment of 100 US Dollars in January 1984. Measured only in terms of the index level, Hong Kong has shown the best performance between 1984 and June 1998, with an index level of 1326 as of June 1998. By the same token, Japan showed the worst performance among the countries under consideration. These two countries have always been most risky, at least when measured by the standard deviation of the monthly returns, which was more than 11%. The United States had the least risky property share market in the sample period.

Apart from the property share data, we also employ MSCI indices for common stocks, both on a global and on a continental level. These indices are monthly total rate of return in US Dollar terms. We also use interest rate data. We take the US 1-year interbank rate as the risk free rate, since we use the perspective of a US Dollar-based investor, and to calculate conditional variables we use the 1-year interbank rates and the 10-year swap rates for all the countries in the data set.

3. METHOD

We focus on the annual returns, which is the standard in most cross-sectional studies like Fama and French (1992) and Ferson and Harvey (1996). We calculate the return in year t as the total rate of return (including dividends) over the whole calendar year t. We define the size s(i,c,t) of property company i listed in country c in year t as the company's market equity in US Dollars observed at the end of December in year t-1. We define $\beta(i,c,t)$ as the beta for company i in country c valid for year t. The beta is calculated from returns observed for the 50 months preceding January in year t. If less then 50 months of data are available, we use the returns from the available months only if at least 24 observations are available; if not, the property company is discarded for this particular year. Note that each firm included in our tests needs to have a size observation in December of year t-1 and a total return for year t, and each firm must have at least 24 months of return data preceding year t to calculate the β estimates. Table 3 provides summary statistics about the pooled excess returns used in the subsequent regressions.

We examine the cross-sectional variation of excess returns on global property shares in the following way. We relate the simple dollar total return r(i,c,t), realized in year t for property share i based in country c in excess of the US 1-year inter-bank rate observed on the last trading day in year t-1, in a factor model to variables with potential explanatory power for the cross-sectional variation in the excess returns. If factor k is denoted by $f_k(i,c,t)$, the factor model is formulated as follows.

$$r(i,c,t) = \sum_{k=1}^{n} \gamma(k) f_k(i,c,t) + \varepsilon(i,c,t) \tag{1}$$

The error term $\varepsilon(i,c,t)$ is assumed to be iid. Note that we pool the data observed over various years to increase the power of the cross-sectional regression.

We consider the following factors. First, we introduce country dummy variables constructed in such a way that, for example, d_{USA} equals one if country c is the USA and zero otherwise. The country dummies control for country-economic specific differences in the return process between the countries. The motivation for this comes from the big differences in the total return index values and the average monthly returns given in Table 1. The dummies disentangle country-specific influences and the influences of the variables that we consider. Thereby, we assume that these influences are independent. In addition, we examine the power of potential

Table 3. Summary Statistics

This table reports summary statistics on the yearly simple returns in US dollars we use on the left-hand sides of the regressions. The data is a pooled sample over both the property shares in the sample and the yearly time periods available (1990 through 1997). The numbers can therefore not be interpreted as time series statistics. They reflect the characteristics of the samples we used in the regressions.

	Mean Return	Standard Deviation	Skewness	Kurtosis	n
Australia	10.00%	29.10%	2.34	10.87	113
France	−3.21%	26.33%	0.21	0.83	262
Hong Kong	21.33%	79.53%	4.57	41.20	278
Japan	−15.85%	36.34%	0.44	1.18	221
United Kingdom	14.27%	88.67%	10.43	160.60	412
United States	12.40%	33.61%	2.61	22.35	498

risk factors beta, β(i,c,t), and size, s(i,c,t). Beta is measured in four different ways. The first, denoted as β-all(i,c,t), reflects the sensitivity of the return of property share i to changes in the GPR world index; i.e. the sensitivity to global movements in the property share market. The second, denoted as β-cont(i,c,t), reflects the sensitivity of the return on share i to changes in continental movements; i.e. the sensitivity to changes in the return of the total return index of the continent the country of share i's origin. The motivation to include this factor comes from the result that the return correlations within continents have increased in the past decade in Europe and North America as shown by Eichholtz, Huisman, Koedijk, and Schuin (1998). The third and fourth way to calculate beta are analogous, but differ with regards to indices used: the MSCI common stock indices on the global and continental levels, in stead of the GPR indices.

Besides the betas we introduce interest rate variables as conditional factors in the model. We look at the 1-year interbank interest level and the first differences in this rate, and at the term structure. For the return in year t on property share i in country c, we observe the 1-year interbank rate ir for that country at the beginning of year t. The first difference d ir is constructed such that it reflects the absolute change of the 1-year local interbank interest rate in the year before a return is observed. The term structure is the difference between the 10-year swap rate and the 1-year interbank rate at the beginning of year t. These conditional factors reflect the country allocation process; they explain the variation in returns across the different countries considered.

4. RESULTS

Table 4 presents the OLS parameter estimates for the parameters in four variations of model (1). We include the country dummy variables, the betas and size as factors, but leave the conditioning variables for later. The betas used to obtain the results in Table 4 are calculated using property share indices. A priori, we expect a positive relationship between return and beta and a negative one between return and size. The first row in Table 4 shows the results for the beta based on the global index. The coefficient associated with that beta equals −0.001 and is not significant. The country dummies vary from −0.144 for Japan, reflecting the poor performance of the Japanese real estate market compared with the others, through 0.196 for Hong Kong. Except for France, these country dummies are significant at the 95% confidence level. The coefficient associated with beta indicates that the beta as defined here has no power in explaining cross sectional variation in returns on property shares. The R^2 equals 0.034, which is low but typical for such models. Recall that we relate the excess returns in one year on variables observed in the previous year. This forecasting aspect of the setup causes the poor fit and therefore the low R-squares. We therefore stress the importance of variables only instead of discussing the model as being a potential forecast framework.

The betas we used in the first regression reflect the sensitivity of property share returns relative to changes in the returns in global property market. The growing continental influence on property shares, as shown by Eichholtz, Huisman, Koedijk,

Table 4. Cross Sectional Results—Property Share Betas

In this table, we report the estimates of the parameters for the models 1 through 3. These models relate the observed risk premium to dummy variables that indicates the country of origin and to beta and size as potential risk factors. The parameter estimates associated with the risk factor can be interpreted as the market price of this risk factor.

	Country dummies						Factors				
	Austr.	France	HKG	Japan	UK	USA	β-all	β-cont	size	n	R^2
1	**0.112**	–0.035	**0.196**	**–0.144**	**0.144**	**0.112**	–0.001			1,850	0.034
	(0.027)	(0.039)	(0.043)	(0.055)	(0.037)	(0.026)	(0.027)				
2	**0.114**	–0.024	**0.202**	**–0.135**	**0.159**	**0.122**		–0.012		1,850	0.034
	(0.054)	(0.047)	(0.038)	(0.047)	(0.049)	(0.035)		(0.030)			
3	**0.426**	**0.280**	**0.526**	**0.219**	**0.433**	**0.410**			**–0.056**	1,850	0.048
	(0.080)	(0.070)	(0.071)	(0.079)	(0.617)	(0.062)			(0.011)		
4	**0.429**	**0.271**	**0.516**	**0.200**	**0.416**	**0.407**	0.014	0.010	**–0.058**	1,850	0.048
	(0.081)	(0.073)	(0.075)	(0.087)	(0.070)	(0.066)	(0.049)	(0.054)	(0.011)		

Standard errors are given between parentheses.
All bold-faced numbers represent significant values at the 95% confidence level.

and Schuin (1998), could imply that betas measured relative to changes in the continental property share market might explain the cross sectional variation better. Test results can be found in the second row of Table 4. Country dummies are similar to the ones for row one and again the coefficient associated with the continental beta is not significantly different from zero. Continental betas are no significant risk factors for international property shares.[2]

These results are similar to those found for US equities; examples of which are Fama and French (1992) and Ferson and Harvey (1996). Many studies have suggested alternative systematic risk factors such as size, the book to market ratio, and price earnings ratios. The latter two are not included in our dataset unfortunately, but we did examine the effect of size, approximated by the log of the market capitalization, in explaining the cross sectional variation. The results are presented in the third row of Table 4. The country dummies have higher coefficients than those in the first two rows but again reflect the differences in performance over the countries. More interestingly, we find that the coefficient associated with size is significantly different from zero and equals –0.056. This suggests that smaller property companies offer higher excess returns. Small fund investors are thus significantly rewarded for their risk exposure. Note that the R^2 improved to 0.048 in the regression with size.

The last row in Table 4 shows the results of a summarizing regression in which we include all the factors we included in the previous rows. As expected, size is the only significant factor explaining cross sectional variation and betas have no effect. One can conclude that size is a globally prized risk factor that has explanatory power for the performance of property companies. This implies that portfolio managers would be able to obtain higher expected returns by increasing their exposure to small companies.

The weak statistical link between the betas and the excess property share returns may be caused by the fact that we calculate the betas on the basis of property share returns indices. Using common stock indices may yield different results. To investigate this issue, we have repeated the analysis, with betas measured on the basis of global and continental common stock indices. The regression results are reported in Table 5. In essence, these results confirm those reported in Table 5: the betas have very low explanatory power, and size is very significant. Only when all the factor loadings are estimated simultaneously do we see that the global beta becomes statistically significant, but with a negative sign. The similarity in the results reported in Tables 3 and 4 is not very surprising given the fact that the correlation between the MSCI β-all and the property share based β-all equals 0.867.

Since we deal with international investments, country allocation is a relevant issue. To investigate this, we include interest rate variables in the analysis. We examine three variables: the nominal one-year interbank interest rate, the first differences of this rate and the term structure, as defined by the difference between the 10-year government bond rate and the 1-year treasury bill rate. Test results are given in Table 6. We extended the model given in the fourth row of Table 4, with all the risk factors we consider, by including the interest rate variables step by step.

In the first row of Table 6, we include the one-year interbank interest rate level in addition to the other factors. The expected negative relationship is confirmed. The coefficient associated with the interbank rate level is significantly different from zero and equals –0.026. Property shares listed in countries where interest rates are low relative to other countries are expected to offer higher excess returns. The other results are equal to those reported in Table 4; size is again significant and negative and beta has no power.

In the second row we show the effects of changes in the one-year interest rates. We relate the excess returns of the property shares in a specific year to the first difference in the interest rate observed in the previous year. The coefficient associated with this factor, denoted by d ir, is significant and equals –0.044. Property shares listed in countries where interest rates have declined last year are expected

Table 5. Cross Sectional Results—MSCI Betas

In this table, we report the estimates of the parameters for the models 1 through 3. These models relate the observed risk premium to dummy variables that indicates the country of origin and to beta and size as potential risk factors. The parameter estimates associated with the risk factor can be interpreted as the market price of this risk factor.

	Country dummies						Factors				
	Austr.	France	HKG	Japan	UK	USA	β-all	β-cont	size	n	R^2
1	**0.126**	–0.014	**0.230**	–0.084	**0.181**	**0.126**	–0.035			1,850	0.035
	(0.054)	(0.039)	(0.042)	(0.058)	(0.039)	(0.027)	(0.025)				
2	**0.114**	–0.026	**0.200**	**–0.128**	**0.158**	**0.119**		–0.015		1,850	0.034
	(0.054)	(0.042)	(0.035)	(0.057)	(0.047)	(0.031)		(0.035)			
3	**0.451**	**0.276**	**0.583**	**0.259**	**0.433**	**0.403**	**–0.079**	0.086	**–0.057**	1,850	0.050
	(0.081)	(0.072)	(0.076)	(0.089)	(0.070)	(0.063)	(0.040)	(0.056)	(0.011)		

Standard errors are given between parentheses.
All bold-faced numbers represent significant values at the 95% confidence level.

to offer higher returns on average this year. Furthermore, the other results still hold. The results from the simultaneous analysis of the interest level and first difference variable in one regression imply that relatively high expected dollar returns can be expected from property companies listed in countries where interest rates are low and/or declining and small caps offer the highest expected returns. The R^2 of the latest regression equals 0.078, which is still low but higher than those for the regressions in Tables 4 and 5.

In the fourth and fifth rows of Table 6, the results for the term structure variable are included. However, the correlation between the term structure and the 1-year interbank interest rate equals −0.905 and for multicollinearity reasons, we drop the interest rate levels when we include the term structure as a variable. The results show a significantly positive relationship between the term structure and the excess property share returns. The R^2 of the model increases to 0.084 when both the term structure and the interest changes are included in the analysis.

5. PRACTICAL IMPLICATIONS

The results of this study have implications for the international allocation of a property share portfolio. The results show that the risk factors we set out to examine are indeed real. The excess returns an international property share investor can expect compensate for the risk he runs: there is no free lunch. Of the factors we examine, the beta appears to be the least important. Judged by our model, beta does not play an important role in explaining excess international property share returns, and it does not matter very much whether we define beta on a continental or on a global basis, or relative to a property share or a common stock index. The practical implication of this finding is straightforward: since beta is not a priced risk factor, it is not a very good idea to pursue a high beta investment strategy. Investing in high beta property shares internationally would entail higher risk without any extra gain.

The risk factors that do drive excess property share returns are interest rate variables and the size of the property companies. Especially the interest rate variables appear to be important. Both the level of interest rates and the change in that level have a significantly negative impact on excess property share returns. The term structure is related to excess property share returns in a positive way. This means that portfolio managers can improve their performance by focusing on interest rates and by investing in those countries where these rates are low or declining, and where the term structure is upward sloping. Furthermore, the negative relationship between size and expected excess property share returns would suggest that a focus on the smaller property companies could be beneficial for performance.

6. CONCLUDING REMARKS

In this paper we have analyzed some factors explaining the cross sectional variation in excess returns on global property shares. The literature has found evidence for the weak performance of beta in explaining cross-sectional variation. Instead,

Table 6. Cross Sectional Results with Conditional Variables—Property Share Betas

In this table, we report the estimates of the parameters for the models 1 through 3. These models relate the observed risk premium to dummy variables that indicates the country of origin and to beta and size as potential risk factors. The parameter estimates associated with the risk factor can be interpreted as the market price of this risk factor.

	Country dummies						Factors			Conditional variables				
	Austr.	France	HKG	Japan	UK	USA	β-all	β-cont	Size	ir	d ir	TS	n	R^2
1	**0.664**	**0.454**	**0.688**	**0.299**	**0.657**	**0.562**	–0.000	0.022	**–0.058**	**–0.026**			1,850	0.059
	(0.096)	(0.083)	(0.083)	(0.089)	(0.087)	(0.074)	(0.049)	(0.054)	(0.011)	(0.005)				
2	**0.375**	**0.210**	**0.546**	**0.174**	**0.383**	**0.388**	–0.028	0.036	**–0.055**		**–0.044**		1,784	0.076
	(0.083)	(0.075)	(0.077)	(0.089)	(0.07[illegible])	(0.067)	(0.051)	(0.055)	(0.011)		(0.007)			
3	**0.517**	**0.327**	**0.651**	**0.240**	**0.529**	**0.484**	–0.034	0.041	**–0.056**	**–0.014**	**–0.037**		1,784	0.078
	(0.104)	(0.091)	(0.090)	(0.093)	(0.096)	(0.079)	(0.051)	(0.055)	(0.011)	(0.006)	(0.007)			
4	**0.312**	**0.193**	**0.333**	0.073	**0.346**	**0.301**	–0.006	0.051	**–0.057**			**0.072**	1,492	0.075
	(0.089)	(0.081)	(0.098)	(0.097)	(0.080)	(0.077)	(0.056)	(0.059)	(0.012)			(0.013)		
5	**0.285**	0.151	**0.348**	0.053	**0.307**	**0.290**	–0.010	0.051	**–0.054**		**–0.029**	**0.060**	1,492	0.084
	(0.089)	(0.082)	(0.098)	(0.097)	(0.081)	(0.077)	(0.056)	(0.059)	(0.012)		(0.007)	(0.013)		

Standard errors are given between parentheses.
All bold-faced numbers represent significant values at the 95% confidence level.

other potential risk factors like size, book to market, price earnings ratios, interest rate variables and consumption have been examined and have been proven to be priced.

Concentrating on property shares listed in Australia, France, Hong Kong, Japan, the United Kingdom, and the United States, we confirm the results put forward in the literature for United States stocks in general and REITs in particular. Size is a significant risk factor and beta is shown not to be significant at all. This implies that risk preferences should be translated in terms of the market value of a property company instead of its beta. Lower market value companies have offered higher returns in order to compensate for the higher (default) risks investors face. Interest rate variables have also been found to have an important impact on excess property share returns, especially changes in interest rates and the term structure. Decreasing interest rates imply high excess returns, and a positively sloped yield curve does the same.

NOTE

1. These data are also used in Eichholtz, Huisman, Koedijk en Schuin (1998).
2. This could be attributable to the fact that we use country dummies. If international capital market segmentation would be an issue, then country effects would dominate global capital market effects, and the country dummies would be more important in explaining property share returns than the global and continental betas. However, this is not the case. We have estimated equation (1) also without country dummies, and have found regression coefficients for the betas with the same value and statistical significance as in the regression with the country dummies.

REFERENCES

Chan, K.C., P. Hendershott and A. Sanders (1990), "Risk and Return in Real Estate: Evidence from Equity REITs", *AREUEA Journal* 18, no 4, 431–42.

Eichholtz, P.M.A. (1996), "Does International Diversification Work Better for Real Estate than for Stocks and Bonds?", *Financial Analysts Journal*, January/February.

——R. Huisman, K. Koedijk, and L. Schuin (1998), "Continental Factors in International Real Estate Returns", *Real Estate Economics* 26, no 3, 493–510.

——M. Schweitzer and H. Op 't Veld (1999), "REIT Outperformance: Does Managerial Specilization Pay?", in S. Zenios, *The Performance of Financial Institutions*, Cambridge University Press.

Fama, E.F. and K.R. French (1992), "The Cross-Section of Expected Stock Returns", *Journal of Finance* 2, 427–65.

Ferson, W.E. and C.R. Harvey (1996), "Conditioning Variables and the Cross-Section of Stock Returns", *working paper.*

Geltner, D. (1989), "Estimating Real Estate's Systematic Risk from Aggregate Level Appraisal-Based Returns", *AREUEA Journal* 17, no 4, 463–81.

Giliberto, S.M. (1990), "Global Real Estate Securities: Index Performance and Diversified Portfolios", Salomon Brothers Real Estate Research.

——and B. Testa (1990), "Global Property Share Performance by Geographic Region", Salomon Brothers Real Estate Research.

Ling, D.C. and A. Naranjo (1997), "Economic Risk Factors and Commercial Real Estate Returns", *Journal of Real Estate Finance and Economics* 14, no 3, 283–307.

——(1998), "The Fundamental Determinants of Commercial Real Estate Returns", *Real Estate Finance* 14, no 4, 13–23.

Peterson, J.D. and C.H. Hsieh (1997), "Do Common Risk Factors in the Return on Stocks and Bonds Explain Returns on REITs?", *Real Estate Economics* 25, no 2, 321–45.

Sanders, A.B. (1997), "The Historical Behavior of REIT Returns; A Capital Markets Perspective", Chapter 12 in R.T. Garrigan and J.F.C. Parsons, *Real Estate Investment Trusts, Structure, Analysis and Strategy*, McGraw Hill.

Titman, S. and A. Warga (1986), "Risk and the Performance of Real Estate Investment Trusts: A Multiple Index Approach", *AREUEA Journal* 14, no 3, 414–31.

6. EVIDENCE OF CYCLES IN EUROPEAN COMMERCIAL REAL ESTATE MARKETS—AND SOME HYPOTHESES

ANDREW BAUM

Henderson Investors, London, UK and The University of Reading, Reading, UK

1. INTRODUCTION

Economists are forced to forecast in the knowledge that they will be criticised by the users of their forecasts for the inevitable inaccuracies they will contain. Historians, on the other hand, look at economists with envy. The perceived repeatability of economic and property cycles, for example, suggests a degree of usefulness which historians would be keen to associate with their own profession.

The only chronological predictions I know which command some confidence are those based on some regular periodicity behind which we suspect an explicable mechanism, even when we don't understand it. Economists are the greatest searchers for such periodicities . . .

Eric Hobsbawm (1997)

But, perversely, not all economists are believers in the cycle. The concept is embedded in psychology, but not necessarily in the higher reaches of academic—and real estate—economics.

Even though it may not be enough to convince the statistical purist, we believe the historical record supports a cyclical view of property markets. On that score, the property cycle is akin to the economic cycle, which a hard-core of economists refuse to believe in, but remains a central feature of how people perceive and experience economic events. The final test is, perhaps, linguistic rather than statistical: it is hard to imagine describing the course of property history without recourse to the term "cycle".

IPD (1999)

If the issue is "linguistic", how can we usefully define cycle in this context? Most modern commentators simply avoid the question. Burns and Mitchell suggested in 1941:

Cycles consist of expansions occurring at about the same time in many activities, followed by similarly general recessions, contractions and revivals.

More useful is the following (Parker and Beade, 1988):

Business cycles are recurrent but non-periodic fluctuations in aggregate economic activity as measured by fluctuations of real GDP about its trend.

Or: (Begg, Fischer and Dornbusch, 1987)

The business cycle is the tendency for output and employment to fluctuate around their long-term trends.

Adopting this now-standard definition of the business cycle gives us the following (Investment Property Databank (1999)):

Property cycles are recurrent but irregular fluctuations in the rate of all-property total return, which are also apparent in many other indicators of property activity, but with varying leads and lags against the all-property cycle.

Or, a personal simplification:

The property cycle means the tendency for property demand, supply, prices and returns to fluctuate around their long term trends or averages.

Whether a universal definition can be suggested or not, the concept of cycles is firmly embedded in European real estate. The sine wave representation of the property cycle and the clock format are equally ubiquitous, suggesting not only highly simple and symmetrical patterns of property market behaviour, but also perfect predictability. It is also noticeable that there is a common omission of any definition of what the patterns describe. This common variable may be development, it may be rental values, it may be capital values, it may be returns: it may be an amalgam of any of these.

In our attempt to be a little better focused in this chapter, we seek to achieve four objectives. First, we provide some contextual material concerning the performance of the UK real estate market relative to stocks and bonds over a long period. Second, we provide UK—and some non-UK European—evidence of the tendency for property demand, supply, prices and returns to fluctuate around their long term trends or averages. Third, we briefly examine some hypotheses which suggest institutional contributions to property cycles in European markets. Fourth, we suggest some reasons why the future may not be as cyclical as the past.

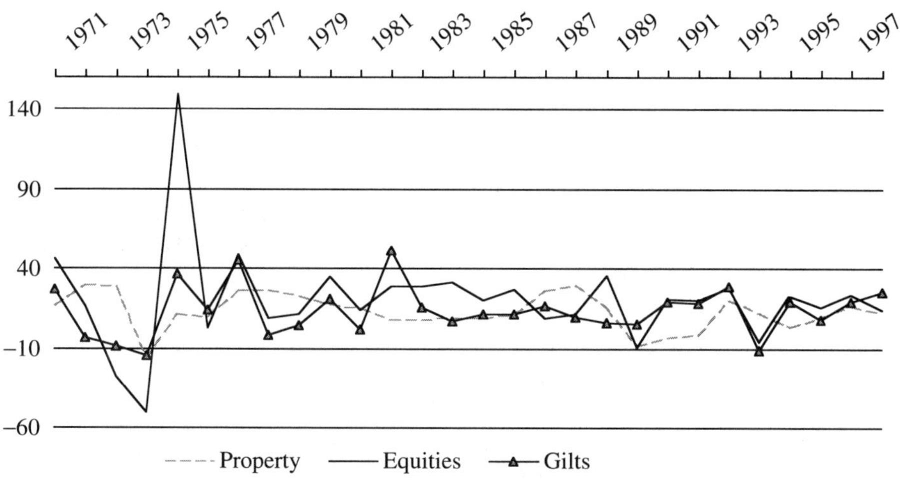

Figure 6.1. Total returns, UK property, equities and gilts, 1971 to 1998

2. THE PERFORMANCE OF UK COMMERCIAL PROPERTY INVESTMENT, 1971–1998

The Investment Property Databank, based in London, provides excellent property data for several countries, the best of which is derived from the UK. Combining this factor with the status of London as a global financial centre, the UK provides an excellent laboratory for a study of the relative performance of real estate, stocks and bonds.

Over the period 1971 to 1998, equities, real estate and government bonds delivered nominal returns of 17, 12.5 and 12% respectively (real returns of 10, 5.5 and 5%). Volatilities were 34, 16 and 11%. The assets were not quite mean-variance efficient over this period. Property and gilts were negatively correlated (−5%), while property and equities were positively correlated (20%) and gilts and equities were strongly positively correlated (67%).

Property's performance characteristics are clearly different from those of stocks and bonds (figure 6.1). There are several reasons for this. UK property is a combination of stock and bond: long leases (15–25 years) with upward-only rent reviews provide long term minimum fixed incomes, while the 5-yearly rent reviews allow owners to benefit from economic and locational growth. However, this is too simplistic a view of the asset class. Property has characteristics which are not common to stocks or bonds. Quite apart from the unique characteristics imposed by the lease contract, it is highly illiquid and lumpy; it depreciates physically, technologically and aesthetically; the supply side is highly regulated by national and local government;

valuations, not transactions, dominate performance estimates; and there is no centralised, regulated market. These factors all contribute to the shape of commercial property performance in the UK.

It would be a mistake, however, to think that there is a single European property market or that there is likely to be convergence of performance across European markets. The very factors which distinguish property from stocks and bonds vary sufficiently between European markets to mean that even if European economies were in harmony European property markets need not be. In particular, lease contracts vary from the UK model at one extreme to the shorter (3, 6 and 9 year) indexed lease common in France, and the supply side is very loose in some markets and very tight in others.

Bearing this in mind, what is the evidence of cyclicality in European property markets?

3. EVIDENCE OF CYCLES IN EUROPEAN COMMERCIAL REAL ESTATE MARKETS

The UK

It has been suggested (MacGregor, 1994) that three UK cycles can be demonstrated. Different cycles are apparent in the development, occupier (rent) and investment markets. Later, MacGregor and Schwann (1999) produced strong evidence for common cycles across different regions and sectors within one national property market. This suggests that regional and sectoral real estate returns are dominated by national occupier, investment and development cycles.

Development

MacGregor *et al.* concluded that a 4–5 year cycle in property development is apparent, but this is not coincident with the rent cycle. Current development profits have been a good explanatory variable of development activity.

Barras (1994) identified four types of real estate development or construction cycles, each of different length. These were: short cycles (4–5 years, the classic business cycle operating on occupier demand), long cycles (9–10 years, creating a tendency for severe over-supply which by-passes every second demand cycle), long swings (20 years, associated with major speculative building booms) and long waves (50 years, technologically-driven).

In conclusion, UK property development has been highly pro-cyclical with GDP growth and property values, but exhibits sharper rises and falls. The evidence suggests adaptive behaviour. A period of excessive optimism is followed by a period of excessive pessimism. Adaptive behaviour can explain much of the late 1980s supply. As prices rise, prices are more likely to be expected to continue to rise; development profits are a function of continued price rises; hence price rises lead to ever-increasing supply levels, which create the conditions for lower prices (disaster myopia). The time lag involved creates an inevitable supply cycle.

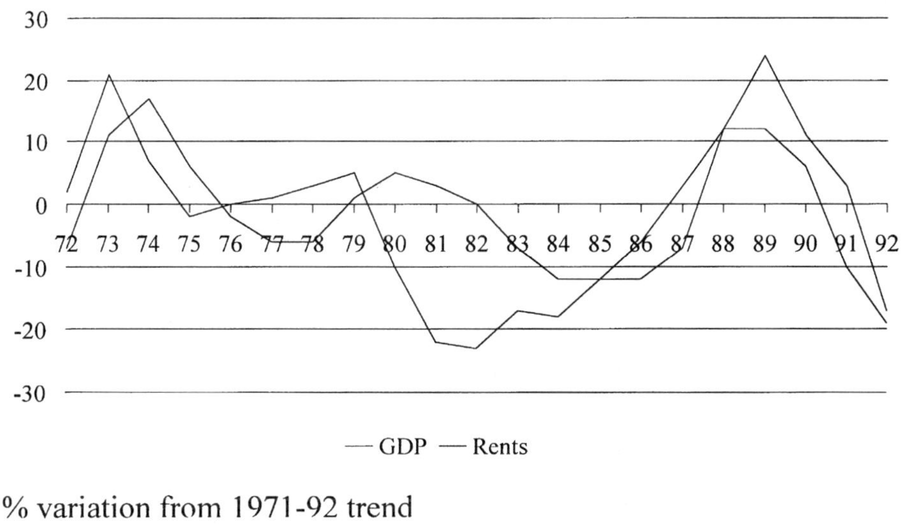

Figure 6.2. Change in GDP and rents, 1971–1992

Rents

MacGregor *et al.* suggested that the demand side is pro-cyclical with economic indicators, but inelasticity of supply means that even highly regular demand cycles can generate irregular rental cycles.

Nonetheless, a simple demand/supply regression model can achieve a very strong explanation of national rental movements over a 30-year period. Typical R-squared results are in the range 90% to 97%; typical variables are rent n − 1, rent n − 2, consumer expenditure/GDP/manufacturing output, floorspace stock and construction orders.

Barras also concluded that rents have clearly been strongly pro-cyclical with GDP. The % deviation from the 1971–1992 trend in rental growth and GDP growth are very strongly correlated. Barras (1994) shows how growth in GDP above the long term trend growth is mirrored in growth in rents above long term trend growth (figure 6.2).

Tsolacos and McGough (1995) confirm the strong relationship between macroeconomic variables and rental data. They found a strong relationship between office development and changes in rents, suggesting a degree of adaptive behaviour among lenders, investors and developers.

Investment: Returns, Capitalisation Rates and Capital Values

Tsolacos and McGough suggested that the linkages between the investment market and financial variables were unclear. MacGregor *et al.* also found investment per-

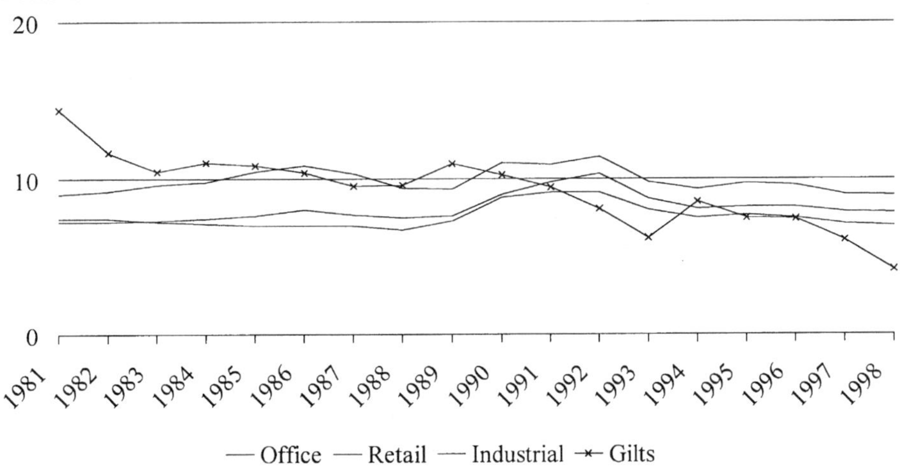

Figure 6.3. Yields, 1981–1998

formance, expressed as rates of total return or changes in capital values or even capitalisation rates, harder to model. Nonetheless, they identified a 4–5 year cycle in the rate of all-property return.

There is no clear relationship between yields (capitalisation rates) on UK property and other asset and money market yields and rates. Figure 6.3 shows the flat performance of UK property yields related to a continued decline in gilt yields. There appears to be no evidence of cyclicality.

The flatness of yields results in an extremely strong relationship between rental growth and capital value growth, both strongly pro-cyclical.

There is some relationship between returns and the business cycle, but this is less strong than the relationship between changes in capital values and economic growth simply because income returns have been reasonably invariant from period to period.

Recent work by IPD (RICS, 1999) provides the fullest picture of long term UK performance yet available. Data assembled from various sources covering the period 1921 to 1998 shows 16 "fairly distinct" peaks and troughs describing total returns delivered in the market. IPD identify six completed cycles, with peaks in 1925–28, 1935, 1950, 1954, 1960–64, 1973, 1979–81, and 1989. They suggest that those cycles have ranged in length from 4 to 12 years, with an average of 8 years; upswings have run from 2 to 7 years, and downswings from 2 to 9 years.

These "recurrent but irregular" patterns are not necessarily the result of a single cyclical process. They could be the product of overlapping cycles of different lengths (5 and 9 years). It is tempting to see a shorter cycle as demand driven, linked to the business cycle in the economy, and a longer one as supply driven, linked to slower fluctuations in new development.

The property cycle is linked to the economic cycle, but the precise nature of the relationship varies from one cycle to another.

IPD (1999)

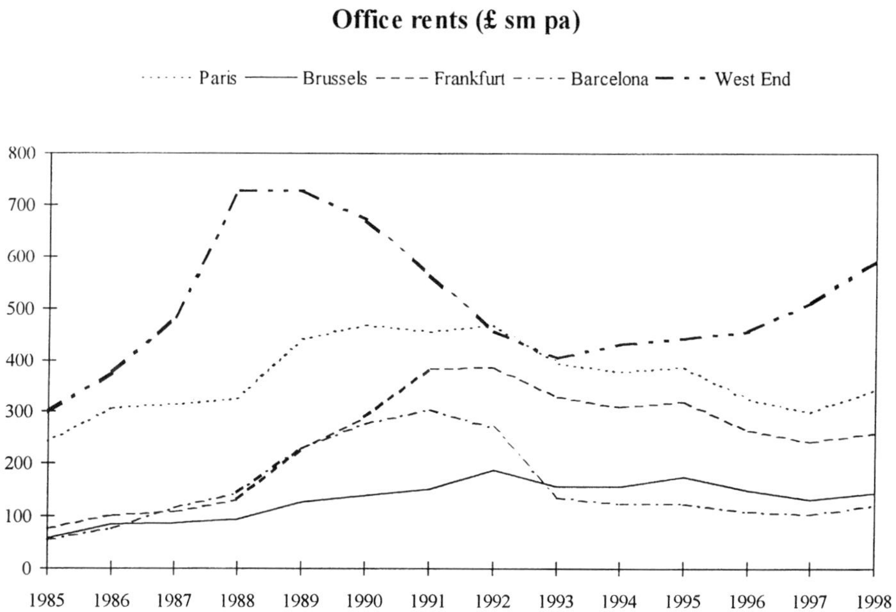

Figure 6.4. Rent cycles in European real estate markets

Continental Europe

Evidence for non-UK markets in Europe is more elusive. Figure 4 shows evidence of office rents in 5 city markets, including London West End. There is some evidence of common cyclical movement, with an apparent lag for the non-UK markets.

Laposa, Barkham, Ashton and Gilbertson (1999) examine supply, demand, vacancy, rents, capitalisation rates and investor behaviour as the six significant indicators of the real estate cycle. They applied this US-based classification to 8 continental (non-UK) European city office markets, concluding broadly that real estate markets in Europe tend to move together although with different lags in the contraction and recovery phases of the cycle. They also suggest that the expected relationship between aggregate vacancy rates and rental rises may not always hold because of splits in sub-markets for different quality of space. This may question any generalised analysis of "the" real estate cycle, even within a single city/sector.

4. HYPOTHESES

Bank Lending and Cycles

There is a costly and understated dynamic relationship between property crises and banking crises.

Renaud, 1998

The relationship between property crises and banking crises is described by Renaud, 1998 and by the same author in another chapter in this book. Despite powerful evidence of this relationship, Thomas, 1998, demonstrated the reluctance of the UK's central bank to regulate the commercial property market.

Beardsley (1997) discussed the adaptive behaviour of lenders which, coupled with the adaptive behaviour of investors, led to an inevitably exaggerated cycle of UK (and French) real estate performance in the late 1980s and early 1990s. The following quotation states the hypothesis very concisely.

Property booms occur in times of rising economic activity with increases in rentals feeding rapidly into increases in collateral value. Both adaptive behaviour and herd behaviour are powerful forces at work as bankers anticipate further rental increases and further increases in capital values . . . banking officers are motivated . . . by means of incentive payments based . . . on the amount of loan business achieved.

. . . Managerial ambitions to grow firms are accommodated by surges in property lending at critical times in the economic and competitive cycles.

(from Baum, Beardsley and Ward, 1999)

In his PhD work, Beardsley (1997) found much evidence to support this hypothesis.

Cycles: The Result of Market Inefficiency?

Prices in all markets go up and down. Inefficiency in real estate markets makes these up and down movements look like a repeatable, cyclical, pattern. We have bull and bear periods in stock markets, but cycles are less often talked about. In property, auto-correlation, valuation smoothing and sticky prices elongate the ups and downs.

Bjorklund and Soderburg (1997) suggested that auto-correlation affects real estate returns to the point that a speculative bubble can be proven to have formed. Antwi and Henneberry (1995) identified what they called habit-persistent (another term might be adaptive) behaviour by lenders and by developers (see above).

In efficient space markets, rent differentials across different locations are quickly eradicated through substitution or a rapid supply response in an extremely efficient market for space (Hendershott, 1995). However, neither substitution nor a price-elastic supply response is likely across European real estate markets. Planning permissions can be slow to obtain; equally significantly, the time delays involved can vary greatly across markets, which are not therefore efficient enough for price adjustment to take place. It may take three months to obtain permission to build a London office building; it may take 2 years in Frankfurt. Both the resulting lack of substitutability across markets and the long supply response within particular markets can act to elongate and exaggerate cycles in space markets.

Grenadier (1995) examined the way owners of space will restrict supply in an upswing. Letting space at a market rent on a five-year lease involves the giving up of a five year American option. In an auto-correlated occupier/rental market, it is easy to see how letting at market rents may appear to be a sub-optimal financial decision, especially when the supply side is slow to respond to demand and price. Withholding space in this way exaggerates the supply shortage and the cyclical upswing.

Renaud (1998) also suggested that endogenous causes of real estate cycles include the inertia (auto-correlation) of rents in a changing environment.

These concepts—auto-correlation and adaptive behaviour—are related, as they indicate inefficiency or irrationality in real estate investment decision-making. They affect the way space is developed, the way rents are agreed for space and the way prices are paid for real estate investments. They exaggerate and elongate upturns and downturns, and create the appearance of definable cycles in real estate markets. Sticky prices affect occupier, investor and developer markets, elongating and exaggerating real estate cycles.

Rates of change in rental values and vacancy rates are slow, due to the actions of intermediaries or agents and the costs of re-locating. Development cycles are slow to reverse due to the commitment created by the large amounts of sunk (human and physical) capital required to complete a project.

Rates of return are also auto-correlated, due to valuation smoothing. Many commentators (for example Barkham and Geltner (1995)) demonstrate the lower volatility which results from the replacement of transactions by valuations as the basis of return measurement. De-smoothing the UK price series produces less cyclical returns on UK property over the period 1981–1997. This challenges conventional views of the volatility of real estate returns, the correlation of the main asset markets, and the cyclicality of real estate rents, values and returns which may be partly the creation of intermediaries and real estate service providers.

5. THE FUTURE FOR EUROPEAN REAL ESTATE CYCLES

Cycles in UK and European real estate can clearly be demonstrated, especially in the construction/development and rental markets. Possible explanations include the inefficiencies introduced into these markets by lenders and other intermediaries and service providers. But times are changing. Will European property markets become more efficient, and cycles less prolonged and pronounced, in the new Europe?

Direct reasons for change would include changes in property financing away from bank debt, and a reduced role for intermediaries such as appraisers and brokers. Some of these changes are underway, created by changes in the way property investment is undertaken and in particular by the globalisation of investment activity and the increasingly securitised property market.

In a recent paper (Baum, 1999), the author sets out to describe changing styles of real estate investment. In doing so, the paper draws on a personal view of the global economic forces which have been unleashed as part of the latest industrial revolution, and examines reasons for increased levels of securitisation.

Globalisation

The historic self-containment of domestic property markets is unlikely to continue. The growth of multi-national companies, increased cross-border trade and communication, the dominance of international stock markets and the increasing importance of cross-border benchmarks will all have an impact on the way real estate is leased, bought and sold.

A Case Study: the City of London

Recent research carried out at Reading University in the UK (Baum and Lizieri, 1999) has shown that foreign ownership of the City of London office market has grown from 5% to 22% in 10 years. In 1972, over 94% of the floor space in the City database was owned by UK firms. Just less than 3% of space was owned by Middle Eastern interests and around 2% was European owned. None of the sample properties was owned by German, Japanese or USA firms. By 1997, 21.9% of the sample buildings were in overseas ownership. 7% of the properties were in Japanese hands, 5% were German owned, 4% were owned by US firms and just under 3% was, as in 1972, in Middle Eastern ownership.

This growth was supported by mid-1980s de-regulation. In 1975 the New York Stock Exchange abolished minimum commission rates: 35 broking firms went out of business but turnover exploded. In 1979, UK exchange controls were abolished, allowing capital to move freely around international markets—a move paralleled in other developed economies. By 1986 ("Big Bang") the implementation of the Parkinson-Goodison accord and financial deregulation meant that merchant banks, jobbers and brokers could combine to become full capacity investment banks, and overseas players could join in. Financial business had become global.

Over the period 1991–96, market globalization intensified, so that the overseas ownership of UK equities increased from 12% to nearly 17% over the five years from the end of 1991 to the end of 1996. The overseas acquisition of UK operations, culminating in 1994–7 in the purchases of Warburgs, Morgan Grenfell, Barings, Kleinworts, Smith New Court, BZW and Mercury by Swiss, Dutch, German, French and American banks, is explained by the need of the City economy to access wider markets.

At the same time, saving-based liquidity in Japan, the relaxing of Swedish and German cross-border investment restrictions and changes in German tax policy pushed funds out from these savings-oriented countries, much into UK property. DTZ estimated that overseas investment in UK commercial property rose from £0.2bn in 1987 to £1.9bn in 1988, £3.1bn in 1989, and £3.3bn in 1990, remaining well above £1bn every year thereafter. According to DTZ overseas owners accounted for around 12.5% of all UK commercial property transactions over the period 1988–1995: clearly, the City has taken a larger than average proportion of this investment. In tune with this change, the overseas ownership of City office property has increased in line with levels of foreign equity ownership.

The Single European Currency

London offers a wonderful case study; so does the wider geo-political structure of Europe. European Monetary Union (EMU) is another process of radical change which has been gathering momentum since the Maastricht Treaty made 1992 and the completion of the Single European Market a significant date in European history. The movement towards a single European currency appears determined to establish the 1999 introduction of the Euro as a second major economic event.

If the UK and other EC countries currently outside the Euro block eventually take part, currency risk will disappear for Euroland investors and will become much simplified for non-Europeans. Regulation and taxation rules will slowly begin to converge. Investment benchmarks will become pan-Eurobloc. This will create a significant change in investor behaviour: from a position where any exposure to overseas assets is a risk against a domestic benchmark, growing recognition of a wider non-domestic benchmark would lead to a need to invest overseas to *reduce* risk relative to the competition.

As the global pension industry grows and international trading is positively encouraged, international property is likely to become a major asset class. In addition, owner-occupiers are likely to fuel growth in cross-border property investment. This is highly likely to change the nature of property cycles.

Securitisation

In an unpublished survey carried out for Henderson Investors in 1996, European institutional investors suggested that the greatest deterrent to real estate investment was illiquidity. The best solution for illiquidity was thought to be a public market quotation. Other surveys suggest similar desires among global investors, and the natural demand for securitised real estate product appears to be enormous. The growth in global securitised property investment appears to be inhibited only by a lack of supply, largely created by taxation and regulatory problems in markets outside a small number of markets including the USA and Australia.

In the US, the REIT market has grown from tiny market capitalisations to more than $180bn in 8 years, much of it held by overseas investors. In Sweden, from what approximated to a standing start in 1995, there are now more than 30 listed property companies with an active international shareholder base. In Australia, rapid growth in the listed property trust market over a 10 year period since 1989 has resulted in $26bn of market capitalisation at March 1999, representing around 25% of the institutional real estate market.

Growth in the universe of securitised property has been rapid. Nonetheless, the total market capitalisation of the 400 companies in the Salomon Smith Barney index, worth $US250bn, represents around eighth of expected net new pension fund investment over the period 1997–2002.

The potential for development of this market is particularly great in Europe. Germany, France, Italy and Spain (all relatively immature institutional property markets, but all part of a single currency area which has been recently and rapidly projected onto the global screen) have less securitised product per unit of GDP than any other country. The relatively mature markets of the USA, Australia, UK and Hong Kong have more. The correlation is powerful, and suggests potential rapid growth in European securitisations.

A securitised market reduces the power and influence of the intermediary. The appraiser/valuer is largely replaced by market pricing, so valuation smoothing has much less impact. The cycle and its strength will, consequently, become less easy to discern.

Property as Private Equity/Venture Capital

A second new style of international real estate investment vehicle has emerged over the 1990s decade. This is the transfer of much real estate investment into venture capital or private equity format. The type of investment vehicle now common to this format (closed end, limited life co-mingled private funds) was commonly used for domestic investment in the US in the 1980s—and largely since discredited.

However, this is now seen as an acceptable form of international property investment, largely because the returns advertised are high, usually in excess of 15% on equity. Gearing is common, at levels as high at 60–80%; the fund manager often has an investment alongside clients, and includes a performance element in the fee charged. This vehicle explains much of the 1990s investment in Poland, Thailand and China. It may be a flawed investment format, but it accesses the diversification potential of private real estate. This is broadening the source of capital for real estate investment and reducing the likelihood of periodic surges and withdrawals of that capital.

CONCLUSIONS

Cycles in UK and European real estate can clearly be demonstrated, especially in the construction/development and rental markets. Possible explanations include the inefficiencies introduced into these markets by lenders and other intermediaries and service providers. But changes are underway. Direct reasons for change would include changes in property financing away from bank debt, and a reduced role for intermediaries such as appraisers and brokers. These very changes are now being created by the twin forces of globalistion and changes in the sources of property capital.

It is possible that the broadening of the base for real estate investment, from traditional pension fund diversification into a mix of private equity, listed product and good old-fashioned private real estate portfolios will broaden the sources of capital to the point where the capital value cycle becomes much less easy to observe.

The sources of capital will broaden both internationally and by type. As a result, we may begin to observe a smoother cycle, with cyclicality expressed more in changes over time in the natural suppliers of capital rather than in changes in price determined by single-source floods of capital into and out of the market.

Globalisation will open up both the suppliers of capital and the markets in which they invest, to the point where more efficient capital flows, implying a less pronounced cycle, can be anticipated.

The global property market which awaits us is likely to be more efficient than the national markets we are familiar with. A highly efficient European property market—or even a single market—is not something we should take for granted, and the cycle may well re-appear in many sub-markets. Nonetheless, the real estate analyst may find it harder in future to produce models of market behaviour with the level of explanatory power which, thanks to the extreme cyclicality of the past, now lies at his/her disposal.

REFERENCES

Antwi, A and Henneberry, J (1995), *Developers, non-linearity and asymmetry in the development cycle*, Journal of Property Research, 12, 3: 217–239

Ball, M, Lizieri, C and MacGregor, B (1998), *The Economics of Commercial Property Markets*, London, Routledge

Barkham, R and Geltner, D (1995), *Price discovery in American and British property markets*, Real Estate Economics, 23: 21–44

Barras, R (1994), *Property and the economic cycle: building cycles revisited*, Journal of Property Research, 11, pp 183–197

Baum, A (1993), *Quality, Depreciation and Property Performance*, Journal of Real Estate Research, Volume 8 Number 4, Fall, pp 541–566

Baum, A (1995), *Can Foreign Real Estate Investment be Successful?*, Real Estate Finance, Volume 12, number 1, pp 81–89

Baum, A and Lizieri, C (1999), *Who Owns the City of London?* Real Estate Finance, Vol 16 No 1, Spring, pp 87–100

Baum, A and Wurtzebach, C (1992), International Property Investment, in Hudson-Wilson, S and Wurtzebach, C, Managing Real Estate Portfolios, New York, Irwin (pp 284–308)

Baum, A, Beardsley, CJ and Ward, CWR (1999), *On UK Commercial Property Lending in the 1980s: A Case of Bizarre British Banking Behaviour?*, Department of Land Management and Development/ISMA Centre, University of Reading

Beardsley, C (1997), *Financing the 1980s Commercial Property Boom: A Behavioural Analysis of Lending Decisions by British Banks*, unpublished PhD thesis, Department of Land Management and Development, University of Reading

Begg, D, Fischer S and Dornbusch, R (1987), *Economics* (2e), London, McGraw-Hill

Bjorklund, K and Soderburg, B (1997), *Property cycles, speculative bubbles and the gross income multiplier*, Royal Institute of Technology, working paper no 24

Burns and Mitchell (1941), *Measuring Business Cycles*, NBER

D'Arcy, E, Keogh, G and Roulac, S (1999), *The Internationalisation of US and UK Real Estate Service Providers: Competing for a Global Badge of Quality*, Paper presented to 6th European Real Estate Society meeting, Athens, Greece

Grenadier, S (1995), *Valuing lease contracts: a real options approach*, Journal of Financial Economics, 38, 297–331

Griffin, Mark (1997), *The Global Pension Time Bomb and its Capital Market Impact*, New York, Goldman Sachs

Hendershott, P (1995), *The use of equilibrium models in real estate research*, The Cutting Edge (conference proceedings), 351–358, London, RICS

Hobsbawm, E (1997), *On History*, London, Wiedenfeld and Nicholson

Investment Property Databank and University of Aberdeen (1994), *Understanding the property cycle: economic cycles and property cycles*, London, RICS

Investment Property Databank (1999), *The UK Property Cycle: A History from 1921 to 1997*, London, RICS

Laposa, S, Ashton, B, Barkham, R and Gilbertson, B (1999), *A Descriptive Analysis of European Office Real Estate Cycles: Comparative Modelling with US Real Estate Markets*, paper presented at European Real Estate Society, Athens, Greece

McGough, T and Tsolacos, S (1997), *The stylised facts of the UK commercial building cycle*, Environment and Planning A, 29, 485–500

MacGregor, B (1994), *Property and the Economy*, RICS Commercial Property Conference, Cardiff

MacGregor, B and Schwann, G (1999), *Common feature in UK commercial property returns*, ERES conference paper

Parker, M and Beade, R (1988), *Modern Macroeconomics*, Oxford, Phillip Allan

Renaud, B (1998), *Property cycles and banking crises*, IPD conference paper

Thomas, V (1998), *How to avoid history repeating itself—the Bank of England's role in the commercial property market*, IPD conference paper

Tsolacos, S and McGough, T (1995), *Property cycles in the UK: an empirical investigation of the stylised facts*, The Cutting Edge, 359–373, London, RICS

Tsolacos, S, Keogh, G and McGough, T (1998), *Modelling use, investment and development in the British office market*, Environment and Planning A, 30, 1409–1427

Worzala, E, Newell, G and Lizieri, C (1996), *The convergence of international real estate markets*, AREUEA conference paper

INDEX